The Werewolf Filmography

THE WEREWOLF FILMOGRAPHY

300+ Movies

Bryan Senn

To John, film-finder extraordinaire,

Even a writer who's pure of heart
And scribbles his thoughts by night,
Needs a friend like John to find those films
That will make the book look bright.

Thank you, my friend, for all your help!

—Bryan Senn

McFarland & Company, Inc., Publishers
Jefferson, North Carolina

ALSO OF INTEREST BY BRYAN SENN
AND FROM MCFARLAND

*The Most Dangerous Cinema:
People Hunting People on Film* (2014)

BY BRYAN SENN AND JOHN JOHNSON

*Fantastic Cinema Subject Guide: A Topical Index
to 2,500 Horror, Science Fiction, and Fantasy Films* (2008; paperback 1992)

*A Year of Fear:
A Day-by-Day Guide to 366 Horror Films* (2007)

*Golden Horrors:
An Illustrated Critical Filmography
of Terror Cinema, 1931–1939* (2006 [1996])

BY MARK CLARK AND BRYAN SENN

*Sixties Shockers: A Critical Filmography
of Horror Cinema, 1960–1969* (2011)

Frontispiece: Lon Chaney, Jr.'s *Wolf Man* towers over the werewolf subgenre,
just as the iconic Chaney himself towers over heroine Evelyn Ankers
in this atmospheric publicity shot for the 1941 film.

**ISBN (print) 978-0-7864-7910-8
ISBN (ebook) 978-1-4766-2691-8**

LIBRARY OF CONGRESS CATALOGUING DATA ARE AVAILABLE

BRITISH LIBRARY CATALOGUING DATA ARE AVAILABLE

© 2017 Bryan Senn. All rights reserved

*No part of this book may be reproduced or transmitted in any form
or by any means, electronic or mechanical, including photocopying
or recording, or by any information storage and retrieval system,
without permission in writing from the publisher.*

On the cover: The terrifying wolf-headed horrors created
by Rob Bottin for *The Howling*, 1981; *background* Halloween
Night © 2017 Stanislav Pobytov/iStock

Printed in the United States of America

*McFarland & Company, Inc., Publishers
Box 611, Jefferson, North Carolina 28640
www.mcfarlandpub.com*

For Lynn Naron,
who leads by example through his friendship and generosity.

For the late Mark A. Miller,
an inspiring writer and friend whose support
and encouragement meant more to me than he knew.

And for Gina,
who brings out the wolf in me.

Acknowledgments

A huge howl of gratitude goes to my generous and supportive group of movie-savvy friends and colleagues whose vast cinematic knowledge helped ease this work's sometimes painful metamorphosis (not from man to wolf but from ephemeral idea to written word). They are:

John Gibbon, who once again so generously applied his amazing cinematic detective skills to find the un-findable.

Image-locator extraordinaire (and walking encyclopedia) Ted Okuda, who always goes that extra celluloid mile.

The MillerCon Gang: Anthony Ambrogio, Ron and Margaret Borst, Mark Clark, Dave Harnack, David Hogan, Lenny Kohl, Mark and Teresa Miller, Lynn Naron, Ted Okuda (again), Dr. Nicholas Schlegel, Steve Thornton, and David Walker.

The Fanexians: Anthony Ambrogio, Cindy Collins-Smith, Bruce Dettman, Jonathan Malcolm Lampley, Arthur Lundquist, and Brian Smith.

And the ETP (Eurotrash Paradise) usual suspects: Holger Haase, Bruce Holecheck, Jeff Segal, Adrian Salmon, Bob Sargent, Dan Taylor, Neil Vokes, and David Zuzelo.

A special thank you to the following interviewees for taking the time to answer my lycancentric questions: effects artist Ted A. Bohus, director Freddie Francis, artist Cortlandt Hull (great-nephew of Henry Hull), filmmaker Ricardo Islas, actor Kevin McCarthy, director Fred Olen Ray, actor Germán Robles, screenwriter Curt Siodmak, actress Gloria Stuart, actor Jack Taylor, filmmaker Robert Tinnell, actor William Ragsdale, bestselling author Carrie Vaughn, and propmaker/effects artist George Willis.

Thanks to Erik Wilber, education director at Wolf Haven International (wolfhaven.org), for his illuminations regarding the real *canis lupus*.

Thanks to my son Dominic, just for being himself (and making his father proud).

And many thanks are due (once again) to my patient wife Gina Beretta, whose perspective, editorial skills, and just plain indulgence so often kept me from simply howling at the moon. (Plus, she agreed to watch all the *Twilight* movies with me so I wouldn't feel so utterly, awfully, horribly alone. *That* is true love.)

Table of Contents

Acknowledgments vi

Introduction 1

The Films 21
(Alphabetically)

Pseudowolves 272

Other Were-Beasts 352

Appendix A: Film Chronology 379

Appendix B: Film Series and Subsets 381

Bibliography 383

Index 389

INTRODUCTION

"I think when people go to a horror film, they see a coalescence of their darkest fears in the form of a monster, and it's very, very cathartic. It's a pleasure, no matter how horrible it is, to f**king *define* it, instead of having that amorphous anxiety swirl around you."—Filmmaker Mel Brooks[1]

DR. FRANKENSTEIN (hearing howling): "Werewolf?"
IGOR (pointing): "There—wolf."—Mel Brooks' *Young Frankenstein*

WhereWolf?

When I decided to undertake writing a comprehensive book on werewolf movies, I was woefully naïve in two respects. One was the massive amount of literature on the topic of werewolves. While the lycanthrope subgenre has no seminal literary text like the vampire (with Bram Stoker's novel *Dracula*), the Frankenstein Monster (originating with Mary Shelley's controversial-at-the-time *Frankenstein or the Modern Prometheus*) or Dr. Jekyll and Mr. Hyde (via Robert Louis Stevenson's classic novella *The Strange Case of Dr. Jekyll and Mr. Hyde*), werewolves boast a huge body of work regarding not only their myths and legends, but the possibility of their *reality*. Yes, countless tomes have explored the "real-life" cases of lycanthropy throughout the ages, starting back before the birth of Christ and continuing up until the present day. Such recent titles as *Werewolves: Fact or Fiction?*, edited by Angela Cybulski; *Hunting the American Werewolf*, by Linda S. Godfrey; and even the youngster-targeted *The Making of a Monster: Vampires and Werewolves*, by Kim Etingoff all explore the origin and possible existence of wolfmen. And there are many, many more. Apparently, readers even in this modern age are enthralled by the concept of a man (or woman) transforming into an animal.

The other surprise was the sheer volume of lycanthrope movies that have been made in the last 100 years—far more than I ever suspected before I started digging into werewolf cinema in earnest. I'd seen all the Universals from the thirties and forties, the smattering of independents from the fifties and sixties, and the myriad Paul Naschy imports from the seventies and eighties (a boon decade for werewolves with the release of such lycan-classics as *An American Werewolf in London*, *The Howling* and the underrated *Silver Bullet*). I'd even caught up with a few more recent efforts, such as the lauded *Ginger Snaps* and the thrilling *Dog Soldiers*. But nothing had prepared me for the sheer numbers of wolfmen (and women) that spilled forth in the 21st century. Along with the vampire and zombie, it seems that the werewolf has caught our modern zeitgeist in its jaws and worried it almost to death. More than *half* of all werewolf films have been produced since the turn of the millennium.

While I searched for a title for this book, a witty friend of mine acerbically suggested "*Two Hundred Sucky Movies and Eight Good Ones.*"[2] Though I respectfully declined utilizing said suggestion, I took his point. Quality werewolf films are definitely in the minority, with the subgenre overloaded with subpar specimens. But then, *any* branch of cinema can claim the same. (And don't worry, as you'll see, there are *far* more than "eight good ones.") Making a movie is such a difficult task that involves so many disparate elements, it's a minor miracle that any film sees completion at all, much less one of quality. But back to the point: Why write a book on werewolf cinema if the majority of the films are, shall we say, less than classic? One answer stems from the old "why climb a mountain" bromide: Because it's there. To date there has never been published a comprehensive werewolf filmography.[3] A better response, however, would be that the werewolf mythos is obviously an important one to our culture, given the sheer volume of lycan-centric films produced over the last century (not to mention the explosion of werewolf novels, TV series, and video games). Second only to the vampire subgenre, the werewolf's popularity far outstrips such fellow horror icons as Jekyll and Hyde, the Frankenstein Monster and the Mummy. And werewolf cinema has given us its fair share of classics, too—innovative, groundbreaking and enthralling films like *The Wolf Man* (1941), *Abbott and Costello Meet Frankenstein* (1948), *The Howling* (1981), *An American Werewolf in London*

(1981), *Silver Bullet* (1985), *Ginger Snaps* (2000), *Dog Soldiers* (2002), and, more recently, the excellent 2010 *Wolfman* remake, Spain's delightful *Game of Werewolves* (2011), and the clever *Late Phases* (2014). Then there's the myriad worthy efforts like *Werewolf of London* (1935), *Frankenstein Meets the Wolf Man* (1943), *The Return of the Vampire* (1944), *The Werewolf* (1956), *I Was a Teenage Werewolf* (1957), *Frankenstein's Bloody Terror* (1968), *The Werewolf vs. the Vampire Woman* (1971), *Night of the Howling Beast* (1975), *The Craving* (1981), *The Company of Wolves* (1984), *Ladyhawke* (1985), *The Monster Squad* (1987), *Wilderness* (1997), *Cursed* (2005), *Skinwalkers* (2006), *Blood and Chocolate* (2007), *Audie & the Wolf* (2008), *Never Cry Werewolf* (2008), *Underworld: Rise of the Lycans* (2009), *The Hair of the Beast* (2010), *Night Wolf* (2010), *Monster Brawl* (2011), *Red Riding Hood* (2011), *WolfCop* (2014), *Wolves* (2014) … and the list goes on.

But why a book covering *every* werewolf film—the good, the bad, *and* the howlingly ugly? Because werewolf tales explore that fascinating side of Man that hides beneath our civilized veneer. In all their metaphorical iterations and permutations, every werewolf movie holds out the promise of illuminating our hidden natures, bringing if not necessarily new insight, then at least some novel illustration of same. And while so many lycan-flicks fail on the whole, even dreck like *Blood of Dracula's Castle* (with its ad-hoc backhanded allusion to lycanthropy as an outlet for repression), or the obscure Uruguayan SOV (shot-on-video) backyard horror *Plenilunio* (with its solitary evil vs. collective good thematics), at least present the germ of an intriguing idea about our savage selves.

WhyWolf?

Perhaps a contributing factor to the werewolf's recent surge in popularity can be put down to one of the great themes in horror cinema—randomness. Being in the wrong place at the wrong time. Bad things happening to good people. Much of early fright cinema (right up into the 1960s) reflected the notion that horror stemmed from one's own actions—the mad scientist, the inviting occultist, or those who simply "meddled in things Man should leave alone." More recently, however, particularly as reflected in the slasher boom of the 1980s, and the subsequent serial killer and home invasion subsets, horror comes randomly into characters' lives through no fault of their own. And in post–9/11 America that may truly be the most terrifying "horror" around, as the cultural climate irrevocably changed that day in 2001 when random death literally rained from the skies on thousands of souls. Of all the "classic" horror figures, the werewolf serves as an able personification of this terrifying notion of "randomness." The Werewolf is a more sympathetic Jekyll and Hyde. After all, Jekyll brought about the horrific transformation himself, whereas most lycanthropes have their monstrousness thrust upon them. As *The Wolf Man*'s wise old gypsy woman Maleva intones, "The way you walk is thorny, through no fault of your own…"

In any case, the werewolf makes for such a fascinating figure because it can be seen through a

Cinematic werewolfery exploded in the New Millennium, with 2002's brilliant *Dog Soldiers* leading the lycanthropic pack.

veritable kaleidoscope of interpretive lenses—the psychological ("an expression of primitive *id* instincts being expressed literally on an animalistic level through a splitting mechanism, thereby avoiding guilt feelings,"[4]), the sociological (the individual vs. the masses; fear of "the Other"), the anthropological (the age-old terror of being killed and eaten by predators), and even the ecological (the nobility of/return to Nature).

"[The horror-fantasy genre] is the genre which comes closest to the true essence of the cinema, which is in itself a phantasmagorical phenomenon," wrote Paul Naschy, *El Hombre Lobo* himself, in his autobiography *Memoirs of a Wolfman*. "Horror-fantasy films deal with the terrible frontier between life and death, with a terrifying universe populated by creatures which have troubled men's dreams since the dawn of creation, creatures which remind us that we carry evil within ourselves." Nowhere is this truer than in werewolf cinema.

In the figure of the werewolf, we can, on the one hand, cinematically channel the predator—bring it into ourselves (or let it out). And on the other, the werewolf explores/exploits our fear of that very predator. And these two dichotomous sides of the werewolf coin can feature in the same movie, buying both sympathy and fear—two very powerful emotions.

"As a creature I just love the werewolf because they're so primal," enthused filmmaker James Isaac. In talking of his 2006 film *Skinwalkers*, Isaac pointed out, "The story is about the choice of whether to embrace [the beast inside us] and go with it and be who you believe you are, or whether to allow society to have its filters and have to make moral choices about what you should do and shouldn't do."[5] In essence, the werewolf mythos encapsulates the notion of nature vs. nurture, the conflict between our inner, animalistic selves and the behavioral restraint thrust upon us by the society we have constructed.

For many, Spanish actor/writer/director Paul Naschy simply *was* "The Werewolf," having helped spark the Eurohorror revival in 1968 with his *La Marca del Hombre Lobo* (released in America as *Frankenstein's Bloody Terror*). Naschy reprised his Waldemar Daninsky/Werewolf character in twelve further films, including 1981's *The Craving* (aka *The Night of the Werewolf*) (German lobby card).

When the balance tips too far towards the primal, the werewolf emerges, usually as a rampaging force of nature intent on killing and devouring its fellow humans—the ultimate rebellion against societal bonds. But such a scenario is rife with anxiety, since without society, mankind would become just another beast of the jungle—and one, without all of society's trappings (everything from fire to firearms), that would be far less effective at survival than most creatures. So at the heart of the werewolf theme beats the fear of societal collapse and mankind's subsequent plunge into the chaos of Nature. In this case, it is *nurture* that we most need, with society's structure teaching—and taming—our innate animal natures so that we, as a species, can stay top of the food chain and reign supreme.

Additionally, the werewolf may offer one of the most intimate explorations of horror's great trope—fear of the "Other." With its real-life roots in xenophobia, the horror genre has often focused on how we deal with "otherness." Werewolf cinema takes this to the Nth degree by literally transforming the protagonist (the viewer identification figure—in essence, the viewers themselves) into what we most fear—the Other.

But perhaps lycan-cinema's strongest pull, both in historical and biological terms, comes from something deeply rooted in our subconscious, even in our very genetics—the fear of, and attraction to, the predator. Man did not start out as the world's top predator. That status has come relatively recently in *Homo sapiens*' short history. For nearly two million years, Modern Man's ancestors have been a prey, rather than predator, species. As nature writer David Quammen observes of those dark times in human history, "Every once in a while, a monstrous carnivore emerged like doom from the forest or a river to kill someone and feed on the body. It was a familiar sort of disaster ... that must have seemed freshly, shockingly gruesome each time, despite the familiarity. And it conveyed a certain message. Among the earliest forms of human self-consciousness was the awareness of being meat."[6] Small, weak, and slow in comparison to the myriad dangerous beasts around them, humans were constantly worried about being stalked and eaten alive by the massive predators in the environment they shared, everything from gigantic cave bears to saber-toothed cats to huge pythons to the 300-pound dire wolf which stalked North America as recently as 8,000 years ago and possessed the longest and most powerful teeth ever found in a canid. (So prevalent was this deadly wolf-like predator that its bones outnumber any other species in the famous La Brea Tar Pits of Los Angeles.) In such an environment, fear would be Man's primary emotion.

Ultimately, Man, through intellect and sociability, did rise to the top of the food chain. But going from *Homo praeda* ("Man the fearful") to *Homo necans* ("Man the killer") was not an either/or proposition but a *merger*, leaving mankind steeped in fear. As cultural historian Paul A. Trout observed, "We can never escape this fear [of being ripped apart and consumed by animals]. Our brains are wired to detect threat on the flimsiest pretext, to be afraid even when there's nothing to be afraid of."[7] A child's irrational fear of the dark (which many people take into adulthood) is evidence of that. Or perhaps such a fear is not so "irrational" after all—at least to our more distant ancestors. It's a safety mechanism, a survival tool. After all, which specimen will survive to breed—the one that fears nothing and strolls out into the savanna at night, or the one who sees danger lurking in every shadow and prudently acts accordingly?

But humans must be able (both now and in the distant past) to control, to manage, this fear; otherwise our species would be paralyzed into inactivity—and into extinction. Consequently, over the millennia, man has turned to storytelling to both pass on survival strategies and to manage the fear of the predator, turning dangerous animals into monsters, gods, benefactors and even role models. "Storytelling is universal because it reflects an adaptation that helped our species survive," explains Trout. "We became a storytelling animal to deal with our predicament as a prey species—to address our fear of being hunted, killed, and eaten by predators."[8] Many cultures contain myths of animals teaching man how to hunt and kill for themselves; and most feature humans that have taken on animal characteristics, even *becoming* said animal (at least metaphorically), in order to hunt and kill more efficiently. *The Wolf Man* screenwriter Curt Siodmak summed it up concisely: "Lycanthropy goes back to the stone ages when people wanted to get as strong as the strongest animal, which was a wolf in Europe, a tiger in

In October 1997 the Wolf Man truly arrived as one of the "Big Five" of Monsterdom, receiving his own U.S. postage stamp alongside Dracula, the Frankenstein Monster, the Mummy, and the Phantom of the Opera.

India, a snake in the Pacific. They tried to identify themselves with that."[9]

Predators hunted, ate, and terrified our ancestors and proto-ancestors for several million years. Evolution insured that survival fear, thought and actions became ingrained in our species. Such genetic hard-wiring is not something that can simply be turned off and forgotten in a few millennium, no matter how "civilized" we've become. True, we are now more likely to be killed by a carelessly-driven car than a predatory big cat. But predators still haunt our existence, if nothing else than in the form of fellow humans (reflected cinematically in the slasher and serial killer subgenres). "Perhaps our greatest moral struggle," posits Trout, "is not so much with our innate homicidal impulses—though some people do have them—but with the excessive and bloody counter-offensive that springs from our displaced fear of being consumed, a fear that has roots—like storytelling and mythmaking—in the deep Paleolithic fear of the predator."[10]

And from these roots grew strange fruit. "The early human mind was inclined to attribute human traits to predators as part of a sophisticated predator-defense program," explained Trout. "This crucial ability to anthropomorphize predators became more pronounced as the human mind became increasingly more creative and imaginative. By giving humanlike mental and emotional traits to predators, our ancestors came to believe that they could 'understand' and negotiate with them.... In short, our ancestors thought they had placed terrifying creatures under some measure of control."[11] Hence the various predator-centric myths and even animal-worship cults that sprang up around the world.

"To survive, early humans not only had to think *about* predators; they had to think *like* them," continued Trout, "viewing themselves from the perspective of the animals that hunted them. This seeming mind-reading ability provided the foundation for the later phenomena of mythic identification."[12] And for the werewolf mythos.

Few things are as frightening as the idea of being hunted, killed and eaten. In the generally safe and insular world our modern society has created for us, such a notion has become a thing of fantasy. But take away our technological trappings, and this becomes a very real possibility. (Of course, such fear still has a very real basis. As anthropologist Donna Hart relates, even today "tens of thousands of people throughout the world fall victim to animal predation."[13] In African myths, humans are referred to as the "meat without hair.") Man has always had an uneasy relationship with Nature—paving over forests, fencing in the wilderness, keeping predators at bay. That's why we find natural disasters so fascinating—and frightening—they remind us of just how little we can affect, can control, Nature. And the werewolf figure does the same thing, albeit on a more intimate level: it shows us just how dangerous Nature can be, and how terrifying it becomes when unleashed directly upon our individual selves. As psychotherapist Anthony Stevens states, monsters "related us directly to our primeval origins. They are hideous manifestations of the archetype of the huge-jawed, slavering, heavily clawed predator, capable of seeking us out wherever we hide."[14]

If the vampire figure embodies our fear of death, then the werewolf embodies our fear of Nature—more specifically, the fear of our own animalistic (or "natural") tendencies. Humans are, after all, part of the natural order of things, with our roots in the animal kingdom (reactionary clergy's desperate claim to the contrary notwithstanding). The werewolf film allows us to explore and conquer these fears of our own inner nature (very often with a silver bullet, a shiny representative of modern civilization). Frank Cawson, author of *The Monsters in the Mind*, observed, "The animal root in our nature has a devastating potential. It is not something that can be played with. Once admitted and invited to take a seat at the table, the animal is like the unwelcomed guest who will not go away and who ends up in possession of the whole house."[15]

It's clear that the human and the animal exist side-by-side within us all. People can be "beasts"—that is, they can behave in a brutal and cruel (or "bestial") manner. Not all the time, and generally not to extremes, but for most individuals those animal urges are there. Humans are corporeal beings borne of the animal kingdom, with all the needs, wants and fears of any other animal. Our intellect separates us from, and elevates us above (at least in evolutionary terms by making us top of the food chain), the rest of the animal kingdom, yet our hardwired needs and urges plant us firmly within the realm of the beasts. The figure of the werewolf, therefore, can be seen as the symbolic freeing of our bestial natures, which we hide beneath our civilized veneer. Folklorist Kathryn Edwards notes, "As both human and animal—the one ideally communable and social, the other solitary and fierce—the werewolf embodies the tensions within humanity itself."[16]

The werewolf can also embody the modern world's disconnect with Nature, which brings with it the fear that we may be thrown back into a more natural state for which we're simply not prepared (reflected cinematically in the popular post-apocalypse subgenre). Because of this disconnect, werewolves have evolved over time—from something evil (in folklore) to something tragic (early cinema) to something heroic (modern cinema, novels and video games). This reflects the tenets of ecology and the more contemporary respect for (and perhaps yearning to return to) Nature. After all, Nature is primal, sensual, healthy, strong. And to ignore this "natural" side of humanity can be disastrous—to the individual as well as the species. As clinical psychologist Richard Noll observes, "When we dissociate too severely from the animal within us all, the biological imperative of human existence, by not allowing its expression

6 • Introduction

in fantasy or behavior and accepting our dual natures, then we pay dearly for it in terms of our emotional and physical health."[17]

WhatWolf?

So what exactly is a werewolf? That depends on who you ask, as there seem to be as many variations in definition as there are methods of becoming (and destroying) a lycanthrope. And this brings up another issue—nomenclature—with some considering the term "lycanthrope" a mental illness designation in which a person merely believes him or herself a wolf, versus an actual transformation into a "true" werewolf. Former priest and occult scholar Montague Summers states in his 1933 volume *The Werewolf*, "Precisely to define the werewolf is perhaps not altogether easy. We may, however, say that a werewolf is a human being, man, woman or child (more often the first), who either voluntarily or involuntarily changes or is metamorphosed into the apparent shape of a wolf, and who is then possessed of all the characteristics, the foul appetites, ferocity, cunning, the brute strength, and swiftness of that animal." The cause? "Werewolfery is hereditary or acquired; a horrible pleasure born of the thirst to quaff warm human blood, or an ensorcelling punishment and revenge of the dark Ephesian art."[18]

The term "werewolf" first appeared in English some time between 1017 and 1035 in the ecclesiastical ordinances of King Canute, though its use in the Teutonic languages dates from much earlier. *Were* or *wer* is the Old English word for man (derived from the Latin *vir*). "Lycanthrope" comes from combining the Greek words for wolf, *lycos*, and man, *anthropos*. So werewolf literally means man-wolf or wolf-man.

Author and researcher Richard Noll suggests that the notion of the werewolf stands for what he labels our "shadow self." "The creature represents the dark animal instincts that society has taught us to suppress in favor of a more civilized demeanor. Such suppression of the beast within, so to speak, can be costly in terms of our emotional health, and can ultimately surface in unacceptable, even violent behavior."[19]

Wolves have played an important part in the history of the western world, even beyond their link to the werewolf legend. Our very civilization is inextricably linked to the animal, with legend telling us that Rome itself was founded by the brothers Romulus and Remus, who as infants were suckled and raised by a she-wolf. The

Werewolf fever permeated more than just the movies, as a lycanthrope even earned his own Marvel comic book, *Werewolf by Night*, which lasted 43 issues from 1972 to 1977.

ancient Greeks included wolf cults among their worshippers; and the Roman poet Ovid wrote that the god Jupiter, displeased with King Lycan, changed him into a wolf—thus giving rise to the term "lycanthropy." (This particular myth can be traced back even further—to the ancient Greeks, who have Zeus transforming the devious King Lycaon into a wolf as punishment for attempting to trick the god into eating human flesh.) Irish folklore posits that St. Patrick punished Venetius, King of Gallia, by transforming him into a wolf.

Throughout the Dark and Middle Ages, no animal in Europe was feared—and respected—more than *Canis lupus*, the apex predator of that time and place. Even today wolves can still inspire terror in man—and rightly so.[20] Though hunted to extinction in England and France in the 1700s, they remained a viable species in places like Spain, Italy and the Balkans. In 1927 the Siberian village of Pilovo was besieged by hungry wolves that knocked down doors to attack the inhabitants. By the time the army reached their town, nearly every family had lost someone to the ravening predators.

More recently, a 2013 *Telegraph* news article noted that "the governor of Russia's largest region has declared a state of emergency after a surge of wolf attacks…. Last January [2012] a 'super pack' of 400 wolves laid siege to the remote town of Verkhoyansk, forcing locals to mount patrols on snow mobiles until the government could send in extra help."[21]

Even wolf expert Shaun Ellis (founder of Wolf Pack Management at Combe Martin Wildlife Park), who lived with a group of wolves for two years, admitted, "There's something innately terrifying about a wolf. First there is their sheer power. I've experienced the fangs of an angry she-wolf hovering above my neck. I've had my head held vice-like in a wolf's jaws. These are animals which can crush a human skull and snap thigh bones, with a bite twice as strong as a German Shepherd dog. When chasing prey, they run at around 40 mph; not particularly fast compared with big cats. But they can keep going for an hour, chasing and chasing until their quarry is shattered. They listen to their prey's heartbeat from several meters away with their uncannily powerful hearing and can judge when it is petrified—the moment they decide to go in for the kill. Then there is their intelligence. I have known of packs where wolves fill their mouths with snow when stalking so that their breath does not steam in the cold—which might give them away to their prey."[22]

Beyond the fear they inspire, wolves were (and are) important animals to many cultures. Unlike bears and most big cats (such as the jaguar and tiger), wolves are extremely social creatures. The pack members bond, communicate (their howling being a conspicuous example), and work together (when attacking an elk, for instance, one will go for the legs, another for the neck, a third for the belly, and so on). Thus, they're easier to humanize than many other species. But perhaps most importantly, they were the first animals to be domesticated, about 15,000 years ago in East Asia. Today their relatives reside in millions of households throughout the world as Man's Best Friend. In medieval Europe (where wolves were common before man hunted the species to the brink of extinction), wolves were often the bane of country folks' existence, preying on their sheep and cattle—their very livelihood—so that the wolf and starvation became enmeshed (hence the popular saying about wanting to "keep the wolf from the door"). Add to this the animal's natural ferocity, and, more pointedly, the cyclical outbreak of rabies (often carried by wolves) that figuratively transformed people into violent beasts, and the "werewolf" legend proliferated. As British researcher Ian Woodward explains, "Frothing at the mouth, which characterizes the human rabid patient, has been a distinguishing factor of the werewolf for thousands of years…. The foaming jaws, the animal rages, the crooked limbs, the savage eyes, the rabid countenance—these are the symptoms of one of the most terrifying and hideous diseases ever to afflict humanity … rabid wolf, the head and jaws all splattered with foam, is a frightening enough sight; but the wild ferocity of its attack on man is chilling in the extreme…. To the rustic mind, a rabid wolf would more than likely be seen as a werewolf, especially if that person was attacked by the diseased animal and subsequently developed all the symptoms of rabies."[23]

Additionally, one of the more curious (and strangely prevalent) ways to become a werewolf according to classic folklore is to drink water from a footprint made by a werewolf. Rabies can be transmitted through eating infected food or drinking infected water. As Woodward observes, "As wolves fastidiously lick their paws after eating a meal, could not the footprints be simply the saliva-infected impressions of rabid wolves?" Woodward continues, "Rabies was certainly raging in the Middle Ages—and so, of course, was werewolfery…. A great many of the reported werewolves were undoubtedly rabid wolves: sufficient in number (as indeed were their rabid human victims) to sow the seed for many a good werewolf story."[24]

HowWolf?

Folklore tells us so many ways to become a werewolf that one could easily wonder how anyone ever stayed human. As mentioned, drinking water from a wolf print—or even from a stream visited by wolves—can bring out one's inner lycanthrope. Committing crimes against the Church or being excommunicated can result in werewolfery. Even falling asleep outdoors during a certain night and letting the moon's light shine on one's face can lead to lycanthropy. One medieval legend has it that in Livonia (a Baltic region), reciting a particular spell while drinking a cup of specially brewed *beer* made one a werewolf. Donning a wolf skin, or wearing a belt made of wolf's hide, will transform the wearer; and eating flesh from a wolf's kill can also do the trick, as well as wearing a special flower. It has been said that heredity plays a part as well—the offspring of a werewolf may inherit the lycanthropy. Even the accident of birth can curse one with werewolfism. According to some folklore, the seventh son of a seventh son undoubtedly becomes a wolf; while being born on Christmas night, or simply under a new moon, makes it a likely prospect as well. But the most prevalent causes involve various spells and incantations, linking lycanthropy to the Devil, with witches and sorcerers actively seeking to become a man-beast for the power that it gives them, or afflicting others with an unwanted curse.

Surprisingly, being bitten by a werewolf doesn't play into most folklore (perhaps because folk tales rarely see a lycanthrope's victim survive an attack). It took Hollywood to codify this most common cause of lycanthropy in pop culture.

The moon, of course, is closely tied to the werewolf, with many films positing that the transformation only comes during the three nights of the full moon. This is quite a departure from the legends of old, which most often claim that the lycanthrope can change at will; in fact, like so much of "accepted" lycan-lore, the notion of the full moon transformation sprang directly from a screenwriter's pen. But could the moon indeed have some sinister pull on our human—or, more precisely, *animal*—nature? Many people think so. Studies have been conducted on the possible effects of the moon on man, including a 1998 investigation of 1200 inmates at the maximum security wing of the Armley jail in Leeds, England. Over a period of three months, researchers found that violent incidents measurably increased during the first and last quarter of each lunar cycle—in other words, the days on either side of the full moon. While some researchers agree that crime does rise during a full moon, one simple hypothesis holds that a full moon simply provides more light for criminal activity: increased visibility leads to increased villainy. But, of course, such a prosaic explanation seems far less romantic than the notion of a mysterious lunar force bringing out our bestial natures each month. A decade before, in 1985, psychologists Rotton and Kelly published an overview of recent studies into the effects of the lunar cycles. In it, they concluded that none of the research demonstrated a reliable link between the phases of the moon and psychiatric incidents.[25] Moreover, as to the idea of dogs and wolves howling during a full moon, park rangers and animal control officers have observed that a full moon actually tends to *calm* canines, as (again) it supplies better visibility to their surroundings. So much for baying at the moon.

During the Enlightenment, the medieval notion of werewolves as a manifestation of witchcraft and Satanism largely gave way to the idea of lycanthropy as a mental illness, as illustrated by an 1857 column in the popular periodical *Household Words* (vol. 15, no. 370): "That many people have been executed, owing to the popular impression that they were wehrwolves [sic], is … only another instance of the fatal facility with which superstition has turned disease itself into food for her love of cruelty."

So what makes the werewolf such a popular figure in today's *modern* world? "I started writing about werewolves because they aren't vampires," declared best-selling author Carrie Vaughn, creator of the popular "Kitty Norville" werewolf book series. "I think a lot of people don't relate to the aristocratic, modern, well-dressed, well-groomed, very powerful vampire. For people who are more naturalistic, they feel more kinship to the werewolf. It is a more shamanistic view. In pop culture the werewolf is often the ravening monster, but I think a lot of people don't see it that way; they see it as being close to Nature—more powerful, more spiritual than something like a vampire."[26]

"I definitely think there's a working class [connection]," added Vaughn, "and the werewolves are often viewed as the servants of the vampires. And they are more rebellious—there's a rebellion about werewolves, the downtrodden. To be a rebel and to fight against that; whereas vampires are seen as a little more Establishment—they have the nice houses, they're more civilized, and they represent this power structure. And I think for a lot of people this just doesn't appeal to them. The wild, untamed, chaotic nature of the werewolf appeals to them more."[27]

And then there's the simple matter of viewer identification. "Werewolves are alive," points out Vaughn. "So many supernatural creatures are not human or dead. Vampires are technically dead; zombies are technically dead; ghosts are *really* dead. Werewolves are still alive—that sets them apart. That makes them more appealing. That makes them more vibrant, powerful."[28]

As evidence of said vibrant power, werewolves have even made the grade at that most definitive of cultural indicators—the theme park. In 2014 Universal Studios Hollywood added a "Halloween Horror Nights" maze based upon *An American Werewolf in London*, featuring such iconic settings and moments from the film as a recreation of the Slaughtered Lamb pub, the bloody werewolf attack on the moors, the groundbreaking transformation sequence, and the porno theater scene, complete with "Zombie Jack." "The team at Universal Studios Hollywood has gone to great lengths to recreate the mood and details of the movie," praised the film's director, John Landis. "I want [visitors] to really absorb the elaborate sets, makeup and special effects custom-designed for this experience."[29]

Another thing that makes the werewolf figure so fascinating is its twist of perception. With the lycanthrope, nothing is as it seems. On the surface this monster looks human, and may even be a friend or lover. But underneath lurks a savage beast, one that we cannot outwardly perceive until it is too late (or until

The popular appeal of lycanclassics such as *The Howling* and *An American Werewolf of London* remains undiminished, as evidenced by this clever display (right) honoring the latter film and its director, John Landis, at the Science Fiction Museum in Seattle, Washington, in 2015. Also pictured at the left is the Nazi werewolf mask utilized to such startling effect in the film's terrifying dream sequence.

the moon is full), which makes it even more dangerous than other, more readily spotted monsters, such as the mummy, zombie, or very often the vampire. The werewolf is a veritable wolf in sheep's clothing. "These are cultural fears that go back 100 years," observed Werewolf-movies.com creator Noel Clay. "When you boil down the vampire, he's essentially a rapist. And when you boil down the werewolf, you basically have the betrayer. It's the friendly face with the knife behind the back."

Of course, as a monster, the werewolf is steeped in pathos—with a capitol "P"—thus providing a strong emotional connection between the pro/antagonist and the viewer. Sociologist Andrew Tudor writes in his cultural study *Monsters and Mad Scientists*, "The monster and the principal character with whom we are invited to identify are one and the same, and our concern is as much for the werewolf as for its victims. Thus most of *The Wolf Man*'s narrative drive depends on our being involved in Talbot's progressive awareness of his fate and his desperate attempts to protect the movie's heroine from his own likely actions."[30]

The werewolf can also raise a very powerful attraction-repulsion dichotomy in the viewer, in which one can be both horrified by, but at the same time attracted to, the notion of transformation. Special effects artist George Willis (*Cursed*, *Underworld: Evolution*) commented on "the idea of transformation—the Jekyll and Hyde aspect of it—being a normal person, even a shy or mild-mannered person by day that's very in-your-head, intellectual, and then by night becoming this feral, muscular, athletic creature that runs around in the wild and physically can defeat any normal human or animal foe. I think the idea of becoming this alter ego is one of the things that makes it most attractive. When this comes out and you are suddenly more powerful than those enemies that during the day would have dominion over you."[31] But like most things in life, such power comes with a price. In fact, the cost can be devastating. "Another thing I think that is attractive about the werewolf genre," continued Willis, "is the idea that it's something you can catch. Like zombies, like vampires, the idea that if you are bitten you'll become one of them. So the fear of them, and trying to avoid them or kill them, then flips once you become one of them because now you are imbued with these powers, but you are simultaneously an outsider that can't ever be part of your original community or village because you know that in a few days you're going to change and eat some of them. So your choices are eat your friends, become an outsider, or be killed. So it creates a lot of emotional dynamics between the characters."[32] As celebrated horror novelist Anne Rice wrote, "The werewolf in many instances embodies a potent blending of masochistic and sadistic elements. On the one hand, man is degraded as he is forced to submit to the bestial metamorphosis; on the other hand, he emerges as a powerful sadistic predator who can, without regret, destroy other men." She astutely concludes, "The werewolf as both victim and victimizer, wrapped in magic, may arouse emotions in us that are hard to define."[33]

WhenWolf? (or ... Larry Talbot's History Lesson)

The very first werewolf film (made, aptly enough, by the fledgling Universal film company, who a generation later codified the subgenre with the first two werewolf talkies, *Werewolf of London* and *The Wolf Man*) was probably *The Werewolf* (1913), a lost 18-minute silent short based on a Navajo Native American legend. Universal followed this up the next year with another two-reeler, *The White Wolf*, in which a captured wolf transforms into a medicine man. This short film has also followed its elder lupine sibling into the Land of the Lost. France entered the lycanthropic fray in 1924 with *Le Loup-Garou*, a movie about the killer of a priest cursed to become a werewolf. (And yes, this too has been lost to the ravages of time—early cinematic werewolves were nothing if not unlucky.) Back in the New World, *Wolfblood: A Tale of the Forest* hit American theaters in 1925, becoming the first feature-length (and currently the oldest extant) specimen. But *Wolfblood* proved to be less than, er, full-blooded in lycanthropic terms, as it featured a man who only *thought* himself a wolf (rather than the genuine wolfman

article). Werewolves remained in hibernation for the next decade until the subspecies howled again (for the first time actually *heard* by audiences after the transition from silent to sound cinema) in Universal's moderately successful *Werewolf of London* (1935).[34] It wasn't until six years later, however, with the release of the 1941 blockbuster *The Wolf Man* (which earned over a million dollars—a fortune in those days, when a movie ticket cost just 25 cents), that werewolves really sprang to life as a legitimate subspecies of horror cinema. As previously noted, unlike the vampire, Frankenstein, and Jekyll and Hyde cinematic subsets, the werewolf has no seminal text. (Guy Endore's little-read *The Werewolf of Paris* stands as, at best, a literary footnote.) Consequently, it fell to the subgenre's first big hit, 1941's *The Wolf Man*, to don the mantle of lycan-template. In essence, *The Wolf Man* (and its sequels) *became* that text, predicated on the illusory notion that the film's lycanlore was based on ancient wisdom and folkore. (*The Wolf Man*'s opening shot—of a heavy volume removed from a shelf and opened to an entry on "Lycanthropy"—reinforces this fallacy.) At this point the werewolf subgenre was born. As film historian Lee Gambin, in his book *Massacred by Mother Nature*, so concisely defines it, a subgenre is "something derived from the archetypal model but coming into its own and existing as something on an entirely different plateau, developing its own stock standards, plot devices, character types, etc." And *The Wolf Man* did just that by establishing the basic standards, devices and character types that permeate the werewolf film to this day (many of them emerging directly from the imagination of screenwriter Curt Siodmak). Things like the full moon, silver, and the tortured-soul characterization became stable tropes for the subgenre.

After *The Wolf Man*'s fiscal success, Universal brought the film's doomed pro/antagonist Larry Talbot back four more times over the next seven years, while other studios, great and small, jumped on the hairy bandwagon with entries of their own (such as Twentieth Century–Fox's *The Undying Monster* [1942], PRC's *The Mad Monster* [1942], and a pair of Columbia entries, *Cry of the Werewolf* and *The Return of the Vampire* [both 1944]). After Larry Talbot's encounter with Abbott and Costello in 1948's *Abbott and Costello Meet Frankenstein*, the brief lycan-flurry was over, and the wolfman lay dormant for another eight years until revived by our old friends at Columbia in the form of 1956's *The Werewolf*. Lycanthropes subsequently loped across cinema screens only sporadically during the Eisenhower Era, with only two further installments—AIP's *I Was a Teenage Werewolf* and Allied Artists' *Daughter of Dr. Jekyll*. Tellingly, during this Decade of the Atom—when alien invaders, big bugs and atomic mutants ruled the genre roost—two of the three features (*The Werewolf* and *I Was a Teenage Werewolf*) offered wolfmen created by *science* rather than the supernatural (and even the *Daughter* remained rather vague about its origins).

For the next decade the werewolf kept relatively quiet. In

After 1941's *The Wolf Man*, silver became an indelible part of lycan-lore. Here a handy heroine (Fabiola Falcón) sharpens a silver crucifix in the Paul Naschy starrer *Curse of the Devil* (1973) (German lobby card).

fact, you can count the number of full-on werewolf features during this period on one hand, with all but one finger pointing towards imports (and the sole home-grown entry, the "nudie-cutie" *House on Bare Mountain*, existing only as a fringe player). Then in 1968 there began the longest-running lycanthropic movie series in history, and it came not from the cinema-rich land of Hollywood but the repressed environs of Madrid, where the dictatorial Generalissimo Franco regime and strict cinema censorship had all but stifled the horror genre. After Lon Chaney, Jr.'s Larry Talbot, Spaniard Paul Naschy's Waldemar Daninsky stands as the most prolific—and important—werewolf figure in cinema history. Daninsky growled and slashed with delicious enthusiasm through thirteen films from 1968's *La Marca del Hombre Lobo* (released in America as *Frankenstein's Bloody Terror*) to 2004's *Tomb of the Werewolf*. "Unlike the films about Lawrence Talbot (Lon Chaney, Jr.)," noted Naschy in his autobiography, "which had a certain continuity, Waldemar Daninsky can move freely through space and time."[35] And move he did. Unhampered by something so mundane as continuity between entries, Naschy's werewolf met everything from vampires and demons to Dr. Jekyll and even the famous Yeti. Though not all of his celluloid misadventures made it to America (at least on the big screen), Naschy's films not only breathed new life into screen lycans, they helped spark an interest in Euro-horror that eventually permeated even the often-insular American market.

While Paul Naschy almost single-handedly kept the wolfman alive in Europe, the werewolf fell on hard times in 1970s America, with the lycan-torch kept lit (just barely) by such low-budget oddities as *Werewolves on Wheels* (1971), *The Boy Who Cried Werewolf* (1973), and *The Werewolf of Washington* (1973); plus a few TV terrors in the form of *The Werewolf of Woodstock*

The terrifying wolf-headed horrors created by Rob Bottin for *The Howling* (1981) changed the face of cinematic lycanthropy forever.

(1975) and *Deathmoon* (1978), and, worst of all, a pair of atrocious grade–Z Andy Milligan movies (*The Rats Are Coming! The Werewolves Are Here!* and *Blood*). Fortunately, a lycanthropic lifeline lay just around the corner…

In 1981, not one, not two, but *three* werewolf classics howled through the cinemas (well, two true werewolf films and one "pseudowolf" entry, anyway): *The Howling, An American Werewolf in London,* and *Wolfen*. The first two modestly-budgeted but well-produced pictures literally changed the face of werewolf cinema forever via their startling make-up and transformations (courtesy of the special effects genius of Rob Bottin and Rick Baker, respectively). These two successes quickly became the yardstick by which all modern lycanflicks are measured. The '80s proved a watershed decade for werewolves because the science of special effects had finally caught up with the transformative concepts of lycanthropy. No longer dependent on simple lap dissolves and cutaways to allow further makeup applications, werewolves in the eighties could bubble and bend and elongate in full view for their horrifically graphic transformations from man to beast. The development of prosthetics, bladders and animatronics allowed for in-your-face metamorphoses that startled, shocked, and horrified audiences, bringing home the full terror of transformation. Add in such '80s near-classics as *Silver Bullet, The Craving* (arguably Paul Naschy's best), *Ladyhawke*, and *The Monster Squad*, and the decade proved a boon to all things lycanthropic.

The Nineties seemed to offer more or less a holding pattern for the lycanthrope, until the subject appeared to stall out, taking a nosedive into such disappointing dreck as *Werewolf* (nee *Arizona Werewolf*), *The Werewolf Reborn!* and *Rage of the Werewolf*. The best the decade could offer was the big-budget disappointment of *Wolf*, the wackiness of *Project: Metalbeast*, and the above-average made-for-TV terrors of *Full Eclipse* and the two-part *House of Frankenstein*.

Fortunately, werewolves recovered (and how) with a seeming explosion in the 2000s that, like some lycanthropic Big Bang, continues to expand outwards to this day. More full-on werewolf movies have been produced in the last decade and a half than in the entire twentieth century. Why the proliferation of werewolves in the 00s and beyond? First off, the horror film in general made a resurgence post–9/11, with the werewolf riding that new wave of popularity. Though some have dismissed any possible link between horror's popularity and the cultural trauma of the 2001 tragedy as mere coincidence, others, like filmmaker Stuart Gordon (*Re-Animator, From Beyond*) saw a definite connection. "After 9/11 horror became even more popular than ever," said Gordon. "I think what that says is about the importance of horror, and how some people need horror as a way of dealing with real-life horror. There's something very healthy about horror movies."[36] George Romero (*Night of the Living Dead*) agrees. "When people feel threatened, they either go to pure entertainment or to something that might strike a chord with the fears they have in real life."[37]

Additionally, the first decade of the New Millennium saw, like the 1980s before it, a significant breakthrough in special effects—computer generated imaging, or CGI. As the decade progressed and this groundbreaking technology improved (and became cheaper and cheaper—to the point that special digital effects could be created on a home PC), the fantasy, sci-fi, and horror genres proved to be major beneficiaries. Now every filmmaker with a werewolf in mind could hang ten on this new techno-wave, creating images of transformation and otherwise impossible (or impossibly expensive) lycanthropic monstrosities.

Then there's the cyclical nature of cinema. Horror-loving filmmakers whose formative years came during the lycan-boom of the 1980s were now making their own movies, and naturally turned toward their childhood influences. For instance, *Wolves* (2014) director David Hayter noted, "*An American Werewolf in London* is one of my top ten favorite films of all time … it's the greatest telling of the classic tale that's ever been."[38] And, truthfully, that's a hard point to argue.

Reel vs. Real Werewolves

Before delving further into the cinematic world of moon-monsters and shapeshifters, let's make one thing clear—lycanthropy *does* exist. It is a recognized, documented condition, generally considered to be a symptom of schizophrenia in which a person believes him or herself to be a wolf. A 1988 article in the British journal *Psychological Medicine* titled "Lycanthropy: Alive and Well in the Twentieth Century" documents twelve cases of lycanthropy "among approximately 5000 psychotic patients treated at McLean Hospital within the last 12 years," with the dozen sufferers' diagnoses ranging from bipolar disorder to schizophrenia to borderline personality disorder. The article's authors conclude that lycanthropy appears to be a nonspecific sign or symptom occasionally seen in severe functional psychosis or, less commonly, as a factitious psychological symptom." On the plus side, they observed that "prognostically, lycanthropy does not appear to represent an ominous sign: seven of the 12 patients experienced a complete remission of their primary disorder [and] three had a partial remission," with only two remaining unresponsive to treatment. In effect, "the delusion of being transformed into an animal may bode no more ill than any other delusion."[39]

Beyond such obvious cases of psychoses, there's also a group of people who identify themselves as "therianthropes." As author Carrie Vaughn describes them, "they feel more lupine than human; they feel they have more in common with wolves and dogs than humans. The ones who've gotten in touch with me, they feel a kinship with wolves; they feel more like wolves than they do people…. They're really polite, and they're fully aware that what they're saying sounds crazy. But this is their reality, this is what they live with. And they just really appreciate when

This Japanese poster for *An American Werewolf in London* (1981) illustrates the combination of horror, comedy, romance, and ground-breaking makeup/transformation effects that spearheaded the reinvigoration of the werewolf subgenre in the early 1980s.

there's somebody out there who *listens* to them and can talk about their condition a little bit."[40]

However, there is no conclusive evidence that human beings have ever *physically* transformed into wolves or wolfmen, with the few documented sufferers changing solely in their own minds. Much like the Loch Ness Monster, Bigfoot and even Little Green (or gray) Men from Mars (Area 51 conspiracy theorists notwithstanding), the existence of physically-transforming humans remains the realm of speculative fantasy. Like with those other supposed monsters, "eyewitness accounts" are the only indication of these creatures' existence. And eyewitness accounts, it has been proven time and again by studies in the medical and psychology fields, are woefully unreliable, given the human mind and memory's problems with observation, perception and interpretation (not to mention individuals' possible ulterior motives). Stretching back nearly a century, scientists have noted, tested, and confirmed the unreliability of human observation. For example, as far back as 1918, psychologist G. M. Whipple commented that "observation is peculiarly influenced by expectation, so that errors amounting to distinct illusions or hallucinations may arise from this source…. We tend to see and hear what we expect to see and hear."[41] Expect to see a werewolf, and one may indeed interpret something seen as that very beast. More recently, research psychologist and memory specialist Elizabeth Loftus concluded in her book *Eyewitness Testimony*, "One thing is clear and accepted by all: expectations have an enormous impact on what a person claims to have seen."

Still, much like with the rest of these fascinating yet unproven phenomena, volumes have been written on the supposed "reality" of werewolves—despite a complete lack of hard (physical) evidence for same. So why do some people persist in believing that werewolves—the fanged, clawed, baying-at-the-moon manbeasts—do exist? Because human beings fear the unknown. And throughout our existence as a species we have interpreted, reasoned, and just plain made up explanations when we had none. The existence of supernatural beings explains the heretofore inexplicable, and though perhaps frightening in themselves, we find such things far less terrifying than the complete unknown. And in the case of werewolves, we've even made up a set of rules by which they behave, thus codifying and extracting at least some of the terror from them. Before the Enlightenment, Medieval authorities concocted all sorts of explanations for the bizarre, often violent behavior of the mentally ill. They were possessed by a demon, cursed by a witch—or were a werewolf.

See Larry Run

Returning to cinema … why are there so many less-than-satisfying werewolf flicks? If clothes make the man, then yak hair makes the werewolf (Universal's makeup genius Jack P. Pierce famously employed this unlikely substance to create *The Wolf Man*). Makeup is critical to the cinematic lycanthrope. As my writer friend Brian Smith pointed out, it's quite difficult to create a convincing original wolfman makeup (hence the frequent reliance on variations of the classic Pierce creation); and a poor makeup simply looks cheesy and ridiculous. All it takes to create a vampire, on the other hand, is a pale complexion and a set of fangs; while a Frankenstein's Monster can be as elaborate or as simple as the budget allows (merely a shaved head and a few stitches produces a credible specimen—just ask Robert DeNiro). But a werewolf needs a head completely covered in hair, along with some kind of canine snout, a mouthful of fangs, and wicked-looking claws. It's not an easy job concocting a convincing lycanthrope … though apparently it's an inspiring one. Makeup effects artist Emersen Ziffle (*WolfCop*) labeled the werewolf "the character we all dream of making. Creating werewolves for cinema is still popular, and will continue to be. For an effects artist, werewolves let you tap into the crazy, wild side of the craft. There is so much to learn and put into practice when given this task; it is so inspiring."[42]

Also requiring inspiration—and this is key—is the all-important metamorphosis. A werewolf movie needs to at least *suggest* a transformation (the very bedrock of the werewolf mythos). Such a transformation personifies—and visualizes—the conflict between light and dark, the inner turmoil of right vs. wrong, the shift from good to evil (or at least civilized to savage). This primal element stretches back to the beginning of storytelling itself. As Paul A. Trout observes in *Deadly Powers*, "In myth and folklore, the most dramatic shape changing entails the transformation of a human into a predatory hybrid creature both human and animal, such as a werewolf, were-bear, were-shark, were-lion, and so on (*were* meaning 'man'). For tribal peoples, such creatures seem to be everywhere because it is natural to assume that a particularly intelligent animal—one that displays the remarkable cleverness of a human—is animated by a human spirit lurking within, or that it is at least under the control of a human whose identity may be hidden."[43]

Beginning with Paul Naschy's *Frankenstein's Bloody Terror* in 1968, transformation often came with demonstrable pain, as the afflicted—the *conflicted*—suffered untold agonies, writhing and moaning as the metamorphosis came over him or her. This metaphor for Evil ripping and tearing through Good to claim the body (and soul?) became fully visualized with Rick Baker's groundbreaking special effects on *An American Werewolf in London*, as joints popped painfully, fingers elongated agonizingly and the face bubbled and twisted to screams—then howls—of pain from the tortured protagonist.

So let's say a filmmaker has overcome the odds and brought their inspiration to life, so to speak, via an impressive lycanthrope and convincing transformation. Once you've covered your lead actor in hair and fur, there's little s/he can do but snarl and growl and perhaps rip out a few throats. Talking werewolves rarely work well (just ask the *Werewolf of London*), seeming more silly than sinister. Perhaps what often differentiates a good werewolf movie from a mediocre or even bad one is what the lycanthrope does while in *human* rather than lupine form. This is where the crucial element of pathos comes in—the sympathy, the tragedy, the humanity. And this means character development, dialogue, and story—things that every film needs to excel at in order to transcend mediocrity. In short, a werewolf movie is a movie like any other, but with a few *additional* challenges necessitated by its lycanthropic nature. So it's little wonder there may well be only "eight good ones" (hyperbolically speaking).

About the Book

As noted, metamorphosis is key to lycancinema; consequently, vicious wolves or wolf-monsters that do not transform fail to qualify for inclusion here. That lets out such creatures as the frightening monster-wolf from *The Neverending Story* (a fantastically articulated oversized puppet), the grotesquely oversexed (and over-endowed) rat-bear-wolf creature from Walerian Borowczyk's *The Beast* (1975), the hyena-like monstrosity from *Brotherhood of the Wolf* (2001), and the red-eyed canines of the hilariously non-p.c. *Helen Keller vs. Nightwolves* (2015).

Despite what this humorous publicity still implies, it wasn't actress Eveyln Ankers who created Lon Chaney, Jr.'s Wolf Man but makeup maestro Jack P. Pierce, whose painstaking efforts gave birth to the iconic figure of *The Wolf Man* in 1941.

In this book I'm sticking strictly with *feature* films, as the inclusion of the myriad shorts and near-countless TV episodes would require another full volume. I do cover made-for-TV movies, however (as long as they reach feature length). Additionally, I've studiously avoided—for both my sanity and yours—those amateur productions that failed to find a legitimate distributor. In other words, self-promoting basement mail-order operators need not apply. This criteria lets me (and you, gentle reader) off the hook for such excruciating claptrap as David "The Rock" Nelson's *Miss Werewolf* (2001) and Bill Zebub's aptly-titled *The Worst Horror Movie Ever Made* (2004). You're welcome. And while I've included sexploitation films that offer werewolfery along with its softcore antics, I've decided to eschew the flat-out hardcore porn variations (such as *Leena Meets Frankenstein* [a sex-infused remake of *Abbott and Costello Meet Frankenstein!*], 2009's *This Isn't The Twilight Saga Eclipse*, and the amusingly slavish *An American Werewolf in London XXX Porn Parody* [2012]), as that's a whole other, er, kettle of lupines. Even with all these judicious exclusions, however, there still remains well over 300 lycan and lycan-related films to discuss, dissect, devour, delight in or denigrate.

Films are listed alphabetically by their English-language title (U.S. theatrical or, if no such release, their most common video/DVD moniker). Purists may cry foul and point out that movies should be designated by their original country-of-origin names, be it in Spanish, Cantonese or Swahili. While such an approach might bring a smug smile to the faces of a few hardline cineastes, most of us in the English-speaking world (specifically the United States) recall Paul Naschy's original wolfman outing as *Frankenstein's Bloody Terror*, not *El Marca del Hombre Lobo*. And who among us would recognize *Meng gui zue tang* as *The Haunted Cop Shop II*? (Of course, who among us would even recognize *The Haunted Cop Shop II* at all?) Each film's original language title, however, plus any English-language alternate or re-release appellations, are listed alphabetically in the text for cross-referencing purposes.

Each full-on werewolf entry will close with a "Morphology" listing (indicating the type of werewolf showcased); "Demise" (detailing how it met its fate); and "Full Moon Rating"(to encapsulate the film's merit—or lack thereof—via a concise zero-to-five-moons rating system).

The "Pseudowolves" chapter details all those films that offer up a werewolf "cameo" (rather than spotlighting a lycanthrope as a main character), as well as anthology movies that feature a werewolf in just one of several episodes. Likewise included here

The funny yet terrifying lycanthropes of the 2011 Spanish horror-comedy *Game of Werewolves* light the way for the future of lycan-cinema.

are those pictures in which the werewolf turns out to be a hoax, and foreign lycan flicks that failed to make their way into the English-language market (i.e. were never dubbed or subtitled in English). Note: Vampire films in which a bloodsucker turns into a wolf (such as the original *Fright Night*, *Dracula 2000* and *Bram Stoker's Dracula*) are not included, the reasoning being that vampires are already "monsters" rather than human beings.

While the wolf remains by far the most common form of shapeshifter in popular culture, a variety of were-creatures have crossed the silver screen as well. The "Other Were-Beasts" section spotlights those films in which humans transform into animals or animal-hybrids other than wolves (or wolfmen). Such lycan-cousins as Cat-Creatures, Wasp-Women, Gorilla-Men, and even a Turkey-Monster are all represented here. Keep in mind that in order to make the cut, there has to be transformations back and forth from man to beast (i.e., those films in which said change is a one-time-only, permanent affliction—*The Fly* or *The Beast Within*, for instance—are excluded). Likewise, the transformation has to be into something recognizable (more or less) as animal in origin. Consequently, were-demons, such as those found in *Cry of the Banshee* and *The Beast of the Yellow Night*, and non-specific monstrosities like *The Man and the Monster*, *The Hideous Sun Demon* and *Atom Age Vampire* (not to mention any Jekyll and Hyde iteration) will have to wait for their own book.

Two appendices—"Werewolf Cinema Chronology" and "Werewolf Film Series and Subsets"—offer listings that delineate the chronological evolution of the cinematic werewolf, and show how certain films group together in terms of sequels, subject, and format.

The Big WereQuestion

"We've all got both light and dark inside us," proclaims werewolf Sirius Black in *Harry Potter and the Order of the Phoenix*. "What matters is the part we choose to act on—that's who we really are." Indeed, as human beings we are truly defined by our actions. But do we always have a choice? Like so many homilies and philosophical bromides, there's an opposing viewpoint that sounds just as valid ("strike while the iron is hot" vs. "look before you leap"; "out of sight out of mind" vs. "absence makes the heart grow fonder"). Curt Siodmak wrote that "the Wolf Man knows that his fate might change when certain circumstances come together and that he is powerless to fight fate. It dawned on me that all of us are 'Wolf Men,' that fate rules our destiny."[44] Do we truly choose or does fate indeed choose for us? Werewolf films force us to ask this Big Question, with the best of them exposing and exploring along the way our dichotomous nature as human beings.

Real Evil celebrates Reel Evil: oil painting created in prison by serial killer John Wayne Gacy (responsible for the deaths of at least 33 young men). Among this real-life monster's favorite screen monsters are Freddy Krueger, Jason Voorhees, Count Dracula, the Frankenstein Monster … and the Wolf Man (The Crime Museum, Washington, D.C., 2015).

"The most wonderful thing about horror is that it endlessly gives pleasure as the world continues to change," observed Oscar-winning director Mike Nichols, who took a detour down the lycan-highway with *Wolf*. "There are basic, terrifying stories that we want to hear again and again. The variations give us great satisfaction and help us to understand our lives a little better. We never get tired of ghost stories around the campfire."[45] Nor of werewolf tales on a full moon night.

The evolving nature of cinematic werewolves reflects the evolving nature of our culture, our society, even our day-to-day existence. Modern consumer society has become disposable, as have to some degree our personal bonds. When we uproot ourselves on an almost periodic basis (not only in terms of locale but in our evolving interests and pursuits), our friendships become disposable as we "move on." With such increased mobility, and such a segmented culture, our "packs" have become liquid, malleable. Consequently, we may find (subconsciously at least) the idea of a lifelong "pack" (symbolizing unconditional bonding) and lifelong "mates"—both attributes of the wolf—quite appealing.

Further, the very American focus on individuality often comes at the expense of cultural belonging. Now that individualism—rather than conformity—has become a valuable commodity, werewolves can become heroic; they don't always need to be destroyed. Such an attitudinal shift has been reflected by recent films like *Dylan Dog* (2011), *Wolves* (2014), *WolfCop* (2014) and the *Twilight* series (2009–2012). Of late, far more avenues have opened up for the figure of the werewolf. Where once it was merely a creature to be feared and pitied, now it can be admired and even hero-worshipped.

Richly thematic, in addition to their basic functions of exploring notions of self-control, loss of identity, and alienation,

Today werewolves are serious business (or business, anyway), as shown by "Howl Con," an annual two-day convention celebrating all things lycanthropic.

werewolf films can wear subtextual coats woven from such fascinating threads as ethnic and class differences (the *Underworld* series), the pain of adolescence (*I Was a Teenage Werewolf*, *Ginger Snaps*), and even coming to grips with old age (*Late Phases*).

"In my screenplay," observed *The Wolf Man* scripter Curt Siodmak, "I delineated the character of the Wolf Man, a figure that has haunted people's fantasy for two thousand years."[46] And it has haunted the silver screen ever since, with no sign of the lycan-theme slackening any time soon. As author Brian J. Frost observes in *The Essential Guide to Werewolf Literature*, "There is, after all, nothing more effective than the werewolf story for exploring the murky realm of the unconscious and revealing the awful deeds it can inspire."[47]

"I don't think interest in werewolves is dying," opined *Wolf-Cop* director Lowell Dean. "I believe that—as with most things in popular culture, be they other monsters or superheroes—popularity is cyclical. There may be lulls in which we have fewer werewolf films, but since the release of the original *Wolf Man*, the character has been a staple of cinema. There will always be some form of dual-identity character on the big screen—be it a new *Dr. Jekyll and Mr. Hyde* or *The Incredible Hulk*. In my personal opinion, the werewolf is underused right now, and has great potential—not just as a CGI puppy or as sidekick to a vampire. The concept is ripe for development."[48] And now it's time to explore that development so far … and perhaps do a little howling at the moon along the way.

Notes

1. "The Love Bug," by David Edelstein, *Rolling Stone* 484.
2. That would be one Mr. Mark Clark, erudite film critic and historian, and author of such works as *Smirk, Sneer and Scream: Great Acting in Horror Cinema* and *Star Wars FAQ*.
3. Author Stephen Jones put together a slim volume entitled *The Illustrated Werewolf Movie Guide* back in 1996, but its brevity and haphazardness makes it far from definitive and of limited use.

4. "Lycanthropy Lives On," by Patrick G. Coll et al., *British Journal of Psychiatry*, vol. 147.
5. "Director James Isaac Talks *Skinwalkers*," by Todd Brown, Twitchfilm.com.
6. *Monster of God: The Man-Eating Predator in the Jungles of History and the Mind*, by David Quammen.
7. *Deadly Powers: Animal Predators and the Mythic Imagination*, by Paul A. Trout.
8. Ibid.
9. "An Outspoken Interview with the Sultan of Speculation: Curt Siodmak," by Dennis Fischer, *Filmfax* 13.
10. *Deadly Powers: Animal Predators and the Mythic Imagination*, by Paul A. Trout.
11. Ibid.
12. Ibid.
13. "Humans as Prey," by Donna Hart, *The Chronicle of Higher Education*, April 21, 2006.
14. *Aridadne's Clue: A Guide to the Symbols of Humankind*, by Anthony Stevens.
15. *The Monsters in the Mind: The Face of Evil in Myth, Literature, and Contemporary Life*, by Frank Cawson.
16. *Werewolves, Witches and Wandering Spirits: Traditional Beliefs and Folklore in Early Modern Europe*, by Kathryn Edwards (ed.).
17. *Vampires, Werewolves and Demons: Twentieth Century Reports in the Psychiatric Literature*, by Richard Noll (ed.).
18. *The Werewolf*, by Montague Summers.
19. *Vampires, Werewolves, and Demons: Twentieth Century Reports in the Psychiatric Literature*, by Richard Noll (ed.).
20. Arguably history's most evil and hated individual aligned himself with the dread figure of the wolf. As noted in Barbara Ehrenreich's *Blood Rites: Origins and History of the Passions of War*, Adolf Hitler identified strongly with *Canis lupus*, naming his favorite dog Wolf, labeling the SS his "pack of wolves," feeling the strong appeal he exuded for the masses stemmed from his "wolfishness," and even ordering Mimi Reiter, an Austrian teenager he was briefly involved with in 1926, to call him "Wolf."
21. "Wolf Attacks Lead to a State of Emergency in Russia's Siberia Region," by Roland Oliphant, *The Telegraph*, January 6, 2013.
22. "As 400 wolves lay siege to a village … have these ruthless killers lost their fear of humans?" by Shaun Ellis, DailyMail.com, February 10, 2011.
23. *The Werewolf Delusion*, by Ian Woodward.
24. Ibid.
25. "Much Ado About the Full Moon: A Meta-Analysis of Lunar-Lunacy Research," by J. Rotton and I.W. Kelly, *Psychological Bulletin* 97.
26. Carrie Vaughn interview with the author, February 2014.
27. Ibid.
28. Ibid.
29. "Universal Adds 'American Werewolf in London' to Halloween Horror Nights," by Austin Siegemund-Broka, Hollywoodreporter.com, August 11, 2014.
30. *Monsters and Mad Scientists: A Cultural History of the Horror Movie*, by Andrew Tudor.
31. George Willis interview with the author, February 7, 2014.
32. Ibid.
33. "Whither the Werewolf," by Anne Rice, *The New York Times Book Review*, April 5, 1987.
34. Some sources cite a 1932 German film called *Loup-Garou* as the first sound lycanthrope, but this obscurity is now lost—if it even existed at all.
35. *Memoirs of a Wolfman*, by Paul Naschy.
36. *Reel Terror*, by David Konow.
37. Ibid.
38. "Interview with David Hayter for his film *Wolves*," by Joseph Falcone, Gonewiththemovies.com, December 27, 2014.
39. "Lycanthropy: Alive and Well in the Twentieth Century," by Paul E. Keck, et al., *Psychological Medicine*, vol. 18.
40. Carrie Vaughn interview with the author, February 2014.
41. *Vampires, Werewolves and Demons: Twentieth Century Reports in the Psychiatric Literature*, by Richard Noll (ed.).
42. "Where Are the Wolves?" by Craig Anderson, *Fangoria* 329.
43. *Deadly Powers: Animal Predators and the Mythic Imagination*, by Paul A. Trout.
44. *Wolf Man's Maker: Memoir of a Hollywood Writer*, by Curt Siodmak.
45. "Who's Afraid of Nichols' *Wolf*," by Chuck Crisafulli, *Fangoria* 131.
46. *Wolf Man's Maker: Memoir of a Hollywood Writer*, by Curt Siodmak.
47. *The Essential Guide to Werewolf Literature*, by Brian J. Frost.
48. "Where Are the Wolves?" by Craig Andersen, *Fangoria* 329.

THE FILMS

Abbott and Costello Meet Frankenstein

(1948; Universal-International; b&w) Director: Charles T. Barton; Producer: Robert Arthur; Screenplay: Robert Lees, Frederic I. Rinaldo, John Grant; Cinematographer: Charles Van Enger. Cast: Bud Abbott, Lou Costello, Lon Chaney, Bela Lugosi, Glenn Strange, Lenore Aubert.

> The Monsters of Menace vs. The Masters of Mirth!—ad line

Many have argued (and continue to do so) that horror and comedy don't mix, a debate that began here, with this first ever out-and-out "horror-comedy." (It took John Landis ten years to get *An American Werewolf in London* made for this very reason. Said Landis, "Everyone who read the script had one of two reactions: 'This is much too scary to be funny' or 'This is much too funny to be scary.' They could never see that it was meant to be both.") Lon Chaney, Jr., the Wolf Man himself, weighed in by opining, "I used to enjoy horror films when there was thought and sympathy involved. Then they became comedies. Abbott and Costello ruined the horror films; they made buffoons out of the monsters." But Chaney and the other naysayers failed to realize that the best horror-comedies (*A&C Meet Frankenstein* included) treat their monsters with respect, utilizing them for genuine chills as well as occasional chuckles. And *Abbott and Costello Meet Frankenstein*, one of the best horror-comedies ever made, offers both in abundance.

While Lou Costello often receives the lion's share of credit as the humorous heart of the famous comedy duo, one shouldn't overlook straight man Abbott's considerable contribution. Many of the pair's laughs arose from verbal routines, honed to perfection during years on the vaudeville circuits (as evidenced by their most famous bit, "Who's on First"), rather than slapstick. Abbott's perfectly-timed delivery and often-flustered persona proved indispensable. As frequent A&C director Charles Barton observed, "In his last years, Lou tried to work without Bud—but he knew damn well he couldn't."

By 1947, Abbott and Costello had fallen out of favor with their home studio, Universal, which had just merged with William Goetz's International Pictures to form Universal-International. The comedians had made 20 hit films for Universal, but their most recent efforts, while still profitable, failed to pull in the punters like before. The days of Abbott and Costello's Top Ten Box Office star status had gone, and Goetz "wanted nothing to do with Abbott and Costello" (according to Barton). Fed up with the duo's antics (including epic, production-delaying poker games and prodigious practical jokes), it was rumored that Abbott and Costello were not long for the Universal lot.

Then producer Robert Arthur came up with the idea of having the Boys 'meet' Universal's stable of monsters, including Frankenstein's Monster, Dracula and the Wolf Man (and originally Kharis the Mummy, Dracula's son Alucard and the Invisible Man as well). Veteran A&C writers Frederic Rinaldo, Robert Lees and John Grant pounded out a script entitled *The Brain of Frankenstein* (dropping the Mummy and Dracula's offspring) in which the Count (Bela Lugosi, playing his most famous character for only the second—and final—time) works with female mad scientist Dr. Mornay (Lenore Aubert) to revive the Frankenstein Monster (Glenn Strange). To this end they need a brain "so simple, so pliable, it'll obey like a trained dog," and settle on the cranium of baggage handler Wilbur (Costello). It's up to Wilbur, his friend Chick (Abbott), and Lawrence Talbot, the Wolf Man himself (Lon Chaney, Jr.), who's trailed Dracula from Europe, to foil the vampire's plans.

Upon reading the script, Costello reportedly commented, "You don't think I'll do that crap, do you? My five-year-old daughter can write something better than that!" But the lure of a $50,000 advance on his percentage, and a name change to the more flattering *Abbott and Costello Meet Frankenstein*, brought Lou around, and the production went ahead.

Good thing too, for, from the wonderfully spooky-yet-comical dungeon-and-graveyard cartoon animated opening credits to the final "sight" gag with the Invisible Man (cameo-voiced by Vincent Price), this is a treat for classic monster and comedy lovers alike. Taking the terror seriously, Barton and company fashioned imposing castle sets, a wonderfully creepy grotto, chilling torture chamber (complete with hellish glowing pit) and atmospheric swamp for their monsters to prowl. One element that sets this film apart from lesser horror spoofs is that it takes its monsters seriously, the laughs arising from Abbott and Costello's *fear* of the creatures, not from poking fun at them. In fact, the picture offers one of the most startling sequences seen in any of the Wolf Man movies when Chaney transforms into a werewolf while sitting in a chair and then vents his demonic fury by viciously ripping at the upholstery in a frightening display.

The picture begins with a bang (or growl), when, only five minutes in, Talbot transforms into the Wolf Man. (With Jack Pierce having fallen victim to the Universal-International merger a year earlier, it was up to new head of makeup Bud Westmore to recreate Pierce's iconic Wolf Man look.) The scene opens with Talbot (in London) staring pensively through some window blinds as he tries to get a call through to a Florida baggage company and stop delivery on the two crates containing Dracula and the Frankenstein Monster. But the moon rises and he transforms. Wilbur, hearing snarls and growls on the other end of the line, admonishes, "You're awfully silly calling me all the way from London just to have your *dog* talk to me." But the laughter changes to shudders when the sequence ends with the Wolf Man savaging the chair.

"I am not an artist," claimed Chaney, "I am a useful actor." And useful he was. By this point in the series, however, there wasn't much left for

Wilbur (Lou Costello) unwittingly makes a narrow (and comical) escape from Larry Talbot's vicious Wolf Man (Lon Chaney, Jr.) in *Abbott and Costello Meet Frankenstein* (lobby card).

his Talbot character, and Chaney had to make do with adopting an earnest, almost hangdog demeanor and spouting lines like "I came all the way from Europe because Dracula and the Monster must be destroyed" and "You think I'm mad." Fortunately, he receives better treatment as his alter ego, with a quartet of scenes giving full athletic reign to his bestial portrayal of a savage manbeast. (Here the scripters made something of a lunar gaff, however, as they have Talbot transforming on *four* consecutive nights; even a schoolboy knows the moon remains visibly full for only three.) Chaney received $10,000 for his five weeks work (the same amount he earned on his last outing in the yak hair, *House of Dracula*).

Though director Charles Barton characterized Lon Chaney, Jr., as "a hell of a guy" and "excellent" actor, he noted that "Chaney was unpredictable. He could really hit the bottle sometimes. He was a Frankenstein when he was on the bottle." Ironically (given Barton's metaphor), he was also a Frankenstein (Monster) in the movie itself. When Glenn Strange broke his foot towards film's end, Chaney volunteered to don the Monster makeup for the scene in which the creature tosses Lenore Aubert (actually Aubert's stunt double, Helen Thurston) out a window.

While making *Abbott and Costello Meet Frankenstein* offered its fair share of fun (including impromptu pie fights started by Bud and Lou—"we had a pie bill of $3800 a picture," recalled Barton, "which they just charged to the studio"), things were not so joyous for Lon Chaney, Jr., in real life. Following shooting, but before the film's release, the actor, after a fight with his wife Patsy on April 22, 1948, attempted suicide by downing 40 sleeping pills. Found unconscious in his truck by his son Ron, Chaney spent time in the Van Nuys Receiving Hospital in critical condition before recovering and reuniting with his wife and family.

Filled not only with classic monsters, but with genuinely funny dialogue (Talbot: "In half-an-hour the moon will rise and I'll turn into a wolf." Wilbur: "You and 20 million other guys.") and A&C set-pieces (a hilarious variation on the team's 'Moving Candle' gag, for example, this time involving Dracula's coffin lid), the film couldn't help but be successful.

And successful it was. *Abbott and Costello Meet Frankenstein* proved to be the best earning Frankenstein film since the 1931 original—*and* the most successful werewolf effort since 1941's *The Wolf Man*, becoming one of the biggest hits in Universal's history to this point. The studio's second-cheapest production of that year, it was their second-biggest moneymaker, resulting in a string of 'Meet the Monsters' pictures, beginning with *Abbott and Costello Meet the Killer, Boris Karloff* (1949) and concluding with *A&C Meet the Mummy* (1955). Arguably the best horror-comedy ever made (and definitely the best of A&C's 'monster meetings'), *Abbott and Costello Meet Frankenstein* stands as a joyous, funny and fitting tribute to Universal's classic comedy team *and* their famous roster of movie monsters, the Wolf Man included.

With quotes from: *Reel Terror*, by David Konow; *It's Alive!* by Gregory William Mank; *Bud & Lou: The Abbott and Costello Story*, by Bob Thomas; "The Life Story of Lon Chaney, Jr.," by B. Gelman Jackson, *Monster Fantasy* 1, no. 4; "Lon Chaney, Jr., Part Two," by Jack Gourlay, *Filmfax* 21.

MORPHOLOGY: Classic Wolf Man
DEMISE: Fatal fall into the sea (with Dracula in tow)
FULL MOON RATING: ****½

Alvin and the Chipmunks Meet the Wolfman!

(2000; Universal) Director/Producer: Kathi Castillo; Screenplay: John Loy; Animation Director: Karen Peterson. Cast (voices): Ross Bagdasarian, Janice Karman, Maurice Lamarche, Miriam Flynn, Rob Paulson, April Wynchell, E.G. Daily.

Something's up with Theodore…—trailer

Yes indeed, that "something" being that he turns into a werewolf! Everybody's favorite trio of "mischief-makers" (as the trailer dubs them) returns in this direct-to-video animated feature follow-up to the previous year's *Alvin and the Chipmunks Meet Frankenstein*.

This time, Simon, Theodore and lovable troublemaker Alvin, along with their manager/surrogate father Dave and their gal pals the Chippettes, run afoul of a lycanthrope when a certain Mr. Talbot moves in next door (voiced by ubiquitous voice artist Maurice Lamarche, whose seemingly endless credits include *The Simpsons, Futurama, Team America: World Police*, and the pseudowolf entry *Big Top Scooby Doo!*). Though monster-obsessed Alvin suspects the mystery man (who always carries a silver wolf-headed cane) of being a werewolf from the get-go, it takes a lot of convincing before anyone believes—and only after the youngest, Theodore, is bitten one night and thereafter transforms into a cute, friendly lycanpuppy. It all comes to a head at the premier of their school play, "Dr. Jekyll and Mr. Hyde," when the chipmunks face down the rampaging werewolf and save the day.

Alvin and the Chipmunks were created by Ross Bagdasarian, Sr., for a novelty record in 1958. Bagdasarian (whose stage name "Dave Seville" was utilized for the group's human manager/adoptive father) voiced all three Chipmunks. After a couple of records, the Chipmunks earned their own comic book and cartoon show in the 1960s. When Bagdasarian died in 1972 of a heart attack, his son, Ross Bagdasarian, Jr., took over, providing the voices alongside his wife, Janice Karman. Further records, TV specials, and a series followed in the 1980s. In 1996 Universal purchased the rights to the characters and produced the direct-to-video feature *Alvin and Chipmunks Meet Frankenstein* in 1999, followed by this entry. The 2000s brought a trio of live-action/CGI Chipmunk movies, but without the participation of Bagdasarian and Karman.

With *Alvin and the Chipmunks Meet the Wolfman!* being a pre-teen-friendly feature-length cartoon, it's little wonder that much of the film's already brief (76-minute) running time is taken up by various "cute" or "meaningful" subplots involving Alvin's monster-mania, the chipmunks' travails in putting on the school play, or Theodore being bullied at school. Oh, and there's a trio of songs, too. Consequently, after a brief (black-and-white) prologue that sees Alvin chased through a very Universal-esque forest by a growling beast (which turns out to be a dream), a long time passes before any werewolfery rears its hirsute head. And this comes in the form of the painfully cute Theodore's nightly transformation into what looks like a cross between a wolf cub and a teddy bear that lopes about on all fours in his jammies, and who acts like a cuddly puppy (even licking his brothers' hands and playing with a roll of toilet paper!).

The *real* manbeast (Talbot's genuinely imposing werewolf) only appears at the climax (though he bit Theodore, this earlier attack occurs off-screen). This cartoon werewolf looks fairly impressive, with its muscular, hair-covered frame, sharp talons, and fierce fanged face framed by a leonine mane of fur.

Like Paul Naschy's *Dr. Jekyll and the Werewolf*, this film juxtaposes the Jekyll and Hyde theme (via the school play Our Heroes are rehearsing) with lycanthropy—though in a kids' movie context. Consequently, the script makes very little of the duality theme, apart from Dave at one point advising Theodore how to play the monster half of his Dr. Jekyll character. "Just think about Mr. Hyde," Dave says, sympathetically, "part man, part monster, angry at the world, different from everyone else." Such compassion can be carried over to the figure of the lycanthrope. Though frightening when finally seen, the werewolf isn't truly evil, just an ill-tempered outsider. In fact, when the transformed were–Theodore defends his brothers and friends from the rampaging monster, he ends up biting the huge beast-man on the hand, resulting in them both transforming back to normal. At this, Talbot sincerely thanks Theodore … before revealing that he is their new school principal (another type of monster?).

The lycanthropy "cure" affected here is novel, if nonsensical. As Simon (the smart one) explains, "Mr. Talbot bit Theodore and turned him into a werewolf. Then when Theodore bit him back, it reversed the process and cured them both." Indeed. But at least scripter John Loy (who penned episodes for a number of cartoon series, as well as various *Land Before Time* sequels and the Chipmunks' earlier *Meet Frankenstein* feature) adds a few more accepted bits of lycan-lore (at least of the cinematic variety), such as the notion that a werewolf will bear in his palm "the Mark of the Wolf" (a paw print–like mark), and how wolfsbane "keeps werewolves away" (which makes little sense here, actually, given the fact that Talbot grows the plant in his garden). Alvin even reads *The Wolf Man*'s "Even a man who's pure of heart…" ditty in his "*Monster Book of Monster Facts*."

Of course, Loy is not above taking a few potshots for a laugh, or shamelessly playing up the cuteness factor. For instance, TV horror hostess Madame Raya, whose show Alvin watches religiously, at one point nonsensically quips, "Did you know that werewolves are allergic to spandex? Maybe that's why you've never seen your mailman wearing bike shorts, ha ha ha ha." Later, when Alvin and Theodore seek her out for advice on how to deal with their werewolf brother, she explains, "A were-chipmunk is unusual but not unheard of. Of course, it's different from a human werewolf. For one thing, your brother is already closer to the primitive animal state." This explains why Theodore changes *every night* and not just during the full moon, like Talbot.

Loy also includes a subplot that might bring a rueful smile to the faces of former "Monster Kids." With the monster-obsessed Alvin scaring himself by watching horror movies, then accusing various people of being monsters (ironically, he turns out to be spot on with Talbot, but by then he's become "the Boy Who Cried Werewolf"),

Dave finally announces, "This monster mania of yours has gotten completely out of control. As of now, your monster days are over. No movies, no models, no 'Dr. Jekyll and Mr. Hyde.' You're going cold turkey." With that, Dave pulls the monster posters off Alvin's walls and sweeps his models and figures into a box. It's a bittersweet scene that many a monster-loving kid can relate to. Comically, Alvin later goes into "monster withdrawal" in his bare room. "The walls are closing in on me; I can't breathe," he gasps. "How can I survive?!"

Still, even former Monster Kids viewing *Alvin and the Chipmunks Meet the Wolfman!* will find themselves wishing for far less "cute" and far more "bite" from this meeting. Fine for the under-10 set, this silly werewolf tale will have most everyone else howling—not with laughter but with frustration.

MORPHOLOGY: Cuddly, puppyish were-chipmunk; massive, fur-covered biped
DEMISE: None; they're both cured
FULL MOON RATING: *

An American Werewolf in London

(1981; Universal; UK/US) Director/Screenplay: John Landis. Producer: George Folsey, Jr.; Cinematographer: Robert Paynter. Cast: David Naughton, Jenny Agutter, Griffin Dunne, John Woodvine, Brian Glover, Lila Kaye, David Schofield.

A different kind of animal—trailer

Indeed it is—a cinematic animal as unique, innovative and groundbreaking as it is frightening, funny and entertaining. "This was my attempt to make a movie dealing with the supernatural in a completely realistic way," explained *An American Werewolf in London* writer-director John Landis. "What do you do when the unreal is real? That was my premise." To that end, Landis set his monster movie in contemporary London, staging pivotal scenes in Trafalgar Square, Piccadilly Circus, and even a seedy downtown porno theater. Landis likewise abandoned the traditional lycan-notion of silver bullets (when David asks Jack about needing silver ammunition, his undead friend dismissively—and amusingly—responds, "Get serious, David") and eschewed the typical horror movie music, replacing it with moon-themed classics like Credence Clearwater Revival's "Bad Moon Rising," Van Morrison's "Moondance," and Bobby Vinton's "Blue Moon." ("I wanted to use [Cat Stevens'] song 'Moon Shadow,'" noted Landis, "but he wouldn't let us use it. ...He was very religious and he disapproved of the film.") In effect, Landis dragged the Gothic figure of the werewolf into the harsh light of modern day—and made it that much more terrifying.

College friends David Kessler (David Naughton) and Jack Goodman (Griffin Dunne) begin a three-month backpacking tour of Europe in Northern England. In the small village of East Proctor they encounter unfriendly locals who warn them to "Beware the moon" and "Keep off the moors." But as they set out that full-moon night they're attacked by a huge beast. Jack is killed and David wounded before the locals arrive and shoot the animal. But just before David passes out he sees the body of a naked *man* in place of the beast. David awakens after three weeks in a London hospital and begins a romance with his nurse, Alex (Jenny Agutter), while at the same time trying to hold onto his sanity after his dead friend Jack starts popping up to warn David of his impending change into a monster, and to urge him to "sever the wolf's bloodline" by committing suicide. When the next full moon comes, David indeed transforms into a four-legged beast that savagely claims the lives of six people before he awakens in the wolf pen at the London Zoo (!) with no memory of the night before. Finally realizing he's not crazy, and that Jack was right, a frantic David flees from his newfound love ("I'm not safe to be with," he tells Alex in a panic) to face his destiny.

While most assessments of this acknowledged lycan-classic focus on such elements as the brilliant blending of humor and horror, the self-reflexive music, the innovative shocks, and the groundbreaking special effects, the film's core still remains, like its *Wolf Man* model, tragedy. Here are two young men venturing out to see the world, whose Grand Adventure ends—through no fault of their own—with death and ... worse. Having been in that situation myself (a young man backpacking around Europe, *not* having become a werewolf), I know how it feels to see the world as nothing but prospects, and how thrilling, how alive it makes you feel. At that point in your life, and in that situation, every day truly *is* a new adventure, and the future stretches before you like a vast sea of possibilities. To have that ripped away—to, in fact, be urged to choose to take it away yourself—might just be too great an ask. This is the great tragedy at the core of *An American Werewolf in London*. It's not merely the loss of life, it's the loss of youth, of possibilities, of what makes life a truly amazing and marvelous gift. And what keeps the film from collapsing into a rubble-strewn emotional warzone for the viewer is Landis' brilliantly-timed use of gallows humor. The scene in which David's various victims cheerfully suggest all the myriad ways in which he can kill himself, for instance, offers some welcome cathartic humor with a black-as-pitch tone.

Rather than ad-hoc jokes or cheap laughs, the film's comedy springs primarily from the juxtaposition of the terrifying and the absurd. At one point David's doctor tries to reassure his patient with, "Now I'm sure if there were a monster roaming around northern England we'd have seen it on the telly." Then there's the almost surreal scene of David awakening naked in the London Zoo's wolf cage (a rather logical place for a werewolf to bed down in the middle of an urban metropolis, actually) and having to steal a little boy's balloon bouquet to hide his nudity until he purloins a woman's coat as he sprints past a park bench, leading to uncomfortable stares as David stands barefoot (and bare-assed) beneath the lady's garment while waiting for a bus. (Shooting the zoo sequence offered a few extra challenges to the naked Naughton, apart from the cold. "The female [wolf] was, as they say in England, 'in season,'" recalled the actor. "She would come over and sidle up to me. Well, I was a little nervous. Her boyfriend is right there watching, and he's a wolf! I was delighted to get out of that cage.") And the sight of David desperately trying to get arrested by standing in Trafalgar Square and shouting "Queen Elizabeth is a man!" and "Shakespeare was French!" at the top of his lungs can't help but raise a chuckle. ("I was quite embarrassed [while shooting] it," admitted Naughton, "and, in fact, you can see that—it was done with a lot of energy, with me spinning away from the camera shouting, 'Queen Elizabeth is a man.' I thought they might want to dub all that, which is why I spun away from the camera. 'Surely they won't use that?'")

The sharpest humor, however, involves the easy interplay between David and the undead Jack. As co-star Jenny Agutter observed, "John [Landis] wanted me to be absolutely honest. The comedy doesn't work if you're not completely sincere about something." When the gory Jack, bits of tattered flesh dangling from his face and neck, initially appears to David, the first words out of his undead mouth as he glances at David's unappetizing hospital breakfast tray are, "Can I have a piece of toast?" Later Jack complains, "Have you ever talked to a corpse? It's *boring!*" When David protests to his gruesome friend, "You're not real," Jack dismissively answers "Oh, don't be a *putz*, David" and con-

An American Werewolf in London • 25

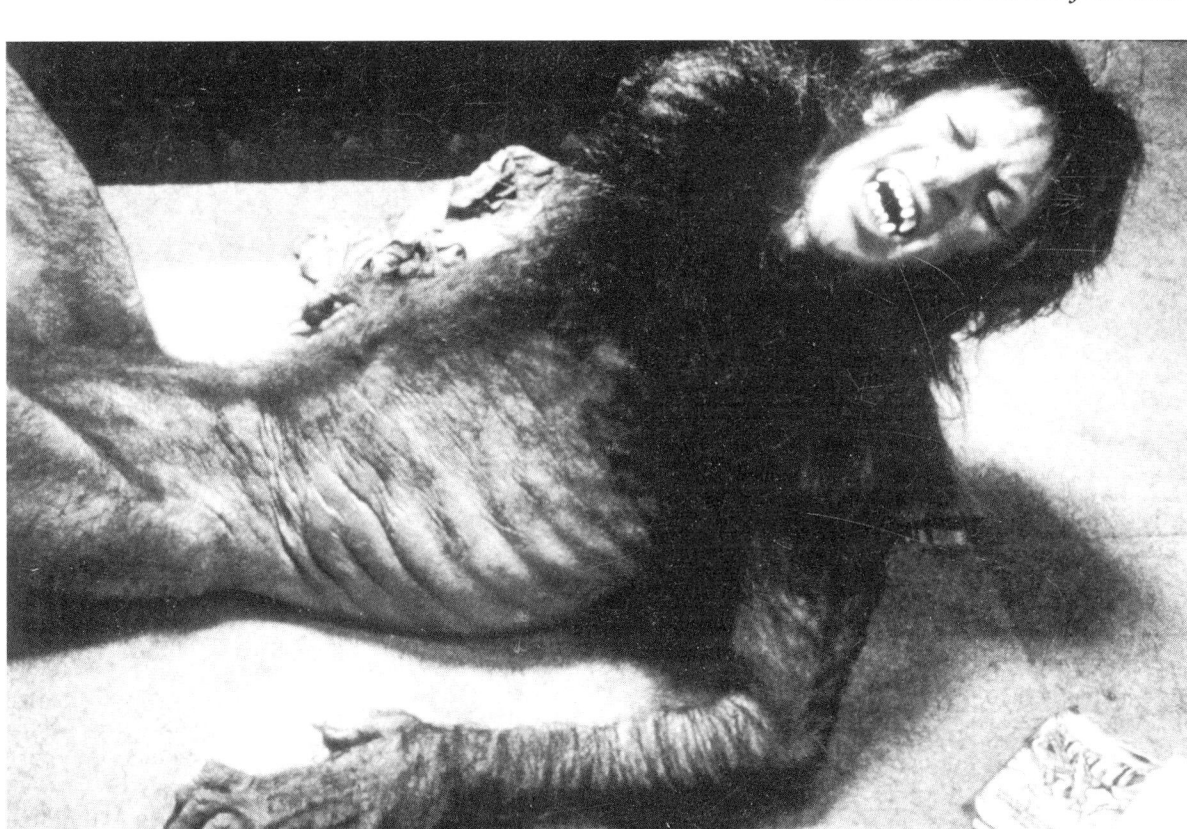

tinues on with his exhortations. "*Goddammit* David, please believe me," pleads Jack, "you'll kill and make others like me; I'm not havin' a nice time here."

Though the source of much of the film's black humor, the decaying Jack still remains a darkly ominous figure, but one whose ghastly green complexion is tempered by the pale hue of compassion. "Take your life, David," he bluntly urges at one point, "kill yourself—before you kill others." Jack then offers to his distressed friend, "Please don't cry. Beware the moon, David."

Despite the periodic comedy, *An American Werewolf in London* remains first and foremost a (highly effective) horror movie. As Landis himself observed, "*American Werewolf* is a very straightforward horror film that happens to be very funny." The sudden and visceral attack scenes are particularly shocking, and powerfully disturbing, beginning with Jack's death, when we see the beast violently ripping into Jack's chest and throat as the young man

Top: The *An American Werewolf in London* extended transformation sequence, courtesy of effects genius Rick Baker, forever raised the bar for werewolf cinema. Baker earned a Best Makeup Oscar (the first ever awarded by the Academy of Motion Picture Arts and Sciences) for his groundbreaking efforts. Pictured: David Naughton in mid-transformation. *Bottom:* Transformation complete: This behind-the-scenes snapshot shows off Baker's quadruped beast in all its glory.

screams and pleads. "My intention at the time was to make that violence truly horrific, and it is," said Landis. "Jack's death is particularly horrible, and it was meant to be."

Landis noted that "one of the film's functions [is] to surprise you. I wanted to keep the audience constantly off balance, as much as David and Jack are when they face the supernatural." One way he does this is by seamlessly blending fantasy with reality. Plagued by bad dreams (of roaming the forest naked, slaughtering a deer with his bare hands, even waking up as a monster in his hospital bed), David's dreamscapes become hyper-real so that both he and the viewer can't distinguish them as such until their bloody and horrific conclusion, leading to several gruesome shocks that come one after the other as startling nightmares *within* nightmares. As a shaken David exclaims upon awakening from one particularly terrifying dream-within-a-dream, "Holy shit!" Holy shit indeed.

The writer-director also provides one of the most action-packed, chaotic, and shocking scenes of climactic mayhem ever to grace a lycanthropicture. And he did it by filming for two consecutive nights (between two and four a.m.) on one of the busiest and most iconic urban landscapes in the western world—London's Piccadilly Circus. When the werewolf breaks out of a theater onto the street, it causes mass chaos as cars—and a double-decker bus—crash into one another, sending bodies flying through windscreens and storefronts. (One of the bystanders thrown through a plate glass window is Landis himself, who started in films working as a stuntman.) As the beast charges down the street, snapping at fleeing pedestrians, pandemonium ensues as out-of-control vehicles ram, run over or crush anything—and anyone—in their careening path in a series of shocking stunts that brilliantly encapsulate the carnage.

Landis writes his characters as three-dimensional figures, with the actors bringing them to realistic, even poignant, life. The beautiful yet vulnerable English-girl-next-door Jenny Agutter (who spent a week in a hospital as a nurse's aide in preparation for the shoot) noted of her role, "It was a solid part. These are real characters in real situations, and that's what's funny about it. That's what's frightening about it, too, when the nightmare becomes real."

By having their lycanthrope move on all fours (rather than walk upright), and erasing all vestiges of human-like features (from its hulking quadruped body to its snarling wolfish visage to its unthinking, vicious nature), Landis and creature designer Rick Baker makes this American Werewolf not merely a melding of man and animal, but a terrifying erasure of all humanity. This is no Wolf*man*, for *nothing* even remotely human remains, either in its form or its behavior, so that it becomes the ultimate loss-of-identity nightmare. Other lycanfilms have taken this tack as well, but few have brought the horror to such involving, palpable life as *An American Werewolf in London*.

Landis plays with the usual werewolf tropes, keeping some (the full moon), discarding others (silver), and creating new ones out of whole cloth, such as the original—and brilliantly cinematic—notion of having the werewolf's victims become "the undead" (which gives rise not only to some horrific images but some of the film's edgiest comedy). As a gruesome-looking Jack solicitously tells a distraught David, "Now I'm really sorry to be upsetting you, but I have to warn you … I was murdered—an unnatural death—and now I walk the earth in limbo until the werewolf's curse is lifted.… The last remaining werewolf must be destroyed; it's you, David." Jack looks more decayed, more ghastly, each time he appears to David, until by film's end he's nearly a talking skeleton (a frighteningly realistic Baker-built puppet).

The film's centerpiece—the amazing Rick Baker-designed two-and-a-half-minute transformation sequence—took a week to film and was all done "in camera" on the set (with no dissolves or optical work). Not only that, it took place in a brightly-lit room, with no shadows to cover potential flaws and hide the effects. "My intention was no tricks," said Landis. "In the whole sequence, there's only one cutaway. That was all in the script, and it was all designed to make it as visceral and realistic as possible, to take something patently absurd and make it realistic."

Not only does this transformation look utterly convincing, it appears horrifyingly *agonizing*. Though other lycan-films had depicted the transformation as painful, *American Werewolf* took the metamorphosis to new hellish heights, casting the change from good to evil in an excruciatingly protracted light as flesh split, bones twisted, and joints cracked, leaving the afflicted to endure minutes of pure agony while his inner beast fought its way to the surface. And because of our identification with the likable David, we can almost feel his agony ourselves. "I envisioned the metamorphosis from man to beast as a violent and painful one," explained Landis. "I also specified that the sequence take place without cutaways and in bright light. The gifted makeup artist Rick Baker accomplished this with an elaborate combination of makeup, foam appliances, and what he called 'change-o' body parts. These were elaborate puppet reproductions of parts of Naughton's body (including his torso, hands, feet, head and face) that could actually stretch and transform into the wolf monster in real time on camera. This sequence took five days to shoot. I ended up using one cutaway: of a toy Mickey Mouse silently watching. Rick won the first of his many Academy Awards for his groundbreaking work."

At times actor David Naughton felt like he was indeed undergoing a form of torture. "After eight or 10 hours in makeup," recounted the actor, "we would finally get out on the set and shoot for 45 minutes. That would be it. One day, I was in makeup for 16 hours. It was the longest day of my life. We shot for three or four hours, different angles, all kinds of moves, so that they would have anything they needed in editing. I was a complete vegetable by the end of that day. After all that, I really wanted people to come away saying, 'Maybe werewolves *do* exist.'"

John Landis wrote his *American Werewolf* script back in 1969 at age 19, while he was working as a production assistant on *Kelly's Heroes* in Yugoslavia. "It was very ahead of its time in so many ways," praised Rick Baker, "and the fact that John had written it ten years before he made it, it seems that much more amazing." Impressed by the film's then-unconventional mix of humor and horror, Baker enthused, "I think John made a unique movie that makes people still talk about it today. If it was a straightforward horror movie with horror movie lighting and horror music, I don't think it would be remembered as well."

After the $100-million success of *Animal House*, Landis was handed carte blanche to make any movie he wanted, but his *American Werewolf* script still proved a tough sell to the studios—particularly since he wanted to avoid casting "stars" as the leads. "I wanted you to accept the complete reality of these people," explained Landis. "It's a complicated issue with name actors, with stars, because now, with marketing, it would be very difficult to get the money but also to sell it with total unknowns, because marketing costs are so high and so important. …At that time, I had made three films that had made a lot of money—*Kentucky Fried Movie*, *Animal House* and *Blues Brothers*—and based on that I was able to do *American Werewolf* the way I wanted, and was able to hire unknowns."

"Of all the movies I've made," concluded John Landis, "*American Werewolf* comes closest to my original intention. …With *American Werewolf in London*, I accomplished what I set out to do. The film works. It's funny and frightening. And I'm proud of it."

Shot for $10 million over the course of nine weeks, the movie earned three times that at the box office, becoming the most successful horror film of 1981 (based on North American rentals). Over the years it has developed an ardent following and garnered accolades from many industry leaders and institutions.

Horror movie maestro Wes Craven (*A Nightmare on Elm Street*, *Scream*), who went on to make his own lycan-flick with *Cursed* (2005), labeled *An American Werewolf in London* the perfect werewolf movie. "[Landis] introduced a state-of-the-art transformation, which had never been seen before. The other great thing is that he introduced this weird combination of terror and humor. And the humor made it incredibly human. …If you look at what came for the next twenty years, there was nothing really like it."

Director Edgar Wright (*Shaun of the Dead*, *Hot Fuzz*) introduced a screening of *An American Werewolf in London* in April 2013 for the "BFI Screen Epiphanies" series. He labeled it his "favorite film," going on to say, "It was the first kind of cross-genre film that I'd ever seen, and it's influenced everything *I've* done ever since. And *Shaun of the Dead*, even though it's a zombie film, the film Simon [Pegg] and I always looked to would be *An American Werewolf in London* because it's really scary and it's really funny and you care about the characters."

In 2008 *Empire* magazine named *An American Werewolf in London* the 107th greatest film of all time. Not *horror* film, mind you, but the 107th greatest *film*, period. That's quite an accolade, and one thoroughly deserved, as *An American Werewolf in London* may very well be the greatest werewolf movie ever made.

With quotes from: *Monsters in the Movies*, by John Landis; *Minds of Fear*, by Calum Waddell; "When the American Werewolf Howled," by David McDonnell, *Fangoria* 129; "An American Werewolf's Girl," by Tony Earnshaw, *Fangoria* 313; "Bad Mood Rising," by W. Brice McVicar, *Fangoria* 307; *Reel Terror*, by David Konow.

MORPHOLOGY: Huge wolfish quadruped
DEMISE: A hail of (ordinary) bullets
FULL MOON RATING: *****

An American Werewolf in Paris

(1997; Hollywood Pictures; UK/Netherlands/Luxembourg/USA/France) Director: Anthony Waller; Producer: Richard Claus; Screenplay: Tim Burns, Tom Stern, Anthony Waller (based on characters created by John Landis); Cinematographer: Egon Werdin. Cast: Tom Everett Scott, Julie Delpy, Vince Vieluf, Phil Buckman, Julie Bowen, Pierre Cosso, Tom Novembre, Thierry Lhermitte.

THINGS ARE GOING TO GET A LITTLE HAIRY—trailer

And that about sums up the level of sophistication in this belated (16 year) follow-up to the classic *An American Werewolf in London*. Though not the worst were-sequel to howl at the screen (several *Howling* entries vie for that "honor"), *An American Werewolf in Paris* does its parent production no favors—to the point where the original's creator completely disassociated himself from it. "I was really disappointed when I saw that [film]," said *An American Werewolf in London*'s writer-director John Landis (who had nothing to do with the sequel). "I thought it was lousy." Indeed.

Andy McDermott (Tom Everett Scott), travelling to Paris with two friends, Chris (Phil Buckman) and Brad (Vince Vieluf), sneaks into the Eiffel Tower after hours in order to bungee jump (!) off the top. But they're interrupted by a beautiful French girl intent on committing suicide. Andy saves her (via an improbable bungee-jumping feat), and the two quickly fall in love. The problem: the girl, Serafine (Julie Delpy), is a werewolf. Andy is bitten, and while he suffers the effects of the curse, the two were-lovers must face down a vicious pack of eager lycanthropes, led by Serafine's former boyfriend Claude (Pierre Cosso), who intend to use their "gift" to rid Paris of riff-raff (such as Americans).

Competently shot, with evocative lighting, atmospheric sets (built in a studio in Luxembourg, as Paris' restrictions and costs relegated shooting in the City of Light to just a few days), impressive locations (including a Gothic graveyard), and fluid camerawork, *An American Werewolf in Paris* admittedly *looks* good. But beneath the glossy skin lies a disappointingly insubstantial skeleton, despite a few thematic points of interest. For instance, while Serafine (and, of course, Andy himself) sees lycanthropy as a curse (with Serafine falling into despair after the "cure" her stepfather had been working on turns out to be just the opposite), Claude and his small gang see it as a "gift"—which he uses to stage "Full Moon Parties" at which his pack dismembers and eats all those attending. "We have a mission," Claude tells Andy, "to purify the world. That's why we pick our victims from the scum of society … the stupid, the lazy, who breed and multiply, weakening the human race." Here lycanthropy serves as a grisly eugenics tool. Then there's the notion that Andy's only hope of a salvation lay in his beloved—literally, as he can only be cured by *eating* the heart of the werewolf that made him. But rather than exploring these intriguing themes, the script tosses them off so perfunctorily (each in one brief scene) that they become mere superficial cogs in an action-generating machine. And with this preoccupation with the (often ridiculous) stunts and running about, the film loses its heart (and head), so that the out-and-out horror of Andy's tragic situation becomes lost in all the noisy CGI-heavy set-pieces.

The production's problems extend past the shallow script. The two leads spark zero chemistry, coming off as nothing more than a pair of actors in the same shot. Rather than the self-reflexive, clever and often subtle black comedy of the first film, *Paris*' tone is one of goofy incredulity (right down to the predictable—and silly—happy ending that slaps the tragedy right off the film's face). None of the three male leads take much of anything seriously, meaning the viewer can't either. Despite this unserious approach, the film's attempts at outright comedy fall flatter than a Parisian crepe, including a ridiculous Inspector Clouseau–like policeman, Alex's two buddies wrestling for change while sifting through some trash, and dialogue along the lines of "How'd you do that—do you work out?" (after the diminutive Serafine easily tosses aside a belligerent thug). The sole amusing moment comes when Claude stages another killer party, but for "Americans Only" (reflecting the general French antipathy towards the U.S.). But perhaps most disappointing of all, at least to lycan-fans, are the werewolves themselves…

John Landis had penned a sequel script (with many of the original characters returning), but Polygram Pictures, who held the sequel rights at the time, rejected his screenplay. "They hated it," recalls Landis. "It was really odd—it was not conventional in any way. They were horrified, and I thought that was a good reaction to a horror script. But they were aghast; they thought it was too outré." So Landis effectively walked away. "They said, 'We still want to make a sequel.' I told them, 'OK, I don't want to know. Just send me a check.'"

Scripting chores then fell to writers Tim Burns and Tom Stern, with the latter also attached as director. "I've always felt that the Achilles' heel of the werewolf genre is the fact that the monsters are sort of awkward-looking," pronounced Stern. "They're always half-man and half-beast, and they don't look organic; they don't look like well-engineered predators. For that reason, the movies have fallen short of reaching into that primal fear that reminds us that we're prey, the sensation that *Jaws* or *Alien* gave us." Stern consequently developed "a 100 percent killing machine, an awesome, huge, 600-pound werewolf.

We decided to use the biggest, meanest predator on land as our model, so we designed our creature around lions and tigers, keeping the facial characteristics of a wolf." However, with *Paris* conceived as a $10–12 million project, Propaganda Films (the original production company) decided to up the ante, meaning that an untried director like Stern was out, replaced by "name" director Marco (*Demolition Man*) Brambilla. Eventually, Brambilla gave way to Anthony Waller—as did Stern's original werewolf concept, which morphed into a biped beast (that could stand upright yet still lope on all fours) when Waller bought the property from Propaganda and rewrote the existing screenplay. What emerged was an ungainly-looking creature with sparse hair strewn over its large, lumpy body; big splayed feet; and a boxy face that looks more feline than lupine (complete with a leonine mane of hair around the head and shoulders). And while the CGI utilized to bring the beast to life was state-of-the-art at the time, it possesses that subtle incorporeal feel that jars terribly with the occasional animatronic insert.

In a drastic departure from the first film, *Paris*' transformation sequence offers none of the protracted agony of the original, lasting mere seconds. Through CGI morphing, Serafine's face takes on a demonic cast, her ribcage changes, then hair grows on her legs and her knees bend backwards into elongated wolf feet. Though the company handling the CGI, Santa Barbara Studios, developed some new software specifically for this project, it still fell well short of the weremark.

Paris carries over *London*'s innovation of making the werewolves' victims the "undead"—rotting manifestations cursed to wander in limbo until the werewolf that killed them is destroyed. But in trying to up the ante by providing Andy with *two* haunting apparitions, *Paris* abandons the blackly comic yet compassionate byplay between David and his undead friend Jack in the original, leaving only a dour Brad and a ditzy bimbo (Andy's first victim) to deliver exposition and annoyance, respectively.

Paris provides something new to lycanlore, however. Here werewolves must eat human hearts to survive (Serafine does so by "acquiring" them from the hospital at which she works, while Claude and his pack's parties supply their victims). And lycanthropy can be cured by consuming the heart of the beast that made you. The film also introduces a drug (concocted by Serafine's stepfather) that was supposed to suppress the change but instead causes a lycanthrope to transform instantly, regardless of the moon. This allows for the two "good" lycanthropes (Andy and Serafine) in human form to go after the "bad" werewolves (Claude and his cronies) in wolf form, ending in a werewolf-vs.-werewolf climactic smackdown when, cornered by a werewolf and out of bullets, a desperate Serafine injects herself with the serum. Unfortunately, the resulting rolling and grappling of these cartoonish, not-quite-substantial CGI monsters proves highly unsatisfactory, as the occasional brief close-up inserts of animatronic muzzles contrasts and points up the artificiality of the computer-generated creatures.

"We didn't want people in theaters noticing the changes and saying, 'This is CGI and this is prosthetics,'" noted FX supervisor Bruce Walters. "The idea was for the werewolf to look the same in both worlds, whether an actor in a costume or a monster created by computer." At this they failed, since the viewer simply can't help but notice the differences.

"I'm a fan of the first *American Werewolf*," stated director Anthony (*Mute Witness*) Waller, "which I've seen many times, but this movie will be even funnier and scarier." Not by half. Nor does it have any real connection to *An American Werewolf in London*. Originally, the script cast Serafine as the daughter of Alex, the nurse (played by Jenny Agutter) who fell in love with David in the original. She became pregnant, left London, and passed the lycanthropic curse down to her French-born daughter. But all references to this (or anything else from the original) were excised from the release print, leaving this *American Werewolf* adrift on its own in Gay Paree. Also omitted were the first film's involving characterizations, genuinely funny black humor, startling shocks, imposing beast and amazing physical effects work.

An American Werewolf in Paris took in $26.5 million upon its release—and received a critical drubbing. Given its $22 million budget, this proved a less than successful return. And it's a sure bet that few of those ticket buyers went away happy. This is one trip to Paris a discerning cinematic traveler would do well to skip.

With quotes from: "Bad Mood Rising," by W. Brice McVicar, *Fangoria* 307; "A Lycanthropic Sequel in Limbo," by Mark Salisbury, *Fangoria* 129; "The American Werewolf That Wasn't," by Michael Gingold, *Fangoria* 134; "French Kills with *An American Werewolf in Paris*," by Caroline Vié, *Fangoria* 167; "Monster Invasion: *An American Werewolf in Paris*," by Caroline Vié, *Fangoria* 162.

MORPHOLOGY: Seven-foot-tall biped
DEMISE: Ordinary bullets; the claws and fangs of another werewolf
FULL MOON RATING: **

Angel Warriors 2 see Werewolves on Wheels

Arizona Werewolf see Werewolf, 1996

Assignment Terror

(1970 [Germany]/1972 [US TV]; Hispamex/AIP; Spain/West Germany/Italy) Original Language Title: *Los Monstruos del Terror*. Alternate Title: *Dracula Versus Frankenstein* (UK). Directors: Tulio Demichelli, Hugo Fregonese (uncredited); Producer: Jaime Prades; Screenplay: Jacinto Molina Alvarez (Paul Naschy); Cinematographer: Godofredo Pacheco. Cast: Michael Rennie, Karin Dor, Craig Hill, Patty Sheppard, Angel del Pozo, Paul Naschy, Ella Gessler.

The Ultimate in HORROR!—ad line

Spain's Paul Naschy, who both scripted and acted in *Assignment Terror*, is the combined Christopher Lee and Peter Cushing of Continental cinema. In fact, to carry the Hammer analogy further, he's also the Terence Fisher (or at least Freddie Francis) of Eurohorror. In addition to starring in nearly three dozen terror films (in which he plays everything from werewolves and mummies to hunchbacks and vampires), Naschy also directed over a dozen of the features himself.

A professed lover of Gothic horror in general and the Universal classics in particular ("All the marvelous films made by Universal Studios in the 1930s are the main source of inspiration for all my work," he stated), Naschy almost single-handedly began a Gothic revival in Spanish cinema in the late 1960s and '70s with his scripting, acting in, and ultimately direction of the Waldemar Daninsky/Werewolf series. Though few Americans know his name or have seen his films, the dedicated Eurohorror aficionado and offbeat cineaste have been seeking out his movies for years. While the plots are sometimes trite, the production values often suspect, the acting usually bad, and the dubbing always atrocious, Naschy's films show an eccentric enthusiasm and appeal in a quirky, almost quaintly exploitative fashion that no American or British-produced horror film of the same era can duplicate.

What sets Naschy's movies apart from (and *above*) the often mean-spirited and cynically exploitative product of his contemporary countrymen is Naschy's respect and outright affection for the cinematic horror tradition. Though Naschy's budget-conscious and sometimes puerile journeys into Gothic fantasy are no better *cinematically* than most of the genre Eurotrash of the decade, their story lines possess an appealing dose of almost wistful nostalgia—spiced, of course, with the requisite dashes of sex and blood. "I wouldn't say that Paul Naschy was marvelous nor that he was very good," admitted the writer-actor-director himself, "but for any person who sits down to watch a film of mine on the big screen or on television, I believe it will communicate to him that what he is watching was made with love." And in the Spanish/West German/Italian co-production *Los Monstruos Del Terror* (which became *Assignment Terror* when released to U.S. television in 1972), Naschy wears this affection on his monstrous sleeve.

Alien Dr. Varnoff (Michael Rennie, a long way from Klaatu in *The Day the Earth Stood Still*) comes to Earth from the planet Ummo on a mission to destroy the human race by unleashing all the classic monsters upon humanity: Dracula, the Frankenstein Monster, the Werewolf, and the Mummy. (Naschy had also included the Golem in his original script, but the production had to pare down the monster roster for financial reasons.) To this end Varnoff inhabits a human body, sets up his lab in a castle, and goes about collecting his supernatural specimens.

"The idea occurred to me to make the definitive 'monsterthon,'" explained Naschy (who reprises his signature character, Waldemar Daninski the Werewolf, from *Frankenstein's Bloody Terror*) about the movie's genesis, "including some extraterrestrials as well. The idea was that an alien agent would reunite all the monsters who had occasioned our most ancestral fears, and bring them to life in order to dominate mankind. The idea, that later was not in the film because we weren't able to finish it as we had wanted, was that he was going to create authentic clones of these monsters in order to help the extraterrestrials to dominate and colonize the Earth. It brought the most classic Gothicism to the modern-day theme of UFOs."

The first thing to strike the viewer on *Assignment* (apart from its outré plotting) is that the film definitely appears "of its time." The go-go

This German lobby card showcases the quartet of monsters (and their poor makeups), including Paul Naschy as Waldemar the werewolf, revived by aliens in *Assignment Terror*.

dancers, mini-skirts, sideburns, bright garish lights and generic psychedelic music traps it firmly in the amber of the Love Generation. This "mod" feel contrasts jarringly with the impressive authentic castle settings, cobwebbed torture chambers, creepy catacombs and general attempt to build a Gothic atmosphere around the classic monsters.

Makeup artist Rafael Ferrer wasn't quite up to the task of Naschy's ambitious monster-laden script. Waldemar the Werewolf (Naschy in his second lycanthropic outing—unless one counts the unfinished/unreleased *Nights of the Werewolf*) appears far less impressive here than in his previous incarnation in *Frankenstein's Bloody Terror* (1968). His wild-haired Lon Chaney, Jr.–style makeup ends with coarse fur hanging off his head and cheeks, leaving the center of his face bare, with nary a nose-piece in sight. Consequently, despite an impressive set of sharpened teeth, he looks more ape-man than wolf-like. Worse, the "Living Mummy" (as he's referred to by several characters), from the way his head is bandaged, appears more like a skinny man with a splitting headache than a 3000-year-old walking corpse. The Frankenstein Monster (referred to as the "Franksillian Monster" for no discernible reason) is a ridiculous ersatz copy of the Universal creation. The actor, in green face and with half-closed eyes, looks more like a fatigued costume party-goer than a creature stitched together from dead bodies. "I had the bad luck," complained Naschy, "of having to count on the worst makeup man of my entire career, Rafael Ferrer, who defrauded us all."

Surprisingly, Naschy didn't give himself much dialogue, nor does the film develop much personality for Waldemar—apart from the tragic curse of his lycanthropy. He spends most of his few human scenes as the unwilling pawn of Varnoff (silently wielding a pickaxe and doing the heavy lifting while digging out the Living Mummy from his tomb, for instance). In fact, it's nearly 50 minutes into the picture before Waldemar utters his first line. But at least he gets the girl, as he asks the obviously adoring Ilona, "Why are you helping me?" and she answers, "I don't really know—perhaps because I'm a woman." Indeed.

Assignment Terror puts a new notch in the old silver bullet. After Varnoff and his helpers retrieve Waldemar's body from his family tomb, they operate to remove the bullet from his heart (cue some real-life open heart surgery footage). Varnoff announces, "The bullet in his heart only immobilized him, left him seemingly dead. His death is permanent only if the bullet is fired by a woman who loves him enough to die for him." A technicality, perhaps, but a decidedly romantic one. And a later dialogue exchange concisely coalesces the very nature of the beast, so to speak:

> ILONA: "Is [Waldemar] a man or a monster?"
> VARNOFF: "Both. The eternal dilemma of mankind—good and evil—the paradox."

According to Naschy, this *Assignment* did not go at all smoothly. "Filming took several months and was fraught with financial difficulties," he recalled. "Work on the film was halted numerous times for financial reasons, only to continue as the Italians and the Germans put in their part of the money." And then the original director quit. "After a few weeks [director Hugo] Fregonese walked off the job and was replaced by Tulio Demicheli, a good friend and wonderful director, who had to deal with all sorts of problems." Though Fregonese receives no on-screen credit, according to Naschy, "the bulk of the film was directed by Fregonese; percentage-wise, it was more or less 70 percent Fregonese and 30 percent Demichelli." Naschy also related how, during the shoot he became acquainted with an occult-obsessed German actress named Barbara Muller who turned out to be a Devil worshipper. She took him to a genuine Black Mass (involving animal sacrifices), which, said Naschy, was "something which has long haunted me and given me many sleepless nights."

Despite its rather rambling and disjointed feel (with numerous characters coming and going, and various plot threads unraveling into tangents that rarely weave back into the whole), and the disappointing appearance of its classic monsters, *Assignment Terror* still has plenty to offer the classic (and not-so-classic) horror and werewolf fan. First off, Naschy homages the movies he loves in the very names of his characters. The girl who ends up falling for Waldemar is named Ilona, sharing the same moniker as the female star (Ilona Massey) of Naschy's self-professed favorite horror film, *Frankenstein Meets the Wolf Man* (1943). And Varnoff's helpmate is called Maleva, a nod to the gypsy woman who guided and protected Larry Talbot's *Wolf Man* through his first two films. Most impressively, Naschy brings to malevolent life every little monster-lover's dream of pitting the classic creatures against one another—in this case treating viewers not only to a longer, more satisfying version of the battle royale between the Wolf Man and the Frankenstein Monster as seen (disappointingly briefly) in *Frankenstein Meets the Wolf Man*, but the novel sight of a Werewolf battling a Mummy—a first in monster history. "The film has a double climax," enthused Naschy, "the Wolfman (Waldemar Daninsky) engages in almost surreal combats with the Mummy and the Frankenstein Monster in two scenes which clearly pay homage to the classic *Frankenstein Meets the Wolf Man*." Naschy fills this nightmare-come-to-life with appropriate energy, as he snarls and leaps and slashes at his undead bandaged foe, who, despite occasionally tossing the Werewolf aside, appears to get the worst of it. Unfortunately, this ground-breaking encounter ends in something of a cheat when the Werewolf goes against his lupine nature and grabs a torch to set the Mummy ablaze. Every monster-loving *child* knows that no self-respecting savage werewolf would ever go *near* an open flame.

Assignment Terror turned out to be Michael Rennie's last genre outing. In his autobiography, Naschy wrote, "Very few people know that Robert Taylor, the great Robert Taylor, phoned me at home, much to my surprise. Somehow he'd read the script and was very keen to play the part of Odo Varnoff. …I was full of enthusiasm and the next day I rushed to tell [producer Jaime] Prades the great news: Robert Taylor wanted to be in the picture. Prades, to my amazement, frowned and told me that Warners had insisted on the part being given to Michael Rennie. When Rennie turned up he was suffering from severe asthma and could only shoot very brief scenes at a time." The actor died the following year. Let's give one last "Klaatu barada nikto" before we bring the curtain down.

Though released (and re-released) successfully across Europe (and even Mexico and South America), *Assignment Terror* never saw the inside of an American movie theater. According to Sam Sherman (whose company Independent International unleashed *Frankenstein's Bloody Terror* on America), he sought to secure the U.S. distribution rights. But, said Sherman, "the owners of the film wanted a ridiculous sum of money for it … fifty thousand dollars for theatrical rights to it, even though it was due to be on TV in five or six months. … I offered them $10,000 and not a penny more. Of course they refused and they ended up being stuck with it, and it just went right to television."

With quotes from: "Interview: Paul Naschy," by José Luis González and Michael Secula, *Videooze* 6/7; *Memoirs of a Wolfman*, by Paul Naschy; *Fright Night on Channel 9*, by James Arena.

MORPHOLOGY: Two-legged classic wolfman
DEMISE: Silver bullet (fired by a woman who loves him enough to die for him)
FULL MOON RATING: ***

Attack of the Werewolves see *Game of Werewolves*

Audie & the Wolf

(2008; Brooklyn Reptyle) Director/Screenplay: B. Scott O'Malley; Producers: Christo Dimassis, Roger M. Mayer, Karol Tafolla Ballard, Jeffrey J. Orgill; Cinematographer: Kenneth Yeung. Cast: Derek Hughes, Tara Price, Christa Campbell, Rance Howard, Richard Riehle.

THERE'S NO SUCH THING AS WEREWOLVES.
BUT WHAT IF A WOLF TURNED INTO A MAN?—trailer

It doesn't take a lot of money to make a great film. All it takes is a clever script, well-drawn characters, a unique tale to tell, a talented cast and crew that will work for next to (or exactly) nothing, and the superhuman determination to pull it all together. Yes, that's "all" it takes to make a low-budget winner. And one wonders why they come so few and far between…

But it *can* be done. Just look to the likes of George Romero (*Night of the Living Dead*), Tobe Hooper (*The Texas Chain Saw Massacre*) or John Sayles (*Return of the Secaucus Seven*). Writer-director B. (Brian) Scott O'Malley (a Roger Corman alumnus) may not have that pedigree, but lightning definitely struck on his third feature film, *Audie & the Wolf*, a fresh, original, and clever low-budget romantic horror-comedy filled with engaging characters brought to likable life by excellent (if largely unknown) actors.

The story of a "reverse werewolf" (as lead actor Derek Hughes put it) opens on a Native American man (Atticus Todd) building a homemade bomb. When a quartet of armed thugs—carrying a dog crate—arrive, the Indian proclaims, "Shit, he found me," and tells his pet wolf, "Remember what I taught you. During the full moon you *hide*. During the full moon you are *dangerous*. Remember to stay in the trees until the hunger leaves you. Don't go among people—they will hurt you and you them." He sends the wolf trotting off into the woods before engaging the men in a deadly firefight. As his master dies, the wolf heads deeper into the trees.

That night, driving home from a party, starlet Rachel Brock (Christa Campbell) hits the wolf with her car and takes it home (unhurt) to her Hollywood mansion, leaving the canine on the porch with food and water. But when the clock strikes 12 that full moon night, the creature enters the house and approaches her bedroom. Panicked, Rachel repeatedly fires her pistol. The next morning the wolf wakes in the woman's bedroom—as a naked man (Derek Hughes)—with bullet scars on his chest, dried blood on his mouth, and the woman dead in the bed with her throat ripped out. Attempting to flee, the man panics at the street traffic and retreats back inside. Having no memory of who he is, he gradually figures out his surroundings and calls up a grocery delivery service, proclaiming, "I need meat!" When punk rocker grocery delivery girl Audie Bantam (Tara Price) arrives, the man (dubbed "John Doe" by Audie) tears into the raw meat and asks Audie for help.

Charmed by his odd manner (not to mention all the cash he gives her—found in the starlet's bedside table), Audie promises to help him regain his memory, even sending for a drunken doctor who'll make house calls. But while Audie is gone, John, ravenous for meat, can't keep himself from attacking anyone coming to the door, including the doc, the maid, the actress' agent, and even a pair of occultists Audie brings around to help, resulting in a basement full of zombies (each of Audie's victims rise from the dead). Can John avoid the clutches of his undead victims (which he keeps locked in the cellar), as well as overcome his insatiable thirst for meat to protect his newfound love?

"This dark comedy/horror," began a Filmmakers Forum call for production personnel for the April 9 to May 3, 2007, shoot for *Audie & the Wolf*, "in the spirit of *Shaun of the Dead*, *American Werewolf in London* and *Evil Dead 2*, offers a topsy-turvy take on the classic werewolf legend." Indeed it does. Apart from the fact that it features a *wolf* transforming into a *man* during the three nights (and days) of the full moon (for John retains his human form for the entire three-day period), the movie offers a number of other lycan-variations.

Like in one of the film's obvious inspirations, *An American Werewolf in London*, John's bloody victims return from death—though here they are corporeal (talking) zombies rather than ghosts. And these undead not only *wish* John harm, they can do something about it, attacking him at film's end with the intent to "chop and burn." As his Indian "spirit guide" (his dead master) tells John, "I'm here to warn you: the people you killed, they walk the earth as the living dead—until they chop you up and burn you." When John reasonably asks, "Why?" the Indian amusingly admits, "You got me. I don't understand it either. But I recommend you chop them up *first*, before they chop you."

Trying to learn more, Audie takes John (safely travelling in her car's trunk) to see an old priest, Father Bailey (Tom Carey). The aged clergyman splashes a bit of holy water on John, which burns his skin (which he then licks, only to talk like he'd just come from the dentist because his tongue now hurts!). The aged Father concludes, "You are one of the minions of the Serpent … a creature of nature perverted beyond all hope by witchcraft and darkness, a terrible beast that preys upon the living. …You are what civilization calls—a werewolf."

Besides the holy water gambit, a magical amulet (brought by the occultist) wards off John. When Audie returns on the third night, she finds John (having just subdued and chopped up all his zombie victims) subtly transformed, with glowing eyes and scraggly teeth—and an uncontrollable rage. Audie flashes the amulet, from which John recoils. But then, betting her life on his love, she tosses the medallion aside. John struggles to control himself, then picks up the amulet and puts it on—despite the searing pain—resulting in him returning to his full human self.

More elucidating is a visit from John's dead master. After John has tied himself up, the Indian appears to him to explain, "I'm your maker and you are a wolf. I tell you this every full moon. Your name is Bainbridge. You hunted Indians. My grandfathers captured your spirit at the battle of Little Big Horn. They bound your spirit to a wolf, as they did to many other white men that day. My grandfathers built a great army of wolf braves." As an aside, he adds, "They almost managed to capture back Montana." He continues, "You're the last of them, the last of the wolf braves," and concludes with a comically dismissive, "Blah blah blah." (Of course, this causes one to question the wisdom of these "grandfathers," for if all their victims returned as the living dead, these "wolf braves" would make pretty poor soldiers after all. No wonder the Indians failed to "capture back Montana.") The obviously exasperated Indian concludes, "It sucks. Tell me about it. You know what sucks worse? It's having to re-explain this to you *every fucking month*!"

Stage magician, stand-up comic and sometime theater and film actor Derek Hughes does a marvelous job portraying an animal-turned-man, adopting all kinds of canine mannerisms, both subtle (sniffing, tilting his head) and outrageously overt (peeing on the indoor houseplants, licking himself in the bath, howling during sex). And more importantly, he effectively conveys the intense confusion and dismay at his surroundings and his own actions—inspiring the pathos that's so important even in a "reverse werewolf" tale. "There's something inside me," he wails to the doctor, "you have to help me!" Later he desperately tells himself, "I'm a man, not a monster," and tries to prove it by forsaking meat to wolf down some tofu potato salad (with a priceless look of horrified disgust on his face). John is terrified of "hurting people"—even as he brandishes a large kitchen knife at the doctor, for instance. And when the maid walks in to see him taking a bite out of the dead doc's throat, Hughes' panicked pleading, "It's not what you think!" (when it so obviously *is* what we think) is both sincere and comical. "You have to believe me—this isn't who I really am," he frantically exclaims; and, all evidence to the contrary, one can't help but believe, or at least believe that *he* believes. "I have a thirst—a thirst for meat," he admits. "No matter how much I eat, I still crave it." It's a nightmarish situation that leads to all sorts of tragedy—cleverly disguised, thanks to the engaging playing of the actors and the humor-filled scenarios—as farce.

More interested in clever comedy than cheap exploitation (as evidenced by Audie keeping her bra on during sex, and the amply-endowed Rachel keeping her top firmly in place), *Audie & the Wolf* succeeds more often than not, even with its judicious use of blood and gore. Never gruesome for gruesomeness sake, the violence comes mostly implied (with just enough bloody-wound aftermath to be convincing)—and when overt, its over-the-top depiction comes laced with comedy. John's attack on the gardener, for instance, begins with the two running at each other with electric weapons—John with a chainsaw and the gardener with a weed-whacker. But their respective cords pull them up short just out of range, as they stare and wave their implements impotently at one another. Then the gardener's plug gives way, and he stumbles forward to his knees. Triumphantly, John shouts, "Let me ask you something" as he cuts off one of the screaming man's arms. "You ever seen a *wolf*," he continues, slicing into the man's other arm, "operate a chainsaw?!" At this he decapitates the poor man, laughing hysterically. The next scene sees John dragging the gardener's body into the house to toss in the basement with the others. The overhead shot shows John holding the body's wrists to laboriously pull it across the entryway floor. But in a laugh-out-loud reveal, as he moves further into frame we see he's only pulling the two *severed arms*—with no body attached.

One of the film's real delights is the appearance of character actor Rance Howard (father of actor Clint Howard and actor/director Ron Howard) as the boozy doctor (who asks for more ice for his drink even as he examines John). When John finally confesses, "I think I might have killed the woman who owns this house," Howard pulls up short and offers, "Well, that kind of *skews* the evening in a different direction, doesn't it?" Given to folksy exclamations like, "In the name of sweet strawberry Jesus, boy, don't kill anybody else," Howard's naturalistic delivery and calm underplaying helps ground the outrageous scenario in a semblance of reality.

Of course, logic sometimes fails to raise its calculated head. For instance, why do the police never arrive to investigate, particularly after John lets his sole living captive—the maid's young son—go. One would think he'd head straight for the cops. Also, when the half-monster John attacks Audie, she dials 911 and, though interrupted, manages to blurt out the house's cross-streets; yet nobody arrives to investigate, and the two leave together peacefully the next morning.

Audie & the Wolf carries a professional gloss missing from most ultra-low-cost efforts. With a miniscule budget under $50,000, keeping locations to a minimum (mostly a large Hollywood home and its well-manicured grounds), the gore realistic, and the gags flowing (but flowing naturally from the story and characters, not grafted-on jokes flying willy-nilly) proved imperative. The witty dialogue at times softens the horror of the situation and at others intensifies it. For instance,

Audie tells the occultist, "[John is] afraid to leave the house, he doesn't know anything, and he can't stop eating meat." At this, the woman quips, "Sounds like a typical American." At another point a shocked witness to one of John's killings exclaims, "You were going to eat her!" A crazed John shouts back, "If she didn't want to get eaten, she shouldn't have been made of *meat*!"

"It's never about the ego or cash or money or whatever you're paying me," concluded actress Christa Campbell, "it's like, oh this is a really cool group and a really cool project, and I really want to be involved in it." *Audie & the Wolf* did indeed turn out to be a "really cool project," one that demonstrates that an innovative script, excellent crew and inspired actors can be worth far more than mere money.

With quotes from: "Crew Needed: *Audie & the Wolf*, Shoots April 9–May 3, CA," studentfilmmakers.com; "Int: Christa Campbell," by JimmyO, *Arrow in the Head*.

Morphology: Normal looking man; (real) wolf
Demise: None; he lives to pant another day
Full Moon Rating: ****

Bad Moon

(1996; Morgan Creek/Warner Bros.) Director/Screenplay: Eric Red (based on the novel *Thor* by Wayne Smith); Producer: James G. Robinson; Cinematographer: Jan Kiesser. Cast: Mariel Hemingway, Michael Pare, Mason Gamble, Ken Pogue, Hrothgar Mathews, Johanna Marlowe Lebovitz.

When they invited him in, they let in something they could never imagine—or ever escape—trailer
---

"Him" being Uncle Ted, and "something" being a werewolf. You see, photojournalist Ted (Michael Pare) and his girlfriend Marjorie (Johanna Marlowe Lebovitz) were on a working expedition in the jungles of Nepal and attacked by a vicious werewolf that killed the girl and bit Ted before he could blast the creature with his shotgun. Ted returns to the isolation of his mountain trailer in the Pacific Northwest to deal with his new curse. On the brink of despair, Ted reaches out to his older sister Janet (Mariel Hemingway), a lawyer and single mom to Ted's 10-year-old nephew Brett (Mason Gamble). Janet convinces Ted to come stay with them for a while at their woodland home, but their family dog, German Shepherd Thor (played by "Primo"), sees the beast beneath the veneer and determines to protect his family from the monster that Ted has become.

Kind of a cross between Hitchcock's *Shadow of Doubt* (with serial killer Uncle Charlie replaced by werewolf Uncle Ted) and the typical boy-and-his-dog story … with a lycanthropic twist, *Bad Moon* was filmed on a moderately healthy-for-the-time $8 million budget and 40-day shooting schedule in the environs of Vancouver, Canada. It opens with a pre-credits bang as Ted and Marjorie's nudity-filled jungle tryst is bloodily interrupted by a werewolf ripping through their tent, violently pulling Marjorie out, holding her screaming form upright, and savagely slashing her to death until the wounded Ted crawls to his shotgun and literally blasts the beast's head off. This blood-and-thunder beginning then takes a schizophrenic turn when the opening credits roll over aerial shots of forests and mountain homes as melodic violins play like in some family-friendly Dreamworks movie.

Despite its sex-and-violence opener, writer-director Eric Red claimed (with no trace of irony), "I'm not going for pointless or just cheaply lurid violence for a quick jolt to the crowd" (which is *exactly* what the opening sequence provides). "This is a character-driven horror film with some thematic complexity, not another simple-minded shocker." The remainder of the film does indeed offer up its grue rather judiciously, and focuses primarily on the dynamics between the characters. Unfortunately, said dynamics and character arcs remain too sketchy to fully work. "There's an almost sociopathic manipulation to Ted's dealings with his family," said Red. "I believe that the werewolf myth can be taken as a metaphor for schizophrenia. Ted is an intense character throughout the movie, and he becomes increasingly schizophrenic. The werewolf is a force of bloodthirst and savagery. Uncle Ted naturally changes at night, but even during the day, this monster begins to creep into his personality." Red fails to properly build this up and flesh it out onscreen, so that one has little inkling about whether Ted was "sociopathic" even before his affliction. One never senses any real affection between him and his relatives. Not particularly sympathetic even from the start, Ted gets downright mean, acting standoffish to his caring sister, harshly barking orders at his young nephew, and, worst of all, scheming to blame a mutilation murder on the family dog (even smirking as the animal is dragged away by Animal Control, then "marking" his victory by pissing on the loyal hound's doghouse!). While engendering a sense of menace in the character, this negates the tragedy inherent in the scenario, so that when Ted finally transforms right before Janet's terrified eyes, he's just another cardboard movie monster/villain, even barking out mid-metamorphosis, "Come back here you stupid bitch!"

Admittedly, this monster looks both convincing and imposing. A huge, shaggy, barrel-chested bipedal beast with a broad wolf's head ending in articulated jaws that move and snarl in a mostly convincing fashion (revealing its robotic origins only when the camera lingers a tad too long). One certainly sees this monster as capable of inflicting the shockingly bloody carnage seen in the opening sequence. "I hired Steve Johnson's XFX company after a long search," said Red, "because I found them to be the most realistic in terms of [the current technology]. Steve's company built an incredibly detailed werewolf head with an amazing range of movement. The eyes roll and nostrils flare during close-ups. When the werewolf and dog go jaw-to-jaw at the climax, it really grabs you." Indeed it does—emotionally as well as viscerally, with the canine hero Thor taking hit after bloody hit and the viewer wincing each time during the impressive canine-a-lupo battle.

Family dynamics with a lycanthropic twist.

However, the film's sole transformation sequence, which Red saves for the end, disappoints. Rather than painful-looking physical changes, à la *An American Werewolf in London* or *The Howling*, Red opts for a few bits of cheap-looking primitive computer-generated-imagery, as Ted morphs in sections, looking like a CGI funhouse reflection. The crunching and snapping noises on the soundtrack are incongruous with the visuals, since Ted appears not only to feel no pain, but to *enjoy* the change—chuckling and smiling as it happens.

Regarding the beast, Red refused to be constrained by typical werewolf lore. "Don't expect any silver bullets," warned Red. "I figured if you blew a werewolf's head off with a shotgun, it would probably do the trick." And it does just that—a wet, gory trick. And despite the movie's title, it eschews the full moon trope. "Why a full moon?" asks a knowing Uncle Ted, amused by the movie *Werewolf of London* Brett watches on TV. "Any moon will do the trick, werewolf-wise," he states. This means that Ted must tromp into the woods seemingly every night (this point—and the movie's timeline—remains a bit hazy) to chain himself to a tree (or, conversely, eat a few hikers). Ted has also seen a doctor, who can't identify the strange mutation in his blood—or treat his condition, leaving Ted to write in his diary, "Perhaps if I spend time with [Janet], with my family, this disease will go into remission. Medicine will not stave off this disease, but perhaps love—the restorative powers of love, family love—will save me. It's my last chance." This notion of love overcoming the beast within, first explored back in 1960's *The Curse of the Werewolf*, here smacks of flimsy reasoning and wishful thinking, given Ted's lack of demonstrable affection for his "family" from the get-go.

"This is also a family story," insisted Red. "The family bond is confirmed against incomprehensible violence and evil, so the overall effect of the picture is affirmative, whereas the usual werewolf film tends to be somewhat nihilistic. A good man is doomed to turn into a creature driven to kill and ultimately die. We certainly preserve that element in *Bad Moon*, but there's another involving the potentially tragic conflict between his affliction and responsibility to his family." Here Red is either being disingenuous or simply ignorant, as *many* werewolf films through the years have explored this affliction-responsibility conflict, often within the context of the family (the original *Wolf Man*, for instance, was a tragedy set against the backdrop of a son's strained relationship with his father). In any case, Eric Red's script and direction, and Michael Pare's performance, fail to bring this familial conflict fully to the fore (with little in Ted's characterization or Pare's acting indicating he is "a good man"), leaving it a mere implication that remains all-but-hidden in the background.

Both Mariel Hemingway (an Oscar nominee for her work in Woody Allen's *Manhattan*) and youngster Mason Gamble (*Dennis the Menace*, *Gattaca*) breathe life into their determined characters, with Hemingway in particular showing both terror and strength at pivotal moments. "Mariel was my first choice as the mother," said Red. "There'll be a great deal of rooting for Jan due to the depth and feeling of Mariel's performance." Hemingway indeed makes for a strong, likable and ultimately courageous heroine. Unfortunately, Michael Pare (*Village of the Damned*, 1995; *Komodo vs. Cobra*) fails to convey the inherent tragedy of his situation. "Michael usually plays heroes, and you still like him here despite his potential for violence," stated Red. Despite the filmmaker's claim, Pare, under Red's direction, does little to make him likable. "We wanted to have someone the audience could sympathize with in view of the pathos of Ted's losing battle with the psychotic beast inside him," continued Red. But neither actor nor director offers much to engender such sympathy (no scenes of Ted grieving over his lost love, no shots of him railing against his condition, and precious few instances of his ever addressing the problem at all).

Eric Red (born Eric Durdaller), who wrote the scripts for the cult favorites *The Hitcher* (1986) and *Near Dark* (1987), has had a problematic and tragedy-plagued career—and life. Red filed for bankruptcy—twice (in 1995 and 2001)—and in 2000 he caused the death of two people in a bizarre collision in which he sent his Jeep crashing into a bar. Immediately following the accident Red picked up a shard of glass and attempted suicide by slitting his own throat, putting him in the ICU. Though he recovered and escaped criminal prosecution, he lost a drawn-out civil suit. "It was a tragic accident," Red said in 2004. "There's nothing I can do to undo it. ...You want someone to blame, you need there to be a reason, but I've had to accept that sometimes tragedies happen where there is no reason. ...My heart goes out to these families and I hope they find a way to move on, as we all must do."

Bad Moon saw bad times at the box office, taking in just over a million dollars (against its $8 million cost). Perhaps not quite deserving of its "bomb" status, *Bad Moon* offers an impressive werewolf, some startling attacks and gore effects, solid acting (both human and canine), some boy-and-his-dog-meets-a-werewolf novelty—and a passel of wasted opportunities.

With quotes from: "*Bad Moon* Rising," by Thomas Crow, *Fangoria* 158; "Death Race 2000," by Paul Cullum, *L.A. Weekly*, January 13, 2006.

Morphology: Wolf-headed biped
Demise: Shotgun blast; German shepherd
Full Moon Rating: **½

The Band from Hell see Neowolf

Battledogs

(2013; The Asylum) Director: Alexander Yellen; Producer: David Michael Latt; Screenplay: Shane Van Dyke; Cinematographer: Justin Duval. Cast: Craig Sheffer, Dennis Haysbert, Kate Vernon, Ariana Richards, Wes Studi, Ernie Hudson, Bill Duke.

THE POPULATION OF MANHATTAN
IS UNDER QUARANTINE ... FOR NOW—poster

Battledogs begins with a bang as a woman suffers what looks like a seizure in a JFK airport bathroom stall but emerges as a huge wolf-creature that runs rampant through the terminal (cue throat-ripping and various gore effects). Those victims left alive immediately transform into wolf-monsters themselves, and soon it's mass lycanthropy. And this all comes in the first five minutes.

The authorities and military subdue the various lycans trapped in the terminal with gas, with the creatures reverting to human form. These newly-minted werewolves are then isolated and confined to a facility on nearby Ward's Island (in what looks like an abandoned train station) where the military, led by General Monning (Dennis Haysbert), intends to utilize this "lupine virus" to create super-soldiers. Opposing their clandestine plan are CDC doctor Ellen Gordon (Kate Vernon) and CDC liaison Major Brian Hoffman (Craig Sheffer), who are soon on the run with "patient zero" Donna Voorhees (former child star Ariana Richards, of *Jurassic Park* and *Tremors*), who may just have the cure to the werewolf disease inside her.

Though casting classic lycanthropy in the role of disease, and exploiting the modern-day fear of mass contagion (forget Bird Flu, this Werewolf Flu is much more terrifying), *Battledogs* never lives up to its startling opening, both in terms of story and execution, with too many subsequent shots of the obvious CGI creatures looking flat and two-dimensional. It's also plagued by pacing issues, including too much time spent with Hoffman and the doc initially talking about, and searching for, patient zero—when we already know who said patient is, and that she fully intends to reveal herself as soon as the chance arises. Poor story construction and over-convenient plotting has all the "canines" suddenly escape to invade Manhattan, leaving the three good-guy leads alone in the facility to face down the bad guys, led by Monning.

The film eats up more running time as the heroic trio make their escape from Monning and his military henchmen, improbably zip-lining over their prison's electric fence and then leading a ridiculous boat chase involving slow, unwieldy tenders. The "canines" all gallop through the amazingly deserted Manhattan streets to conveniently converge on Central Park. Cue the brief, small-scale confrontation between soldiers and werewolves. Moving beyond the silly and improbable into the realm of utter ludicrousness, at one point a werewolf suddenly leaps through a skyscraper window to take out a helicopter firing on its brethren below. After yet another anemic chase involving Our Heroes (this time in an S.U.V.) comes a scene in which a werewolf jumps onto the wing of a cargo plane Hoffman attempts to fly, miraculously causing the engine to fall off (!). Then the hero lands the laboring aircraft on a suspension bridge (!!), shearing off the wings but keeping the fuselage intact—with all three protagonists coming through unscathed (!!!).

Some awful dialogue compliments the poor plotting. As the (topically African-American) President of the United States contemplates bombing Manhattan to keep the werewolf virus from spreading, he melodramatically intones, "Heavy is the head that wears the crown." And when Monning finally meets his comeuppance, the doc asks Hoffman, "Where's Monning?" to which Our Hero replies, "Dog food."

The oddly-designed beasts, when seen full-view, look like oversized mutant wolves with elongated, ridged snouts (reminiscent of a horse skull) and overly-muscular limbs (including a set of powerful but awkward-looking hind legs), coming off as a cross between a giant rat and deformed wolf. Once bitten, victims begin to transform almost immediately via a cleverly edited series of snippets integrating simple physical effects—shirts ripping to reveal coarse hair underneath, mouths opening to show them overstuffed with jagged fangs, eyes widening to reveal greenish orbs—and CGI (nails morphing into claws, faces darkening and rippling). For a low-budget production (particularly from The Asylum, who brought us the likes of *Snakes on a Train*, 2006; *Mega Shark vs. Crocosaurus*, 2010; and the immortal *Sharknado*, 2013), the effects work relatively well, including a later transformation showing a wolf-face morphing back to human via seamless CGI.

Viewing lycanthropy as a disease rather than a supernatural curse, the film eschews the typical silver bullet-and-full moon tropes to make up a new set of (pseudo)scientific-minded rules about werewolves, including having the transformation triggered by increased heart rate brought on by heightened emotion or stress (à la *The Incredible Hulk*). "We need to keep these people calm, keep their heart rates down," warns the doc, with a rate of 150 being the breaking point. Afraid of a worldwide outbreak, the CDC desperately wants to keep the lupine virus quarantined while they search for a cure, while the military intend to use the virus to create "the most significant advance in warfare since the predatory drone" (according to the General). Oddly,

Major Hoffman (Craig Sheffer) makes nice with one of the *Battledogs*.

the term "werewolf" never arises, with Monning contemptuously referring to the beasts merely as "canines."

The heroic Major Hoffman, however, sees the creatures not as monsters but as afflicted people. "No bullets unless it's completely necessary," he admonishes, "remember they're human beings." At one point Hoffman tries to reason with one of the creatures, saying, "There's still part of you that's human," and even reaches out to pet it. Patient Zero, Diana Voorhees, a wildlife photographer bitten by a black wolf in Canada, shows true remorse, as do even the more aggressive of the afflicted. After killing four men and being tranquilized, a now-human perpetrator pleads, "I couldn't help it. I'm sorry, I didn't mean to kill them." This adds the potent element of pathos so intrinsic to the werewolf subgenre.

First-time director Alexander Yellen was no stranger to the werewolf theme, having worked as a cameraman on 2009's *Wolvesbayne*. Filmed in Buffalo, New York (a far cheaper place to shoot than New York City), under the innocuous shooting title of *Ward's Island*, as a made-for-TV SyFy Channel production, *Battledogs* fails to do justice to its intriguing concept, sabotaged by a sometimes tedious execution and simplistic characterizations bordering on the cartoonish (General Monning is impossibly heartless, while Major Hoffman stands as the stereotypical bleeding heart good-guy who transforms into a bad-ass action hero by film's end). Though better than many a CGI-laden SyFy Channel movie, and better executed than most Asylum knockoffs (damning with faint praise, really), *Battledogs* remains yet another middling lycanthropic time-waster.

Morphology: Large, four-legged mutant wolf-creatures
Demise: Any old bullet will do
Full Moon Rating: **½

The Beast Must Die

(1974; Amicus/Cinerama Releasing; UK) Alternate Title: *Black Werewolf* (video). Director: Paul Annett; Producers: Max J. Rosenberg, Milton Subotsky; Screenplay: Michael Winder (based on the novella *There Shall Be No Darkness* by James Blish); Cinematographer: Jack Hildyard. Cast: Calvin Lockhart, Peter Cushing, Charles Gray, Anton

36 • *The Beast Must Die*

Not only did *The Beast Must Die* offer cinema's first sporting hunt of a werewolf, it created the "Werewolf Break" (in which viewers were invited to guess the lycanthrope's identity).

Diffring, Marlene Clark, Cairan Madden, Tom Chadbon, Michael Gambon.

> CAN YOU GUESS WHO IT IS WHEN WE STOP
> THE FILM FOR THE WEREWOLF BREAK?
> SEE IT ... SOLVE IT ... BUT DON'T TELL!—poster

Here's a real novelty in the lycanthrope subgenre: A wealthy big game hunter is obsessed with hunting a *werewolf* for sport. To this end he gathers half a dozen suspects—one of whom is a werewolf—at his palatial estate (the wild grounds of which he's rigged with all manner of cameras and sound devices for tracking purposes) to ferret out the hairy culprit in order to hunt him (or her) down like a ... er, dog.

Such a clever premise is so rife with possibilities that it becomes almost criminal to see it wasted so badly in the hands of neophyte director Paul Annett and lead actor Calvin Lockhart (*Cotton Comes to Harlem*). As millionaire sportsman Tom Newcliffe, Lockhart can't seem to say his dialogue without shouting and posing, as if he's playing some low-rent dinner-theater Othello. His wide-eyed, forced delivery of lines such as "In this world you're either the hunter or the hunted," "One of you sitting here in this room is a werewolf," and "[I] dream of hunting and facing what no man has ever trapped before" rings more of strained desperation than the intended intensity. Lockhart lacks anything remotely resembling charisma (and cuts a pretty poor physical specimen as well, with his slight frame sheathed in a black leather pantsuit), so that his pivotal obsession carries little weight. (Reportedly, Robert Quarry [*Count Yorga, Vampire*] was originally set to play the lead, but the producers went with Lockhart instead to capitalize on the then-current blaxploitation craze. Pity.)

Two other major issues keep this *Beast* from becoming a true beauty. First is the meandering and repetitive script, which, when not forcing its players into repeated parlor games of pass-the-silver-candlestick or breathe-the-wolfsbane-fumes (as Newcliffe tries repeatedly—and unsuccessfully—to learn the identity of the lycanthrope), offers three tiresomely repetitive "hunts" on the three successive nights of the full moon, utilizing everything from security cameras seemingly mounted on every tree to a helicopter equipped with infrared camera and machine gun (so much for "sport"). The other major blunder comes in the form of the monster itself. Rather than a slavering man-beast straight out of a nightmare, this werewolf looks no more menacing than what it really is—a shaggy-maned German Shepherd straight out of the kennel. For the scene in which this lycanthrope supposedly rips out a victim's throat, the man desperately clutches the beast and holds it upright against his chest, making it look more like a doggy dance than a life-and-death struggle.

"The problem with that picture," admitted co-producer Milton Subotsky, "was that I didn't know what to do with it. I liked the idea, but if you read the story and ask yourself how am I going to film this, the story begins to have too many elements. It has a fairy tale element and a fantasy element and it never ties them together. We never licked that problem or got the script right. The director was Paul Annett, who was basically a TV director, and he didn't do a very good job."

One of the film's few memorable moments comes not during any attack but in its *aftermath*, when the camera reveals a victim's gruesomely bloody face—complete with a hole where his left eye should be (with the camera zooming in for grisly effect). Oddly enough, this shocking bit of grue was only included *because of* the censors. In some Bizzarro-World scenario, co-producer Subotsky—and U.K. distributor British Lion—were desperate for *Beast* to earn an "X" rating in the U.K. (their equivalent of America's "R"), but the British Board of Film Censors passed the picture with an "AA" rating for all audiences (not so marketable for a purported horror flick). Subotsky went to the Board: "I said I didn't want to put unnecessary material in the picture and would they please give me an "X," but they refused. The Board said that audiences expected certain things from an 'X,' so I had to put outtakes of werewolf attacks Paul Annett had shot that I didn't like into the print to get the rating. The gore was redundant." Well, said redundancy went a long way towards providing what few thrills and bits of excitement the film could muster.

Also injected into the movie at the last minute was the (in)famous "Werewolf Break," added by Subotsky as a William Castle–style gimmick intended to beef up viewer enthusiasm for this hirsute "detective story" (as the narrator labels it). With about 15 minutes to go, the film freezes, and an unseen narrator announces "This is the werewolf break" and invites the viewer to guess the beast's human identity. Over shots of the various suspects, he asks, "Is it Paul Foote, Jan, Davina, Dr. Lundgren, Caroline? You have 30 seconds to give your answer.… Made up your mind? Let's see if you're right." And the film resumes. "I put in this 'Werewolf Break' at the end," recounted Subotsky, "which I really stole from William Castle's *Homicidal* [1961], because I'd always admired that bit. Castle has his 'Fright Break' and after the clock ticked around, he said, 'Still here? You're a brave audience.'" While such a cheesy ploy can't fail to bring a smile to the face of the seasoned horror fan, the hoary device brings the already creaking carriage of a scenario to full stop.

One of the few joys of the picture is (with the one obvious exception) its cast. Such wonderful character actors as Charles Gray, Anton Diffring, and the inimitable Peter Cushing go a long way towards grounding this outrageous premise in some manner of believability. Unfortunately, Diffring and Gray are literally the first to go, and Cushing, as the werewolf "expert," is saddled with too much expository claptrap. Still, ever the professional, Cushing brought something special to his difficult task. Said director Paul Annett to interviewer Jonathan Sothcott: "I have never before or since worked with an actor so diligent in his preparation for a role. Before filming started and whilst he was still on another picture, envelopes containing little color crayon drawings arrived for my approval. He was playing a Norwegian professor of lycanthropy and had worked out exactly how he would like to appear, from the sandy crew cut wig to the colors in his knitted sweater. 'But only if you approve, my dear.' Approve? I loved him for it."

Cushing was equally beloved by his fellow actors. "The first day I was on the set," recalled Marlene Clark, "Peter Cushing came over to me, and he was holding something behind his back. It was a nosegay [a small bouquet]! He gave me a nosegay to welcome me to the film, and to England. It was such a wonderful gesture. He really was a gentleman." In addition to cultivating friendships by delivering flowers, Cushing went the extra mile to cultivate his character's Norwegian accent by studying language tapes. While a testament to his professionalism, he really needn't have bothered, given the caliber of the production—though, admittedly, the viewer is truly grateful whenever Cushing is onscreen (and Lockhart is not).

The final horror movie produced by the English film company Amicus (best known for their many portmanteau horrors, such as *Tales from the Crypt* and *The House That Dripped Blood*), *The Beast Must Die* took the company rather limply over the finish line with this unique but disappointingly tepid combination of blaxploitation horror, Agatha Christie's *Ten Little Indians* and werewolfery. Audiences thought so too. In the U.K., *The Beast Must Die* was released on a double bill with Brian DePalma's far superior *Sisters* (retitled *Blood Sisters*)—and die it did at the box office, both in Britain and America.

With quotes from: "The Amicus Empire: An Interview with Milton Subotsky," by Dennis Fischer, *Filmfax* 42; "Scream and Scream Again: The Uncensored History of Amicus Productions," by Philip Nutman, *Little Shoppe of Horrors* 20; "Slinking Through the '70s," by Chris Poggiali, *Fangoria* 191.

Morphology: German Shepherd
Demise: Silver bullet
Full Moon Rating: **

The Beast of Bray Road

(2005; The Asylum) Director/Screenplay: Leigh Scott; Producers: David Michael Latt, David Rimawi, Sherri Strain; Cinematographer: Steve Parker. Cast: Jeff Denton, Tom Downey, Sarah Lieving, Joel Hebner, Tom Nagel.

On October 31, 1989, a strange beast was spotted in southwestern Wisconsin. Since then, several eyewitnesses and a single photo have surfaced. The Beast has never claimed a human victim. Until now…—trailer

---

"BASED ON A TRUE STORY" says the screen before the film proper starts. Yeah, right. Almost immediately, a young woman flees through the woods from a barely-glimpsed hulking creature only to pause under a tree after everything goes quiet. She looks up, and suddenly a clawed, hairy hand descends to grab her by the head and haul her upwards. The camera stays on her kicking legs while she screams, before they abruptly drop out of frame as her entire lower half—severed at the waist—falls to the ground, followed by coils of red viscera. With this very first pre-credit scene of unassuming gore, *The Beast of Bray Road* announces its intentions—to offer up a grue-infused stalking-monster movie. In that respect, it more or less succeeds. But it fails at just about everything else (from its unconvincing characterizations, unfathomable motivations, subpar acting, and, most disappointingly, the less-than-impressive "Beast" itself).

Big-city cop Phil Jenkins (Jeff Denton) takes a job as a small-town sheriff right as a string of brutal murders hits the backwater burg. Everyone in town (including his ragtag local deputies) begin talking about the "Beast of Bray Road," a local werewolf legend that dates back to the 1800s. More cattle, horses and people go missing; a crypto zoologist named Quinn (Tom Downey) shows up to help; and Phil finds time to romance the proprietress of Kelly's Roadhouse (Sarah Lieving). Finally, Phil and his team whip up some silver bullets and go on a werewolf hunt, leading to a surprise revelation as to the identity of the lycanthrope at the blood-soaked, fiery climax.

Wisconsin-born writer-director Leigh Scott based his story on some much-publicized werewolf "sightings" in Walworth County, Wisconsin, though he took little more from the supposed real-life reports than the location. For instance, to date, no attacks (much less deaths) have been attributed to the Beast, whereas the movie monster rips open chests, bites off limbs, and splatters heads with abandon. And that may be the film's biggest (only?) asset—a penchant for amusingly over-the-top carnage. It takes a certain kind of sensibility—and chutzpah—to film a scene of a beautiful girl fleeing through the woods after *half* of her boyfriend ends up tossed on the hood of their parked car, only to have the monster tackle her, rip off her leg, and then hunker down to gnaw on the severed limb as she agonizingly tries to crawl away.

Of course, such outrageous episodes (and there are many more, including entrail-ripping, head-biting, and the old arm through the chest gag), coupled with the foolish actions of the cartoonish characters, dilute whatever inherent prey-fear (evoking the primal horror of being stalked and eaten) the film might engender, as one just can't take it seriously.

From the beer-and-libido-driven backwoods yokels to the goofy deputies (who seem more interested in drawing tourists to their little town with some werewolf publicity than stopping the ghastly killings), nobody in this picture behaves in a reasonable manner. Even the usually calm-to-the-point-of-parody Sheriff engages in some very un-sheriff-like behavior, like immediately inviting civilian Quinn to join their investigation (despite the lawman stating time and again he doesn't believe in werewolves) and even instigating a half-assed bar fight.

The actors can do little with the silly script. Jeff Denton projects nothing more than a dull neutrality, his bland demeanor making no real impact as the ostensible hero. Tom Downey at least seems mildly animated, displaying more personality as the crypto zoologist simply by dint of comparison. And pivotal female lead Sarah Lieving, as Kelly, is pretty and vivacious but stays mostly in the background until the unlikely climax.

Leigh Scott's competent though colorless direction (excepting the gore scenes, which he pulls off with gruesome aplomb) doesn't help. Under Scott's hand, cinematographer Steve Parker over-lights nearly ever scene, so that even the nighttime woodland stalking sequences appear flat and uninteresting. No shadows, no fog, no atmosphere, no suspense.

Of course, Scott might just have been suffering from filmmaker's fatigue. The writer-director, who got his start in the business working for Roger Corman's Concorde Pictures, not only had to shoot his entire movie in a mere two weeks, he helmed two other films for The Asylum this same year, *Frankenstein Reborn!* and *King of the Lost World*. But that proved just a warm-up for the prolific filmmaker, as he directed (and often wrote) *six more* the following year.

Scott's simplistic script pulls out the old bromide of the protagonists learning all the "rules" of werewolfery from an old book. Reading from the tome, Quinn ticks them off in a stop-the-movie-I-wanna-get-off moment of unimaginative exposition: "Werewolves possess the power to regenerate … any injuries inflicted with silver will stop this power of regeneration"; "If one is bitten by a werewolf and survives, he or she is now doomed to become a werewolf"; "In time the werewolf can learn to control his metamorphosis, to no longer be bound by the cycle of the moon"; "Werewolves are smart predators, relying on their animal instincts and human sensibilities." And there you have it. Oh, except that later Quinn produces a syringe full of wolfsbane (from where, exactly, is anybody's guess). "It's Ebola for werewolves," he pronounces. "It may not be strong enough to kill it, but it may force it back into its human form." And how does Quinn know this? No idea, as he didn't even read this bit in the book. (At film's end he goes one better by handing over a fistful of syringes to one of their number who was bitten during the fracas, announcing that this "should be able to keep it under control.")

The film's threadbare budget peeks through at times like an ill-placed hole in an old pair of jeans. For instance, the sometimes poorly modulated sound nearly ruins several scenes and mocks the moment when Quinn stops to dramatically announce, "There's no birds, no insects—silence." This supposedly suspense-inducing observation is nearly drowned out by the heavy traffic noise from the road so obviously behind them.

The production's straightened circumstances (Tom Downey not only co-starred as Quinn but served as the film's production designer; creature creator Danny Russo did double duty by playing trouble-making yokel Zeke; while actor Joel Hebner played not only Zeke's beefy brother but wore the Beast costume as well) no doubt contributed to the movie's disappointing lack of a transformation scene. The closest it comes is a point near the climax when we see the lycanthrope in human form (but with glowing eyes and fangs) chewing hungrily on a victim's entrails. A cutaway shows the woozy Phil looking on, before the camera cuts back to the creature—now in full Beast mode. And, as mentioned, perhaps the biggest disappointment, given the film's monster-centric nature, is the Beast itself. With its humpbacked bulky form covered in thick fur; long, stringy, unkempt hair around its face; slightly protruding dog snout; pointy ears; oversized incisors; and neon-green eyes, it looks like some bizarre Rasta-Quasimodo-Yeti mixture that stands on its legs yet awkwardly bounds on all fours (trying—and failing miserably—to emulate a quadruped).

Still, the film keeps things moving, with plenty of behaving-stupidly Beast-fodder periodically wandering into the woods for a date with another gruesome set-piece. An unpretentious, mildly entertaining monster movie, *The Beast of Bray Road* stands as one of the better films to emerge from the low-budget fringe-film factory known as The Asylum. Admittedly, coming from the company most famous for derivative shlock like *Supercroc* (2007) and *Mega Piranha* (2010), not to mention the ludicrous-but-entertaining *Sharknado* series, that's not saying a whole lot.

Morphology: Bulky hunchbacked Beast
Demise: Silver bullets
Full Moon Rating: **½

Beast Within see Uncaged, 2016

The Big Bad

(2011; Phase 4 Films) Director: Bryan Enk; Producers: Jessi Gotta, Bryan Enk; Screenplay: Jessi Gotta; Cinematographer: Dominick Snilli. Cast: Jessi Gotta, Jessica Savage, Timothy McCown Reynolds, Patrick Shearer, Alan Rowe Kelly.

LITTLE RED HAS A BIG PROBLEM—tagline

Frankie Ducane (Jessi Gotta) is on a mission: to find a man named Fenton (Timothy McCown Reynolds). Her search leads first to a dive bar, where she encounters a drug addict, Molly (Jessica Savage), who she becomes friendly with and then is forced to kill after Molly "turns." You see, Molly had encountered Fenton herself, leading to her becoming infected with lycanthropy. Next, Frankie is kidnapped by a mysterious man (Patrick Shearer) and taken to the dungeon-like lair of the freakish Annabelle (Alan Rowe Kelly), who Frankie also kills after Annabelle tortures her and takes one of her eyes. Finally, Frankie tracks Fenton down to his woodland cabin, where a full moon confrontation ensues and their inextricable ties are revealed.

Filmmakers care. Nobody sets out to make a bad movie (well, unless your name is Jerry Warren). Like all artists, moviemakers, whether backyard amateurs or high-priced professionals, have an ideal in mind and use whatever talent, technique and resources they possess to try and fulfill that ideal. Moviemaking is such a difficult, time-and-resource-consuming process that, while some succeed, many more fall well short of their goal. So while one can't fault a filmmaker for trying, and even applaud his or her efforts, one *can* fault—and boo—the results. Though the low-budget *The Big Bad* displays plenty of effort, and looks far better than its straightened circumstances should allow, the results rarely warrant anything more than an occasional polite golf clap.

The Big Bad starts out slowly. The first thing to strike the viewer is the film's obvious technical affectations—extreme close-ups, shaky hand-held photography, and an overall gauzy, washed-out, filtered look to the visuals. Rather than "edgy," it all just feels oppressive, with a depressing color palette dominated by grays and browns. Then, of course, there's the fact that we're following the actions of a young woman (Frankie) we don't know and don't yet care about, and who does nothing of import for the first 10 minutes anyway—until she throws an inexplicable temper tantrum by beating on an old tire with a baseball bat. The next 15 minutes consists of Frankie hanging out with Molly in the dive bar where they drink, talk about their "shitty lives," and snort coke. Screenwriter/co-producer/star Jessi Gotta admitted that "Quentin Tarantino and David Lynch are two of my all-time favorite [filmmakers]"; and this interminable, talky opening third strives hard to be "cool," à la Tarantino, but fails miserably.

Consequently, the first third of this 78-minute film could be excised without significant impact. At the half-hour mark something finally does happen. After Molly passes out, having slashed her wrists in the toilet, Frankie carries her outside. In a back alley Molly suddenly awakens with a vicious growl, glowing eyes, a misshapen nose, and fangs. When she attacks, Frankie manages to draw a knife and stab Molly to death. Afterward Frankie looks up and notices it's a full moon.

"I think werewolves appealed to me from the standpoint of it being an average person who is 'infected,'" said Gotta, "and how that infection affects/can destroy a person's family." To this end, Gotta grafted a revenge story onto the classic tragic Wolf Man tale, with Frankie seeking to destroy the man-monster that killed her mother and tore apart her family. In the end, though, she finds she can't bring herself to do it. As Gotta explains, "The year before we started working on this film my dad was diagnosed with cancer, so there was much to pull from. In the film the character I play, Frankie, does not hate the person infected; she hates their disease…" This adds an extra emotional layer to the proceedings.

For the majority of the film the werewolf is indeed the Big Bad a monster whose presence is revealed only by shaky p.o.v. camerawork accompanied by growling and bone-crunching sound effects (as he feeds off his victims, out of sight). But once Frankie finally catches up with him (in human form), we learn that this werewolf is very much the tortured soul. As he tells Frankie before the full moon rises, "I need you to know that I never thought I would ever hurt you or your mother. …This was not malicious, this was not a choice." Resigned to his fate, Fenton then tells her, "If you're gonna do it, do it now." But Frankie demurs, saying, "You're not who I want." She doesn't want to kill the man, she wants to kill the *monster*. Frankie is determined to face down the *beast*, and that night she follows him into the misty woodlands, silver knife in hand. There ensues the film's centerpiece, a suspenseful stalk and slash sequence in an effectively eerie setting. "The forest was a set," noted director Brian Enk, "which we preferred to actually shooting on location so we could control the lighting and the environment. Director of photography Dominick Sivilli and I worked out a lot of what that would involve before the set was even built. We looked at a lot of forest scenes from horror movies—we wanted something that was kind of a cross between the theatrical style of the original *The Wolf Man* and the pretty-grungy look of the 2009 remake of *Friday the 13th*." It makes for an atmospheric setting that, unfortunately, the filmmakers fail to fully exploit, mostly due to an unlikely—and unconvincing—change in the heroine's demeanor.

Strangely, the heretofore highly capable, badass Frankie (who not only battled and killed the Molly-wolf but also the freaky Annabelle) suddenly turns from vengeful monster-hunter (who coolly dons an eye patch before immediately resuming her search) to frightened victim. First thing, she panics and runs blindly—right smack into a tree, impaling herself on a branch! After painfully pulling it out (off-screen, of course), she yells, "Come and get me!" into the night. Hearing low growling sounds, she sees a shape race past her. Frankie lunges and stabs with her knife, striking home. It's not the werewolf dead on the ground, however, but some innocent person (out for a woodland stroll, perhaps, only to be chased by the creature?). Struggling to pull out the weapon stuck in the unfortunate's chest before the monster pounces, Frankie finally retrieves the knife and stands to face the beast. But then her eyes go wide, and she holds her hand in front of her mouth as if to suppress a scream. Frankie next runs away and barricades herself in Fenton's cabin, defeating the very purpose of her being there (to hunt and kill the werewolf). This marks an incongruous and unconvincing sea change in her character—from cool, determined and laconic (even when kidnapped and mutilated) to terrified, near-hysterical, and cowardly—that smacks of clichéd woman-in-peril expediency rather than true character development.

Only in the final five minutes, when the two finally go at it hand to claw, do we get a good look at this lycanthrope. He's a more-or-less satisfying update of the classic Wolf Man, with fanged (bloody) mouth, built-up canine nose, angry-looking ridged brows, and gray hair covering his head and cheeks. At one point the beast seeks her out by sniffing and lapping at a small pool of her blood on the floor. This immediately affects the werewolf, weakening him—due to the silver supplement we saw Frankie take earlier, the metal having permeated her blood (a clever use of the silver trope).

Apparently, werewolves are an organized lot, as it's intimated that the man who kidnaps Frankie is a lycanthrope himself, one working for the sadistic, eyeless Annabelle to keep Frankie from fulfilling her mission and attracting any more attention to the lycan-community. A few cryptic comments like "some of us don't want change; some of us are happy being off their radar," and "some of us are a little sick of being in the closet, so to speak," and "we have systems in place to handle such *incidents*" raise plenty of questions—which the script doesn't bother to answer. The film immediately drops these intriguing notions like a hot silver potato to instead take an uncomfortable detour down the torture-porn highway when the bizarre Annabelle (who spouts vague witticisms like "the great omelet of social change demands the breaking of a few eggs; it just sucks to be an egg"), an overweight, middle-aged woman with no eyes, torments the strapped-down Frankie and gouges out one of the girl's eyes to wear on her own face! When Frankie finally escapes (after another confrontation with some barely-seen "thing" in the basement, and the ridiculous demise of Annabelle when Frankie tosses some water on her, causing the woman to inexplicably dissolve in a gooey mess like some mutant Wicked Witch of the West), she leaves behind any potential answers along with her missing orb.

"The script very distinctly has three acts," explained director Brian Enk, "and we approached these as having three different 'looks' and vibes." Act One offers the dive-bar scenario with Molly, Act Two encompasses Annabelle and her lair, and Act Three consists of Frankie finally catching up with Fenton and their final confrontation. To achieve these "'looks' and vibes," Enk employs far too much precious technique, including splicing in some 8mm home movie footage to illustrate a flashback—which has nothing to do with said recollection; inter-cutting shots of lapping waves with Fenton's apologetic reminiscence (again, *nothing* to do with the story he's telling); random slow-motion; hair-blowing-in-the-wind shots; stutter-step photography (suggesting, perhaps, some kind of instability?); rapid edits; extreme close-ups; and a roving camera revealing only bits and pieces of a scene. Used judiciously, these can all be effective at generating mood or enhancing a point, but through overuse they become merely tedious and attention-drawing.

At the finale, one can almost make a case for lycanthropy as a metaphor for domestic abuse, with the vengeful stepchild tracking the abusive surrogate parent who destroyed her family with his violence. But Gotta's script eschews such explorations in favor of ... well, bizarre twists and turns and characters. The finale sees both Frankie and the werewolf beaten and battered but ultimately unwilling to finish the job. "I just miss you both so much," Frankie tearfully tells the creature, referring to both her mother *and* him. Then, in either a moment of clarity or self-loathing (or both), the werewolf raises up Frankie's hand holding the silver knife and pulls it into his own chest.

"Jessi and I originally set out to make a 'horror movie,' but *The Big Bad* ended up being a more complex animal," observed Enk, "it's also a dark fairy tale, a supernatural melodrama, a mystery, lots of things." It's also far too constrained in its action, diffused in its look, and uneven in its pacing, so that in the end, *The Big Bad* has only a Little going for it.

With quotes from: "An Interview with Jessi Gotta and Bryan Enk," by Gary Conley, Roguecinema.com.

Morphology: Standard (gray-haired) wolfman
Demise: Silver knife
Full Moon Rating: **

Big Bad Wolf

(2006; Rainstorm Entertainment/Screen Media Ventures) Director/Screenplay: Lance W. Dreesen; Producers: Clint Hutchison, Lance V. Dreesen; Cinematographer: Stephen Crawford. Cast: Richard Tyson, Kimberly J. Brown, Sarah Aldrich, Christopher Shyer, David Naughton, Trevor Duke.

WHERE MAN ENDS, EVIL BEGINS...—ad line

Reflecting the duality of lycanthropy, this *Big Bad Wolf* looks to be a simple (though polished) gore and sex-filled werewolf exploitationer. But like the werewolf figure itself, below the surface lurks a theme that proves far more dark and dangerous than any hairy, fanged monster.

At the urging of two obnoxious frat brothers and their girlfriends, pledge Derek (Trevor Duke) reluctantly steals the keys to his stepfather Mitch's (Richard Tyson) isolated cabin for some "partying." Convincing his tough goth-chick platonic friend Sam (Kimberly J. Brown) to accompany him, Derek and co. reach the cabin just as the full moon rises. Soon, a werewolf attacks the group, viciously slaughtering (and in one case *raping*) the four college kids, with only Derek and Sam escaping with their lives. Putting two and two together, the duo suspect Derek's mean-spirited, abusive stepdad is the monster and, with the help of Derek's Uncle Charlie (Christopher Shyer), set about proving it. But things go awry when Mitch discovers their plan, culminating in a final showdown back at the cabin.

"We don't pull any punches," enthused writer-director Lance W. Dreesen. "The wolf wracks up a pretty big body count in our film, and does so with bloody, maniacal glee! We have legs being shredded off, stomach-churning eviscerated torsos, decapitations, blood-drenched maulings, throat rips, impalings, and a really nasty castration!" Indeed, from the very first scene (a suspenseful nighttime stalking sequence that ends with the monster ripping off a hunter's leg and holding it above its head to let the blood drain into its gaping maw), this Big Bad Wolf commits all manner of alarmingly realistic-looking mayhem. But besides the gruesomely convincing limb, head, and entrail-ripping, this werewolf enjoys *raping* its (female) victims as well. "I've always felt that the werewolf is, or should be, the incarnation of the primal id—the beast within man," explained Dreeson. "And if that beast was unleashed, it wouldn't just go around devouring people—it would rape and pillage as well. So we didn't want to shy away from that. Our beast has a strong lascivious side—and acts upon it. It might make some people a little uncomfortable, but he doesn't go through the entire film raping people. [No, but he does so onscreen *twice*, with a third off-screen assault implied.] But it is part of the film—one I believe is true to the nature of the werewolf myth. The original Brothers Grimm version of 'Little Red Riding Hood' has a strong sexual subtext, and many people feel the wolf in that story is a metaphor for predatory rapists."

Apart from this "uncomfortable" sexual violence aspect, it becomes even more disconcerting (and, unfortunately, a little silly) when the werewolf starts tossing off macabre one-liners like a hirsute Freddy Kreuger. "Little pigs, little pigs, let me in," he half-growls/half-coos at the teens trapped in the cabin. "Or by the hair of my chinny-chin-chin, I'll huff and I'll puff—and I'll rip your guts out!" After raping and killing a girl, he growls at her boyfriend, "Oh, I'm sorry, was that your bitch, Champ?" Worse still, the largely unfunny and tasteless wisecracks spill over to his human persona (when Mitch breaks into Sam's trailer and kidnaps her, he quips, "Let's go to the cabin and get in a little bestiality, waddayasay?").

On the lighter side, director-screenwriter Dreesen was obviously well-versed in cinematic lycan-lore (*and* possessed a healthy sense of humor). For instance, he names his werewolf "Mitch *Toblat*," an anagram of "Talbot"; while the DNA lab to which Uncle Charlie sends the sample is called "Namflow"—"wolfman" spelled backwards. The local who tries to warn the kids off going to the cabin (a cameoing Clint Howard) is named "Fulton Chaney." And as a cameo kicker, David (*An American Werewolf in London*) Naughton appears in one throwaway scene as the sheriff.

For the most part, Mitch, as played with menacing relish by Richard Tyson, comes off as the clichéd evil, abusive stepfather who threatens Derek and verbally abuses Derek's mother (with intimations of physical violence) at every turn. Such a one-note characterization (coupled with a few telling "hints") makes more than obvious the identity of the werewolf, negating the "mystery" angle that takes up the film's middle third. When a shell-shocked Derek clings to the absurd notion that a bear or wolf attacked them at the cabin, Sam rightly insists it was a *werewolf*, pointing out, "It was a full moon; it was walking on two legs and wearing pants. Oh, and it was fucking *talking* to us! What the hell else could it have been? The question isn't what it is, it's *who* it is." It's a question with an obvious answer from the get-go. Consequently, as the protagonists run around trying to learn/confirm what the viewer already knows, the only drama or suspense comes from the rather mundane methods they use to go about securing their evidence. Of course, this does lead to one unusual—and disturbing—method of evidence gathering.... When Mitch catches Sam in his bedroom searching for hair samples, Sam must pretend to be interested in him sexually, telling the aroused Mitch that he needn't force her because she's a willing partner, and proving it by giving him a blow job (thus securing the DNA "sample"). Rather than "edgy," however, this comes off as creepy and tasteless—descriptors applied to most of the film's sexual encounters (not just the rapes but also some kinky role-playing in the woods between a frat boy and his less-than-enthusiastic girlfriend).

One exchange between Mitch and Derek breaks the clichéd mold to offer a solitary moment of pathos, which stands out for its slightly humorous beginnings that blend into a genuine expression of self-pity. When Derek, who now knows the truth, points a gun at his stepfather, Mitch states, "There's no silver bullet in there."

DEREK: "What if I shoot you in the head, huh?"
MITCH: "I dunno, I never tried that."
DEREK: "You should have."
MITCH: "Maybe I should have. Why don't you do it for me—right now. You put me out of my misery. Pull the trigger. Pull it! Goddamn it, pull it!"

But it's a moment set in stark relief due to its isolation, since for the rest of the film Mitch appears at ease with—and even to revel in—his savage alter-ego.

Though there's nothing particularly innovative about the werewolf's appearance, it still makes for a fairly impressive beast-man. Wearing a full body suit covered in coarse hair and a ridged chest, its human-wolf hybrid face, with angular cheekbones, protruding brows, mottled skin, leonine nose, wolf ears and wicked set of protruding fangs gets the point across that this monster means business. Disappointingly, the film's sole, too-rapid transformation looks cartoonish as Mitch's skin darkens and morphs via some unconvincing CGI.

This werewolf not only retains its full human faculties and talks, he also transforms at will (at one point changing in the middle of the day to deal with the meddling Uncle Charlie). Additionally, emotional surges can effect a metamorphosis as well. "One of the first things I learned when I was infected," says Mitch to the captive Charlie, "was that on a full moon I was compelled to change—needed to, wanted to. But on the other nights I felt the urge, especially when I was hungry or tired or just a little too horny. But I could resist it. But the one thing that got me was *stress*." Yes, this is definitely a *modern* werewolf.

Filming in Los Angeles and California's Simi Valley, director Dreesen imbues his movie with a professional polish, masking its low-budget roots with some evocative technique—circling camera, monster-eye view shots (complete with iris effect), misty woodland lighting—to go along with its convincing gore.

Intriguingly, beneath *Big Bad Wolf*'s hairy exterior lurks a far more insidious theme than lycanthropy—domestic violence. Mitch is not merely a werewolf, he's an abusive husband and stepfather, with several scenes involving Derek and his mother hammering home the notion of the *human* beast lurking beneath Mitch's outwardly civil exterior.

Along these lines, several times Mitch claims that his victims' predicaments are their own fault rather than his. Like a typical abuser he transfers the blame for his violent actions, informing Charlie it's his own meddling that demands his death; and telling Derek that his four slaughtered frat friends' demise "was *your* fault. I have a cabin so I can isolate myself so I can't hurt anyone. That's why no one is allowed up there. But you—you brought 'em right to me."

The film's ending even reflects one of the most perfidious aspects of domestic violence—that those who grow up in an abusive household are more likely to become abusers themselves. With his dying words, Mitch tells Derek, "My curse is now your curse." On the surface he means lycanthropy, but on a deeper level perhaps it's a warning.

Though this imperfect *Big Bad Wolf* doesn't exactly blow the house down, beneath its gory, wisecracking huffing and puffing, it offers something a little deeper, a little worthier, a little more thought-provoking: lycanthropy as a metaphor for domestic violence.

With quotes from: "Director Talks *Big Bad Wolf* Gore," HorrorDigital.com.

Morphology: Talking, hairy biped
Demise: Silver-tipped arrow
Full Moon Rating: ***

The Black Harvest of Countess Dracula see *Curse of the Devil*

Black Werewolf see *The Beast Must Die*

Blood

(1974; Bryanston) Director/Screenplay/Cinematographer: Andy Milligan; Producer: Walter Kent. Cast: Allan Berendt, Hope Stansbury, Patti Gaul, Micheal Fischetti, Pamela Adams, John Wallowitch.

Sickening horror to haunt your nightmares!—ad line

New York–based gutter auteur Andy Milligan returns to the lycan-well once more (after 1972's *The Rats Are Coming! The Werewolves Are Here!*) with *Blood*, a torpid tale of married couple Regina, the daughter of Dracula (Hope Stansbury), and Lawrence Talbot, Jr. (Allan Berendt), the son of the Wolfman, setting up house in America in the late 1800s. There Lawrence intends to continue his experiments with man-eating plants, from which they extract a serum needed to keep Regina alive. A dull series of encounters with servants' relatives, nosy estate agents, crooked lawyers, and blackmailing harridans ensues before it all goes up in smoke (literally).

Though slightly more accessible than the usual Milligan hate-fest (including his vitriol-laced yet still dull *The Rats Are Coming! The Werewolves Are Here!*), *Blood* offers its fair share of bitchiness and unpleasant characters. (When Regina, frustrated with her husband's apparent lack of affection, angrily tells him, "Oh, go to hell!" he wearily replies, "We're there already.") One of Milligan's more polished productions, *Blood* presents a better (re: almost competent) level of lighting and photography, with some occasionally effective low-key illumination and a shot or two featuring actual depth of field. It also features a more professional (or at least slightly less amateurish) level of acting, led by a just-starting-out Patti Gaul as the servant Carrie (who, *un*like every other Milligan actor, actually went on to a real career, appearing in such features as *The Big Chill* and *Silverado*, and on numerous popular television series). The film also contains Milligan's usual abrupt, garden-shears editing and some muddy nighttime photography that obscures whatever (non)action takes place onscreen (including the sole werewolf killing). Worst of all (at least for animal lovers and those viewers of conscience), Milligan repeats his reprehensible real-life rodent snuff act from his earlier *The Rats Are Coming!* when Regina decapitates a live mouse with a cleaver—for real.

Blood remains just as light on werewolfery as it is on entertainment. We first see the werewolf only in the final 15 minutes, as the transformed (off-screen, of course) Talbot bursts in and attacks a maid. Before any damage can be done (or excitement generated), however, Carrie quickly subdues the ineffectual beast with a hypodermic. Though lasting only a few seconds, it's long enough to reveal the mask-and-makeup for the subpar job it is, with this bulbous-nosed lycanthrope

When Dracula's daughter marries the son of the Wolf Man, one might expect more than the unpleasant snooze-fest that is Andy Milligan's *Blood* **(ad from a double-bill with** *Legacy of Satan***).**

looking like a cross between W.C. Fields and an ape-man. The only other time we get a (brief) look at the werewolf comes at the film's climax, which merely consists of a bit of grappling between the wolfman and his angry vampiress wife during a small-scale conflagration. Before any resolution can be found, the film abruptly cuts to a new couple looking at the house some time after the apparently cleansing fire. Their names? Baron and Baroness Von Frankenstein…. Though an amusing conceit, this last-minute joke falls far short of making up for all the earlier tedium.

Clocking in at just over an hour, *Blood* barely qualifies as a feature film. In fact, it barely qualifies as a *film* period, plagued as it is by a talky, near-actionless script, with little happening until the half-way mark, when one unfortunate receives a cleaver to the head. This crude but effective gore effect stands out from the other few bits of violence—an impromptu double hand amputation, for instance—which are all of the obvious mannequin variety.

Given a bigger budget than usual for this movie (reportedly a still-meager $20,000), Milligan abandoned his trusty 16mm Auricon camera and shot his stilted story on 35mm, though still using his own dilapidated Staten Island home as the primary (only) location (as he did with so many of his other shoestring shoots).

Milligan claimed he never saw the finished film, yet boasted he sold *Blood* to Bryanston Pictures for double its cost. Bryanston, run by Louie "Butchie" Periano (who had ties to the feared Columbo mafia family), had released the groundbreaking hardcore breakthrough *Deep Throat* in 1972, as well as *The Texas Chainsaw Massacre* in 1974. Whatever its other underhanded activities, Bryanston's releasing of *Blood* truly was a crime against cinema.

Morphology: Big-nosed, nattily-dressed wolfman
Demise: Fire (and a vampire)
Full Moon Rating: *

Blood and Chocolate

(2007; MGM; USA/UK/Germany/Romania) Director: Katja von Garnier; Producers: Hawk Koch, Richard Wright, Wolfgang Esenwein, Tom Rosenberg, Gary Lucchesi; Screenplay: Ehren Kruger, Christopher Landon (based on the book by Annette Curtis Klause); Cinematographer: Brendan Galvin. Cast: Agnes Bruckner, Olivier Martinez, Hugh Dancy, Bryan Dick, Katja Riemann.

TEMPTATION COMES IN MANY FORMS—tagline

Filmed, and set, in Bucharest, Romania, *Blood and Chocolate* tells the story of Vivian (Agnes Bruckner), a young member of a secret pack of "Loup Garou," a close-knit community living in the shadow of Bucharest society. "If Man suspects we are still here he will exterminate us," says Gabriel (Olivier Martinez), the pack leader. "We must rule this city from the shadows." Into Vivian's life comes traveling artist Aiden (Hugh Dancy), doing research for his graphic novel about werewolves. Sympathetic to the legends, he tells Vivian that the Loup Garou "were revered. They were the best of Man, the best of Beast. Kind of shapeshifters, I guess. Until they were wiped out." Not quite, as Aiden soon learns when Gabriel, to whom Vivian has been promised as his new mate, decides that Aiden must be silenced. Now Vivian must choose between her pack and her newfound love, which may mean death for herself and others.

While perhaps sounding familiar, *Blood and Chocolate*'s scenario and characters carry far more weight than that other romantic young-adult take on lycanthropy—the vapid *Twilight* series—as do the principal actors (Jennifer Love Hewitt was attached to *Blood and Chocolate* early on but thankfully gave way to the more accomplished Agnes Bruckner). Bruckner, Dancy and Martinez all bring their characters to palpable life, grounding the frequently fraught situations in a semblance of verisimilitude.

Though loosely basing the movie on the best-selling young adult novel by Annette Curtis Klause, the filmmakers did not involve the author. "The producers don't keep me up to date," admitted Klause in a 2006 interview (while the movie was in post-production). "I find my information on the Web." But she took this philosophically, stating, "I knew there was a good possibility that the film wouldn't resemble my story, but how often do you get a chance to have something you wrote made into a movie? It had to be a laugh, at least, right? A glimpse into a whole new world. We can at least pray that the movie works on its own terms, and hope that it inspires the viewers to read the book. It might be fun, despite being different." Fortunately, *Blood and Chocolate* turned out to be far more than just "fun," offering up a lycan-alternative that cast werewolves in a far more sympathetic light than most.

These werewolves are not monsters; they are a separate subspecies of humanity. They don't even *look* like monsters, for when transformed they become wolves. One cannot be *made* a Loup Garou; one must be born into it. In fact, *Blood and Chocolate* posits that werewolves can be just as appealing as the traditional, eroticized vampire. "Wouldn't it be sexy and thrilling" asked co-scripter Ehren Kruger (who did double duty as an executive producer), "to experience half your life in the wild as an animal? It's hard to do that in werewolf movies because they're presented as so monstrous and horrifying and savage, so we tried to depict the allure of that culture." They also did that by casting a cadre of attractive actors (who, unlike in the *Twilight* films, possess substantial acting chops), and using real wolves, rather than some FX-created monstrous man-wolf hybrid, to portray their lycanthropes.

"I really liked the idea of exploring the werewolf myth in a way that had similarities to tribal human cultures that are being squeezed out as modernity rolls along," continued Kruger. "[In the film] lycanthrope culture has to exist in hiding, and has rules that they don't stir the pot or kill humans or mess with mankind, because they nearly wiped them out." (Kruger was no stranger to werewolves, having inserted one into his script for *The Brothers Grimm* two years before.)

Kruger adapted an existing script by Christopher Landon (son of Michael Landon, of *I Was a Teenage Werewolf* fame), changing (among other things) the setting from Maryland to Romania. "In exploring the idea of a culture that may predate humanity," explained director Katja von Garnier, "we wanted to set the story in a locale that felt a little closer to the origin legends of werewolves." The ancient, ornate buildings, cobblestone streets and medieval churches of Bucharest create an evocative, even bewitching Old World setting for this tale of a secret lycan-society.

In the movie, lycanthropes are more blessed than cursed. "Traditionally, the werewolf is created by a curse, but here it's an ability," explained Von Garnier. "These characters are shapeshifters who can change into animals, and how great is that—it's liberating!" It's also portrayed as beautiful. When the Loup Garou want to shift, they break into a run and then leap into the air. A golden light envelopes them, and they hit the ground in wolf form. Loup Garou generally do not kill humans (with the exception of the occasional organized hunt in which Gabriel carefully chooses a victim—a despicable criminal, for instance—that he sets loose in their sacred woodland). Nor does Gabriel condone any "lone wolf" activity ("We hunt as a pack or not at all"). Vivian, who has "never killed anyone," tells Chase, "It's not the hunt that I live for, it's the running—the being free."

Like in actual folklore, the moon has no particular sway over these beings (who shift at will). But like in Hollywood folklore, silver will kill them. This becomes clear during a well-staged, edge-of-the-seat attack on Aiden by Vivian's troublesome cousin Rafe (Bryan Dick) in an old church. When a panicked Aiden takes shelter in a confessional booth, the wolf Rafe breaks through the wooden screen to snap at Aiden's throat, accidentally biting down on Aiden's silver medallion. Backing away, the wolf smacks its lips and paws at its smoking muzzle as if stung. This exposition-through-action approach typifies the film's fluid visual emphasis—rather than relying on dialogue to lay out the ground rules (like so many lesser lycan-flicks), Von Garnier and company opt to *illustrate* this key plot point. *That* is cinema.

"I really wanted a completely different approach," explained Von Garnier, "and that's possibly what makes this film special—because

Blood and Chocolate: a more romanticized (but still relevant) take on lycanthropy.

of the real wolves, for one, but also by focusing on the love story, and on aspects of the characters as well. I wanted people to understand every character's perspective—even Gabriel, who is anti-human." Gabriel considers Man to be the monster. "This thing before you is called Man," he announces to his pack before setting loose a slimy drug dealer to be hunted. "But I call it 'Menace.' The rest of Man is corrupt at its core. The only thing it's good at is destruction. So once in a while we must make an example, to show this Menace that one may be outnumbered but we will never be out-*hunted*."

Beyond this Man-as-monster theme, *Blood and Chocolate* speaks to its youthful audience with a powerful voice. When Vivian tries to send Aiden away for his own safety, stating, "My family has plans for me," Aiden responds with, "But your future is your own, isn't it? I know what it's like not to want what *they* want for you. But it's *your* life—you don't get another." Such a freedom-to-choose sentiment can't help but appeal to the film's target demographic (or to anyone who seeks to chart his or her own course through life). Gabriel, as charismatic and good looking as he is, represents the Old Order, with questioning Vivian and Aiden representing youth in this generational conflict in wolf's clothing. It's almost *The Graduate* with fur.

Blood and Chocolate is not all (blood) pudding and bon bons, however. The middle section becomes terribly angsty as Vivian and Aiden fall in love (cue the make-cute montage), then wallow in anguish when Vivian tries to break it off to protect her new paramour. And the picture runs out of steam towards the end, with too many climactic confrontations that, rather than build, merely become repetitive. Fortunately, there's enough thematic richness, engaging character development, involving acting, and exciting set-pieces (including a thrilling chase through the woods as the pack hunts Aiden, who survives only through his own resourcefulness, coupled with a well-concealed silver knife and timely intervention by Vivian) to sustain interest.

A commercial failure, *Blood and Chocolate* grossed only $6 million worldwide theatrically. It also failed to please most critics. "I want this to be a romantic experience [for the audience]," concluded Von Garnier. "And I want them to root for our couple. …And I want audiences to feel awe from the wolves, and exhilarated during the hunt scenes. Ultimately, I want them to feel heightened emotions—to be thrilled, to laugh and to be sad. I always want a rich emotional experience from a film." And Von Garnier and co. delivered just that. It's just unfortunate that so few critics recognized this, and, more importantly, so few patrons experienced it.

With quotes from: "Author Update: Annette Curtis Klause," by Cynthia Leitich Smith, *Cynsations*; "*Blood & Chocolate*: Young Werewolves in Love," by Paul Gaita, *Fangoria* 260.

Morphology: Four-legged wolves
Demise: Silver (in any form)
Full Moon Rating: ***½

Blood Moon (1971) see The Werewolf vs. the Vampire Woman

Blood Moon

(2014; Uncork'd Entertainment; UK) Director: Jeremy Wooding; Producers: Michael Vine, Jeremy Wooding; Screenplay: Alan Wrightman; Cinematographer: Jono Smith. Cast: George Blagden, Raffaello Degruttola, Shaun Dooley, Jack Fox, Corey Johnson, Eleanor Matsuura, Amber Jean Rowan, Anna Skellern.

WHEN IT'S RED, YOU'RE DEAD—ad line

What's rarer than a *mariphaisa lumina lupina* flower blooming in the moonlight? A werewolf *Western*. That's why *Blood Moon* is both so welcome and so disappointing. Apart from *Ginger Snaps Back: The Beginning* (actually set in 19th century Canada rather than the American Old West) and one third of the cheap Mexican horror anthology *Rider of the Skulls*, *Blood Moon* features the only werewolf to prowl the dusty trail. And while the film walks tall as a character-driven visit to the Old West, it stumbles like the town drunk leaving a saloon when it comes to lycanthropy.

In 1887 Colorado, a stagecoach carrying a disparate group of passengers makes a pit stop at the abandoned mining town of Pine Flats. They find the caretaker there (played by David Sterne, who faced *The Wolfman* in 2010) dead, brutally slain by a "skinwalker," a werewolf. Arriving soon after is a pair of outlaw brothers who murder the stage driver and take the passengers hostage. It's up to a deputy returning from his honeymoon (Tom Cotcher), a mysterious gunslinger (Shaun Dooley) who hitched a ride on the coach, and a neighboring town's marshal tracking the two criminals to not only subdue the outlaws but defend the rest against the marauding beast intent on killing and eating them all.

Mixing the Western and horror genres is always a tricky proposition. Few have tried, and fewer have succeeded. Though injecting horror into a Western milieu *can* work (1999's *Ravenous* comes to mind), more often than not it turns into something like *Billy the Kid vs. Dracula* (1966). Fortunately, *Blood Moon* borrows from the best of both genre worlds, conjuring images from John Ford's *Stagecoach* (1939) and the Quentin Tarantino–scripted, Robert Rodriguez–directed *From Dusk Till Dawn* (1996). In *Blood Moon*'s early scene of gunslinger Calhoun standing in the road to flag down the coach, saddle in hand (having had to shoot his injured horse in the film's striking opening sequence), one can't help but see echoes of John Wayne's *Stagecoach* introduction. When Calhoun boards the crowded stage, he takes his place on the floor, just like Wayne's Ringo. Later, when the two outlaws take the Good People hostage, only to seek sanctuary in a bar (Pine Flats' abandoned saloon) and (sort of) band together when supernatural forces lay siege, one can't help but think of *From Dusk Til Dawn* (particularly when the psychotic younger outlaw brother is killed early on, just like Tarantino's psychotic younger brother character in *Dusk*).

Amazingly, with just over half a million pounds (less than a million dollars), and shooting in *England* with a British cast and crew (at the "Loredo Western Town" in Kent—24 buildings built over the last 40 years by a group of Western enthusiasts), *Blood Moon* clinically captures the mud and the grime and the cold and the harshness of the American Old West (Colorado chapter). Director Jeremy Wooding had made only two (very British) features before this, having working mainly in television. So it becomes doubly impressive that he could so ably inject the feel of an American Western into his werewolf tale. And thanks to cinematographer Jono Smith's evocative lighting and mobile camerawork (including some intense p.o.v. shots), the film looks far more polished than its straightened circumstances should allow. There's even the occasional bit of artistry, such as when a shot of spindly tree branches goes out of focus to bring the background of a full moon behind them into sharp relief as one character speaks of the Beast Within. "It was tough making a period piece on a budget," admitted Wooding. "But as I have worked with many of the Heads of Department before, I knew they were great at keeping production values high in spite of having limited resources."

"The key to it for me was making a 'Gothic Western,'" explained Wooding. "I am a big fan of English Gothic in literature, film, fashion, architecture etc. So, my English 'Gothic sensibility' informed my approach to the material. And I did a lot of research into the comic book and graphic novel precursors to this genre mix. Those comic strips showed me that the mix could work, and that fed into my vision of the movie—a comic book tale come to life." Fortunately, *Blood Moon*'s characters prove far more substantial than most comic book examples. From the two squabbling outlaw brothers to the timid preacher to the stoic lawman with his new bride, to the laconic gunslinger with a secret past (asked repeatedly by different characters where he was from, Calhoun would always mysteriously reply, "I'd tell you, but you've never heard of it"), Alan Wrightman's script fleshes out the potential stereotypes into full-fledged characters that involve the viewer in their plight. A cadre of talented jobbing English actors, led by the steady, enigmatic presence of Shaun Dooley (*The Woman in Black* [2012], TV's *Broadchurch*) as Calhoun, adds depth, bringing them to vivid life. So when someone dies (whether by gunshot or werewolf claw), it makes an impact.

In keeping with its Western setting, the werewolf here is not some Satanic-cursed beast from Eastern Europe but a Native American skinwalker. Through the feisty female Native American tracker Black Deer and her prickly relationship with the marshal, we learn that "a skinwalker is a Navajo warrior banished from their tribe for learning the forbidden secret of shapeshifting." During the blood moon, "skinwalkers are at their strongest." And though silver is necessary to stop a skinwalker, it takes a little something extra to truly finish the job: "White ash, prepared by my father," says Black Deer. "If a skinwalker is shot in the heart with a silver bullet it might *appear* to die. White ash sends it to the Land of the Dead." And, in fact, at film's end a shot of silver does topple the monster, but the werewolf only writhes in pain until Calhoun sprinkles the sacred ash over it, upon which it transforms (via cutaways) first into a human covered in fuzz, then a naked (dead) brave.

During their ride to Pine Flats in search of the outlaws, Black Deer admits to the Marshal, "Some of us are only *part* skinwalker. But if the beast within is too strong, I turn into something half-human, half-skinwalker, hated and hunted by both." Overcome by the power of the full (blood) moon, she transforms as she talks. Sharp claws poke through her fingertips, and the skin of her calf splits open to reveal the hairy wolf pelt beneath. When she turns to him, she's become a she-wolf—though not a particularly convincing one. Her blackened face, dog nose, bushy eyebrows, and oversized fangs protruding in a pronounced overbite conjures visions of a Halloween haunted house. Most disappointingly, this potentially intriguing notion of full werewolves vs. half-wolves comes to naught, since after initially attacking the marshal, she stops herself and then simply runs off into the woods, never to be seen again. But this is only the first of several lycancentric disappointments.

The manbeast's motivations remain a mystery. Is the skinwalker's unprovoked attack a form of Native American retribution? Is it something more personal? Is he merely hungry? The script ignores such potentially intriguing issues, making this werewolf merely a one-dimensional monster.

The werewolf siege doesn't begin until the 50-minute mark. Fortunately, the characters are well drawn—and the human scenario intriguing—enough to hold one's interest while waiting for the skinwalker to make its hirsute appearance. While Wooding and co. capture an Old West feel with their colorful characters and clever dialogue (as well as some more-accurately-staged-than-most gunfights resulting in several realistically nasty head shots), when it comes to the horror side of their Western equation, they sometimes end up in the negative column. Keeping their beast largely unseen for the first hour works fine, letting the tension of the situation build through character interaction and the occasional teasing glimpse of a furry shoulder (as it watches its prey), or wicked claws (as it slices open a man's throat), or a massive broad back covered in dense hair (as a shotgun blast opens a red patch of flesh, only for the gaping wound to miraculously close up and heal in a startling, and very convincing, bit of localized CGI work). Finally, a split-second flash of the monster's huge wolfish face, all angry green eyes and sharp yellow teeth gives the viewer a jolt as it lunges towards the protagonists. Unfortunately, the illusion melts away like human flesh on a transforming werewolf when a few seconds later the camera reveals the creature in full. With a protruding muzzle ending in a bat-like nose; pointy, elf-like ears; a tuft of coarse hair sprouting from its head; and an impossibly wide, oversized, grinning maw filled with pink gums and fangs, it resembles a cross between a wolf, a bat, and The Joker. But at least its huge, hairy, and threateningly solid physical presence marks it as more convincing than many an insubstantial CGI lycan.

Worst of all, however, the heretofore near-unstoppable (regular bullets hurt and even divert it, but can't kill it) manbeast's demise proves woefully anticlimactic. After the creature has decimated their ranks, the survivors, armed with a shotgun loaded with silver shot, stride down the street towards the werewolf. The skinwalker, whose lethality up to now has been surpassed only by its cunning and stealth, simply stands on a roof waiting while its enemies approach. Calhoun then stops, takes careful aim, and fires. The werewolf topples off the roof to lay writhing on the ground until the white ash sends it to its Happy Hunting Ground. Staged with little suspense and less action, it proves a poor demise for what had been a terrifyingly dangerous werewolf.

A final denouement, obviously aimed at franchise potential, implies that Calhoun might just be some all-knowing monster hunter, as he indicates he's moving on to his next job—helping to eradicate some "varmints ... with six-inch claws and bat wings" down in Santa Clara. Such a cheap and cheesy conclusion doesn't sit well with the heretofore realistic character's (and film's) tone.

Premiering at the London Frightfest Film Festival in August of 2014, *Blood Moon* made its American debut on DVD the following year. While it stands tall as a unique addition to lycancinema, with its novel Old West setting and involving characters, its poorly-handled werewolf marks it as something of a wasted opportunity.

With quotes from: "Interview: Jeremy Wooding—Director (*Blood Moon*)," by Janel Spiegel, horrornews.net.

Morphology: Hulking, hairy biped
Demise: Silver shotgun shells (with a white ash kicker)
Full Moon Rating: ***

Blood of Dracula's Castle

(1969; Crown International [theatrical]/Paragon International [TV]) Alternate Title: *Dracula's Castle* (TV). Directors: Al Adamson, Don Hulette (extended TV version, uncredited); Producers: Al Adamson, Rex Carlton; Screenplay: Rex Carlton; Cinematographer: Leslie Kovaks. Cast: John Carradine, Paula Raymond, Alex D'Arcy, Robert Dix, Gene O'Shane, Barbara Bishop, Vicki Volante, Ray Young.

HORROR BEYOND BELIEF ... LIES WAITING FOR ALL WHO DARE ENTER THE VAMPIRE'S DUNGEON!—poster

Replace the word "horror" with "boredom," and the above tag-line would be far more accurate. That said, at least this slow-moving low-budgeter is better than its even cheesier co-feature, *Nightmare in Wax* (damning with faint praise). And *Blood of Dracula's Castle* is also one of producer-director Al Adamson's (*Dracula vs. Frankenstein*, *Blood of Ghastly Horror*, etc.) better looking efforts (damning with even *fainter* praise).

A professional photographer (Gene O'Shane) inherits a castle out in the California desert(!) and takes his fiancée (Barbara Bishop) to inspect his new property. There he ultimately learns that the castle's genteel renters (Alex D'Arcy and Paula Raymond) are a pair of vampires (Count and Countess Dracula actually, though they employ the alias Townsend) who, along with their butler George (John Carradine), deformed hunchback caretaker Mango (Ray Young) and escaped psychopath helper Johnny (Robert Dix), kidnap young girls to keep in the dungeon as their own personal hemoglobin taps. They also occasionally sacrifice one of the captives to the Moon god "Luna."

So why is this low-rent vampire flick in a book about werewolf movies? Well … when Crown International decided to package the film for television in the early 1970s via Paragon International, they concluded its 84-minute running time was too short and decided to film an additional seven minutes to extend its length. With Al Adamson no longer involved (the picture, along with its co-feature *Nightmare in Wax*, had been wrested from Adamson and Sam Sherman's Independent International company when the double-bill ran into financial difficulties with the lab during post-production), Don Hulette purportedly shot the additional footage. (Hulette was something of a padding specialist, having done similar duties for *They Saved Hitler's Brain* and about thirty other low-rent features.) With all the talk about the "the great god Luna" and Johnny's loss of control when the moon rises, it was a natural to transform Johnny the psychopath into Johnny the *werewolf*. "Something happens to me when that damn moon is full," reports Johnny. "I do things I don't want to. It's almost like I'm obeying an order from—somewhere. I want to kill, I have to kill." (Of course, the sociopathic Johnny does plenty of killing during the day, without the benefit of the "damn moon," but apparently that's beside the point.) Anyway, one hirsute mask and three added scenes later, and *Dracula's Castle* (the film's new TV moniker) now houses a lycanthrope. The first werewolf moment comes when Johnny escapes from prison by bribing a duplicitous guard (played by production manager John "Bud" Cardos). In the original version, the guard insists Johnny clobber him to make it look like a legitimate jailbreak, but Johnny, possessed by bloodlust, goes far beyond the "one swift stroke" to pound away at the hapless guard. For the TV version, as Johnny strikes the guard, a shot of the moon triggers a freeze-frame of Johnny's hate-maddened face, which dissolves to that of a werewolf visage. The manbeast then continues to rain blows down on the guard (out of frame) for a few seconds before the scene cleverly cuts to the Countess in their castle happily speaking of Johnny and saying, "He's so wild and carefree…" The second lycan-scene (lasting twenty seconds) begins with an obvious day-for-night shot of Johnny the wolfman running through the woods before coming upon a stream, drinking from it, and crawling away. Johnny then wakes up next to the water in human form. The final bit of lycanthropy comes via a totally self-contained four-and-a-half-minute sequence in which the wolfman stalks a random girl through the woods. Close-ups of the frightened victim alternate with shots of the werewolf looking around before the girl sprints off across a field, with the beast-man in hot pursuit. More footage of the werewolf rushing, tearing and even crawling through the brush in search of his terrified prey pad out the running time before the girl finally stumbles into a clearing and falls to the ground. Then, in the movie's sole truly effective lycan-moment, the werewolf steps from the bushes, and we, like the cornered girl, gaze upwards at his savage countenance. With wild, coarse hair, deep-set dark eyes, bestial wolf's nose and vicious fangs, this Johnny-wolf makes for a fairly menacing-looking wolfman.

Naturally, the werewolf notion fits into the scenario only, er, fitfully. During the full moon sacrifice ceremony later in the film, for instance, Johnny stays human rather than transforming. And in the end he's shot and killed (again in human form) with his own gun—sporting lead, rather than silver, bullets. There's also a snoot full of continuity errors, such as when the wolfman sports the same prison garb he originally wore a full day and night *after* he's made his successful escape and settled in at the chateau.

At one point Johnny states, "I don't fight my impulses. Therefore I don't have any problems. Except when that damn moon is full. Sometimes I seem to lose my control and my power of reasoning." Given the new footage, such a line takes on new meaning, almost surreally positing lycanthropy as an answer to repression and the "problems" that come along with it. Later, Johnny elaborates further: "All of us are affected by the full moon. It affects our blood. We must satisfy our lustful desires." Hedonistic werewolfery as therapy? Hmmm.

To its credit, despite a reported eight-day shooting schedule, the picture looks fairly professional (thanks to the competent lighting and solid photography of Leslie Kovaks [*Easy Rider*, *Ghostbusters*, *Two Weeks Notice*]) and is generally well-acted, both by old pros Carradine, D'Arcy (*Horrors of Spider Island*) and Raymond (*Beast from 20,000 Fathoms*)—each of whom add a touch of class and some droll humor to the silly proceedings—*and* by likable newcomers O'Shane and Bishop. (Adamson originally wanted Carradine for the Dracula role, but the production's money men demanded that D'Arcy play the Count, so Adamson had to settle for Carradine as the butler.)

Consisting mostly of talk, or long stretches designed solely to eat up some much-needed running time (a photo shoot at Marineland; the protagonists swimming in the ocean; two lengthy driving-in-the-car sequences, etc.), the film offers little in the way of action. Admittedly, some of the dialogue *is* amusing (Count to Johnny: "How about your psychotic desire to kill?" Johnny: "Oh well, we all have our little shortcomings"), but most sounds simply banal. And worst of all, the picture's one "money" shot (the dissolution of the vampires) was filmed for pennies. Too cheap even for some dissolves and a couple of prop skeletons, Adamson keeps the camera locked down on the hero and heroine as they stare and exclaim, "They're getting old" and "They turned to dust"—without ever *showing* it.

While the movie's exteriors (filmed at a real castle purportedly shipped over from Ireland and rebuilt in Lancaster, California) appear impressive, the interior sets (shot at the Santa Monica Sound Stage) look shoddy in comparison, including what has to be the world's tidiest plywood-and-Styrofoam castle dungeon (two token rats appear; but, despite the captive girls' screams of disgust, the rodents make little impact when they scurry across a floor so clean you could eat off it).

"Al was not what you would call a good director," concluded production manager John "Bud" Cardos (who also had a small role as a security guard). "He could raise the money for these little shows, and put them together, but he shot everything so fast he could have made 'em a lot better … [they were] sloppy." (Cardos later went on to direct his own features, including the entertaining William Shatner-starrer *Kingdom of the Spiders*.) Retired from moviemaking since the early 1980s, Adamson was murdered in 1995 and his body entombed in cement under his own Jacuzzi by a live-in contractor remodeling Adamson's Indio, California, home. It proved a tragic denouement bizarre enough for one of the filmmaker's own tawdry movies.

With quotes from: "Motorcycle Maniacs, Fantastic Fights: John 'Bud' Cardos," by Bob Plante, *Psychotronic Video* 24.

Morphology: Chaney-esque wolfman
Demise: Plain old lead bullet (fired, embarrassingly enough, from his own gun)
Full Moon Rating: **

Blood of the Werewolf

(2001; Brimstone Productions/Delta Entertainment) Directors/Producers: Bruce G. Hallenbeck, Kevin J. Lindenmuth, Joe Bagnardi; Screenplay: Bruice G. Hallenbeck, Keven J. Lindenmuth, Stephen C.

Steward, Joe Banardi; Cinematographers: Joe Bagnardi, Kevin J. Lindenmuth. Cast: Tony Luna, Mary K. Hilko, Mia Borrelli, Sasha Graham, Bruce G. Hallenbeck, Helen Black, Bill Chaput, Ron Rausch, Mike Gingold, Dan Bailey, Tom Nundorf, Ted. V. Mikels.

> Things get a little hairy when the moon is full...—tagline

Blood of the Werewolf illustrates a prime axiom of the horror movie industry: *Anything* can secure a home video release, particularly from a company that specializes in combining various disparate shorts made by amateur filmmakers into a like-themed anthology. One such company is Brimstone Productions, run by Indy moviemaker Kevin J. Lindenmuth. Lindenmuth typically conscripts his like-minded backyard moviemaking friends into adding a couple of their camcorder creations to his own micro-budgeted short to produce a feature-length product for undiscriminating, I'll-buy-any-DVD-with-a-genre-slant patrons. Here Lindenmuth cobbles together a werewolf-themed trio of stories, the middle tale being his own.

"Blood Reunion" (directed by Bruce G. Hallenbeck) centers on a horror writer who returns to his home town and looks up old flame Jane, who's kept under the tyrannical thumb of her cranky "Granny Radford." Granny is determined to keep men away from her granddaughter, and for good reason—if she "feels the stir of the flesh her beast blood will take over." The second tale, "Old Blood" (by Lindenmuth, who also helmed the almost-as-bad *Rage of the Werewolf* in 1999), focuses on a lesbian couple, one of whom is a "shapeshifter." Charlene is fascinated by her girlfriend's "power" and wants to share in it. But when her partner finally acquiesces, Charlene learns that one should be careful about what one wishes. The final segment, "Manbeast" (by Joe Bagnardi), stars the first story's director, Bruce Hallenbeck, as a man on the run from a pair of hunters determined to kill him. "I used to be just like them," he intones in voiceover, "before I was attacked by the wild beast." Now he is "cursed to change into a creature, cursed to attack others and make them like me." Unfortunately, due to clumsy camerawork and obvious scripting, the viewer is cursed to glean the story's Big Twist within the first five minutes, leaving a half-hour of running through the woods before the unsurprising "payoff."

Amateurish with a *lower-case* 'a,' this inept-in-all-departments anthology of awfulness takes the occasional clever idea ("Old Blood"'s shapeshifting twist on ambition and vanity; the 'eye of the beholder' lycan variation in "Manbeast") and strands them on a desert island of boredom. Transported on a wave of cheap videography (characterized by focus issues, lighting problems, and seasickness-inducing hand-held camerawork); hollow, inconsistent sound; stilted "acting" from friends and family; and seedy, low-rent locations (including a sand quarry standing in for the final tale's "Forbidden Zone"), the shipwreck proves inevitable.

Bereft of wit, charm, or even mildly interesting characters, and saddled with a dowdy, milquetoast lead (in Mary Kay Hilko), the all-too-predictable "Blood Reunion" buries whatever insight into the relationship between sexuality and humankind's animal nature ("I must die a virgin," she sadly states, "or die violently") it might have offered in a mud hole of ineptitude. "Old Blood," filled with disjointed, talky scenes that make little sense (with characters yakking about making a "spirit," transferring power, the lineage, the pack—all with zero follow-through), offers a mildly amusing twist that's undone by its abrupt handling and a ridiculous-looking papier-mâché mask. The final tale, "Manbeast," the most ambitious and competently-shot of the three, is so ham-fisted and awkward that it loses whatever impact its *Twilight Zone*–esque premise with a lycan-twist might have offered.

And despite the film's "…when the moon is full" tagline, none of the three stories feature lunar-induced lycanthropy. The only notable surprise the movie holds is the blink-and-you'll-miss-it pre-credit cameo by low-budget auteur Ted V. Mikels (*The Astro-Zombies*, *The Corpse Grinders*) staring into the camera to utter nonsense like "We are the ancient ones" and "We must never forget that we were the first," apropos of nothing at all.

Offering nothing but a few ill-defined and ultimately wasted variations on werewolfery, the bungled backyard boredom of *Blood of the Werewolf* just goes to show that a camcorder and a few willing friends does not a movie make.

Morphology: Dog-faced woman; bushy-headed wolfmen
Demise: Pointy silver crucifix; ordinary gunshot
Full Moon Rating: ½

Bloodz vs. Wolvez

(2006; I.E. Entertainment) Director/Producer/Screenplay: John Bacchus (as Z. Winston Brown); Cinematographer: Paul Swan. Cast: Malik Burke, Richard Carroll, Jr., Kardiss Marie, Jenicia Garcia, Raymond Spencer, Jakeem Sellers.

> Only the survivor will see the daylight—ad line

Director John Bacchus (as Z. Winston Brown), maker of such derivative no-budget trash as *The Erotic Witch Project* (2000), *Play-Mate of the Apes* (2002), and *Kinky Kong* (2006), turns his sleazy sights on the old vampires vs. werewolves conflict in a sort of no-budget ghetto version of the *Underworld* series. The story pits the well-to-do vampire clan the Bloodz, headed by Asiman (Richard Carroll, Jr.), against the ghetto-dwelling werewolf pack the Wolvez, led by Loup Garou (Malik Burke). The "Asiman Corporation" has bought up a number of derelict buildings in Wolvez territory to turn into upscale condos. Consequently, Asiman wants a truce with Loup (vampires have been at war with werewolves for centuries) in order to complete the project. Seeking a better life for his pack, Loup agrees, but when Asiman's duplicitous wife betrays her husband *and* Loup, the Wolvez call off the truce and take the war to the Bloodz.

Though shot on video in New York City (primarily in half-finished, still-under-construction apartments), the movie at least looks professional, with adequate lighting and proper focus. The same can not be said of the often poorly modulated sound, however, with voices ringing hollow in the mostly empty rooms, and a barely audible narration ("…an ancient rivalry of rare semi-human species comes to a crossroads…") under the opening credits that fades in and out. And triple-threat producer-director-screenwriter Bacchus, abetted by videographer Paul Sawn (returning from Bacchus' *Vampiyaz* [2004] and *Zombiez* [2005], and who normally works as a grip on *real* movies and TV series), employs the handheld shaky-cam to an epileptic degree.

Bacchus' script fares no better in trying to make up for its lack of import and wit with street-talk and vulgarity, perhaps best summed up when a vampire underling calls together a small group of blood-suckers to determine how to kill werewolves (despite the fact that they've supposedly been at war with the lycans for hundreds of years, and have dispatched several of Loup's pack already). She reads the classic *Wolf Man* ditty—but Bacchus carelessly gets it wrong: "Evan a man who is puritan [rather than "pure"] in heart and says his prayers by night, may become a wolf when the wolfsbane blooms and the moon is pure and bright," rather than the original's final line of "and the Autumn moon is bright," or the minor change from *Frankenstein*

Meets the Wolf Man of "and the moon is full [rather than "pure"— whatever a *pure* moon might be] and bright." In any case, none of the vampires know what wolfsbane might be(!), so one suggests kryptonite(!!)—"I know that kills werewolves," he assures the group. Another pipes up with, "I heard that if you hold their dick really tight and slice it off at the base, it kills them instantly." Nice.

These urban gangsta werewolves prove to be an uninteresting lot— even their leader, the groan-inducingly named "Loup Garou" (a moniker only slightly more obvious than his packmates' "Cujo," "Rex" and "Lobo"). Though actor Malik Burke (who also served as one of three "associate producers") gives it the old homeboy try, he must make do with building his clichéd character with dialogue like, "I'm a werewolf, bitch! You a vampire. We ain't human. I don't give a fuck about 'legal.' Don't give a fuck about your 'business.' I don't play by those rules." Burke does have one arresting moment, however, when Loup tries to explain to Asiman how he can never truly fit in with humanity. "I tried to assimilate," Loup says sadly. "I had a wife, a daughter. I ate them. I have killed everything I have ever loved. 'Cause when that full moon glows, I'm just a werewolf. And I'll always be. So fuck all that 'assimilation' shit." But another round of ghetto-gab quickly extinguishes this brief flicker of pathos. Besides, his sympathetic plea makes no sense given that these Wolvez retain their human faculties while in lycan-form (meaning he knew exactly what he was doing when he "ate them").

Throughout the picture the lycanthropes do very little of note, mostly sitting (or laying) around their under-construction apartment building (which not only lacks furniture but interior walls) and occasionally meeting with the vampires for more pointless posturing. One amusing moment arrives when Garou invites a (stereotypically gay) "etiquette expert" over to instruct him in the ways of polite society, only to have his impatient lieutenant shove his fist into the hapless man's stomach to pull out his guts (unconvincingly represented by a few butcher shop leftovers). The most memorable weremoment (for all the wrong reasons), however, comes when one of the pack slyly looks around, then lays down some newspapers on the floor and *defecates* on them—with the camera moving in for a close-up of what turns out to be an apt metaphor for the movie as a whole.

These lycanthropes' werewolf form consists of some delicate-looking fangs, a set of long fingernails, and intermittent glowing red eyes. That's it. With no fur, no facial hair, nor even a wet dog nose in sight, the only way to distinguish the vampires from the lycans is their mode of dress—the Bloodz wear suits and ties while the Wolvez dress like bandana-sporting gangbangers. Though perhaps not unexpected in a production that apparently can't even afford blood squibs (most of the conflicts involve gunplay, with victims dancing around pretending to be hit by bullets, without a drop of blood in sight), such monster minimalism makes it that much harder to buy whatever claptrap the script is selling.

The potentially intriguing thematic conflict between the haves (Bloodz) and have-nots (Wolvez) within the black community proves as superficial as the Wolvez' hairless appearance. When Asiman asks Loup at their initial meeting "What will it take to bring this [war] to an end?" the werewolf answers, "Jobs. Housing. Free rent." Later, Loup observes, "The Jews and the Palestinians can't get it together, what makes you think we're any different?" And that's about it, unless one sees symbolism in the lyrics of a background rap song playing in one scene: "I think best when I rip flesh, mmmm / I should really try to kill less / And yet there's no regrets, you can't domesticate us / Don't make good pets." Or not.

Z-grade in more than just its urbanized title, the nihilistic and pointless *Bloodz vs. Wolvez* should be avoided at all cost.

Morphology: Homeboys with pointy incisors and long fingernails
Demise: Silver bullets
Full Moon Rating: ½

The Boy Who Cried Werewolf

(1973; Universal) Director: Nathan H. Juran; Producer: Aaron Rosenberg; Screenplay: Bob Homel; Cinematographer: Michael P. Joyce. Cast: Kerwin Mathews, Elaine Devry, Robert J. Wilke, Scott Sealey, Bob Homel, Susan Foster, Jack Lucas.

POSSIBLE IN THIS DAY AND AGE? THOSE WHO DIDN'T BELIEVE … ARE DEAD!—ad line

---

The Boy Who Cried Werewolf is one of those films that leaves a deep impression—on those under the age of thirteen. Anyone older seeing the movie for the first time might have difficulty getting past its 1970s stereotypes (and fashion), dated dialogue, bloodless (and largely action-less) action, made-for-television sensibilities (despite its theatrical pedigree), and disappointing werewolf. As illustration of the film's impact on the younger set, future filmmaker Mike Davis, creator of 2012's *President Wolfman*, noted, "My dad took me to that movie when I was little and it freaked the hell out of me. …As a young kid that terrified me. I don't know if it was an analogy for child abuse or what. But seeing that movie sitting next to your dad is really scary, and it affected me."

When recently divorced Robert Bridgeston (Kerwin Mathews) takes his young son Ritchie (Scott Sealey) to their mountain cabin for some fishing, they're suddenly attacked by a werewolf in the woods. Robert fends off the manbeast, sending it over an embankment to its death (impaled on a post)—but not before his attacker has bitten him on the arm. When Ritchie tells the local law, "It was a real werewolf, Sheriff; it attacked us," no one believes him, not even dear old dad. "Ritchie, stop this monster business," admonishes Robert (it was too dark to see properly, he claims, and the body had reverted to its human form after death). But Ritchie doesn't stop, and his concerned mother, Sandy (Elaine Devry), takes him to see a psychiatrist (George Gaynes), who advises Robert to bring Ritchie back to the cabin as therapy. Once there, a full moon transforms Robert into a werewolf who attacks and kills several people (even causing a fatal road accident). Ritchie now suspects that his dad has become a monster, yet still no one will listen. Finally, Ritchie's mom agrees to accompany her son and ex-husband to the cabin for a possible reconciliation. But after a disturbing encounter with some Jesus freaks (whose "holy circle" Robert seems unable to enter), Robert transforms that night and carries off Sandy. A sheriff's posse (out hunting the "animal" that's been doing the killing) runs across the lycanthrope and, despite Ritchie's heartfelt protestations, blasts the creature, who falls backwards onto a splintered post that pierces his heart.

Like some hirsute Afterschool Special, the mild-mannered, PG-rated *The Boy Who Cried Werewolf* takes the themes of separation anxiety and parental betrayal and covers them with wolf hair. The two parents obviously still love one another but can't live together (he resents her devotion to her career, and she [rightly] labels him a chauvinist). Little Ritchie can't understand this and, like most young offspring of divorced parents, wants them back together. If such emotional trauma weren't enough, *Boy* becomes a true child's nightmare when one parent changes into a monster (literally). Compounding the matter is the fact that no authority figure, no adult at all (including his own father), will believe him when he tells them what he saw. "He's a monster, Mom," pleads Ritchie, "a real werewolf, but he

The Boy Who Cried Werewolf (1973) • 49

The generation gap turns monstrous in *The Boy Who Cried Werewolf*. Under the hair and dog nose is Kerwin Mathews, who retired from acting after making this movie. Coincidence? (American lobby card)

doesn't remember it." At this, his shocked mother warns, "Ritchie, you can't make up stories like that about your Dad."

Despite the now-dated Seventies speech patterns, stereotypes and fashions (the werewolf runs around in sport coat and yellow turtleneck sweater), *The Boy Who Cried Werewolf* can't help but invite comparisons to its (far superior) model, *The Wolf Man* (1941). Like the original, *Boy* revolves around the father-son dynamic and the dangerous disconnect between the two generations. Here, however, it is the father who becomes the bestial monster rather than the son, which adds elements of parental betrayal and mistrust of authority. Unfortunately, rather than exploring and expanding upon these key psychological issues, screenwriter Bob Homel (in his only produced script) addresses them only obliquely, leaving such tasty thematics buried in a vat of cinematic cheese.

Rather than *The Wolf Man*'s roving band of gypsies, *The Boy Who Cried Werewolf* offers a roving band of hippies. This group of VW-driving Jesus freaks, led by Brother Christopher (played by screenwriter Bob Homel himself), generates most of the film's (unintentional) laughs. When the redneck sheriff attempts to roust the "mobile commune" and addresses them as "you freaks," Brother Christopher shoots back, "We're freaked out on God, man." Indeed.

Reflecting European legends, the film ties lycanthropy to Satanism, most overtly through the fanatical hippies, whose leader, after hearing a howling in the woods, enthuses, "Hey, a demon is comin' to test us!" When Robert and family stop to gawk at the "Jesus encampment" (behaving as if it were some roadside attraction—"We've only come to watch"), Brother Christopher has his followers form a circle and dance around the large wooden cross they've planted in the ground. "It shields us from Satan," he explains. "Enter, enter—it's only a pentagram, sir.... Only a demon of Hell cannot enter." But Robert, in fact, can *not* enter the circle, stopped by an invisible barrier.

Even Ritchie's psychiatrist gets in on the demonic act when he meets with Robert to discuss the boy's "werewolf fixation." "Legend has it that the werewolf's index fingers become longer than the center fingers," he tells Robert. "The longer a person is possessed, eventually his hands may *stay* deformed—a kind of Mark of Satan." A subsequent scene shows Mathews dismayed when he notices his index finger has indeed become longer than his middle digit, indicating the "possession" has taken a strong hold.

Boy adds a few wrinkles to the usual werewolf lore, however. Like vampires, here werewolves can be killed with a stake (or handy signpost) through the heart. As Ritchie says (he's read a book about werewolves),

"You know, Dad, we're lucky that werewolf got stuck through the heart with that road sign. Because there's only three ways you can kill a werewolf—by being struck through the heart, or being bashed in the head with something made of silver [an obvious nod to *The Wolf Man*], or with wolfsbane—that's a mysterious plant that suffocates werewolves, and it only blooms in the full moon."

Unlike with most werewolf movies (which usually make the viewer wait patiently for the first glimpse of the monster), the wolfman appears from very nearly the first frame, as it skulks in the foliage watching a car approach. While this would normally be a plus for most lycan-fans, here it only reveals from the get-go the disappointingly non-threatening look of the manbeast. The less-than-frightening wolfman, more terrier than terror, sports a well-groomed halo of thick, straight hair sprouting from a canine face with a wet dog-nose and protruding muzzle reminiscent of the simian countenances from *Planet of the Apes* (1968). Such a resemblance is unsurprising, given that *Boy*'s werewolf creator, Tom Burman, had assisted makeup pioneer John Chambers on *Planet* (and later partnered with Chambers to open up a makeup effects studio). After *Boy*, Burman went on to much bigger (and better) things, working on such films as *Close Encounters of the Third Kind* (1977), *Invasion of the Body Snatchers* (1978), and *The Godfather Part III* (1990). Burman also handled the transformation effects makeup for the were-creatures in *Cat People* (1982), and turned Michael J. Fox into *Teen Wolf* (1985). He even received an Academy Award nomination for Best Makeup in 1988 for *Scrooged*. Obviously Burman got a lot better.

The first werewolf (who attacks and infects Robert) was played by stunt coordinator Paul Baxley, and the fight between Mathews and the Baxley beast remains refreshingly energetic and violent. Unfortunately, cinematographer Michael P. Joyce (in his only theatrical credit as DP, the rest of his work being for television) lights the scene so poorly that the viewer often has merely the dimmest outline of the figures with which to follow the action. After this first encounter, director Nathan Juran immediately abandons this more active tack to keep the rest of the werewolf attacks discreet and bloodless (and largely unseen), and the killings completely off-screen.

Juran handles the film's sole transformation sequence simply but effectively, adding a few details to flesh out the standard metamorphosis. First, the horrified Robert sees that his fingers have elongated and the nails have turned black. Then, touching his sweat-drenched face, he feels fangs in his mouth. As he (and we) look into a mirror, a series of dissolves show him becoming the beast.

Mathews' lycanthrope engages in some very un-werewolf-like behavior, such as sneaking in to bury a victim's head in the cabin's basement with a shovel—more the actions of a human serial killer than an animalistic beast-man. (Said notion, like everything else in this mild movie, comes across merely as suggestion, however—no severed head, nor any other overt gore, is seen, just implied through dialogue.)

A decidedly lightweight actor, Kerwin Mathews, as the oblivious, doomed Robert, turns in his usual earnest yet superficial performance (his characters rarely appear to have much going on under the surface). Consequently, while offering the occasional moment of pathos (such as when he finally accepts the truth of his affliction and implores his son to lock him in the basement before he changes), the werewolf figure takes an emotional backseat to the desperate boy whom no one believes. This would be fine, except that twelve-year-old newcomer Scott Sealey (in his first and only film) gives a performance more irritating than ingratiating. The rest of the cast do little better, including the annoying Bob Homel as the hippie leader, and the somnambulistic George Gaynes (from TV's *Punky Brewster*) as the boy's dull psychiatrist.

Famous for his title role in the Ray Harryhausen fantasy *The Seventh Voyage of Sinbad* (1958), Mathews had to submit to four hours in the makeup chair for *Boy*. "The torture was immense," complained the actor. "I couldn't even eat during the day because I couldn't move my face. The first time I saw myself in the full werewolf makeup, I thought, 'Kid, this is definitely your *last* film.'" Not quite—but almost. After *Boy*, Mathews retired from acting and moved to San Francisco to run an antiques business, but stepped in front of the camera once more for a one-day cameo in John Stanley's near-amateur *Nightmare in Blood* (filmed in 1975 but released in 1978). Mathews died in 2007 at age 81, survived by his partner of 46 years, Tom Nicoll.

Boy was Romanian-born director Nathan Juran's final film. Juran had directed Mathews fifteen years earlier in what would be both men's most famous (and beloved) movie—*The 7th Voyage of Sinbad*—as well as in the 1962 musical-fantasy *Jack the Giant Killer*. Juran also helmed such sci-fi cult favorites as *The Brain from Planet Arous* (1957), *Twenty Million Miles to Earth* (1957) and *Attack of the 50 Foot Woman* (1958). "I approached the picture business as a business," admitted the unpretentious Juran. "I always did pictures for the money, and for the creative challenges. I wasn't a born director. I was just a technician who could transfer the script from the page to the stage and could get it shot on schedule and on budget. I never became caught up in the 'romance' of the movies." With *The Boy Who Cried Werewolf*, it shows.

Paired with the far-better *Sssssss* ("Don't say it, hiss it"), *Boy* comprised the bottom half of the last double-bill released by Universal. Coincidence? The film's punny title was deemed clever enough to be recycled for a 2010 made-for-Nickelodeon-TV movie.

With its two-dimensional characters, flat acting, flatter lighting, perfunctory direction, meandering story, and poorly-realized lycanthrope, *The Boy Who Cried Werewolf* can easily inspire the viewer to cry uncle.

With quotes from: *President Wolfman* DVD commentary; "Kerwin Mathews: Part II," by Steve Swires, *Starlog* 120; "Nathan Juran," by Steve Swires, *Starlog* 141.

Morphology: Turtleneck-sporting, wet-nosed wolfman
Demise: Impalement through the heart
Full Moon Rating: **

The Boy Who Cried Werewolf

(2010; Nickelodeon; US/Canada) Director: Eric Bross; Producer: Scott McAboy; Screenplay: Art Brown, Douglas Sloan; Cinematographer: Robert McLachlan. Cast: Victoria Justice, Chase Ellison, Brooke D'Orsay, Matt Winston, Steven Grayhm, Brooke Shields.

> She's going through some changes, and nothing will ever be the same…—trailer

Not a remake of the 1973 Kerwin Mathews vehicle of the same name, but a family-friendly Nickelodeon made-for-TV movie about a pair of teen siblings going through (admittedly drastic) "changes," *The Boy Who Cried Werewolf* adds little to the lycanthropy-as-puberty theme explored by far better films like *I Was a Teenage Werewolf*, *Ginger Snaps*, and *Trick 'r' Treat*.

Awkward high-schooler Jordan (Nickelodeon teen TV star/singer Victoria Justice) lives with her fourteen-year-old, horror-loving prankster brother Hunter (Chase Ellison) and widower father David (Matt Winston) in California. When the family unexpectedly inherits a castle from their late Uncle Dragomir, they fly to Wolfsberg, Romania, to see their new property. Met by the castle's sinister housekeeper,

Madame Varcolac (Brooke Shields), they take up uneasy residence in the castle, where Jordan and Hunter discover a hidden laboratory. There Jordan accidentally cuts herself on a vial of blood labeled "L.B. 217" and soon transforms into a werewolf. Now the siblings must find a cure before the end of the lunar cycle, or Jordan will remain a lycanthrope forever. At the same time they become embroiled in a centuries-old conflict between the werewolves and the local vampires, who seek possession of the castle as the start of their reign on earth.

With Vancouver, Canada, standing in for Romania, authenticity takes a back seat to "cutesy." Wolfsberg is the kind of sunlit, squeaky-clean European town right out of EuroDisney, a place where everybody speaks English at all times. The perky blonde local real estate agent, Paulina (Brooke D'Orsay), even looks and sounds like a grown-up Valley Girl. Brooke Shields, as the severe and imposing Madame Varcolac (whose name is Romanian for "werewolf") glowers and scowls in a caricature of the already-parodic Cloris Leachman from *Young Frankenstein* (1974). The film even steals the "Frau Blucher" running gag from that earlier horror-comedy classic by having a wolf howl every time someone says "Madame Varcolac" aloud. When she joins forces with Hunter in trying to find a cure for Jordan, Mme. Varcolac answers the girl's questioning look with a heavily accented "Izz okay, I'm cool." Ugh.

The vampires are more cartoonish than ghoulish, with the lead vamp's minions generally making goofy faces and looking confused. Fortunately, the werewolves look and act rather more impressive, courtesy of veteran creature creators Greg Nicotero and Howard Berger (*Hostel*, *Grindhouse*, *The Mist*). (The duo also worked on the 2005 werewolf feature *Cursed*.) It's 45 minutes of lame jokes and superficial characterization, as well as a truly embarrassing musical interlude when Jordan walks the streets despondently while the song "Not Somebody Else" (sung by Victoria Justice herself) plays on the soundtrack ("Breathtaking, frightening, these feelings inside me..."), before the first transformation scene. Fortunately, if not exactly worth the wait, it offers one of the film's few startling moments. While the CGI metamorphosis itself occurs almost instantaneously, it's seamless and given added impact by Justice twisting her head like an afflicted animal, then abruptly thrusting her half-transformed face towards the camera. The mid-stage makeup creates an impressive interim she-wolf, with long, flowing hair, a ridged face, prosthetic nose, sharp fangs and bushy whiskers. Chasing her brother down the hall, she becomes a fully transformed, hair-covered beast with a powerful torso, wolf-shaped head, canine muzzle, and glowing blue eyes. The second (male) werewolf looks even more menacing, with a darker, more wolfish appearance to its countenance to go along with its imposing, hair-covered body.

Despite the presence of two classic monsters (werewolf *and* vampire), this Tween-targeted terror tale focuses more on social horrors (Jordan bullied by the cool kids, hopelessly stammering in front of her new crush, etc.) than any actual frights, though it occasionally offers up the sporadic moment of near-frisson (such as when Jordan first transforms and corners her cringing brother—tension that completely evaporates when their Dad yells upstairs for them to keep the noise down). "Nobody's ever going to go to prom with me," wails Jordan, feeling monstrous and ugly after recovering from her first transformation—a line that gets to the heart of this Ugly Duckling tale. "And you know why—because boys don't want to go to prom with a *werewolf*!" Perhaps not, but Jordan soon adapts to her newfound power (which includes heightened senses, increased strength and agility, and, of course, a taste for meat that baffles the previously vegetarian girl). Like others before it (*Ginger Snaps*, *Blood and Chocolate*), the film equates female lycanthropy with sexual awakening/self-confidence, with the initially nerdy, klutzy, and awkward Jordan looking stunning and dressed to kill after becoming infected. Obviously, coming of age means getting in touch with one's inner animal.

When the siblings finally learn that "werewolves are good" (as Jordan marvels)—humanity's champions in an eternal struggle to suppress the "purely evil" vampires—the film finally ups the action ante by pitting first the Jordan-wolf against a coven of the bloodsuckers (well, half-a-dozen anyway), and then offering an admittedly exciting and energetic climactic battle between the vampires and *two* lycanthropes (Jordan and her brother Hunter, who, it turns out, has inherited the lycanthropy gene from their uncle and has fortuitously just come of age). Of course, this being family-friendly fare, violence never really rears its ugly head—apart from some werewolf/vampire grappling as they toss each other around the Disney-ish catacomb and graveyard sets. Deaths only occur indirectly, as the werewolves push the vampires into shafts of sunlight, causing them to flame up and disappear. (Of course, this begs the question as to why, since dawn has obviously come, the two werewolves don't immediately change back to human.)

Overall, however, these lycans do little to live up to their fierce-looking appearance. Never a threat to humans, they only attack vampires (and apparently big game—"I ate a wild boar last night," bemoans Jordan after her first transformation). Though at one point Jordan worries that she might lose control and hurt her brother or father, this never seems a serious threat (while she initially intimidates Hunter after her first transformation by staring him down, nose to snout, she then simply lopes off after her dad calls to them upstairs). And later the two sibling werewolves even bear (wolf?) hug their human father upon escaping their chains in the vampires' lair.

Unlike with the best horror comedies, in which the (often black) humor arises directly from the horrific situations, *Boy*'s puerile and forced comedy appears intended to *diffuse* whatever terror might possibly appear. When Hunter's monster-knowledgeable friends advise him that he must kill his own sister with "a silver bullet straight through the heart, that's the only way," Hunter reacts to this horrific notion with, "I can't shoot my sister—you know how much trouble I'd get in?"

Like with puberty itself, the initial fear of "horrific" changes prove largely unfounded, as it turns out that "werewolves are good." In fact, Jordan's new beau (the local butcher boy) sums it up at the end with, "Sometimes change is good"—even if said change involves hair growth and mood swings, and be it caused by transforming from girl to woman or man to wolf. Ultimately, *The Boy Who Cried Werewolf* remains a comforting yet disappointingly vapid excursion into the concerns of The Boy Who Cried Puberty.

No doubt due to the popularity of its teenaged TV star with the younger set, the Halloween-themed movie scored a ratings hit, catching 5.8 million television viewers upon its October 23rd premier on the Nickelodeon channel. Caveat emptor.

Morphology: Fur-covered, wolf-headed biped
Demise: None (these are family-friendly werewolves)
Full Moon Rating: *½

Cannon Movie Tales: Red Riding Hood see Red Riding Hood (1989)

La Casa del Terror see Face of the Screaming Werewolf

Castle of Desire see Tomb of the Werewolf

The Company of Wolves

(1984; ITC/Cannon; Great Britain) Director: Neil Jordan; Producers: Chris Brown, Stephen Woolley; Screenwriters: Angela Carter, Neil Jordan (story: Angela Carter); Cinematographer: Bryan Loftus; Cast: Angela Lansbury, David Warner, Graham Crowden, Brian Glover, Kathryn Pogson, Stephen Rea, Tusse Silberg, Micha Bergese, Sarah Patterson.

> Neither child nor adult, wolf nor human … this is the twilight world which lies between the pages of any fairy tale.—trailer

A beautifully photographed and cleverly directed (by future Oscar winner Neil Jordan), if sometimes obtuse and heavy-handed, Freudian take on the "Little Red Riding Hood" fairy tale, *The Company of Wolves* begins in the present day but quickly moves into a medieval dreamland to follow the uneasy fantasies of a 13-year-old female protagonist on the cusp of womanhood sleeping away an afternoon. During said dream, her bitchy older sister is killed by wolves in the forest, and Rosaleen (Sarah Patterson) seeks solace from her "Granny" (Angela Lansbury), who tells her various sexually-charged cautionary tales about wolves that are "hairy on the *in*side." It culminates with Rosaleen meeting her own seductive "wolf" before the dream world bursts through into reality.

"This isn't a werewolf movie in the accepted sense," opined producer Stephen Woolley, "as the characters don't turn into the type of creatures seen in *The Howling* or *American Werewolf*—they transform into large wolves." (Apart from a pair of real wolves employed for close-up shots, most of the "wolves" in the film were played by Belgian shepherd dogs with dyed fur.) And they do so in a strikingly original fashion, thanks to the vision of director Jordan and the wizardry of special makeup effects artist Christopher Tucker (*Quest for Fire*, *She-Wolf of London* TV series).

Matching Tucker's singular transformations are the film's highly imaginative sets. Cobweb-shrouded trees and giant mushrooms fill a claustrophobic forest populated by wolves with glowing red and yellow eyes. Even the village, with its almost organic-looking cottages, seems sprung from the rich woodland setting itself. This large, surreal forest (created by production designer Anton Furst [*Flash Gordon*, *Alien*]) covered nearly an entire sound stage at Shepperton Studios.

Much of the movie's dialogue, generally uttered by Angela Lansbury's hyper-critical Granny, carries strong sexual connotations. "Don't stray from the path," she warns Rosaleen. "Once you stray from the path you're lost entirely." Said path being chastity, with her virginity being what's lost. "The wild beasts wait for us in the shadows," continues Granny, "and once you put a foot wrong, they *pounce*." The "wild beasts" being sex-obsessed men, naturally. She also becomes rather more blunt at times, warning of men in general: "They're nice as pie until they've had their way with you. But once the bloom is gone, the beast comes out." Throughout, the film equates lycanthropy with sexual predation.

While Lansbury's Granny comes off as harsh and bad-tempered, particularly given her frequently sour delivery, she occasionally leavens her dour portrayal with a bit of humor. "You can't trust anyone, least of all a priest," she warns Rosaleen while they sit in the village churchyard, then quips, "He's not called 'Father' for nothing."

Jordan fills his film with visual symbolism that underscores the sexual themes—and politics—of the stories, though not all of it works. At one point Rosaleen finds some eggs in a bird's nest, along with a hand mirror and red lipstick (vanity and worldliness?). When Rosaleen puts on the lipstick (entering womanhood?) the eggs hatch to reveal tiny human fetus–like figures. She brings one home to show her mother, who smiles with joy before the tiny figure expends a solitary tear in a ridiculously heavy-handed representation of lost innocence. Toward film's end, when the werewolf beats Rosaleen to Granny's house, he strikes out at Granny, causing her head to fly off(!) and then shatter like a porcelain doll against the fireplace(!!). Why? Freud himself might struggle with that one.

The self-contained stories within the main story (dream) gives the film an anthology feel, but the anchoring sameness of place and theme creates a solidity that binds it all together into a compact whole. Granny's first tale proves to be the most memorable. "Once upon a time," she begins, "there was a woman of the village who married a travelling man…" Cue scenes of a forest wedding romp, after which the new bride and bridegroom (future Oscar nominee Stephen Rea [*The Crying Game*]) retire to their cottage. But before they can consummate their union, the man is lured outside, ostensibly by the call of nature (to "make water") but actually by the call of the full moon. He never returns, and the disappointed bride fears he was taken by the wolves prowling about that night. Years later she has remarried and borne three young children. Overburdened by the drudgery of her domestic life, she seems no less pleased than astonished when her first husband, though gaunt and disheveled, walks through the door. But when he sees her brood, he grows angry and labels her "whore." He then literally rips away the skin of his own face, leaving nothing but red sinew and exposed muscle. Suddenly, before her horrified eyes, his face elongates into a muzzle and becomes more and more canine-like. As fur sprouts and be becomes a full wolf, the terrified woman's current husband walks in, sees the beast, grabs an axe, and decapitates the creature. In slow motion, the wolf's head lands in a cauldron filled with milk, but when it bobs to the surface of the now-pink liquid, it's the head of a man. The likable Rea; the gruesome, visceral, unique transformation; the daily-grind and careful-what-you-wish-for thematic underpinnings; and the beautifully-crafted, near-poetic portrayal of the lycanthrope's demise all combine to make this the film's most coherently powerful cautionary tale.

Effects artist Christopher Tucker broke down the Travelling Man transformation into six distinct stages. The first sees Rea in contact lenses and prosthetic facial pieces that he could rip away from his face. The second stage involves the skinless animatronic head and torso (affectionately dubbed "Bert"). Bert 1 evolves into Bert 2, who takes on a lupine character as the bones elongate. Bert 3 then shows the ears growing and the snout projecting, before transitioning to Rover 1, a canine minus the pelt. Rover 2 completes the transformation into a fur-covered wolf. "I wanted to ring the changes and to make the whole thing macabre in keeping with the rest of the film," said Tucker, "so I decided to remove the character's skin and hair and develop it from there. I wasn't being gratuitous for the sake of it, as to rid the skin helps to remove certain appendages that get in the way, such as the ears, nose, and lips. It was logical to get all that stuff out to the way and to get on to the real business of the bones and muscles rearranging themselves."

"Believe it or not, it took over seven long, uncomfortable hours," complained Stephen Rea (who, despite said "long, uncomfortable hours," went on to make nine films with director Neil Jordan to date) on the show-stopping flesh-ripping scene. "It was horrible, but the scene turned out really, really well. And I had a blast in postproduction, dubbing all sorts of screams and growls and whatnot over it."

Unfortunately, the film's disjointed narrative falls short of its imaginative technical accomplishments. Not all of the stories-within-stories (or the main narrative, for that matter) measure up to the punchy "Travelling Man" tale, with some, including a dull and predictable telling of a "she-wolf" visiting the village in the form of a young woman, seeming like mere time-filler. Even Rosaleen herself gets in on the act when she relates a "true" tale to her mother about a woman scorned who crashes the wedding feast of the nobleman that misused her. Somehow she causes the entire wedding party to transform into wolves. "The wolves in the forest are more decent," she sneers as they all start to change (clawed toes push through patent-leather shoes, corseted bosoms turn hairy, and women sprout canine snouts before pulling off their powdered wigs. (This proves to be Tucker's sole make-up misstep, as he utilizes some goofy-looking canine-like masks to portray the interim metamorphoses before dressing up some real wolves in fancy clothes.)

Fortunately, the main dream concludes with Rosaleen confronting, Little Red Riding Hood–style, the very thing her Granny has always warned her about—a wolf that is "hairy on the *inside*." After the man has killed Granny, Rosaleen shoots him in the arm with his own gun, causing him to writhe in pain and then transform. Amazingly, from the man's wide-open mouth emerges a fully-formed wolf muzzle. Then a wolf's hide rips through the splitting skin on his naked back before a lupine head thrusts itself all the way out, shedding the human hide as it emerges. It's a second unique and marvelously realized transformation that remains in the mind's eye long after all the sledgehammer symbolism has faded.

Of the pivotal transformations, Jordan said, "We wanted to get away from the usual effects sequence wherein you see the first stage, then cut to a reaction shot, cutting back to the next stage in the transformation. I tried to compose the scenes so that the metamorphosis takes place in the foreground while the actors could react in the background. I think it works very well, but without Chris Tucker we'd have been stuck."

Yet the perfectionistic Tucker was not fully satisfied with his groundbreaking work. "The transformations we ended up with never came up to expectations," complained Tucker, who also designed the make-up for *The Elephant Man* (1980), "because we never had the budget to do what was originally envisaged. Very often things were ready the day they were shot." Still, Tucker and his crew pulled off some amazing metamorphoses. "I have never liked the Lon Chaney Jr. concept of the wolf-man," Tucker explained, "as I think it's rather stupid and very disappointing. ...It's the idea that's wrong; if

American poster for the U.K. Freudian fantasy feature *The Company of Wolves*.

you're going to do a werewolf picture then you should have people turning into wolves, not wolf-men. I was even disappointed by *The Howling* and *An American Werewolf in London*. Technically the effects were good, but again I felt the concepts were wrong. One film had a group of creatures that looked like a grotesque Disney vision of the Big Bad Wolf, and in the other, when you finally saw the werewolf, it was nothing more than a bear-like beast. I relished the opportunity presented by *Company of Wolves* to do something different." And despite what some might consider his shortsighted, even blasphemous opinions of previous screen werewolves, Tucker accomplished just that—something *very* different.

In only his second feature, Irish writer-director Neil Jordan displayed much of the talent that took him to the heights of Hollywood (an Academy award nomination for Best Director—and a win for Best Original Screenplay—for *The Crying Game* in 1992), employing slow-motion, a mobile camera, and startlingly imaginative special effects to tell his tale(s). Jordan went on to helm such diverse projects as *Interview with the Vampire* (1994), based on the Anne Rice bestseller, and the historical biopic *Michael Collins* (1996).

Unfortunately, not knowing how to end this coming-of-age nightmare, Jordan and co-scripter Angela Carter merge the dream world with the real one by having the modern Rosaleen finally awaken, only to see the wolves of her dream tearing through a painting on the wall and come through the window of her bedroom. She screams, the credits roll over a shot of fallen toys (more lost innocence symbolism), and the voice of Rosaleen intones a pointed poem: "'Little girls,' this seems to say, 'never stop upon your way / Never trust a stranger, friend, no one knows how it will end / As you're pretty, so be wise, wolves may lurk in every guise / Now, as then, 'tis simple truth: sweetest tongue has sharpest tooth.'" Though yet another striking visual, the scene (like much of the picture) makes little narrative sense.

Principal photography on *The Company of Wolves* began on January 9, 1984, and lasted nine weeks (the various makeup effects and transformations took a full six weeks to shoot). "I don't think of *Company of Wolves* as a horror film; I think it's an allegory," concluded Rea. Making its world premier in Canada on September 15, 1984, the British "allegory" saw wide release (to 995 theaters) in America on April 19, 1985. Costing $3 million to make, the picture took in only $4.3 million during its U.S. run. Apparently, American moviegoers would rather have had a true "horror film." Had Jordan and co. offered more of the sublimely horrific than the sledgehammer allegorical, perhaps *The Company of Wolves* would have indeed been company worth keeping.

With quotes from: "Chris Tucker in the Company of Wolves," by Philip Nutman, *Fangoria* 42; "A Wolf in Rea's Clothing," by Chris Alexander, *Fangoria* 30; *The Illustrated Werewolf Movie Guide*, by Stephen Jones.

Morphology: Large gray wolves
Demise: Decapitation; (regular) bullets
Full Moon Rating: ***

The Craving

(1981/85; Dalmata Films/Film Concept Group; Spain) Original language title: *El Retorno del Hombre Lobo*. Alternate Titles: *Return of the Wolfman*; *The Night of the Werewolf* (DVD). Director/Screenplay: Jack Molina (Paul Naschy); Producers: Modesto Herez Redondo, Julia Saly; Cinematographer: Alejandro Ulloa. Cast: Paul Naschy, Jully (Julia) Saly, Silvia Aguilar, Narciso Ibanez Menta, Azucena Hernandez, Beatriz Elorrieta, Rafael Hernandez.

IT USED TO BE ONLY A MYTH—poster

Released in Spain on the same day (April 10, 1981) as *The Howling* in America, *The Craving* proved to be far less conspicuous than its American cousin but nearly as important, since it straddles the apex of Paul Naschy's long-running Waldemar Daninsky/Wolfman series.

More polished, more eventful, and more coherent than most entries, this (superior) remake of Naschy's most successful film, *The Werewolf vs. the Vampire Woman*, saw Naschy not only writing and starring, but directing as well.

Naschy failed to realize, however, that time marches on, as had the werewolf film (with the innovative lycanthropes of *The Howling* and *An American Werewolf in London* soon leaving Naschy's Chaney-esque wolfman mired in the amber of nostalgia). The ever-romantic filmmaker could not, or stubbornly would not, see the innovations on the horizon and opted to return to his greatest success of the previous decade, thereby letting the lycanthropic sea change then taking place wash over and all-but-drown him. By the time *The Craving* hit American shores in 1985, the subgenre had morphed so drastically that Waldemar Daninsky seemed a quaint anachronism, a 40-year throwback. Consequently, it failed financially. Now, however, with the benefit of distance and perspective, modern viewers can enjoy *The Craving* for the enthusiastic, entertaining, and artistically nostalgic endeavor it is.

Closely following the plot of 1971's *The Werewolf vs. the Vampire Woman*, *The Craving* sees a trio of college students—Karen (Azucena Hernandez), Barbara (Pilar Alcon) and Erika (Silvia Aguilar)—searching for the grave of the legendary Elizabeth Bathory to validate their research. In "a wild place in the Carpathians" they encounter the revived Waldemar Daninsky (recently resurrected when a pair of grave robbers removed the holy silver cross from his chest), whose courtly ways and primitive castle lodgings mark him as a man apart. The duplicitous Erika, however, has her own agenda. "I gave myself up to Satan and black magic a long time ago," she tells her aged mentor—before murdering him for a magical medallion. "I have communicated with the tormented spirit of Elizabeth." So while Karen and Waldemar are busy falling in love, Erika uses the medallion to entrance Barbara, and then employs Barbara's blood to revive the vampiric Elizabeth Bathory (whose tomb Erika has finally found). Elizabeth immediately vampirizes both Erika and Barbara, and the trio of vampire women prowl the countryside, while at the same time Waldemar's werewolf adds to the body count during nights of the full moon. Karen, knowing that only she can give her beloved Waldemar peace, determines to plunge the silver cross back into his heart. But first they must try to find and stop Elizabeth and her acolytes, leading to a final full-moon confrontation between werewolf and vampire on Walpurgis Night.

Paul Naschy considered this his most personal Daninsky picture. "*El Retorno del Hombre Lobo* [*The Craving*'s Spanish title] contains all the coordinates of my own life," stated the filmmaker, "fitting together like the pieces of a jigsaw puzzle: the claustrophobic castle, the Gothic tombs, the ill-fated love affair, the menace of the undead, the ostracism of someone who is despised for being different and the all pervading shadow of death. All of these elements go to make up my personality and my work." Naschy revealingly went on to explain, "My personality was forged by the war, by my exposure to religion, by a partially frustrated sexuality, by my family and social background, by the people I knew, by love and by the ever present shadow of death." With *The Craving*, all this angst and passion went into producing what may be Naschy's most polished film (certainly among his Daninsky efforts).

Rather than a slavish remake of the previous decade's *Werewolf vs. the Vampire Woman*, however, *The Craving* offers enough changes—and improvements—to raise it above its seminal model. *The Craving* begins with a tone-setting pre-credit Medieval sequence that shows nobleman—and werewolf (responsible "for devouring hundreds of poor innocent people")—Waldemar Daninsky, whom Elizabeth Bathory had "dominated with her Satanic arts," put to death (a scene echoing—albeit faintly—Mario Bava's famous *Black Sunday*, as the executioner places a baroque metal mask over Waldemar's face and then hammers a silver cross into his chest, resulting in blood pouring grotesquely from the mask's mouth slit). *Vampire Woman* opens with a pair of doctors accidentally reviving the werewolf when they remove two silver bullets from Waldemar's chest. *The Craving* handles the wolfman's resurrection in a far more atmospheric manner—by having a pair of graverobbers invade the medieval Daninsky tomb and remove the "sacred cross, forged with the silver of the Mayenza Chalice" from Waldemar's heart. *The Craving* eschews the first film's rather contrived accidental resurrection of the vampiric Elizabeth by careless innocents, replacing it with the intentional (and atmospheric) revival by evil acolyte Erika. *The Craving* wisely dispenses with the heroine's boyfriend character from *Vampire Woman*, whose tedious searching needlessly slowed the proceedings. This also ups *The Craving*'s tragedy quotient by having the heroine succumb to the werewolf's bite at film's end after freeing her beloved from his curse—with the two doomed lovers united in death—rather than letting her simply walk away with her human beau as in the earlier film. Romantic as well as tragic, *The Craving*'s Waldemar "can only be freed from his eternal curse if a woman who loves him is willing to sacrifice her life by thrusting through his heart the holy silver on the night of the full moon." Not just courage is required here, but the ultimate sacrifice for the one she loves. And the *Vampire Woman* heroine's dream in which she succumbs to the vampiric Elizabeth becomes reality in *The Craving*, resulting in further incident and suspense when, for a time, the bewitched Karen acts in secret opposition against Waldemar's efforts (even braining him with a silver-tipped cane at one point) before he can free her from the vampire's evil influence. But perhaps most tellingly, the remake's climax sees the werewolf battling not one *Vampire Woman* but two—Elizabeth and Erika—in a far more energetic and satisfying confrontation (during which Elizabeth at one point uses her Satanic powers to make her own coffin rise into the air and fly towards the lycanthrope, only to shatter impressively against the beast-man's powerful claws). Here writer-director Naschy takes a page from *Vampire Woman* director León Klimovsky's playbook by inserting moments of slow-motion into the violent battle that add an otherworldly feel.

Original Spanish poster for *The Craving*, writer-director-star Paul Naschy's most polished lycan-effort.

Of course, *The Craving* didn't manage to escape all of its inspiration's odd peccadillos. For instance, *The Craving* is nothing if not expedient. Karen falls madly in love with Waldemar—and professes that love—in the very first scene we see them interact together! And like in *Vampire Woman*, incongruity runs rampant. At one point Karen asks Waldemar why they don't try to find Elizabeth's hiding place during the daylight hours. Waldemar responds with, "Only during the night of the full moon will I have sufficient power to destroy her." So... a mere stake through the heart won't do? But after the vampiress menaces Karen that night, Waldemar changes his tune and the two begin searching the ruins for her resting place after all. Additionally,

The Craving includes an unfortunate (original) comical interlude with a pair of buffoonish traveling preachers (though it turns out they're just thieves casing the joint) who talk with Waldemar about the region's recent vampire-murders. One tells Waldemar, "There's only one solution [to the vampire problem] if you ask me—garlic. A *lot* of garlic. Garlic up to your *ass*!" The laughable line speaks for itself.

The wonderfully authentic settings (castle ruins, stone outbuildings, creepy crypt), the occasional swift and vicious werewolf attacks, and the Gothic lyricism of the vampire women scenes help paper over the cracks. Under Naschy's direction, cinematographer Alejandro (*Horror Express*) Ulloa's mobile camera and evocative lighting show the undead women, their pallid complexions stark against their shroud-like black nightgowns, gliding through the fog-filled night, accompanied by a choral cacophony on the soundtrack that transforms them into eerie, unholy creatures.

Naschy obviously learned from *Vampire Woman* director Leon Klimovsky (with whom the actor collaborated on numerous occasions). Though Naschy largely eschews the eerie slow-motion of the vampires' presence Klimovsky pioneered for *Vampire Woman* (except for a few select moments during the climactic battle), he still captures their preternatural essence by employing fog and a steady, unearthly movement as they advance, the camera retreating before them as they glide effortlessly forward. Naschy also offers the occasional flourish that betrays his artistic ambitions. For instance, at one point a shot of the moon reflected in a puddle suddenly includes the upside-down image of the werewolf's face looming into view. The creature pauses and snarls before moving forward, closing—and ending—the shot as the monster steps into the puddle.

While the film offers the expected nudity (at least for horror movies of the time), it comes off as almost incidental, as if Naschy had matured beyond the merely exploitative, salacious elements so often showcased in his earlier efforts. The camera doesn't dwell on naked female torsos like in previous Daninsky outings, instead presenting occasional nakedness in an offhand, matter-of-fact manner that actually fits into the scenario (e.g., a long shot of Barbara's bare body hung upside-down over Elizabeth's crypt, or Erika simply getting ready for bed). Even Waldemar's solitary love scene (Naschy usually scripted himself *multiple* dalliances) is shot simply, tastefully, and quickly, with barely a breast exposed.

Naschy called *The Craving* "one of my fundamental works; I believe that its values are quite evident. It's a Gothic film where there are very good special effects for the time, with a very well created atmosphere and one of the best make-ups of the Wolf Man." Indeed, this iteration of the Waldemar wolfman looks more feral and ferocious than ever before, with coarse, shaded hair covering his face and head (providing texture and depth), large pointed ears protruding from behind his temples (for a more lupine look), an angry-looking ridged forehead, darkened nose piece, and vicious-looking, frequently drooling mouthful of fangs. With a fur-covered torso beneath his open shirt and hairy hands ending in wicked-looking claws, he truly looks animalistic, but with an almost demonic cast. When the beast attacks, he bites into his victim's neck, savagely jerking their body like a rag doll in a vicious display. "The superb makeup was the work of Ángel Luis de Diego, with photography by Alejandro Ulloa," recounted Naschy. "I really enjoyed making this picture, giving full rein to my love of heavy Gothic imagery, blended with both real historical detail and unbridled flight of fancy."

The Craving was Naschy's first Waldemar Daninsky movie in five years (and his ninth time beneath the yak hair). The movie failed at the box office, leaving the filmmaker without a funding source until he found some Japanese backers a few years later after directing a string of documentaries for Japanese television. This Eurasian partnership ultimately yielded *La Bestia y la Espada Mágica* (The Beast and the Magic Sword), another fiscal failure that effectively ended the Daninsky saga (relegating Naschy's beloved character to cameo status in *Howl of the Devil*, and guest-starring roles in the disappointing *Licantropo* and the awful American sexploitationer *Tomb of the Werewolf*).

Naschy labeled *The Craving* "a fundamental title in my filmography (one of the three or four which I consider great) and among the best that the Spanish Fantastic Cinema has produced." Though far from perfect, and not really in the same league as such superior Spanish specimens as *The House That Screamed* (1969), *Horror Express* (1972), *The Living Dead at the Manchester Morgue* (1974), *Who Can Kill a Child?* (1976), and Naschy's own *Horror Rises from the Tomb* (1972), *The Craving* still stands as a solid addition to the lycan-canon and perhaps the best overall example of a Naschy werewolf movie.

With quotes from: *Memoirs of a Wolfman*, by Paul Naschy; "Paul Naschy Filmography," by José Luis González and Michael Secula, *Videooze* 6/7.

Morphology: Fierce-looking, black-clad wolfman
Demise: Silver cross-dagger
Full Moon Rating: ***½

Creature of the Night

(2006; Brain Damage Films) Director/screenplay: Diana Curry; Producers: Diana Curry, Michael Branch; Cinematographer: Dan Kote. Cast: Doug Grady, Shannon Greer, Mark Schell, Kurt Azaroff, Cheri Christian.

Half MAN, Half WOLF, ALL ANIMAL!—tagline

"*Creature of the Night* is my attempt to make werewolves sexy," declared first-time writer-director Diana Curry. Gauging the result of this micro-budgeted ($15,000) feature, she failed utterly.

Rock star Rob Parker (Doug Grady), of the popular band V14, has more on his plate than making albums, touring, and avoiding paparazzi—he's also a werewolf. Though he locks himself up in his basement "lair" on nights of the full moon, he somehow manages to get out and stalk the night, with the occasional mutilation murder appearing in next day's paper. One morning he awakens naked in the woods next to a beautiful young girl, Laura (Shannon Greer), whom he had chased the night before but miraculously left unharmed. Panicking, he abducts her and keeps her in his basement while trying to decide what to do with her now that she knows his secret. Finally talked into letting her go by his friend and band mate Ben (Mark Schell), Rob finds that he has become consumed by thoughts of Laura. Surprisingly, the feelings are mutual, and they soon consummate their newfound love. But Rob's bitter ex-manager Cliff (Kurt Azaroff), who also knows his dark secret, determines to thwart this happy ending…

Cheap, cheesy and amateurish in every way, *Children of the Night* offers little more than flat videography, overwrought acting, a muddled story and uninspired direction. The videocam look and inadequate lighting gives the no-budget game away from the get-go, not helped by the terrible faux media "profile" of the band V14 that opens the film (including a laughable chat-show interview scene shot on a set that even a porn production would find embarrassing). The meandering movie then slows to a crawl by settling into Rob's cramped basement lair, as he alternately drinks, indulges in tiresome outbursts, and attempts to kill Laura (*three times*—via suffocation by pillow, drowning in a sink, and revolver to the head—but each time he can't bring himself to finish it). As Rob's friend later apologizes to Laura, "Rob really is a good guy. It's just, when he changes—he tries to stay away from people but sometimes he just doesn't handle it the right way." Really? Cheesy montage scenes of the two protagonists contemplating their feelings for each other, an awful music video stuck smack-dab in the middle for no real reason, and a protracted sex scene (with clothes *on*) take up the bulk of the rest of the picture until the admittedly surprising (but small-scale) climax that sees psycho Cliff holding both Laura and Rob captive in Rob's own lair (which Curry and co. constructed inside a rented storage unit).

One of the picture's few effective elements is the intriguing twist of making the werewolf a pure victim rather than victimizer. It turns out that Rob has killed no one after all; the bitter, psychotic Cliff has been perpetrating the mutilation murders in order to make Rob *think* he's responsible. ("I don't know what I do when I'm the wolf," whines Rob. Well, not much, apparently.) "Hell," sneers Cliff at the climax, "[Rob] can't even be a proper werewolf. Stupid bastard only catches small animals like rabbits and pets. I've been following him around for months now, and nothing."

Curry's direction veers from sheer banality (just pointing the camera and letting the scene play out) to pointless trick work (filming Rob carrying the tied-up Laura from *upside-down* for no discernible reason). Her idea of subtlety is superimposing the rear view mirror–like image of a pair of eyes over the scene of a woman walking at night to indicate the stalker's presence, and some shaky-cam, red-tinted, double-vision photography for the wolf's p.o.v. (perhaps lycan–Rob is in need of Lasik surgery?).

Curry handles her lycanthropic elements no better than anything else. For instance, Rob's Big Reveal to Laura about his curse has him matter-of-factly relate, "I wasn't always a werewolf. I was on vacation in the jungle. I got attacked. I thought I was gonna die, but I didn't." So much for drama. For most of the movie, Rob's werewolf form consists of nothing more than a pair of colored contact lenses and vampire fangs. Transformations occur off-screen, with only a bit of audio to indicate the change. At the climax, however, when Rob transforms during the day—*before* the full moon rises (perhaps an emotional response to Laura being threatened by Cliff, though this remains unclear)—he goes into full-on German Shepherd mode (played by a real dog and a pathetic hand puppet for a frenzied close-up).

In an onscreen interview (included as a DVD extra), Diana Curry relates how she moved from West Virginia to Atlanta to pursue her dream of making movies—not as a director but as a screenwriter. She states how she's "not a technical person," and only directed and co-produced *Creature of the Night* to showcase her scriptwriting skills (using the film as a calling card), and that she'd much rather have *others* direct her screenplays. Looking at the inconsequential result, so would the viewer. (*Creature* proved to be just as ineffectual a calling card as a movie, since to date Curry has made no further features, either as director *or* screenwriter.)

With quotes from: "Your [sic] Watching Caught in Clapper," *Children of the Night* DVD.

Morphology: German Shepherd
Demise: None; this rock star lycan lives to rock 'n' transform another day
Full Moon Rating: *

Cry of the Werewolf

(1944; Columbia; b&w) Director: Henry Levin; Producer: Wallace MacDonald; Screenplay: Griffin Jay, Charles O'Neal (story: Griffin Jay); Cinematographer: L.W. O'Connell. Cast: Nina Foch, Stephen Crane, Osa Massen, Blanche Yurka, Barton MacLane.

WHEN THE BELL TOLLS AT MIDNIGHT…
WEREWOLVES PROWL THE EARTH!—poster

Despite the misleading tagline, only *one* (less-than-impressive) werewolf prowls the earth here, taking the form of a rather petite, unimposing canine that nonetheless commits several gruesome murders. When the resident scholar (Fritz Lieber) at the New Orleans LaTour Museum (the former home of the infamous Marie LaTour, which legend claims was a werewolf) is brutally murdered, investigations ultimately lead to the gypsy princess Celeste (Nina Foch), leader of a gypsy tribe camped nearby. Celeste, Marie's daughter, has inherited her mother's lycanthropy, and remains intent on destroying anyone close to the secret housed in the LaTour mansion—a hidden sacred altar built around her mother's revered resting place.

Even before Columbia's first werewolf film, *Return of the Vampire*, hit theaters on January 1, 1944, the studio announced in December 1943 their intent to make a sequel, *Bride of the Vampire*. Though *Return* did indeed prove to be a modest hit, the proposed sequel ultimately metamorphosed into the unrelated—and inferior—*Cry of the Werewolf*.

Cry starts out with a (verbal) bang, thanks largely to the steady presence and mellifluous-voiced delivery of veteran character actor John Abbott (*The Vampire's Ghost*), playing a museum guide lecturing his patrons on the occult: "The tradition of werewolves and vampires dates back almost to the world's earliest recorded history. Of the two, the werewolf is perhaps the most horrible because the instinct for evil is so strong that they willingly and cunningly assume the shape of a beast in order to kill."

Right off the bat, *Cry* takes a different tack from its few lycanthropic predecessors, marking werewolfism not as a moon-triggered curse endured by an unwilling victim (à la *Werewolf of London* and *The Wolf Man*), but a condition embraced by the possessor, who can transform at will "in order to kill." Additionally, this she-wolf possesses hypnotic powers (much like the classic vampire), as she places the heroine in her control at one point to turn her against the hero. Even beyond these bits of lycan-innovation, *Cry of the Werewolf* offers the screen's first *female* she-beast (a lycanthropic ancestor, perhaps, to the classic femme fatale of the nascent film noir subgenre, which was just then finding its footing before leaping to the forefront of American post–World War II cinema).

However, though presenting the screen's first she-wolf, this *Cry* turns out to be not one of women's liberation but of longing for traditional gender demarcation. Made during the height of World War II, when women across America had entered the work force en mass for the very first time, *Cry of the Werewolf* seems a backhanded reaction to the patriarchal society's wariness towards this new breed of independent female. As such, the film casts the woman in power—the leader of her tribe—as a literal monster, one who willingly sacrifices the notion of love and support to instead walk the path of brutality and evil, a perverted feminine form who wields her power with a murderous fist (or paw, as the case may be). Here, female strength and independence equates to savagery. It's almost a reactionary plea to restore the patriarchal status quo—which the authority figures (the police) do at the end with a hail of bullets.

But lest one get carried away in musings on the movie's inadvertent sociological import, it's important to note that at the end of the day, *Cry of the Werewolf* stands primarily as a rather mediocre and generally *un*-impactful entry in the fledgling werewolf subgenre. In fact, it was

"As a Woman She wanted LOVE! As a Werewolf She wanted BLOOD!" So proclaimed the ads for Columbia's *Cry of the Werewolf*, which offered the screen's first female lycanthrope (double-bill trade ad).

a further two-plus decades before another hirsute honey loped across the screen—and this not in Hollywood but down Mexico way in *Santo vs. the She-Wolves* (1976). In America, the screen's next female lycanthrope didn't arrive until 1985's *Howling II*. So much for influence.

One of the biggest problems with *Cry of the Werewolf* is its slow pace and labored structure, as the first half is taken up by the police inspector (Barton MacLane doing his patented bull-in-a-china-shop bit) and his men dully trying to suss out the suspects, while the hero, Bob (son of the murdered museum scholar), attempts to learn the same things on his own. Then, at the 31-minute mark (half-way through the film) comes the first transformation, as Celeste becomes a wolf in order to attack and kill the museum janitor (formerly in her service) for his blundering. This pivotal moment too, however, is botched. It begins as the camera moves from Celeste to her shadow on the wall. The shadow slowly sinks down and, via a quick dissolve, abruptly becomes that of a wolf, its jaws open. Unfortunately, the elegance of this metamorphosis is marred by director Henry Levin holding on the wolf shadow for several seconds, revealing it to be an obvious still life, with no malevolent movement whatsoever. (Additionally—and amusingly—this she-wolf somehow incorporates her clothing into her new wolf-pelt, as she transforms from fully-clothed woman into a fur-bearing wolf in the blink of an eye, or camera cutaway, leaving nary a stitch in sight.)

Still, if there's very little substance to its slight story (little more than a murder mystery with a few unusual set-pieces), *Cry* tries to make up for it with an excess of style. Cinematographer L.W. O'Connell's (*Return of the Vampire*) low-key lighting and use of shadows, bathing the sets in pools of light and darkness, adds some much-needed visual interest to the dull proceedings. Likewise, director Levin seemingly takes a page out of the Val Lewton playbook with some clever use of sound and suggestion right out of *Cat People* (1942). As Bob explores a dark cellar, the camera follows Celeste's legs in close-up as she slowly advances towards him, and we hear the steady click of her high heels. Suddenly, the noise of her shoes becomes the click of claws on cement, and the camera next reveals not her legs but the wolf's paws padding down the corridor towards Bob. In another scene, the heroine (Bob's love interest), deep in thought, suddenly hears the scrabbling of paws on the floor near her. When she turns towards the sound, there stands Celeste. Unfortunately, *Cry* sorely lacks *Cat People*'s layered story and nuanced characters, making do with simplistic plotting—and padding—and one-dimensional protagonists.

A real liability is the tepid Stephen Crane as the "hero" Bob, a petulant dullard who's about as dynamic as his name. Fortunately, Nina Foch brings some welcome intensity to her role of shapeshifting murderess, even adding a (brief) note of pathos when she tells the heroine, whom she intends to make a werewolf like herself, "You will learn to live as I must live—apart, beyond the reach of men and mortals." Her voice, tinged with sadness, then hardens as she bitterly continues, "And for that love which once shone in a man's eyes, loathing will be substituted."

Nina Foch, who made her screen debut by facing down a werewolf (and vampire) in Columbia's earlier *The Return of the Vampire*, here dons the wolf skin herself as Celeste, the princess and leader of her gypsy tribe. Third-billed in *Return*, she earns the top spot in *Cry of the Werewolf*. Despite her exalted status here, in a 1999 interview she recalled little of the film, dismissively noting that "it was still very much a low-budget picture," and that "the best thing about playing a werewolf is you get to rest while the wolf works."

As well as Foch, *Cry* recycled some of Mario Castelnuovo-Tedesco's atmospheric musical compositions from *Return of the Vampire* in an attempt to bring some much-needed atmosphere and suspense to *Cry*'s less-than-scintillating scenario.

With quotes from: "A Werewolf Prepares: Nina Foch," by Danny Savello, *Scarlet Street* 33.

Morphology: Small four-legged wolf
Demise: Bullets (of the mundane lead variety)
Full Moon Rating: **½

Crying Wolf

(2015; Uncork'd Entertainment; UK) Director: Tony Jopia; Producers: Dominic Took, Tony Jopia; Screenplay: Andy Davie, Michael Dale, Tony Jopia (story: Tony Jopia, Andy Davie); Cinematographer: Gwyn Hemmings. Cast: Caroline Munro, Gary Martin, Kristofer Dayne, Gabriela Hersham, Ian Donnelly, Joe Egan.

The Moon is HIGH, and so is the body count—trailer

While the first part of the above tagline for this low-budget British horror-comedy rings hollow (since the moon has nothing to do with these werewolves, who can shapeshift at will), the second is spot on, with dozens of victims (and lycanthropes) meeting their bloody fates over the course of the overstuffed story's 91 minutes. Though chock full of grue (everything from the expected throat-slashings to decapitation, impalement, head-squashing, a heart ripped from a chest and fed to its victim[!], and somebody cut in two with a chainsaw), it's also filled with flashbacks and unrelated vignettes that leave the central tale a disjointed mess.

When a group of "friends" embark on a camping expedition to the Cotswolds, it quickly becomes apparent that this will not be an ordinary outdoors outing, as these folks are a pack of werewolves on the hunt for a little lupine bonding (and prey—"No lone wolfing around," orders their leader, "we hunt as a pack"). Complicating things are a (human) sister who horns in on the group, a pair of sexy hitchhikers picked up along the way, and the ostensible camping guides, Charlie (David Sellicks) and Ricky (Marco Radice, who affects an atrocious American accent for no discernible reason), who turn out to be werewolf hunters luring the pack into a trap.

A pre-credits opening sees a private investigator going to a small village to look into the disappearance of a friend. There in an antiques shop he finds an ancient book titled *Crying Wolf*, which the proprietress (former Hammer starlet and Bond girl Caroline Munro in a two-minute cameo) is reluctant to sell him. After an oddly out-of-place James Bondian credit sequence (complete with naked female silhouettes and gun-toting superimpositions), the detective settles into a pub to read the tome. He narrates, "The shopkeeper was right—this book was so much more than ink and paper. The evil bound within its pages was terrifying, but utterly intoxicating. I had to read on." Incongruously, the P.I. then relates the main narrative by reading from this oversized leather-bound book that looks like it's kin to the ancient Necronomicon—despite the fact that the story it relates took place less than six months ago. Even more inexplicably, the book (and film) derails itself through side-trips to multiple flashbacks and vignettes that prove tangential at best, with many even wholly unrelated to the main tale. "What this film was about," noted director/co-producer/co-scripter Tony Jopia, "was a lot of wind-ups, was about the people telling stories that you never knew whether they were real, and playing with the perception of making people sort of just enjoy them for what they were but also wonder how its part in the film is relevant." Unfortunately, so many of said side-trips are completely *irrelevant*, including vignettes about two caricatured gangsters meeting the Devil; a pair of sunbathers imagining killers everywhere; and a "mad ninja" stalking the village streets. Even some of the lycan-centric flashbacks prove disappointing, such as a modern-day "Little Red Riding Hood" variation that devolves into nothing special—just a werewolf stalking and killing a (grown) woman in a red dress. And even after the film's proper (admittedly exciting) climax, it slaps on a misplaced and nonsensical *zombie* coda. Rather than exploring the potentially fascinating group (werewolf) dynamics of this lycan-band ("They'll do whatever I command once I've had them kill in the wild," posits the alpha, "this trip is going to solidify us as a pack once and for all"), Jopia and co. spend their time on tangential asides.

Jopia tries to hold things together with periodic narration like, "From now on, they were a pack; they'd hunt and kill in unison—organized, controlled, and far more deadly," and "Tensions among the friends grew, along with their deepening hunger." Such interjections, intended to illuminate the characters' motivations and states of mind, merely smacks of last-ditch desperation to disguise the poorly rendered characters and even poorer story construction (since so little of said "unison" and "tension" is on display).

None of the characters offer much in the way of characterization; most are too thin even to qualify as "cardboard," and nearly all prove unlikable. Even the two "innocent" female hitchhikers turn out to be conniving con-artists, while the werewolf-hunting Charlie shows himself to be a deranged, vengeance-seeking psycho who laughs maniacally as he cuts a man in half with a chainsaw! Consequently, one has little emotional investment when a character dies (which nearly all of them do), with nothing to hang one's interest on other than the novelty of the kill or the arc of the bloodspray.

While the carnage they cause can be quite impressive (some ropey CGI blood and stretchy effects notwithstanding), the werewolves' appearances fail to match. Rubbery mutant dog faces surrounded by an unruly mop-top 'do are the order of the day, topping the shaggy, less-than-convincing body suits that look more bear-like than lupine.

Crying Wolf features nearly as many naked breasts as gore scenes. It seems as if every female in the film was instructed to get her kit off at one point or another, even if just to change clothes (for instance, the two hitchhikers disrobe after someone spills soup all over them). While some might applaud such devotion to the female form, it's clearly pure exploitation here (the old "boobs and blood" mantra coming to the fore).

At least Jopia the director does better than Jopia the screenwriter, as he evinces some deft handling of the various set-pieces. For example, one nighttime attack flashback shows a woman screaming as two hairy arms grab her by the shoulder. The camera moves forward to focus on their shadows on the brick wall. The beast raises her arm and *pulls it off*, with blood spraying everywhere. The camera shows the two shadows merge, as crunching sounds play on the soundtrack, before pulling back to reveal the beast's (actual) arms holding a now headless torso. A brief burp on the soundtrack ends the scene. Amusing, suggestively gory, and cleverly shot, such scenes as this make one wish Jopia had taken as much care with his script as with his staging.

Goofy rather than funny, *Crying Wolf* fails to capture that delicate balance between humor and horror exemplified by such lycan classics as *The Howling, An American Werewolf in London, Dog Soldiers*, and *Game of Werewolves*. The level of comedy becomes manifest from the outset—by naming the town "Deddington." Clever? Not by half. Then it continues when a creepy customer makes a purchase from the shopkeeper for the amount of £6.66 Get it? 666…

About the best it can do are a few amusing bon mots for the gore sequences. At one point Charlie has a pack member chained up in a barn ("Diluted silver nitrate stops you from transforming," he explains to his confused captive). Charlie then brings out a chainsaw, to which the alarmed lycan asks, "What are you going to do with that?" Charlie gleefully responds, "Funny you should ask—I'm gonna fucking *neuter* ya!" and lays in.

Australian actress Rosie Pearson, who played pack member Emma, enthused, "I really enjoyed running through the woods, wearing all the makeup, the prosthetics, the hair—once you get all those things on, then you feel more like a wolf." But becoming a werewolf has its hazards too. Towards the end, she rips off her shirt to expose strands of wispy hair between her breasts. "When the hair was ripped off, the glue got stuck on there for about a week, so I had a very very dirty looking chest for about a week." While the disappointing *Crying Wolf* may not leave any marks on the viewer, its convoluted story, dearth of characterization, and myriad missed opportunities won't leave much impression either.

With quotes from: "Barking Up the Wrong Tree: The Making of *Crying Wolf*," *Crying Wolf* DVD; "Rosie Pearson, *Crying Wolf* Interview," by Victoria Stedeford, Youtube.com.

Morphology: Shaggy, dog-faced bipeds
Demise: Everything from (regular) bullets and crossbow bolts to chainsaws and bombs
Full Moon Rating: **

The Curse

(2001; Arrow) Director/screenplay: Jacqueline Garry. Producers: Trent Tooley, Heidi Reinberg; Cinematographer: Bud Gardner. Cast: Amy Laughlin, Mike Dooly, Sara Elena Knight, Matthew Arkin, Ken Garito, Michael Leydon Campbell.

> Pray you're not her type … blood type that is—tagline

Lycanthropy as PMS? That's the premise of this feminist black comedy by first-(and last)-time writer-director Jacqueline Garry, who was directly inspired by the case of English barmaid Sandie Craddock. No, Craddock was not a werewolf; rather, in 1980 the Crown reduced her murder charge (for stabbing to death a fellow barmaid) to manslaughter due to Craddock's "diminished responsibility" because of severe premenstrual tension. The Court decided that "years of diaries and institutional records indicat[ing] a cyclical pattern to her violent behavior," supported the argument that PMS (premenstrual syndrome) "turned her into a raging animal each month and forced her to act out of character." Craddock received probation along with progesterone treatment. That same year, a British woman named Christine English employed the same defense to escape incarceration for crushing her boyfriend against a utility pole with her car, killing him. The murder charge was reduced to "manslaughter due to diminished responsibility," resulting in nothing more than a one-year driving ban. Though mentioned in medical journals as far back as 1931, PMS had finally arrived in the courts—and the media, with British tabloids concocting headlines like, "Once a Month I'm a Woman Possessed," "Dr. Jekyll and Ms. Hyde," and "Premenstrual Frenzy."

Garry took this "premenstrual frenzy" notion to the extreme in her tale of mousey New Yorker Frida (Amy Laughlin), who suffers monthly from severe PMS (which appears to tie in with the full moon) and has little luck with men, despite the efforts and encouragement of her sexy best friend Jennifer (Sara Elena Knight). One day at a lingerie sale, a woman bites Frida on the hand when they both grab the same pair of panties. Soon, along with Frida's monthly irritability and bloating comes excessive hair growth on her arms and legs, a new appetite for meat (she's a vegetarian), and a glowing green eye color. Also, she experiences black-outs and awakens in her bed stained with blood (the first time is the result of her period; later it appears to be blood from her "dates"). Things become even more complicated when an investigating detective, Peter (Mike Dooly), becomes smitten with Frida, and she with him. Can Frida find a way to combat her premenstrual lycanthropy before she does something terrible to her newfound beau?

Shot in New York City on 16mm for a miniscule $37,000, *The Curse* looks far more polished and professional than it has a right to. Clever camerawork (including some steadicam-like werewolf p.o.v. moments) and beautiful New York City cinematography (courtesy of DP Bud Gardner and director Jacqueline Garry herself, who served as her own solitary second unit to capture some gorgeous shots of the New York skyline at dawn and dusk), along with the real-world locations (including Frida's apartment furnished with some spectacular antique furniture) add production value as well as verisimilitude.

A sly feminist treaty, *The Curse* puts forth its viewpoints via a number of amusing incidents and dialogue exchanges. Thankfully, rather than forcing obvious jokes into the mouths it its characters, Garry's script has the comedy arise naturally from the situations. At one point late in the film Frida, desperate to stop the killings, determines to commit suicide. This heavy theme (which only serves to engender further pathos for the likable lead character) is handled via a quick, blackly-comic montage of Frida stepping off a ledge, gulping down a bottle of cleaning fluid, and trying to hang herself. It concludes with Jennifer bursting into Frida's apartment to find Frida's head in the oven. But rubber-gloved Frida is only *cleaning* the appliance. "You scared the shit out of me," cries Jennifer, "I thought you were trying to kill yourself." Frida replies, "I tried it—it doesn't work. I think I need silver bullets."

When Frida reveals to Jennifer her fear that she's become a lycanthrope, her friend sarcastically responds, "A PMS werewolf? Of course! Frida, are you on drugs?" After falling for Peter, Frida bemoans, "I finally meet a guy that I like, and I find out I'm a fucking werewolf!" At one point Frida tells Peter, "There's something I have to tell you. It's about—PMS. I get it really bad." Peter reassures her with, "I'm sure your bark is worse than your bite," to which Frida responds, "I think my bite's a lot worse."

Garry's script often pokes fun at male-dominated institutions, including the psychiatric and medical professions. When Frida tells her (male) shrink, "I had a dream last night that I was a doormat," the psychiatrist asks, "What do you think that means?" Frida reasonably answers with the obvious, "That I'm a doormat, of course." At another session she confesses that she thinks she's a werewolf. "Let's explore this," he suggests, "what makes you feel like a werewolf?" Frida's response: "I ate a guy last night."

Frida also seeks help from her medical doctor, telling the elderly male physician, "I'm worried about my next PMS spell. It's gotten much worse, and I'm not myself lately. I get bloated and irritable, and my breasts get larger, my nails turn into claws, my teeth get sharper, and I have more facial and body hair." The nonplussed doc dismissively answers, "Sounds all stress-related to me; is that all?" Frida continues, "I have nightmares and I black out." At this the doctor waves a hand, "Diet and exercise, that's all there is. I'm not a big proponent of this PMS craze"—as if the condition is just some passing fad.

The film stutters at times due to pacing issues, with too many slow spots that can't be fully sustained by scenes of Frida and Jennifer shopping, walking, dining and talking. (Fortunately, the two likable leads are engaging enough that these time-filling sequences don't feel too protracted or painful.) Also, the near-complete lack of special effects disappoints on the lycan-front. We never see Frida's full werewolf-self. The closest we come is a pair of glowing green contact lenses, a wispy patch of hair on her arm, claw-like fingernails, and the suggestion of a set of delicate fangs to indicate the change is coming. (This minimalism was not necessarily an aesthetic decision but one arising out of the near non-existent budget; Garry and co. could not afford to employ a special effects artist, so they did the work themselves. For instance, the woman who bites Frida at the film's beginning to infect her with lycanthropy was played by a production assistant who served as a makeshift makeup artist, applying the hair to Frida's arms.) All the attacks, save one, are implied rather than shown, the exception being Frida's killing of her callous ex-boyfriend in the shower, which becomes an amusingly accurate parody of Alfred Hitchcock's famous *Psycho* murder. This was "a turning of the tables," noted Garry of the gender-switch, "the whole script is. The shower scene was our little homage; that was fun." The other two attacks offer either a quick p.o.v. chase ending in the victim falling and screaming; or nothing at all—completely unseen and only coming to light the next day when Frida awakens with a severed arm in her bed after another unsuccessful date. This leads to one of the more amusing sequences, which begins with a shot of Frida in bed with an arm draped lovingly over her hip. But the initial notion that Frida has finally experienced a tender night of lovemaking evaporates when a trickle of blood suddenly flows down the motionless hand, causing Frida to sit up and reveal it to be a *severed* arm. She then must deal with the unwanted appendage—first poking it with a broom handle, afraid to touch it, then delicately picking it up by the fingers with rubber gloves and holding it at arm's length before placing it upright in the garbage disposal, shoving it downwards, and squeamishly crimping her eyes shut.

Apart from this one (comically employed) severed arm and a couple of otherwise intact bodies splashed with red paint, the victims of Frida's savagery offer little visceral impact (which perhaps works in favor of the film's comedic tone, but at the expense of any possible horrific/tragic implications).

Werewolf-wise, *The Curse* (a term here which, of course, carries a female-centric double meaning) may be one of the strongest feminine tracks in the annals of lycancinema. While researching Frida's new condition, Jennifer comes upon an old book from the nineteenth century in which author "Madame Sconce" writes: "The original werewolves were females. They became werewolves on the lunar cycle because it corresponded to the woman's cycle. My suspicion is that the only cure is true love. The female cycle werewolf only kills men, and never kills someone she truly loves." Lycanthropy—and PMS—can only be cured by tender understanding, by true love.

More an ironic comedy about modern dating and feminism than a horror movie about a werewolf and its victims, *The Curse* does include the occasion sequence of straight-up suspense. For Frida's third (and final) victim, she becomes a true (sexual) predator, luring an East Village musician into bed before ripping him to pieces. Unlike the two previous seemingly accidental (and unwanted) killings, here Frida seems far more intent, as if she has finally embraced her lycanthropy, or at least the inevitability of it all. Garry stages the brief scene in dim lighting, so it becomes a shot of tangled, struggling silhouettes, accompanied by distressing sounds, before the dying victim's bloody hand manages to hit the bedside light to reveal his staring, dead eyes and bleeding body.

Though comparisons to the previous year's much bigger-budgeted—and far better known—*Ginger Snaps* (2000) might seem inevitable, *The Curse* was actually made prior to that now-acknowledged lycan-classic. "We shot our film in September 1998," recounted Garry. "Unapix [a producer of *Ginger Snaps*] had seen the trailer we made to get finishing funds. Since that was the goal, it showed almost the whole story. They kept calling us as we were editing; checking in, asking when they could see the film … and then a year or two later, there's *Ginger Snaps*, a menstrual werewolf movie. It really pissed me off. I felt like they actually stole some stuff."

The Curse climaxes with a confrontation between Peter and Frida at her apartment. Peter (tellingly wearing a red hoodie), now convinced of his love's lycanthropic (PMS?) nature, goes to Frida's apartment (lair) to try and comfort her, asking, "Can't you bite me, and then I'll be like you?" She responds that this curse (gift?) is only for women ("It doesn't work that way; men don't get PMS"). Discordant violins playing on the soundtrack, the mobile camera circling warily as they talk, and Frida's green animal eyes and cold smile (like that of the Big Bad Wolf) add tension and a palpable sense of danger to the moment. Despite Peter insisting they can work it out ("Other couples have worse problems—cheating, lying; what's a little werewolf a few days a month?"), Garry ends on a decidedly uneasy note. Can lycanthropy—can PMS—truly be tamed? And, more to the point, *should* it? (Perhaps it's down to male envy of the female and her empowerment. After all, the male—in the form of Peter—wants to be like the woman in the end, but cannot.) Offering a darkly comical take on such issues and questions, the film (which premiered on the festival circuit in 2001, but took two more years to see a broader video release) leaves it open as to whether lycanthropy—womanhood and all that entails—is a blessing or, indeed, a *Curse*.

With quotes from: "Hormone Hostages: The Cultural Legacy of PMS as a Legal Defense," by J.C. Chrisler, in *Charting a New Course for Feminist Psychology,* edited by L.H. Collins, et al.; "*The Curse*: Blood Moon Rising," by Christine Allen, *Fangoria* 225.

Morphology: Unknown; the beast's appearance remains a mystery
Demise: None; she finds true love … maybe
Full Moon Rating: ***

Curse of the Devil

(1973/77; Izaro Films/Goldstone; Spain/Mexico) Original Language Title: *El Retorno de Walpurgis.* Alternate Titles: *The Black Harvest of Countess Dracula* (video); *The Return of Walpurgis* (video). Director: Charles Aured (Carlos Aured); Producers: Ramiro Meléndez, Luis Méndez; Screenplay: Jack Moll (Jacinto Molina, aka Paul Naschy); Cinematographer: Frank Sanchez (Francisco Sánchez). Cast: Paul Naschy, Faye Falcon (Fabiola Falcón), Vinc Molina (Mariano Vidal Molina), May Oliver (Maritza Olivaras), Joe Martin (Jose Manuel Martin), Maria Silva.

> Can man be turned into an animal? Do animals become men? Is it possible to exorcise the powers of Satan? Does the love of a woman really conquer all?—trailer

The answers: Yes. No. Maybe. And 'It depends on how you look at it.' This sixth released entry in Paul Naschy's Waldemar Daninsky series (with each film unrelated to the next) is the first to offer a truly detailed account of the werewolf's origin. Rather than acquiring the curse by simply being bitten (as in *Frankenstein's Bloody Terror* and *The Fury of the Wolfman*) or simply arriving on the scene already afflicted (like in *Assignment Terror, The Werewolf vs. the Vampire*

Woman, and *Dr. Jekyll and the Werewolf*), *Curse of the Devil* spends its entire first half detailing how vengeful gypsies transformed Waldemar into a rampaging lycanthrope.

A medieval prologue features an armor-clad Daninsky ancestor righteously killing the Satan-worshipping Count Bathory, then burning Bathory's wife Elizabeth (Maria Silva) as a witch. From the flames she proclaims: "I curse you, Daninsky, and all your descendants. And Satan will see that you pay. Until one day one of your kin will again kill one of my kin, spill blood in what seems an accident, and from that time on all those who bear your name will live a hell on Earth." With this oddly convoluted curse hanging over the Daninsky household, the film leaps forward three centuries to the 1800s, where aristocrat Waldemar Daninsky (Paul Naschy) and his gamekeeper Boris (Fernando S. Polack) hunt a wolf (looking suspiciously like a German Shepherd) on his wooded lands. The superstitious (or knowing?) servant surreptitiously loads Waldemar's shotgun with silver shells. Waldemar shoots as the beast runs into some brush. But when he parts the bushes, a horrified Waldemar sees a naked man lying dead with a wound in his chest. (Strangely, this takes place in full daylight, though the implication is clear: the man was a werewolf. And even stranger, afterwards, a dazed, guilt-ridden, and perhaps none-too-bright Waldemar refers to the animal as "a wolverine," asking "where did it disappear to?") The dead man's kin, gypsies (and apparent descendants of the Bathorys), then perform a ritual to summon the Devil (a tall figure covered head to toe in a black leotard—with visible zipper) who has congress with several willing gypsy girls before choosing one to carry out their diabolical plan. "He has selected you, Ilona," intones the old witch-woman presiding over the proceedings, "to mark Waldemar Daninsky with the Devil's Teeth. The skull of the wolf will create his hell on Earth." To this end, Ilona (Inez Morales) worms her way into Waldemar's bed, then, on Walpurgis Night, drips her own blood over the "unholy relic" and uses the wolf skull to bite Waldemar's chest while he sleeps. Henceforward he will become a murderous werewolf during the full moon.

The film's second half focuses on the townspeople's growing suspicions; an escaped axe-wielding lunatic roaming the countryside (who the local inspector blames for the recent rash of killings); Waldemar's burgeoning romance with a young woman, Kinga (Fabiola Falcón); Waldemar's faithful servant attempting to protect her unknowing master; and Kinga's promise to help Waldemar (by wielding a pointy silver cross).

Sprinkled in among scene after mundane scene of nearly every character walking in the woods (Waldemar alone, Waldemar with Kinga, Kinga's sexually precocious little sister Maria, various servants, the inspector, and finally a handful of the *de rigeur* torch-wielding villagers), are a few striking scenes and incidents, some of them downright bizarre. For instance, after attacking Waldemar with the unholy wolf's skull, Ilona flees Waldemar's castle into the forest where she's abruptly dispatched by the axe-wielding madman. Later, Kinga's attention-starved younger sister tricks Waldemar into meeting her at a hunting lodge and attempts to seduce him by saying, "I came here a virgin; I'm not gonna leave that way." This segues into Waldemar's first transformation, it being the night of the full moon. As the two embrace, the moon rises. Waldemar pulls back from on top of the nubile girl, and from her point of view we see him half-transformed, with hair covering much of his face. He lowers himself towards her again; then, after a close-up of the screaming lass, he pulls back once more to show his full wolfish visage, with bright red blood dripping from his mouth onto the countenance of the now-dead girl. The scene draws a disturbing parallel between sex and violence.

The salacious and violent sequence also showcases the superior Wolfman makeup (better than in any previous Naschy film), with its face covered in coarse, realistic-looking hair, wolf ears (towards the top of the head to add that lupine look), wicked set of fangs, and dark, leathery skin under the yak hair. Unfortunately, this werewolf iteration skulks far more than it rampages, and Naschy fails to imbue his beast-man with the brutal energy seen in previous outings. Acting more human than animal—walking normally (even tiptoeing forward to launch a surprise attack on a blind

Striking German poster for *Curse of the Devil*, sixth in Paul Naschy's long-running Waldemar Daninsky series.

woman), quietly watching potential victims from behind a tree, even smashing the inspector's head in with a rock rather than slashing with claws and fangs—it appears that Naschy's were-heart just wasn't in it.

"It's a good-looking film," opined Naschy himself, "very carefully constructed, with an interesting plot and that strange search for love that turns Waldemar into a kind of libertine ... not exactly, since what he's searching for isn't sex, but rather the love that can free him from his curse." Well, Waldemar finds far more than his fair share of sex over the course of the film, as *Curse of the Devil* displays more female pulchritude than any previous Daninsky outing. It seems that nearly every young female in the cast gets buck-naked at one time or another, with several offering full-frontal nudity.

"There are some real high points in the film," continued Naschy, "an attack in which the werewolf is really impressive, and later when he kills the blind woman who is trapped inside of a house with him." The attack Naschy mentions is indeed one of the more memorable in the film, with the werewolf breaking into a cottage by ripping the bars from a window then leaping onto the man inside. The peasant grabs up an axe and swings several times, with the werewolf weaving and ducking before the weapon finally connects. But instead of drawing blood, the blade supernaturally *breaks* on the wolfman's abdomen, since silver is the only metal than can hurt the werewolf. It's a startling and effective visual that underscores the creature's preternatural dangerousness and invulnerability.

But perhaps the film's most baroquely disturbing sequence doesn't even involve the werewolf. At one point the villagers have collected the bodies of three victims, and their leader goes to each corpse and gently gouges out the eyes(!), collecting the gruesome orbs in a bowl. "That the werewolf shall be forever blind, these eyes are offered," he intones before tossing them into a fire. Just then the Inspector bursts in, shocked (naturally) by what's taking place. "We do what we have to do," justifies the village elder. "Sometimes the victims of the werewolf return from their tombs to haunt the living, thirsting for blood." It's a clever inversion on the medieval folk belief that some vampires, after being killed, may return as werewolves.

Director Carlos Aured worked with Naschy several more times, most successfully on *Horror Rises from the Tomb* (1973), which many (this author included) consider Naschy's best film, and the excellent *Blue Eyes of the Broken Doll* (1974; aka *House of Psychotic Women*). Unfortunately, his leisurely-paced and largely pedestrian work here more closely resembles what he brought to the dismal *The Mummy's Revenge* (1973). Some stilted dialogue ("You're not culpable; you didn't invite this malediction"), toneless dubbing, and a bland (and rather horse-faced) leading lady in the form of Fabiola Falcón (who abandoned acting the following year to go behind the camera as a producer) fail to improve matters.

Given its original language title of *El Retorno de Walpurgis*, one might think this a direct sequel to *La Noche de Walpurgis* (*The Werewolf vs. the Vampire Woman*). Such was not the case. Rather, the like-minded moniker was employed simply to evoke that earlier film's success. Of course, even more misleading was the English language title, intended to capitalize on *The Exorcist* phenomenon. In fact, the film's American advertising included taglines like "Damn the Exorcist! The Devil won't let go!" and "Prepare Yourself for The HORROR of *PSYCHO*! The TERROR of *EXORCIST*!" with nothing alluding to the fact it was even a werewolf movie.

Despite its focus on the werewolf origin, some disturbingly weird moments, and more naked nubiles than you can shake a silver crucifix at, the *Curse of the Devil* turns out to be a curse of general dullness. While not the worst Daninsky outing, it's far from the best.

With quotes from: "Paul Naschy Filmography," by José Luis González and Michael Secula, *Videooze* 6/7.

Morphology: Fierce-looking wolfman
Demise: Sharpened silver cross
Full Moon Rating: **½

The Curse of the Werewolf

(1961; Hammer/Universal-International; UK) Director: Terence Fisher; Producer: Anthony Hinds; Screenplay: Anthony Hinds (as John Elder) (based on the novel *The Werewolf of Paris* by Guy Endore); Cinematographer: Arthur Grant. Cast: Clifford Evans, Oliver Reed, Yvonne Romain, Catherine Feller, Anthony Dawson.

HALF-MAN ... HALF-WOLF—ad line

Filmmaker John (*An American Werewolf in London*) Landis called *The Curse of the Werewolf* "an extremely handsome picture" and "probably the best looking Hammer film." He further noted, "Oliver Reed is an excellent werewolf," before cheekily adding, "as he proved the

Oliver Reed in full (wrinkly) regalia for *The Curse of the Werewolf* (1961), Hammer Films' sole entry in the lycanthropic arena.

rest of his life." (Indeed, Reed earned a reputation as a notorious hellraiser, as fond of brawling and engaging in shocking behavior as he was of drink. He died of a heart attack during a bender—while filming *Gladiator*—in 1999, age 61.) While Landis' plaudits ring true, what doesn't is the oft-touted label of "classic" some critics have pasted onto this *Curse*. Though it certainly looks good (with period sets and costumes surpassing even the usual Hammer opulence), and the young Reed is everything one could wish for in a lycanthrope (intensely charismatic and sympathetic in human form, and forbidding and ferocious as the wolfman), *The Curse of the Werewolf* proved to be a meandering lycan-tale whose admittedly impressive werewolf action comes too little and too late to fully overcome a general air of overstuffed dullness.

In 18th century Spain a beggar (Richard Wordsworth) ends up locked in the dungeons of an evil Marques (Anthony Dawson) and forgotten for decades. When a beautiful mute serving girl (Yvonne Romain) spurns the grotesque Marques' lecherous advances, the despot tosses her into the cell with the near-animalistic beggar, who rapes her. After killing the Marques and escaping the castle, the girl ends up in the home of kindly Don Alfredo Carrido (Clifford Evans). When she dies in childbirth, Alfredo raises the child, Leon, as his own. But evidence indicates that as a young boy, having been born under a full moon on Christmas Day, Leon transforms into a wolf and attacks the local goat herds. Given advice from the local priest (John Gabriel), Don Alfredo's affection for the boy temporarily tames the animal inside him, and Leon grows into a strapping young man (Oliver Reed). Getting a job at a vineyard, Leon falls in love with the winemaker's daughter, Christina (Catherine Feller). But a full moon night on the town brings out the latent beast in Leon, and only Christina can sooth his savage breast. Unfortunately, before they can run away together, the authorities incarcerate Leon, leading to lycanthropic mayhem—and tragedy—at the next full moon.

Curse follows its classic predecessor *The Wolf Man* in its tragic character-driven approach, with the man taking precedence over the monster (though it lacks its progenitor's linear sense of excitement and immediacy). *Curse*'s opening credits give the game away, as the names roll over an extreme close-up of a set of staring eyes. The raised, malformed brow ridge and fine hairs across the bridge of the nose (not to mention the eyes themselves—a dark golden color surrounded by bloodshot whites) reveal that these orbs belong to the werewolf. The film's intentions immediately become clear when several *tears* seep from the inhuman eyes. In *Curse*, pathos will be the order of the day.

Like most Hammer films, *Curse* is populated by a cadre of talented character actors (and a riveting lead in the smoldering Oliver Reed) who bring to vibrant life its Gothic story among well-dressed settings, and it shares the major flaw evinced by a number of said productions—a bloated length. (Many a Hammer horror stands as a wonderful 70-minute movie … that takes 90-plus minutes to play out.) In *Curse*'s case, the entire opening half-hour (detailing first the beggar's saga, then the servant girl's) could have easily been excised, or at least truncated into a concise flashback, with no ill effects apart from missing out on Anthony Dawson's ridiculous Snidely Whiplash characterization as the impossibly dastardly Marques. This would have sped up the film's glacial pacing, and quickly gotten at the meat of the matter (as it were), rather than forcing us to spend the first half-hour with characters we care little about and never see again.

Curse draws more upon medieval folklore for its lycan-rules than most productions. Leon becomes a werewolf simply by being born at the wrong time (with the animalistic rape sowing the unhallowed ground). As Don Alfredo's knowing housekeeper says, "For an unwanted child to be born then [on December 25th] is an insult to Heaven, Senor, that's what I was taught." While it tips its hat to Hollywood by including the silver bullet and full moon tropes, *Curse* posits its werewolf as an evil spirit invading a human body, as well as harkening back to the Spanish Inquisition in its methods of dealing with lycanthropes. A jailed Leon pleads with Don Alfredo and the priest to tell the Mayor that "he must have me executed—now. And Father, you must tell him how it must be done—burned alive." It's an obvious reference to the notorious auto de fey, the Inquisition's punishment for heresy, witchcraft—and werewolfism.

The initial trigger comes when the young Leon inadvertently tastes blood for the first time (as the gentle lad picks up a wounded squirrel and tries to "kiss it better"). After that, says little Leon, "I dream I'm a wolf, like in a picture book, drinking blood." His guardian turns the boy's hand over to reveal patches of coarse hair on his palm and forearm. Don Alfredo seeks counsel from the priest, who tells him of "elemental spirits about us at all times—spirits, without bodies, of creatures that have never lived." These "roaming spirits," continues the priest, invade a body, "usually at the moment of birth. The soul and the spirit war with each other to gain mastery of the body…. A werewolf is a body with a soul and a spirit that are constantly at war. The spirit is that of a wolf. And whatever weakens the human soul—vice, greed, hatred, solitude—especially during the cycle of the full moon when the forces of evil are at their strongest, these bring the spirit of the wolf to the fore. And, in turn, whatever weakens the spirit of the beast—warmth, fellowship, love—raise the human soul." Dismayed, Don Alfredo asks, "Is there no cure?" The priest answers, "Only love. When he's older, he may meet a young girl who he'll love very deeply. But, what is more important, she should love him very deeply. Then he may be saved."

Director Terence Fisher (who helmed many of Hammer's most lauded productions) and co. were obviously much more interested in the human relationships than in their monster. In fact, the build-up to Reed's first appearance as the werewolf (83 minutes in) takes longer than the entire running time of *any* previous werewolf movie. Until then, the viewer must make do with the largely superfluous preamble; another quarter-hour of little Leon's travails (and Don Alfredo's horrifying discovery about his young charge); and then another forty minutes of the adult Leon making friends, falling for Christina ("Run away with me"), and partying with his pals, 18th century-style. The only action comes from Leon's first nocturnal lycan-rampage in which he kills three people—all *off-screen* (with only a shadow and hairy hand to indicate the change, brought on by Leon's visit to a local den of iniquity, as his baser instincts, coupled with the rising full moon, release the beast within).

Despite its flaws, *The Curse of the Werewolf* proved groundbreaking in several respects. It was the first *color* werewolf movie, and also the first to draw blood in vivid (though still somewhat reticent) fashion. (At film's end, when shot with a silver bullet, bright red blood spurts from the hole in the beast-man's chest—a shockingly realistic effect for the time.) *Curse* also made far more explicit the link between love and salvation which the Universal werewolf series merely implied. Here the very human qualities of "warmth, fellowship, love" keep the beast at bay: Christina sitting up with Leon on the second night of the full moon prevents him from changing.

The 22-year-old Oliver Reed lied about his age (tacking on several years) in order to secure the part, his first starring role. The job paid him about a thousand pounds for eight weeks' work, and it was makeup man Roy Ashton who helped him secure it. "I suggested Oliver Reed [to producer Tony Hinds]," said Ashton. "He was exactly right: his powerful bone structure was just right for the appearance, and his gifts as an actor were perfect for the part. In addition, he resembled a wolf when he was angry." The makeup (including a leotard covered with yak hair to simulate his wolf-coat torso) took two hours to apply.

"No, no, no!" desperately shouts Reed's Leon when confronted with the truth of his affliction. "I don't believe! I can't!" But Reed's anguished sobs indicate otherwise, for deep down he knows the truth. The actor's likable demeanor, his barely-held-in-check fiery intensity, and his tortured denials brings the character to vivid, tragic life.

The wolfman, when he finally appears during the film's final eight minutes, makes for an effective blending of man and monster, thanks to Ashton's makeup and Reed's animalistic performance. Coarse gray hair covers his cheeks and chin, a built-up nose hints at the creature's animal origins, pointy wolf's ears near the top of its head lend a canine caste, and realistic-looking fangs cement its savagery. A fur-covered torso completes the picture of a dangerous beastman, with Reed's athletic strength and aggressive ferocity imbuing the creature with deadly vibrancy.

Disappointingly, the film's sole transformation isn't worth the long wait, with the monster emerging via a set of simple dissolves—of his *hands*. Recalled Ashton, "I suggested the wolfman's transformation by only showing his hands. To do this we had to lock the cameras off in the same position for each shot of the stop-motion photography: I prepared a cast out of plaster with their imprints, so that, every time they stopped the camera, we could take Oliver away to apply more hair and to make the nails a little longer. When he came back he put his hands in the cast again, as it had been before." Fortunately, once transformed, the werewolf then engages in some acrobatic rooftop leaping and fierce snarling that, while offering scant recompense for the previous hour and a quarter of general inactivity, at least leaves the viewer with a *taste* of were-action.

"I liked that [film]," noted director Terence Fischer, "because of the tremendous interrelation between the characters, between Reed and the girl. Hell, anyone can turn into a werewolf, can't they? But it was his *situation* that made it exciting. The horror of him knowing that this was happening to him and the conflict between this and his love for the girl. And audiences, I think, will respond to this because they can understand the emotional pull between people rather than the fact of someone turning into a werewolf, or Dracula wanting to bite someone's neck. Of course, Oliver Reed was very good as the werewolf. In my opinion he's never done anything better."

While no lycan classic (despite the claims of some avowed "Hammer-heads"), *The Curse of the Werewolf* still offers a pathos-driven plot, some thought—and emotion—provoking lycan-situations, a fiery and sympathetic lead, and a ferocious wolfman. But it takes a whole lot of patience to get there…

With quotes from: "Trailers from Hell: Curse of the Werewolf," by John Landis, trailersfromhell.com, 2013; *Evil Spirits: The Life of Oliver Reed*, by Cliff Goodwin; *The Horror People*, by John Brosnan.

Morphology: Hairy-chested wolfman
Demise: Silver bullet
Full Moon Rating: **½

Curse of the Wolf

(2007; Brain Damage Films) Director/Screenplay/Cinematographer: Len Kabasinski; Producer: Lisa McQuiston. Cast: Lanny Poffo, Darian Caine, Brian "Blue Meanie" Heffron, Pamela Sutch, Renee Porada, Todd Humes, Katie Russell, Alex Bolla, Leon South.

When the Moon is Full…. Beware of the CURSE!—tagline

Erie, Pennsylvania, native Len Kabasinski likes making movies. Since 2005's *Swamp Zombies*, he's been taking vacation time and weekends to churn out micro-budget epics like *Fist of the Vampire*, *Ninja: Prophecy of Death* and *Skull Forest*. (No, he hasn't quit his day job.) *Curse of the Wolf* was Kabasinski's sophomore effort, and while miles above his unwatchable *Swamp Zombies* debut, it's still terrible.

When twenty-something werewolf Dakota (Renee Porada) tries to break away from her poor white trash pack, alpha Michael (Todd Humes) and his three underlings track her down to drag her back. Escaping a second time, Dakota successfully starts a new life working in a veterinary office. She also has found a way to suppress her monthly transformations by using drugs stolen from the vet. However, six months later her pack picks up her scent again, kills her new friend, and tries to bring her back into the fold once more. But circumstances see her befriending a shady bar owner (Lanny Poffo) and his high-kickin' pistol-packin' henchman (played by Kabasinski himself) and henchwomen, leading to a bloody showdown between the werewolves and Dakota and her new gangster friends.

A self-professed lover of "low-budget martial arts movies," Kabasinski, who holds two black belt degrees, fills his flicks with small-scale martial arts scenes (he serves as his films' "fight choreographer" and often participates in the brawls himself). Consequently, his movies' heroes, villains and even monsters all throw karate punches and reverse kicks. Yep, in Kabinski's films, truly 'everybody was kung fu fighting'…. Naturally, *Curse of the Wolf* features far too many of these repetitive fight scenes (it seems as if *every* encounter ends with low-grade punches and kicks), making it feel much longer than its already protracted 105-minute running time.

Another curse on this *Curse* is its nearly across-the-board junior high–level acting. Kabasinski stacks his cast with former pro wrestlers (Lanny Poffo, Brian "Blue Meanie" Heffron), porn starlets (Darian Caine, *Batbabe: The Dark Nighty*, *Kinky Kong*) and various amateur martial arts enthusiasts (including the director himself, whose emoting makes Chuck Norris look like Sir Laurence Olivier). Consequently, there are very few (if any) accomplished—or even competent—actors in *Curse of the Wolf*.

Grainy videography, dim lighting, choppy editing and a music/sound track that at times feels more than a little random (though it does offer its own driving garage-band theme song: "It's the curse of the wooooooolf!") complete the amateurish picture. The werewolf makeup looks poor, with very little continuity among the werewolf visages. Some look like a rubber dog's head mask, while others appear to be a man (or woman) in black face with bits of hair and a few primitive prosthetics pasted on.

These lycanthropes can change at will, with their strength increasing the closer it gets to the full moon. Kabasinski raises the age-old "curse-vs.-gift" notion of lycanthropy by casting Dakota in the "tortured soul" mold, while the rest of her pack revel in their animalistic tendencies. Kabasinski also offers the intriguing notion of Dakota controlling the change through drugs. "I found a way to live a normal life—that's all I wanted," she tells Michael. Unfortunately, the simplistic script remains more interested in martial arts than character themes, so that these potentially weighty issues merely float on the surface of a sea of cheap karate kicks. In any case, the actors, each straining to add forced emphasis to even the most mundane line, can't invest their characters with anything deeper than a paper cut.

The one effective bit of werewolfery comes via the Big Transformation Scene, which Kabasinski shoots (though not particularly *well*) as a messy, gruesome spectacle. The man falls to his knees and bloody bits of his face begin dropping off, landing with a squelchy splat on the floor, until he grabs the top of his head with his hands and peels back his scalp, revealing the moist wolfish head underneath. (Here the ocular-challenging lighting and shaky camerawork might actually be a blessing—at least for those with more delicate sensibilities.)

Gratuitous nudity (shower scene, bubble bath) and two different soft-core sex scenes spice things up (or at least give the teen, and teen-at-heart, viewers what they want). In fact, every primary female cast member gets naked except for Renee Porada as Dakota (but even she strips down to her lacy unmentionables at one point for no particular reason). Of course, these sexploitation elements, like the werewolf scenes, don't fare particularly well due to the flat lighting and poor camera choices.

Kabasinski directs no better than he writes or acts. At one point he attempts the now-clichéd dream-within-a-dream shock pioneered by *An American Werewolf in London*, but he stages it so poorly (with the big gotcha simply someone placing their hand on the protagonist's shoulder) that it makes no impact. And he tries the same thing *twice*. The climactic battle between the humans and werewolves (who've augmented their ranks by recruiting winos and changing them into wolfmen ... all off-screen, mind you) likewise offers little impact, as combatants appear from nowhere and disappear just as abruptly, so that one is never sure just who is doing what to whom and where. Suddenly, someone is in the house; suddenly someone else is in the woods; suddenly someone is now in the barn. And suddenly the viewer no longer cares.

Morphology: Dark-skinned, hairy wolfmen (and women)
Demise: (Regular) bullets and bombs
Full Moon Rating: *

Cursed

(2005; Dimension Films) Director: Wes Craven; Producers: Kevin Williamson, Marianne Maddalena, Jennifer Breslow, Dan Arredondo, Dixie Capp, Julie Plec; Screenplay: Kevin Williamson; Cinematographer: Robert McLachlan. Cast: Christina Ricci, Joshua Jackson, Jesse Eisenberg, Judy Greer, Scott Baio, Milo Ventimiglia, Kristina Anapau, Portia de Rossi, Shannon Elizabeth, Mya.

BEWARE THE FULL MOON—ad line

Such an unoriginal and banal tagline seems symptomatic of this protracted production, which became a veritable poster boy for "Studio Interference." Not only did Dimension Films drop the ball marketing-wise, the Bob Weinstein-led conglomerate appeared to have little idea about the true nature of the project, since the moon has nothing to do with those *Cursed* (these lycanthropes can change at will). Fortunately, two of the prime movers behind the camera were screenwriter Kevin (*Scream*, *I Know What You Did Last Summer*) Williamson and director Wes (*A Nightmare on Elm Street*, *The Serpent and the Rainbow*) Craven, who rode the interference wave to produce something far better than the studio-spawned tsunami should have allowed.

When young professional Ellie (Christina Ricci) and her kid brother Jimmy (Jesse Eisenberg) are involved in a car accident one night in the Hollywood Hills, they're both bitten by a huge beast that drags off the driver of the other car. Soon, both Ellie and Jimmy must deal with heightened senses, increased strength, and "unnatural sexual allure," in addition to their everyday problems (Ellie's difficulties with her reluctant-to-commit boyfriend Jake [Joshua Jackson], and the nerdy Jimmy with *everything* about high school, including a set of jock tormentors). The mark of the pentagram appearing on both their palms, and Ellie's run-in with a psychic, convince the siblings that they have indeed been cursed. "You've been infected," proclaims the fortune teller to Ellie. "You gotta sever the line of the beast—that's the only way to break the curse." Complicating things is the fact that "the beast is human too ... and it's closer than you think." Is the monster the oddly-acting Jake, Ellie's obviously smitten coworker, one of Jimmy's tormentors, or is it someone else entirely? All is revealed in a climactic confrontation at the opening of Jake's new wax museum/nightclub "Tinsel," where Ellie and Jimmy must face down the monster.

Like with screenwriter Kevin Williamson's previous efforts, *Cursed* offers a new yet still-familiar milieu covered in a layer of self-awareness that plays more referential and witty than mocking and jaundiced. For instance, the morning after the attack, with Jimmy convinced they've been cursed with lycanthropy (and Ellie naturally skeptical), Ellie tells her brother, "You should get to school."

> JIMMY: "Hey, I was bitten by a werewolf. If that's not good enough for a sick day.... I could be cursed."
> ELLIE: "Everybody's cursed, Jimmy; it's called life."
> JIMMY: "No, I mean by the Mark of the Beast."
> ELLIE: "Is that what kids are calling it these days?"

Williamson's clever script offers several red herrings—in various shades of crimson. And the surprise revelation at the climax truly is one (a surprise), with its own internal logic. Even after the beast meets its demise in a hail of police bullets (à la *An American Werewolf in London*), the film features a second, more intimate climactic confrontation that satisfyingly ties everything together.

Williamson fully acknowledged his script's references, stating, "*Cursed* is a classic werewolf story that is sort of a throwback to *The Wolf Man*, with a little bit of *An American Werewolf in London* thrown in, with a little bit of *Teen Wolf* thrown in. We took great care to do something different but at the same time reminiscent of all the previous films." The *Teen Wolf* moment comes when the nebbish Jimmy reluctantly tries out for the wrestling team, where he bests—and humiliates—the bullying team captain who's been tormenting him throughout high school. This sets the stage for one of the film's most amusing moments when said wrestler, Beau, shows up on Jimmy's doorstep afterwards to admit all the homophobic slurs he's hurled at Jimmy over the years simply masked the fact that Beau himself is gay. And thinks Jimmy is too...

> JIMMY: "I'm not gay, I'm cursed."'
> BEAU: "I know, it sure feels like that—not being able to tell anyone, talk to anyone about it."
> JIMMY: "No, no, I'm cursed by the Mark of the Beast. I'm a—a werewolf."
> BEAU: "C'mon Jimmy, you don't have to pretend anymore, not with me."
> JIMMY: "No, no, it's part of the curse. I'm appealing—I have an unnatural sexual allure."
> BEAU [appraisingly]: "Yeah, yeah you do. I know."

While homaging earlier lycanthropictures, Williamson offers a few tweaks to the typical werewolf lore. For instance, silver won't necessarily kill a werewolf. "You actually have to separate the head from the heart," announces Jimmy (after doing some on-line research). "Silver just hurts a lot." (When Jimmy touches a silver cake server, it burns his hand.) Then there's the notion of the sign of the pentagram on one's palm giving the were-game away—though rather than the mark appearing on the victim (as in *The Wolf Man*), here it materializes on the lycanthrope itself. And the way to cure lycanthropy? Sever the attacking beast's bloodline. Said beast was not made but born. As the unfortunate admits to Ellie near film's end, "I was born with this curse, [but] I learned how to control it." These werewolves can change at will, can reason, and can even talk after a fashion (with the monster amusingly growling "Shit!" at the climax when it hears a cadre of cops approaching).

Apparently the curse is not limited to humans, for Jimmy inadvertently passes it on to his dog when the golden retriever, frightened by his changed master, bites Jimmy and draws blood. Later, the mutt transforms into a shaggy devil hound that trashes the house and chases Jimmy out the door.

Williamson is smart enough to keep some things open-ended, however, rather than providing a series of pat answers. When Ellie mockingly asks, "When do we sprout hair and pointy ears," Jimmy admits, "It's all a little sketchy. Maybe never, maybe tomorrow. The experts can't really agree on that one." In fact, the pair never fully transform, leaving that to the creature that stalks and kills those around them.

The sole transformation scene begins well, showing hands sprouting claws, then its human legs and feet bending and warping as they extend into canine limbs and paws. But as the camera pans up the body, the primitive CGI (this *was* the early 2000s) becomes painfully apparent. Its artificial video game look turns the heretofore physically impressive beast into a 2-D animated figure. Fortunately, the monster—with its extended legs, muscular hair-covered body, and snarling wolf's head—looks imposing when played by 6'5" actor Derek Mears in the werewolf suit ... but not so much when Craven and co. resort to CGI to show the creature leaping, climbing, and bounding over cars.

Unconvincing CGI aside, Wes Craven offers up the same engaging, edgy, and sometimes startling direction he brought to such films as *The Hills Have Eyes* (1977), *Red Eye* (2005), *My Soul to Take* (2010), and the *Scream* series, staging the violence in sudden, startling, and disturbing bursts. The initial werewolf attack, for instance, comes without warning. After the tension of the car crash dissipates when Jimmy finally frees the driver trapped upside down by her seatbelt, the beast suddenly crashes through the window, latches onto the shoulder of the screaming woman, and drags her into the woods, with Jimmy and Ellie hanging on, only to be dragged with her. Then, after the two finally let go and scrabble away to apparent safety past the car, the victim's body comes hurtling over the vehicle to knock Ellie to the ground. With horror, Ellie—and we—see that there's nothing left of the woman below her waist. Even more horrifying, her staring eyes suddenly move—she's still alive and momentarily tries to crawl further away before finally dying. It's a powerful and gruesomely terrifying tone-setter, made more so by Craven's camera drawing Ellie towards itself to emphasize her horrified expression.

The second werewolf attack (in a parking garage) comes with another jolt—but after a suspenseful buildup this time to indicate the monster's presence, including some low-angle p.o.v. shots and the victim noticing an oil stain with human footprints leading from it that abruptly turn into animal tracks. Suddenly, the beast appears, grabs the girl, and throws her *over* an adjoining car. Stunned and lying on the ground, she looks underneath the car to see two oversized wolf legs on the other side, which suddenly leap upwards as the creature lands on the automobile's roof. She scrambles away, and Craven offers a few close-ups of the beast's ear as it listens for its victim, then the monster's upper face while its eyes move this way and that, searching for its prey. In a nod to Craven's own Freddy Krueger, the stalking monster then runs its claws along the car's metal, tormenting the terrified girl with a sound like fingernails on a blackboard. It's a compact, clever sequence that showcases the creature's immense strength, senses, and terrifying—and evil—intelligence.

Ad for Wes Craven's *Cursed*, a clever, self-reflexive, and thoroughly enjoyable postmodern take on lycanthropy that deserves better than the critical bashing and box-office indifference it garnered.

The wax-museum-themed bar/nightclub "Tinsel" makes for a macabre—and self-referential (in keeping with Williamson's script)—setting for the ostensible climax. Its wax figures (such as Frankenstein's Monster on a full lab set and Chaney's Wolf Man in a faux forest setting), movie props (including a replica cane from *The Wolf Man* "donated by the Chaney estate," as Jake boasts), and Hall of Mirrors centerpiece lend atmospheric ambiance to the exciting and gruesome battle between man, half-man and monster.

68 • *Dark Moon Rising* (2009)

Aptly named, *Cursed* proved to be a seriously troubled production. First, filming began without a satisfactory script, as Dimension failed to allot sufficient pre-production time for their werewolf opus. Then, eight weeks into the scheduled 12-week shoot, special effects master (and lycan-pioneer) Rick Baker left the production, to be replaced by Greg Nicotero's KNB EFX company, fresh off the back-to-back *Ginger Snaps* sequels. ("Rick just stepped back and decided not to work for a while," said Craven, due to rumored burnout brought on by the truncated preproduction time and underdeveloped script.) "Wes and the studio decided they wanted the creature to have more musculature and less hair," said Nicotero. "The only thing we were unable to change was the face, because it had already been scanned digitally into the computer [for CGI shots]. ...The only thing left of Rick's original conception is the face." But what a face—all snapping, toothy jaw, angry yellow eyes, and massive wolfish cranium that's well articulated to come alive with natural movements and expressions. (Note: Baker still retains a "Special Make-Up Effects Designed By" credit.)

Curse was scheduled to wrap in June 2003, but due to various production problems—rewrites, recasting, the deletion of entire characters (including those originally played by Skeet Ulrich, Omar Epps and Corey Feldman), the werewolf overhaul—the production shut down until November, when reshoots commenced, continuing on into February 2004 (with 90 percent of the original footage discarded and/or reshot, as estimated by Craven). After *another* ten days shooting in April, the film finally debuted on February 25, 2005. Much of the tortuous route from pen to screen can be laid at the feet of Dimension Films. When the studio ultimately decided they wanted a PG-13 rating, Craven threw up his hands. "I can't win at this point," lamented the director in December 2004 after completing the final mix on *Cursed*, "so I'm just going to walk away. I'm way past what my contractual obligations are to this film." (Fortunately, *Cursed* can be viewed in its full, unrated version on DVD, restoring its considerable, er, bite.)

Craven, sitting in the director's chair for the first time in four years (since *Scream 3*), was awarded a hefty budget of $35 million. (After all the problems and reshoots, this figure reportedly ballooned to $75 million.) "I thought Kevin [Williamson] had a good idea for the story," said Craven about what drew him to the project, "and I had always wanted to take a shot at a werewolf movie. I liked the idea of humanizing it more and making it much more realistic. Yes, there's a monster, but this is as much a film about three people finding their new selves, their true selves, while dealing with their emerging werewolfism."

Upon its release, *Cursed* took in only $30 million worldwide, earning less than half its final cost. It was an expensive lesson for Dimension Films. Apart from its ridiculously ineffective, primitive-by-today's-standards CGI effects, and a rather abrupt about-face by one of the primary characters (in order to provide a secondary climactic coda), however, *Cursed* proved to be a fine addition to the werewolf genre, and deserves far more respect than its tortured history has allowed.

With quotes from: "*Cursed*: Where Wolf?" by Marc Shapiro, *Fangoria* 237; "The *Cursed* Is Over?" by Marc Shapiro, *Fangoria* 241; "Second Time Hairy," by Marc Shapiro, *Fangoria* 241.

Morphology: Massive, hairy, wolf-headed biped
Demise: Bullet to the brain (and decapitation)
Full Moon Rating: ***½

Dark Moon Rising

(2009; Grindstone Entertainment/Lionsgate) Alternate Title: *Wolf Moon* (video). Director: Dana Mennie; Producers: Dana Mennie, Julie Snider Mennie, Lance H. Robbins, Richard Cueto; Screenplay: Dana Mennie, Ian Cook; Cinematographer: Mark Ream. Cast: Max Ryan, Maria Conchita Alonso, Chris Mulkey, Chris DiVecchio, Ginny Weirick, Sid Haig, Billy Drago, Lin Shaye.

Within each of us there hides a dark side; most of us can control it, but some are consumed by it—trailer
---

Director/co-writer/co-producer Dana Mennie (along with his co-producer/casting director wife Julie Snider Mennie) worked for twelve years to bring the "romantic thriller" *Dark Moon Rising* (as characterized by its star, Chris DiVecchio) to the screen. While few will say that this small-scale indie (filmed on a purported $3 million budget) was fully worth the wait, *Dark Moon Rising* (which morphed into *Wolf Moon* when released on video by Lionsgate after its limited theatrical run) turned out to be an uneven yet not unworthy addition to the New Millennium werewolf canon.

When hunky drifter Dan (DiVecchio) drives his muscle car into the small Texas desert town of Pahrump, straight-laced local girl Amy (Ginny Weirick) takes notice. Amy soon draws the quiet and brooding Dan out of his shell, and the two fall in love. Unfortunately, Dan harbors a dark secret—on the nights of the full moon he transforms into a werewolf, sometimes slaughtering local livestock. Dan has never killed a human, however, unlike his estranged father, the bloodthirsty lycanthrope Bender (Max Ryan). Now Bender has come to Pahrump, a trail of corpses in his wake, to claim his son. Can Amy, her rancher father (Chris Mulkey), the local sheriff (Maria Conchita Alonso), and a vengeance-fueled former cop on Bender's trail (Billy Drago) help Dan resist and defeat his vicious progenitor?

Shot in a little over five weeks on location in Beatty, Nevada, *Dark Moon Rising* comes across as a rare (for the modern millennium anyway) character-driven werewolf story—and sometimes suffers for it. If a bit too earnest in its yearning teen love theme (particularly in virginal Amy's portentously heartfelt narration that strikes uncomfortably close to *Twilight* territory), at least the film offers a pair of well-rounded werewolf characters that embody the lycanthropic "gift" and "curse" dichotomy. Slow to get started (it's 38 minutes before we get a good look at the werewolf—and 50 minutes before the first transformation), the film takes its time to introduce its characters and build their relationships. Such a patient approach works well when dealing with well-rounded characters in intriguing situations brought to life by talented actors; unfortunately, the principals here lack the depth necessary to fully pull off such a leisurely build-up, leaving the viewer yearning for a bit of lycanthropic action as they're forced to watch Amy and Dan "make cute" while getting to know one another; Amy's over-protective father worrying about his daughter's new beau (while at the same time sort-of/kind-of rekindling the relationship with his old flame, the Sheriff); and, worst of all, a vapid getting-to-know-you/falling-in-love montage, complete with generic power ballad. "Even though there is a little bit of horror in this film, that isn't the driving catalyst of the plot," admitted DiVecchio. "The storyline is really about the love between these two characters who are so oddly matched but who find companionship together."

Fortunately, the patient viewer is finally rewarded once the lycan-ball gets rolling, thanks in large part to the terrifying characterization of Max Ryan as the charismatic, vicious Bender. He makes for a truly frightening villain, even (and particularly) when in human form. Embodying the stillness that can erupt at any time into savage violence, Ryan uses his deep voice and menacing tones to paint a portrait of a true killer, one who fully embraces the notion that his lycanthropic nature has given him the "right" to kill whenever and whomever he chooses. "Take a look around," Bender contemptuously tells his son. "Look at this cattle—they're clueless. Sittin' in front of their TV and computer, numbing themselves to *life*." Bender personifies the arrogance of Evil, and the evil of arrogance. "Don't fight it," he orders, "enjoy it. Have beautiful women. Kill mercilessly. That is your right." Adding yet another layer, Bender possesses a decidedly dark sense of humor, at one point mockingly quoting Warren Zevon's "Werewolves of London": "Ladies, gents—I saw a werewolf at Trader Vic's drinking a pina colada, and his hair was *perfect*; ah-ooo."

Then there's the impressive look of the savage wolfmen themselves, refreshingly accomplished by clever makeup and (mostly) physical effects. The first transformation shows the shirtless Dan raising his face to the night sky and howling in pain as he rises up into frame. Suddenly his skin darkens and he morphs (in a smooth, quick and impressive moment of CGI trickery—one of the few instances in the film to eschew physical effects) into the snarling manbeast. With long hair covering his head, arms and torso; and a ridged, demonic face with a slightly extended muzzle, a skeletal nose opening, and wicked protruding fangs; he looks fiercely powerful.

The two actors do well to bring out their inner beasts, especially DiVecchio, who stretches, lopes and leaps in a convincingly animalistic manner. "I'd seen *Wolf* with Jack Nicholson plenty of times," said the actor about what werewolf films inspired his performance. "But because I knew I had to do a lot of work in a creature suit, it was important for me to understand the embodiment of this animal. I didn't want to imitate. I wanted to make him unique to my own style and to make it something I connected with. I followed up on an idea suggested by my acting coach and drove up to Joshua Tree [National Park] about three times with my dog. I parked myself in the middle of the desert and let the dog loose. I'd follow my dog around and imitate and mimic everything my dog would do. The reactions of an animal versus the reactions of a human differ because an animal's senses are more heightened." DeVecchio, with his crouching gait, tilt of head, and rapid movements, embodies this human-canine hybrid well. And Mennie makes his beasts perform, staging an impressively energetic and violent werewolf confrontation for the film's climax, with the two lycanthropes going lupo-a-lupo in a vicious display of primal power.

Taking a page from classic folklore, the film posits werewolfery as the result of witchcraft, with the curse passed down through one's bloodline. A fortune teller informs the couple that "[Dan's] father was cursed by sorcery. ... You are his beta." And while embracing the Hollywood tropes of the full moon and silver bullet, the movie adds a few new wrinkles of its own. "He hasn't tasted human blood," continues the palm reader. "But once you have ... nothing may redeem you—except to become that which you already are." Apparently, when a werewolf embraces his dark side through killing humans, his awareness increases, and he reaches his full potential as a monster, as it were. "Your father," explains the psychic, "he cherished the curse. He can kill anytime, anywhere that he wants, and retain human intelligence—clear mind and knowledge of his acts."

Despite the slow start and sometimes cloying and clichéd dialogue ("There's a storm brewin' and it's comin' down heavy; better realize what side of the fence you're on…"), *Dark Moon Rising* remains an intermittently successful and engaging, character-driven ride down the lycan highway. One could do much worse than to throw a little light on this *Dark Moon*.

With quotes from: "Hunks of Horror: *Dark Moon Rising* (aka *Wolf Moon*)—Interview with Chris Diveccio," by Michael Guillen, Twitchfilm.com.

Morphology: Shaggy, bipedal wolfmen
Demise: Silver bullets
Full Moon Rating: ***

Dark Moon Rising

(2015; Uncork'd Entertainment) Director/screenplay: Justin Price; Producer: Jennifer George; Cinematographer: Khu. Cast: Stasi Esper, Cameron White, Eric Roberts, Khu, Lisa May, Matthew Simmons, Greg H. Trevino, Eliza Roberts.

PRAY FOR THE SUNRISE—ad line

Things don't bode well when a werewolf film (or *any* movie, for that matter) opens with a shot of a tanker truck engulfed in obvious CGI flames. Trepidation only deepens when such an inauspicious beginning devolves into some wobbly, dimly-lit p.o.v. footage that concludes with a shot of a phony-looking manbeast posing in the moonlight. So begins this near-unwatchable muddle of a movie about a pack of werewolves searching for a mysterious girl, and the college student who comes to her aid. Apart from a few pack-attacks (on some amorous teens in a car, on a group of cops in the woods, at a rave), the film focuses on Dawn (Stasi Esper) and her would-be paramour Chase (Cameron White) as they come to grips with what's happening (neither have much of a clue—just like the viewer) and try to avoid packmaster Sin (writer-director Justin Price himself) and his followers.

"As creatives and fans of great cinema," commented Price, "it becomes important to understand that our job is to try and put forth what is on our hearts and in our souls down to the bones as best we can." Price's heart and soul must be filled with confusion, for that's about all his film "puts forth."

Tellingly, Price is a fan of the *Twilight* series (almost unbelievably, he labels Kristen Stewart a "fearless actress"), though he notes that for *Dark Moon Rising* "we were actually inspired by Japanese animation." That might explain the black-clad emo hero with a mop of carefully mussed black hair hanging over his face to match his downcast demeanor. As Chase, Cameron White speaks so softly and offers so little expression—even when confronted by magical mystery worlds and venom-spewing monsters—that he becomes a mere hole in the screen blacker than his own dyed 'do. "You're weird," Chase tells Dawn at one point. "And I'm weird. You're a killer, a wolf, a fairy, I don't know. But it scares the hell out of me." Given White's bland, toneless delivery, one would never know.

Like the film's myriad confusing events themselves, the unilluminating dialogue ranges from pretentious to nonsensical. "I've spent my whole life chasing shadows," pronounces Dawn, "something you'll never fully comprehend." Nor will the viewer. Pointless lines float through the film like flotsam on a red tide. "I can see everything you're hearing right now," announces Dawn. Come again? "You'll never speak freely again," she concludes. Er … why? The scattered script even sends a veteran thespian like Eric Roberts (playing a werewolf expert … or something; predictably, this remains vague) down the muddy rabbit hole when he's forced to pointlessly ramble on about the ins and outs of "making hooch" before seguing into a diatribe about 'Nam ("Just one big brew—of white lightnin'!").

To its credit, *Dark Moon Rising* features not one but two types of lycanthropes—a smoothly muscular dog-headed biped and a full-on wolf. To its *dis*credit, however, neither do much of anything (most of the "action" involves the werewolves in human form), and the slapdash CGI used to bring both types to life (real wolves need not apply) transform them into risible cartoons. Still, the film does offer one particularly inventive transformation when the group's female werewolf, Kai (played by "Kuh," the cinematographer!), turns into a column of flame that flies down into the bonfire below it, out of which then steps a large wolf. Sadly, said wolf's incorporeal, herky-jerky, disembodied-from-the-background movement turns this potentially winning mystical effect into yet another dismal failure.

Silver, like the moon, remains a non-issue, for there's never any mention of the lycan-killing metal, though the wolfsbane plant apparently does affect them (*how* exactly, like just about everything else in the film, remains unclear).

Apart from the ability to shapeshift at will (the lunar cycle has no pull here—despite several pointed allusions to the dreaded upcoming "Red Moon" … which never materializes), these werewolves possess mystical powers, some of them quite odd. For instance, at a dance club, alpha werewolf Sin extends his hand towards the dance floor and releases what appears to be a fistful of sweat beads, which cause the dancers to suddenly rip into their partners and beat each other to death. (Unfortunately, like with most everything else in this miserable misfire, Price botches this intriguing release-the-beast-within concept with a vague and cheap-jack execution … so to speak.) And Sin's right-hand wolf, Gecko(!), can breathe out what looks like fire extinguisher smoke in something he grandiosely labels a "venom strike."

Time after time Price makes poor directorial choices. Twice he flashes an introductory label onto the screen next to a posing villain: "Kai, of the One" (whatever that means) and "Gecko of the Titans: Celestial" (whatever … again), that makes the movie look like some live-action Pokémon game, despite the fact we've already seen these characters multiple times and need no further "introduction" (written or otherwise). More take-the-viewer-out-of-the-moment film school preciousness comes in the form of multiple voiceovers. Seemingly every character, no matter how tangential, is awarded an internal monologue at one time or another. And the thoughts they articulate—"What is April thinking?"; "This bitch is truly crazy"; "What have I gotten myself into?"—add *nothing* to the film but risibility.

At one point Chase tells Dawn, "I don't think you understand that I don't know what you're talking about." This could be *Dark Moon Rising*'s anthem. Though the pack appears to be searching for Dawn, it's never made clear *why*. We don't even know if she's a werewolf or not, as she never transforms. She does possess super strength and speed, as well as the bizarre ability to transport herself—and Chase—into fantasy worlds (composed of rocks, floating lights and a gigantic moon). And how Chase fits into the picture (and where his latent powers come from) also remains ambiguous.

Price intended this to be the first part of a trilogy. But with critical reception nearly one-hundred-percent negative, it'll be a marketing miracle if any further installments materialize. "I remember sitting down with the distributors and telling them that the first film would be more of an epilogue, sort of a history lesson before we can really start fighting and blowing minds." Never mind that this first movie would actually be a *prologue* rather than "epilogue" (of course, such confusion in Price's mind might explain quite a lot…), but *Dark Moon Rising* offers nothing coherent in the way of a "history lesson," except, perhaps, a history of *in*coherence.

(Note: Be careful not to confuse this *Dark Moon* with the 2009—and actually watchable—film of the same name; you'll live to regret it.)

With quotes from: "*Dark Moon Rising* Director Thanks *Twilight* Franchise, Kristen Stewart in Exclusive Interview," by Jessica Harmon, moviepilot.com.

Morphology: Hairless, muscular, dog-headed biped; full (CGI) wolf
Demise: Throat-ripping, perhaps (it's difficult to tell)
Full Moon Rating: *

DarkWolf

(2003; 20th Century–Fox) Director: Richard Friedman. Producers: Richard Friedman, Steve Hirsch, Lawrence Silverstein, Diane Cornell; Screenplay: Geoffrey Alan Holliday (story: Geoffrey Alan Holliday, Chuck Scholl); Cinematographer: Stuart Asbjornsen. Cast: Samaire Armstrong, Ryan Alosio, Andrea Bogart, Jamie Bergman, Alexis Cruz, Stephen Williams, Tippi Hedren.

HALF MAN. HALF BEAST. PURE EVIL—tagline

Sex and violence: long the province of low-budget, independent exploitation filmmakers. Yet, ever since the summer blockbuster was ushered in by the mammoth success of *Jaws* in 1975, major studios have co-opted what heretofore had been forbidden fruit, joining their low-rent brethren in the pursuit of dollars via undraped women and severed heads (or split-pea soup in the case of Warner Bros.' prescient *The Exorcist*). Twentieth Century–Fox, a longtime player in big-budget Hollywood, was no different, and their *DarkWolf*, while *low*-budget (under a million dollars), reflects this exploitation mindset from frame one—in which a topless woman performs a lap dance in a strip club.

A hulking biker (Kane Hodder) bursts into a busy strip joint (literally breaking down the door), only to be subdued by the pursuing police. But just after he's placed into the waiting police van by the two detectives on the case, a hairy creature emerges through the vehicle's steel walls, kills two cops and makes its escape. Detective Turley (Ryan Alosio) reveals to new recruit McGowan (Jaime Bergman) that their suspect is a werewolf. "A werewolf?" she asks, incredulous. "Half man, half wolf," he answers, "try to keep up, McGowan." Confused, she responds, "I don't understand." Impatiently he shoots back, "Stop trying to understand. Listen. Yes, I know, 'werewolves.' They exist, they're real. Get over it." After she's gotten over it, they head to a local diner to seek out bag-lady Mary (a slumming Tippi Hedren, a long way from Alfred Hitchcock's *The Birds*), who seems to have all the answers when it comes to lycanthropes. That's because she is the last of a race of near-immortals tasked with protecting the werewolves' blood-line. According to Mary, the creature who killed Turley's partner is the DarkWolf, a hybrid lycanthrope intent on mating with "the next matriarch pure-blood." Said matriarch is unknowing waitress Josie (Samaire Armstrong), who will be going through some significant changes this night. When Mary dies at the DarkWolf's claws, she passes on her mission to Turley, who must now protect Josie from the tracking lycanthrope. Turley, Josie, Josie's friend Stacey and her photographer boyfriend Wayne, take refuge at Turley's station house. But the DarkWolf lays siege, culminating in a final rooftop confrontation.

"*DarkWolf* had an amazing amount of special effects at the time when CGI was pretty much in its infancy," recalled director Richard Friedman. "It was incredibly costly to do, and we did it unsuccessfully." *That* is an understatement. The computer-generated shots of the shaggy quadruped sprinting away present that artificial, blurred, indistinct look that immediately screams primitive CGI. Worse, the full-on metamorphosis sequences turn the characters into literal cartoons in a cut-rate video game. "The CGI is horrific," concurred Friedman. "I mean, it's terrible! We shot it in seven weeks, all in one studio in downtown L.A. Everything you see in that movie, except the exterior street scenes, was done in that one studio on a standing set."

Fortunately, the physical effects (highlighted by its disturbingly gruesome body count) and the impressive creature itself (designed by John Buechler) provide far more than one might expect from a low-budget outing. "The creature came out looking pretty good," opined stuntman/actor Kane Hodder, who plays the human form of this DarkWolf. He's right. "Sometimes it's hard to do something like that and not have it come out looking hokey, and I think it came out fine." Fine indeed, with its imposing shaggy body (save for a bare, gorilla-like chest and shoulders, the result of Buechler modifying an existing ape suit—"a very *expensive* ape suit, about $90,000," claimed Friedman—for their werewolf) and huge wolf's head. Said head, which Friedman frequently shoots in extreme close-up to emphasize its power and savagery, comes alive via its blinking eyes, twitching snout, and naturally moving fang-filled maw. But lest one become momentarily convinced of this terrifying beast's reality, there's another awful CGI ramble or cartoonish metamorphosis (five in all) lurking just around the corner to burst the realism bubble.

Buechler and co. didn't do as well by their female werewolf, however. At the film's midpoint, Josie begins to transform (in Turley's bathroom). She doubles over and falls into the tub, only to emerge in some intermittent lycan-stage, her fine blonde hair now a coarse brown, her brow ridged and raised, her ears pointy (with fingernails to match), and a set of run-of-the-mill fangs filling her mouth. She immediately falls back into the tub, and when she rises again, her composure—and human appearance—have been restored. Later, however, she goes full-on lycan (in another horribly unconvincing CGI metamorphosis), but she looks no more impressive. Though supposedly a "pure-bred" werewolf, she appears far less wolfish than the hybrid DarkWolf. With her nude body covered in skin-darkening makeup, a back-length cascade of dark hair, fangs, claw-like fingernails, and a face that appears more simian than canine, she looks like a half-made-up *Planet of the Apes* extra. Worse, she does very little while in her lycan-form. While she slinks about and literally sniffs at Turley, he reads from a handy book that "on the night of the first transformation she must be led into the light of the full moon, or else she will be locked forever in the limbo between human and werewolf form." Turley then manhandles this docile she-beast out onto the fire escape and into the moonlight, where Josie immediately resumes her human appearance. Odd. And disappointing.

DarkWolf offers a few twists and turns on the standard lycan-tropes. For instance, yes, it takes silver to kill a werewolf (Turley keeps a box of silver bullets in his desk for just such an occasion), but this special "DarkWolf" must be shot in the *eye* (a dart to the heart just won't cut it). Though the proceedings take place over the course of a full-moon night, the lunar cycle seems to have little effect on the DarkWolf, who can change at will. There are two types of lycanthropes. "There's 'werewolves' and there's 'hybrid werewolves,'" explains Turley to his new partner during one of the film's overabundant and overlong expository scenes. "Now, 'werewolves' are normal—normal werewolves. [Whatever *that* means.] Nine hundred years ago a human Saxon knight mated with a werewolf. Boom—we got hybrid werewolves." And now "that hybrid werewolf is out there searching for the next matriarch pure-blood. He needs to mate with her, breed out the next generation of pure-blood werewolves." To this end he follows her scent, and ends up killing anyone who's crossed her path ("Don't let her touch anyone," warns Mary, "if she touches the skin, DarkWolf will follow that scent, and it will kill them"). Of course, while a novel notion (much werewolf mayhem resulting from lycanthropic lust), this makes little sense; for instance, how could crossing a "hybrid" with a "pure-blood" result in another pure-blood?

Apparently, not all hybrid werewolves are created equal, as there's only *one* "DarkWolf." "The beast you encountered tonight," explains the oh-so-talkative Mary, "is like no other—he's much stronger and much more dangerous. He's a dark prince—a king in waiting—the DarkWolf." Another surprise: most major metropolitan police forces have special units to deal with werewolves! "The fact is," explains Turley to his incredulous new partner, "there's a quiet little office in the back of this detective's bureau dealing with them." Who knew?

The script tries to make this rather small-scale and intimate tale of a mate-maddened beast into a worldwide epic of global and apocalyptic proportions (à la the same year's *Underworld*)—not by actions or visuals, but (as is its sad, sad way) via a few lines of dialogue. Mary (who else?) relates, "If he tracks her down and mates with her, my race will perish and there will be more soldiers of darkness coming. And without us, they will conquer your race as well. Humans will be no more." Mary apparently belongs to a long-lived "race" of "Protectors," though Mary herself, a rather well-dressed bag lady, does a poor job of that (dying at the first encounter with DarkWolf and passing on her sacred mission to an ordinary cop). Worst of all, Mary admits she's the last of her kind, so … what exactly was the plan in this apocalyptic scenario again? Mary—and the screenwriter—apparently hadn't really thought this through.

First (and last) time scripter Geoffrey Alan Holliday admitted that if he had the chance, "I think I would make the dialogue shorter, because there were some times when it got awfully long." Turley and Mary both engage in scene after scene of extended exposition to try and cram in all the facts we need to know about werewolves in general and DarkWolf in particular. Continued Holliday, "And in some cases it was necessary to get long. We couldn't write around it—the history had to be told, the back story was necessary." Actually, one *can* write around it, since such history/back story can always be *shown* rather than told (flashback anyone?); or relayed over time via a few incidents that tie it to the present; or, conversely, related in a far more cinematic—and engaging—manner than one character just ticking off the bullet points to another. And this doesn't necessarily require a lot of money. For instance, *Game of Werewolves* utilized a set of stylish drawings to accomplish the same end. As it is, *DarkWolf*'s various history-filled monologues only serve to slow the proceedings to a talk-filled crawl and rob the film of its impetus (not to mention visual momentum, which Friedman had been at obvious pains to build up).

Holliday also dropped the idea ball when he introduced the intriguing "touch of death" notion—and then did nothing with it. The horror of inadvertently killing with one's touch ("Anybody you touch tonight will be imprinted; he'll seek them out, looking for you") is ripe with existential, alienating angst (dating all the way back to the 1936 Boris Karloff vehicle *The Invisible Ray*). But rather than having Josie agonize over her terrible plight, and exploring it further, the movie offers her one brief moment of distress before the script launches her into the next bit of action.

Speaking of action, director Friedman (*Doom Asylum*, *Scared Stiff*, *Phantom of the Mall: Eric's Revenge*) infuses his flawed film with far more visual energy than it warrants. The werewolf attacks come fast and furious, all frenetic close-ups and spraying blood. He even attempts a very *Terminator*-esque assault on a police station, in which the DarkWolf leaves an impressive tangle of mangled corpses strewn about the squad room after a brief montage of swiping claws, ripped throats, gunshots and screams (it *is* a low-budget effort, after all).

It's not all (cut-rate) action and gory killings, however. Apart from the aforementioned talky stretches, the proceedings grind to a screeching halt when, half-way through the film, Friedman indulges in a lengthy erotic lesbian photo shoot interlude. Granted, the sight of the two beautiful naked models sexily cavorting on the rooftop in body paint may set the blood pumping, but it does nothing to advance the story or delineate the disappointingly one-note characters. Friedman tries to tie things together by cutting in scenes of the werewolf attacking a victim during the erotic sequence. But shots of the two girls passionately nibbling on each other's necks juxtaposed with those of the werewolf ripping out a victim's throat, as blood spills and flesh tears while the women prance and fondle and pant, exposes, along with the pulchritude and viscera, the base exploitation underpinning the sequence.

Kane Hodder (who first played a lycanthrope in 1995's *Project: Metalbeast*) called *DarkWolf* his favorite werewolf movie. "I always wanted to work with the director, Richard Friedman, who always puts quality work together for less money than he should have, and the part was basically the main bad guy of the movie before he becomes the werewolf. So I play the character as a human without any makeup, and that appealed to me. The character itself was also very one track–minded and violent … so I'm used to that." (Hodder's big claim to fame is having played unstoppable killing machine Jason Voorhees in four *Friday the 13th* movies.)

Inside the beast suit itself, however, was stunt coordinator Rick McCallum. And though he sells the illusion well with his imposing frame and quick, animalistic movements, he had no easy time of it. "You try and start walking like a [four-legged] wolf with leg extensions that weigh 15 pounds apiece and a 25-pound suit and a head on top of you—it's difficult," admitted McCallum for *DarkWolf*'s making-of featurette. "And it's even more difficult doing stunts in that. But the suit's great—it's real flexible."

"There were a lot of werewolf films around that period of time, and they're probably all better than *DarkWolf*," concluded Friedman, "but it did go out on the shelves among some very large movies. Fox kind of forced video stores to buy *DarkWolf* if they were buying any other, bigger films. It had a lot of firepower behind it. … Fox ended up making about $6 million on that $650,000 movie."

With quotes from: "Friedman's Frights," by Jason Bene, *Fangoria* 331; "The Arrow Interviews.… Kane Hodder," by John Fallon, JoBlo.com; "*Darkwolf*, a New Breed," *DarkWolf* DVD.

Morphology: Shaggy, wolf-headed quadruped
Demise: Silver bullet (to the eye)
Full Moon Rating: **½

Daughter of Dr. Jekyll

(1957; Allied Artists; b&w) Director: Edgar G. Ulmer; Producer/Screenplay: Jack Pollexfen; Cinematographer: John F. Warren. Cast: John Agar, Gloria Talbot, Arthur Shields, John Dierkes, Mollie McCarth, Martha Wentworth, Marjorie Stapp, Rita Greene.

> IS THERE A RAVAGING BEAST
> HIDDEN IN HER BODY?—trailer

Note: Those unfamiliar with this low-budget horror entry from the 1950s may want to seek out and watch the film (if so inclined) before reading further, as detailing its lycanthropic qualities can't help but answer the above question and provide major spoilers. For those who already know the answer … read on.

Called back home by her guardian Dr. Lomas (Arthur Shields) upon her twenty-first birthday, Janet Smith (Gloria Talbot) brings her fiancé George (John Agar) along. "You, my dear," reveals the kindly Lomas (who Janet formally refers to as "*Doctor*" throughout), "are an heiress to a sizable estate and fortune." He also reveals, somewhat reluctantly it seems, that she is not a 'Smith' after all but a *Jekyll*—the daughter of the infamous doctor-turned-killer. And "around here," Lomas explains, "they still believe that Dr. Jekyll, in the form of a werewolf, prowls thirsting for blood every time the full moon rises." This causes Janet to question whether she can marry George after all. Worse, she begins having nightmares in which she, in the form of an alluring, violent alter-ego, viciously attacks and murders people—waking up the next morning with blood on her nightdress! After several locals turn up with their throats torn out, Janet is on the verge of hysteria. George finally discovers, however, that the duplicitous Lomas has been inducing these dreams via hypnosis, and plans to make her kill herself so that *he* will retain control of the Jekyll fortune. And most terrifying, George learns that Lomas is the werewolf who has been committing the murders.

One of only three lycan titles from the 1950s (the other two being 1956's *The Werewolf* and 1957's *I Was a Teenage Werewolf*), *Daughter of Dr. Jekyll* distinguished itself as the only werewolf film of this science- (and science fiction-) minded decade to take a Gothic approach to its lycanthrope. Unfortunately, that's about the only thing that does distinguish this impoverished (though not entirely uninteresting) entry from its two superior siblings.

Though set in England at the turn of the twentieth century, anachronisms and just plain carelessness tend to destroy the illusion of time and place. Not only does this manor house possess incandescent lights, but one can see 1950s cars whizzing by outside a lightly curtained window! And, remarkably, none of the principals sport even the hint of a British accent (Janet and George sound American, while Lomas affects an Irish lilt).

The film's trailer proclaims, "A vampire drawing sustenance from bestiality!" Apart from its rather unfortunate verbiage (due, one hopes, to simple ignorance regarding the connotations of "bestiality"), such publicity lines illustrate the picture's confusion regarding vampirism and lycanthropy. In speaking of his old friend and colleague Dr. Henry Jekyll, Lomas says that after Jekyll's death, "The villagers broke into his tomb and drove a stake through his heart—the only safeguard, according to ancient tales of witchcraft, that keeps a werewolf from rising out of the grave when the moon is full to hunt for human blood." (Whether Dr. Jekyll was truly a werewolf or the locals merely mistook him for one—due to his personality-altering experiments—remains unclear.)

Besides conflating lycanthropy with the vampire mythos, this muddled *Daughter* deigns to provide any explanation for its werewolfery. Is it drug-induced? A logical assumption, given the Dr. Jekyll connection, though nothing truly points in that direction. Is it a curse? Again, the script provides no evidence. Does Lomas bring on the transformation himself or is he a slave to the moon? The murderous doctor simply transforms, though apparently he still retains all his human faculties, given his calculated murders while in wolfish form. In fact, Lomas takes full advantage of his condition (whatever its cause, and whether voluntary or not) in his convoluted plotting to drive Janet mad and steal her inheritance. Most disappointingly, all these unaddressed issues create a decidedly shallow werewolf characterization, leaving only a standard villain who hides behind a kindly facade. No pathos, no self-doubt, no moral questioning, not even any relishing of savage freedom—only *greed* characterizes this one-note lycanthrope. Still, the drive-the-heiress-mad plot—perpetrated by a *werewolf*—remains novel, if nothing else.

Said werewolf's appearance, however, proves as disappointing as the film's confused lycan-lore. Sixty minutes into the seventy-minute movie we finally see Dr. Lomas transform. It begins with a close-up of his hand as it subtly grows hairier through some simple but clever

A well-groomed werewolf (note the slightly hairy cheeks and tiny fangs) menaces the *Daughter of Dr. Jekyll* in this American lobby card.

changes in lighting (courtesy of "special photographic effects" men Jack Rabin and Louis DeWitt, who provided the effects for many a low-budget '50s entry, including *Cat-Women of the Moon*, *The Black Sleep*, *Pharaoh's Curse*, and *The Atomic Submarine*). Then Lomas' face darkens as *it* becomes hairier. Unfortunately, this is accomplished through some too-obvious face paint that only becomes visible under special lighting (a technique that harkens all the way back to the 1931 version of *Dr. Jekyll and Mr. Hyde*, where it was utilized to far better effect). With his back to the camera, Lomas now turns around, fully transformed. Sparse hair on the sides of his face and temples, a pair of somewhat pointy fangs, slightly elongated ears, and a mad gleam in his eye are the only flimsy indications that man has become animal. And this were-Lomas, well-dressed in full suit and tweed coat, acts quite un-wolf-like. Rather than leaping and snarling and biting and clawing, he fights like an ordinary man, grappling with George and pushing him down a set of stairs before delivering a swift kick to the head to finally knock his opponent unconscious. The beast-man then rushes back up the stairs, exits the tomb, and *locks the door behind him*. Almost humorously, this werewolf then becomes a rather metaphorical "wolf" when he spies through a farmhouse window an attractive young woman dressing *and pauses to watch*—yes, he has now become a peeping wolf. A recovered George ultimately tells Janet that Lomas is "mad—worse than that, he changes into something; he isn't human." By this werewolf's actions (and even his appearance), however, one could barely tell.

"Yearning for love," describes the film's trailer, "and discovering on the eve of her marriage the monstrous inheritance that was her birthright of fear." If one were so inclined to look deeper into this 'B' potboiler, one might conclude that said fear has its roots in the dark recesses of sexuality. The female "monster" of Janet's nightmares, with her exotic beauty and low-cut, diaphanous nightgown, looks more sexy than monstrous (and far more alluring than the demurely dressed and rather plain-looking Janet). She's almost like a subconscious representation of Janet's repressed sexuality. Or perhaps it's a manifestation of her *fear* of sex, spawned by her impending marriage. Janet even tries to break off her engagement with George, ostensibly because she believes her bloodline to be tainted—though maybe it's something deeper.... Of course, such a reading remains pure conjecture, as nothing else in the film explicitly points in this direction. (Director Edgar G. Ulmer shot the dream scenes—the most evocative sequences in the film—in some recently burned-out woodlands, using ultraviolet film, off-kilter angles, and a far sexier double for Gloria Talbot to generate a nightmarish atmosphere.)

"I did that picture strictly for the bread," admitted John Agar. "I didn't fluff it—I did the best I could with what I had to work with—but it wasn't my cup of tea, I just didn't believe it." Nor does the viewer. Agar, with his bland, corn-fed persona, never looks too comfortable in his Victorian Gothic surroundings (particularly when wearing a ridiculous striped leisure jacket that makes him look like he just stepped away from a barbershop quartet).

Gloria Talbot does better with her pivotal role of the confused, tortured Janet. "I'm mad," she concludes, exhorting George, "You've got to do something—lock me up or put me in a madhouse!" her tormented hysteria rising to become both unnerving and heartbreaking. "I had some good lines in the film," fondly recalled Talbot, "like, 'If you love me, you'll kill me'—I really felt it, and I can still make myself cry when I watch that scene." Of course, she also had some real clunkers to deliver. At one point she answers George's pleas to leave with him then and there with, "I can't make a decision—I'm not capable of it," painting her character as quite the shrinking violet.

Fortunately, at the helm of this muddled mess stood a man with both the ability and experience to make a silk purse out of a cinematic sow's ear. If anybody could save this *Daughter*, that person was director Edgar G. Ulmer. Ulmer helmed one of the greatest films of horror cinema's Golden Age—*The Black Cat* (1934), starring Boris Karloff and Bela Lugosi. During production of that dark, multi-layered classic, however, Ulmer fell in love with script girl Shirley Castle. Unfortunately, she was married to a Universal studio executive at the time, who had Ulmer blacklisted for having stolen his wife. Consequently, Ulmer never made another studio picture and toiled for the next quarter-century in the land of low-budget independents. Even without major studio backing, however, Ulmer still produced a number of excellent low-budget films, including *Bluebeard* (1944), *Detour* (1945), and *The Man from Planet X* (1951). Of course he also directed the awful *Beyond the Time Barrier* and *The Amazing Transparent Man* (both 1960). In between these two polar-opposite subsets rests *Daughter of Dr. Jekyll*.

Ulmer employs plenty of fog to add atmosphere and a modicum of scope to the cramped settings and soundstage "exteriors" (much as he did with *The Man from Planet X* six years earlier). Working with cinematographer John F. Warren (*The Colossus of New York*, TV's *Thriller* and *Alfred Hitchcock Presents*), Ulmer fills the manor house (a real mansion in Los Angeles, near Hancock park) with evocative shadows to match the baroque Victorian brick-a-brac. (Sadly, no amount of studio smoke can obfuscate the obvious table-top model used to represent the house and grounds' exterior in longshot.) Ulmer often moves his camera to good effect, slowing dollying in to punctuate a bit of dialogue, for instance. Of course, when said dialogue consists of awkward lines like, "I still shudder when I recall that face, like some perverted mask of evil out of a legend of horror," all the fluid camerawork in the world can't save it. Fortunately, veteran player Arthur Shields (*How Green Was My Valley*, *National Velvet*, *She Wore a Yellow Ribbon*) delivers such dialogue with a naturalness that *almost* sells it.

According to *Daughter* writer/producer Jack Pollexfen, "Ulmer was an excellent director, at his best when he had his back up against the wall budget-wise." It's a rather disingenuous, self-serving statement by the tight-fisted Pollexfen, given that, post–*Black Cat*, Ulmer never had the chance to show what he *could* have done with a more generous budget.

"Edgar Ulmer—I liked him a lot," enthused Gloria Talbot. "He was [laughs] kind of insane, and I love people who are quirky and funny. He just was easy to work with—he was not a Douglas Sirk, who thinks he can get a performance out of somebody by scaring them to death. He was affable and fun—a pixie, sort of." Affable and fun—remarkable, given this put-upon pixie's tight schedule (about a week) and impoverished budget.

Though by no means a classic, this *Daughter* deserved better than becoming the bottom half of a double with the impoverished Bert I. Gordon effort *The Cyclops* (also starring Talbot); as, in truth, *Daughter of Dr. Jekyll*, with all its flaws, still remains the more accomplished picture of the two.

With quotes from: *Interviews with B Science Fiction and Horror Movie Makers*, by Tom Weaver.

Morphology: Follicle-challenged, well-dressed wolfman
Demise: Stake to the heart
Full Moon Rating: **½

Death Hunter: Werewolves vs. Vampires

(2011; Sunstream Motion Pictures/MTI) Director/Screenplay: Dustin Rikert; Producers: Sam McConkey, Dustin Rikert; Cinematographer: Andrew Robertson. Cast: Sam McConkey, Paulino Hemmer, Mike Lawler, Rich Williams, Shari Wiedman.

> NOW ONE MAN WILL USE THE POWER OF THE WEREWOLF TO FIGHT THE KING OF ALL VAMPIRES—trailer

John Croix (played by co-producer Sam McConkey) and his wife (Shari Wiedman) become lost on a backwoods desert road when they take a nighttime shortcut. Ending up at a roadside bar, they're set upon by the owner and patrons—all of whom are vampires. The bloodsuckers take his wife, but John manages to escape, only to be attacked in the desert by a werewolf. Though saved by a mysterious, crossbow-wielding older man named Van Ness (Mike Lawler), John has been bitten. Van Ness administers some kind of werewolf "antidote," which leaves John with the powers and abilities of a lycanthrope but without the nasty, moon-triggered side effects. Van Ness labels John "the Chosen One" and trains him to battle the "creatures of the dark night." But when the old man succumbs to wounds inflicted by a werewolf, John must wage war on his own, going off to beard the head vampire in his den, with a trio of teens he rescued from a lycan in tow.

Filmed in the Arizona desert, *Death Hunter: Werewolves vs. Vampires* is not near as imaginative nor engaging as its synopsis might suggest. First off, despite its subtitle, there are no "werewolves vs. vampires," as the two supernatural camps remain stubbornly separate. John first battles the beasts, then later takes out the vamps. Second, writer-producer-director Dustin Rikert throws every (cheap) thing he can think of at his plywood set wall to see what sticks; and not much does. Besides including both vampires and werewolves, there are werewolf victims "doomed to walk the Earth in an in between state" (à la *An American Werewolf in London*); talk of a "prophecy" and "Chosen One"; a low-rent *Karate Kid*–like montage training sequence (that parsimoniously recycles previously-seen footage); the idea, highlighted in *Fright Night*, that faith is needed to battle the supernatural ("The cornerstone to fighting all evil is the Good Book," pronounces Van Ness); a $1.98 version of a vampire bar right out of *From Dusk Till Dawn*; and some third-act typical teens (jerky jock, hot chick, sweet girl, nervous nerd) stolen from a hundred different '80s horror flicks.

Whatever (copycat) ambitions the movie had, however, are completely undone not only by a lack of originality, but by a dearth of imagination and resources. For instance, the film features the worst tavern set ever. An obvious storage unit housing a plywood bar, a few cheap tables and chairs, and some scaffolding hung with plastic sheets as a "stage," the establishment ("Shamus' Bar"), with its handful of overweight patrons and pair of skinny "dancers," is a trailer trash shadow of *From Dusk Till Dawn*'s impressive "Titty Twister." A few bits of over-obvious greenscreen work creates some cartoonish backgrounds (including a ludicrous-looking mountain of bones outside the vampires' lair), while Rikert utilizes the same shot of a substandard CGI werewolf *five times* over the course of the movie. And the brief Big Battle with the amassed werewolves (all four of them) sees John and a wounded Van Ness repetitively shooting the few wolfmen in the head with crossbow bolts backgrounded by a not-fooling-anyone blue tinting serving as a cheap day-for-night process. Most laughably, when Van Ness tosses some holy water onto a CGI lycan, Rikert simply reverses the film to show the beast leaping back *up* to the clifftop from which it first leapt *down*.

Talk is cheap, and Rikert fills his film with plenty of it. Sequences of John and his wife blathering on in the car, the quartet of teens talking through a (chaste) game of "strip poker" in their car, and John listening to Van Ness' interminable pronouncements in scene after scene after scene sink the movie in a morass of banal verbiage. The cloak-wearing, abandoned house–dwelling, pretentious prophecy–spouting Van Ness serves not only as John's healer and mentor, but as a walking exposition machine, filling us in on more than we want to know about werewolves and vampires, thereby saving the time and expense of actually orchestrating exciting or impactful scenes to illustrate said points. As noted, talk is cheap, and this character becomes a metaphorical miser. In fact, had actor Mike Lawler been paid by the word (if paid at all), he could have comfortably retired after spouting the reams and reams of dubious dialogue here.

Death Hunter does offer the occasional amusing reference (to much better movies), such as when John and his wife pull up to a menacing looking establishment, and she cautions John, "Wait, wait, wait—don't you remember that movie *Motel Hell*?" At this, John locks the car doors and replies, "I didn't see *Motel Hell*, but *Wolf Creek* scared the crap out of me." Too bad the rest of the overly talky script offers little more than substandard one-liners like "How 'bout some fire, scarecrow?" (as Van Ness splashes some holy water on a werewolf) and "funny" moments such as the three young people scarfing the jerky John offers them only to learn it's dried "desert rat" (cue the grossed-out spitting and gagging).

The films starts fairly strong, with an opening sequence in which a young couple preparing to make love in the desert are attacked by not one but two werewolves—of varying stripes. While the man searches his backpack for a condom, a werewolf springs upon his waiting partner. The young stud emerges from the tent with the prophylactic, only to have his lover literally drop at his feet, dead at the hands of the clothes-wearing wolfman: wooly wig, bushy whiskers, prosthetic nose, raised brow and cheek bones, and sharp fingernails (on normal hands). After a brief tussle, the man manages to retrieve a shotgun from his car's trunk and blast the beast. But the lycan just gets up and keeps coming, even after the man runs him down with his BMW. Finally, the man takes out the wolfman by blowing up his car with the creature next to it. But then he comes face to face with a full (CGI) werewolf: a hair-covered, big-chested biped with wolf face, big ears, claws, the works. Unfortunately, the scene ends there, so we've no idea how he handled (or didn't) this powerful beast. Also unfortunately, despite the coitus interruptus nature of the scene, Rikert appears to have shot his wad right out of the gate, for nothing else in the movie lives up to the promise of the opening, including how he handles his lycanthropes.

The computer-generated beastie sports a typical overstuffed, muscled torso and rounded wolf head, and a grinning maw filled with razor-sharp teeth. This adequate, if unimaginative, design can't overcome the cartoonish look of its primitive CGI origins, however, leaving the viewer longing for an appearance by one of the cut-rate wolfmen instead. At least these half-human monsters have some substance.

Disappointingly, Rikert includes no transformation scenes (not even at the creatures' deaths), instead presenting his various lycanthropes simply as personality-less crossbow bolt fodder (oddly, nearly every werewolf meets its fate this way, probably so that Rikert could re-use his bolt-to-the-head prosthetic). Consequently, apart from another (by now expected) long-winded exposition from Van Ness stating "a werewolf is a damned soul—doomed to walk the earth until put to rest," there's no presentation of pathos nor exploration of the tortures experienced by these "damned souls." We never see their human side; they're just hairy monsters.

Rikert offers some arbitrary variations on the typical werewolf "rules"—arbitrary because he rarely follows up on them or incorporates them into the story. For instance, just like vampires, werewolves are "allergic" to holy water. But only silver will truly kill them. "Silver is poison to their blood," explains Van Ness. "Holy water will slow them down, but it will only buy you time." Another odd twist on lycan-lore springing from the vampire-werewolf dichotomy: "There's only one thing that holds true for both [vampires and werewolves]—kill the leader and you stop them all." While this plays into John's battle with the bloodsuckers, it seems to have fallen by the wayside regarding the lycanthropes, as nothing comes of this during John's (short and impoverished) showdown with the beasts (in fact, we never even learn just which lycan is indeed their "leader"—if they even have one).

One-man-band Dustin Rikert, in addition to scripting, co-producing and directing, also provided the "special makeup F/X" (in conjunction with his brother Wade), as well as co-editing the feature. Rikert, a USC film school grad, helmed a fistful of other low-budget movies you've never heard of, such as *Ghost Rock* (2003), *Haunted Airplane* (2009) and *Easy Rider 2: The Ride Home* (2012).

Death Hunter features a pivotal play stolen right from the *An American Werewolf in London* playbook. "A lycan, like a vampire, is a damned soul," pronounces Van Ness. "To die by one of them is to become a damned soul yourself, doomed to walk the Earth in an in-between state until the killers are stopped and the spirit set free." Of course, Rikert offers no examples of these "damned soul" victims, like *American Werewolf* did so wittily and impactfully. Here the characters simply *talk* about this disturbing notion rather than enact it. And that about sums up *Death Hunter: Werewolves vs. Vampires*—a sketchy playbook without the personnel or resources to adequately run the plays.

Morphology: Fuzzy-headed wolfmen; muscular, hair-covered CGI biped
Demise: Exploding BMW; silver crossbow bolt
Full Moon Rating: *½

Death Moon see Deathmoon

Deathmoon

(1978; EMI Television) Alternate Title: *Death Moon* (video); Director: Bruce Kessler; Producer: Jay Benson; Teleplay: George Schenck (story: Jay Benson, George Schenck); Cinematographer: Jack Whitman.

76 • Deathmoon

Cast: Robert Foxworth, Joe Penny, Barbara Trentham, Dolph Sweet, Charles Haid, Debralee Scott, France Nuyen.

> An island of pleasures terrorized by a werewolf cursed to kill!—ad line

Premiering on the *CBS Wednesday Night Movies* back in May of 1978, this made-for-television film offers up the novelty of a *tropical* werewolf ... and little else. Shot on the beautiful island of Kauai, Hawaii (and at the Coco Palms Hotel), *Deathmoon* begins with an off-screen narrator (France Nuyen) reading from an opening scrawl: "Wherever fearsome beasts have roamed, the legend of the Werewolf persists ... even in the tropical Paradise of the Pacific where, it is said and believed that—when the shadow of the moon is cast—he who is cursed will be transformed from an ordinary man into a vicious beast." Enter one ordinary man—overworked businessman Jason Palmer (Robert Foxworth)—whose dreams have been troubled by visions of a mysterious Polynesian ceremony. On the advice of his doctor, Jason takes a vacation, choosing Hawaii because his great grandfather served there as a missionary a hundred years earlier. In between relaxing in the sun and striking up a new romance with the attractive Diane (Barbara Trentham), Jason suffers nocturnal blackouts. Not so coincidentally, a rash of murders in which the victims are "torn apart" plagues the resort. It turns out Jason's ancestor had defiled that sacred ceremony of Jason's dream and destroyed an alter; and now "a curse, it is said, haunts the descendants of the defilers."

Confusion and pathos are the order of the day here, as Jason doesn't even realize he's the unwitting man-monster until the very end. TV stalwart Robert Foxworth (star of made-for-television features like *The Questor Tapes* and *Ants*, and the long-running series *Falcon Crest*) makes for a likable, if rather bland, central figure, whose bewildered demeanor generates just enough sympathy to hold a viewer's interest. The same cannot be said of his lady love, however, as Barbara Trentham's one-note performance falls as flat as a Hawaiian surfboard.

George Schenck's teleplay takes far too long to get the werewolf ball rolling, with nearly forty minutes passing on uninteresting characters, and a going-nowhere subplot about a hotel thief, before the first (largely off-screen) werewolf attack. Further time filler consists of the hotel detective *and* the real police doing their investigative thing, and some dull getting-to-know-you footage as the two leads fall for each other, with the tedium broken only by the poorly staged and generally unseen werewolf attacks (one per night).

Director Bruce Kessler does the production no favors by keeping just about anything of interest hidden (with most of the attacks discovered only afterward, and then represented by little more than a bit of dialogue and the sight of a body bag being carted away). Kessler was a near-ubiquitous television director in the 1970s and '80s, helming episodes of everything from *I Dream of Jeannie* and *Adam-12* to *Marcus Welby, M.D.* and *The Rockford Files*. He even oversaw a (rather weak) episode of *Kolchak: The Night Stalker* ("Chopper"). He directed a few theatrical features as well, including the biker flick *Angels from Hell* (1968) and the offbeat horror *Simon, King of the Witches* (1971).

Deathmoon has that washed-out, too-dark '70s photographic look, which criminally fails to take advantage of the gorgeous tropical surroundings, making the Garden Island of Kauai look no more enticing than a So-Cal backyard. And Kessler spends far too much time in the cramped-looking hotel rooms and offices, as well as keeping his camera tight on his actors rather than letting it roam or explore the expansive natural wonders of the environs. Cinematographer Jack Whitman lights the scenes so poorly that at times one can see nothing through the nighttime murk. Of course, some

Amazingly, the pedestrian made-for-television *Deathmoon* saw theatrical release overseas. Granted, it did feature the world's first (and only) *Polynesian* werewolf, but still ... (Turkish poster).

might say this is a blessing when, after our long (52-minute) wait, we catch a first brief glimpse of the werewolf in question. With bushy hair all around the edge of his makeup-darkened face, which remains rather bare apart from some heavy brows (and lacking any particular canine features—no snout or dog nose, for instance), and a pair of moderate-length fangs, this lycanthrope looks more like an ape-man than wolf-monster. And this werewolf creeps about disappointingly slowly and silently, with its animal ferocity displayed only in the few sudden and swift attacks that last so briefly they barely register, with the darkness and dim photography further obscuring whatever might be seen. The film's climax comes with one effective "gotcha" moment, but otherwise it consists of a bunch of ill-defined running about in the dark.

The nature of this beast remains maddeningly indistinct as well. At one point the house detective goes to the local island witch to try and learn more—and she turns out to be the priestess of Jason's dreams (France Nuyen). But this potentially intriguing thread remains woefully unraveled, leading only to the hotel dick stupidly suggesting to the skeptical police lieutenant that they have a werewolf on their hands. "Werewolves?" laughs the man. "You've been smokin' too much of that Maui Wowie." At this reasonable response, the hotel detective retorts, "It's not exactly a werewolf—it's an Ileoha-Uakopua" (whatever *that* means). And who knew that the lunar cycle in Hawaii involved *five* consecutive nights of the full moon?!

Still, despite its wasted opportunities and dearth of lycanthropic activity, *Deathmoon* deserves *some* credit, if for nothing else than the novelty of offering up the world's first (and only, to date) *Hawaiian* werewolf.

Morphology: Bipedal wolfman
Demise: Ordinary bullets
Full Moon Rating: *½

Dr. Jekyll and the Werewolf

(1972 [Spain]/1973 [US]; Arturo González Producciones/Filmaco; Spain) Original Language Title: *Dr. Jekyll y el Hombre Lobo*. Alternate Titles: *Dr. Jekyll and the Wolfman; Doctor Jekyll vs. the Werewolf*. Director: Leon Klimovsky; Producer: Arturo González; Screenplay: Paul Naschy (as Jacinto Molina); Cinematographer: Francisco Fraile. Cast: Paul Naschy, Shirley Corrigan, Jack Taylor, Mirta Miller, Jose Marco, Luis Induni, Barta Barry, Luis Gaspar, Elsa Zabala, Lucy Tiller, Jorge Vico, Adolfo Tohus.

> To destroy the Monster was to destroy the one she loved!! Could she? Could you?—ad line

When Robert Louis Stevenson's famous novella *The Strange Case of Dr. Jekyll and Mr. Hyde* was published in 1886, he probably never dreamed of the bizarre permutations his characters would undergo in the future. One of the oddest is this Paul Naschy European import.

Dr. Jekyll and the Werewolf is the fifth outing for Naschy in his four-decade-spanning series featuring the tragic character of Waldemar Daninsky, the Wolfman. Naschy, Spain's undisputed "king of horror," was involved in nearly 70 productions since 1967, both in front of and behind the camera. Like for many of them, here he not only starred but wrote the script as well (using the moniker Jacinto Molina, an abbreviated version of his real name: Jacinto Molina Alvarez).

Dr. Jekyll and the Werewolf's convoluted story involves a descendent of Dr. Jekyll (Jack Taylor, a regular player in the films of the prolific Jess Franco) attempting to cure Waldemar Daninsky (Naschy) of his lycanthropy by using his grandfather's infamous "personality chang-ing" serum—with the expected disastrous results (thanks to the evil machinations of Jekyll's jealous assistant, played by Mirta Miller). Now, instead of two personalities, the poor wretch has three to deal with: Waldemar, the Werewolf *and* Mr. Hyde.

A film of two halves, *Dr. Jekyll and the Werewolf* focuses on the latter during its initial stages, as we follow newlywed Justine (Shirley Corrigan), who's older husband Imre (Jose Marco) takes her on a honeymoon to his rustic childhood village in Transylvania, wanting to visit the graves of his parents. (What a romantic.) After the requisite ominous warnings from the local innkeeper ("Nearby that cemetery is the black castle; the man who lives there is a monster"), they run afoul of a trio of bandits at the dilapidated cemetery. The criminals murder Imre and attempt to rape Justine, but Waldemar intervenes, dispatching the ruffians and taking Justine to his castle to recuperate. There she discovers his horrible secret, and, of course, falls in love with him. It's an all-too-familiar (and unlikely) scenario in the Naschy canon, but director León Klimovsky infuses the proceedings with enough Gothic atmosphere (particularly when Justine, clad in a black nightgown and with candelabra in hand, explores the forbidding castle) to hold one's interest, as well as providing a simple but effective introduction for the werewolf. When the surviving bandit recruits two more cronies to rob the castle and kill Waldemar on a full moon night, the hunters become the prey. First revealing the monster's presence via a clawed, hairy hand, Klimovsky then cuts to a close-up of the werewolf's snarling face before the camera zooms in on its open, fang-filled mouth, making for a startling, dramatic intro.

Unfortunately, Gothicism ultimately gives way to modernity when Justine, having fallen for Waldemar, takes him back to swinging London to see her good friend Henry Jekyll, hoping Henry can cure her newfound love. At this point the film settles down into some rather dull interplay between the various characters, as Justine tries to convince Jekyll to help, Jekyll finally acquiesces and performs various experiments in his makeshift attic lab, and Waldemar frets. Until Hyde finally breaks free towards film's end and engages in a bit of woman-whipping, prostitute strangling, and nightclub prowling, the only thing livening up the proceedings is an all-too-brief lycan-rampage when the amazingly unlucky Waldemar is trapped in a stuck elevator as the moon rises. "Why? Why must this happen?" whines Waldemar as he begins to writhe in pain. Three cutaways to the startled nurse trapped in the lift with him reveal an increasingly hairy beast-man. Finally, the repairmen get the lift going. But when the door opens, Waldemar's bloody victim falls out, and the suit-wearing werewolf, crimson-tinged drool dripping from its mouth, rushes forward, scattering the onlookers.

With Stevenson's Jekyll and Hyde creation an almost spiritual cousin to the werewolf (both involve personality—and physical—transformation, and both reflect the two sides of man's nature), combining the two monsters seems a natural, even inevitable, pairing. (One might even see the lycanthrope as *Nature's* very own Jekyll and Hyde.) Such a juxtaposition presents the possibility of delving deeply into the duality of man, and even into the nature of evil itself—or the evil of Nature in all its amoral savagery. While the werewolf personifies discord between the civilized and the bestial (moral man vs. savage animal), Jekyll and Hyde represent a more sophisticated, more refined conflict (moral man vs. immoral evil). The lycanthrope offers an internal battle between primary forces: civilization and nature; whereas Jekyll & Hyde struggles between the constructs of man: morality vs. immorality. While the bloodlusting beast that is the werewolf may be amoral, Mr. Hyde is *im*moral, embracing evil for evil's sake. Yet both figures—the lycan and Hyde—seek personal gratification at the expense of all else. Hence, both fly in the face of society's codes; the difference being that the werewolf does so by nature (with ties to Nature with a capital 'n'), while Hyde does so by choice (representing the self-centered, hedonistic, impulsive side of humanity).

Beyond this dichotomy, *Dr. Jekyll and the Werewolf* highlights a struggle between the supernatural (Waldemar's werewolf) and science (via Jekyll's chemical serum), or, on a less fantastical level, nature (the werewolf) vs. nurture (the artificially-molded Hyde). Intriguingly, while science initially triumphs over nature (with Jekyll effectively curing Waldemar of his lycanthropy by injecting him with his Hyde serum, watching as the apparently stronger Hyde persona overcomes the inner werewolf, then administering the antidote to vanquish Mr. Hyde and thereby leave Waldemar as himself), in the end, nature reasserts its dominance when Hyde runs out of Jekyll's serum and can no longer keep the Waldemar side in check. When the serum wears off, Hyde weakens, and Waldemar becomes himself once more—but almost immediately the full moon rises and Waldemar again transforms into the Wolfman. Nature has proven to be the strongest force after all—stronger than science, and stronger than societal constraints (personified by the "normal" Waldemar).

"[*Dr. Jekyll and the Werewolf*] established a kind of liberation from the bestial, unthinking level of the werewolf, only to unleash the consciously evil Mr. Hyde," enthused Naschy. "It's a pirouette within the world of these multiple personalities. I think it's an interesting film, above all for the re-creation so unique of Mr. Hyde." Of course, the term "interesting" doesn't necessarily translate to "good."

While combining two such classic monsters in one movie (and in one body) is a concept rife with possibilities, in the hands of director León Klimovsky it turns rather dreary and dull—at least in the film's second half. It's almost as if the director lost interest after sending his wolfman to London and letting loose Hyde in the beast's stead. The werewolf's few brief London appearances come with little vitality or suspenseful staging, the attacks listless and perfunctory (a quick grab, a bite, and off he goes). "This picture had the captivating novelty of a triple personality," opined Naschy. "It could have been quite good, but the short-sightedness of León Klimovsky made for some careless moments." Such moments extend even to the disappointingly mundane climax, in which Justine waits, armed with silver bullets. When the werewolf arrives, she loses her nerve; it lunges for her, knocks the gun from her hand, and bites her throat. Dying, she manages to reach the pistol and, as the beast-man walks away, shoots him twice in the back (though no bullet holes nor blood splotches mar his pristine light grey sweater). It's not much bang for one's lycanbuck.

Unlike in most of his previous (and subsequent) outings, Naschy makes for a disappointingly lackluster werewolf here. (Perhaps the struggle with Hyde sapped him of his wolfish ferocity?) He moves slowly, almost lethargically; and he walks in a very human-like manner that lacks the athletic, savage momentum of his usual lycan-portrayals

The subpar werewolf makeup matches Naschy's subpar wereplaying: coarse hair covering his entire face (disappointingly, no prosthetic nose piece differentiates it from a human proboscis), a mouthful of stained fangs, and small protruding wolf's ears. With drool dripping from his chin, he looks rather like a rabid victim of hypertrichosis (abnormal hair growth) and bad dentistry. He initially sports a black shirt and pants à la Naschy's beloved role model, Larry Talbot, though later he looks far nattier in sport coat and stylish sweater.

Both Klimovsky and Naschy do better with their *other* monster, however, as demonstrated by Hyde's introduction. When Jekyll injects Waldemar, strapped to a gurney, with his grandfather's serum, a sweating Waldemar momentarily loses consciousness. Then his eyelids slowly open, his nostrils flare, and his eyes widen. Klimovsky shifts to a Hyde point-of-view shot, with the camera looking upwards into the concerned faces of Jekyll and Justine. A green filter clouding the image gradually clears as Hyde comes fully awake, with the picture finally taking on color to show Jekyll and Justine in stark relief, indicating Hyde has now entered our world. It's a clever visualization of evil (often represented by the color green) invading our realm. The Hyde makeup, though simple, is equally effective. A close-up of Waldemar/Hyde's face reveals a lank-haired fiend with yellowish eyes and pasty, veined skin. "Set me free!" Naschy's Hyde hisses, grinning evilly. "I must be free!"

Naschy infuses his version of Mr. Hyde with enough evil to choke a corpse, neatly strangling his latest female conquest just for the fun of it, and gaining real pleasure in flogging a half-naked bound beauty. But he becomes laughably old-fashioned walking around a mod 1971 London in a top hat and cloak. "The anachronism of [Hyde] going about modern-day Soho in his cape and top hat appealed to me," Naschy explained. "Had he been dressed as any normal city-dweller, I don't think the character would have been as effective." Effective? Well, the best laid plans of mice and werewolves...

This did result in a rather amusing incident during filming. "Dressed and made up as Mr. Hyde, filming in Soho, [London]," recalled Naschy, "these people in a sex shop started hurling insults at me. So I took my walking stick and went after them [laughs]. They were so scared they locked themselves inside the shop. They couldn't see the cameras that were hidden inside a car.... They just thought I was a nutcase."

Argentinean-born Leon Klimovsky (1906–1996) originally trained as a dentist before cinema's siren song enticed him to trade the dental drill for the director's baton. Relocating to Spain in the 1950s, he worked on comedies, dramas, war films and Westerns through the 1960s. In the 1970s his career took a turn toward the macabre when he was hired to direct Naschy's *The Werewolf vs. Vampire Woman* (1971) and *Dr. Jekyll and the Werewolf* in quick succession. He then went on to a string of Eurohorrors like *Vengeance of the Zombies* (1973; again with Naschy), *The Dracula Saga* (1973), *The Vampire's Night Orgy* (1974, starring Jack Taylor), *Devil's Possessed* (1974; with Naschy), *Strange Love of the Vampires* (1975), and *The People Who Own the Dark* (1976; Naschy again) before retiring in 1979.

According to actor Jack Taylor (Jekyll himself), Klimovsky was "a very kind, educated gentleman" who "realized the limitations imposed at the time, budget, censorship, etc., and produced acceptable products. He was always courteous to his actors and crew. There wasn't much time for artistry or direction" Taylor went on to note that "shooting conditions were a bit primitive … no caravans for costume or makeup. However, this was done at an eighteenth century complex near Madrid, and at least we had a roof."

"Everyone likes a fright, as long as you can be sitting in your favorite chair or are protected by the audience surrounding you in the theater," continued Taylor about the appeal of these films. "The werewolf is a victim of destiny, a sensitive creature who suffers just like Pearl White and a long line of male or female characters. Have you ever considered that perhaps Hamlet could have been one during his off moments? It would be difficult to be invited for dinner at some aristocratic event or Fourth of July picnic and suddenly realize that the moon is getting fuller and fuller." Or, as shown here, stuck in an elevator.

Two versions (select scenes, actually) of *Dr. Jekyll and the Werewolf* were shot—one for the homegrown Spanish market, and another for international distribution. The difference? In Spain at the time, under the repressive Franco regime, nudity in films was forbidden. So Spanish producers would shoot a clothed version for domestic consumption, and then have the actresses drop their nighties for the export version. *Dr. Jekyll and the Werewolf* featured several scenes of this nature.

"I never thought of it as one of my better films," admitted Naschy. And he's right. Despite Klimovsky's uneven direction and disappointing werewolf action, however, *Dr. Jekyll and the Werewolf* still offers some effective Gothic atmosphere, the occasional moment of horrific artistry, and a boatload of novelty in linking the two (three?) classic horror figures—the werewolf, and Jekyll & Hyde—together, making it worth a look not only for Naschy completists but for were-lovers everywhere.

With quotes from: "Interview: Paul Naschy," by José Luis González and Michael Secula, *Videooze* 6/7; "Paul Naschy: Memoirs of a Wolfman," *Dr. Jekyll and the Werewolf* DVD; Interview with Jack Taylor conducted by the author, March 2015.

Morphology: Larry Talbot–like wolfman
Demise: That pesky silver bullet
Full Moon Rating: **½

A werewolf sporting a turtleneck sweater? Well, it *was* the '70s … (German lobby card for *Dr. Jekyll and the Werewolf*).

Dr. Jekyll and the Wolfman see *Dr. Jekyll and the Werewolf*

Doctor Jekyll vs. the Werewolf see *Dr. Jekyll and the Werewolf*

Dr. Jekyll y el Hombre Lobo see *Dr. Jekyll and the Werewolf*

Dog Soldiers

(2002; Pathé; UK) Director/Screenplay: Neil Marshall; Producers: Christopher Figg, Tom Reeve, David E. Allen; Cinematographer: Sam McCurdy. Cast: Sean Pertwee, Kevin McKidd, Emma Cleasby, Liam Cunningham, Thomas Lockyer, Darren Morfitt, Chris Robson, Leslie Simpson.

SIX MEN, FULL MOON, NO CHANCE—poster

"It's a monster movie full of outrageous blood and guts but given some truly unique twists," said *Dog Soldiers* star Sean Pertwee. "It begins like an Army documentary, develops into a scary chase movie and then becomes *Zulu* with werewolves…"

A platoon of British soldiers on a training exercise in the Scottish Highlands become prey for a pack of werewolves. The soldiers hole up in an isolated farmhouse and try to find a way to defend themselves against the seemingly unstoppable lupine marauders. It's a simple, straightforward action/horror scenario that springs to vivid life due to an electric pace, crisp writing, well-drawn characters, intense human conflict, brilliant acting, evocative direction, atmospheric photography, thrilling action set-pieces, a shocking (and judicious) use of gore and black humor, and absolutely *the* most terrifying lycanthropes ever to slash across the silver screen. (These werewolves mean business: at one point a beast literally rips the head off one soldier and *throws it* at another one!)

Writer/director Neil Marshall characterized it as "[*Saving*] *Private Ryan* with werewolves instead of Germans; it's that intense." Indeed, the early twilight battle/chase through the woods features quick shots of the fast-moving creatures in silhouette intercut with brief black-and-white werewolf-POV footage, while the (un)steadicam photography, tracer bullets, shouting and organized chaos of the retreating soldiers heightens the adrenaline pumping excitement. Add to that the horrifying yet blackly funny concept of one soldier (a lead character, no less) trying to run while literally holding in his own guts (after having his stomach ripped open by werewolf claws), and it becomes unforgettable.

Marshall cites such siege-oriented films as *Rio Bravo* and *Zulu* as influences, but, curiously, not *Night of the Living Dead* (which the film's second half most resembles—with lightening fast, intelligent werewolves standing in for slowly lumbering, mindless zombies), a film he'd never even seen. (*Night of the Werewolves* was considered as a title at one point, but thankfully discarded.)

First-time writer/director Marshall had worked in the British film industry since 1992, as editor, storyboard artist and director's assistant. His *Dog Soldiers* script had been germinating, evolving and (ahem) transforming for six years, honed to near-perfection. (Said screenplay features character names based on genre figures. Sargent Wells, for instance, was named after H.G. Wells, while Private Bruce was named after *Evil Dead* actor Bruce Campbell.) As a boy Marshall used to spend family vacations in the Scottish Highlands. "It struck me as being a country full of beauty as well as underlying menace.... I thought, here was the perfect atmospheric location to have something wild and ferocious running around.... The sad thing is, we couldn't shoot in Scotland because it was impractical and expensive. We ended up in Luxembourg, which was a good enough substitute."

Shot in six weeks in the Spring of 2001 in Petite-Suisee, Luxembourg (due to that country's advantageous tax laws), the *Dog Soldiers* production built a farmhouse exterior, with interiors shot at the local Carousel Studio. Filming was almost as arduous as, well, an Army maneuver in Scotland, with rain pelting the film company almost continuously. "Just standing up proved difficult," recalled Pertwee, "as our sloped location turned into a mudslide.... We truly became a tight ensemble during this difficult period, and that was exactly what Neil wanted to convey in the movie. It added to the realism."

The film features no CGI, just animatronics and the tried-and-true man-in-werewolf-makeup/costume. "Apart from the *Jurassic Park* movies, nothing created digitally looks good to my mind," said Marshall. "The industry has never been able to get hair or fur right, and everything from *Anaconda* to *The Mummy* looks too much like a video-game cartoon.... I wanted my werewolves in the same frame as the actors to convey the physical terror of their presence." FX veteran Bob Keen (*Hellraiser*) created the nearly eight-foot-tall werewolves. "The werewolves are based on animal kingdom fact rather than anything too fantasy-oriented to keep them as realistic as possible," said Keen. "It was important to Neil that the werewolves looked like bloodthirsty creatures that could tear you apart." Played by stuntmen with stilt extensions on the legs and sporting a headpiece that took two operators to work the various eye, nose, ear and jaw movements, these beasts look like a scarier, steroids-enhanced version of *The Howling* lycanthropes.

"*Dog Soldiers* isn't about tortured human souls condemned to turn into wolves every cursed full moon," explained Marshall. "It's about nasty, ferocious, wild beasts that must kill and eat people at whatever cost, though using silver is still the main method of eradication. The werewolves aren't treated in any major fantasy context, either. They are just another enemy, like Nazis or terrorists, that this platoon of rookies must contend with. That's important to the success of the overall piece, in my mind. Having a solid base in combat realism means that when certain fantastical elements are introduced, they still remain utterly realistic. Believability can't be shattered so easily with that strong foundation."

Filmmaker John Landis labeled *Dog Soldiers* an "exciting, action-packed horror movie." The *American Werewolf in London* director (and avowed horror fan) is right on the money. What *Aliens* did for the hoary old otherworldly B.E.M.s (bug-eyed monsters), *Dog Soldiers* did for werewolves—transforming the generally solitary tortured-soul creature into a group of lightning-fast, cunning, vicious, and near unstoppable killing machines.

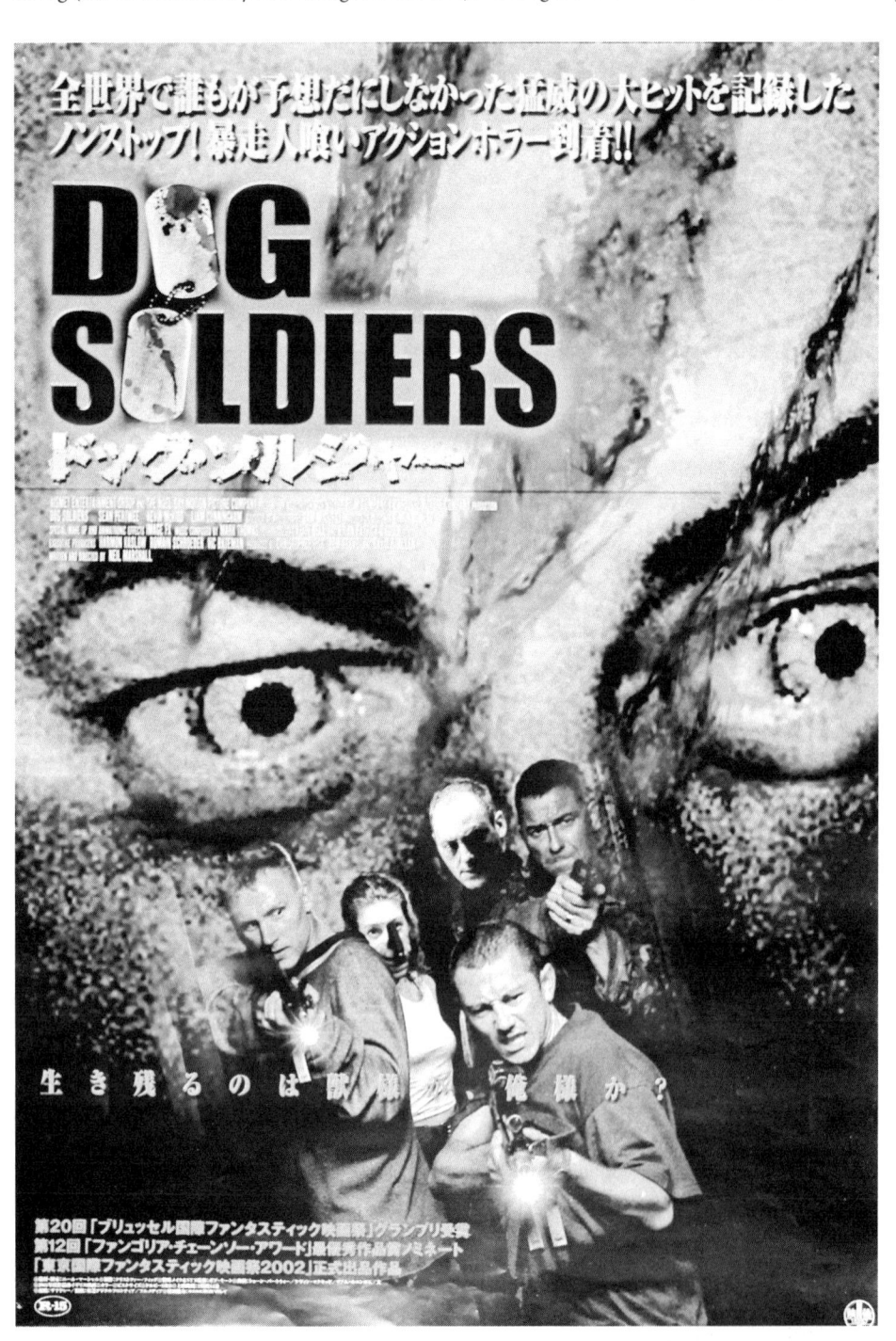

A hit in the U.K., as well as Europe and Japan, the innovative, action-packed yet character-driven *Dog Soldiers* inexplicably failed to find a theatrical distributor in the U.S., going straight to video (Japanese poster, courtesy Armin Junge).

Despite some American funding, *Dog Soldiers* was made specifically for the British market. Its opening weekend gross was the biggest for a horror film released in the U.K. Unfortunately, it failed to find an American theatrical distributor and ended up premiering (in an edited version) on the Sci-Fi channel. Perhaps these short-sighted executives found it to be *too* British. Sean Pertwee, in a forward for the book *Urban Terrors*, called *Dog Soldiers* "about as British as roast beef. It wears the Union Jack on its sleeve and flaunts it with pride. I do believe that *Dog Soldiers* and its director Neil Marshall helped lead the way for the biggest horror resurgence in this country [Great Britain] since the Hammer House of Horror films in the 1960s, and I'm extremely proud to be part of that charge."

"I absolutely love horror movies," concluded Marshall, "but it's also the genre I'm least satisfied with.… For example, I adore *An American Werewolf in London*. It's scary, it's funny and it features the best transformation scene ever. Yet the actual werewolf itself is a bit of a dog. Take *The Howling* too. It's great and the werewolves are spectacular—except you hardly see them! So I wanted to make a werewolf picture that didn't fall short in any area." And Marshall did just that, as *Dog Soldiers* stands hairy head and shaggy shoulders above every other modern-day werewolf effort.

With quotes from: "The Bark & Bite of *Dog Soldiers*," by Alan Jones, *Fangoria* 212; *Monsters in the Movies*, by John Landis; *Urban Terrors*, by M. J. Simpson.

Morphology: Two-legged, towering Big Bad Wolves
Demise: Immolation via explosion … and one silver letter opener
Full Moon Rating: *****

Dracula (the Dirty Old Man)

(1969; Whit Boyd) Director/Producer/Screenplay: William Edwards; Cinematographer: William Troiano. Cast: Vince Kelley, Ann Hollis, Libby Caculus, Joan Pickett, Bill Whitton, Sue Allen, Adarainne, Ron Scott, Bob Whitton, Rebecca Reynolds.

> From out of a time-rotted tomb crawls…—tagline

… *Dracula (the Dirty Old Man)*, the kind of movie in which non–descript jazz guitar and piano music plays monotonously through *every* sequence, regardless of the scene's tone; and so much time is taken up by characters walking to and fro, entering and leaving buildings, crossing streets, driving, or just standing around that the filmmakers insert inane stream-of-consciousness narration in a desperate attempt to make it at least *sound* like something is happening. Oh, and there's a half-dozen naked women, too.

Originally shot straight (well, as straight as a no-budget soft-core sex flick advertised as the "SHOCK NUDIE SHOW OF THE CENTURY" *can* be), *Dracula* became a comedy when producer-director-writer William Edwards (who also produced and wrote *Ride the Wild Stud* and the pseudowolf entry *The Mummy and the Curse of the Jackals* the same year, his only other credits) decided to insert a new soundtrack with "funny" voices (Dracula becomes a Jewish stereotype) and prattling "comedy" dialogue. While an occasional line might raise a smirk ("It was a day just like any other day," the hero narrates, before deadpanning, "which doesn't say much"), most of the blathering musings are more fatuous than hilarious ("As I sped towards that mineshaft, little knowing what awaited me there, I knew I felt like I was going to get shafted"). And the obviously ad-libbed dubbed-over dialogue never matches the actors' mouth movements; in fact, characters frequently speak without even moving their lips. Amazing.

The plot (such as it is) has Count Alucard ("Dracula spelled backwards," as the opening credits so helpfully explain) occupying an abandoned mine (played by the ubiquitous Bronson Canyon), where he fondles and feasts on naked girls brought to him by his thrall, hypnotized reporter Mike Waters, who periodically transforms into a talking werewolf newly named by Dracula as "Irving Jackalman" (wearing the same ridiculous werewolf mask seen in *The Mummy and the Curse of the Jackals*). "I want for you bring me a girl every night," this Yiddish Count tells his wolfish procurer, "and I'll make you from a novice jackalman—I'll promote you as you do good."

Dracula (the Dirty Old Man) steals from Columbia's *Return of the Vampire* the notion of a werewolf serving a vampire (with the bloodsucker's hypnotic power triggering the transformation) but fails to take anything else of value from that earlier near-classic. Rather than Bela Lugosi's imposing Count, here we have a pancake-faced, goateed Dracula (played by first- and last-time actor Vince Kelley) sporting a white stripe through his slicked-back hair that makes him look like the bastard love-child of a lounge lizard and a skunk. Constantly muttering inanities in a Jewish accent like some third-rate Catskills performer, Dracula does little but paw the captive women before biting them on the breast. The lazy bloodsucker (who periodically transforms into the worst cardboard cutout bat this side of a ten-year-old's monster-themed birthday party) leaves his werewolf slave to do all the heavy lifting, which includes several bloody attacks (resulting in red paint smears on faces and necks) and two unpleasant instances of were-rape in which Jackalman has his hairy way with the women while muttering tasteless comments like "Yummy" and "Is this really how they give artificial respiration?" Though it might seem somewhat disingenuous to paint a low-budget soft-core sex film with the "tasteless" brush, violent-rape-as-good-clean-fun simply goes beyond the pale.

Said werewolf—with its furry dog-face, a muzzle full of snaggle-teeth, wild unruly hair, and big ears on top of its large shaggy head—looks like a cross between a schnauzer and Fozzie Bear. And the pivotal metamorphosis occurs with actor Ron Scott ducking down below frame only to pop up after a cutaway as fellow actor Billy Whitton sporting the crude werewolf head and hairy hands.

Just as in *Return of the Vampire*, the werewolf slave turns on his vampiric master at film's end. Here he finally balks at Dracula "keeping the best ones for [him]self" and tries to pull the amorous Count off his latest naked female (who happens to be Waters' girlfriend). At this, an annoyed Dracula merely pushes him away, sending the man-beast reeling. The Count then takes a large rock and (off-screen) knocks his disobedient servant unconscious. (Tellingly, when Dracula raises the rock, he inadvertently reveals the pre-painted "bloodstain" on the rock's underside *before* he even strikes; two takes apparently were one too many for this shoddy quickie.) By this time, however, the sun has risen, and Dracula staggers back to his coffin only to disappear, replaced by a pile of ash. At this, the prone werewolf writhes on the ground and suddenly displays an intermediary look (human face with bushy eyebrows, bits of sparse hair, and fangs) that, while no great were-shakes, is still far more effective than the ludicrous full-on lycan-head. In the next shot he's back to being Mike Waters—and none the worse for wear, since he's soon getting it on with his nude girlfriend ("Ever done it in a cave?" asks Mr. Smooth…).

Pathetic in all categories (even the pulchritude on display is spectacularly below-average), *Dracula (the Dirty Old Man)* will sorely try the patience (and fast-forward button) of anyone not already enamored of *The Mummy and the Curse of the Jackals*. And that's *everyone*.

Morphology: Suit-and-turtleneck-wearing, bipedal, big-headed wolfman

Demise: None; he returns to normal when Dracula meets his doom—and then has sex with the girl!
Full Moon Rating: zero moons

Dracula Versus Frankenstein see *Assignment Terror*

Dracula's Castle see *Blood of Dracula's Castle*

Dylan Dog: Dead of Night

(2011; Omnilab/Freestyle Releasing) Director: Kevin Munroe; Producers: Ashok Amritraj, Scott Mitchell Rosenberg, Gilbert Adler; Screenplay: Thomas Dean Donnelly, Joshua Oppenheimer (based on the comic series *Dylan Dog* created by Tiziano Sclavi); Cinematographer: Geoffrey Hall. Cast: Brandon Routh, Sam Huntington, Anita Brien, Brian Steele, Kurt Angle, Peter Stormare, Taye Diggs.

LIVING INVESTIGATOR. UNDEAD CLIENTS. ZOMBIE PARTNER. NO PULSE? NO PROBLEM—poster

---

The best-selling Italian comic book series *Dylan Dog* by Tiziano Sclavi has sold over 60 million copies worldwide. Few of those sales occurred in America, however, where the title—and character—remain largely unknown. So it's a little surprising that a U.S. production company should want to make a (moderately expensive) film adaptation. Surprising, but not unwelcome.

The film's opening narration sets the scene: "New Orleans can be a tough town to die in. But when you die and come back—you call me, Dylan Dog…. The undead are out there, hiding in plain sight. And in my day I was the line between you and them. I was the peace, the cork in the bottle, the line in the sand." Now working as a cut-rate private eye in The Big Easy ("where else would you hide if you were a creature of the night," he reasonably asks), Dylan (Brandon Routh) has left his supernatural-soaked past behind after his fiancée was killed by vampires. Turning down a potential client, Elizabeth (Anita Brien), when it becomes clear that werewolves are involved, Dylan is drawn back to the case after the death of his only friend and sort-of partner, Marcus (Sam Huntington). "I thought I'd left my past behind," he says, "but sometimes it has a way of sneaking up and punching you square into the present." But Marcus, killed by a massive flesh-eating zombie, comes back as the undead, and the two, along with Elizabeth, set about unraveling the convoluted case, which involves a stolen talisman containing demon's blood, and the intended resurrection of a 5000-year-old demonic vampire that may mean not only the subjugation of the supernatural world but of humankind as well.

The movie begins on a lycan-high note when Elizabeth sees a massive creature flee the scene of her father's murder. "My father was killed by some kind of monster," she later tells Dylan. "He was huge, thick fur, massive claws." Unfortunately, we catch only a glimpse of the large shape as it leaps past her and through the window of the murdered man's study. But Dylan, once on the case, is able to track down the killer werewolf by analyzing a strand of its hair. "There are four werewolf clans in the city," he tells her, adding, "They're pretty territorial—like the mob…. These families, like any wolf pack, have identifying colors in their coats." Dylan can also determine that the hair strands are from a "female, between her second and third coat, which means she's probably about 18." This leads Dylan to the Cysnos werewolf clan, whose headquarters reside (naturally enough) in a meat packing plant. Dylan's questions and veiled accusations anger the clan leader, Gabriel (Peter Stormare), whose eyes glow red while his fangs protrude. Recovering himself, Gabriel, due to their former friendship, spares Dylan. But Gabriel's hulking, hotheaded son, Wolfgang (Kurt Angle), is not so understanding. Muttering, "You're nothing but a lousy Breather," he begins tossing Dylan around the plant. Ominously, he asks Dylan, "You know the last time I tasted human? They say we ain't allowed no more. But hey, rules were made to be broken." After another punch that lands Dylan across the room, Wolfgang transforms. Closing his eyes in concentration, a quick close-up shows his ear extending to a point as the hair around it grows longer, before his eyes suddenly open wide to reveal green animal irises. Long hair rings this wolfman's face, which consists of a wide, flattened nose, angry-looking ridged brows, and a wicked set of fangs. Dylan insults him with, "You hit like a vampire," before taking out a pair of brass knuckles—made of silver—and knocking him senseless. This leads to a simple but cleverly-filmed metamorphosis that harkens back to the original *Werewolf of London* transformation technique. With the camera holding on a close-up of the dazed creature's face, it begins moving forward past his supporting arm as he tries to rise, and emerges on the other side to show he's human again, with a line of four smoldering scars where the silver has contacted the side of his face.

Unfortunately, there's precious little further lycan-action until the film's climax, with the bulk of the picture taken up by Dylan's search for the "Heart of Belial" (the talisman), and run-ins with the vampire clan, the True Bloods, and the near-unstoppable mutant uber-zombie. Subplots involve Dylan's flashback to his fiancée's death, his obligatory hook-up with Elizabeth, and poor Marcus comically trying to come to terms with his new undead status (including a disgusting diet of worms and maggots, a pervasive rotting smell, and a new—*black*—arm grafted onto his body ["They were out of caucasian arms in your size"]).

Regarding werewolves, Dylan quips, "They're not just in grandma's cabin out in the woods—or only in London" (mouthing the script's self-aware reference to *An American Werewolf in London*). "They're here in the city, living and working among us. Most have learned to control the change, to control the beast inside, but sometimes the beast gets loose." Dylan ultimately tracks down this "loose" beast, only to find the teenage girl dead—killed for the talisman by the monster-zombie. It turns out that werewolves are on the side of the Angels here (the were-girl who killed Elizabeth's father to get the talisman intended to use it to put a stop to the conflict between the lycanthropes and vampires). A half-dozen werewolves, led by Wolfgang, even serve as the cavalry at film's end, coming to Dylan's aid by taking down the *real* villain—and thereby stopping the symbiotically-linked reanimated Devil-monster that's about to destroy Dylan.

"The most common way to become a werewolf is inheritance," Dylan explains, "like a genetic disorder passed down from parent to child." The "parent" of this werewolf clan is played with stylish panache by Swedish-born actor Peter Stormare (who had previously faced a werewolf in the pseudowolf entry *The Brothers Grimm* in 2005, and who subsequently leant his voice talents to another pseudowolf entry, 2012's *Big-Top Scooby-Doo!*). "Peter is a cool dude, he's really fun," enthused *Dylan Dog* director Kevin Munroe. "We called him up for the role of the head of the werewolf clan. We were trying to really cast everybody according to type, so all the werewolves are very working class, dock worker types. I love the idea that their eyes were really focused, and Peter has this real focused face. We talked and he really loved the role and he said, 'Of course, I'll come down and do it.' His wife was almost going into labor, but he came down for the three days and was such a good sport about it."

Director Kevin Munroe (2007's animated *TMNT*), making his first live-action film, took full advantage of his New Orleans shooting locations, juxtaposing the city's architectural charm with dilapidated factory settings (which house the hungry undead) and a particularly atmospheric graveyard. "Because of Katrina," recalled co-star Sam Huntington, "there was a lot of damage done to the cemetery we shot in. All the cemeteries in New Orleans are above ground and that one had been hit pretty hard. I think it was in the 9th Ward, in a bad part of town. A lot of their crypts were open, so you would see stuff in them. And then, I had to crawl on top of one. It was so awful and gross. That was creepy." Nothing beats realism.

Refreshingly, Munroe made sure practical effects (rather than CGI) were the order of the day. "My first pitch about directing the movie had all practical effects in it," the director stated, "and that was when the budget was much more. If I had had more money, I would have just put more people in suits in the movie. I wouldn't ever have gone to CG, for that stuff, specifically.... There's a reality to it, and there's also a humanity to it, too. I think that's why I like the practical effects. You can look at a creature and still see vulnerability or the character behind the creature. To get character behind CG creatures, that's so few and far between." Star Brandon Routh agreed. "It's always great to have something real. It's better to be staring at somebody than an X on the camera's matte box, for any kind of scene. It's great to have a living, breathing beast lunging for me and swinging at me."

And these beasts do plenty of lunging and swinging, so much so that Dylan becomes something of a human punching bag, as he's continually beaten up by werewolves, vampires, mutant zombies, and ultimately the oversized winged demon. Dylan even admits at one point, "For someone who thinks he's pretty smart, I certainly get the crap kicked out of me a lot." He takes hits (which not only send him flying across a room but that would kill a real man) so often that he ought to have his local ER on speed-dial. "He does get the shit kicked out of him a lot," admitted Munroe. "I love that. That's just my taste, and I know that I'm in a minority. A lot of people have watched it and said, 'Is he Superman? He's just getting kicked.' And I'm like, 'That's funny. I love that he gets uppercut.' I like it comic book. That was the tone of this." Things move from comic-book improbable to downright ridiculous, however, for the climactic battle with the revived Belial demon. Set in a wonderfully evocative dilapidated theater, sans roof, the fight involves Belial tossing Dylan 25 feet into the air onto the upper balcony, with Dylan falling back down, flat on his back (something that, if it didn't kill him outright, would certainly leave him incapacitated). Later the monster tosses him into the balcony once again, then flies up to throw him back down—*through* four levels of scaffolding. That kind of physical punishment should have killed Dylan three times over. "There might be something going on underneath there with Dylan," conjectured Routh. "I think there is some backstory that he may not be totally mortal." If so, the film fails to even *hint* at it. "And, realistically," continued Routh, "you're going to get the crap beaten out of you by these monsters. He probably shouldn't be getting up from some of the fights." Indeed.

Improbable punishment scenarios aside, the often ingenious script, offering both action (full of impressive monster battles involving convincing wire-work) and comedy (mostly involving the genuinely funny Sam Huntington as the reluctant zombie Marcus, who at one point even attends a zombie support group!) keeps the viewer guessing, and even features a truly surprising twist regarding the identity of the villain pulling the undead zombie-strings. Dylan's hard-boiled, borderline tongue-in-cheek narration periodically spices the proceedings. Sample: "The thing about werewolves is that they don't take too well to being accused of murder—especially those they commit."

Unfortunately, the clever chuckles and exciting monster-brawls can't fully overcome the film's fatal flaw: lead Brandon Routh (a television actor best known for his tepid turn as the titular character in the overblown *Superman Returns* [2006]). As Dylan, pretty boy Routh lacks the presence necessary to pull off the role. Rather than worldweary and cynical, his disaffected playing and inflectionless tone simply falls flat. Dylan's zombie sidekick acts far more animated than he, as Routh goes for deadpan but mostly just manages dead.

On the plus side, Routh and Huntington display an easy chemistry together. They became good friends on *Superman Returns* (Huntington played Jimmy Olsen to Routh's Clark Kent) and it shows. "We were friends," recounted Huntington, "that really, really helped the onscreen relationship. The most important thing for these two characters was that they had that chemistry. " But on his own, Routh can't sustain anything close to interest. With a more charismatic and comedically-talented lead, *Dylan Dog* coulda been a contender; as is, it's more of a second-string also-ran.

"I would love to do a sequel where we go back to London and the character roots," exclaimed Munroe. Given that *Dylan Dog* made a paltry $1.2 million domestically (and only $4.6 worldwide) against its $20 million budget, it seems highly unlikely we'll see this character again (at least in this iteration).

With quotes from: "Director Kevin Munroe Exclusive Interview, *Dylan Dog*," by Christina Radish, collider.com, April 28, 2011; "Brandon Routh and Sam Huntington Exclusive Interview *Dylan Dog*," by Christina Radish, collider.com, April 27, 2011.

Morphology: Large wolfmen
Demise: None; they're the *good guys*
Full Moon Rating: ***

An Erotic Werewolf in London

(2006; Seduction Cinema) Director/Screenplay: William Hellfire; Producer: Michael Raso; Cinematographer: John Fedele. Cast: Misty Mundae, Anoushka, Darian Caine, Julian Wells, Zoe Moonshine, Ruby LaRoca, Linda Murray.

"My animal spirit is set free upon the rising of the full moon"
—the Erotic Werewolf in London herself

Obviously intent on capitalizing on the John Landis werewolf classic *An American Werewolf in London*, this camcorder concoction of lesbian lust, with a thin (*very* thin) veneer of lycanthropy thrown over its softcore Sapphic sex scenes, fails in nearly every department. From the cheesy opening credits, to the first protracted lesbian lovemaking scene (coming out of nowhere, with nary a preamble in sight), to the blank-as-a-plank acting from the titular titillating terror (played by the sexy but emotively-challenged Polish-born "actress" Anoushka), to the not-fooling-anyone ordinary bedroom masquerading as a hospital room, to the barely-inches-above-amateur camerawork and "effects" (not to mention visible boom mike shadows), it goes without saying that this film's director, cut-rate video maven William Hellfire, is no John Landis.

More along the lines of the 1976 Italian oddity *Werewolf Woman* (Hellfire admits to this Euro-obscurity being his "inspiration" on his film's DVD commentary track), and with a nod to Hammer's *Curse of the Werewolf* in its linking of sexual arousal with lycanthropy, *An Erotic Werewolf in London* began production in 2001 (it being an excuse for director/writer Hellfire to squeeze a free plane ticket from tightfisted producer Michael Raso) but wasn't completed until 2006.

Microbudget softcore siren Misty Mundae (nee Erin Brown) toplines the film, though the title role really belongs to Anoushka, whose voluptuous figure isn't voluptuous enough to hide the fact that she couldn't invest a heavily-accented line of dialogue with anything close to emotion (or even inflection) to save her life. That said, her enthusiasm for the "action" scenes (re: lesbian sex) certainly shines through.

With titles on his resume like *Orgasm Torture in Satan's Rape Clinic* (2004), *Bikini Girls on Dinosaur Planet* (2005), and *Cloak and Shag Her* (2008), one can't expect much from videographer William Hellfire. And "not much" is just what the viewer gets with *An Erotic Werewolf in London*. Well, not much in the way of competent filmmaking anyway, as Hellfire et al. utilize their cheap video camera, tacky bedroom sets and low-rent lighting to offer up an *over*abundance of softcore lesbian action, so much so that all the repetitive nipple-nibbling, tongue teasing, and body bumping flies straight past *Erotic* into *Boredom*. The various girl-on-girl and solo sex sessions last anywhere from five to ten minutes each, so that the actual plot of *An Erotic Werewolf in London* boils down to little more than a 10-minute short. Said plot has two bar owners/lesbian lovers encounter a heavily accented (and heavily bosomed) blonde stranger (Anoushka), who seduces the brunette (Misty Mundae) and then bites her. (Like in many a sexual fantasy, these characters remain nameless; no one over the course of the movie ever mentions a single name, underlining the fact that they're all just ciphers—mere bodies rather than actual characters.) While her victim recovers in the hospital (and transforms into a killer herself during lesbian rubdowns with two separate nurses), Anoushka journeys to London, contacts a reporter, tells her lycanthropic story (shades of *Interview with a Vampire*), and seduces and slaughters her gorgeous neighbor. Misty sneaks out of the hospital and heads home to her true love, who ties her up and makes love to her until Misty fully transforms, forcing her paramour to shoot her. Meanwhile, Anoushka is still on the prowl for more sex and flesh…

Werewolf-wise, apart from a few multiple exposure shots of Anoushka sporting fangs, long fingernails, and a few wisps of golden hair on her arms, the only transformation scene comes at the very end when a tied-up Misty goes full-on (minimalist) werewolf. With her lower arms and hands covered in hair, her nose blackened, and her teeth now a set of fangs (lower jaw only), she sports heavy eyebrows, pointy ears, and a ridiculous-looking strip of fur crisscrossing her abdomen (the rest of her naked body remaining hairless). She growls like a dog, breaks her S&M bonds, and advances on her lover, who sobbingly shoots the were-bitch with a handy loaded gun retrieved from the bedroom bookcase.

In between all the fondling and heavy breathing, the film manages to make a few comments on the nature of this eroticized lycanthropy. When the reporter asks Anoushka why she chooses a large city like London to inhabit rather than the countryside, she answers, "You'll never find such an abundance of prey as that of a major city. My apartment is my den." Said "den," incidentally, features a framed *Texas Chainsaw Massacre* poster up on the wall, showing that, along with hairy hands and an appetite for human flesh, lycanthropy also brings with it some unusual decorative flair (and perhaps good taste in fright films).

"I'm always a wolf," Anoushka further explains, "but on the night of the full moon I cross over completely to the animal world." Though this erotic werewolf appears happy with her "nature," it begs the question of why she confesses all to a reporter, even going so far as inviting her to her "den," and allowing the woman to witness her seducing and killing her neighbor.

One of the few intriguing aspects of this threadbare scenario has lycanthropy linked to sexual desire—and fulfillment. "Once I've chosen my prey, I attract, seduce it, and devour it," Anoushka declares. With sex being the preamble to feeding, orgasm triggers the change. "I assume the body of the wolf—but only at the climax—it's an extension of my orgasm." But with *An Erotic Werewolf in London*, this provocative notion of female empowerment perversely serves the male gaze by merely providing an excuse (time after time after time) to satisfy the movie's decidedly male-oriented view of two women having sex. Perhaps Hellfire and co. felt that indeed it is the thought that counts … but more likely they just enjoyed filming lesbian sex scenes over and over again to, er, flesh out the film's scant 68 minutes (that nonetheless feels much longer).

Morphology: Nude lesbian wolfwoman
Demise: (Lead) bullet
Full Moon Rating: *

Eyes of the Werewolf

(1999/2003; Sterling Entertainment) Director/Screenplay: Tim Sullivan; Producer: David Sterling; Cinematographer: Jeff Leroy. Cast: Mark Sawyer, Stephanie Beaton, Jason Clark, Eric Mestressat, Deborah Huber, Tim Sullivan.

"I have memories of the murders—vague and dreamlike"—cursed protagonist
---

Shot in February 1999 on a budget of $5,000, but not released (on video) until 2003, *Eyes of the Werewolf* tells the story of Rich (Mark Sawyer), a research chemist who receives an eye transplant after a terrible acid accident destroys his original orbs. Unfortunately, the unscrupulous doctor (woodenly played by director Tim Sullivan himself) who performs the experimental procedure procures his body parts illegally, and Rich's new eyes belonged to an unwilling donor hunted down and killed by a band of organ-harvesting rednecks. And worse, unbeknownst to Rich, the doc and even the clueless killers, this latest victim was a *werewolf*! Consequently, as the DVD box describes it, "all hell breaks loose when Rich, with the help of his horny nurse, a midget and a lesbian detective, tries to extract revenge during the next full moon." Exploitative hyperbole aside, what really happens is that Rich, in his animal form, seemingly targets those who've wronged him, including his cheating wife, her lover, and the duplicitous doctor. He does indeed seek help from a sympathetic nurse (Stephanie Beaton) who soon comes to love him, a midget with an affinity for the occult whose shack he stumbles upon in the woods, and a writer friend. The "lesbian detective," however, tries to track down Rich, the prime murder suspect, while also attempting to put the moves on Rich's girlfriend.

This all sounds far more eventful than anything this backyard camcorder production delivers, however, as the sub-porno level settings (cheap apartments and offices stand in for the progressive private hospital), grainy shot-on-video photography (dirty lenses included), and amateurish acting (leaden Mark Sawyer is never believable in his tortured Lon Chaney role) close these *Eyes* before they ever fully open. The meandering script, full of awkward dialogue and all-too-convenient contrivances (including a moon—represented by a cheesy painting—that stays full for *four* nights in a row), offers little but a few poorly-staged werewolf attacks, and two pointless and protracted soft-core sex scenes obviously designed to focus the Eyes of the Viewer on no-budget scream queen Stephanie (*Bikini Planet, Evil in the Bayou*) Beaton's two surgically-enhanced assets. The best any hapless viewer caught staring into these *Eyes* can hope for is a knowing chuckle at Sullivan, an obvious fan, naming his mad medico "Dr. Atwill" (after Lionel Atwill, who appeared in the Universal werewolf entries *House of Frankenstein* and *House of Dracula*) and Rich's writer friend "Siodmak" (after Curt Siodmak, screenwriter of *The Wolf Man* and *Frankenstein Meets the Wolf Man*); and perhaps the not-unexpected-but-still-novel and cartoonishly gruesome "If thine eye offends thee…" denouement.

Lycanthrope-wise, apart from its unique premise of the curse of lycanthropy being carried along by a transplanted body part, *Eyes of the Werewolf* posits a closer tie between the human and the beast than most werewolf films. Here, rather than the wolfman becoming an indiscriminate killing machine, as in most lycan-flicks (or even "seeking to kill the thing it loves best," à la *Werewolf of London*), the manbeast instinctively targets those who have wronged it while in human form. "Your animal self wanted to kill Craig," explains Siodmak about why the monster zeroed in on Rich's wife's lover. And later the creature dispatches Rich's cheating wife, and then the evil doctor who refused to help Rich. Conversely, when the beast could easily kill Rich's loving nurse/girlfriend at film's end, it passes her by—positing the beast within as much closer to the civilized human side, with the Monster acting on the wishes of the Man. "I have memories of the murders," comments Rich, "vague and dreamlike." Here lycanthropy seems more akin to the Jekyll-Hyde dynamic than the more diametrically-opposed man-beast relationship found in most werewolf films, with the beast released to carry out the wishes of the Id.

Cinematographer (and editor) Jeff Leroy does triple-duty by also providing the film's make-up effects, serving up an unconvincing wrinkled rubber mask to create an oversized wolf's head, complete with obvious L.E.D. glowing red eyes and mechanically-moving jaws, along with some Styrofoam body parts. The sole transformation scene involves a few fades, with more and more hair applied to actor Mark Sawyer's face as he writhes on the couch, before cutting to the full-head mask. Though looking cheap and unconvincing, at least the production made the effort. Leroy went on to direct his own ultra-low budget lycanthrope movie in 2006—*Werewolf in a Women's Prison*.

Though possessing a rather unique and intriguing premise, little in these homemade *Eyes* are worth (ahem) seeing. The discerning viewer should answer an unqualified "nay" to these *Eyes*.

Morphology: Bipedal, wolf-headed lycanthrope
Demise: Impromptu self-surgery
Full Moon Rating: *

DVD cover showcasing the two major assets (hint: *not* the eyes) of the micro-budgeted S.O.V. horror *Eyes of the Werewolf*.

Face of the Screaming Werewolf

(1959/64; A.D.P. International; Mexico/U.S.; b&w) Original Language Title: *La Casa del Terror*; Director: Jerry Warren, and (uncredited) Gilberto Martinez Solares (werewolf footage) and Rafael Portillo (mummy sequences); Producer: Jerry Warren; Screenplay: Gilbert Solar (Gilberto Martinez Solares, werewolf scenes), Alfred Salimar (Alfredo Salazar, mummy sequences); Cinematographers: Richard Wallace (Enrique Wallace, mummy scenes), Raúl Martínez Solares (werewolf sequences, uncredited). Cast: Landa Varle (Yolanda Varela), Lon Chaney, Donald Barron, Raymond Gaylord (Ramón Gay), Steve Conte, Jorge Mondragon, Emma Roldan, George Mitchell, Chuck Niles, Bill White, Fred Hoffman.

The Mexican werewolf-comedy *La Casa del Terror*, starring Lon Chaney, Jr., metamorphosed into the humorless (and near-unwatchable) *Face of the Screaming Werewolf* after low-budget American schlockmeister Jerry Warren got his paws on it.

A TERROR-CADE IN THRILLS!
A NIGHTMARE IN CHILLS!—trailer

In the early 1960s, American fringe filmmaker Jerry Warren (*Man Beast, Teenage Zombies*) acquired the rights to a 1959 Mexican horror comedy, starring the popular Latin comedian Tin Tan (*and* featuring Lon Chaney, Jr., as a werewolf!), called *La Casa del Terror*. Warren excised nearly all of Tin Tan's scenes (thus eliminating the original movie's *star*) and inserted footage from the 1957 *La Momia Azteca* (which he'd already cannibalized to create the atrocious *Attack of the Mayan Mummy* in 1963). But Warren didn't stop there; *Face of the Screaming Werewolf* is really a combination of *four* different film snippets. In addition to the *Momia Azteca* and *Casa del Terror* footage, Warren recycled some of his own scenes shot with American actors for *Attack of the Mayan Mummy*, and included a few scraps of *new* footage lensed specifically to bridge some of the expository gaps in *Face*.

As might be expected from such a patchwork pastiche, *Face of the Screaming Werewolf* makes little sense and provides even less entertainment, offering only a few nostalgic moments of Lon Chaney in his trademark Wolf Man makeup (though a bit shaggier here than in his halcyon days at Universal) for those diehard fans desperate enough to sit through this painful 60 minutes (which feels like *twice* that length).

The story has a young woman, the reincarnation of an Aztec maiden, lead a scientific expedition to an ancient pyramid on the Yucatan peninsula where they find two bodies—an ancient mummy and a modern man in some sort of mummified condition ("placed in the pyramid only recently after an exchange of body fluid with the mummy in an effort to achieve an apparent state of death," as one character unhelpfully explains). The Aztec mummy comes to life, but the expedition subdues the creature and brings it—and the still-dead 'modern' mummy—back to the city for study (all, disappointingly, off-screen). A rival scientist steals the modern mummy and restores it to life, only to find that the man (Lon Chaney, Jr.) is actually a werewolf! Meanwhile, the living mummy escapes, abducts the reincarnated girl, and is promptly killed when hit by a car (again, off-screen).

The two story lines have nothing to do with one another, and a paucity of dialogue (synching the dubbing was obviously too big a strain on Warren's grade-Z budget) insures that the viewer often has no idea who is doing what to whom. Many of the scenes appear to be thrown in at random just to pad the running time (and the few new shots of Warren regulars—like Chuck Niles and Steve Conte—answering the telephone or delivering radio broadcasts eat up further time without adding anything appreciable to the confusing proceedings).

The first 20 minutes of *Face of the Screaming Werewolf* (a full third of the picture) consists of *La Momia Azteca* footage lifted from

Warren's earlier *Attack of the Mayan Mummy* (1963). It didn't improve with age, for the long ceremonial flashback sequence quickly grows tiresome, and the mummy only pops up in the last minute.

In an interview with Tom Weaver, Jerry Warren referred to his doctoring of Mexican imports as "a natural, easy way to make movies without an exceptional amount of work." Well, with *Face of the Screaming Werewolf*, Warren put in even less work than usual—and it shows.

The *Casa del Terror* footage provides *Face*'s few highlights, including seeing Chaney Jr. in his black-shirt-and-trouser Lawrence Talbot get-up once more (he even leaps over a lab table at one point with a bit of the old Wolf Man ferocity); atmospherically-lit and unsettling insert shots of creepy wax figures (the villain's secret lab is at a wax museum—though this isn't made clear in *Face*, resulting in more confusion); and the boffo lab set itself, with a giant pressure cooker/tanning bed contraption (used to try and revive the mummy), various banks of electrical equipment, bubbling beakers, and a giant spinning apparatus of undetermined origin.

Working 12 to 14 hours each day, Lon Chaney, Jr., completed all of his scenes for *Casa del Terror* in just two days. Director Gilberto Martinez Solares shot with three cameras to capture Chaney from various angles, as Chaney rapidly switched from normal makeup to mummy makeup to werewolf makeup. "He was a drunk," said Solares of his American star. "That was the first thing to say about him. All day long, every day. He had a small doctor's case that was supposed to contain make-up. But hidden in the middle, he had a tequila bottle—with a straw sticking out. Whenever he'd need a makeup change, he'd go for that straw. Also, Chaney didn't speak any Spanish, so his voice had to be dubbed in later. But the producer forced me to use him because of his status as a horror star." Solares' preferred genre was comedy, and his favorite comedian was Tin Tan, with whom Solares made an amazing 40 films and who Solares considered "a genius." Solares made one further foray into werewolf territory with the deliriously entertaining *Santo and Blue Demon vs. the Monsters* (1970).

The nonsensical (but not in a good—nor entertaining—way) *Face of the Screaming Werewolf* is chock full of people we don't know doing things for reasons we don't know involving other characters we don't know. Why watch *Face*? I honestly don't know.

With quotes from: *Interviews with B Science Fiction Stars and Horror Heroes*, by Tom Weaver; "Director Gilberto Martinez Solares," by Brian Moran, *Santo Street* 18.

Morphology: The original Wolf Man himself (south-of-the-border style)
Demise: Bludgeoning with a flaming torch
Full Moon Rating: *½

The Feeding

(2006; Lionsgate) Director/screenplay: Paul Moore; Producer: G. Scott Tanner; Cinematographer: Todd Gilpin. Cast: Courtney Hogan, Dione J. Updike, Andrew Porter, Roderick Shephard, Jennifer Leigh, Kara Marin Amedon, Robert Pralgo.

> As the Full Moon Rises, They're About
> to Discover a New Breed of Terror—trailer

Actually, the full moon has nothing to do with this "new breed of terror," for the *Feeding* lycanthrope stalking the two rangers and a group of campers is a "theriomorph—something that can change shape at will," as one character explains. Never mind that a theriomorph is actually an artifact (such as a vase) in the shape of an animal and has nothing to do with lycanthropy or even general shapeshifting—that would be closer to a therian*thrope* (a being partly human and partly animal in form). Fortunately, that little etymological detail is one of the few things this low-budget (about $160,000) but surprisingly effective lycanflick gets wrong.

When all the game disappears from an Appalachian forest, the local rangers suspect a rogue predator has been decimating the fauna. The Wildlife Department in Washington, D.C., sends Special Officer Jack Driscoll (named, no doubt, in a nod to Bruce Cabot's heroic character from the original *King Kong*), played by Robert Pralgo, along with animal behaviorist Aimee Johnston (Dione J. Updike) to track and kill this dangerous animal before human casualties ensue. Too late; the beast has already claimed two hunters, and it subsequently slays a local ranger. Jack and Aimee soon realize that this is no rogue cougar, bear or wolf, but a creature with almost human intelligence. The beast sets its lycanthropic sights on a group of twenty-something campers in the area, killing several in one go, then picking off the rest one by one as the rangers try to lead them out of the forest, culminating in a final confrontation with the massive man-wolf at a hunting cabin.

The film opens promisingly with a well-constructed, atmospherically-staged scene of two rednecks doing a bit of nighttime hunting out of the back of their pickup. Rather than startling a deer with their flashlights, however, they encounter the creature. Afforded only brief glimpses of a large, hairy shape moving towards their truck, they fire, sending the huge silhouette to the ground. When the first hunter cautiously approaches the creature, it suddenly revives and slashes the man's throat. With the second hunter scrambling for the supposed safety of the truck cab, he (and we) see a huge, toothy muzzle in the rear view mirror before the sequence concludes with a long shot of the truck rocking back and forth as the man screams and the monster growls—and rips and shreds.

After this the movie settles down to introduce its characters—Jack and Aimee, who evince an easy chemistry in their intelligent banter and faintly antagonistic interactions, and the seven twenty-something campers (three couples and a female third wheel). The script takes the time to flesh out what could be simple monster fodder figures into individual characters. While attractive enough, they're not the typical Hollywood bimbos and pretty-boy jerks one sees in the average slasher flick. And while sex and weed *are* on the menu, they interact in a playful yet refreshingly adult manner. Even the seemingly obligatory skinny-dipping scene, in which all four actresses reveal their charms, sees them unaffectedly chatting amongst themselves rather than coquettishly flirting like oversexed adolescents. Consequently, when the beast begins its attacks on these well-rounded characters at the film's half-way mark, it brings with it a heavy dose of genuine shock and suspense to go along with the blood and guts.

At this point the film ratchets up into a taut, gripping run-and-fight scenario, with the surviving characters trying to hold it together and think their way out of this terrifying situation as the beast methodically separates them and brutally picks them off, causing the final trio to make a stand at a hunting cabin. The characters act believably, even intelligently. Forced to make difficult choices, both practical and moral, as they run and battle for their lives, they display enough courage—and make enough reasonable mistakes—to make them seem genuinely human rather than sudden superheroes or simply stupid. There's nary a Rambo-wannabe in sight; instead, normal people react to an abnormal situation the way normal people might (i.e., terrified and confused, and finding inner strength that doesn't automatically imbue them with Navy Seal or Ninja skill sets). It makes for a refreshingly realistic scenario (well, as realistic as an oversized-werewolf-stalking-campers-through-the-woods scenario *can* be anyway).

Director Paul Moore stages scenes simply but effectively, and employs some clever technique to enhance the expected monster-movie tropes, including a distorted iris effect for the *de rigeur* beast-vision p.o.v. shots (thankfully used sparingly) and even mounting an *effective* false scare. Cinematographer Todd Gilpin's efficient lighting in his ambitious night-for-night photography gives the film a far richer look than its meager budget should allow. Unfortunately, in a rare misstep, Moore and Gilpin sometimes shroud the creature in a gauzy glow via filtered photography, as if they have little faith in the monster's appearance. At other times they photograph the beast with crystal clarity, resulting in the odd dichotomy drawing attention to itself.

Moore need not have worried about his werewolf, however, for this massive monster appears both imposing and frightening (if not always entirely convincing), particularly given the up-angle shots of it standing and snarling and breathing heavily that emphasize raw power and terrifying presence, as well as the revealing glimpses of its vicious, gruesome actions (which include gory throat-ripping, hearts pulled from chests, and a nasty bit of impromptu spine removal). Moore eschews the easy out of cheap CGI to employ only practical effects, including utilizing an animatronic werewolf head to augment the man-in-a-suit monster. Said suit looks striking. Standing seven feet tall, with a huge mutant wolf's head—all leathery ridged skin over what looks like exposed jaw tendons, and long muzzle full of huge fangs—topping its powerful, shaggy body, it sports a raised spinal ridge along its hirsute back and a (somewhat unfortunate) rat-like tail.

Though the moon remains a non-issue (as does nighttime itself, as one kill takes place in broad daylight), the film adheres to the notion of silver being deadly to lycanthropes by cleverly incorporating a character's "lucky silver dollar" into the werewolf's eventual demise. More importantly, the movie adds a monstrous twist to the notion of lycanthropy by making the werewolf into a thinking predator who hunts in cycles and always covers its tracks. Jack and Aimee ultimately glean that this creature follows a pattern—a pattern Jack has encountered twice before (while tracking a rogue bear in Washington State and a wild cougar in Arizona). As he tells Aimee, "This thing is migrating. As near as I can tell, it feeds off the game animals until an area is dry. Then it just kills whatever it can find. After that it goes into hibernation for the better part of a year. Also, each time so far the killings stopped each time we bagged a rogue. But the tracks never matched up. It's like this thing—it knows to move on once we've made our kill. Basically it's framing the other animals." And this monster, who, observes Aimee, "doesn't act like a predator, it acts like a serial killer," cannot afford to leave witnesses. "Now that we've seen it, if we escape it can't hide anymore."

But writer-director Moore nearly drops the ball at one point when Aimee and her companion stumble across some wild wolfsbane as they desperately try to make their way back to her jeep. She identifies it as "a poisonous plant the Germans used to kill wolves back in the Seventeenth Century." Unfortunately, the film—and Aimee—does nothing with this notion, leaving it lying right where she found it (rather than trying to utilize this seeming botanical windfall as a bit of protection or even a weapon). "But it's not indigenous to this continent," continues Aimee. How did it get here? She has no idea, but does comment that "It's also associated with the presence of..." before leaving the word "werewolf" hanging. So this potentially intriguing twist on classic folklore becomes a mere throwaway discovery to provide the heroine with the opportunity *not* to say aloud what the viewer already knows.

In fact, oddly, no character *ever* utters the "w" word, though they dance around it on several more occasions. Perhaps that's intended to make the notion more believable—as if they were all too afraid to say the word and so perhaps make it true (though, really, in such an obvious situation, when each and every survivor has been convinced they're being stalked by a genuine lycanthrope, wouldn't *someone* be shouting "werewolf" to the rooftops rather than coyly alluding to it again and again?).

For much of the movie's running time it seems that this might not be a true werewolf film after all, but merely a movie about some mysterious hybrid beast (à la 2012's *Dogman*, for instance), but the suspenseful, clever finale puts paid that notion when the mortally wounded creature transforms (off-screen) back into a man. This does point up a weakness in the movie's structure, however—that it might just as well have been a rampaging bigfoot movie, or a story about *any* intelligent stalking predator. "Who was he?" asks a survivor about the dying man-wolf, to which Aimee answers, "Does it matter?" Well, only if you want to play up either the mystery or tragedy angle inherent in the werewolf mythos. But taken on its own terms, and given *The Feeding*'s broader focus, then no, it really doesn't matter here.

Filmed for three weeks in August and September 2004 on location in Virginia under the shooting title *Wolfsbane*, the re-titled *The Feeding* made its inauspicious debut on the SyFy Channel (then still utilizing the more prosaic "Sci-Fi" spelling) in 2006. It really deserved better. Director of photography Todd Gilpin compared *The Feeding* with *Jaws*, his all-time favorite film, by stating, "It's the same kind of thing, except it's a werewolf instead of a shark." Well, not *quite* the same thing. Though one can't fault Gilpin's enthusiasm, realistically, his film is more sand shark than great white. Still, even with its minor flaws, *The Feeding* stands as an intelligent, character-rich, well-acted and suspenseful addition to the werewolf canon, which becomes particularly notable given its low budget *and* the fact that the mid–2000s were less than kind, quality-wise, to lycan-cinema.

With quotes from: "Wolf's Tale," by Beth Jones, *The Roanoke Times*.

Morphology: A "Big Bad Wolf" (as described by one character)—huge, hairy biped topped with mutant wolf's head
Demise: Arrow tipped with silver
Full Moon Rating: ***½

Frankenstein and the Werewolf Reborn! see *The Werewolf Reborn!*

Frankenstein Meets the Wolf Man

(1943; Universal; b&w) Director: Roy William Neill; Producer: George Waggner; Screenplay: Curt Siodmak; Cinematographer: George Robinson. Cast: Ilona Massey, Patric Knowles, Lon Chaney, Lionel Atwill, Bela Lugosi, Maria Ouspenskaya, Dennis Hoey.

IT'LL SCARE THE YELL OUT OF YOU!—ad line

Well, probably not. Not only has the film's three-quarter-century patina lost much of its terrifying luster, its at-times-juvenile script significantly interferes with the fright factor. Even so, this first ever pairing of two classic creatures still contains enough atmosphere, action, and out-and-out artistry to secure it a place in the werewolf pantheon. And despite its peccadillos, there's no denying its milestone status. *Frankenstein Meets the Wolf Man* can stand toe-to-toe (or paw-to-paw) with the original *The Wolf Man* in terms of importance to lycanthro-cinema. Though not as successful artistically as the original, it surpasses its progenitor in terms of werewolfery, not least because it features the first time Larry Talbot transforms into the Wolf Man

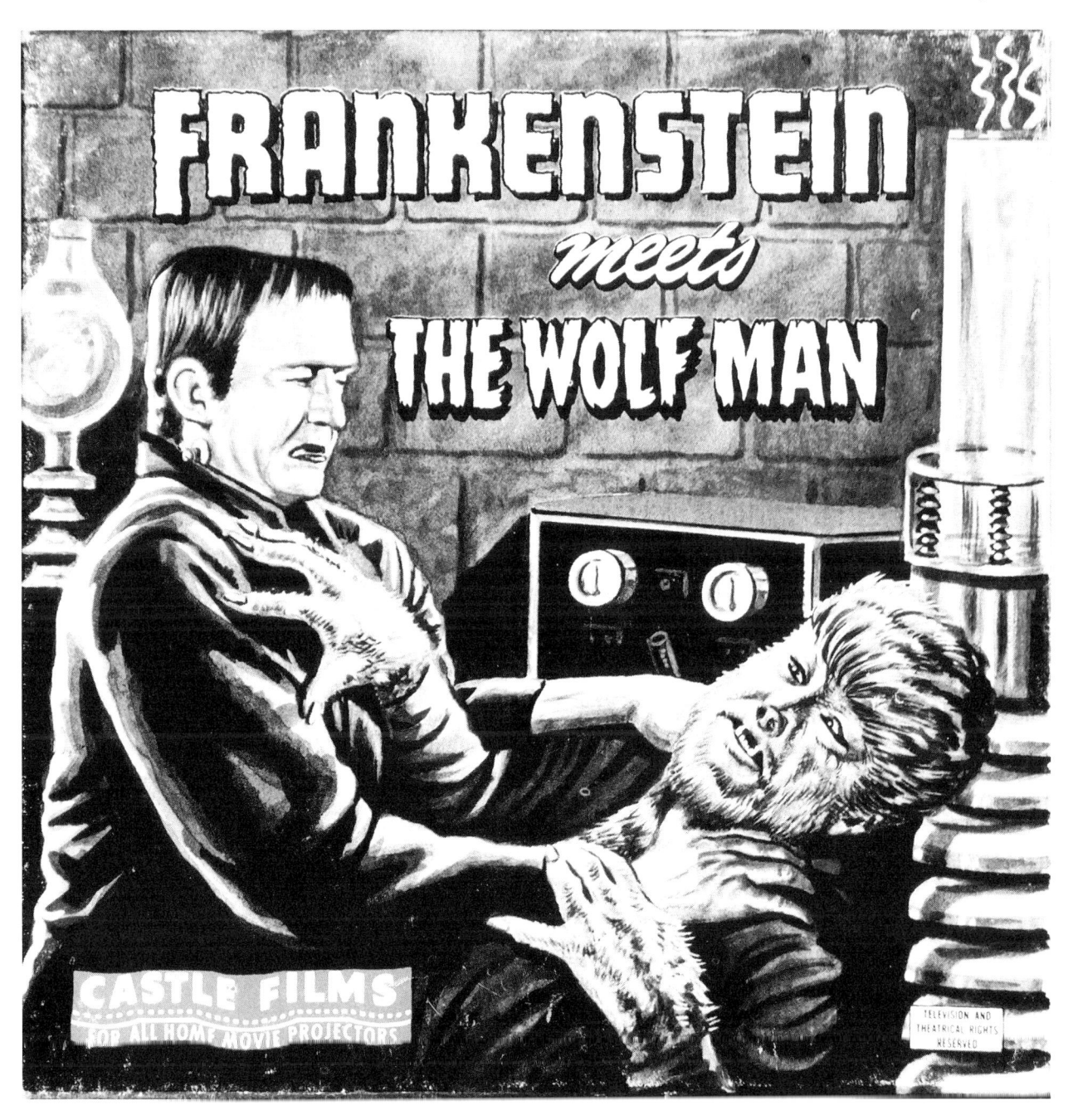

Though the box cover art for the 1960s Castle Films 8mm abridgment of *Frankenstein Meets the Wolf Man* **portrays the climactic battle between the two titans of terror, nearly three-quarters of the digest's running time consists of the eerie opening sequence in which grave robbers inadvertently reawaken the Wolf Man.**

onscreen (in the original we only see him change from werewolf back to man, and then only in death). *Frankenstein Meets the Wolf Man* (or *FMTWM*) also offers such superior scenes as the stunning opening graveyard sequence (arguably the most atmospheric of the decade), the Wolf Man's vicious attack on the Cardiff constable, and the lycanthrope's acrobatic climactic brawl with the Frankenstein Monster (billed as "the battle of the century" by Universal's PR boys). Additionally, this was the movie that inaugurated the "monster rally" concept that carries through werewolf cinema to this day (as evidenced by the successful *Underworld* and *Twilight* franchises).

But perhaps most importantly, at least to lovers of lycanthropic mayhem, *FMTWM* indirectly led to the birth of Waldemar Daninsky,

the most prolific werewolf character in cinema history. This was the film that inspired Paul Naschy to pursue his own destiny as a big-screen werewolf. Naschy wrote that after seeing *Frankenstein Meets the Wolf Man* as a young boy in Madrid, "from that day on Larry Talbot was my hero. After all, he was a good man whose only desire was to find a cure to free him from his need to kill. The stunning transformations brought on by the full moon really made an impact on me. I even recall that, on one occasion when my mother asked me what I wanted to be when I grew up, I replied, 'A werewolf.' You should have seen the look on her face!"

"In 1942, with the war raging," recounted screenwriter Curt Siodmak about how *FMTWM* came about, "I was having lunch in

Universal Studio's commissary when George Waggner, my producer, passed me on the way to the executive table. I was sitting with Yvonne de Carlo and Mary MacDonald. I wanted to show off my wit and said, 'George, why don't we make a picture, *Frankenstein Wolfs the Meat Man*—I mean, *Frankenstein Meets the Wolf Man*.' To 'wolf' somebody had the connotation of sexual harassment. I laughed, Yvonne laughed, Mary laughed, but not George. He only looked at me quizzically and walked on." Later, Waggner summoned Siodmak. "'Here is your assignment,' George said. '*Frankenstein Meets the Wolf Man*.' 'But it was a joke,' I said. 'Not anymore,' George said. 'I give you two hours to find a brilliant idea.'"

Said "brilliant idea" begins four years after the events of *The Wolf Man* when a pair of grave robbers break into the Talbot family crypt on a full-moon night and inadvertently free a revived Larry Talbot (Lon Chaney, Jr.) from his entombment. Found unconscious in the street the next day, Talbot ends up at Queen's Hospital in Cardiff as a head-injury patient (the result of his father's alacrity with a silver-headed cane at the climax of *The Wolf Man*). Talbot's attending physician, Dr. Mannering (Patric Knowles), only thinks him mad when Larry tells him he's a werewolf. So Talbot makes his escape and searches Europe for the old gypsy woman Maleva (Maria Ouspenskaya), "the only one who understands." When he finds her, she tells him, "I know a man who can help you," and takes Larry to Vasaria in search of Dr. Frankenstein. But, of course, Frankenstein is dead (after the events of *The Ghost of Frankenstein*). The full moon transforms Larry into the Wolf Man, who kills a local girl, then falls into an ice cavern beneath the Frankenstein Castle ruins while fleeing a mob of angry villagers. Waking the next day, Larry discovers the Frankenstein Monster (Bela Lugosi) frozen in the ice and thaws him out, hoping the brute can lead him to Frankenstein's diaries (which, he believes, will provide Larry with a way to die). But the weakened Monster cannot help, and Larry turns to Elsa, Frankenstein's daughter (Ilona Massey), and Dr. Mannering, who has trailed Talbot to Vasaria, to restore Frankenstein's laboratory and "drain off the energies" of both the Monster and himself, thus ending both creatures' reigns of terror. But at the last moment, Mannering has a change of heart and fully restores the Monster. Just then the moon rises, and Larry transforms. With the two creatures battling to the death, a villager blows the dam above the castle. Mannering and Elsa escape, but the resulting flood waters wash the two monsters to their doom.

When one thinks of *Frankenstein Meets the Wolf Man*, one can't help but think of "Poor Bela"—Bela Lugosi, that is, whose straightened circumstances in the 1940s saw him taking on the role of the Frankenstein Monster, a part he'd so famously spurned back in 1931 (paving the way for Boris Karloff to rise to stardom and ultimately supersede Lugosi in the horror actors pantheon). Now donning the famous head piece and asphalt spreader's boots himself, Lugosi failed to cover himself with thespian glory as the Monster. His stiff-armed, straight-legged gait, his bewildered expressions, and his too-round, too-fleshy face makes him the object of caricature rather than chills. To be fair, blame must be shared with screenwriter Curt Siodmak. As a sequel to both *The Wolf Man* and *The Ghost of Frankenstein*, Siodmak's *FMTWM* script called for the Monster to be nearly blind *and* to talk (like he did at the close of *Ghost*). Though three scenes of Monster dialogue were shot, the studio nixed them all ("with Lugosi [the dialogue] sounded so Hungarian funny that they had to take it out," claimed Siodmak), leaving the actor's stumbling portrayal unexplained—and inexplicable—to viewers. (Despite Siodmak's aspersions on Lugosi's delivery, in truth, the lines were so ludicrous that *no one* could have carried them off with any semblance of seriousness.) In some scenes, such as when the Monster leads Talbot to Frankenstein's lock box, you can even see Lugosi's lips silently moving. Beyond Lugosi's artificial awkwardness (a stark contrast to Karloff's expressive, loose-jointed movements), the 60-year-old actor frequently looks tired (and was doubled by stuntman Eddie Parker for much of the picture).

Universal originally intended that "The Screen's New Master Character Creator" (as their publicity dubbed him)—Lon Chaney, Jr.—play *both* monster roles. As *Variety* (May 6, 1942) reported: "Universal is playing double-header in spinal-chills. Studio is tossing its *Wolf Man* and *The Ghost of Frankenstein* into one horrendous grapple. Lon Chaney Jr. ... is slated to clinch with himself in a duplex monstrosity titled *Wolf Man Meets Frankenstein*. General idea is that two monsters are better than one when they work on the same salary, even though there are no priorities on monsters."

Such was not to be, however, as cooler heads prevailed, leaving room for Lugosi to step into the Monster's shoes.

But a bigger problem than a wobbly Monster is Siodmak's slipshod screenplay, which features not only some unlikely plotting, but poorly motivated characters spouting near-risible dialogue. Siodmak appears to have exhausted himself on his original *Wolf Man* script and expends little creative energy on this sequel which Waggner thrust upon him. With *FMTWM*, Siodmak, who thought of himself as a novelist first, let his disdain for Hollywood screenwriting seep through. Several ciphers—er, characters, behave oddly for no apparent reason apart from simple convenience. For instance, when Elsa meets Talbot, who's masquerading as a buyer for her late father's estate, she responds to his duplicity with a calm smile and a pleasant inquiry as to what she can *really* do for him! Any reasonable individual would at least become a bit peevish, if not violently angry, at having been lured all the way to Vasaria under false pretenses just to be grilled by a churlish oaf wishing to acquire her father's scientific secrets. Then there's Dr. Mannering, who, by his own admission, has abandoned his practice in Cardiff to follow Talbot "all across Europe" for months because he ... er ... wants to bring Talbot back to England and lock him in an insane asylum. Of course, given the claptrap Siodmak forces the doctor to speak, it's no wonder Mannering has no sense of reason or proportion in his actions. "People with brain injuries sometimes develop super-normal mental powers that are quite extraordinary," he pronounces. No they don't. Never in the history of medicine has a brain injury resulted in *any* improvement in "mental powers." (In a thirty-year health-care career working with head-injured and neurologically-impaired patients, this author has never seen any indication of a brain injury improving *anything*.) And, of course, after Mannering promises to destroy the Monster by "draining off his energies," he abruptly changes his mind at the last second because "I can't destroy Frankenstein's creation; I've got to see it at its full power." What?! Where did *that* come from (apart from the expedient pen of a tired scriptwriter)?

Balancing out Siodmak's and Lugosi's shortcomings are the deft direction of Roy William Neill (best known for guiding Basil Rathbone through his prolific Sherlock Holmes film series, as well as directing Boris Karloff in his remarkable double role from 1935's *The Black Room*); the fluid camerawork of cinematographer George Robinson (*Dracula's Daughter*, *Son of Frankenstein*, and the two subsequent Wolf Man sequels *House of Frankenstein* and *House of Dracula*); the impressive Gothic settings of John Goodman and R.A. Gausman (*Son of Dracula*, *Phantom of the Opera*); and the breathless beauty of (top-billed) heroine Ilona Massey, whose curvy form in her diaphanous nightgown nearly steals the show from the headlining monsters. Then there's the impeccable work of effects genius John P. Fulton, whose flawless transformation scenes stand as the best of their kind; and, of course, the sympathetic presence of Lon Chaney, Jr., juxtaposed with his animalistic savagery when sporting the iconic Jack

Pierce makeup. With its final cost of $238,000, Universal spent a third more on *Frankenstein Meets the Wolf Man* than its progenitor, the original *Wolf Man*. Consequently, the film certainly *looks* good.

"With an idea like that [Frankenstein meeting the Wolf Man] you need a gimmick to write the story around," noted Siodmak. "So I had the Wolf Man meet the Monster while he is looking for Dr. Frankenstein—because the doctor knows the secret of life and death, and the Wolf Man wants to die. But the Monster wants to live forever. It's ironic. That's the gimmick." Fortunately, it was a bit more than a simple gimmick, for Siodmak, despite his obvious case of writer's weariness, further develops his central Talbot character; with Lon Chaney, Jr., who considered the Wolf Man his "baby," making the most of it. Talbot's bewilderment in *The Wolf Man* has now evolved into grim resignation. After Larry revives in the Cardiff hospital, he recognizes, "I can't die." Chaney's mixture of awe and despair at this horrific realization—that he is doomed to go on killing forever—and his subsequent desperate determination to end his life, codifies the tragedy of the lycanthrope, of someone who has lost control of his very nature to the point that death has become the only option. It's potent stuff, brought nightmarishly home by Chaney's sincere playing. When Larry tells Mannering, "I only want to die," or, later, "I don't want to live through another spell," Chaney's simple honesty hammers home the heartbreak of his situation.

"Lon played the part of Larry Talbot with a sincerity that gave that film a value of fear and pity," observed Siodmak." The writer, who befriended the actor and worked with him on several subsequent occasions, went on to conjecture that "being cruelly mistreated as a child by his famous father, Lon Chaney Sr., Lon suffered from clinical depression, which he tried to overcome by his addiction to alcohol. I knew Lon until his premature death in 1973, a tragic character who couldn't adjust himself to life. He was the Larry Talbot in *Frankenstein Meets the Wolf Man*, who wanted to die. In that picture, Lon played himself, which made his part frighteningly believable."

Fortunately, it was not all doom and gloom on the set. "I think Lon Chaney is one of the nicest, sweetest people in the world," recounted co-star Ilona Massey. "It was a great deal of fun." (Unlike with Evelyn Ankers in *The Wolf Man*, Chaney and his *FMTWM* leading lady got along swimmingly.) "You know it took four hours to put on his makeup and when it was on, it was hot under the lights, it was very difficult for him to eat. He mostly had soup which he sipped through a straw, and just for fun we put hot peppers in it! We had a lot of fun ... everyone had fun in the picture."

Regarding the much-heralded climactic battle between the Wolf Man and the Frankenstein Monster ("*Diabolical Murder Monsters.... Lusting for a* DEATH-DUAL!" heralded the ads), such hyperbolic labels as "TITANIC COMBAT" and "THE BEAST BATTLE OF THE CENTURY" rather overstated the point. The admittedly furious fray (as the lithe Wolf Man athletically lunges, leaps and slashes at the hulking Monster, who tosses the manbeast around like a doll) is sweet but short, taking up little more than a minute of screen time. And, disappointingly, it ends before any conclusion can be reached, as the water from the blown dam cascades onto the combatants, leading to an exterior shot of the (model) castle crumbling under the tidal wave onslaught. Still, it makes for an exciting—if not wholly satisfying—monster-clash conclusion that can't help but appeal to the inner Monster Kid in all of us.

Supported on a double-bill by *Captive Wild Woman* (another shapeshifting saga), *Frankenstein Meets the Wolf Man* made a huge splash at the box office, reaping great financial rewards for Universal and paving the way for more monster rallies to come, including that studio's own *House of Frankenstein* and *House of Dracula*. And despite its obvious flaws, it also provided additional depth to one of lycancinema's founding characters, further cementing the Wolf Man's place in the annals of horror history.

With quotes from: *Memoirs of a Wolfman*, by Paul Naschy; *Wolf Man's Maker: Memoir of a Hollywood Writer*, by Curt Siodmak; *Universal Horrors*, by Michael Brunas, John Brunas, and Tom Weaver; "An Interview with the Outspoken Sultan of Speculation: Curt Siodmak, Part Two," by Dennis Fischer, *Filmfax* 14; "Interview: Ilona Massey," by James Miller, *Varulven* 4.

Morphology: *The* classic Wolf Man (of course)
Demise: Raging torrent ... though only until the next sequel
Full Moon Rating: ***½

Frankenstein's Bloody Terror

(1968/71; DC Films/Independent International; Spain/W. Germany) Original Language Title: *La Marca del Hombre Lobo*. Alternate Titles: *Hell's Creatures* (UK); *Mark of the Wolfman* (unofficial DVD). Director: Henry L. Egan (Enrique L. Eguiluz); Producer: Maximiliano Pérez-Flores; Screenplay: Jacinto Molina (Paul Naschy); Cinematographer: Emilio Foriscot. Cast: Paul Naschy, Diana Zura (Dianik Zurakowska), Michael Manza (Manual Manzaneque), Anita Avery (Aruroa De Alba), Rosemarie Winters (Rosanna Yanni), Gilbert Granger (Julián Ugarte).

> SEE—THE "WOLF MONSTER" attack—LUSTING, SLASHING, RIPPING in a Gory, Flesh-Hungry, Blood-Mad Massacre!—ad line

Subtlety in advertising was never Sam Sherman's forte (American patrons were promised a free burial for anyone who died of fright during the film's showing; the undertaker is still waiting...). Sherman, co-founder of the distribution company Independent International, was in trouble. He'd promised a group of exhibitors that he'd have a Frankenstein film for them by a certain date ("Frankenstein" still being deemed box office at the time), but had nothing along those lines. The solution? Take a recently acquired import, an atmospheric 1968 Spanish werewolf-and-vampire flick called *La Marca del Hombre Lobo*, and re-title it as a Frankenstein movie. To at least pay lip-service to the Franken-notion, Sherman commissioned animator Bob Le Bar to create a brief prologue that showed a cartoon Frankenstein Monster changing into a fanged Paul Naschy and then into a werewolf! Adding some bombastic narration ("Now, the most frightening Frankenstein story of all, as the ancient werewolf curse brands the family of monster-makers as 'Wolfstein'"), Sherman had F. Neumann re-edit the Frankenless film to become *Frankenstein's Bloody Terror* ("in Super 70mm Chill-O-Rama") for 1971 drive-in patrons.

This first introduction of Waldemar Daninsky (Paul Naschy) as the Wolfman has him slaying a revived werewolf (with a sharpened silver cross) and in the process becoming infected himself. In desperation, he contacts a strange couple, Dr. Janos Mikhelov (Julián Ugarte) and his wife Wandessa (Aurora de Alba), experts in the occult, for help. (As evidenced by a pre-production document housed at the Spanish Instituto Nacional de Cinematografía, sixties Continental scream queen Barbara Steele was initially slated for the role of Wandessa; that would have been a casting coup indeed, though De Alba delivers an appropriately sinister and erotically-charged performance.) The pair turn out to be vampires, leading to a supernatural showdown, with Waldemar's friend Rudolph (Manual Manzaneque), and Waldemar's true love, Janice (Dianik Zurakowska), caught between a vampire and a were-place.

Paul Naschy's first Waldemar Daninsky werewolf film, 1968's *La Marca del Hombre Lobo* (Mark of the Wolfman), made it to America in 1971 as the nonsensically titled *Frankenstein's Bloody Terror*, courtesy Independent International, who needed a Frankenstein film to fulfill booking commitments. Company head Sam Sherman simply tacked on a bogus opening narration to justify the Frankenstein-less film's title change. Ironically, this ad features a rendering of a Frankenstein Monster (not to mention a photograph of Boris Karloff from the original 1931 *Frankenstein*!) *and* a vampire—but no werewolf (though note the fangs and wolf ears on comic book artist Gary Morrow's drawing of the Monster).

Despite its deceptive marketing strategy and living-in-the-past advertising ("See—The Wolf Monster! The Vampire-Doctor! The Ghoul-Woman!" hyped the film's trailer in ballyhoo straight out of a 1940s monster-rally), *Frankenstein's Bloody Terror* proved innovative in several ways. It introduced Paul Naschy and his signature Waldemar Daninsky the Werewolf character (who rampaged through a dozen subsequent films) to America. It opened the door for the coming Spanish horror boom. It melded the Gothic atmosphere of Universal with the eroticism of Hammer. And it brought the werewolf into the gory limelight by letting the blood flow freely for the first time in lycan-cinema history. "Moreover," observes Spanish horror film expert Nicholas Schlegel in his groundbreaking *Sex, Sadism, Spain and Cinema*, "in a storytelling strategy that predates (by thirty-five years) the popular and extremely lucrative movie and novel franchises *Twilight Saga* and the *Underworld* series, *La Marca del Hombre Lobo* features multiple werewolves pitted against multiple vampires."

"My first starring role was in *La Marca del Hombre Lobo*," recounted el Hombre Lobo himself, Paul Naschy. "Once the script was completed, they needed someone to play the werewolf part. Basically, they wanted Lon Chaney Jr., but he was too old and refused their offer. So, because I'm an actor first and foremost, I immediately accepted this role, which the German co-producers offered me."

"The Germans wanted an Anglo-Saxon sounding name for the film's overseas distribution," continued Naschy, who was born Jacinto Molina Alvarez. "They didn't want a Spanish name. They called me from Munich, telling me they needed a pseudonym within an hour, or they would pick one themselves for the publicity materials! I grabbed a newspaper, found an article on Pope Paul VI and chose Paul as the Christian name. Then I remembered a dear weightlifting friend of mine—I was the Spanish weightlifting champion some time ago—whose name was Naschy [actually Hungarian Imre Nagy], and this is how I became Paul Naschy."

Labeled "the first real Spanish horror film" by Eurocinema scholars Cathal Tohill and Pete Tombs, *Frankenstein's Bloody Terror* was also the first Paul Naschy–starring movie, a subset that went on to encompass over 75 feature films (nearly half within the horror genre) and four decades. "The film was a big budget effort for the time, shot in 3D and 70mm widescreen."

Penned by first-time scripter Naschy himself (under his real name of Jacinto Molina), "the screenplay," observed Schlegel, "written by a fan rather than a professional, lacks the finesse or sophistication of a seasoned screenwriter, but this potential detriment becomes the film's greatest asset; impassioned enthusiasm compensates for amateurism (and this came to define Naschy's early work)." And while the dialogue (abetted by some unfortunate, stilted dubbing) and simplistic plotting does indeed smack of "amateurism" for the film's prosaic first half, once Daninsky turns wolf, the script takes a hard right into near-surreal brutality and erotic Gothicism. At this point the heretofore straightforward werewolf tale (obviously patterned after the original *Wolf Man*) offers up such unique elements as a pair of Satan-worshipping vampires plotting to control the lycanthrope ("Prince of Darkness," intones Janos, "possess this man soul and body!"), the bloodsuckers erotically entrancing the two young protagonists as their anguished fathers frantically search for their missing offspring, and the manipulating undead reviving the original werewolf (yet again) in order to test the strength of their new lycan-pet in a lupine-a-lupine battle to the death.

With all this taking place within authentic medieval settings, lit with atmospheric artistry by cinematographer Emilio Foriscot (*Face to Face* [1967], *The Case of the Scorpion's Tail* [1971]), the film becomes a visual Gothic delight. In addition to the dusty, rubble-strewn catacombs (to which Waldemar has retreated while searching for a cure) festooned with cobwebs, chains, skeletons and torture devices, the producers secured such stately Madrid locations as the Marquis of Cerralbo estate (today the Cerralbo Museum) and the Castle of San Martin de Valdeiglesias, their impressive halls bedecked with tapestries, suits of armor and ancient weaponry that offer authentic production values which Hollywood at the time simply couldn't replicate. As Schlegel notes, "Although set in the present day, the film benefits from its stately locations, which lend the work a distinct 'period piece' aura."

Under Enrique Eguiluz' assured direction, Foriscot's camera moves frequently, often dollying in towards characters to generate a claustrophobic feel within the imposing settings, as if trapping the protagonists (and the viewer) within its gaze—and perhaps within the ever-tightening noose of destiny. And the talented cinematographer employs an atmospheric color palette that would make even Mario Bava proud, with swirling fog picking out shafts of green, blue and orange light to enhance the eeriness—or shock, in the case of the transformation scenes, which see Waldemar illuminated in an angry, savage red.

Said metamorphoses reflect the film's very nature—simple but with added details that raise them above the mundane and render them surprisingly effective. As Waldemar clutches his chest and writhes in pain, the lighting dims, then goes red, while the picture grows hazy and distorted (via some carefully-placed Vaseline on the lens) before clearing to reveal the Wolfman. Though less complicated than the expected lap-dissolves (which subsequent Daninsky entries embraced), it's more creative than the usual cutaways. Enhanced by angry-sounding drumbeats and otherworldly choral chanting on the soundtrack (replacing—and improving—the repetitive bombast of the original Spanish score here), and underscored by the fiery red lighting on the creature's hirsute countenance, the change becomes one of horrific proportions.

Naschy cuts an impressive lycan-figure (patterned after his self-professed "hero," Lon Chaney, Jr.) with his wild eyes, prominent protruding fangs, and face fully covered in dark coarse hair. The actor immediately crashes through a closed window, leaving the red-lit, confining interior for the blue-tinged wilderness outside, like a beast seeking the cool sanctuary of nature. Once again, the evocative color schemes add visual and emotional texture. Naschy's energetic performance manifests itself with his Wolfman's first attack. The beast impressively bursts through the door of a gamekeeper's hut, splintering the wood, to viciously attack the man, tearing at his throat before tossing him into the fire, then leaping upon the man's grown daughter to leave *her* throat a scarlet mess while her father helplessly spits up blood and writhes in the flames. It's a brutal, pitiless, and gruesome introduction to the monster Waldemar has become. (Though somewhat truncated for the American release, it still remains powerfully disturbing in its ferocity).

This marks a turning point in the film, as the heretofore rather tame bit of Eurogothic shows it means business. Never before in a lycan-flick had the blood been so red and flowed so freely. Not to mention the burning alive of a dying victim. This alone marks *Frankenstein's Bloody Terror* as a watershed werewolf movie, as it became the first to drag the werewolf's nature from the darkness of suggestion into the blood-spattered light of undisguised savagery.

Curiously, Naschy fills his script with religious references. "Please pray, Rudolph," the tormented Waldemar implores after his first horrific night as the beast. Stumbling into a church, he splashes holy water onto the pentagram-shaped wound on his chest, as if trying to ward off the coming change through the power of God. At one point Janice takes up a crucifix by her bedside and kisses it, again referencing the protagonists' appeal to—and trust in—the divine for help. But all this religious observance and supplication avails them naught, reflecting, perhaps, the Catholic-raised Naschy's ambivalent views about the Church.

Unfortunately, it's not all fun and (werewolf) games, as the film falters at the finish line, offering a disappointingly tame vampire-vs.-werewolf climactic confrontation (something Naschy would correct—with relish—in his later *Werewolf vs. the Vampire Woman* and even more so in *The Craving*). When the Wolfman catches up with the fleeing Janos, they grapple perfunctorily for a few seconds before the beast abruptly bites Janos' neck. Vaseline goes back onto the lens, and a few flames spring up in the foreground to consume the vampire, leaving only a smoldering cloak on the ground. Cue Janice, who "loves him enough to die for him" and a date with some silver bullets. Abandoning the glorious eccentricities of the movie's second half, the film returns to the prosaic as the tragic music swells on the soundtrack and the camera reveals the dead Waldemar, human once more, freed from his curse.

Though he doesn't proffer much personality in human form (character development consists of a taciturn delivery and a perpetual look of mild concern), Naschy's Waldemar Daninsky, like any good lycanthropic antihero, is bursting with pathos. After recovering from his first horrific transformation, Waldemar implores Rudolph, "When this happens to me, you must use that pistol. You've got to shoot me. Please don't let me murder again." And Waldemar isolates himself in the catacombs beneath an abandoned monastery, locking himself into a cell at night to protect others from what he's become.

By Naschy's own admission, he went through "five interminable hours of torture" under makeup man Jose Luis Ruiz' steady hand to become the werewolf. And playing a bloodthirsty lycanthrope was not easy. "I remember a violent scene in which the Wolfman is on the rampage," wrote Naschy in his autobiography. "Craving fresh human blood he smashes his way through the door of a gamekeeper's house. Instead of making a false door frame out of balsa wood, the SFX people, with a laudable sense of economy, merely made a few cuts in the real, massively compact door. On hearing the magic word 'action!' I went hurtling at the door like a meteor and nearly smashed myself to a pulp. I broke through the door but the impact left me black and blue all over. On another occasion while filming in the underground tunnels of the Conde Duque barracks in Madrid, I nearly suffocated amid all the smoke that we were using for atmospheric fog."

Despite such trials and tribulations, Naschy possesses a real affection for his character. "Daninsky is a Polish name I gave to my werewolf, thinking of the oppressed people of Poland," explained the writer-actor. "My character is bitter, persecuted and misunderstood, the bearer of a curse he cannot shake off. In the end, he is forced to kill without wanting to. Aware that his romantic affairs have no future, he seeks them out only to get rid of his curse."

Naschy has obviously taken his troubled character to heart. "Quite simply, it's me. The pity is I can't become a werewolf in true life. All too often I would like to. It's obvious that in the works of every man there is much of his true self. Like Waldemar, I too have been left aside and misunderstood. I have spent all my life swimming against the current."

Though he may not have made a particularly big splash in said current (American current, anyway), Naschy has his following—those fans who appreciate and enjoy his endearing enthusiasm and heartfelt affection. As the 1970s progressed, Naschy's continuing werewolf series opted for increasing dollops of nudity and gore (not to mention outlandish plotting), culminating in the delicious delirium of such entries as *The Werewolf vs. the Vampire Woman* (1971) and *Night of the Howling Beast* (1975), arguably the best—or at least most entertaining—of the bunch.

"Some people like my work and others do not," Naschy observed philosophically in an early 1990s interview, "but that is a matter of personal taste. In life, you cannot keep everyone happy, and it is pointless to try. Instead, you must do what you feel.... It is sad that many modern directors are exploiting and abusing this audience [of horror fans] with bad films. They try to appeal to them by title, take their money, and leave them disappointed. In my prime, I always gave the public what I thought they wanted. I was a horror fan myself before I became an actor, director and screenwriter, so I knew first hand what some of their tastes were. I'd like to think I reached my goal in keeping horror fans happy and entertained. If not, at least I gave them my best effort."

With quotes from: *Sex, Sadism, Spain and Cinema*, by Nicholas G. Schlegel; "Paul Naschy: Spain's Greatest Horror Star," by Lucas Balbo, *Psychotronic 7*; *Immoral Tales*, by Cathal Tohill and Pete Tombs; *Memoirs of a Wolfman*, by Paul Naschy; "Horror with a Spanish Twist: Paul Naschy," by Dale Pierce, *Filmfax 33*.

Morphology: Savage Chaney-esque wolfman
Demise: Silver bullets
Full Moon Rating: ***½

Full Eclipse

(1993; HBO Pictures) Director: Anthony Hickox; Producers: Peter Abrams, Robert L. Levy; Screenplay: Richard Christian Matheson, Michael Reaves; Cinematographer: Sandi Sissel. Cast: Mario Van Peebles, Patsy Kensit, Bruce Payne, Anthony John Denison, Jason Beghe, Paula Marshall, John Verea.

A SECRET ELITE PACK WITHIN THE L.A.P.D. ARMED, OUT OF CONTROL … AND OUT FOR BLOOD—tagline

The beautiful Patsy Kensit takes on a Wolverine sheen in the werewolf-cop actioner *Full Eclipse*.

Hotshot L.A. police officer Max Dire (Mario Van Peebles) is near burnout, with the cynicism and depression engendered by the street violence he witnesses every day spilling over into his troubled marriage. After his partner commits suicide under mysterious circumstances, Max is offered a position on an elite team, backed by the mayor and headed by Captain Adam Garou (Bruce Payne). "Adam isn't just a detective," explains sexy team member Casey (Patsy Kensit), "he's also a scientist." Well, he's actually a werewolf who has mastered his "condition" and who has created a "drug" that enhances his team members' abilities, making them stronger, faster, and impervious to harm (apart from silver). Reluctantly drawn into the "Pack," Dire discovers the truth (they carry out clandestine vigilante attacks to decimate the gangs and drug lords of L.A.) and, with help from the smitten Casey, sets about bringing down the now-out-of-control Garou.

A wild, bloody, excitingly-staged shootout at a nightclub opens this made-for-HBO production, indicating the movie's action-oriented roots, which wind throughout the various violent free-for-all raids by the Pack, and culminates in a Max-vs.-full-on-werewolf climax. "I love action movies and I love werewolves, so it was just perfect!" enthused director Anthony Hickox, who brought another werewolf to the screen (briefly) in *Waxwork* (1988).

More than just a series of near-balletic action set-pieces, however ("I'd been watching all the John Woo," admitted Hickox, "this was before everyone else started doing it; and I'd been watching all these crazy Hong Kong action movies, and I was like, 'well this would be a great thing' about all the slow motion and all the double gun stuff"), *Full Eclipse* offers involving characters brought to realistic life by charismatic actors. With his cool confidence, measured intensity, and penetrating gaze, Bruce Payne (*Passenger 57*, *Howling VI* [playing a vampire rather than a werewolf]) makes for a magnetic and seductive villain that can hold his own even against Van Peeble's likable, scene-stealing presence. They make a perfect study in contrasting pro- and an-tagonists.

Like with the far more famous (and groundbreaking) *Night of the Living Dead*, *Full Eclipse*'s hero being African-American was merely a happy accident. "I'd just seen that cowboy movie he'd made," recalled Hickox, "*Posse* [which Van Peebles also directed], and I thought he'd be great. And I sent him the script, and he said, 'I love it.' It's funny because the part was never written for a black guy and, even when I sent it to Mario, it was written for a white guy. He said *Full Eclipse* was the first script he'd ever got that didn't outright say 'a black guy' in it."

Van Peebles was drawn to the project by what he called "man's fascination with his animal nature, or his animal side. We've always been curious about our evolution from beasts, and our connection to them. I always wanted to play a werewolf or a vampire, or something of that nature. It's very cathartic to be these different people, see what they feel and let that part of you go. It's healthy to do this." He also appreciated the multi-layered nature of the script. "You can read this on several different levels. That's what I find attractive. You can look at it on the drug level, you can look at it on a sexual level, on all kinds of sociological levels. Or just roll with it as a film."

Also multi-layered is the character of alpha male Adam Garou, who revels in the power (and license for violence) his lycanthropy brings, and enjoys dominating those around him. The scene in which he completely subjugates a quaking Casey through his mere will remains a disturbing standout. At one point Garou complains, "I hated being at the mercy of the lunar cycle. So primitive. Pathetic." Garou employs "biofeedback, drugs" to overcome this monthly cycling (and, by extension, *feminine*) trait of lycanthropy. Lest one become too excited about the intellectual potential of *Full Eclipse*, however, this intriguing feminism subtext remains unexplored, buried under all the gunfights and macho posturing, with the female characters, including Casey, largely leaving it to the males to sort things out.

But the film does take on another social issue more directly—that of drug addiction. Garou's serum, which temporarily elevates the taker to near-superhero status, carries with it both a psychological and physical toll. His pack members become like addicts craving the rush, and he even cows Casey by threatening to withhold her dose. When Max encounters the sole surviving member of Garou's previous pack from Miami, the man is a physical wreck, his features disfigured (crystal meth–like) and his mind consumed with hatred for Garou. "I took it too many times," he laments. "I can't go back; it strips your glands." Even the dialogue slyly ties lycanthropy to addiction, with Max resisting temptation by jokingly responding to Casey's urgings with, "I gonna have to 'just say no.'" And later, when he confronts Garou and his Pack as they prepare for yet another bloody raid, Max rails at them, "This neo–Nazi supercop bullshit—you're swallowing his insanity right now. Go ahead, shoot up." When Max finally learns that the mysterious drug is not a product of chemistry but is actually Garou's own cerebral fluid extracted directly from his brain, Garou mocks dismissively, "This is my brain. This *is you* on my brain. Any questions?"

Richard Christian Matheson and Michael Reaves' script, originally titled *The Pack*, offers more depth than many a were-story, both in terms of character and thematics. "I've never been a fan of werewolf movies," admitted the prolific Matheson (son of famed novelist and screenwriter Richard Matheson). "As soon as they transform, they seem kind of benign to me." (Obviously he hadn't been watching the *right* werewolf movies.) "If the script was going to be about werewolves, I also wanted it to be about addiction and overcoming the controlling influence of the lunar cycles." And *that* he and his writing partner accomplished in spades, for it's not a curse or a bite that creates werewolves here, but the injection of a drug.

The Pack members don't grow fur or transform into canines like typical lycanthropes, however; rather, Wolverine-like claws sprout from their knuckles, their brow ridges become somewhat distended, their ears take on points, and their teeth elongate into fangs. Also, though enjoying enhanced physical abilities, they maintain their human faculties, employing guns as well as claws. This look stemmed from a combination of director Hickox' love of comic-book characters and classic horror. "I'm a huge comics fan; I read a lot of Marvel Comics, so I had a look I wanted," explained Hickox. "Superheroes gone wrong, the whole Marvel mutant thing." Hence the Wolverine-like claws. "I wanted the wolves to look like the first actor [Henry Hull] who played one in *Werewolf of London*," continued the director. "We were going for a cross between him and Oliver Reed from *Curse of the Werewolf*."

Keeping within the lycan-traditions (at least the cinematic ones), these werewolves can be hurt by silver (it causes their flesh to bubble and burn). And though full moons need not apply (it's the serum, coupled with adrenaline as they go into "battle," that triggers the transformation), a lunar eclipse is a special case. During said climactic event, Max shoots Garou with a silver bullet—to no effect. "Didn't you get my memo?" sneers Garou. "A full eclipse protects me from *everything*—including silver." And here is when the more traditional Big Bad Wolf comes out to play. "Now you wanna see something *really* scary?" taunts Garou (a famous line lifted from *Twilight Zone: The Movie*). Walking purposefully towards Max, Garou raises his arms and morphs into a huge, fur-covered, wolf-headed biped. Though imposing in its massive size, this shaggy were-beast seems a little too bear-like in appearance to fully satisfy. Hickox wasn't particularly happy with it either. "The thing with the end werewolf is that it was done very late so we couldn't really work and refine it," lamented the director. "It's like a first draft of what it was meant to be, and it kind of just always pissed me off that we didn't get into it earlier…. It's the fact it's so unmovable. It's kind of like wearing a suit of armor…. Like the guy inside couldn't even move the wolf's hand, it was that heavy!" As a consequence, the long-looked-for battle between Max and the Garou-beast seems hurried, with too many quick cuts giving it a disjointed feel. Still, it fittingly concludes on an emotional note, with the now-human-again, dying Garou imploring, "Max, don't let it all end here. Lie down in my blood. Take my power. Protect the innocent" (a novel, if odd, notion—that the werewolf can pass on its power to someone who basically bathes in its blood). Garou, though a monster, was not necessarily "evil." He truly did feel he was on a mission to fight crime, and he wants what he started to continue past his own existence. This quality adds further layers to what could have been a simple power-mad villain character. As actor Bruce Payne observed, "I found a lot of undercurrent issues within this character of a police officer who really feels he's a shining knight. This bad guy thinks he's a good guy; he believes he's on a good quest."

And those open-minded viewers wishing to see a different, multi-layered, actionful (if not altogether perfect) take on the traditional cinematic lycan-tale would do well to make a quest of their own and track down *Full Eclipse*.

With quotes from: "Cops and Werewolves: A *Full Eclipse* Retrospective with Director Anthony Hickox," by Matty Budrewicz, *UK Horror Scene*; "*Full Eclipse*: Police Lycanthropy," by Anne Moore, *Fangoria* 129.

Morphology: Fanged, pointy-eared humans; furry, wolf-headed biped
Demise: Silver nitrate
Full Moon Rating: ***½

Full Moon High

(1981; Filmways Pictures) Alternate Title: *A Transylvanian Werewolf in America* (Australia); Director/Producer/Screenplay: Larry Cohen. Cinematographer: Daniel Pearl. Cast: Adam Arkin, Roz Kelly, Ed McMahon, Joanne Nail, Bill Kirchenbauer, Elizabeth Hartman, Kenneth Mars, Alan Arkin.

> HE'S TODAY'S TEENAGE WEREWOLF … ONLY THE RULES HAVE CHANGED!—poster

Director/writer Larry Cohen makes good, quirky mutant-killer-baby movies (*It's Alive* [1974] and *It Lives Again* [1978]). He makes good, quirky giant monster films (*Q, the Winged Serpent*, 1982). And he even makes good, quirky blaxploitation flicks (*Black Caesar*, *Hell Up in Harlem* [both 1973]). But if *Full Moon High* is any indication, what this low-budget indy auteur can *not* do is make a good horror-comedy, quirk or no quirk.

In 1960, Tony (Adam Arkin) is the star quarterback of the Full Moon High School football team. Looking forward to the big game against their rivals, Tony ends up accompanying his CIA-employed father (Ed McMahon) to Romania on a trip to pick up some secret microfilm. "Romania," enthuses his dad, "it's quite a country. It's deep behind the Iron Curtain. It's steeped in the superstitions of the Dark Ages. A country warped by ignorance and fear. You'll love it." Once there, Tony encounters a mysterious woman who reads his palm and tells him he will live forever—and that "when the moon is full, don't make any appointments, you'll be busy." Laughing it off ("I am not one of those types to believe in things like vampires and werewolves and virgins—I've never seen any of those"), Tony walks home alone, only to be attacked by a huge, wolfish creature. Returning to America, Tony now periodically transforms during the full moon into a hirsute, slobbering teen who goes about gently biting the locals, resulting in newspaper headlines like "WEREWOLF ANNOYS COMMUNITY" and "PLAYFUL NIPPINGS CONTINUE." After his father is killed in a freak accident in his basement bomb shelter, Tony drops out of school and leaves town, abandoning his team before the big game. Twenty years later Tony returns, having aged nary a day. With the town in disarray and his beloved high school nearly in ruins, Tony poses as his own son and re-enrolls, intending to restore the good name of Full Moon High by helping to beat their rivals for the first time in two decades.

Full Moon High takes a "spoofy" tack in its humorous course, rather than letting the laughs arise more naturally from situations and characters, à la *An American Werewolf of London*. (At one point Cohen ill-advisedly mocks that werewolf classic, whose agonizing, prolonged transformation scene broke new ground in werewolf cinema, by having Tony declare during his first transformation, "God, this is worse than a root canal.") Consequently, *Full Moon High*, unlike *American Werewolf*, offers no real horror nor suspense, nor even drama, along with its gags and giggles, since nothing is taken seriously. Such an approach *can* work (Mel Brooks' *Young Frankenstein* being a brilliant example), but Cohen is no Brooks, and the various jokes and comical set-pieces fail more often than they succeed. Most of the laughs arise from the playing of a few veteran performers— Kenneth Mars (who, incidentally, featured in Brooks' *Young Frankenstein*) as the closeted gay football coach, an over-the-top but genuinely funny Ed McMahon (yep, Johnny Carson's sidekick) as Tony's anti-commie and sex-obsessed dad, and, most particularly, Alan Arkin (Adam's real-life father) as the insulting psychiatrist (whose breath-of-fresh-air appearance comes all too briefly only at the end). Unfortunately, the film offers them only limited screen time, with the majority of the picture taken up by the strained comedy and unfunny antics of the other performers. While Adam Arkin brings a laid-back likability to the role of Tony, he often can do little with the desultory dialogue and silly situations. For instance, walking home alone on a dark Romanian night, Tony seeks directions at a lonely farmhouse, only to be startled by some sinister violin music. As the violinist looms into view, breaking the fourth wall, Arkin reacts in fear. Silly. Then, when he spies the approaching werewolf's silhouette, he calls out, "Hey, is anybody here with this dog? Don't dogs have masters here, or only musical accompanists?" Finally, after getting a good look at the snarling beast, he deadpans, "*The Call of the Wild*—I got a B-plus on

Before *Teen Wolf* there was cult filmmaker Larry Cohen's *Full Moon High*, a spoofy (and far less successful) effort to make high school werewolves hip.

that report. I'm very big on wolves—very very big. Nice wolf, nice wolf. I'm sorry I called you a dog before." The sophomoric dialogue and Arkin's calm delivery drains the scene of whatever menace it might have held—which is too bad, given that this werewolf stands as a striking specimen. With its glowing red eyes, furry wolfish face (complete with huge, snapping jaws), hulking body suit covered with hair, upright posture, and throaty growls, it could be *The Howling*'s lycanthropes' younger half-brother (or at least second cousin). Alas, Cohen's script and Arkin's can't-take-it-seriously attitude makes a mockery of this potentially frightening manbeast, particularly when Tony tells it, "Alright, pee on me and let's call it a night, ok? Ruin a pair of shoes but leave the throat alone." Worse, once the creature pounces on him, Arkin continues to feebly protest and then starts to act like he enjoys the nipping—as if receiving some kind of lycanthropic hickey.

After this solitary scene, all further werewolfery is handled by Arkin himself, who sports a *Werewolf of London*–lite makeup (though lacking the satanic quality of that Jack Pierce creation) that sadly reflects his lycanthrope's ridiculously mild demeanor. (As Tony declaims in human form, "I've never killed anyone—I nibble!") Tony's sparse wolfman visage completely lacks the all-important wolf-nose appliance, and offers only bushy eyebrows, long sideburns, and a set of elongated teeth to indicate he's anything other than an ill-kempt highschooler with hygiene issues. And Tony-wolf does little but run about advancing on screaming coeds, who invariably show up with a tiny bandage on their derrieres the next day. His nocturnal noshings do offer Cohen the opportunity to include a clever montage of amusing newspaper headlines to represent Tony's 20 years of globe-trotting before his return: "HAIRY FIEND BOTHERS NEW YORKERS," "JACK THE NIPPER STILL AT LARGE," "WOLFMAN EATS CHINESE. THIRTY MINUTES LATER, HUNGRY AGAIN."

In terms of werewolf lore, the film adheres to the common cinematic rules of the full moon triggering the transformation, the afflicted's lack of conscious control while in bestial form, and the notion of the werewolf's immortality—barring a silver bullet. However, it glosses over the very important notion of transmission. While Tony is infected by being bitten by a werewolf, *his* various nips and nibbles result in no more than sore backsides for his victims. By rights, the countryside should be overrun with werewolves by now, though perhaps his wolfman-lite affliction has been diluted enough so that he's no longer infectious. In any case, such considerations—as well as consistency itself—take a back seat to the various kitchen-sink, hit-and-miss gags. Even the sanctity of the tried-and-true silver bullet falls foul of the cheap laugh. At film's end, though shot and ostensibly killed by the silver loaded-gun-wielding psychiatrist, Tony eventually opens his eyes, sits up, and looks directly at the camera to tell us, "Don't worry, with today's inflation, it takes more than six shots to kill a werewolf," before romping off into the brush in search of Miss Montgomery, who apparently *was* infected by Tony ("It's your turn to bite *me* now…"). It all closes on a family photo of the pair of them with a quartet of hairy werewolf babies.

Star Adam Arkin has commented, "We all look to have transcendent experiences that lift us out of the everyday, and fear is a good one. But, I think it's the same reason why people want to laugh their heads off." Unfortunately, with *Full Moon High*, the viewer experiences precious little of either.

With quotes from: "Adam Arkin," *buddy TV* website.

Morphology: Lightly hirsute two-legged wolfman
Demise: Silver bullets … but not really
Full Moon Rating: **

La Furia del Hombre Lobo see *The Fury of the Wolfman*

The Fury of the Wolfman

(1972; CIC; Avco Embassy; Spain) Original Language Title: *La Furia del Hombre Lobo*. Alternate Title: *Wolfman Never Sleeps*. Director: J. M. Zabalza (José Maria Zabalza); Producer: Maximilian Pérez Flores; Screenplay: Jacinto Molina (Paul Naschy); Cinematographer: Leopoldo Villaseñor. Cast: Paul Naschy, Perla Cristal, Veronica Lujan, Michael Rivers (Miguel de la Riva), Mark Stevens, Diana (Pilar Zorilla), Jose Marco, Francisco Almoros, Javier Rivera, Ramon Lillo, Fabian Conde.

WAS IT MAN … ANIMAL … OR WOLFMAN?—ad line (whose question, given the film's title, seems to have a rather obvious answer)

Though produced in 1970, this third Waldemar Daninsky film—after 1968's *Frankenstein's Bloody Terror* and 1970's *Assignment Terror* (and not counting the never-finished/released *Nights of the Werewolf*)—was shown theatrically only in Spain and Argentina, and then not until two years later. It made it to America only via television, when Avco Embassy packaged it for the product-hungry airwaves in 1974.

When Walter/Waldemar (the name inexplicably changes during the dubbing) Daninsky (Paul Naschy) returns from an ill-fated expedition to Tibet, during which he barely survived an attack by a strange beast he thinks was a yeti, he learns that his beloved wife has been unfaithful. During the next full moon he transforms into a werewolf, kills his wife and her lover, and then ostensibly dies from electrocution when he encounters a downed power line. Daninsky's scientific colleague and old flame, Dr. Ilona Alman (Perla Cristal), realizing he's not really dead (he'd confided in her about his fear of transforming into a werewolf), digs up Waldemar's body and takes it to her ancestral castle home, where the obsessed mad scientist intends to dominate her old lover with sound waves and "chemotodes." But Ilona's sympathetic assistant Karen (Veronica Lujan) has fallen for Waldemar and tries to help him escape, with the two battling a bevy of "mutant" experiments Ilona keeps in the castle dungeons. Finally, after Ilona has revived Waldemar's dead wife, now also a lycanthrope, and set the two werewolves against each other, Waldemar turns on Ilona, who fires a silver bullet into his heart before dying herself at his side.

Paul Naschy himself labeled *Fury of the Wolfman* "a nonsensical movie" whose many failings lay at the feet of "a half-crazy director and an alcoholic named José Maria Zabalza." Of course, Naschy also called it "a film that didn't work too badly." Didn't work *at all* is more like it, thanks to its confusing storyline, mismatched footage, poor staging, stilted dialogue, and bizarre kitchen-sink approach (though sometimes this offers moments of near-surreal delirium that, while not at all credible, at least holds the boredom at bay).

This Werewolf's *Fury* remains as uneven as the picture itself, partly because of the unfortunate choice to a) insert poorly-matched werewolf footage from the earlier *Frankenstein's Bloody Terror* to pad the running time; and b) utilize a double for Naschy to save further time and money. "The fellow swaggered around more like a Madrid city pimp than a ravening beast," complained Naschy. Actually, he walks about more like a somnambulist in search of a bed, his slow, tentative movements at odds with Naschy's more vigorous and energetic demeanor. For instance, at one point the wolfman double quietly opens

98 • *The Fury of the Wolfman*

a window and calmly climbs over the sill; whereas Naschy's werewolf had earlier leapt through a closed window. The mismatched insert shots stolen from the earlier film prove far more atmospheric as well, the evocative lighting and energetic staging underlining the banality of the new, inferior footage.

Lycan-wise, this *Wolfman* goes beyond the expected full moon and silver bullet tropes to inject a few novelties into the notion. Strangely, the curse of lycanthropy here originates in the wilds of Tibet rather than its usual haunts in the dark forests of Transylvania (a notion that Naschy would revisit—to far greater effect—in the superior Waldemar Daninsky entry *Night of the Howling Beast*). Further, the victim of a werewolf may become a lycanthrope even if he or she is *killed* in the attack—*if* the victim's heart is pierced by the claws of the beast. As Ilona tells the horrified Waldemar upon presenting the revived corpse of his dead wife, "When you clawed through her throat you also clawed through her heart, and so the curse you brought back from Tibet has been transferred to her now." Additionally, though a silver bullet will do the trick, a werewolf can also be killed by another lycanthrope. Waldemar himself tragically tells Karen, "I have to be destroyed either by another beast or the hands of a woman who loves me enough to kill me using a silver bullet."

Naschy's makeup here remains far from the best of the series. Though sporting a wicked-looking set of fangs, and thick hair covering his head, cheeks and chin, a sparsely-covered nose and almost bare center of his face negates this *hombre lobo*'s usually more savage look. The picture does boast a decent time-lapse transformation sequence, however. As he lay in his bed next to his wife, Waldemar professes his love to her—just before he metamorphoses into a violent monster. Unlike in many a Naschy werewolf movie, however, the change comes quickly and painlessly—one minute he's talking to her ("Erika, you're mine—why can't you realize it?—for you I'd die a million times just so you'd love me"), then seconds later he's a werewolf biting into her throat.

Ilona's castle houses various oddities, including a group of hippie hedonists; a gaggle of filthy men chained in a dungeon; a cape-wearing Phantom-of-the-Opera figure prowling the corridors; a man in a full suit of armor who attacks Waldemar for no apparent reason; someone—or some*thing*—hiding in some bushes who reaches out to grab Waldemar's legs, only to be met by the business end of Waldemar's axe; "hermetically sealed" doors that trap our protagonists within the castle; and a pair of corpses hidden behind a freshly painted wall. Though sounding rather eventful, it's all presented in such a disjointed and poorly-staged manner that the only impression made is one of confusion.

The film that made Paul Naschy cry—*The Fury of the Wolfman*, arguably Naschy's worst Waldemar Daninsky outing (Argentinean poster).

A raft of nonsensical, stilted dubbed dialogue completes the picture of a disorganized production. For example: "You know about my investigations.

And if I succeed, all of the violence, all the instincts that are lack of love, will disappear. Mankind is wrong in its thinking, and these things will change." Or: "But after the doctor's preliminary phase, they'll be authentical mutants, and always they'll live in darkness." At the very end, the inspector wraps things up with, "Not even the most fervent imagination could conceive of even half the horrors that we've seen," before, without skipping a beat, adding, "Look what a beautiful day it is."

"I wrote this film," stated Naschy, "with the intention that it would be directed by Enrique Lopez Eguiluz, who had helmed the first film in the series [*Frankenstein's Bloody Terror*]. As a matter of fact, the opening superimposed Tibetan scenes were filmed by him. All of a sudden the producers discharged Eguiluz and replaced him with José Maria Zabalza…. We began shooting, and what happened was that this gentleman, from the very moment that he arrived on the set, was completely drunk. What's more, he began re-writing my script, eliminating much of my role." Naschy characterized Zabalza as the Spanish film industry's very own Ed Wood; and given the muddled mess that resulted, he may not have been far wrong.

The picture does offer some rather unique and twisted sexual dynamics, however (though the characters' behaviors and motivations frequently make no more sense than the rest of the confused story line). "Very soon you'll be the beast that I dominate," Ilona enthuses at one point, before donning an elegant evening gown and whipping the transformed Daninsky, who's chained to the wall. She then embraces the apparently-cowed wolfman and passionately *kisses* the beast—who enthusiastically responds by gently sliding down her dress as she pushes herself upon him, marking him as the screen's first lycanthropic lothario.

At another point the werewolf escapes the confines of the castle and ends up in the bedroom of a naked village girl (or *nightgown-wearing* village girl in the censored version). But rather than leaping upon her and tearing out her throat (as the wolfman previously did with his own wife), the lycanthrope simply lays down beside her. The next shot shows the manbeast calmly rise up and depart, leaving the girl breathing heavily (in agony or ecstasy?)—just before a police inspector bursts in and tells her to "calm down," covering her nakedness with a sheet. Did the werewolf ravish her? Did the wolfman engage in a bit of hirsute snogging? Did the beast simply cuddle? Even Naschy has no answers here, as this was undoubtedly another supercilious sequence filmed without his participation.

The version of *Fury of the Wolfman* commonly available in America (on several bargain-bin DVD labels) is a truncated TV print, taken from 16mm, which deletes all of the nudity and most of the sexual undercurrents. For those truly interested, the full-length version (taken from a Swedish print) can be had on grey market DVD under the title *Wolfman Never Sleeps*. While the uncut version sheds no more clarity on the story, it at least ups the interest level with its bizarre sexual subtext.

The Fury of the Wolfman is the only film that ever made Paul Naschy cry. "I can tell you," the actor admitted, "it was one of the few times in my life that I've cried—only with the death of my father, and also that of a friend—but with this film, I came to cry out of helplessness for the tragedy of what this man [Zabalza] had done to me. That included the impudence of shooting scenes without me; for example, those scenes of the Wolfman walking along the street like a normal person—that is not me!… This man crippled a film that could have been quite good. This is the most unfortunate title in my filmography."

"Once the film was completed," recalled Naschy, "a private screening was arranged for a potential distributor. When this man arrived in his car, his headlights focused upon a guy urinating in the street. The distributor asked who it was, and was informed it was the director of the film, José Maria Zabalza; whereupon the man left without ever seeing the screening." With *Fury of the Wolfman* being the worst of Naschy's vintage Waldemar the Werewolf efforts, perhaps that was just as well.

With quotes from: "Interview: Paul Naschy," by José Luis González and Michael Secula, *Videooze 6/7*; *Memoirs of a Wolfman*, by Paul Naschy.

Morphology: Upright-walking wolfman (and wolfwoman)
Demise: Silver bullet, and strangulation by a fellow lycanthrope
Full Moon Rating: *½

Game of Werewolves

(2011; Vertice Cine; Spain) Original Language Title: *Lobos de Arga*. Alternate Title: *Attack of the Werewolves* (UK). Director/Screenplay: Juan Martinez Moreno; Producers: Tomás Cimeadevilla, Emma Lustres; Cinematographer: Carlos Perro. Cast: Gorka Otxoa, Carlos Areces, Secun de la Rosa, Mabel Rivera, Manuel Manquiña, Luis Zahera, Marcos Ruiz.

ONE VILLAGE, THREE HEROES, LAUGHTER
OF TERROR—(Spanish) trailer

Though somewhat awkward in translation, the trailer's trumpeting of "LAUGHTER OF TERROR" turns out to be right on the money when it comes to the Spanish horror-comedy *Game of Werewolves*, whose laughs, many of them pitch-black, perfectly complement its terrors.

Struggling writer Tomas Marino (Gorka Otxoa), who's authored one book ("and nobody read it"), returns to his ancestral village of Arga after fifteen years to try and pen his second novel—and to attend a "tribute ceremony" as the guest of honor (he being a published author and all). It soon becomes clear that here "guest of honor" translates as "sacrificial lamb" when the villagers truss him up, along with his literary agent Mario (Secun de la Rosa), and dump them through a trap door in a forbidding barn into a warren of underground tunnels that run beneath the local graveyard. With the help of Tomas' sheep-loving childhood friend Calisto (Carlos Areces), they escape the clutches of the massive werewolf (!) imprisoned in the catacombs. A century ago a persecuted gypsy placed a curse on the tyrannical (and pregnant) Marchioness Marino, wife of the local lord. "At the age of ten," recounts Calisto, "her son would become a wolf and bring death and evil to the village. Only when 100 years had passed, 100 years exactly, if the beast devoured a male Marino, with the same blood in his veins, then the curse would disappear and the beast would return to its human form. But if that didn't happen, an even greater evil would fall on the village." Tomas is that male Marino. Avoiding both the bloodthirsty villagers and the now-escaped werewolf, the trio, aided by Tomas' tough grandmother and a stoic local cop, must face down the "even greater evil" that arrives the next night when the "second curse" takes effect and all hell breaks loose.

Writer Kurt Vonnegut once said of the concept of black humor, "The biggest laughs are based on the biggest disappointments and the biggest fears." And few fears are bigger—or more primal—than that of being dismembered and eaten. In this "Comedia Bestial" (Bestial Comedy), as the film's Spanish poster proclaims it, black comedy gallops through the film like a mighty were-steed.

The werewolf's initial appearance is, like so much in the movie, a winning combination of horror and humor. When the camera first

The best werewolf film since *Dog Soldiers*, the clever, suspenseful, frightening and funny Spanish horror-comedy *Lobos de Arga* became *Game of Werewolves* in America. Note how the overt comedy portrayed in the original Spanish poster was toned down in favor of a more menacing image for the American version.

zooms in on its savage countenance, the creature opens its maw and roars. The scene then cuts to a reaction shot of Tomas and Mario standing stock still, eyes wide in frozen terror. Up above in the graveyard, Calisto opens up a hole beneath a grave (led there by Tomas' dog Vito), with the tombstone crashing down upon the hairy form directly below. "Calisto, help us! Do something!" Tomas shouts up to his friend. Suddenly the worm-riddled arms of a rotted corpse drop down through the hole, causing Tomas and Mario to scream. "Grab on!" cries Calisto, who uses the disinterred cadaver like a ladder to pull them up from the tunnel—and beast—below!

The film's lycanthropic set-pieces reflect both comedy and terror, beginning with the very first attack. Not knowing the werewolf has escaped the tunnels, two armed villagers stand shoulder to shoulder guarding the barn's entrance. As one casually glances to his left, two huge, hairy hands silently drop down from above, wrap themselves around his companion's head and yank him upwards out of frame. His oblivious compatriot then turns back only to find his friend gone in a moment both disturbing and comical.

The next lycan set-piece continues the pattern. The village innkeeper and his wife awaken to noises coming from the bar below. As the man creeps downstairs with his shotgun, the creature rises up from behind the bar (having eaten their pet rabbit). Mere feet away, the man raises his gun, takes careful aim at the monster's head, and pulls the trigger—just as his wife calls out, "You forgot the cartridges."

Click. The beast then lashes out and with one blow decapitates the forgetful barkeep. Timing is indeed everything.

And the movie's final coda—regarding the protagonists' "little problem" (two of them have been bitten)—is as funny as it is clever. But far from a silly spoof or lightweight comedy, this *Game* is played straight, as are the truly terrifying monsters. The comedy arises naturally from the characters' reactions to the horrific absurdity of the situations. This *Game* has bite, too, leaving most of the characters either dead or maimed.

The clever script offers some amusing word play (often at the expense of the local yokels) that works even in translation. When Tomas meets his uncle, he tells him, "One of the reasons I'm here is to get back to my roots, look for inspiration in the past, give the muse a call, you know." At this, his puzzled relative helpfully volunteers, "We've still got a mutual exchange here, but if you're patient you can call anyone." Later, after the protagonists lock themselves away in a house against the rampaging werewolves, Calisto notes, "They'll be back. They're half animal, half man. They may be villagers, but they've got a bit of a brain." And at the climax, the protagonists barricade themselves in the church. "This is a sacred place," observes a hopeful Mario. "I bet they can't come in; they're cursed." Just then two werewolves violently crash through the stained glass windows to land right in front of them. So much for *that* theory.

When a pair of policemen arrive in the village that night, they're confronted by a gang of werewolves standing near their police car. The elder cop tells his rattled younger partner to lower his weapon and then calmly addresses the creatures. "Hello, good evening," he says evenly. "Please remain where you are, with your hands over your heads. Thank you very much, boys." To his partner he says, "We don't know if they're violent; we'll give them the benefit of the doubt." But when one lunges forward, the cop rapidly raises his gun and shoots the beast in the head! "Doubt resolved," he deadpans. At this, his junior partner rapidly empties his pistol magazine in a panic. But the next shot shows all the remaining werewolves standing right where they were. "Very good, Joaquin," says his partner wearily, "you've just wrecked the engine and probably the radio." The young man has shot their car multiple times but missed all the monsters.

Writer-director Juan Martinez Moreno effectively builds an atmosphere of menace right alongside the humor. When Tomas first arrives he finds the villagers decidedly unwelcoming, drawing curtains against him and staring with stony faces, unspeaking. As Tomas walks along a path, a man suddenly rushes at him with a huge scythe. Tomas panics and runs but immediately trips and falls. The menacing man stands over him and raises his wicked-looking blade to strike … and then merely lifts the tool's strap over his head and carefully sets it down before helping the lad to his feet. It turns out this is his Uncle Evanisto (the village's mayor and self-proclaimed priest) there to welcome his prodigal nephew. Like nearly everything in the film, things are not quite what they seem, as the ostensible menace turns out to be benign. But, cleverly, the paradigm soon shifts, and the now-benign turns out to be truly menacing after all (with this self-same uncle being the village leader that's lured Tomas into their sacrificial trap).

Moreno's screenplay gets to the heart of the matter quickly, when after only 20 minutes the villagers truss up Tomas and Mario for sacrifice (tying them to wooden crosses) and drop them into the tunnels to meet the dreaded werewolf. "I'm sorry, boy," his uncle apologizes. "If it's any consolation, think of Jesus. His sacrifice saved humanity. Yours will save a village." He tips the cross forward and cuts Tomas loose to fall screaming through the trap door. Through Moreno's deft direction, however, this puzzling, terrifying sequence ends on a very funny note. The stationary camera focuses on the stone wall of the tunnel as Tomas' flailing body passes in front of it to land with a thud below frame. Then, as Tomas struggles to his feet and rises back up into the picture, *Mario's* body comes tumbling down on top of him, taking Tomas out of frame again. They both immediately pop back up, with Mario complaining, "What a whack! It could have killed me!"

The laughter quickly gives way to fear once more, however, as the two skittishly explore the dank, creepy tunnels, leading to a horrifying discovery. Tomas and Mario spy what looks like a body beneath a burlap shroud, with bones strewn all about the byre. "Take a closer look," urges the timid Mario. "You fucking do it," snaps back a recalcitrant Tomas. "It's your village," answers Mario, to which Tomas responds, "No way! Madrid is my village." But, ultimately, Tomas hesitantly approaches and slowly reaches out for the sack cloth. As the tension mounts, a dirty hand suddenly shoots out to grip his wrist. While Tomas screams like a little girl the hand suddenly changes— the fingers elongate and grow hair, while dark nails spring forth from the fingertips, accompanied by gruesome snapping sounds, like bones twisting and breaking. Tomas rips himself away, and the form expands beneath the raggedy cloth; then, still covered, it rises up to tower over them like some filthy ghost-creature. "Run!" shouts Tomas, and the duo flee down the tunnel. The mobile camera—moving with them, letting them pass, then following behind—visually captures their sense of panic before a split-second shot shows a huge shape loom behind and then leap *over* them, plunging them (and us) into darkness as their torch goes out. It's a tension-filled, heart-stopping lycan-introduction indicative of how seriously the film takes its monster(s).

Though taking the standard werewolf-stalking-the-village approach for the first half, the movie turns things upside down when the "second curse" kicks in and the *entire village* transforms en masse into vicious lycanthropes who then chase and attack the small group of humans. Such a clever switch not only ups the lycan-ante but the action (and horror) quotient as well, leading to an exciting werewolf car chase (with the old auto driven by Tomas's tough *grandmother*), some impressive stunt work as werewolves leap twenty feet through the air to pounce on their victims, and a desperate final stand in the old church that ends with a literal bang.

The attacks come fast and furious, vicious counterpoints to the dark humor of the situation. As the protagonists try to flee in the grandmother's car, a werewolf leaps upon the hood and smashes its fist through the windscreen. When it grabs his grandmother's throat, Tomas sticks the monster in the eye with the car's red-hot cigarette lighter, sending the creature flying backwards. But the car stalls out, and the protagonists flee on foot. In the foreground, the wounded beast suddenly sits up from the pavement, its ferocious face filling the frame and its bloody, ruined eye socket *smoking* as it roars its rage after them.

The three quirky main characters—dim-bulb Mario, "yokel" Calisto, and city-wise but cowardly Tomas—though mildly buffoonish, each appear endearing in their own way. And when called upon, they come through (Calisto especially is quick with a plan and handy with a shotgun). Even Tomas steps up at the end, becoming a vengeful, determined hero after the shocking death of his beloved grandmother. Toss in a heroic, no-nonsense elderly policeman, and Tomas' cute and clever Jack Russell terrier (part "Asta" from the old *Thin Man* films and part "Gromit" from the British *Wallace & Gromit* series), and one can't help but root for these likable lunkheads.

Moreno, aided by cinematographer Carlos Perro, sets the stage beautifully through mobile camerawork and atmospheric lighting, the full moon eerily illuminating the old graveyard, for instance, and torchlight casting just enough flickering illumination in the tunnels to conjure all manner of shadowy horrors from the protagonists' (and viewers') imagination. Speaking of the lunar cycle, the full moon triggers the werewolves' transformation, with the creatures reverting back to normal at dawn (even the dead ones). Silver, however, remains a non-issue, as these lycanthropes succumb to everything from a shotgun blast to a shovel to the head.

Thankfully, Moreno wanted his werewolves to have substance, heft, and therefore eschewed CGI in favor of stuntmen in impressive-looking werewolf suits. These creatures, with their hulking hirsute bodies, sport striking red eyes set deep in a wolfish, fang-filled face. "Many movies just use CGI for budget reasons to save money," Moreno explained, "and sometimes to me when you have an action scene or a transformation scene and the CGI party starts, to me it looks like the Warner Bros. cartoons: like Wile E. Coyote and the Roadrunner. I still see the transformation scene in *An American Werewolf in London* and shit my pants! So from the beginning we tried to do it that way. We have a little CGI for the werewolf jumps to erase the cables and cranes, and in the last scene where [a character] becomes old. But most of the creatures and the action sequences we made for real."

Game offers more than just laughter and chills, as pathos comes into play when Calisto discovers the monster in its true form the next day—a cringing, frightened *ten-year-old child*. "None of this was his fault," observes Tomas' kindly grandmother, "the poor thing has been a victim all his life." This, along with the realistic—and likable—characterizations of the foible-prone protagonists, covers the film with the oh-so-important cloak of humanity worn by so many of the better werewolf movies.

When push comes to shove, none of the protagonists can bring themselves to kill the cursed boy. "So what do we do?" asks an exasperated Tomas. "It'll be night soon, and then Dennis the Menace here, or whatever he's called, will turn into a monster." It is indeed quite the conundrum, one solved in a gruesome, disturbing, and darkly comical fashion (of course) when Calisto has an idea. "Look, to break the curse, the beast has to eat a male Marino, right? As far as I know, the curse doesn't say he has to eat *all* of you. Maybe a finger would do." There then ensues a blackly comical sequence in which the two hold down an unconvinced, struggling Tomas. "One—two—" counts Calisto as he raises a cleaver over Tomas' forcibly extended pinky, then *shunk*! and the finger's off. At this Tomas screams in pain and cries out, "What happened to *three*, you bastard?!" As Tomas nurses his bandaged hand and downs a bottle of liquor, Calisto and Mario stare down at the severed digit. Calisto says, "I guess we give it to the kid." At this Mario asks, "Like that? Raw? It's a bit creepy." Calisto agrees, and the next shot shows the little finger frying in a pan, with Calisto reaching for garlic and parsley. But the kicker comes when they set the fried finger down on a plate in front of the boy, and Vito the dog suddenly snatches up the digit and eats it. The next scene shows Thomas pulling the cork from a bottle of booze with his teeth because *both* hands are now wrapped in bloody kitchen towels! The visual punchline comes with a few further verbal bon mots as well, with the drunken Tomas bitterly offering, "Go on, give my other finger to the dog. And give the kid my *balls* if you want to." The darkly hilarious sequence concludes when the boy finally eats the (second) finger, causing the watching Tomas to vomit. "Come on," offer a jovial Mario, "it's not that bad. You're lucky. Not many people can say they saw themselves being eaten." Indeed.

Why did Moreno choose to make a film about werewolves? "I think the reason is that Spain was conducive to werewolf movies," explained the writer-director. "I don't know if you know an actor/director called Paul Naschy, but he also made werewolf movies in the '60s and '70s. It's a big tradition. And there are so many movies and television series about vampires and zombies at the moment that I decided to go with this instead. Also, as a horror fan, I'm tired of watching these vampire and werewolf movies where they're cute and they fall in love and have children. That's crap! These things were created to scare, so I try to get that back a little bit."

Fully cognizant of his film's antecedents, Moreno was a fan of the werewolf subgenre. "There are some very clear influences on the movie," he explained. "I love the movies from the '80s, like John Landis [*An American Werewolf in London*] and Joe Dante [*The Howling*]. But also the classics, like the Universal films from the '30s, and *Curse of the Werewolf*, by Terence Fisher. That's a masterpiece, and it was wonderful for us because it was set in Spain!" But it took considerable effort to see his project to fruition. "It took five years to make *Lobos De Arga*," noted Moreno, "and four of those were looking for the money." Thank goodness he found it and gave to us this lycanthropic neo-classic.

Moreno filmed *Game* in the region of Galicia in Northwestern Spain. Galicia is "the only place in Spain where you can still find these kinds of magic traditions," said Moreno. "They have these old traditions about witches and about ghosts, and they don't only keep their traditions but they're very proud of them. It was the right place to locate the story."

Game of Werewolves did for lycanthropes what *Shaun of the Dead* did for zombies ... except *Shaun* was a big hit and received wide distribution in the U.S., whereas *Game* remains woefully—and unfairly—obscure to most American viewers. Don't let the nonsensical title fool you ("In America it's *A Game of Werewolves*, I guess because of *A Game of Thrones*," posited Moreno); for those looking for a funny, scary, affecting, and highly entertaining werewolf outing, this *Game* is one well worth playing.

With quotes from: "*Playboy* Interview: Kurt Vonnegut Jr.," by David Standish, *Playboy*, July 1973; "Night Visions 2012: Juan Martinez Moreno and *Attack of the Werewolves*," by Owen Williams, Empireonline.com.

Morphology: Fierce, shaggy manbeasts
Demise: Ordinary bullets, sharpened stakes, dynamite, even a shovel
Full Moon Rating: *****

Ginger Snaps

(2000; Motion International/Unapix Entertainment; Canada) Director: John Fawcett; Producers: Steve Hoban, Karen Lee Hall; Screenplay: Karen Walton (story: Karen Walton, John Fawcett); Cinematographer: Thom Best. Cast: Emily Perkins, Katharine Isabelle, Kris Lemche, Jesse Moss, Danielle Hampton, Peter Keleghan, John Bourgeois, Mimi Rogers.

They don't call it the *curse* for nothing—ad line

Fangoria magazine (the veritable Bible for contemporary horror fans) labeled *Ginger Snaps* not only "the most important horror film of 2001" (the year of its American release) but "the most fiercely original and intelligent social commentary ever to grace the genre." And it's a hard point to argue. Brimming with subtext on everything from the objectification of women to the soul-sucking conformity of suburban life, *Ginger Snaps* utilizes lycanthropy as a metaphor for the transformation of girl into woman, with all the hormonally induced confusion, rage and, yes, blood that entails.

"My first feature film, *The Boy's Club*, made in 1996, was a coming-of-age drama that featured 14-year-old boys," said *Ginger Snaps* director John Fawcett, "and I thought maybe it would be fun to work with girls next. Then I realized I had never come across a girl werewolf. It was a concept I had never seen before, and once I got into the writing process with Karen Walton we realized there were all these things that made it important the characters were female. Werewolves are linked to the cycles of the moon. We compared that with the menstrual cycle, and as soon as that clicked we realized it was deadly important the film be about women."

Two outsider sisters, 16-year-old Ginger (Katharine Isabelle) and 15-year-old Brigitte (Emily Perkins), spend their time photographing each other in staged death scenes (even making a pact: "Out by 16 or dead on the scene—together forever"). Meanwhile, a rash of horrible dog mutilations have plagued their suburban neighborhood, giving rise to rumors of the "Beast of Bailey Downs." While walking on a full moon night, Ginger gets her first period ("I just got the curse," she tells her sister, disgusted). Suddenly, a huge, misshapen beast, drawn by the scent of blood, attacks Ginger. The sisters fight it off and run screaming across a road, where the pursuing monster is splattered by a passing van, driven by doper Sam (Kris Lemche). Ginger's wounds immediately begin to heal, and her personality alters. She even seduces Jason (Jesse Moss), a callous jock for whom she previously had nothing but contempt. As the month progresses towards the next full moon, Ginger not only develops odd physical characteristics (more hair, sharper nails and teeth, and even a tail stub), she becomes more violent, killing a dog and then threatening those around her. Can the worried Brigitte, with help from Sam, keep her sister from fully transforming into a monster?

Filmed in the Toronto suburbs on a budget just under $5 million Canadian, *Ginger Snaps* almost didn't make it off the starting block. Canadian director John Fawcett (2005's *The Dark*, TV's *Orphan Black*) was casting his film when the massacre in Columbine, Colorado, took place. The timing proved unfortunate, to say the least. "We had sent the script to a number of casting directors, and a few of them were so offended by the material in the light of Columbine that they organized a boycott of the film," said Fawcett. "They went to the press. It freaked a lot of people out. Here we were with a movie with kids killing other kids. All of a sudden we became an exploitation movie. It was in all the national newspapers. No one cares about Canadian cinema in Canada, yet here we were taking taxpayers' dollars to make a sensational exploitation film with no artistic merit whatever. That is how we were perceived in the press. It hurt us in fairly large ways—there was a poor turnout for casting calls because agents were not sending out the script. The public school board wanted absolutely nothing to do with us. That made our lives extremely difficult. I thought it was hilarious at first until I realized it was hurting us in Toronto. But possibly it was fortunate, because I was forced to go elsewhere for my cast, and that led to Vancouver where I found Katharine Isabelle, who plays the 16-year-old Ginger, and Emily Perkins, who is her 15-year-old sister Brigitte." Both young actresses bring to vivid life their disparate characters, providing the (heavy) heart and (damaged) soul of the story.

Ginger Snaps is all about Girl Power. The major male characters are either bewildered (the girls' clueless dad), victims (Ginger's horny boyfriend Jason), or ineffectual (the luckless Sam). One sequence even cleverly turns the gender tables when jock Jason, bragging about nailing Ginger in his car the night before, is humiliated by spots of blood seeping, menstrual-like, through his pants (his "infected" penis leaking blood). Ginger has passed the "curse" onto him—both literally and metaphorically.

In *Ginger Snaps* lycanthropy becomes a symbol of female empowerment: with this "curse" comes a blessing. All four of Ginger's victims are male (with the lone survivor—Jason—metaphorically metamorphosed into a menstruating girl). The film's lone female casualty—mean-girl Trina—dies accidentally when she slips on a puddle of milk while wielding a knife in Ginger's kitchen (illustrating the old adage "Never *die* over spilled milk"?).

Pointing out the double standard surrounding sexuality, Ginger wallows in some morning-after guilt about sex with Jason, noting,

Girl Power in a werewolf suit: the gender-bending *Ginger Snaps*.

"He got laid—I'm just the lay." Later, when Ginger and Brigitte hide the body of the accidentally-killed Trina, Brigitte worries about being caught. But Ginger remains confident that society's prevailing attitude towards the *commodity* of women will keep them from suspicion. "Girls don't do this shit," she answers dismissively. "A girl can only be a slut, bitch, tease or the virgin next door."

Unconventional in nearly every respect, *Ginger Snaps* avoids the typical werewolf movie tropes like a highschooler evading parental questioning. Beginning with its monster's unique appearance—a huge, pale-skinned, dog-like creature with a malformed wolf's head ending in huge, slavering jaws (courtesy of creature creator Paul Jones) that walks on four legs rather than two—the film makes its own rules. Silver has no bearing on lycanthropes. As Sam points out to Brigitte, "That thing on the road—my van did a pretty good job on it, without the benefit of silver. So let's forget Hollywood rules." (Despite this, Sam postulates that "the ancients thought pure metal purifies the blood," causing Brigitte to try and halt Ginger's developing lycanthropy via some homemade belly-button piercing with a silver ring. It has no effect.) Likewise, rather than the expected solitary abrupt metamorphosis, Ginger experiences a more gradual change from human to animal, exhibiting lupine traits along the way. The transformation comes on incrementally rather than all at once on the full-moon night, with each passing day bringing more changes—first a small, tail-like appendage appears at the base of Ginger's spine; a few days later her fingernails are noticeably sharper; later the tail has grown long enough so that she must tape it to her leg for gym class; and later still her teeth become pointy. "I was very interested in the biological transformation, in making a metamorphosis movie," noted Fawcett. "The idea that you wake up every morning and look at your body and see something has changed, has mutated, that interested me and led me to the idea of actually making a werewolf film." The script does concede to the full moon (that is when the final, fully-realized metamorphosis occurs), but, as Fawcett pointed out, this underlines the crucial link between the lunar and menstrual cycles. And, with a nod to European tradition, Sam "compared homeopathic treatments to folklore" and comes up with distilled monkshood as a potential cure. (Since wolfsbane and monkshood are closely related—both belonging to the aconite plant family, and both contain powerful toxins—they've sometimes become intertwined in folklore.)

Ginger's change is not merely a physical one. Discovering her sexuality—and the power that comes with it—the misfit outsider becomes a sexual predator, with director Fawcett emphasizing this "transformation" by shooting her seductively walking down the school hallway in slow-motion, turning every boy's head as she passes. Here it is the female that is both the werewolf and the sexual threat. At one point Brigitte (amusingly) warns off the now-sexually provocative Ginger's new love interest, Jason, with "She's ovulating!" But the traditional fear of unprotected sex resulting in teenage pregnancy has been shifted into the realm of the supernatural, with the curse not of unwanted pregnancy, or even of the Clap, but of *lycanthropy* being passed along to Jason. "You gave it to Jason," accuses Brigitte. "You had unprotected sex and infected him." Ginger's offhand response: "Oops."

"I think there is an aspect in the transformation from child to adult," observed producer Steve Hoban, "that is similar to transformation from a moral human with conscience into an immoral creature capable of terrible things. Part of maturing is learning to control unsocial behavior. Brigitte learns this but Ginger, of course, does not. I think this kind of story using werewolves had never been done before."

Ginger's behavior becomes more and more animalistic as the full moon draws near. She has rough sex with Jason ("You taste so good!"), then kills her neighbor's dog ("I get this ache," she says miserably, "I thought it was for sex but it's for tearing everything into fucking pieces"). Finally, she kills two people (the meddling guidance counselor and the unfortunate janitor who stumbles upon the bloody scene). After gleefully murdering the janitor, Ginger announces to a horrified Brigitte, "It feels so good—it's like touching yourself," equating the awakening lycanthropy with her burgeoning sexuality. Fawcett visualizes this connection beautifully when Ginger takes control of their coupling in Jason's car. She tosses Jason down and bites him, the spine of her exposed back rising up under the skin to indicate her heightened lycanthropic/sexual arousal as she usurps the traditional male role of the sexual aggressor.

Fortunately, Fawcett and company lay a hugely entertaining veneer above their multiple layers of feminine-themed subtext, so that *Ginger Snaps* never devolves into a feminist polemic. The werewolf framework, punctuated by moments of suspense and violence, keeps things moving. For instance, the werewolf attacks—all screams, quick flashes of the grotesque creature, and hand-held camerawork—are both chaotic and frightening, generating the frisson of a wild animal attack. The script's witty (and salty) dialogue, coupled with the involving acting and fleshed-out characterizations, grounds the proceedings in bemusing reality. At one point a worried Brigitte asks her doubled-over sister, "Are you sure it's just cramps?" At this Ginger replies, "Just so you know—the words 'just' and 'cramps' don't go together." Later, the worried Brigitte tells Ginger, "Something's wrong, like more than you just being—female." When Ginger discovers hair sprouting from her healing shoulder wound, she laments, "I can't have a hairy chest, B—that's fucked!" Such interactions amuse, enlighten, and entertain, drawing the viewer into the sisters' plight.

Ginger Snaps focuses not just on the girls' world, but on their *teenage* girls' world, with the various adults having all the significance of those in a Charlie Brown cartoon (one almost expects to hear "wah wha wha-wha wha" whenever one opens their mouth). Parents have little input—and less effect—in this teen-centric world. As *New York Times* writer Alex Pappademas argues, "The teenage-monster movie works with more evergreen subtextual materials, making metaphorical the weirdness of adolescence—of waking up one morning with uncontrollable urges, new and troubling growth, and a sense that the world hates and fears you." And *Ginger Snaps* cleverly literalizes this with its werewolf motif. As Hoban noted, "I really liked the idea of a movie that dealt with the difficulties of growing up but [was] told using the metaphor of a bloody werewolf yarn." Hoban and Fawcett consequently looked long and hard to find the right performers—the right *teenage* performers—to bring their tale to life. "From the outset we decided it was crucial to have actors who either were teenagers, or would be completely believable as teenagers. We felt much of the strength of the movie depended upon our teenaged girls and the other kids feeling like teenagers. If they had been actors in their 20s pretending to be teenagers, then I think the whole movie would have felt less honest. A 28-year-old Ginger would have killed our audience's suspension of disbelief more than our five-foot, two-inch ex-jockey in the rubber werewolf suit."

About said werewolf, Fawcett said, "I knew I was going to have to show the monster eventually, but it is not just a monster, it is Brigitte's sister. I shot as much as I could of this rubber thing we had created, and then used as little as I could get away with." The less-is-more dictum works here, as the film only falters in its final twenty minutes, when Ginger fully transforms into a ravening beast. With Ginger's complex and fascinating character now fully subsumed, it leaves only the expected chase sequence as the monster tracks and attacks first Sam and then Brigitte. Though shot in an exciting and suspenseful manner, all quick cuts, sudden starts, and chaotic camerawork, it can't help but feel like a return to convention in a brilliantly *un*conventional cinematic lycan-world.

"We knew we were making a good movie," recalled Canadian actor Kris Lemche (who played Sam), "and during that era, Canadian independent cinema—if I can even use that term, because most films in Canada rely on government funding—it was just a dismal time. There weren't a lot of interesting movies coming out of Canada that the average person could watch and enjoy…. On *Ginger Snaps*, we were all kind of excited that perhaps we were trailblazing in the Canadian market, making something that was going to be accessible and enjoyable not only to young Canadians, but U.S. audiences, Europeans, whoever wanted to watch it. We were excited about making a fun, quality film, finally—with no money!—in Canada." Though attaining theatrical success in its home country and Europe, *Ginger Snaps* didn't even make it into American theaters, going straight to DVD in the U.S. Nevertheless, this lycanthropic groundbreaker found its audience on home video and cable, culminating in the production of two sequels.

With quotes from: "*Ginger Snaps*," by Michael Rowe, *Fangoria* 234; "Girls Get Their Teeth Into a Hairy Moment," *The Herald* (London), June 28, 2001; *Minds of Fear*, by Calum Waddell; "We Are All Teenage Werewolves," by Alex Pappademus, *New York Times Magazine*, May 20, 2011; "Dead in Cold Climates," by Michael Gingold, *Fangoria* 324.

Morphology: Pale-skinned quadruped
Demise: Speeding van; butcher knife
Full Moon Rating: ****½

Ginger Snaps 2: Unleashed

(2004; Seville Pictures/Lions Gate; Canada) Director: Brett Sullivan; Producers: Grant Harvey, Steven Hoban, Paula Devonshire; Screenplay: Megan Martin; Cinematographers: Gavin Smith, Henry Less. Cast: Emily Perkins, Tatiana Maslany, Eric Johnson, Janet Kidder, Brendan Fletcher, Katharine Isabelle.

IT ONLY DIES IF YOU DO—tagline

The (deserved) success of the Canadian lycan-femme classic *Ginger Snaps* on DVD and cable television encouraged the production of two sequels—*Ginger Snaps 2: Unleashed* and *Ginger Snaps Back: The Beginning*, shot back-to-back in Edmonton, Canada. Unfortunately, the original film's principal architects, writer Karen Walton and director John Fawcett, stepped aside (Walton ostensibly busy with other projects, and Fawcett taking a "been there, done that" attitude, though he did serve as one of the executive producers for the sequel tandem). As a result, *Ginger Snaps 2: Unleashed* proved far less successful than its progenitor, both commercially and aesthetically.

In the first *Ginger Snaps*, high schooler Brigitte (Emily Perkins) became tainted with her sister Ginger's lycan-infected blood before she was forced to kill Ginger, who had fully transformed into a ravening beast. Now Brigitte lives a bleak, lonely existence in some snowy town where she takes periodic injections of monkshood extract to keep her growing lycanthropy at bay. With the treatment slowly losing its potency, she desperately takes a double dose and winds up in a dingy drug rehab facility after her "near-fatal anaphylactic reaction." Meanwhile, a mysterious werewolf has been tracking her, killing whomever it encounters. Brigitte must find a way to escape the facility and secure enough monkshood extract in time to fend off the coming change, as well as face down the monster dogging her every step.

Eschewing the multi-layered subtext of the brilliant original (which addressed everything from adolescent angst to suburban ennui), *Ginger Snaps 2* takes the well-worn were-path laid by Larry Talbot himself by focusing solely on Brigitte's desperate attempt to avoid the inevitable transformation and hold onto her humanity. Though she realizes that the monkshood injections she periodically takes offer only a temporary delay rather than permanent cure ("It doesn't stop it; nothing will stop it"), the film has her continue on, spinning her were-wheels until she winds up in the dismal, ironically-named Happier Times Care Center. There the scenario spends most of its time on Brigitte's ineffectual escape attempts and her pleas for her "fix" as the gradual transformation process accelerates. Tossed into the mix is the odd character of a comic book–obsessed 13-year-old girl named "Ghost" (Tatania Maslany), an obviously off-kilter pre-adolescent whose bizarre behavior serves more as a distraction than augmentation. It feels as if neophyte scripter Megan Martin (penning her first produced screenplay) had nothing new for the Brigitte character and so concocted a diversion.

"It's really great coming back to this role," enthused Emily Perkins, returning as the troubled Brigitte. "This movie is scarier than the first one, it's funnier—everything's just up a level." Everything except story, character, and subtext, that is. As a result, *Ginger Snaps 2* becomes just another Monster Movie, with far more emphasis on the carnage and grue than on the characters and themes. "We're pushing the gore, pushing transformation speeds," enthused director Brett Sullivan. Indicative of this is the mysterious beast that stalks Brigitte, literally sniffing around outside wherever she appears. "It wants to mate with me," she announces disgustedly. Where this lycan lothario came from, or even who it is (or used to be) remains undetermined—it's just a monster lurking out in the dark to make things more difficult for our beleaguered heroine and to provide some (admittedly suspenseful) stalking scenes culminating in gruesome bloodshed.

"That whole suburban thing had been done already," said scripter Martin. So she set the sequel in a rundown drug treatment facility, complete with unlikely detritus-littered abandoned hospital wing through which the characters can wander to be attacked by the monster. To her credit, however, Martin cleverly brought back the first film's title character by having Ginger (Katharine Isabelle, reprising her role) periodically materialize to comment upon, and even taunt, the heroine. A manifestation of Brigitte's anxiety, "[Ginger is] the dark voice hanging over Brigitte's subconscious," noted Martin, who gives Ginger many of the film's best lines. "It all starts innocently enough," warns Ginger, "today you want to fuck him, tomorrow you want to bite a hole in his sternum." Later Ginger quips "Don't you just love the sound of nature" as Brigitte listens to the screams of a (deserving) werewolf victim. But Martin generously saves the best dialogue for her prime character. In therapy group, the psychiatrist asks Brigitte, "What's your best-case scenario?" Brigitte darkly, sarcastically, replies, "My best-case scenario, *Eleanor*, is hair everywhere but my eyeballs, elongation of my spine until my skin splits, teats, and a growing tolerance—maybe even affection for—the smell and taste of feces, not just my own. And then excruciating death." First-time director Brett Sullivan (who served as editor on the original *Ginger Snaps*) adds a comical exclamation point by showing the disgruntled doc writing on her notepad, "Lesbian?"

Unfortunately, we never get to see what Brigitte's "best-case scenario" might truly look like, for she serves merely as the tormented hero of the piece who battles the marauding monster. As such, her gradual transformation consists of baby were-steps: first an ear grows pointed (which she gruesomely attempts to hide by slicing off its tip); then a few days later wisps of hair appear on her palm; later she sports red around her irises; and then subtle fangs appear (which she attempts to file down). Such an incremental transformation had been done far better, more subtly, and with greater impact in the original. Near the film's climax, the skin on Brigitte's forearm bubbles and warps, and her face becomes grotesquely distorted. Keeping with the sequel's more gruesome emphasis, Brigitte's interim were-form abandons the sleek, almost feline look of Ginger's in the first film for some skin boils and warped features that make her look more leprosy victim than wolfwoman. Fortunately, the full-on werewolf that Brigitte and

Ghost must face down marks an improvement (the only one) over that seen in the original. Rather than the pale-skinned, prominent-ribbed, dog-like creature from the first, this lycanthrope (created by respected Hollywood FX veteran Howard Berger, of KNB Effects, and his assistant Scott Patton) appears as a more formidable, furry, muscled hybrid that impressively launches itself through the air with its powerful hind legs to tear into a victim with its snarling wolf-like jaws. "The effects are more visceral on this film than in the first *Ginger Snaps*," noted Berger. "The werewolf feels more real to me." And it certainly looks more real, particularly given its expressive, articulated head. (This "reality feel" led to some amusement on the set. "When Howard is operating the puppet head," divulged Sullivan, "he unwittingly makes werewolf noises. He doesn't even know he's doing it. He'll be like, 'Rrrf, rowwwr, rowwr.'")

Unlike in the original, there's no mention of the moon this time, with Brigitte's burgeoning transformation seemingly just a slow, inexorable progression. And the werewolf stalking her has nothing to do with the lunar cycle; in fact, it seems that this creature remains permanently in its were-form, never changing back to human (the script offers no clue as to its origin or identity—it's just a beast in the night).

As a generic werewolf movie, *Ginger Snaps 2: Unleashed* proves more or less competent, with a decent lycanthrope and several exciting, bloody attack sequences. But as a follow-up to the multi-layered, character-rich *Ginger Snaps*, this lycan-rehash fails to *Unleash* anything particularly noteworthy.

With quotes from: "*Ginger Snaps II: Unleashed*—Howling for More," by Scott Rollans, *Fangoria* 230; "Berger Sez Bigger's Not Better," by Scott Rollans, *Fangoria* 230.

Morphology: Man-sized furry quadruped
Demise: Pointy implements
Full Moon Rating: **½

Ginger Snaps Back: The Beginning

(2004; Seville Pictures/Lions Gate; Canada) Director: Grant Harvey; Producers: Steven Hoban, Paula Devonshire, Grant Harvey; Screenplay: Christina Ray, Stephen Massicotte; Cinematographer: Michael Marshall. Cast: Katharine Isabelle, Emily Perkins, Nathaniel Arcand, J.R. Bourne, Hugh Dillon, Adrien Dorval, Brendan Fletcher, David LaHaye, Tom McCamus, Matthew Walker.

An evil that is born in the blood—trailer

Set in the Canadian wilderness of 1815, this second sequel to the lycan-classic *Ginger Snaps* is more accurately a prequel. Rather unusually, it offers no linear tie to its progenitor; instead, it simply takes the two main characters 200 years into the past to recreate the first film's main plotline: Brigitte dealing with her beloved sister Ginger's gradual change into a werewolf. While offering an atmosphere-rich setting, some well-formed secondary characters, exciting attack set-pieces, a tense siege milieu, and better-realized werewolves, *Ginger Snaps Back: The Beginning* fails to live up to the original's rich thematics. In lieu of the multi-layered coming-of-age text (as well as the various suburban blight, teen angst, and progressive feminist *sub*texts), *Ginger Snaps Back* stands (like its sister sequel) as a more straightforward monster movie, with subtlety and humor giving way to more lycan-action and gore. While much of this marks the film as a cut above the average werewolf movie, given its impressive pedigree one can't help but wish for a bit more thought-provoking bark to go along with its gruesome bite.

Teenage siblings Ginger (Katharine Isabelle) and Brigitte (Emily Perkins) are rescued from wandering in the wilderness by Native American warrior "Hunter" (Nathaniel Arcand), who takes them to the nearby Northern Legion Trading Company fort. Now manned only by a skeleton crew, the stockade has been awaiting overdue supplies while the men fend off attacks from a pack of huge, wolf-like beasts—werewolves. After Ginger is bitten by one (the commander's young son, who he secretly keeps locked away as the boy undergoes his slow transformation), Brigitte must find a way to cure her sister's gradual change and stave off her growing bloodlust. As the werewolves continue to attack outside and tensions boil over within the fort, Brigitte, guided by Hunter and an Indian seer, must choose between her sister and the remaining survivors.

Scripters Christina Ray and Stephen Massicotte populate their story with well-defined, intriguing characters (brought to vivid life by a cadre of fine Canadian character actors): the weary, grieving commander; the bigoted, brutal lieutenant; the crazed cleric obsessed with the wages of sin; the alcoholic, despairing doctor; the French trapper steeped in the lore of his home country's *loup garou*; the Noble Savage armed to the teeth with tomahawk, bow and knife. Though they may not be original characters, they work well within the roughhewn setting and taut siege scenario.

What doesn't work so well, however, are the two female leads—both in terms of character and realization. "To me," said director Grant Harvey, "it's a Gothic love story between the two sisters. We've embraced a really romantic idea, but it's very dark. It's quite different from the first film. That movie was very gritty and real, and 'street.' This one is certainly more fantasy, but it has similar attitudes." Unfortunately, those "attitudes" don't translate well here. Though the two-against-the-world Ginger and Brigitte encapsulate the disaffected youth of modern suburbia in the original *Ginger Snaps*, their hostile teen personas seem sorely out of place in the Canadian wilds of 1815 (exemplified by Ginger, clad in period corset and gown, cynically sniping, "These people are fucked"). "Every once in a while," observed star Katharine Isabelle, "we pop out with things that are very, like, first *Ginger Snaps*. But it still works in this time period." Truthfully, it doesn't. And while perfectly cast in the original, Emily Perkins, with her sucking-on-a-lemon sullenness, and Isabelle, with her cocky, chip-on-her-shoulder demeanor, can't carry the heavier burden of straight drama here, their snarky sensibilities coming across as awkwardly incongruous in a period wilderness setting.

Fortunately, director Harvey (promoted from second unit director on the original *Ginger Snaps*) keeps things moving, with various well-staged werewolf attacks, suspenseful set-pieces, tension-filled human interactions, and even the odd creepy dream or vision to distract from the occasional awkwardness. The impressive fort setting (all wood, mud, blood and death as the creatures lay siege); the snowbound, fog-shrouded forest; and the costumes and earthy characters make for a far more involving atmosphere than the previous sequel's drab drug clinic setting. Filming took place at Fort Edmonton, an impressively detailed replica of a fur-trading post. "As soon as I saw it I flipped," noted Harvey, "It is this incredible set that you can shoot in 360 degrees. It really is like a wooden castle surrounded by forest wilderness." Added producer Paula Devonshire, "The great thing about Fort Edmonton is that it's a replica. It was built in the 1970s, so it's heated and has plumbing. It's a little more production friendly. And because the furnishings aren't real, historical artifacts, it isn't as horrendous a deal if something gets damaged." Cinematographer Michael Marshall (*Wrong Turn 4*, *Curse of Chucky*) illuminates this "incredible set" as if by candle or firelight, completing the authentic frontier feel.

The multiple werewolves (courtesy of KNB EFX) also impress,

with their large bodies, shaggy coats, elongated limbs, and malformed wolf heads faintly reminiscent of *The Killer Shrews* (though far more convincing). This sequel apes the original in its portrayal of Ginger's creeping lycanthropy revealing itself in incremental physical changes: hair sprouting from the rapidly healing bite wound; irises taking on an animal hue; fingernails lengthening unnaturally; eye teeth becoming fangs; and streaks of white appearing in her red hair. And there's her behavior, beginning with statements like, "I can smell your blood," and culminating in the evidence of Ginger's blood-smeared mouth.

Also like in the first feature (but *un*like the second), these werewolves seem tied to the moon. The creatures attack on full-moon nights (presaged by atmospheric shots of the luminous orb); and the French trapper warns of the loup garou, "Beware its bite, or we might become a slave to the full moon too." Despite this lunar emphasis, the werewolves seem to be in a permanent state of beastliness, as we never see any transform back to human (remaining in their lupine state even after death). The Frenchman also explains that killing the creature that bit you can effect a cure ("[If] you kill it before you turn, the spell will be broken"). This results in an emotionally—and morally—charged subplot in which Ginger must decide whether or not to kill a young boy (the Commander's slowly-changing son).

Adding a new (period-appropriate) were-wrinkle, the film posits *leeches* as a way to uncover werewolfism. The fort's doctor uses these creatures to test for lycan-infection among the men. If a leech is placed on someone afflicted with lycanthropy, the victim reacts in pain, and the leech instantly swells to grotesque proportions. Though a seemingly out-of-left-field concept, these creepy, wriggly, bloodsucking lycan-detectors certainly up the film's squirm factor.

The script ties werewolves to Native American folklore, particularly the Wendingo legend. Trying to have its lycan-cake and eat it too, the picture also suggests lycanthropy as an infection brought to North America by the invading Europeans. "The English and the French brought with them their diseases to plague our land," states Hunter. "And with them came the Wendingo." So along with smallpox and the clap, the whites brought the disease of lycanthropy to the New World.

Delving far more into the supernatural than the previous two films, *Ginger Snaps Back* opens with the following narration: "The Indians say the curse began in the time of the Ancients and was passed down through the blood of generations. There are legends of the Wendingo, and the coming of the Red and the Black." (Note that Ginger has bright red hair, while Brigitte sports raven black tresses.) "Legends of the day of reckoning, when death would consume the land, and good would face evil, of the day the curse would be broken forever, or grow stronger and live on to plague generations to come." Later, the Indian warrior intones, "I've known you before I found you in the woods. Since I was a boy I've seen your face in dreams…. The dreams told me to protect you." Things pass the point of logical return, however, when Hunter begins spouting further mystical claptrap like, "It is believed amongst our people that those who lived always lived; do not fear death" (whatever *that* might mean).

While *Ginger Snaps II: Unleashed* at least received a theatrical release in its native country, *Ginger Snaps Back: The Beginning* (shot back to back with its sister sequel) suffered the ignoble fate of going straight to video. Which is a pity, given that, while falling short of its progenitor, *Snaps Back* offers enough involving characters, well-realized milieu, and exciting lycan-action to make it the better of the two sequels.

With quotes from: "*Ginger Snaps Back*: Historical Howls," by Scott Rollans, *Fangoria* 236.

Morphology: Fur-covered, misshapen quadrupeds

Demise: Arrows, knives and (ordinary) musket balls
Full Moon Rating: ***½

The Hair of the Beast

(2010; Seville/Les Films Christal; Canada) Original Language Title: *Le Poil de la Bête*. Director: Philippe Gagnon; Producer: Real Chabot; Screenplay: Stephane J. Bureau, Pierre Daudelin; Cinematographer: Steve Asselin. Cast: Guillaume Lennay-Thivierge, Viviane Audet, Gilles Renard, Patrice Robilaille, Antoine Bertrand, Michel Barrette.

A HAIR RISING TALE—trailer

The Hair of the Beast is unique in two respects: it's the first (and only, to date) French-Canadian werewolf movie, and it's the first (and, again, only) to posit lycanthropy as a result of *bestiality*.

In 1665 New France (Quebec), upon escaping from prison after being condemned to death for taking liberties with the wrong woman, Joseph Côté (Guilloume Lennay-Thivierge) stumbles across the body of a dead priest in the woods, dons his cassock as a disguise, and takes the cleric's bag. Said priest was Father Brind'amour, a local hero who, legend has it, vanquished a werewolf 20 years before. Taken in as Brind'amour at a local hamlet, Joseph becomes embroiled in a werewolf hunt after several killings take place. When a villager is savaged by a lycanthrope, Joseph drives it off by stabbing it with a sharpened crucifix he finds in his priest's bag, but is bitten before the creature flees. Despite the priest's diary noting that "beasts, like humans, are born of a female, and their bite is not contagious," several locals truss Joseph up and decided to burn him at the stake just in case. But another werewolf attack interrupts their efforts, and Joseph must face down the monster(s) to save the villagers.

From Father Brind'amour's diary: "He stumbled upon his friend mating with a female wolf. And Father Brind'amour prayed that no offspring be born of that union. But it wasn't enough. One day a werewolf appeared. And then another." Yes, these werewolves are the result of the local Seigneur (Lord) having had sex with a wolf! Possessing no qualms about his depravity, the haughty Seigneur (archly played by Gilles Renaud with equal parts assured arrogance and bemused bile) tells the shocked Joseph, "Like you and the inquisitors from the Old World, [the real] Brind'amour was prejudiced against those who like animals." *Like* animals indeed. For this horrible perversion, this great sin, his offspring were born as werewolves. (Fortunately, director Philippe Gagnon conveys this perversity quickly and tastefully via silhouette figures in an artistically-rendered shadow-puppet forest flashback.) Lycanthropy reflects an unnatural melding of man and beast.

Ironically, when the lord finds one of his werewolf sons preparing to rape a girl, he snarls, disgusted and incredulous, "You want to take her like a *man*?! But you're better than that!" The film ties such underlying perversity to the Unholy, with the villagers talking of the werewolves as "possessed," and looking to the imposter priest as a soldier of God sent to rout Satan's servants. Then, as a trio of villagers wait after nightfall in a clearing ringed by torches, a howl sounds from the darkened wood, and the torches abruptly extinguish as if blown out by a supernatural wind. This attitude fits in well with the film's period setting, with the principals taking the idea of werewolves as a matter of course, reflecting the widespread French—and general European—belief of that time in the existence of the Satanic *loup garou*.

The production's excellent period costumes and sets make the film appear far more sumptuous and authentic than its reported $4.5 million Canadian budget should have allowed. And director Gagnon (who worked almost entirely on made-for-TV productions) keeps the story focused and swiftly moving, while Stephane J. Bureau and Pierre Daudelin's tight screenplay quickly and efficiently imbues the various characters (brought to life by a bevy of fine Quebecois actors) with distinct personalities. A veteran of French-Canadian cinema and television (having appeared in over 40 movies and TV series), Guillaume Lennay-Thivierge, as Joseph, plays the likable rogue, who becomes a hero almost in spite of himself, to a T.

The isolated woodland setting, the rustic buildings and furnishings, the peasantry and period dress, all suggest an almost Little Red Riding Hood/fairytale milieu as the Big Bad Wolves stalk innocent girls ("My sons usually prefer eating women," states the sinister Seigneur, "the thigh is firm, the filet tender"), and the brave (and not-so-brave) woodsmen try to fend off (or cowardly appease) the beasts. In keeping with this tone, most of the carnage remains implied rather than overt, with the brutal attacks portrayed through reactions and suggestive shots, such as screaming victims being abruptly dragged out of frame into the darkness by the unseen monsters. Even the final battle between Joseph and the last werewolf is portrayed more through sound effects, bookended by a few quick edits, than visuals. Though gorehounds might find this lack of visible carnage disappointing, the clever use of suggestion makes for a more richly involving viewing experience by enhancing the intimacy of the film's storybook qualities.

With nary a *Hair* out of place on this cinematic *Beast*, the film sports one unsightly bald patch. Unfortunately, it's a big one, and in such a critical position that it becomes impossible to comb over: the werewolves. For the first hour the lycanthropes remain a mysterious—and frightening—presence, glimpsed only in long shot as shadowy shapes in the forest, or as a hairy arm ending in sharp claws that suddenly enters the frame. But when finally seen full-view, they immediately lose their potency—for two reasons. First, their design—roundish heads with protruding snouts set atop a muscular hairy frame—makes them look more like skinny *bears* than looming lycanthropes. And second, their obvious CGI origins negate whatever physical presence even a subpar wolfman might possess, so that they lose their sense of weight, their feel of reality. That said, the film's sole transformation sequence proves cleverly effective. The camera first shows an arm and hand darken before morphing into a clawed appendage; then, as the man slowly turns his face towards the camera, his nose and lower jaw smoothly extends into a wolfish snout (thus demonstrating how localized CGI can truly work, whereas a complete reliance on computer imagery often results in disappointment).

These werewolves stand upright but can move swiftly on all fours. In keeping with the general folklore beliefs from the time period, the moon remains moot, as they can transform at will. They obviously retain their human intelligence, obeying commands from their human father while in wolf form (even chaining a victim up in the basement of their manor house). And they can be killed by any ordinary weapon. This last results in a climactic demise for one of the creatures that proves both horrific and mildly humorous: when a group of women take shelter in the rustic chapel building, a werewolf breaks in. Spying the menacing creature in the rafters above them, the terrified nun in charge exclaims, "Pray, girls!" But the heroine shouts, "No, grab anything that could hurt it!" When the beast then drops to the floor, the women all rush forward en masse and overwhelm the creature, stabbing and bludgeoning it over and over with tools, knives and scissors.

With better realized lycanthropes, *The Hair of the Beast* might have become another nouveau classic, like *Game of Werewolves* or *Late Phases*. As is, it remains a unique, engrossing but flawed addition to lycancinema.

Morphology: Man-shaped hairy body topped by mutant wolf's head
Demise: Any sharp implement
Full Moon Rating: ***½

Half Moon

(2010; Vicious Circle Films) Director/Screenplay: Jason Toler; Producers: Warren Sheppard, Will Alexander IV, Matt Barnes; Cinematographer: Andy Patch. Cast: Tori Black, Marek Matousek, Torey D. Sutton, Nicki Hunter, Shawna Lenee, Jack Lawrence, Joy Ashley, Zander Kane.

There's something more dangerous
prowling the streets tonight—tagline

What do you call a movie that consists of two actors sitting in a room talking for the entire time? *My Dinner with Andre*. What do you call a movie that consists of two actors sitting in a room talking for the entire time before one of them turns into a monster for 10 seconds? *My Dinner with a Werewolf*? No, *Half Moon*.

Prostitute Rose (Tori Black) meets a "special trick," Jacob (Marek Matousek), at his cheap motel room for the night, but the man seems more interested in talking than anything else. For example, when she tries to give him a lap dance he doesn't respond (resulting in Rose angrily labeling him a "faggot"). Finally, she drops her hard-boiled street attitude and shows some tenderness towards him (after he relates how his girlfriend was "killed by a bear"), and they make love. But upon finding his bag in the bathroom afterward—filled with such items as rope, duct tape, and a gun—she panics and ends up injecting him with a tranquilizer (also in the bag). Calling her abusive pimp, Kevin (Torey D. Sutton), she and Kevin tie the unconscious Jacob to a chair and formulate a plan to obtain the cash Rose saw Jacob stash in the room safe. When Jacob awakens, he pleads to be let loose so he can call his "doctor"—for whom the money is earmarked for treatment of his "disease." He cryptically warns, "If I don't make it to my doctor I'm going to kill you both." As they talk, Jacob finally reveals that he suffers from lycanthropy, and he must obtain one final treatment in order to affect a cure. Rose doesn't believe at first and, more afraid of her pimp than Jacob, continues to hold him (while Kevin is off securing tools to open the safe). But finally Jacob begins to change, and she decides to release him so that they can escape to his doctor. Too late, as Kevin returns and the pull of the full moon proves too strong for Jacob to resist…

With a reported budget of $100,000, *Half Moon* looks like it was made for *Half That* (or less). Beginning with some grainy nighttime videography that appears far too much like the old VHS camera look than it should (given the film quality of even inexpensive video equipment in 2010), it offers the same cartoonish-looking CGI shot of clouds passing across the full moon not once, not twice, but *four* times. Add in some uneven, muddy sound, and the feeling of cheapness is complete.

Lead actress Tori Black appeared in over fifty movies released in 2010. Apart from *Half Moon*, however, all of them were porn flicks (with titles like *Pretty Little Lesbians*, *Legs Up Hose Down*, and *Panty Pops*). "The role of Rose was a hooker with a heart of gold," explained writer-director Jason Toler about his search for the right actress. "In my mind, someone who understood the sex trade, but isn't a dirty or negative stereotype. It was hard to find the right person to play that role. When an actress came in to audition they were either too innocent or too over the top. We met with twenty-six different girls. Tori came to the audition and I thought let's give her a chance. To be honest, I thought she was too tall and would give a bad read, but she blew the other people out of the water. She understood the pain of Rose and her innocence. She was really a good actress." Well, not by half. The beautiful, slim brunette (real name Michelle Chapman), a former *Penthouse* Pet of the Month and two-time AVN (Adult Video News) Female Performer of the Year, gives a performance here—in her first "legit" role—that could charitably be called "uneven." Her voice often becomes abrasive as she balks and scoffs and talks trash (pushing the Ebonics-style dialogue far too hard). Marek Matousek, looking like a low-rent Treat Williams, comes off better, with a more modulated, naturalistic portrayal that engenders some sympathy for his character. Unfortunately, neither can carry an entire film, particularly one whose script relies so heavily on page after page of hit-and-miss dialogue between two characters.

Said dialogue, littered with "bitches" and f-bombs, frequently proves tiresome and pointless, as the pair, while eating their paper-plate dinner, engage in rambling, pseudo-philosophical discussions ("The truth hurts; lies are less painful"; "It's not the lies that are easy, it's the way that you lie that gets easier") or argue over who knows more about Pete Rose's career. It's a full half-hour into this 80-minute movie before *anything* happens—and this is just an aborted lap dance leading to *another* conversation and a brief soft-core sex scene. Then, for the remainder of the film (up until the final eight minutes), Jacob, tied to the chair, tries to talk Rose into letting him go. That's it. Spinning their verbal wheels, the two keep going over the same ground: "Let me call my doctor," he begs, while Rose obstinately comes up with objections and conjectures ("Maybe you were gonna call another hooker for seconds after you killed me."..).

"The story and the characters keep the movie interesting," claims Toler. "The story is just as much of a thriller as it is a balls to the wall blood fest horror film. I wanted the characters' story to keep people interested. I compare it to the old *Twilight Zone*, *Tales from the Dark Side* and *Monsters*. Those shows weren't huge gore fests, but the stories kept you interested. *Half Moon* is like that, but on a bigger scale." No, it's not, as the only time the endless conversation comes even close to "interesting" is when Jacob finally reveals the nature and details of his "disease." "I handle [lycanthropy] in a realistic way," claimed Toler. "Werewolfism or lycanthropy compared to zombies or vampires is a more believable disease. When Jacob is tied to the chair and is trying to convince Rose to let him go, he gives her a back story and scientific facts that I researched. It's believable that this man could have a mutation based off of the environmental change and that there would be a doctor out there to exploit it." Believable? Well, in a low-rent horror movie, maybe.... But at least Toler took this novel notion and ran with it. "I have a special condition," explains Jacob, "and a special doctor. He's underground—his methods are fuckin' mad and dangerous. But he helps. I have to take the medicine at a certain time" (just before the transformation). And what happens if he doesn't take said medicine? "I suffer from a rare disease," continues Jacob, "it's called lycanthropy. My metabolism is affected by the changing cycles of the moon. Sometimes I lose myself; I go into fits of rage. My body won't listen to my mind." Beyond this, he takes tranquilizers, pain killers, and even cocaine ("to dull my [heightened] sense of smell") in the hours leading up to the change to keep him calm and to placate the "growing hunger." Where did this mysterious "doctor" come from, asks Rose. Apparently, the doc "was infected once, but he found a way to cure himself." Now he helps others—for a price ("the substances he uses are expensive and hard to find"). So here we have a scientific treatment, and ultimately a cure, for lycanthropy. Said treatment consists of "enzymes, nitrates, antibiotics, muscle relaxers, and silver nitrates." "But I thought silver was bad for werewolves—didn't I see that in some movie?" asks Rose, reasonably. "It is," answers Jacob, "but in small doses it can stop, and in my case reverse, the effects."

But even much of the film's lycan-centric discourse falls flat, particularly Jacob's rambling monologue about how he became a werewolf. He begins by saying, "We were in a car accident..." and meanders on and on, proffering far too many tangential details before the viewer realizes this accident has *nothing* to do with the subsequent werewolf attack (which occurred while they were hiking in Montana). Finally getting down to brass tacks, Jacob's recounting of the vicious struggle is about as evocative as a meatloaf recipe: "Suddenly this thing attacks her [my fiancée]. At first I thought it was a bear. It turned and took a huge part of my forearm..."

At the 72-minute mark, Jacob finally starts to exhibit physical signs of the coming transformation—foaming at the mouth and showing a little more hair on his arm. Next he sports a pair of contact lenses and fangs as he writhes in the chair before some cartoonish CGI morphs him almost instantaneously into a shaggy, lumbering, big-eared, wolf-headed biped with big white teeth set in an immobile muzzle. For this pivotal metamorphosis, Toler "wanted to do something that would be easy to shoot, but still exciting to see. We shot the actor clean, in half make up and then the creature suit and morphed it with little after effects. It doesn't look bad, and I hope the audience enjoys it for what it's worth." Truthfully, it *does* look bad, or at least amateurish. Consequently, it's worth very little, particularly given the paucity of werewolf screen time, which lasts all of *10 seconds*. Lumbering to his feet, the werewolf attacks Kevin, who arrived mere minutes before and began beating on Rose for having loosened Jacob's bonds. A swipe of the monster's hairy arm sends Kevin's rubbery severed hand to the floor. Then, after a brief shot of the creature biting Rose's leg for no discernable reason (except to provide a coda in which Rose is back walking the streets on a full moon night to earn money for *her* cure), it ambles off down the hall. That's it.

"We shot the film in a week," revealed Toler. "We had a very tight shooting schedule, and my style is pretty straight to the point." Toler's "straight to the point" direction proves no more convincing than his tiresome script or lead actress, as he alternates pointless camera angles (why are establishing scenes of the city streets shot *diagonally*?) with a locked-down camera that makes the visuals as dull as the endless palaver.

Toler came from a music video background, and this was his first feature. "I've always *loved* horror movies," enthused Toler. "I was that kid that would take the bus to the $1.00 theater (when there still were dollar theaters) and stay all day or until they kicked me out." *Half Moon* failed to set the indy horror world on fire for Toler, who has produced nothing else since then—though he reportedly has a new film in the offing. The title? *Crack House of the Dead*. Hmmm. With its talky structure, cheap camerawork, cheesy effects, and disappointing lycanthrope, this *Half Moon* comes off as half baked.

With quotes from: "Interview with Jason Toler of *Half Moon*," by Brandon C. Sites, Brandonsites.blogspot.com.

Morphology: Bulky, shaggy, wolf-headed biped
Demise: None; it just wanders off
Full Moon Rating: *½

Hall of the Mountain King see *Night of the Howling Beast*

Hammer of the Gods see *Thor: Hammer of the Gods*

The Hammond Mystery see *The Undying Monster*

Hell's Creatures see *Frankenstein's Bloody Terror*

Horror of the Werewolf see *Night of the Howling Beast*

Horrors of War

(2006; Hollywood Wizard) Alternate title: *Zombies of War* (UK); Directors: Peter John Ross, John Whitney; Producers: Peter John Ross, Sean Reid, Philip R. Garrett; Screenplay: Peter John Ross, John Whitney, Philip R. Garrett; Cinematographers: Greg Sabo, Scott Spears. Cast: Jon Osbeck, Joe Lorenzo, Daniel Alan Kiely, C. Alec Rossel, Chip Kocel, Jason Morris, Louie Cowan, Sean Velie, David Carroll.

In War, Death Is Not The Only Thing To Fear—poster

Combining the Horror and War genres in one film presents plenty of possibilities. Unfortunately, like many battles fought during World War II itself, the aptly-named *Horrors of War* turned out to be a cinematic bridge too far, as its ambition far outstrips its abilities. Shot on film (some 35mm, but mostly 16mm and even 8mm) in three weeks in Ohio in July 2005 for a reported $300,000 (though this figure seems rather … optimistic, given what appears onscreen), the story posits that towards the end of World War II, Hitler stepped up his plan to unleash a new secret weapon—zombies! When Allied intelligence learns of this, they send Lt. Schmidt (Jon Osbeck), Captain Russo (Joe Lorenzo), and their small squad of men, including Sgt. Gary (Daniel Alan Kiely), who just happens to be a werewolf(!), on a mission to capture the doctor in charge of the project and blow up the secret zombie-making lab.

A film of two halves, *Horrors of War*'s first part covers Lt. Schmidt and his platoon's encounter with a werewolf in Occupied France (the brother of a pair of French women assaulted in a woodland cottage by some brutal GIs), resulting in Sgt. Gary being bitten, thus becoming a *loup garou* himself. This comes in handy when Schmidt teams up with Captain Russo to attack the "supersoldier" facility in the film's second half. Unfortunately, at the climactic showdown, the Allied werewolf proves no match for the Axis super-zombie, as the lycanthrope ends up shish kebabbed on a protruding pipe during their brief battle. It takes *another* zombie (this one on the side of the Allies)—Captain Russo, who injects himself with the secret serum—to destroy the evil undead Nazi. (Such self-sacrifice, while admirable, makes little sense, however, as all one need do to kill the enemy creature is shoot it in the head—which these selfsame soldiers had done during several previous zombie encounters. But there's not much drama in *that* …)

Sgt. Gary's werewolf apparently can change at will (no full moon needed) and retains its human intelligence while in wolfman form—at least enough to differentiate between Allied green and Axis grey. "When things go down, when I change," Gary tells his comrades, "just be glad you're not a Kraut." Of course, such a transformation proved beyond the film's limited budget, leaving a scene in which Gary jumps on the back of the Zom-Nazi, yells at his comrades to get out, and then, after a quick cutaway, stands in full were-mode ready to do battle with the undead supersoldier.

The initial French werewolf (ultimately dispatched with the traditional silver bullet—proffered by one of the grateful women after Lt. Schmidt shows her some kindness) offers a different but not wholly effective makeup that eschews the traditional hairy face and snout for a molded countenance that looks more like a demonic bat (complete with large pointy ears) than a man-wolf. Reportedly, the other actors were not allowed to see Joseph Shaw (playing the *loup garou*) in his werewolf makeup until filming the actual attack scene. *Why* is anybody's guess, for his greyish, wrinkled bat-face; oversized gremlin ears; and long scraggly hair looks less than imposing (not helped by his skinny physique). And the filmmakers shoot said attack in such a mundane, matter-of-fact manner that his supposedly striking appearance barely registers.

Conversely, the transformed Sgt. Gary, at the wolf-vs.-zombie climax, sports a more traditional hirsute look. *Horrors of War* was originally conceived as a three-part anthology film. Before production began, however, the middle story was dropped completely and the character of Lt. Schmidt was created as a bridge between the werewolf and zombie stories, with the climactic meeting of the monsters added as well. Hence the differences in appearance between the Sgt. Gary werewolf and the creature that bit him.

Co-directors Peter John Ross and John Whitney employ plenty of cinematic tricks, such as handheld camerawork, zooms, and quick edits, to try and capture the chaos of battle—with varying levels of success. Despite these efforts, many of the skirmishes appear to be just what they are—a handful of guys running around the woods shooting blanks at one another. On the plus side, the actors sport authentic-looking uniforms and World War II–era weapons that add some much-needed verisimilitude to the scenario. "We used World War II re-enactors in the film as featured extras," explained co-director Peter John Ross. "They in turn brought tanks, armored cars, authentic weapons and uniforms, and more. We shot a D-Day re-enactment on Lake Erie with 300 extras and even a real P-51 Mustang buzzing overhead. This made our movie look a whole lot bigger and better." Obvious exaggerations aside (nowhere in the film are there anywhere *near* 300 battlers), given the too-frequent small-scale firefights and long scenes of the squad tramping through the woods or holing up in some farmhouse, the filmmakers would have done better to emphasize their tale's *Horrors* over *War*. "'More monsters, more guns,' that's the dictum for the movie," stated Ross. "It's tough to find a balance between that and a good character story, but we've managed to do that with our film." Not really. The werewolf appears far too briefly during the film's first half, and the zombies follow suit in the second section. (It *could* have been even more lycan-lite. "We had a dictum from our executive producer to have more of the werewolf in the film," recalled Ross. "'Maybe attacking something in the woods' because Blockbuster needs at least 8–10 specific horror elements. So we scoured the film for a place for anything we could do and have it make sense.") And the climactic battle between lycanthrope and walking corpse—in which the two engage in a very un-monster-like tussle, punching and kicking like they're in some drunken barroom brawl, lasts only a minute before the zombie easily dispatches the werewolf with the business end of a pipe.

A run-down factory in Youngstown, Ohio, stands in for the run-down factory in occupied France that houses Hitler's "Project Osiris." Amazingly, Der Fuhrer saw fit to entrust this game-changing secret weapon project to one reluctant doctor, guarded by a mere three soldiers, at a cut-rate laboratory, which consists of a corpse strapped to a gurney, a solitary table with a few beakers and test tubes, and a syringe full of the glowing green zombie-making formula (perhaps the doc was a *Re-Animator* fan?).

"We made a 'Grindhouse' style movie, like *Planet Terror*, or a 'B' movie you would have seen on a Saturday matinee," said Ross. *Horrors of War* proved not nearly that competent, however, as evidenced by one frenetic firefight in a graveyard (with soldiers sprinting and diving behind tombstones) that sadly reveals the gravestones' Styrofoam nature. Add in some over-the-top acting (particularly in its final third), and poor, sub–SyFy Channel CGI for when the transport plane is hit by flak and the troops parachute one by one to safety, and the cheese factor rises to limburger level.

"It's not every day you get to make a period World War II movie with zombies and werewolves and have this much fun," beamed co-director John Whitney. Too bad it's just not all that much fun to *watch*.

With quotes from: "Wikinews Interviews Author and Filmmaker Peter John Ross," by Joseph Ford, wikinews.org; *Tales from the Front Line of Indy Filmmaking*, by Peter John Ross; "Ohio Based Feature Film *Horrors of War*," by Mitchell Wells, horrorsociety.com.

Morphology: Two-legged wolfmen
Demise: Silver bullet; skewered on a metal pipe at the hands of a Nazi zombie
Full Moon Rating: *½

House of Dracula

(1945; Universal; b&w) Director: Erle C. Kenton; Producer: Paul Malvern; Screenplay: Edward T. Lowe; Cinematographer: George Robinson. Cast: Lon Chaney, John Carradine, Martha O'Driscoll, Lionel Atwill, Onslow Stevens, Jane Adams, Ludwig Stossel, Glenn Strange, Skelton Knaggs.

ALL *NEW* Sensations!—ad line

Despite its tagline, *House of Dracula* was anything but "new." Recycling the monster rally concept from *House of Frankenstein*, this "new" *House* is furnished with the same old monsters—Dracula, the Wolf Man, the Frankenstein Monster, a mad scientist and a hunchback—as well as much of the same personnel both in front of and behind the camera (including director, producer, screenwriter, and cinematographer). That said, it *is* fairly "sensational," standing as a marked improvement over its prototype.

Though filmed over a year after its immediate predecessor, *House of Dracula* actually began life before *House of Frankenstein*, conceived as a sequel to *Frankenstein Meets the Wolf Man* called *Wolf Man vs. Dracula*, with Lon Chaney, Jr. (naturally) returning as Lawrence Talbot and Bela Lugosi slated for a long-overdue reprise of his famous vampire role. But after Lugosi's disastrous turn as the Frankenstein Monster in *Frankenstein Meets the Wolf Man*, Universal perhaps thought twice (or possibly scheduling conflicts were to blame, with Bela touring extensively at the time in the play *Arsenic and Old Lace*). In any case, this, coupled with some censor-dictated script changes and Boris Karloff's return to the studio on a two-picture deal (the other being *The Climax*), prompted Universal to rush ahead with *House of Frankenstein* instead (with 38-year-old John Carradine twirling the Dracula cape rather than the 61-year-old Lugosi). A year later the discarded script landed in the lap of *House of Frankenstein* writer Edward T. Lowe, who revamped it (ouch) into *House of Dracula*.

One night just before dawn, Count Dracula (John Carradine) pays a call on respected Visarian physician and philanthropist Dr. Edelmann (Onslow Stevens). It seems the Count wants "release from the curse of misery and horror against which I'm powerless to fight alone." Yes, Dracula seeks a cure for his vampirism. Edelmann agrees to help and prescribes a course of blood transfusions. Meanwhile, Lawrence Talbot (Lon Chaney, Jr., receiving top billing for the only time in his five Universal Wolf Man films) arrives on Edelmann's doorstep seeking treatment for *his* affliction—lycanthropy. The doctor determines that by re-shaping Talbot's cranial cavity (utilizing an experimental mold the scientist has been cultivating that can soften bone) he can affect a cure. Meanwhile, Edelmann finds the Frankenstein Monster in a cave beneath his castle-home and sets the brute up in his laboratory for study. Things quickly go awry when Dracula has a change of heart and puts his vampiric moves on Edelmann's beautiful nurse Meliza (Martha O'Driscoll). Edelmann disposes of the vampire (by dragging his coffin into the rising sun), but not before the duplicitous Dracula has contaminated Edelmann's blood with his own. Edelmann becomes a murderous Jekyll-and-Hyde creature. But the doc manages to perform the curative procedure on Talbot before the evil in his blood has him restoring to full power the Frankenstein Monster—just as the expected throng of torch-wielding villagers show up, ending it all in a fiery conflagration.

Though only slightly more plausible than *House of Frankenstein* in its potty plotting, *House of Dracula* offers a stronger sense of conviction than its predecessor, primarily due to a significant improvement in the "mad doctor" department, the solid playing of the expert cast (both Carradine and Chaney reprise their roles to great effect, with Onslow Stevens standing as the scenario's solid center), and heightened sense of Gothic atmosphere.

The philanthropic Dr. Edelmann makes a far more level-headed and sympathetic character than *House of Frankenstein*'s brain-crazed Dr. Niemann, with Onslow Stevens' steady presence adding gravitas to the outlandish proceedings (a vampire and a werewolf, neither of which the science-minded Edelmann believes exist, each seek the doctor's help in the same week—what are the odds?). Stevens' kindly demeanor and calm underplaying makes it all the more terrifying when his tainted blood transforms him into an evil imp who murders for fun and plots to unleash the Monster on the world (with Stevens pulling out all the stops to malevolently glare and maniacally grin). Consequently, it becomes *more* than simple diversion when the tainted Edelmann becomes Hyde, with Stevens' subsequent anguished torment at the actions of his alter-ego transferring to him the tragic monster mantle usually reserved for Talbot's Wolf Man. Edelmann's tortured confession to Talbot, whom he knows will understand, underscores his torment: "My soul and mind have been seized by some nameless horror, a lust which changes me into the thing that killed Siegfried tonight." It's a neat twist that keeps the pathos and tragedy (not to mention body count) high while giving Talbot a much deserved break.

Better constructed than the previous *House* (*of Frankenstein*), the film more smoothly integrates its characters into its overstuffed scenario. For instance, rather than pure chance bringing Dracula to the attention of the Mad Scientist, here the Count seeks out Edelmann for treatment. Likewise, Talbot, who, rather than simply reviving and taking up his "I want to die" shtick (as in *House of Frankenstein*), becomes proactive in his search for a cure, seeking out, like Dracula, the beneficent doctor (Edelmann must have *some* reputation across Europe).

And Stevens' gleefully fiendish alter-ego, with his malicious manner, evil glint, and sudden, snake-like strikes of violence, becomes more frightening than any of the classic monsters. When the possessed Edelmann calmly menaces the kind, self-sacrificing, hunchbacked nurse Nina (played with great sympathy by Jane Adams), only to suddenly pounce and strangle her before tossing her limp body through a trap door like a discarded rag doll, it inspires more shock than anything seen in the film's predecessor.

While *House of Dracula* offers little more Wolf Man screen time than the lycan-impoverished *House of Frankenstein*, it makes more of what it has. Though one of only two Wolf Man sequences, the beast-man's first appearance is a doozy. Talbot shows up (with no explanation as

112 • *House of Dracula*

"ALL NEW... ALL TOGETHER!" This half-sheet poster is half-right anyway, as the same old monsters are once again all together in Universal's (improved) follow-up to their *House of Frankenstein*.

to how he survived his death by silver bullet at the close of *House of Frankenstein*) and gets himself locked up in the town jail, where he transforms (in a near-flawless series of dissolves that prove far superior to the truncated metamorphosis seen in *House of Frankenstein*) before the shocked eyes of both the police and Dr. Edelmann. (A moment before, Edelmann had remonstrated with Talbot that "I believe that anything can happen—in a person's mind"; well, take *that*, Mr. Skeptic.) Chaney then demonstrates why he has been, and always will be, the screen's preeminent Wolf Man. He snarls and lunges through the bars at his onlookers, straining and battering against the cell door. Unable to reach his prey, he turns suddenly and flings himself at the window, savagely yanking on the metal bars blocking his escape. Returning to the door, he pulls and struggles in a frenzied animal rage before collapsing from exhaustion and frustration. Chaney delivers a ferocious, athletic and potent portrayal of a caged animal.

Later, the Wolf Man appears for the second (and final) time in the tidal cavern below the castle and attacks Edelmann. But with the werewolf's paws wrapped around the doc's neck, choking the life out of his would-be rescuer, the moon sets and Talbot transforms back to himself in the nick of time, thus sparing Edelmann (and furthering the plot). It's another exciting and savage (albeit brief) display by Chaney's werewolf.

For the first time in the Universal series, the Wolf Man kills no one (the Production Code would not permit a murderer—even a *were*-murderer—to escape punishment). And, of course, the tormented Talbot finally escapes his curse—not through death, as he'd so desperately sought in the two previous pictures, but through a medical miracle. Talbot even gets to act the hero, shooting the tragically tainted Edelmann at film's end and setting fire to the lab to destroy the Frankenstein Monster. (This last sequence, pointing out the budget-conscious film's parsimoniousness, is comprised mainly of fiery footage taken from the climax of *The Ghost of Frankenstein*, in which the Monster was played by ... Lon Chaney. Consequently, Lawrence Talbot spends the film's final moments trying to evade himself!) Of course, poor Larry was back for *Abbott and Costello Meet Frankenstein*, once again afflicted with his terrible werewolf curse. Perhaps the cure simply didn't take...

In the meantime, Chaney demonstrates once again that he was a better actor than many gave him credit for. During the Big Test following his treatment, Talbot stands in the garden as the moon rises and illuminates his face. Chaney's expression of trepidation changes to subtle wonderment as he brings the back of his hand up to his face, feeling for hair that isn't there. His hunched shoulders straighten as he raises himself up ever so slightly, and a look of joyous disbelief creeps into his eyes. To the actor's credit, it all remains very subtle—the mildest of metamorphoses—and all the more effective (and affecting) for it.

The castle sets, all stone arches and heavy furnishings, the laboratory chockablock with esoteric equipment, and the steamy cave beneath the castle contribute to a dark, almost nightmarish milieu. The fact that nearly every scene takes place at night, with candle (or moon) light generating pools of darkness and light, allows the skill of veteran cinematographer George Robinson (*The Invisible Ray, Son of Frankenstein, Tower of London*) to shine (so to speak). Even the rare daylight scene offers shadows and depth in Robinson's multi-layered lighting and photography (with plant leaves creating planes of darkness in the foreground of a room, for instance).

Director Erle C. Kenton's excellent use of said shadows (particularly to heighten the Evil Edelmann's menace) adds to the Gothic ambiance. Kenton appears to have taken greater care here than with *House of Frankenstein*, harking back to his more imaginative work on *Island of Lost Souls* (1932). For example, when Larry convalesces after his treatment, he sorrowfully tells Meliza, "Time after time people have tried to help me; time after time they've failed. If *this* fails, I—" he trails off. The camera shoots the scene through an iron railing, a visual metaphor for the prison of his curse. But when Meliza urgently reassures him, "It won't fail, Larry," the camera angle changes. No longer are the bars in the foreground; it's as if she (and Edelmann) has freed him.

Intriguingly, *House of Dracula* offers a decidedly scientific take on its supernatural beings. Vampirism, concludes Dr. Edlemann, is caused by "a parasite in the blood." Talbot's lycanthropy, however, seems more complicated. "The examination discloses one condition," explains Edelmann, "pressure on certain parts of the brain. This condition, coupled with your belief that the moon *can* bring about a change, accomplishes exactly that." So apparently the medical abnormality (pressure on the brain) must be augmented by *belief* in order for one to become a werewolf. "During the period in which your reasoning processes give way to self-hypnosis," continues the doc, "the glands which govern your metabolism get out of control, like a steam engine without a balance wheel. When this happens the glands generate an abnormal supply of certain hormones—in your case, those which bring about the physical transformation which you experience." Whew. Always the pragmatist, Talbot comes straight to the point: "Explaining it doesn't help—what can you do about it?" Edelmann proposes to enlarge Talbot's cranial cavity and thus relieve the pressure. All he needs is his special bone-softening mold in sufficient quantities. And, to Talbot's great relief, he succeeds.

House of Dracula scripter Edward T. Lowe was a veteran scenario writer (and sometime producer) whose hundred-plus credits stretched all the way back to 1912. Along the way he penned the 1923 Lon Chaney Sr. starrer *The Hunchback of Notre Dame*, 1933's *The Vampire Bat* (starring Lionel Atwill, who plays the police inspector in *House of Dracula*), and, of course, this film's antecedent, *House of Frankenstein*. Retiring from Hollywood in 1946, Lowe "burned all his scripts, clippings and mementos accumulated through his 35 years in the industry in what he called 'the great cleansing,'" reported *Variety* (May 23, 1973 obituary), and "kept his vow never to write again." *House of Dracula* was his final screenplay. Coincidence?

House of Dracula produced waves whose ripples reached the unlikeliest of shores. French horror filmmaker Jean Rollin, who went on to create a veritable cottage industry in vampire-centric sensual cinema with films such as *The Nude Vampire* (1970), *Requiem for a Vampire* (1971) and *Lips of Blood* (1975), was greatly inspired by this *House*. "When I was a kid," recalled Rollin, "I happened to see *House of Dracula*, and those images have haunted me for years. That, I consider a scary film, by all standards. Perhaps my movies are a way of exorcising those fears." Not particularly "scary" these days, *House of Dracula* still offers up enough stylish atmosphere, monstrous mayhem, and incident and pathos (not only from the expected Talbot/Wolf Man character, but from the tormented good doctor as well) to make it a genuine House of Entertainment.

With quotes from: *Shock Masters of the Cinema*, by Loris Curci.

Morphology: Universal's Wolf Man
Demise: None; Larry Talbot is cured!
Full Moon Rating: ***

House of Frankenstein

(1944; Universal; b&w) Director: Erle C. Kenton; Producer: Paul Malvern; Screenplay: Edward T. Lowe; Cinematographer: George Robinson. Cast: Boris Karloff, Lon Chaney, John Carradine, J. Carrol Naish, Anne Gwynne, Peter Coe, Lionel Atwill, George Zucco, Elena Verdugo.

FIVE TIMES MORE TERRIFYING, FIVE
TIMES MORE THRILLING—trailer

…And FIVE TIMES the wishful thinking. Given the financial boon of *Frankenstein Meets the Wolf Man*, which featured not one but *two* famous monsters, wouldn't bundling *all* their creatures together reap even greater rewards? So must have reasoned the Universal brass in 1944 when the studio announced their upcoming *The Devil's Brood* (changing it to *House of Frankenstein* during production) which would feature not only the Wolf Man and Frankenstein's Monster, but Dracula, a mad doctor, a hunchback, and the Mummy (ultimately dropped from the roster). As it turns out, five heads are *not* better than one (or even two).

A film of two halves, *House of Frankenstein* opens with escaped convict (and mad scientist) Dr. Niemann (Boris Karloff) murdering, then impersonating, the owner of a traveling Chamber of Horrors that just so happens to contain the skeletal remains of Count Dracula. Niemann revives the vampire and forges an unholy alliance with Dracula (John Carradine) in an effort to destroy Niemann's old enemies. The film's second half (after Dracula's sunrise demise) details Niemann finding the frozen Monster (Glenn Strange) and Wolf Man, Lawrence Talbot (Lon Chaney, Jr.), in the ice cave beneath Frankenstein castle, and the mad doctor's subsequent plans involving various brain transplants. The revived Larry becomes the third point of a lopsided triangle between Niemann's hunchbacked servant Daniel (J. Carroll Naish) and tag-along gypsy girl Ilonka (Elena Verdugo)—with tragic results.

This third appearance of Universal's Lawrence Talbot the Wolf Man (following *The Wolf Man* and *Frankenstein Meets the Wolf Man*) serves Larry well but does his werewolf half no favors. In fact, we see very little of the Wolf Man. First the manbeast thaws from the ice and immediately changes back into Larry. Then Talbot transforms at the next full moon only to slink off into the night, with a subsequent attack on a villager mentioned but not shown. Finally, Larry transforms once again, only to be shot to death by Ilonka a few seconds later. So we see the werewolf wake up, we see him go for a stroll, and we see him die—the only were-action being a brief mauling of the gypsy girl. It's a pretty poor return on our lycan-dollar.

Ever the pro, Chaney imbues the sole werewolf attack (on Ilonka) with his trademark vigor, crashing through a glass door, then pouncing savagely on his prey. "When that happened I had never seen him

114 • *House of Frankenstein* (1944)

before as the Wolf Man," recalled Verdugo about the sequence. "I remember the scene was done on Stage 25. He was supposed to burst through a glass door, which was made of sugar or something. They had a professional screamer on the set to dub in my screams, but when he came through the door and jumped out at me I let out a blood-curdling scream. It was the most frightening moment of my life! They didn't have to use the professional screamer because I was pretty convincing."

While a werewolf for only a few moments, Chaney receives more screen time as Talbot, and Lon makes the most of it. Though singing the same old tune from *Frankenstein Meets the Wolf Man* ("I only want to die"), the actor carries it with conviction. Universal paid Chaney $10,000 to don the yak hair for a third time (second in cost only to Karloff, whose mad scientist role earned him double that amount), and it proved money well spent. "What's your name?" Ilonka bubbles at their first meeting. "Lawrence," Talbot answers glumly. "They call you Larry?" she coquettishly queries. After a pause, Chaney's eyes drop and his mouth hardens before he answers grimly, "They used to." With a few gestures and his expressive demeanor, Chaney speaks volumes with only a few words. "Lon Chaney was a damn good actor," concluded co-star John Carradine. And in his work here it shows—and proves that he was capable of more subtlety and nuance than many gave him credit for.

Of Chaney, Peter Coe (who plays the young hero in the opening Dracula vignette) recollected, "We went fishing and hunting together many times up at his ranch near Placerville. He had a beautiful ranch. He and I both loved to drink. He drank three or four quarts of booze a day. I couldn't keep up with him! He was a great guy, I loved him.... We were like two lost buddies. He was a drunk and I was a drunk."

Elena Verdugo called Chaney "a very sweet, nice, big oafish guy. And he was always so hot in those things he wore. I remember feeling a touch of empathy for him. It was as if he wanted something more, something better than the film he was doing."

While Chaney's tortured Talbot role fits him like a glove, not all the thespians in this *House* cover themselves in glory. Elena Verdugo (only 18 at the time) paints a vivacious picture, but her lack of depth makes Ilonka more silly schoolgirl than tragic heroine willing to die for her newfound love. And Boris Karloff, though given little to work with in terms of either character depth or decent dialogue, stalks through in single-minded mad doctor mode without the sympathetic subtleties he brought to so many of his better roles. According to studio publicity, J. Carrol Naish spent time studying the mannerisms of a hunchbacked derelict in L.A. Naish imbues the murderous Daniel with heartfelt genuineness as the doomed outcast longing for a "normal" body and love. "I've killed four men for you, Master," he proclaims, trying to get Niemann's attention.

The film's technical aspects fall well below the level established by the previ-

"MONSTER, WEREWOLF, DRACULA together for the first time in the same film!" crowed this atmospheric Swedish poster for *House of Frankenstein* (1944). Fortunately, it wasn't the last, with *House of Dracula* appearing the following year.

ous *Frankenstein Meets the Wolf Man*. For instance, the Wolf Man's shift back to human (after thawing from the ice) is accomplished via a single, unimpressive dissolve, the crude, one-shot transformation indicating a general lack of care. The third and final werewolf sequence offers a full-fledged transformation, with Larry staring into the mirror as he becomes the Wolf Man. But this, too, proves cut-rate, with fewer stages than in previous efforts, resulting in a far less smooth (or convincing) metamorphosis than those seen in the film's two technically rich predecessors. The more economical approach works, however, in the film's first transformation from man to wolf. Rushing outside to look at the moon, Larry grimaces, holds his face, and then starts walking. The camera pans down to his bare feet as he steps forward, moving out of frame. The camera follows, revealing his footprints in the dirt that suddenly change from human to wolf-prints. The camera then raises its lens to reveal the Wolf Man moving off into the misty woods. Though obviously staged with an eye towards economy, it's an effective—and clever—metamorphosis.

Then there's Edward T. Lowe's disjointed, serial-like plot construction and unwieldy dialogue ("Why have you freed me from the ice that imprisoned the beast that lived within me?" Talbot awkwardly asks of Niemann after his thaw). The much-touted combination of creatures turns out to be something of a cheat, as they never meet. Dracula is destroyed long before the Wolf Man and the Monster show up, and the Wolf Man is dead before the Frankenstein Monster revives. Only getting up off the lab table for the film's final minutes, Glenn Strange's Monster is more a moving prop than actual character.

Perhaps most disappointingly, the screenplay makes hash out of Boris Karloff's pivotal character (a shame, given that Karloff was returning to the series that had made him a household name a decade before). To secure his aid, Niemann promises Talbot, "I'll build a new brain for you—I'll lift this curse from you forever." From his introduction in prison, during which he goes over a childish chalk diagram on his cell wall detailing the transfer of a human brain into a dog's body, Niemann has brain transplants on the, er, brain. Niemann's convoluted plan to revenge himself upon his enemies (those who sent him to prison 15 years ago) involves multiple brain swapping. "I'm going to give that brain of yours a new home," he tells a terrified Ullman (*King Kong*'s Frank Reicher), "in the skull of the Frankenstein Monster. As for you, Strauss [*Frankenstein*'s Michael Mark], I'm going to give you the brain of the Wolf Man, so that all your waking hours will be spent in untold agony, awaiting the full of the moon which will change you into a werewolf." He also plans to plop the Monster's brain into Talbot's body (why?), even though he'd sort of/kind of promised that body to Daniel. Whew. Not only is all this cerebral folderol needlessly complex, it's just plain silly.

Though obviously cranium-obsessed, Niemann seems a little vague on just where a person's mind (or personality) lay—in the brain or the body—as he waffles back and forth on this point (terrorizing Ullman by threatening to place his brain in a monstrous body, while threatening Strauss with a new werewolf brain). In any case, Niemann soon has Ullman's and Strauss' brains floating in jars awaiting their new bodies (though he's rudely interrupted by the mob of torch-wielding villagers before he can do anything with them).

A depressingly somber ending (resulting in death for *every* major character) concludes the serial-like scenario, striking a surprisingly dire chord. Considering this symphony appeared to be aimed at the younger crowd (given its chapter-play construction and focus on multiple monsters), such nihilism seems almost mean-spirited. (Incidentally, this was the first time the tried-and-true silver *bullet* came into play as a werewolf slayer.)

Yet even an inferior Universal monster rally remains worth seeing, with its occasional wisps of Gothic atmosphere, colorful players, rousing musical score and classic creatures—particularly when it features Lon Chaney's tragic Wolf Man. It's just too bad the foundations of this *House* proved so shaky.

With quotes from: "A Man, a Myth, and Many Monsters: Lon Chaney Jr.," by Jack Gourley and Gary Dorst, *Filmfax* 20; Carradine to interviewer Ted Newsom (quoted in *John Carradine: The Films*, by Tom Weaver); "Peter Coe Interview," by Conrad Brooks, *Cult Movies* 8.

Morphology: Larry Talbot's Wolf Man
Demise: Silver bullet
Full Moon Rating: **½

House of Frankenstein

(1997; NBC) Director: Peter Werner; Producer: Michael R. Joyce; Screenplay: J. B. White; Cinematographer: Neil Roach. Cast: Adrian Pasdar, Greg Wise, Teri Polo, CCH Pounder, Miguel Sandoval, Jorja Fox, Richard Libertini, Karen Austin, J.A. Preston, William Converse Roberts.

> Man's three most feared predators have returned—vampires, werewolves, Frankenstein loose in L.A.—promo spot

Originally broadcast in two parts on November 2 and 3, 1997, this 168-minute made-for-TV movie takes nothing from the original 1944 *House of Frankenstein* but the name—and the combining of the three classic monsters into one story (which, actually, is *more* than the rather-segmented '40s film did).

In modern-day Los Angeles, wealthy developer and owner of the Gothic-styled "House of Frankenstein" nightclub Crispian Grimes (Greg Wise) sends a team to recover the body of the Frankenstein Monster for display in his club. He also employs his lackey Klaus to take care of any "loose ends" in his various business ventures. A gray wolf attacks and kills one of Grimes' uncooperative business associates after a party, witnessed by Grace Dawkins (Teri Polo), who fends off the beast with some mace—but not before it scratches her leg. As the wolf retreats, leaping over a rock to escape, it begins to transform so that it hits the ground running as a *man*. You see, Klaus is a werewolf, and Grimes his vampire master. The detective investigating the killing, Vernon Coyle (Adrian Pasdar), soon falls for Grace, and vice-versa. Grace has been infected with lycanthropy, however (as a knowledgeable professor later explains, "If the werewolf hurt her in any way, even a scratch, then he's made her—she's a werewolf now too"). She and Coyle attempt to elude Grimes, who, having had to eliminate the unstable Klaus, has set his undead sights on making Grace his own. "Vampires love lycanthropes," explains the professor (CCH Pounder), "a little homo sapien, a little savage beast—you know how men are." After the vampire kidnaps Grace and installs her in his fortress-like mansion, Coyle, aided by the professor and a revived—and sympathetic—Frankenstein Monster (angry with Grimes for having killed the only human to have befriended him), must try to rescue Grace and destroy the evil bloodsucker.

Given its extended nature, it's rather disappointing that so few in-depth characterizations can be found in this *House*, with the protagonists seeming rather shallow and one-note (shrinking heroine, skeptical-but-brave hero [who at least drives a vintage mustang], strident know-it-all professor). But then, in a film like this it's the monsters that really count, and *House of Frankenstein* does a better job with *them*—at least the master vampire (played with delicious deviousness by Greg Wise) and the sympathetic Frankenstein Monster (brought to imposing yet poignant life by Peter Crombie). The werewolf, Klaus (Carsten Norgaard), has only a few scenes and even less personality, but the lycan-torch is soon passed on to Grace for the second half, which proves far more eventful than the movie's somewhat staid first 90 minutes.

After a slow start *House* takes off with one monster confrontation, attack, or all-out-assault after another, culminating in the protagonists' storming of Stone Manor ("played" by the famous Frank Lloyd Wright–designed Ennis-Brown house, the original *House on Haunted Hill*). Surprisingly, this ostensible climax—bearding the monster in his den—ends rather perfunctorily, with a simple fall from the balcony incapacitating the heretofore invincible vampire, allowing the Frankenstein Monster to unceremoniously drive a wooden railing into the bloodsucker's chest. Quite cleverly, however, things aren't what they seem, and there's bigger and better monster mayhem to come.

"Lycanthropes are a funny breed," states the professor at one point, "half human, half not." Taking a scientific approach to this supernatural phenomenon, she continues, "I like to think of the lycanthropic virus as a kind of chronic viral infection." Still, "to kill the lycanthropic virus once and for all you have to kill the host with a silver bullet."

For werewolves, the full moon does indeed affect a change, but they can also transform at will. "Lycanthropes are pretty normal most of the time," continues the professor, "but when the moon is full the virus gets a wake-up call and takes over. But if the lycanthrope chooses to wake up the virus he can do it every night he wants to." Lest one deem it a gift rather than a curse, however, she goes on to say, "Lycanthropes generally don't survive very long; it's a horrible existence. You're mortal like the rest of us—with all the same longings, fears and doubts in your heart—but you're a monster too."

After short-changing the werewolf in Part 1 (and after offering up such in-depth explanations for lycanthropy), it proves doubly disappointing that the script's second half keeps the newly-minted werewolf Grace largely locked up in Grimes' mansion where the besotted vampire tries to convince her to love him while attempting to kill her "true" love, Coyle. ("I need you to love me," insists Grimes, to which Grace disdainfully replies, "You're just like everyone else—you only want what you can't have.") This has the unfortunate result of turning this werewolf into a doggie-damsel in distress needing rescue from her detective prince.

But at least *House of Frankenstein* takes the same road as its namesake's sequel, 1945's *House of Dracula*, by allowing its werewolf to be cured—while providing a novel twist. During the fracas at Stone Manor, Grace goes over the balcony and transforms mid-air into a wolf (a *white* wolf rather than the gray beast that turned her). Grimes then commands the wolf to attack her would-be rescuers, forcing Coyle to shoot her with a silver bullet. After the Frankenstein Monster subdues the vampire, Coyle and the professor rushes the still-breathing wolf to a hospital. At gunpoint Coyle forces the medicos to take the animal into an operating theater, where he orders the docs to let the wolf flatline, returning Grace to her human form. The doctors then revive her (and remove the bullet), thus killing the lycanthrope virus but sparing the human. She is now cured.

It's almost a pity that, with the services of veteran werewolf creator Greg Cannom (*The Howling*, 1987's *Werewolf, Fright Night Part 2, Meridian, Van Helsing*) at their beck and call, *House*'s filmmakers decided to utilize a real wolf for their lycanthrope(s) rather than a wolf-man hybrid. But at least they allowed Cannom to create a credible makeup version for the Frankenstein Monster, as well as an excellent *Gargoyles*-like winged bat-devil creature for Grimes while in vampire form. Couple these impressive makeups with some surprisingly effective for the time CGI transformations (with the werewolves and vampires smoothly morphing almost instantaneously), and add in some mobile camerawork (highlighted by some vampire "flight-cam" heat-sensitive photography), involving action set-pieces (climaxed by a frenetic and exciting assault on the eponymous nightclub), and monsters you come to either love or hate, and this *House of Frankenstein* is definitely worth a visit for monster fans in search of a clever update on these classic creatures.

Morphology: Normal-looking wolf
Demise: Silver bullet to the heart
Full Moon Rating: ***½

House of the Wolf Man

(2009; Taurus Entertainment) Director/Producer/Screenplay: Eben McGarr. Cinematographer: Royce A. Dudley. Cast: Ron Chaney, Dustin Fitzsimmons, Jeremie Loncka, Sara Raferty, Cheryl Rodes, Jim Thalman, John McGarr, Michael R. Thomas.

THE MOST TERRIFYING, THE MOST CHILLING, THE MOST DIABOLOICAL HOUSE OF ALL…
—1940s-style trailer

In the 1940s Universal brought us the entertaining monster rallies *Frankenstein Meets the Wolf Man*, *House of Frankenstein* and *House of Dracula*. Perhaps disappointingly, they closed the cycle (with the comedic *Abbott and Costello Meet Frankenstein*) before they could produce what would have been the next logical entry—"*House of the Wolf Man*." Well, such an egregious oversight was rectified in 2009 by low-budget producer-director-screenwriter Eben McGarr. Unfortunately, it came a day late (actually half a century) and (far more than) a dollar short.

Dr. Bela Reinhardt (Ron Chaney, grandson of Lon Chaney, Jr.) invites five young strangers to his castle on a proverbial Dark and Stormy Night to choose an heir. "You are all very special in your own way," he tells them. "As a scientist, I'm curious to see how special." He concludes, rather menacingly, "My heir will be chosen through the process of—elimination." The quintet then have to deal with such melodramatic clichés as eyes watching from behind portraits, a hulking mute butler (à la Boris Karloff in the 1932 classic *The Old Dark House*), a washed-out roadway, a strange old woman hidden away in a secret room, and monstrous footprints outside the castle. After much bickering and poking about, they learn that Dr. Reinhardt is actually Dr. Frankenstein, that they're all his illegitimate offspring, that his famous monster is chained up in the basement, and, worst of all, that Reinhardt is a werewolf!

The first thing to strike the viewer is the film's picture-perfect 1940s horror atmosphere, with the various characters arriving one at a time in a driving rainstorm, pulling up in front of the castle in period automobiles to enter the impressive foyer. Several wonderfully evocative sets—ornately furnished bedrooms, long dark hallway, dungeon-like laboratory—almost become characters themselves due to the carefully crafted black-and-white photography and lighting (courtesy of veteran indy cinematographer Royce Dudley) right out of the classic Universal playbook, all planes of shadows and depth. Unfortunately, little of import happens in this wonderfully re-created environment, with nearly an hour of creeping about punctuated by windy exposition and stilted dialogue. Sample: "If he is to blame you shall have your pound of flesh, I assure you. But let us have the truth of it first." Even in the 1940s nobody talked like that. Consequently, until the film's final ten minutes, *House of the Wolf Man* comes off like an atmospheric but rather turgid stage play. The movie's last reel, however, is another matter...

It begins when Reinhardt gathers them all in the dining room to proclaim, "Tonight you are all part of my greatest experiment. To see if your gifts and your skills are the result of my blood running through your veins. If the moon intensifies your abilities and sharpens your survival instincts, or if my mother is right and it is not a biological mutation transferrable by blood, but a *curse*." At this, the full moon rises and Reinhardt transforms—in a simple but cleverly staged sequence. Sitting at the head of the table, Reinhardt drums his fingers impatiently as his potential heirs bicker amongst themselves. A close-up of his hand shows that his digits have become unnaturally hairy. After a cutaway, another close-up reveals that his still-drumming fingers are now tipped by wicked-looking claws. Noticing the change, the protagonists flee the room, and we see Reinhardt half-transformed, with facial hair and fangs. After another cutaway to the heirs' panicked flight, the camera returns to show Reinhardt even hairier than before. A shot of the full moon precedes his final appearance. Bushy hair sprouts from his head and cheeks, while a wrinkled forehead, canine nose, pointed ears and fangs, coupled with a powerful chest and muscular torso under a tattered white shirt, makes him look like a cross between one of Dr. Moreau's manimals and Oliver Reed from *Curse of the Werewolf* (this Universal-centric production's sole nod to Hammer horrors). He roars, leaps onto the table, and scrambles, almost simian-like, across it to bound over a chair and lope up the stairway after them. Such an impressive introduction, coupled with the animalistic athleticism of Billy Bussey as the Wolf Man, emphasizes the power and ferocity of this man-beast.

The monster readily dispatches most of the characters in a flurry of new-age nihilism that never would have passed muster with 1940s sensibilities. McGarr films these attacks, however, in keeping with his classic models—bloodless and either below frame or in silhouette. Ultimately, the Wolf Man goes mano-a-mano (lobo-a-cadáver?) with the mottle-faced Frankenstein Monster (another impressive variation on a classic horror figure, well played by Craig Dabbs clad in a sheepskin jersey à la *Son of Frankenstein*). It's an impressively brutal knock-down/drag-out that includes such sights as the Wolf Man nearly scalping the Monster, and the Creature tossing the lycan-

Promo for the 1940s-style, fan-centric *House of the Wolf Man* (2009), starring Ron Chaney, grandson of Lon Chaney, Jr.

thrope clear across the room (a nice bit of wire work). More energetic (and longer) than the much-heralded confrontation in *Frankenstein Meets the Wolf Man*, this battle of the titans ends, like its predecessor, before a resolution—this time not because of a blown dam but because Dracula (Michael R. Thomas doing a decent Lugosi impression) inexplicably shows up (for no apparent reason apart from completing the classic monster rally triumvirate of Wolf Man, Frankenstein's Monster and Dracula), resulting in the trio hissing, grunting and growling at each other before an abrupt "The End" closes it all out. Disappointing, to say the least.

The non-monster cast makes a far worse impression, however. While one can see why producer-director-screenwriter McGarr wanted neophyte Ron Chaney for his picture, casting the grandson of Lon Chaney, Jr., in a pivotal role proved to be the equivalent of shooting oneself in the foot (with a silver bullet). Though a nice man, Ron Chaney is no actor—and it shows. Such stunt casting rarely pays off, and it backfires here when it quickly becomes apparent that Chaney inherited none of his famous relatives' thespian talents. His awkward dialogue delivery, for which he employs a deep monotone in a vain attempt to disguise his rather milquetoast voice (and demeanor), reveals just how uncomfortable he is in front of a camera. "It was something that just popped up, I thought it would be a lot of fun," said Chaney about acting for the first time (and paying tribute to his grandfather). "It's something I've wanted to do all my life—a little boyhood fantasy come true." Good for him. Not so much for the viewer. The remainder of the cast (all amateurs or unknowns with few significant credits) are zealous yet unconvincing. Their hearts were obviously in the right place, just not the talent. Though one can applaud the efforts behind this earnest homage, *House of the Wolf Man* remains closer to a cinematic hovel than impressive movie mansion.

With quotes from: "Interview with House of the Wolfman's Ron Chaney," by Robert Hood, *Undead Backbrain*, July 20, 2010.

Morphology: Hairy, wolf-faced biped
Demise: No idea; the film ends before the battle of the monsters concludes
Full Moon Rating: **

House on Bare Mountain

(1962; Olympic International Films) Directors: R. L. Frost (Lee Frost), Wes Bishop (uncredited). Producers: David Andrew (Bob Cresse), Wes Don (Wes Bishop); Screenplay: Denver Scott; Cinematographer: Greg Sandor. Cast: Bob Cresse, Laine Carlin, Leticia Cooper, Laura Eden, Connie Hudson, Dan Hyland, William Kirk, Ingrid Lind, Virginia Mark, Ann Meyers, John Nada, Betty Peters, Laura Sanders, Roc Shannon, Fran Sinatra, Millie Stewart, J.J. Watson, Angela Webster.

EVERYTHING'S OFF! WHEN THE HOLLYWOOD
MODELS MEET THE MONSTERS!—ad line

Indeed, everything *is* off—in more ways than one. "*Filmed in* NUDERAMA *& Sexicolor*," this intermittently amusing, almost quaintly naughty "nudie-cutie" from the early 1960s is definitely "FOR *ADULT* ADULTS ONLY!" (as noted in the film's advertising). "$72,000 worth of sex, sin, seduction and laughter," promises the film's hyperbolic pressbook. While it does offer a few giggles now and then (depending upon how forgiving one's funny bone might be), as far as "sex, sin, and seduction" goes, this *House* is pretty bare indeed. Yes, a bevy of semi-nude (generally topless) young women frequently prance about (undressing, dressing, showering, jumping rope, sunbathing, showering again…), but, as was the custom of "adult" films in the early '60s, actual sex and seduction need not apply. As far as can be determined, the "nudie cuties" occupying the *House on Bare Mountain* are as chaste as they are well-endowed. Only later in the decade did (simulated) sex enter the cinematic lexicon of adult entertainment.

"Starring Lovable Bob Cresse as Granny Goode" (as the opening credits proclaim), the film begins with Granny Goode (Cresse in drag) behind bars, narrating the unfolding tale of "how a nice, kindly, white-haired old lady like myself wound up in this—*situation*." It begins (and ends) at "Granny Goode's School for Good Girls," which Granny runs as a front for her bootlegging operation housed in the basement. Presiding over her still is chief liquor-maker and bottle washer "Grackow," who just happens to be a werewolf! We discover this when Granny, annoyed with all the howling from the night before, storms into the locked cellar and proceeds to chastise Grackow by slapping his hand … er, paw. "Half-moon, full moon, blue moon—I don't care. You gotta stop buggin' the broads!" she admonishes before stomping on his foot for emphasis. Immensely tall, we only see Grackow's torso and hairy hands at first, until Granny climbs a stepladder so she can grab his shirt and finally look him in the eye. With bushy whiskers, a pompadour-like 'do and pointy ears, he makes for a rather benign looking lycanthrope, particularly given his makeup-free nose and lack of fangs. Given that the werewolf makeup (which ends at the neck—when Grackow lifts his head we see pale human skin) was provided by cut-rate veteran Harry Thomas (*Frankenstein's Daughter* [1958], *Plan 9 from Outer Space* [1959], *The Navy vs. the Night Monsters* [1966], etc.), it's little wonder Grackow looks so goofy.

Granny then proceeds to threaten Grackow with "the outside world. You remember the outside world, huh sweetheart? That's right—silver bullets, people chasing you all over the place, stakes in the heart. It was a real bad scene, wasn't it, sweetheart?" Grackow acts more like a lapdog than a werewolf, hanging his head in shame and uttering inarticulate mumbling sounds. Also, he apparently stays hirsute at all times, never changing back to human form.

With Grackow suitably cowed, Granny then goes about her business of running the school, which means extended scenes of the topless (and sometimes bottomless—at least from behind; back then, pubic exposure garnered attention from the pornography police) girls dressing, showering, performing calisthenics, etc. Often said "titillation" sequences are accompanied by Granny Goode's comical narration (she is, after all, telling us this story). For instance: "Sally was president of our Literary Society; and I tell you, her dramatic reading of *Tropic of Cancer* was something you'd never forget!" Or this: "The girl bouncing the beach ball is little Sandra. The poor child came from a broken home—her house slid off a cliff and cracked right in two."

The plot (such as it is) reveals that the new girl at the school is an undercover (though uncovered) policewoman, resulting in a raid during the school's annual "Masque Ball" (which devolves into topless dancing after various characters over-spike the punch). Granny gets the drop on the cops, however, after they sample her debilitating hooch. But there's one more twist to this tail-filled tale: Granny's escape is blocked by a man who declares he's from the UWA, Local 17—the "United Werewolves of America" union. Grackow has turned Granny in for paying him a mere 13 cents a day and "working him overtime without paying him overtime." So Granny ends up behind bars after all, declaring, "Well, that's how it all happened." But looks can be deceiving, and the camera pulls back to reveal the union man, the cops, and Grackow all chained in the basement making bootleg liquor. *They* are the slave-labor captives behind bars, and Granny goes upstairs to "greet the new freshman class … he-he."

"This film is the *Cleopatra* of the nudies," promised the *House on Bare Mountain* pressbook (referring to the then-most expensive film ever made). "Its total budget cost of $72,000 represents the most expensive professional nudie to date." While said figure may very well be the result of an inflated imagination, *House on Bare Mountain* does offer better production values than most of its ilk, with rich color photography, competent lighting, and even some camera movement. Also, the sets are fairly elaborate. Star Bob Cresse recounted:

A very dear friend of mine named Wes Bishop started that [film], and he'd done everything first class. He'd written the script which was a very clever idea, and as you know it turned out to be the first girlie film to include the monsters. He'd rented a huge studio and built big elaborate sets, he'd gotten expensive camera equipment and booms, cranes, dollies, and spent a lot on preparation, and thereby blown all his money. He was able to do one day's shooting, and then he had no more cash to finish the film. He came to me and told me the situation.... At that time, Lee Frost was my director, and the two of us were in the production and distribution of films. We told Wes, "Here's what we'll do. We'll pull you out of it. We'll put up the money to finish the picture, and take that money back out of the film rental, and we'll distribute the film for you, but we've got to film it our way." He said, "What's your way?" And I told him that we'd ad lib it and shoot everything in two days. He said, "It can't be done!" And I said that it could be done, with Lee and I working together and adding our scenes to the one day Wes had already shot. And that's what we did.... When Lee would get ready to shoot the scene, he'd ask, "Are you ready?" And I'd say, "Give me a minute to think of something." And I'd just ad lib the scene and we'd do it in one take each time.

Though there's little original in Cresse's Old Mother Hubbard act, he still makes for a likable enough pro/antagonist. "I put myself in the film doing a comedy part as Granny Goode," said Cresse, "which is my take-off on Jonathan Winters doing that old lady bit of his. Physically I do resemble Winters quite a bit."

"In combining three of the top gross attractions, nudity—comedy—and horror," assured the film's exhibitor manual to potential theater bookers, "*The House on Bare Mountain* should prove to be your biggest gross in many a year." It does indeed offer oodles of the first, and a generous (if not always palatable) helping of the second, but only the barest pinch of the third. In fact, the picture's one true "horror" figure (apart from a few poorly-costumed partygoers at the "Masque Ball" sporting Dracula makeup and a Don Post Frankenstein mask) is Grackow the werewolf. And he is played strictly for laughs. Even so, Cresse and company apparently gave their audience what they wanted, as, according to Cresse, "that film made money hand over fist."

With no hint of sexuality, but with plenty of pulchritude on display, *House on Bare Mountain* seems quaint, almost charming. And unlike its later nudie-cutie (pseudo)werewolf compatriot *Orgy of the Dead* (1965), it rarely outstays its welcome, even inspiring the odd chuckle here and there. Besides, how can one fail to appreciate a nudie film

"The Nudies Meet the Nasties"—and a werewolf—in *The House on Bare Mountain*.

whose opening credits include "Hair Styles by Hoover Vacuum" and "Body Makeup by Everybody!"

With quotes from: *House on Bare Mountain* pressbook, Olympic International Films; "Cult Movies Interview: Bob Cresse," by Mike Vraney, *Cult Movies* 9.

Morphology: Very tall, semi-hairy wolfman
Demise: None (unless one counts forced labor as a "demise")
Full Moon Rating: **

Howl

(2015; Metrodome; UK) Director: Pal Hyett; Producers: Ed King, Martin Gentles; Screenplay: Mark Huckerby, Nick Ostler; Cinematographer: Adam Biddle. Cast: Ed Speleers, Shauna Macdonald, Elliot Cowan, Holly Weston, Amit Shah, Rosie Day, Duncan Preston, Sean Pertwee.

> LAST TRAIN. FULL MOON. ALL CHANGE—ad line

We've had *Snakes on a Plane*, so how about Werewolves on a Train? That's the premise of this direct-to-video British effort. "I'd like to think there is more to it than that," laughed director Paul Hyett. "There's other things going on, we have our zero to hero train guard that has to step up emotionally and physically and has a character arc that shows him having to dig deep and step up in ways that he didn't think he could, to be an alpha male after another character in the film so clearly held that mantle. But saying that, it is supposed to be just a fun, popcorn type movie, an enjoyable creature romp." And in that, *Howl* at least partially succeeds.

Turned down for promotion, discontented train guard Joe (Ed Speleers) pulls a double shift on the midnight run from London to Eastborough. But while passing through some heavy woodlands (played by England's famous Black Park, home to many a Hammer horror), the train makes an emergency stop after hitting a deer. Something kills the investigating driver, leaving only Joe, trolley girl Kate (Shauna Macdonald), and a handful of disparate passengers to discover that a band of creatures—werewolves—are intent on making them their next meal. Needing to repair a damaged fuel line to get the train going again, the protagonists barricade themselves in a carriage, argue, sacrifice and die as they try to fend off the monsters.

Up until the 55 minute mark, all we see of the werewolf (at that point there's only one we know of) is a pair of oversized, muscular wolf legs (seen from underneath the other side of the train as the monster holds aloft a kicking victim) and a massive, hairy arm ending in a clawed hand (which drags a screaming woman through a shattered window). Once the beast finally steps into full view, however, the imaginative hopes raised by such tantalizing partial glimpses slide into dire disappointment. Long, lank hair frames a distorted, craggy, furless face and mouthful of ragged fangs. Its professional wrestler's physique consists of a thick, veined neck above a corded, muscular torso (again with little hair). About the only lycan-qualities on show are the oversized canine feet (accomplished via some surprisingly effective CGI applied to the creature's lower half) and a pair of wolfish pointy ears. "I wanted to get away from big furry werewolves with big snouts," proclaimed Hyett. He succeeded, as these werewolves look more like mutant cavemen than typical lycanthropes.

Werewolves on a train: *Howl* (2015)

Discarded along with the classical were-look are the usual lycan-trappings. Despite several foreboding shots of the full moon, the werewolves remain in their were-state even after dawn breaks, countermanding the typical nocturnal lunar laws of lycanthropy. In fact, we never see them change, even after death, so their condition may be permanent (there's no indication one way or the other). "I wanted to get away from the mythology of silver bullets and instant transformations," announced Hyett. Indeed, silver is not an issue, as a sharp axe—or even a fire extinguisher (used to cave in a beast's head)—will do the job. "My idea," continued the director, "was that it takes years to transform, from a bite, that it was a virus-like disease, bones would take a long time to transform, breaking and then reforming, muscles snapping and re-fusing." Though a unique take on lycanthropy (which, unfortunately, Hyett fails to put across in the film), the lack of a *human* side to these lycanthropes—or any individual personality, for that matter—removes from the creatures much of what makes werewolves such memorable monsters. Consequently, the creatures-trap-people-on-a-train scenario could just as easily have featured mutant cannibals, zombies or even Bigfoot.

"To be honest, it wasn't really the werewolf subgenre that influenced me on *Howl*," admitted Hyett, "more the '70s disaster movies like the *Poseidon Adventure*, *The Towering Inferno*, mixed in with John Carpenter, films like *The Thing*, *The Fog*. And there's references to *Elm Street* [the creature dragging its claws along the side of the train to terrify the inhabitants with the awful sound, for instance] and even *Irreversible*. I tried not to be influenced by other werewolf films but wanted *Howl* to be a retro type creature feature with a classic feel." Hyett didn't even mention what surely must be the film's foremost influence—George Romero's *Night of the Living Dead*. Aided by cinematographer Adam Biddle's atmospheric lighting (making the surrounding woods pregnant with menace) and claustrophobic photography, Hyett manages to effectively capture that horror classic's siege vibe, as the protagonists desperately try to secure their position to keep the creatures out, while dealing with the deteriorating group dynamics within. This was not sophomore director Paul Hyett's first lycan-rodeo. Having worked for two decades as a makeup and prosthetics effects artist, he previously helped bring to life the lycanthropes in *Werewolf: The Beast Among Us* (2012).

Howl starts slowly as it introduces the various characters but fails to adequately develop them, leaving only superficial impressions. Ed Speleers (of *Downton Abbey* fame, and who played the hero in yet another UK werewolf movie, 2012's *Love Bite*) makes for a likable enough lead, but there's little characterization left for the rest, who must make do with the standard Fat Guy, Bookworm, Alpha Male, etc., templates. And the film's best actor—Sean Pertwee (who in 2002 ran afoul of a far more impressive pack of werewolves in the excellent *Dog Soldiers*)—is completely wasted, as he falls victim to the creature almost immediately. Playing the train's driver, Pertwee appears in only one sequence, in which he creeps down the track for a few moments, checks the train for damage, and finds a deer under its wheels. He mutters a line or two, then abruptly meets his maker (*and* the unseen werewolf). Obviously the budget couldn't support Pertwee's salary for more than a one-day cameo, which is too bad, as his special brand of naturalness and intensity could have added some welcome (and much-needed) depth.

The film's best spell remains the twenty-minute patch in the middle when the terrifyingly mysterious creature traps them in the railway car, pounding the carriage walls, breaking through a window to grab a screaming victim, and generally ratcheting up the suspense and siege terror. Once the werewolf enters the car in full view, however, the tension dissipates drastically due to the monster's disappointingly man-like appearance and subsequent quick demise. Said demise does come in an impressively chaotic fashion, however, which remains far more convincing than the standard Hollywood action-hero set-piece. As panic erupts among the protagonists, the little band grab whatever they can find and lay into the creature with various wrenches, pipes and axes. Afterwards, viewing the bloody carnage, they're suitably hushed, even distraught, at what they've done, their realistic reactions highlighting the true horror of extreme violence. Suddenly, the battered creature sits up, but a resolute Joe simply grabs a fire extinguisher and repeatedly bashes its head until there's little left, concluding the sequence with a pragmatic—and refreshing—response to the old the-monster-isn't-really-dead-after-all bromide.

Before implementing their danger-filled plan to repair the fuel leak and get the train moving again, an exhausted Joe says a few words. "A few hours ago we were strangers. And most of you probably wish we still were. But we're going to try and get out of here now. We're gonna do whatever it takes to survive—*together*—all of us." The sentiment underlines the humanity that can save them, and defines the underlying strength of humankind—the ability to work together that has allowed our species to more or less master the planet and rise above the better equipped beasts around us … including, apparently, werewolves. But such self-sacrifice comes with a cost, and the film concludes on a satisfyingly somber note that's just light enough to avoid descending into nihilism.

Still, had *Howl* paid more heed to both its human characters and lycanthropic aspects, it could have become far more than just an "enjoyable popcorn movie that was funny, exciting and scary in places" (as characterized by Hyett).

With quotes from: "Interview with *Howl* Director Paul Hyett," by Matthew Kaiser, punchdrunkmovies.com; "*Howl* and *The Seasoning House* Director Paul Hyett," by Lisle Henderson, theslaughteredbird.com.

Morphology: Wolf-legged, loose-skinned bipeds
Demise: Brain-bashing; pole-skewering
Full Moon Rating: ***

The Howling

(1981; Avco Embassy) Director: Joe Dante; Producers: Michael Finnell, Jack Conrad; Screenplay: John Sayles, Terence H. Winkless (based on the novel by Gary Brandner); Cinematographer: John Hora. Cast: Dee Wallace, Patrick Macnee, Dennis Dugan, Christopher Stone, Belinda Balaski, Kevin McCarthy, John Carradine, Slim Pickens, Elisabeth Brooks.

> WHEN THE HOWLING STARTS … THE HORROR BEGINS!—poster (UK)

The year 1981 changed the face of werewolves forever—literally. Until then, Jack Pierce's *The Wolf Man* had served as the cinematic template for all things lycanthropic. But with the appearance of Rob Bottin's Big Bad Wolves of *The Howling*, werewolves would rarely harken back to the now-quaint man-covered-in-yak-hair prototype. Henceforward, lycanthropes would be measured against the towering wolf-headed nightmare creatures of this bonafide lycanclassic.

Los Angeles TV newscaster Karen White (Dee Wallace) puts herself on the line in order to lure out serial killer "Eddie the Mangler" (who's become obsessed with her TV personality). After a terrifying confrontation in a porn shop booth, in which Eddie (Robert Picardo) dies under the bullets of a spooked rookie cop, a traumatized Karen suffers from nightmares and amnesia. Karen seeks help from media guru and "behavioral expert" Dr. George Waggner (Patrick Macnee), who sends her to his woodland retreat up the coast called "The Colony" (an "experimental living community" that offers "seminars, group therapy … to try and tackle this amnesia thing"). Once there, Karen hears strange and terrifying howling in the surrounding woods, her husband Bill (Christopher Stone) falls prey to the seductions of "very elemental" Colony member Marsha (Elisabeth Brooks), and Karen's co-worker and best friend, Terry (Belinda Balaski), learns the truth—the Colony is actually a colony of *werewolves*, with Eddie being a former member (and brother of Marsha). Dr. Waggner has been helping his fellow lycanthropes integrate into the modern world, but Karen's presence threatens to end it all in death and destruction.

Not only did *The Howling* prove to be one of the most well-constructed (thanks to the multi-layered scripting of John Sayles), technically adept (courtesy of Rob Bottin's groundbreaking effects work) and entertaining (due to the deft and slyly humorous direction of Joe Dante) werewolf movies of all time, it stands as one of the most insightful, with ideas and issues writhing beneath its skin like a lycanthrope waiting to burst forth from its human shell.

"Repression is the father of neurosis, of self-hatred," pronounces Dr. Waggner on a TV talk show that opens *The Howling*. "Stress results when we fight against our impulses. We've all heard people talk about 'animal magnetism' and 'natural man,' 'noble savage'—as if we'd lost something valuable in our long evolution into civilized human beings…. We should never try to deny the beast, the animal, within us." So posits the clever, thought-provoking screenplay that brings to life this very "beast within."

In the end, the beast cannot be tamed, merely kept in check—and only for a short time. As elderly werewolf Erle (John Carradine) so succinctly puts it, "You can't tame what's meant to be wild, Doc; it ain't natural." Continues Erle, "We should have stuck with the old ways. Raising cattle for our feed—where's the life in that? Humans are our *prey*—we should feed on them like we always done. Screw all this channel your energies crap!" The pitiful psychobabble of modern society is no match for the natural order of things. In other words, it's true: you can't fight Mother Nature. Even Waggner himself capitulates at the close, forcing his foe's hand by steadily walking towards him and causing him to shoot. "Thank God," utters the weary doc as he falls, finding relief in death.

Sexuality plays an important role in *The Howling*—just as it does in nature. As personified in the figure of the wild, untamed, "nymphomaniacal" Marsha (enticingly encapsulated by newcomer Elisabeth Brooks), sexuality sits side-by-side with lycanthropy. Giving in to one's primal urges—as Bill does when he ventures into the moonlit forest to mate with Marsha—results in the emergence of his inner beast. Here sex, as much as violence, remains firmly linked to lycanthropy. Werewolf Eddie's first appearance comes backgrounded by a violent sex film playing in a porno shop booth (in which Eddie terrorizes heroine Karen White). Our animal natures are not merely comprised of bestial violence but equally of unbridled sexuality. This connection is literalized when Bill first transforms while making love to Marsha in the screen's *first* werewolf sex scene (culminating in a less-than-convincing special effect involving an obvious cartoon wolf silhouette—one of the film's few missteps). And it's sex that helps rip apart the human relationship between Karen and her husband Bill. After her trauma, she finds it difficult to make love to him. Rather than showing patience and understanding, however, Bill gives in to his baser animal instincts and consummates his new relationship with Marsha. Sex, as much as lycanthropy, has sundered their relationship.

Apart from a pair of largely unseen (at least in English-speaking territories) Mexican Santo flicks from the previous decade, *The Howling* was the first film to present werewolves in a communal setting, the first to reflect the pack mentality of real wolves. Up to now, werewolves had been decidedly solitary creatures, which goes against the true nature of wolves, who hunt and live—and succeed, like humans—through bonding and cooperation with others of their species. Such a sociologically relevant turn adds further dimension to an already thematically rich lycan-scenario.

Director Joe Dante, a film fanatic himself, filled his movie with referential in-jokes, such as placing a copy of Alan Ginsberg's "Howl," or a can of "Wolf Chili," in the background, having Disney's "Three Little Pigs" cartoon play on a television, and naming characters after earlier werewolf movie directors, such as George Waggner (1941's *The Wolf Man*) and R. William (Bill) Neill (helmer of *Frankenstein Meets the Wolf Man*). Other character names include Erle C. Kenton (*House of Frankenstein* and *House of Dracula*), Jerry Warren (*Face of the Screaming Werewolf*), Terry Fisher (*The Curse of the Werewolf*), Fred Francis (*Legend of the Werewolf*), Lew Landers (*The Return of the Vampire*), Sam Newfield (*The Mad Monster*), Charlie Barton (*Abbott and Costello Meet Frankenstein*), and Jack Molina (an Anglicized Jacinto Molina, aka Paul Naschy).

Beyond the obvious homages, Dante uses references to (and clips from) his hairy predecessors as cinematic shorthand (characters watch clips from *The Wolf Man* that concisely relay pertinent werewolf lore) and to underscore the action with knowing irony (cutting to Maria Ouspenskaya reaction shots from *The Wolf Man* at choice moments). And rather than relaying his movie's rules via the expected stuffy professor or werewolf expert exposition, Dante employs Dick Miller's cynical bookstore owner's offhand, amusing flippancy ("Silver bullets or fire—that's the only way to get rid of the damned things. They're worse than cockroaches").

But it's not just the expected tropes here, for *The Howling* adds a few fillips of its own, cleverly integrating them into the story. Not only can a werewolf "change shape anytime it wants, day or night, whenever it gets a notion to" (as Miller's bookseller informs), but "they come back from the dead if you don't kill 'em right. Plus they regenerate … three days later they're as good as new." This explains the "deceased" Eddie's terrifying—and unexpected—return toward the film's end.

"We had discussed which rules we were going to use," recounted scripter John Sayles (who cameos in the film as a sandwich-eating morgue attendant), "settling on a combination of Hollywood and traditional folklore—but I think we were among the first to create horror-movie characters who had seen horror movies." In other words, *The Howling* was "meta" before such a term even existed.

Continued Sayles, "We talked about the original shapeshifter myths, which usually involved somebody able to willingly turn into a predator to kill their enemies and have it blamed on an animal. This brought me to the idea of free will and all the other psychosocial experiments that were bubbling on the West Coast at the time—EST, Synanon, Reichians, primal screamers—and how some were about sublimating the id and some were about letting the inner child/beast out into its fullest expression." Under Dante's assured direction, Sayles' script pokes fun at all this "channel your energies crap" by playing up the quirks of the Colony's residents, their superficial cheeriness (or, alternatively, obvious broodiness) either masking or betraying their characters' dark undercurrents.

"We didn't want to do the Lon Chaney–style werewolf for *The Howling*," said Dante about his lycanthropes' new look. "We all loved those films, but here we wanted to do something severely different." And different they were, with latex, prosthetics, animatronics, puppets, air bladders, and even condoms pressed into service. "We looked at

16th-century woodcuts featuring wolves and werewolves," continued Dante, "we wanted the lean, hungry 'big bad wolf' look."

Dante originally hired Rick Baker to create his lycanthropes, but when John (*An American Werewolf in London*) Landis found out about this, he held Baker to a promise he'd made to Landis to do *his* werewolf movie (a promise made way back in 1971). Consequently, Baker recommended his protégé, Rob Bottin, to Dante for *The Howling*. Bottin was only 21 when he did the groundbreaking effects on *The Howling*, his first makeup job in charge (with an effects budget of $50,000). "He was wonderful," enthused Dante, "although the makeup took like two days to apply. We were woefully behind schedule all the time." But the patience paid off—handsomely. *The Howling* transformations were done in long takes (just as in *An American Werewolf*) that saw the actors twisting and contorting, with air bladders bubbling under latex skin to change man (and woman) into werewolf. "We kept [the transformation] in shadow," said Dante, "because it's scarier. It's also to hide the flaws. When you're dealing with latex and rubber, it's better not to see that it's latex and rubber." (Bottin also created several full-size dummy creatures that could be shot from air cannons so that it looked like the monsters were leaping through the air, though Dante ultimately cut this footage from the release print, feeling it didn't integrate well with the other werewolf scenes.)

Makeup man Steve Johnson, who worked on both *The Howling* and *An American Werewolf* (though going uncredited on *The Howling* because, he claims, "I was supporting Rick Baker, [so] Bottin had my name taken off the credits"), maintains that it was all Rick Baker's idea to film the transformations in real time. Johnson states that "Baker had told Rob about his ideas on how to transform the man into monster, and they were so excited.... Rob ripped off Rick's ideas, and *The Howling* was released first."

Either way, it works a treat. The show-stopping sequence of Eddie's transformation begins with his face beginning to *bubble*. His eyes go white, then become a luminous green. He holds up his hand and sharp nails emerge from the fingertips. His shirt splits on his chest as his torso, covered in fine hair, expands. Eddie's mouth, now filled with fangs, pulls back in a hideous rictus grin as his face pushes outwards into a wolf muzzle, while pointy ears emerge from beneath his matted hair. "Our werewolf transformations are so much better than the one in *An American Werewolf in London*," opined star Dee Wallace. While some might take exception to this, they are indeed amazing. Dante agreed with Wallace. "Less is more," opined the director. "There is so much light in *American Werewolf*'s transformation that what are really brilliant effects don't come off as well as they might."

When it comes to moviemaking (or anything, really), serendipity is a quality not to be undervalued. It was intended that Eddie's

Poster for the terrifying, wittily self-aware, and groundbreaking *The Howling*, which, in tandem with *An American Werewolf in London*, kick-started the moribund werewolf subgenre in the 1980s.

transformation be smooth and fluid, but as Dante recalled, "When we came to do it on the set, we would press buttons, or pull things, and sometimes things would pop. We tended to view it as a mistake, and when we were editing the scenes we tried to cut around the parts that changed abruptly." But with bone-cracking sounds added (at the suggestion of the sound effects editor), "all of a sudden they were on purpose. So the whole concept, instead of being this sort of supernatural, smooth, gliding change, became this torturous, painful, bone-cracking metamorphosis. In addition to covering up our mistakes, it improved the whole scene."

John Carpenter (*Halloween*) hired Bottin to do the effects for his remake of *The Thing* on the strength of the artist's work on *The Howling*. Carpenter told Bottin, "Rob, I just saw *The Howling*, that's the scariest stuff I've seen in my entire life. How is anyone ever going to top that? Can you top that? Can you?" Given Bottin's subsequent visually stunning, award-winning effects work on *The Thing* (1982), it's safe to say the answer was "yes."

Director Joe Dante came up through the ranks at Roger Corman's New World company (a kind of informal hands-on film school). Said Corman, "We had a kind of training program that not everybody goes through, but Joe Dante is a good example. Joe started as an assistant editor, went on to be a trailer editor, then a feature editor, then a second director, and finally a director. So by the time he was a director, he had learned our style of work." And he put this style to good use on *The Howling*, as evidenced by his handling of the first full-on werewolf appearance.

It begins when Karen's friend and co-worker Terry arrives at the Colony to check on some leads. As she walks through the foggy woods in late-afternoon light towards Marsha's cabin, a hairy, clawed hand startlingly rises up into the foreground, indicating the stalking has begun. Then as she cautiously enters the shack, a shot of two wolfish legs, walking upright, following her ratchets up the unease. After Terry finds some incriminating drawings and gruesome bone-sculptures that tell her Eddie has been here, the beast's powerful arm suddenly breaks through the wood wall to grab at her. A frantic Terry manages to chop off the limb with a hatchet, gazing in horror as it bubbles and changes to the disembodied arm of a *man*, before she panics and flees back to the deserted Colony offices. There she regains her composure, calls her lover (another co-worker), and begins going through the doc's files. Just when she finds a file on Eddie, a clawed hand abruptly enters the frame (echoing the previous scene) and takes the folder from her. We then see the beast in all its imposing glory—a huge, upright, powerful, hairy torso topped by an elongated wolf's head sporting long ears and a toothsome muzzle. It opens its huge maw and swipes at the side of Terry's head, knocking her to the floor. The searching eyes, the brows knitting in a snarl, the muzzle wrinkling as it howls brings the creature to convincing life as it lifts the terrified girl by the neck, her feet frantically kicking the air while the elongated, clawed wolf-legs stand unmoving in an image of horrific power incarnate.

With *The Howling*, Dante managed to create not only an artistically significant werewolf movie, but, by all accounts, a fantastic working environment for those involved. "*The Howling* was a blast," enthused star Dee Wallace (whose affecting, vulnerable portrayal of Karen anchors the film in the here-and-now), "and my all-time favorite film to do! My fiancé at the time, the late, great Christopher Stone, played my husband. We were in love and working together!" In fact, it was Wallace who suggested Stone for the role. "It was once again like, 'Let's put on a show,'" continued Wallace, "everyone in one trailer, working ungodly hours—and having a *blast*." (And what was Wallace up to during her fiancé's sex scene—with another woman? "The night they shot that, I went off to a local bar and drank!" said the actress.) Christopher Stone tragically died of a heart attack in 1995 at age 53.

"Working with Joe is a joy!" confirmed Wallace's co-star Belinda Belaski. "First of all he allows everyone his or her creative freedom…. As far as John Sayles and his writing, I just feel he is an absolute genius. He told me on the set of *The Howling* that he loved my Betsy character so much from *Piranha* that he created my Terry Fisher role based upon her!" And frequent Dante collaborator Kevin McCarthy (here playing Karen's gruff newsroom boss) told this author, "Working with Joe is always a delight. He's very inventive. Whimsical, sardonic, sparky. Loads of fun."

Joe Dante might very well have passed on directing *The Howling* had things gone a little differently. At the time, Dante had signed on to direct a proposed *Jaws* sequel for Universal, tentatively titled *Jaws 3: People 0*. But with feuding producers pulling the project in different directions, Dante jumped ship when offered *The Howling*, described by a producer friend as an innovative and unique werewolf movie. "The worst thing you can do as a director is work for people who don't know what kind of movie they want to make," said Dante. "I thought it would be great to once again work on an independent film, a film where I'd have complete artistic control rather than being at the mercy of a major studio, like Universal. So I left *Jaws 3: People 0*, which was shelved and made way for the legit *Jaws* sequel *Jaws 3-D*. I went on to do *The Howling*, which was a superb career choice I must say!" Indeed it was.

Of course, this same year saw the release of another groundbreaking were-classic, *An American Werewolf in London*, which hit theaters a mere four months after *The Howling*. Both films are smart, witty, and very frightening, and both feature excellent special effects and terrifying werewolves. Many fans consider one or the other to be their favorite lycan-film, but it boils down to a matter of personal preference between the two quality productions. Of the two watershed werewolf movies, *The Howling* went into production first in 1980, and was completed much faster and cheaper than *American Werewolf*. *The Howling* took 28 days to shoot, at a cost of $1.6 million (though, according to Dante, "a lot of [that] money didn't get up on the screen" due to having to "pay off a number of other people who owned rights to things"). Dante feels *The Howling* actually forced *American Werewolf* helmer John Landis' hand. "It galvanized John into action," claimed Dante. "I don't know if he would have done *An American Werewolf* if he didn't have this other movie competing."

Scheduled to come out in October 1980, *The Howling*'s release was pushed back when Dante decided to add some post-production effects. After principal photography wrapped, Dante told Avco Embassy, "If you could give us a couple of more bucks, we can do better." The execs agreed, and Dante added a week of re-shoots with a full werewolf suit. "We went back and replaced a lot of things in the movie with this new stuff, and it made all the difference," recalled Dante. Finally released in April of 1981, the film was a, er, howling success, earning nearly $18 million in the U.S. alone. (Note: *An American Werewolf* brought in $30 million domestically, but cost six times what *The Howling* did to produce, giving *The Howling* a far better profit ratio than its rival.)

In any case, *The Howling* stands on its own two were-feet as the film that reshaped the modern werewolf, creating *the* new image of an iconic monster within a self-aware, frightening and funny milieu that remains a beloved, and much-copied, template to this day.

With quotes from: "Back to the Colony," by Lee Gambin and Ki Wone, *Fangoria* 307; *Reel Terror*, by David Konow; *Shock Masters of the Cinema*, by Loris Curci; "The New Breed of Werewolf FX," by Mark Salisbury, *Fangoria* 134; *Voices from Twentieth-Century Cinema*, by Wheeler Winston Dixon; *Massacred by Mother Nature*, by Lee Gambin; Interview with Kevin McCarthy conducted by the author, 1996; *Horror Film Directors*, by Dennis Fischer.

Morphology: Towering Big Bad Wolf on two legs
Demise: Silver bullets and fire
Full Moon Rating: *****

Howling II see *Howling II…Your Sister Is a Werewolf*

Howling II: Stirba—Werewolf Bitch see *Howling II… Your Sister Is a Werewolf*

Howling II…Your Sister Is a Werewolf

(1985; Hemdale; UK/USA) Alternate Titles: *Howling II: Stirba— Werewolf Bitch* (UK); *Howling II* (US video). Director: Philippe Mora; Producer: Steven Lane; Screenplay: Robert Sarno, Gary Brandner (based on the novel *Howling II* by Gary Brandner); Cinematographer: Geoffrey Stephenson. Cast: Christopher Lee, Annie McEnroe, Reb Brown, Marsha A. Hunt, Sybil Danning, Judd Omen, Ferdinand Mayne.

It's the rocking, shocking, new wave of horror—trailer

What is it with werewolf sequels? Is there some mysterious force that, like the inexorable pull of the moon, transforms a lycan-classic's follow-up into something hideous? Looking at the likes of *An American Werewolf in Paris*, *Teen Wolf Too*, and the first of these abysmal modern missteps, *Howling II…Your Sister Is a Werewolf*, one might be forgiven for thinking so. Poor in nearly every respect, the only enjoyment to be gleaned from *Howling II* is its camp value as a swirling whirlpool of ineptitude.

Tenuously tying itself to the original, *Howling II* opens at the funeral of the first film's heroine, Karen White, attended by her brother Ben (Reb Brown), her friend and colleague Jenny (Annie McEnroe), and the mysterious "occult investigator" Stefan Crosscoe (Christopher Lee), who comes right to the point when he tells Ben, "Your sister was a werewolf." Ben reacts as any normal person would, but that night he and Jenny return to the cemetery and witness Stefan fending off a werewolf attack, as well as dispatching Ben's sister (the silver bullets were removed during an autopsy, allowing her to revive). Ben and Jenny then join Stefan on a trek to Transylvania in search of the Queen of the Werewolves, Stirba (Sybil Danning), hoping to put an end to the evil lycanthropes' reign before they take over the world … or something.

From its first expository scene, in which Stefan takes Ben and Jenny back to his home (the Frank Lloyd Wright–designed Ennis-Brown house, better known to horror movie fans as the *House on Haunted Hill*) to watch a video of Karen's final broadcast (a slipshod reenactment of the scene from *The Howling* in which Karen turns into a werewolf on national TV) to the cheesy light show climactic demise of Stirba, *Howling II* simply reeks of ridiculousness. In between it offers such dubious "delights" as a castle guarded by men wearing ludicrously large medieval helmets; a passel of dominatrix-dressed women serving as Stirba's retainers; a werewolf "orgy" in which a gaggle of extras writhe around on the floor in front of Stirba's throne in various states of dress and transformation (consisting of the odd pointy ear and set of fangs); a ménage à trois involving Stirba herself in which the trio, their bodies covered in downy hair ("I had to endure eight hours of them gluing hair onto my body," complained Danning), snarl and pose and wave their claws in a laughable attempt to convey lupine passion without actually touching each other; a creepy hotel clerk who gleefully announces the protagonists will be occupying "room 666" (for no discernable reason); dialogue on the level of "I told you we'd get these fuzzballs"; an uncomfortable looking Christopher Lee trying his best to stay stentorian in a punk night club while wearing blue jeans and new wave plastic sunglasses; and a passel of flat-faced wolfmen that look like escapees from a high school adaptation of Pierre Boulle's *Monkey Planet*.

"It was a werewolf movie, and after two weeks, the werewolf suits had not arrived," explained director Philippe Mora about why the sudden drop from Rob Bottin's groundbreaking lycanthropes of *The Howling* to the new film's bargain-basement monkey costumes. "When they finally turned up, they were in crates stenciled 'Planet of the Apes.' They'd sent me monkey suits. Christopher [Lee] said to me, 'Dear boy, I have an idea for you. Tomorrow, do a close-up on me, and I will explain that before man turns into wolf, he goes into a monkey phase: man, monkey, wolf.' I said, that's brilliant, that's exactly what we're going to do."

The "Howling" theme song, performed by UK composer Stephen W. Parsons in a faux-nightclub in Prague (but with a real audience of Iron Curtain punks), can be heard on four different occasions throughout the film, and its driving beat and dark pulse remains one of the picture's few positives. "Originally I was not going to be in the movie," recalled Parsons, "but then everyone was like, 'Ah! Now we have this rock theme and we're going to recreate a club in Prague; how about you come over and form a band to do the scene?' I thought that would be fun. So we put a group together, and it was a great time."

If *Howling II*, made for a mere $2 million (though even that seems considerably more than what appears onscreen), is remembered at all by those who saw it back in the 1980s, it's for two things—both of them belonging to Sybil Danning. The spectacularly-endowed Austrian-born actress was at the time the queen of exploitation cinema. Unfortunately, her limited acting ability couldn't match her limitless figure. Though she looks good in her poofy blond '80s hair and physics-defying outfits (looking like they'd just fallen off the *Battle Beyond the Stars* wardrobe truck), she carries little weight when she speaks, sounding more kitten than lioness (or more pup than she-wolf). Mora and company apparently recognized this and kept her dialogue as minimal as her leather-and-latex ensemble. At one point, "inspired" by the were-mating of her two underlings, she oh-so-dramatically rips off her top to expose her ample breasts in a moment sure to make male viewers sit up and take notice. The film's producers did as well, for during the movie's closing credit montage, composed of shots from the film interspersed with the faux new wave band performing (yet again) the "Howling" theme, they play this bodice-ripping scene again, and again, and again—*seventeen times*! And so the filmmakers divulge the level of respect they have not only for their material (and lead actress), but for their audience as well.

Writer Gary Brandner, upon whose novel *Howling II* the film was (loosely) based, and who wrote the first-draft script (later changed significantly by Robert Sarno), recollected that after an initial screening, "Danning ran out in tears because they kept flapping her breasts like that!" "Oh, she was absolutely mortified," agreed Mora. "I had done it five times because I thought it was funny. Unbeknownst to me, the producer saw it and thought it was the greatest thing he'd ever seen. He said to the editor, 'Re-print that!' So *he* has to get a lot of the credit." Danning, though indeed perturbed, has apparently since made peace with it. "The next day," recalled the actress, "I went straight to the producer's office and asked them to cut the ripping-dress bits. He reduced the number of times that shot appeared [given that seventeen remained in, one wonders how many they took out!], but he wouldn't take them out completely. The producer thought they looked great, the buyers loved it, fans love it, so how can I argue with that?" Well...

"It could hardly be dignified with the label 'horror movie,'" concluded Christopher Lee of the film, "since it apparently wanted to send up the lycanthropic genre, but failed to frighten or amuse." *Howling II* could hardly be dignified as a *movie*, period. While Lee brought his trademark dignity and gravitas to his poorly-scripted part, he had to make do with absurd expositional dialogue like, "At the next full moon it will be the tenth millennium of Stirba's birth; at midnight on that day, all werewolves will reveal themselves. The process of evolution is reversed. Before that happens, Stirba must be destroyed, and I will do it." Mr. Lee's commanding demeanor *almost* makes you believe it.

Absurdisms abound when it comes to *Howling II*'s werewolves. Apart from their threadbare simian appearance, these lycanthropes are "immune to silver—only titanium will kill them." Why? Luckily Stefan and the Transylvanian locals have a plethora of *titanium* bullets, knives and axes lying about. At one point Stefan gives Ben and Jenny a pair of "holy medals," saying, "They will protect you." Later Stirba simply removes the medal from around Jenny's neck and sends it back to Stefan to lure him to her; so much for "protection." (By the way, the film's Big Reveal indicates that Stefan is Stirba's *brother*, though apparently *not* a werewolf. Again—why?)

Here lycanthropy definitely falls on the Satanic side, with Stirba being something of a sorceress. (She even keeps an inverted crucifix—the international symbol of Satan—in her castle lair.) Sitting on her throne festooned with human bones and wolf pelts, she strokes a stuffed wolf(!) and grasps a staff topped by a two-foot gargoyle. At one point she pulls a Moses and brings the staff-topper to rubbery life to attack an interloper. Stefan arms Ben with a pair of "blessed" earplugs to protect him against Stirba's evil spells, which sees her spouting gibberish and shooting red lights from her fingertips in order to make a confederate's eyes literally pop from his head (a poorly-realized gore effect that wouldn't be amiss in an H.G. Lewis movie).

This Satanic origin for lycanthropy is completely at odds with the nature-themed werewolves of the original *Howling*. In the first film, the lycanthropes were all about embracing one's true nature; here it's about giving in to hedonism via the unholy, the Satanic (hammered home when a werewolf hunter tosses some holy water onto a wolfman, causing it to scream and smoke).

Director Philippe Mora and cinematographer Geoffrey Stephenson over-light their authentic Czechoslovakian castle settings and woodlands to an alarming degree. Given the brightness of their nighttime settings, Transylvania must have some extra powerful stars shining in its skies. Consequently, Mora's desperate attempt to build atmosphere consists of randomly inserting shots of Gothic architecture, gargoyles, and the famous skeleton clock from Prague's town square. And to suggest the werewolf transformations, he simply repeats a few close-ups of pointy ears, hair growing from skin, and rubbery muzzles pushing forward—over and over (and over) again.

"This was far from my favorite," deadpanned Christopher Lee to authors Tom

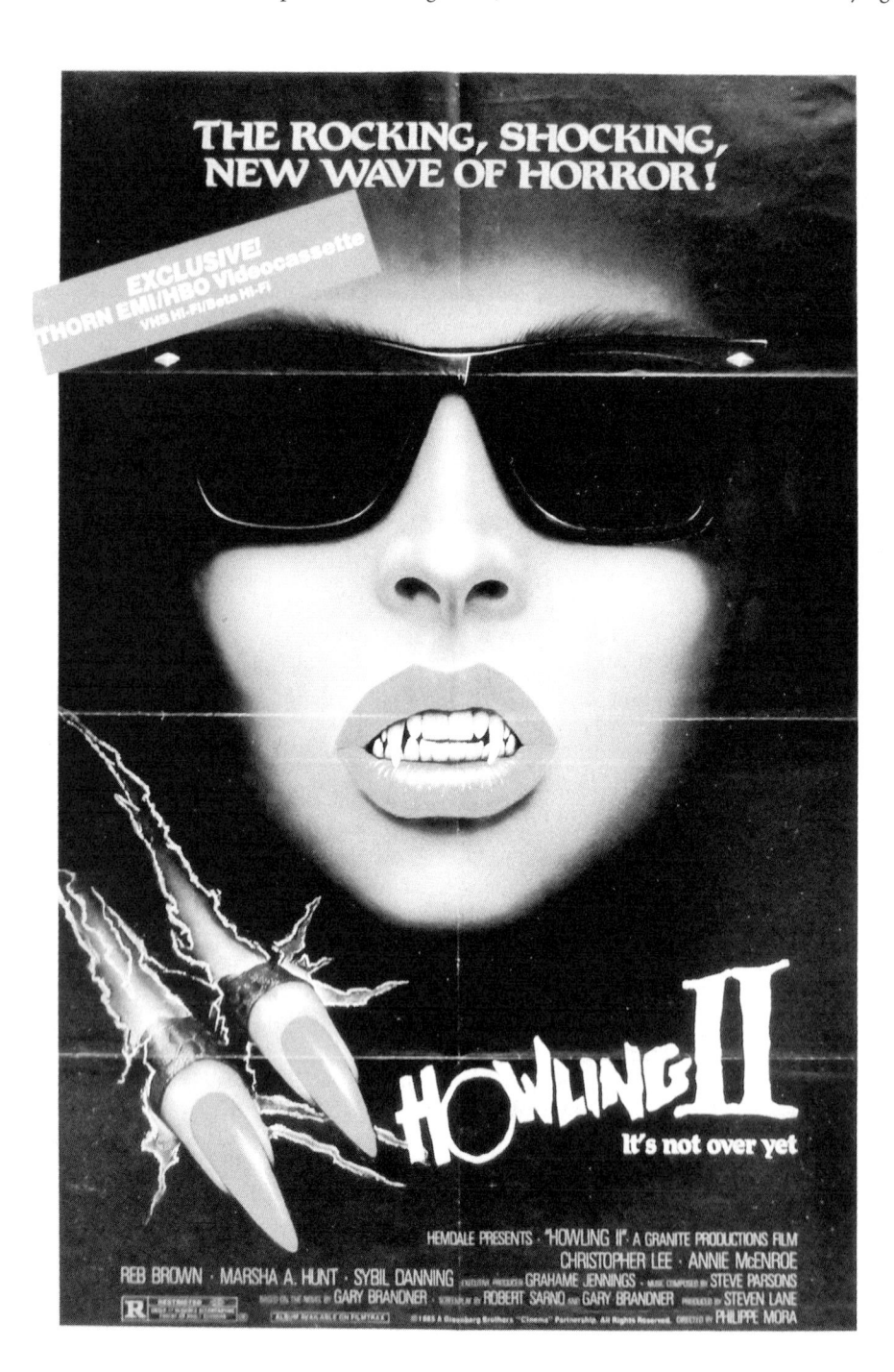

One of the worst sequels to one of the best werewolf movies—the campily inept *Howling II... Your Sister Is a Werewolf* (U.S. video poster).

Johnson and Mark A. Miller. "Dreadful. I'd done just about every possible horror movie, so, I thought, why not a werewolf film? I read the script and thought it would be okay. Most scripts do look okay. It's putting them on the screen that's difficult.... Also, it offered me the chance to see Czechoslovakia." At least he got *something* out of it (it certainly wasn't professional satisfaction). Unfortunately, this sorry specimen turned out to be the only lycan-foray made by the late, great Sir Christopher Lee, last of the classic horror stars.

Amazingly, *Howling II* failed to kill the *Howling* franchise, which gave birth to six more entries to date. "It's not over yet," warned the film's trailer. Looking at the results, perhaps it should have been…

With quotes from: "Interview: Sybil Danning," by Santos, horrornews.net; "Christopher Lee: Dracula, Nazi Hunter and Much More Says Filmmaker Philippe Mora," by Philippa Hawker, *Sydney Morning Herald*; "Pet Sounds: The Music of *Howling II*," by Kristian Day, *Fangoria* 340; "Horror in Print: Gary Brandner," by Stanley Waiter, *Fangoria* 72; *Showgirls, Teen Wolves, and Astro Zombies*, by Michael Adams; "Danning with Praise," by Lianne Spiderbaby, *Fangoria* 302; *Lord of Misrule: The Autobiography of Christopher Lee*, by Christopher Lee; *The Christopher Lee Filmography*, by Tom Johnson and Mark A. Miller.

Morphology: Hairy, primate-like wolfmen (and women)
Demise: Titanium (knives, axes, bullets)
Full Moon Rating: *

Howling III see *Howling III: The Marsupials*

Howling III: The Marsupials

(1987; Bancannia/Square Pictures; Australia) Alternate title: *Howling III* (UK). Director/Screenplay: Philippe Mora (based upon the book *Howling III* by Gary Brandner); Producers: Charles Waterstreet, Philippe Mora; Cinematographer: Louis Irving. Cast: Barry Otto, Max Fairchild, Imojen Annesley, Dasha Blahova, Leigh Biolos, Ralph Cotterill, Barry Humphries.

JUST WHEN YOU THOUGHT IT WAS SAFE
TO GO DOWN UNDER…—ad line

What if a race of werewolves evolved along the same lines as humans? And what if in Australia they evolved from *marsupial* wolves (mammals who raise their young in a pouch)? "We Australians have a marsupial version of everything, including the wolf," noted director Philippe Mora. "Why not put that into the pop zeitgeist? It was comedic—werewolves with pouches!—but I wanted to be *pro* these creatures."

Beautiful Jerboa (Imojen Annesley) runs away from her abusive stepfather Thylo (Max Fairchild) in the tiny outback town of Flow ("Wolf" spelled backwards). In the big city of Sydney she meets Donny (Leigh Biolos), assistant director for the in-production horror movie "Shape Shifters Part 8." Getting Jerboa a part in the production, Donny and she fall in love. But it soon comes to light that Jerboa is a lycanthrope—a marsupial werewolf. Meanwhile, scientific investigators Beckmeyer (Barry Otto) and Sharp (Ralph Cotterill) have been searching for a werewolf study subject, and find one in defecting Russian ballerina Olga (Dasha Blahova). With the (were)cat now out of the bag, the government begins a crackdown on lycanthropes, taking everyone in Flow prisoner and chasing Donny and Jerboa (who now carries their newborn son in her pouch), and Olga and Beckmeyer (who's become sympathetic to the persecuted werewolves' plight) into the Bush, where they must evade or destroy the military operatives sent in after them.

Writer-producer-director Philippe Mora returned from the disastrous *Howling II* to bring this second sequel to life—meaning one should keep expectations *low*. As author Gary Brandner, whose book *The Howling III* was adapted (at least the title, anyway) for this film, succinctly put it, "Unfortunately, the same guy who botched up *Howling II* directed *Howling III*!" Surprisingly, Mora actually exceeded expectations here, turning out twice the film as *Howling II* for less than half the money. Which just goes to show that everything starts with the script. That said, *Howling III* is still not a particularly tasty shrimp on the barbie.

It's all well and good to make a plea for tolerance, even within the context of a cheap horror movie. Mora and company in *Howling III*, however, in making their "plight of the werewolf" film, present lycanthropes who (apart from Jerboa) are shown as brutish, uncouth primitives that, when transformed, do nothing but maim and kill. While this serves the cause of exploitation, it weakens the film's underlying theme—that just because someone is different does not mean they should be persecuted, much less hunted down and killed. And, truthfully, the film's painfully obvious low budget (less than a million dollars) doesn't allow for much in the way of convincing exploitable material anyway (with its PG-13 rating—making it the only *Howling* entry to sidestep an R—keeping things bloodless). The werewolves' appearances are at best amateurish and at worst laughable, often looking like actors sporting large papier-mâché dog heads. This works just fine in the more comedic moments during its first third (such as the appearance of a trio of goofy-looking were-nuns with mutant snouts protruding from their habit-framed faces), but when the movie gets down to business and takes a more serious turn as it explores the plight of this persecuted species, one's willing suspension of disbelief bounds away like a startled kangaroo.

Mora does his best to sell it by keeping shots of the various werewolves minimal, utilizing split-second slices of fur and snout to try and preserve some semblance of believability. Unfortunately, he doesn't always succeed. For instance, Mora shoots Thylo's transformation scene (in which the two docs induce the change by subjecting their strapped-down subject to a strobe light) as a chaotic, visceral, and frightening experience, all flashing lights, exploding equipment (the transforming lycanthrope emits huge amounts of energy, thus disrupting the electronics), and agonized sounds emitted from the werewolf mingling with the panicked screams of the terrified scientists. But the scene's impact is undercut by the subpar effects, with simple cutaways indicating several stages of change until a shot of the rubbery snout stretching like a sock puppet completely bursts the lycan-bubble.

Though misleadingly advertised in the UK with ad lines like "The agent of SATAN is at large…," *Howling III* eschews the Satanic evil of the *Howling II* werewolves to return to the more lycanthrope-as-creature-of-nature underpinnings of the original *The Howling*. Unfortunately, that's about all this sequel shares with the classic first film, apart from a healthy dollop of humor. While not nearly as sly in its comedic elements as the original, *Howling III* nevertheless manages a few amusing moments. For instance, when Beckmeyer meets with the President of the United States (played by Australian veteran actor Michael Pate of *Curse of the Undead* fame) and tells him, "We possess evidence that werewolves exist … in the Soviet Union," the President interrupts with, "Look, Beckmeyer, I am as anti-communist as the next man, but this is preposterous." Later, three female werewolves come to the city searching for Jerboa disguised as *nuns*. And Mora is not above sending himself up as well, by having the effete movie director (Frank Thring, sounding—and looking—a bit like Alfred Hitchcock) tell his new starlet, "This movie is about pop culture. In the sixties Andy Warhol shows us how pop could be high art. In fact, everything is high art—that's what this is all about. For example, in your first scene you'll be gang-raped by four monsters."

These lycanthropes (with their outback camp festooned with human skulls and ribcages) can change at will. "It's not the full moon that turns you—that makes you wild," Jerboa informs Donny during their post-coital embrace (as a slowed-down cover version of John Fogerty's "Bad Moon Rising" by The Reels plays softly on the soundtrack). When Beckmeyer asks the captive Thylo, "How do you turn yourself into your animal self?" Thylo answers, "I just think about it and it happens. If I get mad sometimes it'll happen. If we're frightened we change. Flashing lights can make us like animals." So strong emotions and strobing light (like with epileptic seizures) can induce the transformations.

The scientists link these lycanthropes not to European wolves but to the Tasmanian wolf (extinct since 1933). "Look at those stripes," observes Sharp, "they're identical to the markings of a Tasmanian wolf, one of the few marsupial carnivores." This leads to the lycanthropes' spiritual origin legend, with Thylo telling how, long ago, "when the hunters killed him [the Tasmanian wolf], his spirit came into us. He's in us now. We are him." This mystical notion becomes literal when Thylo calls on "the Phantom," a wolf spirit, to "make me the Big One." The next we know, a (ridiculous looking) giant wolf-rat head bursts into the tent of the two military assassins sent to kill the lycans, ending in a bazooka-caused explosion that obliterates everything. Jerboa, however, offers a different, more romantic, take on this "Phantom." "He once was a man who loved a beautiful wolf," she says. "They had children—half wolf and half human—us. When he died he turned into a big wolf and visited us in our dreams."

Beckmeyer, appalled at the government's genocidal attitude toward this "new species," learns that in the 1800s several governments, including Britain and the U.S., went on a campaign to wipe out the lycanthropes around the world. "The Pope believed they were a Satanic manifestation," explains a high-ranking military man, "and asked both governments to keep the matter secret for all time." The military now intends to wipe them out completely. Beckmeyer then escapes into the Bush with the few remaining lycanthropes. Twenty years later, Sharp finds Beckmeyer and informs him, "The Pope came out and declared that lycanthropes were not the Devil's work, and we were all God's children. He declared an amnesty. The President endorsed it." This leads to the film's unlikely Disney-ish happy ending coda, in which the protagonists' twenty-year exile in the Bush ends when the world decides to accept the werewolves as human and live in harmony with them. This in itself is one thing—if the filmmakers want to put forth these pie-in-the-sky sentiments to the audience, then do it—but to insert a final cheap and cheesy "oh-no-it's-happening again" closing shock ploy only negates this tone and leaves a sour taste in the viewer's mouth (not sweetened by the generic '80s glam-rock soundtrack that both audibly annoys and seriously dates the film).

The Australian *Howling III* featured the screen's first (and only) *marsupial* werewolves (U.K. DVD cover).

On the plus side, Mora proves inventive at times, employing a p.o.v. fish-eye lens, for instance, when the heroine tries to stave off a transformation triggered by some flashing lights. And when the ballerina involuntarily changes during a rehearsal at the Sydney Opera House, Mora makes clever use of the camera to both add urgency and disguise the subpar effects. As she spins on her toes, the camera periodically cuts to the few shocked onlookers, each time going back to the ballerina to show her having grown hairier and more wolfish with each twirl. Finally, she sports a furry body and full wolf's head, with Mora offering quick edits of muzzle and hair to mask the cheesiness of the, er, mask.

"You're damned if you do and damned if you don't," said Mora about making *Howling* sequels. "If you copy the first one, they say 'Big deal.' If you don't, they say 'Why did you do it?' With *The Howling* series, every single film is different. I intended *III* to be a parody of the whole genre." Unfortunately, *Howling III* fails as a parody, as its humor lacks both consistency and bite (with the film's final half turning serious and, worse, saccharine). Mora *did* succeed in creating something "different," however, via his presentation of *marsupial* werewolves. That's *something*, anyway.

With quotes from: *Showgirls, Teen Wolves, and Astro Zombies*, by Michael Adams; "Horror in Print: Gary Brandner," by Stanley Waiter, *Fangoria 72*; "*Communion*, an Interview with Writer Director Philippe Mora," by Irv Slifkin, moviefanfare.com.

Morphology: Hairy, wolf-headed *marsupial* bipeds
Demise: Ordinary bullets
Full Moon Rating: **

Howling IV: The Original Nightmare

(1988; IVE; UK) Director: John Hough; Producer: Harry Alan Towers; Screenplay: Clive Turner, Freddie Rowe (story: Clive Turner; based on the novels *The Howling I, II*, and *III*, by Gary Brandner); Cinematographer: Godfrey Godnar. Cast: Romy Windsor, Michael T. Weiss, Antony Hamilton, Susanne Severeid, Lamya Derval.

A TERRIFYING JOURNEY INTO THE GAPING
JAWS OF DEATH…—ad line

Shot in South Africa on a reported $2 million budget, and released straight to video, *Howling IV: The Original Nightmare* returns to its roots as more of a remake of the original *The Howling* than a sequel. In fact, it adheres closer to Gary Brandner's first *Howling* novel than the original film did. It didn't help.

Troubled best-selling novelist Marie Adams (Romy Windsor) suffers from hallucinations (ghostly nun, fiery wolf's head, bleeding eyes). Her doctor prescribes rest, telling her husband Richard (Michael T. Weiss), "She needs to go somewhere where her imagination won't be stimulated." So the couple rent a remote cabin near the tiny mountain town of Drago (a highly unlikely hamlet so small that its one street remains unpaved yet still manages to boast a general store, bar, tow truck service, doctor, sheriff, art boutique and even massive bell tower). That night they hear howling in the woods, which frightens Marie. She makes friends with Janice (Susanne Severeid), an ex-nun come to Drago to investigate the mysterious trauma that resulted in the lingering death of her friend Sister Ruth. It turns out Sister Ruth is the nun of Marie's "hallucinations," and their further investigations leads them to conclude that Drago is populated by werewolves—a conclusion confirmed when Richard succumbs to the charms of a dusky local beauty and becomes a manbeast himself. The two terrified women set a trap for the townsfolk, leading to death and fiery destruction.

Apart from the original's Joe Dante, *Howling IV* features the most accomplished director to get behind a *Howling* camera—John Hough. But the Curse of the Howling Sequel apparently struck down even this proficient filmmaker, as Hough brought little of the talent (and none of the enthusiasm) he displayed on films like *Twins of Evil* (1971) and *The Legend of Hell House* (1973). Defeated by the uneventful script, wooden acting, and dearth of werewolfery, Hough's by-the-numbers direction makes the film a listless exercise. "I was very disappointed with the director of *Howling IV*," complained producer/co-writer Clive Turner, "but I thought we ended up with a reasonable film, and the special effects by Steve Johnson were just stunning." Obviously Turner (who cameos as a tow truck driver) thought wrong about the "reasonable film," though he was closer to the mark about the effects—what there are of them.

"There's something so sinister about these woods," observes Marie. Perhaps that's due to the overworked fog machines that fill the surrounding woodlands with clichéd mist every night. Talk and fog are about all the film has to sustain itself for its first forty minutes. When something finally does happen, it's a hiker attacked by … a subjective camera. We don't actually see a werewolf until the 65-minute mark, and it's onscreen for only a second (when his lover instantly transforms and bites the cheating Richard on the shoulder, thereby making him a lycanthrope too). We must wait another ten minutes for anything else of import. This also proves to be a blink-and-you'll-miss-it attack consisting of some parting bushes, a rushing shape, a brief shot of a muzzle latched onto the victim's neck, and a glance at the subsequent wound. But then comes the Big Scene—Richard's (and the film's only) transformation. And it's a doozy. As Richard walks through the woods, he suddenly stops and doubles over in pain. Straightening up, he begins to *melt*. Dripping goo and bits of flesh (reminiscent of the vampire bodyguard's ghoulish demise in *Fright Night*), Richard dissolves into a gooey skeleton sinking into a puddle of slime. Suddenly—and inexplicably—out of the woods pop several half-transformed wolfmen (and women) to rhythmically chant "Satan calls you" (to speed up the metamorphosis, perhaps?). Then from the puddle rises a wolf-shaped figure, a pale canine muzzle emerging from its misshapen face. While not particularly convincing (and too abrupt in its conclusion), at least this showstopper evinces some grisly imagination.

Even so, FX artist Steve Johnson was disappointed in the way his werewolf effects were utilized. "Lennie MacDonald, Bruce Zahlava and Eric Feidler did a wonderful job," enthused Johnson. "However, the final effects look nothing like we intended. The producers wanted something really new for the transformation, so we had the man *melt* into a big pool of ooze in several different stages. Then we zoom in on the pool and it forms into a wolf. But take a look at the edited film; I don't think that idea gets across, through no fault of our own."

While stingy with its werewolf sightings, *Howling IV* at least offers lycan *variety*, with one wolf-headed biped (whose huge toothy muzzle ringed by coarse hair harkens back—albeit faintly—to the original *Howling*'s lycanthropes), several clothes-wearing wolfmen, and finally a pack of red-eyed German Shepherds. And as a bonus, the town doctor becomes something that looks like a big-eared, wide-mouthed gargoyle.

But no amount of last-minute were-scrambling can offset the film's fatal structure. Its mystery angle is an obtuse one, since the movie spends most of its time following the two women as they try to figure things out, when *we* know from the get-go it's … werewolves. And by saving all its were-action for the final ten minutes, the film hobbles to the finish after shooting itself in the foot. Add in two leaden leads (Windsor and Weiss) who possess about as much charisma as their big, blow-dried hair, and the film topples over from its own ennui.

More a remake than a true sequel, *Howling IV: The Original Nightmare* **actually hues closer to its source novel than** *The Howling* **did back in 1981. Unfortunately, it falls well short of its model in every *other* respect.**

While *Howling IV* lives up to its subtitle in terms of revisiting its literary origins, it fails (miserably) to measure up to its cinematic model. Rather than *The Original Nightmare*, it proves to be The Original Dud.

With quotes from: "*Howling VII*: Long in the Tooth?" by Anthony C. Ferrante, *Fangoria* 134; "The Comeback Kid," by Gregory Nicoll, *Fangoria* 76.

Morphology: Sparsely made-up wolfmen (and women); hairy wolfish biped; and a pack of four-footed canines
Demise: Fire
Full Moon Rating: *½

Howling V: The Rebirth

(1990; IVE/Vestron; UK) Director: Neal Sundstrom; Producer: Clive Turner; Screenplay: Clive Turner, Freddie Rowe (story: Clive Turner; based upon the series of books *The Howling I, II and III* by Gary Brandner); Cinematographer: Arlege Armenaki. Cast: Philip Davis, Victoria Catlin, Elizabeth Shé, Ben Cole, William Shockley, Mark Siversten, Stephanie Faulkner, Mary Stavin.

> The Beast Returns!—ad line

What do you get when you mix two parts *Ten Little Indians*, one part *The Beast Must Die*, and a smidge (and I do mean smidge) of lycanthropy? *Howling V: The Rebirth*. Cynically tying their rehashed hoary-old-mystery plot to the lucrative (at least on video) *Howling* franchise, screenwriters Clive Turner and Freddie Rowe concoct a tale of eight individuals invited to the opening of "a Hungarian castle that's been closed for 500 years." (Five centuries ago, all the inhabitants of said residence were killed or committed suicide, leaving only a single baby alive.) A snowstorm strands them at the castle, and soon some mysterious killer/beast begins picking off the guests one by one, as they try to piece together the mystery. It comes to light that all eight have the same birthmark, which relates them "directly to the events that occurred in this castle 500 years ago," according to their enigmatic host, the mysterious Count (Philip Davis). It transpires that the Count, a member of "an ancient religious order," has lured each of them there to discover which one is "the werewolf, and to kill it."

Populated by under-developed ciphers (amorous tennis pro, bubbleheaded actress, enigmatic Swedish star, charming playboy, scholarly professor, mysterious Count, and even a sinister butler) rather than realistic characters, and brought to "life" by a cadre of unknowns whose acting ranges from competent to flat to plastic, it takes far too long for the plot to get up and running. For the first half-hour the various protagonists chit-chat, deliver sketchy back stories, and wander about the castle for no discernable reason. Despite all the palaver, the script fails to provide enough substance to make us care about any of these cardboard caricatures. Consequently, when the principals finally begin turning up dead, one can hardly be bothered to take notice—particularly given the repetitive nature of these (off-screen) killings.

"You can shake a piece of fur fabric at the camera for those guys and they'd be happy," said FX maven Steve Johnson (a former assistant of Rob Bottin's) dismissively about *Howling V*'s producers. And that's about all one gets from *Howling V*. "I loaned [*Howling V* effects artist] Kevin Brenna my wolf suit [from *Howling IV*] and suggested they use him." And they did ... barely. For all the werewolf "action" seen onscreen, the film could just as easily have been shot as a straight mystery melodrama. (In fact, the practicalities of a murdering werewolf in this setting comes into serious question, as this secret were-killer, rather than simply killing and immediately resuming its benevolent guise, must first undress, then transform, then transform back, and then get dressed again each and every time it claims a victim—all unseen, of course) Never once does the camera capture the creature for a good look, leaving only two split-second shots of gaping jaws, one hairy clawed hand, and a brief backlit outline of Johnson's hairy body suit to convey the central menace. We never see an actual attack, just the occasional panicked victim as *something* comes for them. And this werewolf kills exactly the same way every time, leaving identical neck wounds on the various bodies the protagonists stumble across. Consequently, these supposedly horrific aftermaths, rather than inspiring shock or terror, simply induce yawns—not only from their tameness but their sameness.

Like installments *II* and *IV*, *Howling V* drops the Return-to-Nature thematics of the original *Howling*'s werewolves to give its beast a Satanic origin, with dialogue even intimating that this werewolf may be directly linked to the Devil himself. "Have you ever heard of Satanic possession," the Count asks one of the final survivors, "where the Devil inhabits the soul of a human being?" Earlier, one of the guests related, "About 1000 years ago in Hungary, packs of savage wolves actually terrorized this area. And legend has it that Satan was in control, taking the guise of men by day and running with the wolves at night." His gullible listener exclaims, "The Devil was a werewolf! Wow, that's incredible." Indeed.

The notion of silver never raises its metallic head. In fact, according to the Count, this werewolf is immune to *everything*—except its blood-relations. "There is only one werewolf," he proclaims, "and it can only be destroyed by one of its own, one who has the mark." Such an odd notion goes nowhere, however, as nobody ever mounts a decent defense against the (unseen) terror. Nor is there any sign of a metamorphosis (something perhaps beyond the impoverished budget). Obviously this werewolf can change at will, though at the end, the Count informs a fellow survivor that "in a moment, when the moon breaks through the clouds, you will see. He will transform—he cannot help himself." So the full moon triggers an involuntary transformation, though ap-

This British DVD cover for *Howling V: The Rebirth*, which has more in common with Agatha Christie's *Ten Little Indians* than *The Howling*, shows far more of the werewolf than the lycan-lite movie itself.

parently only when it peeks from behind the clouds (a ridiculous notion, actually, meaning that all a lycanthrope need do is avoid the moon's direct light—by staying indoors, for instance). Of course, it turns out Mr. Know-It-All Count is quite wrong, for in the final shot the moon does indeed emerge, and the culprit, rather than transforming, simply smiles knowingly into the camera.

While the authentic Hungarian castle settings look stark and impressive, director Neal Sundstrom (who went on to make sexploitation flicks in France) underutilizes this rich setting by confining his cast to a few rooms, and repeatedly going over the same handful of spots to represent the supposed "endless labyrinth" beneath the castle.

"I like *Howling V*," said Clive Turner (who not only co-wrote and produced *Howling V*, but cameoed as one of the doomed guests). Well, that makes one. "But one of our biggest problems," he continued, "was that Murphy's Law operated while we were shooting. We shot it in Hungary in January, when it was supposed to snow; it had snowed there every year for the past 50 years. But whenever we did a scene requiring snow, it was always sunny and bright, so we had to import it in." Uncooperative weather proved the least of the film's problems, however. With its cardboard characters, stilted script-of-convenience (which has the mortally endangered protagonists stupidly *split up* to endlessly wander the maze-like secret tunnels beneath the castle; while one even takes a bath "to feel better"), dearth of action, near-invisible werewolf, and poor photography (with lighting sometimes too dim to even make out which character is in frame, much less show what they're doing), rather than "The Rebirth," *Howling V* should have been subtitled "The Stillborn."

With quotes from: *The Illustrated Werewolf Movie Guide*, by Stephen Jones; "*Howling VII*: Long in the Tooth?" by Anthony C. Ferrante, *Fangoria* 134.

Morphology: Hairy biped (at least in outline, as the film never displays it clearly)
Demise: None
Full Moon Rating: *

Howling VI: The Freaks

(1991; Allied Entertainments/Avid Home Entertainment; UK) Director: Hope Perello; Producer: Robert Pringle; Screenplay: Kevin Rock; Cinematographer: Edward Pei. Cast: Brendan Hughes, Michele Matheson, Sean Gregory Sullivan, Antonio Fargas, Carol Lynley, Jered Barclay, Bruce Martyn Payne.

> Vampire vs. Werewolf: The Ultimate Clash
> of the Forces of Evil—ad line

Unfortunately, this promised "ultimate clash" comes too little and too late to save yet another *Howling* sequel from its bargain-bin destiny. Like most of the others, *Howling VI* is a sequel in name only, taking nothing from any previous *Howling* entry but the theme of lycanthropy. It follows the travails of drifter Ian (Brendan Hughes) who walks into the small town of Canton Bluff just before the arrival of "Harker's World of Wonders" traveling carnival. Immediately hired by town preacher Dewey (Jered Barclay) to help fix up the dilapidated church, Ian, though keeping to himself, makes a favorable impression on the locals, not least of all Dewey's beautiful daughter Elizabeth (Michele Matheson). But Ian has a dark secret—not only is he tracking the sinister Harker (an evil vampire who had wiped out his family years ago), he's also a werewolf. When Ian's lycanthropy is exposed, Harker (Bruce Martyn Payne), with the sanction of the townsfolk, puts him in a cage to exhibit as his latest attraction. But when several citizens turn up dead (killed by Harker), the town targets Ian, culminating in the promised vampire vs. werewolf showdown.

Howling VI offers a rare appearance by a woman in the Man's World of horror movie directors. First-time director Hope Perello had plenty of production experience at Empire Pictures, where she'd worked her way up from assistant to the head of production to VP in charge of production (producing both *Puppetmaster* and *Catacombs* herself). "I felt kind of stupid at the beginning," admitted Perello about directing for the first time, "because although I had lots of production background in horror movies, I hadn't seen many of them. I never knew you could do so much with horror movie material until I delved into *Howling VI*." Sadly, Perello actually does very little with the material—at least for the movie's first half. It takes that long for Ian's lycanthropy to finally show itself, with the bulk of the time spent watching Ian repair the church, finger his notes and clippings about Harker, and try to avoid falling in love with Elizabeth. Intended to engender sympathy and develop Ian's goodhearted and tragic character, these mundane scenes, rather than inspiring pathos, simply instill impatience (not helped by Brendan Hughes' complete lack of personality as Ian).

Wasted opportunities and head-scratching incongruities rise quicker than a full moon. Ian tells of how Harker had murdered his family and changed him into a lycanthrope (*tells*, rather than shows, with Perello eschewing a golden opportunity for a portentous flashback), yet Harker ridiculously fails to recognize Ian (noting only that he "looked familiar"). "Harker was part of some strange cult," recounts Ian, "my father was obsessed with destroying it." Harker wiped out Ian's entire family and "left me like this—with this curse." That's all we're told (again, not shown) of how Ian became a werewolf. Such lazy scripting and corner-cutting direction is emblematic of the contrived nature of this tepid tale.

Other moments of inane expediency come when the heretofore cool-as-an-undead-cucumber Harker, leading the werewolf hunt for the persecuted Ian, becomes impatient and indulges in a ridiculous vampiric hissy-fit (tipping over a parked pickup truck during his tantrum) in front of the townspeople, stupidly exposing himself as the monster he is. And Harker's motivation remains hazy at best. Why frame his self-proclaimed "prize attraction" for murder? Then Harker begins destroying his own carnival as he pursues Ian, intent on killing him no matter the cost. Again, why? If he's had some change of heart about utilizing Ian as his new carnival freak, the film doesn't deign to let us know.

To their credit, Perello and screenwriter Kevin Rock try to infuse their werewolf movie with loftier themes than the expected Tragedy of the Lycanthrope trope. Most notably, the script addresses the plight of those different from the "normal." Harker himself explains his "Museum of Oddities" in terms of succor for its denizens. "This world serves many purposes," he says. "To the curious—it is a source of fulfillment; to the weak—it is a source of strength; and to those that live in it—it is a source of sanctuary." This "Normals are the *real* monsters" theme harkens back to Tod Browning's *Freaks* (1932). To the filmmakers' *dis*credit, however, this sentiment rings hollow given the cruelty and murderous malignancy exhibited by Harker's trio of goons, "oddities" all—a murderous dwarf with a third arm (Deep Roy), a sadistic she-male (Christopher Morley), and a bloodthirsty geek (Antonio Fargas, "Huggy Bear" from the old *Starsky and Hutch* TV series!).

Perello does little better by her werewolf, though she introduces him via a memorable (if brief) full moon metamorphosis. Taking a page out of the *American Werewolf* playbook (or at least a line or two), she shows Ian groan in agony while his fingernails painfully pop upwards as claws protrude from beneath them. He then falls to the floor, and his back tortuously arches and cracks and moves under his shirt, while his bubbling face becomes more angular. Fully transformed, however, Ian-wolf makes for a poor lycan-specimen, as he looks more like an unkempt Frankenstein Monster than a savage wolfman. With sparse hair on his oversized chest, and most of his face bare (fringed by a scraggly beard and lank hair), he sports a Neanderthal-like brow and nose. About the only wolfish characteristics are his furry arms and clawed hands, his sharp teeth, and his extended canine-like feet.

"Todd Masters [*Nightmare on Elm Street 5*] devised an effect using short stilts that would allow the werewolf to walk on its haunches without being supported by wires," enthused Perello. "The guy in the suit was on those stilts every day at least a month before we began shooting so he could really work with them, and it was so hot he was getting an Olympic workout. Ultimately, he could only stay up for a few minutes at a time." For all we see of this fancy footwork (a solitary scene lasting only a few seconds in which the were–Ian merely traipses off into the woods), the "guy in the suit" (Tony Snegoff) needn't have bothered.

Worst of all, this lycanthrope does nothing of import until the final, over-too-quickly battle with the evil vampire. After transforming, we see nothing more of the werewolf until Harker exhibits the captured Ian in his freak show the following night. At the show, Harker fingers a magic crystal and mutters a mysterious incantation, which triggers the chained Ian's transformation (a novel notion that reinforces the lycanthrope's Devilish origins). Harker then tosses a cat, befriended earlier by the sympathetic Winston the Alligator Boy (Sean Sullivan), to the were–Ian to demonstrate the beast-man's ferocity. But the wolfman sees Winston's horrified, silent pleading and releases the cat rather that eating it. Harker had earlier told Ian, "You are the worst kind of freak—one who tries to control it. But you can't deny your true nature." Apparently, Ian's lycanthropic nature isn't much different from his human one.

The more impressive monster turns out to be Harker when he vamps out, with his dark blue skin, demonic face and bald nosferatu pate, but he only appears at film's end for The Big Battle. It begins with the vampiric Harker tossing about the now-human Ian. Winston grabs Harker's magic crystal and recites the incantation, causing Ian to change for the vampire vs. werewolf smackdown (since it's not a full moon, Ian needs this little diabolical "push" to transform). Disappointingly, it lasts less than a minute before were–Ian grabs a wooden shaft and stakes the vamp, then rips the tent flap open to expose his enemy to the rising dawn, resulting in a dusty disintegration. Ian is obviously still Ian while in wolfman form, able to out-think (and stake) the vampire, and never hurting anyone (even the cat) except said bloodsucker.

"I just love the characters," exclaimed Perello. "The werewolf is tragic—he's cursed, he doesn't want to be the way he is and there's nothing he can do about it. And, to a lesser degree, the same is true of the vampire. They're not born evil; they're made that way." Here Perello articulated one of mankind's age-old questions: Destiny or Free Will? (which, in today's modern parlance—and biological bent—can be recast in light of Nature vs. Nurture). "The difference" continued Perello, "is that the vampire's given in to evil, while the werewolf is still fighting." This, too, like so much in the film, comes across in only muddled half-measures, as one never gets the impression that Harker has *any* regrets whatsoever. Betraying nary a hint of the supposed tragedy about which Perello speaks, he is fully comfortable in his own evil skin, with Bruce Martyn Payne (providing the movie's sole convincing performance) playing the Devilish Monster to a tee. Payne went on to play a werewolf himself two years later in the far superior *Full Eclipse*.

Like in several previous *Howling* features, Satanism once again sits at the root of lycanthropy. Harker, during his carnival barker's spiel before unveiling his new werewolf exhibit, intones, "The very heart of Satan beats within him. Only God's purity can kill him—silver, forged from a holy chalice blessed by a man of God. This is the only way he will know death." So ordinary silver bullets just won't do; they must be crafted from a holy relic and further blessed by a minister—not that this point ever gets tested.

"The producers might have liked something with a little more emphasis on the gruesome aspects of the story," admitted Perello. "But, to be honest, the heavy gore wasn't in the script and I wasn't about to go out of my way to put it there." Nor did she put in much in the way of horror, either, or just plain excitement, making *Howling VI: The Freaks* just another desultory denizen of the *Howling* ghetto.

With quotes from: "Scare Sisters," by Maitland McDonagh, *Fangoria* 102.

Morphology: Barrel-chested, bearded wolfman
Demise: None
Full Moon Rating: *½

Howling VII see The Howling: New Moon Rising

Howling VII: Mystery Woman see The Howling: New Moon Rising

The Howling: New Moon Rising

(1995; Allied Entertainment/LIVE Entertainment) Alternate titles: *Howling VII*; *Howling VII: Mystery Woman* (UK). Directors: Clive Turner, Roger Nall (uncredited); Producer/Screenplay (based on the series of books *The Howling I, II* and *III* by Gary Brandner): Clive Turner; Cinematographer: Andreas Kossak. Cast: John Ramsden, Ernest Kester, Clive Turner, John Huff, Elizabeth She, Jacqueline Armitage, Jim Lozano, Robert Morwell, Jim Brock, Claude "Pappy" Allen, Harriet Allen, Romy Windsor.

SOMEWHERE OUT THERE A NEW
TERROR IS BREEDING—ad line

Up in the high desert hills above Yucca Valley in California, near Joshua Tree National Park, stands a small community called Pioneertown. Its unique history began back in the 1940s when Roy Rogers, Gene Autry and the Sons of the Pioneers banded together to construct a Western town movie set with real buildings in which they could live while filming. Over 50 motion pictures and countless television shows (including *The Cisco Kid*, *Annie Oakley*, and *Judge Roy Bean*) have been filmed there.

What has all this got to do with werewolves? Well, just ask Clive Turner, writer, producer and star of *Howling IV*, *Howling V* and this one, the seventh in the loosely-related *Howling* film series. Turner set *The Howling: New Moon Rising* in Pioneertown, utilizing the real-life locations (including the famous Pappy & Harriet's Pioneertown Palace bar) and hiring various non-actor residents to play themselves. "Clive had been visiting there for years and decided to set the story there, and just grafted on the werewolf plot," revealed *New Moon Rising*'s original director, Roger Nall.

Though tying together the events (via "flashback" footage) from *Howling IV* and *V*, the film ignored *Howling VI* altogether (despite Turner serving as post-production supervisor on *VI*), with Aussie biker Ted Smith (Turner) apparently having survived the events of *Howling V* to come riding into Pioneertown. Landing a job at Pappy & Harriet's Pioneertown Palace bar, he quickly ingratiates himself with the locals (including Pappy and Harriet) through his wit and charm. Ted's late-night pronouncements into a tape recorder, however, indicate an agenda beyond slinging drinks and telling jokes. Meanwhile, a human skeleton has been found in the desert, and the detective on the case (John Ramsden) for some reason seeks out Father

John (John Huff), who specializes in bizarre phenomenon, for consultation. After reviewing the file, Father John pronounces, "The being that killed that man is none other than our adversary the Devil—in a lycanthropic manifestation. The killer is a werewolf." Though skeptical, the inspector continues digging into the case, particularly after several people around Pioneertown turn up dead, apparently savaged by a wild animal. Circumstances point to Ted, and the townsfolk take up arms against the perceived werewolf. But a clever ruse perpetrated by the inspector, in collusion with Ted himself, exposes the lycanthrope's true identity, with the silver-armed locals at the ready.

Full disclosure time. I've been to Pioneertown (and spent many pleasurable hours at Pappy & Harriet's) and have a fondness for the place and its quirky denizens. (*Billboard Magazine* named Pappy & Harriet's Pioneertown Palace one of the "Top Ten Hidden Gems in the Country" for its 2012 "Best Clubs" issue. Among the performers who've taken the stage there are Robert Plant, Eagles of Death Metal, and Vampire Weekend.) My father lived in Pioneertown (in a house my grandfather built) as a boy, and even ended up sitting on Roy Rogers' knee one time for a photo-op. So while I like to think I can separate nostalgic warmth from critical thought, one might make a claim to some bias on the part of this author. That said, I fully realize this film's shortcomings. Yet I also see the underlying charm that filmmaker Turner brought to the production via his obvious affection for the town and its people. Consequently, I can't agree with *New Moon Rising*'s general reputation as the worst of the lot (*Howling V* wins that "honor," with *Howling II* a close second, despite the latter's admitted camp entertainment value).

Though sometimes touted as the nadir of the *Howling* series, the straight-to-video *The Howling: New Moon Rising* is actually better than most of its brethren. Which, admittedly, is damning with faint praise. Like *Howling V*, it offers a novel setting, though this time a Western town rather than Hungarian castle. Also like *V*, the film is constructed as a who-is-the-werewolf mystery, though with more engaging characters and a better constructed script. And while it offers no more original werewolf action than *V* (and its beast, when momentarily revealed at film's end, is more trite than terrifying), it at least takes the best of *Howling IV* by swiping nearly all its lycan-footage (including the startlingly gooey metamorphosis scene) to illustrate the flashbacks.

Still, this *New Moon Rising* falls flat in many respects. The first half-hour consists largely of "local color," with scene after scene of the regulars drinking and line dancing; and Ted sweeping up, telling jokes or romancing the waitress. Sample "comedic" exchange:

JIM: "You ride in from Australia?"
TED: "I flew most of the way."
BROCK: "Your arms tired?"
TED: "Only when I flap 'em."
JIM: That could give you *arm*ritis.
TED: "It's alright, I just had a bout of *hip*atitus."
JIM: "Yeah? A little bit further down your leg, it'd probably get *knee*monia."
BROCK: Hell, I'd be more worried about small*cox*."
TED: "Well, I'm pretty lucky there—I've already had *dick*theria."

We're not talking sophistication here.

In between these exchanges and various country music numbers (several of them performed by Pappy and Harriet themselves) come periodic cuts to the Inspector talking with Father John, which segues into scenes from either *Howling IV* or *V*, with the priest offering narration like, "The Inquisition believed that Satan had taken the castle under his protection." Back and forth the film goes from Pioneertown shenanigans to recycled *Howling IV* and *V* footage as the priest drones on and on to tie things together. For instance, he says that back at the Hungarian castle (cue part *V*), "Ted, the only Australian, became the fall guy—and he was never seen again." (Actually, in *Howling V* Ted *was* seen again—lying dead in the snow.) At one point the detective snidely asks Father Exposition, "Is this going to be a *long* story?" and the viewer can only wonder the same.

New Moon Rising plays fast and loose with its werewolf mythos as well. The lycanthrope can alter its human shape—or possess a human host (this point remains hazy). Referring to the events in part *V*, Father John says, "The spirit of the werewolf had already assumed the identity of one of the group," and has now "taken over the body of another person." The creature also possesses mind-control ability, thus explaining the discrepancies told by the returning *Howling IV* character Marie Adams (Romy Windsor), who claims Ted is the werewolf tow truck driver (he was) in the recycled part *IV* flashback footage—lies planted in Marie's head by the lycanthrope to throw further suspicion on Ted. Additionally, the priest gravely intones, "Very soon it will be three years to the day since that Hungarian castle burned to the ground. Three years is the time it takes a werewolf to grow to full strength, to reach maturity." Such an odd bit of lycan-lore serves only to close the time gap between *Howling V* and this film. (Of course, it makes little sense because three years ago the beast went on a decimating rampage in part *V*, so it was obviously *already* "mature.") Amusingly, the inquisitive inspector asks, "How do you know all this?" with the old priest delivering the evasive, crackpot *non*-answer, "I've always known the theories of werewolves."

The two (new) werewolf attacks are filmed in an almost identical fashion. They consist of nothing more than red-tinted p.o.v. footage rushing at the victim, then a shot of the body (with a few red splotches around the neck) being dragged out of frame. But perhaps that's just as well, for when the guilty party finally transforms (a quick-and-cheesy CGI morphing moment) into the ravening beast at the very end, its big-eared, rubbery-faced mutant wolf appearance as it bursts through a door in slow motion only to face a gaggle of gun-totin' townies inspires more giggles than gasps. "They didn't even originally have a werewolf budgeted for the film," complained Nall. "They were either going to allude to one or maybe get some werewolf paws made." So Nall rewrote the script to get more werewolf action "and a final confrontation scene where the good guys actually face it down." Unfortunately, said face-down played up the sorry state of its werewolf, exposing it for the ridiculous ad hoc creation it was.

"It is really, completely, utterly unique," pronounced Turner of *New Moon Rising*, before adding, "You can't always do justice when you have a very limited budget." Given its unusual setting (not to mention its obsession with line dancing), the film does indeed fall into the "unique" category in lycan-cinema. Unfortunately, it's not all that good.

Originally, *The Howling: New Moon Rising* (alternatively labeled *Howling VII*) was to be shot back-to-back with *Howling VI*, from a continuous script by writer Kevin Rock (following the further exploits of Ian the werewolf and Winston the alligator boy from *VI* as they travel to Budapest), but budgetary issues nixed that notion. "They ultimately opted not to spend the money to go to another country and make *Howling VII*," explained Turner. "So they simply shelved the project and left *Howling VI* to ostensibly be the last of the series." Later, LIVE became interested in reviving the series, and decided to make *New Moon Rising* a collage of the best scenes from the earlier films, with new footage shot to bridge the gaps. "LIVE wanted to somehow integrate elements from the previous *Howlings*, even if we didn't cut an entire movie out of them," recounted Nall, "because for some reason they wanted to tie the pieces of the films together. This was hard, of course, as you know if you've seen the previous films. I believe we've done a pretty interesting job; it does relate to the others without looking like a bad *Star Trek* episode when they ran out of money at the end of the season."

Writer-producer-actor Clive Turner (who also served as editor and *accountant*—Turner was a CPA!) frequently clashed with original director Robert Nall (a visual effects veteran whose only directorial credit was the 1996 thriller *Hard Time*). "They both had very different visions of what they wanted," said creature creator Jerry Macaluso. "Roger was making a werewolf movie and Clive was making a very character-driven thing. He really wanted to make a movie about the people of this little town, and the werewolf was completely secondary." Nall basically walked away. Turner ended up reshooting "about 50 percent" and collected the sole directing credit for his troubles. "It's Clive's world," conceded Nall, "so I let him have it because it's his baby from the start—he created the idea and was married to the town."

The duo even differed on the look of the werewolf. "Clive wanted it to look like the one Steve Johnson had done in *IV*," recalled Macaluso, "and Roger didn't want it to look anything like that.... So we started to go for a middle ground nobody liked and finally ended up doing some of our own thing. We also tried to keep some of Rob Bottin's style form the original *Howling* in there." Tried ... and failed.

Despite the Turner-Nall conflict, it looks like the participants (who, though occasionally awkward in front of the camera, do a decent job overall by playing themselves) had a ball making their little movie, and, truth be told, Clive Turner and his fun-loving demeanor makes for an engaging, unconventional lead. There are far worse characters (including nearly all those from the previous five *Howling* sequels) one could spend 90 minutes with than the inhabitants of Pioneertown.

Though definitely delivering a "homegrown" vibe, the production at least looks professional, with competent (if unspectacular) lighting and sound. As the end credits explain, "The events depicted in this motion picture are fictitious. The characters depicted in Pioneertown are real." Sadly, one of these real characters, Claude "Pappy" Allen, passed away just before *The Howling: New Moon Rising*'s release. Turner dedicated the film to this unique country western legend and Pioneertown stalwart.

"There has never been the intent to make a bad film," Turner said, defending the *Howling* series in general. "We've always intended to make a good film, and the stories were always well-written. They didn't necessarily come out that way, but sometimes it was beyond our control." Though his claim of having "well-written" stories smacks of wishful thinking, his point is well taken. And while *The Howling: New Moon Rising* can by no means be labeled a "good" film, the thin vein of high desert small-town charm that runs through this block of celluloid cheese makes it at least palatable—which is more than can be said of several of its *Howling* compatriots.

With quotes from: "*Howling VII*: Long in the Tooth?" by Anthony C. Ferrante, *Fangoria* 134.

Morphology: Big-eared, wolf-faced (clothed) biped
Demise: Silver bullets (lots of them)
Full Moon Rating: **

The Howling Reborn

(2011; Anchor Bay; US/Canada) Director: Joe Nimziki; Producers: Joel Kastelberg, James Johnston; Screenplay: Joe Nimziki, James Johnston (based on the book *The Howling II* by Gary Brandner); Cinematographer: Benoit Beaulieu. Cast: Lindsey Shaw, Landon Liboiron, Ivana Milicevic, Jesse Rath, Niels Schneider, Frank Schorpion.

FULL MOON. NEW BLOOD—ad line

Touting *The Howling Reborn* as "*Twilight* with bite," production-distribution company Anchor Bay made its intentions obvious with this reboot of the overextended *Howling* franchise largely through the man chosen to oversee the project (and hopefully jump start the "new" series): first-time writer/director Joe Nimziki, a former studio *marketing* executive (at New Line, MGM, and Sony). Though original *Howling* producers Steven Lane and Robert Pringle served as *The Howling Reborn*'s executive producers, that's about all the ties the film can claim to the original. Shot under the working title of *Howling VIII*, the movie has nothing to do with either 1981's *The Howling* nor any of its subsequent sequels. "I was a fan of the original when I was young," noted Nimziki, "but I never saw any sequels." Neither did he read any of the Gary Brandner *Howling* novels (despite the movie's misleading credit "based on the book *The Howling II*").

"I always thought werewolves could be such a great way of telling a coming of age story," said Nimziki of what drew him to write the script in the first place. To this end he penned a scenario calculated to appeal to the *Twilight* set, though (thankfully) with more "bite" than that watered-down, angsty teen-fest. Told from the point of view of 18-year-old Will Kidman (Landon Liboiron) on the eve of his high school graduation, *The Howling Reborn* has the latent curse of lycanthropy start to manifest in the confused teen. As he finally summons the courage to pursue the girl of his high school dreams, Eliana (Lindsey Shaw), he must not only battle his own inner urges but also the unwanted attentions of a pack of werewolves, led by his own long-thought-dead mother (Ivana Milicevic), intent on inducting him into her pack. With them all trapped in his locked-down high school building on graduation night, Will must not only protect Eliana from the monsters, he must stop their plan to spread their lycanthropy and create a werewolf army.

"I think sometimes werewolves get a bad rap," explained Nimziki. "People think they're not as sexy or whatever as vampires. But hopefully this film will debunk that a bit. The urge to lose control and live just by instinct can be dangerous, sexy ... the very things that I think people like vampire flicks for." Indeed, the pack's alpha, as played by the beautiful and exotic Bosnian-born Ivana Milicevic (a former Bond girl from 2006's *Casino Royale*), very nearly epitomizes "sexy." And the beasts themselves prove oh-so-dangerous indeed. Though filming on a relatively low budget in Quebec, Canada (where shooting is cheap), Nimziki and his producers thankfully took the time and expense for a more realistic, hands-on approach to their werewolves than so many New Millennium filmmakers. Eschewing the easy path via the often two-dimensional, weightless-looking CGI, Nimziki employed Academy Award nominee Adrian Morot (*300*, *Night at the Museum 2*) to bring his lycans to touchable, physical, dangerous life, resorting to computer imagery only briefly (for some quick and smooth morphing). There's nothing like a full man-in-a-suit werewolf for realistic-looking physical interaction. Morot individualized each werewolf as well, creating two basic types—the lesser wolves that look like mutant lycans (smooth torsos, hairy arms and legs, a mix of human-demonic features and huge bat-like ears); and the primary wolves, which resemble the impressive creatures from the original film (complete with full-on, articulated wolf's head and toothy muzzle atop a towering, hair-covered physique). And these creatures leap and move with startling speed, engaging in all manner of vicious mayhem that culminates in one of the most satisfying lupo-a-lupo physical battles ever committed to celluloid. The slow-motion scene of one werewolf using the other as a monstrous battering ram while it literally runs *through* wall after solid wall, bludgeoning its opponent into insensibility, is an inventive show-stopper.

Reborn gives birth to a few new twists on the usual werewolf lore. As his exposition-providing friend explains, only silver or fire can kill a "garden variety werewolf," but these have little effect on the "alpha wolf," who can only be destroyed by *another werewolf*. Also, lycanthropes, like vampires, apparently live forever. Will's mother hasn't aged a day in 18 years. And Will philosophizes at film's end, "Most of us don't have the option of waking to eternal life or experiencing undying romance. Our lives and loves are painfully finite. But maybe that's how it *should* be. Because the parts of the human condition that we suffer from the most are the very things that make us what we are. We appreciate time because of our lack of it." Indeed.

Unlike the namby-pamby superhero wolves of the *Twilight*-verse, here "real werewolves are hard-frikkin-core. They're doomed to struggle between their humanity and their animal natures." Like so many things in life, lycanthropy, whether "curse" (as Will views it) or "gift" (as his mother corrects), is all about "choice." His mother has embraced her inner animal. She enthuses, "Just image having the power over all the things you feel you can't control—it's *amazing*." She continues, "Forget your books [as she literally rips one in half] and your technology [as she crushes Will's phone in her fist]. That's not life. That's a series of distractions *from* life." Her view posits lycanthropy as an answer to the disconnect—not only from nature but from one's fellow man—so often engendered by modern "civilization" and technology. Of course, this entails also returning to the morality of an *animal*. "It's a cruel world," she explains, "and the only morality in a cruel world is 'every being for themselves.'" But to embrace this Luddite anti-intellectualism, one must literally become a monster. As Will says during his closing narration, "While we can all be monsters, we're always at our most monstrous when we ignore our humanity." Such surprising depth helps separate *The Howling Reborn* from much of its inferior and superficial *Twilight*-ish brethren.

Unfortunately, not everything in the film is as well thought out. The frequent (and frequently pretentious) philosophizing voice-overs by Will about life, love, human nature, free will, ad infinitum, ad nauseum, quickly grow tiresome. Sample passage: "We let moments pass, opportunities pass, our lives pass—day after day—until before we know it, and without ever realizing it, the best versions of ourselves have become a distant memory."

Also, the movie sometimes threatens to collapse under the weight of incredulity—not over its fantasy elements, like werewolves and curses, but in its handling of mundane reality (which, ironically, is crucial to "selling" the fantasy factor). For instance, Will's New York high school features a daily security/lock-down system that would be overkill in a maximum security prison (including impenetrable automatic steel shutters slamming closed

Though an obvious teen-targeted *Twilight*-like reboot, the action-packed, werewolf-heavy *The Howling Reborn* generally works in spite of itself.

over every door and window). And Will and Eliana pop into the school's chemistry lab to whip up a pair of homemade flamethrowers in less time than it takes for homeroom roll-call. Likewise, Will also manages to find some sliver nitrate *and* a gun(!), so that he can paint bullet tips with the deadly-to-werewolves silver substance (so much for this school's vaunted "security"). Most ludicrous of all, right in the middle of Will and Eliana's fight for their lives through the maze-like building's vast corridors and rooms, the nascent couple decide it's time to finally consummate their burgeoning love affair and fall into a steamy embrace. While this might appeal to the hormone-ravaged teen viewing audience, it's a ridiculous betrayal of the two characters and their situation, which both Nimziki and the two engaging lead actors have been at such pains to create. But such are the dangers of pandering strictly to the youth market. In fact, an amusing—if totally off-base—dialogue exchange early on in the movie encapsulates the filmmakers' misguided attitude. When Will's cinema-savvy friend Sachin (Jesse Rath) incredulously asks him, "Have you never seen a werewolf flick?" he receives a sheepish "No" in reply. "Can't blame you," Sachin concedes. "That's what studios get for casting geezers in their lead roles. I mean, if I want to see people in their forties, I'd just go home and look at my parents."

"We truly believe this picture will re-launch the franchise and lead to even bigger and better new chapters ahead," enthused Anchor Bay Senior Vice President of Marketing Jennifer Roberts in a 2011 press release. Alas, it was not to be, as so far no further installments have materialized (despite the closing credits offering a few snippets of footage indicating the bigger story may have already begun). Though the flawed *The Howling Reborn* proved to be far from the perfect lycanthropic offspring, it featured enough quality and substance to make werewolf fans wish for further, more mature siblings.

With quotes from: "Interview: Joe Nimziki Talks *The Howling: Reborn*," by Karen Benardello, shockya.com; "Anchor Bay Films 'Bays' at the Moon with *The Howling Reborn* on Blu-Ray and DVD," anchorbayentertainment.com.

Morphology: Bipedal hybrids and wolf-headed beasts
Demise: Silver, fire, and another werewolf
Full Moon Rating: ***

I Married a Werewolf see *Werewolf in a Girls' Dormitory*

I Was a Teenage Werewolf

(1957; American International Pictures) Director: Gene Fowler, Jr.; Producer: Herman Cohen; Screenplay: Ralph Thornton (Aben Kandel, Herman Cohen); Cinematographer: Joseph La Shelle. Cast: Michael Landon, Yvonne Lime, Whit Bissell, Tony Marshall, Dawn Richards, Barney Phillips.

> TEENAGE GUYS 'n' DOLLS ... *TERRIFIED*,
> FOR DRIVING THIS BOY IS A *SAVAGE*
> *LUST* ... TO KILL!—trailer

This was the film (and title) that opened the floodgates of teen-targeted terror that washed over the drive-ins in the late 1950s. At the time of its release, *I Was a Teenage Werewolf* sparked a lot of controversy with its provocative advertising campaign. A Senate subcommittee even discussed the film, which (according to director Gene Fowler) cost $82,000 to make (though producer Herman Cohen put the figure at $150,000), was shot in six days (others claim a more generous but still rushed two weeks), and earned over two million dollars before the year was out. Its tremendous cult appeal and success encouraged AIP (and others) to churn out dozens of other "teen" monster movies in the years to come, such as *I Was a Teenage Frankenstein*, *Blood of Dracula*, *Teenage Caveman* and *The Blob*.

But beyond its obvious exploitation value, *I Was a Teenage Werewolf*'s incisive script, inventive direction and excellent cast set it above its contemporaries and imitators. Without the werewolf angle, it would have been a tight and engrossing teen drama; with the lycanthropy, it became a superior sci-fi/horror entry; and with that *title*, it evolved into a cult classic. (Said title alone insured the film's success, with comics across the country making it the butt of their jokes, while an Illinois senator provided the picture a million dollars' worth of free publicity by publicly labeling it "scandalous and immoral.")

The story centers on Tony (Michael Landon), an angry, sullen, but ultimately likable and well-intentioned high-schooler whose hair-trigger temper gets him into trouble with his school, his girl and the law. When Tony unthinkingly beats up a friend, he realizes he needs help. The troubled teen goes to see psychiatrist Dr. Brandon (Whit Bissell), who, unfortunately for Tony, has been seeking the perfect human guinea pig for his secret experiment. And Tony indeed has "the proper disturbed emotional background" needed. "Through hypnosis [and a special serum]," the mad medico explains to his assistant, "I'm going to regress this boy back, back into the primitive past that lurks within him. I'm going to transform him and unleash the savage instincts that lie hidden within." The result? No, not a primitive Neanderthal but a werewolf! (Apparently, all those evolutionists and anthropologists got it wrong, and we're more lupine than primate.) Brandon's reasoning for such a bizarre achievement: "Mankind is on the verge of destroying itself; the only hope for the human race is to hurl it back into its primitive dawn, to start all over again." A bit reactionary, perhaps, but heartfelt. After killing several people as a werewolf, the confused Tony is identified as the monster and goes on the run, finally seeking out the doctor, leading to a climactic creation vs. creator confrontation.

Though low budget, *Teen Werewolf* shines in nearly every department, from the thoughtful scripting and well-drawn characters to the carefully staged technical aspects and spot-on thespians. The werewolf slant is an added bonus (at least for those horror enthusiasts among us), its lycanthropy a symbol-made-flesh of the changes teens face—in their own bodies, in their emotional regulation (or lack of same), and in their desire to fit in with their peers. In short, *Teenage Werewolf* stands as a hirsute fairy tale exploring the dangers of adolescence and puberty itself, becoming the first film to link lycanthropy to the "troubled teen."

"I tell you what a werewolf is," says police station janitor Pepe (who just happened to come from a "little village in the Carpathian mountains") to the night sergeant. "It's a human being possessed by a wolf. When the evil eye is on you the savage beast somehow gets inside and controls you, makes you look and act like a wolf. Makes you hunt down your victim and kill like a wolf." Though providing a bit of ominous background, this supernatural "legend" fails to fit with the Teenage Werewolf's decidedly *scientific* origin (via a special serum and hypnosis). And neither the moon nor silver has anything to do with it, with Tony's first onscreen transformation (via a few wavy dissolves) occurring during the day, triggered by the shock of a school bell suddenly sounding in his ear.

The look of the beast follows the general template set by Lon Chaney, Jr.'s *The Wolf Man*, but adds some variations, such as thick, coarse hair built up to subtly suggest a pompadour; a black nose;

138 • *I Was a Teenage Werewolf*

Lycanthropy as teen angst in the seminal *I Was a Teenage Werewolf* (American lobby card).

pointy wolf's ears; and a wicked set of jagged fangs that protrude not from the bottom (like with the Wolf Man) but the top of its drooling maw. With its hairy, clawed hands and telltale letterman-style jacket, the Teenage Werewolf cuts an iconic cult figure.

Though many "stars" who got their start in low-budget fare like this tend to try to sweep their early days as a take-anything-offered actor under the rug, Michael Landon (who came to prominence via such television megahits as *Bonanza*, *Little House on the Prairie* and *Highway to Heaven*) regarded his debut effort with fondness, and always talked about it freely, even affectionately. And no wonder, considering the fine performance he delivered. Landon (who, according to producer Herman Cohen beat out Scott Marlowe and Jack Nicholson [!] for the role) is fresh-faced and eager in his big-screen debut, full of energy and charm and possessing a winning smile—in contrast to his violent temper. The fledgling actor makes his character both real and intense. When Tony responds violently to an innocuous Halloween prank by viciously beating a friend and pushing his own girlfriend to the floor, the look of pained confusion and self-loathing on his face when he realizes what he's done speaks volumes. And when, toward the end, he realizes what he's become, his almost violent pleading with the duplicitous Dr. Brandon to "Help me! Please!" becomes almost heartbreaking.

Landon is just as effective in hirsute form. Running, snarling and leaping with a wild energy, he *becomes* the savage beast. In the attack in the gym, he lunges at the girl, heedless of the stack of folding chairs he crashes into in his frenzied bloodlust. It's an impressive physical performance that perfectly matches his intense emotional one. "We thought he had almost killed himself in that gym scene," recalled Cohen, "when he ran after Dawn Richards and jumped right into that bunch of iron chairs. That was Michael. It's funny, but when he had that makeup on, he said he felt like he *was* a werewolf. He was excellent. There was nothing he didn't do that we wanted him to do; in fact, he always wanted to do more." Director Gene Fowler concurred: "You could ask him to do anything and he'd do it.... I loved Michael—he was a very young kid at that time, maybe twenty years old, but he was good, a hard-working guy, always knew his lines."

According to co-star Ken Miller, however, Michael Landon "*hated* the makeup—he *hated* it so much! We had this wonderful old makeup man who did it, Philip Scheer—an old veteran—but he just took his time. It just took an eternity, and it *had* to be very uncomfortable." Even so, Landon still gave his all while under all that "hated" greasepaint and hair.

As Dr. Brandon, reliable character actor Whit Bissell (*Creature from the Black Lagoon*, *Invasion of the Body Snatchers*, *I Was a Teenage*

Frankenstein) takes a rather ridiculous, one-note character and makes him utterly convincing. Far from the raving madmen found in the mad doctor melodramas of the previous decade, Bissell's "mad scientist" is cold and calculating, replacing bombast with a frightening single-mindedness. When Bissell rhetorically asks, "What is one life, compared to such a triumph?" his tone of cold determinism both convinces and chills. Bissell's natural delivery and quiet intensity transforms this one-dimensional character into a 3-D villain, one who fully believes in what he's doing and whose demeanor communicates that belief to the viewer.

Former editor and first-time director Gene Fowler, along with veteran cinematographer Joseph LaShelle (*Laura*), do wonders with the paltry budget and inadequate schedule, taking the time and effort to build upon and enhance the solid script with fine technical touches. In the now-classic scene of the attack on the high-school gymnast, the leotard-clad young lady stretches and hangs upside down on the parallel bars while Tony watches. The school bell next to Tony suddenly sounds, triggering a transformation. The girl then notices Tony, and we see—upside down—the snarling beast advancing towards us in a clever and disturbing victim's point-of-view shot.

Unfortunately, after the careful character build-up and the highlight of the gym sequence, the film begins to flag, and we must make do with a few poignant scenes involving Tony's confused and concerned father, some police procedural sequences, a rather listless dog attack on the werewolf (involving Fowler's own dog) and some tramping in the woods (complete with torch-wielding posse) until the final, admittedly exciting, confrontation when the monster turns on its maker. There's also a rather tepid (though obligatory, considering its target audience) teen party sequence, complete with silly song ("Eeny, Meeny, Miney, Mo") and goofy dancing. And scripter "Ralph Thornton" (a pseudonym employed by novelist Aben Kandel and—claims the man himself—producer Cohen) hauls out that hoary old chestnut (which was creaking with age even in the 1950s) for the film's closing line: "It's not for Man to interfere in the ways of God."

But overlook these few foibles, and *I Was a Teenage Werewolf* stands as a shining example of artists and technicians taking an exploitable (if preposterous) premise and constructing an engrossing film suffused with themes and subtexts that (much like Fowler's other genre entry, *I Married a Monster from Outer Space*) belies its absurd title. And who can fail to love a movie that uses werewolfery as a metaphor for teen angst?

With quotes from: *Attack of the Monster Movie Makers*, by Tom Weaver; *Science Fiction and Fantasy Film Flashbacks*, by Tom Weaver.

Morphology: Letterman jacket–clad biped
Demise: Ordinary bullets
Full Moon Rating: ***½

Iron Wolf

(2013; Generation X Group/Anchor Bay; Germany) Alternate Title: *Werewolf Terror*. Directors: David Brückner, Jens Nier; Producers: Jens Nier, Nico Sentner, Dominik Starck, David Brückner; Screenplay: Marco Theiss; Cinematographer: David Brückner. Cast: Carolina Rath, Roland Freitag, Hannes Sell, Catarina Döhring, Michael Krug, Dominik Starck, Urs Remond, Nico Sentner.

HOWL HITLER!—tagline

"*Iron Wolf* was created under the most unfavorable conditions," recalled co-producer/star Dominik Starck, "i.e., low on budget, with a very young and partly still quite inexperienced team, including myself. But despite all the limitations, this film has a certain something captured and immortalized." And that "certain something" is a *Nazi werewolf*…

"Germany 1945." With Russian troops approaching Berlin, German Major Schilling (Nico Sentner) pays a visit to Dr. Berger (Urs Remond) at his Nazi research lab to see the results of the doc's latest experiment—a werewolf conditioned to attack only the enemy. "He is programmed to react to optical as well as sensory stimulus," explains the doctor. "Even a less Aryan soldier will be identified by his uniform, his language or his smell." In other words, this werewolf is trained to recognize insignia (and, apparently, blonde hair) and sniff out non–Aryans! The Major, impressed by a bloody demonstration utilizing two Russian prisoners, beams, "Create an army of these creatures; we have a war to win!" But before the doc can put said plan into action, the Russians overrun the facility, and the Major hastily blows it all up (including the doctor) to keep it from falling into enemy hands. "65 years later," a homeless man scavenging in the now-abandoned building finds an old German military coat and rifle, and hears banging coming from behind the laboratory's metal door. Oddly, he takes it upon himself to become an impromptu sentry and guard the trapped creature. Fast forward another few years, to "Present Day," and the members of a punk rock band decide to hold their reunion concert in the old research facility. They set about cleaning up the mess, but the band's leader, Spike (Dominik Starck), runs across the tramp and ends up releasing the monster, which immediately starts picking off the punks, then lays siege when the survivors barricade themselves inside.

A low-budget German independent horror film (shot in English in two weeks in an abandoned slaughterhouse), *Iron Wolf* promises much but delivers little. While director David Brückner, making his sophomore feature, shows some inventiveness in his (and "co-director" Jens Nier's) technique, employing different angles and set-ups to create some visual variation, ultimately he relies too heavily on the "immediacy" of the shaky-cam to set the tone (and mask the settings' impoverished nature). The very first scene betrays the picture's straightened circumstances. As a squad of Russian soldiers creep towards a building, it becomes obvious that several of these infantrymen are actually *women* (friends of the filmmakers, no doubt, hastily pressed into service and squeezed into makeshift uniforms to fill out the platoon). And the closing credits reveal that many of the movie's "stars" worked behind the camera as well (both Dominik Starck and Nico Sentner served as producers *and* executive producers, for instance), while co-director Jens Nier donned the hairy suit and uniform to play the Iron Wolf himself (which he co-designed with effects supervisor Stefan Forberg). Brückner himself even stepped in front of the camera to play the Nazi doctor's crippled assistant (a role that appears to be a nod to, of all things, *The Brain That Wouldn't Die!*).

But more disappointing than its less-than-epic production values is the shallow scripting that transforms a potentially fascinating lycan-twist into just another subpar monster-stalking scenario. "Creature?!" exclaims the doctor's overzealous (and probably insane) assistant during the World War II prologue. "That is not a 'creature'—that is the next step to a superior German race." Disappointingly, the script immediately drops this eugenics wackiness like a hot potato. And despite laying the initial groundwork, the film almost immediately abandons its issue-laden notion of the werewolf targeting everyone *except* those sporting Nazi regalia. The found German military coat inadvertently saves Leon, Spike's put-upon brother, from the monster when Leon hides beneath it; but otherwise the punks make no decision about whether or not to don the raiment of the Third Reich in order to ward off the beast and save their lives. Rather than forcing these modern German youth, who profess to abhor fascism and actively mock their country's Nazi past at every turn (even literally pissing on some painted swastikas), to face the sins of their fathers, the film takes the simpler path to become just another monster-on-the-loose tale. So much for exploring the issues of fascism and how a society deals with its collective ghosts.

The haphazard screenplay not only lets its subtext slip away like an SS officer heading to Buenos Aires, it takes numerous illogical turns and raises far more questions than it answers. For instance, why on earth would the tramp stick around for years to "guard" the potential horror behind the door (and how did he even know it *was* a "horror" and not some fellow bum stuck in a room)? The Berlin "Nazi research facility" is played by a derelict Glauchau slaughterhouse in Saxony, Germany, with no sign of any fire, much less a supposedly lab-leveling explosion, on its walls. Even more astounding, the seventy-year-old rifle they find still *works perfectly*, and the World War II gas cans still contain viable fuel (convenient for whipping up some Molotov cocktails)! On the other hand, though the creature's final demise proves just as unlikely (and decidedly unspectacular), it at least sparkles with novelty: Our Hero stabs the beast with a Nazi knife, then shoves a *silver ring* his girlfriend found into the wound. At this the creature clutches its stomach and topples over dead. Yes, Iron Wolf offers the screen's first lycan-death-by-jewelry.

Regarding its lycanthrope, this *Iron Wolf* turned out to be a paper tiger. The film never shows the beast in its human guise. With no human identity behind the creature, the werewolf is just a generic monster. We've no idea if it was a former prisoner, a volunteer soldier, or simply someone whisked off the street to become the Nazis' guinea pig. Of course, this cavalier handling dispenses not only with the need for characterization but for that potentially expensive and time-consuming metamorphosis scene. Instead, the only thing to characterize the pivotal figure of the werewolf is a split uniform and some cheap bloodletting. Pathos, tragedy, and even irony (could they have transformed an anti-fascist freedom fighter into a Nazi-loving monster?) need not apply. Late in the film, the doctor's notes reveal, "Werewolves … heal quickly and can only be killed with silver…. We have trained the werewolf to kill our enemies, and we control the re-transformation." *How*, exactly, remains undisclosed.

It's forty minutes into the film before the band members finally release the beast, and then it stays more or less hidden for a further quarter-hour, with only a hairy arm, a shadow on the wall (looking stiff and immobile) and an indistinct, ill-lit shape moving behind a hedge to mark its presence. When it finally steps into full view, one can only wish it hadn't. An oversized poodle-head with pointy bat ears, an immobile rat muzzle, and linebacker-like shoulder pads under its swastika-festooned uniform give the cheap game away. Even Brückner's dim lighting (he served as his own cinematographer) still proves too revealing for this risible monster.

"We all know what that beast out there is," notes one terrified bandmate. "We've seen it—and it was not a goddamned German Shepherd!" Well, it kinda was. As a protagonist later reads from the doctor's notes, "The real breakthrough came when we spliced the werewolf genes with a German Shepherd. Suddenly the beast was tamable. Like a dog, we could train him." So this creature is half werewolf and half *dog*.

In Dachau, apparently, a "Romanian gypsy" prisoner turned into a werewolf (and "killed eight men before he was trapped"). "The next day," writes the Nazi scientist in his notes, "he was transferred to my lab in his human form. The following night I was able to witness the transformation for myself. It was a breathtaking event." The viewer has to take this on faith, however, since, unlike the doc, we never witness it for ourselves. In fact, we witness very little during this lengthy exposition sequence, as the flashback footage shown under the doctor's narration reveals none of the action described. We must make do with mundane (and cheap) scenes of the doc talking with his assistant, looking at his notes, and speaking on the phone!

The actors' performances vary from toneless to over-the-top. Of course, it couldn't have been easy for them, as they're forced to deliver their dialogue not in their native German but in English, some with accents so thick you could cut them with a Henckel. With the verbally hobbled actors playing sketchily-drawn, unlikable characters, the viewer has little investment in them and cares less for their fates.

In the end, half-baked ideas and wasted opportunities turn this *Iron Wolf* into a pot metal dog.

With quotes from: "Interview: Dominik Starck (BGT-Exclusive)," *bereitsgetestet.de*.

Morphology: Uniformed, dog-headed Nazi
Demise: Silver ring (stuffed into an open wound)
Full Moon Rating: *½

Ladyhawke

(1985; Warner Bros./20th Century–Fox) Director: Richard Donner; Producers: Richard Donner, Lauren Shuler; Screenplay: Edward Khmara, Michael Thomas, Tom Mankiewicz (story: Edward Khmara); Cinematographer: Vittorio Storaro. Cast: Matthew Broderick, Rutger Hauer, Michelle Pfeiffer, Leo McKern, John Wood, Ken Hutchison.

A magical, mystical adventure—poster

Like the ads proclaimed, *Ladyhawke*, though offering as a main character a *werewolf*, is more "mystical adventure" than horror film. A medieval fantasy of tragedy and romance, it follows the plight of warrior knight Navarre (Rutger Hauer) and his lady love Isabeau (Michelle Pfeiffer). When the all-powerful Bishop (John Wood) sets his lecherous sights on Isabeau, she spurns his advances. At this, the jealous and corrupt clergyman vows that the two lovers would be "always together, eternally apart." To wit: he casts a diabolical spell that causes Isabeau to transform into a hawk by day, while Navarre becomes a black wolf at night. Thus, they can never be together, can never touch, in human form. When a young thief, dubbed "Mouse" (Matthew Broderick), escapes from the Bishop's dungeons and crosses Navarre's path, the downcast knight, wandering alone with his beloved "Ladyhawke," sees a way to enter the Bishop's heavily fortified castle and put an end to his tormentor, and perhaps the curse itself.

Medieval Man often looked upon werewolves as the willing servants of Satan, or, conversely, as the result of a curse caused by witchcraft. Keeping within the film's medieval milieu, Navarre's nightly transformations are the result of the evil Bishop "calling upon the powers of Darkness for the means to damn the lovers." Beyond this nod to authentic folklore, however, *Ladyhawke* adds several entertaining layers—poignant romanticism and thrilling adventure—to the classic cinematic notion of the tragic lycanthrope. A romance, a tragedy, a medieval adventure, and a unique werewolf tale, *Ladyhawke* makes for an entertaining "amalgam of themes," as director Richard Donner dubbed it. "It's adventurous, outrageously romantic, and pure escapism."

Filled with beautiful, majestic scenery; authentic stables, hovels and castles (three of which were owned by Italian film director

Luchino Visconti); atmospheric lighting; and lush, fluid photography, it's a truly sumptuous looking production. Star Rutger Hauer credits much of the movie's success to Italian cinematographer Vittorio Storaro (*Ladyhawke* was filmed in Italy with an Italian crew). "With Dick [Donner]'s instincts and Storaro's camera work," said Hauer, "*Ladyhawke* became not only a beautiful story, but also a beautiful visual adventure." Though receiving a mixed critical reception overall, one thing the critics agreed on was the picture's gorgeous visuals. London's *Time Out* magazine called it "beautifully photographed," while Vincent Canby, in the *New York Times*, singled out the movie's "visual splendor."

The film's score was composed by Andrew Powell and produced by Alan Parsons. Richard Donner said that he was listening to the Alan Parsons Project while scouting film locations and naturally tied the two together. The dated music, however, all driving drumbeats and synthesizer rhythms, is very much of its time, aurally transforming the 13th century into the mid–1980s. Perhaps one should be grateful, however, that Donner wasn't listening to Culture Club…

As "Mouse," the unimposing, slightly comic Matthew Broderick is likable enough, despite his distracting comes-and-goes-like-the-wind attempt at a British accent. A young Michelle Pfeifer brings an ethereal beauty to her tragic role. And Rutger Hauer offers a stoic, manly presence that becomes heartbreakingly tragic at times.

Donner (*The Omen* [1976], *Superman* [1978], the *Lethal Weapon* films) originally wanted Hauer for the role of the Bishop's villainous captain of the guard, but Hauer balked. "Earlier, Dick had offered me the role of a bad guy, the Captain of the guards," the Dutch actor recalled. "I said, 'Forget it. I want to play the hero.' He wanted someone younger. So, I asked why would you consider young people for this role? There is more to this than just a teen picture. If you want to tell a story about someone who is about strength, endurance and love, you need an actor with balls. I act from my guts and I know I have the balls. I know I can do it. Dick wasn't convinced." Donner's first choice for the tragic and heroic Navarre was Sean Connery (not much youth there), but the Scottish superstar was in the Bahamas playing Bond for the last time in *Never Say Never Again*. Then, two weeks before shooting, Donner settled on Kurt Russell. But when Russell dropped out ("each of them [Russell and Donner] just didn't feel comfortable with the other," claimed Hauer), Donner finally handed the Navarre role to Hauer. "Dick Donner calls me up in Holland. He asked me to come to Italy in one week. I asked for what role? And he said, 'Navarre.' I was there in 24 hours."

The shoot wasn't easy for Hauer. After losing 20 pounds during the protracted climactic fight scene in the Cathedral (the first sequence shot), Hauer had to contend with "a sword poking you in the ass, there are these saddlebags and crossbows sticking the horse in the ass, and there's this hawk sitting on your arm. So, you're out of control. You just have to hope the horse is feeling OK."

We first see Navarre transform only after 70 minutes, and the simple and quick metamorphosis, though eerie and effective, seems hardly worth the wait. Like everything else in *Ladyhawke*, however, it's beautifully shot. With the soundtrack consisting of a series of heartbeats, Navarre moves through the shadow-filled forest at twilight, discarding his clothing as he walks. A lightning flash reveals his pale torso as he steps towards the camera before the image fades and a large black wolf trots forward.

Navarre in wolf form was played by four different Siberian wolves—Kollchek, Levi, Akeela and Sasha—imported from California by animal trainer Ron Oxley. Oxley chose this subspecies because Siberian wolves are larger than their European counterparts.

Like with his handling of the transformation, Donner plays up the story's romance and adventure more than its horror elements. Though menacing looking as the large black wolf, Navarre only kills while in *human* form. One suspenseful sequence, however, sees the intelligent animal leading one unctuous character—a coarse wolf-hunter hired by the Bishop to trap and kill the Navarre-wolf—to his poetic-justice demise in the jaws of his own vicious traps.

Though the film's publicity claimed the story was based on a famous medieval legend, it all came from primary screenwriter Edward Khmara's imagination (Khmara ultimately won a settlement from Warner Bros. over the false claim). It took nearly four years for producer Lauren Shuler to bring everything together after optioning Khmara's original script. Shot in August of 1983 on a reported $20 million budget, *Ladyhawke* grossed only $18 million domestically, though foreign and ancillary sales pushed it into the black. But beyond any financial return, *Ladyhawke* brought two lovers together in real life, for Shuler and director Richard Donner fell in love while working together on the film and eventually married. "*Ladyhawke* was the spark to their romance," recalled Hauer.

With quotes from: *All Those Moments*, by Rutger Hauer; "Rutger Hauer, Knight Wolf to a Ladyhawke," by Lee Goldberg, *Starlog* 95.

Morphology: Large four-legged black wolf
Demise: None; cured of the curse, he lived happily ever after with his lady love
Full Moon Rating: ***½

Late Phases

(2014; Dark Sky Films/MPI) Alternate Title: *Late Phases: Night of the Lone Wolf*. Director: Adrian Garcia Bogliano; Producers: Brent Kunkle, Zak Seman, Greg Newman, Larry Fessenden; Screenplay: Eric Stolze; Cinematographer: Ernesto Herrera. Cast: Nick Damici, Ethan Embry, Lance Guest, Erin Cummings, Rutanya Alda, Tina Louise, Al Sapienza, Caitlin O'Heaney, Karen Lynn Gorney, Dana Ashbrook, Tom Noonan.

> IN THIS IDYLLIC COMMUNITY A CLEAR NIGHT IS A BLESSING. BUT FOR ONE MAN IT'S A CURSE—trailer

Here's a unique take on werewolves—lycanthropy as a metaphor for aging. With the American population becoming older (as the baby boomers move into their "golden years"), such a representation becomes both topical and poignantly powerful. With *Late Phases*, Spanish-born director Adrian Garcia Bogliano (*Here Comes the Devil*, *The ABCs of Death*), working from an insightful script by Eric Stolze (*Under the Bed*), brings the aging issue to palpable life via an emotionally rich, character-driven tale … with werewolves.

Elderly blind Vietnam vet Ambrose McKinley (54-year-old Nick Damici in convincing old-age makeup) moves into the gated Crescent Bay Retirement Community. The no-nonsense, ex-military widower (who has hung onto his collection of firearms despite his blindness) reacts gruffly to those around him, such as the nosy neighborhood "welcoming committee" (among them a ghastly-looking Tina Louise, whose frog-lipped face simply screams Botox-gone-wrong). "I'd see you ladies to the door," snaps Ambrose, "but I'm blind." He also has an uneasy relationship with his grown son Will (Ethan Embry), who works hard at being helpful and vainly seeks approval from his embittered, closed-off father. On Ambrose's very first night in his new place a hulking werewolf kills his next-door neighbor and then bursts into Ambrose's own house. His loyal German shepherd bravely attacks the beast, however, and fends it off, leaving a distraught Ambrose to put a bullet in the brain of his mortally wounded seeing-eye dog. While the police and the rest of the community put the vicious assault down to the work of a wild animal, Ambrose pieces together the evidence (including monthly dog disappearances) and concludes that a lycanthrope stalks Crescent Bay every full moon. While sussing out the likely suspects, he prepares to take down the beast at the next lunar cycle. But the culprit, a tortured soul driven mad by his affliction, learns of Ambrose's plan and intentionally infects several other residents, leading to a bloody battle between the sightless ex-soldier and a pack of vicious werewolves.

"Back when I was writing this in 2011," explained scripter Eric Stolze about the film's genesis, "my grandparents were quite ill and sort of on their last legs, and so while I was dealing with that it was sort of a cold splash of water in my face that everybody gets at various points in their life where they realize there is so little dignity in this part of it. There's so little dignity in the places that you're put, in the treatment that you're receiving and the sort of out of sight, out of mind mentality that you're faced with. It occurred to me that that's really something horrifying about the real world that you really don't see in a lot of horror movies. Especially not since the '80s when teenagers became more and more excited about horror so they started to populate horror more and more."

More than a simple horror movie or even basic lycan-tale, *Late Phases* tackles the topic of aging head on. "People don't come to places like this to live, they come here to die," notes Ambrose about his new "community." The film cleverly links the protracted, inexorable transformation that comes with growing old to lycanthropy. The slow but inescapable metamorphosis of aging contrasts with the quick but no less inexorable change into a monster, with both transformations ultimately ending in death (or at least the death of one's dignity, one's humanity). In effect, the protagonist's battle with the geriatric werewolves becomes a metaphorical fight against aging itself. And though on the surface he prevails (dispatching the monsters), he cannot outrun or outfight his own inevitable demise at the film's bittersweet conclusion.

Lurking in the story's background, like a beast in the shadows, is the truly frightening specter of dementia, when someone loses their very identity, becoming something alien—almost a monster—to their friends and loved ones. Though the dreaded identity-stealing Alzheimer's disease is only mentioned once in the film, the underlying implication remains chillingly present.

Beyond the aging themes, *Late Phases* explores the often difficult father-son dynamic. Ambrose and Will share an obvious history of pain and regret, with what remains unspoken just as important as the few words uttered between them. Eric Stolze's thoughtful script, along with the subtle emotional playing of Nick Damici and Ethan Embry, makes one care about the two characters, thereby involving the viewer more deeply in Ambrose's plight. Said director Bogliano, "I felt like it was interesting to approach the father and son relationship from the point of view of a son watching his father grow older." And Bogliano consistently puts his money (shot) where his mouth is. When the proud Ambrose ("I'm blind; I'm not crippled") barks at his son to go live his own life, Will, feeling hurt and betrayed, answers back, "If you ever need anything from me, don't come calling because I'm gonna *go live my own life.*" At this, Ambrose, sitting in a doorway, gradually leans back, his stricken face melting into the shadows to finally disappear into the darkness—the darkness of isolation and loneliness.

The heart of *Late Phases* lay in its character relationships, offering a protagonist who's dealing with/overcoming a physical handicap. But with a vicious werewolf in the mix. (At the climax, Ambrose uses a hearing aid to track the werewolves outside his house and zero in on their location.) "I think this had a story," noted lead actor Nick Damici. "You take the werewolves out of it and the story was still there. Ultimately I think that's more important than the genre element." This proved far from accidental. Revealed Bogliano, "The one [werewolf movie] that's my favorite is *Silver Bullet*. I found a lot of things in the script that were similar. The community, the relationship with the priest, there were some elements there. The leading character having a handicap. You've got a boy in a wheelchair, and here you have this blind man. There were a lot of elements, and Eric [Stolze], the writer, he was a big fan of *Silver Bullet*."

"I always appreciated that *Silver Bullet* was a whodunit," said writer Stolze. "I appreciated that they utilized that fundamental concealed identity of the werewolf to make it into this really interesting story of who in this town is not who they say they are? Who's more than they appear to be? That's such a fun element to play with as a writer that always kind of got my imagination going. It seemed like a really fun opportunity to play around with the mystery element in the script and it helps people focus on the characters as well."

But lest one mistake this for some slice-of-life Hallmark Channel drama, the film bookends its thought-provoking issues with thrilling—and frightening—werewolf action. Less than 15 minutes into the movie the monster makes its first appearance, terrifying Ambrose's next-door neighbor Gloria (*The Deer Hunter*'s Rutanya Alda) before leaving her a grisly, disemboweled corpse. The creature then crashes through Ambrose's door, wreaking formidable destruction before finally retreating in the face of the determined canine. And at the hour mark the monster returns—along with four more fresh lycan-converts, resulting in all manner of mayhem. One particularly arresting set-piece sees a terrified victim flee to his car. Panicked, he starts the engine, and the headlights reveal the hairy monster standing in the road. The creature suddenly leaps ten feet onto the hood and smashes its arms through the windshield. The werewolf's gaping maw then thrusts through the shattered windscreen, and a crimson splash onto the side window suggests the occupant's grisly fate, hammering home the horrific, near-unstoppable power of these monsters.

Unlike the standard action hero, Ambrose takes a horrific beating, which heightens both the sense of realism and empathy. On the night of Ambrose's confrontation, he dons his dress uniform and prepares his weapons (for which he's commissioned a handful of silver bullets). But at his first were-encounter a vicious blow slices his side to ribbons before he can kill the beast, resulting in him having to tape his abdomen together with surgical gauze. Next, when a werewolf jumps him from behind in his own kitchen, Ambrose throws it over his shoulder and aims his gun at the creature on the floor. But the beast knocks the pistol aside just as Ambrose pulls the trigger, and the bullet shatters his own foot! And finally, as a hobbling Ambrose is reduced to swinging at the final monster with a sharpened shovel, the creature lunges and sinks its fangs into his shoulder, leaving shredded skin visible beneath his shredded uniform.

Though sticking to the conventional lycan-tropes (full moon, silver bullets), the beasts themselves appear anything *but* conventional. Apart from the fact they're all geriatric werewolves (some with missing teeth, others with sagging chests, and even one with an egg-sized cataract), their shaggy grey hair–covered limbs, ribbed bare chest, oversized heads, huge pointy ears, and squarish snouts with massive lower jaw make them look like a cross between a wolf and a gremlin. But there's nothing comical about these septuagenarian beasts, as they slash and bite with an abrupt ferocity that leaves their victims awash in their own blood and internal organs. (Thankfully, director Bogliano doesn't dwell on the grue, holding just long enough on the grisly aftermath to register the full horror of the brutal deeds without wallowing in the gore.) Though the creatures can stand and walk upright, they frequently drop down to lope on all fours. And they seem to possess at least a rudimentary intelligence while in wolf form, as one werewolf holds the now-human corpse of his dead mate (his wife) and howls in anguish.

"In the script, there was a description of the werewolves as having white hair and missing teeth," noted Bogliano. "It was really interesting because it was like having these old werewolves. That was the basic thing that I brought to the [special effects] guys. They started designing from there, and they knew what they were doing." Indeed they did.

Late Phases does lycan cinema proud by focusing on a central werewolf character that inspires both pity and terror (once his identity has been revealed). This man, cursed, like Larry Talbot himself, for performing an heroic act (stopping the original beast that stalked the local woods—"I killed it, but it got to me first"), has been driven mad by his malady, a psychosis that has taken the form of religious mania. (In one scene he engages in self-mutilation—"acts of contrition" he calls them—to cope with the horror of what he's become.) He is not an evil man, just a hopelessly desperate one. "Father, I need absolution," he pleads with his priest, "I need it before it's too late." He continues, "I have tried everything and nothing works. All I want to do is live in worship, and kill in solitude, and die in peace." Chillingly, just before he transforms he concludes his plea to the priest with, "I tell you this because I want you to know that when I kill you it's out of love. It's an act of mercy." The mercy being to spare the padre from his own cursed fate.

The subsequent transformation stands as one of the best in werewolf cinema. It starts with the man literally ripping the shirt off his chest, his skin coming right along with it, exposing the hairy torso beneath. The camera pans down his body to show coarse fur bursting through the split skin of his calf. He falls forward on all fours to show his mouth bristling with fangs and his hand a clawed appendage. The camera moves upwards to reveal his writhing hairy back, then glides away and turns as he stands to reveal his face—which he literally rips away to release the wolfish visage beneath. The moving, swooping and gliding camerawork smoothly ties the snippets together to create the illusion of a seamless, continuous, and shockingly gruesome metamorphosis.

This practical werewolf transformation, courtesy of Robert Kurtzman (*From Dusk Till Dawn*) and his team utilized a computerized motion-controlled camera rig programmed to dip and swirl in a certain way, with the metamorphosis coming in one fluid sequence rather than choppy edits as in so many lycan-flicks. Said Bogliano, "We're trying to create the illusion that it all happens in one single take, which is very complicated. But it's worth it, because this way you can believe everything that you see. If you can see the tricks of a transformation, it's more difficult to believe that the creature actually exists."

Filming in upstate New York, Bogliano worked with cinematographer Ernesto Herrera to create an oppressive "late afternoon" atmosphere to match the late phase of the disillusioned protagonist's life. Herrera utilized diffused lighting to underscore the drabness of the endless beige of this depressing enclave. Even the wallpaper and lawns are painted in shades of brown.

But not everything falls neatly into these *Phases*. The pace lags in the middle, as Ambrose follows a few leads, visits a shady gunsmith (played by co-producer Larry Fessenden) to secure some silver bullets, and even tentatively unburdens himself to the priest ("When I went to 'Nam, I honestly thought I was gonna save lives"). Fortunately, this proves to be a mere speed bump, and the film soon picks up speed to finish with an action-packed and emotional bang.

"I like werewolf movies," concluded star Nick Damici, "but I don't think I've ever seen one that really nailed it. There are some definitive vampire movies I really love, but I don't think they've quite done that great werewolf film. Hopefully this is it." Well, it may not quite be "it," but *Late Phases*, with its involving characters, compelling story structure, and multi-layered screenplay, not to mention impressive practical effects and one of the most striking metamorphosis scenes since *An American Werewolf in London*, comes fairly close.

With quotes from: "Writer Eric Stolze Talks *Late Phases*," by Evan Dickson, Collider.com, December 5, 2014; "Director Adrian Garcia Bogliano and Star Nick Damici Talk *Late Phases*," by The Wolfman, TheWolfmanCometh.com, March 14, 2014; "*Late Phases* and Hairy Faces," by Michael Gingold, *Fangoria* 338.

Morphology: Fur-covered gremlin-wolf monstrosities
Demise: Silver bullets
Full Moon Rating: ****

Legend of the Werewolf

(1975; Tyburn/Rank; UK) Director: Freddie Francis; Producer: Kevin Francis; Screenplay: Anthony Hinds (as John Elder); Cinematographer: John Wilcox. Cast: Peter Cushing, Ron Moody, Hugh Griffith, Roy Castle, David Bailie, Lynn Dalby, Stefan Gryff, Renee Houston, Norman Mitchell, Mark Weaves, Marjorie Yates, David Rintoul.

HORROR STALKS … THE STREETS OF PARIS—ad line

Given its similarities to the far better known Hammer film *Curse of the Werewolf* (period setting, parallel plot/central character, monsters that could be twins)—and the fact that both scripts were written by the same man, Anthony Hinds—it's perhaps inevitable that this generally overlooked *Legend* be compared with its much-lauded predecessor. Though lacking the iconic presence and brilliant pivotal performance of *Curse*'s Oliver Reed, *Legend of the Werewolf* in many ways remains a more *entertaining* film than the heralded *Curse*—thanks largely to its more streamlined story, increased level of action, and a thoroughly engaging portrayal by Peter Cushing.

Produced by the fledgling Tyburn Film company, and headed by Kevin Francis (a former Hammer employee and son of *Legend*'s director Freddie Francis), *Legend of the Werewolf* follows Etoile, who, after being raised by wolves as a child, ends up as the "wolf boy" in a cut-rate traveling show. Upon reaching manhood, Etoile (David Rintoul), when the full moon rises, transforms into a ravening beast who kills a fellow carnival worker. Aghast at what he's done, Etoile flees. Ending up in Paris, he stumbles across a rundown zoo, complete with a pair of decrepit old wolves. When the zookeeper (Ron Moody) notices his "way with the animals," he hires Etoile as an assistant and gives him a place to sleep on the premises. Soon Etoile falls for Christine (Lynn Dalby), who comes to the zoo for lunch every day. When Etoile learns the truth about Christine (she's a local prostitute), he flies into a rage. On the next full moon, he once again transforms, this time killing a customer of Christine's. Inspector Gerard (Stefan Gryff), aided by his police surgeon friend Professor Cataflanque (Peter Cushing), investigates the murder, and several more that occur in quick succession. As more of Christine's customers die horribly, and as Etoile sinks into despair, it's up to Cataflanque to follow his hunch and find Etoile, ending in a tense, poignant, and tragic confrontation in the Parisian sewers.

Freddie Francis, a very visually-oriented director (he made his

Looking very much like Oliver Reed in *The Curse of the Werewolf*, David Rintoul lives the *Legend of the Werewolf* (British pressbook).

name as an Oscar-winning cinematographer), sets the tone beautifully from the first post-credits shot. The camera stares upwards at the woodland trees, the dappled sunlight illuminating their leaves. It then pans across this bucolic vision of nature to tilt downwards and suddenly bring into close-up a gruesome skeletal corpse hanging from a gibbet alongside the country road. Here things are not always what they seem, and darkness often lurks beneath the surface—reflecting the film's major themes and characters.

Francis employs red tinting and a gliding, mobile camera to indicate the wolves,' and later werewolf's, point of view. He stages the werewolf attacks with a minimum of gore but a maximum of suspense. This werewolf doesn't simply pounce and rip and shred, it *stalks* its victims, with Francis' camera gliding after its prey until the unfortunate turns and sees the snarling face of his own death. As a kind of representational punctuation to the bloodshed, Francis occasionally inserts an extreme close-up of the creature's fang-filled mouth, the maw oozing freshly-spilled, bright crimson blood, to shockingly fill the screen.

Francis films Etoile's first transformation with an imaginative economy (no doubt dictated by budgetary restrictions) that remains no less effective for its simplicity. As wolves howl in the surrounding forest, Etoile thrashes in his sleep, grimaces as if in pain, and drags his hands up to his face to reveal them covered in hair. Then a close-up of his blood-shot, animal-like eyes gives way to red-tinted POV shots as he moves through the woods. Later in the film, Francis is afforded a full metamorphosis, which producer Kevin Francis played up in publicity and interviews. "It has always struck me that nobody has ever done a werewolf film properly," opined Kevin. "Universal had a go, but their version is creaky now in terms of the technique they had. You see, I believe that no matter how good the film is, you've got millions of people sitting there waiting for this bloke to turn into a werewolf. So we spent a lot of time and money developing a new photographic technique that can do this absolutely marvelously." Exactly where the money went, and just what this "new photographic technique" might be remains a mystery, for, while Francis stages the transformation well (filming his subject violently ripping open his shirt and moving about while the change occurs in order to sidestep the typical static nature of such a scene), Etoile becomes the wolfman through the same use of "creaky" cutaways and increasing makeup stages that served Larry Talbot so well back in the day.

Unfortunately, the script, by former Hammer producer/screenwriter Anthony Hinds (*Kiss of the Vampire*, 1963; *The Reptile*, 1966; *Dracula Has Risen from the Grave*, 1968; etc.), doesn't always offer Francis the sturdiest of frameworks, and leaves many questions unanswered. At one point Cataflanque tries to convince his inspector friend that they're seeking a werewolf, resulting in a risible exchange:

> INSPECTOR: "But a man that turns into an animal—how can you believe that?"
> CATAFLANQUE: "A tadpole turns into a frog. We all believe that because we've seen it—it's one of nature's miracles. Now is it that strange if at a certain time a man turns into an animal?"
> INSPECTOR: "And just because of the moon?"
> CATAFLANQUE: "But why not? The moon controls the oceans; it drives some men insane; and tribes all over the world still worship it."

Fortunately, Peter Cushing's natural and impassioned delivery almost sells this hollow claptrap, but the script generally does him few favors, with the veteran actor forced to build his characterization with his clever use of props and natural intelligence, compassion and humor.

During the pre-credits sequence, in which a group of refugees flees through the wilderness, a narrator (Cushing) intones, "In the forests it was not uncommon to be attacked by wolves. And for the wife to die in childbirth was commonplace." When these very things happen to infant Etoile's parents, the narrator continues, "This particular child, instead of being torn to pieces by the wolf pack that killed its father, was accepted by them—warmed by the females, even protected by the males. Why this should have been we can only hazard a guess. Perhaps it was the time—midnight on the eve of Christmas when, traditionally, the wild beast is said to guard the cradle of a newborn child." As to why Etoile later developed into a lycanthrope, the script remains equally vague. Was it because he was raised by wolves (if so, then why did he not transform until reaching adulthood—and long past puberty, by the look of him)? Was it because he was born at the stroke of Christmas Day (some folk legends equate this with vampirism and werewolfery)? We never learn the answers and must simply take his developing monstrous nature as a matter of course.

This werewolf, though apparently hurt by regular bullets (as evinced by his pain when shot by the police near the film's end), must be killed by silver (as Cataflanque's assistant reminds him, "We know we must have a silver bullet, sir"). Etoile seems fully aware of his lycanthropic condition from his first transformation. ("Aware of his terrible legacy," says the narrator after his first metamorphosis, "the boy fled.") After his first killings in Paris, Etoile pitiably pleads to no one in particular, "Help me, somebody—please help me." But there is nobody to help, and he continues his wolfish rampage. In beast form, Etoile truly is half-man, half-animal. He can still reason somewhat (targeting those "customers" sullying his lady love, for instance), yet possesses the savage impulses of an animal. This leads to a tense final confrontation in the Gothic-styled sewers beneath the Paris streets, when Cataflanque goes down alone in order to save Etoile. When he sees the wolfman's shadow, Cataflanque calls out, "If you come out and show yourself, I won't shoot—you have my word." When the monster steps forward, as if it understands, Cataflanque soothingly speaks to the beast-man like any fugitive: "If you give yourself up, I'll try to help you. Otherwise the police will track you down. They'll find you wherever you hide and destroy you." Cataflanque goes even further, telling the werewolf, "I'll throw my gun away. I know I can trust you, Etoile." Peter Cushing's sincerity and compassion shine through, and his use of the monster's human name seems to strike deep into the heart of the beast to find the humanity still residing there. At this, the wolfman, who had only ever snarled and growled and killed, speaks, pleading, "Help me, please." But just then the inspector and his men arrive, causing Etoile to attack and the police to fire on him. "You fools!" shouts Cataflanque. "Blundering idiots! Must you always kill?!" Shots of the wounded werewolf fleeing and plaintively calling "Christine!" paint a portrait of tragedy and unnecessary loss, making this one of the most powerful denouements in the werewolf canon.

Sadly, newcomer David Rintoul, in his first film appearance (he went on to forge a career in television), is no Oliver Reed (nor even Lon Chaney), and his overly intense playing comes off as alternately sulky and near-psychotic (when angry). It doesn't help that the script paints him as almost moronic in his naiveté. The scenes between Etoile and Christine carry little conviction (and the script fails to provide any real basis for this relationship), and one wonders why Etoile has fallen so hard for the young prostitute. His abrupt infatuation, even to the point of asking her to marry him after only a few brief interactions (not to mention discovering her true profession), shows Etoile to be foolish, emotionally immature, and clingy. This proves a significant, though not completely debilitating, weakness in an otherwise strong production.

Kevin Francis started the Tyburn film production company with the aim of reviving the Gothic horror films he loved. Tyburn produced only three theatrical pictures, all released in 1975—*Persecution*, *The Ghoul* and *Legend of the Werewolf* (the latter two directed by Kevin's father, Freddie Francis)—before folding, having succumbed to the changing public tastes for big-budget horror like *The Exorcist*, or cutting edge indies like *The Texas Chainsaw Massacre*, over Hammeresque Gothics.

"Basically what we're doing," concluded Kevin Francis about *Legend of the Werewolf*, "is making a jolly good horror yarn with some good people in it, and we're doing what the people want to see better than anybody has ever done it before." While that last point is certainly open to debate, *Legend* does indeed qualify as a "good horror yarn" that's definitely filled with "good people." First and foremost among them is Peter Cushing. Then there's Ron Moody as the seedy zoo keeper, who fleshes out what could have been a mere caricature into a fully-formed, even complex, human being, equal parts repellant (the way he always licks the rim of his glass to get the last drop), crude, and endearing (his hesitant patting of Etoile's shoulder, his anger and squeamishness when ordered by the police to kill the wolves in his charge, and his sometimes softening expression and pity in his eyes demonstrate that a heart does indeed beat beneath his uncouth exterior). An amusing cameo by Roy Castle as a nervous photographer hired to photograph some corpses at the morgue, coupled with the easy, affectionate, and humorous banter between Cushing's surgeon and Stefan Gryff's likable police inspector, adds further interest to this *Legend*.

Apparently, having your son as your boss was not an altogether easy thing for Freddie Francis, as he and Kevin purportedly experienced some friction during both *The Ghoul* and *Legend*. (Some years later, Anthony Hinds commented that "the father and son don't get on too well, but I like both of 'em.") In any case, Freddie had become disillusioned with the role of "horror" specialist, and after *Legend* he gave up directing for nearly ten years, working solely as a cinematographer. "I was really so bored with those sorts of films," he admitted.

Two days into filming, a timber wolf used for the movie's opening escaped and took refuge in nearby Black Park (scene of many a Hammer horror), resulting in a media frenzy (it made the front page of the August 22, 1974, issue of *The Times*) and the unfortunate death of the animal. "Runaway Wolf Shot," read the *Times* headline. "A police marksman yesterday killed a wolf which escaped on Tuesday [August 20, 1974] from Pinewood Film Studios near Iver, Buckinghamshire." "I loved the publicity," recalled Kevin Francis, "but I was sorry the whole thing happened. The only reason the animal had to be killed was because the stupid journalists stampeded all over the place and kept frightening the poor thing. If we'd been left alone, as we asked, we would have been able to tranquillize it and get it back in its cage."

All this publicity availed this *Legend* little, however; though released theatrically in Europe, it failed to find a distributor in the U.S. and only saw the light of day in America via video. Which is a pity, as *Legend of the Werewolf* deserved—and deserves—better.

With quotes from: *The Horror People*, by John Brosnan; "Anthony Hinds, Prince of Hammer: Part Two," by Bruce G. Hallenbeck, *Fangoria* 75; *The Films of Freddie Francis*, by Wheeler Winston Dixon.

Morphology: Bipedal wolfman (in the Oliver Reed mold)
Demise: Silver bullet
Full Moon Rating: ***

The Legend of the Wolf Woman

(1976; Dimension; Italy) Original Language Title: *La Lupa Mannara*; Alternate Titles: *Werewolf Woman* (UK), *She Wolf* (video), *Terror of the She Wolf* (video); Director/Screenplay: Rino di Silvestro, Tony La Penna (English language edition); Producer: Diego Alchimede; Cinematographer: Mario Capriotti; Cast: Annik Borel, Frederick Stafford, Dagmar Lassander, Tino Carraro, Elio Zamuto, Osvaldo Ruggieri, Andrea Scotti, Howard Ross.

A TRUE STORY SO BRUTAL AND HORRIFYING
it was kept from the public for over a century!—poster

This low-budget Italian exploitation film starts with an interesting premise but immediately degenerates into a morass of dull soft-core sex and pointless sadism. The story revolves around Daniela (French actress Annik Borel), who resembles a distant ancestor that, legend has it, was burned alive as a werewolf. As a result of being raped at age 13, Daniela identifies sexuality with beastliness and violence. After learning about her lycanthropic ancestor, Daniela becomes violent whenever aroused or propositioned, and ends up biting and murdering her victims (though *without* turning into a wolf). As her doctor puts it, "She's suffering from ancestral complexes" (try and find *that* in any psychology textbook).

Poorly photographed, filled with ridiculous stilted dialogue, and offering a This-Really-Happened narration for its anticlimactic (non)

146 • *The Legend of the Wolf Woman*

ending, *Legend of the Wolf Woman* has little to recommend. The copious nudity and often protracted sex scenes are anything *but* erotic, and only inspire the desire to hose off. Upping the sleaze factor is the film's organ-and-drum porno-style jazz score. The wolf woman in question (the ancestor) appears only during the film's opening—about the only worthwhile seven minutes found in the movie. It begins as the camera zooms in to the image of the full moon, filling the frame. This dissolves to a shot of a woman's face (Borel) suddenly rising up to emit a startling scream. The next shot shows a woman (Borel again, playing Daniela's ancestor) completely nude, standing inside a circle of campfires, her arms raised to the heavens as the credits roll. This opening gambit concisely sums up the film's proclivities—shock and nudity. As the credits continue, the woman dances and writhes naked (to the point of looking like she's having a seizure). Next a narrator intones: "And on the night of the full moon the howl of the werewolf will be heard. Its terrible cry will make men *tremble*! They will close their shutters and bolt their doors. Then the werewolf will begin searching for food, tearing to pieces whomever crosses its path." The camera subsequently pans across the spent ashes of the fires to come to rest on the prostrate form of the nude woman—now covered in hair! She slowly rises to reveal a darkened face, red eyes, a built-up dog nose, and a mouth full of oversized teeth (but curiously lacking true fangs), all framed by flowing blonde locks. Also revealed are the creature's hair-covered breasts and dark, *inch-and-a-half-long* nipples (one almost expects to see a credit for "nipple prosthetics"). The she-wolf rises and stretches towards the sky, emitting a half-growl/half-cry at the moon. Next a band of torch-bearing villagers in period dress (it's supposedly 200 years ago) chase the beast through the darkness. She hides behind some trees and attacks a man who'd become separated from the mob. Knocking him to the ground, she bites his throat. As blood gushes from the screaming man's wound, this tool-using werewolf grabs up the axe he'd dropped and buries it in his skull, resulting in gouts of bright red stage blood. The next we see of the she-wolf, she's tied to a stake and struggling vainly as the villagers solemnly surround her squirming form (with no indication of *how* the mob caught the she-beast). But before anything further happens, the scene shifts to a woman sitting up in bed and screaming (Borel … again), obviously jolted from a nightmare. Were the scenes we just witnessed merely a dream, were they a vision, were they historical reality? We'll never know, as the rest of the film follows the mentally unbalanced Daniela as she attacks and kills anyone who crosses her sexually-phobic path.

When Daniela's concerned father takes her to see a psychiatrist, the doctor offers, "It would be ridiculous to think that anyone could turn into a wolf on the night of the plenilunium [full moon] and act like a beast, committing animalistic acts, sexual and demoniacal. And yet lycanthropy exists." This doctor considers lycanthropy to be a purely mental condition, with Daniela's werewolfism a manifestation of her "sexual phobia" in combination with her learning about the legend of her lookalike ancestor. It's an intriguing premise that, unfortunately, director-screenwriter Rino di Silvestro decides to exploit rather than explore

Equating lycanthropy with mental illness, "Ancestral complexes" give rise to *The Legend of the Wolf Woman* in this low-budget Italian sleaze-fest (American poster).

by offering up scene after scene of soft-core sex and cheap violence in lieu of character or plot development.

Borel, with her angular features and deep-set eyes, possesses a distinctly sinister beauty (like a sleazy, low-rent, blonde Barbara Steele). Unfortunately, about the only convincing thing about her is her voluptuous figure and the allure it offers her numerous victims. When enmeshed in her "werewolf" rage, however, she truly looks, acts and sounds like an animal. Losing control—biting, scratching, and screeching like a banshee as she bangs her victim's head against a steering wheel or bedpost—the anything-but-shy Borel makes for a convincing maniac. But during her character's "sane" moments she comes off as either blank (even near-catatonic) or whining. In either form she engenders little sympathy, so her unwanted transformation to homicidal beast carries little weight (and no pathos).

Born Anne Borel in France in 1948, Annik Borel made a handful of mostly exploitation films in Europe and America in the 1970s (plus a few appearances on TV series like *The Odd Couple*, *Police Story*, and *Love—American Style*) before dropping from sight at the end of the decade. She appeared as a topless hooker in the blaxploitation entry *Truck Turner* (1974), and as a persecuted witch in Ted V. Mikels' threadbare *Blood Orgy of the She Devils* (1972). Reportedly, Borel spoke German, French, Italian and English fluently (she delivered her *Wolf Woman* lines in English but was dubbed by another actress for the film's American release). Publicity claimed she was the illegitimate granddaughter of Mussolini!

"Without makeup she was incredibly similar to a wolf," said writer-director Di Silvestro of his star. Di Silvestro is best known for his trashy, leering women-in-prison and Nazploitation flicks like *Women in Cell Block 7* (1973) and *Deported Women of the SS Special Section* (1976), in which he mixes queasy doses of sex and violence. Though he only directed eight films in a dozen years, he kept busy as a ghostwriter, authoring over 200 screenplays. "Sex is a natural thing," he said, "but it also gives you an uncontrollable desire, like murder for the serial killer who begs to be caught. We have an irresistible desire to make sex." *And*, so he apparently thought (if this sexploitative *Legend* is any indication), an irresistible desire to *watch* it.

Early on, the doctor handling Daniela's case, in an incredible non sequitur, tells her worried father, "My dear Count, when science decides to contribute more time to the study of extra sensory phenomena, I think that within 50 years we will make more progress in the understanding of the mental ills and psychological problems of mankind than our men of culture have done throughout the centuries." Well, "that's a very interesting theory, and somewhat fascinating" (as another character so repetitiously puts it). Later, the same doctor talks about "a perversion of facts that are heterogeneous, the components of which can be sought by psychiatrists or the phenomenon of parapsychology." It's as if he's just tossing out random ten-dollar words! Pseudo-psychological claptrap like this litters the film like Daniela's string of victims. "It is clear that her personality has been shattered because of the influence of a violent neurotic charge," the muddled medico pontificates. And it's equally clear that this "doctor" has no idea what he's saying. "It's utterly imperative to make sure her brain's energy isn't released due to tension, the cause of which we don't really know." Don't really know indeed. Finally, the doc seems to abandon all attempts at scientific gibberish to move on to *occult* babbling. "We are all cells belonging to one immense entity that is universal and to us remains unknown," he tells an attentive police inspector, apropos of nothing. "It seems we're surrounded by the occult, and so occult are [sic] also the processes of reincarnation." But wait, later he posits that Daniela is "possessed by lycanthropic fury. She kills her brother-in-law—her mind breaks down at this point. What happens: disassociation, schizophrenia." It seems this doc wants to have his mental illness cake and eat his occult slice too.

In the last quarter of the picture, Daniela, on the run from the police after leaving a trail of slaughtered men (and women), finally meets a fine young fellow who doesn't pressure her for sex. As unlikely as it sounds, they're soon frolicking through a romantic montage—holding hands, walking on the beach, kissing at sunset. Has the Wolf Woman finally found love? In a month the full moon returns, and along with it her homicidal urges. But Daniela forces them down, conquers them, and triumphs. She calls her bewildered father and says, "I ask forgiveness for what I've done to you and [my sister] Irena. It was my illness, father, that made me do all those horrible, despicable things. But now something's happened, something wonderful—it's making me well again. I met a man, and I love him, and he's made me really happy." Ah yes, lycanthropy (or at least mental illness) cured by the love of a good man. But it doesn't last, as a trio of criminals break into the house they're sharing, brutally rapes Daniela, and kills her lover. At this point the film takes one final detour—into nasty rape-revenge territory—as Daniela tracks down and cold-bloodedly murders her three assailants (not with the fury of the wolf woman but by more conventional means—using heavy machinery to crush two of them at the junkyard where they work, and setting fire to the third's hovel to watch him burn). This final, sudden turn down yet another exploitation side road proves to be an exceedingly unpleasant coda to a generally unpleasant film.

Aside from an occasional moment of involuntary whimsy engendered by the outrageously inept dialogue, there is little here to appeal to anyone but the S&M heavy breathers in the audience. Incidentally, Quentin Tarantino loves this film.

With quotes from: "Maestro … di Silvestro," by Massimo F. Lavagnini, *Nocturno* 4.

Morphology: Hair-covered, dog-nosed, naked female; and ordinary woman with an extraordinary reaction to sexuality
Demise: None; captured by the police, her fate remains uncertain (though her wolf-woman ancestor was burned at the stake)
Full Moon Rating: *½

Leviatán see Monster Dog

Light of Blood

(2014; Cult Movie Mania Releasing) Director/producer/screenplay: Gustavo Perez; Videographer: Gustavo Perez (and *nine* others). Cast: Rebecca Holycross, Gustavo Perez, Josey Heston, Michael Chomick, Ray Nelson, Laura Kennedy, Louise Barrett, Jack Barrett.

> Tony Luna was on the verge of execution—until his communist captors hatched a better plan…—trailer

Said plan? To make Cuban soldier Tony (played by writer-director Gustavo Perez himself) a werewolf. Actually, they intended to use him as a human guinea pig to test their "supersoldier serum," but the chemical concocted by a group of Havana scientists led by Colonel Ramos (Michael Chomick) turns prisoner Tony (scheduled to meet the firing squad simply for sleeping with the Colonel's wife!) into a Lon Chaney–style wolfman. After a series of murders committed by the unknowing Tony, the local authorities seek help from Colonel Ramos, with the Colonel sending his man Tony (now apparently forgiven for his indelicate indiscretions) to aid the investigation! After a few more random killings, the various scientists and finally the Colonel meet their fate at Tony's paws before the Colonel's wife puts this Cuban wolfman out of his (and our) misery.

Extraordinary enthusiasm and superhuman perseverance are two central ingredients in creating any successful film. Others include an engrossing story, intelligent script, believable actors, technically proficient crew, and visionary director. Unfortunately, *Light of Blood* offers only the first two. Though an occasional extra or bit player in *real* movies, Cuban-American Gustavo Perez, who wrote, produced, directed, and starred in *Light of Blood* (not to mention providing "Lighting," "Set Design," "Makeup," and "Special Effects") may possess enthusiasm and perseverance, but he can't rise above his no-budget and, worse, no-talent limitations to produce anything but a painful exercise in amateur moviemaking.

Deficient in every way, *Light of Blood* offers grainy, shaky, focus-challenged video travelogue footage of visually uninteresting Cuban locales mixed with flatly-lit, poorly staged, and worse acted interior sequences. The faux accents affected by the amateur actors (when the hollow, muddy sound lets you *hear* them) comprise a mix of American, Latino and vaguely Eastern European, with one character even sounding *Cajun*. Mismatched footage (even mismatched video stock), inappropriate music, and random shots—of city streets, people walking, dogs barking, weird paintings (this last because a [minimally] re-dressed low-rent art gallery stood in for most of the interior settings)—abound.

Light of Blood's plotting is as nonsensical as its title ("light of blood" means ... what exactly?). Characters come and go without introduction and for no apparent reason, and things happen for even less reason (at one point a floating decapitated head on a string appears before the Tony-Wolf to bob up and down, with the beast-creature next seen running down the sidewalk carrying the phony-looking prop in his paws). Elements are introduced then dropped (an entire sequence focuses on an apparently werewolf-wise Russian maid talking about tales from the Old Country and emphasizing how it must be *silver* that kills the beast, yet Tony ultimately falls beneath the blade of an ordinary sword). Towards the end, when the werewolf is out of the bag and the Colonel, police inspector, and doctors all pow-wow about how to stop the rampaging Tony, one doc haltingly tells them, "The formula has affected him so much that he probably mutated to, completely to a beastly form. He is always probably in his wolf form; he's never in his human form." The very next scene shows Tony—*in his human form*—sitting in front of a wall.

Light is no better werewolf-wise. This lycanthrope transforms seemingly at random, with all of his listless (and generally bloodless) rampages occurring in broad daylight (night shooting was apparently beyond Perez' abilities). To Perez' credit, he makes the pivotal metamorphosis ubiquitous, if not effective, by providing *five* transformation scenes (all of them accomplished the same way). It begins with Tony strapped to a gurney (*why* is anyone's guess) as the camera zooms in on his face, then zooms out again (after an obvious cut) to show shoe polish–darkened eyes and nose, and a few wiry whiskers. The camera zooms forward a second time and pulls back to display yet more whiskers. One more rapid zoom-in/zoom-out reveals Tony's final wolfman appearance: wiry grey hair covering his head and most of his face, a black dog nose and plastic-looking fangs (with the makeup ending abruptly at the neck). A pair of store-bought gorilla hands completes the ensemble.

While in wolfish form, Tony retains the power of speech (telling one victim "I'm your worst nightmare!" before she faints and he carries her off to do ... whatever—the next we see of her she's simply a body under a sheet). Despite this, he apparently has no memory of what he does in lycan-form (even complaining about "blackouts"), at one point attempting to aid the police investigating the murders his own alter wolf-ego committed! (Perez simply pushes through this potentially intriguing subplot without a hint of irony, tragedy, or exploratory aplomb.)

Perez likens his lycan to several classic antecedents. "This is a chemical werewolf," explained the filmmaker, "like *I Was a Teenage Werewolf* was a chemical werewolf. The movie *The Werewolf* from 1957 [sic] with Stephen Ritch, that was a chemical werewolf." True. A big difference being that those two were also *good movies*. While Perez claims inspiration from both Michael Landon's Teen Werewolf ("He was a real ferocious werewolf") and Paul Naschy's many lupine portrayals, it never translates to his own lackluster lycanthrope. Perez' wolfman walks, moves, and even runs in a disappointingly ordinary fashion, with little to differentiate this decidedly *non*-ferocious "monster" from some pudgy guy in desperate need of electrolysis (and direction) ambling down the street.

Taking nearly two years to complete, *Light of Blood* was finished in 2005 (using travelogue video footage Perez and his brother shot in 2003 while visiting relatives in Cuba as background, with interiors and actor scenes later filmed in Perez' home state of Florida). After making its "world premier" at the Romeo Coffeehouse in Ybor City, Florida (a free screening), the movie languished unseen until the tiny indy outfit Cult Movie Mania Releasing put it out on DVD in 2014. They needn't have bothered.

"YOU AIN'T NEVER SEEN A WEREWOLF MOVIE LIKE THIS!" proclaims this amateurish film's amateurish trailer. Nor would you *want* to, for it's simply a case of bad grammar, worse movie.

With quotes from: "An Interview with Gustavo Perez," *Light of Blood* DVD.

Morphology: Gray-haired Lon Chaney wannabe
Demise: Sword to the chest (or at least held under the arm)
Full Moon Rating: ½

Little Dead Rotting Hood

(2016; The Asylum) Director: Jared Cohn; Producer: David Michael Latt; Screenplay: Gabriel Campisi; Cinematographer: Laura Beth Love. Cast: Eric Balfour, Bianca A. Santos, Romeo Miller, Patrick Muldoon, Marina Sirtis, Heather Tom.

SHE'S *NOT* AFRAID OF THE BIG BAD WOLVES—tagline

A young woman sprints through the forest at night, back-lit fog and frantic camerawork emphasizing her panic as she flees from a large wolf. The creature brings her down and brutally savages her. Called off by a middle-aged woman in a red cloak, the beast retreats. As the older woman approaches the mauled girl, she says, "We're running out of time.... The people have to be protected. It's your turn now. This is the only way." The girl dies from her bloody wounds, and the older woman whispers, "I'm so sorry; I love you," then tearfully buries her body, leaving a sword in the grave. She then intones, "As the moon grows over the coming days, may the tide of its light illuminate your path, so that you may fulfill your destiny, my child." Cutting her wrist, the woman drips her own blood over the earth and collapses, dead.

So begins *Little Dead Rotting Hood*, a modern mixing of the old Brothers Grimm fairy tale ... with swords and zombies and werewolves (oh my!). Soon after this pre-credits sequence, the dead girl claws her way out of the earth, but she's changed—along with her gaping wounds, she sports strange eyes, fangs, and claws at the ends of her fingers. It turns out that this hitherto normal high-schooler,

Samantha (Bianca A. Santos), has been chosen as the next "Keeper of the Forest"—an undead heroine charged with keeping the (were)wolves at bay. The local sheriff (Eric Balfour) and Samantha's confused boyfriend Danny (Romeo Miller) investigate not only Samantha's disappearance but the recent spate of wolf killings (a dozen in the last few months), leading to a showdown with a gigantic "den mother" megabeast in which Samantha must use her newfound powers to save the day.

"Just about everyone has heard the fairy tale 'Little Red Riding Hood,'" noted screenwriter Gabriel Campisi. "Everyone is familiar with the girl in red, the grandmother, and the big bad wolf. But no one really knows anything about these characters, their back stories or where they come from. What if they were nothing like who we thought they were? What if there was a lot more to Little Red, to the grandmother, and to the wolf than we imagined?"

Indeed, what if Little Red was actually an ass-kicking zombie-girl; grandma was the ninja-skilled "Keeper of the Forest" passing her powers onto her granddaughter; and the Big Bad Wolf was an entire pack of werewolves lorded over by a fifteen-foot-tall mega-lycan? Yep, we've obviously passed through the gates of that over-the-top, often ridiculous cinema domain that is The Asylum (purveyors of such celluloid wackiness as *Mega Python vs. Gatoroid*, *2-Headed Shark Attack*, and, of course, the infamous *Sharknado* series).

But don't let that scare you, for the imaginative and entertaining *Little Dead Rotting Hood* manages to surmount its trashy pedigree to become something more than its impoverished parts. For one thing, it's competently acted, with the standouts being the naturalistic playing of Romeo Miller (as Danny) and the entertainingly goofy turn by Patrick Muldoon as Deputy Henry. It moves at a rapid pace, with resurrections, wolf attacks, and giant werewolves coming at a fast and furious pace. The CGI effects, though uneven, are miles above most Mega Shark/Piranha/Croc/Python productions. The action-packed finale, involving the Big Beast, countless gunshots, and even a flame thrower (not to mention Samantha-zombie whose red cloak and shiny sword are the source of her power), proves far more ambitious—and effective—than most cut-rate Asylum efforts. And it possesses the out-and-out fun factor of a *15-foot-tall werewolf*. Giant monsters have been a popular cinema staple since the 1950s, and combining the oversized menace with the werewolf subgenre can't help but raise a smile for those enamored of either.

"Not every horror movie has to encompass the same things," noted director Jared Cohn. "We try to not be so formulaic. That said, there definitely are some familiar elements that the audiences come to expect, and we don't want to let anyone down. The Asylum is successful for a reason in that they deliver those expectations. The goal, though, is to deliver above and beyond. Sometimes it works better than others." Indeed, *Little Dead Rotting Hood* definitely works "better than others" as it molds the disparate elements into a uniquely entertaining pastiche.

Still, the film can't wholly escape its cheesy roots. For instance, the supposed high-school-age leads look to be about 28. It follows the hoary old '80s slasher bromide of "have sex and die" (the werewolves' first two victims are a teen couple fooling around). Unfunny dialogue peppers the script ("Why aren't they attacking?" "They're waiting for their orders." "What is this, a fucking drive-through?"). The characters, even the "authorities," accept the idea of marauding werewolves—as well as a wolf-fighting zombie-girl—rather too readily. And the film betrays its derivative nature by making Samantha a sort of "Buffy the Werewolf Slayer" ("There are other 'Keepers' out there too," she tells the sheriff at film's end, just to cement the notion).

Also, the script seems hazy about its werewolf lore. While there's much talk of the full moon, it appears the orb isn't really a factor, as the creatures can shift at will. Confusingly, sometimes ordinary bullets work, killing the wolves, while at other times (such as the confrontation at their den) the protagonists pump lead into the creatures with no appreciable effect. And while the regular werewolves keep their wolf-shape after death (the sheriff even drags one into the office for examination), the oversized "den mother" transforms back to its human form upon its demise (a surprising character reveal).

Said den mother, "a megawolf—will rise when the hunter's moon falls on the equinox," reads Samantha in her grandmother's diary. "She'll lead her army of wolves to kill everyone in sight." All we see of said army, however, are a trio of black-clad men who quickly transform into wolves. The low-key lighting and evocative bone-crunching noises on the soundtrack can't completely mask the low-quality CGI morphing effect, but at least it lasts only a few seconds before the real wolves step in, with close-ups of their snarling faces generating an air of savage danger. "I love when the real wolves we had brutally attack people," enthused Cohn, "and we intercut the real wolves and actually had military attack dogs spray-painted black—Belgian Malinois go to town on people. It was nuts. Those dogs could easily murder most any human. Vicious and beautiful."

"At the heart of the movie," claimed Campisi, "there's a love story between Samantha (Little Dead Rotting Hood) and her boyfriend Danny. It's what drives all the characters' motivations and turn of events from start to finish, why the story evolves the way it does, despite the external forces at work." While such romantic character development is to be applauded (particularly on a rushed two-week shoot), the *real* heart of the movie is its gigantic uber-werewolf (a huge bipedal monster with hairy arms and legs, massive torso, and misshapen wolf-human hybrid head). *This* is what really sets *Little Dead Rotting Hood* above Asylum's two previous lycan-efforts, *The Beast of Bray Road* and *Battledogs*.

With quotes from: *Little Dead Rotting Hood*: A Reimagining of the Red Riding Hood Story—Exclusive Interview with Writer Gabriel Campisi," by Sachin Trivedi, ibtimes.com; "Interview: Director Jared Cohn Talks *Little Dead Rotting Hood*," by Travis Anderson, shocktillyoudrop.com; "Interview with *Little Dead Rotting Hood*'s Jared Cohn," by Chad Armstrong, leglesscorpse.com.

Morphology: Real wolves; 15-foot-tall bipedal megabeast
Demise: Shotgun blasts; fire; and a magical sword
Full Moon Rating: ***

Lobos de Arga see *Game of Werewolves*

Lone Wolf

(1988; Prism Entertainment) Director: John Callas; Producers: Sarah Liles, Doug Olson, Michael Krueger; Screenplay: Michael Krueger (additional material by Nancy M. Gallanis, John Callas); Cinematographer: David Lewis. Cast: Dyann Brown, Kevin Hart, Jamie Newcomb, Ann Douglas, Siren.

A COMPUTERIZED TRAIL TO MONSTROUS,
MOONLIT MURDER…—ad line

There's no denying that the 1980s was a watershed werewolf decade, what with the lycan game-changing *The Howling* and *An American Werewolf in London*, not to mention the popularity of the comedic *Teen Wolf*. There's also no denying that the 1980s saw its fair share of forgettable were-fare as well (*My Mom's a Werewolf*, *Teen Wolf Too*, a pack of inferior *Howling* sequels, etc.). Unfortunately, the obscure, Colorado-shot, direct-to-video *Lone Wolf* falls with a snow-muffled thud into the latter category.

One full moon winter night a rash of bloody murders puts a crimp in the attendance records of Fairview High School. The police pass the killings off as the work of "wild dogs," but a month later, on the next full moon, the mutilation murders begin again. Computer nerd Joel (Kevin Hart) teams up with nice girl Julie (Dyann Brown), whose boyfriend was an early victim, to try and solve the mystery, in the process catching a glimpse of the killer—a werewolf. When the cops dismiss their claim, Joel fashions some silver bullets (out of his father's old trophies!) and, going on predictions made by his computer analysis, lays in wait at the Fairview High Winter Costume Ball to confront the monster.

Filmed in and around Denver, Colorado, over a two-week period, *Lone Wolf* opens well with a clawed hand suddenly silhouetted against a full moon as a terrifying growl trails off into an unearthly howl. Unfortunately, the film immediately devolves into eighties cliché as the scene shifts to blonde Julie in a parked car asking, "What was that?" while her preoccupied boyfriend continues to nibble on her neck. For the next 90-plus minutes we're bombarded with Big Hair (on the boys as well as the girls); stock high school characters (jerky jocks, brainy nerd, slutty chick, silly sidekick, sweet girl, overbearing teacher, uptight matron) played by 10-years-too-old regional theater actors; and a preponderance of early computer technobabble.

Werewolf-wise, the film offers only brief glimpses of its beast (designed by Paul C. Reilly, Jr., whose brief career climaxed with work on the short-lived *Monsters* TV series, 1989–1991), which might just be for the best. With an elongated, goblin-like face and pointy ears, oversized fang-filled mouth, and flowing mane of scraggly hair, this lycanthrope looks like a mutant hair band front man. The film does offer one fairly impressive transformation, however, coming in its final 10 minutes. In a sort of low-rent *Howling* riff, it features close-ups of fangs growing from distended gums, ears elongating into points, brows bubbling and stretching, and the jaw painfully protruding into a muzzle. While nothing new or innovative, it's a decent, if brief, effort at a physical transformation. "The prosthetics effects were kinda neat for that low budget a film," opined special effects coordinator Ted A. Bohus, who put the effects crew together and flew out from New Jersey for a week at his producer/screenwriter friend Michael Krueger's behest. "There was some cool werewolf effects in there. We really tried to mimic *The Howling*–type thing, where you have the ears moving and the mouth moving and everything. We had the big animatronic mask that went on the guy, and he could actually open his mouth, which was pretty cool. For that low budget a film there was some decent prosthetic effects."

There were also some amusing behind-the-scenes moments to go with the gruesome on-screen gore. Bohus himself played the mutilated victim the gang stumbles across at the school. "That was me laying in the snow, with a mangled face. And they thought to do something really funny, to leave me out there in the snow. They said they would take the takes, and don't move; and I had to hold my breath and not breathe. And then they broke for lunch, and they weren't gonna tell me. Of course, I had a lot of people that were very loyal to me on that crew because I hung out with these guys, took 'em out for beers. So a guy comes over and says they're gonna try to pull a trick on you. So I went with it, because the director wanted to get a laugh."

Though structured as a whodunit (i.e., who is the werewolf?), the script eliminates all but one of the prime suspects half-way through by throwing them all together in a sort of low-key Scooby-Doo werewolf hunt at the school. So the Big Reveal at the climax becomes small potatoes. Still, the big question may not be 'Who is the werewolf?' but 'Why is this script so computer-centric?' An inordinate amount of screen time is spent on Joel, Julie, et al. sitting in computer class, breaking into computer labs (the school's and, unlikeliest of all, the police department's!), researching on a computer, running computer analyses, and simply *talking* about computers. Joel even uses some magical computer program to track and predict the monster's movements! Perhaps screenwriter/producer Michael Krueger (*Mindkiller* [1987], *Night Vision* [1987], *The Amityville Curse* [1989]) held a secret ambition to become a computer programmer? Was he an early Microsoft stockholder? Had he just discovered the wonders of DOS? In any case, one would think that Bill Gates executive produced this public-service-announcement-for-the-computer-industry-disguised-as-a-werewolf-movie. (Note: Krueger tragically succumbed to cancer in 1990, age 39, leaving whatever ambitions he held—computer-linked or otherwise—sadly unfulfilled.)

Versatile film crewmember John Callas (dialogue director on *Young Lady Chatterly* [1977], production manager and first assistant director for *The Happy Hooker Goes to Hollywood* [1980], and second unit director for *The Hills Have Eyes Part II* [1984]) made his directorial debut on *Lone Wolf*. It also proved to be his swan song, as he made no further features. Callas does his best to create suspense, such as when a girl goes to her friend's house late at night and knocks on the door. Suddenly, a p.o.v. shot and growling on the soundtrack indicates the monster's presence. Then, as she repeatedly knocks, to no avail, a shadow rises up the door, growing larger and larger as the camera—the beast—moves in closer until the girl finally turns and screams. Likewise, Callas tries to generate a semblance of fright with a few sudden flashes of the snarling werewolf face before each attack. Unfortunately, a preponderance of medium shots lit in the flat, over-bright style of so many low-budget '80s features leaves it to the actors—and a few choice shots of grue (throat slashing, heart ripped from chest, head severed from shoulders, and a particularly nasty face ripping)—to carry most of the show. Too bad the band of enthusiastic but amateurish Denver thespians reveal why they were never heard from before *Lone Wolf* or since. The standouts are Dyann Brown as Juile (only because her impossibly big hair out-bigs everyone else's) and Jaime Newcomb as bad-boy rocker Eddie (because his impossibly big hair out-bigs ... well, you get the point). "The whole idea of Michael Krueger's production company was to use local people," recalled Bohus. Of course, even seasoned pros (no matter what their 'do) might fall flat given lines like "She probably doesn't know a microfiche from a tunafish." Add in a quartet of ersatz '80s rock songs (by the never-heard-of-them local band Tyxe) performed by Eddie and his group at the local low-rent nightclub to augment the schmaltzy synth score, and this *Lone Wolf*, far from a cinematic alpha, takes its place near the bottom of the pack.

With quotes from: Interview with Ted A. Bohus conducted by the author, 2015.

Morphology: Large-headed, clothes-wearing wolfman
Demise: Silver bullet
Full Moon Rating: *½

Love Bite

(2012; West End Films/Creative Scotland; UK) Director: Andy DeEmmony; Producers: Robert Bernstein, Douglas Rae, Paul Ritchie; Screenplay: Ronan Blaney, Chris Cole; Cinematographer: Tat Radcliffe. Cast: Jessica Szohr, Ed Speelers, Luke Pasqualino, Adam Leese, Kierston Wareing, Robert Pugh, Timothy Spall.

> **For the virgins of Rainmouth, things are going to get hairy!**—ad line

With its unique (and amusing) lycan-premise (werewolves stalk and eat only *virgins*) and self-deprecating, likable lead (*Downton Abbey*'s Ed Speelers doing his best twenty-something Hugh Grant impression), this UK horror-comedy promises much but (like most of its hapless, sex-starved protagonists) fails to fully deliver.

In the dreary seaside town of Rainmouth-on-Sea, young Jamie (Speelers) waits for true love, while his mates, led by Kev (Luke Pasqualino), simply look to get laid (and fail spectacularly time and again). A rash of disappearances sets the local constabulary on edge, and a mysterious, unsavory man named Sid (Timothy Spall) checks into Jamie's mum's B&B. Meanwhile, Jamie meets a beautiful young American woman, Juliana (Jessica Szohr), at a party and is instantly smitten. Though it appears the attraction is mutual, Juliana has the habit of running off at inopportune times—particularly on nights of the full moon. It turns out that Sid is a werewolf hunter, and he's been tracking Juliana across Europe. Sid explains that lycanthropes "kill and eat the virgin on the night of the full moon. They can smell 'em a mile off." Can Jamie protect his skeptical (and virginal) friends? Will Jamie himself be next on the menu? Will he have to kill his newfound love? Will *any* of these dopes ever "break their duck" (as Sid so tactlessly puts it)?

Like *The Company of Wolves* before it, *Love Bite* casts (indirectly) the werewolf in the role of sexual predator. Here the beast only hunts virgins, literally feeding on their innocence. Unfortunately, rather than exploring this intriguing avenue, *Love Bite* ducks down the grimy boulevard of crudity and cheap sex jokes (e.g., Sid warns Jamie, "You've got 24 hours to dip your pickle" and "The hornier you are the more delicious you are"). Apart from Jamie, these innocents are clueless, sex-obsessed ninnies, not likeable enough to engender any real sympathy. Consequently, one cares little whether they get their "pickle" dipped in time, or whether it (and everything else) will be bitten off by the prowling beast.

Also disappointing (once we get a decent look at it—over an hour into the film) is said beast. With its relatively low budget of two-and-a-half million pounds (about four million dollars), *Love Bite* was never going to become a lycan-spectacular. But the almost cartoonish, two-dimensional CGI werewolf, seen clearly only at film's end, looks cheap and absurd by *any* standard. Though standing eight feet tall, its rat-shaped head and giant, grinning, toothy maw conjure images of an animated mutant Tasmanian Devil.

The disappointment of its appearance aside, *Love Bite* offers an intriguing mix of traditional and novel notions about its monsters. Like most cinematic werewolves, these lycanthropes are governed by the lunar cycle and can only be killed by silver—though, perhaps taking a page from the popular zombie playbook, only a shot to the *head* will bring it down. Anywhere else and the beast, though smarting, will keep on coming. Also, rather than the expected bite being needed to infect a victim, lycanthropy is passed on by any scratch from the monster's claws—and the change comes almost immediately, that very night. Then, of course, there's the unique concept of werewolves seeking out and eating only *virginal* flesh—a first in lycan-cinema.

Unfortunately, the few split-second werewolf encounters before the final smackdown allow for little exploration of this creature's human-animal dichotomy. We never learn just how much of the Man (or woman) remains in the Beast, whether it's governed by reason or instinct, and whether the afflicted considers it a gift or a curse. All we know is that it sniffs out virgins because "such inflamed tenderloin flesh is the sweetest meat of all," explains Sid. Werewolf-wise, *Love Bite* offers little more than a nibble.

Despite its salacious subject matter (and dialogue), veteran TV director Andy DeEmmony (*Red Dwarf*), making only his second theatrical feature, admirably refuses to give in to exploitative temptation. Utilizing suggestion rather than full-on nudity, he keeps the viewers' gaze focused on the characters instead of their naughty bits, allowing the actors to flesh out their roles rather than simply roll out their flesh. Though this works a treat for the well-written, likable Jamie and the mysterious yet appealingly down-to-earth Juliana, the script casts his friends as little more than sex-obsessed cretins with whom we must spend far too much time.

But the movie truly jumps the shark with its tacky, supposedly comical, finale that sees two werewolves in silhouette having sex (doggy style, naturally), and a jokey final coda that negates the very nature of the only two characters we care anything about. Even the admittedly clever eleventh hour twist can't quite counteract this ill-conceived, character-canceling denouement.

"We found a nice balance of making people laugh, and jump, and a little bit heartfelt at the same time," opined co-star Luke Pasqualino. Wishful thinking perhaps, as it's not all that funny (the constant bombardment of hit-or-miss sex jokes wears thin pretty quickly), and there are precious few "jumps," given its ludicrous lycanthrope. But indeed it does offer some heart in the seemingly doomed relationship between the two likable leads—at least until it goes off the rails at film's end.

"It's a bit of a throwback to an eighties movie," chimed in Ed Speelers. "It's very bright, it's very glamorous in some respects. It's got a cool, uplifting vibe to it even thought it's got people being eaten by werewolves in a little seaside town. I think it's fun and bright." Only intermittently fun, *Love Bite*, like far too many of its characters, proved to be not all that bright after all.

With quotes from: "*Love Bite*: Ed Speleers and Luke Pasqualino Interviewed by Holly Patrick," *The Fan Carpet*, November 4, 2012.

Morphology: Huge, hairy biped
Demise: Silver (bullet to the head, arrow to the eye)
Full Moon Rating: **½

La Lupa Mannara see *The Legend of the Wolf Woman*

Lycantropus see *Werewolf in a Girls' Dormitory*

The Mad Monster

(1942, PRC, b&w) Director: Sam Newfield; Producer: Sigmund Neufeld; Screenplay: Fred Myton; Cinematographer: Jack Greenhalgh. Cast: Johnny Downs, George Zucco, Anne Nagel, Glenn Strange, Sarah Padden, Gordon Demain, Mae Busch, Reginald Bralow, Robert Strange, Henry Hall, Edward Cassidy, Eddie Holden, Jon Elliott, Charles Whitaker, Gil Patrick.

> One minute a harmless country boy ... the next moment a snarling, ferocious Wolf Man!—ad line

Taking note of *The Wolf Man*'s (ahem) howling success, low-budget specialists PRC (Producers Releasing Corporation) concocted their own werewolf variation—in the form of a hirsute Glenn Strange, the product of mad doctor George Zucco's nefarious experiments. Directing/producing brothers Sam and Sigmund Neufeld (Sam having anglicized his name to "Newfield" while sibling Sigmund elected to keep the family's Teutonic surname intact) had their *Mad Monster*

152 • *The Mad Monster*

prowling cinemas less than five months after *The Wolf Man*'s premier, making this the first film to jump on the werewolf bandwagon set rolling by the Universal classic. Unfortunately, the haste shows in its slapdash script and threadbare production values. Still, it offers one point of originality, as *The Mad Monster* marks the first appearance of a *scientific* werewolf.

Discredited scientist Dr. Lorenzo Cameron (George Zucco) has sequestered himself and his sympathetic grown daughter Lenora (Anne Nagel) in a swampland mansion to continue his experiments on the mixing of animal and human blood. Utilizing his simpleton handyman Petro (Glenn Strange) as his human guinea pig (the insensitive Cameron even refers to him as such in just those words), Cameron employs a serum extracted from wolf's blood to transform the unwitting Petro into a wolfman. Why? "This country's at war," the mad doctor explains (to a group of colleagues conjured from his own fevered imagination). "Our armed forces are locked in combat with a savage horde who fight with fanatical fury. That fanatical fury will avail them nothing when I place my new serum at the disposal of the War Department. Just picture an army of wolfmen—fearless, raging—every man a snarling animal." But there's more behind Cameron's scheme than just an altruistic wish to produce a super-soldier. Bitter about how he was ridiculed in the press for his outlandish theories and forced to resign from his position at "the University" by his skeptical colleagues, Cameron decides to use Petro to murder his main detractors one by one. So, in essence, it's a tawdry tale of revenge. Into the savage scenario comes young reporter Tom (Johnny Downs), Lorena's beau, until the wolfish Petro finally turns on Cameron, and the two meet their doom in a fiery finale.

The film's werewolf makeup, by Harry Ross (*Dead Men Walk* [1943], *Mesa of Lost Women* [1953]), is simply not in the same class as Jack Pierce's *Wolf Man* creation. As Petro, Glenn Strange (Universal's fourth Frankenstein Monster) looks more silly than savage, with long Amish-style sideburns, fluffy, combed-back hair, and heavy cheekbones and nose that make him appear more ape-like than wolfish (resembling Bela Lugosi in *The Ape Man* or, worse, a male version of Paula the Ape Woman from *Captive Wild Woman*). Strange becomes what may be the screen's most lethargic werewolf, acting quite un-wolf-like as he slowly walks about in an upright posture exhibiting none of the animal intensity that made Lon Chaney's Wolf Man so memorable. "He's no longer human," observes Cameron. "He's a wolf—snarling, ferocious, lusting for the kill." Strange's lackluster, hesitant playing, however, makes this "wolf" into a tame lapdog.

Glenn Strange (left) proves that werewolves and overalls don't mix in the poverty-row horror *The Mad Monster* (Lobby card).

Adding insult to injury, this poor man's Larry Talbot initially sports a pair of Farmer Brown overalls, then later a cheap sport coat and felt hat, giving him the appearance of an unkempt derelict with a bad overbite. Strange does better in his human guise, delivering his simple dialogue in a slow, almost sing-song manner, so that Petro becomes an almost Lennie-like gentle giant. Though lacking subtlety, Strange's poor dupe engenders sympathy for his plight and underscores the dastardliness of Zucco's mad medico.

Speaking of which, the cultured, ever-malignant (and seemingly omnipresent—at least at PRC) Zucco is, as usual, superb, bringing as much understated menace to his role as the alternately vapid and bombastic script would allow. When Petro, not knowing that Zucco nightly transforms him into an wolfman (thinking only that he suffers from sleepwalking), innocently asks the "good doctor" if he can cure him of his nocturnal wanderings, Zucco tells him no and that he may have to be locked up at night. When Strange laments, "It don't seem fair to lock a man up—like an animal," Zucco's sardonic smile at the irony of the statement is truly chilling. And Zucco makes the most of his You-Think-I'm-Mad speech as he rails at his imaginary denouncers conjured up out of his own twisted imagination.

Though obviously a product of Poverty Row, the film boasts some decent (if cramped) sets, including Cameron's lab (with its entrance secreted behind the bookcase, naturally), all stone walls, shelves of chemicals and bubbling beakers, and an atmospheric mist-shrouded swamp (that cleverly obfuscates the lumbering man-monster). Likewise, director Sam Newfield occasionally leaves off his standard medium shots to insert something a little more evocative, such as when Leonora opens the secret lab door to reveal the wolfman advancing towards her—and the camera—as the low-key lighting (finally) makes him look fiercely menacing rather than risible.

The film wastes no time getting right down to business, busting out the Mad Monster a mere four minutes in with the first transformation, the metamorphosis captured efficiently if unimaginatively through a few simple dissolves. Of course, this marks the sole onscreen transformation (unless one counts the reverse shot of same a mere five minutes later when Cameron delivers the antidote to change Petro back to human form). After this, the metamorphosis occurs either off-screen or is completely obscured by that ridiculous felt hat. Unfortunately, after transforming, this Mad Monster does very little (in fact, the first time we see him he remains securely tied to a couch). When Cameron does send his wolfman out into the night, the man-monster typically wanders around the cramped swamp set a bit before scaring a bystander or creeping through a window. The few sparse murders remain coyly off-screen (with the final attack on Carmeron relayed through the old shadows-on-the-wall ploy). Surprisingly, the script has the beast's first victim turn out to be a six-year-old girl, murdered (off-screen, of course) in her own bedroom. Even more surprisingly, though, the supposedly grieving parents, interviewed later, seem strangely nonchalant and unaffected by their loss.

Other scripting headscratchers include the convoluted way Cameron sets up his scheme of vengeance (somehow talking his victim into delivering the final injection to Petro himself and so sealing his own doom) and the motivation behind his grown daughter Lenora's devotion to her obviously potty papa (despite the fact he constantly flies off the handle and keeps her a virtual prisoner, with little contact allowed with the outside world). Despite its scientific origin, the werewolf itself appears to be supernaturally invulnerable, as one backwoods denizen fires both barrels of his shotgun at the beast at close range, with no effect. Later, when a group of villagers gather to discuss the recent murder, an old crone labels the beast a "werewolf" and declares, "You can't kill him no ways, 'cept with a silver bullet." (Perhaps she'd seen the Universal film?) And the fiery finale is even more contrived than usual, with the expected conflagration started by a providential bolt of *lightning*.

Though not particularly clever, veteran low-budget scripter Fred Myton was nothing if not prolific, with more than 150 screenplay credits stretching all the way back to 1916. Up until the early 1950s he worked steadily, penning mostly low-end Westerns for Poverty Row outfits like Supreme, Republic, and, of course, PRC. He wrote one other horror film (also for PRC, and again starring Zucco and directed by Sam Newfield)—1943's *Dead Men Walk*.

Like Myrton, busy director Sam Newfield's career began in the silents and lasted into the 1950s, over which time he helmed close to 300 films. According to his nephew, Sigmund Neufeld, Jr., Sam suffered from a gambling addiction throughout his adult life that kept him near penniless most of the time, spurring on his prodigious output (Newfield directed 20 pictures in 1942 alone, typically earning $500 a film). Newfield made so many movies for PRC that he utilized two different pseudonyms (Sherman Scott and Peter Stewart) to disguise the fact that most of PRC's output was directed by one man. Upon Newfield's retirement, he was so destitute that his brother Sigmund (the head of PRC from 1940 to its merging with Eagle-Lion in 1948) purportedly paid off his gambling debts and set him up in an apartment in Hollywood.

Though featuring the first scientifically-created werewolf, *The Mad Monster*, with its poor script and poorer wolfman, adds little to the lycanthrope canon. Saved only by a few atmospheric moments and Zucco's entertainingly villainous performance, it merely crouches in the shadow of the Universal classic.

Morphology: Two-legged wolfman
Demise: Fire
Full Moon Rating: **

La Maldición de la Beastia see *Night of the Howling Beast*

La Marca del Hombre Lobo see *Frankenstein's Bloody Terror*

Mark of the Wolfman see *Frankenstein's Bloody Terror*

Metalbeast see *Project: Metalbeast*

Monster Among the Girls see *Werewolf in a Girls' Dormitory*

Monster Brawl

(2011; Image; Canada) Director: Jesse Thomas Cook. Producers: Jesse Thomas Cook, John Geddes, Matt Wiele; Screenplay: Jesse Thomas Cook (story: Jason David Brown, Jesse Thomas Cook); Cinematographer: Brendan Uegama. Cast: Dave Foley, Art Hindle, Robert Maillet, Jimmy Hart, Herb Dean, Kevin Nash, Lance Henriksen.

IT'S THE FIGHT OF THE LIVING DEAD!—poster

Ever since Frankenstein met the Wolf Man back in 1943, creature feature fans have been treated to monsters (both classic and new) battling one another on the big (and small) screen. For those who always felt a bit disappointed at the all-too-brief and inconclusive climactic battle royale between those two classic creatures in *Frankenstein Meets the Wolf Man*, the Canadian horror-comedy *Monster Brawl* scratches a monstrous itch.

During the opening credits, an unseen narrator (Lance Henriksen) announces, "Tonight, the most highly anticipated extreme sporting event ever. Eight deadly monsters summoned to the ring from all corners of the earth, fighting to the death to determine the most powerful ghoul of all time." Yes, it's time for the *Wrestlemania*-like television event called "Monster Brawl." As one of the show's two color commentators explains, "The tournament consists of two conferences—the 'Undead' and the 'Creatures.'" The Undead roster features "the Mummy," "Lady Vampire," "Zombie Man," and "Frankenstein." Making up the Creature conference are "Cyclops," "Witch Bitch," "Swamp Gut," and "Werewolf." A series of bouts—fights to the death—ensues, with the two champions of each conference meeting for the final Heavyweight match.

Fortunately for this low-budget production shot entirely in Collingwood, Ontario, a shortage of funds didn't translate into a shortage of ideas, as *Monster Brawl*'s amusing set-up and clever script match the cast and crew's (many of them volunteers) obvious enthusiasm and dedication to the production. Ontario-based director/screenwriter/co-producer/editor Jesse Thomas Cook rightly called *Monster Brawl* "a $5-million movie for about one-tenth of that," as it does indeed look like a (multiple) million bucks. (Note: The film's actual cost has been estimated to be as low as $200,000 Canadian.) Its graveyard setting ("We're coming to you live from the abandoned and overgrown Hillside Necropolis in Central Michigan," states the announcer)—housing the wrestling ring, two tombs that serve as locker rooms for the contenders, and a dilapidated, open-front shack for the announcers' booth—provides the proper atmosphere for the fast-paced, funny and occasionally gory action (heads *will* roll).

But even as clever a concept as *Monster Brawl* would fall flat on its monster face without a) monsters that look menacing rather than silly; and b) actors good enough to run with the satirical scenario without looking foolish. Breathing life into lines like, "Somebody better call the humane society because we're witnessing extreme animal abuse here" (as Frankenstein pummels the Werewolf), and "Weighing in at 225 pounds, the Man in the Moon, the Howler, the Disemboweler.... Werewolf!" are veteran Canadian actors Dave Foley (co-founder of the "Kids in the Hall" comedy troupe) and Art Hindle (*Black Christmas*, *The Brood*) as the tournament's color commentators, and real-life wrestling manager/leg-

Promo ad for the clever Canadian horror-comedy *Monster Brawl*, which graphically answers the question tantalizingly raised but coyly dropped by *Frankenstein Meets the Wolf Man* in 1943: Who would win a battle between the Wolf Man and the Frankenstein Monster?

end Jimmy Hart (playing himself) as ringside announcer. According to Cook, most of the money he had went towards casting. "We wanted to invest in getting people from the horror genre and the wrestling world that people will recognize," explained Cook. "On the wrestling side we've got Jimmy Hart and Kevin Nash, and a wrestler named Robert Maillet [*300*], who's playing Frankenstein's Monster. We've also got Herb Dean, a UFC ref. Beyond that, our announcers are Dave Foley and Art Hindle. We also have Lance Henriksen." Henriksen plays "the Voice of God" (according to the credits, anyway); in fact, his stentorian tones offer occasional narration and intermittent critical commentary on the fights.

The monsters were created by brothers Jason and Jeff Derushie, whose The Brothers Gore company provided solid variants on the classic creatures. The Werewolf, for instance, features darkened skin; angry-looking eyes; ridged forehead; demonic pointed ears; long hair framing the satanic face; and a mouth full of wicked fangs. Hairy arms and hands further reveal the beast beneath the flannel shirt and ragged jeans. Though not particularly unique or innovative, it's a very credible wolfman that steps into the Monster Brawl ring.

In keeping with the movie's parodic nature, this Werewolf can talk—and talk *trash* at that. Before his opening bout with Swamp Gut (a unique-looking—and disgusting—"Swamp Thing" variant), Werewolf tells his opponent (and, as per WWF tradition, the viewing audience): "Swamp gut, I know you've been hearin' it, walkin' through the swamp with that big gut of yours. You must have been hearin' it. The frogs have been sayin' it, all the toads, all the creepy crawlers have been sayin' it: 'Here comes the *wolf*!'" Rather than ripping and tearing and slashing with teeth and claws like most lycanthropes, however, this wrasslin' wolfman employs headlocks, rabbit punches, and chokeholds. After polishing off Swamp Gut (via a flying leap from the top rope to explode the swamp monster's insides in a "lunar belly buster" move), Werewolf, the heavyweight champion of the Creature Conference will meet Frankenstein, leader of the Undead Conference. Before the championship bout, Werewolf's trash-talk takes on a bit more thematic weight, reflecting (if obliquely) the tragedy and pathos inherent in this doomed creature. "What makes me think I have a chance in *hell* of beating Frankenstein?" the underdog Werewolf asks rhetorically. "One word: vengeance. It was a monster that took my wife. It was a monster that took my child. It was a monster that took my life away. So I guess you could say I don't like monsters very much."

At one point, color commentator "Sasquatch Sid" (Art Hindle) gives his pre-match assessment of the wolfman: "Werewolf possess incredible agility, speed and those keen animal instincts. He can take a ton of abuse, and he'll be in turbo moonshine mode tonight. And we're basically looking at a tremendous athlete, well-conditioned and powerful." Indeed, as energetically played by local wrestler R.J. Skinner (who did double duty by playing the Mummy as well), this lycanthrope leaps, dodges, punches, and moves with impressive agility and power, taking on opponents much larger than himself. Unfortunately for lycan-fans, the werewolf action, though energetic, remains relatively brief, with the beast-man's first bout lasting a mere four minutes, and his second marking a mere five.

Also unfortunately (for everyone), the film falters when it leaves the satirical spin of the "Monster Brawl" broadcast and steps out of the ring for a series of straightforward backstory vignettes about each monster. Nearly as impoverished as they are short, these brief interludes come as more typical low-budget horror rehash than innovation (with the exception of the Cyclops and Swamp Gut bits, whose novelty makes them stand out among the rest). Werewolf's two-minute tale follows a man hunting in the woods at night before a flashback shows him discovering his mutilated wife while camping. Now stalking the beast that killed her, the vengeance-seeking hunter is surprised by a lycanthrope, who bites him before the man shoots the creature dead. Bleeding from his wound, the man almost immediately transforms into a wolfman himself and howls. (Said transformation, though simple, remains quite effective due to some clever staging and camerawork: the wounded man struggles to rise to his knees next to a large tree; the camera moves in towards him, then swings around the other side of the tree to reveal the crouching victim, now a werewolf.)

Fans of the monster rally concept originated with *Frankenstein Meets the Wolf Man* will be happy that *Monster Brawl*'s climactic battle between those two titans of terror goes on longer, and remains far more satisfying in its conclusion, than the original's far-too-brief and interrupted conflict. After nearly seventy years, the clever and entertaining *Monster Brawl* finally provides some monstrous closure by showing us who would win (and how). Thanks, *Monster Brawl*. Successfully walking that fine line between homage and ridicule, *Monster Brawl* satirically skewers—while at the same time affectionately honoring—both classic monsters and Big Time Wrestling. In that respect, *Monster Brawl* is a monster success.

With quotes from: "*Monster Brawl*: Gruesome Grappling," by W. Brice McVicar, *Fangoria* 302.

Morphology: Bipedal, wrasslin' wolfman
Demise: Decapitation
Full Moon Rating: ***½

Monster Dog

(1984; Continental/Trans World; Spain/US/Puerto Rico) Original Language Title: *Leviatán*. Director/Screenplay: Claudio Fragasso (as Clyde Anderson); Producer: Carlos Aured; Cinematography: José Garcia Galisteo. Cast: Alice Cooper, Victoria Vera, Carlos Santurio, Pepeita James, Emilo Linder, Jose Sarsa.

> The Fear…. The Terror…. The Nightmare….
> They Will Never Forget It!!!—tagline

Shock-rocker Alice Cooper as action hero? "Welcome to My Nightmare" icon Alice Cooper as a werewolf suspect? Bite-the-head-off-a-chicken-onstage legend Alice Cooper as a Eurotrash star? Yes indeed, thanks to the Spanish-American co-production *Monster Dog*, the hard-rocking, hard-living, horror-loving Mr. Cooper can lay claim to all of these.

Cooper (born Vincent Damon Furnier) plays Vincent Raven, a rock star who returns after twenty years to his dilapidated family home in the country to shoot his latest rock video, complete with a small crew of attractive young people, including his director girlfriend Sandra (Victoria Vera). With the remote area plagued by wild dog attacks, things soon go awry after an encounter with what seems to be a monstrous killer dog. A quartet of locals arrives at the rundown mansion, intent on killing Vincent (and his friends), who they think has inherited the curse of lycanthropy from his long-dead father (an accused werewolf killed by the villagers decades before). Though Vincent successfully defends his friends from the murderous locals, most of his party still fall prey to the mysterious monster. Is Vincent indeed cursed with lycanthropy, and if so, will Sandra be able to destroy him?

Like many a low-budget European production of the time, *Monster Dog* was shot MOS (without sound), with the multinational actors speaking their various native tongues, their characters' voices to be recorded later. Surprisingly, Cooper did not dub his own voice, as that job fell to frequent dubbing actor Ted Rusoff. The voice in the two songs ("Identity Crisis" and "See Me in the Mirror") Cooper sings in the film, however, is all his own. (Note: Neither song appeared on any of Cooper's albums until he included them in the 4-CD box-set *The Life and Crimes of Alice Cooper* in 1999.) After opening with a cheap but rather engaging music video of Cooper performing "Identity Crisis" (with the rocker dressed as everything from Billy the Kid to Jack the Ripper), *Monster Dog* goes straight for a Eurogothic flavor, as demonstrated by the hand-held camerawork, misty backlighting, ominous music, and snippets of shocking grue. The off-kilter Eurovibe continues in how everyone casually accepts the notion of a roving pack of killer dogs, how the rundown mansion seems bathed in a perpetual fog, how the house's caretaker has mysteriously disappeared, and how one female crew member becomes hysterical at the drop of a hat.

The creepy nighttime drive to the mansion provides not only an ominous warning by a crazy old man (in bloody, tattered clothing) who staggers out of the fog, but the first brief glimpse of the titular Monster Dog, its face seen amongst the bushes for a split-second. In fact, this remains the pattern for all the creature attacks—a momentary glimpse of a demonic dog head atop a huge body standing upright, its slavering jaws lunging toward the camera (and victim). Such brevity serves the beast well, as it not only underscores the brutal swiftness and mysterious nature of the monster, but also helps obfuscate its rather unconvincing, plastic appearance.

At one point Vincent reads from an old book called "Werewolves: Myths, Legends and Scientific Reality" that features a full-page photograph of Lon Chaney as the Wolf Man! When a skeptical Sandra asks about the werewolf's supposed "scientific reality," Vincent tells her, "There's a disease, a heart disease, that transforms the patient into some kind of madman, a beast that goes howling at the moon like a wolf." He then relates how this affected him personally: "Twenty years ago something terrible happened here, and it's happening again. Entire families were wiped out by a pack of killer dogs.... The people needed a scapegoat, so they accused my father." Why? "My father was afflicted with that disease I was telling you about. Sometimes when the moon was full he'd leave the house and go wandering through the fields like an animal.... The neighbors slaughtered him—stabbed him with pitchforks, doused him with gasoline and set him on fire." (With neighbors like these, it's no wonder Vincent has kept his distance for two decades.)

When a quartet of gun-toting locals show up (looking like bandito refugees from a Spaghetti Western), the film veers into *Straw Dogs* territory, as the four lay siege to the house and terrorize the inhabitants, with Vincent desperately (and bloodily) fighting back (resulting in a truly gruesome shotgun-blast-to-the-head moment). The leader of the gang states, "When Vince gets back I'm gonna shoot him right through the heart with this silver bullet. That's how you kill werewolves." He also believes that Vincent controls the pack of wild dogs roaming the countryside. "It's him who commands them, controls them. Those are the powers of

Alice Cooper as werewolf? (American poster for *Monster Dog*).

werewolves." This introduces a new wrinkle to the lycanthrope tapestry: werewolf as alpha dog to a pack of wild canines. (The vicious dog pack, who at one point break into the house, do seem calmed by Vincent's presence…) Of course, these yokels—and the film itself—seem a little hazy on the more standard werewolf lore. For instance, if pitchforks and fire worked just fine on his lycanthropic father, why the need for silver bullets for Vincent? In fact, the werewolf finally meets its death via an ordinary shotgun shell.

Metamorphose-wise, we never see the Monster Dog change from human to werewolf. Without giving away the beast's identity (or the tragic twist at the film's close), we do finally see at the end one mid-transformation stage in which the afflicted first sports some light facial hair and then a rather rubbery deformed dog-head mask. Though less than impressive visually, the actors and atmospheric, quick-cut photography carry it off fairly well.

Though in no danger of taking the Academy podium come Oscar night, Cooper exudes both an easygoing charm and laidback intensity as the take-charge Vincent, who bravely defends his house and friends against the brutal gang of self-proclaimed werewolf hunters. He's perfectly adequate in his heroic yet potentially sinister persona. Spanish actress Victoria Vera, who played Vincent's girlfriend, recounted, "The movie was wretched and unpleasant, but I had a tremendous time together with Alice; he is a very fabulous and funny person. Everybody at the shoot knew him as 'The American.' He didn't think of himself as a superstar." Cooper accepted the role in order to get back working after a disastrous year in which he was hospitalized for alcoholism, narrowly avoided divorce, and was dropped by Warner Bros. Records after his latest album underperformed. "I was so out of my comfort zone on that," admitted Cooper about his first starring movie role. "I had just gotten out of the hospital and told my manager Shep that I had to find something that would let me prove to myself that I could work sober. I had never done a concert sober, never done anything. He said, 'What if we take a movie?' And we found that movie in Spain." Not wishing to make another *Citizen Kane*, Cooper knew exactly what he was getting with *Monster Dog*. "I wanted to make the kind of movie I like to rent. Really a great C-movie. I don't like A-movies or B-movies. I wanted to do a C-movie where there's so much blood in it it's stupid, and the story is stupid. I had to do it sober, and it worked. I am very proud to say I am in two of the all-time greatest turkeys: *Monster Dog* is one of them, and *Sgt. Pepper's Lonely Hearts Club Band* is the other one."

"I developed a good working relationship with Cooper," declared *Monster Dog* director Claudio Fragasso, "he's a good man. Cooper has a passion for horror movies, and every night we would watch them together as if we were little boys! Even then, Cooper had a love for golf. So much so that he even had a miniature golf course constructed in his hotel room." *Monster Dog* was the directorial debut of Claudio Fragasso, co-author of (and assistant director for) a number of Bruno Mattei horror films, such as *Hell of the Living Dead* (1980) and *Rats, Night of Terror* (1984). Fragasso remains most (in)famous for directing the so-bad-it's-good cult oddity *Troll 2* (1990). He later shifted his directorial gears to make a number of critically lauded political films in his native Italy, as well as working extensively in Italian television.

Monster Dog marks the second time the bear-like actor Ricardo Palacios (playing the gruff local sheriff) fell beneath the slavering jaws of a werewolf, the first coming in Paul Naschy's *The Craving* (filmed in 1981 but not released in America until 1985), in which he appeared as an ill-fated gravedigger. He made a living playing bartenders and bandits in Spaghetti Westerns, including such notable entries as *For a Few Dollars More* (1965), *The Good, the Bad and the Ugly* (1966), and *Day of Anger* (1967). Another actor, Barta Barri (who plays the crazy old man warning Cooper and co. of their impending doom), was a veteran of lycan-cinema as well, having appeared in both *The Werewolf vs. Vampire Woman* (1971) and *Dr. Jekyll and the Werewolf* (1972).

Filmed in the Spring of 1984 in Torrelodones, Spain, just outside of Madrid, *Monster Dog* debuted in Italy in December 1984 but didn't make it to American shores until two years later, where it went straight to video. Despite its obvious budget constraints (typified by the small cast, single location, and oftentimes cheesy creature effects), *Monster Dog* remains a fairly engrossing werewolf tale. The Is-he-the-beast? mystery and *Straw Dogs*-meets-*The Wolf Man* vibe, coupled with some moody music, suspenseful staging, likable characters and convincing acting (particularly when things go wrong), make this *Monster* more than just your typical Eurodog.

With quotes from: "Monster Dog," by Sergio, *SickthingsUK*; "The Man Behind the Mask," by Justin Beahm, *Fangoria* 307; "Rats and Creeping Flesh," by Jay Slater, *Darkside* 73.

Morphology: A … well, monster dog (bipedal beast with demonic dog head)
Demise: Shotgun blast (sans silver)
Full Moon Rating: ***

Monster Mash

(2000; DiC Entertainment/Rai Fiction; US/Italy) Director: Guido Manuli; Voice Director: Paul F. Quinn; Screenplay: Guido Manuli, Judy Rothman Rofe. Cast (voices): Ian James Corlett, Robert O. Smith, Janyse Jaud, Jim Byrnes, Patricia Drake, David Sobolov, Scott McNeil, French Tickner.

It's a Graveyard Smash!—tagline

This direct-to-video animated special starts promisingly enough with a skeletal dog narrating (in a Boris Karloff voice): "Yorick is the name. I live here at the Drac Castle with three of the most terrifying monsters of all time: Frank—a wretched creation from parts unearthed from the dankest depths of the graveyard; Drac—a dashing bloodthirsty tyrant from Romania, a creature of the night; and Wolf—once an ordinary man, now cursed by the full moon and transformed into a hideous, tormented beast." Unfortunately, nothing in the subsequent Saturday morning cartoon–level story or simplistic animation matches this darkly evocative opening.

The three famous Universal monsters have fallen on hard times, as Frank has lost his juice, Drac wears dentures, and Wolf is gray and balding. No longer deemed scary, the trio become mere "entertainers," juggling pumpkins on the TV show *Foolish Monster Tricks*. The Ghoul Guild Tribunal summons them to answer for their lack of fright, where the judge ("His Ogreship") decrees: "You must succeed in terrorizing a typical family. If you fail, you will be sentenced to an eternity of— working children's birthday parties!" The judge chooses the Tinklemeisters, an obnoxious (and overweight) American family of four. When their first efforts to frighten fail, the trio lure the Tinklemeisters back to their castle, where they succeed in terrifying the two parents (who still fear the old-school monsters) but have more difficulties with the younger generation. Can Drac, Frank, and Wolf pull off the scare, or will nefarious forces within the guild derail their efforts to save their frightful reputations?

Though naturally aimed at the kiddie crowd, *Monster Mash* offers a few nuggets of interest among its silly jokes and subpar musical numbers. For one, it contrasts the old-guard monsters with the new generation of horror icons by pitting Drac, Frank and Wolf against a villainous trifecta comprised of "Freddie DeSpaghetti," an amalgam of Jason and Freddie Kreuger, with flesh-eating pasta(!) for hair; a creepy living doll named "Chicky" (an obvious takeoff on *Child's Play*'s Chucky); and the *Alien*esque "Alien Eater." When Wolf says to the Tribunal, "We were once the scariest monsters around," His Ogreship counters with, "That was a different era. There is now a more *effective* generation of fiends," indicating the Freddy/Jason, Chucky, and Alien knockoffs. To the older monster lovers among us, this stings; so it becomes rather gratifying when the classic monsters end up besting the modern upstarts. And one can't help but smile when the littlest Tinklemeister (the one most difficult to scare) concludes at the end, "Give me an old-fashioned monster any day. Give me a monster with *passion*.... Give me a monster who knows there's a time to frighten and a time just to be a friend." A bit heavy on the schmaltz, perhaps, but a worthy sentiment nonetheless.

Monster Mash also presents its werewolf with a bit of wit and wisdom. In his defense at the Tribunal, Wolf (voiced by Scott McNeil, an Australian-born Canadian voice actor who, by his own estimation, has provided voices for over 8,500 characters) labels the new breed "monsters without a history, monsters without a soul, monsters created by toy companies rather than arising spontaneously from folklore and mythology reflecting Jungian archetypes filtered through the collective unconscious." Then, to his now-dumbfounded audience, he admits, "Well, that's what I heard."

During the flashback sequences showing the monsters in their heyday, the film cleverly switches to black and white, emulating the creatures' original medium. And one transformation sequence shows Wolf, in human form, walking past castle windows and gradually changing between each one in a clever homage to *Werewolf of London*'s seamless metamorphosis effects.

Of course, the cartoon also includes plenty of silly bits, such as when Wolf, snarling and growling, attempts to scare little Spike, only to have the tyke produce a ball and toss it, causing Wolf to gleefully chase it like a puppy—right out the window. And later the kids complain of Wolf's body odor, then dump him into the bath and subsequently make him up to look like a poodle!

Monster Mash's threadbare budget shows through not only in its short 64-minute running time but in its mediocre animation (with scenes often "recycled" during songs, flashbacks, end credits, etc., to save on costs). Scooby-Doo need have no worries.

Though adequate Halloween fare for the kiddies, adult viewers may find themselves hitting the fast-forward button, particularly during the four god-awful songs (Bobby Picket's "Monster Mash" excepted). Still, it deserves a point or two for making an affectionate case for the classic monsters, the Wolf Man included, something sure to appeal to one's inner Monster Kid.

Morphology: Cute cartoon wolfman
Demise: None—"Wolf" regains both his hair and his "scariness" in a happy-monster ending
Full Moon Rating: **

The Monster Squad

(1987; Tri-Star) Director: Fred Dekker; Producer: Johatnan A. Zimbert; Screenplay: Shane Black, Fred Dekker; Cinematographer: Bradford May. Cast: Andre Gower, Robby Kiger, Stephen Macht, Duncan Regehr, Mary Ellen Trainor, Leonard Cimino, Tom Noonan.

> You know who you call when you have ghosts. But who do you call when you have monsters?—tagline

"Never send a man to do a kid's job," advises the ads for *The Monster Squad*, a funny and scary (though uneven) homage to classic monsters (and monster-loving kids/kids at heart). The movie announces itself (and its tone) from the opening scrawl: "One hundred years before this story begins, it was a time of darkness in Transylvania. A time when Dr. Abraham Van Helsing and a small band of freedom fighters conspired to rid the world of vampires and monsters, and to save mankind from the forces of eternal evil.... They blew it." After an atmospheric Transylvanian-set prologue to illustrate this point (complete with armadillo marching across Dracula's crypt, à la Tod Browning), the film takes us to present day and introduces a quintet of kids who "have a sort of monster club" where they sit around and discuss/argue about monsters in their elaborately-decorated treehouse (complete with a *Vampire Circus* poster on the wall). Sample exchange:

SEAN: "Look, Wolfman doesn't go to work—he's not like a *guy*."
PATRICK: "What are you talking about? He walks around; he wears pants."
SEAN: "He *had* to wear pants. Those movies were made in the Forties. He had to wear 'em so you wouldn't see his—wolf dork."

When their leader, Sean (Andre Gower, sporting a "Stephen King Rules" t-shirt), receives Abraham Van Helsing's diary as a gift (his mom found it at a garage sale!), this triggers the arrival of Dracula and his cadre of classic creatures (the Mummy, the Creature from the Black Lagoon, the Frankenstein Monster, and the Wolfman), who seeks the diary and a magical amulet that will somehow let him rule the world. When the adults around them refuse to listen, the self-proclaimed "Monster Squad" must take up arms (stakes, silver bullets, etc.) against the evil creatures and, with the help of a change-of-heart Frankenstein's Monster (who abandons his "master" to befriend little five-year-old Phoebe), try to thwart Dracula's evil plan.

"I always loved the Universal Monsters—Frankenstein, Wolfman, Dracula ... particularly the monster rallies of the '30s and '40s," said director/co-writer Fred Dekker about where he took his inspiration for what he termed "the Little Rascals meet the Universal Monsters." Continued Dekker, "I went to [*Lethal Weapon* scripter] Shane Black, who was my college chum, and I said 'You love *Abbott and Costello Meet Frankenstein*?' and he said 'Yeah,' and I said 'That's kinda what I want to do, but with kids.'" And while not quite attaining such a lofty goal, the 26-year-old Dekker came close with this, his sophomore effort as director (his first being the even better *Night of the Creeps*).

With its obvious target being the pre-teen set (apart from Sean's cop father and the "Scary German Guy" who helps out, all but one of the titular protagonists are pre-pubescents), the film surprisingly turns rather dark at times. In between the politically incorrect juvenile insults ("good luck, butt-love") and scatological humor ("Fat Kid farted!") come some creepy touches and frightening set-pieces. For instance, when lightning suddenly illuminates Dracula's face, it momentarily reveals a living skull beneath his countenance.

"This is a comedy adventure, but it has a harsher edge than something like *The Goonies*," admitted Dekker. "There's death in this movie." Indeed there is, as shock and tragedy rub shoulders with cuteness and comedy in a sometimes uneasy alliance. For instance, Sean's police detective father, Del (Stephen Macht), eventually comes to believe in—and battle—the monsters alongside his son. Racing with his partner to his own home when he learns that Dracula intends to kill Sean to obtain the diary and amulet, Del watches in horror as the vampire strolls out of Del's house and coolly tosses a stick of dynamite under the police car—with Del's partner still inside the vehicle. As his panicked friend screams "Del!" the car explodes. It's a shockingly brutal slap in the face for what some might term a "kid's movie." "Something's out there and killing people," grimly states Sean. "And if it's monsters,

For *The Monster Squad*, creature designer Stan Winston had to update the classic Universal monsters while making sure not to get too close to the copyrighted makeups of the originals.

nobody's going to do a thing about it—except us." It's quite a weight these kids take upon their skinny shoulders.

More subtle adult themes creep into the film as well. As the kids take their leave of the "Scary German Guy" (Leonardo Cimino) after he translates the diary for them, one observes, "You sure know a lot about monsters." "Now that you mention it," the elderly man replies sadly, "I suppose I do," and we see a concentration camp serial number tattooed on his forearm as he shuts the front door. Such a subtle moment conjures the ghosts of *real* monsters.

In addition to its adult approach, one key to *The Monster Squad*'s success (just like with its *Abbott and Costello Meet Frankenstein* model) is the filmmakers' respect for their monsters. While the occasional joke comes at the creatures' expense (for instance, Fat Kid [yes, that's the character's accepted non–P.C. moniker] slams a pizza slice into Dracula's face to ward the vampire off with the garlic in the pie), these classic creations are portrayed as serious, terrifying, and dangerous. Though as Dracula, Duncan Regehr affects an Hungarian accent, he's no parodic Lugosi imitator but an imposing figure who brings death with him. The film's aquatic Creature looks like a meaner, nastier version of its Black Lagoon cousin, and the Wolfman looks and acts as feral and savage as a rampaging Lon Chaney or Oliver Reed. "The original Wolfman was much more of a man, and ours is very much a wolf," observed Dekker. "It's how you would expect [FX artist] Stan Winston to approach it, which is, 'what if a man actually turned into a wolf?' The shape of his head resembles a wolf, whereas Lawrence Talbot was a guy with fuzz on his face. It's halfway between Lon Chaney Jr. and the Rick Baker [*American Werewolf in London*] approach."

To avoid any potential lawsuits, the filmmakers had to walk a fine line between homage and originality, crafting their creatures so that they'd be instantly recognizable as Monsterdom's Big Five, but different enough so that they didn't infringe on Universal's copyrights. Makeup maestro Stan Winston succeeded admirably. According to co-writer Shane Black, Dekker "wanted to make [the monsters] as spooky as they were in the originals." But, continued Black, the film also "has a tremendous amount of heart, due primarily to the amount of care Fred put into it."

Jonathan Gries plays the unnamed tortured soul in the Larry Talbot mode, while Carl Thibault takes over to inflict fear while in Wolfman form. This John Doe Talbot's introduction sees Gries at the local police station frantically pleading, "Officer, please, lock me up! I'm a werewolf!" Of course, they don't believe him; but the moon rises and Gries goes crazy, grabbing a policeman's gun and firing it into the ceiling, screaming "Lock me up!" until another officer shoots him. This immediately invests the character—trying to protect others at his own expense—with crucial sympathy. Later, as the coroner's ambulance hauls his body away, he transforms under the sheet covering him. A shot of a hairy hand with its flesh bubbling, and clawed toes suddenly poking through shoes, heralds the change. Next, the werewolf suddenly springs up to attack the driver—and end the scene, leaving the carnage to our imagination. The beast's appearance, with its wolf-shaped head and ears, hairy torso, and demonic, almost cat-like face, stands tall as an imposing lycanthrope. And his subsequent actions only cement this frightening image, despite the fact that when in werewolf form he's obviously under the thrall of Dracula. (While human, the bloodsucker must keep him drugged and tied to a chair—a clever reversal of expectations.) Just before the moon rises, Dracula archly tells him, "I'll go have a bite while you change into something more—comfortable." But the man escapes (having palmed the pills the vampire had used to sedate him) and calls the police from a payphone to alert them to the villain's whereabouts (a groan-inducing address of "666 Shadowbrook Road"). But as he talks on the phone, the moon rises, and the camera moves in and begins circling to the left. After the roving camera passes behind a stanchion, momentarily obscuring our vision, we see the man is half-changed, with hairy cheeks and fangs. Spraying drool, he desperately shouts (to Sean's detective father on the end of the line), "He's gonna kill your son!" He then drops the phone, screaming in agony. We see his nose suddenly protrude and his cheekbones shift beneath his skin before he doubles over. His shirt abruptly splits up the back to reveal the hairy torso beneath, which shifts and expands. Now fully transformed, the werewolf crashes out of the booth, howling. It's a quick but very intense and convincing transformation.

This lycanthrope lies at the heart of the film's most impressive—and tragic—denouement. As Del battles the beast-man in an upstairs warehouse room during the climactic confrontation, Sean arrives and distracts the monster long enough for his father to light a stick of dynamite, stuff it down the creature's pants and send the lycan crashing through the window to explode mid-air in a graphic (though curiously bloodless) mess. But everyone knows, including the Monster Squad, that only silver can kill a werewolf—even one blown to pieces. In the alley below, the lycanthrope's severed limbs and assorted body parts slide towards the ripped-open torso to reattach themselves, and soon the Wolfman is up and rampaging once again. As various cops ineffectually shoot and attack the revived creature, the eldest Monster Kid, Rudy (Ryan Lambert), grabs up a fallen policeman's gun and loads it with a silver bullet (which he'd made in shop class). Rudy takes aim, shoots, and the werewolf goes down. Now in human form, his chest bloody, he gasps "Thank you" and dies.

Of course, the Wolfman also inspires the movie's signature comedic line. When the lycanthrope suddenly springs upon the kids investigating the old mansion, Fat Kid panics and kicks him between the legs. As the manbeast doubles over in pain, Fat Kid marvels, "Wolfman's got nards!" Crude, admittedly, but funny.

On the distaff side, the script sometimes sacrifices verisimilitude for expediency. For instance, how did the magical amulet travel from Transylvania (where it opened a vortex in the 100-years-past prologue) to a secret basement room of a dilapidated old mansion in America? And why does the Creature suddenly pop out of the swamp next door (was it always there, just laying low until Dracula summoned it)? Likewise, is it mere coincidence that the Wolfman shows up in this same town's police station begging to be locked up before the moon rises? Though unaddressed issues like these, along with an over-reliance on McGuffins (the biggest being the Van Helsing journal that explains all, and the amulet itself), smacks of screenwriter's convenience, Dekker and Black provide enough incidents to go with the scripting accidents to allow the viewer to tag along for the monster ride without too many bothersome longings for logic. And many of these incidents will bring a smile to the face of classic monster movie fans, such as the sequence in which little Phoebe sits playing by a pond when the Monster approaches—conjuring images of the tragic "Little Maria" incident from the original *Frankenstein* (1931). (Fortunately, *this* Monster doesn't try to make Phoebe "float," and instead accompanies her to their clubhouse where he makes friends with the gang, learns a few new words ["Bogus"], and even indulges Phoebe's whim to play dress-up.)

Costing a hefty-for-the-time $12.5 million to make, *The Monster Squad* earned a paltry $3.8 million at the box office (compared to the same year's *Predator*, which took in nearly $60 million). Fortunately, time has been kind to *The Monster Squad* (as well as to Dekker's other underperforming cult classic, *Night of the Creeps*), as it's developed a strong following in the years since its release, rightly becoming a firm fan favorite of monster-loving viewers everywhere.

With quotes from: "*The Monster Squad* 20 Years Later: Wolfman's Still Got Nards," by Aaron Crowell and Nathan Hanneman, *HorrorHound* 6; "*The Monster Squad*," by William Rabkin, *Fangoria* 66; "*The Monster Squad* and Me," by William Rabkin, *Fangoria* 67.

Morphology: Two-legged, hairy, pants-wearing wolfman
Demise: Silver bullet
Full Moon Rating: ***½

Los Monstruos del Terror see *Assignment Terror*

Moon of the Wolf

(1972; Filmways/ABC Television) Director: Daniel Petrie; Producers: Everett Chambers, Peter Thomas; Teleplay: Alvin Sapinsley (based on the novel by Leslie H. Whitten); Cinematographer: Richard C. Glouner. Cast: David Janssen, Barbara Rush, Bardford Dillman, John Beradino, Geoffrey Lewis, Royal Dano.

A left handed wolf stalks the bayou!—tagline

First broadcast on September 26, 1972, as an *ABC Movie of the Week*, the Southern Gothic *Moon of the Wolf* places a werewolf in modern-day (well, modern-day 1972 anyway) Louisiana bayou country. When a local girl in the rural town of Marsh Island turns up brutally slain, her throat ripped out and body mutilated, wild dogs are blamed. But when an autopsy reveals she was killed by human hands, Sheriff Aaron Whittaker (David Janssen) sets his investigative sights on several locals. But the leads go nowhere, and it appears nearby plantation owners, brother and sister Louise and Andrew Rodanthe (Barbara Hale and Bradford Dillman), may be somehow involved. With the elderly Cajun father of the murdered girl babbling about a "lukaruk," and evidence mounting that the murderer possesses inhuman strength, the no-nonsense sheriff must seriously entertain the notion that something supernatural has invaded his parish.

Coming off as a small-town crime melodrama in the tradition of *In the Heat of Night*, complete with socioeconomic class distinctions (poor white trash vs. landed gentry)—but *sans* Sidney Poitier and *with* a werewolf—*Moon of the Wolf* accomplishes its modest goal of drawing the viewer into its Southern hothouse of murder and violence (at least at the made-for-TV level) via genuine location shooting and some colorful characterizations from a cadre of excellent character actors (including Royal Dano and Geoffrey Lewis as backwoods denizens).

Regarding the rules of lycanthropy, *Moon of the Wolf* remains a pastiche of old and new. A bed-ridden old Cajun with seemingly prescient powers (though unable to effectively relate said premonitions, given his inability to say more than "mon dieu" and "loup garou"—mispronounced as "lukaruk," no less) sees a pentagram in the palm of the werewolf's next victim, taking a page right out of *The Wolf Man* handbook (copyright 1941). And while the dialogue makes no explicit mention of the full moon, shots of the bright lunar orb visually establish the link between the lunar cycle and the beast within. (And, of course, there's the title...)

But this being the modern world of 1972, lycanthropy is defined as "a disease you can take pills to control." Though remaining somewhat vague on the exact nature of these "pills," Louise reads in a book on lycanthropy that "true lycanthropy might also respond favorably to the drugs for a time, then the disease develops an immunity to the drug." Hence the recent rash of full-moon murders. Further departures from the norm "has it that werewolves are repelled and rendered temporarily harmless by the smell of sulfur" (a notion that at one point pretty much gives the mystery game away). And apparently there's two methods of dispatching a werewolf: death by burning, or death by a bullet that has been blessed (bringing a decidedly non-scientific bit of theology to the otherwise rationality-based table). So forget the silver and grab the priest.

The beast itself fares better when kept *off*-screen, with the mystery aspect and the various local characters remaining far more intriguing than the cut-rate manbeast itself. Once revealed, this unstoppable monster looks like a nattily-attired man (neatly-pressed slacks and dress shirt) with well-coiffed hair, a dog nose, sideburns and beard, a modest set of fangs, and hairy hands ending in sharp nails. It makes for a rather refined-looking werewolf (to go with his refined Southern aristocrat demeanor, perhaps). So it's just as well that veteran film and TV director Daniel Petrie (*A Raisin in the Sun*, *Sybil*, *Cocoon: The Return*) keeps his creature under wraps for the film's first hour, using p.o.v. shots of the terrified victims-to-be, accompanied by breathy growls on the soundtrack, to suggest the horror of the infrequent werewolf attacks.

This well-dressed wolfman exhibits amazing strength that would put even Lon Chaney, Jr., to shame, as at one point it rips a huge iron door right off a jail cell to get at its next victim. And for its big reveal, this wolfman energetically attacks the doc and tosses around some orderlies before leaping through a (closed) window to make his escape in a reasonably exciting display of animal savagery.

Actor Bradford Dillman (*Bug*, 1975; *Piranha*, 1978) called the wearing of heavy makeup, and particularly spirit gum, "the devil's punishment for taking up the profession [of acting]. It smells worse than ether and, once applied to the lace that's patted on your face, it itches worse than hives.... And if any physical exertion is required, perspiration causes the gum to run, making the itching nigh unbearable. In *Moon of the Wolf* I impersonated a werewolf, and came to have an appreciation for the trials of Lon Chaney, Jr., who made a career of playing lycanthropes. The unfortunate man had hair pasted all over his body and he was always running, so the temptation to scratch away what had been so painstakingly applied must have been overwhelming. His solution to deadening the nerve ends, I'm told, was to drink. Having gone through what he did, I don't blame him."

While the film's structure precludes any focus on pathos (since the cursed creature's identity remains hidden—more or less—for the first three-quarters of the picture), it introduces a somewhat ad hoc element of tragedy after Ellie shoots her rampaging brother with a gun

The smartly-dressed (though ill-mannered) Southern werewolf affected by the *Moon of the Wolf*.

found in his dresser drawer. When the bullets do the job, she tearfully remarks, "The bullets—he must have had them blessed. He knew," indicating that Andrew suspected what was coming and prepared for the inevitable end.

TV star David Janssen (*The Fugitive*, *Harry O*), as the local sheriff, plays a methodical and contemplative crime-solver unwilling to rush to judgment, letting us see behind his gruff, prickly exterior to a man of thought and obvious intelligence, and one possessing a rather wry sense of humor. He exudes a weary amiability as evidence disqualifies his three prime suspects and things start to point toward something preternatural.

Unfortunately, the climax comes rather perfunctorily—and with some poorly superimposed, artificial-looking flames (no wonder they fail to do the trick), with the manbeast finally stopped by mere bullets. Even worse, after literally falling into a fiery inferno, this werewolf inexplicably emerges with nary a smudge on his clothes or a wolf's hair out of place. Likewise, onscreen transformations need not apply, saving time and expense; at the end, after Ellie shoots him down with the blessed bullets, she says, "Aaron, look," and the camera reveals her brother lying on the floor, back to normal (though still quite dead).

In the end, an uncluttered, linear story that, at a quick 75 minutes, never outstays its welcome, combined with its genuine location shooting (in Burnside, Louisiana, with Clinton, Louisiana, standing in for downtown Marsh Island) and its well-acted murder mystery structure, makes *Moon of the Wolf* one of the more engaging made-for-TV movies of its time. Unfortunately, its less-than-impressive—and easily dispatched—werewolf makes it a decidedly lesser lycanthropicture. Still, thanks to the authentic atmosphere and local characters effectively portrayed by a cadre of fine actors, *Moon of the Wolf* works as a melding of made-for-TV sensibilities and Southern Gothic charm, with a bonus werewolf tossed into the mix.

With quotes from: *Are You Anybody? An Actor's Life*, by Bradford Dillman.

Morphology: Well-dressed man with slightly wolfish features
Demise: (Blessed) bullets
Full Moon Rating: ***

Moonchild

(1994; Asylum Home Video/Englewood Entertainment) Director/Producer/Videographer: Todd Sheets; Screenplay: Todd Sheets (story: Todd Sheets, Roger Williams). Cast: Auggi Alvarez, Kathleen McSweeney, David Miller, Rebecka Rose, Julie King, Cathy Metz, Kyrie King, Harry Rose, Stefan Hilts, Jody Rovick.

A FULL MOON CAN BE FATAL!—tagline

And when it comes to one's aesthetic sensibilities, so can watching amateurish shot-on-video dreck like *Moonchild*. Written, produced, directed and photographed (as well as just about everything else) by Missouri-based no-budget VHS auteur Todd Sheets (*Zombie Bloodbath*, *Biker Babes from Beyond the Grave* and about two-dozen other obscurities), *Moonchild* does for werewolves what Watergate did for the Nixon Administration—terminally embarrass itself through its own ineptitude. And just like with that disgraced former president, one can perhaps appreciate Todd Sheets' ambitions but *not* his methods.

"Inspired by the book of 'Mark,' Chapter 13 of the King James Bible and the song 'Moon Child' by Iron Maiden" (according to the opening credits), *Moonchild* posits a world taken over by the Sodality Corporation and run by Dictator Kronos, a mutant sicko (with "666" carved on his belly) who sends his mind-controlled soldiers and cyborgs out to quash what little remains of the untainted human race. Or so we're told, since the film's $1.98 budget wouldn't support more than a few "soldiers" in homemade uniforms and cardboard armor to battle Our Heroes (a misfit band of resistance fighters) in various Kansas City loading docks, junkyards and parking lots. Lycanthropy (sort of) enters the equation when Jacob Stryker (Auggi Alvarez) escapes from a Sodality prison. Jacob is the victim of "the Moonchild Project ... a gene-splicing experiment mixing animal and human cells together." With wolf cells added, Jacob now has "superhuman strength and the ability to shapeshift," though he remains ignorant of his powers. Jacob intends to rescue his young son Caleb (Stefan Hilts), taken by Sodality for study because Caleb's blood can cure disease and save mankind (or something). Aided by a handful of freedom fighters, Jacob must battle his way through mutant cannibals, cyborg bounty hunters and Kronos himself to save his son.

Moonchild offers a strictly sci-fi take on lycanthropy, as illustrated by this sophomoric dialogue exchange between Jacob and a Resistance doctor who's just examined him.

JACOB: "I'm a werewolf—a friggin' goon who howls at the full moon and runs around pissin' on fire hydrants?!"
DOC: "No, you are a hybrid being. There's no such thing as a werewolf. They've combined your cells with those of a wolf."

Jacob shapeshifts only twice, with the first resulting in a sort of intermittent stage that looks like a square-faced Elephant Man with sharp teeth. Then, for his climactic battle with the deformed Kronos himself, Jacob abruptly morphs (via primitive cartoonish graphics) into a hulking, furry humanoid that looks like a body-building Muppet with an immobile, hairy face and fangs. This Big Battle lasts all of 45 seconds before Jacob defeats his mighty opponent and morphs back to normal. So much for werewolfery.

Filled with cheesy costumes; cheesier acting; half-speed fights; ten-mile-an-hour car "chases" (which no amount of pounding ersatz metal music can invigorate); stilted dialogue ("he could be the hero we've been waiting for; his son could help save our people who are dying of unknown diseases; we will help him on his quest"); sparsely decorated plywood sets; and a desperate need for tighter editing (a long scene showing each and every character climbing down a ladder is soon followed by a scene of each and every character climbing back *up* that ladder) makes *Moonchild* more of a *bastard child* entertainment-wise.

The sole scrap of amusement to be gleaned from this amateurish mess are the closing thank-you credits. Sheets concludes his lengthy scrawl of acknowledgments with a thank you to "Jesus, the main force for life and freedom." Then, without skipping a beat, he adds a litany of then-topical (and decidedly *un*–Christian) vitriol, in which he attacks everyone from Kurt Cobain and Tonya Harding to Tipper Gore and the Clintons. And all without a trace of irony.

Morphology: Musclebound, fur-covered, pants-wearing biped
Demise: None; this werewolf is the triumphant *hero*
Full Moon Rating: ½

My Mom's a Werewolf

(1989; Crown International) Director: Michael Fischa; Producer: Steven J. Wolfe; Screenplay: Mark Pirro; Cinematographer: Bryan England. Cast: Susan Blakely, John Saxon, Katrina Caspary, John Schuck, Diana Barrows, Ruth Buzzi.

Every daughter's mother goes through a change of life, but no mother's daughter ever tried to stop that change with a silver bullet—and an electric razor—trailer

---

The 1980s were filled with box-office comedy hits like *Airplane!* (1980), *Caddyshack* (1980), *Porky's* (1982), *Back to the Future* (1985), and *Ferris Bueller's Day Off* (1986). Several films even successfully grafted comedy onto a horror scenario, producing such genre winners as *Ghostbusters* (1984), *Gremlins* (1984), *The Return of the Living Dead* (1985), *Night of the Creeps* (1986), and *Beetlejuice* (1988). And a few even brought werewolves into the comedy fold, as witnessed by the popular *Teen Wolf* pictures. Even the groundbreaking *An American Werewolf in London* offered numerous laughs along with its horrific screams. Coming at the end of the decade, *My Mom's a Werewolf* decided to race ahead with the comedy aspect, leaving its horror elements as non-starters. Unfortunately, rather than edgy and clever, most of said comedy proved silly and cornball, full of sitcom-level situations and misunderstandings. Though the PG-level film feels like it could be something spawned on the Lifetime or Nickelodeon networks, the various adult-oriented sex jokes (sleazy dentist who turns teeth filing into a near-orgasmic encounter, fat neighbor who enjoys bondage, etc.) leaves one wondering just who the movie's target audience might be (sexually precocious pre-teens? sophomoric adults?).

Volvo-driving, health food–cooking homemaker Leslie Shaber (Susan Blakely) has become mildly dissatisfied with her neglectful husband (John Schuck). Going out to buy flea collars for their dog, she meets mysterious, handsome pet shop owner Harry Thropen (John Saxon, with pointy incisors and hypnotic eyes), who thwarts an attempted purse-snatcher and ends up taking Leslie to lunch. There he first kisses her hand, then *licks* it. Luring her back to his pet-shop lair, Thropen hypnotizes Leslie and begins to seduce her. Sucking on her toes(!), he gets carried away and *bites* her big toe, bringing her out of her hypnotic reverie and sending her fleeing in indignation. With little memory of what transpired, Leslie awakens the next morning with fangs of her own. Soon her ears grow pointy, and the long, wispy hair on her legs grows faster than she can shave it. With Thropen intent on making her his "were-wife," Leslie's teenage daughter Jennifer (Katrina Caspary), aided by her horror movie–savvy friend Stacey (Diana Barrows), must find a way to kill Thropen before the full moon wanes and Leslie's curse becomes permanent.

The script borrows from both *Fright Night* and *An American Werewolf in London* (both of which successfully blend comedy into their horror) but with none of the involving characterizations or clever and suspenseful plot constructions of either, leaving only a stream of unfunny jokes and silly "misadventures" to fill the time. For instance, when Jennifer and Stacey visit the fortune teller Madame Gypsy at the beginning, they see not one but two crystal balls on her table; "I like a second opinion," the psychic offers as explanation. During the reading, a perturbed Madame Gypsy cries, "I see the sign of the pentagram on your face!" to which Stacey helpfully retorts, "Uh, I think that's just a zit." Towards the end of the movie, Stacey explains to Jennifer, "You got to find the werewolf that infected her," before adding, "Maybe we should just call a vet." And these are a few of the *funnier* exchanges…

German poster for the '80s horror-comedy *My Mom's a Werewolf*.

The only horror in this supposed "horror-comedy" arises from one *American Werewolf in London*–style dream-within-a-dream monster shock scene. The film offers no onscreen werewolf murders (leaving the radio to mention a few earlier "animal attacks"), and the final tussle between the Harry-wolf and the reluctant Leslie-wolf in her bedroom involves only mild grappling and the beasts hitting each other with pillows as the feathers fly. Jennifer's dispatching of the evil beast with a silver fork taped to the end of a broom handle remains perfunctory, bloodless and transformation-less, as this werewolf retains its hirsute form after death (the better to avoid those pesky potential murder charges, no doubt)—just a quick jab while the monster is on its knees, followed by the creature squirming on the floor a bit before melodramatically expiring.

It's little wonder the screenplay turned out so poorly, given it was penned by no-budget auteur Mark Pirro, writer-director of *A Polish Vampire in Burbank* (1985), *Deathrow Gameshow* (1987, a poster of which adorns Stacey's bedroom wall) and the (sort of) werewolf entry *Curse of the Queerwolf* (1988). First time Austrian-born director Michael Fischa's resume isn't any more impressive, with *Death Spa* (1989) and a segment of the 2009 anthology *Deadtime Stories* (not to be confused with the 1986 pseudowolf film of the same title) proving to be career "highlights." Fischa adds nothing of interest to the sorry scenario, staging scenes in a humdrum fashion (including the botched climax). Apart from Harry's jungle-like backroom lair (filled with plants, animals, wolf pelts and jungle sounds), the settings consist of mundane suburban households, with little of visual interest (apart from some token fog on the climactic full moon night).

As the werewolf who starts it all, John Saxon's smarmy, smiling presence is one of the film's few assets, as he plays his smooth, womanizing character with appropriate "animal magnetism" and an undercurrent of self-assured menace. Unfortunately, his screen time remains short, and the movie suffers for it. Fashion model-turned-actress Susan Blakely (a Golden Globe winner and Emmy nominee) mostly looks confused about her condition or exasperated by her new fangs and rapidly-growing body hair. Bland and uninteresting, her dissatisfied housewife takes her husband's neglect with little more than a sigh and a wistful "oh well." And there's little chemistry or affection between her and Katrina Caspary as her teenage daughter, who becomes the film's focus after Jennifer learns the truth about her mother and determines to free her from the curse. A few pointless cameos from the likes of *The Bob Newhart Show*'s Marcia Wallace (as the hairdresser who sees Leslie's wolfish appearance as "the ultimate challenge") and Grammy-winning singer Marilyn "One Less Bell to Answer" McCoo (in her first film role) as a bossy TV reporter who won't let her interviewees get a word in edgewise do little to liven things up. Then there's Ruth Buzzi (of *Laugh-In* fame) in the throwaway role of money-hungry Madame Gypsy, who sets the stage at the beginning (à la Maria Ouspenskaya's Maleva in *The Wolf Man*) and then ... does nothing else.

Speaking of *The Wolf Man*, this *Mom* offers a few odd (and often pointless) updates to cinematic werewolf lore. These werewolves can apparently change during the day and at will (though Leslie doesn't go the full lycan–Monty until the full moon rises). Intriguingly, while in human guise lycanthropes possess several tell-tale signs (along the lines of medieval legends such as hairy palms or index fingers the same length as middle fingers). Here, both Thropen and Leslie sport noticeably sharp incisors, while Thropen also possesses reddish eyes (which he hides behind sunglasses) that are all the better to hypnotize you with, my dear. This brings up one of the film's more unusual notions—that werewolves can hypnotize their victims/prey (a talent usually reserved for vampires). As Stacey tells Jennifer, "Werewolves have the power of hypnotizing people into believing they're friends." Also along vampiric lines, werewolves live forever, with Thropen telling the confused Leslie, "You're becoming immortal." But the oddest notion of all is that killing a werewolf will make the perpetrator into one him/herself unless an exorcism is performed over the body.

Where on earth did *that* come from—and, er, *why*? (Obviously, it's merely an excuse for one final, predictable joke.)

The werewolves prove even less impressive than the movie's human characters. When fully transformed, Leslie-wolf sports fluffy blonde hair, pointy ears, an angry brow ridge, extended canine muzzle, and an oversized mouth filled with fangs. She might actually look rather fierce if the bubble wasn't burst by the obviousness of the immobile rubber mask. Her male counterpart looks even more demonic, with his dark fur and ferocious dried-apple monkey-wolf face. Too bad it, too, projects about as much vitality as a Halloween mask.

Transformations prove conspicuous solely by their absence. We never see Thropen (or Leslie, for that matter) transform—just boom, they're werewolves. The only onscreen change comes after Thropen's death, when the Leslie-beast, cowering in a chair, returns to normal via one simple dissolve (another distant echo of the original *The Wolf Man*, which saw Lon Chaney transform only at the end when he changes from beast to man).

For uber-fans, an early sequence has horror-loving Stacey dragging Jennifer to a "sci-fi convention." There she gushes over "issue number 12" of *Famous Monsters* magazine (with a price tag of $175!) as real-life *Famous Monsters* editor Forrest Ackerman ("Mr. Sci-Fi" himself) wanders past in a Hitchcock-like cameo. Later, while perusing another monster mag, Stacey announces to a disinterested Jennifer, "I bet you didn't know that Lon Chaney Jr. was the only actor to play all of the monsters—Frankenstein, Dracula, the Wolf Man and the Mummy." And as a final coda after the climax, Stacey calls Jennifer on the phone to tell her, "We got a big problem. *Fangoria*, issue 43, October 1978: 'Unless a formal exorcism is performed on a deceased werewolf, the one who killed it will transform within 24 hours.'" (Of course, *Fangoria* didn't even *start* publishing until 1979 ... but it's the thought that counts.) Though such inside references might warm the cockles of a horror nerd's heart, they prove an ephemeral and fleeting respite from the inanities surrounding them.

Said Susan Blakely of her starring role, "I've always wanted to do a comedy. That's, in fact, what I trained for. Plus, the chance to play one of the only leading female werewolves in history was definitely different and intriguing." Though such enthusiasm may be admirable, Ms. Blakely apparently forgot about such earlier female-centric lycan-flicks as *Cry of the Werewolf* (1944), *Werewolves on Wheels* (1971), *The Legend of the Wolf Woman* (1976) and 1985's *The Howling II* (not to mention the two south-of-the-border entries *La Loba* and *Santo vs. the She-Wolves*). While none of these could be considered lycan-classics, the weak, unfunny and horror-lite *My Mom's a Werewolf* does nothing to supplant *any* of them.

With quotes from: "Susan Blakely Bio," *My Mom's a Werewolf* DVD, Rhino Video.

Morphology: Hairy-limbed, rubber-faced wolfman (and wolfwoman)
Demise: Silver fork
Full Moon Rating: *½

Nature of the Beast

(2007; ABC Family) Director: Rodman Flender; Producer: Steve Solomos; Screenplay: David Kendall, Bob Young; Cinematographer: Kim Derko. Cast: Eddie Kaye Thomas, Autumn Reeser, Paula Boudreau, Dave Nichols, Gabriel Hogan, Mary Ashton, Eric Mabus.

Every relationship has its issues, but this one is a real beast—promo spot
---

Eddie Kaye Thomas plays Rich, whose wedding to his fiancée Julia (Autumn Reeser) fast approaches. There's just one problem (well, apart from choosing the flatware pattern): Four years ago Rich was bitten by a werewolf while in college, and now once a month he must hole up in a cabin in the woods to sit out the full moon. But when Julia becomes suspicious about his "writing time" (he ostensibly shuts himself up to work on his long-overdue dissertation) and schedules a weekend at her parents' estate during the cycle, things go horribly wrong and Julia learns the truth. While trying to help her hirsute hubby-to-be, they stumble across the information that if the alpha wolf who made him (a beta) can be destroyed before the beta takes a human life, the curse will be lifted. So Rich goes back to his college stomping grounds to try and track down the beast that turned him, with Julia (and her gun-happy family, who made their fortune in firearms) close behind.

Coming off like an overlong sitcom pilot, the Toronto-lensed, made-for-TV horror-comedy *Nature of the Beast* offers plenty of comedy but very little horror. The two leads, Thomas (the *American Pie* films) and Reeser (TV's *The O.C.*), make for a likable couple, and the script provides them with plenty of amusing dialogue to sink their comedic fangs into. For instance, when Julia first learns of Rich's condition, she's understandably upset, commenting, "I just found out my fiancé is a werewolf—I'm about to marry Len Chaney!" "*Lon* Chaney," offhandedly corrects Rich. "*Dick* Cheney," she exasperatedly shoots back, "I don't care!" Later she asks him, "Were you always like this? Were your mom and dad ... 'wolf-people?'" He answers, "No, they're accountants—hairless, repressed accountants."

"In this film, the comedy is what makes the horror work, and vice-versa," opined co-star Autumn Reeser. "You can become desensitized quickly during a horror/gore film because you're always on the lookout for the next big scare, so you're bracing yourself. With a film like *Nature of the Beast*, you become invested in the characters because they're endearing and you like them, so it's much more effective when horrifying things happen to them." Indeed it is, yet very little "horrifying" does happen. The various sitcom staples—quirky relatives, silly misunderstandings (often involving body hair and dogs), put-upon fiancée, snide quips—and comedic situations (at one point Rich wages a losing battle with his speedily-growing facial hair by shaving every few minutes) take center stage, leaving very little time or energy for the *true* nature of the beast. Only twice does the film veer towards straight horror—during the flashback sequence showing the sudden werewolf attack in which Rich's friend is killed (a brief splash of blood) and Rich bitten, and when the monster leaps atop Rich and Julia's speeding car and peels the roof back like a can of sardines. The rest of the picture takes the tone of a family-friendly comedy, with one never feeling the goofy leads to be in any real danger. This results in a general lack of suspense—even during the climactic battle between the evil alpha and Rich's beta. Said smackdown, again tinged with comedy (courtesy of various relatives' comical reactions), ends when a well-aimed silver cake knife causes the alpha to literally burst into flames, leaving nothing but a smoldering wolf's skull.

Lycanthropy-wise, *Nature of the Beast* offers some intriguing twists on the ... er ... nature of its beast. The film posits two distinct types of werewolves—the alpha (a creature born a lycanthrope) and the beta (one bitten by an alpha and thus infected with lycanthropy). The alpha looks lean and mean, a full wolf's head (complete with oversized jaws and fangs) atop a hairy, powerful body that runs upright on a set of extended canine legs. Rich's clothes-wearing beta, however, resembles a scowling *Teen Wolf*, with long hair on its head, face and arms, a slightly protruding snout, and a set of modest fangs. Apart from their difference in appearance, the alpha can transform at will (the beta only during the full moon) and possesses significant animal magnetism (with the alpha quite the ladykiller—figuratively as well as literally). The alpha, who "can live for hundreds of years," appears to retain its full faculties while transformed, while the beta becomes an unreasoning animal (though at film's end, Rich does ultimately overcome his bestial nature to refrain from harming Julia, his true love). The alpha also exercises considerable power over the beta; in fact, at one point the alpha, through sheer force of will, makes Rich transform, even though it's not a full moon. Fortunately, that old standby silver works on both.

Reeser saw the film as more than just a lightweight horror/comedy, thinking it "a metaphor for all of the big and little realities that come to light when you have decided to spend the rest of your life with someone. There's suddenly no more hiding because there is someone who will be in your life 24 hours a day, seven days a week, year after year after year.... Julia really believes in marriage and understands what it takes to make it work. It's always work and there is always a problem to be overcome, so I feel like in some ways, the movie is a love-letter to marriage and the energy it takes to have a successful relationship. I'm also a believer in mating for life." Just like wolves...

Reeser called *Nature of the Beast* "the perfect movie to watch at Halloween, and there are lots of chills and scares, [but] the comedy means you won't go to bed and feel like you have to keep the lights on! And it all turns out OK in the end, so you and your family can end the night on a cheerful note." While the "lots of chills and scares" may be mere wishful thinking, the film does indeed offer plenty of comedy, some of it even funny. Still, in the end, this *Beast* needed far more *bite*.

With quotes from: "*Nature of the Beast* Autumn Reeser Interview," by Seat42F, Seat42F.com.

Morphology: *Teen Wolf*–type hairy biped (*and* a more imposing wolf-headed furry alpha beast)
Demise: Silver wedding fork and cake knife set
Full Moon Rating: **½

Neowolf

(2010; Lionsgate) Alternate title: *The Band from Hell*; Director: Yvan Gauthier (as "Alan Smythe"); Producers: Daneile J. Suissa, Nicholas Thomas, Alessandro di Gaetano; Screenplay: Alessandro di Gaetano, Michale Januara (story: Allesandro di Gaeano); Cinematographer: Kevin Atkinson. Cast: Michael Frascino, Heidi Johanningmeier, Agim Kaba, Ryan Ross, Megan Pepin, Tiffany Shepis, Veronica Cartwright.

A Love Story Between A Girl And A Werewolf—tagline

Nascent rocker Tony (Michael Frascino) returns home to his small desert town from chasing his musical dream in order to reconnect with his girlfriend Rosemary (Heidi Johanningmeier), a botany student at the local college. Winning her back with a song he'd written for her and performs at the local nightclub's open mic night, Tony is noticed by Vince (Agim Kaba), front man for the popular Romanian rock band Neowolf, there for the following night's gig. Vince invites Tony to party with the band, and Tony soon falls into the clutches of the band's "talent scout," Paula (Megan Pepin), who seduces and bites Tony. You see, Neowolf not only rock, they transform—into werewolves. And Vince has set his glowy-eyed sights on making Tony the newest member of their band—and pack. Rosemary, with help from a werewolf-savvy local nursery owner, Mrs. Belacov (Veronica Cartwright), must fight to free her boyfriend from the band's clutches.

Given the marketing trajectory reflected in the above ad line, and the fact that the film is populated by impossibly good-looking, hip young twenty-somethings (all models and soap opera actors), *Neowolf* was obviously aimed at the *Twilight* crowd. But lacking the built-in audience engendered by a popular book series, and with nothing behind it but some surface prettiness, it's no wonder *Neowolf* disappeared straight into video purgatory (and even *that* downsized distribution came nearly two years after filming in and around Palm Springs was completed in 2008).

Despite its tagline, the "love story" aspect rings as false as these werewolves' phony contact lenses. Though hip and handsome, Tony is about as deep as a desert creek in July, and he treats Rosemary abominably. He can't even talk to her about getting back together without his eyes noticeably wandering to a curvy coed walking past. And then he chooses to party with Vince and his band rather than spend time with his newly-reconnected girlfriend, despite the fact that the Neowolf members are all obviously a**holes. Worse, Tony immediately succumbs to the slutty charms of Paula. So much for true love. So when Rosemary goes all out to try and save Tony from the pack, one simply wonders, "Why?"

In addition to its shallow characterizations (even the charming-but-crude Vince comes off as a one-note villain), inconsistencies and plot contrivances stampede across the screenplay like buffalo fleeing a pack of wolves. After Rosemary begins to suspect the band's lycanthropic nature (when some mutilated bodies turn up), she breaks into a nursery in order to steal some wolfsbane plants. (Why she didn't just *buy* them like a normal person remains a mystery.) Anyway, when the shotgun-wielding nursery owner Mrs. Belacov catches Rosemary red-handed, instead of calling the police she serves this thief a cup of coffee and asks about her troubles! Later, Rosemary goes back to Mrs. Belacov for advice, and the older lady lays down the skinny on werewolves (her mother was from the Old Country). Even more convenient than a handy gardener/lycan-expert is the fact that Mrs. Belacov decides to take up arms and help Rosemary beard the beasts in their tour bus den. To this end she just so happens to have a handy bullet-making kit ready to melt down the family silverware and conveniently whip up a batch of silver shotgun shells! And speaking of shotguns, when Mrs. Belacov shoots a werewolf roadie to begin the final showdown at film's end, none of the other nearby band members take notice of the loud blast. Apparently, along with sharp canines and some minor hair growth, lycanthropy also brings deafness.

To the film's credit, director Yvan Gauthier shoots in a competent fashion, providing varied angles and set-ups, and occasionally some inventive visuals. For instance, when Rosemary researches the sinister band on her laptop, Gauthier films the scene as if the camera were inside her computer looking out at Rosemary (and her friend) past the various web pages on the screen. Not only does this up the uneasiness factor (with the implication of a sentient internet watching them), the reversed Google logo and various images superimposed over their faces cleverly allow us to simultaneously see the information relayed on the websites *and* the principals' reactions to it.

Unfortunately, Guathier becomes self-indulgent and frequently succumbs to Film School 101 flashiness-for-flashiness sake. Speeded-up photography to show the passage of time; slow-motion photography to, well, perhaps extend the running time; skip-frames; dissolves; green-lit billowing smoke.... Gauthier pulls them all out of his self-conscious bag of tricks to no particular advantage. He also includes far too many musical numbers—five, to be exact, with the same song done *three* times! While these repetitive numbers serve to stretch the lightweight script out to feature length, they add nothing to the story or sketchily-drawn characters.

The werewolves' slight appearance perfectly reflects the shallow orientation of the rest of the picture. With built up brows, a slightly enlarged nose, glowing eyes, delicate fangs, minimal wispy facial hair, and a carefully teased moptop, these lycans look more like salon-bound Neanderthals than wild beast-creatures. And when Tony transforms at film's end (via the expected split-second morphing effect) his sideburns and tousled blonde 'do completes the image of a surfer dude after a rough night.

As far as werewolf lore goes, *Neowolf* buys into the typical full moon and silver bullet tropes. The only thing "Neo" regarding this *wolf* is the notion that wolfsbane acts like acid on a werewolf's skin (though it "only works when they're in their cursed form," so it's useless as a means to prove a werewolf's identity). The film also posits that someone bitten can be cured—if caught in time. As lycan know-it-all Mrs. Belacov relates (taking a page from the 1987 *Werewolf* TV pilot book), "To release a werewolf, one must destroy the source of evil which affected them; you have to kill the one who passed on the curse." But this must be done before the full moon cycle ends, or the initiate (in this case, Tony) will remain a werewolf forever.

The acting is about what one might expect from a group of newcomers (Johanningmeier), models (Frascino), soap opera players (Kaba and Ryan Ross), and ballerinas(!) (Pepin)—proficient but uninvolving, with enough surface gloss to look professional but lacking any real depth. What legitimate thespian Veronica Cartwright (*The Birds*, *Alien*) is doing here is anybody's guess.

French-born director Yvan Gauthier had his name removed from the film, with "directed by Alan Smythe" appearing in the credits ("Alan Smithee"—here changed to "Smythe" in a pretentious gesture that matches the movie's self-important tone—is the name used by directors wishing to disown a project). One has to wonder, though, what Gauthier, whose indifferent resume includes a short film called *F**king Zone*, might have to complain about…

Like its pretty, plastic leads, *Neowolf* is all looks and no substance.

Morphology: Mildly wolfish wolfmen (and women)
Demise: Silver shotgun shells
Full Moon Rating: **

Neuk-dae-so-nyeon see *A Werewolf Boy*

Never Cry Werewolf

(2008; Peace Arch Releasing; Canada) Alternate Title: *Uncaged* (UK rerelease); Director: Brenton Spencer; Producer: Aaron Barnett; Screenplay: John Sheppard; Cinematographer: Curtis Petersen. Cast: Nina Dobrev, Peter Stebbings, Spencer Van Wyck, Melanie Leishman, Sean O'Neal, Kim Bourne, Kevin Sorbo.

> THE MORE SHE LOOKS, THE MORE SHE SEES. THE MORE SHE LISTENS, THE MORE SHE HEARS. AND THE MORE SHE FEARS, THE MORE HE KILLS—trailer

One of the better made-for-television movies to debut on the Sci-Fi (later SyFy) Channel, *Never Cry Werewolf* takes the boy-next-door scenario and makes it extra hairy (literally). When hunky new neighbor Jarrod (Peter Stebbings) moves in next door, high schooler Loren (Nina Dobrev) senses something strange about him. And when several women Loren sees him with subsequently disappear, Loren concludes that Jarrod is a werewolf (besides, he has *hairy palms*). Indeed, the deathless lycanthrope Jarrod sees in Loren the image of his long-lost love, and sets his wolfish sights on making her his new "mate." After the police refuse to help, Loren seeks aid from washed-up TV hunting show host Redd Tucker (Kevin Sorbo). It all comes to a showdown when Jarrod kidnaps Loren's little brother, forcing Loren and Tucker to face the wolf in his own lair.

Filmed in Ontario, Canada, on a purported $1 million (Canadian) budget, *Never Cry Werewolf* offers up a compact yet intriguing tale of The Beast Among Us. And if it seems oddly familiar … it is, for *Never Cry Werewolf* could just as easily have been called *Always Cry Fright Night*. Aping that 1985 vampire hit right down to specific sequences (such as Loren spying on Jarrod seducing a topless prostitute at the window before he turns off the light, leaving only glowing eyes and a sudden scream) and individual shots (Jarrod staring up at her window menacingly from the yard below). Instead of high schooler Charlie from *Fright Night*, there's high schooler Loren; instead of hunky Jerry Dandridge the vampire, there's hunky Jarrod Martin, the werewolf. Loren bears a striking resemblance to Jarrod's long-lost love (as seen in an antique locket), just like Charlie's girlfriend Amy did in *Fright Night* (as seen in an antique portrait). After taking the police to Jarrod's house (just as Charlie did in *Fright Night*), a desperate Loren seeks aid from cheesy local "TV star and sportsman" Redd Tucker—just like Charlie when he sought help from cheesy TV horror host Peter Vincent. And like Vincent in *Fright Night*, Tucker initially refuses to help (being nothing more than a frightened phony) but ultimately shows up just as Loren is about to confront the monster in his lair. Then when the going gets tough and Loren falls into the creature's clutches, Tucker runs away (just as Vincent did), only to encounter a newly-turned minion (a local delivery boy Steve, whose crush on Loren leads him into Jarrod's clutches, vs. Charlie's friend "Evil Ed," who was vampirized by Dandridge). And they need to kill the werewolf before midnight in order to save Steve, otherwise he'll stay a half-human/half-werewolf hybrid forever—just as Charlie needed to Kill Dandridge before dawn in order to save Amy from permanently becoming a vampire in *Fright Night*. "The curse can be lifted in two ways," Loren reads during her internet research, "by slaying the [werewolf] victim with a silver knife or bullet, or if the werewolf that caused the curse is killed by midnight of the *first* full moon."

Fortunately, Canadian cinematographer-turned-director Brenton Spencer, aided by DP Curtis Petersen's (*Death Wish V* [1994], *Lake Dead* [2007], *Hyenas* [2011]) roving camera and evocative lighting, makes the most of the '80s-classic-rehash scenario. (If you're going to copy something, copy from the best—and as far as '80s horror goes, one could do far worse than the witty and entertaining *Fright Night*.) Frequently filming the shaggy monster in slow motion or in back-lit silhouette, Spencer plays up the dangerous nature of this beast-on-two-legs.

The cast also serve the familiar scenario well. Much like William Ragsdale in *Fright Night*, Nina Dobrev makes for a likable and resourceful young protagonist (even fashioning makeshift silver arrows for her crossbow by duct-taping the family silverware to the shafts); and Peter Stebbings exudes both the charm and the dangerous attraction necessary to pull off the central role. And while no Roddy McDowell, Kevin Sorbo (TV's *Hercules*) brings some heart to what could have been merely a cartoon caricature. The actor projects depth into the shallow figure of washed-up, phony TV "big game hunter" Redd Tucker. "That's pretty much what my character is," said Sorbo. "You know he's struggling with alcoholism, and he's got a lot of things going on in his life, and he sees this teenage girl who is going to go risk her life and he kind of has a change of heart. He decides he needs to do something with his life, so I come in and try to help save the day. Well, she really is the one who saves the day, but my character definitely helps."

Like the charming and self-assured vampire in *Fright Night* (played with alluring aplomb by Chris Sarandon), werewolf Jarod (personified by the cool, confident Peter Stebbings) cuts a magnetic central figure with his masculine presence and charming bad-boy image (he's good with his hands and even rides a Harley). Jarrod is no Larry Talbot clone whining about wanting to die and seeking to end his curse. No, this lycanthrope revels in his bestial side, enjoying the kill and savoring some long pig stew in his kitchen. He even goes so far as to take a strip of skin off a hanged criminal (a neighborhood sex offender under house arrest for whom Jarrod throws a private necktie party) that he can wear in order to induce the transformation at will (no more waiting for that full moon to trigger his change). As such, Jarrod becomes the beast personified, not a figure of pathos but the Big Bad Wolf of our collective nightmares. Intending to transform Loren into a werewolf like himself, Jarrod tells her, "No, not a monster—you'll be better, stronger, faster" (a perhaps unfortunate echo of the famous *Six-Million-Dollar Man* TV series intro). "We'll run in the night together, and you'll taste the thrill of the hunt, the rapture of the kill.… It's not a curse, it's a gift."

Fortunately, creature creator Paul Jones (*Resident Evil: Apocalypse* [2004], *Survival of the Dead* [2009], *The Thing* [2011]) fully realizes this Brothers Grimm nightmare come to life with his physically-imposing werewolf creation. The huge, upright, fur-covered biped with massive torso topped by a snarling oversized wolf's head makes for an imposing monster indeed. And it's only fitting that a monster movie patterned after an '80s classic feature a werewolf patterned after the impressive lycanthropes from that decade's pivotal, image-changing *The Howling*. *Never Cry Werewolf* marked British-born special makeup effects artist Paul Jones' *fifth* foray into werewolf territory. Jones helped create the more humanistic wolf-men (and women) found in a trio of New Millennium lycan-flicks—the groundbreaking *Ginger Snaps* (2000), the disappointing *Blood Moon* (2001), and the worthy *Skinwalkers* (2006), as well as starting down the lycan-path by contributing to the *Waxwork* anthology back in 1988 (see *Pseudo-Wolves* chapter).

Despite its copycat nature, *Never Cry Werewolf* adds a few new wrinkles to the tried and true werewolf tropes. First off, Jarrod is accompanied by a faithful black German shepherd, which turns out to be his "familiar." As Loren learns (again from the internet), "A werewolf is often accompanied by a demon familiar, usually in the form of a black dog." At one point, Jarrod and his dog corner Loren and her potential paramour Steve in a local gun store, where his "demon from hell" pet transforms (via CGI—the one major instance in which director Spencer eschewed physical effects for computer imaging) into a spike-backed, skinless mutant hellhound that rampages through the store until Loren grabs a shotgun and fires a fistful of handy novelty silver bullets to take down the beast.

Additionally, "werewolves never age … and have hypnotic power over the opposite sex" (animal magnetism taken to the extreme, no doubt—or perhaps just a borrowing from the "sexier" vampire sub-genre). But most interesting is the notion that the werewolf transformation, generally governed by the moon's cycle, "can be made at will using a charm which is made from the skin taken from the neck of a hanged criminal." This echoes (and adds a gruesome twist) the medieval legends of people becoming werewolves by wearing belts made of wolf-skin or transforming after donning full pelts.

Though derivative as all get out, *Never Cry Werewolf*, modeled after a winner, offers decent, even amusing characterizations; some suspenseful set-pieces involving an imposing monster; a few dollops of humor (Loren's bedroom is littered with VHS tapes of faux werewolf movies with titles like *Katts & Werewolves* and *The Werewolf's Bris*); and enough production—and entertainment—value to forgive its overall lack of originality. For its DVD debut in Japan, *Never Cry Were-*

wolf was called *School Girl vs. Wolfman*—a not-inaccurate yet still rather amusing retitling.

With quotes from: "Exclusive Interview: Kevin Sorbo," by The Fan Girl Next Door, House of Horrors.com.

Morphology: Shaggy, wolf-headed biped
Demise: Silver-plated shotgun barrel impalement
Full Moon Rating: ***½

Nhong Werewolf see Werewolf in Bangkok

Night Drop see Night Shadow

Night of the Howling Beast

(1975/77; Profilmes/Constellation Films; Spain) Original Language Title: *La Maldición de la Beastia*. Alternate Titles: *The Werewolf and the Yeti*; *Hall of the Mountain King* (video), *Horror of the Werewolf* (TV); *Werewolf* (DVD). Director: M. I. (Miguel Iglesias) Bonns; Producer: Modesto Pérez Redondo; Screenplay: Jacinto Molina (Paul Naschy); Cinematographer: Tomàs Pladevall. Cast: Paul Naschy, Grace Mills (Mercedes Molina), Silvia Solar, Gil Vidal, Luis Induni.

> You feel your Heart POUNDING, You know It's out there, You can't SCREAM, NOW IT'S AT YOUR THROAT—ad line

This seventh released entry (of twelve) in Paul Naschy's Waldemar Daninsky the Werewolf series may be the most entertaining of the bunch. It's certainly the most eventful, and uncategorically the wildest, tossing Tibetan bandits, sexy cannibal she-demons, a beautiful sorceress, and yes, the Abominable Snowman into its lycan-mix. Leaving off his beloved Gothicism (which permeates nearly all his other Daninsky films), writer-star Naschy penned a tale of anthropologist/psychologist Waldemar Daninsky (Naschy) joining an expedition to search for the fabled Yeti in Tibet. While on an ill-fated scouting trip for a secret mountain pass, Waldemar becomes separated from his comrade and seeks shelter in a cave, whereupon a pair of gorgeous sisters offer succor—and their beautiful bodies—before revealing themselves as cannibalistic, fanged demons. Though Waldemar dispatches them both, one bites him in the chest, passing to him the curse of the werewolf. Meanwhile, the rest of Waldemar's expedition run afoul of a group of mountain bandits, led by the evil Sekkar Kahn (Luis Induni). With several of the party now imprisoned in Sekkar Kahn's fortress (including Waldemar's lover, Sylvia [Mercedes Molina]), Waldemar must find a way to defeat the bandit, rescue his girl, and cure his lycanthropy—but not before facing down the Yeti himself in a hairy struggle to the death.

"Paul Naschy ... is considered to be the world's foremost screen horror star today," grandiosely claimed the American pressbook for *Night of the Howling Beast*. With Britain's Hammer Films all but a dead issue by the mid–1970s, relegating both Peter Cushing and Christopher Lee to subpar, often-puerile efforts like *At the Earth's Core*, *Dracula and Son*, and *Starship Invasions*, and with Vincent Price largely settling for guest spots on TV, there *is* a point to be made. But, truth be told, following *Night*, Naschy entered a fallow period horror-wise just like his better known brethren. Following 1976's *Inquisition* (marking the actor's directorial debut), it took five more years for another out-and-out Naschy horror to see international play, that being the Daninsky follow-up *The Craving*. In any case, it was nice to see Naschy get a little ballyhoo in America after toiling so long in general obscurity (at least in regards to the U.S. market). For his work in *Night of the Howling Beast*, Paul Naschy earned a Best Actor award at Spain's Sitges Film Festival (celebrating fantasy and horror films) in 1975. And while there was never any risk of Paul Naschy mounting the Oscar podium steps, in *Night of the Howling Beast* he seems less stiff and far more comfortable in his own skin (and werewolf hair) than he did during many other thespian outings. In wolf-form Naschy never looked livelier, leaping from atop boulders, jumping onto a horse-and-rider to bring down both man and beast, and engaging in an energetic grapple with the oversized yeti, rolling in the snow, slashing and biting, before finally overpowering the gigantic brute.

While Naschy always infused his beloved Daninsky character with enough pathos to choke a lycanthrope, here he goes that extra mile to turn the sympathetic Waldemar into a veritable action hero. Though Naschy litters his script with werewolf attacks, never does his Wolfman kill an innocent. This manbeast is not so much a danger to the protagonists (as in so many other iterations) but a heroic monster pitted against evil. In fact, each and every throat-ripping assault results in the death of either bandits, drunken rapists, or monsters (cue the yeti). The werewolf even directly rescues Waldemar's lady love from the clutches of three lecherous brigands, killing her assailants and leaving the fainting girl without a scratch. And while in human form, Waldemar has never been more noble. Sure, he's stopped a few sexual assaults and killed a couple of backwoods bandits before, but here he becomes a regular Erroll Flynn, dispatching palace guards with swords, and besting the Khan himself in an intense and lively battle involving knives, furniture, a spear and finally an ill-placed pit of spikes.

Naschy also turns *Night of the Howling Beast* into his own personal *House of Dracula* (and not just because the film employs multiple monsters). An avowed Universal horror fan (Naschy even names one of Waldemar's fellow expeditioners "Larry Talbot"!), he lets his character finally live at the end, cured of his malediction (just like the original Wolf Man in *House of Dracula*). Not only that, incurable romantic that he is, Naschy sends Waldemar walking off into the sunrise with the girl. "I'm free," he marvels. "It's true—I'm free!" Regarding this miracle, Naschy took inspiration from another Universal film—the first werewolf talky, in fact—*Werewolf of London*. "There exists a magic plant," a helpful monk tells Waldemar. "When its petals are mixed with the blood from a young girl, they can cure those like you who have been contaminated by the demons of Karakarahn." So at film's end, when the exhausted but triumphant werewolf collapses after his fierce battle with the yeti, Sylvia, Waldemar's lover, conveniently spies said plant, cuts her palm, mixes her blood with the petals, and feeds them to the unconscious lycanthrope. The monster immediately transforms back to Waldemar, and all is right with the world.

Naschy later admitted some dissatisfaction with this happy ending. "To be honest," he said, "I was not in favor of his survival. I think the werewolf should die in each film, only to be reborn in the next. It was done for commercial reasons." Commercial or not, it makes for a refreshingly upbeat and well-deserved conclusion for our intrepid hero.

"A Naschy film is always sure to be a blood-thirsty shocker," continued the movie's PR boys, and in terms of the violent and inventive *Night of the Howling Beast*, this turned out to be more than mere hyperbole. Containing nearly as many outré elements as there are yak hairs on a wolfman, this *Night* offers the following: cannibalistic nympho-demons; Tartan banditos; outdoor gunfights (in which a trio of brave Europeans take down more bad guys with their tiny revolvers than a score of bandits manage with machine guns!); a brutal despot who skins girls alive as "treatment" for nasty boils on his back; a beautiful "foreign" witch whose sadism and lust for power leads her to offer her own body to Waldemar while intoning "You will obey me—as a man and as a beast—and no one will oppose me!"; a prisoner revolt of half-naked nubiles—led by a captive *princess*, no less; half a dozen werewolf attacks; several naked women with the flesh from their backs peeled off in sheets (a sequence that earned the film a spot on the infamous "video nasties" list in England in the 1980s); and, of course, a cameo by the Abominable Snowman himself, culminating in an exciting monster-vs.-monster showdown between our heroic lycanthrope and the enraged yeti. With all that going on, there's little time to notice the film's flaws (the overuse of unconvincing day-for-night photography; the fact that the Himalayan landscape is sometimes snowy and sometimes not—even in the same locale; and the occasionally silly dialogue ("No, this nightmare can't be true, I hope that soon I'll awaken"; "Your goodness and your love will help overcome the bad within him, and conquer pain and death"). And, admittedly, the yeti really has no place being in this movie. Seen very briefly at the beginning when it abruptly attacks an expedition (leading to Waldemar's reconnaissance mission) and at the very end when it attacks the Wolfman, it merely serves as a monster McGuffin—more a creature of expediency than substance. Even so, it provides the oddly entertaining coda of a minute-long battle between a werewolf and the Abominable Snowman—something inventively bizarre enough to bring a smile to the face of any lover of the unusual.

With so much of the film set outdoors (with the mountains and woodlands near Barcelona standing in for the wilds of Tibet), the film takes on a bigger scope and sense of adventure (enhanced by the bandit scenario) than most of Naschy's werewolf films. Here Naschy eschews his standard Gothic (the closest Waldemar comes to a castle setting are the stone-walled dungeons of Sekkar Kahn's palace) for a more epic adventure feel. It marks a refreshing—and entertaining—change of pace for the series.

Naschy himself characterized this anomalous film as "a comic-strip brought to the screen; with the Wolf Man, Tartars, the Yeti, action, the ever-present curse of the werewolf, and the Tibetan flower which frees Waldemar from this curse. In short, a film that I find very amusing." And so will most werewolf fans, particularly those with a taste for offbeat Eurohorror.

Still, Naschy admitted, "I am not entirely satisfied with the movie. I believe the director, Miguel Iglesias Bonns, had a splendid film in his hand of which he didn't take full advantage. The final result is nothing more than an entertaining adventure film, when what I had in mind was much more ambitious. This meant I was in constant confrontation with Bonns." Despite Naschy's reservations, however, Bonns offers plenty of moments of unease and outright horror along with

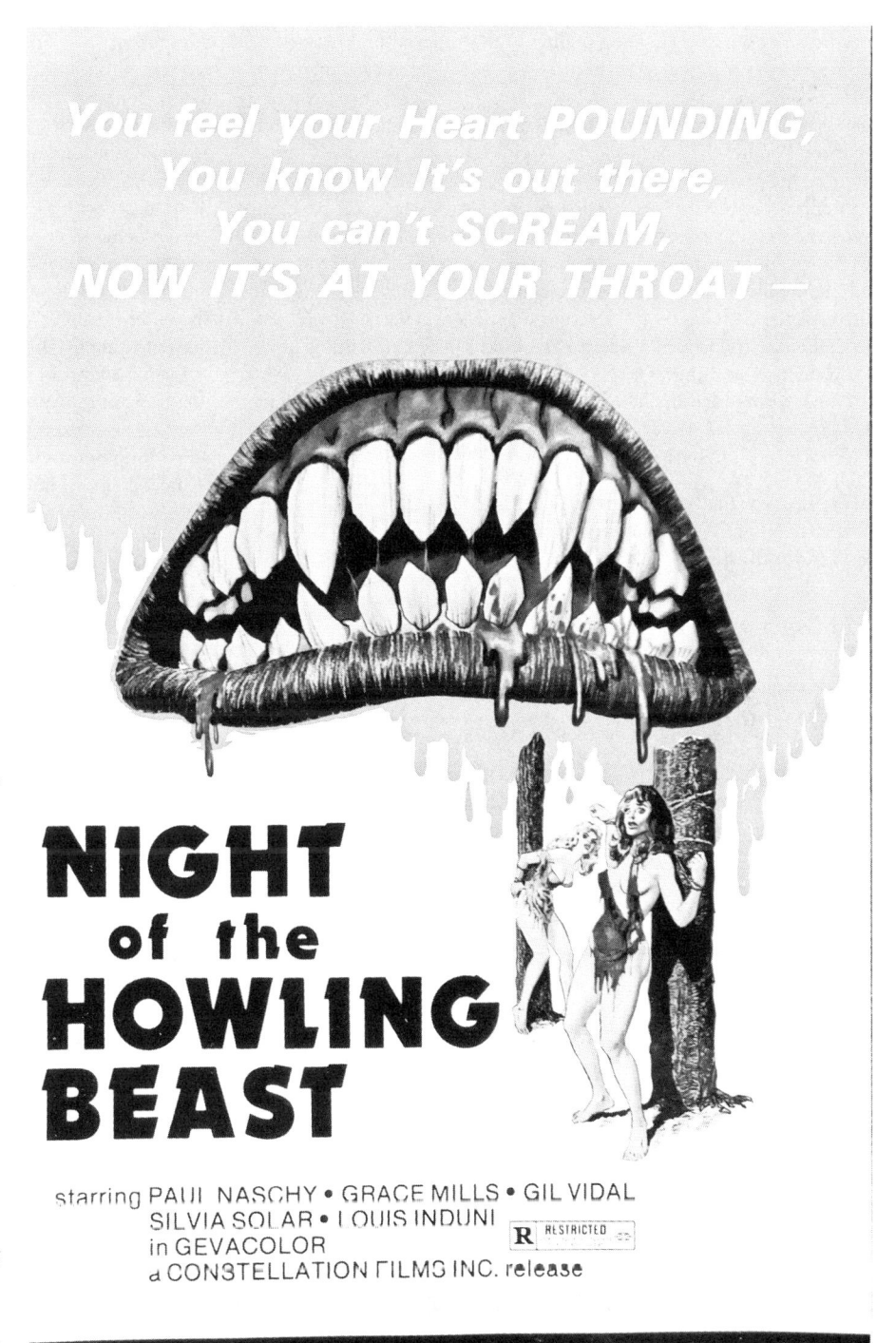

While perhaps not the aesthetic pinnacle, the epic, action-filled *Night of the Howling Beast* stands as the most entertaining entry in Paul Naschy's long-running Waldemar Daninsky/ Werewolf series (American pressbook).

the movie's action-adventure focus. For instance, when Waldemar and his local guide become lost searching for that elusive mountain pass, his superstitious companion panics. "The demons of the Red Moon, I hear them!" he cries, and races over a ridge and screams. When Waldemar catches up with him, he sees only his companion's footprints, which end abruptly in the middle of a snowfield(!)—as if the man has simply vanished into thin air. Discordant sounds and faint, echoing laughter on the soundtrack hammer home the moment's preternatural eeriness. It's a first disturbing inkling of the supernatural terrors to come, terrors which arrive full force when Waldemar, having been rescued by two sexy women living in a cave, witnesses his two gorgeous conquests gnawing like animals on severed human limbs. Bonn likewise handles the werewolf attacks with verve and panache. For instance, one encounter begins from the werewolf's point of view as the camera rushes towards the startled victim. A cut to the man's p.o.v. reveals the snarling Wolfman visage closing in, before a final switch back to the lycan-view shows the victim falling backwards, his throat now a horrific, bloody mess. The scene comes off as quick, startling, effective and involving ... apt descriptors for *Night of the Howling Beast* as a whole, marking it as Waldemar Daninsky's most entertaining hour (and thirty-four minutes).

With quotes from: "The Howl from Overseas," by Jose Ignacio Cuenca, *Fangoria* 134; "Paul Naschy Filmography," by José Luis González and Michael Secula, *Videooze* 6/7.

Morphology: Shaggy Talbot-esque wolfman
Demise: None; Waldemar finally finds his cure
Full Moon Rating: ****

The Night of the Werewolf see *The Craving*

Night Shadow

(1989; Quest Entertainment) Alternate Title: *Night Drop*. Director/Screenplay: Randolph Cohlan; Producer: George Temple; Cinematographer: Sean McLin. Cast: Brenda Vance, Stuart Quan (as Dane Chan), Kato Kaelin, Orien Richman, Tom Boylan, Mike Hamilton, Aldo Ray, Rick Scott.

> Where Evil Lurks...—tagline

In the late 1980s the home video phenomenon was booming, with mom and pop rental shops springing up seemingly on every street corner in America. With customers clamoring for new titles every week, store owners became desperate for product. Consequently, wannabe indie filmmakers and would-be auteurs often had little difficulty finding financing to fund their low-budget efforts—particularly if said opus fell within the ever-popular horror genre. First (and last) time director Randolph Cohlan's *Night Shadow* was one such out-of-nowhere production, serving its function to help fill video shelves before disappearing into (deserved) obscurity.

Returning to her home town of Danford (the film was shot in Hanford, and Fresno, California) for a brief vacation, up-and-coming TV newscaster Alex Jung (Brenda Vance) sees a sinister stranger on the side of the road who stares meaningfully after her. When he opens the trunk of his car, bits of dismembered corpses threaten to tumble out. Soon a rash of mutilation murders strikes the small town, with local sheriff Adam (Tom Boylan), Alex's old flame, nonplussed. Alex's martial arts–practicing brother, Tai (Stuart Quan, nee "Dane Chan"), and his two mullet-headed, practical-joker friends (Orien Richman and Kato Kaelin), soon become targets of the murderous drifter when Tai, a motel maintenance man, finds his secret diary in one of the rooms there. Worse still, it finally becomes clear that the killer is actually a *werewolf*!

Shot in abandoned factories, back alleys and cheap motel rooms (much of the film takes place at a real, cut-rate motel), and definitely of its 1980s time period (mullets and blow-dried bottle blondes abound), *Night Shadow* simply screams "low budget." Its surprisingly competent (if unspectacular) lighting and photography, however, coats it with an unexpectedly professional-looking sheen. Unfortunately, such surface gloss can't keep the glacially paced and poorly constructed script from placing boredom front and center. *Night Shadow* is the kind of movie that shows a man pulling up in a car, parking, exiting the vehicle, and ambling all the way up a long walkway to the porch—with a locked-down camera capturing every tedious step. Other scenes offer plenty of pointless dialogue exchanges about how terrible the murders are, how the authorities are in the dark, etc., culminating in a dull press conference conducted by the sheriff that adds absolutely nothing—no information, no development, and no point (except to eat up some running time).

Even the film's big "suspense" set-piece (which, like everything else of import in this molasses-drenched movie, doesn't come until well after the hour mark) is so drawn out as to leech away every bit of interest long before its predictable conclusion. As Tai's friend Dean (Kato Kaelin, who went on to earn his 15 minutes of fame as a notoriously unreliable witness in the O.J. Simpson trial) walks through an alley alone, he hears noises, becomes worried, nervously cracks some jokes, then creeps ever so slowly for ever so long that it engenders more relief than shock when the werewolf finally steps up behind him to claim his prey.

Very little happens during the first hour (apart from the sheriff finding a few mutilated bodies—which are more suggested than shown), though real-life karate instructor Stuart Quan (as Tai) gets to show off his martial arts skills in one scene when he takes out a band of rowdy bikers at the motel in a middling kung fu melee. Unfortunately, this little bit of welcome action elicits more guffaws than gasps due to the ridiculously clichéd pan flute music playing on the soundtrack that's right out of the old *Kung Fu* television show. Quan also gets to show off his six-pack abs—over and over again—as Tai wears nothing but a series of ludicrously short half-shirts and cut-off man-bra tank tops. (Stuart Quan was a sometime stunt man/bit player in films like *License to Kill* [as "ninja"] and *Big Trouble in Little China* ["Chang Sing #4"]. He died in 2006 of a heart attack at age 43.)

None of the so-called actors (few of whom did anything before or since) can muster up much inflection in their monotone deliveries, much less expressions on their faces. The only thespian with any life (and the only name actor in the cast) is a wasted Aldo Ray, who appears in a couple of unimportant scenes as an irrepressible novelty salesman. Wearing a silly fish-hat, he has little to do except enthusiastically extoll the virtues of novelties like the "Squid Scraper." Of course, the poor script helps them not at all by offering only bland, two-dimensional characters defined by little more than practical jokes, drinking beer in abandoned factories, or working out with a punching bag.

Night Shadow was writer-director Randolph Cohlan's debut. It also proved to be his swan song, and it's not hard to see why. In addition to his dull, unwieldy script, time after time Cohlan makes poor directorial choices. For instance, several times during the film the drifter, who appears to be attracted to Alex, sits at a nearby table and simply stares at her creepily. At this, Cohlan superimposes storm footage over his face so that it looks like lightning shoots from his eyes. Cohlan repeats this ill-conceived, pretentious, and *silly* effect not once but twice more. Yet another odd choice comes when the rather perfunctory car-motorcycle chase (the picture's one major action set-piece) ends in a less-than-spectacular crash that sees Tai falling off his bike. Apparently, this pedestrian stunt so pleased director Cohlan that he replays it *three* times in succession—in slow motion—to close out the scene (and ensure that nobody missed it the first—or second—time).

At about the hour mark, something finally happens—and that

something is the Big Transformation scene. Finding his precious diary stolen from his motel room, the drifter lashes out in anger, sending a tabletop fan crashing to the floor. He then begins to growl, revealing a mouth full of fangs. His hands darken and become hairier, and the skin under his brow seemingly bubbles (in a primitive but not ineffective bladder effect). He falls to his knees, and the film cuts to a shot of the blank wall as the shadow of an elongated wolf's head rises up into frame and howls. Filmed in rapidly-edited, tight close-ups, the minimal effects offer maximum impact. Unfortunately, the movie quickly bogs down again in a series of uninteresting, time-killing scenes (deputy making his rounds, the trio of friends sitting around, etc.) until the last five minutes, when the protagonists finally go toe to claw with the lycanthrope.

When we finally get a good look at the beast at film's end, the wait proves hardly worth it. With long fur covering every inch of its body, and a mane of dark hair surrounding its dog-like face, this werewolf looks disturbingly like a huge, unkempt Shitzu. Ridiculously, its eyes periodically flash with a red glow. Still, walking upright on two legs, its barrel-chested physique and snarling maw cuts an imposing if not particularly convincing figure.

Though ironically titled *Lycanthrope* during shooting, there's no reason at all why *Night Shadow* should be a werewolf film. Given its story structure and the way Cohlan shoots the movie (keeping the manbeast largely unseen until the very end), it could just as easily (and more believably) have been a standard serial killer story.

Regarding lycanthropy, *Night Shadow* provides even *less* characterization for its werewolf than for its cardboard protagonists. The nameless lycanthropic drifter just arrives in town with a car trunk full of body parts and starts killing people. We know nothing about his background, his motivations, or his feelings. He rarely appears onscreen (in either human or animal guise) and never speaks a word. Apart from the brief transformation and a couple of scenes in which he simply stares at heroine Alex, effects technician turned actor Rick Scott (in his only role) has next to nothing to do as the mysterious drifter.

Also having nothing to do is the full moon, nor any other bit of lycan-lore, as this manwolf transforms in full daylight and apparently at will. Ordinary bullets appear to have little effect, for after the sheriff shoots the beast at the climax several times it still keeps coming. The only variation on/addition to the werewolf canon comes in this creature's implied hunt for a mate (the man's diary mentions a "nuptial song"), though this remains so vague and muddled that the notion comes to naught. Apart from the staring scenes (accompanied by the ridiculous storm/lightning superimpositions), Alex and the drifter never interact, even at the climax. Additionally, the picture seems to allude to the creature's supernatural power when, at one point, the enraged drifter's eyes glow red, resulting in blood bubbling up from the clogged drain Tai works on in the room next door—for no discernable reason. But, again, nothing comes of this potentially interesting notion.

Despite the gruesome nature of the various killings, *Night Shadow* remains light on the gore. Most of the attacks occur off-screen, with little bloodshed. Just one flash of bloody body parts in a car trunk, and one impalement by steel pipe, with the rest of the victims shown in a body bag or simply being dragged out of frame. Eschewing shocking grue in favor of suggestion is just fine—*if* the film offers something in its place (excitement, pathos, character involvement)—none of which *Night Shadow* does.

At least the climax finally presents a bit of excitement, when Tai rams into the beast with a police car, pinning it to a wall. As the creature writhes and howls in pain and rage, it pushes at the vehicle to try to free itself, even moving the heavy automobile slightly. Tai then picks up a fallen deputy's gun and fires at the car until it explodes in flame, engulfing the werewolf. But then, of course, Cohlan drags out the film with a dull epilogue montage showing the wounded Tai being treated by paramedics, Alex hugging her brother, and Alex and the sheriff embracing and talking while schmaltzy music plays. Roll credits and roll zzz's. Ultimately, five minutes of activity can't erase the previous 85 of tedium.

Fresno native Darrell Mapson served as stunt coordinator on *Night Shadow* (he also played one of the hell-raising bikers who receives a beat-down from Tai). "We had a couple of good fight scenes, chases, high fall, a crash and car explosion," he recalled. "The acting was surprisingly good without any big names or budget. It was fun to work on. Kato Kaelin was natural in his acting and should have been made known from this instead of the O.J. Trial." Well, that's debatable…

With quotes from: "*Night Shadow* Reviews and Ratings," *Internet Movie Data Base*, June 1, 2005.

Morphology: Bipedal, long-haired, dog-faced beast
Demise: Exploding police car
Full Moon Rating: *½

Night Wolf

(2010; Eyeline Entertainment/Lionsgate; UK) Alternate Title: *13 Hrs.* (UK). Director: Jonathan Glendening; Producers: Duncan Napier-Bell, Nick Napier-Bell, Romain Schroeder, Tom Reeve; Screenplay: Adam Phillips; Cinematographer: Jordan Cushing. Cast: Isabella Calthorpe, Tom Felton, Gemma Atkinson, Joshua Bowman, John Lynch, Cornelius Clarke, Simon MacCorkindale.

> ON A FULL MOON NIGHT, FIND OUT WHY
> HOME WILL NEVER BE SAFE AGAIN—trailer

"From a producer of *Dog Soldiers*" trumpets the American ads for the British *Night Wolf*. Drawing parallels to that modern-day were-classic might not have been the best marketing idea Lionsgate ever had. First off, apart from those cinematic lycan-lovers among us, most Americans probably have never even *heard* of *Dog Soldiers* (given its lack of a U.S. theatrical release and inauspicious American debut on the cheese-loving Sci-Fi Channel). Second, while the suspenseful, well-acted, and engrossing *Night Wolf* stands as a cleverly-constructed horror nail biter, its unique-but-underwhelming lycanthropes (when finally revealed at the film's climax) can't hold a were-candle to the Big Bad Wolves laying siege in *Dog Soldiers*.

Sarah Tyler (Isabella Calthorpe) returns home from living in L.A. to Crowhurst Hall, her ancestral estate in England, in order to reconnect with her family (consisting of her mother, stepfather, and several brothers and half-brothers). But as the siblings' uneasy reunion progresses into a drinking/smoking party, a vicious creature invades the manor, kills Sarah's stepfather, and begins picking off the rest. As the survivors are forced to take refuge in the attic and try to think their way out of their terrifying predicament, the family members' complex interpersonal dynamics come to the fore, setting up even more obstacles to overcome than a ravening monster.

Filmed on location in Surrey, England, at an impressive—and oppressive—country house that had obviously seen better days, *Night Wolf* takes the time to develop its cadre of characters, and their strained relationships, at the outset, so that the viewer comes to see as individuals, with real histories and personalities, what many movies introduce as mere werewolf bait. As director Jonathan Glendening so concisely put it, "The thinking is that if you know who the characters are properly you'll care when they are ripped apart." Indeed, the discovery of the father's gruesomely mutilated corpse (which heralds the near-non-stop action to come) arrives as a real shock not only to the horrified characters but to the viewer as well. "Also, we're trying to set up a human normality before tearing it apart with something supernatural," continued Glendening. "The creature is also a metaphor for the seething resentments and sibling rivalries, so you need to set those up for the later revelations to work. You always need a calm before the storm, and I think these family scenes help lull the viewer into a false sense of expectation about the rest of the film."

With the familial lines sketched and the viewer-lulling stage set, *Night Wolf* then launches into a savage, terrifying siege scenario, as the handful of siblings and friends seek refuge in a cramped attic from the fast-moving, unstoppable "thing" below. In trying to work out how to escape, or at least call for help, they formulate—and execute—various plans. And when things go bloodily wrong, the characters' true colors (some of it blood-red) come out, further revealing the seeping emotional wounds beneath the various surface ones. *Night Wolf* takes on something of a *Night of the Living Dead* tone (a small group trapped in an enclosed space over the course of one [full moon] night), but with a faster pace, bloodier results, and even more involving characters. Glendening's precise direction offers only indistinct flashes of the vicious creature, with terrifying sound effects and bulging doors (as the monster tries to crash through them) signifying its powerful presence. The truly gruesome eviscerated remains of its victims—all blood, viscera, and torn-open ribs—become visual testaments to its deadly efficacy. The actors, led by a strong Isabella Calthorpe (who, incidentally, should have felt right at home on an aristocratic estate, given that she's a true blueblood herself, a direct descendant of King Charles II, and fourth cousin to Prince William and Prince Harry) and an almost unrecognizable Tom Felton ("Draco Malfoy" himself from the *Harry Potter* series), bring their well-rounded characters to believable life so that the viewer indeed does care when they are "ripped apart."

Shot and released as *13 Hrs.* in England, the film was retitled *Night Wolf* by U.S. distributor Lionsgate for its American debut. "I prefer *13 Hrs.*," complained Glendening, "as it's a discussion point and draws the audience in rather than just telling them straight what you get: it's set at night ... with a wolf. I've found people who don't know it's a werewolf movie prefer the movie and its revelation than people who know in advance." Given the script's dearth of werewolf references for most of its running time (until the exciting finale)—no talk of the moon, or silver, or even the term "werewolf"—this *Night Wolf* indeed might just as well have been some massive, unstoppable rabid dog as a murderous lycanthrope (in fact, one of the characters postulates just such a theory early on). But Glendening tosses us a lycan-bone towards the end when he offers up a brief but highly effective transformation scene that involves claws pushing out of fingernails, growing fangs, darkening skin, glowing eyes, and a spine painfully raising up beneath a shirt. This last proved to be Glendening's "favorite FX ... when [the] transformation happens and [the] spine is 'cracking' vertebrae ... all that was was a line of socks dragged under a T-shirt and then reversed in the edit, but with a few cracks on the sound track it looked painful and brilliant." Indeed it does.

Not quite everything works out well for this *Night Wolf*, however. Glendening wanted something "different" in his werewolf—and he got it. Unfortunately, "different" does not always translate into "effective." "The creature was a representation of an inner disease that was ripping a family apart," noted Glendening. "It was furless, white, opal and luminescent, and looked as though it had been birthed through pain ... it is a savage beast." Yes it is, and it remains a terrifying one—so long as it stays out of the spotlight. "Like with *Jaws*," revealed Glendening, "we tried our best not to show the creature until the very end"—a wise choice, as it turned out. Once fully revealed at the climax, we see something that looks far too human—more like the albino mutants from director Neil (*Dog Soldiers*) Marshall's excellent follow-up *The Descent* (another tie-in to that superior lycanflick, perhaps?) than a half-man/half-wolf creature. Bald, hairless, and white-skinned, the only nod to its canine connection is a fang-filled, misshapen muzzle protruding from its face. This leaves us with a fantastically-realized werewolf scenario that lacks an effective werewolf. It's like an NFL team quarterbacked by a college rookie. That such an otherwise swift and nimble production should drop the lycan-ball on such a critical play as this becomes a major disappointment.

Also, while the Big Reveal at film's end regarding the werewolf's identity remains thematically on point, there's nothing particularly revealing about it (despite the lead actress' best efforts to appear heart-wrenchingly horrified), since the astute (or even awake) viewer has figured it all out by the midway point. So the denouement feels expected, even forced, and carries far less weight than it should. Still, even with these nocturnal blemishes, the well-paced, exciting, and involving *Night Wolf* howls as one of the better entries from the busy were-year of 2010.

With quotes from: "Interview with *13 Hrs* and *Strippers vs. Werewolves* Director Jonathan Glendening," LoveHorror.com.

Morphology: Hairless, pale, dog-faced biped
Demise: Throat-ripping
Full Moon Rating: ***½

La Noche de Walpurgis see The Werewolf vs. Vampire Woman

Planet of the Werewolves see Rage of the Werewolf

Plenilunio

(1993; Halven/Sub Rosa; Uruguay) Director/Screenplay: Ricardo Islas. Executive Producer: Ruben Sosa; Camera: Marisel Ayala. Cast: Martin Cabrera, Ricardo Islas, Ana Cecilia Garcia, Sebastian Rivero, Manuel Charbonner, Daniel Elola.

DON'T PLAY IN THE WOODS, FOR THE WOLF
IS COMING ... *AND THE WOLF IS HUNGRY*...—ad line

This early, micro-budgeted, shot-on-video effort by Uruguayan filmmaker Ricardo Islas offers a faint glimmer of the promise that brought him to America in the late 1990s for a PBS producing career in Chicago, and subsequent directorial turns on genre fare like *Headcrusher* (1999), *Night Fangs* (2005), and *Zombie Farm* (2009). Though still low-budget (under the $1 million mark), these later productions are miles away from the peso-pinching backyard effort that is *Plenilunio* (which translates as "Full Moon").

When a man is killed by a "wild dog" (at least according to the clueless police) during a full moon, the friendly group of kids who like to hang around the small local cable TV station run by cameraman Roberto (writer/director Ricardo Islas himself) surmise it to be the work of a werewolf. Joining forces with the murdered man's two young sons, the kids explore the woods near the crime scene and barely escape an encounter with a tall, enraged "guy with white hair" (an albino who always wears dark glasses) who's just bought an isolated house in the woods. After the beast slaughters several people rehearsing at the local theater during the next full moon, the kids induce Roberto to go check out the sinister stranger. This only results in the suspect (Martin Cabrera) viciously attacking Roberto, ending with the albino taking a fireplace poker through his cheek while Roberto escapes. The man subsequently traps Roberto and the children at the large, isolated house to which the cable station has recently moved, intending to keep them there until the moon rises. "No one gets in, no one gets out," the killer ominously intones through the house's locked door before beating a reporter to death before their very eyes. (Note: Illustrating the trials and tribulations of no-budget filmmaking, this location change arose from necessity. "We went through a big setback when the TV station where we started shooting the movie moved its operation to a different place," recalled writer-director Ricardo Islas. "The whole plot about Roberto getting hired to work in a new cable station was made up as a solution to having lost our main location.") Roberto and the kids prepare for the monster's coming assault as best they can, hoping they can fend off the beast by setting an electrified trap.

One of the great pleasures of watching foreign films is seeing a different set of sensibilities shape and mold familiar themes. Filmmakers from other cultures often bring an unusual (and frequently fascinating) perspective to their storytelling, not only in purely technical terms but in tone and approach. For American viewers raised on predictable Hollywood fare, with its expected rhythms, characters, and tropes, this can add the spice of novelty, and, more importantly, unpredictability—an "anything-can-happen-at-any-time" quality. In *Plenilunio*, director/screenwriter Roberto Islas stars himself alongside a group of tween and teen children. Obviously not professional actors, this rag-tag bunch overcomes their awkwardness to react, and interact, like real children would in such a bizarre and frightening situation. Consequently, they seem far more real than the typical pint-sized Hollywood action hero tykes. Likewise, Ricardo himself eschews the clichéd he-man role to portray a man whose fear is palpable but who does what he can with his limited skills to try and save the children whom circumstance has thrust into his care. This adds some much needed verisimilitude to the climax in which an average adult and group of everyday kids must try to save themselves from a horrible (and horribly unconvincing) situation. "The kids were (still are) a group of friends that used to get together in real life with me at the old TV station where I was working in actuality when we shot the movie," recalled Islas. "There's a lot of truth to that group of kids and the older 'brother' type that I was, simply because in real life I had been their teacher in either English as a second language (which I taught for a living for years in Uruguay) or in art (I used to teach comics). So the group was real, and that's probably why the interaction works pretty smoothly. I even recorded them talking about werewolves and then wrote my dialogue trying to be faithful to the way they talked." This natural, real-life rapport shines through in the film. At one point the killer taunts, "You are weak, and that weakness is my strength." But he is wrong, as Roberto's and the children's strength comes from the fact that they care about one another. And, unlikely as it seems for such an impoverished and often unbelievable production, so does the viewer.

That said, *Plenilunio* is *not* a good werewolf movie. First there's the technical limitations, with the cheap-looking, flat videography screaming "camcorder commando" from frame one. Second, since talk is cheap, Islas fills his film with it, offering a plethora of trivial conversations between the kids and Roberto, the gang of tykes, the victims-to-be at the theater, etc. Likewise, plenty of unedifying tramping through woodlands, children perusing werewolf comics and film magazines (including a Latino edition of *Fangoria*), a superfluous visit to a dance club, and an unfunny practical joke (involving a condom baked into a pizza) act like an anchor on the film's pacing.

Islas indicates the werewolf's presence through handheld p.o.v. shots and what sounds like a dog panting on the soundtrack. The first (highly unfortunate) inkling of its true form comes during the attack at the theater when what looks like fuzzy white slippers advance down some stairs. The subsequent attacks are so choppily edited that one becomes disoriented trying to keep track of the sequence's Where and Who and What. The occasional split-second shot of unconvincing ketchup-laden gore fails to smooth over the confusion.

Never shown clearly, even during the climax, the werewolf resembles not so much a vicious manbeast as a cheap, oversized stuffed dog, the kind you might win at some travelling carnival after spending 50 bucks on the ring toss. Though anything but convincing, this lycan-beast at least possesses one unique quality—a snow white pelt, making it the first (and only, to date) *albino* werewolf in cinema history. Why this unusual look? "I could lie [about the reason]," laughed Islas, "but I didn't know how to effectively change the color of that material, so I decided it was easier to turn the man into an albino." The beast, which Islas built himself, "was made out of sponge with a wire frame. The hair was similar to cotton ... it's the stuff they use to stuff jackets when they're not using feathers. The teeth and claws were hand made out of clay, and the eyes were stuffed animal glass eyes." Islas admitted that "the reason not to show it [much] were mainly two: because I don't like to show monsters a lot, even when well made. And because this one wasn't precisely a successfully crafted creature." Indeed, this homemade puppet-monster stands as one of the least convincing werewolves to ever curse ... er, cross, the screen.

When one of the kids observes, "We need silver bullets," Roberto retorts confidently (for no discernible reason), "No, that's just a legend." Hmmm, so is the notion of a man turning into a wolf at the full moon. In any case, this werewolf can be hurt (in man or beast mode) just like any other creature, as evidenced by the open wounds his human face sports after a nasty encounter with a fireplace poker. And in the end it wasn't silver killed the beast, it was electricity (a nod to the original *The Thing*, perhaps).

In the positive column, the finale, which sees the killer/werewolf lay siege to the TV station, generates a modicum of suspense—largely due to the empathy the cast has engendered, placing the viewer in their shoes to ask "What would *I* do in this desperate situation?"

Upping the horror factor, Roberto has several brief conversations with the killer, who stands outside the locked door, barring the kids' escape. When Roberto pleads with him to at least let the children go, he refuses—"because I'm *hungry*." Yikes. He continues ominously, "You will be locked in there until the moon comes out. You will feel the fear as you imagine the pain. You will wonder who's first, and desperation will finish off your stupid friendship. You will become animals. That's what we were and will be." But what this lone wolf fails to take into account is his intended victims' humanity, the love of one's fellow man engendered by the fellowship of society. In the end it becomes a contest between the solitary beast and the collective humans—nature vs. society, amorality vs. brotherhood, savagery vs. love.

"I believe that in desperate moments is when you can see the true nature of people," opined Islas. "And when the werewolf has them all trapped in the house, some will chicken out and others will brave up. I was trying to make sort of a primitive statement about human nature overshadowing animal instincts. But I guess the crazy wolf overshadowed them all" [laughs].

As the human form of that "crazy wolf," Martin Cabrera's hard, whispery voice, coupled with his dark glasses and torn face, makes him a truly frightening figure (even had he *not* been able to turn into a ravening beast during the plenilunio). Just before the moon rises he drives a metal rod through Roberto's hand, pinning him to the ground!

As Roberto writhes in agony, the heartless killer taunts him with, "When the wolf is here you'll be the last one [to die]—so you can year [the children's] screams." Cabrera was so menacing that Islas regrets not utilizing him more. "Martin Cabrera, who played the werewolf in its human shape, was very effective," agreed Islas. "He came up with the whisper, and it was very well used. My mistake (one of them) was not to trust him enough to have him play a conventional wolf man with make-up as opposed to creating a gigantic puppet. Yet, to many, it's the crazy creature that makes the movie 'memorable.'" Memorable for the wrong reasons, perhaps…

The film's sole transformation (coming about ten minutes from the end) is no better than the rest of the impoverished effects. First, a couple of cutaways show Cabrera's face becoming hairier. Then what looks suspiciously like cotton candy begins to spread over his arms until one quick shot reveals the beast in all its goofy glory—looking like a Saint Bernard covered in snow flock, with a pair of beady eyes sitting in mounds of white "fur." "The wolf was falling apart towards the end of the movie," revealed Islas, "and it was beyond repair. To man it, it took three people, one for the head and one for each claw. I remember very long nights to get a few shots."

Far from the tortured soul of so many lycanthropictures, this wolfman revels in his animal power and the evil he can inflict. Even in human form he tries to kill Roberto and one of the older boys when he finds them snooping around his house. Later, while taunting Roberto through the locked door, he chillingly relates a horrifying little story about how he "once f**ked a girl, she got pregnant. I loved her. That's why I couldn't let her give birth to that thing. Unfortunately, she didn't survive the abortion—maybe because I ate her belly." Brrrr.

Amazingly, *Plenilunio* actually played a few select theaters and festivals in Uruguay, as well as being released on video and cable television there. Its distribution to the more sophisticated U.S. market proved far more problematic, however, with the small company Sub Rosa issuing a limited-release subtitled VHS version, now long out of print.

With a miniscule budget of only $500, *Plenilunio* may be the cheapest werewolf movie ever made. Fortunately, it's not the worst. Even though making *Plenilunio* "was quite a challenge," concluded Islas, "we enjoyed every damn minute of it…. When I'm making a movie, I feel like I'm walking on clouds." This ethereal happiness in just "putting on a show" shines through the unique, if amateurish, *Plenilunio* and makes it almost watchable … almost.

With quotes from: Interview with Ricardo Islas conducted by the author, January 2015.

Morphology: Big, white-furred quadruped
Demise: 6000 volts of electricity
Full Moon Rating: *½

Le Poil de la Bête see *The Hair of the Beast*

President Wolfman

(2012; Wild Eye Releasing) Director/Screenplay: Mike Davis; Producers: Mike Davis, Miles Flanagan. Cast: Dean Stockwell, Clifton James; (voice): Marc Evan Jackson, Anthony Jenkins, Chris Smith, Del Stetson, Ashley Ann, Amanda Abel, Casey Robinson, Amy Trinth.

HAIL TO THE TEETH—tagline

"Filmed in Stag-o-Vision—no lights, no camera, all action!" announces *President Wolfman*, "a 'green' movie using all recycled public domain and stock film footage" (as characterized by writer-director Mike Davis). A so-called green movie, explains Davis, is "a film made out of 100 percent recycled materials. These include public domain stock film footage taken from grainy old industrial shorts, weird classroom educational films, outdated advertisements, non-copyrighted features and vintage stag loops. The footage is chopped up, re-dubbed and re-edited to create an entirely new movie with new sound and dialogue." The obvious advantage, Davis notes, is that it comes "complete with film stock, production value (explosions, monsters, crowds, spaceships, exotic locations and stuff), [all] without having to spend tons of money or be at the mercy of studio executives." The "non-copyrighted feature" (fallen into the public domain) utilized by Davis as the framework for his *President Wolfman* is the 1973 political satire/horror hybrid *The Werewolf of Washington*, starring Dean Stockwell as a presidential press aide in Washington, D.C., who becomes afflicted with lycanthropy. "Discovering the 1973 film *Werewolf of Washington* supplied me with the trunk I needed to hang my branches on to make *President Wolfman*," said Davis.

As *President Wolfman* begins, the biggest thing on incumbent U.S. president John Wolfman's (Dean Stockwell) political plate (besides the upcoming election) is the "Chimerica Bill," a proposal by certain members of Congress—spearheaded by the duplicitous Vice President—to merge America with China in order to salvage the U.S.'s faltering economy. While on a hunting trip on an Arizona Indian reservation, the President is attacked and bitten by a wolf (coyote stock footage). Upon his return to Washington, the President periodically transforms into a werewolf and roams the D.C. streets, stalking and killing. With the media alerted to his tragic condition, the President goes on the run, but finally determines he must return to veto the Chimerica Bill—as well as save his eight-year-old son from the murderous clutches of the evil Vice President.

"I never sat and watched *Werewolf of Washington* all the way through," stated Davis, "because I didn't want to be influenced by the dialogue in that movie, what happens in the story. I wanted to just be completely free to imagine what I thought they were saying and what I thought they were doing." The original *Werewolf of Washington* became a werewolf after being bitten while on a junket to Eastern Europe, for instance, while *President Wolfman* becomes a werewolf when an Indian chief (who speaks with an *Eastern* Indian accent) summons up the spirit of the "dire wolf" (more mangy coyote stock footage) and commands, "Make revenge!" After that, whenever the full moon rises the President transforms into the less-than-impressive Chaney-esque manbeast of *Werewolf of Washington*. After the attack, the President ends up at the amusingly named Lon Chaney Memorial Hospital, where the doctor makes the crude announcement, "Good news, Mr. President—you're a fuckin' werewolf; you're cleared for discharge."

The kitchen-sink approach taken by Davis results in plenty of over-the-top stupidity to accompany the often disappointingly vulgar-rather-than-funny dialogue. But it also offers the occasional bit of biting satire and moments of truly inventive comedy. For instance, the Chinese dictator (portrayed by an Asian character in a vintage Coca-Cola promotional short!) intent on buying out America says at one point, "I will force the people of North Dakota and the people of South Dakota to *switch places*! That would be hilarious!" Frequent teletype-style messages on the bottom of the screen helpfully inform us not only of the setting ("Apache Indian Reservation"; "The White House") but, amusingly, the general scenario ("A Curse on the Paleface"; "Another W.T.F Flashback").

More knowing chuckles come from the film's funky blaxploitation-style theme song. "*President Wolfman* features library music, and a score that I composed myself and gathered several talented friends together to record it, which is another cheap way to go…. The song is an homage to blaxploitation themes of the 1970s, which is the aesthetic I chose to go with for the movie. Not that this is a blaxploitation movie by any means, but I'm a huge fan of the energy, vibe and pacing of that genre and thought it would compliment the footage."

Obviously inspired by the deadpan humor of *Airplane!*, many gags involve word play. Says President Wolfman to his political adviser, "I don't listen to poles, Ed, because poles can't talk— they're tall pieces of wood used for hanging telephone wires and escaped bears." When the werewolf stalks a woman in the streets, she shouts, "Stay away, I have a black belt!—and shoes and a bag to match." Unfortunately, Mike Davis is no Jim Abrahams or David Zucker, so much of it falls flat, coming off as more stupid-dumb than stupid-funny (e.g., President: "I can't veto that bill if I'm behind bars." Aide: "I thought you gave up bartending.").

"It looks like a movie you would find in an old shoebox," described Davis, "all dusty and dirty, that your uncle left there, and put in the VCR to see what it was." As such, *President Wolfman* is comprised of 112 different sources: educational films, industrial films, promotional films, public service announcement films, even some Junior Miss pageant footage. Among the most memorable are some oogey dental surgery footage and a real childbirth scene (cops delivering a baby in the back seat of a car in a police training film called *Sudden Birth*). Not everything integrates smoothly, but the sheer number of disparate elements keeps the wackiness factor high and the movie moving briskly. "The script for *President Wolfman*," stated Davis, "must be the following things (in order of importance): entertaining, funny, exciting, scary and shocking." Whether he succeeded or not on all or none of those counts will be a matter of personal taste for each viewer, though it's a safe bet that at least *some* of the throw-them-against-the-wall-and-see-what-sticks gags will generate a smile.

Davis got his start in the stock footage business by piecing together old movie and TV clips to accentuate the pre-taped spots for the *NBC Today* show. For *President Wolfman*, Davis' second "green" movie (the first being 2008's *Sex Galaxy*), he employed a handful of professional voice artists to portray over 100 different characters.

The movie concludes on a clever "meta"-note via a final kicker after the credits roll. Over public service announcement footage of a young African American girl in front of the White House, she says: "The film you have just seen is a representation of what could happen if our current president, John Wolfman, is not reelected for a second term in office. Luckily, there are no such things as werewolves in real life. But China is real. And so are black people. So this November vote to reelect the President and keep a real Wolfman in the White House." Indeed, President Wolfman has *my* vote…

"My sincere hope is that other filmmakers will be inspired to try the same thing, and that a new, recycled, 'green movie' genre will

Lobby card–style ad for the horror-comedy *President Wolfman*, a "green" movie (comprised of public domain and stock footage re-edited with a new soundtrack) about a U.S. president who becomes, well, a wolfman. Inset: Dean Stockwell in footage from *The Werewolf of Washington*.

emerge as a subcategory of a subcategory," concluded Davis about his unique lycanthropic offering. "That is my dream." Striving for that dream, this *President* campaigned through the film festival circuit in 2012 before making its DVD debut in 2014.

With quotes from: "*President Wolfman*: Making of a Green Movie," by Mike Davis; *President Wolfman* DVD commentary track.

Morphology: Political manbeast
Demise: Silver bullet
Full Moon Rating: **½

Project: Metalbeast

(1995; Prism Pictures) Alternate Titles: *Project Metalbeast: DNA Overload*, *Metalbeast* (UK); Director: Alessandro de Gaetano; Producers: Frank Hildebrand, Timothy E. Sabo, Michael Carazza; Screenplay: Alessandro de Gaetano, Timothy E. Sabo; Cinematographer: Tom Callaway. Cast: Kim Delaney, Barry Bostwick, John Marzilli, Musetta Vander, Dean Scofield, Kane Hodder.

THEY WANTED A SOLDIER AS HARD AS STEEL.
THEY CREATED A CREATURE THAT COULD
NOT BE DESTROYED—ad line

A seven-foot-tall metal-skinned werewolf? Indeed, that's the culmination of *Project: Metalbeast*, one of the more enjoyable lycanthropictures of the 1990s (an admittedly fallow decade after the fantastic bumper crop of the 1980s). *Project: Metalbeast* takes its sci-fi/horror hybrid premise and runs with it, stirring covert government programs, cryogenic freezing, super-soldiers, (not-so) mad scientists, classic

Hungarian werewolves and a science-enhanced lycanthrope with metal-based synthetic skin into a hearty stew that should satisfy the appetites of most monster movie fans ... or at least those with a taste for cinematic mac 'n' cheese. And besides, it offers one of the most outrageous ways to kill a werewolf in lycan-history.

Before the credits roll, a teletype message flashes on the screen to nicely sum up the film's premise:

Project: Operation Lycanthropus
Agency: U.S. Military Intelligence
Destination: Carpathian Mountains, Hungary
Objective: Sample werewolf blood
Purpose: Create superior combat agent

It's nice to know that back in 1974 our government was well-versed in all things lycanthropic, and, more importantly, had a concrete plan to exploit werewolves! In any case, two agents steal into a Hungarian castle in search of some werewolf blood. When the creature attacks, Butler (John Marzilli) shoots the monster and then claims the precious bodily fluid sample. Later, at the "U.S. Secret Operations Center," Butler becomes impatient with both his boss, Miller (Barry Bostwick), and the science team assigned to study the monstrous hemoglobin. Butler injects himself with the blood, transforms, and kills a man before Miller puts him down with some silver bullets. After consigning Butler's (now-human-again) body to the cryogenic unit in the building's basement, Miller bides his time for twenty years until the opportunity arises to reactivate "Operation Lycanthropus" in 1994 as "Project Metalbeast" (though such a sobriquet remains merely implied rather than stated outright). It seems that Dr. Anne de Carlo (Kim Delaney, later of TV's *NYPD Blue*) and her team, under the command of Brigadier General Hammond (William G. Clark), are on the cusp of developing a metal-based synthetic skin they hope will aid burn and skin cancer victims. Miller, of course, sees their research in terms of potential weaponry and, after taking charge of Anne's project, assigns Butler's thawed corpse as a "safe" cadaver test subject for the experimental grafts. ("These so-called scientists don't know it yet, but they're going to give you a skin of steel," Miller tells the corpsesickle when no one's around, "You'll be indestructible and under *my* control.") The result: when Anne removes the silver bullets from their subject's body during the grafting procedure, Butler partially revives (though in a confused, near-helpless state). During the night of the full moon, however, Butler recovers fully and transforms into an unstoppable beast, now with skin so hard that even silver bullets can't penetrate it. As it moves through the facility, slaughtering everyone it encounters, Anne and her team must find a way to stop the killcrazed monster. (One word: *bazooka*.)

Project: Metalbeast presents not one, not two, but *three* impressive lycanthropic iterations. The first, a "natural" werewolf (seen in the Hungarian castle and later as the creature Butler becomes back at the base), stands tall as a burly, hair-covered, bipedal beast topped by an imposing wolf's head with deep-set, angry-looking eyes; a muzzle stuffed with oversized fangs; and pointed wolf's ears. The second version is a human-werewolf hybrid when Butler appears stuck in a semitransformed state after having been subdued and returned to the lab. Half his face remains human, while the other half shows wolf-like features in s disturbing Siamese twin/werewolf Janus creation. Later, when the moon rises fully he takes his final shape—that of the Metalbeast. A huge, toothy wolf muzzle; red-glowing orbs for eyes; mottled, rippled, veined skin showing through tufts of dark hair; wicked claws like razor-sharp knives; a massive muscled torso; and long, quilllike hair cascading down the back of its huge frame make the Metalbeast one of the most striking werewolves of this (or any) decade.

Wearing John Buechler's seven-foot-tall metal-skinned werewolf suit was stuntman/actor Kane Hodder (who played Jason in four of the later *Friday the 13th* films). Hodder also served as this *Project's* stunt coordinator, and the creature leaps from rooftops and tosses men aside in an impressive display of strength and agility.

The film takes the usual werewolf lore as a matter of course—full moon transformation, silver bullets—while employing the novel notion of creating wolfmen super-soldiers, and adding the uniqueness of the metallic skin grafts that make this lycanthrope nearly indestructible. It's *The Mad Monster* meets *The Indestructible Man*! Oddly, in one scene the Metalbeast appears momentarily stymied when it faces Anne and sees the crucifix she wears around her neck. Is this a *Satanic* werewolf? (If so, this is the first—and last—inkling, as nothing further develops along these lines.)

Alessandro de Gaetano and Timothy E. Sabo's screenplay tosses out plenty of *other* half-baked ideas strictly for convenience sake. (De Gaetano would carry on this tradition of expediency with his other ill-thought-out werewolf script—for 2010's *Neowolf*.) For instance, when the beast begins its killing rampage through the facility, why does no one think to call for outside help? And why, when Anna decides the military base must be placed in lock-down to keep the Metalbeast from escaping—and pushes a convenient button that automatically does just that—does nobody come from outside to investigate? So much for military efficiency. In any case, this must be the most understaffed army base in history. When the Metalbeast escapes the lab and goes on its (small-scale) rampage, the film's low budget becomes painfully evident, as this massive facility supports only half a dozen scientific staff, one brigadier general, and a couple of MPs.

Fortuitously, General Hammond happens to collect vintage silver dollars—enough to allow the nominal hero, Phillip (Dean Scofield), to melt them down and create silver tips for three *bazooka* shells (since ordinary gunfire won't penetrate the Metalbeast's, er, metalhide).

The careless scripting extends to ill-defined character motivations as well. For example, why does Miller think the creature will be under his control after the team inadvertently revives it, especially given that it had *never* been obedient to him (in fact, he'd had to shoot the monster himself back in 1974)? How does Miller think he'll get away with shooting a brigadier general—which he does, in the knees—and then leaving him *alive*? And Miller forbids the scientists to do anything that might harm the beast, yet he carries a gun filled with silver bullets (perhaps thinking of his encounter 20 years ago—but then again, he expects to "control" the monster).

But the worst sin committed by the script is poor pacing. After the first 20 minutes, which include two well-staged werewolf attacks, the movie bogs down as the scientists butt heads with Miller, fret over various ethical considerations, and try to discover the identity of their test subject—something the viewer already knows—causing interest to flag considerably until the Metalbeast finally rises and rampages. Apart from an oogey skin-grafting sequence, the film's middle third is all verbal confrontations and playing cards (*two* scenes' worth of poker).

Fortunately, as the duplicitous Miller, actor Barry Bostwick (best known as Brad from the cult phenomenon *The Rocky Horror Picture Show*) serves as a breath of fresh air in this stagnant atmosphere. Bostwick's dynamic villain obviously enjoys the secret knowledge he possesses *and* the power he wields over the team of scientists. Bostwick delivers his sometimes acerbic lines with a tongue-in-cheek arrogance in his tone and a humor-appreciating twinkle in his eye. After dictating his new terms to Anne's obviously perturbed team, Miller asks, "Why are you all so glum? You're scientists—isn't this how you people have fun?" Even more than his underhanded actions, Bostwick's glib, condescending attitude makes Miller a villain you love to hate. Later he tells the protesting General, "Here I am trying to make your job easier and all you do is resent me for it. It's just so confusing, isn't it?" with a bemused condescension that speaks volumes about how he considers people mere pawns in his grand game.

Even for Miller's (fitting) demise, Bostwick keeps his haughtiness intact. After the Metalbeast has tossed Miller across the cryogenics chamber several times, the creature hauls him to his feet. Bloodied and battered, Miller, unperturbed, uses his final seconds to arrogantly smooth back his hair one last time—just before the towering monster rams his claws all the way through Miller's torso. If nothing else, you gotta admire this villain's misguided chutzpah.

Director/co-writer Alessandro de Gaetano keeps the film visually appealing with some mobile camerawork and varied set-ups, disguising as well as he can the factory basement and working warehouse settings with atmospheric lighting and multiple camera angles. He also creates an almost Hammer-like Gothic ambiance for the werewolf-in-a-castle prologue. Surprisingly, De Gaetano did very little else in film (making only two other movies—the amusingly titled *Bloodbath in Psycho Town* in 1989 and *Butch Camp* in 1996), though he did co-write/produce another lycanflick in *Neowolf* (2010). De Gaetano ultimately went into advertising, specializing in writing and directing infomercials.

Though restricted by a low budget, hampered by a contrived script, and restrained by an action-less midsection, this *Metalbeast* still manages to break away and stand tall, due to its engaging, tongue-in-cheek human villain; a fantastically imaginative and well-realized werewolf (in three different phases); and ... death by silver-tipped bazooka shell (brilliant!).

Morphology: Seven foot-tall bipedal, wolf-headed manbeast (with skin as tough as steel)
Demise: Silver bazooka shell
Full Moon Rating: ***

Rage of the Werewolf

(1999; Brimstone) Alternate Title: *Planet of the Werewolves*. Director/Cinematographer: Kevin J. Lindenmuth; Producer: Santo Marotta; Screenplay: Kevin Lindenmuth, Santo Marotta. Cast: Santo Marotta, Tom Nondorf, Joe Zaso, Sasha Graham, Debbie Rochon.

> There is no escape...—tagline

Well, that's not exactly true. One *can* escape the *Rage of the Werewolf*—merely by hitting the eject button on the DVD player. And it's a fair bet that many viewers, even diehard werewolf fans, will do just that before the closing credits roll on this shot-on-video micro budgeted mess filmed in and around New York City (including Brooklyn and Coney Island) mostly on weekends from January to March, 1999.

The movie opens on some cheap and unconvincing computer graphics as a narrator (Debbie Rochon) intones: "On August 12, 2001, scientists discovered that a meteor was on a collision course with the Earth. Nuclear weapons were used in an attempt to destroy the deadly meteorite. Although they did not destroy it completely, they did manage to knock it off course, sending it crashing into the Moon's surface. The impact was so powerful that it changed the Moon's orbit, bringing it closer to Earth. The result: The weather was affected, tides increased. But the most astounding thing that happened was the strange biological change certain people underwent..."

Said change? Every full moon sees them transform into werewolves. Apparently (according to a scientist on TV), "a certain percent of the population possesses a latent gene that can cause lycanthropy—a sort of unbalance between human and animal. Now the shifting of the Moon has caused this dormant gene to accelerate." A TV reporter adds that "the disease has been contained to several major cities—Las Vegas, Houston and New York." Consequently, Manhattan has become a werewolf quarantine zone. Two of its denizens, however, "good" brother Jake (Santo Marotta) and "bad" brother Lazlo (Joe Zaso), were "natural" werewolves long before the calamity, meaning they can transform at will. Jake just wants to be left alone to deal with his "curse," while Lazlo intends to exploit his "gift" and create an army of lycanthropes to do his bidding. To this end, Lazlo kidnaps a vampire (Debbie Rochon) in order to create vampire-werewolf hybrids, with Jake out to stop his sinister sibling, culminating in a final lupine-a-lupine battle between the lycan-brothers.

Director/co-writer/videographer Kevin J. Lindenmuth called *Rage of the Werewolf* "sort of a cross between *Escape from New York* and *Planet of the Apes*, but with werewolves instead of apes." And with talk instead of action; dirty back alleys and Brooklyn basements instead of a rubble-strewn Manhattan; and a handful of puma-growling dime store werewolves instead of scores of articulate and convincing simians. *Rage* also comes with flat, grainy camcorder videography; amateurish performances by friends and filmmakers (the movie's producer takes the starring role); and creatures that look like they came from the Halloween aisle at Walmart.

Biting off far more than it can chew, *Rage* is big on ideas but small of scale, meaning the notion of a whole city transforming into lycanthropes under the full moon is realized by a brief montage of one-on-one attacks, and a solitary scene in which a quartet of mismatched werewolves take down a bounty hunter. (Hunters "can get 1000 bucks for a wolf pelt on the black market"; never mind the fact that these werewolves revert back to human form when killed....) Likewise, though there's plenty of talk of vampires descending en mass to reclaim their captured kin, no other bloodsucker ever shows up. And the only way we know that New York has become a huge werewolf prison is that a character *says* so.

Half-speed fight scenes, one cartoonish fire effect, and too many dingy basements and tiny apartments give the film an impoverished feel. While one might forgive a certain cheesiness at this level of camcorder cinema, what *can't* be overlooked is poor pacing. Scene after scene of the two unlikable leads (the morose Jake and his wannabe-werewolf sycophantic friend Ralph) constantly bickering and arguing not only raises the question as to why these two stick together, but why the *viewer* sticks with them as well. Rule number one of home-grown horrors: never *bore* your audience (a rule Lindenmuth and co. appear to have forgotten). Things don't improve via flat-looking VHS videography (with lighting so poor that scenes often become monochromatic); muted sound (with dialogue sometimes drowned out by ambient noise); acting that varies from watch-my-lips to can't-be-bothered; and the sorriest werewolf costumes this side of a trailer park Halloween party.

When fully transformed, the werewolf brothers sport furry rubber-and-plastic bat-faces, with extended muzzles, and what appears to be a large set of mutant Spock ears. Their bodies consist of spook show gorilla costumes, complete with plastic-looking belly and pecs.

The handful of once-a-month werewolves on view wear a variety of cheesy Halloween masks, each more pathetic than the last. Typical is a woman sporting orange hair and a mutant dog muzzle, complete with rubbery teeth and huge bat ears (with fuzzy paws and feet failing to help the goofy image). The dreaded were-vamp fares no better, given the silly, goggle-eyed mutant mask whose rubbery nature shows up all too clearly in close-up.

On the plus side, Lindenmuth stages the film's sole transformation sequence simply but effectively, filmed as a black-and-white flashback. Jake walks in front of a pillar, then emerges on the other side in werewolf form—just like the clever metamorphosis scene in *Werewolf of London* (had that near-classic been shot with a VHS camcorder, that is).

Rage tries to have its were-cake and eat it too. While positing werewolfery as a genetic disorder, it also brings in the classic supernatural "curse" aspect, with Our Hero (Jake), and The Villain (his brother Lazlo) being "natural" werewolves, the result of their father being bitten by a wolfman in the Old Country and passing the curse down to his offspring (though curiously—and inexplicably—their sister didn't inherit the condition). Unlike the newly-minted genetic werewolves (who can be killed just like any regular human), the two brothers are impervious to nearly everything (including bullets) except silver.

When the change first hit Jake, he couldn't control it and transformed only at the full moon. Now, however, he can metamorphose at any time and control his animal instincts (and even talk) when in wolf form. "The werewolf usually has two personalities, sort of like Dr. Jekyll and Mr. Hyde," said producer/co-writer/star Santo Marotta. "One is a good-natured person, the other a savage animal. This makes for a tortured soul and an interesting character different from the usual monsters portrayed in books and movies because the character wants to be rid of this curse. The classic Wolf Man has always been one of my favorite monsters. In doing this film on werewolves it gave me the opportunity to show a different kind of werewolf, someone who can change at will and retain some portion of his human persona and memory, depending upon the degree in which he transforms."

Though often falling back on the crutch of the uninspired by trying to shock with four-letter words, Lindenmuth and Marotta's script at least touches on moral issues when Jake, enraged at the actions of a bounty hunter, tells the man, "We hunt because of the genes in our blood. But you scum of the earth hunt only for greed, sport." And at one point Lazlo, trying to win Jake over to his way of thinking, tells his brother, "You've only begun to see the cruelty of man—the selfishness, the insolence." Lazlo tells him their lycanthropy is a gift: "I don't want a cure; I want to embrace it. I want to lead the others who are like us. I want to crush the humans into the ground until only our kind remain." Still, such brief surface comments come off as little more than self-righteous lip service, and only momentarily distract from the tedium and cheese enveloping them.

The movie stars micro-budget "scream queens" Sasha Graham (a Lindenmuth regular who also faced more furry fiends in 2001's *Blood of the Werewolf*) and Debbie Rochon (*Tromeo and Juliet*). "They were both friendly and very much into the characters they played," said Marotta. "Both actresses were extremely professional, and we had a lot of laughs along the way." Which is more than can be said for the viewer.

Noted Rochon, "I'm a big fan of the horror/sci-fi/fantasy genre, ever since I was a little girl, and I enjoy working with 'creatures'! You just simply do the best job possible under the circumstances that are presented to you. If a movie is very rushed and doesn't have the script to showcase your talents or range, then you just go with the flow and do your best and that's it. I always try and enjoy myself regardless." Which, again, is more than can be said for the viewer, as the *Rage* engendered here is likely to be anger felt at having wasted 90 minutes of one's life.

With quotes from: "Interview with Santo Marotta," by Brimstone Media Productions, Lindenmuth.com; "Debbie Rochon: An A+ B-Queen," Filmthreat.com; *The Independent Film Experience*, by Kevin J. Lindenmuth.

Morphology: Shaggy, big-eared, bat-faced, gorilla-bodied bipeds
Demise: For most, any old method will do; for the villain, decapitation, with the still-living head and body finally destroyed by a hand grenade
Full Moon Rating: *

The Rats Are Coming! The Werewolves Are Here!

(1972; Constitution Film) Director/Screenplay/Cinematographer: Andy Milligan; Producer: William Mishkin. Cast: Hope Stansbury, Jackie Skarvelis, Noel Collins, Joan Ogden, Douglas Phair, Ian Innes, Berwick Kaler.

A GRUESOME TALE OF MAN-EATING RATS
and BLOOD-SUCKING WEREWOLVES!—poster

When the soft-core sexploitation subgenre turned hard in the late 1960s and early '70s (with the arrival of such pictures as 1969's *I Am Curious Yellow* and 1970's *Sexual Freedom in Denmark*), low-rent filmmakers who made their professional home on New York's notorious 42nd street needed to change with the times. Director-writer-cinematographer-editor Andy Milligan, a fringe player among fringe players, declined to go the triple-X route and so turned his sweaty sights towards horror and gore. *The Ghastly Ones* was the first of his $1.98 homegrown horror productions, quickly followed by *Torture Dungeon* and *Bloodthirsty Butchers* (both filmed in 1969 but not released until 1970). Milligan would pay his actors $25 a day, film in his own run-down Victorian-style home in the wilds of Staten Island, make the costumes himself (using his "Raffine" pseudonym), and shoot on short ends with a 25-year-old 16mm newsreel camera. The question is not why his pictures are so bad, but why they are watchable at all. And the answer is that Milligan's movies contain a raw, often perverse energy that's never conventional, as he wears his misogynistic ("Women are basically monsters," he claimed), misanthropic, conflicted heart on his sleeve. (By all accounts Milligan had a horrible childhood and loathed his mother, angrily shouting out "Bitch!" at her funeral; such anti-family vehemence frequently breaks through in his films.)

Taking his ancient Auricon camera to London in late 1968, Milligan contracted with a wealthy young British swinger named Leslie Elliot to make movies for Elliot's Compton Cinema Club, a series of small, private theaters that showed uncensored films to its members. But after two productions, Milligan fell out with Elliot's father (who turned out to be the money behind the operation) and was on his own. Milligan subsequently contacted low-budget producer/distributor William Mishkin, for whom he'd made a number of movies back in New York, and ended up making three more pictures in England, one of which was *Curse of the Full Moon*, the tale of a dysfunctional aristocratic family in the 19th century who harbors a deadly secret. Upon its release in 1972 (over two years after it was filmed)—on a double-bill with Milligan's *The Man with Two Heads*—the film had become *The Rats Are Coming! The Werewolves Are Here!* The first part of the ludicrous title came as an afterthought when Mishkin deemed the movie too short (and too dull). Milligan hastily shot a few additional scenes back in New York of leading lady Hope Stansbury (who also starred in Milligan's *other* werewolf film, *Blood*) interacting with some rodents in order to cash in on the then-current popularity of *Willard* (she even names two of her rats "Ben" and "Willard"!). "Andy couldn't get any gray rats," recalled cast member Eric Concklin, "so he bought white rats and sprayed them with gray Krylon paint. Of course, the rats didn't like that very much, so they started licking it off as we were shooting. By mid-afternoon they were white again, so he sold them back to the pet store." The ploy failed to inject much more than some additional confusion and one stomach-churning scene in which Stansbury's character tortures and mutilates a mouse *for real* (when Stansbury refused to participate in this, Milligan hired a teenage boy to don her dress, and then shot just his hands as he brutally stabbed and hammered a nail into the live animal).

In 19th century England a young woman, Diana Mooney (Jackie Skarvelis), returns to her family estate with both a new husband and a medical degree. The bedridden patriarch (who claims to be 180 years old thanks to "a formula he discovered when he was a doctor") refuses to sanction his daughter's surprise marriage, and runs roughshod over the rest of the household, which includes two sons (one of which "has the instincts of an animal" and must be kept chained in his room), and daughters Phoebe (Joan Ogden) and Monica (Hope Stansbury) (whose hobbies appear to be torture and murder). With tensions boiling over, the family "curse" finally manifests itself when nearly the entire household transforms into werewolves during the full moon.

Filled with talk, talk, and more talk—much of it about horrible childhoods, sibling rivalries, and family poisonings—delivered by venomous and hate-filled characters, *The Rats Are Coming! The Werewolves Are Here!* is an ugly film filled with ugly characters saying ugly things. Worse, it's also a boring one. Nothing much happens (apart from two poorly-staged murders) until the final ten minutes. All the mysterious palaver about the Mooneys' "condition" ("Our family is like no other family, as you know"; "This family is doomed"; etc.) and coy references to the full moon inspires tedium rather than suspense, since the movie's very title gives the game away before the first desultory frame unspools.

Milligan shoots the endless dialogue scenes (which eat up most of the picture's running time) in static medium shots and close-ups. The constant talk and a general lack of eventfulness makes it seem like a stilted stage play (which is how Milligan got his showbiz start—by

The Rats Are Coming! The Werewolves Are Here! **And the Audience Has Left (if they're prudent). Two years later, gutter auteur Andy Milligan revisited the lycanthropic theme with** *Blood* **(sans rats this time).**

producing avant-garde plays in New York bars and coffee houses). But the brief and infrequent "action" set-pieces (the few murders and the climactic werewolf melee) have Milligan bobbing and weaving with his hand-held camera to such an extent that it not only obscures the action but induces seasickness.

Milligan purportedly made *Rats* for a mere $18,000, but one wonders where even *that* much went, as it doesn't appear onscreen. Though Milligan shot on location at a large country house and stately grounds, he rarely takes his camera outside. And he tightly frames his actors—sometimes uncomfortably so—rather than taking advantage of his sumptuous surroundings. The harsh, grainy 16mm photography, and the melodramatic (and often intrusive) canned library music, generates a cheap and unpleasant atmosphere. Milligan's idea of a tracking shot is to simply walk in front of his moving actress, which gives a herky-jerky quality to the queasy image. And the scene in which Monica attacks her "friend" with a cleaver looks like it was edited with one ("choppy" indeed). *Rats* is the kind of shoestring "period" production in which you can hear car horns honking in the background. While admittedly unusual in its warped sensibilities, *Rats* is still strictly home-movie stuff.

Though decked out in proper clothes and elegant gowns (some courtesy of Milligan himself, an accomplished dressmaker and former owner of a New York dress shop), this cursed family can't hide its beastliness, as the venomous and hate-filled characters constantly engage in verbal (and sometimes even physical) abuse (with Monica torturing her mentally-challenged, chained-up brother with hot candle wax and a belt!), so that the final revelation of lycanthropy seems an almost natural outgrowth of their all-pervasive inner bestiality. Here werewolfery becomes the brutal icing on this dysfunctional family cake.

But it takes 75 minutes for Milligan to finally tip his lycanthropic hand—via another overlong dialogue sequence in which the verbose patriarch explains to his new son-in-law: "Three centuries ago my great-grandmother was bitten by an animal. This animal was afflicted with a dreaded disease which was passed on to all members of the family through the birth of each new child." That's it—explanation (and exploration) over.

The first glimpse of a werewolf comes in the last 10 minutes—and then passes so quickly as to barely register. And forget any transformation; these werewolves metamorphose on a dime, simply turning around to reveal a fake nose, a few clumps of hair stuck to their faces, and a set of oversized plastic fangs, with their hands ending in long press-on fingernails. During the grand lycan-finale, one by one the family members all transform and then attack and kill one another, with newly minted silver bullets dispatching the last lycan standing. It all sounds more exciting than Milligan's abrupt staging and chaotic camerawork makes of it, however. And, tellingly, the film closes on an old woman blathering on about baby names!

Rats marks the only time over the course of 25 shoestring productions that Milligan appeared in one of his films, here playing a rather effete gunsmith who sells the heroine a pistol (anachronistically looking like a weapon that should be in James Bond's hand rather than one from the 19th century) who drones on and on about nothing at all in order to extend the running time. Milligan died of AIDS in 1991 at age 62 in California (where he'd been living since the mid–1980s). Destitute at the time of his death, he was buried in an unmarked grave somewhere in Los Angeles.

With quotes from: *The Ghastly One: The Sex-Gore Netherworld of Filmmaker Andy Milligan*, by Jimmy McDonough.

Morphology: Sparsely made-up, well-dressed wolfmen (and women)
Demise: Silver bullets (and fellow lycanthropes)
Full Moon Rating: *

Red Riding Hood

(1989; Cannon; US/Israel) Alternate Title: *Cannon Movie Tales: Red Riding Hood*. Director: Adam Brooks; Producers: Yoram Globus, Menahem Golan; Screenplay: Carole Lucia Satrina; Cinematographers: Yuri Neyman, Ye'ehi Shnegur. Cast: Amelia Shankley, Isabella Rossellini, Craig T. Nelson, Rocco Sisto, Helen Glazary.

Rediscover the magic—tagline

This first cinematic "Little Red Riding Hood" adaptation to feature a *shapeshifting* Big Bad Wolf (i.e., a werewolf) was part of Cannon Films' *Movie Tales* series—"lavish, feature-length new versions of the world's best-loved storybook classics" (as their promotional materials dubbed this set of nine movies). But after their preceding fairy tale entry, *Rumpelstiltskin* (1987), tanked at the box office, the studio opted to forego a U.S. theatrical release for *Red Riding Hood* and sent it straight to video in 1989. Though indeed "feature-length," one would be hard-pressed to apply the term "lavish" to this small-scale, impoverished production. Filled with cut-rate costumes, high school–level sets, and simple, cheesy songs, *Red Riding Hood* looks more like a tired community theater production than a "lavish new version" of the storybook classic. Producing partners Menahem Golan and Yoram Globus no doubt spent most of their budget on bringing the film's two recognizable "names" to film at their G.G. Israel Studios in Jerusalem in 1987. Unfortunately, TV stalwart Craig T. Nelson (*Poltergeist*) and international actress Isabella Rossellini (daughter of actress Ingrid Bergman and director Roberto Rossellini, and star of films like *Blue Velvet* and *Death Becomes Her*) leave little impression with their walk-through performances. The miscast Nelson's banal, everyday delivery and general non-presence makes for a very poor villain in a role that simply cries out for some blackguard bombast. When he tiredly breaks into his solo musical number "I'm Good at Being Bad" ("It's sweet how sour I am"), one cringes not only at how poorly he talk-sings through the song but at just how off-base his claim appears to be, as the milquetoast TV star is *terrible* at being bad. And director Adam Brooks, known more as a screenwriter (*Practical Magic*, *Bridget Jones: The Edge of Reason*) than director, exhibits little inventiveness on this, his sophomore directorial turn.

Set in medieval times, *Red Riding Hood* centers on the carefree and fearless young Linet (Amelia Shankley), daughter of the local lord, Percival (Craig T. Nelson). Percival went off to war and has not been heard from in seven years. During his absence his conniving twin brother Godfrey (Nelson again) has become the land's feared and hated ruler. Obsessed with Percival's beautiful wife, Lady Jean (Isabella Rossellini), Godfrey, with the aid of his supernatural spy Dagger (Rocco Sisto), who can transform himself into a wolf, intends to forcibly make Lady Jean his queen while doing away with the pesky Linet, the one person in the land he cannot intimidate.

Linet becomes "Red Riding Hood" after her grandmother (and local "healer") Nanny Bess gives her a magical red cloak that will "keep her from harm." This cloak comes in handy when Dagger impersonates a supposedly sick Nanny Bess at her cottage to try and fool Linet ("My, what big teeth you have, Grandma") before literally eating her up (off-screen, of course). Fortunately, Linet's father Percival has finally returned that very day and races to the cottage to cut open the wolf—who lolls half-delirious on the bed, his belly distended with his recent meal—and free a still-intact Linet, who was indeed "kept from harm" by her enchanted scarlet cloak.

To stretch out the slow-rolling, paper-thin story, every few minutes there's an awful song or sappy ballad (seven in all), with only one approaching even mediocre standards. When Linet meets the wolf Dagger (in human guise) in the woods, they engage in an amusingly ironic duet called "Never Talk to Strangers." In it, Linet takes the "pro" and Dagger the "con" side of the issue. "These days wickedness is on the rise / Things could happen to a kid your size," sings the wolf-in-human's-clothing; while the smiling Linet warbles back, "If you never talk to Strangers / You may never make a friend / And a friendly-looking stranger / Is no danger…" Well, we know how *that* one turns out.

In addition to the subpar production values, amateurish songs, and uninspired performances, *Red Riding Hood* falls short in the werewolf department as well. It begins promisingly enough, with a four-legged wolf seemingly stalking Linet through the woods. But after being all-too-easily scared away by an approaching villager, we see that this "wolf" looks like nothing more than your average German Shepherd. We soon learn, however, about this canine's diabolical nature. Back at Godfrey's castle, the wolf rests on a divan. Godfrey stares at it and pointedly intones, "Wolf into man, fast as you can"—and a still shot of the wolf dissolves into a still shot of a reclining man. Though cheap and obvious, this cut-rate "transformation" does lead into an intriguing revelation about lycanthropy, when Godfrey tells his subservient man-wolf, "I gave up my heart and soul for you—to spy for me, to do my will, to kill—the power of the wolf," the implication being that Godfrey has sold his soul to the Devil to acquire this werewolf familiar. Later, a villager confirms that Godfrey has indeed employed "black magic." This linking of lycanthropy to Satanism and witchcraft harkens back to the medieval legends about werewolves, though making the manbeast a servant of a black magic practitioner adds a unique wrinkle to the standard myth. And like pre–Hollywood werewolves, neither silver nor the full moon comes into play here, with Dagger changing from man to wolf and back at will (even without the benefit of Godfrey's "Wolf into man..." ditty).

The true nature of this beast-man remains frustratingly vague, however, with it never made clear whether Dagger began as a man who was given the power of the wolf, or started as a wolf and was given human faculties and form. He may even be a magical being conjured up out of whole cloth. In any case, Dagger does disappointingly little—as either wolf or man—besides skulk about spying for his master. At one point he even takes a pratfall into the mud while trying to peer in a window. Consequently, this clumsy werewolf becomes neither imposing nor frightening.

Dagger does receive the film's best line, however. When Godfrey admits that he can no longer feel love, he asks Dagger if *he* loves anything. Dagger wistfully answers, "I love to run with the pack under a full moon. I love a romantic dinner by the sea." He then drops his thoughtful tone to acerbically observe, "The two don't seem to go together, though." This self-aware wolf also suffers a moment of existential angst when he admits to himself "the miserable creature I've become. I don't know myself anymore. I'm not really an animal, not really a man." But the script drops this tortured tack as quickly as it picks it up, and Dagger simply goes about his business, never to be troubled again. As Dagger, Rocco Sisto (*The Sopranos* TV series) shows more spark than the rest of the cast put together, so it remains a real shame that the potentially fascinating facets of his character remain undeveloped and unexplored.

The final sequence with Dagger remains the film's single most disturbing image—that of the half-transformed werewolf lolling on the bed after having consumed Linet. The oversized dog-body, its belly swollen and undulating, topped by a half-human head (all bushy beard, dog nose, ridged eyebrows, pointy ears and fangs), though not a particularly convincing sight, still inspires a shudder nonetheless, particularly in contrast to the banality of every other scene in the movie.

Refreshingly—and perhaps surprisingly, given its target audience—the film doesn't shy away from the gruesome aspect of the classic fairy tale: the rescue of Red from *inside* the wolf's belly! Though presented as a bloodless, er, operation, Percival's slitting open of the (were)wolf's body (resulting in the death of the lycanthrope) and the subsequent emergence of Linet still remains a grotesque and disturbing concept. Unfortunately, there's little else to recommend in this bland and ironically toneless (given the plethora of singing) take on "Little Red Riding Hood."

Morphology: Average-looking German Shepherd
Demise: Common hunting knife
Full Moon Rating: *½

Red Riding Hood

(2006; 20th Century–Fox) Director: Randal Kleiser; Producers: Steve Austin, Jonathan Bogner; Screenplay: Timothy Dolan (based on a story by The Brothers Grimm); Cinematographer: David Stump. Cast: Laine Kazan, Henry Cavill, Morgan Thompson, Sam Stone, Daniel Roebuck, Cassandra Peterson, David Kaufman, Debi Mazar, Joey Fatone.

A Classic Tale with Some Modern Magic!—tagline

Originally envisaged as a 16mm soundstage production, the experimental *Red Riding Hood* was ultimately shot in HD at director Randal Kleiser's (*Grease*, *The Blue Lagoon*, *Big Top Pee-wee*) suggestion, breaking new ground in utilizing digital technology, including the then-untested Viper Filmstream camera. Recalled production executive Jack Serino, "We shot 18 days on a stage. We never had locations. We basically shot the Redwood forest in the middle of the San Fernando Valley."

A babysitting grandma (Laine Kazan) reads the story of "Little Red Riding Hood" to siblings Claire (Morgan Thompson) and Matt (Sam Stone) from a magical book of fairy tales—a book that changes the story according to the reader's whims (making the Big Bad Wolf a werewolf, for instance) and incorporates the listeners into the tale. Striking close to home for the twelve-year-old Claire, who dons heavy makeup in anticipation of sneaking out to join her friends at the mall, Red, reads Grandma, "was beginning to go through changes, and see the world differently. Her parents still treated her like a little girl; no one seemed to understand her." Red's mother sends her off on her bike to her ailing Granny's house with some chicken soup, admonishing her to stay out of the woods because of the wolf lurking there. Red's response: "Mother, please; the wolf is just an urban legend made up by adults to scare little kids." The defiant Red takes a short cut (conveniently labeled "short cut") through the forest, where she encounters a strange man (Joey Fatone) who runs off when a hunter (named, obviously, "Hunter") approaches. Hunter (Henry Cavill) tells Red, "He was a werewolf. But he could transform himself into the human form of anyone he had eaten." Hunter knows this because he saw the werewolf kill both his parents, and has been on the beast's trail ever since. Though skeptical, Red is smitten with the handsome Hunter. She soon becomes lost in the woods, however, and must be rescued by her little brother Rusty. The pair finally arrives at Grandma's house, but the werewolf (who has been consuming everyone from a TV reporter to a Boy Scout troupe) has beaten them there and gobbled up Granny. Hijinks ensue until Red finally uses the silver bullet Hunter had given her to put a stop to the werewolf's rampage.

A comical, self-aware, kid-friendly musical version of the classic fairy tale, *Red Riding Hood* creates an at-times surreal artificiality through a backdrop that mixes music video sensibilities with video game visuals for its tale of burgeoning adolescence and listen-to-your-parents morality. (According to camera operator Sean Fairburn, the production utilized "computer generated sets and backgrounds or composited, location backgrounds for almost every shot in the film.") Though it doesn't always work, the film offers enough novelty and points of interest to make it worth a look—especially for lovers of lycan-cinema.

Lycanthro-wise, the movie presents the clever idea of having the werewolf take on the form of whomever it has eaten last. To illustrate the point, director Kleiser first introduces the beast-man as a pair of wolfish, clawed feet walking through the grass which morph into brown shoes mid-stride. "The werewolf lived inside a big redwood tree," reads Grandma. "When he was alone he'd take on his wolf form," intriguingly implying that werewolves are more wolf that becomes human than human that becomes wolf. The werewolf's sparse appearance—pointy ears, long sideburns, goatee, bushy eyebrows, dog nose, delicate fangs, and hairy, clawed hands and feet, all wrapped up in a long leather coat, frilly green tuxedo shirt, and striped trousers—captures the creature's beastliness without making him too frightening. While disappointing for a horror film, it's perhaps appropriate for a fairy tale. This werewolf not only talks, it sings, offering up a somewhat disturbing (given the circumstances) rendition of the sexually-charged sixties Sam the Sham and the Pharaohs classic "Little Red Riding Hood," as well as a food-centric number called "I Need Her Now" that features a colorful, surreal montage of the wolf imagining cooking up Little Red in a variety of scrumptious dishes—Red Meatballs, Red pizza, Red cake, Red turkey, etc.

Amusingly, the wolf frequently argues with himself, with Kleiser showing his human form schizophrenically squabbling with his werewolf half in a comical visual representation of the lycanthrope's dichotomous nature. "The curse of the werewolf," complains his human side, "is that no matter how much you eat, you're never satisfied." "We wouldn't be cursed," shoots back his wolf-half, "if you hadn't gypped a gypsy fortune teller out of five bucks."

At one point Red queries Hunter, "Hey, I saw *The Wolf Man* on TV, and doesn't there have to be a full moon for him to turn into a wolf?" Hunter responds with, "That's only in the movies. A werewolf can transform at will. It can also assume the appearance of its last victim." And when the werewolf eats said victim, his mouth expands to impossibly large (CGI) proportions as he lunges forward. Though not particularly realistic looking, it remains appropriately disquieting.

Hunter tells Red, "Silver is toxic to a werewolf. Killing it is the only way to save the souls of the people it's consumed." And at film's end, when Red does just that, the werewolf explodes to reveal all those said souls, now returned to life, in its place (and ready for the grand musical finale).

The uneven but intermittently clever script by Timothy Dolan (*Trailer Park of Terror*) references other fairy tales as well. For instance, crossing a bridge, Red must face not the "Three Billy Goats Gruff" but the "Three Ashleys"—a trio of trash-talkin' bully-girls. Grandma watches occasional TV news bulletins, labeled "Wolf-Watch One," that announce the tally of "the Timberland Wolf's" victims (at one point reaching a total of 23).

The two juvenile leads, though sometimes overly cute, come off as likable enough, and Joey Fatone (formerly of the band NSYNC) appears personable and amusing as the gregarious, schizophrenic werewolf. "Real sorry for eating everybody in sight and all, but if I had to do it all over again…. I'd use more salt," he mocks deliciously. Cassandra Peterson (better known as sexy horror hostess "Elvira, Mistress of the Dark") cameos as Hunter's mother in a brief flashback sequence, though she only delivers a couple of lines before the werewolf reaches out and pulls her into his mouth "in one gulp" in a cartoonish, creepy effect.

Disappointingly, the "what big eyes you have" climax falls flat, not only because it comes in the form of a semi-rap duet(!), but because the atmospheric lighting and danger-infused set-up is undercut by speeded-up photography right out of the Keystone Cops, goofy sound effects, and Three Stooges–like slapstick (with Red shoving an electric toothbrush up the werewolf's nose, while Rusty sticks a plunger onto his face). It does offer up this amusing exchange, however:

RED: "You're not my grandma!"
WEREWOLF: "Duh."
RED: "Where is she?!"
WEREWOLF: "I'm a werewolf. You do the math."
RED: "You ate my grandma?" That's so *rude*."
WEREWOLF: "You're tellin' me. She gave me gas."

Eight different musical numbers periodically bring the proceedings to a screeching halt, though some are blessedly short. Much of the more overt comedy devolves into silliness, illustrated by Hunter's silver bullets fired from his blunderbuss-like rifle taking a slow, wobbly trajectory that the werewolf can simply sidestep.

Beyond the sometimes puerile comedy and tedious musical numbers, *Red Riding Hood* feels downright uncomfortable at times, given the cusp-of-pubescence status of its female lead. Kleiser, no stranger to the sensitive topic of underage love/sexuality (he was a veteran of *The Blue Lagoon*, after all), doesn't shy away from the classic tale's sexual awakening metaphor, having Red sing a romantic song about the far-too-old-for-her Hunter, and scampering about in a provocative short skirt and red go-go boots.

In a case of six-degrees-of-werewolf-separation, Kleiser credits actress and teacher Nina Foch with shaping his career. "When I took Nina Foch's directing class at USC way back in 1965," said Kleiser, "it was the most amazing class I had ever taken and, in retrospect, I'd say it still is the most valuable film-school course I have taken…. There are so many things of value that actors and directors can learn, and so much knowledge to be accrued from her classes and her teachings." Nina Foch had played a cinema lycanthrope way back in 1944 in *Cry of the Werewolf* (as well as facing one down in *Return of the Vampire* in 1943).

If you can look past the general goofiness and silly songs, *Red Riding Hood* becomes a sometimes imaginative, intermittently amusing, and mildly entertaining take on the classic tale of childhood innocence and burgeoning adulthood. If you can't, then it's just an uncomfortable bore.

With quotes from: "Red Riding Hood," by Jack Serino, *Highdef*; "*Red Riding Hood* HD Tech Report," by Sean Fairburn, *Highdef*; "The Master of On-Screen Chemistry: Randal Kleiser," by Shannon Luster and Sharon Jordan, *Cultscoop Magazine*.

Morphology: Talky wolfman
Demise: Silver bullet
Full Moon Rating: **

Red Riding Hood

(2011; Warner Bros.) Director: Catherine Hardwicke; Producers: Jennifer Davisson Killoran, Leonardo DiCaprio, Julie Yorn; Screenplay: David Leslie Johnson; Cinematographer: Mandy Walker. Cast: Amanda Seyfried, Gary Oldman, Billy Burke, Shiloh Fernandez, Max Irons, Virginia Madsen, Lukas Haas, Julie Christie.

BELIEVE THE LEGEND. BEWARE THE WOLF—ad line

"Little Red Riding Hood" meets *Twilight*? On the surface, one could be forgiven for expecting such a travesty here, given the premise of a teenage girl torn between two hunky young men in a supernatural milieu, *and* the fact the film is helmed by original *Twilight* (2008) director Catherine Hardwicke. Then, of course, there was the early publicity promoting it as a "Gothic retelling" of the fairy tale with "a teenage love triangle at its center." Fortunately, *Red Riding Hood* proved to be far more than "Little Red *Twilight* Hood," as it takes a darker and thankfully more adult turn (despite its PG-13 mandate). And it doesn't hurt that this time Hardwicke had a few *real* actors to work with (including Oscar nominee Gary Oldman and Oscar winner Julie Christie) rather than a handful of *Tiger Beat* cover models (and it goes without saying that lead Amanda Seyfried is miles above one-note Kristen Stewart).

Seyfried plays Valerie, a headstrong girl living in a medieval village "on the edge of the Dark Forest." Though she loves woodcutter Peter (Shiloh Fernandez), her mother has betrothed her to wealthy young blacksmith Henry (Max Irons, son of Jeremy). But just as Valerie determines to run away with Peter, the murder of her younger sister sends the village into a frenzy. For twenty years they've had an uneasy truce with a werewolf in the forest, offering sacrifices of livestock to the beast every full moon. But now things have changed, and the village priest sends for Father Solomon (Gary Oldman), who "has destroyed werewolves and witches throughout the kingdom." The arrogant Solomon locks down the town and sows discord among its inhabitants, turning neighbor against neighbor. "The wolf lives here in this village," he announces. "The real killer can be your neighbor, your best friend, even your wife." With Valerie seemingly targeted by the werewolf, can the obsessive Solomon and his soldiers defeat the beast or at least uncover the werewolf's true identity before it decimates the populace—or the villagers decide to sacrifice Valerie to the monster?

Recounted Hardwicke, "I didn't figure out who the Wolf was when I read [David Leslie Johnson's script]. I liked the un-peeling of the secrets and the lies in the town…. If I could really keep that mystery of who the Wolf was until the end, and create that feeling that you are suspicious of your friends and family, and have that growing paranoia, I thought that would be a fun challenge, and also relevant to current day." Hardwicke does just that, and with great aplomb. Building on Johnson's (*Orphan* [2009], *Wrath of the Titans* [2012]) clever screenplay, the film becomes an involving mystery as to the identity of this Wolf in sheep's clothing.

Hardwicke brings the visual style and sense of atmosphere she displayed on *Twilight* (one of that puerile picture's few assets) to bear fully on this dark fairy tale. Valerie's obligatory red cloak (an impressive garment made by her grandmother), for instance, stands out in symbolic contrast to the stark snowy landscapes. High angle shots and close camera work (during a tense chase scene, for instance) contrast with sweeping vistas captured in swooping movements. "From the beginning, we take the viewers over with the helicopter shot and I wanted to add the castle and the town, so that you feel like you're really in a different kind of world," said Hardwicke. "It was important to control the sunlight and the clouds, and just the feeling and the mood, to surround you in that world." And surround us it does, enveloping the viewer in the near-claustrophobic feel of the beleaguered village and forbidding woodland.

Enhancing the atmosphere is the impressive medieval hamlet itself, all rough-hewn logs and wood planks encircled by an imposing wall, courtesy of production designer Tom Sanders (an Oscar nominee for *Bram Stoker's Dracula* and *Saving Private Ryan*). Hardwicke, a former production designer herself, explained, "I wanted to create a sense that the paranoia the town feels from being menaced by this beast for 20 years is expressed in the architecture." To this end the houses are raised on stilts with ladders leading to their doors, while their rooftops and exterior walls are studded with protective spikes. Even the church itself reflects the hope-and-terror dichotomy under which these people live, with one half of its door painted with an angel, while the other half sports a wolf-headed devil. In the forest, the huge trees, often leaning at ominous angles, sport what look like massive thorns rather than living tree limbs.

Though the monster appears in only three sequences, its presence permeates the film from the beginning. Constant reminders of the terror the Wolf holds over the village—from the dialogue that often references it, to the actions of the villagers (even during a celebration they don pig and sheep masks and jovially play the parts of victims), to the church decoration—the beast is always felt, always near.

This aura of fear and the notion of appeasement ("we sacrifice our best livestock every full moon") strikes an almost genetic chord, recalling the time when early man not only feared the predator but turned that terror into veneration, making the beasts that preyed upon them into deities—creatures to be feared but also to be *appeased*. Deifying the predator was a way to assuage the fear by creating the illusion of control (if we sacrifice to it, it will not harm us), and this bleeds over into *Red Riding Hood*, the sacrifices inflating the monster's presence by turning it, in the eyes of the villagers, into a near-unstoppable dark demi-god.

Red Riding Hood's treatment of its werewolf reflects the intelligence of its script, adding novelty to its lycan-lore, but with purpose. One line of dialogue, for instance, establishes the ground rules: "We know the weaknesses of the werewolf—it can't come out in daylight; it can't step on holy ground; and there's silver." The "holy ground" restriction not only plays an important part in the scenario later on, it ties the werewolf to the medieval belief of lycanthropy being an offshoot of witchcraft, and Satan himself. (Father Solomon being a witch hunter, as well as werewolf killer, only reinforces this connection.)

Screenwriter Johnson also cleverly incorporates one of the best known werewolf folk tales into Solomon's backstory. Upon his arrival in the town, Solomon tells the celebrating villagers (who think they've killed the beast) that the wolf head their hunting party has mounted on a stick belongs to an ordinary gray wolf rather than *the* Wolf. He relates how werewolves revert to human form after death, and as proof he tells the spellbound revelers how years ago he survived his first werewolf encounter by hacking off the beast's front paw, causing it to flee. Upon returning home, however, Solomon found his wife "with a bloody rag wrapped around her wrist." And in place of the severed wolf's paw he had retrieved and placed in a box was a severed human hand…

Adding further elaboration on lycanthropy, Solomon explains the importance of the "Blood Moon." "The Red Planet," he explains, "converges with the Moon once every 13 years. This is the only time a new werewolf can be created. During the week of the Blood Moon the werewolf may pass his curse on with a single bite." Consequently, "During a normal full moon the wolf bite will kill you, but during a Blood Moon your very souls are in danger." This novel notion cleverly addresses the practical question (so often ignored or glossed over): If its bite is so contagious, why is the world not overrun with werewolves (and vampires, for that matter)?

This beast can talk—sort of. Coming face to face with Valerie after rampaging through the village, the monster stares at the frightened girl and in a low voice growls, "You can't escape from me…. I'm coming back for you before the Blood Moon wanes." Though her equally terrified friend Roxanne hears only growls, Valerie hears the creature's words/thoughts (the reason for this becomes clear at the end during the Big Reveal). In any case, the werewolf retains its full human faculties while in beast form, targeting its victims with deadly accuracy, thereby making it an even more terrifying figure than simply some supernatural animal.

Huge (twice the size of an ordinary wolf), with bright yellow eyes, coarse pitch-black fur, and a snarling muzzle filled with gleaming fangs, this impressive beast runs, leaps and springs with amazing speed. At one point two soldiers throw ropes around its powerful neck, only to be tossed into the air with a shake of its head. The convincing CGI creature animation matches the efficacy of the wolves in the *Twilight* films (this technical prowess being that series' sole outstanding accomplishment), though with the improvement of a far more threatening—and imposing—appearance and demeanor.

Unlike the oversized teen-friendly wolves of the *Twilight* films, "the [*Red Riding Hood*] wolf does some pretty nasty shit," points out Hardwicke. "Our wolf is different [from the *Twilight* wolves]. He only comes out at night, so you don't see him in the day, and he's ferocious; he's not like the good guy you can go up and pet…. He has some pretty good attack scenes." Indeed he does. Springing forward, its blink-of-an-eye passing leaves slashed corpses in its wake. Though the actual bloodshed is kept to a minimum (as dictated by the studio-mandated PG-13 rating), with one severed hand being the sole disembodied representative of its violent potential, this wolf is lethal.

A near-political subtext adds another layer to this already rich confection, personified by the ruthless Solomon who determines to discover the beast's human identity at all costs, trampling on the villagers' freedoms ("Your homes will be searched, your secrets brought to light") and even their very lives (torturing one simpleton to death for "conniving with demons" because "his speech is twisted" and he enjoys card tricks). "Look for the signs," he urges them, "isolation, witchcraft, the black arts, abnormal behavior, strange smells." He sows the seeds of discord among the villagers, with neighbor suspecting neighbor, friend suspecting friend, even lover suspecting lover. With the Wolf having told Valerie things echoed by those closest to her, at times she even suspects her own Grandmother and her true love, Peter. Solomon turns his quest into a literal witch-hunt, showing how easily fear turns to suspicion, which turns to betrayal, which turns to unreasoning action. Torturing one poor soul by tossing him into a great iron pot shaped like an elephant, a fire burning beneath its belly, he sanctimoniously announces, "We do this for the greater good." The ends justify the means, while "the means of pleasing God is sometimes flawed." Indeed—at least for those who let their arrogance and self-righteousness blind them to their own humanity. Here Solomon almost becomes worse than the Wolf, the cure turning out worse than the disease. Such a metaphor solidifies when seen through the fear-clouded lens of the post–9/11 climate. As Hardwicke observes, "Father Solomon pits everybody against each other, kind of like Homeland Security coming to town. You know, 'Turn in your neighbors!' 'Suspect everyone!' So

Far more than just a teen-targeted *Twilight* take, the 2011 *Red Riding Hood* offers up a dark, adult, lycan-heavy interpretation of the classic fairy tale.

you're looking at everything from the point of view of every person, through new eyes, imagining, 'Could he be the killer?' And every word they say, you hear echoes of them later on in what the Wolf says."

The clever screenplay keeps the viewer guessing right along with the characters (even Valerie, who suspects first one person, then another), and concludes the absorbing mystery with a truly surprising reveal in the final 10 minutes, one that falls in perfectly with previous events.

The ending shows the resourcefulness and intelligence and strength of the lead character—*without* making her into a standard Hollywood Rambo-ette performing all manner of impossible action heroine feats. Unfortunately, Hardwicke's *Twilight* sensibilities got the better of her at this point and she didn't stop there, instead choosing to continue on into a maudlin, faux-romantic/tragic epilogue (complete with ill-advised voiceover narration) that gives the well-crafted Valerie character an unwanted Bella-esque sheen. It's an unfortunate misstep in an otherwise surefooted production.

Shot in Vancouver, Canada, from July to September 2010 on a budget of $42 million, and released towards the beginning of 2011, *Red Riding Hood* kicked off one of the best years in werewolf cinema since the subgenre's 1981 revitalization. Hot on the film's cloak-tails came a bumper crop of superior lycan-flicks like *Game of Werewolves*, *Monster Brawl* and *The Howling Reborn*. Though *Red Riding Hood* can't quite match the deliriously entertaining *Game*, its beautiful fairytale setting, forbidding atmosphere, clever screenplay, intriguing subtexts, superior cast and well-realized werewolf mark it as one of the better fruits of this excellent harvest.

Many critics, however (including Roger Ebert, who gave it only one out of four stars), could not see the clever wolf beneath its *Twilight*-sheep's clothing and panned the picture. Most *viewers*, fortunately, weren't so blind, and the film earned over $89 million worldwide during its theatrical run.

With quotes from: "Director Catherine Hardwicke Exclusive Interview: *Red Riding Hood*," by Christina Radish, Collider.com; "Red Riding Hood Grows Up," by Michael Gingold, *Fangoria* 301.

Morphology: Huge black wolf
Demise: Silver (in the form of sharpened metal *fingernails*)
Full Moon Rating: ****

Red: Werewolf Hunter

(2010; Syfy; US/Canada) Director: Sheldon Wilson; Producer: Robert Vaughn, Teleplay: Brook Durham (story: Angela Mancuso); Cinematographer: Russ Goozee. Cast: Felicia Day, Kavan Smith, Stephen McHattie, Greg Bryk, Rosemary Dunsmore, David Reale.

> What big eyes they have. What big teeth they have.
> What big guns she has—promo spot

"Red Riding Hood isn't little anymore," promises the promo for this made-for-television Syfy Channel movie filmed near Toronto, Canada. It begins promisingly enough with an elderly woman and her granddaughter attacked by a hairy beast in their quaint cabin in the woods. As the terrified little girl hides and looks on, her gruesomely mauled grandmother summons her dying strength to stab the creature, causing the beast to burst into flame, leaving only a pile of ashes for the shocked girl to step around. After this promising intro to the Little Red Riding Hood theme, the horrific fairytale ambiance gives way to the cheap modern clichés in which the SyFy Channel specializes—a handful of nondescript characters in a small-scale situation battling unconvincing CGI monsters in cheesy locales with weapons galore.

Virginia Sullivan (ne "Red"), played by Felicia Day, brings her fiancé Nathan (Kavan Smith) home to meet her family—her grandmother and two brothers. But when Nathan is bitten by a werewolf in the woods, Virginia must convince her family not to kill him. You see, the Sullivans are all werewolf hunters charged with keeping the local lycanthropes in check. Their uneasy truce has been broken by a rogue werewolf named Gabriel (Stephen McHattie), who, unlike the rest of the lycans, can transform at will without the stimulus of the full moon. He has gathered together the previously peaceable werewolves, killed their pack leader, and set about teaching them to shift, with the intention of destroying the Sullivans once and for all.

"The [Red Riding Hood] fairytale itself," said star Felicia Day, "was only like a jumping off point about the idea that if the first Red Riding Hood killed the first wolf then what if they felt like the responsibility was to kill all wolves forever and keep them away from the world." Too bad the filmmakers "jumped off" in all the wrong directions. While the notion of the descendants of the original Red Riding Hood taking it upon themselves to train as werewolf hunters and keep humanity safe from the Big Bad remains rife with imaginative possibilities, writer Brook Durham, director Sheldon Wilson, and a cadre of bland actors (led by Day and Smith, who rarely change expressions and exhibit zero onscreen chemistry) sink those possibilities into a morass of poorly-drawn caricatures, predictable scenarios, and clichéd acting. The constant squabbling among the siblings over what to do about the infected Nathan soon grows tiresome, as does the repetitive nature of the werewolf hunts/encounters, with each ending in a silver bullet or knife to the heart and the resultant fiery immolation. Taking a page from the *Buffy the Vampire Slayer* handbook, these werewolves, when killed, spontaneously combust, leaving only a pile of ash.

Worst of all, scripter Brook Durham goes for quantity over quality with his werewolves. Though numerous lycanthropes populate the script, none, save Gabriel himself, has *any* distinguishing personality. These interchangeable clothes (and fur-)-hangers offer no tortured remorse, no conflicted agonizing over the "curse" or the "gift," and no interest whatsoever. This lack of substance takes a literal turn with the substandard CGI creatures (there's nary a werewolf suit nor yak hair in sight), who look flat and two-dimensional with their awkwardly-moving, elongated bodies and misshapen faces. Framed by tufts of hair, their pinched countenance and oversized toothy mouth makes them look like a cross between Gollum and a mutant possum. And the hunters dispatch these cartoon creatures so handily that suspense need not apply.

The only bright spot comes in the form of actor Stephen McHattie's charismatic portrayal of the evil Gabriel. McHattie's measured intonations and malevolent stillness, coupled with a subtle gleam in his eye and a wry, mirthless smile, bring some gravitas even to awkward dialogue like "There is a beast in all of us waiting to be summoned." Co-star Felicia Day labeled McHattie "a great actor, like really just immersive really in the part. Sometimes I didn't know if he was in character or not off the set. He is definitely inspirational in that he took what was on the page and just kind of made it his own in a way that you could never have scripted honestly.... He was actually pretty frightening, to be honest with you."

Reveling in his evil power, Gabriel comes off like some lycanthropic motivational speaker, urging his lycan-brethren to master the ability to shift at will. "When you are in the throes of transformation," he enthuses, "it is such joy, such ecstasy. Think that you can have that sensation whenever you want it. Let that desire drive you." Equating metamorphosis with drug use or even sexual release—rather than the

A less-than-convincing CGI werewolf from SyFy's *Red: Werewolf Hunter*.

"torture of the damned" (as Larry Talbot calls it) or the physical/mental pain seen in so many werewolf movies—remains a daring take on lycanthropy. One character states, "Once you are bitten, it's like a disease or a drug you can't kick." Sadly, the film drops this transgressive idea like a hot potato, abandoning any possible explorations of these novel notions in favor of more bickering amongst the uninteresting protagonists and a few cut-rate action scenes (culminating in a small-scale attack on Red's house and the perfunctory dispatch of the movie's sole character of interest—Gabriel).

While *Red* adheres to the Hollywood standards of the full moon and silver, it adds a few wrinkles to its werewolf lore. If one is bitten by a werewolf, "there's a slim chance the effect can be reversed—but only if you kill the wolf that bit you, and only if you do it before you make your first human kill." In other words, one must wash away the original sin (by killing the original beast) and rise above one's bestial nature to keep to the moral high ground ("If you kill a human, you are cursed for as long as you live").

According to Day, the shoot "was a whirlwind. And being able to do the stunts, you get one take and we'd move on. And at the end of the day we'd just be always—it's always the filmmaking mantra that you never have enough time to do what you want." That may be so, but with *Red: Werewolf Hunter*, what the discerning viewer may want is to pass on it altogether.

With quotes from: "Felicia Day Interview," by Pattye Grippo, *Pazsaz Entertainment Network*, October 25, 2010.

Morphology: Tall, spindly, hair-covered werewolves
Demise: Silver through the heart
Full Moon Rating: *½

The Return of the Vampire

(1943; Columbia) Director: Lew Landers; Producer: Sam White; Screenplay: Griffin Jay (story idea: Kurt Neumann; additional dialogue: Randall Faye); Cinematographers: John Stumar, L. William O'Connell. Cast: Bela Lugosi, Freida Inescort, Nina Foch, Miles Mander, Roland Varno, Matt Willis.

MAN? or MONSTER? or BOTH?—ad line

Columbia, who for so long had been rather circumspect about producing horror films (relying on a series of scientifically-focused Boris Karloff "mad doctor" movies as their ticket in the horror sweepstakes), finally broke down in 1943 to create a true Gothic terror picture. From the opening pre-credit sequence (a terrified woman backs away from a sinister cloaked figure and screams when a cloud of fog envelopes her) we *know* that this is indeed a horror movie. If any doubts remain, the opening narration—"This is the case of Armand Tesla, vampire"—dispels them.

Originally titled *Vampires of London*, the story begins in 1918 London with the staking of bloodsucker Armand Tesla (Bela Lugosi). One World War later and the Blitz uncovers the undead fiend's body. When two well-meaning Civil Defense men remove the iron stake from Tesla's corpse (thinking it a piece of shrapnel), the vampire resumes his reign of terror and sets about revenging himself on those responsible for his staking and their descendants. In his plans he uses a poor thrall, Andreas (Matt Willis), who, under the vampire's spell, becomes a werewolf-like creature (but one that can still converse and think like a man).

Director Lew Landers (*The Raven* [1935], *The Boogie Man Will Get You* [1942]) provides some subtly effective and frighteningly evocative staging for this macabre tale. For instance, when the vampire invades the bedroom of a little girl, the scene begins with mist swirling outside her French doors. The doors suddenly fly open of their own accord and wisps of fog flow into the room. The camera follows the invading mist and pans across the floor where we see a moving shadow take the shape of a caped figure. As the shadow rises against the opposite wall and the silhouetted arms raise ominously, the little girl awakens and screams when a cloud of mist suddenly surrounds her. Throughout the film, Landers makes use of shadows, the dark shapes letting the viewer's imagination work its wonders. Note: writer/director Kurt Neumann (1958's *The Fly*), who penned *The Return of the Vampire*'s original story, was originally set to direct as well, but delays caused him to leave the project. The same thing happened to him on *Werewolf of London*, meaning he lost out on not one but *two* lycan-flicks.

After Universal passed up Bela Lugosi for the title role in *Son of Dracula* (1943), opting instead for the jowly, flat-toned Oklahoman Lon Chaney, Jr. (with disastrous results), the proud Hungarian jumped at the chance to play Drac—er—Armand Tesla in Columbia's *The Return of the Vampire* (for a Dracula by any other name beguiles just as sweetly). Lugosi appears to relish his role, bringing all the power of his hypnotic voice and stately presence to bear on this vampiric reprisal. Considering the quality of his other recent assignments (Poverty Row abominations like *The Ape Man* and *Ghosts on the Loose*, or, even worse, his embarrassing turn as the Monster in *Frankenstein Meets the Wolf Man*), Lugosi must have thought he'd died and gone to undead heaven. (To illustrate how low his fortunes had sunk, the actor received a paltry $3,500 for starring in *The Return of the Vampire*.)

"Bela was a funny guy," remembered *Return*'s assistant director, Earl Bellamy. "You never knew what he was gonna do. He would come in in the mornings with that cape on, and flourish it around, and then go get the white makeup. He didn't talk much to anybody, he just was kind of within himself.... He gave us tickets to come up and see the play [*Arsenic and Old Lace*] that was on Hollywood Boulevard, that he was starring in. We all went, and we all had the first and second row of seats, 'cause it involved all the crew. And when intermission time came, we all wanted to go, it was so terrible [laughs]! And we couldn't, he'd stiffed us by putting us in the first two rows, so we had to sit through the whole play!"

From the look of this half-sheet poster, the film *should* have been called *The Return of the* Werewolf. In any case, *The Return of the Vampire* marks the first cinematic pairing of lycanthrope and bloodsucker (courtesy Lynn Naron).

Lugosi is ably supported by a well-chosen cast who go a long way toward bringing believability to this rather unlikely tale. Particularly effective are Miles Mander as the doubting Scotland Yard inspector, who provides just the right mix of officiousness and sardonic humor (even venturing the occasional double-take), and Matt Willis as the tortured Andreas, who alternates between convincing anguish when in human form and an evil glee while in his werewolf guise.

The picture offers a novel take on lycanthropy by casting its wolfman in the role of lapdog to a vampire (a notion that 60 later became the foundation of the *Underworld* series). Rather than the uncontrollable savage beast seen in previous werewolf outings, Andreas becomes the pawn of pure evil, retaining his powers of speech and reason while in wolfman form, while seemingly reveling in the evil he's ordered to do. Instead of the internal struggle between man and beast—civilization and nature—that so many screen werewolves personify, Andreas embodies the more theological struggle between good and evil (much like the classic Jekyll and Hyde character ... but with far more hair).

As introduction, the camera shows this wolfman walking into a crypt and approaching a coffin. Then, surprisingly, the manbeast speaks: "Master, it's night again—beautiful, dark, silent night, with the fog creeping in. Time for you to awaken, Master." Not only does this werewolf talk, he all but waxes poetic. Another departure from the tried-and-true rules of lycanthropy has Andreas' transformations tied not to the lunar cycle, but to the whims of his vampire overlord. Tesla's hypnotic control seemingly induces the change, though at one point Andreas, when threatened by a pair of policeman while on an errand for his master, transforms from human to wolfman (off-screen) on his own in order to escape. Likewise, apart from the occasional growl, Andreas exhibits little wolfish behavior. In fact, when battling the two policemen, he resorts to decidedly human fisticuffs, throwing punches and grappling rather than biting and slashing (though the growling and occasional barks on the soundtrack aurally remind us of his canine condition).

On the technical end, *The Return of the Vampire* is top-drawer (looking much better than its slight $138,545.54 final cost should allow). Louis Diage provided some wonderfully detailed and moody graveyard sets that measure up to Universal's high standard. Makeup man Clay Campbell rendered some effective werewolf makeup (which he repeated 12 years later for Columbia's 1950s entry in the lycanthrope sweepstakes, *The Werewolf*), and special effects coordinator Aaron

Nadley created convincing transformation scenes (with the image subtly distorting over a series of 10 separate dissolves, and the light changing so that the hair seemingly grows before our very eyes) that look smoother than those in many of the much-heralded Universal Wolf Man movies. And director Landers orchestrates some gritty bombing sequences, complete with convincing explosions and debris, and neatly inserted bits of actual war footage that add a nice touch of authenticity.

All is not perfect with this vampire's *Return*, however. While providing some masterful atmospheric lighting on the marvelous graveyard sets, cinematographers John Stumar and L. W. O'Connell don't always photograph Lugosi to that actor's best advantage. In scenes which simply cry out for some moody low-key lighting, his face often appears over lit so that the ravages of age (not to mention those of long-term drug use) become all-too-apparent on the sexagenarian actor's countenance.

Since *The Return of the Vampire* really is a Dracula film in all but the name, it's unsurprising that it suffers from the same ills that plague that seminal classic—namely an overly talky latter half. After a strong 30 minutes, *Return*'s story bogs down, with characters running about discovering (or seeking to convince others of) what the audience already knows. While all is not lost (there's still plenty of atmosphere and an occasional chill), the film's latter half proves disappointing. Fortunately, *Return* avoids the anti-climax Tod Browning laid on *Dracula* and instead provides the viewer with an exciting—and rather grisly—denouement, including a brief but effective vampire meltdown.

In the 1940s, Columbia made only one other (half-hearted) stab at traditional horror, the weak *Cry of the Werewolf* (1944, with *Return*'s imperiled heroine, Nina Foch, taking the lycanthropic lead). With *The Return of the Vampire*, however, the studio not only provided a rare worthy vehicle for Lugosi (the last time a major studio would grant him a starring role in a serious picture), it created an effective and entertaining (if flawed) Gothic-style chiller. Though certainly not on the level of the Val Lewton pictures or of such prestige productions as *The Uninvited* (1944) and *The Picture of Dorian Gray* (1945), and falling short lycan-wise of *The Wolf Man* and subsequent Larry Talbot entries, *The Return of the Vampire* still remains one of the better horror films of the 1940s—one equal (and even superior) to many of Universal's offerings of the decade.

With quotes from: "I Remember Bela! Earl Bellamy on Bela Lugosi," by Tom Weaver, *VideoScope* 44.

Morphology: Bipedal wolfman
Demise: Regular bullet and the latent effects of a bomb blast
Full Moon Rating: ***½

El Retorno de Walpurgis see *Curse of the Devil*

El Retorno del Hombre Lobo see *The Craving*

Return of the Wolfman see *The Craving*

The Return of Walpurgis see *Curse of the Devil*

Sabrina, Secrets of a Teenage Witch: A Witch and the Werewolf

(2014; Lionsgate) Director: Trevor Wall; Producer: D. S. Kulkarni; Screenplay: Pamela Hickey and Dennys McCoy, Peter Lawrence, Darren Jones (Head Writer: Dean Batali). Cast (voices): Ashley Tisdale, Ian James Corlett, Tabitha St. Germain, Erin Mathews, Maryke Hendrikse, Kathleen Barr, Matthew Erickson, Andrew Francis.

Everyone's favorite half-witch, half-human is back for an all new movie adventure—trailer
---

Truth in advertising? Hardly. This "all new movie adventure" is actually just three episodes from the short-lived (2013–14), digitally animated series *Sabrina, Secrets of a Teenage Witch* grafted together ("Dances with Werewolves," "Return of the Werewolf," and "Creatures and Caves") to make a (barely—at 63 minutes) feature-length "new movie."

Sabrina starts with a bang (or howl) as the titular teenage witch (voiced by Ashley Tisdale) and a rival warlock flee through the woods from a pair of werewolves. But it quickly turns out that this is only a contest staged by Enchantra, ruler of Witch-World. After Sabrina outsmarts her competitor (and the lycanthropes—mere pets of the witches), she heads back to Earth and resumes her role of typical teen. When Sabrina gives her horror movie/werewolf-loving friend Harvey (Matthew Erickson) a letterman's jacket just like the one worn by "Rupert the Werewolf" in "*Breath of the Werewolf 3*," the garment makes Harvey a werewolf for real (Sabrina didn't realize it hadn't been "de-magicked" yet, and that it carried the curse of lycanthropy). Now Sabrina must try to keep Harvey-wolf out of trouble whenever the full moon rises.

Though lasting a little over an hour, the movie's ADD freneticism and tiresome characters make it seem much longer. Sabrina sighs and complains about having to live in two worlds ("Some day I'm supposed to be queen of the Witch-World, but I'd rather be a regular teenager—which, honestly, is hard enough"), and makes cracks on the level of "This stuff smells worse than nuke-juice" after were–Harvey drenches her in drool. Typical of the script's level of wit: When Sabrina's witch-guardian explains that Harvey's lycan-dition is now permanent, she quips, "Every full moon things are gonna get—hairy, hahahahaha." Ha ha indeed.

Apart from the visual throwback to Michael Landon in *I Was a Teenage Werewolf*, the notion of a magic garment—in this case a letterman's jacket—transforming its wearer into a beast harkens back to medieval lore. But lest one draw too close a parallel between this Teenage Werewolf talisman and the classic folklore trope of wolf pelts and wolf-skin belts changing their wearers into werewolves, Harvey's magicked jacket serves as mere McGuffin. Once he puts it on, the curse has been passed to him—done deal—and whether he wears the coat or not becomes immaterial (though Harvey, being a hardcore horror nerd, rarely takes it off). Now a permanent werewolf, Harvey's transformations are triggered solely by the full moon.

At one point a witch friend informs Sabrina that, unlike the friendly lycan-pets of the Witch-World (who, oddly, sport identical lettermen's jackets), human werewolves are "mean, mindless eating machines." But Harvey-wolf seems more interested in eating snack foods than people, doing nothing more menacing than waylaying a pizza delivery truck and consuming every pie onboard. With its oversized wolf head, pointy ears, long snout, bushy tail, and big hairy hands and feet, this lycanthrope looks like a cartoonish Big Bad Wolf. Not particularly scary (several gags involve Harvey's friends assuming he's just in costume), were–Harvey runs about chasing cats or searching for more snacks.

The transformations (of which there are three—one per episode) remain as perfunctory and disappointing as the rest of this lycan's activity. The first merely shows a split-second change in Harvey's shadow on the wall, while the second fails to even offer up a silhouette (instead inserting a cutaway to the full moon, then back to the fully transformed Harvey). The third and final metamorphosis is yet another quick shadow-change. So much for imaginative use of the wide-open possibilities of digital animation.

At the close of the third episode ... er, movie, Sabrina discovers a cure for lycanthropy—and it's just as random and nonsensical as the high-school-jacket cause: If a human werewolf finds the secret treasure of the Trolls in Witch-World, he'll be cured. Really. So after a bit of Troll-baiting, Sabrina uses her magic wand to dunk were–Harvey into a pink pond (apparently the Troll's treasure), and Harvey is human once more.

Over-bright (primary and secondary colors painfully saturate the screen), over-frantic, and over-cute, *A Witch and the Werewolf* makes the viewer wish this *Teenage Witch* had kept her *Secrets* to herself.

Morphology: Bipedal Big (Not So) Bad Wolf
Demise: None; he's cured!
Rating: *

Santo and Blue Demon vs. Dracula and the Wolf Man

(1973; Cinematográfica Calderon; Mexico) Original Language Title: *Santo y Blue Demon vs. Dracula y el Hombre Lobo*. Director: Miguel M. Delgado. Producer: Guillermo Calderón Stell; Screenplay: Alfredo Salazar; Cinematographer: Rosalio Solano. Cast: Santo, Blue Demon, Aldo Monti, Agustin Martinez Solares, Jr., Nubia Marti, Eugenia San Martin.

A brutal power struggle between good and evil
—(translated) tagline

Though not as monster-heavy as the spectacular *Santo and Blue Demon vs. the Monsters* (1970), *Santo and Blue Demon vs. Dracula and the Wolf Man* is no slouch in the Mexican monster rally department either. On the plus side, the film features Dracula (Aldo Monti, his '70s haircut and sideburns contrasting amusingly with his classic penguin suit); the Wolf Man "Rufus" (Agustin Martinez Solares, Jr.), who serves the Vampire Lord in the bloodsucker's plan to rule the world by turning all humans into either vampires or wolfmen; and a kindly professor turned creepy zombie menacing his own granddaughter. Co-starring with the heroic "El Enmascarado del Plata" El Santo (playing himself) is his pal and near-equal in the crime-fighting superhero wrestler business, the blue-masked Blue Demon (also as himself). In the minus column, however, sits a meandering, mundane subplot in which the revived Dracula seeks vengeance on the descendants of those who initially staked him hundreds of years ago, while the Wolf Man—in human form—woos one of said female descendants in an ill-conceived and illogical vengeance scheme.

Then there's the overabundance of flatly staged wrestling action (three full bouts). Disappointingly for those Santo and Blue Demon fans who enjoy watching their heroes' energetic acrobatics in the ring, the locked-down camera and obvious studio staging (plain blue background, no visible audience) robs the movie's many wrasslin' moments of their sense of immediacy and excitement. In fact, it looks as if the brawny contests take place in some disconnected other dimension, with the piped-in sounds from the unseen crowd only underlining the feel of isolation. This is a real shame, because a well-shot Santo and/or Blue Demon bout (versus "The White Angel" and "Renato the Hippie," respectively) with a frenzied audience can get the blood pumping by showcasing the duo's agile abilities and their immense popularity with the crowds.

South-of-the-border werewolves apparently play by a very different set of rules. For instance, Rufus is revived from the dead just like his master, Dracula—by blood dripping onto his skeletal remains in his sarcophagus. Unlike Dracula's onscreen revival, however, the Wolf Man's resurrection occurs off-screen (no doubt to save on yet another round of special effects), after which the restored Rufus sits up in his Wolf Man guise (wearing what looks like a freshly-ironed yellow silk pirate shirt). He then calmly walks over to Dracula to declare, "I'm ready, Master." Obviously this werewolf retains his full human faculties while in hirsute form, displaying not the savagery of the beast but the calculated coldness of a human villain. Appearance-wise, this Wolf Man sports a rather primitive Lon Chaney get-up: coarse hair covering every inch of his head and face save for his (brown colored) nose, and a pair of tiny fangs protruding from between his lips. Rufus' lycanthropy appears to extend only to his head and hands, though, as his neck and partially bare chest remain free from any unsightly wolf hair.

Rufus' half-dozen wolfmen underlings (who come into play during the film's climax) vary in appearance and completeness of their makeup. Some have a full face of hair like Rufus, while others just a simple fright wig and bushy beard. One boasts little more than heavy eyebrows and a scraggly goatee. The two heroes battle the lycanthropes with punches and wrestling throws—and the wolfmen respond in kind, acting more like hairy henchmen than animalistic monsters. The film completely foregoes all the tortured, conflicted possibilities inherent in the man-into-beast concept and opts instead to utilize its werewolves as mere punching bags and wrestling fodder for the eponymous masked heroes.

After the brief resurrection scene, Rufus, "chief of the terrifying breed of the beast men" (as an old tome describes him), never again becomes a wolfman—at least until the very end when he battles with Blue Demon. (One sequence does offer an *implied* transformation, however, when Rufus escorts a woman on a nighttime stroll: over the shot of the full moon we hear a few grunts and growls, and then the girl's scream, but the metamorphosis, attack and assumed bloody result remain unseen.) At the climax, when tussling with Rufus in his human guise, Blue lands a punch that sends Rufus reeling to the ground. After a brief cutaway, Rufus rises as the Wolf Man, only to be dispatched shortly thereafter when Santo simultaneously kicks him and Dracula into the waiting pit of spikes. Furthering the lycan-disappointment, we never see just *how* Rufus transforms that cave full of captives into wolfmen (nor, for that matter, do we see Dracula working on his assembly line producing vampire minions).

Apparently any pointy object will do when dispatching these werewolves, with silver being superfluous. During the climactic free-for-all, as Santo and Blue Demon battle the wolfmen horde in their cave lair, Santo hurls a spear into one wolfman—who promptly falls to the ground and vanishes in a puff of white smoke, leaving the spear standing upright in the soil! And, of course, Rufus himself expires when the Silver Masked Man tosses him into the pit of spikes (*sans* smoke).

As well as the taint of lycanthropy (at least in *this* film), Wolf Man actor Agustin Martinez Solares, Jr., had movies in his blood, being the son of cinematographer Agustin Martinez Solares (*100 Cries of Terror*), and nephew of both cinematographer Raúl Martínez Solares (*Night of the Bloody Apes*, *Santo and Blue Demon vs. the Monsters*) and director Gilberto Martinez Solares (*Face of the Screaming Werewolf*, *Santo and Blue Demon vs. the Monsters*).

Even with its various pacing peccadilloes and lycanthropic lapses, *Santo and Blue Demon vs. Dracula and the Wolf Man* contains enough

Wrestlers vs. werewolves: *Santo and Blue Demon vs. Dracula and the Wolf Man* (Mexican poster).

monstrous or outré elements to keep ennui from creeping into this cinematic ring, including a bloody resurrection scene right out of *Dracula Prince of Darkness* (bleeding out a victim suspended over Dracula and the Wolf Man's bones) and a Dracula demise sequence borrowed from *The Return of Dracula* (did someone say "pit full of spikes"?). The movie also offers bright comic-book lighting (chock full of primary colors) contrasted with wonderfully shadowy Gothic illumination (particularly in some misty woodland settings). Then there's the lycan-heavy climax in which the two heroes face off against not only Drac and Wolfy, but a whole pack of savage werewolves. Never before was so much yak hair seen in one place at one time.

"The movies I make are not art," admitted Santo himself, "they are made to entertain. People go to see them to have fun." And those who come to see *Santo and Blue Demon vs. Dracula and the Wolf Man* with than in mind will not be disappointed.

With quotes from: "On Monsters and Imposters: Santo's Final Say," by Ruben Sano, *Santo Street* 13.

Morphology: Clásico hombre lobo (wolf man)
Demise: Pit full of stakes
Full Moon Rating: **½

Santo and Blue Demon vs. the Monsters

(1970; Cinematografica Sotomayor; Mexico) Original Language Title: *Santo y Blue Demon contra los Monstruous*; Director: Gilberto Martinez Solares; Producer: Jesús Sotomayor Martinez; Screenplay: Rafael Garcia Travesi; Cinematography: Raúl Martínez Solares. Cast: Santo, Blue Demon, Jorge Rado, Carlos Ancira, Raúl Martínez Solares, Jr., Hedi Blue.

> FROM THE MANSION OF HORROR ESCAPES
> THE BLOODTHIRSTY CREATURES YOU
> MOST HATE AND FEAR...—poster (translated)

Santo and Blue Demon vs. the Monsters opens, like *Abbott and Costello Meet Frankenstein*, with our two heroes and each of the featured monsters introduced during the credits. Except *Santo and Blue Demon vs. the Monsters* is not a comedy—well, not intentionally anyway.

The Mummy, the Cyclops, "Franquestain," the Wolf Man, the Vampire, and the Vampire Woman all receive their 15-seconds-of-fame introductory billing. But that's forgetting a diabolical bald hunchbacked dwarf named Waldo; a cadre of green-faced zombie henchmen; a big-domed alien-like creature with exposed brain (who merely stands around as background decoration), and the evil, cackling mad scientist who creates/revives all these monsters in his laboratory cave located beneath an abandoned castle!

Said scientist (himself revived from death by Waldo at the film's beginning) captures masked wrestler and all-around good guy Blue Demon, uses a "duplicating" machine to create an evil double, then sends the doppelganger, along with the scientist's mind-controlled monsters, out to attack the locals and kidnap the scientist's hated brother (who scoffed at his sibling's evil experiments) and niece. Of course, masked wrestling hero El Santo, the Man in the Silver Mask (friend of Blue Demon, boyfriend of the niece, and heroic defender of all), has something to say about this, and numerous set-to's with various monsters (including one ringside wrestling bout in which the Vampire disguises himself as a masked opponent named—get this— "The Vampire") ends in a free-for-all between Santo and the good Blue Demon on the one side, and the evil Blue Demon and all the monsters on the other.

Things move at a *rapido* pace (with monster attacks coming at frequent intervals), allowing little time for the frequent filler found in many a Santo and/or Blue Demon feature (one exception being a nightclub sequence in which the principals watch a silly south-of-the-border Gene Kelly–style number that's obviously lifted from a completely different—and much older—movie). Plenty of day-for-night photography adds to the kitsch quotient (and contrasts comically with the occasional real nighttime shot).

The monsters prove more amusing (unintentionally so) than terrifying. Santo himself admitted, "In the film there are some monsters that didn't look quite right." For instance, the Vampire (nobody uses the 'D' word, but it's pretty obvious on what famous Count he is patterned) sports not only the expected evening dress, top hat and cape, but a set of oversized fangs and gigantic pointed ears. The elfin bloodsucker does impressively launch himself into the air in bat pose, however.

The Mummy sports clean bandages and a five-day growth of beard; and the poor, inept sap never accomplishes anything more than serving as Santo's 3000-year-old punching bag. "The mummy was a poor skinny man, an actor," dismissed Santo. The Frankenstein Monster is a tall gentleman in an obvious—and crude—mask (with a goatee!), but he does a nice job of crushing one victim's head under his asphalt-spreader's boot in the movie's one moderately gruesome scene. Best of all is the Cyclops (recycled from the 1959 sci-fier *La Nave de los Monstruos*)—an unwieldy rubber-suited steroid-monster with one glowing eye, an oversized guppy-mouth, and big fuzzy ears.

The Wolf Man (played by Vicente Lara) seriously disappoints, with his bushy gray beard, lanky hair, oversized ears, sparse nose piece, and inch-long fangs. Sporting a dark suit, and walking about and opening doors like any normal person, he looks more like an elderly man in dire need of orthodontia than a bloodthirsty werewolf. He does receive more than his fair share of screen time, however, and takes pride of place when he becomes the first of the various creatures to see action—attacking and killing a farmer and his wife (for no apparent reason), leaving their young son horrified at their bloody corpses. Yet after this initial savage display, for the rest of the picture he behaves decidedly un–wolf-like, mostly standing around with the other monsters patiently awaiting orders or entering one fracas after another at the behest of the Blue Demon doppelganger. At one point he does try to bite Santo's throat, but for the most part he makes do with throwing punches and executing wrestling moves. At the climactic battle in the underground lab, this *hombre lobo* even grabs the torch waved at him by the good Blue Demon and tosses it aside—then picks it up *himself* to use as a weapon. A werewolf wielding *fire*? But *Santo and Blue Demon vs. the Monsters* remains unconcerned with such trivialities as lunar cycles, silver bullets or werewolf motivation, so that this lycanthrope becomes more of a supernatural henchman than a tortured soul or brutal blending of man and beast. No transformations, no human guise, no agonizing over his curse ... this wolfman merely takes orders and throws punches. Such a no-nonsense, nuance-free approach does lycan-cinema no favors, but it fits in perfectly with the movie's central theme—the battle between good and evil for Truth, Justice and the Mexican way.

Starring the two most popular luchadores (masked wrestlers) in the history of Mexican wrestling (and Mexican wrestling cinema), *Santo and Blue Demon vs. the Monsters* was the first true pairing of these two titans (Santo made a brief appearance in the Blue Demon–starrer *Blue Demon vs. the Satanic Power* in 1966, but only in a cameo role). Though they played "best friends" in *Vs. the Monsters*, they were anything *but* in real life, with Blue Demon being particularly resentful of Santo's number-one status in the ring and on the screen (Blue frequently being relegated to sidekick for Santo's hero). "We did have a fierce rivalry because we were both very popular," commented Blue Demon, "but I feel I was the superior wrestler.... Outside the ring, our rivalry wasn't as strong. We weren't enemies, but we weren't exactly friends either." When asked which wrestlers he considered good actors, Blue Demon pointedly replied, "I don't like to be disrespectful, so I'd rather not answer that question." While Blue Demon (real name Alejandro Munoz Moreno) made 28 films over the course of his career, El Santo (real name Rudolfo Guzman Huerta) starred in nearly twice that number. Whatever Blue's opinion of his rival's acting, Santo was nothing if not popular on the silver screen, and he and Blue Demon went on to make seven more movies together, including the werewolf-filled *Santo and Blue Demon vs. Dracula and the Wolf Man* (1973). (Note: Though *Vs. the Monsters'* closing credits lists Alejandro Cruz as playing Blue Demon, this isn't entirely accurate. Better known as the masked wrestler Black Shadow, Cruz, a friend and partner of the real Blue Demon [Alejandro Moreno], sometimes doubled for Moreno on the screen, including playing the "evil" Blue here.)

"*Santo y Blue Demon contra los Monstruos* is not bad," concluded Santo, the Silver Masked Man himself, "only some of the monsters don't look very scary." No, but they *are* quite entertaining. Finally subtitled in English and released in America in the early 2000s, and chock full of cheesy fun, *Santo and Blue Demon vs. the Monsters* is not to be missed by those enamored of south-of-the-border psychotronica.

With quotes from: "On Monsters and Imposters: Santo's Final Say," by Ruben Sano, *Santo Street* 13; "Meet the True Blue Demon," by Brian Moran, *Santo Street* 7.

Morphology: Sparsely-haired, suit-wearing wolfman
Demise: Fiery conflagration (implied)
Full Moon Rating: ***

Santo vs. las Lobas see *Santo vs. the She-Wolves*

Santo vs. the She-Wolves

(1976; Estudios Jiminez Pons Hermanos; Mexico) Original Language Title: *Santo vs. las Lobas*. Directors: Jaime Jiménez Pons, Ruben Galindo; Producer: Jamie Jiménez Pons; Screenplay: Ramón Obón, Jaime Jiménez Pons; Cinematographers: Raul Dominguez, Victor Gaitan. Cast: Santo, Rodolfo de Anda, Gloria Mayo, Jorge Rusek, Nubia Marti, Erika Carlson.

El Santo and Blue Demon, those two defenders of Truth, Justice and the Mexican Way, face off against a bevy of monstrous minions, including El Hombre Lobo (the Wolf Man), in *Santo and Blue Demon vs. the Monsters* (Mexican poster).

"You will signal the beginning of the eternal rule of lycanthropes!"—dying werewolf queen Luba to her successor

Santo vs. the She-Wolves marks the fifth and final time the Mexican masked wrestling superhero/crime fighter El Santo tangled with werewolves (the others being *Santo and Blue Demon vs. the Monsters* [1970] and *Santo and Blue Demon vs. Dracula and the Wolf Man* [1973], and, more tangentially, *Samson vs. the Vampire Women* [1962] and *Samson in the Wax Museum* [1963]). In *Santo vs. the She-Wolves* the Man in the Silver Mask faces off against an entire tribe of lycanthropes, led by a rejuvenating werewolf queen and her king.

Cesar Harker (Rodolfo de Anda) contacts masked wrestler and all-round-hero El Santo for help. Harker, who comes from a long line of werewolf hunters, has discovered that a local gathering of lycanthropes plan to create a new queen and thereby rule the world of men. After Santo is attacked by wolves, he journeys to Harker's village, where the werewolves lay siege. Harker tells Santo, "You must help us end the curse of the werewolves.... We must succeed before the accession of the Red Moon." (Of course, nobody ever explains just what a *red* moon might be.) But Santo has been bitten, and "anyone who's bitten by one becomes a werewolf on the first Red Moon." After Cesar falls prey to the werewolf queen, Santo joins Eric, Cesar's twin brother, and the likable "Gipsy," Harker's bald-headed, bare-chested, leather-vested he-man servant (deftly enacted by Santo's real-life friend and manager Carlos Suarez), to battle the she-wolves and their male counterparts, led by Licar, King of the Werewolves, and save not only Santo himself but all of humanity.

Santo vs. the She-Wolves was shot towards the end of the *lucha libre* cinema cycle, when masked wrestler movies, popular for two decades, had lost much of their appeal (time marches on—even in wrestler-loving Mexico). Consequently, budgets for these productions shrank, and those few *luchadore* movies (never lavish to begin with) that *were* being made in the mid-to-late 1970s could charitably be called impoverished. *Santo vs. the She-Wolves* overcame this by taking a rather gritty turn, emphasizing bleak, seventies-style horror more than the candy-colored, kid-friendly tone of previous Santo films (even from only a few years before, like in *Santo and Blue Demon vs. Dracula and the Wolf Man*). Via hand-held photography, echoing sound effects, dim lighting (with silhouettes of hulking beast-men at twilight rising up into frame), an emphasis on real settings rather than artificial sets, and an absence of distracting, out-of-place time-filler, like sappy nightclub musical numbers and/or dance routines (almost a staple of the *lucha libre* subgenre), *Santo vs. the She-Wolves* makes itself over into a fairly effective low-budget horror entry—with the added attraction of everyone's favorite Silver Masked Man at its center.

Mexican poster for *Santo vs. the She-Wolves*, the fifth and final time the silver-masked wrestling hero tangled with lycanthropes.

Directors Jaime Jiménez Pons and Rubén Galindotake every opportunity to underline this new emphasis on horror. At one point the werewolf queen tilts back her head and laughs—a sinister, hollow sound that echoes into the next scene, drawing the eeriness forward. When the wolves attack Santo, the point-of-view photography alternates between the backpedaling masked man desperately kicking at the canines, and close-ups of the slavering jaws snapping and lunging at the camera—at us. It's a cheap but involving horror trope that conveys the immediacy—and danger—of the situation.

At Harker's village, an outdoor dinner party turns into a chaotic, bloody brawl when the lycanthropes attack. The hand-held photography and rough, abrupt editing emphasize the chaos and highlight the bloody victims, as people flee in terror, leaving Santo and Gipsy to brutally battle the beast-men (and women). Perhaps the most effectively disturbing sequence comes when Gipsy and the heroine (who, of course, has fallen for Santo—"I love you," she tells him, to which the stalwart hero dismissively replies, "We'll discuss that later; right now we need to save those children's lives!") attempt to drive a station wagon full of village children to safety. As they drive through what appears to be an abandoned quarry, a gang of savage werewolves hurl rocks and flaming bundles of hay at the car before viciously assaulting the vehicle. The evil creatures paw at the windows and rock the car back and forth trying to get in, generating an almost *Night of the Living Dead* feel.

This darker, grittier tone continues even into the portrayal of the beloved central character, cracking the heretofore invincible El Santo's bulletproof persona—to the point he high-tails it up into the arena rafters to escape a pair of snarling wolves and screams for help until two guards arrive on the scene. Unlike in most Santo outings, Our Hero looks and acts genuinely frightened at times. And the final mano-a-lobo battle between Santo and Licar, though ending with Santo tossing the werewolf king over a cliff, remains surprisingly melancholy. Santo's victory is met by a thoughtful Santo simply staring after his victim while the lonely sound of the wind plays over an otherwise silent soundtrack. No triumphant music swells, no grateful bystander utters, "God bless Santo"; the curtain closes on this image of a solitary, introspective Silver Masked Man contemplating the horror and tragedy of the situation.

At first glance, the she-wolves look like big-haired, bearded ladies, though a closer look reveals slight variations, with some resembling cute Pekingese pups and others appearing more like fanged Lhasa Apsos. The queen herself sports a hairy face, long eyelashes, wavy locks of long werewolf hair, a mouth full of large (plastic-looking) fangs, and long (but still pretty) fingernails. Werewolfism apparently ends at the neck, though, for she boasts smooth skin wherever her fur bikini fails to cover.

Beyond these minor differences, there are two distinct types of werewolves—the human hybrid wolfwomen (and wolfmen) and full-on wolves (played by German Shepherds), who attack and bite Santo, opening the potential of Santo himself becoming a werewolf. In any case, all the werewolves retain their human faculties and have no ties to the moon. They are able to take on their lycanthropic guise whenever it suits them (one hirsute wolfwoman even peeks over a wall to spy on Santo in broad daylight). At one point, the local sympathetic doctor reveals that he, too, is afflicted with the curse of lycanthropy. But he somehow remains on the side of Good, staying friendly towards Santo even while in reluctant werewolf mode—which consists of a bushy beard, hairy hands and moderately long fingernails.

Of course, along with the various she-wolves, this tribe of lycanthropes features a number of male werewolves as well, including "Licar, King of the Lycanthropes," who arrives at their village sealed in a box sent from Transylvania. (Mexican actor Jorge Russek, who played Lican, appeared in a number of Hollywood productions, including *The Wild Bunch*.) "I've come to join you to eliminate the last of the Harkers," he tells his followers after they kill the train station attendant and liberate His Hairiness from the crate. Consequently, *Santo vs. the She-Wolves* marks the first portrayal of a werewolf *community*, years before the concept coalesced in the classic American entry *The Howling* (1981).

The film's one transformation scene consists of a simple dissolve when Licar, after being knocked unconscious by Santo at the attack on the party, reverts back to his human form upon regaining consciousness. Amazingly, not only does *he* transform, but the torn purple shirt he sported as a snarling werewolf magically becomes a neat, white dinner jacket, complete with bow tie!

One particular innovation found among these *Lobas* is making their symbolic scourge the protagonist himself. Santo is able to defeat numerous werewolves rampaging through the dinner party by using only his fists and wrestling moves, leaving many of the monsters unconscious or dead (whereas Harker and the rest require silver bullets to dispatch the lycanthropes). Unlike the others, Santo needs no silver bullets, as he himself, due to his legendary status as "The Man in the Silver Mask," is lethal to lycanthropes. As Cesar tells Santo, "The *Book of Licars* says that only a silver symbol can eliminate them [the werewolves]. Your mask is silver." So Santo, the Man in the Silver Mask, stands as the living bane of lycanthropy.

Loaded with grim situations and surprising deaths (nearly all the principal characters, including the She-Wolf queen herself, and the initial hero and heroine, perish within the first thirty minutes, allowing a whole new cast of characters to appear—including the murdered Cesar's twin brother—for the second half), *Santo vs. the She-Wolves* remains a rather bleak, rough-hewn, fascinatingly strange addition not only to Santo cinema but to big-screen lycanthropy.

Morphology: Two-legged wolfmen (and women) *and* four-legged wolves (played by German Shepherds)
Demise: Silver (either in the form of bullets or the fists of El Santo, "The Man in the Silver Mask")
Full Moon Rating: ***

Santo y Blue Demon contra los Monstruous see *Santo and Blue Demon vs. the Monsters*

Santo y Blue Demon vs. Dracula y el Hombre Lobo see *Santo and Blue Demon vs. Dracula and the Wolf Man*

Scooby-Doo and the Reluctant Werewolf

(1988; Hanna-Barbera/Warner Bros.) Director: Ray Patterson; Producer: Berny Wolf; Screenplay: Jim Ryan. Cast (voices): Don Messick, Casey Kasem, Hamilton Camp, Jim Cummings, Joanie Gerber, Ed Gilbert.

> A Howling New Scooby-Doo Movie—ad line

"Over 7 million kids and 6 million adults watch Scooby-Doo each week!" So claimed a promotional ad for the made-for-television Scooby-Doo animated feature film *Scooby-Doo and the Reluctant Werewolf*. Unfortunately, while the movie focuses on Scooby and Shaggy (*and*, much to original series fans' dismay, Scooby's talking nephew-pup Scrappy-Doo), it's not a "true" Scooby-Doo feature. Missing are the rest of the Mystery Inc. gang (Fred, Velma and Daphne), as well as whatever charm the original series possessed, replaced by poor puns, silly slapstick, and moronic monsters—"real" monsters rather than the villain-in-a-mask terrors of the original series. While this sea change from human to supernatural villains *can* work (as in the cleverly self-aware and sometimes creepy *Scooby-Doo on Zombie Island* [1998]), *Reluctant Werewolf* transforms its cadre of classic (and not-so) creatures into bumbling buffoons that serve as the butt of insults and pratfalls (eschewing the lesson taught by every successful horror-comedy since *Abbott and Costello Meet Frankenstein*—that the monsters need to be treated seriously in order for the comedy to work).

The story begins with a goofy auto race in which racecar driver Shaggy (voiced by Casey Kasem), along with his pit crew Scooby-Doo, Scrappy-Doo (both Don Messick), and Shaggy's girlfriend Googie (B.J. Ward), wins when his car drills underground to come up ahead of the leader(!). It quickly switches to "deepest, darkest Transylvania" where, at Castle Dracula, the Count (Hamilton Camp) and his monster minions have a problem. It seems that their resident werewolf has retired (to Florida) "just before the Monster Road Rally." "How can we pick a Monster of the Year without a werewolf?" moans the Mummy. So Dracula decides he needs to make a new werewolf. The undead villain consults an ancient tome (the Grimness Book), which "shows the one who is to become a werewolf"—a drawing of Shaggy! Drac sends a pair of inept hunchbacks, "the Hunch Bunch," on a mission to America to transform Shaggy into a new werewolf and transport him to Transylvania for the upcoming race. After a few failed attempts, the Hunch Bunch finally manages to maneuver Shaggy into "the right position" for a moonbeam to strike him and trigger the transformation (no spells, incantations, or bites necessary—just exposure to the full moon). At this, he instantly turns into a, er, shaggy werewolf (complete with dog-like face, red eyes, and pointy ears). The Hunch Bunch then kidnaps Shaggy and his pals, and delivers them to Dracula's castle, where the reluctant Shaggy-wolf must find a way to thwart his various monster opponents in the Transylvania Road Rally.

Rather than metamorphosing every full moon, Shaggy stays permanently in his werewolf guise—except when he has the hiccups, during which he transforms back and forth after each hiccup. No matter his outward appearance, however, Shaggy remains himself, talking and acting in his usual Shaggy fashion ("Like, totally weirdsville"). He doesn't even realize he's been changing while hiccupping. And how does Shaggy finally shake this lycan-curse at film's end? After winning the road rally against all odds, as the cheating Drac and his monster racers employ all manner of traps (man-eating plant, giant spider web, devious detours and even a shrink ray), Shaggy gets his hands on the Grimness Book and recites the following passage: "Oogley-boogley, wobbly-why / No more werewolf am I / I'm going to be a normal guy." And poof, he's back to normal (or at least what passes for Shaggy-normal). The one bright spot for lycan-savvy viewers comes when at one point the Shaggy-wolf hops into his hot rod to drive off with the girl (Googie), with police in hot pursuit—conjuring memories of the outrageous dune buggy–driving *Werewolf of Woodstock* a decade earlier.

Accidental references to seventies lycan-delirium aside, *Reluctant Werewolf* concisely sums itself up when an exasperated Dracula turns into a bat and flaps disgustedly away after yet another failure, with Vanna-pira (Dracula's game show model–like bride, who looks eerily like a cartoon Barbi Benton) observing, "I knew some day they'd drive him batty." Toss in further groan-inducing gags like flying bat-burgers, plasma pizza and scream beans, not to mention Drac's cadre of bungling monsters typified by the likes of Dr. Jekyll and Mr. Snide, the Schlock Ness Monster, and Ghengis Kong (a giant Gorilla with Fu Manchu moustache), and one can't help but rename this unsightly blemish on the Scooby-Doo franchise "*Scooby-Doo and the Reluctant Viewer.*"

In perhaps the film's sole positive, *Scooby-Doo and the Reluctant Werewolf* at least marked the annoying Scrappy-Doo's *final* appearance in the franchise (until revived as the villain in the 2002 live-action *Scooby Doo* movie). Lesson apparently learned.

Morphology: Skinny, Shaggy-shaped, talking wolfman
Demise: None; Shaggy reverts to his original, slightly less shaggy self
Full Moon Rating: *

Shadow of the Werewolf see *The Werewolf vs. the Vampire Woman*

She Wolf see *The Legend of the Wolf Woman*

Silver Bullet

(1985; Paramount) Alternate Title: *Stephen King's Silver Bullet*. Director: Daniel Attias; Producers: Dino DeLaurentiis, Martha Schumacher; Screenplay: Stephen King; Cinematographer: Armando Nannuzzi. Cast: Gary Busey, Everett McGill, Corey Haim, Megan Follows, Terry O'Quinn, Kent Broadhurst.

> IT STARTED IN MAY IN A SMALL TOWN. AND EVERY MONTH AFTER THAT WHENEVER THE MOON WAS FULL ... IT CAME BACK—ad line

The ever popular Stephen King here adapts his old-fashioned werewolf "novelette" *Cycle of the Werewolf* for the (pardon the expression) silver screen. Set in Tarkers Mills (Small Town USA), *Silver Bullet* (also known as *Stephen King's Silver Bullet*) is every monster-loving kid's escapist fantasy of meeting and ultimately defeating a real live monster, and first-time director Daniel Attias manages to retain much of the small town charm as well as the midnight horror of King's novelette.

"Stephen King," related producer Martha Schumacher, "is one of the most prolific and best-selling authors today. As soon as I read *Cycle of the Werewolf*, I knew it would make a terrific movie because it has all the elements a movie should have: it's heartwarming, it's adventurous, it's scary ... and surprising." Indeed it is.

The basic storyline revolving around a rash of killings devastating this idyllic hamlet and the young wheelchair bound boy who discovers the werewolf's shocking identity is a dark Disney-esque fantasy brought to life via Carlo Rambaldi's monster suits and various severed limbs. Even more important are the excellent characterizations and acting of the three principal players—the boy Marty (a young Corey Haim), his older sister (Megan Follows), and the disreputable but good-hearted Uncle Red (played to colorful perfection by Gary Busey, who utters the film's best line when he exasperatedly exclaims, "I'm a little too old to play 'The Hardy Boys Meet Reverend Werewolf'!"). These characters make the story come alive and involve the audience in the nightmarish proceedings.

Filmed in Wilmington, North Carolina, *Silver Bullet* is more a character-driven film than a moon-driven one, making it an unusually mature monster movie. The three main protagonists (a wheelchair-bound boy, a sister resentful of the attention awarded her handicapped brother, and an alcoholic uncle) all have their own internal demons to fight right alongside the furry external one. "What we tried to deal with, kind of subtextually throughout the film," explained director Daniel Attias, "is the notion that crippledness is more a function of one's own image of oneself than anything else. That fact that the boy is physically crippled does not *make* him crippled. The movie becomes his progress towards accepting himself and gaining acceptance from his family."

Though reserving most of its screen time—and sympathy—for its central protagonists, the film directs a bit of pathos towards its werewolf as well, at least early on. Tormented by dreams of his victims transforming into werewolves themselves (in a disturbing, almost surreal mass metamorphosis sequence), the tortured Reverend Lowe (played by the soft-spoken Everett McGill) wakes up screaming and pleads, "Let it end, dear God. Let it end." But as time progresses and the killings continue, Lowe becomes more a figure of fear than pity, particularly when it becomes clear that he remembers at least some of what he does as the Beast. Targeting Marty when the boy learns his terrible secret, he says, "I'm very sorry about this, Marty…. I would never willingly hurt a child." But he tries to do just that, attempting to run down Marty with his car. A conflicted but obviously weak man, Lowe hypocritically hides behind his collar. "I can't kill myself," he tells Marty (who's been sending him anonymous letters suggesting he do just that). "Our religion teaches us that suicide is the greatest sin a man or woman can commit." And he even goes so far as to justify his monstrousness by claiming to have saved a suicidal woman's soul by killing her himself: "You see how all things serve the will and the mind of God." Such an evolving character arc makes for an intriguing, three-dimensional monster to go along with the well-drawn protagonists.

A cast of quirky characters color the background with deeper hues than most. In among the support are veteran tough-guy Lawrence Tierney (as the tough-guy bartender) and Terry (*The Stepfather*) O'Quinn as the beleaguered sheriff. O'Quinn creates the film's most chilling moment when we see him walking away from a crime scene in a daze, a blood-stained child's kite dangling from one limp hand as he recites a shaky Hail Mary, his voice strained, his face ashen, and his eyes haunted. This subtle reaction scene carries more emotional impact than any of the (admittedly well-done) flying limb sequences that pepper the picture.

Director Daniel Attias (who cut his industry teeth working as assistant director for such cinematic giants as Steven Spielberg and Francis Ford Coppola) and cinematographer Armand Nannuzzi create several standout set-pieces involving striking camerawork and edge-of-the-seat suspense. Utilizing POV shots (as the hitherto unseen monster begins to climb toward an upper window and unsuspecting victim), menacing noises (which one victim-to-be investigates among the shadowy forms in a darkened greenhouse), and quick, frenetic cuts (flashing claws, demonic eyes, snarling fangs) when the monster finally attacks, Attias carefully constructs his scenes for maximum build-up that ultimately explodes in a terrifying frenzy. (Sadly, Attias, who showed such promise in his debut film, soon abandoned movies for the more secure clime of episodic television, working steadily on such hit series as *Northern Exposure, Beverly Hills 90210, Buffy the Vampire Slayer,* and *The Sopranos*.)

This *Silver Bullet* is not completely untarnished, however. While the werewolf kills are handled in a delightfully fast and furious manner in the picture's first half (all claws slicing the air and snarling figures in the mist), once the monster is shown full view it loses much of its impact. "There were several discussions about what sort of a creature we wanted to create," recalled Attias, "and it went through many transformations, if you will—on paper anyway—until we got something that we felt was the right look." Frankly, this "right look" appears more like something from Goldilocks's afternoon nap than a vicious lupine nightmare. Rambaldi's werewolf suit just doesn't cut a terrifying figure in full light, with its roundish bear-like body and stubby snout.

Also, Attias occasionally goes a bit overboard on the "family feature" quality, at times trying to inject a little too much *Afterschool Special* into what is in truth a gruesome R-rated horror film (especially one whose very first scene concludes with a decapitated head flying through the air!). But in the end, it's still an enjoyable monster movie with appealing characters (no easy task considering two of them are pre-pubescents) and a satisfying conclusion. *Silver Bullet* has not received the recognition it deserves, especially since there's always room for an uplifting creature feature.

With quotes from: "Stephen King's Silver Bullet," by Sharon Williams, *Monsterland* 6; "Stephen King's Silver Bullet," by David Everitt, *Fangoria* 48.

Morphology: Bipedal bear-like beast
Demise: Silver bullet (naturally)
Full Moon Rating: ****

Ski Wolf

(2008; SRS Cinema) Director/Screenplay: Chris Seaver; Producers: Leo Belodaeu, Joe Davis, Rachel Lovinger, Chris Seaver; Cinematographer: Jack DeQueaf. Cast: Casey Bowler, Trent Haaga, Billy Garberina, Alix Lakehurst, Saetia Lereoux, Jesse Ames.

> Hairy palms are the LEAST of his problems!—poster

No doubt all the goofy characterizations, silly voices, and scatological jokes in *Ski Wolf* cracked everybody up at the time, and went over like gangbusters with the group of friends making this camcorder quickie, but the "humor" fails to carry over to the third-party viewer. No doubt making *Ski Wolf* was far more fun than actually watching it. Hell, it would *have* to be.

The story (such as it is) has twenty-something Scott (Casey Bowler) and his friends visiting his Uncle Billy (Billy Garberina, who looks no older than his supposed "nephew") at their family-owned local ski resort one last time before Billy is forced to sell. Scott, after being humiliated by Ralston (Trent Haaga), the obnoxious BMOM (Big Man on Mountain) who is set to buy the resort at the end of the weekend, is randomly attacked by an (unseen) werewolf while outside suffering the effects of a laxative prank. Apparently surviving the vicious mauling intact, he soon develops hairy palms and eventually, after being hit by a giant snowball thrown by Ralston, fully transforms into the coolest dude on the slopes—the trash-talking, groovy-walking, babe-stalking Ski Wolf. With the narcissistic Ralston feeling threatened by the newfound popularity and lupine coolness of Ski Wolf, a winner-take-all race down the dreaded "Mt. Doom" is in the cards. But when the self-centered Ski Wolf starts treating his friends like wolf scat, can Scott regain his buddies' trust, win the race, and save their beloved ski resort? More importantly, will any viewer still care after 70 minutes of this excruciating almost–home movie?

Written and directed by video "auteur" Chris Seaver, maker of such no-budget nonsense as *Scrotal Vengeance* (2001), *Heather and Puggly Drop a Deuce* (2005) and *Terror at Blood Fart Lake* (2009), *Ski Wolf* looks, acts, and even *smells* bad (though the last may just be this viewer's imagination). With lighting, photography, script and acting well below even the poorest of porno productions, *Ski Wolf* offers only a couple of cheesy gore effects (a decapitation and baby-eating[!] played strictly for laughs—that fail to materialize), lame pop-culture references and characterizations (including one cast member doing a bad Bill Murray impression from *Caddyshack*, while another talks like a Viking escapee from a Renaissance fair), and a crude but passable *Teen Wolf*-ish lycanthrope. The makeup on said werewolf ends at the neck and hands, however, which means that during the Ski Wolf sex scene (yes, he gets it on with an overweight, over-endowed, all-round unattractive "babe" in the form of self-styled fetishist and fringe porn actress Alix Lakehurst) we're bombarded by the sight of Ski Wolf's pasty-white, doughy body bumping uglies. Shudder. The sole transformation sequence encapsulates this production's quality (using the term loosely), as it consists of Scott writhing around, dropping out of frame, then popping up as the now-transformed Ski Wolf.

But lest one think that *Ski Wolf* is merely an amateurish concoction of pop-culture rip-offs and crude humor, it also imparts a moral lesson to its viewers. At one point an apologetic Scott explains to his friends that "when I'm the Wolf, it's like I'm having sex with a woman and I'm cummin.'" But Scott has learned there's more to life than meaningless metaphorical ejaculation, conceding, "It really took me being a self-centered, arrogant werewolf to realize that my *friends* are what's truly important to me." Awww.

So ... failing as a werewolf movie (and morality play), how does this *Wolf* stack up in the *Ski* department? Well, gentle reader, it doesn't. Beyond the high school-level videography, the puerile script, and the countless boobs and masturbation jokes, the real crime committed by this supposed *Ski Wolf* is the fact that he never really skis. For a story set at a ski resort, the characters rarely leave their cramped house interiors, with only a token scene here and there set in the dilapidated day lodge or on the slopes (even then the actors merely stand around at the foot of the bunny hill). Seaver's camcorder captures only a few moments of actual skiing, with these being decidedly pedestrian (almost literally, as the pace isn't much more than a brisk walk). Even the climactic Big Race down the dreaded "Mt. Doom" appears like the two contestants are simply speed-walking on a green run. This author, a long-time skier, can forgive quite a bit in a ski movie (or a werewolf flick, for that matter)—*except* the absence of actual skiing. With nothing else going for it, without the *Ski*, this *Wolf* is merely a dog.

Morphology: A Teen Wolf wannabe on skis (supposedly)
Demise: None, he lives to ski (or not) another day
Full Moon Rating: Zero moons

Skin Walkers see Skinwalkers

Skinwalkers

(2006; Lionsgate; Canada/US/Germany) Alternate Title: *Skin Walkers*. Director: Jim Isaac; Producers: Don Carmody, Dennis Berardi; Screenplay: James DeMonaco, Todd Harthan, James Roday; Cinematographers: David A. Armstrong, Adam Kane. Cast: Jason Behr, Elias Koteas, Rhona Mitra, Natassia Malthe, Sarah Carter, Kim Coates, Tom Jackson, Wendy Crewson, Matthew Knight.

The Beast Waits Within—ad line

"I love the idea of the beast inside all of us," said *Skinwalkers* director James Isaac (*Jason X*, 2001), "and this script really plays with that, that's what the story's all about." Said story follows the efforts of a clan of werewolves living in a small town to protect a 12-year-old "half breed" (with a human mother and werewolf father) who, legend says, upon reaching his 13th birthday will somehow "bring an end to all skinwalkers." Unfortunately, there are those who revel in their lycanthropy and see it not as a curse but a gift. "A war has been raging between those who want the curse to end and those who embrace the powers of the beast," explains the film's opening scrawl. The latter group, personified by a small band of leather-clad, chopper-riding, badass lycans, come after this "chosen one," intent on keeping their werewolf status intact. The "good" werewolf bunch must flee (in their modified RV) in order to keep the boy alive.

In among all the gunplay and escape sequences, the scenario offers more depth than most. As Isaac notes, "The story's about the beast inside of us and the choices we make, whether to embrace that beast. You can call it your dark side, whatever you want to call it, but we all have that primal animal in us.... Most of us have to make those choices every day." Indeed, at the core of *Skinwalkers* is the notion of *choice*—embrace the animal inside us or embrace society's dictates and give up (or at least control) said beast. This reflects the very core of the werewolf mythos—nature vs. nurture, inner animal freedom vs. regulating society. Though some may posit that society is an artificial construct, one that can even block our individual primal needs, it is that very construct that has allowed us to climb to the top of the food chain. Alone and naked in the wilderness, a human being is nigh on defenseless; but surrounded by others, or even equipped with the collective power of society (everything from the rudimentary mastery of fire to the technological advantage of firearms), s/he becomes the true king of the jungle. So Man must use his intellect to forge societal bonds, allowing the human race to reign supreme. (The many apocalyptic stories and films that deal with the breakdown of society and the resultant chaos illustrate our fascination with—and fear of—this concept.)

It is our intellect that allows us to construct society, and our emotions (compassion, empathy) that allow us to live within it. That makes man an animal of dichotomies (if one chooses to see reason and emotion as opposites). When a member swings too far one way or the other, he or she becomes either a beast relying solely on instinct, or a heartless, cold, calculating "machine." Neither can survive long nor succeed within the society Man has created. *Skinwalkers* pits ordered society (in the form of the "good" werewolves, who assimilate themselves into the community and even physically restrain themselves during the nights of the full moon to ensure they don't break society's rules) against savage nature (the rogue werewolves who ride motorcycles and kill whenever their bloodlust rises). "There's a real story there," enthused Isaac. "You take away the werewolf part of the story and it's still a very dynamic story about family, choice, sacrifice, civil war between family members, and so you've got a lot of depth."

The thoughtful *Skinwalkers* adds some nuance to accepted werewolf lore. It posits that "the first skinwalkers were Native Americans" (as one character explains). "They believed the power of the wolf was a gift, but it mutated. Many couldn't control the lust for power, couldn't fight the beast inside them." Noted co-producer Dennis Berardi, "We made a stylistic choice in this film not to be Gothic, but to base it in North American tribal mythology, rather than the European werewolf tradition which has been done to death." Besides characterizing lycanthropy as a tribal or even familial condition, passed down through generations, the film sees it as akin to an addiction triggered by the taking of human life. "The nature and the craving for human blood is so intense that if they break free and feed they will become the beast forever." Not literally—as these "bad" werewolves only transform during the cycle of the full moon or when their passions are aroused—but internally, with "the lust and desire to consume human blood so overwhelming for them, it's like drugs to an addict." In the modern world,

198 • *Skinwalkers*

One of the "sexy and powerful" *Skinwalkers* **(Natassia Malthe) (courtesy makeup maestro Stan Winston).**

where addictions of nearly every kind are front and center in the zeitgeist, this reflects a very topical updating of the werewolf mythos.

"The creatures themselves are a true blend of human and beast," described Isaac (who began his cinematic career as a special effects technician, working on such films as *Return of the Jedi*, *Gremlins* and David Cronenberg's *The Fly*). "They're very subtle. I wanted them to be very sexy, very powerful, scary when we need them to be." And that they are (courtesy of makeup maestro Stan Winston). Looking like a more bestial Lon Chaney man-wolf hybrid, though with more distortion in the angular face (raised brows, hollow cheeks, yellow eyes), they sport hairy arms and ridged naked torsos, not to mention a set of wicked claws and oversized fangs. In keeping with the attempt at characterization, each werewolf has its own individualized appearance (the female member of the wolf pack sports a smoother, sleeker look, for instance). And when one opens its fang-filled, saliva-dripping mouth to roar its rage, it's a truly unsettling sight. "We wanted to connect with the audience," noted Berardi," to the point that, when [lycan leader] Varek transforms, you still know it's Varek and he still gets to emote and connect.... So we went for a very humanistic design—upright, not ever on all fours—more for story reasons than design reasons."

At one point the head of the good werewolves, Jonas, insist they make a stand rather than continue running. At this, the boy's human mother protests, "I'm not like you, Jonas. I don't have the beast inside of me." To this, Jonas shoots back, "You better find it, or your son will die"—indicating that sometimes we must take our inner strength from the animal inside us, and that perhaps humanity divests itself entirely from its inner beast at its own peril.

Said Isaac about his approach to lycanthropy, "The rules are the same. We're staying very true to the mythology on that level. They use silver bullets, the moon brings them out. We wanted to stay true to the mythology and, not update it but to do what I think it really needs which is to give it some soul." And that it does. The script cleverly pits the two groups against one another, exploring the pathos and humanity of the "cursed" ones, as well as exploiting the savagery and monstrousness of those who embrace lycanthropy as "a gift." As Isaac points out, "there are two sides, one that has made the choice to try to make moral decisions and hopefully end the curse, to try to live normal lives; the other side, of course, embraces being a werewolf and loves the power and the passion and the primal energy that comes with that, and they want to preserve that."

To maintain its PG-13 rating, Isaac, without shying away from the violence and brutality inherent in the story, keeps the gore more suggested than shown, while still making an impact through sound effects and editing.

Not everything works for these *Skinwalkers*, however. The McGuffin of the "chosen one" somehow making everything alright upon turning 13 appears both trite and unsatisfying. The small band of evil lycanthropes come off as low-rent shadows of the vampire clan from the groundbreaking *Near Dark* (even aping a sequence in which the antagonists invade a local bar to slaughter and eat the inhabitants). And, most disappointingly, *Skinwalkers* offers up far more gunplay than werewolf action (until the climactic confrontation), with the villains periodically—and repetitively—catching up with the protagonists for yet another shoot-out/escape. Fortunately, the well-drawn individual protagonists brought to life by a competent cast help move the plot along and keep all that action meaningful rather than just loud (like in so many modern shoot 'em ups). Indeed, when one sympathetic character "turns," it makes for a tense, shocking and emotionally wrenching scene of betrayal and dismay.

One of the better werewolf efforts of the new millennium, *Skinwalkers* offers some food for thought along with its action-fueled carbohydrates, raising it above so many of its empty-calorie (and empty-headed) brethren. Unfortunately, audiences of the time didn't see it that way. A financial failure, the twenty-million-dollar film earned only slightly more than a million dollars domestically, and only $2.5 million worldwide. And, sadly, director James Isaac lost his battle with a rare blood disorder on May 7, 2012, passing away at age 51.

With quotes from: "Director James Isaac Talks *Skinwalkers*," by Todd Brown, Twitchfilm.com; "*Skinwalkers*: Werewolf Wars," by Michael Rowe, *Fangoria* 262.

Morphology: Streamlined, muscular wolfmen (and women)
Demise: Silver bullets
Full Moon Rating: ***½

Stephen King's Silver Bullet see *Silver Bullet*

The Strangers

(1998; Vista Street Entertainment) Directors/Producers: Sergei and Yuri Ivanov. Screenplay: Steven Weller, Sergei and Yuri Ivanov; Cinematographer: Anthony Moncado. Cast: Richard Bent, Shana Betz, Victoria Hunter, Jennifer Marks, Matt Martin, Jimmy Lord, J.J. Denton, Joe Durrenberger.

ONLY THE INNOCENT SURVIVE!—ad line

Which is more than can be said for viewer interest, as that dies out after the very first scene. *The Strangers* is not just another cheap camcorder travesty … it's a *muddled*, cheap camcorder travesty. Confused and confusing, and full of ill-defined characters acting on obtuse motivations, the film remains a boring, nonsensical, technically inept shot-on-video mess with nothing to recommend.

The story follows Trent (Richard Bent), an apparent werewolf who now works as a laborer at a nowheresville roadside store/restaurant up in the mountains, where he flirts with the two waitress stepsisters and steals chains to constrain himself during nights of the full moon (or so one infers, as no overt metamorphosis ever occurs). Enter the evil werewolf Jade (Victoria Hunter), Trent's former wife, and her new paramour, looking to sire a werewolf son via Trent's alpha seed … or something. Apparently, Trent killed the alpha and now Jade must mate with *him*. "You gotta give her a son," says Jade's smarmy new companion. "You give her a son and we live forever. You don't and we die—and you go first." What this means, exactly, is anybody's guess, as no further explanation is forthcoming.

The script's dialogue is just as vague and pointless as its plotting, ranging from banal to just plain stupid. "You know, memories aren't always what we recall," observes one character. Somebody needs to tell him that memories actually *are* what we recall—that's what makes them "memories." Sheesh.

As Trent, Richard Bent broods … and broods … and broods. The rest of the cast offer about as much personality as the ranch house garage that stands in for the supposed backwoods general store. Jennifer Marks, as Trent's love interest Pearl, gives it the old college try but comes off more hysterical than heartfelt.

First- and *last*-time producing/directing brothers Sergei and Yuri Ivanov do not deign to insert any action or suspense, instead filling their film with scene after scene of characters talking (often with the audio levels so low, and/or the ambient background noise so high, that one can barely hear the dialogue—which, truthfully, may be no great loss); characters traipsing through the woods (extending the already excruciatingly dull sequences with meaningless *slow-motion*); or characters having sex (even the two stepsisters inexplicably engage in a lesbian tryst in the restaurant bathroom)—though much of it clothed or filmed in obfuscating long shot. The Brothers Ivanov try to dress up their lifeless mannequin of a movie with some frilly technique, such as the aforementioned slo-mo, hand-held shaky-cam footage, and protracted zooms, but these serve only to annoy rather than enhance. Toss in such desperate, ineffectual distractions as a long, out-of-left-field scene of one character engaging in auto-erotic asphyxiation(!), and seemingly miles of car-cam footage showing the road rushing past a fender, and these *Strangers* overstay their welcome from the get-go.

The few attack scenes end before any actual attack, and the aftermath is always *talked about* rather than shown ("Oh God, look here!" bleats one character, with the camera locked on him rather than the shocking carnage he supposedly sees). The occasional exposed breast is about the only "special effect" seen in the film—until the final five minutes, when the oversized Spock ears and rubber rat-bat-faced werewolf mask comes out.

Which leads to the lycanthropic angle … a decidedly obtuse one, given that the only indication that *The Strangers* is indeed a werewolf movie comes from a bit of stilted dialogue at the hour mark when Trent confesses his condition to Pearl (who first swallows it hook, line and claw; then rejects the notion as delusional; and finally runs screaming when Trent abruptly sports a mouthful of ugly dentures). Like just about every other aspect of this amateurish atrocity, confusion reigns supreme when it comes to lycanthropy. Though Trent indicates that he (and the other werewolves) only transform during the full moon, Jade and her lover occasionally sport a set of snaggle-teeth for no apparent good reason (perhaps simply to remind viewers that yes, there *are* werewolves in this picture). Given this fangs-only look, however, these lycanthropes could just as well be vampires, a notion reinforced by the fact that the method of their destruction is a wooden stake through the heart.

When we finally see a werewolf—or what passes for a werewolf in this impoverished universe—one can only snort in derision rather than shudder in fear. After a brief tussle between Trent and Jade's companion (culminating in the most unconvincing decapitation scene this side of an Andy Milligan movie when Trent literally knocks his opponent's block off with a half-hearted swing of his arm), then between Jade and Pearl (ending in Jade's staking), Trent turns around to finally reveal himself in all his lycanthropic glory—which consists of giant bat ears, heavy brows, hairy cheeks, a flat bat-like proboscis, massive red lips, and an oversized cleft chin that would make even Jay Leno cringe. Then when this ludicrous bat-rat-wolf live-action cartoon begins *talking*, with Trent begging Pearl to kill him ("No Trent, I can't—I love you!" "Then set me *free*! Do it!!"), *The Strangers* turns into a cinematic joke. Unfortunately, the joke is on the viewer who just wasted 89 minutes of his or her life.

Mom told you not to talk to strangers; well, I'm telling you not to *watch Strangers*. Simply put, do not invite these *Strangers* into your home.

Morphology: Bat-faced biped
Demise: Wooden stake to the heart
Full Moon Rating: zero moons

Strippers vs. Werewolves

(2012; Kaleidoscope Film; U.K.) Director: Jonathan Glendening; Producers: Jonathan Sothcott, Simon Phillips, Patricia Rybarczyk, Billy Murray, Gareth Mullaney, Ciaran Mullaney; Screenplay: Phillip Baron (based on *Strippers versus Werewolves*, by Pat Higgins); Cinematographer: David Meadows. Cast: Adele Silva, Ali Bastian, Marc Bayliss, Martin Compston, Sarah Douglas, Alan Ford, Billy Murray, Lysette Anthony, Steven Berkoff, Martin Kemp, Robert Englund.

THIS FULL MOON THE WOLVES HAVE BITTEN
OFF MORE THAN THEY CAN CHEW—trailer

As the opening credits roll, Duran Duran's 1982 pop hit "Hungry Like the Wolf" (covered by the band Wild Moon) plays on the soundtrack while we watch a club explode in London 1984. Moving ahead to 2011, a dancer, Justice (Adele Silva), at the "Vixens" strip club looks on in horror as her private client transforms into a werewolf. Panicking, she stabs the manbeast in the eye with a (silver) fountain pen, killing him. This sets in motion a vendetta by the man's wolfpack, led by Jack Ferris (Billy Murray), which (unknown to the girl) just so happens to include Justice's fiancé, Scott (Martin Compston). It all culminates in a strippers vs. werewolves showdown at the club (involving some of the same players from the 1984 bombing), as Justice and the girls make a stand against Scott and his were-boys.

Very British, and far less sleazy than one might expect from such a title ("The single biggest criticism of the film is that the strippers don't strip enough," noted producer Jonathan Sothcott), *Strippers vs. Werewolves* remains an entertaining melding of the modern British gangster film (as exemplified by such Guy Ritchie entries as *Lock, Stock and Two Smoking Barrels*, *Snatch* and *Rocknrolla*) and the werewolf movie.

Like some overeager club patron tossing out twenties, *Strippers vs. Werewolves* makes its intentions known from the outset. Within the first minute the film offers a stripper—and a werewolf (though neither go too far in their respective departments, with both keepin' it tasteful). As a dancer dressed in a sexy schoolgirl outfit (and suggestively sucking on a lolly) gyrates in front of a suit-wearing gangster-type, the man becomes excited (veritably vibrating in his chair) while quick edits of hair and fangs flash across the screen. Then, as the girl turns around and bends over to gaze at him from between her legs, she—and we—suddenly see an upside-down werewolf visage. The wolfman rises from his chair, the girl's eyes widen in panic, he growls and lunges, and she pulls out a (silver) fountain pen and stabs the monster in the eye before screaming hysterically. It's an inventive and startling opening that perfectly sets the tone for this small-scale but generally clever modern lycantale.

The next werewolf scene further cements the were-gangster bond. It begins with a pair of hard cases torturing a bloodied man strapped to a chair. "Stop bleeding so much, Richard," taunts one menacingly, "you gotta learn to *co-agulate* more effectively. How you gonna cope when we remove your jaw?" Suddenly, a group of werewolves interrupts the "fun" and slaughters the two gangsters. At this, the bleeding victim giddily proclaims, "You're here to save me! You're werewolves who protect the innocent, werewolves on a quest to destroy the evil. You're hero werewolves!" But the still-human leader (Jack) calmly answers, "Sorry mate, we're just regular werewolves, I'm afraid," and his gang commences to eat the trussed-up man alive.

Director Jonathan Glendening utilizes a whole bag of tricks to keep things moving—and hip. For instance, he employs a split-screen technique to not only add a sense of urgency, but to create an often amusing juxtaposition (one side of the screen showing a stripper distracting some customers, for example, while the other reveals the bouncer sneaking a dead body—the fountain pen victim—out the back). Rather than simple fades or dissolves, Glendening employs slash marks or sexy silhouettes to transition from one scene (of the werewolves) to the next (the strippers), underlining the two sides to the story. And at the climactic battle (small-scale though it may be), a scorecard periodically flashes on the screen after each deadly set-piece (e.g. "Strippers 1 v Werewolves 0").

This was Glendening's second werewolf film, the first being *Night Wolf* (aka *13 Hrs*): "It's not really the werewolves that attract me," noted the filmmaker. "I mean the wolves in *SvW* are so different to the creature in *13hrs*. In *13hrs*, the creature was a representation of an inner disease that was ripping a family apart. It was furless, white, opal and luminescent, and looked as though it had been birthed through pain ... it is a savage beast. Whereas in *SvW*, the werewolves are sentient beings, and being a werewolf is a lifestyle choice; it just marks their gang apart as 'a pack.' So both are polar opposite in terms of their takes on a werewolf.... But I can't deny I love a bit of prosthetic fun."

There's actually very little "prosthetic fun" in *Strippers vs. Werewolves*, given the creatures' rather minimalist makeup, and the fact that they're in human form more often than not. With their overgrown sideburns, prominent fangs, heavy brows, and pointy ears, these lycans resemble a simian version of Henry Hull's *Werewolf of London*. Rather than a curse, lycanthropy is something to be enjoyed, with the pack strutting about like geezer gangsters, making such comments as, "I'm going to kill you so slowly your driving license is going to expire before you do." They play with their food (chasing a naked nubile around their lair for fun) and eat their enemies (with the pack taking out some toughs just because they'd scratched Jack's car). While the moon holds no sway—they transform at will, and seemingly instantaneously (the budget obviously didn't include any onscreen metamorphosis money)—silver is a necessity. "The only way to kill a werewolf—," reads one of the girls from a book her occultist boyfriend lends her, "—you must pierce his heart or brain with silver."

The book also tells them that "Werewolves must bite you for the curse to work, or you could bite it." This plays into a subplot in which Justice bites down on Scott's shoulder during sex—hard enough to acquire the "gift" herself. When Jack, a self-professed misogynist, learns of this, he reiterates his strict "no girls allowed" policy for his pack. Consequently, when it looks as if Justice might turn, he tells Scott that at the "first sign of fur, cut off her face." Ouch.

The obviously self-aware film references several werewolf classics. The now–alpha Jack visits his incarcerated former pack master (played with menacing intensity by a cameoing Robert Englund) at the "HM Chaney" prison; while a darts player snarls "You made me miss" in a nod to *An American Werewolf in London*.

Strippers vs. Werewolves generally strikes the right balance of humor and horror, not only through the situations but the characters and dialogue as well. For instance, when one pack member excitedly exclaims, "We're the baddest, meanest werewolves ever! No one messes with us. We fuckin' rock!" Jack peevishly retorts, "Do you have to keep swearing? It's annoying—" before adding, without a hint of irony, "—when there's no fuckin' need." When the girls see the horrific aftermath of a wolf attack at Vixens (bodies—and body parts—strewn everywhere), one laments of a slaughtered colleague, "Poor Saffron, she had such great legs." She then queries, "Have you found the other one?"

The script takes enough time to, ahem, flesh out the character of Justice and her three girlfriends, investing them with enough personality to make the viewer care about their fates (making it an emotional shocker when one of the likely leads becomes a gory meal for the pack half-way through the picture). Likewise, the film delineates the wolves as well, from the brutish simpleton to the psychotic skinhead to the nattily-dressed charmer to the calm yet oh-so-dangerous Jack (played with cool authority by Billy Murray). Then there's a wonderful, laugh-out-loud side-turn from Simon Phillips as the geeky, bumbling vampire hunter boyfriend of one of the girls, who plays a crucial role at film's end.

Said end, unfortunately, proves to be the movie's Achilles heel, as it ultimately runs out of steam, with the impoverished climax offering about as much energy as a fatigued pole dancer at the tail end of her second shift. Despite some quick edits desperately trying to punch up the desultory "action," it proves a disappointing conclusion to an otherwise engaging effort.

According to producer Jonathan Sothcott, the low-budget project was anything but 'easy-peasy.' "The whole bloody film was a living nightmare," he admitted. "Everyone fell out, the money was late, the creative core was pulling in completely different directions, one of the actors was incredibly badly behaved. I fired more people on that film than on all my others put together. We needed another dressing room just to contain all the egos. I have to pay tribute to my producing partner Simon Phillips [who nearly steals the film playing the timorous occultist] because without his level head we wouldn't have had a film at all. But every day it seemed he was calling me with a new crisis—it was just jinxed. For all that it wasn't that bad a film, there are bits of it I love and I really enjoyed working with Robert Englund, Lysette Anthony, Alan Ford, and old pals such as Martin Kemp [the pen-to-the-eye werewolf], Steven Berkoff and Lucy Pinder, who kindly came and did cameos."

At the film's world premier in London, Sothcott enthused, "When a script comes through the letterbox called *Strippers vs. Werewolves* I couldn't do anything other than make it—it's such a slam dunk. It appeals to everyone—boys, girls … werewolves, everyone in between. It's a great, silly throwaway beer and pizza movie." Indeed it is. And had a bit more cash (or inventiveness) been thrown at the climax, it could have been even more.

With quotes from: "Interview: Jonathan Sothcott," by Nicholas Yanes, scifipulse.net; "Interview with *13 Hrs* and *Strippers vs. Werewolves* Director Jonathan Glendening," LoveHorror.com; "*Strippers vs. Werewolves* World Premier Interviews."

Morphology: Big-eared, normally-dressed wolfmen
Demise: Silver bullets; silver high heel through the heart(!); explosion, with the subsequent body parts kept from re-forming by placing them in separate jars(!!)
Full Moon Rating: ***

Teen Wolf

(1985; Atlantic Releasing Corporation) Director: Rod Daniel; Producers: Mark Levinson, Scott Rosenfelt; Screenplay: Joseph Loeb III, Matthew Weisman; Cinematographer: Tim Suhrstedt. Cast: Michael J. Fox, James Hampton, Scott Paulin, Susan Ursitti, Jerry Levine, Jim MacKrell, Lorie Griffin, Mark Arnold, Jay Tarses.

> He's always wanted to be something special,
> but he never expected this—trailer

Teen Wolf opens like a nightmare: strange, disorienting sounds echo ominously against a black screen while the stark credits roll. But when the darkness dissipates to finally divulge the source of this disturbing cacophony, it's not some monstrous horror scene but a high school basketball game in which a sweat-drenched Michael J. Fox misses—in agonizing slow motion—a free throw. Welcome to the terror of *Teen Wolf*, a movie about adolescent transformation taken to the Nth degree. Unlike earlier (and later) teen angst lycan-films, however (such as *I Was a Teenage Werewolf*, the biting satire *Full Moon High*, and the *Ginger Snaps* series), *Teen Wolf* makes gentle comedy out of the real-life horrors of burgeoning adulthood. Following in *The Karate Kid*'s mega-popular footsteps, *Teen Wolf* embraces the underdog-triumphing-through-sports trope as well. Yes, *Teen Wolf* offers the first-ever basketball-playing werewolf…

High Schooler Scott Howard (Michael J. Fox) struggles with his humdrum life—playing on a losing basketball team, yearning after the pretty girl he can't have, and generally trying to rise above his "average" status. One day he begins to experience changes—odd hair grows on his chest, his eyes glow red at times, and his ears lengthen. Soon he transforms completely into a teenage werewolf! His middle-aged dad (James Hampton), also a lycanthrope, explains that this is normal, and that "werewolves are people just like anyone else." When Scott's inner Wolf comes out during a basketball game (giving him Jordan-esque skills), he quickly becomes the most popular (wolf)boy in school. With his newfound notoriety going to his head, Scott ultimately learns that it's most important to be oneself, culminating in Scott and his teammates digging deep to triumph—*without* the Wolf—during the Championship game.

In the world of *Teen Wolf*, lycanthropy isn't contracted by a fateful bite; it isn't the result of a Satanic curse; and it has nothing to do with being at the wrong place at the wrong time. It's simply hereditary. Scott's transition to werewolf comes on gradually, over the course of a few days. It begins with little—and temporary—changes, such as Scott's eyes glowing red for an instant, his ears becoming momentarily pointy under his feathered hair, or wisps of fur suddenly covering the backs of his hands (to his great embarrassment). Finally, Scott fully transforms in front of a bathroom mirror in a brief but effective air-bladder-infused sequence. As he stares at his reflection in dismay, Scott's face becomes more angular and his skin bubbles slightly. His fingernails are suddenly sharp claws, and we watch his ears elongate. Scott covers his face with his now-hairy hands, gasps, and involuntarily draws backwards to reveal—the Wolf. "Jeez Louise," he comically groans at his hairy cheeks, long beard, canine nose and delicate fangs.

This pivotal sequence segues into the film's funniest moment. When Scott's father demands his son open the bathroom door, Scott reluctantly does so. Scott stops short, however, when he—and we—see his father, the man's altered middle-aged face framed by a ring of fluffy gray hair. With his glasses perched on his enlarged dog-nose, Mr. Howard deadpans, "An explanation is probably long overdue."

Said explanation offers more about this film's brand of lycanthropy. "Sometimes it skips a generation; I was hoping it would pass you by," says Mr. Howard. At this, Scott shoots back, "Well, Dad, it didn't pass me by—it landed on my *face*!" His father tries to tell Scott that "It's not all bad. For one thing, you're going to be able to do a lot of things the other guys aren't." Scott isn't having any, however, bitterly shooting off sarcastic remarks like, "I can look forward to a life of stealing babies in the middle of the night, and killing chickens, fearing full moons, dodging silver bullets." His father calmly counters, "Don't believe all that stuff you see in the movies. With certain obvious exceptions, werewolves are people just like everyone else." Mr. Howard also offers that age-old superhero bromide about great power requiring greater responsibility, before concluding, "The werewolf is a part of you, but that doesn't change what you have inside." So rather than lycanthropy subsuming one's personality, here it becomes a metaphor for attaining one's potential—for growing into who you really are. It's

Portrait in werewolf cuteness: The *Teen Wolf* (Michael J. Fox) and his belle du jour (Lorie Griffin), dressed for the high school play.

not surprising, perhaps, that such a were-notion surfaced in the "self-actualization" decade.

After his initial unwanted change, Scott finds he can shift at will—"but sometimes it happens when I don't want it to" (i.e., when angry or excited), though nothing further is made of this potentially dramatic loss of control. In fact, nothing much is made of *anything* weighty, apart from Scott's subsequent growing pains on his journey to discover who he really is, Scott or the Wolf.

A line of dialogue listing Scott's litany of complaints sums up the movie's slight premise: "Dad, I got a bad outside hook shot, I'm allergic to eggs, I got a six-dollar haircut; I mean, I *have* problems—I don't need this one." But, as it turns out, being a werewolf isn't much of a "problem" after all; in fact, here lycanthropy falls firmly on the side of "gift" rather than curse. It begins with Scott (with his temporary glowing red eyes and gravelly voice) inadvertently intimidating a liquor store clerk into selling him a keg of beer for a party. Then, during a scrum after a loose ball at the next basketball game, Scott rises from the floor in full wolf-mode; as everyone gapes, he delivers a slam dunk before leading his team to their first victory in three years. Soon "the Wolf" is the most popular figure at school (with Scott's enterprising friend Stiles printing up "Teen Wolf" t-shirts and bumper stickers). Scott-wolf even gets the girl of his dreams—at least for an afternoon. There ensues further basketball shenanigans, a *Saturday Night Fever* prep scene (complete with white suit), and a high school dance that culminates in the student body doing an impromptu "werewolf" dance—hands held like claws—in the gym.

It's the oldest adolescent story in the book (dressed up in a werewolf suit)—nerdy kid struggles to find an identity, stumbles into popularity, abandons his few true friends (and values), then finds his way back

just in time. Simplistic and unlikely (even *sans* the werewolf bit). Scott works his way back to the straight-and-narrow path far too easily, without any real consequences or soul searching. And the script carefully sidesteps any truly important issues. For instance, while it's implied that Scott's mother has died, Scott's (or his father's) feelings of loss over such a devastating tragedy remain completely unaddressed. As a result, the film (like the Teen Wolf himself) comes off as mere fluff without any real substance.

Fortunately, the production had 23-year-old Michael J. Fox upon which to hang its werewolf suit. (Amusingly, most of Fox's "high-school" costars were in their mid-twenties as well.) Fox's unimposing physique, low-key likability and every-kid quality brands him as the epitome of "nice," and *Teen Wolf* plays off this in its gentle, friendly, nonthreatening look at a high-schooler's growing pains—with the added fillip of lycanthropy tossed into the comical mix.

This popular flick (combined with *Back to the Future*, released a month earlier) made Michael J. Fox a star. *Teen Wolf* grossed over $50 million and led to an inferior sequel, a children's cartoon show, and a long-running television series (starting in 2011). Mild in every way, *Teen Wolf* stands as a silly, safe, and reassuring look at teenage troubles through a lycanthropic lens.

Morphology: Long-haired, cute-nosed, friendly, basketball-playing teen werewolf
Demise: None (the only danger faced by this Teen Wolf is split ends from too much blow-drying)
Full Moon Rating: **½

Teen Wolf Too

(1987; Atlantic Releasing Corporation) Director: Christopher Leitch; Producer: Kent Bateman; Screenplay: R. Timothy Kring (Story: Joseph Loeb III, Matthew Weisman); Cinematographer: Jules Brenner. Cast: Jason Bateman, Kim Darby, John Astin, Paul Sand, Mark Holton, James Hampton, Estee Chandler, Stuart Fratkin.

> Freshman have always had trouble adjusting to college life. But never like this—poster

By 1987 Michael J. Fox had become too big a star (thanks to the original *Teen Wolf* and the *Back to the Future* films), and no doubt carried too big a price tag, to sign on for a warmed-over rehash like *Teen Wolf Too*. So *Teen Wolf* executive producers Thomas Coleman and Michael Rosenblat hired 18-year-old TV child actor Jason Bateman to be their new Teen Wolf. No doubt the sequel's line producer, Kent Bateman, had something to do with the selection—given that Jason was his own son.

More remake than sequel, *Teen Wolf Too* sees Todd Howard (Bateman), cousin of the first film's Michael J. Fox character, Scott, arrive at college on an athletic scholarship (science major Todd has no idea why he's been given a full ride, as the only time he'd been on a field was playing clarinet in the marching band). It turns out Scott's old basketball coach Mr. Finstock (Paul Sand) now coaches the college boxing team. Under pressure from Dean Dunn (John Astin) to recruit a ringer, Finstock recommended Scott's cousin, hoping that Todd, too, will bring the prowess of the Wolf to his sporting endeavors (like Scott did with basketball in the first *Teen Wolf*). While settling in on campus, the same thing happens to college freshman Todd as what happened to High Schooler Scott—he wolfs out for the first time, utilizes his werewolf abilities to excel at his chosen sport, lets his newfound popularity as the Teen Wolf go to his head, chases the beautiful-but-shallow girl while ignoring his real friends (and the nice girl who loves him for who he really is), and finally faces the championship bout as just plain Todd. And with a little advice (and boxing tips) from his Uncle Howard, Scott's dad (James Hampton, reprising his role from the first film), Todd triumphs in the end.

Aptly named, *Teen Wolf Too* turned out to be an also-ran. TV writer (and later producer) Timothy Kring (penning his sole theatrical screenplay) took Joseph Leob and Matthew Wiseman's *Teen Wolf* script and merely changed high school to college, and basketball to boxing, leaving most everything else the same. He even ports over a quartet of returning characters (though two of them—Scott's money-hungry friend Stiles and the laconic Coach Finstock, still fond of non sequiturs—are played by new actors) who do exactly the same thing (Stiles capitalizes on the Wolf's popularity by selling hats and t-shirts; Coach dispenses non-sequitur advice; Scott's father mentors his wolfish nephew; and "Chubbs" makes fat and food funny). Doing just enough to avoid a plagiarism suit, Kring still had to officially (and rightly) credit Loeb and Wiseman with "original story" and "characters."

A subtle—but important—difference between the two films, however, comes in the way *Teen Wolf Too* handles its lycanthropy. Rather than a metaphor for the difficult transition from adolescence to adulthood (as portrayed in the first film), here the Wolf simply becomes a symbol of Todd's inner jerk. Rather than finding his true self via the metamorphosis, Todd regresses, becoming *more* adolescent while in Wolf-form (transforming from responsible nice guy trying to better himself into a self-centered party animal prone to reckless driving and showing off via bad song-and-dance routines). So lycanthropy, rather than helping to find one's inner strength like in the original, here becomes a teen-weight dragging Todd back towards his infantile roots. Though the sequel tried its best to slavishly imitate the first *Teen Wolf*, its ersatz script failed to capture the nuance of the original, which made the Wolf truly seem a part of the protagonist and allowed the two to meld together by film's end into a stronger character. In *Teen Wolf Too*, Jason Bateman's Todd acts, speaks and does little to convey any real growth (even relying on the self-defeating act of conjuring the Wolf—via the overused and cheesy trick of his eyes glowing red during the championship boxing match—to get him up off the canvas and back into the fight). It's just one more disappointment in this dumbed-down retread that offers nothing new, much less anything of substance (either in its thematics or slight entertainment value).

Another, more visually obvious, detrimental difference comes in the shoddy look of the sequel's werewolf. Though not at all frightening, Michael J. Fox's Wolf looked far from human, with prosthetics giving the actor's features a canine cast. Bateman's face, however, is left relatively untouched, it's all-too-human features surrounded by a halo of long hair (appearing like a dark brown Santa beard) and topped by a bouffant-like quiff that looks more ludicrous than luscious.

Shooting at Pomona College in Claremont, California, director Christopher Leitch films the silly story in a straightforward manner; though competent, it lacks visual flair. Leitch made only one other feature film after *Teen Wolf Too* (1990's *Courage Mountain*, a vapid updating of *Heidi*), spending the rest of his career bouncing around television series and making TV movies. No wonder *Teen Wolf Too* has all the gravitas of a tepid sitcom episode.

Justin Bateman has referred to *Teen Wolf Too* as a "low light" of his career, and it's not hard to see why. High school dropout Bateman fails to convince as a brainy science student, and evinces none of the self-effacing charm or innate likability of original Teen Wolf Michael J. Fox. Instead, he projects little more than a general blandness. Consequently, the copycat *Teen Wolf Too* has the same lightweight premise of the original *Teen Wolf* but lacks the dynamic central performance (by Fox) that added some weight to its slight story … leaving nothing for *Teen Wolf Too* but some unfunny "comedy" (pratfalls at a dance reception, students pranking Todd by setting a batch of fleas on him, a "frog fight" in biology lab) and a few admittedly well-filmed boxing scenes. Though Bateman had appeared on various TV shows since the age of ten, this was his big-screen debut. Fortunately, he improved considerably, going on to forge a respectable career in series television (*Valerie, Arrested Development*) and in films such as *Paul* and *Horrible Bosses*. At least *something* good eventually came out of *Teen Wolf Too*…

Panned by critics (Roger Ebert and Gene Siskel gave the film two emphatic thumbs down), the $3 million *Teen Wolf Too* still managed to dupe patrons into shelling out a collective $7,888,000 during its theatrical run (over a third of that coming on its opening weekend—before word got around). Still, it was a long way from the blockbuster first film, and its meager take effectively scuttled whatever further franchise plans might have been in the works. Thank goodness.

Morphology: Hirsute college freshman
Demise: None; this boxing werewolf lives to fight another day
  Rating: *

Terror of the She Wolf see *The Legend of the Wolf Woman*

13 Hrs. see *Night Wolf*

Thor: Hammer of the Gods

(2009; Sci Fi Pictures/Universal) Alternate Title: *Hammer of the Gods*. Director: Todor "Toshko" Chapkanov; Producers: Jeffrey Beach, Phillip Roth; Screenplay: Steve Bevilacqua, Rafael Jordan; Cinematographer: Ivo Peichev. Cast: Zachery Bryan, Alexis Peters, Mac Brandt, Daz Crawford, Melissa Leigh.

> At worlds end, lost and betrayed, he will meet his fate—trailer

Not only will he meet his fate, he'll meet an island full of werewolves. Conceived, no doubt, to ride the publicity coattails of the then-in-development big-budget *Thor* (which took a further two years to finally hit screens), this made-for-TV knockoff took a different, small-scale tack from its blockbuster brother. Said tack: Vikings vs. werewolves—a potentially fascinating concept that, under the budgetary constraints of the SyFy Channel, and the *creativity* constraints of a talent-challenged cast and crew, falls as flat as a hammer blow.

A small band of Vikings, led by Balour (Mac Brandt), his younger brother Thor (Zachery Bryan) and his disgruntled half-brother Ulfrich (Daz Crawford), journey towards the mythical "Midgard" for the honor and glory of claiming new territory for their people. Landing at night on a mysterious island, the Vikings discover a group of cowering villagers, the frightened survivors of an earlier expedition. Soon, a group of "wolf-creatures" begin decimating their meager forces, while Thor experiences visions of a mighty warrior wielding a huge hammer. It turns out Thor is the reincarnation of that "champion of the gods," and he and his Vikings must fight through the myriad werewolves to the cave of Fenris the Wolf, son of the god Loki, who not only controls the werewolves but keeps the magical hammer close (because it's "the only thing in existence that can truly end his immortality").

Vikings against werewolves—what could go wrong? With Bulgarian-born director Todor Chapkanov at the helm ... plenty. Primarily an assistant or second unit director, Chapkanov has taken the full reigns himself on only a few projects, most of them direct-to-TV SyFy Channel offerings (including the following year's even poorer pseudowolf effort *Monsterwolf*). Here Chapkanov gets almost everything wrong, from the (mis)casting of his pivotal lead to the uneven pacing, and from the Renaissance fair–level swordplay to the sub-par CGI and disappointing makeup effects.

Shot in Bulgaria (where filming is cheap), *Thor: Hammer of the Gods* initially entices with some eerily beautiful, mist-laden atmosphere and snow-covered woodlands—before it disappoints with some atrocious CGI landscapes (including what looks like a cartoon mountain). The plot meanders as the Vikings go hither and yon (though never quite getting anywhere) until finally the quintet of survivors make it to Fenris' cave lair. But here the climactic battle with the "wolf god" (a creature flatly realized through more poor CGI) is both perfunctory and unexciting, with Thor simply bashing the beast on the head a few times with the Hammer until the brute lay still. Then, confronted with the remaining werewolf minions, Thor simply strikes the ground with the Hammer, sending out a magical shock wave that literally dissolves the wolf-creatures. No muss, no fuss, and no excitement.

Apart from the over-the-top but admittedly entertaining Daz Crawford as the turncoat Ulfrich, the Vikings (played by low-rent actors reciting their stilted lines like they're doing Shakespeare in the Park) are little more than bland cardboard cutouts. The role playing–level dialogue consists of ridiculous phrasing like "By the skulls, I've no words for that stench" and "Let's make haste, you flat-footed mares."

But the biggest liability comes in the form of the titular demigod himself—the Mighty Thor—as portrayed by the anything-*but*-mighty former child actor Zachary Bryan. With his chubby face and barely-visible beard, Bryan's Thor looks like nothing more than an everyday schlub playing dress-up and wielding an oversized plastic hammer. Embarrassingly, several times Bryan even has to use his hand to hold his ill-fitting helmet in place on his head. Best-known (*only* known) for playing Tim Allen's son on the old *Home Improvement* sitcom, Bryan, with a physique more suited to joystick wielding than swordplay, never looks (nor sounds) like a Viking warrior, much less the *ultimate* Viking warrior.

Despite its obvious flaws, *Thor* manages to generate a modicum of interest—at least early on—via some suggestive shots of menacing figures among the trees and an occasional bloody aftermath. But when the werewolves step forth full view, this *Hammer* misses the nail and hits the thumb. With the body of a man but the head of what looks like a mutant Rottweiler (complete with big, boxy jaws), these "wolf-creatures" (the term "werewolf" never arises) are obviously taken from the *Dog Soldiers* mold, but with far too much emphasis on the "dog." They work best when kept mostly in shadows, or shown only by swiftly moving blurs or a clawed hand invading the foreground.

With its werewolves based on Norse mythology (or the low-budget Hollywood facsimile thereof), silver and the full moon need not apply (in fact, the lycanthropes can transform at will, even during daytime). Uniquely, one becomes a werewolf not from a beast's bite but by drinking the blood of Fenris (who looks like a cross between a giant wolf and an oversized armadillo, and speaks in a growly demon voice)—meaning this version of lycanthropy is a strictly voluntary condition. "Drink from his blood and you'll have power and immortality," enthuses one rapt convert. (Of course, it also means that in order to secure said power, one must serve as minion to a cranky Norse beast-god.) Additionally, these lycanthropes heal almost instantaneously from sword cuts, and even regenerate limbs (several characters mention this, though it was apparently too costly to actually *show*), but they can't recover from decapitation.

Had the filmmakers eschewed the tenuous Thor element (and the horribly miscast Zachery Bryan) and simply called the movie *Vikings vs. Werewolves*, it might have fared better. But without the timely Thor tie-in, the production might never have seen the green light in the first place. Which, come to think of it, might have been for the best...

Morphology: Skinny, loincloth-wearing bipeds sporting oversized wolf heads
Demise: Decapitation (and magic hammer shockwave!)
Full Moon Rating: **

Tomb of the Werewolf

(2004; American Independent) Alternate Titles: *Castle of Desire* (alternate cable TV version), *The Unliving* (extended reissue version); Director: Fred Olen Ray; Screenplay: Fred Olen Ray (as Sherman Scott); Producer: Kimberly A. Ray; Cinematographer: Gary Graver. Cast: Paul Naschy, Jay Richardson, Michelle Bauer, Stephanie Bentley, Kennedy Johnston, Leland Jay, Beverly Lynne, Jacy Andrews, Frankie Cullen, Don Donason.

If you raise the dead prepare to join them—tagline

Paul Naschy comes to America! For Naschy's thirteenth (and final) turn as his signature wolfman character Waldemar Daninsky, low-budget auteur Fred Olen Ray (*Deep Space, Attack of the 60 Foot Centerfold, Dire Wolf*) lured Naschy to Hollywood (or at least the low-rent environs of same). Actually, it was a package deal. Recalled Ray, "Senor Molina [Naschy's real name] was wanting to come to the U.S. for Don Glut's movie [*Countess Dracula's Orgy of Blood*], but it was a one day cameo and too much traveling for too little. Don was looking to see if anyone else could use him, and I had the idea of doing a movie featuring Molina's most famous character. I liked those films, so it sounded like a fun idea."

"I had reservations about whether the market really wanted a wolfman movie," continued Ray, "so we added a 'late night' element to hedge our bets." This "late night element" turned out to be half a dozen soft-core sex scenes more akin to porn than eroticism. (Tellingly, Ray even cast XXX veterans Evan Stone and Monique Alexander as a pair of villagers whose outdoor sexcapade is rudely interrupted by the werewolf.)

Shot in March of 2003, *Tomb of the Werewolf* (filmed as *The Unliving*, its subsequent reissue title) sees Richard Daninsky (Jay Richardson), the last living descendant of Polish nobleman Waldemar Daninsky, inherit a mysterious castle—and its even-more-mysterious (and sexy) housekeeper Elizabeth (Michelle Bauer). Seeking the fabled Daninsky treasure, Richard contacts psychic investigator Amanda Collins (Stephanie Bentley) and brings the reality TV show "Current Mysteries" crew to the castle to try to discover the booty's whereabouts. But the scheming Elizabeth, who's really Satan's servant Elizabeth Bathory, takes Richard to the castle's secret crypt and tricks him into removing the giant silver dagger lodged in Waldemar's heart. Elizabeth intends to use the revived Waldemar to "deliver up a total of six souls to my master [so] I can move on to bigger and better things."

Unfortunately, with this film Paul Naschy moved on to *smaller* and *lesser* things, for *Tomb of the Werewolf* looks far cheaper than most of his Daninsky entries. Shooting in and around the Hollywood Castle, a medieval-style mansion/film rental property in the Hollywood hills (used for everything from *This Is Spinal Tap* to Tom Petty videos), created a decidedly artificial look (unlike in Naschy's Euro-shot efforts, which at least had the benefit of genuine castle locations). Writer-director Fred Olen Ray, who has proven himself better suited to tongue-in-cheek (and cheek-displaying) homages such as *Hollywood Chainsaw Hookers* and *Evil Toons* than out-and-out fright films, does his usual competent-but-no-more job (the impossibly short seven-day shooting schedule left little time for anything else). For instance, when the protagonists meet the castle housekeeper, we see that it's the same evil woman who cursed Waldemar in the flashback sequence—but Ray fails to underscore this in any way, presenting her in such a nonchalant fashion that the sinister revelation carries no weight. Frequent too-tight framing makes the film feel cramped and cheap, and the stilted acting (veteran Jay Richardson being the only thespian to render an even half-way convincing performance) does nothing to alleviate the impression. Adding visual insult to rushed injury, cinematographer Gary Graver (who cut his teeth on Al Adamson flicks) over-lights just about everything, destroying what little atmosphere the faux castle setting might have generated (despite Ray working his rented fog machine overtime). But at least Ray displays a sense of humor about it all, at one point having a protagonist watch *The Mad Monster* on television, and featuring this among the closing credits: "Filmed on location at Digital Blue Studios and The Rolling Hills of Vasaria" (referencing the de facto fictional location of various Universal Wolf Man sequels).

Like in several of Naschy's previous entries, Daninsky's lycanthropy here is the result of a Satanic curse. A flashback shows Waldemar fretting over his beloved wife, who's dying from the Plague. Elizabeth Bathory shows up to offer Waldemar a cure—in exchange for his soul (or something ... this remains vague). As the Daninsky family history tells it, "From that hour on, Waldemar Daninsky's soul was not his own, and he became as one possessed." When the full moon rises, Waldemar grimaces, revealing a set of fangs, and then instantly morphs (via smooth but cheap-looking CGI) into the drooling wolfman. His first victim? His recovering wife. But this tragic irony is nearly undone by the wobbly double-vision werewolf p.o.v. photography Ray employs and the clichéd wolf howls right out of the old *Dark Shadows* daytime serial.

Still, beneath the tawdry veneer beats (faintly) a romantic—and thoughtful—heart. As Amanda says of Waldemar, "He was a man who loved his wife so much that he made a pact with the angel of Satan in order to save her life—only to slay her himself when the spell of the beast came upon him." Tragically, love led to lycanthropy. More accurately, it was the all-consuming fear of losing that love that led to ruin. Because Waldemar could not let go, he became a monster. Which

Advance flyer for Fred Olen Ray's *Tomb of the Werewolf*, the final screen appearance of Paul Naschy as Waldemar Daninsky. Shot as *The Unliving*, the picture saw re-release—in a sexed-up version—a decade later under that moniker.

just goes to show that even a sexploitative slice of cheese such as this can deliver a subtle warning against obsession—one must sometimes accept circumstances or risk losing everything.

By his own admission, Naschy had always wanted to film a "final chapter" for his Daninsky saga (particularly after his disappointment with 1996's *Licantropo*). Naschy had even written his own script, *Eyes of the Werewolf*, but was never able to obtain financing for the project. Unfortunately, Naschy's participation in *Tomb of the Werewolf*, the only Daninsky film *not* written by Naschy, turned out to be little more than stunt-casting. Onscreen for only a few minutes, Naschy has nothing to do (and less to say, given only three words of dialogue) but lurk about the grounds while in human form, appearing slightly uncomfortable in his foppish 16th century garb, and looking more than a little ridiculous in his medieval mullet-wig. As the werewolf, Naschy looks similar to (though bushier than) his earlier incarnations but, again, has little to do. The few attacks appear quick and perfunctory, marked only by Naschy's trademark drooling and the odd dangling bit of bloody flesh.

Even so, Naschy professed to be grateful for the opportunity to play his beloved character once more, stating, "It was a terrific experience; I felt right at home playing Waldemar again, with the same *fuerza* as before. It was as if I'd just made *Mark of the Wolfman* [*Frankenstein's Bloody Terror* in America] the week before!" Well, not quite the same "*fuerza*." As Ray recalled, "He did not speak a word of English beyond 'good morning,' so we worked through an interpreter. He had a bum knee and it was difficult for him to get around, so we did use a stunt double for some of it."

"Fred [Olen Ray] wanted to make this film as an homage to me and to my wolfman pictures," said Naschy. To that end, Ray included Daninsky's old nemesis, Elizabeth Bathory, in his scenario. The vampiric, blood-bathing Bathory had appeared in one iteration or another in three of Naschy's Daninsky movies—*The Craving, Curse of the Devil* and *The Werewolf vs. the Vampire Woman.*

Concluded Naschy, "Maybe [Ray's] films are not classics, but at least they're professionally made. Neither of these movies [*Tomb* and *Countess Dracula's Orgy of Blood*] are super-productions, and I know that they're not going to be as good as my old pictures, but they'll be worthy little features all the same." "Worthy" being open to interpretation…

After *Tomb*'s initial video release, Ray removed most of the blood and extended the sex scenes in order to make a more "erotic" version called *Castle of Desire*, employing the directorial pseudonym of Nicholas Medina (letting his sense of humor—and sense of horror movie history—show). But without the bite (so to speak), and with far too much time taken up by the protracted sex scenes, it comes off as a dull soft-core skin-flick laid over the barest of lycan-bones. A decade later Ray combined the two versions (blood *and* breasts) and re-released "the complete works," as he put it, as *The Unliving* (*Tomb*'s original shooting title). Far from an improvement on the original version, however, the re-insertion of the numerous overlong soft-core sequences slows *The Unliving*'s already sluggish pace to a crawl. For those lycan-lovers wishing for something at least *akin* to horror, put a stake in *The Unliving,* avoid the *Castle,* and head straight for the *Tomb.*

With quotes from: Interview with Fred Olen Ray conducted by the author, October 2015; "A Spanish Werewolf in L.A.," by Mike Hodges, *Fangoria* 234.

Morphology: Classico hombre lobo
Demise: Sharpened silver cross
Full Moon Rating: *½

A Transylvanian Werewolf in America see *Full Moon High*

The Twilight Saga: Breaking Dawn Part One

(2011; Summit Entertainment/Lionsgate) Director: Bill Condon; Producers: Wyck Godfrey, Karen Rosenfelt, Stephenie Meyer; Screenplay: Melissa Rosenberg (based on the novel *Breaking Dawn* by Stephenie Meyer); Cinematographer: Guillermo Navarro. Cast: Kristen Stewart, Robert Pattinson, Taylor Lautner, Billy Burke, Peter Facinelli, Elizabeth Reaser, Kellen Lutz.

FOREVER IS ONLY THE BEGINNING—poster

The fourth (of five) *Twilight* films begins promisingly enough by showing hunky young Native American Jacob (Taylor Lautner) angrily stalking out of his house to immediately transform into a gigantic snarling wolf that races off into the forest (via some excellently rendered CGI). Left behind is the crumpled invitation to Bella and Edward's wedding. Also left behind is viewer interest in this penultimate installment in the ultimate supernatural teen-angst movie series, since, for the next two hours the viewer is "treated" to scenes of Bella (Kristen Stewart) nervously preparing for her upcoming nuptials with her vampire soul mate Edward (Robert Pattinson); the wedding ceremony itself; the expected conflict between the puppyish, pining Jacob and the terminally condescending Edward; the couple's idyllic island honeymoon; and, finally, the discovery that Bella has miraculously become pregnant, with the preternaturally-growing vampiric baby literally sucking the life from her. It all culminates in an overwrought birth scene and Edward's desperate attempt to "turn" Bella into a vampire before she dies. Such a scenario may work well for the teen readers of *Tiger Beat* (the *Twilight* books' and movies' intended demographic), but it only drags on interminably for the discerning moviegoer—and for lovers of lycanthropic cinema.

After the brief opening scene with Jacob, over an hour of glacially-paced screen time passes before any werewolves reappear. It comes when Sam and his wolf pack decide, over Jacob's protests, that they must kill Bella and her unborn child, which they feel poses a dangerous threat to the whole community. Chasing Jacob down in wolf form, the pack corners him in a lumber yard, and then they … *talk*. No vicious fighting, no battles for pack supremacy, no mutinous uprisings, just boring debate. Yes, these gigantic werewolves palaver back and forth telepathically in deep doggy voices, putting a capital "r" in ridiculous and completely removing any awe or mystique the sight of powerful horse-sized wolves might engender. It ends with Jacob loping off to warn Edward and his vampire family of the werewolves' intentions.

Thematically, *Breaking Dawn Part One* may very well be the worst of the *Twilight* bunch—and that's saying something. Continuing on the theme of Bella embracing an abusive relationship with the controlling Edward, and subsuming herself in him rather than finding her own selfhood, their first night of conjugal love results in painful marks and deep bruises. And while Edward is mortified at what he's done to her (and resolves to avoid a repeat performance, so to speak), Bella makes light of her injuries and does all in her power to tempt him further. Then, of course, she insists on becoming a vampire—on literally losing her own humanity and replacing it with Edward's version, making herself over in his own image, as it were. So much for women's liberation.

Even worse, the film becomes one long, drawn-out, thinly-disguised pro-life political polemic. When the couple learn that Bella is pregnant with Edward's baby, and the vampire fetus is growing at such an accelerated rate that "it's breaking your bones now, it's crushing you from the inside out," Bella refuses to even consider an abortion—despite Edward's, Jacob's, Dr. Cullen's, *everybody's* pleas to do just that. "The fetus isn't compatible with your body," explains the vampire doctor. "It won't let you get the nutrition you need." Nevertheless, Bella decides to die trying—and goes about doing just that, wasting away to become little more than a walking skeleton (via a three-hour makeup job and some horrific CGI work that makes her look like a Holocaust survivor). So not only does *Breaking Dawn* advocate marriage at a young age (Bella is only 18, after all), it proselytizes that young girls should completely subjugate themselves to an older, stronger male (changing completely to suit the *man's* needs) and give up everything—life included—for the continuation of the male's bloodline.

Amazingly, such a backwards, near medieval attitude was embraced by legions of teens and young women throughout the world (one poll suggested that nearly 80 percent of ticket buyers were females under the age of 25). Progressive the *Twilight Saga* is not. Which makes it doubly astounding that it was helmed by Bill Condon (who beat out the likes of Sofia Coppola and Gus Van Sant for the coveted director's chair), maker of sensitive, reflective and, yes, progressive films like *Gods and Monsters* (1998) and *Kinsey* (2004).

Filmed back to back, *Breaking Dawn Part One* and *Part Two* were based on the Stephenie Meyer book *Breaking Dawn*. Said producer Wyck Godfrey on how they decided to split the 754-page tome into two cinematic halves, "We basically want to take the audience through the emotional part of Bella's journey as she becomes a vampire. The first part will cover the wedding, the honeymoon and the birth." Unfortunately for *Part One*, Bella, in the form of blank-as-a-plank actress Kristen Stewart, offers up about as much convincing emotion as a two-tiered wedding cake, making Bella's "emotional journey" a very short one indeed.

At one point Bella tells Edward, about her impossible pregnancy, "I know this seems like a scary thing. It's not—it's a miracle." In fact, given her death-warmed-over appearance, it *is* a "scary thing"—the *only* scary thing in the entire movie, since the inevitable (and hoped-for) climactic battle between Sam's lycanthropes and the Cullen clan vampires dissipates like yak hair with the coming of (a breaking) dawn. Occurring at night, making it difficult to even see the little that goes on (and exacerbated by the pointlessly frenetic editing), the confrontation consists of a few leaps and a handful of punches before Jacob shows up and commands them all to cease. After the far more exciting and dramatic battle to the death in the prior film, the tame tussle (there's nary a bloody lip on either side, much less any casualties) is nothing more than a waste of good werewolves.

Like a reluctant participant in a cheesy wedding, the viewer comes away with nothing more than a passel of regrets and a tacky, ill-fitting bridesmaid's dress. Astoundingly, the action-less, retrogressive *Breaking Dawn Part One* grossed $281 million in North America alone, and $712 million worldwide. Apparently, there are plenty of impressionable girls out there willing to don such a disappointing gown.

With quotes from: "What Does the Future Hold for Bella, Edward in *Breaking Dawn*?" by Susan Wloszczyna, USAToday.com.

Morphology: Giant wolves
Demise: None of the lycanthropes perish … or do much of anything, really
Full Moon Rating: *

The Twilight Saga: Breaking Dawn Part Two

(2012; Summit Entertainment/Lionsgate) Director: Bill Condon; Producers: Wyck Godfrey, Karen Rosenfelt, Stephenie Meyer; Screenplay: Melissa Rosenberg (based on the novel *Breaking Dawn* by Stephenie Meyer); Cinematographer: Guillermo Navarro. Cast: Kristen Stewart, Robert Pattinson, Taylor Lautner, Billy Burke, Peter Facinelli, Elizabeth Reaser, Kellen Lutz, Michael Sheen, Dakota Fanning.

THE EPIC FINALE THAT WILL LIVE FOREVER—poster

Not if there's any justice in this cinema-mad world. The whole *Twilight* saga *should* be remembered (if at all) as nothing more than a minor footnote in cinema history. A fad blown out of all proportion to its actual depth or real value. Like the mood ring or pet rock.

This (thankfully) final installment in the bloated but uber-popular series (at least among females under the age of 20) picks up with Bella (Kristen Stewart) having been turned into a vampire to save her from death during the traumatic birth of her and Edward's (Robert Pattinson) half-vampire baby, Renesmee. While mastering her newfound powers and adjusting to married vampire life and motherhood simultaneously (though the script woefully eschews whatever observations and insights such struggles might provide in favor of more silly soul-gazing and love declarations, glossing over the very real challenges marriage and child rearing inevitably bring), Bella and her new extended vampire family, the Cullens, must prepare for a confrontation with the feared vampire overlords the Volturi, who feel Renesmee is a danger to them that must be eradicated. It all culminates in a climactic battle between the Cullen clan and their allies (including Jacob [Taylor Lautner] and his werewolf pack), and the powerful forces of the Volturi.

Though more eventful than the near action-less *Breaking Dawn Part One*, *Part Two* still spends well over an hour on nothing at all, as the Cullens welcome Bella and her baby into their clan, worry over the Volturi's upcoming actions, and gather "witnesses" (Mormon novelist Stephenie Meyer's quasi-religious term for allies) for the upcoming confrontation. Fortunately, the picture occasionally provides a bit of respite from the tiresome Bella and Cullens by offering occasional glimpses of the creepy Volturi (led by the disturbing Michael Sheen, whose intense, dangerous, snake-calm demeanor simply oozes menace in the film's one truly effective portrayal). The ruthless, powerful, merciless Volturi make for a refreshingly sinister presence after all the banal, feel-good schmaltz of Bella and Edward and Jacob and all the rest of the insufferable Cullen clan. (Not to mention the awful dialogue, with Kristen Stewart's deadpan delivery of lines like "I was born to be a vampire" and "Nobody's ever loved somebody as much as I love you" continuing to raise the obvious question of what Edward, Jacob or *anybody* sees in this vapid, insecure girl.) Still, it's a long, long slog to get to an eight-minute battle. Admittedly, said fight offers a fairly thrilling eight minutes, full of impressive hand-to-hand (or hand to paw) combat that (surprisingly) results in several main characters—both vampire and werewolf—meeting their violent demise. At one point even the frozen, snow-covered ground literally opens up to swallow good and evil alike. But wait, (not so surprisingly) it turns out to all be a dream (or vision), which the prognosticating Alice telepathically transmits to the Volturi leader to show what will occur if the Volturi actually *do* attack. Consequently, the mighty Volturi simply turn tail and walk away, leaving all the Cullens and their allies unmolested, and Bella, Edward, Jacob and Renesmee to walk off "blissfully into this small but perfect piece of our forever" (the film's—and book's—final line). Such an unsatisfying it-was-only-a-dream ending is straight out of the original *The Wizard of Oz* (1939); but unlike in that beloved classic, with *Twilight* there's no real change or growth or lesson learned, not even a revelatory "There's no place like home" to ease the disappointment of such an unsatisfying cop-out conclusion (one designed solely to spare the readers/viewers any potential emotional questioning or thought expenditure in having to face sacrifice and tragedy).

Throughout the *Twilight* series the CGI werewolves were created by Tippett Studio, who began work on these impressive lycanthropes in February 2009 for the second film, *The Twilight Saga: New Moon*. The look of the huge wolves altered somewhat over the course of the series, given the input of three different directors. "It's a subtle balance of just how anthropomorphic these wolves are," said [visual effects supervisor] Eric Leven. "[*Breaking Dawn Part Two* director] Bill [Condon] wanted to make sure that we had a sense of the human or the shape shifter in there. Finding that balance of how much of a human performance versus an animal performance was important for Bill." Leven observed that "Bill has always treated the wolves as characters and never as computer generated things, and directs them in the same way he'd direct any actor. He would always give us direction like Sam should be angrier. It's the best way to work. His treating these creatures as characters, instead of just computer bits, was really great."

Phil Tippett himself noted that "because we've been working on this franchise for such a prolonged period of time, we've been able to improve the look from show to show. Wolves generally are pretty darn clean, and since Bill wanted the wolves rangier, that means a lot more fur matting and clumping, like they've lived out in the woods. We edged towards something a bit more feral." But such attention to realistic detail wasn't easy. "There is also a balance between look and technology," added Tippett. "The body count of the wolves escalates, and because we're adding a great deal more hair to get the right texture, that fur really ups the rendering time. We've gone from four wolves to eight to twelve, to sixteen in *Part Two*. So we have to be very careful about that balance, because it takes hundreds of hours to render each wolf." And these unique, realistic, and truly impressive lycanthropes turned out to be the main asset of the series; which makes it a crime against lycanthropy (and cinema in general) that more wasn't done with them.

The Twilight Saga: Breaking Dawn Part Two grossed over $800 million worldwide, making it the most financially successful of the five *Twilight* films. And while the series offered a novel take on werewolfery in the form of Native Americans transforming into gigantic wolves brought to realistic life via the magic of CGI, throughout the five movies—ten hours-plus of screen time—it could offer nothing more than a drawn-out portrait of teen angst and subjugation to the male order in the form of abusive relationships and rabid anti-abortion propaganda. Oh, and plenty of boredom too. Let's hope that the sun has indeed set on this vision of *Twilight*.

With quotes from: "Learn About All the Special Effects That Went into *The Twilight Saga: Breaking Dawn Part Two*," by Shawn Cauthen, ScreenSlam.com.

Morphology: Giant wolves
Demise: Broken neck (via vampire) and fall into a fiery chasm; but wait, it was all merely a vision, so ... none
Full Moon Rating: *½

The Twilight Saga: Eclipse

(2010; Summit Entertainment) Director: Daniel Slade; Producers: Wyck Godfrey, Karen Rosenfelt; Screenplay: Melissa Rosenberg (based on the novel *Eclipse* by Stephenie Meyer); Cinematographer: Javier Aguirresarobe. Cast: Kristen Stewart, Robert Pattinson, Taylor Lautner, Bryce Dallas Howard, Billy Burke, Dakota Fanning.

> Vampires. Werewolves. Humans. It's time to choose a side—poster

Following hot on the heels of the mega-blockbuster sequel *The Twilight Saga: New Moon*, this third entry in the popular teen-targeted series continues the will-they-or-won't-they tortured relationship between "normal" high school girl Bella (Kristen Stewart) and brooding pretty-boy vampire Edward (Robert Pattinson), with hunky (and generally shirtless) young werewolf Jacob (Taylor Lautner) tossed into the mix to complete the third point of this angst-fueled triangle. The ostensible plot has the surviving evil vampire from the previous *Twilights* raising an army of "Newborns" in order to exact revenge on Edward and Bella for the death of her mate. (In contrast to most vampire films, here newly-made vampires are actually *stronger* than their older counterparts because remnants of their human tissue still lingers.) Edward and his vampire "family" must form an uneasy alliance with Jacob and his werewolves in order to protect Bella and their home turf of Forks, Washington, from the invading band of berserker bloodsuckers.

In this hand-wringingly vex-some film series, any time away from the three vapid leads is most welcome, and *Eclipse* offers said respite through a series of flashbacks delineating various secondary characters' origins and backstories, not to mention some attention focused on the army of "Newborns." That said, there's still far too much ridiculously earnest eye-gazing, hand-holding, and teenage love-yearning to make *Eclipse* anything short of risible for the, shall we say, mature viewer.

At one point Edward, in speaking about how he felt when he thought he'd lost Bella, claims, "There are no words." But for endless stretches of this film's 124 minutes there's nothing *but* words—and laughably melodramatic words at that. (Sample: "When you see her everything changes; all of a sudden it's not gravity holding you to the planet—it's her." Ugh.) This overlong angst-fest is chock full of insipid narration (courtesy of Bella's inner monologue), and painfully long stretches of Bella and Edward oh-so-earnestly talking, or Bella and Jacob pouring out their feelings to one another, or Bella attempting to lose her virginity to Edward (who'll have none of it, he being of "a different time"), or Bella continually badgering Edward to make her a vampire. Edward resists, of course, demanding that she marry him first, but one wonders how Edward can cope with such constant nagging. Edward: "Marry Me." Bella: "Change Me." Viewer: "Kill me."

Through it all, Kristen Stewart never alters her slightly constipated, confused expression. The real question behind the *Twilight* films should not be "Edward or Jacob?" but "Why Bella?" Obviously the magic fueling this franchise is not the supernatural forces of werewolves vs. vampires but the impossible mystery of why anyone would want this uninteresting and annoying teenage girl in the first place. Adding insult to injury, said "heroine" is not some strong independent role model that its teen audience can look to and emulate, but a confused milksop completely defined by the two "men" in her life. "This isn't a question of you or Jacob," she tells Edward, "it's between who I should be and who I am." And who she is is nobody, really—certainly not someone who can stand up for and look out for herself, as she's constantly in need of protection or rescue from one or the other of her supernatural "boyfriends." And despite Edward's good intentions, his behavior towards Bella has all the hallmarks of an abusive relationship—he's controlling, he isolates her from other people, he's jealous, and his continually bemused expressions and attitude towards her are condescending as hell.

On the plus side, *Eclipse* features far more werewolf action than the previous installment (and more action period). We learn a bit more about these Native American lycanthropes as well, the chosen "spirit warrior" shapeshifters of the Quiliute tribe, and their relationship to the vampires. "The Cold Ones—our magic reawakens when they are near," explains a tribal elder. The quintet of giant superwolves from the earlier installment has expanded to a band of seven. And we need wait only about 15 minutes before the werewolves show up (unlike the desultory hour in *New Moon*). Unfortunately, their initial appearance remains all-too-brief, as the Cullen clan chases the rogue evil vampire Victoria over into the wolves' territory (only for her to get away yet again). But the beasts are soon back (in a particularly effective flashback detailing the role of these shapeshifting warriors in the tribe's history) and remain a more constant thread throughout the narrative than the little-more-than-cameo bits of *New Moon*. And unlike the two previous installments, *Eclipse* finally offers a *real* climax—a battle to the death between the bloodthirsty Newborns and the good vampires and their werewolf allies. Here the CGI special effects truly shine, as the gigantic wolves leap at their prey in slow motion, their huge jaws gaping wide, to engage in all manner of impressive head-ripping and limb-severing. (Of course, in order to keep the film accessible to its young target audience via a PG-13 rating, these vampire victims don't spurt blood and gore but instead neatly shatter like porcelain dolls when dismembered.) Unfortunately, this welcome bit of imposing lycanthro-fury ends all too quickly, and it's back to focusing on the starry-eyed high school soul-mate melodrama once again.

Though *The Twilight Saga: Eclipse* represents a vast improvement over the previous werewolf-lite installment, that's still damning with faint praise. It's like saying having a tooth pulled is better than a full root canal. And while *Eclipse* offers isolated moments of impressive werewolf action and an admittedly exciting undead-mano-a-lycan-mano climactic battle, for those over the age of consent it still remains the cinematic equivalent of a trip to the dentist.

Morphology: Oversized CGI wolves
Demise: None; once again Jacob and his werebros come through unscathed
Full Moon Rating: *½

The Twilight Saga: New Moon

(2009; Summit Entertainment) Director: Chris Weitz; Producers: Wyck Godfrey, Karen Rosenfelt; Screenplay: Melissa Rosenberg (based on the novel *New Moon* by Stephenie Meyer); Cinematographer: Javier Aguirresarobe. Cast: Kristen Stewart, Robert Pattinson, Taylor Lautner, Ashley Greene, Rachelle Lefevre, Billy Burke.

THE NEXT CHAPTER BEGINS—poster

This movie is, like, totally awesome—if you're a 14-year-old girl. If, on the other hand, you have a Y-chromosome, an ounce of testosterone in your system, or a sensibility that goes beyond texting your BFF about that cute guy in math class, *Twilight Saga: New Moon* remains little more than a repetitive, tiresome, unbelievable (and downright laughable) journey through lovesick teendom. It's like *Tiger Beat* magazine come to life. True, this first sequel to the mystifyingly popular *Twilight* film (itself an adaptation of the best-selling teen book by Stephenie Meyer) tosses werewolves into the angsty mix, but its Romeo and Juliet–themed (the heroine wakes from her pre-credit dream sequence with a copy of Shakespeare's play on her pillow), I-must-choose-but-I-cannot plotline sorely tries the patience of any viewer old enough to drink … or vote … or maybe even drive.

Director Chris Weitz felt no qualms about telling the story of a young girl's first great love. "I feel that on some level, people are the same and have similar needs," he stated. "Like Bella, I've gone through heartbreak, so I have sort of walked in her shoes. And in some ways, I am a teenaged girl. I have a high estrogen count, so that helped a lot." Indeed.

After having come to live with her dad in the small town of Forks on the rain-drenched Olympic Peninsula of Washington State, high school senior Bella (Kristen Stewart) now pines for her lost love, Edward (Robert Pattinson), a vampire who, along with his benign "family" of bloodsuckers, has left town for Bella's own good. Taking solace in her friendship with local Native American boy Jacob (Taylor Laut-

ner), Bella finds herself falling for *him* now, too. The hitch—she still loves the absent Edward; oh, and Jacob has recently discovered he's a werewolf and now (literally) runs with a handful of other young tribesmen with the lycanthrope gene. With some vengeful vamps on the prowl for Bella (she indirectly led to the death of one of their own in the previous film), can Jacob protect her; and—more importantly—who will Bella ultimately choose, vampire Edward or werewolf Jacob?

Bella's depressive narration (sample: "There's nothing now") grates from word one. Add to that line after line of sad, chaste (it was written by a devout Mormon, after all) proclamations of tortured love like "You're everything to me" and "It doesn't makes sense for you to love me," and *New Moon* quickly becomes old hat. It's *so* angst-filled and super-serious that one simply can't take *any* of it seriously. Over and over again comes dialogue like "Bella, you're my only reason to stay alive" (Edward) and "I know that I've been hurting you, and it's killing me" (Jacob), ad infinitum, ad nauseum. If overblown teenage angst were a salable commodity—say, a hamburger—then the *Twilight* series would be the McDonalds of the cinematic world, with over one billion sold.

After two long hours of this, the lack of any real climax adds desultory insult to risible injury, as the expected Major Confrontation between werewolf Jacob and vampire Edward simply drizzles away like a Washington rain. Bella steps between her two angry loves to stop their inevitable fight, and the lycanthrope merely lopes away into the forest. Consequently, the movie ends on the "shock" moment of Edward asking Bella to marry him. Gasp!

In *The Twilight Saga*, lycanthropy is not so much a curse as it is a superpower. It's also a hereditary condition passed down to a few members of a tribe of Native American Indians, a condition triggered by the presence of their hated enemy—the vampire. As Jacob explains to Bella, "A few lucky members of the tribe have the gene. A bloodsucker moves into town and then the fever sets in." These werewolves can transform at will, and do so almost instantaneously and without pain (no tortuous flesh stretching or bone cracking here). "Our werewolves are very much like they are in the book: they're giant wolves," noted Weitz. "There's no waiting around as a guy's hand turns into a paw. It's a lightning-fast transformation. [Effects specialist] Phil [Tippet] has done a great job with them."

These werewolves also appear to retain their human sentience while in oversized lupine form. And rather than wanting "to kill the thing it loves" (or kill anything, really), these super-wolves seek to protect it (Jacob in wolf form tracks and saves Bella from a menacing vampire). Additionally, their main purpose appears to be hunting down evil vamps—not "the harmless Cullens" (as Jacob labels the non-threatening "vegetarian" local vampire clan, who live only on animal blood and enjoy a protective "treaty" with the wolf tribe) but the occasional marauding bloodsucker passing through their territory who feeds on the random hiker here and there (the small town of Forks, population 3000, must have the worst per capita murder rate in the nation!).

In *New Moon* the beast has been tamed, even sanitized—right down to the shorts and tennis shoes consistently worn by these lycanthropes in human form just prior to the change (where these garments disappear to during the transformation is anybody's guess). Consequently, despite their impressive appearance and movements (the detailed CGI truly is excellent, with their beautiful fur rustling in the wind), they've lost much of what makes the werewolf such an intriguing figure. They're now simply eye-candy (in *both* wolf and human form, as the ripped Jacob laughably shuns a shirt in nearly every scene)—all flash and no substance.

First appearing over an hour into the movie, these wolves actually do very little, apart from two scenes in which they chase down a fleeing vampire in the forest (the first they catch; the second gets away). The fight with the first cornered bloodsucker is almost as brief as the split-second transformations, which is doubly disappointing given the excellent CGI renderings of the impressive beasts. The vamp delivers a blow that sends one giant wolf flying through the air, and then the wolves catch up with the bloodsucker, knock him to the ground and descend upon him like a, well, pack of wolves. But the PG-13 film cuts away at this moment, leaving whatever mayhem the werewolves wreak strictly to the viewer's imagination (not necessarily a bad thing, but disappointing given the general dearth of lupine action).

Twilight Saga: New Moon premiered on November 16, 2009—which was, appropriately enough, a new moon. It was a massive hit, grossing nearly $300 million domestically (six times its reported budget), making it, sad to say, the most monetarily successful werewolf movie up to this time (surpassed only the following year by—you guessed it—the next *Twilight* installment, *Eclipse*). So what can we take from this? Apparently there are a *lot* of 14-year-old girls out there.

Author's Personal Note: After viewing the first (werewolf-free) *Twilight* and this initial sequel, I feel that *The Twilight Saga* has become the [wolfs]bane of my existence. I will endeavor to persevere through the three subsequent sequels, but it's going to be hard ... very hard. Your thoughts and prayers, dear readers, will hopefully see me through...

With quotes from: "Under a New Moon," by Jessica Leibe, *Fangoria* 288.

Morphology: Horse-sized but otherwise proportional CGI wolves
Demise: None; Jacob and his four werewolf homeys live through the movie (which is more than can be said for viewer interest)
Full Moon Rating: *

Uncaged (2008) see *Never Cry Werewolf*

Uncaged

(2016; RLJ Entertainment) Alternate Title: *Beast Within* (UK); Director: Daniel Robbins; Producers: Yoni Frager, Adam Werth, Mark Rapaport, Daniel Robbins; Screenplay: Mark Rapaport, Daniel Robbins; Cinematographer: Rasa Partin. Cast: Ben Getz, Kyle Kirkpatrick, Zachary Weiner, Paulina Singer, Garrett Lee Hendricks, Michelle Cameron, Gene Jones.

BEWARE THE BEAST WITHIN—tagline

Indeed. Especially when it breaks out on one's eighteenth birthday. In "Fall 2003" six-year-old Jack, hiding beneath his bed sheets, bears audio witness to the brutal murder of his father and the subsequent disappearance of his mother. Twelve years later, raised by cousins, an eighteen-year-old Jack (Ben Getz) receives a mysterious call from his Uncle Mike, inviting the boy up to his woodland ranch. Bringing his sex-obsessed nerdy cousin Brandon (Zachary Weiner) and their sex-obsessed happy-go-lucky friend Turner (Kyle Kirkpatrick) to the ranch, Zach soon begins waking up naked in the snowy woods with nary a memory of the night before. Borrowing Turner's Go-Pro camera (which Turner likes to use for his sexcapades), Zach learns that he nightly transforms into a werewolf, in which form he kills a man. When he goes to see a witness, Rose (Paulina Singer), to his earlier attack, he becomes embroiled in the machinations of Rose's jealous gangster husband, Gonzo (Garrett Lee Hendricks). It all culminates in tragedy, as those close to Zach alternately try to help (locking him in a cage at night, for instance) or destroy him.

Uncaged starts poorly, as a birthday party for Zach devolves into vomit jokes and endless palaver about "pussy" and "dick sucking." The crude humor falls flat and fails to endear one to the three protagonists (excepting, perhaps, for Jack, who looks rather uncomfortable with it all). Fortunately, things get far more interesting when the trio take up residence in Uncle Mike's woodland home (with Mike away for the moment), and Jack becomes more and more worried about his amnesiac nocturnal activities. A viewer looking for the next *Howling* or *American Werewolf*, however, will be sorely disappointed by the more minimalist portrayal of said activities. Apart from one brief head-ripping shot towards film's end, the attacks are mostly implied (werewolf p.o.v., screaming victim, dead body aftermath), though *suspensefully* staged with intimate camerawork. Likewise, the transformations remain more suggested than revealing, albeit fairly artful (implied by a few clever cutaways and one effects shot of Jack's ridged, undulating back ripping through his shirt). Still, subtlety has its place, and neophyte filmmaker Daniel Robbins does wonders with a few simple tricks, involving camerawork, and creative editing (not to mention clever use of the Go-Pro p.o.v. cam), making the attacks and transformations appear both frantic and violent. Robbins also offers a few visual flourishes, such as utilizing colorful graphic novel–style drawings not only as scene transitions but to illustrate Jack's troubled family history (one of bloodshed and killings).

As the film progresses, Zachary Weiner (a less hyper, more likable Eddie Deezen–type), as Brandon, provides most of the amusement (some of it seemingly ad-libbed). When Jack first shows Brandon the Go-Pro footage and tells him, "I think I'm a Werewolf," Brandon reacts with "What happened to your dick—that's the real question—did it transform?" Then, when a bloody Brandon lay dying after being mauled the night before by were–Jack (a shocking and dismaying turn of events), he tells the now-human Jack, "You shoulda seen yourself—you looked awesome," before adding, "Please call a prostitute—I don't wanna die a virgin. Do you think I'll have enough blood for a boner?"

Unlikely as it seems, the immature Brandon (who actually grows on you as the movie progresses) becomes the film's philosophical voice. When Brandon locks Jack into the cage, he reasons, "If werewolf—you eats me, it doesn't make it evil—it's just a monster, you know. It doesn't have any control over it.... That's what makes it a monster—it doesn't have a choice." This keeps the film firmly grounded in the familiar *Wolf Man* territory of pathos and tragedy by taking the burden of evil off the protagonist's shoulders and placing it firmly on circumstance, or fate, if you will. The way Jack walks is thorny, through no fault of his own ... just his cursed genetic makeup.

Fortunately, the low-key, likable Ben Getz does well to engender sympathy as the quiet, confused, and afflicted Jack (particularly in contrast to the sex-focused nerdiness of Brandon and the sex-focused obnoxiousness of Turner). Consequently, the viewer actually cares about this young man's fate, and roots for him when he decides to help Rose after all and use his curse for good, so to speak, in taking out the gangsters. This intriguing twist, however, nearly comes unraveled due to the unlikely nature and impoverished presentation of the improbable Bad Guy characters. This "mean motherf**king" gangsta and his two homies incongruously occupy what looks like a middle-class suburban home. And when, out of nowhere, Gonzo's wife Rose abruptly appeals to Jack for help (even suggesting he kill her gangster husband!), it seems even less realistic than a young man suddenly developing into a werewolf.

Said werewolf remains as minimalist as most of the film's other qualities. With a black dog nose, fangs, and largely bare face haloed by a mane of long hair, this lycanthrope rather looks like a meaner version of Michael J. Fox's *Teen Wolf*. Fortunately, Robbins beefs up his beast's less-than-imposing appearance by keeping it always snarling, charging forward, or ripping into flesh, the constant violent motion of the creature making it seem more vicious and dangerous than its prosaic appearance might suggest.

Uncaged adheres to most of the accepted were-tropes, though it provides a novel (and sometimes humorous) spin on same. Like in some folklore, here lycanthropy is an inherited trait; though the picture goes Hollywood by allowing the curse to be passed on through the bite (as happens to one major character). While vulnerable when in human form (one of Zach's relatives succumbs to a regular shotgun blast), only silver will do the trick after the beast has emerged. But other, more prosaic methods, still work, as brought humorously home at film's end when a transforming character, confronted by a rifle-wielding Rose, boasts, "Only a silver bullet can kill a werew—" just as she slams him in the face with the rifle butt and then proceeds to cave in the creature's skull. But the oddest new twist (obviously for expediency sake) comes regarding the full moon. At one point Brandon, researching Jack's condition on-line, explains, "I got some bad news—we got like four more days of you turning into a werewolf. The moon only has to be *basically* full for you to transform. And I'm looking at the lunar calendar—it says we have four more nights of basically full moons." So rather than the standard three nights of the full moon, these lycanthropes must contend with *six* ... basically.

Despite its obvious flaws and threadbare budget (the rural landscape sports a thick layer of snow in some shots and appears completely bare in others, even on the same supposed day), *Uncaged* offers enough food for were-thought, involving characters, and overall competence to make it a cage worth opening.

Morphology: (Meaner) Teen Wolf–looking werewolf
Demise: Silver shotgun shell; rifle butt
Full Moon Rating: **½

Underworld

(2003; Screen Gems; UK/Germany/Hungary/USA) Director: Len Wiseman; Producers: Tom Rosenberg, Gary Lucchesi, Richard Wright; Screenplay: Danny McBride (story: Kevin Grevioux, Len Wiseman, Danny McBride); Cinematographer: Tony Pierce-Roberts. Cast: Kate Beckinsale, Scott Speedman, Michael Sheen, Shane Brolly, Bill Nighy, Erwin Leder, Sophia Myles, Robbie Gee, Wentworth Miller.

> WHEN THE BATTLE BEGINS, WHICH
> SIDE WILL YOU CHOOSE?—trailer

Well, for three-quarters of this slick, relatively big-budgeted ($22 million) franchise-starter about "the war between vampires and lycans," it chooses the side of the vampires. But by film's end, viewer sympathies lie firmly on the side of the werewolves. This turnabout offers a gratifying twist to a novel, if flawed, tale of a "thousand-year-old blood feud" in which specially trained vampires, dubbed "Death Dealers," live to hunt down and exterminate lycanthropes. But when death dealer Selene (Kate Beckinsale) spies several lycans tracking a human, Michael Corvin (Scott Speedman), she uncovers a lycan plan "to combine the blood lines" of the werewolves and vampires, and so create a hybrid species that could end the war. "The key was to locate the rarest of blood lines," explains the lycan doctor in charge, "a direct descendent of Alexander Corvinus" (a fifth century warlord who survived the plague and whose "body was able to change the disease, mold it to his benefit"). Corvinus "became the first true immortal. Years later he fathered at least two children who inherited this same trait ... one bitten by a bat, one by a wolf." And so the vampire and lycan clans were born. Now Michael's blood "allows for a perfect union between our species." And Selene, who discovers the truth about her duplicitous vampire overlord Viktor (Bill Nighy), must forsake her own clan to try and protect Michael.

Though werewolves and vampires had opposed one another as far back as 1948's *Abbott and Costello Meet Frankenstein* (with a hint of lycan-bloodsucker dissent captured even further back by the worm-turns werewolf of 1942's *The Return of the Vampire*), never had it been on the scale of *Underworld*'s supernatural species strife. With this film, werewolves truly declared war on vampires (and vice-versa). Consequently, *Underworld* proved to be an action film first, and a werewolf movie second. (Director Len Wiseman himself labels it "an action movie that has vampires and werewolves.") Scenes of chases, shootouts (with the vamps using silver bullets and the lycans employing some kind of ultra-violet ammunition), and various action mayhem dominate the proceedings. Though the script offers some convoluted back story, the plot sometimes becomes lost amongst the myriad characters, double-crosses and *Matrix*-style encounters.

Disappointingly, apart from one short, quickly-edited scene of werewolves slaughtering vampires on a train, and another brief lycan-vamp confrontation near film's end, the action primarily consists of *gun* battles between the two species. This begs the question: Why make them werewolves and vampires at all, if the predominant conflict comes in the form of John Woo–style shootouts?

Such paucity of full-on werewolfery becomes doubly disappointing given the imposing design and convincing portrayal of these lycans, for *Underworld* produced the most impressive, realistic-looking werewolves of the decade (second only, perhaps, to the beasts of *Dog Soldiers*). Indeed, beyond its clan-war mythology, *Underworld*'s greatest contribution to lycan-cinema might be the eight-foot-tall bipeds with taut grey skin, massive neck and shoulders, and elongated head ending in a gaping maw filled with razor-sharp teeth. Creature designer Patrick Tatopoulos even does Jack Pierce proud by utilizing yak hair to create the beasts' Mohawk-like mane. Sparse hair on the body leaves the imposing musculature visible, so that the beasts truly look like powerful creatures that could easily rip a man (or vampire) apart. (Curiously, these monsters—both werewolves *and* vampires—never threaten humans directly. The vamps even feed off synthetic or cloned blood. In directing all their viciousness towards one another, these creatures have little truck with humanity and so create an insular [under]world all their own.)

When Tatopoulos met with director Wiseman during pre-production, they both felt "that practical effects [rather than CGI] were clearly the best way," reported Tatopoulos. "We started to design it as a wolf, and then I remembered what Rick Baker did in *American Werewolf in London*; I felt the last stage of his transformation was a little bit too like a wolf. It was less creative compared to when the guy starts transforming and becomes something halfway between a man and wolf. I thought that looked the coolest."

Actor-screenwriter Kevin Grevioux, who partnered with his friend Wiseman to concoct *Underworld*'s original concept and story, wrote himself into the movie. "I wrote [lycan enforcer] Raze for me," admitted Grevioux. "And I wanted to be a werewolf rather than a vampire, because playing a monster is cooler, so I wrote in two transformations for myself." (Apparently when it comes to self-casting, lycanthropes win out over vampires.) Said transformations proved just as impressive as the werewolves themselves, with the wolfish

212 • Underworld

features pushing out of the human skin before smoothly morphing (via some judicious and convincing CGI) into the massive, physical beast.

Frequent monster-suit performer Brian Steele (*The Relic*, *Hellboy*, *Blade: Trinity*) donned the *Underworld* lycan-suit. "It was a performance that required me to wear leg extensions," he recounted. "This brought a new challenge to my performance. There I was standing over seven and a half feet tall fighting many different actors in this animatronic suit with leg extensions trying to create a performance that was convincing. The last thing any suit performer wants is to look like a guy in a big rubber suit! So I trained for many hours with the leg extensions before leaving for Budapest until they became a part of me. This allowed me to work with confidence and concentrate on other areas of the lycan performance." (Steele went on to play William, the very first lycan, in the sequel *Underworld: Evolution*.)

Creating a new, science-based (DNA) mythology for its monsters, *Underworld* eschews many of the classic vampire and werewolf trappings. For instance, vampires have no problems with garlic or crosses, and need not be staked (sharp swords will do)—though sunlight remains deadly. As for werewolves, they, like vampires, are immortal. And while the full moon triggers a change, they can also transform at will. Silver is deadly, but only if it hits a vital organ. Beyond that, the lycans have created "an enzyme to stop the change" during the full moon. And when the werewolf leader, Lucien (Michael Sheen), bites Michael to make him a lycan, Michael sees images from Lucien's past. 'You've been bitten," explains Selene, "his memories are passed to you." Such memory transference makes for a novel (and handy-for-storytelling) bit of lycan-lore.

Underworld was shot in Budapest, Hungary, by video/commercials director Len Wiseman, making his first feature. Filming for ten weeks in a disused basketball arena-turned-makeshift-studio in a former Eastern Bloc country was no easy task. "Having 15 on-set translators is probably not what you want on your very first film," recounted Wiseman. "Yet Budapest had the Gothic comic-book look I needed, with exotic-looking buildings oozing violent history and cobblestone streets." Wiseman and cinematographer Tony Pierce-Roberts enshrouds the film in a dark, rainy, Gothic milieu that imbues the story's modern gunplay and scientific backbone with the feel of medieval warfare. And Pierce-Roberts "deliberately kept [the werewolves] in the shadows to heighten their menace and make sure they don't look like men in suits."

Underworld turned out to be something of a lycanthropean Peyton Place. Coming into the film, Kate Beckinsale had been romantically involved with co-star Michael Sheen for eight years (they have a daughter together), but by the end of production Beckinsale had hooked up with director Wiseman, with the two ultimately marrying in 2004. (Purportedly they all remained on friendly terms afterwards.)

Kate Beckinsale in all her leather-and-latex glory.

Earning over twice its budget domestically, and nearly $100 million worldwide (plus another $50 million in video sales), the *Underworld* war has raged through three sequels to date: *Underworld: Evolution* (2006), *Underworld: Rise of the Lycans* (2009), and *Underworld: Awakening* (2012).

With quotes from: "The Making of *Underworld*," *Underworld* DVD; "I, Monster Maker," by Carnell, *Fangoria* 230; "Notes from the *Underworld*," by Alan Jones, *Fangoria* 226; "Master of Monsters," by Al J. Vermette, *Werewolf Cafe*; "*Underworld*: Love Be Damned" by Alan Jones, *Fangoria* 222.

Morphology: Huge, muscular bipeds
Demise: Silver nitrate, or silver bullets to vital organs
Full Moon Rating: ***

Underworld: Awakening

(2012; Screen Gems) Directors: (Mans) Marlind & (Bjorn) Stein; Producers: Tom Rosenberg, Gary Lucchesi, Len Wiseman, Richard Wright; Screenplay: Len Wiseman, John Hlavin, J. Michael Straczynski, Allison Burnett (story: Len Wiseman, John Hlavin; based on characters created by Kevin Grevioux, Len Wiseman and Danny McBride); Cinematographer: Scott Kevan. Cast: Kate Beckinsale, Stephen Rea, Michael Ealy, Theo James, India Eisley, Sandrine Holt, Charles Dance, Kris Holden-Ried.

VENGEANCE RETURNS—ad line

If the previous installment in this lycanthropic franchise, *Underworld: Rise of the Lycans*, showed that third time really *is* the charm, then *Underworld: Awakening* embodies the old axiom that you should not go to the well too often.

After a montage of scenes and a bit of narration from vampire warrior Selene (Kate Beckinsale) to catch us up on the events of the previous three installments, she observes that "a new darkness arose" in the form of humanity's discovery of the existence of vampires and lycans. This resulted in "the Purge. Human beings no longer kill each other. We are the enemy they've been waiting for. Escape has become our only chance of survival." But before Selene and her vampire-werewolf hybrid lover Michael can make their getaway, they're taken captive by the authorities. Twelve years later Selene awakens from a deep freeze in a high security laboratory at the Antigen Corporation, run by Dr. Lane (Stephen Rea). Ostensibly developing a "cure" for the vampire and lycan "infections," Lane has his own secret agenda—he's part of a lycan plot to cure not their condition but their aversion to silver, and so let the now underground species rise again and reign supreme. To this end, Lane has delivered (or grew—this remains vague) Selene's hybrid daughter (India Eisley), intent on using her DNA in his experiments ... or something (this remains equally hazy). The escaped Selene first joins forces with a small coven of vampires, and then a concerned police detective (Michael Ealy), to rescue her daughter and bring down Antigen.

Wasted opportunities stumble through this *Awakening* like a sleepwalker shuffling through the halls of a ruined mansion. The film all but ignores the issue-laden potentialities of its genocide subplot in which the humans, now aware of the vampires and werewolves, set about systematically destroying them. Apart from a few references to "the Purge," and one throwaway scene with the superfluous human detective character (who improbably aids Selene in her climactic assault) giving a brief recounting of how his vampirized wife was dragged out into the sun by 'the Feds,' little is made of the topical xenophobic issue. The script even sidesteps the intriguing possibility of the two non-human factions—vampires and lycans—setting aside their "war" to band together against the human world. Instead, the film focuses on a small-scale, simplistic assault-the-bad-guys-to-rescue-someone scenario. Even what should be a primary, pathos-inspiring character—Selene's surprise daughter—comes off as mere plot device.

Producer Richard Wright maintains that "a lot of the film is actually structured as a mystery. [Selene is] trying to piece together what happened, who did this to her and why." And so are the viewers, with limited success. Despite, or perhaps because of, four different screenwriters, *Awakening*'s lackadaisical yet frenetic script is the poorest of the franchise. Loose ends fall like sunbeams on a vampire to explode whatever believability the story might muster. For instance, just how did Selene end up with a daughter while frozen for twelve years? Was she pregnant when captured, then brought to term by the docs to deliver a popsicle progeny? Was her egg harvested and combined with Michael's sperm to generate a test-tube hybrid? Was she simply cloned via her DNA? The script never addresses this issue because it doesn't matter—given that Selene's daughter is not so much a character as a living McGuffin, something that's been placed there simply to power the plot.

"You really want to see stakes that mean something in these kinds of movies," said lead actress Kate Beckinsale, referring to the addition of the daughter character. "Otherwise, it really is just lots of explosions and people running around in tight clothes. That's all very well and I think there is a place for that, but you don't really engage properly unless you feel there are some real stakes there." Ironically, despite the presence of a whole gaggle of vampires, such 'stakes' in *Underworld: Awakening* are nowhere to be found, since the script fails to make anything significant of this new character or Selene's sudden relationship.

"I thought I was going to play a werewolf," complained actor Stephen Rea, "but I didn't actually become one. They just CGI-ed me. I wish I had, actually. I would rather like it." So would we, Stephen, so would we. And that's yet another major problem with the film—too much CGI and not enough practical werewolf effects, so that the lycan-beasts never seem quite real when interacting with the actors. The previous *Underworld* installments sidestepped (or at least deflected) this problem by employing some impressive men-in-suit monsters for close-ups and physical contact. Here, however, the producers took a page out of the *Van Helsing* playbook and just CGI-ed the whole kit and lycan-caboodle. And the movie suffers for it.

The acting comes off as overwrought in its almost comical earnestness, with nary a smile cracked throughout the movie. Even veteran Oscar-winner Stephen Rea can do little to bring his dour, underwritten caricature to life, coming off as little more than a were-version of Grumpy Cat.

The picture has its moments, however, not least of all an admittedly exciting and well-staged action-packed battle between the vampires and the lycans when the werewolves invade the bloodsuckers' hidden lair. It climaxes with the appearance of a super-werewolf—a twelve-foot-tall giant. Unfortunately, the beast's video-game-like CGI look, with its uber-enhanced, wide-as-a-car torso, makes it appear more hairy ogre than werewolf.

Underworld: Awakening does lycanthropes no favors. Unlike in previous installments, the movie casts lycans as the evil villains of the piece. More cyphers than characters (we see only two of the werewolves in human form—Lane and his son, and even they are afforded no real characterization), werewolves are simply the Bad Guys ... because they are. They're present just to give Selene and the Coven something computer-generated to fight. The film offers no significant lycan back story, no development, nothing to hang any discernible characteristics on. Cardboard is thicker than any characterization here.

"I really wasn't intending to do another one," said Beckinsale about her return to the leather and latex Selene suit. "I kind of always heard it was a trilogy, and that was that. I didn't like the idea of rehashing the same thing too much." She should have gone with her original instincts, as rehash is about all this fourth film accomplishes. The poorly-conceived, simplistic story and underwritten characters transform all its gunfire and explosions into sound and fury that signifies nothing.

The most expensive (at $70 million) entry in the series to date (and the only one lensed in 3D), *Underworld: Awakening* also proved, surprisingly, the most successful of the quartet (earning over $160 million worldwide), despite a general panning from critics. In a fair world, the missed opportunities of the flashy but largely characterless *Underworld: Awakening* would have effectively put the franchise to sleep. But as of this writing, series producer and sometime director Len Wiseman has announced a possible fifth *and* sixth installment. Perhaps they should quit while they're behind...

With quotes from: "*Underworld Awakening*: Black Leather and Bloodsucking," by Thom Carnell, *Fangoria* 310; "Howling for More: *Werewolf the Beast Among Us*," by David J. Moore, *Fangoria* 317.

Morphology: More big bipeds, and one huge (12-foot-tall) mega-werewolf
Demise: Silver (blades, bullets, grenades, etc.)
Full Moon Rating: **

Underworld: Evolution

(2006; Screen Gems) Director: Len Wiseman; Producers: Tom Rosenberg, Gary Lucchesi, David Coatsworth, Richard Wright; Screenplay: Danny McBride (story: Len Wiseman, Danny McBride); Cinematographer: Simon Duggan. Cast: Kate Beckinsale, Scott Speedman, Tony Curran, Shane Brolly, Steven Mackintosh, Derek Jacobi, Bill Nighy.

A NEW RACE, A NEW BATTLE, A NEW HERO—trailer

But, unfortunately, the same old problems: convoluted plotting and not enough werewolfery. This first sequel to *Underworld* opens with a 13th century prologue in which a troupe of steed-riding, armored vampires, led by Viktor (Bill Nighy) and Marcus (Tony Curran), the First Vampire, come across a village massacred by Marcus' brother William, the First Lycan. While battling the various newly "turned" werewolves, the vampires finally subdue the massive were-William (making sure to keep him alive and "imprisoned for all time," as they believe his death would destroy all subsequent lycans, which the vampires use as daytime watchdogs). Back in the present, vampire warrior Selene (Kate Beckinsale) hides out with new lycan-vampire hybrid Michael (Scott Speedman), while powerful elder vampire Marcus, now revived from his centuries-long hibernation, destroys Selene's vampire clan and begins searching for her and Michael. Over several encounters with Marcus in his horrific bat-winged form, and gaining aid from the mysterious, immortal Corvinus (Derek Jacobi), Marcus' and William's *father*, Selene and Michael learn that they are somehow the key to Marcus finding his were-brother's place of imprisonment. Should that happen, Marcus will create a race of hybrids that will decimate mankind.

"I never thought *Underworld* would make over $100 million," marveled returning director Len Wiseman. "I just didn't." But it did, which means ... sequel. "There is so much that was developed for the first movie that we weren't able to tell," continued the director. "I'm really excited about being able to reveal a lot of the history and origins of the war. What started it? How did the first vampire and the first lycan ever get into battle? What was that about? What was the power struggle between the elders?... It was thrilling for me to be able to bring this history into *Underworld: Evolution*."

Unfortunately, most viewers will probably be more confused than thrilled, for Wiseman and scripter Danny McBride pack so much of this into their screenplay that the film more resembles a tangled ball of celluloid yarn than a linear action movie. With multiple (and repeated) flashbacks to events from the distant past (as well as to events from the previous film) and several long stretches of exposition to try to connect the lycan-dots, *Underworld: Evolution* becomes distractingly convoluted.

It also plays fast and loose with its own internal logic. For instance, just how his lycan-brother William (nigh on uncontrollable, as he can't change back to human) fits into Marcus' nebulous plan to reign as a god over a new race of hybrids remains vague, as does so many other glossed-over plot points in this poorly-constructed kitchen-sink conglomeration. It even tosses in a head-scratching point at film's end when Selene realizes she can now walk in the sunlight. Why? Who knows (perhaps it has something to do with having drunk Corvinus' blood, or maybe Wiseman was simply tired of shooting only at night and wanted some easier day-shoots for future installments?). As typified by this out-of-left-field daywalking bit, the film seemingly ignores its previously established tenets. For instance, Selene dispatches some lycan watchdogs by stabbing them with a knife, though there's no indication it's a *silver* weapon. And at the climax she kills several more (Corvinus' men, former allies, who've just turned) by shooting them with machine guns—though the men had made a point to inform her they only had ultra-violet bullets rather than silver). Likewise, Selene empties clip after clip of said ultra-violet bullets (designed specifically to kill vampires) into the bat-winged Marcus monstrosity over the course of the movie, producing no more effect than a BB gun (despite these deadly bullets having caused vampires to disintegrate in the previous film).

The overstuffed script limits its werewolves to three active lycan encounters. The first, excitingly staged in a snowbound medieval village in which the slaughtered inhabitants suddenly transform and rise up as ravening lycanthropes, is sorely let down by an overreliance on unconvincing CGI. The thrill of watching werewolves leap from rooftops onto the backs of horses to rip the faces off their riders deflates exponentially with the cartoonish look of the computer-generated beasts. Fortunately, the two subsequent werewolf episodes—in which Selene and Michael battle a trio of lycan watchdogs guarding a monastery, and the duo face off against the massive were-monster William (as well as several newly-made lycans)—rely more on physical effects than CGI, giving the encounters more heft and a weightier reality.

Obviously, though more dependent on CGI here than in the first film, Wiseman and co. didn't completely abandon what makes their werewolves so impressive: physicality. "[CGI] will be heavier this time just because the movie's bigger [with an estimated budget of twice the original's], and we have more luxury to add things," said returning creature creator/production designer Patrick Tatopoulos. "But more or less, the creatures will zip up the side," meaning practical effects still take the lead.

The sequel's werewolves look a bit different than the original's. "There are what we're calling 'first-generation werewolves,'" explained Wiseman, "that have not evolved to the point where we see them in the first *Underworld*. They are more creature-like and have a bit more hair on them ... a longer snout. They're not as refined and half-human as they are in the first movie."

Brian Steele played William, the very first lycan. "The great thing about William," recalled the veteran monster-actor (returning from the first *Underworld*), "was that there were no limits on how to play him. I went into it with the idea of just making him ruthless. A killing machine! We worked on changes with the leg extensions to give him more mobility than what the original wolves had. As you can see in the film, William has the ability to walk almost upright, then attack in a quadruped stance. This gave me many performance variations to draw from. I can't say enough great things about Tatopoulos Studios." Steele got his start in the monster-suit industry playing the Frankenstein Monster for the Universal Studios tour in 1987.

Effects artist/model maker George Willis (who created the claws and fangs for the film's various werewolves *and* vampires) felt that "the most amazing thing about the *Underworld* films was that the suits were very alive. The suit actor that wore them [Steele] was 6'7" and very thin and athletic. And the suit itself had a two-foot prosthetic stilt under the foot which was basically cabled to the back of the knee so that the foot itself ended up being about two feet long, where it really didn't look like a human in a suit. It was almost as if he were running around on his toes." In other words, more wolf-like, as wolves (and dogs) walk on their toes, with the heel (or "hawk") of their elongated foot raised in the air. "The creature ended up being about eight feet tall," continued Willis, "but was very agile and athletic. And it really did look like some feral creature. It didn't move like someone in a suit. I think that's one of the things that really sold the film for me."

But all this good work is once again let down by the script. While the were–William is indeed a powerful monster, he lacks depth, as we never see his humanity (he cannot transform back to his previous form, and we see nothing of him before the change). So while he leaps and growls and slashes impressively, in the end he's just a big bipedal wolf-monster with no discernable personality. Marcus fares better as the main villain, since he can reason and talk even in his grotesque bat-faced guise (whose makeup took four hours to apply). In addition to flying, the monster uses his massive bat wings as weapons, spearing and holding his opponents with their pointed tips. But even Marcus seems rather one-dimensional, as his motivations remain maddeningly vague.

Tellingly, the film's standout scene doesn't even involve a werewolf, but focuses on the flying bat-monster attacking Selene and Michael as they attempt to flee in a large truck. With the creature ripping at Michael riding in the open bed, and Selene driving the speeding truck while shooting at the flapping creature or trying to scrape it off against the rock wall, it generates some high-octane suspense and thrilling effects-oriented action. According to Wiseman, this was one of the hardest sequences to film. "The biggest thing for me," recalled the director, "was how to shoot this massive truck chase in four days. With

A lycan chows down in *Underworld: Evolution* (2006), which features some of the best realized man-in-a-suit werewolves of the new millennium.

an action movie, you've easily got two and a half weeks. But we did it in four days, or five days with 2nd unit, and it was incredibly intense." And that intensity translated well to the screen. Would that the same had happened more often, and with the werewolf characters as well.

Shot in Vancouver, Canada, rather than in Budapest like the first film (primarily to reduce travel time and fit in with the now–higher profile cast's schedules), *Underworld: Evolution* looks fantastic. Evocative art direction, atmospheric cinematography, and impressive sets, including the half-submerged castle dungeons that house William's steam punk–style sarcophagus, entice the eye and fire the imagination. The expansive, three-story, watery, crumbling castle tower interior spanned by a series of rickety wooden rope bridges makes a fabulous setting for the truly thrilling climactic battle that pits Selene and Michael against Marcus and William (along with several of Corvinus' men-turned-werewolves).

Underworld: Evolution proved even more financially successful than its predecessor, grossing $113 million worldwide (with another $61 million in video sales). As far as story quality goes, however, this entry would have been more accurately titled *Underworld: Devolution*.

With quotes from: "Theories of *Evolution*," by Anne Moore, *Fangoria* 250; "*Underworld Evolution*: Monsters in Love and War," by Vince Yim, *Fangoria* 249; "Master of Monsters," by Al J. Vermette, *Werewolf Café*; George Willis interview with the author.

Morphology: Massive wolf-headed bipeds
Demise: (Silver?) knives; decapitation; excessive bullet wounds
Full Moon Rating: **½

Underworld: Rise of the Lycans

(2009; Screen Gems) Director: Patrick Tatopoulos; Producers: Tom Rosenberg, Gary Lucchesi, Len Wiseman, Richard Wright; Screenplay: Danny McBride, Dirk Blackman, Howard McCain (story: Len

Wiseman, Robert Orr, Danny McBride); Cinematographer: Ross Emery. Cast: Michael Sheen, Bill Nighy, Rhona Mitra, Steven Mackintosh, Kevin Grevioux.

EVERY WAR HAS A BEGINNING—ad line

So does every film franchise. *Underworld*'s "beginning," however, didn't come until its third installment. The best of the *Underworld* breed, *Rise of the Lycans* opens, like all its brethren, with a voiceover narration to briefly explain the circumstances surrounding the war between vampires and werewolves: "Two decades have passed since the creation of both species. The war had begun. Viktor increased his army, creating a legion of vampires to protect them from the very first clan of werewolves, a vicious and infectious breed unable to take human form ever again. Until *he* was born.... Lucien."

Featuring a far more linear and coherent story line than its sometimes overstuffed predecessors, the 12th century–set *Rise* sees vampire overlord Viktor (Bill Nighy) using Lucien (Michael Sheen) to create "a new race of immortals—lycans—werewolf but also human." Viktor uses them as both daylight watchdogs and as slaves to shore up the vampires' sanctuary against the "mindless beasts" that lurk outside their fortress walls. These bestial werewolves—"William's kind"—ravage the countryside and threaten both the bloodsuckers and their human vassals. "If we cannot protect our humans—the grass upon which we graze—it makes us look weak," complains one member of the decadent vampire council. Viktor's headstrong daughter Sonja (Rhona Mitra) has begun a forbidden romance with "Viktor's pet," Lucien, and when Viktor turns against the two lovers, Lucien leads both his lycan slave brethren and the savage werewolves of the woods in a rebellion against their vampire masters.

Effects artist Patrick Tatopoulos (who served as creature designer on the previous *Underworld* films) sat in the director's chair for the first time for *Rise of the Lycans*. Tatopoulos' surprisingly assured direction remains refreshingly straightforward and far less frenetic than previous helmer Len Wiseman's (who here took a co-producer role). This makes it doubly disappointing that Tatopoulos has to date abandoned the baton to return to effects work (and was passed over for the next film in the series, *Underworld: Awakening*).

Unlike the two previous *Underworld*s, *Rise* devotes more attention to the lycans than the vampires, offering more werewolf action than its two predecessors combined. "*Rise of the Lycans* is all about the werewolves," confirmed co-producer Richard Wright. "We've spent more time shooting them on this film than we spent shooting the entire first movie." Director Tatopoulos agrees that *Rise* "is not the same as the previous movies. It has been done twice—however, not through the eyes of the lycans. It has always been seen through the vampires' eyes. This is something of a reinvention." Consequently, this entry truly does mark the *Rise of the Lycans*.

Regarding the lycanthropes he helped design and create for the first two features, Tatopoulos notes, "The werewolves are a similar design to those in the previous films; however, we have hundreds of them in this one. I had to work out the balance between suit work and CGI." Fortunately, he gets it right (even the transformational morphing looks convincing). The sheer expansiveness of the narrative (several scenes show scores of lycans converging on the castle) required a heavier reliance on CGI than before. Thankfully, the technology had advanced enough to make these scenes work (unlike in the previous *Underworld: Evolution*). Physical effects still prevailed for the close-up work, with Brian Steele and several others donning the impressive werewolf suits to get down and dirty. "On *Rise of the Lycans*," noted special effects supervisor Jason Durey, "it has been physical and mechanical effects. There have been a lot of rigs for blood-squirting and the opening up of necks, decapitations of wolves and humans, arm amputations, people biting each other.... We've used over 300 gallons of blood on this show."

While the two previous *Underworld*s were shot in Hungary and Canada, respectively, producer Wright and co. took their crew to New Zealand to film *Rise*. "Because of cast availability, we had to shoot from January through March," he explained, "and we didn't want to be outdoors in Eastern Europe then." Also, the Home of the Hobbits featured a "level of craftsmanship [that] is spectacular. It's obviously part of the reason we came here, but it's certainly the reason we stayed."

Though visually stunning sets and evocative atmosphere remain a trademark of the entire series, *Rise* out-atmospheres them all. "One of the briefs here was to go pre–Gothic," noted Oscar-winning (for *Lord of the Rings: The Return of the King*) production designer Dan Hennah. "The traditional Gothic vampire is great, it's a lovely design theme, but this was a chance to do something different." The superbly-realized medieval castle sets, all stone and rock and multi-level dungeons, create a dark world to reflect the story's dark themes. Even the surrounding forests appear to be conjured from shadows, spidery trees, and spiked branches. Pleased to "have had the opportunity to build something nice and big with plenty of character," Hennah created a dark, flinty environment with "plenty of chains and braziers. It's a steel-and-stone world, a pretty nasty little place—lots of fleas on the floor, pretty ugly." Ugly and highly atmospheric, with its skull-and-bone-encrusted pre–Gothic décor conjuring images of a sinister ossuary.

Rise does fall on occasion, however. The "tragic love story" ultimately becomes too overwrought and predictable, for instance, but Michael Sheen's charismatic presence helps sell the scenario, and he becomes a convincing leader. Forget Spartacus ... "Lucien! Lucien! Lucien!" Too bad Rhona Mitra, as his vampire lover Sonja, can't match Sheen's intensity, nor equal villain Bill Nighy's icy, sly presence. (Nighy confessed, "I love vampires and really hate werewolves, which is only right" for his role as head vampire. "Werewolves are messy and hairy," explained the then-59-year-old veteran actor, perhaps best known for his work in *Shaun of the Dead* and the *Best Exotic Marigold Hotel* movies, "but I do really like vampires and everything about them." Though his rather fussy preference in monsters may be questionable, his wickedly commanding and nuanced performance makes a strong impression.)

As compensation for these shortcomings, *Underworld: Rise of the Lycans* concludes with a thrilling battle chock full of medieval mayhem (and werewolves) that sends blood and body parts flying on a massive scale, as well as a more intimate and satisfying final cathartic confrontation between Lucien and Viktor. Consequently, this superior prequel shouldn't fail to get a, er, *Rise* out of appreciative werewolf fans.

With quotes from: "*Underworld Rise of the Lycans*: Bloody Beginnings," by Michael Helms, *Fangoria* 280.

Morphology: Oversized wolf-headed bipeds
Demise: A myriad of medieval weaponry
Full Moon Rating: ***½

The Undying Monster

(1942; 20th Century–Fox) Alternate Title: *The Hammond Mystery* (UK); Director: John Brahm; Producer: Bryan Foy; Screenplay: Lillie Hayward, Michel Jacoby (from the novel by Jessie Douglas Kerruish);

Cinematographer: Lucien Ballard. Cast: James Ellison, Heather Angel, John Howard, Bramwell Fletcher, Heather Thatcher, Aubrey Mather, Halliwell Hobbes.

> IT'S AS WEIRD … AS EERIE AS "DRACULA." IT'S AS THRILLING … AND CHILLLING AS "FRANKENSTEIN!"—trailer

Sadly, no. And it's not nearly as *INVOLVING* nor *EXCITING* as *The Wolf Man* either. The first of the majors to follow Universal into the light of the full moon, 20th Century–Fox's obvious attempt to cash in on the success of *The Wolf Man* (1941) apparently couldn't commit to the Full Horror Monty and so hedged its bets by concocting more of a mystery thriller than a horror film.

The story centers on the Hammond family, primarily a brother and sister (played by John Howard and Heather Angel), who seem to be haunted by the "Hammond Monster"—some kind of horrible family legacy. After an apparent attack on the brother and a local girl by some unidentified (and unseen) beast, a pair of Scotland Yard detectives (James Ellison and Heather Thatcher) are dispatched to the Hammonds' forbidding manor home. Following a long stretch in which the detectives try to suss out what's going on (while the butler and various servants act furtively, and the principals try to impeded the investigation) to pad out the picture's already brief (63-minute) running time, the "monster" abducts the sister and carries her to the sea cliffs, where the one truly exciting sequence in the film takes place. This is the first—and last—time the monster is shown. As he draws himself up over the edge of the cliff we see a man in rather sketchy werewolf makeup who is promptly shot (with common lead bullets) and whose visage changes to that of … well, that would be spoiling what little "mystery" the film can muster.

Twentieth Century–Fox contract player George Sanders took a suspension in order to avoid this assignment, resulting in frequent cowboy actor James Ellison (*The Plainsman*, numerous Hopalong Cassidy entries, and one classic horror—*I Walked with a Zombie*) stepping up to play the Scotland Yard detective/forensics expert. Though the urbane Mr. Sanders made a lucky escape, the audience was not so fortunate, saddled as they were with the stiff and unlikable Ellison whose smarmy, superior air simply grates, particularly when juxtaposed with the more natural playing of the rest of the generally engaging cast.

Werewolf-wise, *The Undying Monster* promisingly harkens back to the medieval connection of lycanthropy with Satanism. At one point

Though its poster promises "horror to make you gasp," *The Undying Monster* offers more mystery than horror, and more yawns than gasps.

the detective confronts the sister about the Hammond legend, which states that "centuries ago one of your ancestors sold his soul to the Devil, and still lives on in a secret room at Hammond Hall, issuing forth at intervals to sacrifice a human life in order to prolong his own." But these notions of Satanic ties and secret rooms become mere time-eating filler. Yes, admits the Hammonds, there is a "secret room" in the cellar, which they keep locked (not much of a secret, really), and the effort expended exploring said room (and its mysterious footprints in the dust) goes absolutely nowhere when the notion fails to tie into anything at all.

Although attempting to follow on the profitable heels of *The Wolf Man*, Fox ultimately seemed unable to cope with the subject's supernatural shadings. At the film's conclusion, the family doctor, played by Bramwell Fletcher (who laughed so hideously when Boris Karloff "went for a little walk" in 1932's *The Mummy*), explains away lycanthropy as a medical condition in which the sufferer merely *thinks* he's a wolf. "It was a form of mania that caused its victim to imagine, consciously or subconsciously, that he was a werewolf," he declares. Never mind the fact that the werewolf in question physically changes before our very eyes, and that the tuft of wolf hair found at the attack scene miraculously disappears before the *detective's* very eyes when exposed to daylight.

On the plus side, *The Undying Monster* offers up some creepy atmosphere and eerie sets. Though obviously stage-bound, the outdoor settings (particularly the "rocky lane") are evocative and atmospheric, the shadowy outcroppings and wind-twisted trees lending it a sinister fairytale-like ambiance. Under John Brahm's sure-handed direction, Lucien Ballard's mobile camera prowls about these sets, both indoor and out, to wring what it can from the largely tepid situations. The opening attack, though kept intentionally vague, benefits from some involving p.o.v. camerawork as the monster closes in on its flailing, screaming victim.

German-born director John Brahm, who created two classic horror-thrillers in the form of *The Lodger* (1944) and *Hangover Square* (1945), not to mention a bevy of notable television episodes for series such as *Thriller* and *The Twilight Zone*, recalled little of his brief lycanthropic foray. Interviewed in 1979, Brahm admitted, "All I remember about *The Undying Monster* was it was shot during wartime, and John Howard and most of my crew got drafted and reported for duty before we were through editing the final product!"

Third-billed John Howard felt *The Undying Monster* "started off with a good premise but just sort of petered out. However, I can't complain about the production, cast or anything like that. It was done rather quickly but I didn't think I was cast correctly. What the hell."

What the hell indeed. Howard was right in that *The Undying Monster* does start well, with the camera taking us inside the ornate Hammond Hall and deftly prowling from one baroque artifact to another—from a grandfather clock to shadowy statuary to forbidding coat of arms to a human hand hanging over the edge of divan, limp in sleep or … death? (It turns out to be the hand of the dozing heroine, Helga.)

Unfortunately, the viewer must wade through 57 of the film's 63 minutes to catch the first shadowy, split-second appearance of the titular monster, as it creeps into Helga's bedroom and carries her off. Then, at the 61 minute mark, we finally get a look at the face of the beast. Disappointingly, it appears more like Jo-Jo the Dog-Faced Boy than the Wolf Man. The head and face, covered in hair, lacks any appreciable nose piece or fangs. Likewise, its hands are hirsute but missing any claws or even elongated nails, making this undying monster appear more carnival exhibit than terrifying manbeast.

As well as bypassing most of the thrills of *The Wolf Man*, *The Undying Monster* eschewed the earlier classic's lunar references. Rather than the moon triggering the transformation, it's simply a "frosty night" that turns man into beast. As the doctor explains, the "curse" manifests itself "only when the victim was out on a frosty night." Time to move to a warmer clime perhaps?

Like everything else it tried to take from *The Wolf Man* (including a little rhyme in the "Even a man who is pure of heart…" mold: "When the stars are bright on a frosty night, beware thy bane on the rocky lane"), the transformation itself falls well short of its model, with the beast reverting to man via a brief, simplistic and crude matte dissolve.

In Britain the film was retitled *The Hammond Mystery* (a far more accurate moniker, given its emphasis on mystery over horror), with the censors deleting the all-important climactic shot of the werewolf (casting the local police in a particularly callous light when they cold-bloodedly shoot what appears to be an unarmed man climbing up over the cliff edge).

Even while possessing many of the elements needed for a first-rate horror—and werewolf—yarn (sinister setting, moody lighting, involving acting, evocative direction), the film can't overcome its meandering, milquetoast script and dearth of werewolf activity. In the end, apart from the opening and closing sequences involving the monster and the dreaded country lane along the cliffs, *The Undying Monster* never quite comes to life.

With quotes from: "John Brahm: The Last Interview," by David Del Valle, Sumishta.com; "The Interview of a Lifetime with John Howard," by Maurice Terenzio, *Filmfax* 31.

Morphology: Hairy (but disappointingly toothless) wolfman
Demise: Bullet (of the regular lead variety)
Full Moon Rating: **

The Unliving see *Tomb of the Werewolf*

Van Helsing

(2004; Universal) Director/Screenplay: Stephen Sommers; Producers: Stephen Sommers, Bob Ducsay; Cinematographer: Allen Daviau. Cast: Hugh Jackman, Kate Beckinsale, Richard Roxburgh, David Wenham, Shuler Hensley, Elena Anaya, Will Kemp, Kevin J. O'Connor, Alun Armstrong.

ON MAY 7TH THE WOLFMAN WILL MEET HIS MATCH—teaser ad line

Said match being not only Dracula but the Frankenstein Monster in this mega-budgeted updating of Universal's monster rally films. *Van Helsing* begins promisingly with an eight-minute black-and-white prologue right out of a classic Universal creature feature—complete with stylized castle, soundstage woodlands, and torch-wielding villagers—as Dr. Frankenstein ("It's alive, it's alive, it's alive!") brings his Monster to life, only to fall prey to an insouciant Dracula (Richard Roxburgh) who has his own plans for Frankenstein's creation. The sequence climaxes in a burning windmill, a visually stunning homage to the original *Frankenstein* (1931). After such a reverential and welcome opening, however, the picture slides into overblown action mode as Gabriel Van Helsing (Hugh Jackman), a sort of 18th century Black Ops agent for the Vatican, battles a CGI ogre that's supposed to be Mr. Hyde in Paris' Notre Dame Cathedral. The only thing more ludicrous than the ensuing over-the-top "action" (more appropriate to an *Avengers* sequel than a Gothic horror redux) is the cartoonish Hyde, a cross between the Incredible Hulk and Shrek who loses an arm without flinching. Soon the Knights of the Holy Order ("the last defense against evil") send Van Helsing, accompanied by his comical sidekick ("Why does it smell like wet dog in here?") Friar Carl (David Wenham), to Transylvania to aid Gypsy princess Anna (Kate Beckinsale, fresh from fighting werewolves in *Underworld*) in battling Dracula and his three Harpy-like brides. Complications arise when Anna's brother, Velkan (Will Kemp), is bitten by a werewolf and, in turn, infects Van Helsing with lycanthropy. Into the monstrous mix steps the Frankenstein Monster, a sympathetic creature which Dracula intends to use to infuse life into a horde of gargoyle-like offspring. The monster hunters ultimately learn that the only thing that can kill Dracula is a werewolf, and Van Helsing, soon to become one, sets his plan in motion…

"A good analogy for CGI would be morphine," observed legendary stuntman and second unit director Vic Armstrong. "Morphine is an incredible drug if you use it for what it was intended for, used sparingly in the right amounts. But when it's used too much, you get addicted and it's a killer. And that's exactly what CGI is. More movies have been killed by CGI than have been helped by it." *Van Helsing* was not only killed by its over-reliance on CGI, it was dismembered and buried under six feet of computer-generated earth.

Shot for a purported $150 million on the massive 500,000-square-foot soundstage at Playa del Rey, California, with location (and some studio) work done in Prague, *Van Helsing* features computer-generated monsters and settings whose two-dimensional look carries even less weight than the unbelievable proceedings. Over and over again, in a near-constant barrage of flashy images and impossible feats, writer-director Stephen Sommers (*The Mummy*) puts his characters—both real and computer-imagined—into ridiculous situations that smack of action-adventure desperation. "I try to make every scene even more complicated," tellingly admitted the filmmaker.

Star Hugh Jackman called *Van Helsing* "an old-fashioned, epic, Indiana Jones type of movie." Sadly, it offers little of the clever, involving characterizations of the Spielberg series, and none of the grounded-in-reality action, choosing instead to present broad caricatures performing impossible feats in a cartoon-looking CG wonderland. The resulting bombardment of broad acting and silly stunts leaves the viewer cold.

Armed with a plethora of gadgetry (automated crossbow, whirling saw blades, telescoping silver spike), Van Helsing becomes an anachronistic James Bond, complete with a Q-like sidekick friar. Sporting a long leather coat and trademark hat (*à la* Indiana Jones), Van Helsing buckles his swash throughout Eastern Europe, swinging from ropes, sliding down zip lines (shot from another of his gadget-guns), jumping chasms with horse-drawn carriages, and defying death through countless feats of derring-do that race past incredulity to leap into the arms of ludicrousness. Hugh Jackman, fresh off his success as Wolverine in the first two *X-Men* movies, offers acting as broad as his shoulders, making this larger-than-life character a caricatured action hero. Under Sommers' overheated direction, the rest of the cast go big as well, sending the proceedings teetering on the edge of camp. This lack of significant character development (Van Helsing falls far short of either Bond or Jones) makes all the overelaborate action little more than sound and fury signifying nothing.

Regarding his film's werewolf, Sommers said, "I watched the

Though impressive in a still shot, this *Van Helsing* werewolf fails to convince when in full CGI-motion.

original, Universal *Wolf Man* and I realized that this guy was really a tormented soul. He wanted to be good but he just couldn't help himself. I felt a lot of sympathy and empathy for the character." Unfortunately, Sommers failed to bring this empathy to the fore, leaving his lycanthrope woefully undeveloped.

"I wouldn't say that the [Wolf Man] design is very different from things you've seen before," admitted Sommers about his beast's look, "but it's certainly quite different from the Universal version, because he's more werewolf than wolf man. It was a matter of being somewhat reverential to the original characters, but at the same time, there's a willingness to do something new." This "something new" turned out to be a cross between a wolf and a superhero, with the wolf-headed beast's steroid-enhanced physique looking like it just stepped off the pages of a Marvel comic book.

British TV actor Will Kemp plays the human half of the film's lycanthrope. "Very early on, when I knew that I was reading for this role," recounted Kemp, "I watched all the old classics and learned about where the Wolf Man comes from. The fact that he's a really important legend among the Universal monsters is great. I watched [*An American Werewolf in London*].... But again, when you're taking on a part that has been played [by others] in the past, you want to make it your own." Swamped by all the CGI and over-the-top thespian antics, rather than making the role his own, Kemp makes next to no impression at all as the supposedly tragic lycan-character. And it doesn't help that Sommers chooses to have direct contact with moonlight be the transformation trigger. So when the moon passes behind clouds, the werewolf suddenly morphs back into the man; and vice-versa when the orb peeks out once again, turning the powerful beast into some kind of lycan-yoyo.

Further missteps come when the protagonists learn that Dracula has a cure for lycanthropy. The vampire has been using werewolves for centuries to do his bidding, "and if any should turn on him, he'd need the cure to turn the beast human before it could destroy him." And what exactly is this lycan-antidote? Just a red liquid in a syringe, with no explanation as to its contents or origin. In other words, it's simply a lycan–McGuffin, there merely for plot convenience.

At one point Sommers has Carl recite the original *Wolf Man*'s "Even a man who is pure in heart..." ditty, though he modifies the ending slightly to "...and the moon is shining bright," and adds another line to encompass the film's vampires: "Or crave another's blood when the sun goes down, and his body takes to flight." But Sommers doesn't confine his borrowings to the Universal classics, he steals from perhaps the most famous Spaghetti Western of all time as well. When Anna finally gains the upper hand on one of Dracula's brides, she admonishes, "I think if you're going to kill someone, kill them; don't stand there talking about it," which is, of course, a clumsy riff on Tuco's "If you're going to shoot, shoot; don't talk" line from *The Good, the Bad, and the Ugly*.

Though Sommers' heart may have been in the right place, his head was a different matter. "The key was to just use the source material," recalled the director. "I went back and watched all the old Universal movies and thought, 'Why did I love these when I was a kid?'" Though the opening reflects that love, the bloom quickly fell off the rose. "The whole opening sequence is in black and white, just because I love that feel," continued Sommers. "And I felt this is a perfect movie to do that—start with an old black-and-white logo. It's going to have that old-fashioned atmosphere. People remember those movies." Indeed they do, and the overblown, soulless *Van Helsing* isn't likely to make them forget the earlier classics, either.

What could have been a veritable love letter to fans of classic horror devolves into a bombastic Bondian mishmash filled with wall-to-wall action set-pieces that quickly grow wearisome through their ridiculous excess and cartoonish effects. An aesthetic failure panned by most critics, *Van Helsing* proved to be a fiscal success, grossing over $300 million worldwide—which only proves the old adage that there really is no accounting for taste…

With quotes from: *The True Adventures of the World's Greatest Stuntman*, by Vic Armstrong; "*Van Helsing* Steps Up to Bat," by Abbie Bernstein, *Fangoria* 231; *Van Helsing: The Making of the Legend*, edited by Linda Sunshine; "Giving 'Em Helsing," by Abbie Bernstein, *Fangoria* 232; "International House of Monsters," by Abbie Bernstein, *Fangoria* 232.

Morphology: Oversized, wolf-headed biped
Demise: Silver bullets
Full Moon Rating: **

War Wolves

(2009; Curb Entertainment/Sci-Fi Channel) Director/Screenplay: Michael Worth; Producers: Mike Curb, Carole Curb Nemoy; Cinematographer: Neil Lisk. Cast: John Saxon, Tim Thomerson, Michael Worth, Natasha Alami, Siri Baruc, Kristi Clainos, Daniel Southworth, Adrienne Barbeau.

> THEY SAY WAR CHANGES YOU …
> THEY HAVE NO IDEA—tagline

In this Sci-Fi network TV movie, a platoon of American soldiers (three men and three women), led by Captain Jake Gabriel (Michael Worth, who also wrote and directed the film) are pinned down in a firefight somewhere in the Middle East when several crazed "dog men" (sporting weird eyes and oversized teeth) set upon them. Back in the U.S., they struggle with the terrible secret of what they've now become—werewolves. Jake has taken the (obvious) alias "Lawrence Talbot" (from *The Wolf Man*) and disappeared into the bottle, self-medicating with alcohol. The three females have banded together, along with one of the men, to form a pack, and now seek out Jake to lead them in their new, savage life. Meanwhile, a pair of grizzled Army veterans (John Saxon and Tim Thomerson, who, along with cameoing Adrienne Barbeau, provide most of the movie's thespian highlights), the unit's former commanders, know the truth and are on the trail of these war wolves, intending to end their existence.

War Wolves begins quite promisingly, particularly in casting lycanthropy as metaphor for PTSD (post-traumatic stress disorder), with the returning war vets reacting to its alienating effects in different ways. Some withdraw (one of the unit becomes a homeless person seeking to stay off the grid), some become violently anti-social (the three she-wolves), and some try to drink the curse away (the alcoholic Jake). Unfortunately, the plot soon devolves into a convoluted mess, with talk of Jake being "the one" (the one *what* exactly is never made clear), and the "pack" desperate to reclaim their former leader (again, *why* they need him so badly is anyone's guess).

Further disappointment comes from these werewolves' appearance, which turns out to be wolf-lite at best, with only a pair of contact lenses, a set of fangs, and the occasional pointy ear designating them as anything other than normal humans. And while in lycanthropic form (which they can effect at will), they appear to possess all their human faculties. Despite Jake's constant worry (and use of alcohol to hold his inner beast at bay), these lycans retain full awareness and willpower. This raises an intriguing point, in that the quartet of "evil" lycans appears to embrace and exploit their new bestial natures, while Jake seeks to suppress it. This adds a nice element of choice to the affliction, so that here lycanthropy stands for the dark path taken by some people. While evil is not necessarily thrust upon them, they embrace it when the opportunity presents itself, making them symbols of the nihilistic selfishness within mankind rather than mere victims of circumstance.

The big problem with *War Wolves* as film is that nothing much really happens over the course of its 104 overlong minutes. While it offers the germ of several intriguing ideas, some occasionally thought-provoking dialogue (speaking of the lycanthropy, the General explains, "It wants to wrestle your soul from you, eat away your heart and your mind—slowly for some, quicker for others—until there's nothin' left of you"), and the intermittently engaging performance here and there (most specifically the quirky turns from veteran B-movie actors John Saxon, Tim Thomerson and Adrienne Barbeau), the movie feels like it's simply spinning its lupine wheels as it crawls from one scene of Jake looking lost and pensive, or the three babes strutting about, or the two aged "jarheads" (as one local dubs them) prepping for a fight to the next. And when the expected climactic confrontation finally comes, it, too, is rather derivative and small of scale, with the women turning on each other (disappointingly off-screen) and hero Jake finally transforming (using the term loosely) to battle the remaining lone male werewolf in a silly, low-rent *Matrix*-style martial arts demonstration.

As a director, Michael Worth indulges in too much film school technique for his movie's own good, filling it with slo-mo flashbacks moments, dimly-lit interiors (perhaps to represent the dark viewpoint of the protagonist?), and self-important unsteady-cam close-ups. It all serves to give the movie a pretentious visual sheen. Matching this is the often pretentious dialogue screenwriter Worth puts into his characters' mouths. They tend not to dialogue but to spout affected monologues. Admittedly, sometimes these turn out to be bon mots, such as when Jake attends an AA meeting and reluctantly tells his "story": "My name is Lawrence and I'm an alcoholic. Well, it's been seven months or something like that since my last drink…" But the subsequent internal narration has Jake revealing what he's *really* thinking: "Hi, my real name's Jake Gabriel. It's been about three hours since my last drink—because if I stop drinking I may kill every single one of you." Or when Adrienne Barbeau's eccentric character tells Jake the following story: "This old Cherokee grandfather was talking to his grandson about the battle that rages inside of people. He said there's two wolves inside each of us. One wolf is a bad wolf, an evil wolf—it's got rage and anger and hatred and jealousy, inferiority, superiority, false pride. And the other wolf is good—love, caring, peace, serenity, faith. And they're fighting this battle to the end. And the little boy thought about it for a minute, and he said, 'But grandpa, which wolf wins?' And the old Cherokee said, 'It's the one you feed.'"

Most often, however, the characters' dialogue makes them appear merely foolish and self absorbed.

Apart from the occasional thought-provoking yarn, *War Wolves* offer a few other bright spots, most of them in the form of Adrienne Barbeau's conspiracy theory/aliens-among-us/Elvis-is-still-alive character. At one point she tells Jake, "Remember, even a man who's pure of heart and says his prayers by night—even he needs a little help from the man upstairs." And she makes this awkward *Wolf Man* homage work. Additionally, John Saxon always makes for a welcome, glowering presence. And here he even gets to tear up for an emotional moment. Such a sight does an exploitation film fan's heart good.

Trying oh-so-hard to be meaningful, however, *War Wolves* ultimately steps off the tightrope of seriousness into the pit of pretension. Even the closing narration, delivered by Jake, now presumably free to be his peace-loving wolf-self, wraps its simple nugget of truth in a cocoon of self-importance: "The true war begins and ends within. The real wins and losses come not from what we can see but from what we can become as a result. And because of that there will always be a war that we must all be soldiers in." Thanks Jake; now go chase your tail…

War changes you indeed … into werewolves (at least according to the SyFy Channel's *War Wolves*).

Morphology: Barely noticeable two-legged wolfmen (and women)
Demise: Regular bullets or fellow lycan's claws.
Full Moon Rating: **

Wer

(2013; Presidio/Universal) Director: William Brent Bell; Producers: Mathew W. Peterman, Morris Paulson, Steven Schneider; Screenplay: William Brent Bell, Matthew Peterman; Cinematography: Alejandro

222 • *Wer*

Martinez. Cast: A.J. Cook, Brian Scott O'Connor, Sebastian Roche, Simon Quarterman, Vik Sahay.

THE LEGEND REBORN—poster

Porphyria: "a pathological state characterized by abnormalities of porphyria metabolism and by excretion of excess porphyrins in the urine and by extreme sensitivity to light." An odd syndrome upon which to center a horror movie, perhaps, but it's one that *Wer* takes in intriguing and effective directions. Filmed in Bucharest, Romania, but set in France, *Wer* follows the story of a man accused of the brutal murders of a family of campers. Big and hairy, the quiet and gentle Talan (Brian Scott O'Connor) lives near the sight of the horrific slaughter which seems to have been perpetrated by a huge animal. The local police, however, due in part to a political agenda, arrest Talan for the crimes. His defense attorney, Kate (A.J. Cook), and her two compatriots, Eric (Vic Sahay) and Gavin (Simon Quarterman), attempt to prove the deaths were the work of an animal, particularly since Talan suffers from a debilitating case of porphyria, which leaves him weak and docile. However, it soon becomes clear than under the influence of the full moon, Talan changes. After a botched medical procedure that results in Talan brutally slaughtering a room full of medical workers, Talan is on the run. Can Kate talk him into giving himself up before the police shoot him down like a dog; and can the police even stop him in any case?

Director William Brent Bell previously helmed the critically polarizing but financially successful "found-footage" feature *The Devil Inside*, and sought to build on that success with *Wer*. "We love the format of crime docs versus just found footage," said Bell. "[*Wer*] will utilize these techniques." Unfortunately, with *Wer* the frequent hand-held camerawork meant to enhance the "crime documentary" feel Bell so loves often simply distracts and annoys, drawing too much attention to itself.

Werewolf-wise, Bell told *The Hollywood Reporter* that the film's title, *Wer*, wasn't necessarily shorthand for "werewolf." "For instance," said Bell, "'wer' can mean 'who' in German but means 'man' in Old High German." Such coyness seems rather disingenuous, particularly given his movie's have-his-werecake-and-eat-it-too approach to lycanthropy. On the one hand, the film intimates

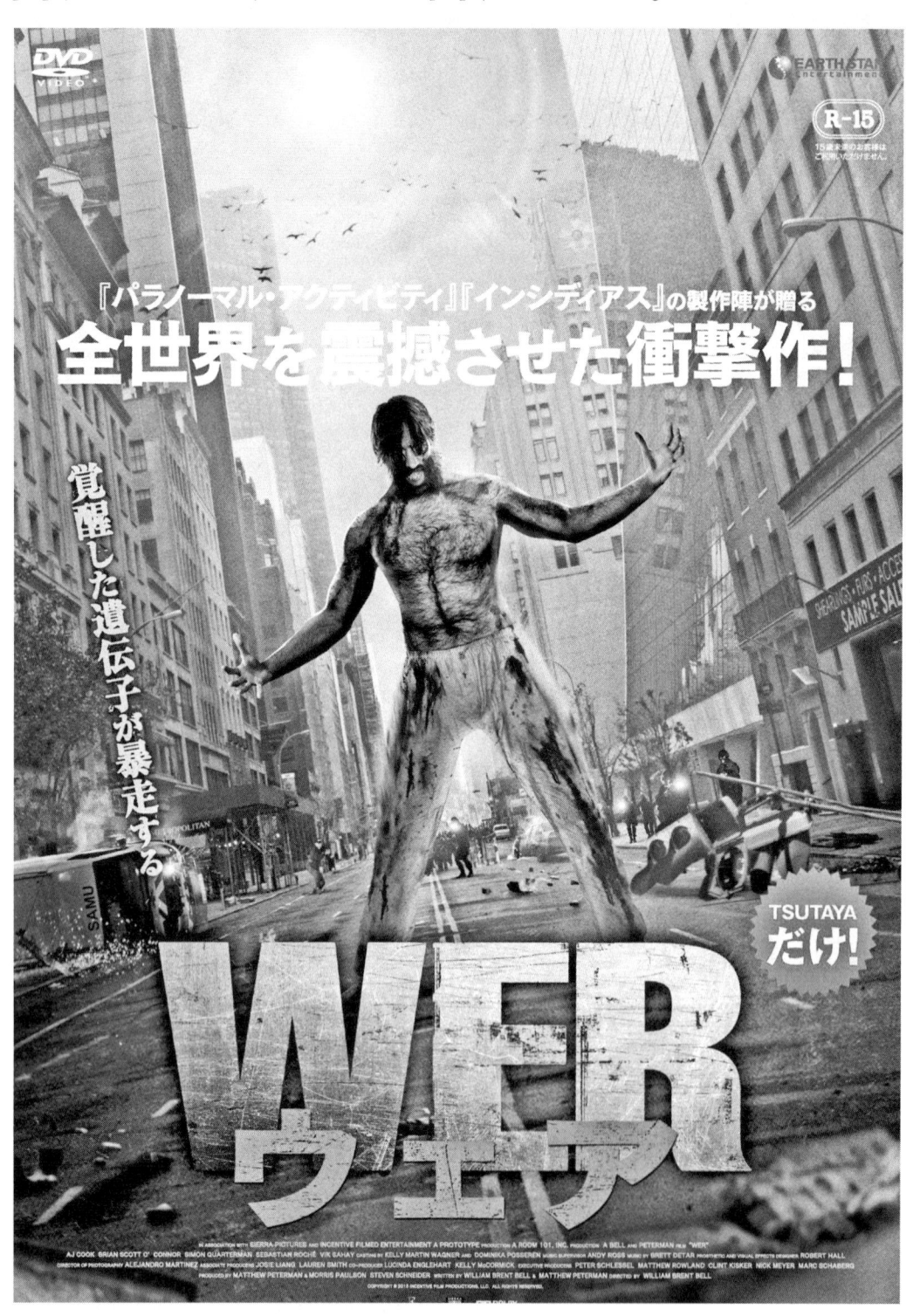

This Japanese poster for the unique and startling *Wer* captures the horrific capabilities of the generally gentle Talan (Brian Scott O'Connor) when under the moon's influence.

Talan suffers from a medical disorder; on the other, he's impervious to bullets, can leap from an eight-story building without injury, lopes on all fours at speeds of 60 mph, and can literally rip a man apart with his bare hands. Then there's the "Lunar Effect," which transforms the weak and docile Talan into an uncontrollable beast during the full moon. At one point a character tries to explain it: "If 500 years ago someone saw a man with Talan Gwyneck's same appearance. And that man was under the influence of the moon—this 'Lunar Effect'—and it made him predatory and made him a killer: 'werewolf.'"

After the initial attack on the camping family, which comes in indistinct snippets of "found footage" taken from their camcorder, it's fifty minutes before the next "action" scene. Unfortunately, the central characters as written (including the strident Kate, an abrasive assistant, and Kate's milquetoast former flame brought in as an animal attack expert) are too shallow and unlikable to sustain interest in the absence of anything else. And Talan himself, when not in violence-mode, says little and does less, simply hanging his head with his hair largely obscuring his face. With long, lanky locks and a heavy beard that covers much of his face (including nearly all of his cheeks), he simply looks like a large, unkempt man (and his physical appearance never changes—it's merely a *mental* transformation that turns him from a docile giant into a ravenous beast).

Of course, the filmmakers take more than a few liberties with their disease of choice. First off, they combine the two types of porphyria in Talan—acute porphyria, characterized by symptoms of muscle weakness, pain, and even hallucinations; and cutaneous porphyrias, among whose symptoms are a sensitivity to sunlight and increased hair growth. And, of course, neither strain induces uncontrollable rage or superhuman strength. Likewise, the enzyme deficiency disease cannot be passed through a bite (as it is in the film), but rather from faulty genetics, too much iron, or diseases such as hepatitis C or HIV.

And then scripters Bell and Matthew Peterman simply make things up. One character cites "studies on epileptics where the full moon triggers these prolonged seizures. They have these violent outbursts and they get almost like this superhuman strength.... They even have a name for it—it's called 'The Lunar Effect.'" Right.

The film's violence is startlingly swift and brutal. One truly believes that Talan can—and will—savagely kill whoever crosses his path. Add in some suspenseful scenes when searching for Talan, ending in several false scares involving birds, bats and even pigs, and *Wer* finally comes alive during its second half. The film closes with the now-infected Gavin telling a TV reporter, "I'm completely serious when I say to you that Talan Gwyneck, by the mere definition of the word, is a werewolf." Taking a more subtle, serious approach to its subject for its first half, *Wer* ultimately presents the viewer with some judicious shocks that leave their mark.

With quotes from: "Film District Takes on *The Devil Inside* Director's *Wer*," by Todd Gilchrist, *The Hollywood Reporter*.

Morphology: Large, hairy man
Demise: None; apparently neither bullets, knives, nor even another werewolf can stop him
Full Moon Rating: ***

The Werewolf

(1956; Columbia) Director: Fred F. Sears; Producer: Sam Katzman; Screenplay: Robert E. Kent, James B. Gordon; Cinematographer: Edwin Linden. Cast: Steven Ritch, Don Megowan, Joyce Holden, Elanore Tanin, Kim Charney, Harry Lauter, Larry J. Blake, Ken Christy, James Gavin, S. John Launer, George Lynn.

Evil Atom-Age scientists turn Man *into deadly, snarling* beast *… Make 10,000-year-old-horror legend* come true!—trailer
---

"Folktales and mythology have many references to the werewolf, a human being who has the power of turning himself into a wolf. The process is, in fact, called lycanthropia in medicine, and the change can be very real, resulting from the bite of a real wolf. There are times when the change has no outward manifestation, but it can also be ghastly, with the victim growing long, coarse hair on the face and hands. Sharp fangs, powerful enough to rip a man to death, jut from the jaws. Just such a change is depicted on the…. Theatre screen, before audience eyes."

So says a patently bogus press article for the first (and arguably best) werewolf film of the 1950s (though *I Was a Teenage Werewolf* has its proponents as well). Like *Teenage Werewolf* after it, the more adult-oriented Columbia 'B' programmer *The Werewolf* posits lycanthropy as a result of science—specifically, *atomic* science (this was, after all, the 1950s).

In a pre-credit sequence, the film focuses on a deserted nighttime street in the small town of Mountaincrest as a man staggers out of the ominous darkness. This initial noirish opening soon steps into standard horror territory, however, when an off-screen narrator (director Fred F. Sears himself) gravely intones, "The word 'lycanthropy' is defined as a human being having the power of becoming a wolf, or of having the power of turning another into a wolf." The man turns out to be Duncan Marsh (Steven Ritch), suffering from amnesia after a car accident. Worse, he's also suffering from lycanthropy, thanks to a pair of local doctors/scientists from whom he sought help after the crash. We don't know this, of course (thought the film's title *might* give an inkling), until after Marsh attacks and kills a man who tries to rob him in an alleyway. On the run from the town's sheriff (Don Megowan), the confused and tormented Marsh seeks help from local sawbones Dr. Gilchrist (Ken Christy) and his nurse/niece Amy (Joyce Holden), but takes to the woods again when the doc suggests contacting the police. Tormented by what he's become, Marsh eludes his pursuers until injured by a bear trap and talked into coming out of hiding by his own wife and young son, who've come to the small mountain town in search of the missing Marsh. Meanwhile, the two doctors who injected him with radiated wolf serum after his accident have also come to Mountaincrest in order to silence their wolfman guinea pig.

In keeping with the story's science-oriented approach (no matter how suspect said science might be), the film eschews standard werewolf mythology, such as the full moon and silver bullets. Marsh's transformations are triggered by emotional turmoil rather than lunar cycles. And though a vicious beast-monster while in hirsute form, he's no more impervious to injury/death than a real wolf. In fact, ordinary *lead* bullets, rather than silver, bring about his demise at film's end.

When one of the pursuing scientists, Dr. Forest (S. John Launer), finds Marsh hiding in an abandoned mine, Marsh pleads, "Please, help me, please." But the doc remains unmoved. "You're going to shoot me?" Marsh asks, incredulous. "But why? What have I ever done to you?" Ritch's plaintive bewilderment here is heartbreaking. But before the doctor can pull the trigger, Marsh transforms (the film's first on-screen metamorphosis). Through a smooth, well-executed series of dissolves, Marsh becomes the wolfman. With large pointed ears, coarse hair covering every inch of his face, a black canine nose, sharp fangs, subtly arching eyebrows, and drool dripping from the misshapen mouth, Ritch sports a rather more sinister version of the Matt Willis makeup from *The Return of the Vampire*, Columbia's previous werewolf

The scientifically created The Werewolf *(1956), played by Steven Ritch, attacks one of his makers (S. John Launer).*

effort thirteen years prior. ("When I would salivate during the transformation," related Ritch, "this was not honey or syrup. This was my own saliva ... partly due to the cold temperatures at Big Bear Lake; saliva would build up naturally and that's when they would shoot the scene for added realism.") With careful attention to detail, the camera also reveals in close-up his impressive wolf-hands, now covered in hair and ending in dark, pointed fingernails reminiscent of sharp claws.

"We shot that film during the latter, colder months of 1955 up at Big Bear Lake, California," recounted Ritch. "The role itself was a challenging and interesting one and turned out to be actually a very difficult two-week shoot. It was very cold up there at the time.... I thought the makeup was very impressive. They had a dentist make special teeth inserts.... The facial hair took a good three hours to apply in gradual tufts over an acetone glue....When they would prepare me for the transformation scenes, I would have to lie down on a six-foot board while in full werewolf makeup, and the [makeup artist] would start to remove small portions of hair ... stop ... shoot it ... remove more ... stop ... shoot it and so on. It was not a pleasant experience, but after seeing the 'dissolves' they did on me, I was really impressed with the outcome."

Though given a special "And Introducing Steven Ritch as The Werewolf" credit, the 34-year-old actor had actually been making films for many years already (including the 1953 Johnny Weissmuller/Jungle Jim outing *Valley of the Headhunters*, and playing Indians in numerous Westerns). But it's the showy role of *The Werewolf* that put Ritch on the radar (at least for horror and sci-fi fans), and the actor, with his large, expressive eyes and everyman face, made the most of the pathos-laden part. For instance, after Marsh wakes up in a culvert he becomes distraught when he sees his bare feet, breaking down fully when he spies the wolf tracks in the snow next to him. "No—I was dreaming!" he half pleads, half sobs. Ritch's confused, desperate demeanor inspires sympathy from the outset.

While in werewolf form, Ritch's abrupt movements, rapid turns of the head, and sniffing of the air complete the picture of a hunted animal. When the beast attacks, Ritch's sudden lunges and snarling viciousness make this manbeast a creature to be feared.

The year after *The Werewolf*, Ritch turned his hand to writing, penning a trio of produced screenplays (including *Plunder Road*, 1957) as well as numerous episodes for a variety of television series. "I felt that I could write better material than what I was being given as an actor," he said, "so I went to UCLA and took a six-month writing course." He continued acting as well, mostly in television, up through the early 1960s. Ritch served five years with the 1st Marine Division in the South Pacific during World War II.

In addition to Ritch's poignant portrayal, *The Werewolf* is an exceedingly well-acted picture all around, particularly given its 1950s "B" horror status. Though everyone appears to accept the idea of a werewolf in their midst rather too quickly, the earnest, even understated playing of all involved nearly sells the unlikely notion. Couple that with Ritch's tortured performance within the wintry tableaux, and *The Werewolf* becomes a highly involving account of one man's spiral into lycanthropic hell.

George Lynn, who plays the evil Dr. Chambers responsible for turning Ritch into a werewolf, had appeared in a lycan-movie before. Lynn played the constable in *House of Frankenstein* who refused to let Boris Karloff and J. Carol Naish park their wagons in his village because of the damage the Wolfman (and the Frankenstein Monster) created in the ruins of the hilltop castle years before.

The Werewolf revolves around a strong moral center, with the authorities, personified by the likable sheriff, needing to catch the creature but reluctant to harm it. The sheriff continually second-guesses his own methods, trying to weigh the safety of the community against the cruelty directed toward this lycanthropic victim. At one point the sheriff even asks the doc and his nurse to talk him out of his rather brutal plan to set bear traps for the manbeast. The lawman desperately tries to take Marsh alive at every turn, at one point using a bullhorn to exhort Marsh to "show yourself, we want to help you. No harm will come to you." Then there's Marsh's wife and young son, who, along with the doc and his niece (the fiancée of the sheriff, by the way), serve as the communal voice of compassion. The one villain of the piece is the cold, Machiavellian Dr. Chambers, as even his partner Dr. Forest balks at Chambers' callousness towards their experimental subject.

This werewolf kills only in self-defense. Until film's end, when he administers some poetic justice to the two guilty scientists, he harms no one except a no-good mugger who tries to rob Marsh at the movie's beginning. Unlike even Larry Talbot in *The Wolf Man*, this lycanthrope never kills an innocent.

Towards the end of the picture, the sheriff finally finds Marsh in the mountains and, with the help of his wife and son, convinces him to give himself up. With Marsh now locked safely in jail, one of the deputies notes that the locals "are scared of what Marsh has become, 'cause it could happen to them—could happen to anyone." This voices a repellant-fascinating aspect of the werewolf mythos—the notion that this horrific condition could be visited on *you*.

After the werewolf (justifiably) kills the two scientists and escapes from his cell, the sheriff concludes, "We can't take him alive this time; he's killed two more men." Then the tragic manhunt is on, with the townsfolk combing the woods with torches—something right out of a Gothic Universal entry. The climax, rather than offering satisfaction and closure, however, brings with it an overwhelming sense of tragedy as the men chase after and shoot down the cornered, wounded animal Marsh has become.

The picture goes a bit off the rails when it leaves Mountaincrest (and Ritch) to introduce the two middle-aged scientists in their mad doctor's lab (complete with flashing lights and buzzing electrical equipment, not to mention several German Shepherds in cages and tanks). Things aren't helped by the standard 'mad scientist' speech delivered by Chambers: "Some day it will happen—the human race will destroy itself—not quickly but slowly. That wolfman is the proof. Radiation creates mutants, people who become monsters, no longer human. They'll make the hydrogen bomb more powerful, then more powerful again—enough to change every person on the face of the earth into a crawling inhuman thing through fallout radiation.... The serum we used from that wolf mutant that died of radiation—that was the answer. By a slow series of inoculations, we can immunize ourselves and a small select group, just as I'd planned. And when the rest of the world is destroyed, we will be the only normal thinking persons left." Though a ridiculous bit of *deux et machina*, this motivational nonsense at least sets the poignant plot in motion.

Filmed largely on location in the mountains near Big Bear Lake, California, and in the San Bernardino National Forest, *The Werewolf* offers an unusual tableau upon which to paint its tragic story. The slushy streets of the small town and the surrounding snow-covered landscapes add an element of cold unfriendliness and frigid isolation to the proceedings.

Well shot by 65-year-old cinematographer Edwin Linden, under Fred Sears' careful direction, *The Werewolf* features a number of subtle, even artistic, touches that creates a thicker cinematic tapestry than what most low-budget werewolf (or general horror) films of the time wrapped themselves in. For the battle in the jail, up-angle camerawork captures the vigorous and brutal attack, while the shadows of the bars on the wall behind them suggests the confines of the trap they—and fate—have created for themselves, adding an ominous underlay to the exciting sequence. The scene ends with the werewolf leaping on Chambers' back, his hairy hands around the man's throat and his head lowering to bite his victim. They drop down out of frame, and the camera holds on the scene while the victim's screams of panic and pain let the viewer conjure all manner of visceral horrors.

Veteran cinematographer Edwin ("Eddie") Linden (who photographed both *King Kong* and *The Son of Kong* in 1933) died just four months after *The Werewolf*'s release. Columbia contract director Fred F. Sears (*Earth vs. the Flying Saucers*, 1956) was a favorite of low-budget producer Sam Katzman because of his ability to bring things in on time and *under* budget. Fast, yes; infallible no: Sears also directed *The Giant Claw* (1957), considered by most to be a Giant Turkey. Sears died of a heart attack in 1957, only a year after Linden. The filmmaker was only 44.

Released on a double bill with the excellent Ray Harryhausen sci-fi extravaganza *Earth vs. the Flying Saucers* (creating one of the best horror/sci-fi double-features of the decade), *The Werewolf* performed fairly well at the box office. "When we went to the preview of it, the response was so positive that the studio decided to film a sequel," recalled Ritch. "Many said that they didn't want me to die.... I managed to touch a sympathetic chord in the audience." Unfortunately, the Columbia head office ultimately decided against a follow-up.

With quotes from: *The Werewolf* pressbook; "Cult of *The Werewolf*," by Paul and Donna Parla, *Filmfax* 62.

Morphology: Classic (though science-induced) wolfman
Demise: Lead bullets
Full Moon Rating: ***½

Werewolf (1975) see *Night of the Howling Beast*

Werewolf

(1987; Tri-Star Television) Director: David Hemmings; Producer: Janice Cooke-Leonard; Screenplay: Frank Lupo; Cinematographer: Jon Kranhouse. Cast: John J. York, Lance LeGault, Chuck Connors, Ethan Phillips, Robert Krantz, Stanley Grover, John Quade.

> There are two kinds of people. Those
> who believe and those who will—tagline

This feature-length pilot for the 1987–88 Fox network television series follows the trials and tribulations of college student Eric Cord (John J. York), whose carefree existence ends when his best friend and roommate Ted (Raphael Sbarge) admits that he is a killer—and a *werewolf*. Wanting it to end, Ted begs the skeptical Eric to tie him up and shoot him with a silver bullet if he changes. But when Ted transforms, he breaks his bonds and attacks. Eric does indeed shoot the beast, but not before being bitten. Now not only must Eric go on the run from an accusation of murder, he realizes that he, too, has been turned, and must find and kill the progenitor of the bloodline (the werewolf who attacked Ted) in order to end the curse.

Though harkening back to the classic *Werewolf of London* and *The Wolf Man* portrayal of lycanthropy as an unwanted affliction—a curse—that the protagonist seeks to cure (or at least escape from via the "final solution" of death), this *Werewolf* also features a lycanthrope that *embraces* the beast within, reveling in the savage power his condition brings. Played with quiet menace by the imposing Chuck Connors in his final television role, Janos Skorzeny (named in honor of the classic 1971 telefilm *The Night Stalker*), the manbeast who attacked Ted, welcomes his werewolfism, thus providing another layer to the savage-inside-us concept. Not only does the film focus on the conflict of man vs. beast within us all, it offers up two battling werewolves—a "good" lycanthrope and an "evil" one—who fight for the life of the heroine at the climax (Eric's sympathetic girlfriend, whom Janos has kidnapped and taken to his woodland cabin lair). This multi-layered set of conflicts, both internal (Eric's struggle to stay human and end the curse) and external (his "good" werewolf fighting Janos' "evil"

226 • *Werewolf* (1987)

The Fox series *Werewolf* began with a two-hour TV-movie pilot. Subsequently, full-moon terror struck every Saturday night for the next eight months.

werewolf), is what makes this modest telefilm at all memorable—that, and the impressive werewolf suits constructed by special effects maestro Rick Baker (unsurprising, perhaps, given that Baker also created the groundbreaking lycanthrope for *An American Werewolf in London* and contributed to *The Howling*). In fact, these thematic dynamics became the hub around which the subsequent series revolved.

Werewolf also borrows the notion of the pentagram from the 1941 *The Wolf Man*. Here, however, the pentagram appears on the palm of the werewolf itself rather than its future victim, indicating an imminent change. Unlike the earlier classic, these lycanthropes transform seemingly at random, with no particular ties to the lunar cycle. As Eric's tortured friend tells him, "It's real random—there's no kind of schedule or cycle. But it's always proceeded by the sign of the pentagram on my palm." He describes the transformation as "a sort of madness; it just seems to well up in me as it gets closer." Conversely, it appears that those who embrace their lycanthropy—such as the evil Janos—can actually control and *induce* the change, releasing their inner beast at will.

Director David Hemmings, aided by cinematographer Jon Kranhouse, offers up an economical but atmospheric transformation sequence that effectively captures the horror of the metamorphosis through select snippets and suggestion. It begins with a shot of the victim's tortured face as a set of fangs (courtesy of *Fright Night Part II*

and *Van Helsing* makeup artist Greg Cannom) protrude from his mouth while he half-growls/half-screams in agony. Then a quick succession of cuts reveals a hair-covered hand, his shirt ripping up the back to expose a deformed hairy torso, and the malformed hand flexing to display elongated fingers that end in razor-sharp claws. Finally, a shadow on the wall of a huge wolf's head suggests the beast stalking on two legs, freed from the confining ropes. When fully revealed, it's an impressive monster possessing a snarling muzzle, long fangs, oversized head and huge shaggy body. The slavering jaws open wide, and the ears lay back menacingly to create a vision of bestial fury. This imposing creature remains one of the film's (and subsequent series') strongest assets.

A second transformation scene towards film's end—this one involving Janos—provides a further jolt. As he begins to change, Janos gruesomely pulls the skin off his own face to reveal the wolf structure underneath just as the elongating muzzle forces itself forward. Though not particularly innovative (similar metamorphoses were utilized in *The Howling* series and, of course, *An American Werewolf in London*), this remains a shocking and grisly standout moment for a television movie of this time.

Speaking of which, *Werewolf* is very much a film *of* its time. Linen jackets and shoulder pads abound, as do '80s rhythms and pop tunes on the sound track (including the now-kitschy "The Future's So Bright I Gotta Wear Shades"). The film also offers up some rather dated optical work in its "werewolf vision" shots of primitive-looking color-negative imagery.

After the first transformation scene and attack on Eric, this *Werewolf*'s pace slows nearly to a crawl, with too much time eaten up by Eric's rather mundanely presented murder rap, and semi-comical interactions with his wet-behind-the-ears lawyer and greedy bail bondsman. Then scenes of him trying to convince his girlfriend of his unbelievable predicament (concluding with her locking him in a storage unit), and the sleazy facility owner complaining about his wrecked door, as well as sequences involving the laconic bounty hunter sent to find Eric, stretch the tedium even further.

But most disappointingly, the climactic battle between the two monstrous werewolves in a flaming cabin remains all-too-brief and inconclusive. After a bit of posturing and grappling, one beast tosses the other outside (it's difficult to tell *which* wolfman is which, as they look nearly identical), the werewolf war peters out, and the scene dissolves to the next morning when the now-human Eric wakes up outside the smoldering cabin, ready to set off on his quest to find and kill the evil Janos.

Werewolf proved to be a big break for future soap opera star John J. York (*General Hospital*). As the cursed Eric, York's naturalistic playing and easy humor makes for a likable and engaging protagonist. "In 1987, I got the title role in the Fox series *Werewolf*," York recalled a few years later. "We did a season and a half—28 half-hour shows. It was a double chase show. I was looking for the head werewolf, and the bounty hunters were looking for me. I used to say it was *The Fugitive* meets *The Incredible Hulk*. The makeup for my role was pretty incredible. They'd do my hands and then my face. That part took the longest, anywhere from two-and-a-half to three hours to put on and over an hour to take off. All that, for a 20-second shot at the end of the day. But it was fun."

As well as this feature-length pilot, British actor-turned-director David Hemmings (*Blowup*, *Deep Red*) went on to direct seven of the series' individual episodes. Hemmings forged quite a career in television, helming multiple episodes of such series as *Magnum P.I.*, *The A-Team*, and *Quantum Leap*.

With quotes from: "Who's New—Mac Attack!" by Janet di Lauro, *Soap Opera World*.

Morphology: Bulky bipedal wolves
Demise: None; both featured werewolves live to howl another day (though the beast that infects the protagonist falls prey to the classic silver bullet)
Full Moon Rating: **½

Werewolf

(1996; A-Pix) Alternate title: *Arizona Werewolf*. Director/Producer: Tony Zarindast; Screenplay: Tony Zarindast, Bard Hornbacher; Cinematographers: Robert Hayes, Dan Gilman. Cast: George Rivero, Richard Lynch, Fred Cavalli, Adrianna Miles, Joe Estevez, Jules Desjarlais.

REST IN … BEAST—tagline

When the big-haired, bigger-chested, marble-mouthed, blank-as-a-plank female lead asks in a thick Eastern European accent, "Wuurwilf? You mean Joel thinks this thing is a wuur-wilf?" you know this is not going to be your average wuur-wilf movie. But when a few minutes later a baseball cap-wearing lycanthrope drives a car(!) into a batch of oil drums inexplicably left in the middle of the road, you know you've either accidentally consumed an illegal substance or passed into the Ninth Level of Lycan-Cinema Hell.

After a digger cuts himself on a werewolf skeleton (complete with wolf's skull topped by bone *ears*) unearthed at an Arizona archeology site, he transforms into a bear-like beast—only to be shot down by his two co-workers handily armed with silver bullets. The two money-and-fame-hungry archeologists in charge of the dig, Professor Noel (Richard Lynch) and Yuri (George Rivero), decide to experiment with their earth-shaking find, and Yuri injects a clueless museum guard (played by director Tony Zarindast himself) with werewolf juice (or something), resulting in the man transforming, only to die in a fiery car crash. With his first subject immolated, Yuri tries again by orchestrating another "accident" with the skeleton in order to infect Paul (Fred Cavalli), a writer come to Flagstaff who's somehow involved in fund raising for the museum, and who becomes romantically entangled with Natalie (Adrianna Miles), a buxom colleague of Noel and Yuri. Paul transforms several times (it seems the full moon occurs on at least five successive nights in this part of the world…) to stalk and kill various victims, while Natalie slowly discovers the truth and determines to help Paul however she can.

The film (made for $350,000 and released directly to video) treats its various werewolves quite poorly, with the first two (the digger and the security guard) allowed little to do before meeting their demise. Only after Paul becomes Werewolf Number Three does a lycanthrope do anything other than *die* (and drive a car). And even then, with his very first attack scene, director Zarindast manages to make lycan–Paul a subject of derision rather than dread. The sequence starts with Paul (in very light makeup—just some wispy hair glued to his face and a set of sharp teeth) ludicrously *crawling* on the ground (with Zarindast utilizing the same silly shot *twice*) before finally rising to (slowly) chase a girl down a dirt road until she becomes bogged down in a *mud puddle*. The Paul-wolf then mauls her by giving her hickies until she collapses—or at least that's what it looks like both during and after the "action."

The following night (a *fourth* straight full moon) Paul transforms again, with his appearance a bit more elaborate this time, consisting of a plastic-looking monkey-faced prosthetic, a full wooly wig, and a pushed-out dog nose.

The script ties this *Werewolf* to Native American folklore, as one of the diggers, half–Indian Joel (ridiculously played by an all-white, over-acting Joe Estevez, younger brother of Martin Sheen and uncle to Charlie) immediately labels the skeleton a "Yalloglanchie," or Navajo "skinwalker." This leads to some of the most stilted dialogue this side of an Ed Wood retrospective. Noel goes on to explain, "The Navajo can tell when a man is Yalloglanchie. He takes on a series of strange body habits, like sleeping like a coyote, nose to anus. The house begins to smell like coyote urine." And then there's this exchange:

NATALIE: "Joel thinks this thing is a werewolf?"
NOEL: "Not exactly, not in our traditional white man's movie monster sense. Yalloglanchie, see, translated, means he who trots here and there on all fours."

Poor Richard Lynch, the only credible actor in the film, does what he can to keep a straight face but is utterly defeated by the risible dialogue. Lynch, obviously there for a quick paycheck, only appears in a couple of scenes, then becomes the forgotten man for the rest of the picture (no doubt counting his blessings). Lynch's distinctive scarred appearance, which made him a popular cinematic villain in the 1970s and '80s, resulted from a 1967 incident in which a drug-addled Lynch set himself on fire in New York's Central Park. After a year of recovery he quit drugs and began studying at the Actors Studio. Among his many notable films are *Scarecrow* (1973), *The Seven-Ups* (1973), *Open Season* (1974), *God Told Me To* (1976), *The Sword and the Sorcerer* (1982), and *Invasion U.S.A.* (1985). Lynch died in 2012 of natural causes.

As primary human villain Yuri, Mexican actor and body builder George (Jorge) Rivero, who looks alarmingly like a buff Boris Karloff from *The Walking Dead* (1936), acts aggressive and uncouth to the point of becoming a living cartoon. Rivero (who got his start making masked Mexican wrestling flicks in the 1960s, including two with the famous El Santo) also starred in the Italian pseudo-wolf entry *Conquest* (1983).

If Rivero's Yuri acts like a live cartoon, Adrianna Miles' Natalie acts like a *dead* one. Polish actress/singer Adrianna Biedrzyńska made two American films under the name Adrianna Miles—Albert Pyun's *Nemesis* (1992) and this one—before resuming her career in Europe under her real name. Hopefully she did better when speaking her native tongue, since in *Werewolf* her bizarre pronunciation and thick accent are the *only* things animating her blank face and general lack of reaction. She acts as if she really has no idea what she is saying.

To label the film's pace "slow" would be an injustice to stop signs everywhere. From the very first sequence, a limply-staged and motiveless fistfight at the dig site, it progresses through a series of random dialogue scenes and lengthy solitary interludes (in which Paul broods or, worse, crawls about on all fours for seemingly minutes at a time to no purpose) to climax in an explosion of ennui with a pace-killing pool-shooting bar sequence. There Natalie first beats Paul in a game, then runs the table on Yuri after he belligerently challenges her, and then plays *another* game with a random, long-haired biker for no particular reason. It's like *The Hustler* dipped in molasses.

Poor directorial choices race through the film like, well, werewolves driving cars. For instance, Iranian-born writer-director-producer Tony Zarindast drags out the protracted pool-playing sequence even further by inserting a slow camera pan across a Western mural on the barroom wall—for no discernible reason and with no payoff (it's not even a particularly *good* mural). The director's minimalist style appears to consist of the mantra 'one scene, one set-up,' as he rarely provides any variation in his camera angles (or *anything* of visual interest, for that matter—unless one counts some blue-tinted day-for-night photography right out of a 1970s TV movie). Then there's the awful nonending that sees Yuri finally meeting his comeuppance in a totally unsatisfactory manner (he runs into the full-on bat-bear beast … is it Paul? no idea], which makes short, unconvincing work of him with a few slaps and a splash of red paint) before Natalie and Paul unite in werewolfery … or something.

These lycanthropes apparently come in stages. The initial werewolf, the digger Tommy, first appears as a long-haired generic wolfman after transforming in the hospital. Later he shows up in full-on wolfish mode—with huge pointy ears, a plastic-looking raised brow ridge, big bug eyes, dog muzzle, and a set of fangs so huge he can't close his mouth. The bulky, hair-covered suit makes him look like a mutant sunbear. At one point the largely immobile jaw manages to open a little wider, emphasizing its rigid artificiality. Of course, his two buddies immediately show up with rifles and silver bullets to take care of the poor Tommy-wolf before he even has a chance to attack. Note that being shot with silver bullets did *not* kill this werewolf, however. A later dialogue exchange (rather than any action or visuals) indicates he's still recovering in the hospital.

The previously mentioned werewolf car crash resulted from producer-director Tony Zarindast having purchased a stock shot of a car driving into a batch of oil drums and exploding. Zarindast had his own car painted to match the color of the car in the stock footage, resulting in a Ford Taurus changing into a Plymouth Acclaim during the crash.

Only two years after its release, *Werewolf* was spoofed by the popular comedy program *Mystery Science Theater 3000*, whose clever riffing worked miracles by transforming a painful viewing experience into an enjoyable one. If you feel the need to watch *Werewolf*, I suggest you let Mike and the 'Bots share—and alleviate—the pain.

Morphology: Rat-bat-bear monster; plastic-faced biped; slightly hairy manbeast
Demise: None (except death by car crash/immolation for one ancillary lycanthrope)
Full Moon Rating: *

The Werewolf and the Yeti see Night of the Howling Beast

A Werewolf Boy

(2012; CJ Entertainment; South Korea) Original Language Title: *Neuk-dae-so-nyeon*. Director/Screenplay: Sung-hee Jo; Producers: Sujin Kim, In-beam Yun; Cinematographer: Sang-mok Choi. Cast: Joong-ki Song, Bo-yeong Park, Young-nam Jang, Yeon-seok Yoo.

LOVE WAS THE FIRST HUMAN
LANGUAGE HE EVER LEARNED—poster

As evidenced by the tag line above, the South Korean *A Werewolf Boy* is more romantic fantasy than tense horror (though a few isolated moments do qualify for the latter). Told in flashback, the story, set in 1965, has teenage girl Soon-yi (Bo-yeong Park) and her family move from Seoul to a house in the country, where they discover a teenage boy (Joong-ki Song) living wild. The lad, whom they dub Chul-soo, moves about on all fours, doesn't speak, lacks social graces, and appears to have been raised by animals. In reality, he is the result of genetic experimentation conducted years earlier on this very farm by a reclusive scientist intent on creating "super-soldiers" by combining human and wolf traits. Slowly, Soon-yi begins to tame the boy's savage ways, developing a close rapport with the gentle but uncivilized youth. But the family's arrogant landlord has lecherous designs on the beautiful Soon-yi, and his nefarious actions bring out the animal in Chul-soo, as well as attracting the attention of an Army colonel and scientist who intend to study and perhaps destroy the wolf boy.

Most of the film focuses on Soon-yi's developing relationship with the smitten wolf boy, as she sets about teaching him table manners, training him to obey simple commands (utilizing a dog manual), and interacting with the few other children from the tiny local village. For the first hour of the film Chul-soo basically behaves like an intelligent dog. But here and there an indication of his Otherness peeks through, such as his ability to throw a ball completely across a pasture or his immense strength (dramatically demonstrated when he protects Soon-yi from a falling beam on a trip to the village). Finally, over an hour into the movie, his true nature emerges when he transforms into the werewolf boy of the title, the metamorphosis triggered by the landlord's assault on Soon-yi. Suddenly, Chul-soo's eyes begin to glow luminously and his breath comes rapidly, accompanied by a deep-throated snarl. In close-up we see his incisors lengthen into (vampire-like) fangs. Another close-up shows his wrist growing (CGI) hair, while his fingers pop and elongate into claws. Then the muscles under his shirt appear to ripple and shift. Next his feet sprout hair and transform into large, paw-like appendages, just as one foot steps menacingly forward toward the camera. Chul-soo then stands full length in his werewolf guise, an unruly mop of hair atop his head and coarse sideburns covering most of his cheeks. Striding forward, he tosses the landlord and his three ruffian companions around like dolls. But after Soon-yi commands him to "Wait!" just as he's about to do something drastic to the cowering villain, the werewolf boy stops and raises up, with the camera showing his hand morphing back to human form once more. Turning towards Soon-yi, we see he is back to normal.

Make-up man Hwang Ho-gyum noted that "werewolf characters are not often seen in Korean movies.... We were thinking of a scary version. But the director, because this film's genre is romance and innocent fantasy, he wanted the werewolf to look sympathetic even after the transformation rather than a terrifying, scary-looking beast." As such, a bit of hair, some hand and foot prosthetics, a set of fangs and some yellow contact lenses to simulate wolf's eyes comprise this "werewolf boy." Explained writer/director Sung-hee Jo, "There are a lot of movies that feature werewolves. Unlike most of them, I wanted our werewolf to keep his human face after the transformation. Instead of transforming into a completely different creature, I wanted there to be some human traits."

This scientifically-created werewolf has nothing to do with the moon or silver. (Oddly, a bit of the seemingly supernatural appears to have crept into the concept, for at the film's close—at which the story returns to modern times—Chul-Soo hasn't aged a day in 47 years.) He transforms only when emotionally provoked, but even then he seems to retain much of his more human thought processes (protecting the girl, targeting only the villains, and obediently stopping when told to do so by his mistress). An innate kindness, gentleness, and love are his predominant traits, and even the beast inside him cannot override his humanity for long.

One of the film's strongest assets is the animalistic yet quite human playing by Korean TV heartthrob Joong-ki Song as the werewolf boy. Song trained in mime for three months before shooting began, and consulted an animal expert to capture the wolf-like movements. Song employed segmented movements—quick, staccato turns of the head, for instance—to mimic animal motion (rather than the smoother motion of a human being). Rapid breathing through the ribcage, so that his chest visibly rises and falls (like with many animals), helped complete the animalistic picture.

Romantic American artwork for the romantic Korean movie *A Werewolf Boy*.

"It was a story about innocence," noted the actor, "and it really resonated with me. I didn't cry my eyes out ... when I read the screenplay], but I felt a lump in my throat." Song's co-star, Bo-yeong Park, labeled the film "a romance" and "a really innocent, good-hearted movie." While that may be, *A Werewolf Boy* doesn't completely work as either a romance or werewolf film. Though beautifully filmed and containing some remarkable scenes (as well as a bravura physical acting job by Joong-ki Song as the wolf boy), its slow-paced scenario tends to replace characterization and suspense with caricatures and saccharine. The local cops and the military men, for instance, are portrayed as impossibly stupid buffoons. And had the villainous landlord sported a mustache, he would certainly have been twirling it.

The public took a far kinder view, however, as *A Werewolf Boy* proved to be a huge hit in its native land, becoming the most successful Korean melodrama to date. Maybe something was lost in translation…

With quotes from: "Making of *A Werewolf Boy*," and "Beautiful Werewolf," *A Werewolf Boy* DVD, CJ Entertainment, 2013.

Morphology: Unkempt, hairy young man with fangs, clawed hands and paw-like feet

Demise: None; the story ends with the solitary werewolf boy building a snowman on a hill

Full Moon Rating: ***

Werewolf Fever

(2009; R–Squared Films; Canada) Director/Cinematographer: Brian Singleton; Producers: Mark Singleton, Brian Singleton, Robin Audette; Screenplay: Brian Singleton (story: Mark Singleton, Brian Singleton, Richard Glasgow). Cast: Heather Duthie, Kevin Norris, Richard Glasgow, Mark Singleton, Megan Fortier, Mark Courneyea, Miles Finlayson, Ian Lloyd.

Terror is on the menu!—tagline

There's something very appealing about a hamburger. Simplicity itself—a bun, a well-grilled piece of meat and a few condiments—it's meant to be eaten quickly, enjoyed in the moment, and then forgotten. One could say the same about *Werewolf Fever*, a low-budget indy filmed on weekends at the real-life Kingburger Drive-In restaurant in Renfrew, Ontario, Canada. Simple, self-contained, and moderately satisfying, *Werewolf Fever* is the cinematic equivalent of a fast food burger.

The straightforward story begins with Odi (Ian Lloyd), cranky owner of the Kingburger drive-in restaurant, berating his various employees before heading out for a hot date (with a hooker, it turns out). Said employees consist of counter girl Mandy (Heather Duthie), roller-skating carhop Sandy (Megan Fortier), fry cook Stubs (Kevin Norris), worker bees Frank (Richard Glasgow) and Ronny (Mark Singleton), and delivery boy—and Ronny's twin—Donny (Singleton again). That evening (a *full moon* evening) Donny pulls his van off the road to relieve himself in the woods, only to be attacked and bitten by some unseen animal, causing him to transform mere seconds later into a ravenous beast! The Donny-wolf then makes its way back to the Kingburger and lays siege, picking off the employees, plus a few after-hours visitors, one by one until finally meeting up with Stubs' silver spatula (a runner-up prize from last year's "Golden Griller Championships"!).

"The story began in April of 2007," recalled writer-director Brian Singleton, "when a group of friends and I stopped for lunch at a classic looking drive-in restaurant in Renfrew called Odi's Kingburger. As we ate our lunch, a joke was made about shooting a monster movie there, with the obvious villain being a werewolf attacking the Kingburger to eat the burgers and the staff. We laughed at first, then I couldn't get the idea out of my head. So, I decided to take the first step and ask. I approached the Kingburger's owner, Robert 'Odi' Audette, to see what he thought about his restaurant being used to shoot a werewolf movie. I soon discovered that Odi was a great guy. Then he introduced me to his daughter Robin, who also happened to love horror." Robin, manager of the restaurant, went so far as to serve as a co-producer on the low-budget endeavor.

Shot at the Kingburger during weekends in the summer of 2007 (it didn't see post-production completion until 2009, when it played the festival circuit before a 2011 DVD release), *Werewolf Fever* starts out somewhat slow, with the first fifteen minutes largely taken up by the impossibly bad-tempered boss Odi barking orders and insulting his staff. But once the werewolf shows up, it's beasts, blood and burgers for the duration. Unlike so many micro-budget efforts, *Werewolf Fever* never outstays its welcome. Jack-of-all-cinema-trades Brian Singleton (director, writer, co-producer, cinematographer *and* editor) avoids that deadly trap into which so many amateur auteurs fall—seeing every shot as a masterpiece. Consequently, Singleton trimmed the footage fat to a lean, easily digested 66-minute running time.

Taking its structure from a far more famous (and admittedly far better) low-budget independent horror—George Romero's *Night of the Living Dead* (1969)—*Werewolf Fever* offers the intimate claustrophobia generated by a group of desperate individuals trapped in a confined locale by an outside force (one werewolf here vs. a horde of zombies in *Night*). The comparison even extends to particulars. When one character suggests they go down in the basement and lock themselves in until help arrives (just like Harry Cooper did in *Night of the Living Dead*), Ronny (like Ben) opposes the idea. Later, Ronny makes a run for a vehicle (the phone is out)—just like Tom and Judy in *Night*—while the others distract the monster (tossing burgers out the drive-thru window). And like in the original, things don't go according to plan. Unfortunately, none of the *Werewolf Fever* characters offer the same depth, nor do their dynamics or interactions carry the same thematic weight, as in *Night of the Living Dead*. Still, it's good to see the film's heart (and guts) are in the right place (at times literally).

While its linear structure and quick pace put the "fast" in "fast food," like most mystery meat sandwiches, *Werewolf Fever* doesn't bear close scrutiny. For instance, whatever happened to the original (unseen) werewolf that bit Donny in the first place? Also, the unstoppable Donny-beast is kept at bay far too easily by flimsy doors and big picture windows; why does it take the werewolf nearly the entire movie before it finally batters down the thin portal in one go? (The obvious answer: Singleton and co. could not afford to damage *anything* at the Kingburger, which had to be ready for business each day after their night shoots. "On the first night of shooting," recounted Singleton, "the werewolf stepped off the dumpster and went through a picnic table. We had to replace the broken boards the next day, but thankfully everything was fine!") And why does Ronny, after making it to a car with a CB radio, simply stand outside, reach through the window, and grab the radio to call for help rather than shutting himself safely in the car's interior as protection against the monster he knows is hot on his heels?

Though featuring only five primary characters, the film offers very little characterization, which might be just as well since the amateur thespians act no more convincing than, say, the Hamburglar. (Brian Singleton's brother Mark played not one, not two, but *three* roles—twins Ronny and Donny, *and* the werewolf.) Alternately toneless and strident, these enthusiastic amateurs give the impression of focusing so hard on simply hitting their marks and remembering their lines that they forget to deliver actual performances. "All I had was a Visa card and a part-time job for funding," admitted Singleton. "I cast familiar actors that I knew would commit to the difficult shooting schedule for the thrill of the project rather than a paycheck." Had Singleton the resources to hire professionals, this *Werewolf* might indeed have induced a *Fever* rather than just a cinematic sniffle.

Fortunately, Singleton displays considerable inventiveness and even some artistic flair in overcoming the many budgetary shortcomings. For instance, the transformation scene (which marks the quickest bite-to-beast metamorphosis in werewolf history, as less than a minute after the encounter Donny changes into a beastman), makes the most of what is *not* shown. After being bitten, Donny stagers in front of his van. Back-lit by the vehicle's headlights, and atmospherically haloed by the drifting fog, he screams in pain and froths at the mouth. In long shot he drops down into a crouch, while brittle snapping and wet squelching noises on the soundtrack, accompanied by his shadowy writhing, indicate the horrible physical transformation. Suddenly he rises up into full furry silhouette and howls—and a werewolf is born. Too bad the look of this lycanthrope can't match the viewer's imaginings engendered by this clever sleight-of-hand metamorphosis.

In fact, after the amateurish acting, it's the *Werewolf* itself that douses most of the *Fever*. Starting at its misshapen oversized were-clown feet still partially encased in sneakers, its goofy hands and oversized immobile mutant rodent mask make it look like a cartoon character come to were-life. The lion-shaped head ringed by a mane of matted hair, elongated ridged face, beady eyes, oversized mouth, and six-inch rubbery ears sprouting from its head (not to mention its thick lumpy tail) make it look more like a rabid were-rodent than a vicious werewolf. Or, as described by the man inside the beast himself (Mark Singleton), it looks like a "mutated beaver." Brian Singleton cleverly employs a few shadow shots early on (the silhouette of a clawed hand moving across a menu board, for instance) to build suspense, but once the beast steps into full view, its silly appearance inspires more giggles than screams. Singleton does what he can by shooting the creature from low angles and, most importantly, keeping the monster active. But while Brian's brother Mark offers plenty of energy in his performance (leaping from table to table, or even from atop the drive-in building itself), he adopts an odd, sideways skipping motion when he runs, his arms hanging akimbo like some ugly primate.

Still, Singleton manages to create a number of memorable moments, the most striking being the "roller skate gag." When roller-skating waitress Sandy goes out to try to talk her obsessed ex-boyfriend out of doing something stupid, she discovers his gruesomely dismembered corpse in the dumpster. Suddenly, the beast lands on the dumpster lid, and as Sandy turns to flee, a swipe of his clawed hand sends her to the ground. As she looks up she sees her own leg, severed at the knee, rolling upright across the parking lot on its solitary skate until finally wobbling and

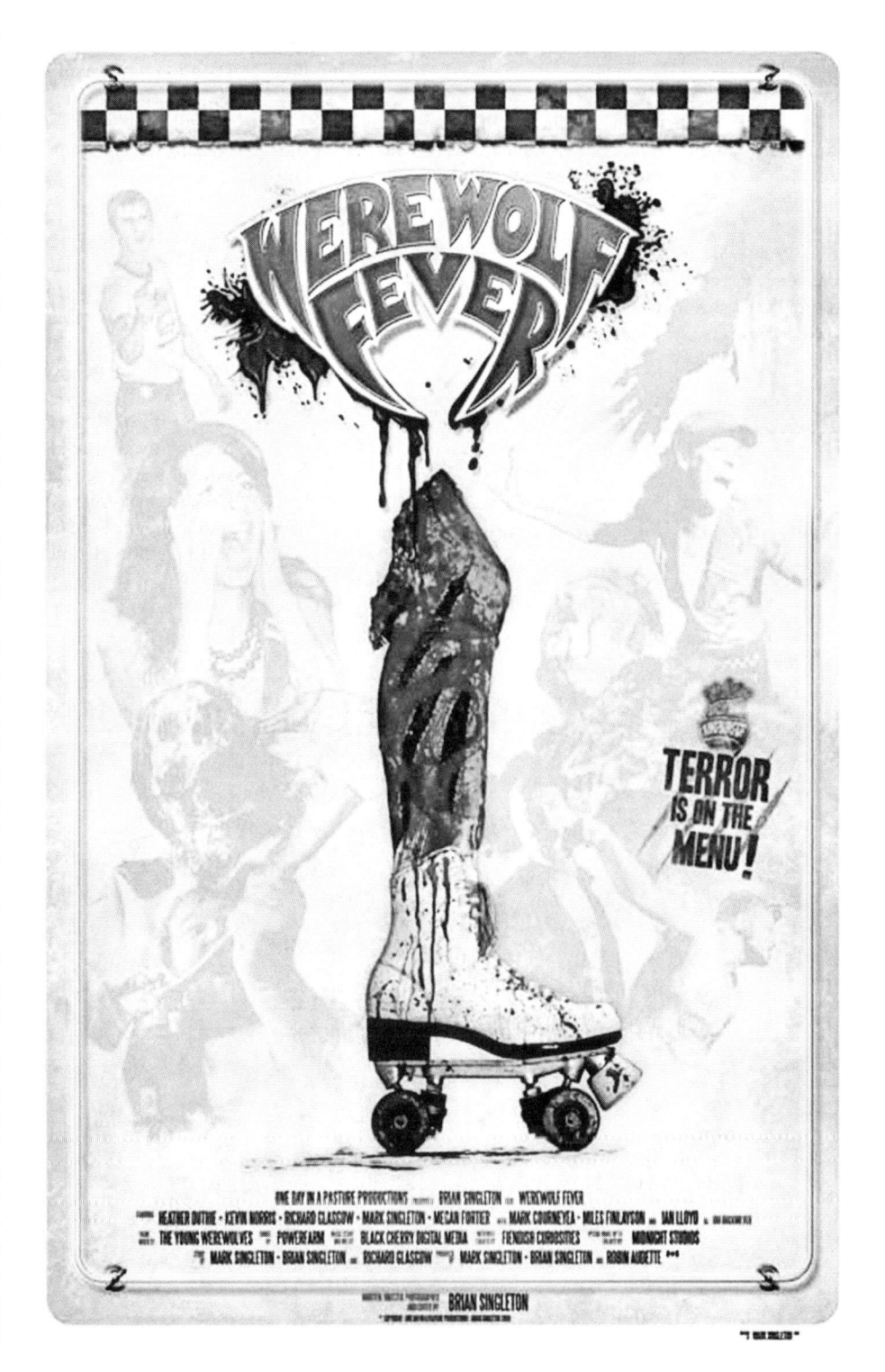

This brilliantly-conceived poster was created by Mark Singleton, who not only co-produced *Werewolf Fever* but played *three* roles, including the werewolf (making this the one and only lycanflick with a poster designed by the werewolf himself!).

falling over. ("We rolled the skate across the parking lot more than 30 times to get the right take," laughed Singleton.) Later, as the survivors creep out to see what has happened to Sandy, they look up to spot the creature standing atop the drive-in gnawing on her severed limb—roller skate still attached—before lifting it above its head like a trophy, roaring in triumph, then tossing it down at their feet. Horrific and humorous at the same time, these scenes encapsulate the outrageous enthusiasm of this hey-let's-put-on-a-werewolf-show production.

"The movie was an exhausting and grueling experience to make," recounted Brian Singleton, "but as usual, it was the time of my life. We had to shoot overnight on weekends, which was very tough on everyone involved, since we all worked full time day jobs during the week…. In the end, I was very lucky to have everything work out for the best." Like one of Odi's kingburgers, *Werewolf Fever* is simple, compact, cheap and cheesy. And while far from a culinary masterpiece, it more-or-less satisfies one's basic craving for cinematic junk food.

With quotes from: "Interview: Brian Singleton, Director of *Werewolf Fever!*" by Zombie King, ZombieInfo.com.

Morphology: Big-headed, bipedal mutant werewolf
Demise: Silver spatula
Full Moon Rating: **½

Werewolf in a Girls' Dormitory

(1961/63; MGM; Italy; b&w) Original Language Title: *Lycantropus*. Alternate Titles: *I Married a Werewolf* (UK); *Monster Among the Girls*. Director: Richard Benson (Paolo Heusch); Producer: Jack Forrest (Guido Giambartolomei); Screenplay: Julian Berry (Ernesto Gastaldi). Cinematographer: George Patrick. Cast: Barbara Lass, Carl Schell, Curt Lowens, Maurice Marsac, Mary McNeeran, Grace Neame, Lucian Pigozzi.

IF YOUR BLOOD CURDLES
EASILY—*DON'T COME!*—trailer

Ditto if your eyelids droop easily. To be fair, this offbeat Euro-take on the werewolf mythos offers some atmospheric nighttime photography (courtesy of cinematographer "George Patrick," an unknown young cameraman who, according to co-star Luciano Pigozzi, died in an auto accident shortly after filming), an impressive Italian villa setting (surrounded by wolf-infested woods), the occasional shock (such as the terrified frozen stare of a young girl's bloody corpse), the bulging-eyed "Italian Peter Lorre" (Luciano Pigozzi) at his most skulkiest, and plenty of pretty girls (including doe-eyed lead Barbara Lass, Roman Polanski's first wife). But this *Werewolf* also sports awkward dialogue (and hollow dubbing), some poor minimalist makeup, and a plethora of dull stretches (including a tedious final 20 minutes that wind down to a perfunctory climax).

Filmed in 1961 near Rome, but released Stateside in 1963 in support

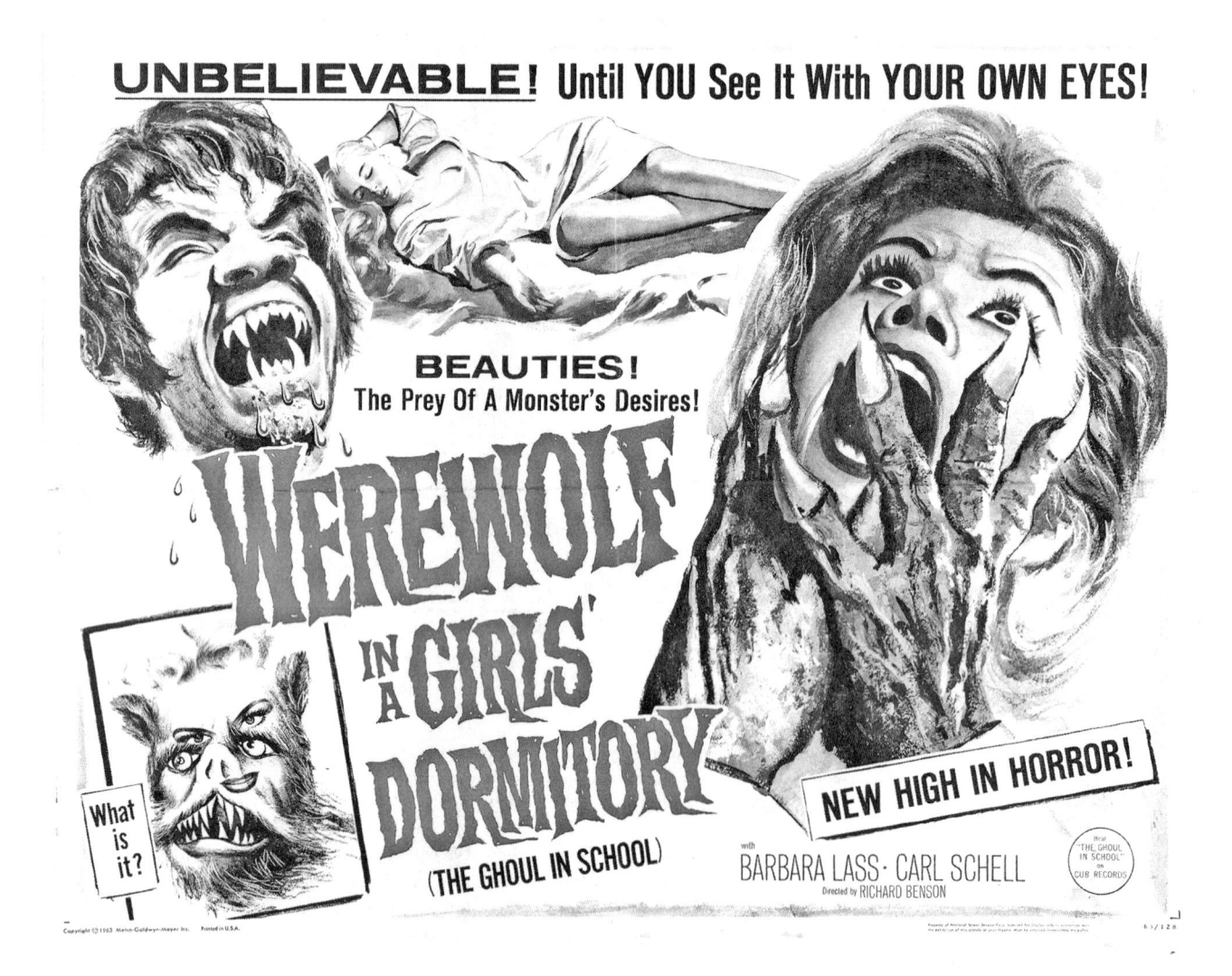

The brilliantly exploitable title may be the best thing about this uneven Euro import.

of the Boris Karloff–starrer *Corridors of Blood*, *Lycantropus* (its original-language title) sees a private reform school for wayward girls plagued by vicious murders. A young disgraced doctor (Carl Schell, lesser-known brother of Maximillian) comes to the school as a teacher and must solve the case of the mysterious murders, finally uncovering a "lycanthropus" in their midst.

Structured like a mystery, the plot involves blackmail, incriminating letters, hypocritical "establishment" figures, and red herrings, as well as a few choice murders (not all at the hands of the werewolf). While this "who's-the-lycanthrope?" angle sustains interest for the film's first half, the lackluster and infrequent werewolf "action" (with the lone transformation sequence consisting of one chintzy cutaway to a single intermittent makeup stage) and dull denouement only engender a sense of disappointment and tedium once the mystery bubble has burst.

Speaking of werewolves, the film sets the mythical beast squarely in the realm of science (or a loose cinematic facsimile thereof), eschewing the supernatural curse, pentagram and silver bullet mumbo jumbo (the creature meets its sad fate at the end of an ordinary lead projectile). "The pituitary gland … can cause a psycho-physical transformation," explains the doc, who happens to be an expert on the dreaded "lycanthropus." For the victim of this rare disease, he continues, "at every lunar cycle the pituitary gland acts strangely and becomes enlarged at the start of the transformation. Our psyche controls upset the balance of the neuro-glandular system, causing incredible distortions in the skin, hair and teeth." This pseudo-medical babble translates into the sparsest werewolf makeup since Henry Hull crossed yak hairs with Jack Pierce in *Werewolf of London*. Decked out in nice slacks and sweater (and at one point even a suit and tie), this werewolf in a girls' dormitory, with its ridged forehead (a silly and obvious prosthetic piece), oversized nose, plastic fangs and three-day beard, unfortunately lacks the sinister satanic quality showcased by Pierce's minimalist makeup from a quarter century before, resulting in what looks like a scarred man with bad teeth after a three-day binge. It's hardly the stuff of nightmares; and the same could be said of the film as a whole.

Note: A movie pressbook can be an amazing thing, as evidenced by the following "article" printed in *Werewolf*'s campaign manual. "A lovely 17-year-old student at an exclusive girls' school outside Turin, Italy, was found pregnant during a routine physical examination. Upon questioning, she revealed that eight weeks before, under the light of the full moon, a werewolf entered her room in the girls' dormitory. Upon further questioning, she claimed that the werewolf had a long, hairy face and drooled at the lips. Local authorities are skeptical of her story, pointing out that the girl might have been influenced by the recent location shooting of the startling new horror film, *Werewolf in a Girls' Dormitory* in and near the city. However, the mayor has decided to adopt a 'wait and see' attitude for the next eight months." Life imitating Art? Right.

Morphology: Well-dressed, lightly-made up wolfman
Demise: Ordinary bullets
Full Moon Rating: **

Werewolf in a Womens Prison

(2006; ME Films) Director: Jeff Leroy; Producer: Tai Chan Ngo; Screenplay: Vincent Bilancio, Jeff Leroy; Cinematographer: Nicholas Melillo. Cast: Victoria De Mare, Eva Derrick, Vincent Bilancio, Domi Arcengeli, Jackeline Olivier.

> When the moon is full, no one escapes
> the fury of the werewolf—trailer

Here's a first—a werewolf in a *women's prison*. Subscribing to truth in titling, micro-budget filmmaker Jeff Leroy (*Creepies*, 2004; *Rat Scratch Fever*, 2011) employs his digital video camera and shoestring sensibilities to create the first ever WIP (women-in-prison)–werewolf hybrid. And given the results, this may very well be the last…

A young woman, Sarah (Victoria De Mare), camping in the Mexican jungle (actually the wilds of Los Angeles' Griffith Park) survives an attack by a werewolf (who kills her boyfriend) only to wind up in a third-world women's prison ("in the great republic of Campuna"). Convicted of murdering her boyfriend Jack (Vincent Bilancio), since none of the corrupt locals believed her werewolf story, she's subjected to the abuse of the prison's degenerate warden, aided by his dominatrix assistant, who farms out his female charges as prostitutes. But Sarah was bitten during the attack, and on the night of the full moon she transforms into a rampaging beast that makes short work of inmates and guards alike. Made doubly remorseful when the ghost of her werewolf-victim boyfriend periodically appears to exhort her to take her own life and so end the werewolf curse, Sarah determines to escape. But the warden has plans to make a fortune by exhibiting her as the world's first captive werewolf…

Small of scale, *Werewolf in a Womens Prison* [sic] is the kind of barely-better-than-backyard production in which the titular institution consists of two plywood cells, a chintzy office, and a medical room hung with sheets; while the prison yard looks like the back alley of a public storage facility.

Writer-director Leroy tosses in plenty of cheesy, over-the-top gore and exposed breasts (truly the cheapest of all "special effects") to try and distract from the amateurish acting, impoverished photography (consisting of that flat, overexposed look that screams "shot-on-video"), and, most disappointingly, dearth of originality. This last is demonstrated by the film's shameless stealing from far better films, most pointedly *An American Werewolf in London*, with Sarah's ever-more-decayed boyfriend periodically appearing to explain how she needs to take her own life. "Until the curse of the werewolf is lifted I'm trapped in this limbo," the unhappy Jack tells Sarah—just like the unhappy Jack tells werewolf-to-be David in *American Werewolf*. But instead of the original Jack's amusing commentary ("You ever talk to a corpse? It's boring!"), we have *this* Jack complaining, "I'm stuck helping psychics and making lame appearances at people's séances." Not only does this blatant theft warrant a visit from the plagiarism police, conjuring the memory of that brilliant earlier lycan-classic does this inept wannabe no favors in comparison.

Werewolf in a Womens Prison fares no better when it tries to be funny. When the two guards pursue the escaping Sarah and her friend, out of the blue the first guard tells the other, "We should wait for the Badger." To this, the second guard sneers, "Badger—we don't need no stinking Badger!" ("Badger," it turns out, is the name of the redneck bounty hunter the warden engages to help track the girls.) So much for a clever script.

The sole werewolf (Leroy employs his one suit for both the nameless lycanthrope attacker and the subsequent Sarah-wolf) looks like a muscular teddy bear with an elongated plastic snout and snaggle-tooth fangs. Ludicrously, it sports bright red L.E.D. lights where its eyes should be. If this ridiculous beast looks familiar, then you've been watching too many S.O.V. (shot on video) werewolf flicks. Leroy recycled (and updated) his monster from the even lower-budgeted (and even less entertaining) *Eyes of the Werewolf* (1999), on which he worked as cinematographer, editor and, most critically, creature creator.

When not going for the goofy grue (including one naked inmate literally torn in half, looking just like what she is—a latex doll), Leroy fills his film with women-in-prison/sexploitation tropes, including leering guards fondling unwilling prisoners; lesbian couplings; and even a slow-motion sponge bath. The topper is a scene in which two women, left chained in the desert as punishment, conclude that "the only way to survive" is to lick the sweat off each others' naked torsos! "I make films that I would enjoy watching," explained Leroy, "and hope there are enough weirdos out there like me." Indeed.

"I always try to make a better movie, no matter what the budget," enthused Leroy. "I'd shoot in a real studio, name actors, a real movie crew, a good script would be great." Since his films have none of those, he goes on to admit, "I cut way too many corners and it usually shows in the final product. I'm wearing all the hats, so the films have a one man band kind of feel." And that feeling is far from good.

About the only innovation found in *Werewolf in a Womens Prison*, apart from the general concept of, well, a werewolf in a women's prison, is the amusing yet improbable notion of silver-laced vodka utilized as a werewolf deterrent. During the beginning, Jack proffers a bottle and tells Sarah, "This is real expensive vodka—it's got real silver flakes in it." Then, during the subsequent werewolf attack, Sarah fends off the beast by bashing it over the head with said bottle, sending the creature reeling as smoke pours from its smoldering hide. She then finishes the job by using a log from the fire to set its silver vodka–soaked carcass alight, with the flaming lycanthrope toppling off a handy cliff (an obvious dummy shot). This indeed marks the first (and only, to date) time a werewolf suffered death by vodka.

Apart from this, the viewer must make do with ridiculously cheesy semi-pro gore effects, exploitative nudity, genre clichés (or outright rip-offs), and a general sense of desperate enthusiasm. Granted, elements such as these *can* be entertaining in their own right, but only when employed in a clever and progressive fashion. Whatever potential resided in this *Womens Prison* escaped long before the opening credits rolled. But really, what can one expect from a film whose apostrophe-challenged title turns the proper "Women's" into the illiterate "Womens"?

With quotes from: "Jeff Leroy: Making Movies for Blu-Ray Drive-Ins," *Guestar, Blog of the Missed.*

Morphology: Bulky, bipedal wolf-creature
Demise: Silver bullet (and silver-laced vodka!)
Full Moon Rating: *½

Werewolf in Bangkok

(2005; Phranakorn; Thailand) Director: Wirote Thongchiew; Producer: Thawatchai Phanpakdee; Cinematographer: Wichien Reungwichayakul. Cast: Nhong Cha Cha Cha (Choosak Iamsook), Natnicha Cherdchubupakari, Debbie Bazoo, Sink Dawksadao, Todsaporn Rottakit.

"I'm a charming werewolf!"—Frank, the Werewolf in Bangkok

In the 2000s Thailand's film industry exploded into action via the amazing stunt work in films like Tony Jaa's *Ong-Bak* (2003) and *The Protector* (2005); JeeJa Yanin's *Chocolate* (2008) and *Raging Phoenix* (2009); and perhaps the

Director Jeff Leroy recycled the werewolf suit from his earlier *Eyes of the Werewolf* (1999) to create a *Werewolf in a Womens Prison*. Being hugged by the musclebound teddy bear–monster is actress Jackeline Olivier.

ultimate stunt-action film from *any* country, the breathtakingly dangerous *Born to Fight* (2004; on which life—or at least the life of a stuntman—was obviously cheap). Often surpassing even the astounding efforts of Hong Kong's Jackie Chan and mainland China's Jet Li, Thai stuntmen and action actors literally put their lives on the line for their art, resulting in exciting cinema that has western viewers gasping at their fearless audacity. Unfortunately, Thai comedy hasn't translated so well, with the culture-centric wordplay and emphasis on scatological/sexual humor seeming either unfathomable or crude (even unfathomably crude). So when *Werewolf in Bangkok* takes a decidedly comedic path for its first half, many a viewer might be tempted to simply step away. But for those who can weather the various fart jokes, bestiality bits ("A woman has only two boobs," compliments Frank, eyeing the row of teats on a potential canine conquest, "you are much sexier") and toilet humor (at one point five-year-old Lilly complains at an inopportune moment, "I need to take a shit," causing Uncle Frank to offer, "You can poop in my backpack"), this first (and only, to date) Thai werewolf export rewards with some impressive lycan-action.

Happy-go-lucky Bangkok trash collector Frank (Nhong Cha Cha Cha) has become guardian of his young niece Lilly (Natnicha Cherdchubupakari). Hoping to earn enough to send Lilly to school, Frank refuses to join the "Digging-Up Gang," who lords it over the local garbage foragers. One night while evading a pair of the gang's henchmen, Frank takes refuge in a creepy "haunted house," where a mysterious cloaked figure chained in a cell ends up biting him. Later, Frank transforms into a werewolf (or "mangy dog," as some label him). Fortunately, all were–Frank wants to do is sniff things and mark his territory. Meanwhile, a pair of werewolf hunters, Singh and Yai, have offered a reward for a lycanthrope, and the Gang sets their sights on delivering wolfman Frank. It all culminates in a surprising reveal about the original lycanthrope, and a vicious, epic battle between the now-fully-wolfed-out Frank and the original evil werewolf.

The film casts back to ancient times with its (awkwardly translated) spoken prologue to explain the origin of werewolves: "In 1004 B.C. a king of Greece had infuriated The Zeus by worshipping him with the wolf flesh. The king was cursed to become a lycanthrope. He changed into a wolf during the war. The werewolf king had bitten many people and transformed them into Wolf-men. Since then, they had disguised themselves as western traders and entered Siam." Following this classical lycan-vein, there's no mention of silver (a Hollywood invention), as the pair of werewolf hunters arm themselves with all manner of (regular) arrows and spears. In addition, one of them, Singh, searches for the werewolf that bit his wife at the film's beginning, needing the creature's heart to effect a cure (a novel—and clever—notion).

Scene after scene offers an uneasy mix of comedy and horror. At the very beginning, a mysterious, largely unseen creature prowls outside the open window of Singh's house. Then a clawed, hairy hand grabs the sill—just as Singh's pregnant wife shuts the window, resulting in a comical yelp of pain. But moments later she turns to see the window wide open again—and the monster behind her. It sinks its fangs into her neck, then bounds away across the nighttime rooftops to howl at the moon—while Singh rushes in, only to howl in anguish at what he finds. This early sequence typifies the film's mix of the comedic and horrific, a blending that sometimes works but oftentimes becomes jarring.

Frank's big transformation sequence begins in a humorous fashion. First he comically beats himself repeatedly in the head with a plastic bottle, unable to control his own movements. Then he lies on the ground howling, while interjecting the occasional "meow." Next he scratches uncontrollably. But then the scene abruptly turns gruesomely serious. As little Lilly looks on, terrified and crying, Frank literally rips the skin off his hands and arms, revealing the mucus-covered fur beneath. He then pulls off his own *face* (a physical effect with some CGI enhancement that, while not altogether convincing, still startles with its squelching sound effects and gooey grotesqueness). But it's once again back to comedy when the fully-transformed Frank turns around and declares, "I'm a charming werewolf."

Rather than the expected hirsute nightmare briefly glimpsed at the film's beginning (and intimated by the skin-ripping shots), were–Frank looks decidedly non-threatening. His face remains smooth, though wispy hair now stands on his previously bald pate, and he sports a cute, black dog nose, pointy ears, and a sharp-toothed overbite that, emerging from a pointy snout, makes him look more rat-like than lupine. His nails have sharpened, and his clawed feet (which he uses to scratch himself) are more wolfen than man-shaped. Lilly, having calmed down, exclaims, "You are a really cute dog; I like it!" Frank is not so pleased. "I'm an *ugly* dog," he wails, "a mangy one. Mommy, help me!" So much for horror.

Oddly, it isn't the full but the *crescent* moon that triggers Frank's transformation (perhaps because he's only half werewolf?). And it takes a "mating" (thankfully, *not* of the sexual kind) between Frank and the mysterious robed figure who infected him to blend into one complete full-on werewolf that can face down the evil lycanthrope at the climax.

Surprisingly, the full beast-man transformation (when the surprise identity of the original werewolf is revealed) proves even less impressive, as its few snippets eschew the (briefly) visceral quality of Frank's change. It begins with a shot of the man's boot, which stretches and then ludicrously evaporates (via obvious CGI) to reveal a wolf-foot. His already clawed hands darken and sprout hair (again through some crude computer morphing), the shirt splits up his back to reveal the hairy hide beneath (this one an effective physical effect), and the man's face extends and pushes forwards (à la *An American Werewolf in London*, but with some poorly-timed CGI enhancement and, incongruously, *steam* shooting from his nostrils).

This full werewolf (like Frank's eventual appearance after he has "melded" with his original attacker) stands tall in a full body suit covered with hair (except for his black, rippled abdomen), with the dark skin of his angular, demonic-looking face contrasting with the white of his fangs. Though skinnier than most movie man-monsters, the lycanthrope growls and slashes and leaps with enough power and ferocity to create an exciting spectacle as the two werewolves battle to the death, all vicious blows, flying bodies, and extensive wire work.

The movie populates its novel milieu (highlighting the "glamour" of the garbage-picking community among the back-alleys and unfinished buildings of Bangkok) with odd characters (some with even odder faces). Though cute, Lilly rarely becomes cloying (in one amusing sequence she even turns her precociousness against the two bumbling henchmen). And despite the best efforts of the script's first half to make Nhong Cha Cha Cha look ridiculous (at which it often succeeds), the actor manages to keep Frank likable through his projection of kindness and simple honesty. (No easy task for a character that cries a lot, gets hit frequently, and at one point even engages in bestiality with a dog!) His interactions with Lilly exude genuine affection, providing a heart for the film's often less-than-attractive body. Though no Lou Costello, the rotund Thai comedian still has us rooting for him by film's end.

The movie is technically competent, even adept at times, with plenty of camera movement, decent (even atmospheric) lighting, and solid editing that generates suspense and enhances the excitement.

And, to be fair, some of the comedy *does* work. Like when Frank, walking with his would-be love interest Shu Shi (Debbie Bazoo), spies the full moon and begins growling and grimacing. "Leave me alone," he warns Shu Shi, "I'm transforming now. I'm a werewolf. I'm gonna eat you up!" But after dramatically ripping off his shirt, he merely sits down, exhausted. "What moon?" snorts Shu Shi, spying a white globe (which Frank has mistaken for the moon). "It's just a stupid lamp, moron!" Then the film suddenly goes Bollywood, with Frank and Shu Shi and Lilly and two-dozen extras breaking into a dance routine— to techno-music with a barking back-beat—for no discernable reason. Ridiculous but amusing.

A film of two halves, *Werewolf in Bangkok* features a frustrating start for the western viewer but offers an exotic (and exciting) vision of lycanthropy by movie's end. As Frank might say, sometimes you have to wade through the garbage to get the prize.

Morphology: Tall, skinny, hairy biped
Demise: Fall from a tall building
Full Moon Rating: **½

Werewolf of London

(1935; Universal) Director: Stuart Walker; Producers: Stanley Bergerman (Executive), Robert Harris (Associate); Screenplay: John Colton (Story: Robert Harris); Cinematographer: Charles Stumar. Cast: Henry Hull, Warner Oland, Valerie Hobson, Lester Matthews, Lawrence Grant, Spring Byington.

WARNING! TO HYSTERICAL WOMEN!
SHUT YOUR EYES!—poster

As early as 1932 Universal began planning cinema's first full-on werewolf film. Set to star Boris Karloff under the direction of Robert Florey (*Murders in the Rue Morgue*), the project never went into production. In 1934 the idea (but not the script) was revived, with Kurt Neumann slated to direct. Stuart Walker eventually landed the directing job after his successes with *Great Expectations* (1934) and *Mystery of Edwin Drood* (1935). Reportedly, Bela Lugosi was briefly considered for the role of Dr. Yogami. Had Lugosi played Yogami instead of Warner Oland, Universal could have saved a good percentage of the film's $195,393 final cost; Lugosi's standard fee at the time was $1000 a week, only one-quarter Oland's salary. Despite its respectable budget (for the time), *Werewolf of London* turned out to be a somewhat stolid and disappointing second-string player on Universal's horror team.

In Tibet, British botanist Dr. Glendon (Henry Hull) is attacked by a strange half man/half-animal creature while searching for a rare flower that only blooms by moonlight, the *mariphaisa lumina lupina*. Returning to England, he meets Dr. Yogami (Warner Oland), who tells him that the mysterious plant is the only known treatment for lycanthropy. Yogami was the original werewolf that bit Glendon in Tibet and now seeks the plant for himself. Glendon refuses to believe, but soon learns the truth as he becomes a murderous manbeast during the full moon, intent on destroying the very thing he holds most dear—his wife (Valerie Hobson). In the end, a transformed Glendon kills Yogami while fighting for the plant's final blossom and dies himself from a policeman's bullet. "Thanks, thanks for the bullet," gasps the lucid lycanthrope. "It was the only way."

"The werewolf is neither man nor wolf, but a satanic creature with the worst qualities of both," explains Dr. Yogami. This first-ever screen lycanthrope evinces few of the tropes that would come to infuse lycancinema. First off, this werewolf still retains the power of reason (to the point that he dons his hat and coat before going out into the night) and even speaks. Yet he also apparently can't reign in his savage nature, as he commits brutal murder each time he appears. Second, "the werewolf instinctively seeks to kill the thing it loves best" (as Yogami warns), an odd yet disturbing proclivity—arising, perhaps, from a perverse sense of self-loathing? Third is the possibility of a cure (or treatment, anyway)—via a rare plant. Few subsequent werewolf films hold out the possibility of treatment, and fewer still offer a botanically-based remedy (Paul Naschy's *Night of the Howling Beast* and the modern *Ginger Snaps* films being rare examples). Fourth, this lycanthrope is brought down by an ordinary lead bullet; silver need not apply. And finally, the Werewolf of London appears more satanic than wolfish. The sharp widow's peak, the pointed ears, the wicked creases around the hollow eyes, and the jutting fangs suggest demon rather than wolf. It's a look that's not wholly ineffective. While Lon Chaney, Jr.'s hairier *The Wolf Man* may seem more bestial and savage, the Werewolf of London is definitely the more evil-looking of the two. Makeup man Jack Pierce deserves high praise here, particularly considering the difficulties posed by a less-than-cooperative Henry Hull, who reportedly objected to an earlier design (more along the lines of what Pierce later concocted for *The Wolf Man*), forcing Pierce to come up with this more streamlined—and devilish—version. "It was a pretty good get-up, wasn't it?" commented Hull in a 1964 interview. "Jack had a special talent for turning men into freaks."

Film historians have intimated that Hull refused to wear Pierce's original makeup due to either vanity or an abhorrence of the makeup chair (Pierce's original concept covered far more of Hull's face and took far longer to apply). Henry Hull's grandnephew, artist Cortlandt Hull (creator/proprietor of The Witch's Dungeon Classic Movie Museum), disputes this. "The only reason Henry wanted Pierce to change the makeup was due to the script," maintains Cortlandt. "Scenes in the film have both the Valerie Hobson and Lester Matthews characters recognizing the werewolf as being 'Dr. Glendon.' As Henry stated it, 'How could they recognize me as Glendon when I was Pierce's Teddy Bear?'" Continued Cortlandt, "The real prima donna was Pierce— he refused to change [the makeup], or even make a slight alteration. But Henry was just as stubborn; he went to [Production Head] Carl Laemmle and explained the situation. Laemmle agreed, and sent a memo to Pierce to tone the makeup down. Pierce was livid. Henry pushed for the widow's peak hairline, to create a more demonic look. As Henry said, 'I had a receding hairline; Pierce didn't even have to use a bald cap!' So, there you have the true story, as told to me by Henry Hull himself."

Added Cortlandt, "You will never find a photo of Pierce making up Henry as the werewolf, as Pierce's vanity was crushed; he refused to let any photos be taken of the two of them together. Pierce was so angry he did not want Hull in his makeup chair any more than necessary. So he made a series of dummy heads of Henry, which were used in two transformations, one when he was asleep in the 'Monk's Rest' tower, and the other at the end of the film, as he dies on the floor."

Playing Mrs. Glendon, the young Valerie Hobson (only seventeen at the time) was frightened to the point of hysterics by Pierce's modified makeup. The actress revealed to the readers of *Famous Monsters of Filmland*: "I knew Mr. Hull was supposed to look horrible, but I had no idea he would look like that. I took one look at him and then started to scream. I couldn't stop. He thought I was joking so he ran towards me and let out an unearthly yell while he reached out a hairy hand as though to grasp my throat. Suddenly he and director Stuart Walker discovered I was in the middle of a fit of hysterics. They rushed me to the studio hospital where they gave me a sedative. When I quieted down I was so weak I could not walk. I had to go home for the remainder of the day."

Ms. Hobson had to contend with yet another horrible visage that same year while playing the *Bride of Frankenstein* (*Doctor* Frankenstein, that is). No further screaming incidents were reported.

On the technical side, *Werewolf of London* is competent enough, with even an occasional flourish to pique the interest. For instance, it contains one of the genre's finest transformation sequences, a moment of sheer beauty and drama as well as exquisite technical precision. It occurs as Glendon walks through the garden toward his laboratory. The camera tracks with him as he moves behind a pillar. When he enters our line of vision again, his face is changed—hairier, more bestial. With a look of tortured confusion he continues walking and passes behind a second pillar, emerging with the full ferocious visage of the werewolf. Accomplished in seemingly one continuous, fluid camera movement, the effect is striking. John P. Fulton's near-flawless effects work affords the scene an elegant simplicity, while the visual movement emphasizes and heightens the metamorphosis, creating a more intense impact than any static transformation.

Stuart Walker's direction is adequate—but only just, with his straightforward approach revealing little inspiration. Cinematographer Charles Stumar (*The Mummy, The Raven*) provides some effective lighting and menacing shadows, particularly in the early Tibetan sequence and in the later low-key illumination of Hull's werewolf countenance, enhancing its diabolical quality. There are some wonderful sets, such as Glendon's private botanical garden. Genteel and pleasant on the surface (all glass partitions and orderly rows of leafy greens), it also contains its fair share of savagery in the form of a carnivorous frog-eating plant and a gigantic Madagascar Carnalia waving its octopus-like tendrils in hope of snatching some unwary creature. This private Garden of Eden can almost be seen as a metaphor for Glendon's own bipolar condition—civilized and proper on the outside, but deadly and savage under the surface.

John Colton's slow moving script blunders badly, however, stepping into the same pitfall that traps many horror pictures from the Golden Age: Comedy Relief (with a capital C and not much "relief"). The unfunny comedic scenes between two drunken old ladies at a Whitechapel lodging house go on far too long to do anything but deaden the pace of an already slow picture.

When one sees a werewolf don a cape and cap to go out "on the town" (as the transformed Glendon does on several occasions), the first response is to chuckle rather than shiver. While a bestial werewolf wearing a hat and slinking about the streets with a collar pulled up to disguise his hairy countenance seems a little ridiculous now, it must be remembered that in the pre–*Wolf Man* days there was no precedent (and no cliché) yet established for werewolf behavior. It wasn't until six years later, in 1941, that *The Wolf Man* revealed what a snarling, savage brute a werewolf can be, and (with the various sequels and variations over the years) established the lycanthropes' credo in cinematic mythology. So, while one might wish for a bit more snarl and savagery from Hull's too-civilized werewolf, and feel disappointment at how easily the characters chase off the rampaging lycanthrope with

Henry Hull as the talking screen's first lycanthrope, the *Werewolf of London* (1935).

a simple knife or a big stick, one cannot come down too hard on this first-of-all-werewolves. Unfortunately, as time has passed and this film has been *sur*passed by its progeny, *Werewolf of London* has dated badly. One cannot critique in a vacuum, and this original comes up short in the monster department.

It is especially lamentable that the two opposing werewolves never meet in lycanthropic form—*that* would have been a climactic fight worth seeing. As is, the final confrontation between the werewolf Glendon and the human Yogami results in a less-than-satisfying exhibition. Even more disappointing is the fact that so little is made of the potential soul-wrenching conflict between the two damned men, each struggling for some brief salvation via the magical plant (the "cure" proves only temporary). Despite ample opportunity for tragic confrontation, the solitary instance consists of one brief line at the very end, when Glendon yells accusingly at Yogami. "You brought this on me!"

Apart from Warner Oland's sympathetic portrayal of the desperate Dr. Yogami, the general acting level is low. Henry Hull's stiff and formal demeanor initially suits his rather aloof character, but Hull proves *too* stiff to be sympathetic and so denies the film much of its power. Letting Hull play his character in such a cold fashion was a near-fatal error on the part of director Stuart Walker, since it precludes the pathos so crucial for a werewolf story of this kind. Simply put, *Werewolf of London* lacks heart. (This element of pathos is what makes 1941's *The Wolf Man* such a success; Lon Chaney, Jr., is infinitely more approachable and likable in that picture than Hull is in this one, and so his tragic fate disturbs the viewer more.)

During production, Universal head honcho Carl Laemmle purportedly offered a $50 incentive to studio employees who could come up with a better title. Some of the (frequently amusing) entries included *Bloom, Flower, Bloom*; *Moon Doom*; *The Whelp from Tibet*; and *What Price Curiosity*. No one collected the reward, however, for the original title was retained.

In a studio publicity article, Robert Harris (the author of the original story and the picture's associate producer) explained why he chose to concoct a werewolf tale: "One of the most prolific fields for motion picture stories has scarcely been scratched [in 1935]. This untapped field is found among the legends and folk tales of the people in the back countries of Europe. These stories have been handed down from generation to generation, stories so weird and bloodcurdling as to send cold chills along the spine.... They are the greatest source for picture stories that exists today, only the film people seem to have passed them by."

Harris went on to ask (and rightly so—at least according to most horror fans), "Why struggle with problem plays and gangster stories when you have this untapped field of stories that are simply packed with all the tense human drama plus almost unbelievable thrills? I believe these folk stories and legends are clean and thrilling entertainment. That's why I decided to write this werewolf story."

Shortly before the picture's premier, Universal's publicity department released an article aimed at exhibitors and theater owners entitled "A Message from the President of Universal Pictures." In it, Carl Laemmle made some rather grandiose claims about his new horror product: "When we produced *Werewolf of London* we gave it all the shock and goosepimples we could jam into it.... *Werewolf of London* is a bloodcurdling thing.... It is as gruesome as *Dracula*—as startling as *Frankenstein*—as much of a soul-shocker as we know how to make." Despite "Uncle Carl's" hyperbole, *Werewolf of London* really is *not* any of those things; it *is*, however, the first full-on werewolf feature film, and as such holds pride of place in the Lycanthropy Pantheon.

With quotes from: "Werewolf of London: Universal's Supreme Shocker Revisited!" *Famous Monsters of Filmland* 86; Interview with Cortlandt Hull conducted by the author, January 2016; "A Message from the President of Universal Pictures," by Carl Laemmle, Universal Pictures.

Morphology: Two-legged manbeast
Demise: Ordinary bullet
Full Moon Rating: ★★★½

The Werewolf of Washington

(1973; Diplomat Pictures) Director/Screenplay: Milton Moses Ginsberg; Producer: Nina Schulman; Cinematographer: Bob Baldwin. Cast: Dean Stockwell, Biff McGuire, Clifton James, Beeson Carroll, Jane House, Michael Dunn.

> IT'S HORRIFIC! IT'S HILARIOUS!—prevaricating poster

"[*The Wolf Man*] was the only horror film I saw [as a kid] ... *The Wolf Man* traumatized me." So pronounced writer-director Milton Moses Ginsberg, who transformed that "trauma" into a satirical stab at the early 1970s political scene in the form of *The Werewolf of Washington*. An editor by trade, this was Ginsberg's second directorial outing (after a commercially unsuccessful 1969 experimental effort called *Coming Apart*). It was also his last.

Seeking to ease out of his clandestine affair with the President's daughter, up-and-coming White House Press Corp journalist Jack Whittier (Dean Stockwell) gets himself reassigned to his paper's Budapest bureau. In Hungary, on his way to the airport to fly back to Washington, D.C., Whittier's car breaks down and he's attacked by what looks like a large black dog. But after clubbing the beast with the silver-tipped cane his Hungarian girlfriend had given him, Jack sees that he's killed a man instead. Back in Washington, the President (Biff McGuire) appoints him Assistant Press Secretary. But Jack has a problem fulfilling his duties on the nights of the full moon.... Jack tries to convince anyone who'll listen, from a Naval psychiatrist to the Commander in Chief, that *he* is the killer rampaging through the Capitol, but no one wants to hear it (thinking it politically inexpedient). Finally, Jack transforms and attacks the President himself in front of dozens of onlookers, leading to a date with a silver bullet.

Unable to raise financing for further features after the fiscal failure of *Coming Apart*, Ginsberg thought, "I'll do a horror film. *The Wolf Man* was hiding in my unconscious. I look at it now and I see why. I was obsessed with werewolves." Why? "[Lon Chaney] is this kind of lumbering guy, the son of this aristocrat. He has no mother. He falls for somebody else's girlfriend, and she falls for him. Immediately it's this heavy Oedipal overlay, with his father finally killing him to save the girl." So Ginsberg sat down and wrote his script in ten days. "I was obsessed with Nixon," continued Ginsberg. "There had been this break-in at Watergate, and at the time Nixon was trying to push through his Supreme Court nominees." The resulting screenplay, a political pitchfork aimed at the White House, scared off Ginsberg's original producers. Finding alternate funding (to the tune of $100,000) through producer (and ex-girlfriend) Nina Schulman, Ginsberg shot his satirical script in about three weeks in and around the environs of Glen Cove, New York (with a few background pickups in Washington, D.C.).

Ginsberg tried to get the likes of Gene Wilder, George Hamilton, and Donald Sutherland for the lead, but ultimately settled for Dean Stockwell, who Ginsberg characterized as "a brilliant choice." (According to the director, Sutherland, who was dating Jane Fonda at the time, "loved the script and wanted to do it. He said, 'I have to see your work.' We had a screening of *Coming Apart* for him, which he loved. He took the film home to Jane Fonda and she said, 'This is sexist. You can't do *Werewolf of Washington*.' So we lost Donald Sutherland.") Ginsberg's loss was our ... loss as well, for Dean Stockwell, never the most dynamic of actors, makes little impression in the admittedly underwritten role, coming off as more simpering simpleton than political animal. During his big scene in which Jack, chained to a chair by the doubting psychiatrist, loses his composure and screams, "I'm just a violent beast! Kill me! I'm better off dead!" Stockwell plays it so abrupt and shrill that it becomes ridiculous (particularly since he'd *just* breathed a huge sigh of relief that he "can finally get some rest tonight knowing I'll be chained").

While in wolf-form, Stockwell acts more like a misbehaving mutt than a marauding monster, ludicrously crawling about on all fours, sniffing at things, gnawing the carpet, panting into the camera, and even licking the hand and face of the diminutive Dr. Kiss (Michael Dunn) when they meet (in an out-of-left-field scene that has were–Jack running across the mini–mad scientist clucking over a Frankenstein-like figure strapped to a gurney in the bowels of a power plant—for no discernible reason). Ginsberg shares the blame with Stockwell, as his dialogue and direction heighten the comically canine comparison (with the panicked President even ordering the werewolf to "sit" and "heel").

Stockwell isn't helped by Ginsberg's scattered script, which fails to offer much character depth either before or after Jack becomes a werewolf. The few scenes set in Hungary paint Jack as a typical Ugly American prone to yelling ("Can't you speak English?!") and only concerned with making his flight. Back in Washington, he just comes off as wishy-washy and confused. Consequently, unlike the movie's obvious Larry Talbot model, the Werewolf of Washington appears terminally unlikable.

"It was the scope of the production—as a scene or three a day in disparate locations, all within a month for a hundred grand, even—that caused me to neglect the artistry of the piece," postulated Ginsberg. "We spent more time driving to and from locations and setting up each morning than actually rehearsing and filming." And it's not as if said locations were all that interesting, with pivotal scenes taking place in front of grubby discount stores, gas stations, or nondescript stone steps. The movie simply looks cheap.

Relying heavily on either shaky hand-held photography or a locked-down camera, Ginsberg fails to supply adequate coverage. Too many instances of characters speaking their lines while off-screen casts an amateurish pall over the production.

Ginsberg had no illusions about his movie's quality. "In the script I tried too hard for laughs and not hard enough at making the characters believable." Indeed, most characters are too buffoonish to inspire believability, including the blustering Attorney General, the pompous psychiatrist, and the muttering President more concerned with image than issues. "And the 'horror' aspect," continued Ginsberg, "I thought was too politically implicit to bother developing cinematically. Both fatal errors, even in a low-budget horror film." Indeed, the attack scenes all end before reaching their fatal conclusion, and blood is conspicuous only by its crimson absence. Apart from the telephone booth sequence (the movie's one standout moment), in which the werewolf finally looks moderately menacing as it lunges and swipes and struggles to get at the terrified woman trapped within the glass rectangle (which at one point tips over to land on its side), the film holds little suspense, much less outright horror.

Though most of the movie's humor falls flatter than a Nixon debate, a rare chuckle escapes to the surface now and again, such as when Jack tries to convince his psychiatrist that he's a werewolf:

JACK: "What about my seeing the signs of the pentagram?"
DOC: "Well, sometimes we see our conflicts in terms of political symbols."
JACK (frustrated): "What's politics got to do with this?!"
DOC (equally frustrated): "Well, what does the *Pentagon* have to do with it?!"
JACK (incredulous): "The *pent-a-gram*, the five-pointed star!"

And the occasional pointed political joke or Watergate reference (the President's penchant for stating, "I would like to make one thing perfectly clear," for instance; and Jack's apartment being located in the *Watergate Building*) can't help but bring a sardonic smile to the face of anyone who lived through the '70s.

Ginsberg relied heavily on *The Wolf Man* not only for his werewolf's appearance (basically a gray-haired version of the Chaney makeup, including hands and feet), but for his film's lycan-lore and set-pieces. For instance, besides adhering to the standard silver and lunar tropes, Jack sees the sign of the pentagram in the palms of his victims-to-be (just like Talbot did in *The Wolf Man*). Like in the Universal classic, Jack becomes a werewolf when bitten by a four-legged lycanthrope, which he dispatches with a silver-headed cane (just as Larry had), yet he transforms into a two-legged wolfman. Then he's chained to a chair by a skeptical authority figure (the Navy psychiatrist standing in for Sir John Talbot) and left alone to face his transformative demons.

Ambitiously, the picture contains three full-on transformation sequences that ape *The Wolf Man*'s classic metamorphoses. "We had to shoot all the transformations in one day," recalled Ginsberg. "The way

Lycanthropy meets politics in the satirical *Werewolf of Washington* (American poster).

I did it was, you only go through the make-up once.... It was all done in that rocking chair, so that I had to put a blue cloth behind him for the transformation in the helicopter, and put a red cloth behind him for the transformation back in the final shot on the floor. The makeup man, who did a brilliant job under the circumstances, would apply a little makeup. I'd shoot it with three different backdrops. Then he'd put on a little more, and we'd do it again with three backdrops hoping that Dean could keep his head in the same place." Too bad Ginsberg didn't apply the same inventiveness to the rest of his movie.

"The film died pretty quickly," recalled Ginsberg about *The Werewolf of Washington*'s poor reception. No one was too satisfied with this unfunny misfire, even its star. "Dean [Stockwell] was very angry with me at the end that the film didn't do better," admitted Ginsberg. "He and his agent felt that I could have edited it differently, and they were right." A horror-comedy misfire, *The Werewolf of Washington* went out not with a transgressive howl but with a disappointing whimper.

With quotes from: *Regional Horror Films, 1958–1990*, by Brian Albright.

Morphology: Black canine; well-dressed, furry manbeast
Demise: Silver bullet
Full Moon Rating: *½

The Werewolf of Woodstock

(1975; ABC Television) Director: John Moffit; Producers: Bill Lee, Hank Saroyan; Screenplay: Bill Lee, Hank Saroyan; Cinematographer: Carl Gibson; Cast: Michael Parks, Harold J. Stone, Meredith MacRae, Ann Dovan, Richard Webb, Belinda Belaski, Tige Andrews.

> After The Festival Was Over … The Music Wasn't The Only Thing That Died—ad line

Premiering on January 4, 1975, on *ABC's Wide World of Entertainment*, this made-for-television attempt to cash in on the Woodstock phenomenon was executive produced by none other than Dick Clark. Which begs the question: Why is the film's music so *awful*?! In any case, it's all here: cheesy rock riffs played on an abandoned Woodstock stage; a hippy chick heroine who keeps re-naming her dog according to the signs of the zodiac; a lycanthropy-causing lightning strike(!); *King Kong/Beauty and the Beast* thematics; goofy cops (including a laid-back detective sporting an ever-present Mike Nesmith beanie); a music-hating werewolf lured out of hiding by a loud rock band; and, best of all, a wolfman making his getaway in a dune buggy! Of course, what's *not* here are Emmy-winning performances, a cogent screenplay, or any semblance of genuine quality. Still, given the right frame of mind (mood-enhancing substances might help), *The Werewolf of Woodstock* can be a deliciously entertaining slice of made-for-1970s-TV cheese that, at a mere 66 minutes, never outstays its groovy welcome.

In 1969, just after the famous music festival, a would-be rock band hops into their flower-powered VW microbus and heads to Woodstock to cut a demo record on the abandoned outdoor stage as an attention-getting ploy. Meanwhile, hippie-hating local farmer Bert (Tige Andrews) gets all riled up one stormy night and sets about trashing the abandoned stage while shouting, "Freaks! Miserable Freaks!!" Suddenly, a bolt of lightening strikes the stage, resulting in Bert taking thousands of volts and ending up in his bed swathed in bandages. "Well, he'll be ok, I suppose," offers the laconic local doc (Richard Webb), before contradictorily adding, "I don't know why he's still alive, though. An electric shock like that would have killed most people." That night the bandaged Bert writhes in bed, then suddenly growls and sits up—having become a werewolf! Out he goes into

A bad acid trip? No, just *The Werewolf of Woodstock* (courtesy executive producer Dick Clark!).

the night, only to attack and kill a passing policeman. Afterwards, the cop's partner describes the killer as having "long hair and a beard; I didn't get a good look at him because it was pretty dark." The authorities' conclusion? "Our killer has to be a Woodstock leftover." Come daybreak and Bert is back in bed in his pajamas, the bandages back on. With the cops now targeting and harassing the hippie band members, Bert transforms again the next night and ends up kidnapping the band's female member, Beckie (Belinda Belaski), taking her to an abandoned building. After more lycanthropic mayhem, the authorities finally conclude that there is indeed a werewolf on the loose and come up with a plan to lure the beast out of hiding by having the band play as loud as they can on the Woodstock stage to enrage the monster. And it works! But the werewolf, with Beckie in tow (the two have apparently bonded), runs from the cops, hops into a dune buggy(!) and races away. Tracking him to the local power plant, the Lieutenant (Harold J. Stone) finally gets a clear shot and fires his sole silver bullet (which he'd had made just in case), causing the Werewolf of Woodstock to fall to his death several stories below.

Co-star Belinda Balaski (playing Beckie) recalled: "We're a part of a band [in the movie]. Andy Stevens—Stella Stevens' son—and myself, and Dennis Weaver's son Rob Weaver, and one other person were the band. And we were practicing to be at Woodstock. Well, the werewolf had a thing about loud music, it drove him crazy. So he goes wacky, and grabs me, and takes off with me. He picks me up and treats me tenderly. It's actually pretty funny, but it was such fun to shoot, because Andy Stevens was such a doll, and Rob was great, and all these people were from such a background."

This werewolf possesses not only the expected full head of fuzzy, fright-wig hair, but an elongated muzzle, a mountain man–style beard and mane, and an oversized mouth full of sharp teeth that would do any *Fright Night* vampire proud. (The werewolf was designed by Joe Blasco, who also created the were-lizard for *Track of the Moon Beast*.) It's a fairly unusual makeup job for an impoverished TV movie (a kind of *Planet of the Apes* meets *Benji* via *Fright Night* look), and Tige Andrews, under all the latex and hair, shows it off to good effect via his energetic performance, racing through the woods, jumping from trees onto his victims, picking up Beckie to carry her off under one hairy arm, and at one point violently tossing the unfortunate doctor through some wood and glass cabinets in a vigorous physical display. "Tige Andrews was in that horrible [werewolf] suit that whole time," recounted Belaski. "That poor man. He was such a dear. [I remember] Tige and I hanging out, combing through his fur, and I was his Fay Wray." Andrews was a vastly experienced TV character actor whose 40 years of credits stretch all the way back to the early 1950s (everything from *Kraft Theatre* to *Murder, She Wrote*), while Belaski went on to face a far more terrifying werewolf in *The Howling*.

Possessing one of the wackiest reasons behind werewolfery ever, *The Werewolf of Woodstock* remains nothing if not novel in its lycanthropic mythology. As the investigating police psychologist (Meredith MacRae) explains, "There's been a lot of research done on the possibility of severe electric shock altering tissue and organs…. Under laboratory conditions, rat skin tissues were found to multiply at unusually high rates in an electrical field. Hair follicles produced hair at five times the normal speed when exposed to the same electrical stimulation." Yes, it's an electro-wolf! Just to make sure the viewer makes the, er, connection, she continues, "After repeated stimulation the changes began to take place without the help of any current at all—until all the cells completely transform themselves into a new, more active variety." Fortunately, the Lieutenant has a sense of humor about all this, and sarcastically observes, "Excuse me, this is 1969 and this is a *modern*, *electrical* werewolf." Indeed.

Veteran TV director John Moffit put some effort into this, at least in regards to the werewolf scenes. At one point we see the moon in the background (it's merely a *half* moon; full moon not essential), and when the focus suddenly shifts it brings the foreground into sharp relief—revealing the face of the werewolf. Later, Moffit shows the wolfman's feet approaching through the dead leaves, then pans upwards to reveal the beast turning his head and snarling, its breath visible in the cold night air. Unfortunately, the more mundane, interior-set scenes too often have a soap opera-ish feel to them, with the camera frequently pulling back from a character to reveal the scene or, conversely, zooming in to focus on the individual speaking. It all serves to remind the viewer that this is indeed a small-scale TV effort after all (particularly as it employs the shot-on-video technique of daytime television for its set-bound scenes). While the laconically likable Michael Parks offers some amusing moments as the detective hero, the hippies remain near-comical caricatures who spout dialogue like, "Oh man, alright, I still think it's a bummer." At one point Dave (Andrew Stevens) snidely dismisses Beckie with, "Why don't you go meditate or something, huh?"—and she actually *does*. The screenplay also disappointingly drops the "long-haired freak" angle almost as soon as it arises, eschewing any generation-gap drama or culture-clash exploration to show the hippies joining forces with the Man to lure out and defeat the beast. So much for counterculture.

The climax atop an unfinished building sees the hero and the beast hopping from girder to girder in a stalk-and-evade dance of death. It's actually quite impressive, given that one misstep would have sent the actors plunging to their deaths. Apparently life was cheap on a Dick Clark production in the 1970s. And given its *King Kong*–esque finale, one almost expects the Lieutenant to gaze at the werewolf's crumpled body (unlike in most lycan films, this wolfman stays in hirsute form after death rather than reverting to human) and intone, "No, it wasn't the silver bullet, 'twas beauty killed the beast." Amazingly, it's all played straight, though the deadpanned lines often inspire chuckles all the same.

It's a shame that, after its initial airing, *The Werewolf of Woodstock* disappeared like some festival crowd after the reefer's run out, and has received no legitimate video release. For those dying to see flower power combat lycanthropy—or who just *have* to see a dune buggy–driving wolfman—it's well worth hunting down this *Werewolf* online or via bootleg DVD.

With quotes from: "Piranhas and Werewolves and Rats…. OH MY! An Interview with Belinda Balaski," by Tony Kay, *Shock Cinema* 33.

Morphology: Dog-faced, big-haired, two-legged, music-hating man-wolf
Demise: That trusty old silver bullet
Full Moon Rating: ★★★

The Werewolf Reborn!

(1998; Full Moon) Alternate Title: *Frankenstein and the Werewolf Reborn!*; Director: Jeff Burr; Producer: Vlad Paunescu; Screenplay: Benjamin Carr (aka Neal Stevens); Cinematographer: Viorel Sergovici, Jr. Cast: Ashley Cafagna, Robin Downes, Len Lesser, Bogdan Cambera, Lucia Maier.

> "A chilling new series that brings classic monsters into your home"—Filmonsters promo trailer

In 1998 Charles Band's Full Moon Pictures (purveyors of the popular, low-budget, direct-to-video *Puppet Master*, *Trancers*, and

In 1998 Charles Band's Full Moon company attempted to reintroduce the classic monsters to youngsters with their direct-to-video *Frankenstein Reborn!* and *The Werewolf Reborn!* When video sales proved disappointing, they abandoned plans for further installments and eventually put both films on one DVD in 2005 titled *"Frankenstein and the Werewolf Reborn!"*

Subspecies franchises) decided to create a series designed to reintroduce classic movie monsters to the younger generation. Thus they announced an initial quartet of direct-to-video films ("for fans of all ages to enjoy") under their new "Filmonsters!" banner—*Dracula Reborn!*, *The Mummy Reborn!*, *Frankenstein Reborn!* and *The Werewolf Reborn!*—with more to follow. After shooting the latter two back to back in Romania (where filming was cheap), however, the series died an early death, with no further installments forthcoming, leaving just "two classics retooled for a new generation" (as the films' combo-trailer describes them).

"I designed that [series] as something that could maybe get me into the cable TV business," related Band. "But I couldn't find a buyer, so as a result we just released them on video and that was that. It was a clever idea. We had about 20 of those projects developed, and we were busy writing scripts because there's so many wonderful classic monsters to bring back and have young kids involved in those adventures."

Aimed squarely at the 12–14 age set, *The Werewolf Reborn!* stars 15-year-old Ashley Catagna (TV's *Saved by the Bell*) as Eleanor Crane, who arrives unexpectedly at her Uncle Peter's rundown estate near a small Eastern European town while her parents attend a conference. Though Peter (Robin Downes) is less than welcoming, circumstances force Eleanor to spend the night. When the full moon rises, Peter transforms into a werewolf and attacks a local in the woods, a member of the posse out hunting the beast that has been terrorizing their village. The next morning Peter staggers back to the house, wounded. But the gunshots miraculously close up and heal, as witnessed by Eleanor. Peter explains that three months earlier he killed a werewolf with a silver knife—but not before he had been bitten. Meanwhile, the local inspector (Len Lesser) follows the trail to Peter's house. Thinking him simply an ordinary murderer ("The only monsters I've ever met are *human* monsters—and you are one of them," states the skeptical policeman), the inspector throws Peter in jail. Eleanor seeks answers from the local gypsies, who give her a gun and some silver bullets. "Nothing kills virkula [werewolf]," the old gypsy woman tells her, "and virkula cannot kill himself. Only silver kill the wolfman." Eleanor goes to visit her uncle in jail but cannot bring herself to shoot him. That night the moon rises again and Peter transforms, breaking free from his cell. Returning to the house, the werewolf attacks Eleanor, but the girl manages to shoot the creature. "This was my destiny," the now-human Peter tells his distraught niece as he lay dying, "to be a thing of wonder—and terror. Do not be sad for me." With this, Peter—and the curse—dies.

This kid-friendly take on *The Wolf Man* offers little real violence and even less gore. The two onscreen attacks come quickly, with the werewolf running out of the darkness to pounce on his victim, and remain brief and indistinct. Just like in the original *The Wolf Man*, *The Werewolf Reborn!* initially reveals its monster via a transforming appendage (feet in the original, a hand in *Reborn*) rather than through a full-on transformation, though artificial-looking CGI morphing in *Reborn* replaces the painstaking and impressive makeup dissolves of *The Wolf Man*. Like in the classic '40s feature, here we see the full transformation only towards the end. Likewise, *Werewolf Reborn!* offers its own "Even a man who's pure in heart…"-style gypsy ditty:

No steel shall slay, no door shall bar / When the full moon shows the mark of the star. / No prayer safe, no curses reprieve / A cursed death and then to grieve. / To silver only, since the world began / Can slay the wolf that walks like a man.

Obviously, screenwriter Benjamin Carr (who penned *Curse of the Puppet Master*, *Thir13en Ghosts*, and the pseudowolf entry *The Creeps*, among others) was no Curt Siodmak.

At least the filmmakers took from the best. Besides its borrowings from the Chaney original, the melancholy yet menacing howl in the night made by this wolfman reborn is the same eerie sound generated by *An American Werewolf in London*. And the notion of the pentagram-shaped scar on Peter's chest where he was bitten by the werewolf comes straight out of the Paul Naschy-Waldemar Daninsky film series.

The beast itself is no more convincing than the movie's primitive CGI. Sporting big fuzzy hair, large wolf ears atop its head, a plastic-looking angular face, and pointy shark-teeth, this lycanthrope looks more like a cut-rate demon than classic wolfman. And it isn't treated terribly well, either. Apart from the two tame woodland attacks, it suffers a rather humiliating confrontation with the teenage heroine. Chased by the beast-man through her uncle's dilapidated mansion, Eleanor runs downstairs, dropping her gun. She then grabs up a blanket and tosses it over the manbeast's head to slow him down (*Scooby-Doo*, anyone?), retrieve the gun, and escape while the uncoordinated monster embarrassingly wrestles with the smothering blankie.

The film's low budget often shows through, not only via the limited and impoverished settings (a few cramped sets and some run-down Romanian exteriors) but in the terrible CGI (including an artificial-looking moonrise and a poor shot of hair growing over the werewolf's hand). Even the boom mike dips into frame during one scene. Such gaffs are perhaps understandable, given the production's inadequate budget and shooting schedule. According to director Jeff Burr (*From a Whisper to a Scream*, *Stepfather II*, *Puppet Master 4* and *5*), "It was shot in 7 days, and for about $25,000. How do I know that? I carried the budget over there, for Charlie [Band], in cash, to be delivered to [producer] Vlad Panescu at Castel Studios. I arrived on a Saturday afternoon in Romania, and we started to shoot on Monday morning. In that time, I cast the Romanian roles, picked the locations, talked to my DP (the great Viorel Sergevici), rehearsed with the American actors, and drank a little palinka (local drink) to steady my nerves."

Much of the acting fares no better. Teen Cafagna (who abandoned Hollywood a few years later to become a successful country/gospel singer under her married name of Ashley Tesoro) appears more abrasive than endearing, and TV actor/voice artist Robin Downes mercilessly chews the scenery as the tormented Peter, alternately trembling and shouting out his lines. As the doubting inspector, however, veteran character actor Len Lesser (*Blood and Lace*, *Papillon*, TV's *Seinfeld*) helps ground the proceedings with his self-assured demeanor and more naturalistic playing.

Given its stated intention of reintroducing the classic werewolf to "a new generation," *The Werewolf Reborn!*'s heart may be in the right place; unfortunately, its head didn't quite follow. Unsubtle and predictable, *The Werewolf Reborn!* might pass muster with the undemanding pre-teen set, but anyone with a cursory knowledge of werewolf cinema will find little to howl at here. With its young protagonist, juvenile-targeted tone, cheap visuals, and disappointing monster, *The Werewolf Reborn!* comes off more like an extended episode of *Goosebumps* than a true terror tale.

After the underwhelming reception of the 1998 video releases of both *Frankenstein Reborn!* and *The Werewolf Reborn!*, Full Moon attempted to squeeze a few more dollars from their failed series by combining the two movies in 2005 into one DVD package and dubbing it *Frankenstein and the Werewolf Reborn!* It fared little better.

With quotes from: "Interview: Charles Band Part II," by M.J. Simpson, *MJ Simpson: Film Reviews and Interviews*; "Exclusive Interview with Director Jeff Burr: Part III," by James Whittington, Horror Channel.co.uk.

Morphology: Typical two-legged Wolf Man (Reborn)
Demise: Silver bullets
Full Moon Rating: *½

Werewolf Rising

(2014; Ruthless Pictures) Director/Screenplay: B.C. Furtney; Producers: Jess Baget, Jennfery Furtney; Cinematographer: Ernesto Galan. Cast: Bill Oberst, Jr., Melissa Carnell, Matt Copko, Brian Berry, Danielle Lozeau, Irena Murphy, Taylor Horneman.

OUT OF THE DARKNESS COMES A NEW
KIND OF BLOOD BEAST—tagline

Well, not really, as *Werewolf Rising* offers nothing new, "blood beast" or otherwise. Emma (Melissa Carnell), a 28-year-old recovering alcoholic troubled by bad dreams, leaves the big city to return to her childhood home in rural Arkansas (where the film was shot). There she meets and falls for a drifter named Johnny Lee (Matt Copco), an escaped convict(!) squatting in a local abandoned church. After fending off the unwanted advances of creepy "Uncle Wayne" (a family friend who's been taking care of the empty house), Emma must also deal with Johnny Lee after he's attacked by a werewolf (his former cell-mate, Rhett, with whom he escaped, and who now prowls the surrounding woodlands), leading to a horrifying discovery about her own family and herself.

Musician/novelist/filmmaker B.C. Furtney wrote the *Werewolf Rising* script in one weekend, and it shows. "The battle for self-control that rages inside Emma exists in direct parallel with the lycanthrope situation in the woods," pontificated Furtney, "and in a sense it's suppressing something else that's going on. I don't want to give anything away, but that monkey on her back simultaneously mirrors and supplants a whole other problem." Despite Furtney's allegorical acrobatics, what comes through onscreen as the *real* "whole other problem" is a group of unlikable characters behaving nonsensically in a muddled scenario. And while only featuring a handful of characters (most of the film exists as a three-person play), the script still manages to pile murkiness upon confusion with its arbitrary happenings and last-minute, desperate attempts to find these werewolves something to do.

Plot holes and inconsistencies pepper the film like backwoods birdshot. For instance, when a werewolf chases Emma through the woods at film's end, she stumbles across a campfire presided over by a woman we've never seen before wearing nothing but a bathrobe. Scoffing at Emma's fear of "the big bad wolf," this mystery woman, Beatrix (Irena Murphy), says she'd been corresponding with "him" in prison (though which "him"—Rhett or Johnny Lee—remains as vague as the identity of the man-monster chasing Emma), and that now he will choose between the two of them. But how does Beatrix know that Rhett (or Johnny Lee, or whomever…) has become a werewolf? When the beast steps into the clearing she drops her robe and offers herself to the monster (as well as offering the viewer the film's one gratuitous nude scene), proclaiming, "Take me!" What?

When it turns out that the beast tearing into Beatrix is Rhett (he transforms—disappointingly off-screen—back to human after ripping out the woman's jugular), one wonders what has happened to Johnny Lee. Sure, Wayne shot him back at the house, but he also shot Rhett too (point blank) after *he* suddenly showed up, so obviously regular bullets don't put these werewolves down. Johnny Lee's abrupt, permanent disappearance from the scenario—particularly given his attraction to, and connection with, Emma, and the fact he's one of only three primary characters—smacks of inept, or at best lazy, plotting.

Then, for no reason at all, Rhett begins talking to the terrified Emma about how "your father had something inside him" and how "it's inside *you*, too," intimating that Emma's father was a werewolf and that she too is a latent lycanthrope. (Did this random convict know her dead father? And if so, how and where? The sloppy script provides no answers.) At this, Emma writhes around a bit, opens her eyes to show her now bestial, glowing orbs, and howls. So yep, *she* is a werewolf. Again … what??

Another question: Whatever happened to the first lycanthrope—the one that attacked Rhett during the pre-credit sequence, leaving him to crawl away to heal and become a wolfman himself? And *who* was it anyway—Emma's dad, perhaps (though Emma had indicated her father was dead)? Who knows—and by this time, who cares.

On the plus side, as Rhett, prolific low-budget actor Bill Oberst, Jr. (*Nude Nuns with Big Guns*, 2010; *Abraham Lincoln vs. Zombies*, 2012; *Circus of the Devil*, 2014) makes for a convincingly creepy hillbilly psycho-turned-werewolf; while newcomer Melissa Carnell gives her all as the contrite, conflicted, and confused Emma. Unfortunately, her earnest efforts can't overcome the muddled motivations of her weakly-drawn character. For instance, after two brief conversations with the obviously homeless escaped convict, she succumbs to his "charms" and invites him back to her house—despite the fact that Wayne had warned her about, and had even given her a gun as protection against, this very same fugitive! Sure, pickings might be slim in this neck of the backwoods, but really—a supposedly sophisticated and beautiful girl falling for a homeless escaped convict lowlife after exchanging a few words? I think not.

Furtney appears to be a better director (here helming his third feature) than screenwriter, as *Werewolf Rising* at least *looks* good (its digital photography in focus and properly lit, in any case) and features the occasional stand-out scene enhanced by clever staging. For example, when Emma first encounters the werewolf (Johnny Lee or Rhett—it's never made clear), she races inside and locks the door as the beast begins a violent attack on her flimsy double-wide. As the growling and pounding assail her ears, in a panic she crawls quickly across the floor, desperately seeking sanctuary against the audio assault that appears to be coming from everywhere, even under the floor. With the camera following her terrified, unheeding movements at near-ground level, she even momentarily crawls up onto the coffee table, as if trying to put further distance between her and the beast that lurks outside—or in an unthinking attempt to distance herself from the insane notion of the nightmare creature itself. Credit both director Furtney and the panicked playing of a near-hysterical Melissa Carnell for making this sequence both involving and terrifying.

Unfortunately, Furtney can do little with the disappointing creature itself once it rears its unconvincing head. (Though there *must* be at least three different werewolves—Rhett, Johnny Lee, and who/whatever mauled Rhett in the first place—there was obviously only one monster suit, as no two beasts ever appear together.) With its slightly protruding muzzle, flattish nose, ridged skin, beady eyes, mouthful of fangs, and huge hairless pointy ears, it looks more like a mutant bat than a man-wolf. And when Furtney, having initially limited it to shadows or shots of a clawed hand, finally reveals the monster full-length, its off-the-rack Bigfoot costume origins become all too apparent (particularly as it lopes awkwardly through the woods). Most disappointingly of all, Furtney completely bypasses that werewolf movie keynote—metamorphosis—by having the creature simply (and almost comically) pop up into frame fully transformed.

Rather than adding ambiance or atmosphere, the bleak woodlands and cheap settings—tiny abandoned church, poor-white-trash prefab (even the bar Wayne patronizes looks like a converted school portable)—simply wrap the unpleasant, lowlife characters in unpleasant, lowlife surroundings. "My hope is simply to provide 80 minutes of escapism for horror and/or werewolf fans who might be hungry for a new beast to emerge from the shadows with an unquenchable bloodlust," said Furtney. Though hope may spring eternal, it doesn't pay the cinematic bills. In the end, uninteresting characters in uninteresting settings doing uninteresting (and inexplicable) things see this *Werewolf* not *Rising* but falling flat.

With quotes from: "*Werewolf Rising* Special Part 2: The BC Furtney Interview," by James Simpson, Ukhorrorscene.com.

Morphology: Bat-faced two-legged beast-man
Demise: None
Full Moon Rating: *½

Werewolf Shadow see The Werewolf vs. the Vampire Woman

Werewolf Terror see Iron Wolf

Werewolf: The Beast Among Us

(2012; Universal) Alternate Title: *Wolfman: The Beast Among Us*. Director: Louis Morneau; Producer: Mike Elliott; Screenplay: Michael Tabb, Louis Morneau, Catherine Cyran (story: Michael Tabb); Cinematographer: Philip Robertson. Cast: Ed Quinn, Stephen Rea, Guy Wilson, Nia Peeples, Rachel Katherine DiPillo, Nadam Croasdell, Ana Ularu, Steven Bauer.

> From the studio that launched a legacy of monster movies, comes an all-new action-packed thriller—trailer

Universal saw *Werewolf: The Beast Among Us* (with its shooting title of *Wolfman II*) as a loose follow-up to their 2010 *Wolfman* redux. Though *The Wolfman* failed to set the box office alight, it proved a big hit on DVD, so the studio gave the green light to this direct-to-video project—as well as a paltry-in-comparison $5 million budget that reflects Universal's scaled-back ambition for it.

In nineteenth century Romania a small band of professional werewolf hunters, led by Charles (Ed Quinn), comes to the village of Dravicu, where a lycanthrope has been decimating the locals. Civic-minded Daniel (Guy Wilson), university-bound assistant to the village doctor (Stephen Rea), joins the hunters in trying to track and kill the monster. After the beast has eluded their traps and appears to be specifically targeting the town "lowlifes," they realize that "this is no ordinary werewolf" but a beast that "thinks like a man." Soon the townsfolk begin to turn on one another, with neighbor suspecting neighbor, until the tragic truth of the werewolf's identity becomes inescapable. But not all the heroic hunters are what they seem either, leading to a monster-vs.-monster showdown, with Daniel's beloved (Rachel Katherine DiPillo) caught in the middle.

Director/co-writer Louis Morneau was obviously hired by Universal because of his extensive low-budget sequel experience, having helmed *Carnosaur 2* (1995), *The Hitcher 2* (2003), and *Joy Ride 2* (2008). A graduate of Roger Corman's informal on-the-job film school (Morneau toiled in Corman's trailer department, where lycan-luminary Joe [*The Howling*] Dante also got his start back in the '70s), Morneau brought with him an action-oriented sensibility that at least keeps this *Werewolf* lively. From the film's opening, in which a young woman frantically flees through the forest, narrowly avoiding all manner of traps and trip wires (bear traps, spiked stakes, crossbow bolts) to plead for sanctuary at a locked cabin door before a vicious werewolf attack, Morneau keeps the exciting action set-pieces coming at a steady pace. Unfortunately, the film as a whole can't keep up, thanks to its underdeveloped characters, disorienting mishmash of modern-vs.-period detail, and unfortunate reliance on cartoonish CGI.

The goody-goody Daniel seems too impossibly altruistic to be real; his doctor mentor simply looks tired; and the band of hunters are one-note cyphers primarily defined by their outfits and weaponry. There's the crude Hyde with his Gatling gun, the elegant Stephan with his knives, the ballbusting Kazia with her crossbow and flame thrower, and the taciturn leader Charles, who, with hat, duster and six-shooter, resembles a laconic Old West gunfighter. A few other, even more nondescript, figures hover in the background as werewolf fodder.

Though populated with competent, if unspectacular, actors, the big name draw goes to Oscar nominee Stephen (*The Crying Game*) Rea as the town doctor whose makeshift morgue can barely hold the mounting tally of mutilated corpses. Unfortunately, the obviously-slumming actor appears more weary than inspired, as if he'd just been woken up and told he would *not* be mounting that Oscar podium after all. (Note: This wasn't Rea's first lycan-rodeo, having appeared in fellow Irishman Neil Jordan's *The Company of Wolves* way back in 1984, as well as *Underworld: Awakening* earlier this same year.)

"Even though it's set in the Gothic period, I'm trying to give it a modern take with some stylistic elements," explained director Louis Morneau. Unfortunately, he goes *too* far in that direction. Like the beast itself, anachronisms run rampant through this 19th century Transylvania town, which seems to be populated by an incongruous mix of Americans, Brits and Slavs—at least if one goes by the various diverse accents on display. Modern-day phrases like "No guts, no glory" and latter-day weaponry abound (the huntress Kazia, for instance, sports aviator goggles and a flame thrower—both very much *Twentieth* century inventions).

Most disappointing of all is the obvious CGI werewolf, who appears awkward and insubstantial, with its hunched back, ungainly hind legs (allowing it to run and leap on all fours) and elongated cranium that's

Professional werewolf hunters in nineteenth century Romania try to expose the *Werewolf: The Beast Among Us* in Universal's scaled-down, direct-to-video follow-up to their 2010 *Wolfman* redux (DVD cover).

neither human nor wolf enough to make it look half as convincing as the far-better-proportioned wolf's head of the physical man-in-a-suit monster employed for close-ups. "CGI can change its entire body structure," explained *Werewolf*'s creature designer Paul Hyett (*The Descent*, *Attack the Block*) about why they turned to the computer so often. "In the computer we can make it double-jointed, which is the idea." They can also make it look very different from the physical effects beast seen up close, which they do—much to the film's detriment.

Fortunately, Morneau at least has a man-in-a-suit take over for the close shots, so that the beast and actors look like they're actually interacting. "I wanted the monster to be quite brutal and strong," noted Hyett. "We looked at werewolves of the ages and wanted to stay away from what had already been done. People tend to sculpt these suits and then put loads of fur on them, and they lose everything when they're trying to shoot it. I really wanted to get away from that. I wanted to present the monster as it is: hard, brutal and tough. At the same time, I wanted it to feel slim, elegant and sleek." Though professing the desire to "stay away from what had already been done," Hyett admitted he was a big fan of the *Underworld* werewolf design. "Not so much the head, but the body, the shape, the colors, the sort of silver grays and blacks." While this werewolf indeed looks "hard, brutal and tough" during those shots involving the physical suit, it looks flat, cartoonish and silly when in CGI form.

The film's solitary transformation sequence remains a disappointingly mixed bag as well. It begins promisingly enough with some subtle prosthetics giving the actor's face a suitably wolfish look. But after these few moments of substantial physicality, it immediately devolves into the usual weightless CGI morphing one might expect from the average SyFy Channel cheesefest.

Regarding lycan-lore, silver is a non-issue (shown by the various weapons wielded by the hunters). The full moon, however, remains paramount, as evidenced by the hunters' skepticism when this particular werewolf kills even on those nights either side of the full moon. "A beast that hunts when the moon's not full—no such thing exists," scoffs one hunter. But he's wrong. This creature is special. As a local gypsy explains, "This beast was not made a werewolf, not infected by a bite, but was *born* one, born of a woman bitten by a beast. This beast is stronger and smarter; the disease is part of its original blood. It gets stronger, too, with each passing moon—until one day it will be able to transform at will."

Most striking, however, is the film's setting—not only the imposing ruins and creepy woodlands of the authentic Romanian locations (where filming is cheap)—but the fact it's a time and place where werewolves are taken as a matter of course. No one, least of all the learned doctor (who "treats" a patient who'd survived a werewolf bite by putting a bullet through his head!), balks at the notion. Death, taxes and werewolves—all are part of ordinary village life here. (In fact, when Daniel pushes a wheelbarrow laden with human limbs and viscera taken from the overflowing morgue—human chum to lure the werewolf into the hunters' trap—down the street, nobody bats an eye.) Professional werewolf hunters roam the land, killing the monsters for money, while more than once someone notes how this particular beast is no "*ordinary* werewolf." Morneau builds a grim atmosphere with shots of mutilated corpses littering the town's main street after a night of lycanthropic rampage, the sheer number of mangled bodies (and body parts) serving as ghastly testament to the all-pervasive presence and horrific power of the Beast.

Several clever twists point the film toward a lively and unexpected climax, which culminates in a battle between the (now sympathetic) werewolf and the (now villainous) hunter, revealed to be a vampire.

Unlike in so many other lycanthropictures (dating all the way back to 1943's *The Return of the Vampire*) where the werewolf plays second fiddle—if not outright slave—to the vampire, here the lycanthrope holds the *primary* monster position. In fact, *Werewolf: The Beast Within* posits vampirism as the mere aftereffect of a werewolf attack! "If they don't torch the bodies [of werewolf victims]," explains one hunter, "they turn into something else." And that something else is a "wurdulak" (vampire). So those killed by werewolves will rise up as vampires if their bodies aren't burned. Unfortunately, apart from a few throwaway lines and one instance of a hunter blasting a newly-risen revenant, this intriguing idea remains little more than a footnote until film's end and the wolf-vs-vamp finale. In any case, it's a unique notion that cements the werewolf's position as top of the monster food chain.

Not all of this *Werewolf* can lay claim to such novelty, however. In fact, the movie begs, borrows and steals from a wide variety of earlier films, becoming a veritable patchwork of lycan-tropes. In addition to the werewolf-battling-vampire climax taken right out of *Van Helsing* and *Underworld*, among others (not to mention *Abbott and Costello Meets Frankenstein*), this *Beast Among Us* features an (admittedly startling) dream-within-a-dream jolt used so effectively in *An American Werewolf in London*; a gypsy who spouts *The Wolf Man*'s "Even a man who is pure in heart..." ditty word-for-word; a vampire who dissolves in a shower of dust when staked, à la *Buffy the Vampire Slayer*; and the old mad-scientist-using-a-werewolf-to-take-revenge-on-those-who-mocked-him scenario right out of the unlikely poverty-row throwback *The Mad Monster*. ("I trained you," rants said scientist to the Beast, "You were born to kill. I just focused your skills on liars, whores and thieves—just practice for when we get to the university. Those pompous idiots—they called my research 'dubious!'") Such borrowings, however, set in its action-packed scenario, serve only to up the fun factor of this unpretentious pastiche. And there's still the occasional wacky detail that makes one sit up and take notice, such as one scruffy hunter popping in a set of metal fangs to turn the tables and literally put the bite on the *werewolf*. (Not particularly practical, perhaps, but an amusing reversal nonetheless.)

"I purposely wrote it with a modern flair," noted *Werewolf: The Beast Among Us* co-writer Michael Tabb, "which is what audiences have come to expect with films like the new *Sherlock Holmes*.... My biggest influences while writing this one were the 1941 *The Wolf Man* and [the non-werewolf] *Brotherhood of the Wolf*."

"This film is a tribute to the old Universal horror films," declared Morneau. "It has all the elements that make it a classic horror story." That may be going rather too far, as its cipher-like characters and sometimes too-convenient scripting force it well off the "classic" path.

Actor Steven Bauer, who plays Hyde, one of the hunters, recalled, "From the first time I saw *The Wolf Man* with Lon Chaney Jr., that image of him transforming has scared me. During my growing-up years, that was an image I couldn't shake. I was always and forever connected to that." And while *Werewolf: The Beast Within* also remains always and forever connected to that classic (as well as the many other lycanfilms from which it shamelessly borrows), it fails to coalesce into a satisfying whole, largely due to its insistence on action over character and shoddy computer effects. Still, it's a lot more fun than the bloated *Van Helsing*…

With quotes from: "Howling for More: *Werewolf the Beast Among Us*," by David J. Moore, *Fangoria* 317.

Morphology: Seven-foot-tall wolf-headed biped
Demise: None; the Beast still lives Among Us
Full Moon Rating: **½

Werewolf: The Devil's Hound

(2007; Synthetic Cinema/Lionsgate) Directors/Screenplay/Cinematographers: Gregory C. Parker, Christian Pindar; Producer: Andrew Gernhard. Cast: Michael Dionne, Tamara Malawitz, Phillip Gauvin, Christy Cignci, Adam Loewenbaum, Michael Wran, Kirsten Babich, Lance Atrik Hallowell.

> SHE'S PART HUMAN, PART WEREWOLF,
> AND ALL EVIL—trailer

She's also tagged with a tranquilizer dart by her concerned German family, placed in a crate, and shipped to America for treatment for her lycanthropy (or something). Unfortunately, the werewolf-containing crate mistakenly ends up at a small, family-run pyrotechnic/special effects business in Connecticut, where the she-beast breaks out, kills a few locals, and bites the owner's son, Kevin (Michael Dionne), intent on transforming him into her werewolf mate. As Kevin struggles with his newfound penchant for sudden violence *and* attraction to the mysterious, accented Christine (Christy Cianci)—much to the consternation of his wife Char (Tarara Malawitz)—the werewolf traps his family in their company warehouse, intent on killing them all. Just then, Christine's father and brother arrive (having learned of the shipping mistake), along with "paranormal bounty hunter" Kwan (Lance Atrik Hallowell), leading to a showdown with the werewolf Christine and the wolfish Kevin.

Shot as *Lycan* in Connecticut on a purported budget of 1.2 million dollars, it's a wonder where the money went. Though looking slicker than most backyard productions (due to the genuine effects house shooting location and some trying-too-hard film school–style direction), it retains that homemade feel through the amateurish acting (alternately over-the-top and awkwardly subdued) and everything-but-the-kitchen-sink smell of desperation (hey, why not throw in a slapstick ninja werewolf expert just for fun ... oh, and an alien abduction joke too?).

The film begins visually strong, with some inventive camerawork and quick edits effectively utilized to set the story in motion. Fluid mobile camerawork, some red-tinted wolf-o-vision p.o.v. photography, and clever suspense-building (after the werewolf escapes its crate, a warehouse door continually banging open has Kevin—and the camera—cautiously approaching, ratcheting up the tension) promises lycan-thrills aplenty. Unfortunately, two-man band Gregory C. Parker and Christian Pindar (who wrote, directed, photographed *and* edited this opus) soon become carried away with their visual gimmicks, to the point of relying on seizure-inducing manic strobe effects and frantic zooms into a victim's bloody, screaming face that obscure, rather than enhance, whatever might be happening. One shot sees the werewolf leaping 40 feet (a less-than-convincing CGI moment), then standing up and roaring next to a gigantic full moon—that suddenly turns blood-red. Though visually striking, such a ridiculous indulgence only serves to take the viewer right out of the story. It all quickly devolves into an exercise in style over substance.

The film offers not one but two (well, one-and-a-half, anyway) werewolves. Unfortunately, both are disappointments. With her white hair–covered body and leonine face, the Christine-wolf looks more Yeti than lycan. And Kevin's wolfishness never progresses past the elongated sideburns and simple set of fangs level. We see neither transform onscreen, though intimations of Kevin's change comes when twice he begins spitting up blood (suggesting—though never *showing*—the painfulness of his growing fangs, perhaps?). Christine apparently changes at will, while Kevin changes, well, whenever the script dictates.

Also disappointing are the werewolf attacks themselves. Though the scenes of lycanthropic mayhem involve throat slashings, limb-ripping, decapitation, and one particularly nasty head-stomping, manic editing and frantic camera movements attempt—but fail—to obscure the unconvincingly stiff prop limbs and basic red paint effects work.

The script offers no backstory for Christine, nor any real character development either, apart from one scene in which she phones her father to complain, "You never accepted me for what I am." Of course, *why* she calls him remains unclear, since she intends to start a new life with a new mate in a new world, and the phone call serves only to let her family track her to Connecticut. But this remains symptomatic of the film's primary weakness—a poorly-thought out and ultimately schizophrenic script.

The screenplay treats Kevin, the ostensible tragic antihero, equally dismissively by building his character with little more than a montage showing him goofing off at the warehouse in true slacker fashion (wrapping scotch tape around his head, jumping off the furniture, bouncing balls off the wall, etc.). The character never engenders any empathy, painting him as an unlikable jerk from the get-go, as he mocks a nerdy co-worker and makes crude sexual advances towards his wife (who miraculously refrains from disdainfully dismissing such juvenile behavior because, well, it's obviously written that way in the script).

Even worse than its poor characterizations, overblown technique, and ADD editing, the film's biggest problem remains its 180-degree tone shift an hour into the movie. For its first two-thirds, this *Devil's Hound* remains a serious one, but at the hour mark it suddenly becomes The Devil's *Jester*, shifting into broad, slapstick comedy. With the arrival of werewolf hunter Kwan, who immediately performs a protracted pratfall routine and employs an outrageous European accent, this *Werewolf* will seemingly do anything for a laugh. Beyond the fact that most of the gags fall flat, the abrupt shift from straight-ahead horror to slapstick comedy kills whatever suspense—and interest—the movie has built. It's as if the filmmakers simply had no idea where to go and so started tossing out anything they could think of. It all culminates in a ludicrous climax in which Kevin's veterinarian *mom* shows up with some kind of laser cannon to dispatch the she-wolf (causing the beast's eyes to literally bug out of her head like some Warner Bros. cartoon character before she vaporizes). Yep, it turns out that mom is a "werewolf hunter" on the side, and she matter-of-factly shoots her wolfed-out son with a tranquilizer dart, resulting in him returning to normal seconds later. "Let's all go get breakfast," she suggests before leading them all away.

Full of camera tricks and gimmicks, *Werewolf: The Devil's Hound* lacks the focus and discipline necessary to make it anything more than a misguided mongrel. What most disappoints is that it appears filmmakers Gregory C. Parker and Christian Pindar possess the tools and imagination to visually bring a story to cinematic life; they just need someone *else* to come up with that story.

Morphology: White fur-covered she-wolf; wolfman with heavy sideburns and fangs
Demise: Laser cannon (or something)
Full Moon Rating: *½

The Werewolf vs. the Vampire Woman

(1971/72; Hispamex/Ellman Enterprises; Spain/W. Germany) Original Language Title: *La Noche de Walpurgis*. Alternate Titles: *Shadow of the Werewolf* (UK); *Werewolf Shadow* (Canada and DVD); *Blood*

248 • *The Werewolf vs. the Vampire Woman*

Moon (VHS). Director: Leon Klimovsky; Producer: Salvador Romero; Screenplay: Jacinto Molina, Hans Munkel; Cinematographer: Leopoldo Villaseñor. Cast: Paul Naschy, Gaby Fuchs, Barbara Capell, Andrés Resino, Yelena Samarina, Julio Penn, Patty Shepard.

Vampire versus werewolf in a battle to the death!—trailer

This fourth Waldemar the Werewolf film (following *Frankenstein's Bloody Terror*, *Assignment Terror*, and *Fury of the Wolfman* [made before but released after *Vampire Woman*]) solidified not only Paul Naschy's position as a horror star but the Spanish horror genre itself. As Spanish film historian Carlos Aquilar observed, "The industrial eruption [of horror films], in effect, began following two commercial successes—*La Residencia* (1969) by Narcisco Ibanez Serrador, and *La Noche de Walpurgis* (1970) by Leon Klimovsky—and one critical success, *El Bosque del Lobo* (1970) by Pedro Olea [a film about a killer who thought of himself as a werewolf; meaning that two of the three watershed films were lycan-centric]. The multiple echoes that arose as a consequence of this phenomenon determined that the Spanish film industry as a whole was interested in cultivating the horror genre."

Financially successful (the highest grosser of Naschy's entire career) not only in its native country (over a million patrons in Spain alone paid to see Daninsky's latest struggle against his lycanthropic nature) but internationally, *The Werewolf vs. the Vampire Woman* truly put Naschy—and his beloved Wolfman—on the cinematic map. Unfortunately, it isn't nearly as successful aesthetically. In fact, it's a rather middle-of-the-road Daninsky entry—greater than most but lesser than several (including Naschy's later remake, *The Craving*).

During an autopsy on the body of Waldemar Daninsky a pair of doctors remove the silver bullets from his heart. Naturally, the werewolf revives, kills the disbelieving medicos, and retreats to an old house in the remote mountains of France. Two beautiful young students, Elvira (Gaby Fuchs) and Genevieve (Barbara Capell), researching their final thesis, arrive searching for the tomb of the legendary Wandesa Darvula de Nadasy, nee Countess Bathory (Patty Shepard), an alleged vampire. With Waldemar's help they find the tomb and open it. Over Elvira's objections, Genevieve removes the silver Cross of Mayenza embedded in Wandesa's skeleton and accidentally cuts herself. The dripping blood later revives Wandesa, who vampirizes Genevieve, tries (unsuccessfully) to do the same to Elvira, and kills various local girls. Adding to the death toll (during the full moon, anyway) is Waldemar's werewolf, who sometimes breaks his self-confining chains to prowl the woods. Meanwhile, Elvira and Waldemar have fallen in love, and she learns of his secret curse. Needing to stop Wandesa before the upcoming Walpurgis Night (or "the vampires will reign supreme"), they finally locate Wandesa's lair. But the full moon rises, and the werewolf battles the vampire woman for the life, and soul, of Elvira.

"A HORROR HIT FOR HORROR FANS": German poster for Paul Naschy's biggest international success, released in America as *The Werewolf vs. the Vampire Woman*.

Like he did in his previous three lycan-films, Naschy (who not only starred but scripted) takes great pains to make his tortured Wolfman the hero—a courageous character to be admired who inspires sympathy as much as terror. At the center of the story is Daninsky's need to control his bestial side at all costs, even having himself chained up to protect his love, Elvira. Tellingly, when Waldemar's unbalanced handyman Pierre knocks Elvira unconscious and starts to carry her off, Waldemar's incensed werewolf somehow breaks his bonds to maul Pierre and save Elvira from a fate worse than death, leaving her recovered and unsullied in the morning. Still, while casting the werewolf in a heroic light, the sequence gruesomely illustrates his savage nature by including shots of bloody flesh dropping from his slavering jaws.

Naschy takes a decidedly romantic view of his lycanthropic antihero. "The only definitive way of eliminating him entirely is through love," observed the writer-actor. "If killed by hatred, he can be reborn as soon as the silver cross [the Cross of Mayenza] is removed." So even though the only cure for lycanthropy is death, it must be delivered by the hand of someone who loves him. Though not a new notion (as far back as 1944's *House of Frankenstein* the silver bullet must be fired by the hand "of someone who loves him enough to understand"), Naschy codified it and took the tragic romanticism to new heights.

But there's more to it than that. As author Nicholas Schlegel points out, "Naschy has structured his werewolf and vampire psyches closely along the Freudian formulation of the id, ego, and superego." Like Larry Talbot before him, Naschy's Daninsky desires death above all else, for only death will release him from his tortured existence (his ego). This desire (to do no further harm) reflects the demands of the moral (and societal) superego. Daninsky's savage impulses—personified by the werewolf—are pure id. As are the vampires themselves: selfish beings devoted solely to the procurement of pleasure (blood). Tellingly, only when in wolf-form can Daninsky stand up to the Countess—in an id vs. id battle. The power of the id is to be both feared and admired—and harnessed, when appropriate, to serve the will of the ego and superego.

In interviews, Naschy often praised Argentinean-born Leon Klimovsky (calling him a "good friend") but complained of the director's parsimonious nature. "The film [*The Werewolf vs. the Vampire Woman*] had the characteristic ups and downs of Leon Klimovsky," opined Naschy, "but I believe that the positive elements stood out above the errors or flaws it might have had. One of those positive elements is the way in which it treated the world of the vampires; I think the movement of the vampires in slow motion is quite successful." Klimovsky collaborated with Naschy on numerous subsequent occasions, including the immediate Daninsky follow-up *Dr. Jekyll and the Werewolf* (1972), and the non–Daninsky films *Vengeance of the Zombies* (1972), *Devil's Possessed* (1974), *A Dragonfly for Each Corpse* (1974), and *The People Who Own the Dark* (1976). "Klimovsky really knew how to move his camera," concluded the actor, "and in the slow motion scenes evoked an eerie, unearthly world of darkness which has since been imitated time and time again."

But it's not the direction nor photography that's the problem (both are more than adequate) with *The Werewolf vs. the Vampire Woman*, it's Naschy's uneven and sometimes baffling script. Characters behave inexplicably at times, and events come out of left field and have little bearing on the pertinent circumstances. For instance, on Elvira's and Genevieve's first night at Waldemar's house (he invited them to stay after their car ran out of gas), a crazed-looking woman (who turns out to be Waldemar's unbalanced sister Elizabeth) sneaks into the girls' room to warn Elvira to leave. But after uttering the warning, she places her hands menacingly around the terrified Elvira's throat, then moves them down to fondle Elvira's breasts! The camera goes out of focus as Elvira faints, coming to on Waldemar's face looming over her as he apologizes for his sister's actions. "Please, try to forget her intrusion." At this, Elvira positively *beams* (despite her earlier misgivings, shared with Genevieve, about how she doesn't trust their host). Quite the forgiving soul. Adding freakish insult to assaultive injury, the next day Elizabeth attacks Genevieve, ripping open her blouse (naturally) and choking her into unconsciousness. But do the girls leave? No.

Later, as Waldemar and Genevieve open Wandesa's tomb, Elvira wanders into the nearby ruined chapel, where she encounters a dried-apple-faced undead monk, Wandesa's former Satan-worshipping cohort, ostensibly revived by Wandesa's power (never mind that Wandesa hadn't reanimated yet—that comes later that night). Hearing Elvira's screams, Waldemar rushes to her aid and stabs the zombie with the silver cross they'd just removed from Wandesa's body, leaving only a pile of smoking robes. Strangely, the two girls sweep this horrific incident under the rug (along with their two earlier violent sexual assaults), as that night they converse normally, with Elvira prattling on about how she loves dancing and "a nice dinner with Marcel," her boyfriend. Such behavior appears incongruous at best and nonsensical at worst.

Then comes the most bizarre interlude of all, when Elvira rides into town with Waldemar's handyman Pierre. Droning on about his village to the bored Elvira, his monologue takes a sudden left turn: "You're very beautiful. I love your long red hair. Don't ever cut it. Why do women cut their hair? Maybe they think it makes them look nicer. But it doesn't, not at all. You know, I think I could like you. You know, there are many women I don't like, not at all." All the while, Elvira gazes ahead blankly, as if Pierre's disturbing diatribe is nothing more than harmless prattle about the weather.

The next scene shows Waldemar disposing of his sister's body (killed by Wandesa). He matter-of-factly drives a stake into his sibling's chest, cuts off her (obvious mannequin) head with an axe, picks it up by the hair, and unceremoniously drops it into the open grave he'd just dug before dumping the headless body in after it, with nary a moment of hesitation, much less a tear or two. So much for family ties.

Waldemar's puzzling lack of sentiment even permeates his big love scene with Elvira. In bed together, he says to her, "Elvira, I know our love has no future, but I want you to know that I'll remember this moment forever, my darling." He then pulls the sheet down to uncover her breasts, which he begins to nibble. The moment becomes almost comical in its artless (mis)timing.

The film slows considerably as Elvira's worried detective boyfriend Marcel (Andreas Resino) tries to trace her whereabouts, interviewing the mayor, the local barmaid, whomever he can find in order to learn what we already know. Once he finally tracks Elvira to Waldemar's home, still more palaver between Marcel and Waldemar (with Marcel insisting Elvira must leave with him and Waldemar finally agreeing), and Waldemar and Elvira (as Waldemar tries to convince Elvira of the same), further bog down the proceedings.

Fortunately, various incidents (and not just of the comically inexplicable variety) keep things moving, particularly whenever the vampire women appear. Ironically, they always move in slow-motion, accompanied by eerie, atonal music. They look otherworldly with their pale complexions, long fangs, and billowing diaphanous shrouds as they seemingly float through a fog-laden corridor or gracefully glide through the ruins near sunrise, escaping into the shadows at the last moment. Echoing laughter and howling winds punctuate the soundtrack as the two vampire women inexorably advance, hands clasped and grinning like demonic children.

Werewolf-wise, Klimovsky's handling of the transformation displays his inventiveness no less than his parsimony. Rather than employing time-(and money-)consuming lap dissolves, he sets Daninsky staggering about his bedroom before falling backward, out of frame, onto the bed. He then cuts to Waldemar lying on the bed, his face now covered with hair, before cutting to a shot of him rising from the bed back into frame, sporting more hair and fangs. Grasping the bedpost, Waldemar falls to the floor. Rising once more, he's now in fully-transformed werewolf mode.

Klimovsky handles the werewolf attacks with equal economical aplomb. When the beast-man comes upon a hobo in the woods, the terrified tramp falls back against a tree. Taking the victim's point of view, the camera stares upward into the hirsute countenance as the werewolf slashes downwards—at us—again and again with his claws, before a final shot reveals the man bloodied and mangled.

"If you can take it, see the most sensational fight to the finish ever filmed," promised a TV promo spot, without the least trace of irony. In fact, said climactic donnybrook between the Werewolf and the Vampire Woman remains an *unsensational* disappointment. Snarling and baring their fangs, the two leap at one another, briefly roll in the dust, then break apart. Then the werewolf simply strides forward and bites Wandesa's neck, resulting in her dissolution (an obvious melting wax effigy) into a maggot-covered skeleton. Meanwhile, Elvira, whom Wandesa had planned to sacrifice to Satan, grabs up the magical silver cross Waldemar had brought with him and, with the (usually energetic) werewolf uncharacteristically standing stock still, walks forward and plunges it into the creature's heart. "Now you're free forever," she tragically intones—at least until the *next* Daninsky film (the following year, as it turns out). And so concludes the most famous—and most successful—Paul Naschy/Waldemar Daninsky movie of all time. Too bad it's not also the best.

With quotes from: *El Cine Fantastico y de Terror Espanol, 1900–1983*, by Carlos Aguilar; "The Howl from Overseas," by Jose Ignacio Cuenca, *Fangoria* 134; *Sex, Sadism, Spain, and Cinema*, by Nicholas G. Schlegel; "Paul Naschy Filmography," by José Luis González and Michael Secula, *Videooze* 6/7; *Memoirs of a Wolfman*, by Paul Naschy.

Morphology: Chaney-esque (including the dark pants and shirt) wolfman
Demise: Silver crucifix-dagger
Full Moon Rating: ***

Werewolf Woman see *The Legend of the Wolf Woman*

Werewolves on Wheels

(1971; Fanfare) Alternate Title: *Angel Warriors 2* (Australian video); Director: Michel Levesque. Producer: Paul Lewis. Screenplay: Michel Levesque, David M. Kaufman; Cinematographer: Isidore Mankofsky. Cast: Stephen Oliver, D. J. Anderson, Deuce Berry, William Gray, Gray Johnson, Barry McGuire, Owen Orr, Anna Lynn Brown, Leonard Rogel, Severn Darden.

> The most eerie, the most chilling, the most terrifying motorcycle horror film ever made—radio spot

A *werewolf*? And it's *on wheels*? Yep, that's what the title promises—and, surprisingly, what the film delivers—though it might be too little and too late for most casual viewers of this horror-biker genre-blender.

While the occasional motorcycle-centric film came before it (e.g., *The Wild One* in 1953), the biker film subgenre truly began when Roger Corman's *The Wild Angels* became a surprise hit in 1966 after the Hell's Angels motorcycle gang came to media prominence. There soon followed a veritable invasion of biker flicks, with titles such as *Hell's Angels on Wheels* (1967), *The Hellcats* (1968) and *Satan's Sadists* (1969) coming fast and furious. When the trend began to fizzle out in the early 1970s, filmmakers looked to extend the life of their cinematic cash cow by combining genres. Thus, *Werewolves on Wheels* roared onto the drive-in screens.

A gang of uncouth bikers called "The Devil's Advocates," led by Adam (Stephen Oliver) and his motorcycle mama Helen (D. J. Anderson, aka Donna Anders, heroine of 1970s's *Count Yorga, Vampire*), go looking for trouble and find it when they encounter a weird group of Satan-worshipping monks at a secluded monastery. Accepting the silent Satanists' offerings of bread and wine, they all fall into a stupor, upon which the monks mesmerize Helen in order to make her a "Bride of Satan" (involving her dancing naked while holding a skull in one hand and a snake in the other). But before the ceremony can be completed, the bikers awaken, bust some Satanic heads, and hit the highway with the confused Helen. Out in the desert to "clear their heads," gang members begin turning up dead—violently killed by some mysterious figure (seen only in silhouette). Eventually it becomes clear that Helen has been cursed by the monks, and through her Adam as well, with the nature of their affliction spelled out in the film's title. It all ends in a fiery confrontation between the gang and the werewolf duo.

Werewolves on Wheels: what a great title—for a disappointing film. For the most part, the characters—among them singer/songwriter Barry McGuire ("Eve of Destruction"), former child actor Billy Gray (*The Day the Earth Stood Still*, TV's *Father Knows Best*), and various real bikers and stuntmen—are obnoxious and dull. The "action" consists of fistfights, male-bonding via wrestling around in the dirt, and monks chanting unintelligibly. The worst these motorcycle mavericks do is rough up one redneck (sending him on his way before he really gets hurt) and mildly mock a gas station attendant. (Though their jackets proclaim them "The Devil's Advocates," they're no Hell's Angels.) Most disappointing of all, viewers must sit through 70 minutes of boring biker behavior before we ever see a werewolf—these lycans (with or without wheels) only show their furry faces in the final five minutes! Fortunately, the makeups prove more than competent, appearing quite similar to the classic Chaney look, though a bit woolier and with longer hair (it *was* the '70s, after all).

*Un*fortunately, when finally fully exposed, these lycanthropes' bark proves worse than their bite, for they are readily dispatched with fire. At least the two fire stunts (the second involving a flaming rider on motorcycle—which explodes mid-air) prove surprisingly polished, exciting and impressive, particularly given the film's straitened circumstances.

"It was shot on a very low budget," recalled actor Billy Gray, "and they were concerned about time, but the atmosphere on the set was much more jovial. People were there not to necessarily advance their careers as much as us to have a good time and have something to do." Ah, the Seventies...

For a low-budget exploitation hybrid, *Werewolves* at least *looks* good, due in part, no doubt, to first-time director Michel Levesque's experience as an art director and production designer. Levesque even comes up with the occasionally arresting sequence. For instance, when the gang, after finally figuring out that those mysterious monks are somehow connected to their "brothers'" deaths ("It's heavy—somebody's controlling the vibes," offers one of the more insightful riders in his oh-so-Seventies vernacular), they head back to the monastery with murder on their minds. But as the gang drives down a desert highway, a fog cloud drifts across the road. Riding into it, they dis-

THIS GANG THOUGHT IT WAS TOUGH...

'til it found a new type of hell... THE BRIDE OF SATAN!

WEREWOLVES ON WHEELS

In COLOR R

STARRING
STEPHEN OLIVER · SEVERN DARDEN Produced by PAUL LEWIS · Associate Producer STUART FLEMING · Music by DON GERE
Written by DAVID M. KAUFMAN & MICHEL LEVESQUE · Directed by MICHEL LEVESQUE · A SOUTH STREET PRODUCTION INC · Released by THE FANFARE CORPORATION

Bikers vs. werewolves—and bikers *as* werewolves—in the deliriously-titled '70s exploitationer *Werewolves on Wheels*.

appear one by one, only to reappear in the middle of a stretch of dunes, bikes mired in the sand. Levesque came up through the Corman school of filmmaking (his first gig involved set designing on *The Trip*). After *Werewolves on Wheels*, Levesque directed only one other film, the women-in-chains sexploitationer *Sweet Sugar* (1972), returning to art directing for the remainder of his career.

Likewise, the movie is well-photographed (filming took place near Barstow and in the California desert), and includes some beautifully composed desert shots, courtesy of cinematographer Isidore Mankofsky (*The Muppet Movie*, 1979; *Somewhere in Time*, 1980; *Better Off Dead*, 1985).

Still, *Werewolves on Wheels* works best as the cinematic equivalent of a novelty item. Not only does it stand as a rare horror-biker film specimen, it features a female werewolf as well as the standard male lycanthrope. It also ties lycanthropy to a Satanic curse, more along the lines of ancient folklore than pop culture werewolfery. And no other movie offers the astounding sight of a wolfman hunched over a speeding Harley. With that deliriously bizarre image (well-captured in its brilliant advertising art), *Werewolves on Wheels* rewards those willing to go along for the ride.

With quotes from: "Forgotten Horrors: *Werewolves on Wheels*," by John Wooley and Michael H. Price, *Fangoria* 242.

Morphology: Harley-riding bipedal wolfman (and wolfwoman)
Demise: Fire
Full Moon Rating: **½

Wild Country

(2006; Jinga Films/Lionsgate; UK) Director/Screenplay: Craig Strachan; Producer: Ros Borland; Cinematographer: Jan Pester. Cast: Samantha Shields, Martin Compston, Peter Capaldi, Alan McHugh, Kevin Quinn, Nicola Muldoon, Jamie Quinn.

There's no escape from the beast within—tagline

When is a werewolf movie not a werewolf movie? When it completely ignores werewolf lore and concocts something totally divested from all previous lycanthropic incarnations—right down to the creatures' appearance. In *Wild Country*, a quintet of troubled Scottish teens (including recent teen mother Kelly Ann, who was bullied by the local priest into giving up her baby for adoption) are dropped off in the desolate Scottish hills for an Outward Bound–type overnight hike. While trekking across the moorlands, they stumble upon an abandoned baby in a castle ruin—as well as a mutilated corpse. With Kelly Ann protectively caring for the infant, the group must try and make their way out of this Wild Country while a huge, wolf-like beast tracks their every move, picking off the hapless teens one by one. Can the survivors find a way to kill the creature before it slaughters them all?

Though admittedly novel, these beasts (it turns out there's more than one) look nothing like what one expects from a lycanthrope. Unfortunately, what they most closely resemble are long-nosed mutant sheep. With their hairless snouts ending in a wet dog nose, jagged teeth, too-small piggy eyes, and a big wooly body, their near-cartoonish appearance is something out of a Muppet's nightmare. First (and, to date, last) time director/screenwriter Craig Strachan smartly keeps his beasties literally in the dark for the film's first two-thirds, building menace and suspense by making the creatures a shadowy presence or offering a mere flash of bloody muzzle as they rip out a throat. A black shape moving among the trees and a pair of eyes malignantly shining in the dark, accompanied by a guttural growl, initially alert the group to its malevolent presence. The first attack comes 20 minutes in (involving a creepy Peeping Tom shepherd), with a brief long shot of something big and indistinct running towards him, then an in-your-face beast-p.o.v. attack, and concluding with a shot of blood spurting from his severed jugular as the body is dragged out of frame.

Sadly, the creatures lose their menacing mystique (as well as any shred of verisimilitude) when dawn comes and we finally see the monsters in all their daylight glory—of which there is precious little, given their ridiculous mutant aardvark appearance and lumbering gait (man-in-suit quadrupeds, with the poor actor inside awkwardly trying to move about on all fours, rarely inspire anything but derision, and this angry Snuffleupagus is no exception).

Eschewing the usual werewolf lore, the film manages to avoid many of the subgenre's pitfalls and clichés. "We decided early on we were going to opt out of the whole corpus of cinema lore about werewolves," noted director/screenwriter Strachen. There's no inkling of the moon affecting a change (the creatures remain in their wolf-form during the day as well as at night), no mention of silver (a wounded monster is effectively dispatched with nothing more than sharpened sticks), and no supernatural shenanigans involving pentagrams or curses. Of course, the film also forgoes any chance at pathos or introspection regarding "the nature of beast," since said nature remains a complete mystery. No one ever uses the "W" word, and up until the very end, there's little inkling that these creatures are anything more than mutant monsters. The pivotal transformation is conspicuous solely by its absence, with only an implied change at the very end (informed by a solitary early-stage makeup shot).

All in this *Wild Country* is not lost, however, despite its disappointing and ill-defined creatures, as the film still has plenty going for it. The sweeping landscape of the Scottish countryside outside Glasgow makes for a very foreboding and isolating setting, one that fully exploits the fear of being out in the open at the mercy of a stalking beast. Believable dialogue and natural performances from a remarkably competent cast (all of them actual teenagers rather than the usual twenty-somethings *playing* teenagers), including first-timer Samantha Shields as Kelly Ann and Martin Compston (*Sweet Sixteen*) as her former boyfriend, establish a refreshingly believable character core. (Compston went on to play a lycanthrope himself in 2012's *Strippers vs. Werewolves*.)

Strachen's screenplay offers up plenty of amusing banter and some downright humorous dialogue exchanges. When talking of how they might kill the beast, one says, "We got a wee knife," to which another exasperatedly responds, "It's got claws and fangs and— killer halitosis for all we know!"

Relying on character and the tension of the situation to carry the straightforward story along, *Wild Country* offers up

The ungainly werewolf (and what's left of its latest victim) stalking the *Wild Country*.

only the occasional bit of gore (including a literal entrails trail and a gruesomely realistic showstopper in which a man is bitten in half), made all the more powerful for its judicious use and brevity. And the quick-paced, tight (72 minute) story never outstays its welcome and includes a nice sting in its tail.

Glaswegian Craig Strachen wrote the script for *Wild Country* in 2001, which was optioned by Ros Borland of Gabriel Films who spent the next three years trying to raise financing, finally finding it through a group of private investors in the U.S. Shooting took place in Scotland in October–November 2004. Aided by steadicam operator-turned-cinematographer Jan Pester, Strachen shot the film on high definition video in and around Glasgow (including Mudgock Country Park, where the ruined castle was located—though the castle's interiors were created on a makeshift soundstage built inside a disused factory in Glasgow).

But back to the beasts.... Strachen approached special effects artist Bob Keen to create the werewolves, but Keen's bid was too high for the relatively low million-pound budget, so several of Keen's Image FX staff (headed by David Bonneywell) stepped in to create a cheaper alternative. It shows. Even so, Keen's name remains prominently featured in the film's credits as "SFX Designer." Said Keen, "All I want to say about *Wild Country* is: I had minimal involvement with it, it was done through the company. And they made the classic mistake of shooting a horror film in broad daylight. Darkness is a great friend. That's all I can say, but in essence there's quite a good piece in there."

The beast's body, with its top-heavy frame, was modeled after the hyena, a truly ungainly looking animal and not a particularly good choice. FX technician Peter Hawkins volunteered to wear the bulky suit. With all this being said, it could have been worse, as Strachen revealed that at one point they had considered putting costumes on dogs(!) to create their monsters (*Killer Shrews*, anyone?). Fortunately, cooler heads prevailed, and the notion was discarded.

Producer Ros Borland relates how "we wanted something that was really big and imposing, something that was really really dangerous—something that you look at it and are absolutely terrified." Well, *that* they didn't get; but thanks to some evocative settings, involving direction, a taut script, and well-drawn and well-played characters, this *Wild Country* still remains a landscape worth visiting.

With quotes from: "Behind the Scenes," *Wild Country* DVD; *Urban Terrors,* by M.J. Simpson.

Morphology: Bulky quadruped
Demise: Stabbed by makeshift spears
Full Moon Rating: ***

Wilderness

(1997; Carlton/Fangoria Films; UK) Director: Ben Bolt; Producer: Tim Vaughan; Screenplay: Andrew Davies, Bernadette Davis (based on the novel by Dennis Danvers); Cinematographer: John Daly. Cast: Amanda Ooms, Owen Teale, Michael Kitchen, Gemma Jones.

> Beauty Is the Beast—tagline

Not to be confused with the (also excellent) 2006 British horror-thriller of the same name, this *Wilderness* is a 1996 three-part British TV miniseries edited down to feature length and released to select European markets the following year (and to video in the U.S. in 2001).

"I'm 31 years old and I want to be able to have children, to have a proper relationship," says sexy university librarian Alice (Amanda Ooms), who has grown tired of meaningless one-night stands. "And to do that I need to get to grips with this wolf thing..." This "wolf thing" sees her transforming into a gray wolf once each month (she shuts herself into a basement room—furnished with a bare mattress, a bowl of water, and some raw meat—during nights of the full moon). Alice seeks help from psychiatrist Luther Adams (Michael Kitchen), who employs hypnosis to try and get to the root of her "problem." Even though at one point Adams sees, for a split-second, the wolf inside her, he passes it off as a "visual delusion." He also develops an unhealthy interest in his patient, and ultimately determines to have her for his own ("It is now agreed that both Freud and Jung had sex with certain patients as a part of the therapeutic process," he writes in his notes as self-serving justification). Meanwhile, Alice, encouraged by the possibility of controlling her inner beast, has met and fallen in love with biologist Dan (Owen Teale), but their burgeoning relationship becomes strained after she reveals her secret to her disbelieving beau. Having learned of a wild wolf sanctuary in Scotland, Alice determines to set her wolf free. Can Dan, now a believer, reach her and bring Alice back to the world of humanity? Will she even *want* to return?

Alice feels isolated from the rest of humanity. She attends a lecture given by wolf expert Jane Garth (Gemma Jones), who notes, "A wolf in captivity, especially a wolf in captivity without access to other wolves, is desperately unhappy." Alice only wants to be "normal." As she tells her psychiatrist, "If I'm in control I can lead a normal life, can't I. I don't need to lock myself up or shut myself in. I don't need to be frightened of harming other people. I'll be free." Alice's yearning encapsulates the fear of losing control and acting upon one's primal urges. If one does that, one can't fit within society, can't lead a "normal life," thus condemning oneself to the role of outsider—a lone wolf, so to speak. And, as the wolf expert says during her lecture, "I don't think it's anthropomorphic or sentimental to speak of the sadness of the lone wolf. No wolf ever chooses to live or hunt alone."

For this she-wolf, not only does the moon trigger the change but so does intense stress. Alice transforms when she feels threatened, not only physically (from would-be rapists, for instance) but territorially as well (she metamorphoses right before the eyes of Dan's soon-to-be ex-wife when she tells Alice that she intends to win Dan back). And finally, through relaxation techniques and self-hypnosis, Alice is able to bring out the wolf at will.

With only one death to Alice's credit (a flashback details how a local lad tried to force himself on the adolescent Alice, triggering her transformation into the wolf that then rips out his throat), the film offers little violence and less gore. But there's plenty of involving angst (thanks to the excellent playing of Amanda Ooms) and moments of heightened tension in which the wolf threatens to break free (and even threatens to attack) to keep things lively. These moments are well-realized by some brief but effective CGI transformations (relatively new technology in 1996), and the use of a live wolf. Of course (like most CGI) the almost instantaneous morphing lacks the weighty, visceral quality of a true physical transformation, but director Ben Bolt (*Doc Martin, Downton Abbey*) stages several of the changes with a sudden fierceness that both distracts and startles (such as when Alice, becoming agitated while under hypnosis, opens her mouth in a snarl which suddenly becomes the fanged maw of a growling wolf).

Alice eventually comes to see that the wolf, her inner animal, is integral to her identity. "I don't think I want to get rid of the wolf," she admits. "I want to control her, rather than feel that she's controlling me." And ultimately she realizes that her inner beast might be even more important than her surface humanity, a notion that drives her to rejoin nature itself. "I used to think that if only I could control the wolf I'd be happy. I was wrong. I missed being her.... Now I realize that the wolf is the best part of me."

All is not perfect in this *Wilderness*, however. Several elements seem forced and abrupt, no doubt due to the telescoping of events from the original 174 minutes to a lean 99. For instance, the almost cartoonishly smug psychiatrist's sudden sexual obsession with Alice develops too abruptly, so that his complete mental breakdown at film's end (after trying to force himself upon her only to be confronted by the wolf) carries little weight. Likewise, the self-professed love between Alice and Dan appears rather contrived and smacks of dramatic convenience, as they apparently become soul mates after only a few dates. No doubt the missing 75 minutes had something to do with these less-than-convincing character turns. Fortunately, there's still plenty of thematic depth to plumb, as well as striking Scottish scenery, well-realized wolf's-eye-view photography as the beast glides through the forest, and the riveting performance of Amanda Ooms, which keeps the viewer interested in Alice's plight.

Swedish actress Ooms (*The Expendables 2*), with her large, expressive eyes and natural sensuality, perfectly encapsulates the appeal of this *Wilderness*, as well as expressing Alice's inner turmoil with her heartbreaking emotional eagerness to attain "normalcy." As with all the best lycan characterizations, Ooms engenders the viewers' sympathy and draws them into her tragic world. According to producer Tim Vaughan, the filmmakers considered over 50 actresses for the role before settling on Ooms. "She was quite natural," said Vaughan. "There was something ... slightly oddly animalistic about that, this natural quality she had. And that was what we thought the role required.... She is completely confident in her own body." This last was critical, given the amount of screen time during which she's completely nude. Said nudity, however, is more natural than exploitative, revolving as it does exclusively around Alice's transformations (in fact, she keeps her clothes *on* during the film's solitary sex scene). Consequently, her nakedness seems a natural outgrowth of her condition rather than mere gratuitous titillation.

"It was amazing sometimes to be on the set when we were doing bluescreen stuff," said Vaughan, "and we had this wolf with us, and Amanda.... She'd be wandering around the set with nothing on, and the wolf would be wandering around the set, and after a certain point the rest of the crew would not take any notice of either of them!" Said wolf was named Ayla, and she'd been rescued and raised by hand.

"We weren't making a horror film," concluded Vaughan, "we were making a film about a wolf." Even more, they were making a thought-provoking film about the animal within us all and our innate need to belong.

With quotes from: "Aaaaaagh, 'Wilderness,'" by M. J. Simpson, *Wilderness* DVD.

In *Wilderness*, a three-part British miniseries edited down to feature length, sexy librarian Alice (Amanda Ooms) struggles to reconcile her humanity with her inner beast.

Morphology: Grey wolf
Demise: None
Full Moon Rating: ***½

Wolf

(1994; Columbia) Director: Mike Nichols; Producer: Douglas Wick; Screenplay: Jim Harrison, Wesley Strick, Elaine May (uncredited); Cinematographer: Giuseppe Rotunno. Cast: Jack Nicholson, Michelle Pfeiffer, James Spader, Kate Nelligan, Richard Jenkins, Christopher Plummer.

THE MOON IS RISING. THE MAN IS CHANGING. THE ANIMAL IS OUT—trailer

When is a werewolf movie not a werewolf movie? When it's a Jack Nicholson movie. And *Wolf* is, first and foremost, a Jack Nicholson movie. Nicholson plays aging book editor Will Randall, who's about to lose his job (due to a corporate takeover), his wife (to an affair with his younger protégé, Stewart [James Spader]), and his self-respect (considered a "nice guy" by nearly everyone, it seems that nice guys do indeed finish last). Then, on a lonely, snow-covered road in Vermont one night, Will hits a wolf with his car. When he moves the body, the beast revives and bites him. From then on, things begin to change. Will's hearing becomes more acute, he no longer needs glasses, and he feels (and looks) 20 years younger. He also finds his backbone and begins taking control of his life. But a few minor side effects have him worried. For instance, he experiences nighttime blackouts after which he awakens in the woods covered in deer blood. Worse, one morning he finds two severed human fingers(!) in his jacket pocket (the result of a run-in with some would-be muggers during one of his spells). Feeling his humanity giving way to the spirit of the wolf inside him, Will seeks solace from his newfound love Laura (Michelle Pfeiffer) before ultimately embracing his true nature after a savage battle with his duplicitous rival Stewart, whom he has unwittingly infected.

Cleverly scripted (by respected novelist, poet, and longtime Nicholson friend Jim Harrison, with tweaks from Wesley Strick and an uncredited Elaine May) and suffused with intriguing ideas, *Wolf* posits lycanthropy as a metaphor for midlife crisis, with the cure being to embrace the change. According to Harrison, the film sprang from his own real-life brush with lycanthropy! "It was during a bad time in my life," recounted the screenwriter, "and I was alone up at my very inaccessible cabin in Michigan. I'd seen a wolf a few days before, and I'd heard them for several nights. I was trying to get some sleep, and I thought I saw a flash of light. I burst out of my cot and hit my head on this deer antler chandelier. I was not myself. I tore off the back door of the cabin, and when I felt my face, it was covered with hair. I was Lon Chaney Jr. for a few minutes. I went out and sat by the river and the change passed. I was back to normal." If one takes his account as anything more than metaphor (or concussion-induced hallucination), this makes *Wolf* the only werewolf film to have been written by one.

A student of Native American legends, Harrison noted, "I really wanted to deal with the Native American idea of transformation—if you need to heal your body or your soul, you go into the body of an animal. That's your medicine." Eschewing the usual Hollywood were-trappings (silver, pentagrams and wolfsbane, for instance), *Wolf* focuses on more metaphysical matters, with talk of the "spirit" of the wolf having fused with Will's own. "Since it happened," says Will, "I feel as though the wolf passed something along to me.... I'm different, more alive, stronger.... [But] I'm afraid it might have a price." The film features a Maria Ouspenskaya counterpart—an aged, retired professor who imparts such knowledge as "Not all who are bitten change;

Jack Nicholson *Wolf*s out.

there must be something wild within," and "The demon-wolf is not evil unless the man he has bitten is evil." While the moon does play a part (the day Will was bitten, observes the professor, "the moon was closest to the Earth it's been in a hundred years"), Will changes after dark whether the moon is full or not ("The wolf rests by day but prowls by night, but is always present"). Not altogether above the hoary old clichés, however, the script has the old man give Will a magical talisman, a medallion that, when worn next to the skin, will prevent the change.

Wolf remains one of the few films to play up the lycanthrope's heightened sense of smell, making it not only an indicator of Will's transmogrified condition but a key plot point. Will smells Stewart's scent on his wife's clothes, leading to the discovery of their betrayal, which sets the rest of the plot in motion (as well as providing a running joke in which he smells alcohol on the breath of those around him).

Transforming megastar Jack Nicholson into a werewolf fell on the capable shoulders of makeup maestro Rick Baker. Though first choice, Baker originally turned down *Wolf* due to another commitment. When that project fell through, he was able to accept the lycan-assignment. "It was challenging to create make-up where you get the impression something is happening to Jack without piling on the rubber. There was talk of computer-generated werewolves in *Wolf*, but you really don't need that in a performance-based film." But you do need *something* wolfish in a werewolf movie, as the disappointingly minimalist makeup here makes clear. Baker's lack of "rubber-piling" results in a lupine protagonist that barely registers as such, with some extended sideburns, mussed hair, and barely discernible canine extensions being the only visual indicators of Will's transformations. And speaking of same, there are no onscreen metamorphoses (apart from one quick CGI shot at film's end when Stewart's dead hand morphs from hairy to human), which becomes doubly disappointing given Baker's participation (his *American Werewolf in London* transformation set the lycanthropic gold standard the previous decade). The final "change" at film's end is simply signaled by a tight close-up of Will's nose and eyes, now completely covered in close-cropped brown hair following his big battle with Stewart (implying that his metamorphosis has progressed much further now). A simple dissolve then shows the fur has darkened, and the creature draws back to howl, revealing a full wolf's head—one whose obvious mechanical origins makes the scene more ridiculous than poignant.

Stanley Kubrick was originally offered the director's baton for *Wolf* but turned it down. Nicholson (who had director approval) then sought out Oscar-winner Mike Nichols (whom the actor had worked with on 1986's *Heartburn*). While Nichols brought a keen visual sense, the slick and glossy *Wolf* ultimately rings hollow, as it lacks the sharpness, grit and edginess Nichols infused into his earlier work like *Who's Afraid of Virginia Woolf?* (1966), *The Graduate* (1967) and *Catch-22* (1970). The director also failed to properly reign in his star, letting Nicholson be Nicholson from the outset. Consequently, rather than a "worm turns" tale of a beaten-down man finding his inner strength (with a little help from a lupine bite), *Wolf* sees Jack Nicholson playing Jack Nicholson (his thousand-yard-stare intact from the get-go) who becomes even more Nicholsonesque as time goes by. The director himself gave the game away when he commented, "None of us could really imagine this film without Jack, because he's sort of halfway towards being a werewolf to begin with." (Of course, even Stanley Kubrick, on *The Shining*, couldn't restrain the Mighty Jack, so perhaps it's not within the power of mere mortals.) As Italian scare-maestro Dario Argento (*Susperia*, *Deep Red*) observed, "That's why *Wolf* didn't work, because Jack Nicholson is Jack Nicholson, you can't just turn him into a werewolf!"

Unfortunately, Nichols compounds this handicap (or perhaps misguidedly tries to divert attention away from it) by relying on technical tricks, the most egregious being an appalling overuse of slow-motion whenever Will wolfs out, which serves to dampen the scene's immediacy and takes the viewer out of the action. (Sound effects from the old *Six Million Dollar Man* TV show pop unbidden into one's consciousness while watching the slo-mo Will chasing down a deer in the forest or grappling with his evil nemesis at the climax.) Nichols does his protagonist no favors by having the fully-clothed, (mostly) human-looking Will bound through the woods (or up a staircase) on all fours in a manner that looks more ridiculous than animalistic (particularly when Will, sport coat intact, leaps atop an eight-foot boulder in Central Park, drops into a crouch, lifts his furless face and howls, causing nighttime joggers and winos to pause—while the viewer simply giggles).

Helping to smooth things over are Michelle Pfeiffer's ethereal beauty and James Spader's hissable smarminess. Unfortunately, neither character comes fully formed, nor do they receive enough screen time to truly balance out Nicholson. (Mia Farrow was Nichols' first choice for Laura, but she had to drop out due to scheduling conflicts. Next up was Sharon Stone, but that actress, riding high from her star-making turn in *Basic Instinct* [1992], turned down the part, resulting in Pfeiffer stepping into the mostly thankless role.)

Wolf does offer its fair share of memorable moments, however. For instance, at one point Will and Stewart have words while standing at the bathroom urinals. Will gets the *last* word by turning and urinating on his rival's shoes. "I'm just marking my territory," he tells his shocked rival, "and you got in the way." And look for a pre–*Friends* David Schwimmer in a bit part as a cop who tries—and comically fails—to handcuff Will for breaking into the zoo at night.

Costing a purported $70 million (with $13 million going to Nicholson alone, and another $6 million to Pfeiffer), *Wolf* was the most expensive werewolf film of its time. It proved to be money well spent (at least on an economic, if not necessarily aesthetic, level), as it brought in a star-powered $65 million domestically, and another $66 million in foreign earnings.

Overly long at 125 minutes, and full of half-realized potential (not to mention an ending that negates all the gains the protagonist has made over the previous two hours), this *Wolf* howls for its missed opportunities.

With quotes from: "The Modern Legends of *Wolf*," by Chick Crisafulli, *Fangoria* 134; *The Illustrated Werewolf Movie Guide*, by Stephen Jones; "Who's Afraid of Nichols' *Wolf*," by Chuck Crisafulli, *Fangoria* 131; *Shock Masters of the Cinema*, by Loris Curci.

Morphology: Minimalist wolfman; full-on wolf
Demise: Ordinary bullets
Full Moon Rating: **½

The Wolf Man

(1941; Universal; b&w) Director/Producer: George Waggner; Screenplay: Curt Siodmak; Cinematographer: Joseph Valentine. Cast: Claude Rains, Warren William, Ralph Bellamy, Patric Knowles, Bela Lugosi, Maria Ouspenskaya, Evelyn Ankers, Lon Chaney, Jr.

> A strange mortal man with the hair and fangs of an unearthly beast ... his hideous howl a dirge of death—trailer

This is the one. Even though the *Werewolf of London* howled over six years earlier, it took the mammoth success of *The Wolf Man* (earning millions, and becoming arguably the best-known—and best beloved—of all werewolf movies) to get the lycan-ball rolling, with several studios, both major and minor, soon jumping on the werewolf bandwagon (as well as Universal itself plugging its new star monster attraction into four subsequent sequels).

When prodigal son Lawrence Talbot (Lon Chaney, Jr.) returns from America to take his place at his ancestral Welsh home, he soon becomes embroiled in forces beyond his control. While taking a local girl, Gwen (Evelyn Ankers), to a gypsy camp to have their fortunes told, Larry is attacked by a wolf. But after Larry beats it to death with a silver-headed cane, the beast turns out to be a man—the fortune-teller Bela (Bela Lugosi). Bela's mother, gypsy matriarch Maleva (Maria Ouspenskaya), relieved that her werewolf son has finally found peace, warns Larry that "whoever is bitten by a werewolf and lives becomes a werewolf himself." Though Larry's concerned father, Sir John Talbot (Claude Rains), tries to reassure his dismayed son, Larry transforms at the next full moon and kills a man. With the locals hunting the "wolf" roaming their woods, and Gwen confused over the distraught Larry's strange behavior, the next full moon brings tragedy, with Sir John wielding the silver-tipped cane against his own son, the Wolf Man.

The Wolf Man's—and cinema werewolves' in general—triumph belongs to three people: a Jewish refugee from Nazi Germany who had to re-start his flourishing writing career not only in another country but in another *language*; a diminutive semi-pro baseball player turned makeup artist who ran his department like "a martinet"; and the troubled son of a silent cinema superstar. Together, Curt Siodmak, Jack P. Pierce, and Lon Chaney, Jr., stand as the head, heart and soul of *The Wolf Man*. Though myriad others contributed significantly to *The Wolf Man*'s status as a horror classic (from George Waggner's well-paced direction, to Jack Otterson's fog-drenched, skeletal-treed sets, to effects pioneer John P. Fulton's immaculate lap dissolve transformations, to impeccable support from the likes of Claude Rains as the calm voice of rationality and Maria Ouspenskaya as a one-woman Greek chorus), it was the Siodmak-Pierce-Chaney triumvirate who propelled the Wolf Man into the classic monsterdom ranks alongside Dracula, the Frankenstein Monster, the Mummy, and the Creature from the Black Lagoon.

"Even a man who is pure in heart / And says his prayers by night / May become a wolf when the wolfsbane blooms / And the autumn moon is bright." The source? Ancient Sumerian tablets? Egyptian hieroglyphics? Old gypsy proverb? No, this classic ditty (delivered by *three* different characters within the film's first fifteen minutes) sprang directly from the mind of screenwriter Curt Siodmak. According to Siodmak, he did "a tremendous amount" of research for *The Wolf Man*, reading "books and books on lycanthropy." Interestingly, despite all this research, Siodmak made up much of his film's lycan-lore from whole cloth, including the pivotal notion that only silver can kill a werewolf (perhaps borrowed from Guy Endore's 1933 novel *The Werewolf of Paris*, though Siodmak never indicated he'd read the book), and linking the pentagram to lycanthropy (in this instance, the shape being seen in the palm of the werewolf's next victim).

Written without reference to Universal's earlier *Werewolf of London* (or to an unfilmed treatment intended as a Boris Karloff vehicle), Siodmak's original script took a more psychological approach to the concept of lycanthropy, keeping his protagonist's (originally named Larry Gill) transformations subjective by showing them only through Larry's eyes. In fact, his first draft kept the eponymous creature off-screen for most of the picture, though Universal brass soon altered that to fit their monster-happy mentality. With the studio demanding a more overt monster, the classic Wolf Man was born. (Note: Siodmak finally got to take a similar psychological tack a decade later with his *Bride of the Gorilla*, which he wrote and also directed, a decidedly smaller-of-scale and inferior-in-result "re-imagining" with a primate rather than lupine monster.)

Beyond its iconic creature, *The Wolf Man*'s impact stems from its multiple thematic layers. "Though Samuel Goldwyn's opinion," noted Siodmak in his autobiography, "was 'If you want to send a message, call Western Union,' he was wrong. Notwithstanding the budget of a motion picture, for me it had to contain a theme, a point of view, opening an avenue of thought, which might induce the public to think." Siodmak unconsciously constructed ("without my knowledge at the time," admitted the writer) a Greek tragedy. "In the Greek plays," he explained, "the gods tell man his fate, and he cannot escape it. In *The Wolf Man*, when the moon comes up, he knows he's going to kill. The influence of the gods over the man is very strong." *The Wolf Man* also serves as something of an inverted Oedipal tale (the father ultimately killing the son in order to preserve an object of desire). But, perhaps most intriguingly—and lastingly—the film explores the terrifying confrontation between rationality and the unknown. With four-time Oscar nominee Claude Rains as its rational center, *The Wolf Man* pits science against superstition, with Sir John, backed by the local doctor, explaining lycanthropy as "a variety of schizophrenia." When Larry, seeking solace from his skeptical father, asks if the older man believes in werewolves, Sir John replies firmly but not unkindly, "I do believe that most anything can happen to a man—in his *own mind*." *The Wolf Man*'s final impact—and much of its lasting power—comes from the tragic consequences of rationality succumbing to (and literally beating to death) the Unknown. Faced with what he's done,

"Even a man who is pure in heart, and says his prayers by night / May become a wolf when the wolfbane blooms, and the Autumn moon is bright..." Lon Chaney, Jr., as *The Wolf Man* (1941).

Rains' horrified, confused, and achingly pitiable reaction to having killed his own son in the form of a werewolf hammers home the horror of rationality's failure. Man, whose intellect has literally *thought* himself to the very top of the food chain, must have explanations, must have cause-and-effect, must have predictability in order to maintain his status. True horror comes when that intellect fails, consumed by the Unknown and forced to face its carefully-constructed paradigm's inadequacies. And the true tragedy of Man (or perhaps his gift, as this striving for knowledge gives mankind purpose) is that he can never know all—there will always be elusive, even frightening mysteries beyond human ken. Though myriad films have followed in its horrific wake, *The Wolf Man* was one of the first—and best—to codify this fear.

But all the thematic richness in the world would have done the film little good if its titular terror had failed to convince. Enter Jack P. Pierce, smartly dressed in his trademark white smock. A longtime Universal makeup mainstay, Pierce had brought monster-level success to his home studio by originating the look of its most famous creations, including Dracula, the Frankenstein Monster, and the Mummy. For his

Wolf Man, Pierce updated his original, more animalistic-looking concept toned-down for Henry Hull's *Werewolf of London*. The result: Pierce's meticulous yak hair and spirit gum creation for *The Wolf Man* became the industry standard by which all wolfmen were measured for the next four decades.

Pierce's intense attention to detail shows in all of his famous creations, not least in his Wolf Man. "It took 2½ hours to apply this makeup," Pierce said of his iconic lycanthrope. "I put all of the hair on a little row at a time. After the hair is on, you curl it, then singe it, burn it, to look like an animal that's been out in the woods. It had to be done every morning."

Lon Chaney, Jr., himself fully realized Pierce's genius, calling him "one of the finest makeup men who ever lived." Not everyone held such a high opinion of the man, however. Gloria Stuart, who suffered under Pierce's strict hand on *The Old Dark House* (1932), complained, "He was very fussy and a martinet. Enormously talented and liked his way of doing things…. He was great with men; he didn't really want to fool around with women."

"Of course I believe that *The Wolf Man* is the best of my horror films—because he is *mine*!" exclaimed Lon Chaney, Jr. Naturally, it didn't hurt that *The Wolf Man*'s success led to the screen's "Master Character Creator" (as the Universal ballyhoo boys labeled him) receiving more fan mail than any other actor on the Universal lot. Chaney was justly proud of his performance as Larry Talbot, the Wolf Man, despite his frequent complaints about the tortuous makeup.

Chaney's werewolf evinces both cunning and animal savagery, spying with anticipation a potential victim; loping, hunched forward, with an animalistic gait; and attacking his prey with furious brutality. But it's his portrayal of Larry's human side that sells the scenario. From his introductory scene, sitting easily in an open car and smoking a cigarette while headed for his homecoming, the eager grin on his open, beaming face immediately conveys his likability and puppyish eagerness to finally close the distance between himself and his estranged father. Getting reacquainted with his father by helping the elder Talbot install some complicated observatory equipment, Larry admits, "I'm all right with tools … but when it comes to theory I'm pretty much of an amateur." Larry is a down-to-earth, self-effacing, guileless guy. And it's Chaney's open, everyman demeanor that draws the viewer to him, allowing the audience to place themselves in Larry's tragic shoes.

No less a thespian heavyweight than Jack Nicholson (who played a werewolf himself over fifty years later in *Wolf*) recognized the actor's performance. "Chaney was very good," commented the modern-day star. "There's a wonderful power he has that sort of comes from the original mythology of the werewolf, which is a very sexual myth. The danger of that legend is that in the course of the cycle of the moon, he's going to kill. Lon Chaney showed a great deal of humanity in that role." Indeed he did.

Of Chaney, Siodmak said, "He was a very unhappy man. His father was one of the great sadists." (Siodmak declined to elaborate further.) One-time co-star Vincent Price (*The Haunted Palace*) concurred. "His father's legacy really haunted him; he was a desperately unhappy man—I felt sorry for him." Chaney Jr. died of a heart attack at age 67 on July 12, 1973, following a battle with throat cancer. His body was donated to the University of Southern California Medical School as an anatomical specimen.

By all accounts, co-stars Chaney and Evelyn Ankers subscribed to a mutual loathing society. Chaney felt the actress had "stolen" his studio dressing room. "On the first day of shooting," recalled Ms. Ankers, "Lon Chaney Jr., my leading man, said to me, 'So you're the gal who swiped my dressing room. You took it away from Broderick Crawford and me—I think that was a hell of a thing to do!'… When I asked the front office about it, they told me Lon had been warned that this would happen if he didn't stop 'misbehaving.' Every Friday or Saturday night, Lon and Brod Crawford would take bottles into their dressing room, get loaded, and then somehow manage to hang the furniture from the ceiling and brawl. On Monday, the cleaning crew was treated to a sight resembling a World War II battlefield." Chaney quickly took to calling her "Evelyn Shankers" (a "shanker" being slang for a syphilis sore). The fact that their onscreen banter and mutual attraction plays as well as it does is a testament to both actors' abilities.

"I have many memories of making *The Wolf Man*," continued Ankers, "but only some of them are pleasant." For instance, Chaney, in full makeup, would "creep up behind me, tap me on the shoulder so I would turn around and then, with his face about an inch from mine, bare his fangs and put his horrible hairy arms and claws around me. After a while I overcame this by sitting with my back against the wall, but he would still catch me sometimes if I were working."

Like fleas on a lycanthrope (or like Lon Chaney to Evelyn Ankers), a few incongruities cause the occasional minor irritation for this *Wolf Man*. Oddly, the bite of the original four-legged werewolf transforms Larry into a two-legged wolf*man*. Perhaps the lycan-curse is diluted when passed on in this manner? And when the authorities find Bela's body in place of the wolf's, he's *fully clothed* (except, as one spectator helpfully points out, for his shoes)—as if the beast's fur coat had transformed into standard gypsy garb. (The Bela-wolf that attacks Talbot was played by a former police dog named "Moose." Chaney ended up taking the German Shepherd home with him. Moose appeared in several subsequent Chaney films, including *Frankenstein Meets the Wolf Man*. Lon's Best Friend died in 1944, hit by a truck on the Universal lot while his master was filming the Arabian Nights–type potboiler *Cobra Woman*.)

Even more puzzling, the first transformation sequence (which cleverly displays the metamorphosis via Talbot's changing feet, saving the full-face transformation for the film's tragic ending) sees Larry stripping down to his white undershirt, and removing his shoes and socks. With the camera focused on his bare feet, we see his lower extremities transform (via a series of flawless dissolves) into a hairy hybrid of human foot and lupine paw. The canine limbs rise and walk (on the balls of their feet, like a wolf), with the scene dissolving to reveal the were-feet outside walking along the misty ground. Except now, the light grey pants Larry had been wearing during the transformation have miraculously changed into dark trousers, and instead of merely a wife-beater, the now-fully-transformed Wolf Man sports a long-sleeved, button-down shirt. Apparently, this werewolf paused long enough to dress more appropriately before embarking upon his inaugural nocturnal prowl.

Finally, at one point the local lawman (played with a scowling sturdiness by Ralph Bellamy) displays a plaster cast of a wolf track taken at the murder scene, with the paw print spanning a good six inches! Strangely, no one comments on how massive the beast that left that imprint must be (perhaps three times the size of a normal wolf). Fortunately, such questionable quibbles dissolve into the woodland fog when juxtaposed against the thematic, visual and thespian richness of the rest of the film.

In the end, it's impossible to overstate how important *The Wolf Man* is to lycan-cinema. Not only did it establish the general ground rules for lycanthropictures, it produced (courtesy of makeup maestro Jack Pierce) the classic werewolf "look" that reigned supreme for the next forty years (until Rob Bottin and Rick Baker finally freed werewolves from the standard dog nose and yak hair with *The Howling* and *An American Werewolf in London*). Thanks to this Universal groundbreaker and its sequels, the Wolf Man rightly took his place as one of the Big Five in monsterdom. Without Lawrence Talbot, werewolf cinema may very well have withered on the vine, or at least taken a very different, less prominent turn. As Curt Siodmak himself concluded, "Lon's *Wolf Man* became the classic werewolf film of all times." Though conflicted about his film's success (feeling Hollywood was beneath him, Siodmak announced, "I'm a writer, not a screenwriter, but was forced to make a living"), he admitted, "In retrospect it makes me believe that I never did anything else of any consistency in my life."

In his book *Lon Chaney Jr.*, author Don G. Smith labeled *The Wolf Man* "the most important horror film of the forties, as well as a triumph for Lon Chaney." Beyond its historical value, however, *The Wolf Man*, conceived as an inexpensive ($180,000) B-picture, has endured, earning its A+ reputation because of its thematic richness, outstanding acting, evocative atmosphere, and technical brilliance. *The Wolf Man* truly deserves the oft-overused sobriquet "classic."

With quotes from: "An Interview with the Outspoken Sultan of Speculation: Curt Siodmak, Part Two," by Dennis Fischer, *Filmfax* 14; "A Man, a Myth, and Many Monsters: Lon Chaney Jr.," by Jack Gourley and Gary Dorst, *Filmfax* 20; "Siodmak's Brain," by Tom Weaver and Michael Brunas, *Fangoria* 44; *Wolf Man's Maker: Memoir of a Hollywood Writer*, by Curt Siodmak; "Wolf Men: Jack Pierce's Incarnations of the Wolf Man," by Scott Essman, *Monsters from the Vault* vol. 18, no. 32; "An Outspoken Interview with the Sultan of Speculation: Curt Siodmak," by Dennis Fischer, *Filmfax* 13; Interview with Gloria Stuart conducted by the author, 1993; "Jack of All Trades," by Anthony C. Ferrante, *Fangoria* 136; Interview with Curt Siodmak conducted by the author, 1993; "Dr. Phibes Regrets: He Is Unable to Lunch Today…. Madam!" by David Del Valle, *Little Shoppe of Horrors* 29; *The Golden Age of B Movies*, by Doug McClelland; *Wolf Man's Maker: Memoir of a Hollywood Writer*, by Curt Siodmak; *Lon Chaney, Jr.: Horror Film Star, 1906–1973*, by Don G. Smith.

Morphology: Bipedal wolfman (of course)
Demise: Silver-headed cane
Full Moon Rating: *****

Wolf Moon see Dark Moon Rising

Lou Garou (Leo Fafard) is … *WolfCop*!

WolfCop

(2014; Cineplex; Canada) Director/Screenplay: Lowell Dean; Producers: Hugh Patterson, Bernie Hernando, Deborah Marks, Danielle Masters; Cinematographer: Peter Larocque. Cast: Leo Fafard, Amy Matysio, Sarah Lind, Corinne Conley, Jesse Moss, Jonathan Cherry, Aiden Devine.

HALF COP, HALF WOLF, ALL WOLFCOP—trailer

A werewolf policeman … who's an alcoholic … and who loves donuts? Yep, the low-budget ($1 million) Canadian horror-comedy *WolfCop* (shot in and around Regina and Moose Jaw, Saskatchewan) features this and so much more.

Lazy, alcoholic burn-out Sargent Lou Garou (Leo Fafard) may be the worst cop in the Woodhaven Sheriff's department. That all changes one night when Lou answers a disturbance call in the woods behind their small town. There he finds a man hanging upside-down from a tree. Before he can free the captive, a group of gowned, mask-wearing occultists knock Lou unconscious. Lou awakens in his own bed the next morning with a pentagram carved on his chest and beard stubble that just won't be tamed by a razor. He also now possesses a heightened sense of hearing and smell, and a newfound love of dogs. That night (a full moon) in his favorite bar, the Tooth & Nail Tavern, Lou transforms into a werewolf and rips apart a pair of thugs sent by the local gang leader to kidnap him. The next night, aided by his gun shop-owning friend Willie (Jonathan Cherry), Lou transforms safely in his own jail cell, but soon dons his uniform and goes out on patrol as WolfCop. In his hirsute form he foils a convenience story robbery, then takes out the local gang at their meth lab headquarters. Researching his new condition the next day, Lou discovers that strange occurrences like this have happened in the town every 32 years, and that lycanthropy is somehow tied to a blood sacrifice ritual taking place during a solar eclipse—an event set to occur the next day…

WolfCop was made because filmmaker Lowell Dean and his crew *won a contest*. As explained by writer-director Dean, "CineCoup is a Canadian competition where filmmakers compete through social media to get their film made. Teams submit their trailer and produce weekly mission videos…. It started with 92 entrants, and every two weeks projects are eliminated. The final winner of CineCoup gets a million dollar budget and the guarantee to have their film screen in theaters across Canada. When we first heard of CineCoup, I already had a first draft of the *WolfCop* script, and we had just shot a concept trailer. It was fate!"

And what a fine fate it turned out to be, as *WolfCop* stands as a superior were-specimen, one of the best of the New Millennium. Much of that comes down to Dean and his attitude toward his admittedly wacky subject. "I hate when werewolves are relegated to the henchman role, like the pet for the main villain," explained the filmmaker. "We're taking a different approach because not only is our werewolf the protagonist, he is arguably a hero, or at least a hero in progress. He's still very much a monster, but you will be rooting for him."

Only his second feature, *WolfCop* showcases Dean's surprisingly sure hand. During the obligatory exposition scene in which Lou relates to Willie what he's learned from a book on lycanthropy, shots of old woodcut illustrations alternate with brief, bloody memory flashes of Lou at the sacrificial ceremony to add visual interest to the dialogue and further tie the character to the events. Dean frequently employs off-kilter angles to enhance the uneasiness of a sequence, and even generates clever visual transitions, such as dissolving from a clock striking ten to a shot of the full moon to reinforce that particular time's import.

"I was about to write a feature script and I couldn't decide between two ideas in my brain—a gritty cop film or a werewolf horror film," recalled Dean about his screenplay's genesis. "I jokingly thought about smashing the two ideas together, and once I pictured it I couldn't stop thinking of that absurd premise. I needed to write it." And thank goodness he did, for lycancinema would be a poorer (and more crime-ridden) place without this WolfCop.

"In terms of tone," continued Dean, "I am inspired by movies like *An American Werewolf in London* and *Scream*, movies that brand themselves horror … but that are two of the funniest films I know of. So [*WolfCop*] will be funny because we will take our absurd subject matter *very* seriously." With the humor arising from the situations and characters rather than any wink-and-nod affectations (all the actors thankfully keep their tongues firmly *out* of their cheeks), *WolfCop* cleverly leavens its horrific moments with naturally-arising humor. For instance, wanting to confirm his suspicions after he finds Lou in the woods, Willie surreptitiously sprinkles some *wolfsbane* into Lou's eggs the next morning (garnering the expected reaction). Later, when the ruthless gang leader admonishes an underling for failing to bring Lou to him by 10 p.m. as ordered (prior to his transformation), he stabs his minion in the eye with his switchblade, pulls out the knife and hurls it to stick into the wall, eyeball still attached. Turning back to the whimpering, bleeding thug, he admonishes, "Next time, keep your *eye* on the time, you dumb fuck." Later, when Wolf-Lou and Willie literally crash the gang's party at their meth lab/barn hideout (with Lou driving his cruiser right through the barn wall), Lou shockingly rips the face off one attacking gang member and carelessly tosses it aside, with Willie, still in the squad car, squealing like a grossed-out little girl when the bloody skin mask *fwaps* onto the car's windshield.

"I think werewolves just aren't given the credit they deserve," opined Dean. "They need more love and care, and have the potential to be just as interesting as other monsters. Werewolves are all about internal conflict. I think *WolfCop* will bring new attention to werewolves because we are going to respect the werewolf mythology but also add a new spin on it." Indeed. And said "new spin" proved just as novel (and strangely appealing) as the notion of a werewolf peace officer that gains strength from liquor and donuts.

The first innovation comes in the werewolf's origin. As the book Lou reads tells it, "Werewolves are created in a baptismal of blood. The sacrifice of an innocent turns another into a beast." So Lou was chosen by the group of robed occultists to be turned for their own nefarious purposes. Which brings up the second unique notion: these Satanists need werewolf blood. Why? They're shapeshifters, and "the blood of one werewolf can maintain their power for decades" (32 years to be exact). "The blood of the beast is drained during the solar eclipse when the wolf is rendered weak" because "the werewolf is pretty much impossible to kill during the phases of the full moon" (Lou is impervious to bullets while in wolf form; though one might wonder about silver, no one has time to test it). And note that the solar eclipse triggers the transformation, just like the full moon.

A third point comes when Lou asks Willie after his first transformation (of which he can remember only snippets), "Do you think I'm myself when I'm the wolf?" At this, his friend amusingly replies, "You and those teeth and those claws. Plus you got that low self-esteem, low IQ, daddy issues. You're an alcoholic so you gotta have some *rage*, right? That's a lethal combo, man." Lethal, yes, but not without humanity or purpose. This werewolf is not an unreasoning, rampaging beast. Lou targets only wrongdoers, and possesses the powers of rudimentary speech. He can even be tender and gentle (as evidenced by a *lycan love scene*).

Intriguingly, the werewolf as pawn, with his blood a simple commodity (the lead villain snorts dried lycan-blood like cocaine), casts the lycanthrope in a different light, more victim than victimizer. Not only does one root for WolfCop due to his conflicted nature (not to mention the fact he's an heroic wolf *cop*), one sees this werewolf as an (ahem) underdog. Yes, he's a monster, but compared to the evil creatures after his blood (who, incidentally, transform into their original shape of ugly reptilian monsters upon their deaths), he's a people-person puppy.

While Leo Fafard, as the low-key, likable Lou, captures his character's laconic, burned-out demeanor perfectly (his introductory scene has him jolted awake by an alarm; stumbling, hungover, to his car; opening the door to vomit; and finally nipping from an ever-present flask), he carries it a bit too far once the fur hits the fan. Fafard rarely changes his weary expression and takes everything in stride. Sure he's an alcoholic used to blackouts, but learning you're now a *werewolf* should at least cause one's eyebrows to raise (if not all-out panic attacks). Still, Fafard's likable, unpretentious characterization captures our sympathies, and the viewer remains 100 percent behind this WolfCop.

WolfCop's appearance carefully walks that line between horror and comedy like a tightrope performer navigating above a circus audience, but with booze and donuts as his metaphorical balance pole. With dark skin, coarse hair, a black canine nose, red-rimmed lips and white protruding fangs (the bottom row prominent à la Lon Chaney's Wolf Man), he appears fierce enough to be taken seriously, yet, with his hulking bulk encased in a now-too-tight cop's uniform, incongruous enough to raise an amused eyebrow.

The juggling act extends to WolfCop's behavior as well. While reveling in his newfound power, which includes brutal and gruesome limb-ripping, head-decapitations, and the aforementioned face-skinning, WolfCop also retains at least some of Lou's humanity, communicating in brief, guttural utterances ("Lou, you're a wolf!" Willie exclaims, to which Were-Lou growlingly adds, "Cop!"); feasting on hooch and donuts (which, like Popeye and his spinach, seems to give him a boost) rather than human flesh; and acting like a cop (well, a cop in the Dirty-Harry-Meets-the-Wolf-Man mode anyway) by thwarting criminals not only with his claws but by using his gun as well. He even has sex while in werewolf form!

This leads to another first in werewolf cinema—consensual were-bestiality. It begins when the sexy bartender Lou constantly flirts with shows up at the station wearing an outfit more than a little reminiscent of Little Red Riding Hood. There she seduces Lycan-Lou, leading to a (tastefully filmed—apart from a few shots of large, clawed hands cupping even larger breasts) were-sex scene. It amusingly concludes with both of them contentedly enjoying post-coital cigarettes, as she says, "I don't want you to take this the wrong way, but I'm glad I waited to sleep with the new, improved version of you."

"[Effects man] Emersen [Ziffle] and I both feel we've come up with a transformation sequence that is referential of classic films but also truly unique," enthused Dean. "It will be done with practical effects, and it will haunt your nightmares." Especially male viewers' nightmares, for *WolfCop* is the first werewolf film to capture an on-screen *penile* transformation. As a drunken Lou urinates in the bar's bathroom, his stream suddenly turns bright red with blood. He then screams in pain and the camera, looking upwards from beneath him, shows his penis bulging outward, elongating and finally *splitting open* to reveal a hair-covered member beneath the shredded skin. Though of questionable taste, this cringe-inducing, body-specific metamorphosis definitely hits home. The transformation next (and thankfully) moves on to the more traditional holding-one's-hand-in-front-of-one's-face-as-it-changes shot—though with a gruesome twist: the skin doesn't simply morph, it sloughs off to reveal the bloody, hairy, clawed were-hand underneath. Shots of Lou's booted feet slipping and sliding on the squishy bits of skin dropping to the floor hammer home the horrific gruesomeness of this physical metamorphosis. The disturbingly grotesque sequence finally ends on a lighter note with a close-up of Lou's foot exiting the bathroom—with hairy clawed toes protruding through the front of his boot.

A second, more detailed (though thankfully phallus-free) metamorphosis occurs when Willie locks Lou in the jail cell the next night. As the clock strikes 10 p.m. (apparently full moon 'magic hour' for werewolves), the shirtless Lou cries out and writhes in pain as his back bulges and the skin along his spine splits to reveal dark, coarse fur beneath. Lou desperately grabs the bars, and the skin on his hand sloughs off as he pulls away, leaving a hand-shaped sheath of bloody skin stuck to the metal. Lou then helps the transformation along by sinking his clawed hands into the flesh in his chest and peeling it back like an orange to expose the moist fur underneath. As the *piece de resistance*, Lou's face literally splits down the middle, with the human halves of this skin mask dangling to either side of the hairy, toothsome visage beneath. Interspersed with a few Willie reaction shots ("Holy shit!") and backgrounded by a series of groans and growls on the soundtrack, the sequence stands as a viscerally affecting and visually impressive man-into-beast moment—that once again ends on a more comical note when an obviously verklempt Willie blubbers, "Lou, that was like the most beautiful thing I ever seen, man!" Picking up the comedic torch himself, the first thing Wolf-Lou does is gesture for a bottle of booze on the desk, and then for a box of donuts…

"We're going the very painful route of shedding a layer of skin," noted special effects makeup designer Emersen Ziffle. "It's not that I dislike the idea of the shape-shift; I just prefer how violent a good ol' skin molt can be. I didn't really draw on any examples I can think of, but Edgar from *Men in Black* keeps popping into my head. I love the way the alien is always fighting against busting out of his skin. The tension of this situation really makes me uncomfortable, and I want the essence of our transformation to be like that." Uncomfortable indeed. Though not as painfully protracted as Rick Baker's groundbreaking transformation work in *An American Werewolf in London*, nor as visually striking as the gruesome metamorphosis in *The Howling*, Ziffle's *WolfCop* transformation may be the most viscerally impressive since that watershed year of 1981.

"It's not just about struggling to retain your humanity when cursed with being a monster," concluded Dean about his feature, "it's about rising above it … and becoming a hero. We are bringing the beast back to the limelight with a vengeance." Given the sometimes scary, sometimes funny, sometimes shocking but always entertaining *WolfCop*, he's not far wrong.

With quotes from: "AICN Horror Talks with Lowell Dean About His New Horror Comedy *WolfCop*," by Kristian Horn, *Ain't It Cool News*; "Where Are the Wolves?" by Craig Anderson, *Fangoria* 329.

Morphology: Liquor-swilling, donut-eating, gun-firing WolfCop
Demise: None; WolfCop lives to chase criminals (and cars?) another day
Full Moon Rating: ****

Wolfman

(1979; The E.O. Corp.) Director/Screenplay: Worth Keeter; Producer: Earl Owensby; Cinematography: Darrell Cathcart. Cast: Earl Owensby, Kristina Reynolds, Sid Rancer, Edward Grady, Richard Dedmon, Maggie Lauterer, Brownlee Davis, Helene Tryon.

A Cinematic Study in Classic Horror—poster

Made just prior to the watershed year of 1981, when directors Joe Dante and John Landis, and makeup men Rob Bottin and Rick Baker, took werewolves in an entirely new direction, *Wolfman* stands as a last glance backwards at the classic notion of the lycanthrope as encapsulated by Lon Chaney and *The Wolf Man* (1941). Even *Wolfman*'s opening credits harken back to the early days of Gothic horror cinema, appearing over shots of a stormy night (all lightning flashes and rolling thunder) as the camera slowly dollies in on an obviously model manor house, followed by a shot of an even more obvious model locomotive (the train ostensibly bringing Colin Glasgow home to meet his tragic fate).

Set in the transitional horse-and-buggy period of 1910 (at least according to the film's poster, which reads, "1910: Colin Glasgow became heir to the Devil's Curse," though late in the movie we clearly see a gravestone dated 1911), *Wolfman* has the globetrotting Colin Glasgow (Earl Owensby) returning to his ancestral home upon learning of the death of his father (secretly murdered by the local Satan-worshipping Reverend Leonard, in cahoots with Colin's conniving relatives). Leonard uses the Black Arts to somehow transfer the Glasgow curse (lycanthropy) onto Colin, the eldest son, so that, after being attacked by a wolf in the graveyard, Colin now transforms into a werewolf on nights of the full moon. After several killings, Colin realizes he is responsible and seeks to be locked up. But transforming once again, the beast breaks out of the jail cell and slaughters Colin's duplicitous family before a silver dagger finally lays his tormented soul to rest.

As becomes obvious by this brief synopsis, this North Carolina–lensed regional throwback is very much structured like its obvious model (and namesake), *The Wolf Man* (1941). An estranged son returns home to the family estate, acquires the curse of the werewolf and kills, tries to convince others, is restrained during one night of the full moon to prove to him that it's all in his mind, transforms (of course) and breaks his bonds, then runs into a hunting party out in the woods where a silver weapon seals his fate.

Beyond its obvious influence, *Wolfman* takes further inspiration from a later source as well. Full of period dress and Gothic trappings—horse-drawn carriage, old cemetery, forbidding manor house, dark drawing rooms (though rather threadbare and obvious soundstage sets)—it resembles a kind of cut-rate, Southern-fried version of a 1960s Roger Corman Poe film. Cementing the analogy, *Wolfman* even features a delirious dream sequence (like most of Corman's Poe entries), complete with distorted soundtrack and roving, woozy camerawork.

Unfortunately, producer/star Earl Owensby, and regional director Worth Keeter, had neither the resources of Universal nor the talent of Corman, so that *Wolfman* falls well short of its inspirational marks. Overlong at 102 minutes, it's nearly an hour before any werewolfery occurs. In fact, most of the first hour is eaten up by much riding around in Colin's carriage as he visits the local tavern, seeks advice from the family doctor or takes solace in rekindling an old flame. Fortunately, the first transformation, though simple, is fairly effective. As Colin gazes out the window at the full moon, the camera focuses on his hand, whose skin gradually darkens before a simple dissolve transforms it into a hair-covered, clawed appendage. Taking only a few seconds, the metamorphosis appears seamless (and apparently painless as well). The next shot directly references (i.e., steals from) *The Wolf Man* (1941) by showing Colin's now-hirsute feet going out a window into the darkness. The following night we get the full-on transformation treatment, as a few simple dissolves show Colin's face turning into that of the Chaney-esque wolfman, complete with canine nose, jutting lower fangs and a covering of coarse hair. This solid rendition of the classic wolfman makeup (co-created, along with Sandy Barber, by director/screenwriter Worth Keeter himself) took four hours to apply, according to Owensby, and another four to remove.

Refreshingly, *Wolfman* steps beyond the shadow of Hollywood tropes (full moon, silver, etc.) by referencing medieval folklore as well. For one, the story directly links lycanthropy to Satanism. It is the sinister Reverend Leonard who sets the curse in motion, intoning, "We ask that the curse of the Glasgow family be the burden of the eldest son. That he should carry out the will of the spirits beholden to Satan, and that he be compelled by our wishes and demands.... I uphold my allegiance to Satan by administration of the curse." For another, the reason Colin re-visits his father's gravesite at night (where he's attacked by the transformative wolf) is to check on something his crazy grandmother told him—that his father carried the sign of the werewolf: an elongated index finger (longer than the middle digit), a notion taken from classic folklore.

Wolfman offers enough to keep most lycan-fans interested, with some decent lighting and nighttime photography, the occasional evocative werewolf p.o.v. shot, competent makeup and transformations, some low-level bloodletting, and an energetic climactic battle culminating in the wolfman and his (villainous) victim crashing through an attic window. Unfortunately, poor pacing, underdeveloped characterizations, and muddled motivation (what was the Reverend Leonard and his conniving accomplices after anyway, and what had they to gain from turning Colin into an obviously uncontrollable werewolf?) largely balance out the good with the bad. Still, given the obvious affection for the classic werewolf character and story evinced here, the production's (silver-pierced) heart was in the right place.

"I'm not an actor," admitted Earl Owensby, who had never even appeared in a high school play before

North Carolina–based movie mogul Earl Owensby offers his best Southern-fried Lon Chaney, Jr., impersonation in the regional throwback *Wolfman*.

casting himself as the star of his own productions. (Owensby initially made his money in pneumatic tools before turning his hand to showbiz. Additionally, he worked as a Sunday school teacher and once unsuccessfully ran for a seat in the state legislature.) "But you know what I am?" he continued. "A salesman." Of course, it's not too difficult to sell *actor* Owensby to *producer* Owensby. And while there's no danger of Mr. O mounting the Academy podium, he possesses an easygoing Southern charm alongside his Elvis-esque accent. As the werewolf, however, Owensby makes a poor Chaney substitute. Rather than moving stealthily and quickly, like Chaney's athletic and animalistic Wolf Man, Owensby moves rather awkwardly, running with his body bent forward and his arms held stiffly at his sides.

Wolfman was filmed at E. O. Motion Picture Studios in Shelby, North Carolina, owned by Earl Owensby himself. Inspired by the Tennessee-shot *Walking Tall* in 1973, Owensby decided to bring the movies to his home state of North Carolina—by building a film studio. Beginning with *Challenge* (1974), Owensby produced (and sometimes directed and starred in) sixteen films through the mid–1980s, most of them actioners released to the Southern drive-in circuit. He also rented out his facilities to outside productions (Owensby built the at-the-time largest underwater sound stage in the world for James Cameron's *The Abyss*—by converting a local abandoned nuclear power plant containment vessel). The 65-acre complex (including on-site hotel, a landing strip, soundstages, an underwater filming pool, recording/mixing studio, editing suites, screening rooms and production offices) is still in (semi) operation as of this writing, though utilized mostly for local commercials. The Earl Owensby Studios official website, however, lists as a "current project" *Wolfman 2!* In 2013, though, the *Shelby Star* reported that Owensby owed $40,000 in back property taxes, and foreclosure on the studio was in process. Let's hope ol' Earl was able to sell his way out of that one and indeed might howl once more…

With quotes from: "Carolinas Filmmaker Earl Owensby Is the Reel Deal," by Dudley Brown, Goupstate.com.

Morphology: Chaney wolfman clone
Demise: Silver dagger
Full Moon Rating: **

The Wolfman

(2010; Universal) Director: Joe Johnston; Producers: Scott Stuber, Benico del Toro, Rick Yorn, Sean Daniel; Screenplay: Andrew Kevin Walker, David Self (based on the motion picture screenplay by Curt Siodmak); Cinematographer: Shelly Johnson. Cast: Benicio del Toro, Anthony Hopkins, Emily Blunt, Hugo Weaving, Geraldine Chaplin, Art Malik, Antony Sher, David Schofield.

THE LEGEND IS ALIVE—tagline

Indeed it is. Unlike with their reboot of another famous monster, the Mummy, Universal's official remake of the lycan-classic that started it all comes close to doing the impossible—following the template of the original while effectively updating the tale for modern audiences. (Universal's *Mummy* series, on the other hand, all but ignored the Karloff classic.) I say "close to" because the movie doesn't always work. Still, apart from a few minor missteps, the 2010 *Wolfman* stands as a surprisingly reverential and enthralling update of the film that truly set the werewolf subgenre in motion.

The Wolfman announces its intentions even before the story starts, with an updated version of the classic Universal "razzmatazz" globe

Meet the *new* Lawrence Talbot: Rick Baker's striking updating of Lon Chaney, Jr.'s werewolf (played by Benicio del Toro) for Universal's excellent 2010 redux *The Wolfman*.

logo from the 1940s before seguing into the original film's "Even a man who is pure of heart…" ditty, here (literally) carved in stone and recited by the gypsy woman Maleva (Geraldine Chaplin). In 1891, prodigal son (and famous Shakespearean actor) Lawrence Talbot (Benico del Toro) returns to his ancestral home at Blackmoor, England, to investigate the mysterious death of his brother, who appears to have been torn apart by an animal. Talbot's estranged father, Sir John (Anthony Hopkins), welcomes his son, though he remains distant. Urged on by his brother's distraught fiancée Gwen (Emily Blunt), Lawrence witnesses a vicious attack by a barely-glimpsed predator at a local gypsy camp. In the process of saving several people, Lawrence is bitten. He soon recovers, but discovers, to his horror, that on the nights of the full moon he changes into a beast, killing whomever he encounters. Finally taken captive by a Scotland Yard inspector (Hugo Weaving) working with the local constabulary, Talbot ends up in an asylum. His mistreatment there, coupled with a disturbing visit from his father (who offers a surprising revelation), results in the Wolfman rampaging through the streets of London before Talbot makes his way back to Blackmoor for a final showdown with the creature that decimated his family and cursed his own life.

"Universal monster movies made me want to do what I do," enthused makeup legend Rick Baker (whose *An American Werewolf in London* transformation remains a high lycan-watermark to this day). "My feelings were that [the makeup] should be an homage, to be like *The Wolf Man*. And Benny [del Toro] also wanted *The Wolf Man*. He wanted to look like Lon Chaney Jr." (In fact, the project started with Del Toro, who, with his manager Rick Yorn, took the remake idea to Universal. A classic monster fan since childhood, Del Toro, who also served as a producer on the film, even has an original *Wolf Man* poster hanging in his house.) Baker's makeup for Del Toro's wolfman (requiring three-and-a-half hours to apply), patterned after Jack Pierce's original (Baker even employed the same basic material as Pierce—yak hair), looks strikingly similar, but with built-up ridges around the eyes (making them appear even angrier), more pronounced fangs, and a fuller mane of hair that hones the image of bestial ferocity. And though Del Toro sports pants and a loose-fitting shirt while in werewolf form, Baker covers his arms, hands, and exposed chest in a convincing layer of fur that completes the picture of the animal inside the man. Add long fingers ending in wicked claws and canine-like feet extensions, and the manbeast becomes an imposing and ferocious figure. For his work here, Rick Baker won his seventh Oscar. On the 83rd Annual Academy Awards show, held on February 27, 2011, Baker and co-winner Dave Elsey (creature effects creative supervisor) took the opportunity to acknowledge the Universal horror legacy, and the groundbreaking work of Jack Pierce, in front of 80 million viewers.

Del Toro's energetic, savage performance, as he stalks, hunched forward like a coiled spring until he explodes into fury, completes the picture. "When you put on makeup," noted the Oscar-winning actor, "all the inhibitions go out the window; anything goes, especially if you're in the makeup of the Wolfman…. You might make sounds you didn't think you'd make, and you take more chances, because it frees you. You might get a little bolder with your choices, and hope they work." And work they do. Like Chaney before him, in human form, the soft-spoken but determined Del Toro weaves a portrait of likable pathos that cements the viewer's sympathy into a foundation of dread at what he's become.

Director Joe Johnston (*Jurassic Park III*, *Captain America: The First Avenger*) lets that dread explode into Gothic-styled mayhem via a number of suspenseful, exciting, action-packed, and disturbingly violent and gory set-pieces whenever the moon rises. "The original *Wolf Man* was one of my favorite films," said Johnston, "and I really wanted to retell the story in a classic form. I didn't want it to be a slasher movie. I wanted to update it and make the characters more interesting and the story much more complex than in the Chaney film. But I wanted fans of the first film to be pleasantly surprised at the fact that they can see that story inside this one." Shooting on the melancholy moors of Dartmoor, England, and at the massive Chatsworth House (dressed with weeds and ivy to create a decrepit look), as well as at Pinewood Studios on authentic-looking, atmospheric interiors (from the grubby, lived-in town tavern to the shadow-filled, cobwebbed Great House), the filmmaker creates a full-blown Gothic atmosphere laced with dread. "[Johnston] sets up the shots in a way that makes them look interesting," lauded co-star Anthony Hopkins. "Lots of smoke, lots of shafts of light … and there's a sense of unease everywhere. It's pretty brutal, it's R-rated, there's a lot of awful stuff that happens, but it's atmosphere, mostly."

A marked departure from the original, Anthony Hopkins' characterization of Sir John strays far from Claude Rains' measured performance. Hopkins, clad in animal-skin coats (Sir John was a big-game hunter whose trophies festoon the gloomy depths of Talbot Hall), and carrying a faraway look in his intense eyes, seems on the brink of a quiet madness. His soft-spoken yet off-kilter dialogue delivery infuses an odd cadence to his pronouncements ("Never look back, Lawrence, never look back—the past is a wilderness of horrors"; or "Look into my eyes, Lawrence—you'll see that I am quite dead"; or "Life is far too glorious [to end it all], especially to the cursed and the damned like myself") that distance himself not only from those around him but from humanity itself. "The script was written in such a way that Sir John Talbot was kind of stiff, and I wanted to make him off-the-wall," explained the lauded actor, "this eccentric aristocrat who has let himself go. A strange man. I based him on a photograph of Samuel Beckett. He's got a wicked, provocative way of dealing with people and setting them off balance with a smile."

Though Rick Baker provided the monster makeup, he had little to do with the several transformation sequences, which were accomplished primarily through CGI. "I hope modern film audiences can accept that," noted Baker. "Kids who go to movies today have grown up on CGI, and that's kind of what they think effects are. That's why there's a lot of digital work in the transformation; it's what people know now." Even for us older folks who grew up on practical effects, the digital work in *The Wolfman* generally appears well-integrated with the physical effects for the metamorphoses. "I wanted this to be a transformation you hadn't seen before," noted Johnston, "and sometimes the very subtle things are the eeriest, whether it's a hand changing shape or teeth being pushed aside. That can be much more painful-looking, and it's a haunting image." The initial transformation begins with just such a subtle, haunting image—a close-up of Talbot's eye, which grows cloudy, then clears to reveal the yellow of an animal's iris. His hands elongate into claws, his feet grow into the paws of a wolf, and he crawls, agonizingly, while his back visibly shifts under his coat. A second transformation (a particularly satisfying sequences laced with irony in which a straight-jacketed Talbot begins to change while his tormenting psychiatrist uses him as a human prop to explain his "delusions" to a full lecture hall) features further disturbing details like his fingers bending sideways(!) at an unnatural angle before elongating into claws, and his mouth going impossibly wide to reveal his teeth shifting and changing.

Perhaps fittingly for a film of the new millennium, *The Wolfman* not only references its 1941 namesake, but pays tribute to a more modern werewolf classic as well. Twice the movie homages *An American Werewolf in London*—first when Talbot's lycanthrope rampages through a crowded London street in a nineteenth-century version of the Piccadilly Circus rampage from *American Werewolf*, complete with horrific (steam-powered) bus crash. Then at film's end, when Gwen confronts Talbot's Wolfman, the creature experiences a moment of recognition right out of *American Werewolf*'s climax in which we see in the monster's softening eyes the man inside the beast momentarily recognize his true love—before furiously springing forward.

When Lawrence confides his inner torment to Gwen, she answers his tragic despair with, "If such things exist, if they are possible, then *everything* is—magic, and God." It's a profound sentiment that neatly sums up not only the film's philosophy, but perhaps some of the appeal of the werewolf legend itself—that everything is indeed possible, that if a dark miracle can turn men into wolves, then perhaps magic, or God, can do even greater things.

Like its titular beast, *The Wolfman* transformed into a troubled production. Original director Mark Romanek left the project (due to "creative differences") a mere four weeks before principal photography was to begin, replaced by Joe Johnston, while various script doctors came and went, reshoots were ordered (including a revamp of the climactic lycanthrope battle), Danny Elfman's moody musical score was tinkered with and rejigged by others, and the film's projected release of November 2008 was pushed back, ultimately to February 2010. Though not a perfect updating (the asylum sequence drags on too long, with a montage of sadistic ice baths, shock treatments and drug-induced delusions that comes perilously close to going over-the-top; while the occasional CGI shot of the Wolfman racing on all fours across London rooftops fails to convince), and despite its various studio-induced trials and tribulations, the film stepped forward to don the mantle of classic remake with remarkable aplomb.

Second unit director Vic Armstrong, who came on at the tail end to supervise some reshoots, didn't necessarily agree. "I watched a rough cut of *Wolfman* several times and thought it needed a lot of work doing to it," recalled Armstrong. "Then I had meetings with the director and the studio and they told me what they wanted re-shooting. It was primarily the climactic fight, though I did lots of other bits and pieces, like the Wolfman running all over London, and through the forest at night. For the big fight they'd shot the werewolves standing up like humans, and they looked like men in furry suits, it just didn't work. So we had them quadrupeding, as we say, where they run along on all fours. Because you can't run at speed in that configuration, we used wires to assist: with wires taking off 35 percent of your weight, you can cover the width of a room in one bound. So we did a really good fight, although in all honesty I don't think the film was ever salvageable." Despite Armstrong's dour assessment, *The Wolfman* turned out to be far more than merely "salvageable," standing as a rare example of Big Budget Hollywood handling a classic property with the proper respect and energy it deserves. It's an engrossing, exciting, and at times frightening updating of a 70-year-old genre icon that earns the admiration of classic horror fans in general, and werewolf devotees in particular. I think Lon Chaney, Jr., himself would have been impressed.

Producer Sean Daniels summed it up best: "It's faithful to the spirit of [Chaney's] performance, and very, very true to the spirit of the great original Universal movie. A lot of effort has been put into that, and I don't believe that's hype. This is a really cool 21st-century version of a 1941 release using a huge amount of craft, but some of it in wonderfully traditional ways."

Receiving a mixed critical reception, and failing to make back its production budget (earning $140 million worldwide against its $150 million cost), this *Wolfman* deserved better. Hopefully, in time, it will be seen for the remarkable achievement it is.

With quotes from: "*The Wolfman*: New Moon Rising," by Mark Salisbury, *Fangoria* 279; "Faces of *The Wolfman*," by Mark Salisbury, *Fangoria* 291; "*The Wolfman*: Hair Today, Gore Tomorrow," by Mark Salisbury, *Fangoria* 290; "Makeup Effects Lab: Baker's New Recipe," by Mark Salisbury, *Fangoria* 291; *The True Adventures of the World's Greatest Stuntman*, by Vic Armstrong.

Morphology: Classic wolfman
Demise: Silver bullet; decapitation (by another werewolf)
Full Moon Rating: ****

Wolfman Never Sleeps see *The Fury of the Wolfman*

Wolfman: The Beast Among Us see *Werewolf: The Beast Among Us*

Wolves

(2014; TF1 International; Canada/France) Director/Screenplay: David Hayter; Producer: Steven Hoban; Cinematographer: Gavin Smith. Cast: Lucas Till, Stephen McHattie, John Pyper-Ferguson, Merritt Patterson, Jason Momoa.

UNLEASH THE BEAST—trailer

Canada: land of the werewolf? One might be tempted to think so given our Northern Neighbor's affinity for producing lycan-movies, and often excellent ones at that. The brilliant *Ginger Snaps* (2000) and its two less sparkling sequels (all three also produced by *Wolves*' Steven Hoban), the inventive *Werewolf Fever* (2009), the clever *The Hair of the Beast* (2010), the outrageous *Monster Brawl* (2012), the hilarious *WolfCop* (2014), and now the involving *Wolves* have all crept forth from the frozen north to warm the cockles of a lycan-lover's heart.

Popular high school football star Cayden Richards (Lucas Till) seemingly has it all—good home, nice parents, cheerleader girlfriend. But one night while making out with said girlfriend he suddenly transforms into a monster (wearing his letterman's jacket in a visual nod to *I Was a Teenage Werewolf*), then awakens in his house to find his parents brutally slaughtered. "My nightmares had come true," he narrates and takes to the road, wandering aimlessly until he meets fellow lycanthrope "Wild Joe" (John Pyper-Ferguson) in a bar, who points him towards the small town of Lupine Ridge. There Cayden takes a job as a farmhand for kindly John Tollerman (Stephen McHattie), who ultimately reveals the truth: Cayden was born into this community of werewolves but put up for adoption for his own protection. Now the town lies uneasy beneath the rule of the violent, half-crazed Connor (Jason Momoa) and his pack of half-Wolves (turned "mutts" rather than born lycanthropes). When Cayden falls for beautiful bar owner Angelina (Merritt Patterson), who Connor intends to take as his mate and so perpetuate his blood line, Cayden must face down the violent Connor and his unruly pack.

Writer-director David Hayter, scripter of *X-Men* (2000), *X-Men 2* (2003) and *Watchmen* (2009), made his directorial debut with *Wolves*. But he came to the subgenre rather reluctantly. "A producer friend of mine came to me and asked me if I would do a werewolf film," noted Hayter. "I didn't want to, because they were very risky and very difficult to pull off. So I thought, 'I need to come up with a take on this that hasn't been done before that I can relate to.' I thought about making it more of a hero's journey rather than a horror film. I thought about my own life, when I was a young man becoming an adult, and you're dealing with issues of sex and rage and violence. In a typical werewolf movie you're looking to destroy all that, but in this film, I wanted it to be something you couldn't destroy. I wanted it to be something you embrace and learn to control and love it, and I felt that would be a very different take on the genre, and something I hope a lot of people will be able to relate to."

About werewolves, Hayter observed, "They're woven into our storytelling DNA. People have been telling these stories for hundreds, possibly a thousand or more, years because they were afraid of the literal wolf in the woods. And I think because there is such an undercurrent of savagery in human beings, it's just a natural comparison to make. I think it speaks to all of our experience in our history, this notion that, yes, we have a thin veneer of civilization on us, but in a dire situation all of that could be stripped away."

Wolves succeeds because of its human—rather than lycan—side. Like with people, there are good werewolves and bad, courageous and cowardly, the searching and the knowing. Here werewolves are not necessarily monsters, though some (like people) are capable of doing monstrous things. Though set in a small rural farming community, *Wolves* does everything it can to bring lycanthropes into the 21st century. Eschewing any sense of the supernatural, *Wolves* posits lycanthropy as a natural condition. "We never use the phrase 'werewolf' in the film," commented Hayter, "and what I'm trying to do was present this creature in the same way that we presented the mutants in the *X-Men* movies. So, it's really a matter of a person—they're not magical creatures, it's just a person—who has intertwined wolf DNA inside them."

Continued Hayter, "Instead of the wolf being the dangerous, insane, monstrous part of you, the film goes to great pains to illustrate that, no, it's the human side that does the really ugly things. The wolf side, if left alone, is a very noble, pack-oriented creature." Tollerman hammers the point home when he disdainfully observes to Connor and his gang, "This isn't a pack. Wolves don't terrorize towns, or kidnap innocents, or brutalize women. You're barely wolves at all."

Wolves features two distinct types of lycanthropes. As Wild Joe tells Cayden, "The bitten ones—they're not pure; they're just mutts. Pure-bred ones, like you and me, we're born this way." The two strains are similar in that they both possess increased strength and agility (though pure-breds prove far more powerful), and both types can change at will. The moon does affect these lycanthropes (as one of the Town Wolves says, "This close to the full moon—shit, even I can barely keep from freaking out"), yet most can control it. Some of the more benign lycans have even more or less abandoned their wolf form ("Some of us ain't even changed in years," says one).

Visually, however, they're poles apart. The impressive looking pureborn Wolves, when transformed, possess smooth, almost leonine features covered in fine fur ("All of the fur you see in the film is actual animal fur," revealed Hayter, "that is put in, hair by hair, by 20 women in California at a table who would sit and punch hair all day into the outfits"). In contrast, the "mutts' (those turned into werewolves by a pure-bred) keep their human features but sport a set of nasty-looking fangs. The Wolves look graceful, powerful, even beautiful; whereas the mutts look like poor white trash with serious attitude and dental issues.

"I think putting a big snout on an actor is a mistake," said Hayter about his creatures' design. "I think, you know, sometimes the ears poking up look like elf ears. If you look at my wolves, their ears angle back because when a wolf is angry, their ears pin back against their head and it just gave it a cooler, sleeker look…. I wanted Angelina to still be beautiful and she was—well, in fact, I really wanted the wolves to be beautiful all the way around because that's how wolves are. They're not ugly, hairy, out-of-control beasts. They're very quiet, sleek, elegant creatures."

But even more important than reflecting the wolf's elegant look, the Wolves makeup allows the human—the actor—beneath it to show through. "The [werewolf] masks are molded to fit on to each individual actor's face," explained Hayter, "and I wanted them glued to the places where the actor's facial muscles move, so that when they twitch, when they frown, when they look at someone in horror, that would translate through the latex. And I think Dave and Lou Elsey, the Academy Award–winning monster makers who created these creatures, pulled that off so beautifully. All the wolves are individually designed so that when the actors are acting, you still feel them. You still feel that is Jason Momoa back there or Lucas Till or John Pyper-Ferguson. They are able to emote." It's these emotional revelations while in wolf form that help keep the characters real and approachable. Rather than simple ravening beasts, these lycanthropes are thinking, feeling manifestations of their human personalities—and this shows through the excellent makeup, displaying their character as a whole rather than in fragments (the human vs. the beast).

Regarding the film's carnage, Hayter took a less is more approach. "For example," said the director, "there's a scene with the bikers where Cayden takes down a guy, and this guy's obviously a bad dude; he deserves whatever he gets. But the point of that scene is that Cayden can't yet control what he's going through, and he tears the guy to pieces. But we framed it very specifically, so you don't see the guy, you see these ropes of blood flying as he's slashing at him. The audience knows the guy is being brutalized in a horrific way, but we're focused on Lucas and the beauty of the creature and the ferocity he is putting into the acting, rather than thinking 'Oh my God, was that a chunk of liver?' And to an extent, that can be more effective when the audience doesn't know what's happening to that guy out of frame. Their own mind can fill it in to wherever they're comfortable." Indeed, one need not always *see* a disemboweling to feel its impact, and such a restrained, cerebral and *effective* approach can be a breath of fresh air in a modern genre that so often favors gory over story.

Hayter and co. fill their film with smart dialogue, laced with subtle humor ("I need a hospital—" groans the wounded Cayden after initially tangling with Connor's pack, "or a vet or something"), tense confrontations (including a vicious throwdown between Cayden and Connor), and some thrilling set-pieces, captured via fluid camerawork and evocative lighting. Cornered by Connor's pack, Cayden desperately leaps off a cliff in a breathtaking, wince-inducing stunt that sends him crashing into the trees far below, leaving him barely alive. "I'm very proud of the jump off the cliff," beamed Hayten, "because that is an in-camera 400-foot-high fall off of the Devil's Punchbowl in Hamilton, and we knew that that one 15-second sequence would probably cost a quarter of a million dollars, but my producers were behind it and we got it, and that was amazing." Indeed it was.

Following the hero's arc, Cayden initially balks at his fate, resisting his true nature (horrified, in fact, by what he's become). Early on he fatefully narrates, "As far as a cure went, all the books agreed: there was only one—suicide." Essentially fleeing from himself, he laments, "I never knew when I'd lose control, so I just kept running, moving from town to town until time lost all meaning to me. I lived in constant fear that I'd kill again. And then one night—I did." Beneath the surface story in which Cayden finally learns he's not the mindless killer he thought he was, but the unwitting pawn of the villainous Wild Joe, lay an involving character arc delineating Cayden's gradual acceptance of his true self, aided by those who come to care about him. As Angelina describes it, "Seeing things the way we see them—the scents, the sounds—this bond with nature…. We use it, learn to control it."

Filmed from September 6 to October 25, 2012, in Toronto, Canada, on a respectable $18 million budget, *Wolves* didn't howl before audiences until two years later. And then it received only a tiny theatrical release before being dumped onto DVD in 2015. A thematically rich, well-produced, involving, and entertaining alternate take on lycanthropic legend, *Wolves* deserved better.

With Quotes from: "Q&A: David Hayter Talks *Wolves*, *Metal Gear*, and *X-Men*," by Victor Medina, cinelinx.com; "Exclusive Interview with David B. Hayter on *Wolves*," by Staci Layne Wilson, dreadcentral.com; "*Wolves* Interview with Writer and Director David Hayter," by W. Andrew Powell, thegate.ca; "Interview with David Hayter for his film *Wolves*," by Joseph Falcone, gonewiththemovies.com.

Morphology: Fur-covered wolfmen (and women); fanged humans
Demise: Slashed throat, gunshot, explosion (basically anything that could kill a human)
Full Moon Rating: ****

Wolves of Wall Street

(2002; Regent Entertainment) Director: David DeCoteau; Producers: Paul Colichman, Andreas Hess, Stephen P. Jarchow; Screenplay: Barry L. Levy; Cinematographer: Horacio Marquinez. Cast: William Gregory Lee, Elisa Donovan, Michael Bergin, Jason Shane Scott, Bradley Stryker, Louise Lasser, Eric Roberts.

Some Brokers Are a Different Kind of Animal…—tagline

Not to be confused with *The Wolf of Wall Street* (which is about a different type of monster entirely), *Wolves of Wall Street* is a well-acted, impressively photographed, but ultimately toothless take on lycanthropy as metaphor for avarice.

Jeff Allen (William Gregory Lee), fresh out of college, moves to New York City wanting to become a stockbroker. "The desire to make money is in my blood," says the over-ambitious but otherwise likable Jeff, who grew up poor and wants to provide for his folks. After striking out at various brokerage houses, he meets bartender Annabelle (Elisa Donovan), who recommends him to the prestigious Wolfe Brothers brokerage (she used to date one of their brokers ... until he was murdered). At the subsequent interview, senior partner Dyson Keller (Eric Roberts, Julia's rather-less-famous brother) tells Jeff, "This is a predatory business; we know what we want and we go after it. I'm looking for someone who's willing to make this job their life." Jeff signs on, but after he's accepted into the small group of young, haughty, immaculately dressed brokers, they get him drunk and one *bites* him. Jeff is now one of the pack, and while material success finally comes his way, so does some disturbing impulses (along with heightened senses and reflexes, and a newfound penchant for steak tartar). "You'll feel the predator in you all the time," warns Vince (Michael Bergin), Dyson's right-hand man, "the beast wanting to get out. But you must control the beast.... If you lose control, in your moments of rage you will cry out with a bloodlust like you've never felt before." When Dyson challenges Jeff over Annabelle's affections (Jeff and Annabelle have fallen in love), Jeff determines to leave the firm. But no one abandons the pack, and a deadly showdown proves inevitable.

Wolves of Wall Street looks far better than one might expect from a fringe filmmaker whose credits include *Creepozoids* (1987), *Beach Babes from Beyond* (1993), and *Bigfoot vs. D.B. Cooper* (2014). But then, director David DeCoteau has had plenty of practice, having helmed over 100 features over the past 30 years (often employing pseudonyms like Ellen Cabot or Julian Breen), many for Charles Band's now-defunct Full Moon company. Given that *Wolves* was reportedly shot in only eight days on location in New York City and New Jersey, the various nighttime cityscapes and opulent interiors look gorgeous, highlighting the surface lure of the Big Apple. About DeCoteau, *Wolves* co-star Bradley Stryker observed, "He's developed an equation for making movies fast and his way that seems to benefit everybody from the producers all the way down through the actors. I think the respect and professionalism he deals with those young actors with is also to be commended. He treats you as a professional, and you thus get your chance to begin your career with that as your perception."

Though the love of money lies at the heart of *Wolves of Wall Street*, love of male beauty (both draped in Armani and undraped in all its glory) is not far behind. For instance, the film's major werewolf attack sequence occurs at an after-hours office party when four of the attractive pack members strip down to their identical black briefs in front of a pair of (fully clothed) admiring women, then march forward on all fours like prancing cats (wolves?) to begin licking and nuzzling the obviously entranced women (who somehow manage to keep a straight face). The sequence ends with the implied eroticism turning deadly—though, disappointingly, this remains implied as well, since we hear the girls' screams (accompanied by snarls) only *after* the camera cuts away from the silly tableau. Given that director DeCoteau is known for various "homoerotic" genre films like *Leeches* and *The Brotherhood* series, which frequently showcase young men shirtless or in their BVDs, this excuse to display male pulchritude makes perfect sense.

Though light on the bite, DeCoteau goes heavy on the bark, filling this morality tale in sheep's clothing with ruthless bon mots like "The key to life is this: focus on what you want, seek it out, and attack; nothing else matters." And "You are a predator now, the old rules do not apply." The supremely confident Dyson (played with smooth, convincing arrogance by B-movie vet Eric Roberts, who went on to appear in the terrible 2015 lycan-flick *Dark Moon Rising*) even leads his pack in pissing off the roof of their building, telling a shocked Jeff, "It's *my* world and I'm just letting everybody else know it." As the film progresses, the lycan allusions become more blatant, with Dyson instructing Jeff, "We are hunters. We hunt money, power, women. We bend humans to our whims, we control their outmoded minds. We are animals, Jeff. We mark territory and we protect it." As Jeff fights against the pull of the moon, Vince tells him, "You've dreamt about the money. You wanted it so badly. We've given you the ability to go for it, Jeff—to claw, scratch, kill for it."

Unfortunately, it's little more than talk. It takes over an hour before DeCoteau shows us any physical change or actual attack, and they're both disappointingly mild. The Big Transformation, when Jeff gives in to his impulses and goes after a belligerent man outside a bar, consists only of an aggressive demeanor and a few blue veins painted on his face, marking these lycanthropes as the most minimalist werewolves ever. And the "attack" sees Jeff lunge at the man only to inflict a minor neck bite, leaving his hickey-victim shocked but relatively unharmed (and leaving the viewer wondering what the man's panicked "Oh my God!" *over*-reaction is all about).

"The moon is a constant reminder of our dominance," explains Vince. "It's our energy, our sustenance." DeCoteau backs this up with frequent shots of said orb (which seems to be eternally full) and talk of its pull, though remaining vague about whether it triggers the change or not. In keeping with the movie's lycan-minimalism, there's little more than these lunar references, an occasional low growl on the soundtrack, and talk of their "pack" to remind one that these *Wolves of Wall Street* really are werewolves rather than just your average yuppie slimeballs.

That said, silver definitely plays into these *Wolves*' mythology; for it's a sterling silver pen (a gift to Jeff from Annabelle) that comes into violent play at film's end. Taking the old axiom "the pen is mightier than the sword" rather too literally, however, the perfunctory and ridiculous climax sees the 110-pound Annabelle dispatching a quartet of healthy young men (werewolves even) by wielding nothing but this small writing utensil!

Wolves of Wall Street offers some style but little substance, beating the greed metaphor into the ground while taking far too long to get to its ultimate point of "be careful what you wish for" and "everything has consequences." With a lot of sound (dialogue) but not enough fury (action), in the end it signifies very little.

With quotes from: "Interview with Actor Bradley Stryker from *The Brotherhood* and *Final Stab*," by Brandon C. Sites, brandonsites.blogspot.com.

Morphology: Ordinary-looking young men with varicose veins
Demise: Silver pen
Full Moon Rating: **

Wolvesbayne

(2009; Active Entertainment/SyFy) Director: Griff Furst; Producers: Ken Badish, Andre Finkenwirth, Leigh Scott; Screenplay: Leigh Scott; Cinematographer: Bill Posley. Cast: Mark Dacascos, Jeremy London, Christy Romano, Rhett Giles, Yancy Butler.

A WAR HAS BEGUN BETWEEN VAMPIRES
AND HUMANS. ONE MAN IS CAUGHT
IN THE MIDDLE—trailer

---

268 • *Wolvesbayne*

And said man just happens to be a (newly minted) werewolf. Self-centered real estate developer Russell Bayne (Jeremy London) survives a chance encounter with a werewolf only to be caught up in a battle between a group of rogue vampires, headed by Vlad Von Griem (Mark Dacascos), and a cadre of vampire hunters, led by Jacob Van Helsing (Rhett Giles, who played the same character in 2006's *Dracula's Curse*, written and directed by *Wolvesbayne* screenwriter/co-producer Leigh Scott). Von Griem intends to restore life to the vampire "goddess" Lilith (Yancy Butler), the first—and most powerful—vampire, and thereby bring a new age of darkness to the world. To do this he needs six magical amulets that were used by the Vampire Council to place the power-mad Lilith in a state of suspended animation 400 years ago ("Not all vampires are bad," points out Van Helsing). And it just so happens that Bayne's great-grandfather was a hunter entrusted with the keeping and protecting of one of these amulets. Now Bayne must master his newfound werewolf powers (with the help of beautiful occult store owner Alex [Christy Romano], an accomplished werewolf herself) in order to join Van Helsing's crew in a showdown with the evil vampires.

"Part human, all terror" claims the ads for the made-for-cable *Wolvesbayne*. While the first part may be accurate, there's little of the latter to be found in this *Underworld*-lite effort. (So "lite" is *Wolvesbayne* that it features only three werewolves in toto to conduct its supernatural "war.") Bayne's silly werewolf look, accompanied by a general lack of lycanthropic activity, precludes much in the way of "terror." The sole passable beast (the full-on, *Howling*-like wolfish biped who initially attacks Bayne) is limited to two brief appearances lasting mere seconds, leaving little more than an impression of a shaggy upright wolf shape. The two werewolf Good Guys/Gals only appear in their humanoid half-stage (and only on a couple of occasions), and these prove none-too-impressive. With a ridged and wrinkled face (*sans* muzzle—or canine features of any kind), bright-colored eyes, fangs, green lips(!), and unkempt biker beard, wolf–Bayne looks like a cross between a ZZ Top roadie and a *Leprechaun* reject. Alex's half-stage appearance ("I haven't changed all the way in years," she boasts) is slightly better—big hair, bushy eyebrows on a heavy brow ridge, mouthful of oversized teeth, fine hair on her arms and exposed abdomen—but still appears more Cro-Magnon than lupine.

Adding were-insult to lycan-injury, after the film's first half focuses on Bayne discovering and dealing with the curse (or "gift" as Alex describes it), and learning about his new superpowers, the film then places Van Helsing and his vampire-hunting team center stage for the remainder, as the two werewolves become mere supporting (sometimes even background) players in their own movie. Rather than *Wolvesbayne*, a more accurate title would have been *Vampiresbayne*, as once again the "cool" bloodsuckers (all dark clothes and darker demeanors) displace the second-fiddle lycanthropes.

The film's ambitions far outstrips its meager resources (a purported $2 million budget), lending an air of

The misleading advertising for the made-for-cable *Wolvesbayne* features a wolfman far more ferocious than the disappointingly goofy-looking werewolf realized in the film.

kitchen-sink desperation to the unfinished-feeling proceedings as Leigh Scott's bloated screenplay tries to fit in far more than its straightened circumstances will allow. Scott (who wrote—and directed—another middling werewolf entry, *The Beast of Bray Road*, in 2005) brings in new characters whenever convenience dictates (including a last-minute addition to Van Helsing's team and a bunch of nondescript vampires for the final melee), and introduces far too many concepts, back stories and superhero tropes to follow (or care about). Consequently, *Wolvesbayne* becomes overloaded with exposition (much of it unnecessary), as characters talk, talk and talk rather than act: introductory narration detailing the history of the vampire clans; Alex explaining (rather than showing) to Bayne his newfound werewolf powers (and weaknesses); Van Helsing relating to Bayne the story of Lilith (covering the same ground we've already tread at the beginning); Alex speaking of her own tragic past; etc.

Likewise, Scott's crowded scenario allows for very little characterization—in either the villains or heroes (apart from self-styled "selfish prick" Bayne)—so that they become more cardboard cutouts than real characters. Consequently, the occasional martial arts and gunplay sequences carry less weight, especially because we often don't even know who these characters are (generic henchmen), while those we do know we care little about.

The characters sometimes act more out of expediency than cleverness. For instance, a museum guard, when he sees on his closed-circuit monitor a man stealing a relic, decides to go confront the thief alone rather than calling for backup or even phoning the police. Later, Van Helsing and co. torture a captured vampire minion until she gives up the information he seeks. But after they leave her in manacles, she simply transforms into mist to make her escape back to Von Griem. Why didn't she just do that in the first place? In addition, Alex seems to have some kind of psychic powers, for she "sees" Bayne in trouble and so arrives in time to thwart the vampire kidnap attempt. But whether this prescient ability is another werewolf trait or just her own special talent remains unclear. And at the end, Van Helsing produces a magic book out of nowhere to read some spells and conjure up a handy vanquishing vortex.

Wolvesbayne likens lycanthropy to superpowers. At one point Bayne tells Alex, "You're making me sound like some kind of superhero or something." These werewolves can reason fully while in wolf-form (Alex even wields a gun while in bestial mode), and possess heightened senses, strength, agility, and recovery ability. Superhero references come fast and furious, with Alex telling Bayne, "You've been given an opportunity, Russell, and with our gift comes many things powers, responsibility, enemies." Then there's the wolfsbane plant, which Alex says "is like our kryptonite." (This cleverly comes into play towards the climax when the vampires truss up the captured Alex in wolfsbane vines to keep her quiet.)

Scott's script isn't all bad, as he obviously put some thought into the werewolf mythos (before largely abandoning the lycan for the vampire in the film's second half). For instance, when Alex tells the confused Bayne, "It's a gift, Russell, not a curse," he shoots back with, "A gift I'd like to *exchange*." Scott deals with the usual full moon and silver tropes just as cleverly (and glibly). "Silver bullets impede our ability to heal," explains Alex. Though these werewolves don't age, and they can change at will, Scott doesn't ignore the lunar link to lycanthropy. "When the full moon comes I get a little crazy," admits Alex. "So I pour a little wine, put on a Sarah McLaughlin CD, and I'm good to go." He also tries to put a more scientific (or at least scientific-sounding) spin on lycanthropy by explaining the transformation as a result of "frustration, aggression—that's where it comes from. The increase in blood pressure stimulates the retrovirus and forces it to become active. With training you're going to be able to control that. You'll feel the changes instead of the anger." Alex tells Bayne that you control it through "relaxation, meditation, just clearing your head." This, apparently, is the New Age werewolf.

Director Griff Furst is an actor furst and foremost (ouch). He even played a supporting role in the pseudowolf entry *Monsterwolf* (2010). Considering his other directorial credits, including such made-for-TV cheesefests as *Swamp Shark* (2011), *Arachnoquake* (2012), and *Ghost Shark* (2013), his work on *Wolvesbayne* stands out for its general competency. He employs some clever visual techniques, such as split-screens to parallel two different simultaneous actions, and a sword stabbing into a body transitioning to an elevator door opening, metal blade dissolving into the vertical door slit. And Furst handles the sole transformation sequence well. It begins as blood suddenly drips from Bayne's mouth. Going into the bathroom to look in the mirror, he suddenly jumps, startled to see that his upper teeth have grown into fangs. Panicked, he runs to the phone but yells and drops it when his hand darkens and elongates. He then screams in pain and drops to his knees, out of sight. A few shots momentarily reveal a bestial, half-transformed face as Bayne writhes and crawls on the floor, as if trying to escape his own body. The camera then captures his shadow on the wall as he rises up and his head elongates into that of a wolf. Just then Bayne awakens in his bed—it was only a dream. Or was it? Bayne notices blood on his hands and discovers an eviscerated pig carcass(!) on his living room rug.

Wolvesbayne premiered on the SyFy Channel's "31 Nights of Halloween" in 2009. While a cut above most SyFy movies seen around this time, its overall technical competence can't overcome poor characterizations, an overstuffed script, and its unsuccessful-TV-movie-pilot feel (not helped by its superhero-like group dynamic and an open ending that sees the happy little band literally racing towards some new supernatural disaster).

Morphology: Bipedal Big Bad Wolf; plus wrinkly-faced, bearded wolfman (and woman)
Demise: Silver bullets (for the Big Bad)
Full Moon Rating: **½

Zombie Werewolves Attack!

(2009; Troma; Canada) Director: Chris Green; Producers: Chris Green, Brendan Whelton; Screenplay/Cinematographer: Chris Green (story: Chris Green, Brendan Whelton). Cast: Marcel Legault, Ginette Gaskin, Dan Gehshan, Tyler Vanderwallen, Michelle Ferguson, Stefan Bitar.

> When a pack of werewolves crash a party …
> stoner becomes the main course—trailer

With an ad line like that, you know that *Zombie Werewolves Attack!* is not exactly reaching for the (full) moon. Shot as *The Howlers Come* (and slapped with the more exploitative title when Troma finally picked it up for distribution), *Zombie Werewolves Attack!* has a group of disaffected 20-something friends (stoners, drinkers, slackers) besieged by ravening lycanthropes when their town is overrun by werewolves. When a quartet of survivors hole up at the local supermarket, they receive assistance from a "bad-ass" werewolf hunter tracking the "alpha werewolf" who started the mess. Can the little band survive until dawn? Will all the werewolves revert back to human form with the coming of the sun? Will any viewer even care by the end of this 71-minute home movie–level horror?

270 • *Zombie Werewolves Attack!*

Director/writer/co-producer/editor/cinematographer/visual effects supervisor (and probably caterer) Chris Green describes *Zombie Werewolves Attack!* as a "horror-comedy," noting, "They [the audience] are gonna laugh first as they get to know the characters, and then they're gonna get scared as the monsters attack them and start chomping them off." Despite Green's claim, there's not a single "laugh" to be found in the film's first half-hour, which consists of little more than excruciating, expletive-laden exchanges (a sure sign of impoverished scriptwriting) between inebriated friends about how they hate their jobs (at "Star Coffee" and "Top Buy"); bitchy, rambling monologues ("I feel like I'm chasing a piece of fuckin' cheese; the so-called 'American dream'—that shit doesn't exist"); and lame, half-mumbled jokes about "eating all the munchies." After that, the only laughs come in the form of derisive chuckles at the foolishness of the characters (such as when the more-or-less hunky hero spots a werewolf and screams like a girl).

Filmed in Mississuaga and Toronto, Canada, on a budget obviously in the four figures (maybe even three), this "self-funded and locally-produced" (as described by Green) feature "has been four years in the making. It was about a year of writing and saving money. Then we shot over 15 days, and I spent about a year editing and a year shopping it around." It was time definitely *not* well spent.

Regarding the all-important lycanthropes, we never see more than four werewolves at a time (and always the same ones), despite the fact that, as the hunter explains, "Most of the town are kibble," meaning that the whole city should be overrun with zombie werewolves. Perhaps this is just as well, however, since those werewolves we *do* see are nothing more than extras sporting dime store Halloween masks and gloves.

The sole transformation scene, though exceedingly brief, is relatively effective, with the victim's face darkening and her incisors elongating. Then, after a cutaway to her oblivious, arguing friends, the camera returns to reveal her fully transformed—all big hair, rubbery mask, and furry arms. "I did the transformation sequences myself using Adobe After Effects," explained Green. "It's a great tool if you have a good home computer."

Green offhandedly injects a bit of lycanthrope history into his screenplay, with the hunter noting that "everyone's heard of the Spanish Inquisition against witches in the middle ages. Most people don't know they burned a lot of werewolves in France and Germany, sometimes whole towns and families—while in human form, of course." The crime of werewolfery (thought to be the result of a pact with the Devil) was indeed punished by death in medieval Europe.

The alpha werewolf "is smart," says the hunter, who's been tracking him for years. "He's been flying from continent to continent avoiding full moons.... This alpha didn't want to change at all. That's when he came up with his flying-to-beat-the-night idea, using time zones." This offers the film's one truly clever original idea, though it's something of a throwaway (and the notion's practicality remains tellingly unexplored). Additionally, this night of terror is "not just a regular full moon. Tonight is a full *blue* moon; it's like a werewolf feeding frenzy. Normally, he would have attacked just a few people; but not tonight." So at least *some* thought went into the werewolf issue here; too bad it didn't carry over into such minor cinematic issues as character development, action, and dialogue.

"Just react when you see a werewolf," advises the hunter at one point to the distraught heroine. "Get 'em before they can get you. *Thinking* will get you killed." Thinking will also get you to ask reasonable questions that the slapdash script simply cannot answer. For instance, what exactly is a "*zombie* werewolf"? The werewolves' victims almost immediately transform into werewolves themselves (like in a classic cinematic zombie outbreak), which offers plenty of lycanthropes but negates any tortured soul-searching or questioning pathos (apart from a few of the protagonists wondering if they should kill their transformed friend or wait to see if she reverts to normal in the morning). The victims are all "half-dead zombie-like werewolves," according to the hunter. What this means exactly is never made clear, as the werewolves neither act nor look anything like zombies, and no distinction is made between the original "true" werewolf and the various "zombie werewolves."

Additionally, Green makes a point of bringing up the notion of using silver as a weapon, having one character remember that "in the movies, like *The Wolf Man*, werewolves are vulnerable to silver," and later arming the werewolf hunter with a silver throwing axe. But these werewolves seem just as vulnerable to ordinary butcher knives.

Adding brain-dead insult to dumb injury, when the "bad-ass" werewolf hunter shows up outside the supermarket, he takes out a couple of lycanthropes but is bitten before being pulled to safety (along with the attacking werewolf)

One of the *Zombie Werewolves Attack!*

inside the store. Once inside, the hunter stabs the offending werewolf to death, cuts off his own arm with his silver Ninja throwing axe, and then picks up his own severed limb and starts beating the dead horse—er, werewolf with it! Then, apparently none the worse for wear, he eschews medical attention to stand around talking, evincing no shock, no pain, nor even any significant bleeding from his freshly-severed stump. "Relax, you've got nothing to worry about now that I'm here," calmly says the now one-armed man. "I'm John Lucas, a hunter." High camp or low stupidity? Given the artless screenwriting and crude dialogue on show throughout (e.g.: "Giant fucking werewolves, like big pissed-off dogs on crack!"; "We're all going to fucking die—giant fucking poodles are going to rip us apart"), one could be forgiven for responding with a less-than-charitable answer.

Though the ludicrousness piles on even further with the protagonists running into and out of, and *back into* and *back out of* the supermarket over and over, at least it's somewhat energetic. And while the half-speed fight choreography, along with the occasional brief and amateurish "gore" sequences (arms torn off, stomachs ripped open, torsos skewered), remains only half-convincing, at least Green and co. give it the old college try. Unfortunately, in the end, *Zombie Werewolves Attack!* barely warrants a D- from Lycan U.

With quotes from: "Interview with Chris Green," by Matthew Toffolo, at the *Wild Sound Horror Film Festival*; "Interview: Chris Green," by Andrew Parker, *Notes from the Toronto Underground*.

Morphology: Bipedal party crashers
Demise: Silver axe, kitchen knife, etc.
Full Moon Rating: *

Zombies of War see *Horrors of War*

Pseudowolves

Here are more briefly covered those films in which the werewolf concept is present but decidedly minimal (i.e., a wolfman "cameo"); anthology movies in which the werewolf appears in just one of the various episodes (thus reducing a feature-length film to a short, werewolf-wise); faux-werewolf tales in which somebody merely *impersonates* or *imagines* him/herself a werewolf; and foreign lycanthropic features that failed to find their way into the English-language market in one form or another.

Las Alegres Vampiras de Vögel

(1975; Titanic Films; Spain) Director: Julio Pérez Tabernero.

In this obscure Spanish horror-comedy, which never saw an English language release, a group of performers become stranded in the Transylvanian town of Vogel when their bus breaks down. Taking refuge at the local castle, they comically run afoul of a vampire count and his equally vampiric servant. A subplot involves a man afflicted with lycanthropy who transforms at inopportune moments into a goofy Paul Naschy lookalike (minus fangs and fierceness). The movie garnered little more than derision from all quarters, even from it's own director, Julio Pérez Tabernero, who labeled it "a dreadful film. There was no script, the gags didn't work, it was insipid. I wouldn't recommend it to my worst enemy as he'd hurl a shoe at my face."

With quotes from: "*Las Alegres Vampiras de Vögel*," Cinemadrome.yuku.com.

Animals

(2010; Maverick) Director: Doug Aarniokoski (as Arnold Cassius).

Animals opens with a narrator explaining, "Each of us carries, buried deep within, the seed of our animal nature. Evolution and civilization have domesticated our impulse to feed and fight and breed without conscience or reason. But there still lurks a rare kind that can change at will. Some follow the natural order and live in peace; others have been corrupted by the taste of human blood, and hunt for flesh and pleasure. They are predators, lurking amidst the human herds. And they lure us across the line that few can cross, and few are [sic] survive—the line between man and animals." Too bad that rather than exploring this intriguing premise, *Animals* decides to spend its time primarily on random sex scenes and aimless poor-white-trash characters.

Jarrett (Marc Blucas) is a failed college athlete who's returned to his small home town to live in a trailer, work a dead-end factory job, and spend his nights at his friend's bar. Into the bar—and into his life—walks Nora (Nicki Aycox), a wild, sexy woman who ends up biting Jarrett during a moment of passion. As Jarrett experiences subsequent changes (rapid healing, heightened senses, increased aggression), the volatile Nora induces him to run away with her. But Nora's "mate," the vicious Vic (Naveen Andrews), finds them, leading to the death of Jarrett's friend and a final showdown in which Jarrett must unleash his inner beast in order to battle the creature Vic becomes.

Shot in Utah and Nevada for an estimated five-and-a-half million dollars, *Animals* is not really a werewolf film. Yes, it's about the "beast within" (or at least within some select people), but said beast, when released, appears nothing like a lycanthrope. In fact, it seems not so much connected to any real animal as some furry mythological dino-beast. And worse, its goofy CGI appearance (upright body, oblong head, huge teeth) becomes even sillier given its ephemeral, see-through form constantly bathed in misty, bright-blue light. (Perhaps we should at least be happy it wasn't *purple*; otherwise thoughts of *Barney* the friendly dinosaur might begin floating through the viewer's head.) The script studiously avoids the "W" word, and never even mentions wolves—employing the generic term "animal" (as in "They're predators that move between man and animal; they survive on human blood"). The film explores no lycanthropic lore, mentions no lunar cycles, and offers no talk of silver (in fact, Nora wears a conspicuous quantity of silver jewelry around her neck, while Vic sports gaudy silver rings on his fingers). The closest the movie ever comes to lycanthropy is a clip from *Werewolf in a Girl's Dormitory* that Jarrett watches on TV.

"The film has to be a fun, fast ride," said star Marc Blucas (*Buffy the Vampire Slayer*), "but if you had to come up with a moral to this story, it's that we all have inner strength and power, and when you let that out, it's then that we're at our most confident, when we can do our most good ... or bad. It's like the superhero analogy—you can use your powers for good or evil."

Unfortunately, *Animals* is far from a "fun, fast ride," given that very little happens for the first hour, apart from the occasional sex scene and various visits to the local bar. And the climactic battle that we've all been waiting for (when Jarrett finally "turns") remains brief and unexciting. One can't tell which cartoonish creature is which, so it remains a mystery as to just who is hitting/clawing/biting who. Even while attacking, these "animals" often (and inexplicably) zap back and forth between human (with glowing blue eyes and a mouthful of fangs) and electric-blue misty beast form.

And as to Blucas' projected "moral" about "inner strength and power," the film's real message could just as easily be: don't have unprotected sex with crazy women you meet in a bar—unless you want to turn into an animal.

Tellingly, it took nearly three years for *Animals* to see release, and then with a pseudonym in place of director Doug Aarniokoski's (*Highlander: Endgame*) real name.

"This is a very real metaphoric mythology," concluded *Animals* screenwriter Craig Spector (who adapted his own novel, co-written with John Skipp, for the script). "It's about relationships. It's about us being animals, and you can do a lot with that." Indeed you can; unfortunately, *Animals* just ... doesn't.

With quotes from: "*Animals* in Heat," by Carnell, *Fangoria* 294.

Aquí Huela a Muerto ... (Ipues yo no he Sido!)

(1990; Warner Espanola S.A.; Spain) Director: Álvaro Sáenz de Heredia.

This Spanish horror-comedy, whose title loosely translates as *It Smells Like the Dead ... (No I Did Not!)*, was a vehicle for the popular (in Spain) comedy duo Martes y Trece. The pair play a down-and-out aristocrat and his faithful servant who unexpectedly inherit an estate ... complete with its monstrous inhabitants in the form of Dracula, the Frankenstein Monster and the Wolfman (though it turns out that said creatures are phonies involved in a plot to wrest the bumblers' inheritance from them). Paul Naschy, Spain's *El Hombre Lobo* himself, plays a supporting role, though not as his famous werewolf character but as the "Comisario."

In his autobiography, Naschy wrote that, when offered the part, "I wasn't too keen, to tell the truth: I read the script and naturally it turned out to be a vehicle to the greater glory of Jose Maria Yuste and Millán Salcedo, the comic duo known as Martes y Trece.... I quickly realized that [director/screenwriter] Alvaro [Saenz de Heredia] intended, to some extent, to follow in the footsteps of the famous *Abbott and Costello Meet Frankenstein*." Naschy also noted how the director intended to use masks for his monsters, but the actor advised him to find a good makeup artist instead, which Heredia did. Naschy claimed the movie was "one of the biggest grossing in the history of Spanish cinema, amazing but true." To date, the picture has not been released to the English-speaking market.

With quotes from: *Memoirs of a Wolfman*, by Paul Naschy.

El Aullido del Diablo see Howl of the Devil

Banpaia Hantâ D see Vampire Hunter D: Bloodlust

The Beast and the Magic Sword see La Bestia y la Espada Magica

La Bestia y la Espada Mágica

(1983; Cinema International Corporation; Spain/Japan) Alternate Title: *The Beast and the Magic Sword* (unofficial). Director: Jacinto Molina (Paul Naschy).

"I believe that in Europe and within the classicism of the genre, this is one of the best films ever made about the Wolf Man." So states writer-director-star Paul Naschy of his tenth, and arguably final "prime," Waldemar Daninsky/Werewolf release. Unfortunately, his inflated opinion doesn't quite bear scrutiny.

Following the box-office failure of Naschy's previous *hombre lobo* film, *The Craving*, Naschy had difficulty raising funding until he hooked up with some Japanese backers after directing a series of documentaries for Japanese television. His first Spanish/Japanese co-production, *Human Beasts* (*El Carnival de las Bestias*, 1980), actually received U.S. distribution and did well enough to lead to five more co-productions in 1983/84, including *La Bestia y la Espada Mágica*. Unfortunately, the latter didn't fare as well and has yet to receive a legitimate English-language release (currently available only as a fan-subbed bootleg DVD).

In "a film that mixed an era of much conflict in Japan—the era of the Shogun, in which the first Europeans began arriving in that country—with the era of medieval Europe" (as Naschy describes it), Polish nobleman Waldemar Daninsky (Naschy) journeys to Japan to find scientist Kian (Shigeru Amachi), whom he thinks can cure him of his lycanthropic curse (placed on the Daninsky family six hundred years before by a vengeful witch). But when Kian's early efforts fail, Daninsky foolishly seeks aid from an evil sorceress (Junko Asahina), who entraps him, pits him against a tiger (!), and ultimately dies at his hands (claws). Now Kian's sister (Yoko Fuji), who's fallen in love with Waldemar, must wield a silver sword to end her lover's torment.

"It was very interesting to film two worlds so opposite and to make them coincide," enthused Naschy, "since it is a voyage which begins on this continent and ends in the Orient.... Artistically it is one of my best films." Well, that's debatable, for even more than a magic sword, this *Beast* falls prey to a weak script (by Naschy himself). Repetitive (Daninsky seeks a cure from a Jewish wise man—it fails; Daninsky seeks a cure from a Japanese wise man—it fails; Daninsky seeks a cure from a Japanese sorceress...) and far too talky (without saying much), rather than "epic," it feels overlong and rambling. Surprisingly, Naschy compounds the issue by failing to fully flesh out his own character, leaving Waldemar as a mostly silent observer during all the palaver. And unlike in so many other Daninsky entries, Waldemar comes off as rather less than sympathetic. For instance, he briefly moans about killing people but does nothing about it. Apparently isolating or chaining himself up during the full moon is too much trouble for this lazy chauvinist (who lets his womenfolk do all the leg work in searching for Kian). The evil sorceress spells it out when she admonishes her captive, "Your great selfishness blinded you. You only looked for a cure for your curse. You couldn't care less about what might happen to the others, just as you don't care about the damage you do when that madness overwhelms your soul." Tellingly, Waldemar doesn't utter a word of denial or protest. Such callousness (or sloppy scripting) lessens the pathos so crucial to the Daninsky (and werewolf) mythos.

Well-produced in authentic castle and Japanese settings (natural baths, temples and paper-walled houses), *La Bestia* looks like a million pesetas. And inserting the European werewolf into a Samurai film (complete with sword fights, bushido code, and tragic seppuku ceremony) brings both visual and thematic novelty to Daninksy's lycan-world. Also novel—and quite impressive—is a sequence in which Waldemar's werewolf must duel to the death with ... a tiger! The sorceress determines to "test our guest's qualities," resulting in an exciting, violent, and surprisingly convincing battle between the werewolf and the big cat, a first in lycancinema. It's a shame such unique action and cross-cultural settings are undercut by poor scripting and characterization (which extends to Naschy "borrowing" from several Universal films when Kian tries to cure Waldemar with a "Tibetan plant" [shades of *Werewolf of London*] and then briefly considers performing brain surgery [!] to "re-establish equilibrium in his brain," à la Universal's two *House* entries).

Naschy's wolfman looks much like his previous iterations, with the added fillip of some striking eyebrow ridges that gives his hirsute visage a more demonic look. And though he makes little impression in human form (with the various Japanese actors taking center stage for much of the picture), Naschy offers his usual energetic take on the savage, drooling monster (particularly during one atmospheric nighttime sequence in which the werewolf decimates a squadron of soldiers in the woods).

here about a successful three-hour Japanese release version may be rather, shall we say, optimistic, particularly given a complete lack of evidence for any theatrical showing outside of Spain.)

With quotes from: "Paul Naschy Filmography," by Jose Luis Gonzalez and Michael Secula, *Videooze* 6/7; "Paul Naschy: Spain's Greatest Horror Star," by Lucas Balbo, *Psychotronic* 7.

Big Fish

(2003; Columbia) Director: Tim Burton.

In this odd, imaginative, quirky drama from odd, imaginative, quirky auteur Tim Burton, five-time Oscar nominee Albert Finney plays Will Bloom, a man on his deathbed who recounts the story of his life through various tall tales, some of which may contain more than a grain of truth. One of his stories has him working at a circus in order to learn the name of the girl he loves and intends to marry (he glimpsed her briefly only once, but knew she was the one). The circus' owner, Amos Calloway (a garrulous Danny DeVito), knows the girl but only doles out bits and pieces of information to Will in lieu of pay. One night Will has finally had enough and goes to Calloway's trailer to demand the name. Hearing a commotion inside, and seeing the trailer rocking back and forth, Will cautiously opens the door, only to have a large black wolf spring at him through the doorway. Escaping the slavering jaws, Will picks up a branch from the ground and hurls it at the beast—who promptly turns and chases after the stick to retrieve it. Realizing the wolf merely wants to play, Will tosses it again, and the animal happily lopes off into the woods. "It was that night," Will explains, "I discovered that most things you consider evil or wicked are simply lonely and lacking in social niceties." The next morning, a tired, muddy and naked Calloway steps out of the trees. "I didn't kill anything, did I?" he worriedly asks Will. "A few rabbits," Will answers, "but I think one of them was already dead." Grimacing, Calloway notes, "That would explain the indigestion." Calloway, now impressed by Will, finally tells him the name of the girl of his dreams—before scratching his ear with his own *foot*. This brief but charming werewolf interlude posits the lycanthrope as being neither evil nor particularly dangerous, but merely misunderstood. It's a refreshing approach, leavened with some understated humor that perfectly fits within the movie's fascinating Southern Gothic fantasy universe.

Set and filmed in Alabama, *Big Fish* began as a project for Steven Spielberg, with Jack Nicholson set to star. After Spielberg left to work

Though Spanish writer-director-star Paul Naschy considers *La Bestia y la Espada Mágica* (The Beast and the Magic Sword) "one of the best films ever made about the Wolf Man," it received no official release outside of its native country (Spanish poster).

"*La Bestia y la Espada Mágica* is more of a fantasy than a horror film, with exceptional photography, which we filmed with a big budget in Toshiro Mifune's studios in Tokyo," recalled Naschy. "We filmed for a week in Spain and five weeks in Japan. It didn't do as well at the box office as *Latidos Pánico* [*Panic Beats*] because the production was more expensive, and *Latidos* was more realistic in tone. In fact, there are two versions of *La Bestia*: a 'continental' version which runs two hours; and another lasting three hours, which was distributed in Japan, where it played to considerable box office." (Note: Naschy has given conflicting accounts about various things over the years, so his claims on *Catch Me If You Can* (2002), the producers approached Tim Burton, who felt drawn to the material after having recently lost both his parents (his father in 2000 and his mother in 2002). The filmmaker injected his own unique sensibilities into the production, such as having Billy Redden, one of the original banjo players from 1972's *Deliverance*, pluck a few notes from "Dueling Banjos" while sitting on a porch. Said Burton, "If you're watching the film and don't recognize the solitary, enigmatic figure on the porch, that's fine. But if you do—well, it just makes me so happy to see him and I think other people will feel the same way."

With quotes from: "*Deliverance*: Billy's Back with his Banjo," by Andrew Buncombe, *The Independent*.

Big Top Scooby-Doo!

(2012; Hanna-Barbera/Warner Bros.) Director: Ben Jones.

The eighteenth direct-to-video Scooby-Doo feature, *Big Top Scooby-Doo* promises to "take viewers on an exciting circus-themed adventure" (so sayeth Warner Home Video publicity, anyway). On a trip to Atlantic City, the Mystery, Inc. gang (Shaggy, Scooby, Fred, Daphne and Velma) discover the Brancusi Circus is in town. Enamored of all things circus, Fred insists they check it out, even though it's closed for the night. Running into the owner (literally), they learn that a werewolf has been terrorizing the big top and robbing local jewelry stores. Promising to help, the gang go undercover as circus performers (with Scooby and Shaggy becoming instant stars for their Dog-and-Shaggy act). Is one of the circus artistes a werewolf seeking a series of jewels that legend says will give him or her the power to transform at will? Or are there human forces and motivations behind the lycanthropic larceny?

One suspect is the Scottish animal trainer being phased out of the show by the owner who considers animal acts passé. After showing Shaggy his troupe of trained baboons, Shaggy inquires if he'd ever trained wolves. "No one works with wolves," answers the Scot. "They're too unpredictable. I'd have better luck trying to train a hurricane." And the werewolves ("He's collecting jewels and making more werewolves," explains Velma after they encounter first a pair and then a trio of lycanthropes)—huge bipedal creatures topped with full wolf's heads—do indeed come on like a hurricane, smashing through glass storefronts, leaping up and over obstacles, climbing buildings, and furiously chasing Our Heroes.

Big Top showcases more intriguing supporting characters than most Scooby-Doo movies, including an insanely jealous trapeze artist, a morose Russian clown with delusions of stage actor grandeur, and a gregarious French strongman. Even more importantly (for nostalgic adults who grew up watching the antics of "those meddling kids" in Saturday morning re-runs, anyway), the film marks a return to the classic Scooby-Doo cartoons of old in that the supernatural menace turns out to be masked *human* villains. And just when it looks like things are all nicely wrapped up, a further sting in the mystery tale results in a heart-pumping action set-piece epilogue. Given its increased production values, richer animation, genuinely scary/suspenseful scenarios, and more sophisticated script, *Big Top Scooby-Doo* stands as one of the best Scooby-Doo features to date.

In 2009, famous *American Top 40* disc jockey and voice artist Casey Kasem, who had been the voice of Shaggy Rogers for over forty years, retired (Kasem died in 2014). Consequently, in *Big Top* Shaggy is voiced by Matthew Lillard, who played Shaggy in the live-action Scooby-Doo films. "I was like, what the hell is my life coming to?" joked Lillard. "I'm a trained actor! I've done Shakespeare, and here I am having farting contests with an imaginary dog!"

With quotes from: "Matthew Lillard: Biography," *Internet Movie Data Base*.

Bikini Beach

(1964; American International Pictures) Director: William Asher.

In yet another teen-targeted entry in AIP's puerile yet popular (at the time, anyway) beach party series, Frankie (Avalon) and Annette (Funicello) and the gang (including a slumming Don Rickles and Keenan Wynn as the token pro- and an-tagonistic adults, respectively) hit the beach, the surf and each other while matching wits (or lack thereof) with Eric Von Zipper (Harvey Lembeck) and his motorcycle gang The Rats. In amongst the sappy songs, surfboard shenanigans, silly slapstick (much of it involving a board-riding, car-driving, super-intelligent simian), and an amusing closing cameo by Boris Karloff as "The Art Dealer" is a throwaway gag in which Von Zipper shoots a game of pool with "South Dakota Slim" (Timothy Carey) while a leather-jacketed werewolf looks on from the sidelines. After Von Zipper departs, Slim, looking for another pool pigeon, settles on the wolf. "How are you fixed for blood?" he asks the seated wolfman. "Wanna play a game before the moon comes out?" The lycanthrope merely growls, and Slim offers a placating, "Alright, take it easy, cool it daddy; I'll play by myself."

Under all the hair was 19-year-old Val Warren, who earned his bit part as the werewolf by winning a makeup contest sponsored by *Famous Monsters of Filmland* magazine. The somewhat crude makeup, along the lines of a shaggier Michael Landon from *I Was a Teenage Werewolf*, was created by Warren himself. In a response to *Famous Monsters* editor Forrest J Ackerman's *Los Angeles Times* obituary in 2008, Warren recalled, "When director William Asher requested that I growl during my brief sequence, my ever-protective agent, 'Uncle' Forry, quickly reminded him that said role had now become a 'speaking part' and, as such, I was entitled to a cast credit as well as the Screen Actors Guild pay standard of an additional 250 bucks. When Asher consented, Forry, like the big kid he was, expressed his delight by turning to face me with a beaming smile and an exaggerated wink."

Blood Moon

(2001; Kushner Locke Company/20th Century–Fox; Canada/U.S.) Alternate Title: *Wolf Girl*; Director: Thom Fitzgerald.

Misleadingly marketed as a werewolf film ("It will rip your heart out"), the made-for-cable, shot-in-Romania *Blood Moon* is actually a stylish, well-acted, character-driven drama about what it might mean to be "normal" and how true beauty comes from within.

A seedy, old-time freak show sets up its tents in the woods outside a small town. Among the sideshow's "delights" (fat lady, she-male [convincingly played by Grace Jones], various midgets) is the star attraction, the "Terrifying Wolf Girl" Tara (Victoria Sanchez). Though she dons false fangs and claw-like fingernails for the show, Tara is actually a sensitive teenage vegetarian ("I don't eat anything with a face") who suffers from hypertrichosis, resulting in excessive hair growth all over her body (think a cute, female Jo-Jo the Dog-Faced Boy). Local misfit teen Ryan (Dov Tiefenbach) becomes smitten with Tara and offers to secretly treat her condition with an experimental depilatory serum his mother, a cosmetics scientist, has developed. Desperate to be "normal," Tara begins taking the injections. When they appear to be working, she demands, over Ryan's concerned protests, that the dosage be increased. Soon the cost of the drug manifests itself in the form of violent mood swings. The more hair she loses, the more savage she becomes, ultimately leading to violence and tragedy.

Tim Curry brings both warmth and wit to his role of Harley Dune, the freak show's owner, ringmaster, and father figure ("Used to be people liked to come see the freaks, now I can barely hold the show together," he laments); while Victoria Sanchez' sweetness and vulnerability shines beneath the hair of the outcast girl who sees beauty in others but yearns so badly for "normalcy" that she sees only ugliness in herself.

In this updating on the Tod Browning classic *Freaks* (1932), the "ugly" characters (the various sideshow attractions, teenage nerd Ryan, and Tara herself) are good, while the "normals" (personified by a quartet of attractive yet mean-spirited teens) are bad. Beauty is only skin deep; you can't judge a book by its cover; true grace comes from within... take your pick, for *Blood Moon* builds upon the classic *Freaks* template to uniquely illustrate said truism. Though not wholly successful (with some lapses in logic and a rather head-scratching, if not altogether ineffective, coda), *Blood Moon* offers an involving, thought-provoking, and ultimately heartrending take on Beauty within the Beast, and the Beast within the Beauty.

Blood of the Man Devil see *House of the Black Death*

The Blood Suckers see *Dr. Terror's Gallery of Horrors*

Bloodspit

(2006; Troma; Australia) Director: Duke Hendrix.

Cheap, tacky, tasteless, crude, vulgar, offensive, and (worst of all) *boring*—these are the adjectives that come to mind when viewing *Bloodspit*, a $4000 Australian slice of awfulness by two guys from Sydney. This SOV obscurity would have (*should* have) remained unseen if not for New York–based Troma (We'll-Pick-Up-and-Release-*Anything*) Entertainment.

With their tongues planted firmly in their cheeks, and their minds planted firmly in the gutter, co-writer/director Duke Hendrix and co-writer/producer Leon Fish create a pastiche of barely related, often-incoherent, usually sexually-oriented, and always unwatchable scenes revolving around the Nosferatu-like Count Blaughspich (played by Hendrix himself) and the wheelchair-bound "Doctor" (co-creator Fish) who's out to end the Count's evil vampiric reign. (The Doctor has dubbed his adversary "Bloodspit" because "he sucks the blood from people and spits them out like an animal!") To this end the Doctor steals the Count's crest from his coffin, thereby barring the vampire's return to the "Mirrorworld" where he can regenerate, causing the bloodsucker to become rather cranky.

Among the Count's vampire minions are his two sisters, several maids, a Scotsman (complete with ginger beard and kilt) and an odd-man-out werewolf named Rufus (played by someone billed simply as "Errol"). Reflecting the bargain-basement production, Rufus' makeup consists of lanky long hair, beard stubble, a dog nose and shoe polish. His introductory scene shows him licking his own (rubber) penis, with the Scotsman admiring, "When it comes to dick-lickin', you're an idiot savant." And things only go *down*hill from there. Appearing in only a few sequences, Rufus (who talks) says things like "My mummy had six titties." With the Count noting, "I don't like werewolves—they are dirty, smelly creatures," Rufus never changes from his (sort of) werewolf state. The "best" the film can do with his underdrawn character is offer the Count a throwaway line—"You know what I like about werewolves? You can cut off their heads and they'll grow back in five minutes"—and provide a silly but sick scene in which the Count's sister cuts off Rufus' (rubbery) phallus with garden shears for no particular reason.

Hendrix and Fish toss in everything but the bathroom sink, with most of the tasteless jokes revolving around sex and toilets (including having Rufus stick his head out of a toilet bowl at one point!). For instance, when the Doctor goes to see the Burgomeister's daughter after she's been bitten by a vampire, the Burgomeister inexplicably sports a beekeeper's hat and makes non sequitur comments like "The bees—they *fuck* me with their sharp little cocks" and "I have learned that the Cock of Man cannot fuck with Nature." Occasionally the film leaves off the toilet humor and spanking scenarios to try something actually funny, such as when the Burgomeister exclaims to the Doctor, "Surely you don't believe in vampires! The Wolf Man maybe. Frankenstein, of course. But *vampires*?!" But never fear, there's another crude joke just around the corner.

Apart from one naked female corpse at the very beginning, none of the players are particularly attractive, so that the frequent fleshy close-ups (bare thighs, bums, etc.) tend to repulse more than titillate. The filmmakers' attitude is summed up by one (thankfully clothed) sex scene between the Count and his ugly sister that culminates in a "facial"—but with blood replacing semen. And with offensiveness replacing artistry, and crudeness replacing wit, *Bloodspit* certainly lives *down* to its name.

Bloody Moon see *Lycanthrope, 1999*

Blue Demon: El Demonio Azul

(1964; Filmica Vergara; Mexico) Director: Chano Urueta.

The only sport in Mexico more popular than lucha libre ("free wrestling") is soccer, and from the 1950s through the 1970s the only luchadore (wrestler) more popular than Blue Demon was El Santo. Both wrestlers wore masks (Santo's was silver, Blue's was, well, blue), which they never removed in public, creating an almost mythic persona that transcended the wrestling ring to invade popular culture in the form of everything from toys to comic books to movies, making them into faux-superheroes. Santo began a highly successful series of films in the late 1950s in which the masked wrestler-cum-crime fighter battled all manner of baddies, from mafiosa to monsters. In 1964 producer Enrique Vergara (maker of many a Santo film) decided to showcase the 42-year-old Blue Demon in his own feature, perhaps as competition for, and a challenge to, El Santo, whose growing popularity caused him to seek higher fees for his film appearances. Blue Demon subsequently starred in 25 features over the next 23 years. Nine of them co-starred Santo, though the two were far from friends in real life (Blue seemed to resent his rival, who nearly always took the lead when they met, both in the ring and on the screen).

The rather redundantly titled *Blue Demon: El Demon Azul* (Blue Demon: The Blue Demon) opens with a couple necking in the woods, only to have their amorous activities rudely interrupted by a rampaging werewolf. Said lycanthrope, nothing if not unique in appearance (sporting big, rounded, fluffy ears to go with its big, rounded, fluffy face), grabs up the man in a deadly bear (wolf?) hug and then tosses his broken body down a hill before chasing the woman through the foggy forest (with the smoke pots obviously doing serious overtime) and squeezing her to death as well. Apparently, this type of lycanthrope has no need for claws or fangs. In fact, this werewolf sports a normal set of human choppers, the filmmakers curiously eschewing the *de rigeur* set of slavering fangs altogether.

The rather redundantly titled *Blue Demon: El Demonia Azul* (Blue Demon: The Blue Demon) introduced (to Spanish-speaking audiences, anyway) the famous Mexican masked wrestler by pitting him against scientifically-created werewolves (Mexican poster).

Here, masked Mexican wrestler Blue Demon, in his first starring role, plays ... masked Mexican wrestler Blue Demon, who, through his learned professor friend, runs afoul of a young scientist attempting to create a "super hombre" via a serum derived from wolves. Unfortunately, those he injects have the nasty habit of transforming into werewolves when the moon rises. This includes one luchadore whom the scientist sends into a bout against the champion Blue Demon as a test of his subject's superhumanness. After the second round, however, the rattled wrassler transforms, causing Blue to execute a few more moves before tossing the hirsute were-wrestler out of the ring (after which the wolfman runs from the arena, his figurative tail between his legs).

The wrestler turned neophyte actor Blue Demon recounted how he was embarrassingly ignorant of filmmaking techniques when thrust into his first starring role: "In my first film I didn't realize that the scenes were shot out of sequence. The first scene I filmed was actually the last scene of the film. There was a character who, in the script, I had been close friends with. We had worked together in defeating the werewolf. But I had never met this man before and didn't realize that our characters were already friends. When filming began, I treated him as a stranger and ignored him. Everyone on the set thought this was very funny."

Blue Demon: El Demonio Azul has never seen release outside of Spanish-speaking territories, which is a shame, as its atmospherically-shot, fog-drenched woodland settings; creepy castle (complete with copious cobwebs, gruesome skeletons, and hidden laboratory); and handful of fuzzy wolfman encounters (not to mention two vigorous Blue Demon wrestling matches) all add up to a fairly fast-paced, engaging luchadore-vs.-the-monsters outing.

With quotes from: "Meet the True Blue Demon," by Brian Moran, *Santo Street 7*.

Blue Demon y Zovek en la Invasión de los Muertos

(1973; Azteca; Mexico) Alternate Title: *La Invasión de los Muertos*. Director: René Cardona, Sr.

Blue Demon y Zovek en la Invasión de los Muertos (sort of) teams masked wrestler Blue Demon with "Professor Zovek," a Mexican escape artist who possesses psychic abilities (he studied in Tibet, he explains), in a *Night of the Living Dead* (or, more aptly, *Invisible Invaders*) zombie scenario.

A fireball lands in the Mexican countryside, disgorging a large black sphere which apparently sends out emanations that raise the dead.

Caught in the middle of this nightmare scenario are a local scientist, his daughter, and escape artist/psychic/all-round hero Zovek (whom they called in to investigate some strange rock paintings that seem to foretell of a cosmic calamity). After numerous altercations and escapes from the walking dead, Zovek manages to destroy the black sphere and deactivate the reanimated corpses. But could this happen again elsewhere, wonders a worried Zovek…

"Professor Zovek" (Francisco Javier Chapa del Bosque), an illusionist and escape artist dubbed "the Mexican Houdini," signed on to do a series of films, this being his second (the first was *El Incredible Profesor Zovek*). But before shooting on his sophomore effort concluded, Zovek died in a fall from a helicopter while performing a promotional stunt for the Suarez Brothers Circus. After Zovek's untimely death on March 10, 1972, the filmmakers hired Blue Demon to appear in a handful of scenes and so bring their production up to feature length. Blue never directly interacts with Zovek (though he supposedly communicates with him via telephone). And while Zovek battles literally scores of the walking dead, Blue faces a mere half-dozen, with one of them (played by Gerardo Zepeda) inexplicably looking like a werewolf. A burly fellow in a tight yellow t-shirt with an overabundant goatee, bushy sideburns, and protruding fangs, he attacks Blue Demon by swinging his muscular arms like a, well, trained wrestler. After Blue Demon delivers a few hits with no apparent effect, the masked hero simply runs off, while the werewolf-zombie is never seen again (though presumably he, too, becomes "deactivated" along with all the rest of the walking dead when Zovek destroys the mysterious orb).

Little happens in the film for the first thirty minutes apart from a whole lot of palaver and a five-minute Zovek nightclub act in which a straight-jacketed and chained Zovek escapes from a flaming sarcophagus. Finally, the dead rise in a creepy, atmospheric sequence set during a nighttime rainstorm. Eerily affecting, the pasty-faced ghouls climb from their coffins and tombs, and stride forth, backlit by atmospheric lighting. They battle Zovek in a smoky cavern, with Zovek then making his escape by jumping into an underground river that nearly takes him over a waterfall. Fortunately, frequent fast and furious encounters with the undead keep the pace and the (low-budget) action level high.

Professor Zovek makes for an impressively active hero, sporting a chest-baring jumpsuit and headband emblazoned with his trademark "Z" as he runs, swims, and fights his way through the various zombies. And though Blue Demon has little to do in his few, largely superfluous scenes, it's always a lift seeing Mexico's number two masked wrestling superhero on the screen. Unfortunately, *Blue Demon y Zovek en la Invasión de los Muertos* never received an English-language release; the late Professor deserved better.

El Bosque del Lobo

(1971; Amboto P.C.; Spain) Director: Pedro Olea.

Loosely based on the real-life story of Manuel Blanco Romasanta (Spain's first documented serial killer, who defended his heinous actions by claiming to be a werewolf), *El Bosque del Lobo* follows epileptic peddler Benito Freire (José Luis López Vázquez), who, due to a childhood trauma, periodically suffers from an irresistible urge to strangle women. Though Freire evinces tortured remorse after each killing, he cannot stop the compulsion. Unlike the 2004 English language retelling of the story, *Romasanta*, this first version focuses not on the famous trial—and the killer's claims of being a werewolf—but on the crimes themselves and the subsequent manhunt (complete with pitchfork-wielding villagers). Though brought to vivid nineteenth century life through its authentic settings, costumes and portrayals, the rather dull *Bosque* spends far too much time on Freire's travels from town to town and the messages he delivers for various characters, punctuated at times by his "spells" of violence.

The only reference to lycanthropy in the film, apart from the folk song bookending the picture, comes during a tavern scene in which Freire and a Bible salesman companion overhear several locals swapping stories of werewolves. Later on the road, Freire's friend puts it all down to superstition and posits, "I think the alleged werewolves probably suffered from epilepsy." Freire merely walks on pensively. To date, *El Bosque del Lobo* has seen no official English language release.

Breaking Wind

(2012; Grindstone Entertainment) Director: Craig Moss.

Though the title suggests a spoof of the *Twilight Saga* entry *Breaking Dawn Part 1* (fourth in the series), this is a (failed) attempt to skewer the third *Twilight* film, *Eclipse*, in which vampire Edward must form an uneasy alliance with rival Jacob (a werewolf) to protect their mutual love interest Bella from a vindictive vampire and her horde of bloodthirsty "newborns." Miles away from the previous year's uneven but far funnier *Twilight* spoof *Vampires Suck*, *Breaking Wind* occupies its entire running time with crude fart jokes and sex references, confusing clever parody with lowest-common-denominator scatological humor.

Breaking Wind handles its werewolfery about as well as it does its humor (poorly). While there's occasional talk of Jacob (and his homeys) being a werewolf, he *never* transforms or appears in wolf guise. In fact, Jacob does nothing but eat constantly and sniff his own flatulence (which perfectly sums up the film as a whole). And the tale told by the Native American chief (Danny Trejo collecting another one-day paycheck) of the tribe's first encounters with the "Cold Ones" devolves into pointless pop culture stupidity: "We were great spirit warriors—shapeshifters. We'd transform into powerful Autobots that fought the Decepticons. Our children turned into Smurfs. And we formed an alliance with Captain Crunch and fought the Hamburglar."

Apart from spoofing the original's hunky Taylor Lautner by casting the tubby Frank Pacheco as Jacob (and having the jelly-roll actor constantly shirtless while frequently going on about "my glorious abs"), there's little wit and less wisdom in this misguided parody. Mean-spiritedly concluding with condescending clips of real "Twi-hards" (hardcore *Twilight* fans), *Breaking Wind* is the cinematic equivalent of a fart in a windstorm.

The Brothers Grimm

(2005; Dimension/MGM; USA/UK/Czech Republic) Director: Terry Gilliam.

"It may not be the deepest film I ever made, but I do think there's real enchantment in it," noted *The Brothers Grimm* director Terry Gilliam, a Monty Python alumnus and creator of such imaginative efforts as *Monty Python and the Holy Grail* (1975), *Time Bandits* (1981), and *Brazil* (1985). Indeed there is, for *The Brothers Grimm* stands as a funny, frightening, and captivating take on classic fairy tales—with a werewolf cameo added to the mix.

In 1811 French-occupied Germany, brothers Will (Matt Damon) and Jake (Heath Ledger) Grimm make a living by posing as monster hunters, preying on the gullibility of the peasantry by exorcising witches and hauntings they themselves stage. But when they encounter a real supernatural menace infesting the forest of Marbaden, they must summon up the courage—aided and abetted by brave local lass Angelika (Lena Headey)—to battle the evil witch kidnapping young girls in an attempt to restore her own youth. Among the monsters they must face are sentient trees that attack with their branches and roots, a possessed horse that spits out spider webs to ensnare and swallow its prey, a blob of black mud that absorbs its victim before transforming into a sinister gingerbread man, and a werewolf—a woodsman (Tomas Hanak) enchanted by the sorceress and forced to do her bidding.

Surprisingly, digital effects supervisor John Paul Docherty drew his inspiration for the movie's lycanthrope from the 2002 remake of *The Time Machine*. "In all honesty, we were not all that impressed by some of the current CG wolves in films," noted Docherty. "We looked at the animation of the CG Morlocks in the *Time Machine* as a nice mix between human and animal behaviors." The CGI werewolf—a huge, shaggy, four-legged wolf with human-looking eyes—isn't entirely convincing, yet it works well enough within the film's dark fairy tale milieu, and its brief screen time (appearing in only three short scenes) insures it doesn't wear out its welcome. First seen in lupine form, it startlingly transforms into a fur-clad woodsman when the beast suddenly stands on its hind legs and painfully snaps its head backwards at an impossible angle. To a cacophony of bone-crunching cracks, limbs contort and change, and a human head emerges from the exposed neck. No mere monster, this werewolf turns out to be Angelika's missing father, adding a touch of pathos to the menace.

Rounding out the film's fantastical scenario (filled with references to the classic folk tales—an old crone peddling apples, a child wearing a red cloak, two others named Hans and Greta...) are a pair of human antagonists on the trail of the Grimms—ruthless French General Delatombe (Jonathan Pryce) and his torture-happy toady Cavaldi (Peter Sormare). The droll Pryce and the buffoonish Sormare offer amusing contrasts in villainy, while Matt Damon and Heath Ledger, as the bon vivant Will and the scholarly Jake, embody a sense of fun that proves critical in balancing the often dark doings.

Director Terry Gilliam originally wanted Johnny Depp for the part of Will, but producer Bob Weinstein nixed that idea, feeling that Matt Damon had more star power. Robin Williams was originally cast in the role of Cavaldi but dropped out, with Peter Stormare landing the part.

Gilliam clashed terribly with executive producers Bob and Harvey Weinstein, heads of Dimension Films, both during and after production, resulting in a ten-month delay in the movie's release. The wait, however, for this incredibly imaginative and visually stunning (with over 800 effects shots) take on classic folklore proved well worth it.

Gilliam shot in the Czech Republic for budgetary reasons ("This is an $80 million movie, which would probably cost $120 million to $140 million in America," noted star Matt Damon). Though *The Brothers Grimm* earned $105 million worldwide, its $88 million production cost (plus the additional expenses for advertising and distribution) made it less than a fiscal success. Fortunately, the engrossing, enchanting, and entertaining *The Brothers Grimm* proved to be an *aesthetic* one.

With quotes from: "Terry's Flying Circus," by Richard Corliss and James Inverne, Time.com; "*The Brothers Grimm*: A Gilliam Fairy Tale," by Alain Blellk, AWN.com; "Damon, Prague, Star in 'Grimm' Fairy Tale," by Carol Memmott, Usatoday.com.

Buenas Noches Señor Monstruo

(1982; Jose Frada Producciones Cinematograficas; Spain) Director: Antonio Mercero.

"For Jose Frade I made a parody of my most emblematic character, the Wolfman," wrote Paul Naschy about *Buenas Noches Señor Monstruo* (Good Night Mister Monster) in his autobiography. "This time it wasn't the legendary Waldemar Daninsky, but a creature called HL [short for 'Hombre Lobo']. It was directed by Antonio Mercero in his usual efficient style.... The unimaginative story related the exploits of a group of retired classic monsters and their encounter with a bunch of unbearable child singers (the juvenile pop group Regaliz). However, the film benefited from high production values and was a big hit with the kids. It's still often shown on TV." In Spain, perhaps, but to date it has yet to make it to America in any legitimate form.

A quartet of children (played by pre-teen pop band Regaliz) becomes lost in the woods during a field trip and stumble across a castle occupied by Dracula, the Wolf Man, Quasimodo, and Dr. Frankenstein and his creature. The famous monsters bemoan their current fate: "No one is scared of us anymore," laments Dracula, "people make fun of our memory." Dr. Frankenstein decides, "We'll show them how wrong they are!... We'll impose fear on the world once again." To this end they decide to "educate the new generation" and set about terrifying the four kids who've stumbled into their grasp. But things don't go quite as planned, as the four tweens end up humiliating the monsters time and again (employing slingshots and fireworks), until finally finishing with a ridiculous "dance-off" and a closing musical number, "The Dance of the Monsters" ("Get down on the floor and start to howl / Swing your arms wildly in the air / And yell like you're a fierce wolf").

The movie's opening credits demonstrate that the filmmakers' hearts were in the right place (if not necessarily their heads), with the names unspooling over tinted stills from classic (and not-so-classic) horror films—everything from Universal's *Dracula, Bride of Frankenstein* and *The Wolf Man* to Hammer's *Phantom of the Opera*, AIP's *How to Make a Monster* and even the Bela Lugosi poverty-row programmer *The Ape Man*. Unfortunately, once the movie proper begins it becomes painfully obvious that lowest-common-denominator humor is the order of the day (with an opening gag in which a 12-year-old rascal shoots a dart at a lizard only to miss and strike the ample backside of his teacher). Things only go from puerile to worse when the kiddo quartet enters the castle domain of the monsters. Silly scenarios and stupid jokes prevail (e.g., whenever the "butler" Quasimodo opens a door, *he* makes a loud creaking sound, explaining, "The doors in the castle don't make noise, so I do it").

As "El Hombre Lobo," Paul Naschy is introduced in close-up holding a human skull—which he then uses as a bowling ball when the camera pulls back to reveal him knocking over a set of human femur pins. Naschy really has little to do as "HL." His best scene comes when they all sit down for a rather uncomfortable dinner. As the moon comes out, HL sprouts hair on his hands and begins to howl. At this, the tykes then break into the terrible "Wolf Man Song," with lyrics like, "He'll howl maniacally / He sounds like an out of fashion singer / It's all just as weird as Tarzan, as Tarzan square dancing." Oddly, after the song, this Hombre Lobo is normal once more, with human hands and no more need to bay at the moon.

Later, the moon appears yet again (apparently if hidden by clouds, it has no affect on this Wolf Man) and HL fully transforms (via a few simple dissolves). Looking like a scaled-down version of his Waldemar Daninsky werewolf (minus the drooling maw and energetic viciousness), Naschy is subjected to one indignity after another. First the two girls think him to be one of their two companions trying to scare them again (after having done so with masks earlier) and begin beating the Wolf Man about the head and shoulders, with one even sticking a flashlight into his mouth and turning it on, making the werewolf's eyes light up! After the beaten beast-man flees, he encounters the two boys, who, thinking him to be one of the *girls* in costume, drops a chandelier on his head!

"Like Boris Karloff, Bela Lugosi, Lon Chaney and Christopher Lee, I had been forced into self-parody," lamented Naschy, "although I had to face Regaliz instead of Bud Abbott and Lou Costello. The film angered my fans, who practically accused me of prostituting their beloved Waldemar Daninsky."

The picture concludes with a song-and-dance number (the film's *fifth*) set in the wax museum where the humbled monsters have now found "work," with the quartet of talentless tykes performing "Buenos Noches Senor Monstruo." The "werewolf" verse: "Then comes the Wolf Man / What a silly fright / He's a good person / He turns into the Wolf Man when the full moon rises / And when he's transformed / He gets excited for any reason / And he's more bestial and criminal / Than Red Riding Hood's wolf." Sigh. Such silly shenanigans will indeed have any viewer old enough to shave wanting to bid "Good Night" to these Monsters.

With quotes from: *Memoirs of a Wolfman*, by Paul Naschy.

The Cabin in the Woods

(2011; Lionsgate) Director: Drew Goddard.

What do killer clowns, vicious mermen and rampaging werewolves have in common? They're all part of the horrific menagerie under *The Cabin in the Woods*. Not a werewolf movie, but a movie that just happens to include a werewolf (along with literally dozens of other supernatural creatures), *Cabin* tells the tale of five college friends who journey to a remote cabin (in the woods, naturally) only to be set upon by a group of "pain-loving hillbilly zombies." But this turns out to be only the tip of the monstrous iceberg, as they're all merely puppets in a much bigger game of sacrifice and appeasement in an ongoing effort to prevent the "old gods" from rising and destroying the world.

The lycanthrope appears in only three brief scenes (and only in full-on wolf form, as we never see the human beneath the hair nor any transformation). It first enters the picture after more than an hour in, when the two surviving protagonists escape the zombies topside only to end up on an impromptu tour of the terrifying menagerie residing in a massive complex beneath the cabin. Huddled inside a clear cube moving elevator-like through the labyrinthine structure, at one point they see the snarling lupine face and massive shoulders of a werewolf looming out of the darkness (looking much like the impressive *The Howling*/*Dog Soldiers* style of lycanthropes). Later, during the first bloody free-for-all after all the creatures have been released and the human inhabitants vainly try to subdue them, in among the attacking giant cobras, bat-monsters, and deadly wraiths, the werewolf takes down a terrified technician. And finally, at the climactic confrontation in which one of the wavering protagonists seemingly turns on the other, the wolf-beast appears once again to attack and disrupt the confrontation.

Though light on lycanthropy, *Cabin in the Woods* remains heavy on both chuckles and chills, not only due to its excellent production values (the estimated $30 million budget appeared to be money well spent, as it looks like every penny ended up on the screen) and inventive monsters, but also to its likable characters—on both ends of the puppet strings. The quintet of imperiled protagonists are painted with a finer brush than in most horror flicks, and the behind-the-scenes string-pullers, personified by a pair of shirt-and-tie office workers with a jaded sense of humor, allow the viewer to identify with those on both sides of this tragic, potentially world-shattering situation. This *Cabin in the Woods* is well worth a visit.

The impressive but all-too-briefly-seen werewolf from the creepy and clever *Cabin in the Woods*.

Capulina Contra los Monstruos

(1973; Panorama Films; Mexico) Director: Miguel Morayta.

Gaspar "Capulina" Henaine was a portly Mexican comedian who specialized in playing lovable imbeciles, generally alongside his partner Antonio "Viruta" Campos. This low-rent south-of-the-border Abbott and Costello–esque team split up in 1967, and Capulina went on to even greater success on his own, while his former partner (who initiated the split) fell into obscurity. With his intellectually-challenged antics aimed at the pre-teen set, Capulina met vampires (*Capulina Contra los Vampiros*, 1970), mummies (*Capulina Contra las Momias*, 1972) *plus* Frankenstein's Monster and the Wolf Man in *Capulina Contra los Monstruos* (Capulina vs. the Monsters). Though highly successful in Mexico,

Capulina remained strictly a Latino phenomenon, and his films failed to break into the English-language market.

In *Capulina Contra los Monstruos*, newsstand vendor Capulina is kidnapped by a mad scientist in order to employ the energy from the timid man's own overweening fear to restore life to the quartet of dormant monsters the scientist keeps in his secret lab. This done, the monsters frighten a few citizens in town, engage Capulina in a pillow fight, and end up back at the lab where they comically face off against Capulina and his quartet of kid friends (who vanquish the creatures with happy thoughts of ice cream!).

With its suitably savage and hirsute appearance (a cross between Jo-Jo the Dogfaced Boy and Paul Naschy's Waldemar Daninsky), the Wolf Man comes off best of the four creatures, as the poor makeup jobs on the Vampire, the Frankenstein Monster, and the Mummy look more silly than scary. This werewolf sports a long furry tail, however, which the contentious Mummy bites at one point. He also incongruously wears a herringbone coat and cape *à la* Sherlock Holmes, and converses quite civilly with his four monstrous *companeros*.

Capulina inadvertently summed up this juvenile film best when he commented, "This [movie] has one of my favorite scenes: when I eat some onions and conquer the monsters with my breath."

With quotes from: "Investigating 'Investigador' Capulina," by Brian Moran, *Santo Street* 14.

Cast a Deadly Spell

(1991; HBO Pictures) Director: Martin Campbell.

In this made-for-cable-TV movie, Fred Ward (*Tremors*) plays Phil Lovecraft, a world-weary private eye (and former cop) in a very different 1948 Los Angeles—a place where magic, monsters and mythical creatures are commonplace. "Everyone uses magic," various characters tell him, but not Lovecraft, who, "for personal reasons," relies on his wits and fists rather than charms and potions. Contracted by a wealthy collector (David Warner) to track down a stolen book, the Necronomicon, Lovecraft soon learns that said demonic tome is the key to bringing about the apocalypse by unleashing the "elder gods" on our world.

At one point, after being targeted by a rune-casting gangster (à la *Curse of the Demon*), Lovecraft ends up at his old precinct house, where his former boss, Lt. Bradbury (Charles Hallahan), is giving the third degree to a suspect in his office—a werewolf (played by Jim Eustermann). Wearing a tatty cap, scarf and overcoat, and sporting mottled skin, huge bat-like ears, scraggly facial hair and an oversized set of choppers, this moth-eaten manbeast looks more like a derelict demon than a classic wolfman. The werewolf merely snarls and howls at the copper's threats, prompting the Lieutenant to retort, "Your buddies can't help you now. And if you think they'd lift a paw to help you, you're an even bigger chump than I figured." As he has the uncooperative werewolf taken away, the Lieutenant wearily comments to the arriving Lovecraft, "God, I hate full moons."

The minute-long werewolf interlude over, *Cast a Deadly Spell* gets right back to the business at hand—cleverly homaging and blending film noir cinema and H.P. Lovecraft mythology. Fans of both subsets will be well pleased with the movie's myriad noirish touches and demonic twists and turns. Everything from hard-boiled narration ("It started that night, and it started with a woman; it always starts with a woman") and duplicitous femme fatales to arcane books and insanity-inducing apocalyptic creatures deftly combine to create a fascinating Chandler-meets-Lovecraft milieu. Though not everything fits together perfectly (a cavorting gargoyle-like demon, for instance, whom Lovecraft kicks in the crotch in order to escape, comes off as more silly than sinister), other more subtle moments of humor, combined with engaging characters brought to vibrant life by a cadre of fine actors (including Ward, Clancy Brown, and Julianne Moore), frequently fills in the cracks, making *Cast a Deadly Spell* a novel and entertaining trip to a time and place that never was but perhaps should have been.

El Castillo de los Monstruos

(1958; Sotomayer; Mexico; b&w) Director: Julián Soler.

In this early Mexican comedy which never found its way north in dubbed or subtitled form, Clavillazo (comedian Antonio Espino) must rescue his lady love from a mad scientist named Dr. Sputnik who creates monsters in his castle lair. Said creatures consist of a Frankenstein Monster (who serves as the butler), a sport coat–wearing apeman kept locked behind bars, a poor man's Creature from the Black Lagoon, a living mummy, a vampire, and a wolfman. The latter sports a dark suit (Mexican monsters are nothing if not nattily dressed), hairy hands with long fingernails, and rather sparse makeup consisting of a mouth full of scraggly teeth, large ears, slicked-back hair ending in a widow's peak, and unkempt beard and whiskers. Completely under the control of the hypnotic Dr. Sputnik (who uses a whistle to summon his creatures), this impoverished lycan doesn't even appear until an hour into the film, and then does little more than grab the misbehaving heroine and carry her to the lab before meeting his fate at the hands of the caged ape-monster, who chokes the life out of this *hombre lobo*.

Shadows, fog, a dank castle (complete with alligator pit and secret laboratory), and a bevy of classic creatures all bode well for some monstrous south-of-the-border entertainment. Unfortunately, the picture primarily focuses on the goofy antics of the comedic hero, with the monsters largely relegated to the film's final third, and then utilized mainly to chase Clavillazo around the *castillo*. On the plus side, director Julián Soler (*Santo vs. Blue Demon in Atlantis* [1970]) managed to secure the services of Mexico's premier vampire, Germán Robles (*El Vampiro* himself), for a bloodsucking cameo. "[Soler] asked me," recounted Robles, "'You are filming right now *Vampire's Coffin* [sequel to the classic *El Vampiro*]. Would it be possible for you to come over and do a cameo part for me? With the same costume?' [*Coffin* producer Abel] Salazar didn't even know about it." Solar also managed to insert some genuinely amusing demises for two of his monsters, having the gill-man devolve into a flopping fish when hit with a mysterious chemical and the Frankenstein Monster dissolve into a pile of bolts and clock parts upon being electrocuted.

With quotes from: "El Vampiro Speaks!" by Bryan Senn, Richard Sheffield and Jim Clatterbaugh, *Monsters from the Vault* 24.

Cazador de Demonios

(1983; Cinematografica Intercontinental; Mexico) Director: Gilberto de Anda.

With a title that translates as "Demon Hunter," *Cazador de Demonios* is rather unique for a Mexican horror movie in that it hangs its horror-hat on indigenous folklore rather than warmed-over Hollywood terrors (at least for the most part).

Like most countries, Mexico has its own version of the werewolf figure. Based on ancient Aztec legends, the "nahual" was an evil warlock who could shape-shift into a dark coyote to drink the blood of its victims. Since the invading Spaniards didn't bring much in the way of werewolf lore when they colonized Mexico in the mid–1500s, the native myths remained largely intact and unaffected by outside influence. The same can *not* be said of Mexican horror cinema, however. Movie Mexi-wolves tended (like the rest of south-of-the-border horror films from the 1950s onward) to follow the lead set by Hollywood, so that shapeshifting warlocks gave way to the more traditional tortured-soul "Larry Talbot" variety of wolfmen. While *Cazador de Demonios* borrowed the traditional Talbot look (sort of) for its monster, it cast the demon-beast in the mold of its ancient homegrown legends.

After a farmer kills a shaman, the locals must deal with a vengeful nahual. While the doubting sheriff tries to pin the rash of grisly murders (all bloody attacks and severed limbs) on a rogue bear, the village priest melts down the church's communion cup to make silver bullets…

Actor-turned-first-time-director Gilberto de Anda shows the beast-man only sparingly (shadows, quick cuts, point-of-view shots), which frequently works in the film's favor, building suspense while obfuscating the somewhat subpar makeup job. Resembling a mangy Lon Chaney knock-off, complete with Talbot-like wolf-feet and clawed hands, the poorly-dressed (but imposingly tall) nahual does offer a rather more wolfish appearance in its hairy head and face, with a protruding snout and mouth full of fangs.

Unfortunately, the atmospheric and unique *Cazador de Demonios* has yet to receive an English-language release.

Chabelo y Pepito Contra los Monstruos

(1973; Alemeda/Azteca; Mexico) Director: José Estrada.

In this Mexican children's film (which never received an English-language release), a pair of mismatched cousins, Chabelo and Pepito, go on an outing with their scout troupe, only to break away from the pack when Pepito's pesky older sister joins them (she's dating the scout leader). Encountering an escaped (man-in-a-suit) gorilla, the two scamps flee to a nearby cave, where they find a living mummy, a second-rate Creature from the Black Lagoon (who battles—and bloodily kills—the gorilla), a Frankenstein Monster (in a crude mask), a blue-faced Dracula, and *El Hombre Lobo* (the Wolf Man). After much running about in the cave and the "haunted" hacienda above it, they discover the monsters are robots created by a supervillain mining some new powerful element in the vicinity.

Aimed squarely at the kiddie crowd, *Chabelo y Pepito Contra los Monstruos* offers the odd—and more than a little creepy—sight of 38-year-old Javier "Chabelo" López playing an oversized kid with a high-pitched voice and a "glandular condition" that causes him to eat almost constantly (cue the numerous hunger gags—including Chabelo chasing after a now-terrified Dracula when informed by Pepito that vampires make good sandwiches!). Childish in every way, the film delivers very little else and particularly short-changes its lycanthropic element. Onscreen for less than a minute, this Wolf Man howls in a couple of shots before being abruptly pushed into a snake pit by a gaggle of boy scouts. *El Hombre Lobo*, decked out in stylish slacks and turtleneck (it *was* the Seventies), boasts effective Lon Chaney makeup, complete with full facial hair, canine nose and prominent fanged under-bite, making him the most impressive-looking monster of the admittedly tatty bunch. Too bad the script gave this token werewolf so little screen time and nothing to do.

El Charro de las Calaveras see *Rider of the Skulls*

Cirque du Freak: The Vampire's Assistant

(2009; Universal) Director: Paul Weitz.

Like the *Harry Potter* and *Twilight* series, *Cirque du Freak: The Vampire's Assistant* is adapted from a series of popular young adult books (this one by author Darren Shan). Unlike those other two mega-successful series, however, *Cirque* failed to take off, despite its open-endedness so obviously tailored toward a cinematic franchise (pulling in less than $14 million domestically against its $40 million budget). The story focuses on teenager Darren (Chris Massoglia), who falls afoul of the traveling freak show Cirque du Freak, one of whose members is a vampire (John C. Reilly). Turned into a "half-vampire," Darren becomes embroiled in an age-old vampire war between those bloodsuckers who kill humans and those who don't.

"I re-watched *Freaks* [1932] right before making this," recounted director Paul Weitz. "It's only about 60 minutes long, but it makes a big impact, that's for sure. The same thing holds true here as in that movie. When you're thinking about portraying strange-looking people, I suppose the questions of political correctness can arise. In this, since we're also including vampires and things that can't humanly happen, like the Wolf Man, there was a weird sort of line to walk where I didn't go in the Tod Browning direction of using people who, in those days, really would have been in a freak show. For me, it was all metaphor." And like that Tod Browning classic, *Cirque* failed to resonate with audiences of the time (though one suspects this to be due more to its vapid lead teen character and rambling story than to the viewers' discomfort with the notion of "human oddities").

Among the various acts and freaks at the Cirque is the Wolf Man (played by special effects artist Tom Woodruff, Jr.), a two-legged hybrid covered in hair and sporting a misshapen, vaguely dog-like head. Said creature is no werewolf, however, as his shape appears to be permanent (i.e., no transformations). Kept in a cage, the savage "Wolf Man" only appears briefly in two scenes—the first during the Cirque's show where the savage manbeast rips the arm off a front-row patron. But wait, the screaming woman is part of the circus itself—and her arm immediately grows back! The second Wolf Man appearance comes when a quartet of evil vamps invades the Cirque's camp, and one of the freaks lets the beast-man out of his cage, resulting in a few seconds of snarling and a couple of vampires sent flying through the air before the Cirque's owner stops the fight.

This same year, *Cirque* director Paul Weitz's younger brother Chris Weitz made *The Twilight Saga: New Moon*, winning this case of box-office sibling rivalry hands down.

With quotes from: "Cirque du Freak the Vampire's Assistant Comes to Town," by Chris Haberman, *Fangoria* 288.

Cold Hearts

(1999; Raven Releasing International/Shifty'z Worldwide Entertainment) Director: Robert A. Masciantonio.

Cold Hearts focuses on twenty-something Viktoria (Marisa Ryan) and her friends Alicia (Amy Jo Johnson, one of TV's *Mighty Morphin Power Rangers*) and Darius (John Huertas), who like to hang out at night at a Jersey Shore boardwalk. Fifteen minutes into the picture we learn that they're all vampires. Big bully vampire Chaz (Christopher Wiehl, who looks and acts more like a cranky frat boy than a bad-ass creature of the night), leader of a gang of *Lost Boys* wannabes, makes their life an (un)living hell until the new boy in town, Seth (Robert Floyd), steps in to oppose Chaz' harassment. Seth also seems to possess preternatural powers. For instance, he can smell the rain coming, moves with lightning speed, and easily manhandles one of Chaz' lieutenants. Is he also a vampire? Nope; at film's end we finally learn he's a werewolf. Unfortunately, so little is made of this novel notion that it comes off as a mere lycanthropic afterthought. (Seth tells Viktoria that one night while hiking in the Appalachian Mountains he was attacked by a "huge gray shape"—the only reference as to how he became a monster.)

While shots of the full moon intimate that Seth's transformation is connected to the lunar cycle, the mechanics remain vague, as Seth appears to choose exactly *when* to change. Said change finally comes at the climactic confrontation with Chaz. "Everything's not what it appears to be," Seth tells the vampire, who's called Seth out for a final showdown. Suddenly, growling on the soundtrack and a bit of shaky-cam photography signals the instantaneous transformation, and there stands Seth—sporting an enlarged prosthetic nose, pointy ears, a light beard, bushy eyebrows, wrinkly skin, a widows peak and a standard set of fangs in a disappointingly minimal wolfman makeup that looks like a plasticized update of Henry Hull's *Werewolf of London*. The subsequent battle lasts a mere 30 seconds before Chaz knocks Seth to the ground (with a stick!), then grabs a flimsy wire-mesh trashcan and raises it above his head in order to crush the prone Seth (or at least give him a headache). Fortunately, Viktoria steps in to plunge her arm through Chaz's chest and pull out his beating heart. Some werewolf…

Apart from this heart gag and a bit of blood spatter, the only real makeup on display is a sizzled vampire who'd stayed out in the sun too long. But the gruesome effect (courtesy of Tom Savini Ltd.) goes begging when the body abruptly turns to ashes via a poorly superimposed (and obviously CGI) dust cloud.

Competently shot in Ocean City, New Jersey, on a $900,000 budget, *Cold Hearts* at least boasts decent lighting and plenty of camera movement, courtesy of first-time director Robert A. Masciantonio, who went on to do … little else.

More a character study of aimless Gen X youth culture than an action or horror film, *Cold Hearts* is short on activity but long on talk. Unfortunately, none of the leads have the screen presence or acting chops to carry the slight story and hold one's interest through the various confessions, soul searchings, and protestations of ennui. Tellingly, the most entertaining part of the film is a genuinely funny post-credits comedy improv "skit" performed by first and second assistant directors Mark Myers and Marlon Grace as officers Felching and Fife, two security guards who find the gooey Chaz remnants on the beach the next day.

In a 2012 interview, Masciontonio stated he was desperate to remake *An American Werewolf in London*. "It's one of the movies that made me want to make horror movies," said the director. "I've already written the spec [script].… I feel like anyone else that makes it is going to eff it up big time. I'll take the responsibility of saying I'm the only one that can do it right." The way Masciontonio handled his last-minute werewolf in *Cold Hearts*, however, makes one think that these sentiments are just so much delusions of lycanthropic grandeur.

With quotes from: "Icons of Fright Interview with Robert Angelo Masciontonio," by Smith, Iconsoffright.com.

Colmillos, el Hombre Lobo

(1993; Torrente S.A.; Mexico) Director: René Cardona III.

Obviously taking its 'lycanspiration' from *An American Werewolf in London* (at least in regards to its *hombre lobo*), this crude but still effective south-of-the-border horror could easily have been dubbed *A Mexican Werewolf at the Horse Track*.

Cristobal (Miguel Angel Rodriguez) works for a wealthy horse breeder but longs to break away from his lowly station in life. A mysterious woman appears in his dreams and leads him to a cave containing a small, gem encrusted, wolf-headed statue. When he awakens, the sacred statue is standing on his dresser. Cristobal sells the gemstones and sets about winning the love of socialite Susana (Olivia Collins). Unfortunately, such largess comes at a cost. Beginning to act strangely, Cristobal inexplicably hunts rats in the stables, finds raw meat irresistible, and breaks a man's arm in a fight with seemingly superhuman strength. Finally, on the night of the full moon, Cristobal painfully transforms into a werewolf that hunts down those who possess the sacred gemstones. And he has given one to Susana…

Though it begins rather slowly, with too much time spent on mundane matters at the racetrack, the film's occasional eerie, fog-shrouded dream(?) sequence, and veteran actor Miguel Angel Rodriguez's tortured portrayal of the likable Cristobal, help hold one's interest until the half-way mark when the beast within finally emerges—in a scaled-down but still impressive *American Werewolf in London*–style metamorphosis. Amid cutaways to the full moon and frightened horses at the stable, Cristobel's face bubbles and distorts as he drops to his knees in agony. In close-up, vertebrae rises under his back, long hair sprouts from his skin, ears elongate, and a muzzle pushes forward from his face. This beast moves on all fours, with quick edits during the attacks designed to obfuscate the obvious man-in-a-suit body and rather unfortunate simian movements. Though a quadruped like its *American Werewolf* counterpart, this Mexican lycanthrope's visage maintains a more half-man/half-wolf appearance.

The film's latter half kicks into high lycan-gear with the brutal, bloody attacks coming fast and furious on the three successive nights of the full moon. Director René Cardona III (grandson of René Cardona, Sr. [*Night of the Bloody Apes, Blue Demon y Zovek en la Invasión de los Muertos*], and son of René Cardona, Jr. [*Night of a Thousand Cats, Tintorea*]) enhances the horrific immediacy of the gruesome, blood-drenched assaults via hand-held p.o.v. shots and rapid cutting between close-ups of slashing claws; the gore-covered wolfish face; blood spattering the wall, hay, leaves, etc.; and the occasional flying severed limb.

More disturbing than the gruesome werewolf violence, however (and for all the wrong reasons), is the fact that the monster's firsts victim is a *kitten*(!), whose eviscerated body looks rather too realistic for comfort (one doubts that the Mexican SPCA was involved in this production). Later, Cristobel awakens naked and covered in blood in a horse stall, with the disemboweled remains of a steed laying beside him. Again, the corpse looks all-too-real, and one suspects, as with the doomed feline, that cheap, expedient reality has supplanted expensive, time-consuming make-up fantasy here.

If one can give the benefit of the doubt to Senor Cardona and co., however, and push the potential real-life animal carcasses from one's mind, then *Comillos, el Hombre Lobo* (which translates as *Fangs, the Werewolf*) stands as a solid addition to werewolf cinema. Sadly, this rare post–1970s Mexican werewolf offering failed to make it north of the border in an English language edition.

Conquest

(1984; United Film Distribution Company; Italy) Director: Lucio Fulci.

What do you get when you cross *Clan of the Cave Bear* with *The Sword and the Sorcerer* and put Italian splatter maestro Lucio Fulci (*The Gates of Hell, The Beyond, House by the Cemetery*) in charge? The muddled, gory ball of confusion that is *Conquest*, that's what. The story (using the term loosely) has a youth with a magic bow set off on a quest through a mystical land ruled by a shapely evil sorceress (sporting a tiny codpiece, metal mask and nothing else). In among the expected Fulci gore-pieces (severed heads, roasted bodies, a woman literally ripped in half), monstrous encounters with everything from cobwebbed critters to friendly dolphins (who save Our Hero from a watery grave), and, of course, a *de rigeur* Fulci zombie interlude (in which a gaggle of shrouded corpses rise out of the lake to battle Our Hero) are a handful (well, four, really) of werewolf-like beings (looking like Chewbacca with a longer snout) who serve as the sorceress' henchm—er,—wolves. Said wolfmen are not lycanthropes per se, as they're not the result of any transformation (yep, apparently they were born that way). They also talk (about on the level of Tarzan, anyway) and follow orders (one who doesn't ends up roasted on a white-hot rock for his failure). An excruciating '80s synth score, photography that often looks like gauze was draped over the camera lens, and ridiculous optical effects (mystical glowing arrows of light anyone?) make this *Conquest* hardly worth the trouble.

Les Contes de la Nuit see Tales of the Night

O Coronel e o Lobisomem

(2005; Natasha Filmes; Brazil) Director: Maurício Farias.

Based on the 1964 novel by Brazilian author Jose Candido de Carvalho, *O Coronel e o Lobisomem* (which translates as "The Colonel and the Werewolf") stars Diogo Vilela as Ponciano, who, at the turn of the twentieth century, inherits a farm (and the title of "Colonel") from his grandfather. His close friend Pernambuco (Selton Mello), son of one of the farm's workers, and with whom Ponciano was raised, receives nothing. Though Colonel Ponciano has a crush on his cousin Esmeraldina (Ana Paula Arósio), he never declares his love. Pernambuco marries her instead, and when the Colonel can't pay the mortgage on his farm, Pernambuco takes it over. Ponciano then goes to court to prove that Pernambuco is a *werewolf*! Even stranger, at film's end the Colonel rides to the sea, where he meets a *mermaid* and then swims off with her!!

This rather talky but beautifully shot Brazilian fairy tale/morality story has never seen an English-language release, which is a pity because its sometimes stunning visuals and impressively atmospheric werewolf confrontation paints it as a unique and worthy lycanthropicture. The wolfman only appears towards the end, as Pernambuco defends himself in court against his former friend's accusations. As Pernambuco insists the ridiculous charges be dropped, the moon rises. Wiping his brow, Pernambuco's hand suddenly darkens. He throws back his head and involuntarily howls, as his hand grows hairy and claws extend from his nails. A supernatural wind springs up, and the courthouse lights flicker and grow dim. Now enraged, Pernambuco rips off his shirt and growls, while the Colonel looks on in horror. Suddenly, the werewolf's now-transformed visage bursts into frame. With its misshapen protruding snout, demonic eyes, and gaping maw filled with pointed teeth and two-inch-long, saber-like incisors, this werewolf looks like evil incarnate. Fur covers its body, and it leaps upon the Colonel as the panicked spectators flee the courtroom. Ponciano desperately shoves a book into its snapping jaws as the beast pins him to the ground. Suddenly an amulet at the Colonel's neck begins to glow with protective power. This sends the werewolf flying backwards, then leaping about the courtroom until it finally breaks through the window to escape. It's an exciting, if brief, confrontation, with the mobile camera, moody lighting, frightening sounds, and impressive makeup augmenting (and disguising) the CGI artificiality of the creature. One only wishes there had been more of this throughout the film. Note: This was not the first cinematic iteration of the story; Alcino Diniz first adapted it to the screen in 1979 as the identically-titled *O Coronel e o Lobisomem*, but this version seems to have dropped into obscurity.

Count Downe see Son of Dracula

The Creeps

(1997; Full Moon Pictures) Director: Charles Band.

Stuttering, chip-on-his-shoulder mad scientist Winston Berber (Bill Moynihan) has created an "Archetype Inducer," a machine that can "transform mythic, cultural and literary archetypes into living entities." To do this, however, he needs the "literary archetypes'" original manuscripts, and he chooses Bram Stoker's *Dracula*, Mary Shelley's *Frankenstein*, Nina Wilcox Putnam's *The Mummy*, and Guy Endore's *The Werewolf of Paris*, stealing several of them from a rare book annex. The young librarian there, Anna (Rhonda Griffin), learns of the theft and hires a video store clerk/private eye wannabe, David (Justin Lauer), to track down the thief. Anna, however, soon ends up as the final ingredient needed to complete Berber's animation process—a female sacrifice. Fortunately, David breaks in during the procedure and frees Anna, leaving the job half-finished, with the newly-animated Dracula, Mummy, Frankenstein's Monster, and Wolf Man as three-foot-tall midgets! The mini-monsters, led by the verbose vampire, set about recapturing Anna in order to complete the process and bring them up to their full size and power.

Phil Fondacaro (who appeared in the 1990 pseudowolf entry *Meridian*, which was also directed by Full Moon founder Charles Band) played the diminutive Dracula. Fondacaro stated that he studied Gary Oldman's portrayal of the famous Count in *Bram Stoker's Dracula* (1992) to "try and get that type of feeling and the way he spoke." Said Fondacaro, "The idea of me playing Dracula to begin with was an amazing opportunity, because, come on, a little person playing Dracula?... It was a very good part. I don't know if it was my best, but it was a part I really sank my teeth into—and that wasn't a figure of speech." The 3-foot-6-inch actor revealed, "I enjoy the evil side [of a character], because when you first see me, the tendency is to either feel sorry for me or laugh at me. So if there's some way I can switch that and make people really be scared of me, I enjoy that." And, surprisingly, as the scaled-down vampire, Fondacaro does just that. Playing the role completely straight, Fondacaro's accented, gravelly voice and menacing demeanor make those rising chuckles stick in one's throat.

Unfortunately, the same cannot be said of the three other half-pint horrors, who mostly stand in the background (none of them ever speak) or occasionally bumble about trying to (literally) trip up the protagonists. While the Frankenstein Monster and Mummy possess passable makeup jobs, the Wolf Man (dressed in an olive drab shirt, black pants and leather shoes) looks disappointingly *un*-wolf-like, with his discolored, lumpy face, small pig/bat snout, red lips and frizzy orange hair. He doesn't even sport fangs. Afforded just a few scant minutes of screen time, the mini-wolf never rises above the role of generic henchman, working in unison with the other "creeps" and never engaging in any lycanthropic or even particularly savage behavior (with nary a transformation in sight). His big moment comes when he stands over a half-naked bound woman brought to the lab and literally *drools* on her. Rather than a "mythic archetype," he's just a silly cypher.

Poorly-paced (it's a half hour of uninteresting interaction between the vapid human characters before the monsters finally show up), the one-joke *Creeps* replaces genuine suspense and eerie atmosphere with cheap shots ("Big talk from a tiny little Dracula") and cheesy settings (comprised of three impoverished sets). Consequently, *The Creeps* remains, er, short on entertainment. (Note: The creepiest thing about *The Creeps* is the off-screen activities of dwarf actor Jon Simanton, who played the Wolf Man. In 2007 the 36-year-old Simanton was arrested in Scottsdale, Arizona, and charged with sexual assault for inappropriately touching his nephew's 15-year-old babysitter.)

With quotes from: "Size *Doesn't* Matter," by Allan Dart, *Fangoria* 202.

CreepTales

(2004; Third Stone Productions) Directors: Ken Mandel, Steve Hegyi ("Howling Nightmare" segment).

This low-budget horror anthology appears more disjointed than most, as each segment was made by different (mostly amateur) filmmakers. As expected, the quality varies wildly, from poorly-filmed one-note entries to a few clever and inventive tales (particularly its last, "Sucker"). The wraparound story opens with a pair of hunchbacked ghouls defiling their Uncle's grave in order to retrieve a video—titled *CreepTales*, naturally—from his cold dead hands. Giggling moronically, they bring it home and show a group of monster friends the six different stories contained therein.

The fifth segment, "Howling Nightmare," is an exceedingly brief (only seven minutes) tale of a group of hunters in the woods tracking a werewolf, with the beast turning the tables on them one by one after their dim-bulb leader suggests, "I got a plan—let's split up." It turns out that it was all a nightmare, with the dreamer awakening in an old house only to look out the widow, see the full moon, and begin to change...

One of the more professional-looking entries, "Howling Nightmare" offers some decent foggy woodland photography and atmospheric lighting, along with some spurting red stuff during the various attacks. The clarity sometimes works against itself, however, by leaving the white-furred full-on wolf-face, with its long snout and even longer teeth, looking just like what it is—an immobile mask. Too brief even to establish characters, much less shed any light on the notion of the beast within, "Howling Nightmare" adds nothing to the lycan canon but a few more vicious werewolf kills and one amusing coda: At the story's end, the half-transformed wolfman steps into the open doorway and howls at the moon—only to stop abruptly when he notices a quartet of hunters outside leveling their weapons at him. He mutters, "Oh shit," and they fill him full of holes.

Filmed between 1986 and 1989, *CreepTales* didn't see the light of day until finally released on video in 2004.

The Curse of the Allenbys see ***She-Wolf of London***

Curse of the Queerwolf

(1988; Pirromount/Raedon Video) Director: Mark Pirro.

Curse of the Queerwolf may very well be the best $6,000, 8mm, gay-themed horror spoof ever shot in Santa Barbara. Inspired by a throwaway character from writer-producer-director Mark Pirro's previous no-budget parody, *A Polish Vampire in Burbank* (1983), the film follows the trials and tribulations of confirmed heterosexual Larry Smalbut (rhymes with "Talbot"; and played by ex–Universal Studios tour guide Michael Palazzolo), who inadvertently picks up a transvestite (amusingly played by a *woman*, Cynthia Brownell) that bites Larry before he discovers the deception. Said tranny was actually a "dickenthrope—a queerwolf," according to the four torch-bearing queerwolf hunters that arrive on the scene. An incidental radio broadcast (from station KBLG—"K-bulge") sums up the situation: "A new strain of venereal disease has just been discovered by doctors at the Turn Head and Cough Institute. The disease possesses men to dress up in women's clothing.... The spit of an infected person causes the victim to take on these incredible emotional changes only during certain times ... one tell-tale sign is the inability of the victim to keep his wrist straight." Now whenever the full moon rises, macho-man Larry turns gay!

Not really a werewolf film (after all, these dickenthropes are more Liberace than lycan), *Curse of the Queerwolf* still manages to mercilessly spoof the subgenre by creating sometimes crude, occasionally offensive but often amusing parodies of various werewolf tropes. For instance, Larry (literally) runs into a gypsy woman who sees a telltale sign glowing on his palm. Instead of the *Wolf Man's* pentagram, however, she sees "the pansygram, the five-pointed flower." And rather than Maleva's "The way you walk is thorny" ditty, she pronounces, "The way you walk is funny, through no fault of your own." The film's take on the "Even a man who is pure of heart" rhyme proves even funnier: "Even a wrist that is strong and firm / And holds up straight by day / May become limp when the moon is full / And the queerwolf comes your way."

The production's big transformation scene, however, leaves off *The Wolf Man* to parody the then-recent lycan-classic *An American Werewolf in London*. When the full moon rises, Larry suddenly begins to groan and writhe. He raises his arms and stares in horror as his wrists suddenly go limp. Then a fishnet-clad foot bursts through his tube sock, while long painted nails grow from his fingertips, a hoop earring appears in his ear, and he howls in anguish. The next morning he awakens naked—not surrounded by wolves in a zoo but by grinning gays in a sauna.

Arguably the film's funniest bit, however, doesn't even involve queerwolfery. It consists of a sequence that sees Larry walking through the woods inexplicably wearing a life jacket and coming across two ugly hillbillies who intend to make him "squeal," *Deliverance*-style. Larry takes off as banjo music begins to play, with the banjo picker (sitting in a tree) singing (to the tune of "The Beverly Hillbillies"): "Now Listen to a story 'bout a man named Lar / A poor little man who was bitten by a q'uar / Then one day he was walkin' by a stream / And met a couple guys that wanted to ream / Sodomy, that is / Black hole / Squealin' pain..." Larry awakens from this dream in his own bed and turns to his girlfriend only to find one of the hillbillies in bed with him! He screams and then awakens for real (a dream-within-a-dream homage to *American Werewolf*).

Cheap shots come faster than towel whips in a Turkish bath. When a police detective arrives to interview Larry, the copper tells him he's "not [from] homicide [but] *homo*-cide; I investigate the murder of homos." The gypsy reveals that there's only one way to kill a queerwolf, and opens a box to reveal ... a silver dildo! "When the moon is full, and yours is too," she instructs, "this must be placed where never was the sun to shine." And as an antidote to queerwolfery, she presents Larry with a magical medallion—of John Wayne. Then there's all the talk of "the torture of the pooftas" and an *Exorcist* parody in which the gypsy offers Larry the services of a ... "fagxorcist" ("The power of Budweiser compels you!").

It's not just lycanthropy and homosexuality (and its attendant reactionary homophobia) that feel the brunt of the script's blunt sarcasm; to this *Curse* nothing is sacred. For example, Larry's aversion therapist friend Dick (who works at the Sweet Holy Mama Therapy Clinic) invariably ends up carelessly killing his clients in ridiculous ways (with two of the doomed patients played by cameoing Forrest J Ackerman and Conrad Brooks), while another running gag has Larry accidently off three different pet dogs (via car, knife and *microwave*), two of them puppies!

Filmed primarily on weekends over the course of six months, the movie looks cheap (the grainy film stock exposes its 8mm roots) but still relatively competent. Though it won't win any cinematography prizes, it's at least adequately lit and in focus (something few DIY efforts can boast). And while the acting varies wildly from amateurish to amusing (particularly Kent Butler as Larry's friend Richard "Dick" Cheese), Michael Palazzolo offers just enough likability to make the hapless, goofy protagonist work. So while this *Curse* remains about as subtle as a rainbow-colored sledgehammer, it offers enough politically *in*correct irreverence to have developed a (small) cult following, particularly among the LGBT crowd.

Dark Shadows

(2012; Warner Bros.) Director: Tim Burton.

From 1966 to 1971 daytime television experienced a new and never-to-be-repeated phenomenon—a supernatural soap opera. Created by Dan Curtis, *Dark Shadows* featured all manner of supernatural storylines over the course of 1,225 half-hour episodes. Everything from werewolves and witches to a Frankensteinian monster and a Jekyll and Hyde clone crossed paths with the benighted Collins family, founders of the fishing town of Collinsport, Maine. But no character made a bigger impact than Barnabas Collins, a tortured 200-year-old vampire who ultimately took center stage at the Collinswood mansion. The extremely popular daily serial inspired books, magazines, comics, and even board games over the course of its five-year run. Towards the end of the series, Dan Curtis even made two *Dark Shadows* feature films (temporarily writing select cast members out of the series for a few weeks to allow the actors to work on the movies): *House of Dark Shadows* (1970), which turned out quite successfully (both financially and aesthetically), and *Night of Dark Shadows* (1971), which didn't (in either respect).

Like many others who grew up in the 1960s, Tim Burton would rush home after school to watch the supernatural soap. *Unlike* most, however, he became a filmmaker with enough clout to indulge his cinematic whims—thus, this *Dark Shadows* redux was born, complete with many Burtonisms, including quirky characterizations, stunningly original visuals, dark whimsicality (sometimes shockingly so, as when a "very thirsty" Barnabas slaughters a whole crew of construction workers, then later a gaggle of VW bus–driving "nice, unshaven young people"), and the "otherness" of a fish-out-of-water protagonist. "I envision Barnabas as a sympathetic, quietly tortured person out of sync with what is—to him, at least—an unrecognizable world," described Burton. This last is brought brilliantly home by leading man Johnny Depp's dignified yet amusing portrayal of the noble, cursed Barnabas. Emerging from his coffin after 200 years, he astoundingly exclaims, "Mephistopheles!" when bathed in the bright illumination of a McDonald's sign (an unintentionally apt oath). Later, upon seeing TV for the first time, he approaches the variety show singer on the screen and demands, "Reveal yourself, tiny songstress!" Reportedly, it was Depp himself (another fan of the original series) who brought the project to Burton and encouraged his favorite director to take the helm. "Listen, there's no way you can get Tim [Burton] and Johnny [Depp] together and *not* have humor," said Burton muse (and domestic partner) Helena Bonham Carter (who plays Dr. Julia Hoffman in the film). "[*Dark Shadows*] was shot and informed by ... [Tim] and Johnny's shared tastes in jet-black humor. And when I say black, at the same time, there is a real innocence there. And that's genuine to their natures."

The story revolves around Barnabas Collins (Depp), a 200-year-old vampire who was imprisoned in a coffin by the beautiful witch Angelique (Eva Green), the spurned lover who cursed him with vampirism. Finally freed in 1972, Barnabas reunites with his dysfunctional descendants at Collinswood, led by matriarch Elizabeth (Michelle Pfeiffer). Barnabas must battle both his bloodthirsty nature and the possessive, vindictive witch to restore his beloved family to their former glory (founders of Collinsport, the Collinses have been supplanted by the supernatural siren Angelique herself, who now runs Angel Bay fishing industries). As Burton describes it, "At its core, *Dark Shadows* is a weird family story, with strong supernatural overtones."

Werewolfery briefly rears its hirsute head at the film's climactic battle between Barnabas and Angelique at Collinswood. At one point Barnabas tosses the witch away from him, and she crashes through the ceiling into the room of Carolyn, Elizabeth's rebellious 15-year-old daughter (played by Chloe Grace Moretz, of *Kick Ass* fame). At this, an affronted Carolyn growls at Angelique, "Get out of my room!" like any terrible teen might do—except Carolyn is up in the rafters sporting sharp teeth and glowing eyes! Angelique obliges and recommences the battle with Barnabas. Then, when it looks like the witch has the upper hand (by bringing the house's woodwork to life and pinning Barnabas to the wall), Carolyn springs down and attacks Angelique. Here we see her face lightly covered in downy hair, her teeth sharp, and, most noticeably, her legs elongated and furry like that of a wolf's. Upon seeing her daughter like this for the first time, a shocked Elizabeth exclaims, "Caroline, my God!" At this, Carolyn snarks, "I'm a werewolf, ok. Let's not make a big deal of it. Woof." Angelique easily tosses the wolf-girl aside, knocking her unconscious, then sarcastically explains to Elizabeth, "Your perfect Collins pedigree lacked a bit of substance, so I sent the werewolf who bit Carolyn in her crib." Though light in the makeup department, this wolfwoman sports a novel (and striking) pair of gams that give her a decidedly bestial appearance while still retaining the bulk of her human features. She also retains her human faculties, including the power of speech. It's a novel take on lycanthropy that unfortunately remains little more than a throwaway concept.

Costing $150 million, *Dark Shadows* disappointed at the box office, taking in just under $80 million domestically. Though it fared better overseas, with foreign earnings totaling another $165 million, the movie failed to live up to its hoped-for franchise potential, so it seems unlikely we'll see any more of the Collinses (including werewolf Carolyn).

This marks the final film appearance of the original Barnabas Collins, Jonathan Frid, who died less than a month before the movie's release. Frid, along with fellow original castmates Lara Parker, Kathryn Leigh Scott, and David Selby, supplied a blink-and-you'll-miss-it cameo as a quartet of party guests at the Collinswood ball. Also at the ball is Alice Cooper, playing himself, hired as the night's entertainment. Cooper starred in the full-on werewolf film *Monster Dog* in 1984, an international co-production whose entire cost could no doubt have been covered by *Dark Shadow*'s catering bill.

With quotes from: "Directing in the Shadows," by Rod Labbe, *Fangoria* 313; "An English Rose Among Dark Shadows," by Chris Alexander, *Fangoria* 313.

Dead Teenagers

(2006; Brain Damage Films) Director: Chris LaMartina.

From *Dark Shadows*' $150 *million* to what looks like 150 *dollars* ... the shot-in-Baltimore horror anthology *Dead Teenagers* is a painfully obvious amateur affair. A man finds a handwritten notebook in his local library dubbed *Book of Lore* that contains four terror tales. "The Boo Men" follows a troubled youth haunted by visions of men wearing sack cloths over their heads; "Full Moonlighting" has a boy turning into a werewolf; "Skeleton Keys" features a ghostly killer with a fondness for piano practice; and "Suckers" is a vampire tale set in a run-down cinema.

"Full Moonlighting" sees teenager Collin (Doug Matthews), recently returned from a trip to Europe where he was "bitten by an animal," trying to avoid his girlfriend Jen (Katie Harris) for her own protection. You see, Collin, now a werewolf, is behind the "rash of vicious wolf attacks" plaguing his home town. After the werewolf kills the two "wolf hunters" hired by the county, Collin attempts to chain himself up in his basement. But Jen disregards his warning to stay away and confronts her boyfriend—only to reveal that she, too, is a lycanthrope. "I'll explain it over dinner," she says, placing a hairy hand on his shoulder as a howl sounds in the night.

Lasting a mere 12 minutes, "Full Moonlighting" has nothing going for it. The lack of characterization and incompetent acting sinks the premise from the start, with the principals' robotic portrayals failing to generate any pathos—or interest whatsoever—in the proceedings. The two brief, all-but-bloodless werewolf attacks fail to even show the lycanthrope, revealing only a hairy paw and the back of what is obviously a Halloween mask. And the story's title is truly a misnomer, as Jen tells Collin, "Any time [the moon] is half-full or greater, you change." This odd, arbitrary lycan-rule was predicated, no doubt, on the fact that the only lunar shot the filmmakers could come up with is of a *three-quarter*, rather than full, moon.

While not quite down to the backyard filmmaking levels of *The Worst Horror Movie Ever Made* or a David "The Rock" Nelson abomination, *Dead Teenagers* offers cheap videography straight out of the previous decade's camcorder era, high school-level screenwriting, predictable tales with little-to-no kick, a sluggish pace that makes its brief 70-minute running time seem *twice* that, embarrassingly amateurish acting from friends and family, and no special effects to speak of (unless one counts pretending to have been stabbed by *holding a stake under one's arm*). Don't be fooled by its enticing (and professional-looking) DVD cover; *Dead Teenagers* is really a dead issue.

Deadtime Stories

(1986; Cinema Group) Alternate Titles: *Deadtime Stories: Tales of Death*; *Freaky Fairytales* (UK). Director: Jeffrey Delman.

This unevenly paced low-budget horror-comedy anthology from Connecticut raked in nearly $3 million on its U.S. theatrical release and was a big hit on video as well (largely due to its impressive video box graphics and the inclusion of the *Deadtime Stories* trailer on a number of compilation tapes—not to mention one of the *pun*niest movie titles of all time). Unfortunately, the film is just not very good, though it deserves points for its intermittently amusing updating of two fairy tale classics.

A disreputable uncle babysitting his young nephew is cajoled into telling a trio of horrific yet comical bedtime stories (poor Uncle Mike just wants to get little Brian to sleep so he can watch the Miss Nude pageant on cable...). The first, "Peter and the Witches," a period yarn about a boy (top-billed Scott Valentine, at the time the only "name" in the cast, having guest-starred on TV's *Family Ties*) enslaved by a pair of witches intent on reviving their dead sister, offers a few bits of inventive grue but little else until it simply, er, peters out. The third story, "Goldi Lox and the Three Baers" (in which the psychic—and psychotic—Goldi bands together with the criminal Baer family), is somewhat better thanks to some broad yet genuinely funny humor and horrific slapstick.

But it's the film's middle tale that shines (well, perhaps a more accurate descriptor would be "slightly glows"). Uncle Mike's version of the beloved tale, here dubbed "Little Red Runninghood," begins like so:

> UNCLE MIKE: "Once upon a time, there was a little girl named 'Rachel.' Actually, she wasn't all that little. She was a hot-looking high school senior with deep blue eyes and fine, firm breasts and—"
> LITTLE BRIAN: "That's not the way Mommy tells it."
> UNCLE MIKE: "Shut up, that's the way I tell it."

One day Rachel (Nicole Picard) goes out running (in a form-fitting red jogging suit) after picking up a prescription at the pharmacy for her grandmother and then meeting her boyfriend for a virginity-losing tryst in a garden shed. Meanwhile, Willie (Matt Mitler) illegally obtains his heavy-duty tranquilizers from the same crooked pharmacist, only to discover that he's mistakenly been given Rachel's prescription, and vice-versa. You see, Willie is desperate to knock himself out tonight—it being a full moon and all. Willie strong-arms Rachel's address from the pharmacist and goes to her house, but nobody's there but Rachel's suspicious grandma ("I've got a meat cleaver and I know how to use it!"). He waits, but Rachel returns after dark, and Willie has already transformed into a beast and attacked grandma. The werewolf kills Rachel's boyfriend and then goes after Rachel herself, who manages to stab the beast with a silver cake server grandma had been polishing. Rachel visits grandma in the hospital the next day, when suddenly granny snarls and shows some rather long canines. At this, Rachel exclaims, "Grandma, what big teeth you have." Freeze frame.

Willie the werewolf sports some imposing fangs and claws, but not much in the way of facial hair—more along the lines of the Henry Hull minimalist mode than the hirsute Chaney version. Still, while less than impressive visually, Williwolf (energetically played by Matt Mitler) snarls and leaps and lunges to good effect (even ripping out the throat of Rachel's hapless boyfriend), making this segment the most lively of the trio. There are still some laughs to be found, however (besides the closing punchline). For instance, when Willie realizes he's transforming (sporting an effective interim makeup), he simply, and amusingly, groans, "Fuck." This being a low-budget production, however, said transformation disappointingly occurs off- rather than on-screen. And while a decidedly minor entry in the werewolf sub-genre, *Deadtime Stories* does present one novel concept: the afflicted attempting to control his "curse" by knocking himself out with tranquilizers until the metamorphosis has passed.

Plagued by some poor pacing, pedestrian direction (helmer Jeffrey Delman went on to make ... very little else), and indifferent acting, *Deadtime Stories* is "saved" by its intermittently witty script and a willingness to go over the top at times. Throughout it all, the cheap and cheesy synthesizer score reminds us that yes, this *is* 1986 after all. But at least the closing song, "The Wolf's Lament" (with lyrics by Delman), sees us out appropriately over the end credits. Amazingly, one *Deadtime* veteran reached the pinnacle of her profession—Melissa Leo (who plays "MaMa Baer" in the flick's final episode) won an Oscar in 2010 (for her role in *The Fighter*).

Note: This *Deadtime Stories* should not be confused with the werewolf-less horror anthology of the same name (executive produced and "hosted" by George Romero) released in 2011. It just goes to show that you can't keep a good title down.

Devil Wolf of Shadow Mountain

(1964) Director: Gary Kent.

Here's a *real* obscurity—a "lost" film that is *so* lost it never even saw release! Announced in some monster movie magazines at the time (accompanied by production stills), this Gary Kent-directed horror western reportedly starred John "Bud" Cardos as a werewolf. "That picture was never even made," laughed Cardos. "It might have been announced, but it was never made. I remember the story well. It was a western with a werewolf in it." Too bad; the world could do with a few more werewolf westerns.

With quotes from: "Motorcycle Maniacs, Fantastic Fights: John 'Bud' Cardos," by Bob Plante, *Psychotronic Video* 24.

Dinowolf see *Dire Wolf*

Dire Wolf

(2009; Retromedia) Alternate Title: *Dinowolf*. Director: Fred Olen Ray.

Modern-day low-budget exploitationer Fred Olen Ray here dips his toe into the werewolf pool a second time (after 2004's *Tomb of the Werewolf*). Sort of—but not really, as the titular terror of this shot-on-video 10-day wonder isn't a lycanthrope per se but a genetically-engineered prehistoric wolf–human hybrid animal. "We took a newly discovered dire wolf skeleton, where the bone marrow was still viable, and introduced human stem cells," explains a surviving employee of the "Clark Bio-Gen Testing Facility." The result: an animal that looks more like a *Howling* reject than "the largest canid that ever walked the earth." The reason: "the perfect battlefield combination—a soldier teamed with a terrifying and intensely loyal attack wolf." Though part (prehistoric) wolf and part man (at least at the genetic level), the creature, despite its werewolfish appearance, lacks the all-important defining characteristic of lycanthropy: transformation (the moon and silver need not apply either). Born a Dire Wolf, the beast dies a Dire Wolf.

Purportedly inspired by the lycanthropes from the 1980s *Werewolf* television series, the creature's rather mangy big-bad-(dire)-wolf appearance (huge ears, long snout, bulky torso, fuzzy fur) screams man-in-a-suit, particularly when it hunches over and "runs" on all fours. Bad-tempered after escaping its lab, this beast eviscerates nearly everyone it comes across in the small-town environs of Santa Mira Spring until the local sheriff, his game warden son, two government agents sent to contain the situation, and a lab worker all band together to track and kill the out-of-control creature (ultimately taking a page right out of Howard Hawks' 1951 classic *The Thing from Another World*).

Eschewing the easy-yet-unconvincing CGI route in favor of the more-difficult-but-still-less-than-convincing practical effects method (the creature never looks like anything more than what it is—a man in a substandard werewolf costume), director/co-writer Ray, an avowed horror and sci-fi fan, offers up a rather old fashioned creature feature—but with some updated gore. The attacks come quickly and often (two in the first ten minutes); and though they're plenty red and wet, the shock of the beast suddenly pouncing to rip out a throat and slash away at a chest until it's a pulpy mass of ribs and red meat wears thin after the sixth, seventh, and eighth repetition. A cadre of low-rent actors, including former Buck Rogers Gil Gerard collecting a one-day paycheck as project head Colonel "Hendry" (another *Thing* reference), and Maxwell Caulfield as the OCD sheriff just as concerned with detailing his cruiser as catching the monster, attempt to breathe life into Ray's serviceable though uninspired script (which is about on par with many a SyFy Channel offering). But despite their best efforts, this *Dire Wolf* never evolves into anything more than a middling time-waster.

Dr. Terror's Gallery of Horrors

(1967; American General) Alternate Titles: *The Blood Suckers*, *Gallery of Horror*, *Return from the Past* (TV). Director: David L. Hewitt.

John Carradine once cited *Billy the Kid vs. Dracula* (1966) as the worst movie he ever made. He must have forgotten about *Dr. Terror's Gallery of Horrors*. Not to be confused with the superior Amicus anthology film *Dr. Terrors House of Horrors* (which undoubtedly the distributors of this pathetic portmanteau intended), *Dr. Terror's Gallery of Horrors* features five short tales of the supernatural, each introduced by onscreen narrator Carradine, and each offering (silly or predictable—or both) twist endings.

The first tale, "The Witch's Clock," has a young couple buy a castle in Massachusetts (!) and find a cursed clock with the power to raise the dead (Carradine appears in this one as a revived 17th century warlock). The second segment, "King Vampire," follows two 19th century police inspectors as they try to stop a vampire killer. In "The Monster Raid," a researcher returns from the grave, thanks to a special "formula," to revenge himself on his cheating wife and murderous colleague. Story four, "The Spark of Life," stars Lon Chaney, Jr., as a doctor delving into the power of electricity whose experiments revive a flabby, middle-aged executed murderer.

The final tale, "Count Alucard," becomes a micro-retelling of *Dracula*, with Mr. Harker arriving at the Count's castle to conclude the deal on Carfax Abbey, only to run afoul of a vampiress and the Count himself. A werewolf comes into play at this episode's "twist" ending when Harker, after dispatching two female vampires, confronts the Count himself. "There's still the vampire that created the two girls," he pointedly tells Dracula, before adding, "I know who he is." The Count answers, "Mr. Harker, you are much too clever for your own good. And now for your meddling, you will have to pay." The Count raises his cloak and advances toward Harker, blocking our view of the intended victim. But Harker answers, "I won't let you drain this village of its blood—I need it for myself." The Count suddenly steps back to reveal Harker as a hairy werewolf! "Aaaaah!" screams the Count, "A werewolf!" Then the Harker–wolfman attacks, pushing Dracula out of frame. The end. This nonsensical two-second "shock" werewolf cameo, featuring Roger Gentry in a cut-rate Lon Chaney/Wolf Man getup, only cheapens an already threadbare episode.

Statically shot on crude plywood sets constructed on a cramped soundstage (with "exteriors" consisting of castle matte shots and coach-driving footage stolen from the Roger Corman Poe films *House of Usher*, *The Pit and the Pendulum* and *The Raven*), *Gallery* looks more like a collection of high-school skits than a feature film. The acting matches the sets in amateurish awfulness, though both Carradine and Chaney give it the old college try, with Chaney (who reportedly earned $1500 for his half-day's work) in particular plowing his way through his underwritten role like a thespian bull in a cinematic china

Ad for the amateurish anthology *Dr. Terror's Gallery of Horror* (**not to be confused with the far superior** *Dr. Terror's* House *of Horrors*), with its blink-and-you'll-miss-it werewolf appearance.

shop. Sadly, this proved to be the ailing horror star's final speaking part in a horror movie.

Carradine's poorly-written, rambling monologues leading into the poorly-written, rambling stories were actually an afterthought. When director-producer-writer David L. Hewitt (*The Wizard of Mars* [1965], *The Mighty Gorga* [1969]) realized his script was too short, he contracted his friend and associate Gary R. Heacock to write intros for each story. "They told me, 'Make 'em as long as you *can*!'" laughed Heacock to interviewer Tom Weaver. "So if John Carradine's introductions to the different scenarios seem a little bit wordy—well, they were, because we had to have [say] 80 minutes, or whatever the running time was, and there just simply wasn't enough in the scenarios." For his long-winded efforts, Carradine received $3,000 of the film's reported $20,000 budget.

Those involved with the wretched project held little illusions about it. Interviewed by Jack Gourlay, co-star Ron Doyle, who appeared in three of the five segments, labeled the film "a piece of shit—pretty disastrous." Another actor, Ron Brogan (from the "King Vampire" story) opined (again to Gourlay), "It was pretty much on the camp side—phony thing.... He didn't go back and correct mistakes as there was no time for retakes."

At least the actors occasionally had some fun with the film (unlike the hapless viewer), as recounted by Doyle: "We were doing a take, and I was supposed to look under a sheet at this dead body. Lon [Chaney] got underneath the sheet and I didn't know it. When I pulled it back, Lon yelled 'Aaarrr' and scared the hell out of me!" That makes *one* person scared by *Dr. Terror's Gallery of* Horridness.

Dr. Terror's House of Horrors

(1965; Amicus; UK) Director: Freddie Francis.

Dr. Terror's House of Horrors proved to be the first (though not the best) in a long line of Amicus anthology films, which included *Torture Garden* (1967), *The House That Dripped Blood* (1971), *Tales from the Crypt* (1972), *Asylum* (1972), *The Vault of Horror* (1973) and *From Beyond the Grave* (1973). Headed by frequent scriptwriter Milton Subotsky and his partner Max J. Rosenberg, Amicus proved to be Hammer's biggest competitor in the British horror arena of the 1960s and '70s.

Amicus' first anthology feature was originally going to be shot in 1962 in black and white with financial backing from Columbia Pictures, but Columbia dropped out when they deemed it too expensive (at a mere $94,000!). It took another two years to obtain alternate financing for the (now-color) project, and even after production finally got underway, the difficult dollar (or, more accurately, problematic pound) reared its ugly head yet again. After two weeks of shooting, the production nearly shut down when part of the American financing was withdrawn (British co-financier Joe Vegoda ponied up the extra cash needed).

Dr. Terror's House of Horrors relates five tales of the supernatural, tying the disparate stories together via Dr. Schreck (Peter Cushing), a mysterious "doctor of metaphysics" who, with a deck of tarot cards, tells the futures of the five men sharing his train compartment. (Subotsky had originally written the five stories back in 1948 as scripts for a planned TV series that never materialized.) The first episode, entitled

"Werewolf," is a rather muddled lycanthrope tale (complete with poorly-lit manor house, skulking servants and easily whipped-up clip of silver bullets); while the second yarn, called "Creeping Vine," has an intelligent mobile plant inexplicably cut phone wires, put out fires, strangle people and trap a family inside their house. The third tale, dubbed "Voodoo," details what happens when a jazz musician (Roy Castle) steals the "sacred music of the great god Damballah." The fourth (and best) segment has pompous art critic Franklin Marsh (Christopher Lee) humiliated by artist Eric Landor (Michael Gough). The spiteful critic then runs down Landor with his car, causing the artist to lose his hand. After the despondent Landor commits suicide, his disembodied hand haunts Marsh, leading to the critic's demise in a bit of poetic justice. In the fifth and final story, Donald Sutherland plays a small-town doctor whose new French bride turns out to be a vampire.

"Werewolf" has architect Jamie Dawson (Neil McCallum) return to his old ancestral home in the Hebrides that he was forced to sell, when the new owner, a "rich, beautiful, lonely widow" (Ursula Howells), contracts him to plan some renovations. In the cellar, behind a false wall, Dawson finds "the coffin of Cosmo Valdemar, the werewolf." He explains that, according to family lore, "over 200 years ago Cosmo Valdemar claimed the house was really his, that my ancestors had stolen it from him." And that Valdemar had been killed by his ancestor with a silver sword, but his burial place remained a secret. Valdemar also uttered a curse. "He swore that his place would be taken by whoever owned the house, and he himself would once again take human shape." That night they find a servant girl clawed to death and a trail of blood leading down to the stone coffin in the cellar. "Something came out of that coffin," concludes Dawson, "something evil." He then melts down a silver cross to make bullets, so that "when that coffin opens tomorrow night, I'll be waiting." But while standing guard in the cellar, he hears a scream from the widow's room. Rushing there, Dawson sees a large canine and fires at it when it flees. But the bullets fail to stop the beast. "I don't understand it," he says. "The legend says the only way to kill a werewolf is a bullet made from a silver crucifix. I had six." Suddenly, the widow's hand rises up into frame (in a bit of effectively dramatic staging by director Freddie Francis), and she asks, "You mean these?" Here we notice her hand is not entirely human, with discolored skin and sharp, claw-like nails. She smiles, revealing fangs; she is a werewolf too! "You see," she continues, "what the legend *really* says is that Cosmo Valdemar will resume human shape again when he's replaced in his coffin not by the owner of the house, but by a descendent of the man who killed him. Now, any dutiful wife would do anything to bring her husband back to life—even after 200 years." She advances, and Dawson screams.

Apart from this amusing twist right out of an E.C. Comics tale, "Werewolf" provides little more than 15 minutes of talk and skulking about an old house. The sole encounter with the Cosmo werewolf consists of a brief close-up of a snarling dog muzzle and a flash of fur as it flees the room. With little characterization and less content, the slight "Werewolf" remains the weakest of the five entries.

The first short tale of this first Amicus anthology film centers on a (barely-seen) werewolf.

"I like anthology films," opined producer/screenwriter Milton Subotsky, "because I feel that in SF and horror the short story format works better than either the novel or novelette." Subotsky's preference notwithstanding, the downside of the anthology format is that there's very little time to develop characters or build and sustain mood—two key components in successful horror films. It's very difficult to fashion a believable milieu or create intriguing characters in less than 30 minutes. When given only half that time, as with most of *Dr. Terror's* segments, it's nearly impossible. In *Dr. Terror's*, the fantastical notions are too abrupt, as characters seemingly take these unlikely happenings as a matter of course (since there's no time for any doubt), allowing for no real credibility.

Fortunately, Subotsky and Rosenberg gathered together a cadre of fine actors who managed to invest some realism in their somewhat stereotypical roles. Peter Cushing, Christopher Lee, Michael Gough, Neil McCallum and Donald Sutherland in particular all bring a believable quality to the unbelievable situations.

In talking of his various anthology movies, director Freddie Francis explained that "my approach to these films is that no one is really going to believe that these sort of things happen ... so I believe that though people may find it horrid for a while, they find it horrid in a giggly sort of way." Of all the segments, "Voodoo" possesses the most of this "giggly" quality. "To my mind," admitted Francis, "it was a fun thing, obviously not to be taken seriously." So while "Voodoo" remains a musically and comedically effective segment (thanks largely to Roy Castle's amiable attitude and Bob Hope–style asides), it fails to generate any real scares. Of the four other segments, only the "Disembodied Hand" episode really works well. "Werewolf" is rather dull, while the "Creeping Vine" remains ridiculously unconvincing, with a poor build-up leading to a weak (anti)climax. Despite the ever-quirky presence of a young Donald Sutherland (in only his third film), "Vampire" also fails to satisfy thanks to its perfunctory plotting and all-too-ready staking (though it does possess an unexpected and amusing final twist). Fortunately, the film's wrap-around is a creepy, suspenseful, well-constructed story unto itself, with the passengers becoming more and more uneasy as Dr. Schreck relates their horrific fates one by one. Of the omnibus format, Francis felt, "The only thing one has to do is to make sure you have a good link. And I think the link has to be able to stand on its own. I think the link we had with Peter Cushing in *Dr. Terror's* was one of the best." Indeed it was.

Thanks to its clever connecting device, the superbly acted and genuinely scary "Disembodied Hand" segment and (to a lesser extent) the flawed but still entertaining "Voodoo" story, *Dr. Terror's House of Horrors* remains a fairly solid entry in the notoriously uneven anthology subset. Too bad it failed to do justice to the "Werewolf."

With quotes from: "The Vault of Subotsky," by Philip Nutman, *Fangoria* 32; *Drums of Terror: Voodoo in the Cinema*, by Bryan Senn.

Drácula Contra Frankenstein see *Dracula, Prisoner of Frankenstein*)

Dracula, Prisoner of Frankenstein

(1972; Chamartin; Spain/France) Original Language Title: *Drácula Contra Frankenstein*; Alternate Title: *The Screaming Dead* (video); Director: Jess Franco.

In the world of cinematic exploitation, the late, prolific, enigmatic and often downright frustrating Spanish filmmaker Jess Franco remains a divisive figure. His low-budget Eurotrash movies range from straight horror to surreal sexploitation to hard-core porn. Some love him, many hate him, but few understand him. Some that do claim that in order to truly "get" Franco, one must see all of his oeuvre—then one can take significant meaning from his films. Most people, even avowed cineastes, however, simply don't have the time (or the patience) for such an undertaking, given that Franco's output encompasses well over 200 movies. While this author has seen perhaps a sixth of Franco's features, the ratio of engaging success (*The Awful Dr. Orlof* [1962], *The Sadistic Baron Von Klaus* [1962], *The Diabolical Dr. Z* [1966], and a few others) to tedious failure (about 30 more) doesn't warrant such a major investment of time and brain cells. Towards the end of his life, Franco himself admitted that he was "disappointed" that people seemed to finally be taking him seriously as a filmmaker. "I don't want to be taken seriously!" he countered. "My films are meant to just be enjoyed, to be fun." Regarding this, one's mileage may vary.

Years after Dr. Seward has dispatched Dracula with a (ridiculously tiny) stake to the heart, the evil Dr. Frankenstein comes to Dracula's castle and revives the Count, as well as a pair of vampire women *and* his own Monster, intending to use them to rule the world ... or something. A now older Dr. Seward must once again don the guise of monster hunter and foil the mad doctor's plans, with the aid of some gypsies and a late-arriving heroic werewolf.

Franco's script matches his disjointed direction (it's over 16 minutes before anyone speaks a word of dialogue) in its lack of logic and outright boredom. None of the characters—protagonist or villain, human or monster—evinces *any* personality whatsoever. Dracula (played by Franco regular Howard Vernon) simply bugs out his eyes and silently stares (never uttering a word); the nefarious Dr. Frankenstein (Dennis Price, just a year before his death) often looks frail and confused, and also speaks nary a word (all his dialogue comes in voiceover, no doubt due to the alcoholic Price's poor health and inability to remember lines); and even the heroic Dr. Seward (Alberto Dalbés) mostly mopes at his desk or lies in bed recovering as the gypsy woman tells him he's destined to vanquish the forces of evil. (Ironically, Frankenstein and the monsters do most of that themselves by turning on one another at the end, with Seward doing nothing but leading a tiny band of torch-wielding villagers to the castle, arriving too late to participate.)

Frequent Franco collaborator Jack Taylor (who starred in eight of Franco's films) labeled the filmmaker "a charming and brilliant conversationalist, with great taste in music, a snake charmer of sorts, a gourmet and, when he wanted to be, a very good director. His only problem was that after the first week, he became bored with what he was shooting and needed a change." In *Dracula, Prisoner of Frankenstein*, a werewolf (played by a one-shot actor billed simply as "Brandy") makes an out-of-nowhere appearance at the movie's climax, and this lycan's abrupt and awkward injection into the mix smacks of ennui-staving desperation. Apparently, the gypsy woman somehow calls forth this wolfman and sends him to attack the castle, where he (briefly) battles the Frankenstein Monster. Just how she accomplishes this remains a glossed-over mystery. At one point the gypsy seer tells Seward, "When the full moon appears and the wind clears the sky, the werewolf will come to help you. The battle will be bloody, but you will win in the end." Then later she reiterates, "I know the wolf will come, and with him fear will be harbored in all evil spirits." This casts the werewolf firmly in a heroic light. Rather than engaging in the usual out-of-control, indiscriminate bloody rampage, he attacks only the forces of evil (in the form of Frankenstein's Monster). Because he simply appears in wolfman form, and we never see him transform from his human guise, he remains more symbol than true

In Canada the werewolf-lite Jess Franco mishmash *Dracula, Prisoner of Frankenstein* was released on a double bill with the full-on Paul Naschy lycanthrope entry *The Werewolf vs. the Vampire Woman* (renamed *Werewolf Shadow*, though mistakenly labeled *Werewolf's Shadow* in the ads).

character. As such, he engenders little empathy, remaining merely a simplistic (good-guy) monster rather than an intriguing figure of tragedy. Even as a monster, this slapdash werewolf disappoints, since his putty nose, plastic fangs, and untidy crepe facial hair and fright wig reveal that just as little care was taken with his appearance as with his, er, appearance. This completely uninspired and uninspiring wolfman specimen logs about two minutes of screen time, during which he makes a few leaps upon the Frankenstein Monster, suffers a couple of judo throws, and once even scampers between the big guy's legs. Sad. The sequence ends with the somewhat scratched and bloodied Frankenstein Monster staggering off back to the lab for some recharging. We see nothing further of the wolfman and remain ignorant of his fate. Franco does not deign to throw this were-dog a bone, failing to show the werewolf lying dead in the corner, licking his wounds, or even scampering out of the castle with his metaphorical tail between his legs. In Franco's world, lycanthropic afterthoughts simply get no respect. And in Canada, *Dracula, Prisoner of Frankenstein* unfairly topped a double bill with the far superior Paul Naschy wolfman film *Werewolf Shadow* (aka *The Werewolf vs. the Vampire Woman*).

"Some of my movies aren't very good, it's true," admitted Franco, "but they are all mine, and all of them have special significance to me." *Dracula, Prisoner of Frankenstein* definitely falls into the "not very good" category. And as for "significance," well, did I mention your mileage may vary?

With quotes from: "Jack's Journey into Perversion," by Kier-La Janisse, *Fangoria* 325; "The Sultan of Sleaze Lives!" by Chris Alexander, *Fangoria* 294.

The Dungeonmaster

(1984; Empire Pictures) Alternate Title: *Ragewar*; Directors: Rosemarie Turko, John Beuchler, Charles Band, David Allen, Steve Ford, Peter Monoogian, Ted Nicolaou.

Eyeing the dollars banked by Disney for their ultra-successful computer-imagery-heavy *Tron* (1982), Empire Pictures head honcho Charles Band decided to combine the computer concept with the then-popular Dungeons and Dragons role-playing game phenomenon for yet another of the company's low-budget cheesefests. He then hired *seven* different filmmakers (including himself) to write and direct short episodes that could be melded together into a feature. The result: *The Dungeonmaster*.

Demon-sorcerer Mestema (the hulking Richard Moll—in long wig and black fingernails) whisks computer programmer extraordinaire Paul (TV actor Jeffrey Byron) and his fiancée Gwen (newcomer Leslie Wing) to his Hellish domain. Looking for a "worthy opponent," Mestema dubs the bewildered Paul "Excalibrate" (in a laughable 'knighting' ceremony, complete with sword and bended knee). Intent on pitting his "diabolical magic" against Paul's "computer magic" (a talking computer on his wrist), the evil sorcerer sets "seven challenges" for Paul, warning, "If you fail just one I'll have your souls." He transports the couple into various scenarios in which Paul must face down (and usually rescue Gwen from) a mini-gargoyle named "Ratspit" and his zombie warriors, a giant stone statue come to life (courtesy of stop-motion animator David Allen), a cave demon with a penchant for throwing rocks, a back-alley serial killer intent on making Gwen his next victim, a machete-wielding heavy metal rock band, and a handful of Road Warrior rejects.

For the first challenge ("Ice Gallery," by Rosemarie Turko), Mestema teleports Paul and Gwen to an ice cavern full of frozen villains and monsters. When Mestema raises the cave's temperature everyone from Jack the Ripper and Genghis Kahn to the Mummy and the Wolfman thaw out and come to life. The werewolf, played by low-end jack-of-all-cinema-trades actor/writer/director/effects artist Ken Hall (whose biggest claim to fame might be having built the *Carnosaur* for Roger Corman in 1993) sports a hairy torso covered in whitish fur (à la Oliver Reed in *The Curse of the Werewolf*) topped by a full wolf's head (muzzle, ears, etc.). Though it *looks* generally adequate, the werewolf appears in only a few split-second shots, and does little more than briefly wave its arms about menacingly before Paul finds a magic crystal that he uses to explode the fiends and send himself and Gwen back to Mestema's lair.

With so many different writer/directors working on so many different segments in so little time (a mere 73 minutes—*including* closing credits) it's no wonder the film fails to hold together, with Paul overcoming each challenge quickly and easily (usually by simply tapping his wrist a few times and firing a laser bolt) before moving on to the next impoverished encounter. About the only enjoyment to be gleaned from this disjointed collage of tired snapshots is the grandiosely over-the-top performance by an obviously-enjoying-himself Richard Moll. Simplistic, broadly acted, and filled with cheap effects, *The Dungeonmaster* is the cinematic equivalent of a bland ham and cheese sandwich at a low-rent diner.

Evil Deeds

(2004; Dark Night Films) Directors: Matt Spease, Bailee Arnett, Isaak Partlow.

"In the tradition of *Creepshow* and *Tales from the Crypt*" touted this micro-budgeted (less than $4,000) anthology's tagline. Well, only insofar as the five-part *Evil Deeds* likewise rides the horror omnibus. There the similarities end, as this hopelessly inept and amateurish camcorder cacophony has nothing *else* in common with those two professional portmanteaus.

A bank robber on the run holes up in what looks like an auto parts storeroom only to find "the Hermit" living there, who tells the thief five terror tales to pass the time: "The Mental Patient," about a female Michael Myers stand-in; the self-explanatory "Vampire at Midnight"; the zombie-centric "Forgive Me Father"; "Hell Beast," a werewolf tale; and the serial killer story "Lamb to the Slaughter."

Despite its five-stories-plus-wraparound format, *Evil Deeds* clocks in at a barely-feature-length 68 minutes—though it feels *much* longer. Sub-wedding-level videography (complete with annoying flares and focus issues), poor sound, poorer acting from a group of Arkansas amateurs (including co-director Matt Spease himself), and poorer still scripting make these *Deeds* nearly unwatchable.

The nine-minute-long fourth tale, "Hell Beast," steps into lycan-territory when Dan tells his girlfriend Helen (played by Harley and Casey Wolfe), "I thought you should get acquainted with the local folklore. I'm talkin' about David Kessler the lycanthope." (Note to no-budget werewolf moviemakers: Referencing one of the best lycan-flicks of all time [in this case the lead character from *An American Werewolf in London*] invites only losing comparisons to your backyard bonanzas.) "Back during the Cold War," continues Dan in a rushed monotone that sounds like he's just trying to get the words out without dropping too many lines, "the Russians decided to experiment. They were going to find a werewolf and genetically enhance them. You see, werewolves are among the most lethal killers out there. But they're only shapeshifters during the full moon. The Russians were trying to find a way to mutate these people so they could shapeshift at will. They searched the whole country looking for werewolves but only found schizophrenics." Cheekily, writer-director Matt Spease runs tinted footage from the Lon Chaney, Jr., vehicle *The Indestructible Man* under this dull diatribe (doctors in a lab, Chaney wandering through the woods). Apropos of nothing seen nor spoken of so far, outside in the woods a mysterious being sporting a long cloak and finger extensions intones, "Arise my Hell Beast; I have work for you to do." At this, a cartoonish superimposed lightning bolt, then flames, herald the abrupt appearance of a beast-man in checkered shirt and hairy mutated dog's head rubber mask (on the level of a middling Halloween prop). The "work" this Hell Beast subsequently accomplishes consists of one quick attack on a wandering drunk, and the mauling of the protagonist (who, it turns out, has "come to kill David Kessler once and for all"). This consists of the beast's hairy paws ludicrously slapping his prone victim's chest over and over while wildly inappropriate foley "punches" play on the soundtrack. A few shots of the Hell Beast leaping at the camera, some pixilated nighttime video footage so muddy as to be indecipherable, and a few yellow-tinted creature's-eye-view shots so oversaturated that they obfuscate everything rounds out the episode. The best part of the tepid tale comes via another flashback in which Dan tells how Kessler had killed his parents—represented by more tinted footage of a *real* (if not particularly good) werewolf movie: *The Mad Monster*. In the end, the nonsensical, footage-thieving "Hell Beast" sheds little light on lycanthropes, leaving one to wonder if werewolves are (a) the product of Commie experiments; (b) tools of demonic forces; or c) bitch-slapping, rubber-masked amateurs.

The true Evil Deed here is Spease and co. inflicting their homemade horrors on unsuspecting viewers. Arkansas auteur Spease made several similarly impoverished direct-to-video "sequels" to this bit of backwoods baloney, as well as a 2012 "remake," though (thankfully) none of them revisited the lycan-topic.

Exhumed

(2003; Frontline Films; Canada) Director: Brian Clement.

This micro-budgeted (reportedly $5,000) Canadian horror anthology written and directed by Brian Clement (2000's *Meat Market* and its sequels) delivers three stories involving zombies, all tied together with a mysterious (perhaps alien) artifact whose glowing blue light raises the dead. The first story, set in feudal Japan, sees a samurai and a monk enter a haunted forest in search of said artifact, only to find more than they bargained for. The second tale (shot film noir–style in shadowy black-and-white, complete with hard-boiled voiceover narration) tells of a female detective stumbling upon a plot to revive stolen corpses, which then segues before its finish into the final episode, "Last Rumble." "Far in the future," our narrator tells us, "our world is engulfed in war. But beneath this war is another battle, fought between immortals for centuries. Only a handful of each side remain, and their fight would soon come to an end." Said fight is a battle between vampire and werewolf gangs that style themselves after the British "mods" (the vamps) and "rockers" (the lycans) of the 1960s. Their immortal rumble is interrupted before it ever really gets started, however, by a platoon of hazmat-suited, gas-mask-wearing soldiers firing silver bullets. ("Silver bullets don't just kill vampires," notes one of the survivors, "they kill werewolves too.") Capturing the lone female vampire (Chelsea "Inka" Arentsen) and female werewolf (Chantelle Adamache), and killing all the rest, the soldiers toss the two into a cell back at their bunker, where they pit them against a few zombies for their own amusement. The general and his head scientist also plan to use them in an experiment (involving the artifact) to transfer "consciousness through the time-space continuum" in order to somehow thwart their enemies and finally win the war. It all concludes back at the close of the second story when a resurrected corpse turns out to house the vampire's consciousness, and an *alien* arrives (our onscreen narrator, Mr. Gray) with his ray gun to try and explain/sort things out (much to the characters' consternation—and the viewers' confusion).

Ambitious but too convoluted for its own good, *Exhumed* does little to explore or advance lycanthropy apart from offering a screen first—a gratuitous lesbian sex scene between a werewolf and a vampire! Yes, despite writer-director Brian Clement's artistic aspirations (as evidenced by the chambara-like first segment and the successfully noirish second), he succumbed to giving the viewers what he presumed they wanted in the form of some prison-cell fanged-girl-on-fanged-girl action. (At least it's relatively brief—and tame—with a few shots of bare breasts and bared fangs lovingly sinking into shoulders.) Apart from this questionable novelty, little illumination falls on the lycanthropic topic apart from some dialogue noting they're immortal and affected by silver, and that they can reason and even talk while in wolf-form. (The general does refer to both the were-girl and vamp-chick as "mutants," but this remains a throwaway line/notion.) This werewolf form remains pretty minimal, consisting of wrinkled skin, a prosthetic dog nose, heavy brows, built-up forehead, a full set of fangs, and, oddly, four-inch-long shaggy eyebrows hanging off to the sides. The transformation (which we never see) apparently ends at the neck, since the rest of them remain human (with nary a claw in sight).

Shot in and around Vancouver, Canada, from January to June 2003, *Exhumed*'s ambition outstrips its intelligence, leaving it an idea- (and homage-) rich pastiche which, like the zombies themselves that form its central notion, can't pull itself together into a presentable whole. And it does the werewolf no favors, either—unless bisexual bitches are your thing.

FDR: American Badass

(2012; Screen Media) Director: Garrett Brawith.

Though technically this puerile spoof *could* be included in the book's main section, I've chosen to relegate it to the *PseudoWolves* category because of its treatment of lycanthropy as little more than an extended throwaway gag. The film would have been little different had the antagonists been men rather than *wolf*men. The supposed manbeasts here behave no differently from humans, sitting behind desks, talking on the phone, even playing beer pong. And their hirsute appearance remains permanent, as they never transform back to human, even after death. "I had been tinkering with making a movie about FDR taking down New York gangsters to end Prohibition," explained screenwriter Ross Patterson. "Then *Abraham Lincoln: Vampire Hunter* came along, and some investors suggested, why don't I have FDR fight werewolves? I wasn't psyched about it initially…" Patterson should have gone with his first impression.

The werewolf bit begins when a wolfman attacks Governor Franklin Delano Roosevelt while he's out hunting. Though FDR gets the better of the beast, the creature bites him on the leg. Instead of passing along the curse of lycanthropy, however, the bite gives him polio(!). After he becomes president, Roosevelt tries to keep America clear of that "trouble" overseas, but a plot to infect the American populace via contaminated booze has ass-kicking FDR take to a tricked-out wheelchair that shoots silver bullets and mini-missiles. The lycan-conceit here being that Hitler, Mussolini and Hirohito (who interact via an early form of the conference call they label "the three-way"—ha ha) are all silly-looking werewolves with big hair, tiny fangs and wet dog noses. "I decided if I could make all the monsters look like Michael J. Fox's dad in *Teen Wolf*, it would be pretty funny," recounted Patterson. "The werewolves look completely non-threatening, which adds to the campiness." But campiness alone does not a feature make; it takes a clever script—something *FDR: American Badass* lacks.

Actor-turned-director Garrett Brawith (making his sophomore directorial effort) wisely cast veteran thespians like Barry Bostwick (doing an excellent FDR impersonation), Bruce McGill and Ray Wise (as Douglas MacArthur), who all do the best they can with the subpar material. Unfortunately, the frequently inane screenplay gives them little to work with. Ross Patterson, as a constantly inebriated, highly articulate Southern congressman, has the best jokes (including several revolving around his nymphomaniac wife), and things get a whole lot funnier when he's onscreen—not surprising, perhaps, given that Patterson was also the screenwriter. Obviously modeled on the *Airplane* and *Naked Gun* movies, *FDR: American Badass* constantly devolves into scatological humor (one character repeatedly squats down and defecates into a vase when excited) and tacky sexual shenanigans (with Roosevelt getting his FDRocks off when his sexy secretary squirts ketchup and mustard all over his wobbly, hot dog–like "polio legs"). And seeing a hallowed historical figure constantly dropping the f-bomb can get one only so far. With crude, cheesy production values (it's almost entirely set-bound) to go along with its crude, cheesy screenplay, *FDR: American Badass* comes off like a poor *Saturday Night Live* skit (with bad language and sex jokes) that just won't end.

With quotes from: *FDR: American Badass*: New Dealing with Werewolves," by Michael Gingold, *Fangoria* 317.

The Feral Man

(2002; Dudez Productions/Tempe Video; Canada) Alternate Title: *Wolf Mania*. Director: Brett Kelly.

At 63 minutes, the Canadian micro-budgeted shot-on-video *The Feral Man* barely qualifies as a feature (particularly since 13 of those minutes consist of the overlong closing credits!). And given its plodding plot, dull characters, toneless acting, mundane videography, frequently tinny sound, and complete lack of monster (or action), it definitely does *not* qualify as entertainment.

Danny (writer-producer-director Brett Kelly himself) is a down-on-his-luck schlub who, after his father's funeral, is attacked by an unseen person (or creature), sustaining a mild head injury. Afterward, he feels different, and begins spending his nights away from his patient live-in girlfriend Linda (Mary Macpherson). As more and more people turn up murdered in the environs, the local homicide squad sets a trap for the killer, leading to Danny's door.

As a character, Danny could not be any less interesting. Self-pitying from the start ("I don't have a car, I don't have any money, and I screw everything up," he whines), he engenders zero sympathy, so that when he begins acting strangely there is little viewer connection—or interest. This only makes the many protracted scenes of Danny brooding while walking through the park, sitting on a bench, drinking in a bar, or complaining to his friends even more boringly pointless.

Worse, Danny is not really a werewolf, or even a "feral man"—he's just a loser who hits his head and becomes a killer (the only outward sign of any change being a hard stare and some eventual blood on his clothing). As the detective in charge (who looks like he's about 20 years old) tells Danny's girlfriend after it's all over, "He recently suffered a blow to the head; this blow caused damage to the lower cortex of his brain. The doctors say this might have triggered something, causing seizures and delusions." Danny leaves a letter for his girlfriend, confessing that "every night I feel the compulsion to hunt and to kill. When I look in the mirror I don't see my own face, I see the face of a wolf." Too bad filmmaker Kelly neglected to visualize this and left such an intriguing notion unfulfilled and tossed off in a *letter*.

Even more plentiful than all the missed opportunities are scene after scene of flat master shots in dull settings (cheap apartments; parking garage; a police squad room that consists of one desk and a computer; etc.), with the camera rarely moving—when not in clichéd p.o.v. mode during the "attack" scenes. Said attacks (five of them) are all staged and shot in nearly identical fashion, as a bit of hand-held shaky-cam signals something watching the victim-to-be, before the camera frantically rushes towards the person, resulting in either the screen going black or a splash of red paint hitting a tree trunk. That's it.

"I kinda wanted to do a werewolf movie, but I didn't want to do a movie that had a guy in a dog suit," explained do-it-yourselfer Brett Kelly (who wrote, directed, produced, and starred as Danny) of his first full feature, shot over nine days in Ottawa. "I interpret it that there was never a werewolf in the movie whatsoever; it was just the guy's instability." Well, *I* interpret it that there was never any interest in the movie whatsoever; it was just the amateur filmmaker's vanity.

With quotes from: "The Feral Man Speaks: Interview with Brett Kelly," *The Feral Man* DVD, Tempe Video, 2005.

Frankenstein and Me

(1996; Malofilm) Director: Robert Tinnell.

For those of us who grew up with cinematic monsters, *Frankenstein and Me* is not only a poignant trip down Memory Lane, but a validation of secret childhood wonder—feelings that monsters *do* exist and, if one believes strongly enough, anything *is* possible. The story, set in 1970, centers on a poor but happy family living in a small community in the California desert (the film carried the shooting title *Mojave Frankenstein*). The father, a likable, soft-spoken trucker (sensitively played by Burt Reynolds, terrible toupee notwithstanding), is a dreamer, a man who loves to spend his time tinkering with impractical gadgets in the garage and indulging his two young sons in their love of fantasy and all things monsters. The mother, however, disdains her husband and sons' penchant for imagination and cannot see past the more "practical" day-to-day drudgery of making ends meet. After the father succumbs to a heart attack (in a truly lump-in-the-throat scene astutely handled by director Robert Tinnell and his actors to evoke the awful pain and loneliness of this tragic moment), the story focuses on the two boys, particularly Earl (Jamieson Boulanger), who feels most keenly the loss of his one validating adult. When Earl visits a cheap traveling carnival that claims to have the "real" Frankenstein Monster—an imposing but lifeless figure—he decides to try and revive the creature. With help from his skeptical friends, Earl builds a primitive lightning rod apparatus (based on a design his father had doodled out for him) in an old abandoned mining building. Everything comes to a head during the climactic storm, and the characters, in this milieu of trying to *create* life, learn something about life itself.

Tinnell's charming story wonderfully captures both the enthusiasm and isolation often felt by monster lovers over the course of their childhood. It also deals thoughtfully with the pain of loss, making the boy's admittedly irrational actions a desperate tribute to his father, who always regretted that he didn't follow his dream. (Dad's dream was to make it big in Hollywood, but he lacked the conviction to stick it out. In one of the film's most heartwarming moments, we see that as a present for their beloved father the two boys have built a makeshift HOLLYWOOD sign up on the rocks behind their house.) To Tinnell's credit, *Frankenstein and Me* remains poignant without becoming cloying, and the script beautifully captures that sense of wonder so strong in childhood that makes such things as Frankenstein's Monster almost magically real.

The hirsute horror from a brief fantasy episode in the surprisingly affecting, family-oriented horror homage *Frankenstein and Me*.

Technically, Tinnell and his crew (filming exteriors on the very edge of the Mojave desert in Victorville, California, and shooting the interiors in Montreal, Canada) put their heart and soul into this production, creating beautiful, finely detailed sets (belying the film's relatively low two-million-dollar budget) which stand as loving homages to such classics as *Frankenstein*, *The Brides of Dracula*, and *Night of the Living Dead*. In these memorable settings, Earl plays out his rich, movie-influenced fantasy life. (Production designer Michael Marsolais transformed an old train warehouse into uncanny replicas of scenes from these seminal horror classics.) During one of Earl's frequent daydreams (for which he's often punished by his shrewish schoolteacher, who forces him to stand with his nose to the blackboard), Earl casts himself as the tragic figure of *The Wolf Man*. The two-minute vignette sees the snarling manbeast chase a girl (appropriately dressed in '40s chic) through a fog-bound forest, only to be felled by a silver bullet. As he dies, he transforms back to his human self (via a series of dissolves—just like in the original) and utters a contented "I will rest now" before expiring. With its stylized woodland set (complete with denuded trees), fog-shrouded atmosphere, and period dress, it makes for a perfect tribute to the 1941 werewolf classic. Tinnell even includes the original's iconic shot of the ferocious Wolf Man eyeing his prey through the spindly branches of a dead tree before attacking.

According to the film's publicity, "Robert Tinnell was able to share his enthusiasm for old movie monsters with [his child stars], who weren't necessarily familiar with Boris Karloff, Bela Lugosi and the other greats of that era." Though one should generally take such press releases with a grain of salt, the director himself related that his young thespians would eagerly gather in Tinnell's hotel room to watch the old classics. *Frankenstein and Me* wonderfully reflects this affectionate enthusiasm.

With quotes from: *Frankenstein and Me* pressbook, Malofilm International, 1996; correspondence with the author.

Frankestein, el Vampiro y Compañía

(1962; Cinematográfica Calderon; Mexico; b&w) Director: Benito Alazraki.

Universal's *Abbott and Costello Meet Frankenstein* (1948) is one of the most beloved horror-comedies of all time. And rightly so. The Mexican *Frankestein* [sic], *el Vampiro y Compania* is one of the most overtly plagiaristic horror-comedies of all time, as it's a nearly scene-for-scene steal from that comedy duo's classic. But while the South-of-the-Border filmmakers lifted the plot, characters, and even a number of gags from the earlier picture, they failed to replicate the truly funny Abbott and Costello dynamics (here substituting Manuel "Loco" Valdés and José Jasso, who display little chemistry and even less comedic artistry) as well as the original's genuinely frightening tone. Rather than treating its trio of monsters respectfully and utilizing their imposing personas to generate an atmosphere of suspense, as in the Abbott and Costello film, the Mexican remake casts its monsters as mere buffoons that serve only as the brunt of a few silly (and unfunny) jokes.

Though slavishly aping the Universal film's plot of two bumbling baggage handlers running afoul of a female mad scientist, Dracula, the Frankenstein Monster, and the Wolf Man (with the latter on the side of the "boys"—when not in hirsute form, that is), *Frankestein, el Vampiro y Compañía* occasionally departs from its chosen model. For instance, the female mad scientist revives both the Monster and the vampire (with the newly-restored bloodsucker then taking hypnotic control of her), rather than Dracula himself having been behind the nefarious plan all along (as in the original). Replacing the A&C film's brain-transplant concept is the notion of a mind-transference, which is actually successful (if temporary), with the Monster hopping around goofily and acting "loco," while Costello stand-in Valdez stumbles about with arms outstretched, trashing the laboratory and menacing the principals. And for some reason, "el Vampiro" is never called Dracula (while, oddly, the Frankenstein Monster drops the "n" to become "Frankestein").

But for lycanthropic purposes, the most interesting change comes at film's end, when el Hombre Lobo battles el Vampiro (just as the Wolf Man fought Dracula in the original). Rather than an exciting chase/battle through the castle, ending in the Wolf Man lunging for Dracula in bat form and taking them both over the cliff to their deaths, the two Mexi-versions simply grapple in a dim basement room, with the werewolf finally choking the bloodsucker into submission before grabbing a handy stake to shove into his chest. The Wolf Man then clutches at his neck and succumbs to wounds apparently inflicted (unseen) by the vampire, while the room goes up in flames (consuming all three monsters) as Our Heroes make their getaway. Such a perfunctory finish for its werewolf, coupled with the curious choice to have the savage manbeast perform such a calculated,

Mexico's plagiaristic answer to *Abbott and Costello Meet Frankenstein*.

PSEUDOWOLVES

premeditated action (the staking), makes for a decidedly unsatisfactory conclusion for the film's lycanthrope.

Each of the three classic creatures prove subpar in every way, particularly the "Frankestein" Monster, whose frog-like features make him look cartoonish. The werewolf's wooly hair and beard, rubbery face, piggish nose, oversized Clark Gable ears, and set of inch-long vampire fangs stands as one of the worst werewolf makeups this side of an Andy Milligan movie. And most disappointingly, this ridiculous-looking Chaney-lite variation displays none of the original's savagery (no tearing the stuffing out of a chair here, for instance). Likewise, in keeping with the cramped sets and cheesy "exteriors" (which are no more convincing than the monsters' silly visages), the Mexican film offers no onscreen metamorphoses. Instead, the actor simply clutches his head, the film cuts away to another character, and then, viola, there stands the werewolf—who generally does very little. Sad.

To date, *Frankenstein, el Vampiro y Compañía* has never received an English-language release, which may be no great loss in the end. Two other horrors directed by *Frankenstein* helmer Benito Alazraki this same year *did* see some screen time north of the border, however—the desultory *Spiritism* and the inferior Santo vehicle *Invasion of the Zombies*—completing a trifecta of Mexican horror cinema disappointment.

Freaky Fairytales see *Deadtime Stories*

Fright Club

(2006; R.D.P.) Directors: Antonio Olivas (as Tyger Torrez), Attika Torrence, Daniel Max Chiu.

Here's another no-budget shot-on-video anthology film that offers up a werewolf tale among its trio of subpar stories. Three friends visit a bizarre art gallery fronting for the underground "Fright Club," a "secret society" founded by and dedicated to turn-of-the-century Gothic artist Sebastian Crowe. The trio wants to join; but first, says the hostess, "You must demonstrate yourselves worthy by going before our eldest member and telling stories.... They must be scary, horrific, terrifying." There ensues three racially-based tales of monsters—Black vampires, an Asian Frankenstein creature, and an Hispanic werewolf.

"Little Red Riding in the Hood" (set in "East L.A. ... once upon a time") has the not-so-little "Roja" ("Red"), after experiencing a disturbing erotic dream (giving filmmaker Antonio Olivas, nee Tyger Torrez, ample opportunity to display actress Cindy Pena's most prominent assets), head out to buy medicine for her ailing grandmother. Carrying a basket of goodies her mother made, and sporting a red shawl, Roja runs across her former boyfriend "Lobo," who wants her back. When Lobo gets a little too physical, a "Mexican FBI agent," who just happens to be at Lobo's tattoo parlor making inquiries, helps her out. Sparks fly. But when Roja arrives at her grandmother's house, she finds only her mutilated corpse—and a shotgun-toting Lobo. But things aren't as they seem, and the FBI agent shows up, shoots Lobo, and promptly transforms into a werewolf ("Rojalita," he tells her, "I like you and want you to join us").

Though only twenty minutes long, the dull and meandering segment still takes time to include plot threads that go nowhere. For instance, Roja goes to the local spiritualist/herbalist to procure her grandmother's medicine, whereupon the disturbed occultist tells Roja, "You have the curse of the wolf upon you" and entreats her to take a small statuette for protection. But this protective amulet never comes into play, with the werewolf vanquished by an ordinary shotgun blast to the head ("Now who's afraid of the Big Bad Wolf," Roja quips before pulling the trigger). Likewise, the proceedings take place during the Dia de los Meurtos ("Day of the Dead"—a big deal in Mexico), but, again, nothing significant comes of this, and the story simply drops this point after taking pains to make it.

The werewolf's appearance disappoints just as badly as the rambling story. With the actor wearing an obvious facial prosthetic that adds angular cheekbones, heavy eyebrow ridges, a distended bat nose, huge pointed ears, a modest set of fangs, and a decided *lack* of fur or hair, he looks more demonic than lupine. The beast can talk while in wolf form (even mocking Roja with the expected "My what big teeth you have—the better to eat you with"), preserving its human faculties. But it's onscreen for such a brief time that nothing else can be learned about this "Big Bad Wolf."

Though some sources put the film's budget at $25,000, one is hard-pressed to see where even a fifth of that went, given the amateurish acting, cheap-looking videography, hollow sound, dearth of action, and paltry special effects (consisting of Halloween masks, a few press-on-fangs, and some stage blood). The biggest effect—the shotgunning of the werewolf—sees the beast's head "explode" via a not-fooling-anyone freeze frame photo.

At film's end, the three initiates are denied entry into Fright Club—which is ironically fitting, as the three tepid tales fail to deliver anything even remotely "scary, horrific or terrifying." The scariest thing in this Snooze Club is an embarrassing sequence in which a corpulent Conrad Brooks (of *Plan 9 from Outer Space* infamy) shows up in a skintight t-shirt for a tryst with Roja's mother. Brrrr...

Fright Night Part 2

(1988; New Century Vista/TriStar) Director: Tommy Lee Wallace.

Three years after high schooler Charlie Brewster (William Ragsdale) and washed-up horror host Peter Vincent (Roddy McDowall) faced down and defeated the vampire Jerry Dandridge in the original *Fright Night*, Jerry's vampire sister comes to town, seeking revenge. In the three-year interim, Charlie, now in college, has just about bought into the notion put forth by his psychiatrist that it was all a fantasy

The unique-looking "Louiewolf" (Jonathan Gries), sadly underutilized in the warmed-over sequel *Fright Night Part 2*.

and there are no such things as vampires. But when a mysterious performance artist named Regine (Julie Carmen) invades his "dreams" and even usurps Peter's place as the host of Fright Night, and people begin disappearing at an alarming rate, Charlie and Peter must once again take up arms against the undead.

Far more overtly comical than the subtly clever and well-liked *Fright Night* (1985), *Part 2* brings little originality in continuing the tale, opting instead for a simple redux with a few minor changes. For instance, this time it's Charlie who falls under the vampire's spell (rather than his girlfriend, as in the original) and must be rescued (by his girl and Peter). And here *Peter* must convince the doubting Charlie of the existence of vampires, rather than the other way round, as before. And the final showdown between the two vampire hunters and the bat-form bloodsucker is merely a scaled down repeat of the original's far-more-exciting climax (with the fiery demise being exactly the same).

While the story's heart remains intact (in the form of the two likable and well-drawn central protagonists of Charlie and Peter), the body of the film lacks the liver and spleen and nearly every other organ, with Julie Carmen making a poor substitute for the charming and malevolent modern-day vampire Jerry Dandrige, so rivetingly realized by Chris Sarandon in the first film. "Regine is definitely a freaked-out personality," opined actress Julie Carmen, "kind of like a cross between Tina Turner and Catherine Deneuve." Unfortunately, as played by Carmen, the character has little of the appeal or presence of either, remaining more a bloodsucking cipher than a full-blown character. Unlike the original's Tom Holland, whom lead William Ragsdale characterized as an "actor's director," *Part 2*'s Tommy Lee Wallace left his actors pretty much to themselves. "I'd have questions and go to him," recalled Ragsdale, "but he was wrapped up in the technical aspect." While seasoned film professionals like Ragsdale and McDowell could cope well enough on their own, this lack of directorial guidance shows in the plastic performance of cinema neophyte Julie Carmen (who'd worked mostly in television).

The script tries to make up for this dearth of villainous quality by upping the quantity, replacing the first film's solitary supernatural henchman with *three* underlings for Regine—a hulking Renfield type, a trendy vampiress, and a rather goofy werewolf character named Louie, played with white trash glee by Jonathan Gries (*Napoleon Dynamite*), who overuses the word "dude" and engages in low-brow antics (when not hitting on Charlie's girlfriend) like playing a joke on a fellow underling by substituting his bowling ball with a human head. We only see Louie in werewolf form in three very brief scenes, two of them played for laughs. With sharp ridges on his misshapen face, long hair trailing down his head and cheeks, and a flat muzzle with a wide mouth and rows of scraggly teeth, the Louiewolf resembles a cross between the Wolfman and the Predator. The full hairy body suit adds some verisimilitude, but this lycanthrope has precious little to do—besides falling off a building (twice).

Fright Night Part 2 did dismal box-office (particularly considering the original *Fright Night* earned more than $50 million worldwide), failing to make back even half its $7.5 million budget upon its initial domestic release. Though not a bad film (it still contains enough of the original's charm—largely realized through the engaging playing of Ragsdale and especially McDowell—to hold one's interest), *Fright Night Part 2* ultimately wasted its opportunities and took the easy, warmed-over rehash route. As Ragsdale himself admitted, "It didn't have the same spark. They tried to update it, but it lost the innocence a bit, and it didn't quite work."

With quotes from: "Fright Night Part 2 Bares Its Fangs," by Marc Shapiro, *Fangoria* 76; interview with William Ragsdale conducted by the author, October 2014.

Gallery of Horror see *Dr. Terror's Gallery of Horrors*

Goosebumps

(2015; Columbia) Director: Rob Letterman.

Based on prolific author R. L. Stine's series of youth-aimed horror novelettes, the cleverly self-reflexive *Goosebumps* follows new-kid-in-town Zach (Dylan Minnette) as he meets mysterious girl-next-door Hannah (Odeya Rush). It turns out that Hannah's misanthropic father is the famous *Goosebumps* author R. L. Stine (Jack Black), living incognito. When Zach and his goofy friend Champ (Ryan Lee) open one of Stine's original manuscripts, a ten-foot-tall Abominable Snowman materializes from the book and goes on a rampage. Though Hannah, Zach and Champ manage to get the beast back in the book, the fracas has released evil ventriloquist dummy Slappy (gleefully voiced by Jack Black) from *his* tome. Slappy steals the rest of the books so he can unleash all the monsters on the hapless town. Stine and the kids must find a way to entrap all the creatures, and save the town and its inhabitants.

Starting like an Afterschool Special—a *dull* Afterschool Special—it's a full half-hour before the first monster appears. And when it does, it's a disappointing CGI Abominable Snowman that looks like a massive white ape. Other monsters fare better, such as a truly amusing—and disturbing—gaggle of malevolent lawn gnomes, a gigantic praying mantis, and the creepy Slappy himself. An hour into the film a werewolf (from the book *The Werewolf of Fever Swamp*) puts in an appearance, encountered by our four protagonists when they temporarily take refuge in the local supermarket. First seen, er, wolfing down steaks at the abandoned meat counter, the wolfman soon gives chase. Though impressively rendered with a hairy, muscular torso topped by a ferocious-looking full wolf's head (complete with drool dripping from long fangs), the goofy athletic shorts and sneakers (with wolf-claws burst through the toes) he wears mitigates the effect. Worse, the obvious CGI gives the were-game away, offering that insubstantial weightlessness so endemic to mediocre computer imaging. This lycanthrope lopes on all fours but can stand upright. Trying to have its cake and eat it too, the three-minute sequence with the werewolf sees the beast alternately menace the protagonists and serve as the butt of their jokes. At one point Stine whispers, "He can smell my scent," and proceeds to douse himself with deodorant spray. At another, Zach distracts the beast by tossing a doggy chew toy down an aisle. This were-mutt growls menacingly, but also barks and emits canine yips of pain when it slides into walls. The encounter ends with our heroes trapped outside on the loading dock before a car careens out of nowhere to slam into the werewolf, knocking it into a dumpster with another doggy yelp.

The werewolf appears once more—for about 30 seconds at the climax (along with everything from mummies and zombies to killer clowns and space aliens)—when it menaces the Pretty Girl at the high school dance. As the beast-man advances, Champ (who has a crush on the girl) springs out of hiding and leaps on the monster's back. As the lycanthrope thrashes around, Champ sinks his teeth into the monsters hairy neck. The flailing werewolf, his neck smoking, tosses champ aside, and turns tail and runs. "Oh my god, how'd you do that?" queries the grateful girl. "Silver fillings," answers Champ. "I had a ton of cavities when I was ten."

Despite all the shouting and running about, and the frequent run-ins with the various monsters, the film's comical tone (and PG rating) never generates any real sense of danger or suspense. Consequently—and disappointingly—*Goosebumps* fails to raise any.

Grindhouse

(2007; Dimension) Directors: Quentin Tarantino, Robert Rodriguez.

Quentin Tarantino's and Robert Rodriguez' double-feature homage to the grindhouse days of the 1970s features a double-bill of the Tarantino-directed *Death Proof* (which focuses on a psychopathic ex-stuntman who kills women with his "death proof" stunt car) and the Rodriguez-helmed *Planet Terror* (revolving around a zombie outbreak). To fill out the full exploitation experience, *Grindhouse* also includes a number of coming attraction trailers—for fake films such as *Don't*, *Thanksgiving*, and *Machete* (which Rodriguez actually made into a real feature in 2010).

Among the faux trailers is one called *Werewolf Women of the SS*, directed by Rob Zombie (*House of 1000 Corpses* [2000], the *Halloween* remake [2007]). According to Rodriguez, "Rob Zombie came up to me in October at the Scream Awards and said, 'I have a trailer: *Werewolf Women of the SS*.' I said, 'Say no more. Go shoot it. You got me.'" Though Zombie filmed for only two days, he shot enough footage for a half-hour short, and reportedly agonized over having to pare it down to trailer-length.

The chaotic, fast-moving preview posits "the Nazis' diabolical plan to create an army of werewolf super-soldiers" during World War II (as the oh-so-dramatic narrator intones). In among the sexploitative snippets of women-in-prison torture scenes, evil Nazi doctors cackling maniacally, and out-of-left-field moments like the one announcing "Nicholas Cage as Fu Manchu," comes a Freudian-fraught scene of a uniformed Nazi werewolf firing off a machine gun while two hairy-but-still-sexy, half-nude she-wolves pose and snarl next to him. And, like all good trailers, the *Werewolf Women of the SS* teaser makes one really want to see the full feature. If only it existed ... (are you listening, Mr. Zombie?).

With quotes from: "House Party," by Mike Cotton, Wizarduniverse.com.

Grotesque

(1988; Empire Pictures) Director: Joe Tornatore.

In this brutal home invasion flick, a gang of crazed punkers break into a mountain home looking for cash and slaughters an entire family. But the kill-crazy punks didn't count on the deformed simpleton, Patrick, who lives in a secret room. After witnessing the atrocities, Patrick decides to come out and exact revenge on those who murdered his kin. *Grotesque* definitely lives up to its name in the unflinching way it portrays the vicious slayings, but the over-the-top acting, first by the psycho punkers and then by a grief-crazed Tab Hunter (who, along with Linda Blair, provides the film its [faded] "star" power), helps leaven the unpleasantness. Also helping to keep things to an almost tolerable level is the picture's self-reflexive approach—in that the head of the family is a Hollywood makeup artist who specializes in monsters (and enjoys scaring his daughter's friends with his latest creation when they come to visit).

Grotesque both begins and ends in a Hollywood screening room, with the opening macabre sequence turning out to be merely the climax of the makeup man's latest picture before the story proper starts and the killings begin. The final sequence has all the principles right back in the screening room, revealing that the previous 80 minutes had *also* been a movie(!), with the makeup man and all his family—actors, obviously—alive and well. But wait—suddenly the film melts, and we cut to the projection booth, where an articulate Frankenstein's Monster (in middling makeup) chats with the Wolf Man (an obvious mask), the latter of which intentionally broke the film because he was less than impressed with what unspooled onscreen. The duo decides to show the audience "what real monsters can do" and stalk into the theater, groaning and growling. After the audience flees, "Frank N. Stein" (as the credits bill him) reassures "Wolf Mann" that "We're still the scariest." Wolf replies, "You're darn right we are." Fade out. With jaunty, comical piano music playing on the soundtrack, it makes for a quaintly amusing but rather jarring final coda to the senseless-violence-and-revenge-filled movie, making it all seem rather ... grotesque.

Halloweentown

(1998; Buena Vista) Director: Duwayne Dunham.

In this Disney Channel TV movie, a trio of siblings (the oldest being 13) follow their kindly grandmother (played by an obviously-needs-the-work Debbie Reynolds) to "Halloweentown," a place where monsters are real and live peaceably outside the purview of the mortal realm. Coming from a long line of witches, the children must help their grandmother (the most powerful witch of all) defeat a mysterious dark force that threatens not only Halloweentown but the whole world. To do this, they must concoct a witches' brew that will reactive the dormant "Talisman of Merlin" and so defeat the dark powers. Needed for said brew are ingredients like "fang of vampire," "sweat of ghost" and "hair of werewolf." So the youngsters pay a visit to the Halloweentown hairdresser—a werewolf—and, with some judicious use of a hair trimmer, end up with the precious ingredient. The one-minute scene is played strictly for laughs, with the non-threatening, makeup-lite wolfman dressed and acting like a stereotypical high-strung hairdresser right out of the 1970s. It ends with the startled lycanthrope feeling the new bald patch at the back of his 'do and saying to himself, "This could be a good look for me." On the other hand, watching the cloyingly cute, painfully predictable, and sickeningly saccharine *Halloweentown* can't be good for *anybody* over the age of 11.

Halloweentown High

(2004; Buena Vista) Director: Mark A.Z. Dippé.

In this third installment in the saccharine-sweet Disney TV–movie series, the now in high school fledgling witch Marnie (Kimberly J. Brown) concocts a plan to bring over a handful of "exchange" students from Halloweentown to go to school in the human realm. Among said students are such supernatural beings as a troll, a goblin, an ogre, and ... a werewolf. Disguised as humans (and masking their quirkiness by claiming to be from *Canada*), the supernatural students try to assimilate into the human world to prove that humans are not the xenophobic monsters that Halloweentown fears them to be. Of course, not everyone wants Marnie's "Kumbaya" sentiments to take root, and nefarious sabotage from a certain Halloweentown sorcerer threatens to disrupt the peace between the two worlds. It all comes to a chaotic head at the town's Halloween Carnival, where the humans and supernaturals ultimately come to accept one another. As one student says, "Sure they look different, but are they really any different on the inside?"

A decidedly secondary character, Pete the Werewolf (Todd Michael Schwartzman) is not, in fact, any different on the inside, being a typical teenager who enjoys playing football (though he tends to catch the ball in his teeth). He's not much different on the outside, either, as each of the Halloweentown students hide their real appearance under a human guise (which they don and doff like a sweater). Seen in only two brief scenes in his natural wolfishness, Pete sports a big head of hair, large goofy ears, and a tiny dog nose to complete the picture of a totally non-threatening, "cute" werewolf. He also behaves quite normally, though in one of the scenes he inexplicably climbs up a wall to catch a tossed apple in his mouth—appearing more like a human fly than a lycanthrope. Oh, and he's also vegetarian.

Haram Alek

(1954; Studio Elgiza; Egypt) Alternate Titles: *Have Mercy* (unofficial); *Ismail and Abdul Meet Frankenstein* (unofficial); *Ismail Yassen Meets Frankenstein* (unofficial). Director: Essa Karama.

Directly translated as *Shame on You*, this Arabic version of *Abbott and Costello Meet Frankenstein* lifts not only the Universal classic's plot and set-pieces, but much of A&C's routines and dialogue. Unfortunately, the Egyptian Abbott and Costello—Abdul Fattah Al-Quasri and Ismail Yassen—possess none of the timing, charisma or innate humor of the original duo. The two simply yell a lot (mostly at each other); while Yassen's rubber-faced mugging and high-pitched squall makes one nod vigorously in agreement when an exasperated character proclaims, "I want to stab you with a blunt knife."

The plot: Baggage handlers Abbott and Costello (er, Egyptian antique shop workers Abdul and Ismail) receive a shipment of crates that contain Dracula (actually, "Farfour XI") and the Frankenstein Monster (though possessing the black suit, big boots and flat-topped head of the classic creature, here he's referred to as the "mummy" of "Bin Bahtour, the greatest scientist the world has ever known in the art of mummification"). Dracula then passes himself off as "the Professor" and plans to use his power, along with a brain transplant (setting his sights on the grey matter of dimwitted Ismail), to fully revive the Monster. The purpose? "It would help him come back to life and tell us the secrets of mummification." The Professor also employs his hypnotic powers to transform his hired-hand surgeon assistant, Dr. Mourad, into a werewolf(!) and thereby obtain his compliance ("Only I can save you," he tells the distraught Mourad). But Mourad (while in human form, anyway) ultimately aids Abdul and Ismail in thwarting the Professor's scheme.

Stealing dialogue and gags wholesale from its Abbott and Costello model (creaking crate gag; revolving wall trick; sitting-on-the-Monster's-lap bit; etc.), *Haram Alek* also offers a few (culturally-induced) variations. Rather than a shadow-filled, European-style castle to house Dracula, the evil Professor lives in a brightly-lit, modernistic mansion (lacking anything resembling ambiance). Instead of the original's clever and amusing Invisible Man coda, a disembodied voice introduces itself to a terrified Abdul and Ismail as "the Angel of Death" in an odd and disturbing closer. But perhaps the strangest variation comes in the form of Dr. Mourad, replacing the original's tragic Larry Talbot. Rather than arriving on the scene already cursed with lycanthropy, à la Talbot, Mourad is made a werewolf by the Professor's hypnotic powers. And when the Professor's innocent niece (and Mourad's fiancée) witnesses Mourad's transformation, the Professor passes it off as "a simple fit of epilepsy" (inadvertently harking back to the Middle Ages' labeling of epileptics as demon-possessed or … werewolves). The Professor informs a horrified Mourad, "Whenever you hear the howling of the wolf, you'll be epileptic!" Yes, rather than the full moon triggering the transformation, Mourad changes whenever a dog barks.

Lacking the original film's talent not only in front of but behind the camera, *Haram Alek* offers a decidedly unimpressive transformation sequence. As Mourad sits in a chair, the light dims until the screen nearly goes black before a jump cut reveals the fully-formed features of the Wolf Man (an obvious, crude mask, with easily discernible eye holes).

Mourad never stays in Wolf Man mode for more than a few minutes (the "epileptic fit" wears off quickly), and he must make do with knocking over some lattice in the garden to display his ferocity, or ripping some stuffing out of a chaise lounge (echoing—faintly—Mr. Chaney's similar but far more frenzied attack on a wingback chair). The butt of jokes rather than an object of fear, Mourad-wolf even steps in a puddle of glue at one point, resulting in a few ineffectual lunges at Ismail while stuck in place. About the only Wolf Man bit that inspires actual giggles of mirth rather than snorts of derision comes when Mourad goes to Ismail and Abdul's apartment to warn them about the Professor. But before he reaches the front door, a howling dog triggers another transformation. Mourad agonizingly pulls off his sport coat and staggers over to a doghouse, falling inside. An unknowing Ismail then goes out to collect his laundry and hears growling coming from inside the doghouse; without looking, Ismail gives the "dog" inside a bone.

In the end, rather than plunging over a cliff to his lycan-death while grappling with Dracula, this Wolf Man is knocked unconscious by the Monster, who then takes the Professor over a balcony to fall to their deaths (only two stories below—apparently Egyptian monsters are far more fragile than their Western counterparts). Upon the Professor's demise, Mourad changes back to his human form, regains consciousness, and rejoices, "Only now, I can enjoy my life."

Though receiving no official English-language release to date, *Haram Alek* can be found as a fan-subbed grey market bootleg—for those masochistic completists among us.

Hard Rock Nightmare

(1988; Olympus Entertainment) Director: Dominick Brascia.

This obscure entry in an obscure mini-subset that flourished during the late 1980s—the rock 'n' roll horror flick, spearheaded by such efforts as *Hard Rock Zombies* (1985, another pseudowolf entry), *Trick or Treat* (1986), *Rock 'n' Roll Nightmare* (1987) and *Black Roses* (1988)—begins on a disturbing note when, in tinted flashback, an old man traumatizes his obviously terrified young grandson by claiming to be a monster. This Meanest Grandpa in the World ends his horrifying diatribe by proclaiming "I'm a vampire, I'm a werewolf!" ("Sometimes you're a total *asshole*!" shoots back his flabbergasted wife) and threatening to creep into the boy's room at night to kill him and his whole family! "Kids love to be scared," harrumphs the sadistic granddad. Some fun. Later, while Gramps naps in a hammock, the boy sneaks up and pounds a stake into his heart! Take that, ya mean ol' bastard! A dozen years later the traumatized tyke, Jim (Martin Hansen), has grown into a twenty-year-old "up and coming rock star" who still has nightmares about the incident (for which he escaped incarceration, having been deemed "temporarily insane," but logged plenty of hours on the psychiatric couch).

When Jim's rock band "The Bad Boys" needs a place to rehearse for their upcoming gig, he borrows his Uncle Gary's (Troy Donahue) motor home and drives his bandmates and their girlfriends to his grandparents' empty farmhouse in the woods, which (an obviously forgiving) grandma had left to Jim in her will. Fine and dandy, except they arrive on the night of a full moon, and soon a werewolf is picking off the interlopers one by one, with Jim believing his grandfather has returned to take revenge. At first nobody believes Jim's exhortations about wolfmen and silver bullets, but it soon becomes evident that he's *not* crazy after all. All is not as it seems, however, for, after Jim's best friend Charlie escapes from a wolf encounter with a handful of fur, Jim realizes the tuft is actually part of a cloth costume. Jim, Charlie, and Jim's girl Sally (the only ones left) lay a trap for the imposter, and Jim shoots the pseudowolf. Suddenly, Uncle Gary shows up wielding a revolver. It turns out Gary put his assistant Dirk in a werewolf suit to pick off his bandmates and drive Jim insane, leaving the farm—and the recently discovered oil deposits beneath it—to Gary.

Unlike most nightmares, this one moves along very slowly, not helped by the "band" performing *three* generic rock songs. Dragging the pace (and plot) down further are several pointless, time-killing dream sequences, including one in which the band members wear their girlfriends' underwear (for no apparent reason) and serve up Tim's decapitated head for breakfast (ending oh-so-tastelessly with the disembodied head vomiting all over Jim).

Characterizations are minimal, relying on genre clichés like the Horny Dude, the Stoner, the Cute One, etc., to distinguish the players (though, amusingly, some of the guys sport bigger hair than the ladies). Dialogue remains on the same level, with lines like, "Oh, I'm so horny," and this exchange:

> CONNIE: "I'm totally against doing drugs."
> SAM (concerned): "Wait a minute—is pot a drug?"
> CONNIE: "No, no, it's an *herb*."
> SAM (relieved): "Oh, ok."

Every once in a while, however, writer/director Dominick Brascia tosses in a joke that hits its mark. After Tina refuses Tim's advances and storms off, he whines, "All I wanted was a little head"—just before being decapitated by slashing claws, with his head sent flying (the one real "effect" in the movie *and* the one truly startling—and amusing—moment).

The characters act even stupider than most horror movie ciphers. After finding Tim's decapitated body and learning that the phone is dead, they all *split up*, with two of them heading back to the motor home to try the CB radio, while another pair decide to hike five miles through the woods to the ranger station. This leaves Jim, Charlie, Sally and Tina back at the house. Later, Charlie charges into the woods *alone* to try to help Paul because—get this—"he's all *alone* out there."

Later, when Jim finds a gun in the house, he tells his girlfriend, "Sally, get some tools—we've got to make some silver bullets." Right. But then he actually *does* it (apparently home metallurgy/ballistic kits are standard issue for farmhouses). Amazing.

At least the film is competently shot, with the backlit, foggy woodlands seen so often in '80s horror flicks creating an appropriate atmosphere for the silly proceedings. And Brascia brings some visual inventiveness to the werewolf attacks, representing the beast with up-angle shots of slashing arms, interspersed with down-angle creature p.o.v. shots of the screaming victims. Effective the first time out, this approach, however, takes on an air of desperation by the third and fourth repetitive attack.

The werewolf itself is initially seen only in extreme close-up, revealing glowing eyes; a hairless, ridged face; and a slightly protruding muzzle ending in a dog nose. This, coupled with the occasional shot of a furry arm and clawed hand, is all we see of the marauding man-beast for over an hour. Once Brascia and co. finally deliver the Full were–Monty, however, one can see why they kept it hidden for so long, as it looks just like what it is—a man in a hairy Halloween costume.

The only performance (and performer) of note comes courtesy of former teen heartthrob Troy Donahue as the villainous Uncle Gary. With only a couple of scenes, Donahue creates a broad, campy characterization that, while neither subtle nor particularly believable, at least remains entertaining, particularly when he's insulting the none-too-bright youngsters. "Why?" asks Jim when Uncle Gary holds the survivors at gunpoint at film's end. "Money, you twit!" impatiently replies a disdainful Donahue. After his career fizzled out in the late sixties, Donahue fell into a morass of alcohol and drugs for the next decade before kicking his addictions to make his living via guest appearances on TV shows and in direct-to-video junk like *Deadly Prey* (1987), *Assault of the Party Nerds* (1989) and, of course, this film.

Wearing his slasher heart on his sleeve, writer/director Dominick Brascia peppers his script with references to the *Friday the 13th* films (unsurprising, perhaps, as actor-turned-filmmaker Brascia had played a victim in 1985's *Friday the 13th: A New Beginning*). After Jim tries to convince the gang that a werewolf prowls the woods, Connie points out that "nobody believes in vampires and werewolves anymore." "Yeah," answers Sam, "if he'd said Tim was killed by a guy in a hockey mask, then I'd have been scared." Later, two of the bandmates walking through the woods make fun of the classic "kill-kill-kill" *Friday* music theme.

The film never takes itself (nor its characters) too seriously, though it remains too low-key to work as either outright parody or straight horror. Often goofy enough to feel stupid but rarely enough to make it particularly entertaining, *Hard Rock Nightmare* is like a live-action, cheap slasher version of a Scooby-Doo episode, with an ersatz '80s hair band standing in for the Mystery, Inc. gang. In other words, it's just not very good.

Hard Rock Zombies

(1985; Cannon) Director: Krishna Shah.

A band of metal rockers rolls into a small town only to run afoul of its bizarre citizens who not only have banned rock 'n' roll music, but harbor an eccentric family consisting of none other than Adolf Hitler, Eva Braun, and their various twisted offspring and followers. After the Nazis murder the whole band, a local girl in love with the lead singer plays a snippet of music that can raise the dead, upon which the now-zombie band members dispatch the Hitler gang, inadvertently transforming them—and most of the town—into zombies themselves, before delivering their promised concert.

Cut-rate in all departments, this mid-eighties misfire's schizophrenic tone changes from serious horror to goofy spoof to rock video and back—again and again and again. But what makes it so exhausting—and exasperating—is not so much the frequent shifts but the poorly conceived and executed set-pieces, the most obvious being the ersatz hair-band rock video-style performance numbers and (worse) musical montages. If there were a hair-band hell, this movie would be it. Then there's the rambling speeches delivered by Hitler—in *German*; various random edits, including frequent insertions of a woman doing a weird interpretive dance in the middle of the road; and ketchup-heavy "effects" and grade-school production values (when the redneck sheriff tosses the band in jail, it's obviously a *horse stall*—complete with hay bales). Occasional nuggets of genuine wit shine through the cinematic iron pyrite (such as having one of the zombies methodically and comically *eat itself* at the dinner table until there's nothing left but a fleshless skull), but they can't save this dopey, screeching mess of a movie.

For no apparent reason (par for the course in this senseless scenario), Hitler's wife (presumably Eva Braun, played by Susan Prevatte) sometimes sits in a wheelchair (though one scene shows her having sex with Der Fuhrer—thankfully under the covers—while allowing their two dwarf sons to watch) and turns into a *werewolf*. In hirsute form she attacks and kills two band members. Onscreen for only a few seconds (and with nary a transformation in sight—she just looks down, and after a cutaway she rises in werewolf form), this wolf-woman (decked out in a dress, with her indistinct head and face covered in close-cropped hair) behaves more like your garden variety Nazi psycho than a savage lycanthrope, stabbing her surprised victims with a switchblade rather than using fangs and claws. It's just one more (tiny) part of the low-rent nonsense that is *Hard Rock Zombies*.

Hard Rock Zombies started out as a 20-minute short to be used as the onscreen film in the comedy *American Drive-In* (1985). But producer/director/writer Krishna Shah decided to invest a little (very little) more time and money and flesh out the short into a feature, thus producing two films instead of one. "Rocker" E.J. Curcio, who played band-leader Jesse, changed his name to E.J. Curse and worked as a model and sometime actor. He also played bass and sang for the Los Angeles–based band Silent Rage.

Harry Potter and the Prisoner of Azkaban

(2004; Warner Bros.) Director: Alfonso Cuaron.

Confession time: I personally don't much like the *Harry Potter* movies. After the novelty of the admittedly imaginative alternate world of magic and muggles quickly wore off in the first film, I didn't find much to hold my interest, as the characters remained broad and one-dimensional, the simplistic situations too black-and-white, and the dialogue often uninteresting or even patronizing. Granted, the amazing special effects throughout the series brings to convincing life this fantastical world of witches, warlocks and magical creatures, but too often there's simply not enough underneath these breathtaking (and breathtakingly *expensive*—this entry, for instance, cost $130 million) visuals.

Third in the eight-film series, *Harry Potter and the Prisoner of Azkaban* follows the continuing saga of young Harry and his friends learning their magical craft at Hogwarts school while fighting the evil machinations of the malevolent Lord Voldemort. This time around, Sirius Black, supposed cohort of the Dark Lord, has escaped from the prison of Azkaban and set his sights on murdering Harry (in retaliation for Harry's deceased parents' role in Voldemort's demise a dozen years ago). But things are not what they seem—and that goes for their new professor as well, for Remus J. Lupin (David Thewlis) turns out to be a werewolf.

Unfortunately, Lupin doesn't appear in hirsute form until 100 minutes in—and then remains so for a mere two minutes of this 142-minute movie. Even more disappointing, this werewolf, with its long, spindly arms and legs, hunched posture, skinny torso, and smooth weasel-like face, looks more like the cringing Gollum from the *Lord of the Rings* movies than a savage manbeast. It's an analogy that only deepens when its first action after transforming is to stand and whimper. The werewolf does ultimately attack our merry band, but it's brief and unconvincing, and over all too quickly after the creature is distracted by a howl in the night and simply lopes away, not to be seen again (except for a 30-second cameo later on during which it sniffs out the source of the howl before being chased off by a flying horse-bird creature called a "hippogriff"). Of course, with Lupin being a sympathetic character, perhaps it would not do to make his hirsute alter-ego too imposing or frightening (these *are* children's books/movies, after all), but given the plethora of imaginative and well-realized creatures populating the world of Harry Potter, it's a pity the poorly-conceived CGI lycanthrope received such short shrift in the design and execution departments. Lupin returned for the last four *Potter* pictures but remained a more-or-less background figure, with his lycanthropy never again addressed (apart from one flippant comment about liking his steak on the rare side).

The Haunted Cop Shop II

(1988; Media Asia; Hong Kong) Original Language Title: *Meng Gui Zue Tang*. Director: Jeffrey Lau.

This sequel to the previous year's Hong Kong hit *Haunted Cop Shop* (made by the same production team and with many of the same actors) carries on the first film's frenetic and uneasy mix of silly slapstick, untranslatable verbal humor, scatological gags, and eerie and sometimes bloody moments to create yet another exhausting hour-and-a-half ride into Asian horror-comedy. After the supernatural shenanigans of the first film, the authorities decide to create a police division "ghostbusting team," pressing into service various police force misfits, including the two heroes from the earlier film, Man-Chill (Ricky Hui) and Kam Mark-K (Jacky Cheung). During their inaugural training retreat at a deserted military base they run afoul of several vampire/ghosts and must find a way to work together to defeat the alternately terrifying and comical menaces.

Lycanthropy rears its shaggy head (sort of) after Man-Chill has been slightly nipped by a bloodsucker in the opening sequence and turns into a kind of half-vamp. As one knowledgeable recruit explains, "There's one kind [of vampire] called were-wolf type of vampire.... He will change when there's moonlight and normal if there's no." As she elucidates further, the moon emerges from behind the clouds, and Man-Chill, unnoticed by his enraptured colleagues, comically acts out the various stages: "First, his brows jump, facial muscles contract uncontrollably. Then, a wolf's tooth comes out. And begin to look for something to bite. And then saliva comes out, limbs cramp. Nerves of the whole body out of control, then shakes all over. Then breathes rapidly, loses its own character ... when it will not behave like a human. Its movements will look like neither wolf nor dog, crawling and jumping ... just like a dog with rabies."

But, of course, Man-Chill only transforms when the moon shines brightly, so he's repeatedly vamping and un-vamping (at the most comically inconvenient moments) as the clouds alternately clear and obscure the moonlight. As she concludes, "It's all right if there's no moonlight. Just like wearing shoes all day if you have athletic feet [athlete's foot]. Who knows if your feet sting [stink]?" Beyond this moon-triggered transformation, the "were-wolf type" sobriquet, and the one protruding "wolf's tooth" (he sports only a solitary fang), there's nothing else in either his appearance nor behavior to suggest a werewolf rather than vampire. No hair, no pointy ears, no snout, no claws, not even any real howling at the moon.

Among all the zany antics (for instance, at one point they all make different animal noises to try and induce a chicken to lay eggs for their breakfast!), there's little time to flesh out the various goofy characters, whose personalities stretch no farther than their nicknames (Miss Bad Luck, Lazy Bone, Romeo, etc.). Crude humor abounds (one vampire suddenly stops her attack to giggle uncontrollably whenever her breasts are touched, while *urination* plays a pivotal role in the main bloodsucker's final demise), as do numerous lost-in-translation verbal quips. While it falls well short of such watershed Hong Kong horrors as *Encounters of the Spooky Kind* (1980) and *Mr. Vampire* (1985), *The Haunted Cop Shop II* offers enough creepy moments, bizarre behavior, and fast-and-furious gags to keep the offbeat cineaste and/or Hong Kong horror fan engaged, and even chuckling on occasion. Native

Haunted Honeymoon

(1986; Orion) Director: Gene Wilder.

The brainchild of director/co-writer/star Gene Wilder, *Haunted Honeymoon* stars Wilder and his real-life wife Gilda Radner as Larry and Vickie, two 1930s-era stars of the successful radio show *Manhattan Mystery Theater*. After Larry develops on-air panic attacks (purportedly due to anxiety over having proposed to Vicki), the couple goes to Larry's castle-like ancestral home to rest and prepare for their upcoming nuptials. There Larry's psychiatrist uncle hatches a plan to cure Larry by "scaring" him healthy. But unbeknownst to those in on the ill-conceived but well-intentioned fright gags, one among them plans to do away with Larry for real in a plot to secure the family fortune.

Haunted Honeymoon opens on a stormy night at a mysterious mansion where a *werewolf* stalks the grounds. But it's soon revealed that this horrific scenario is actually a radio play, "Haunted Honeymoon," being enacted by Larry and Vickie for their listening audience. (Amusingly, the play's inspector informs us, "There's only one way to tell if a man has the werewolf in his blood—he'll give himself away by stammering, ever so slightly, on all words beginning with 'w.'" Indeed.) But there's more werewolfery to come, as, back in the "real" world, the mysterious killer at Larry's family estate dons a werewolf mask to enact his nefarious plot. Additionally, the picture ends on a comical note when the entire scenario turns out to be just a radio play after all—with Larry, Vicki, and the rest wrapping it all up while safe inside their New York studio. But as Larry and Vicki drive off after the show, a figure steps into the road to gaze after them while an unseen narrator intones, "Before you all settle back into the cozy comfort of a happy ending, let me ask you one question: Are you so sure that our story has ended? Until next time, this is your Host wishing you pleasant dreeeeams…" And the figure turns towards the camera to reveal the visage of a werewolf!

This occasionally funny but mostly dull throwback to the Old Dark House mysteries of yesteryear (at one point the overly dramatic Aunt Kate—played by Dom DeLouise in drag—lifts an entire soliloquy from the 1932 James Whale masterpiece *The Old Dark House*) does the werewolf subgenre no favors, as it focuses more on mystery than lycanthropy. Though his hairy face and sharp teeth make him *look* like a wolfman—at least from the neck up (a natty dark suit and black gloves round out this werewolf's ensemble), he doesn't evince any wolfish behavior as he peers in windows, operates complicated trip mechanisms to open secret passages, and does his killing not with claws and fangs but a stiletto. Of course, this all makes perfect sense, given that this creature's curse isn't lycanthropy but *greed*—he's actually a murderous relative who dons a werewolf mask to play into eccentric Aunt Kate's "obsession with werewolves." (At one point the grand dame dramatically announces at dinner, "I know that one of us is a werewolf!" Well, a pseudo-werewolf anyway.)

Technically well-shot and boasting sumptuous production values, the film suffers from a tepid script and meandering story. What the movie really has going for it can be summed up in two words: Gene Wilder. Even when working with subpar material (often the case here), this brilliant comedian, with his likable demeanor, understated expressions and impeccable timing, makes one of the hardest things in show business—comedy—look easy and natural. As a director, Wilder brings his obvious affection for his subject matter—namely, the halcyon days of radio and movie mysteries—to bear on the material, infusing an otherwise silly story with a modicum of charm. Also charming is the obvious bond Wilder shares with his leading lady, Gilda Radner, his real-life wife. Sadly, this was the last picture the actress/comedienne made before her premature death from ovarian cancer in 1989. In her autobiography, Radner wrote of the film, "On July 26 [1986], *Haunted Honeymoon* opened nationwide. It was a bomb. One month of publicity and the movie was only in the theaters for a week—a box-office disaster." The movie ended up earning back little more than half of its $13 million budget.

With quotes from: *It's Always Something*, by Gilda Radner.

The Haunted World of El Superbeasto

(2009; Starz Media/D&E Entertainment) Director: Rob Zombie.

This feature-length adult cartoon by musician/filmmaker Rob Zombie (*House of 1000 Corpses* [2003], *Halloween* [2007]) follows the sex-fueled misadventures of masked-wrestler superhero El Superbeasto (based on Zombie's own comic-book creation), who makes porno films by day and fights evil by night alongside his sexy sister sidekick Suzi-X (voiced by Zombie's real-life wife, Sheri Moon Zombie).

Werewolves appear in two brief sequences. The first comes when El Superbeasto shoots a sex film with two women. When the moon rises, suddenly one girl transforms into a werewolf and the other a gorgon. Quick-thinking "Beasto" grabs a wooden stake and a dildo to form a cross with which to ward off the werewolf (like Peter Cushing in *Horror of Dracula* … sort of) before jamming the stake into the wolf-woman (apparently in *The Haunted World of El Superbeasto* vampire "remedies" work just fine on lycanthropes too). The second wolfish appearance comes when Suzi X steals Hitler's disembodied head from a Nazi castle guarded by zombies and werewolf stormtroopers. Sadly, all the Nazi-wolves do is goose-step through one scene, leaving all subsequent mayhem to the undead Third Reichers.

The Haunted World of El Superbeasto runs the gamut from a brilliant send-up of *Carrie* and genuinely funny riffs on *Planet of the Apes*, to horrid musical numbers with lyrics like "It's all right to jerk off to cartoons / the Japanese do it all the time" and tasteless scenes involving the Bride of Frankenstein receiving oral pleasure from the Creature from the Black Lagoon in a pool of water, with a gravestone nearby bearing the name of James Whale (the director of *Bride of Frankenstein*, who drowned himself in a pool). *Halloween*, *The Shining*, *The Fly*, *They Saved Hitler's Brain*, *The Abominable Dr. Phibes*, *This Island Earth* … none are safe from Zombie's crude humor. Though offering more hits than misses, and even inspiring a few laugh-out-loud moments with its obvious and irreverent homaging, the film never quite lives up to its more understated (and far more clever) opening sequence in which a black-and-white cartoon version of Edward Van Sloan steps onto a stage (à la the original 1931 *Frankenstein*) and intones, "How do you do. Mr. Rob Zombie feels it would be a little unkind to present this picture without just a word of friendly warning. We are about to unfold the story of El Superbeasto…"

El Superbeasto took three years for Zombie to complete, due to various scheduling, production and financial delays, before its straight-to-video release in September 2009 (garnering mixed-to-negative reviews). Zombie characterized his sleazy, one-of-a-kind cartoon oddity as "this little tiny half-a-million dollar direct-to-video movie that expanded into this $10 million animated extravaganza.… It's like an R-rated adult/monster/sex comedy. There's nothing really like it that I can think of. People always say it's like Ralph Bakshi's stuff [the xrated *Fritz the Cat*, 1972; *Wizards*, 1977], but ... it's [more] like if Sponge-Bob and Scooby-Doo were filthy." Most impressive of all was the cast of voice talent Zombie managed to round up (including Paul Giamotti as lead villain Dr. Satan). Among the many celebrity participants were horror film veterans Ken Foree, Tura Satana, Clint Howard, Sig Haig, Danny Trejo, and *The Howling* star Dee Wallace.

Whether one finds the copious nudity and often crude humor irreverent, transgressive, raunchy or just plain obscene depends entirely upon one's personal sensibilities. But horror movie fans will undoubtedly enjoy the innumerable references and rip-offs that pop out more often than the ubiquitous cartoon breasts.

With quotes from: "Exclusive: Zombie Talks T-Rex," by Scott Collura, IGN.com.

Have Mercy see *Haram Alek*

Hellboy Animated: Blood and Iron

(2007; IDT Entertainment/Anchor Bay) Director: Victor Cook.

The second of two animated features based on the *Hellboy* comic book series by Mike Mignola (the other being the previous year's *Hellboy Animated: Sword of Storms*), *Hellboy Animated: Blood and Iron* followed on the heels of the successful 2004 live-action film adaptation directed by Guillermo del Toro. Cast members "returning" from the excellent Del Toro film (in voice form anyway) are Ron Perlman (as Hellboy), Selma Blair (as Liz Sherman), and John Hurt (as Professor Bruttenholm). *Blood and Iron* sees Hellboy (the demon-turned-friend-of-man) and his "Bureau for Paranormal Research and Defense" colleagues tangling with Erzabet Ondrusko, a vampire who bathes in the blood of servant girls (*à la* real-life "Bloody Countess" Elizabeth Bathory) *and* turns out to be a high priestess to Hecate, "a Greek goddess and Queen of the Witches." As well as battling the vampiress, harpies, a minotaur and Hecate herself, Hellboy must face down a werewolf.

In a brief, two-minute sequence, the old ex-priest whom Erzabet had enslaved turns on his hated mistress and reveals her hiding place to Hellboy and co. But after they leave him, two witches (actually disguised harpies) appear and tell the trembling man that "there is no redemption for you tonight. You have betrayed our Queen. She still has work for you." At this, one of the crones produces a wax effigy of the man and scratches a glowing symbol upon it—resulting in his immediate transformation into a huge werewolf (shown via his shadow on the wall morphing into the monster). This bipedal werewolf (complete with tail) looks massive and fearsome with its powerful torso, glowing eyes, shaggy mane of hair, large wolf ears, jutting canine nose, and oversized fang-filled mouth set in a square jaw. The beast viciously attacks Hellboy, giving as good as it gets until Hellboy rips a set of antlers from the wall just as the werebeast leaps at him, resulting in the werewolf's death by impalement. Though an exciting interlude, with some intense and brutal battling (much of it occurring in a red-drenched room of the old mansion Erzabet inhabits), the brief lycanthrope episode has little to do with the film's main storyline. Still, it's good to see this wolf have its day—or two minutes, anyway—in such an excellent animated film series.

Hotel Transylvania

(2012; Sony/Columbia) Director: Genndy Tartakovsky.

In this clever and charming animated monster-mash feature, Dracula (Adam Sandler doing a passable Lugosi accent) has protected his daughter Mavis (Selena Gomez) from the outside world (primarily from humans, whom Drac considers to be the *real* monsters) for a century by building an isolated sanctuary for monsters only, the Hotel Transylvania. "It's a place I built for monsters," explains the Count, "out there lurking in the shadows, hiding from the persecution of humankind." But now the teen vampire (she's turning 118) wants to spread her (bat) wings and see the world. With all the monsters coming to the hotel for Mavis' birthday bash, a young human backpacker, Johnny, stumbles into the place as well, causing all manner of mayhem, fun, and ultimately romance until Dracula learns that sometimes you just have to let your child grow up and make her own choices.

A vast array of monsters arrive at the hotel, everything from a *Fiend Without a Face*–like disembodied brain to Bigfoot to the Blob. Not to mention all the classic creatures, such as the Frankenstein Monster and his bride, the Invisible Man, mummies, witches, gargoyles and zombies. One of the first to arrive is a tie-wearing werewolf named Wayne, along with his pregnant wolfwoman wife and about two-dozen rambunctious were-cubs. After they exit their cab in a cloud of chaos, Wayne apologizes to the pumpkin-headed driver, "Yeah, it's a mess back there," and gives him a big tip. Like all the monsters, the werewolf (who stays in his hirsute form throughout) is drawn for cute rather than fright, with his large fluffy head, pointy ears and long snout making him look more like a bipedal hedgehog than wolf-monster. His bent-forward posture amusingly suggests the fatigue he must feel from constantly riding herd over his bouncy brood. When his cubs bound into the hotel and commence to chew on the drapes, plonk the piano keys, and pee on the furniture ("Housekeeping!" orders Drac), Daddy-wolf sardonically states, "Hey kids, reel it in—you're only supposed to make Mom and Dad miserable." Though a decidedly secondary character, Steve Buscemi voices Werewolf Wayne with just the right levels of exasperation and resignation to generate maximum amusement.

Wayne pops up only now and again, but he features in two particularly funny vignettes. The first shows him in bed, exhausted, his bulging red eyes staring straight ahead as his many cubs lay all over him, snoring and twitching and drooling. Just as his bloodshot orbs finally close in blessed sleep, the alarm goes off and his little ones awaken to join in the howling. Ouch.

The second amusing incident offers a bit more, er, bite. As Drac, Wayne, and several others race their hearse down the road in hot pursuit of the departing Johnny (after Dracula finally realizes that the human and Maven love each other), they come across a herd of sheep blocking the way. "I got this," says Wayne and dashes from the car. A second later he jumps back into the hearse and lets out a huge belch (along with a bit of white fluff). And there are no more sheep in the road.

Insightful ("As a father," says Dracula, "you do everything to keep your family safe, even if you have to break their trust") and touching (Dracula ultimately learns that the only thing worse than seeing a loved one leave is seeing her unhappy), as well as entertainingly funny, *Hotel Transylvania* stands as a worthy cinematic destination for adults as well as kids (just ask Wayne).

Hotel Transylvania 2

(2015; Sony/Columbia) Director: Genndy Tartakovsky.

A direct follow-up to the engaging *Hotel Transylvania* (2012), this animated sequel begins with the marriage of vampire Mavis (voiced by Selena Gomez) and human Johnny (Andy Samberg). Mavis' father, Dracula (Adam Sandler), has accepted the human into his household—and opened up his hotel to the outside world, with monsters peacefully mingling with humans. Soon a child is born to the happy couple, and little Dennis (Asher Blinkoff) grows up among the hotel's resident ghouls, zombies, and werewolves. Yes, the exasperated were-dad, Wayne (Steve Buscemi), is back, with an even bigger brood of rambunctious wolf pups (one of them, the cute Winnie, even providing a childhood crush for Dennis). The plot sees Mavis becoming concerned for Dennis' safety, as the half-human, half-vampire child shows no sign of growing into a monster. She feels they must leave the hotel to let Dennis grow up in the human world. Drac, of course, believes that his grandson will indeed become a vampire (it can take up to five years for the fangs to drop) and does everything he can to see it happen before Dennis' upcoming fifth birthday, including a comically ill-fated trip with his buddies to show his grandson how to behave like a monster.

Once again a supporting character, werewolf Wayne features in only a few (amusing) scenes. The first sees Wayne as the hotel's tennis coach. Unfortunately, when someone hits a ball, he can't keep himself from chasing after it like a golden retriever and then burying it under the clay court. When Wayne's gaggle of werecubs (hyped up on sugar) demolish a birthday party, he resignedly deadpans, "There's a reason they call it a 'litter.'" Dracula takes Wayne, along with the Frankenstein Monster, the Invisible Man, the Mummy, and the Blob, on his outing to show Dennis how to become a monster. "If we don't inspire Dennis, how is he going to find his inner monster?" posits Drac. But Wayne is reluctant to go all monstery, muttering, "We don't need to kill anymore—we have Pop-Tarts." Urged on by Drac, Wayne finally prepares to show Dennis how to kill and eat a deer—but he's immediately distracted by a thrown Frisbee, which he chases and catches and proudly retrieves. "You're a were-wussie," dismisses Drac.

While it starts off cleverly, reintroducing the wonderful characters from the first film, the sequel quickly slides into predictable pap, as "Vampa" Drac becomes obsessed with ensuring Dennis becomes a vampire rather than a human. Early on, Mavis asks her father, "You're really ok with him not being a monster?" Dracula answers, "Human, monster, unicorn—as long as you're happy." It's a virtuous message of tolerance, but one that the film quickly shows to be mere lip-service, as Drac does everything in his power to force little Dennis' development into a vampire. Though comical hijinks ensue (some of them quite funny), real character growth does not. And rather than truly exploring—and reinforcing—its noble theme of acceptance, the movie takes the easy way out at the end, with little Dennis finally getting his fangs after all (becoming a mini super–Drac who almost singlehandedly saves the day when a pack of gargoyle-like evil bat-creatures attack), thereby solving the human-or-monster problem without making the characters truly come to grips with it. So rather than adding anything new, or offering further thematic or character evolution, *Hotel Transylvania 2* just presents more of the same—which, admittedly, is intermittently clever and funny. It just could have—and *should* have—been so much more.

This sequel made nearly half a *billion* dollars against its $80 million budget (significantly out-earning its predecessor's $358 million worldwide take), so one can bet this *Hotel* will be opening its doors yet again.

House of the Black Death

(1965; Taurus) Alternate Titles: *Blood of the Man Devil*; *The Widderburn Horror*. Directors: Harold Daniels, Jerry Warren (uncredited).

In this obscure, no-budget tale of witchcraft, John Carradine and Lon Chaney, Jr., play Andre and Belial Desard, two rival warlock brothers. Carradine is the good warlock and Chaney the evil one, and they engage in a Satanic struggle for control of their ancestral home. Mixed into the mess—er, story—is a blink-and-you'll-miss-it werewolf subplot in which Belial and his coven place a lycanthropic curse on one young member of the Desard family. The film's budget was so low that there was no cash for werewolf makeup; we simply see his back as the supposed lycanthrope escapes the room in which he's been imprisoned, and then his normal face again after he's been killed. Sad.

Cheap looking poster for the even cheaper looking *House of the Black Death* (aka *Blood of the Man Devil*), a production so impoverished that during a brief lycanthropic subplot *it never even shows the werewolf.*

Lovers of *Le Bad Cinema* maintain that the only truly bad movie is a boring movie; given that, *House of the Black Death* is a *terrible* movie. Anything remotely exciting is talked about rather than shown—and often talked to *death*. A better title would have been *House of the Unending Gabfest*. Add to this static photography; dim, uneven lighting; amateurish acting; choppy, often nonsensical editing; and continuity that seems to have sprung from another dimension (despite frequent long scenes of exposition added by schlockmeister Jerry Warren in a desperate attempt to plug some of the plot holes), and the film becomes an unwatchable pastiche.

To add insult to injury, it embarrasses two of the screen's classic horror icons, for Carradine and Chaney hit rock bottom with this pathetic crime against celluloid. Chaney plays Belial as a rather simple-minded devil worshipper (as if Lenny had sold his soul for a rabbit hutch), all amiable grins and obvious expressions. Carradine spends most of his screen time in bed; when up (and awake), he puts on his patented authoritative, crotchety old man persona.

Apparently, making the film was nearly as painful a process as watching it. When producer William White ran into problems, with personnel leaving like rats deserting a sinking ship, the investors turned the half-finished project over to no-budget moviemaker Jerry Warren. "They had a terrible mishmash of a movie," recalled Warren. "It *wasn't* a movie, it was a bunch of film. Somebody took over the project, contacted me and asked if I could make a movie out of it…. The whole thing was laid in my lap and I functioned as *everything*—as producer, as director, as editor, putting music in it, the whole works. It came out *bad* but it came out playable, too, and it did pull out some money for the people who backed it."

When *Jerry Warren* (*Teenage Zombies* [1960], *The Incredible Petrified World* [1961], *Frankenstein Island* [1981]) has to rescue a film, you *know* you're in trouble. Actress Katherine Victor (who Warren brought in for some additional expository scenes) commented, "[Somebody] made a picture called *House of the Black Death* and it wasn't cohesive. So [Warren] took it over and I think he made it *less* cohesive!" Indeed.

With quotes from: *Interviews with B Science Fiction and Horror Movie Makers*, by Tom Weaver; *Science Fiction Stars and Horror Heroes*, by Tom Weaver.

How to Make a Monster

(1958; American International Pictures) Director: Herbert L. Strock.

"IT WILL SCARE THE LIVING *YELL* OUT OF YOU!" proclaimed the punny tagline for *How to Make a Monster*. Well, not really.

How to Make a Monster? Apply hypnosis-inducing makeup that turns a young actor into an obedient pseudo-werewolf—that's how. Unhinged studio makeup man Pete Dumond (Robert H. Harris, right) does just that to actor Larry Drake (Gary Clarke), while Pete's loyal assistant Rivero (Paul Brinegar) looks on (lobby card).

But it *will* bring a nostalgic smile to the face of most 1950s monster movie fans. This AIP follow-up to their successful *I Was a Teenage Werewolf* and *I Was a Teenage Frankenstein* tandem (both 1957) opens on the impressively savage-looking face of the Teenage Werewolf (replicated by makeup artist Philip Scheer from his work on *Teenage Werewolf*) before the camera pulls back to reveal veteran makeup man Pete Dumond (Robert H. Harris) applying the finishing touches to his creation at "American International Studios." Under all the hair and greasepaint is young actor Larry Drake (Gary Clarke), who's starring alongside his compatriot Tony (Gary Conway, sporting the same monster makeup he wore in *Teenage Frankenstein*, also courtesy of Scheer) in the studio's new picture, "Werewolf Meets Frankenstein." Unfortunately, a studio regime change has dictated that monsters give way to musicals, and creature-creator Pete has been handed his pink slip after 25 years of faithful service. Embittered, he determines, "I'll destroy them—and I'll use the very monsters they mock to bring them to an end." Utilizing his new experimental foundation cream ("It makes the subject passive, obedient to my will"), Pete sends his two teenage monsters out to kill the studio executives, and even dons some caveman makeup himself to dispatch a nosy security guard. It all resolves in a conflagration at Pete's home where his enshrined "children" (past monster makeups) are displayed (with the black and white film impressively going to full color for this final reel, allowing us to see the head of *The She Creature*, and the alien masks from *It Conquered the World* and *Invasion of the Saucer Men* in "living color").

The Teenage Werewolf's big scene comes when one of the hated executives runs the rushes for "Werewolf Meets Frankenstein." As he sits sourly watching, the werewolf suddenly rises up from behind his screening chair (had he been hiding there the whole time?) and grabs the man's throat, choking the life from him while literally foaming at the mouth. ("[Actor Eddie Marr] must have had a quart of drool on him," laughed Gary Clarke. "They gave me some fizzy stuff that makes you look like you're foaming at the mouth.") Later, the police coroner notes how the victim's neck was snapped by "fiendish strength" (apparently Pete's mesmerizing makeup also makes its wearer exceedingly strong), and his neck was "clawed and bitten." Recalled Clarke, "I sneak into the screening room and I throttle this studio executive and bite his neck and sever the jugular vein and … disembowel him [*laughs*], whatever they had me do. The actor says to me, 'Take it easy, will ya? I just got a new suit,' and I say okay. Well, then [producer] Herman [Cohen] comes up to me and says [*in a soft voice*], 'This is that guy's last day of work here. I want this to be a *good shot*!' So when the director calls *action*, I throw this guy all over the place! We do a couple of takes, because Herman keeps saying, 'Okay, let's do it again. Gary, gimme a little *more*, will ya?' [*Laughs*] I kept saying to the guy, 'Sorry…!'"

Though rather talky (there are, after all, only three killings, with each monster—including Pete's "caveman"—given only one murderous set-piece) and full of filler (including a terrible song-and-dance number, "You've Got to Have Ee-oo," performed by John Ashley—as himself), *How to Make a Monster* offers a fun glimpse into low-budget studio filmmaking. It also generates a comfortable familiarity by not only creating a screen world that references real-life pictures like *I Was a Teenage Werewolf* and *I Was a Teenage Frankenstein*, but by populating its cast with familiar genre faces. Among them are Thomas Bowne Henry (*Brain from Planet Arous*, *Blood of Dracula*) as the faux film's director, the ubiquitous Morris Ankrum (*Earth vs. the Flying Saucers*, *Beginning of the End*, *The Giant Claw*) as a police captain, Robert Shayne (*The Face of Marble*, *Indestructible Man*, *Kronos*) as Larry's agent, and, of course, Gary Conway from *I Was a Teenage Frankenstein*. Additionally, Malcolm Attenbury takes fifth billing as security guard Richards (he played the well-intentioned but ineffectual father in *I Was a Teenage Werewolf*).

With quotes from: *Earth vs. the Sci-Fi Filmmakers*, by Tom Weaver.

Howl of the Devil

(1987; Freemont-Nasch International; Spain) Original Language Title: *El Aullido del Diablo*. Director: Paul Naschy.

Written, co-produced, directed by, and starring Paul Naschy, *Howl of the Devil* was, said the Spanish horror icon, "like my own howl of anguish, a painful catharsis which finally liberated me from long repressed phobias and obsessions." He went on to say, "I included in the film all the things that had a special significance for me personally: old movie serials, terrifying fairy tales, the legendary Universal monsters, the scorn of certain critics towards my work, the many envious and spiteful characters who had had an adverse effect on my life." While this may have been good work-therapy for the obviously troubled filmmaker, it doesn't do the viewer any favors, as *Howl of the Devil* is so filled with vitriol that even the inclusion of a cadre of classic monsters can't smooth over its overwhelmingly nihilistic unpleasantness. Every character is selfish, mean-spirited and bitter, from the sadistic failed actor and the lecherous priest, to the derelict ex-schoolteacher and foul-mouthed prostitute. Even the three ostensibly "sympathetic" characters turn out to be a necrophile, a gold-digger, and the Antichrist himself! Lines like "Life is stress mostly," and "Today's youth is shit—drug addicts, delinquents, homosexuals!" abound. Unlike with most of Naschy's oeuvre (including his Waldemar Daninsky/werewolf series), *Howl of the Devil* offers nothing and no one worth saving. A victorious Satan himself sums it up at the end with, "Evil will forever rule the human race."

The bizarre story sees troubled one-time actor Hector Doriani (Naschy) soliciting prostitutes for sex games in which he dresses and acts like famous villains (Rasputin, Bluebeard, Fu Manchu). Hector's dead brother Alex (Naschy again, in flashback) was a far-more-famous actor (known for his horror roles), and Hector has become the grudging guardian of Alex's 11-year-old son Adrian (played by Naschy's real-life offspring, Sergio Molina). Helping to alleviate the boy's loneliness are the beautiful housekeeper Carmen (Caroline Munro) and the family butler Eric (Howard Vernon), a dabbler in the Black Arts who periodically conjures up Alex's spirit. But little Adrian relies most on his fantasy friends—the Frankenstein Monster, Mr. Hyde, the Phantom of the Opera, Quasimodo, and Waldemar the Wolfman (all played by Naschy)—who pop up periodically to keep him company. In the meantime, a giallo-esque black-gloved killer has been stalking the grounds and brutally dispatching all who come near this cursed house where "time stands still."

Sixty-three minutes into the film, Adrian, out in the woods after dark, receives a brief visit from a werewolf (Naschy in his expected Wolfman makeup). In the foggy half-light, Adrian greets the monster with, "Hello Waldemar. Poor friend. You're the best. And the least liked of them all. I knew you'd visit me. Have you seen Larry Talbot? He suffers like you." At this, the Wolfman knowingly nods. Lasting a mere 40 seconds, the scene concludes with Adrian being called back to the house. As his most famous character, Waldemar the Wolfman, Naschy does nothing but stand and nod, making this a particularly disappointing lycanthropic cameo.

Shot over four weeks at Naschy's family's country house at Lozoya del Valle (where the better known—and far better—*Horror Rises from the Tomb* was filmed), the picture ran into financial difficulties upon the death of one of its producers and ended up premiering on Spanish

Playing a horror actor disdained by the critics, Paul Naschy saw Howl of the Devil **as his personal howl of anguish (Spanish lobby card).**

television rather than on the silver screen. It was never officially released outside of Spain.

In an interview in *European Trash Cinema* magazine no. 8, *Howl of the Devil*'s uncredited (and disputed) co-writer, Salvador Sainz, labeled Naschy a pirate, an idiot, a megalomaniac and "my avowed enemy." The feeling was mutual, as Naschy, in his autobiography, refers to Sainz as "The Bizarre One" and describes him as "fairly tall, pot-bellied, with acromegalic, Frankensteinish features and a stutterer."

Though not the last screen appearance by Paul Naschy the actor—nor of his famous hirsute creation Waldemar Daninsky—*Howl of the Devil* was the last gasp of Naschy the *auteur*, with his subsequent film work primarily being that of an actor-for-hire. Of *Howl*, Naschy concluded, "I played 12 characters, each well-rounded and all believable. I really had a ball." Unfortunately, the same cannot be said for the viewer of this nasty, misanthropic movie.

With quotes from: *Memoirs of a Wolfman*, by Paul Naschy.

Hybrid

(2007; Peace Arch Entertainment; Canada/USA) Director: Yelena Lanskaya.

What might happen if the eyes of a wolf were transplanted onto the head of a man? Well, not much, if one goes by this slow-moving, uneventful made-for-television U.S./Canadian co-production shot in Winnepeg, Manitoba.

In rescuing a co-worker from an industrial fire, Aaron (Corey Monteith) is blinded. Agreeing to an experimental operation at the Olaris medical research facility (which works hand in glove with the military), Aaron becomes the first transplant recipient of a pair of wolf's eyes. His sight returned, Aaron soon begins experiencing the wolf's memories, and escapes from the heavily guarded facility with the help of Native American schoolteacher Lydia (Tinsel Korey) who'd brought the injured wolf to Olaris in the first place (not knowing it would be killed as a donor). As a ruthless military team desperately searches for their experimental subject, Aaron reconnects with the donor wolf's pack, culminating in a showdown in the woods.

At one point the head doctor tells her military liaison that "the most common problem with organ transplants is something called rejection reaction.... Occasionally this can be experienced on a psychological level.... 'Lycanthropy' refers to a pathological condition of delirium, a type of hysteria where a person believes they are turning into an animal, a wolf." But Aaron is not a werewolf per se, and he never transforms. He does possess increased strength and agility (and the ability to leap from several stories and land unhurt), as well as heightened senses. The only outward physical change, however, is his bright yellow eyes.

So little happens in the film's first half that the "highlights" consist of one small-scale bar fight (more of a "push-around" than actual fight), Aaron running through the streets shirtless accompanied by a small pack of stray dogs, and Aaron making a midnight pilgrimage to the local zoo where he does … nothing. The second half consists of Aaron hiding out with Lydia, going on a spirit journey (or something) under the guidance of Lydia's medicine man godfather ("The spirit of the wolf will help you find who you are"), and trying to elude the (small) military team sent to retrieve him. This last culminates in a protracted stalking sequence in which the quintet of soldiers tracks Aaron through the forest. It drags on and on, however, without any payoff, just shot after shot of the men nervously creeping about and peering tensely through their gun sights. Finally, Aaron takes a few out and confronts the rest, resulting in a perfunctory fight before he wins the day and lopes off with his new wolf pals.

Utterly wasting a novel notion, and trying to paper over its dearth of action and ideas with some superficial Native American back-to-nature lip service, *Hybrid* is indeed just that—neither fish nor fowl, neither a werewolf movie nor an eco-friendly polemic. Like Aaron himself (played with one expression—consternation—by Canadian actor Corey Monteith, who died in 2013 of an accidental drug overdose at age 31), it's a confused, muddled mess that fails to generate any real interest.

In the Midnight Hour see *The Midnight Hour*

La Invasión de los Muertos see *Blue Demon y Zovek en la Invasión de los Muertos*

Ismail and Abdul Meet Frankenstein see *Haram Alek*

Ismail Yassen Meets Frankenstein see *Haram Alek*

It

(1990; ABC/Warner Bros. Television; USA/Canada) Alternate Title: *Stephen King's It*. Director: Tommy Lee Wallace.

Based on the Stephen King novel of the same name, this two-part, three-hour made-for-TV movie, first airing on November 18th and 20th on ABC, concerns a group of misfit kids who band together in the summer of 1960 against an ancient evil that has been murdering local children. "It" takes the form of a sinister clown (menacingly played by Tim Curry), as well as various things that frighten its victims the most—including a rotting skeleton and the titular terror from *I Was a Teenage Werewolf*. ("I'm every nightmare you ever had; I am your worst dream come true; I'm everything you ever were afraid of," rasps the evil "Pennywise" the clown.) Though "the Loser's Club" appears to vanquish the monster, they make a pact to return if ever It comes back. And thirty years later the killings have begun again…

Each of the children encounter Pennywise (and Its other incarnations) at one point or another, and for Ritchie (Seth Green), the group's resident wiseass, It takes the form of the Teenage Werewolf. After the group enjoys a matinee of *I Was a Teenage Werewolf* at their local theater (with the pivotal gymnasium scene playing on the screen), Ritchie has a messy run-in with some bullies in the school cafeteria. Sent down to the basement to secure a mop from the janitor, Ritchie instead finds the monster from the movie (a darker, more demonic-looking variation on Michael Landon's teen werewolf, courtesy of makeup artists Norman Cabrera and Jack Bricker), who grabs Ritchie with Its hairy, clawed hand. Ritchie screams "Help, help!" and breaks away. But when he turns back to look, he sees only a laughing Pennywise. "Beep, beep, Ritchie. Come back anytime," It growls in its faux cheerful gravel-voice. Ritchie flees back to the cafeteria and shouts, "You gotta help me, please! In the basement—there's a werewolf!" But his panicked pleas elicit only derisive laughter from his schoolmates. Later, the gang ponders the horrors they've seen. "It was a werewolf for Ritchie because he saw that dumb movie," observes one. "But it was a clown underneath." Another surmises, "So maybe it's some kind of evil being that can read our minds and take the shape of stuff we're afraid of." One more nod to lycanthropy comes when the children decide to go down into the sewers to beard the beast in Its lair. One of the kids brings along his mother's solid silver earrings as ammo for their slingshot, as he "just knows" that silver will hurt the monster. And it does.

Filmed over two months in the summer of 1990 in New Westminster, British Columbia, *It* proved a ratings bonanza for ABC, with Part I watched by 17.5 million households, while 19.5 million tuned in for Part II. Given the personnel involved, it's little wonder *It* turned out to be as involving and frightening as it did, despite its television roots. Scripters Lawrence D. Cohen (*Carrie*) and Tommy Lee Wallace (*Fright Night*) coalesce Stephen King's engrossing, character-driven, and truly terrifying tale of evil and innocence lost (and found) into an involving, incident-packed three hours. Sitting in the director's chair was scripter Wallace (writer-director of the criminally underrated *Halloween III: Season of the Witch* [1982]). Wallace had previously directed another werewolf in the pseudowolf entry *Fright Night Part II* (1988). And bringing the well-written characters to life were a gaggle of talented and likable TV stars, including Richard Thomas (*The Waltons*), Harry Anderson (*Night Court*), Tim Reid (*WKRP in Cincinnati*), and John Ritter (*Three's Company*). The child actors proved remarkably adept as well, with one of them, Emily Perkins (as the young Beverly Marsh), going on to star in a lycanthropic landmark, *Ginger Snaps* (2000).

Though the telefilm's latter half becomes somewhat disjointed, with too many repetitive flashbacks interrupting the tempo and mounting dread of their coming confrontation, and Its final form—a rather silly-looking stop-motion giant spider-crab-bug monster (with human-like arms)—disappoints, the involving script, insightful characterizations, believable acting, and truly creepy set-pieces make *It* an example of superior made-for-TV terror.

Jack & Diane

(2012; Magnolia Pictures) Director: Bradley Rust Gray.

No, this is not about "two American kids doin' the best they can" (as John Mellencamp put it in his 1982 hit song "Jack and Diane"). Rather, two teenage girls (one visiting from England) meet in New York City and fall in love. The naïve Diane (Juno Temple) fascinates the tomboy Jack (Riley Keough), and vice-versa. But as their rocky relationship blossoms, only to splinter when Jack learns that Diane will soon leave to study in Paris, Diane experiences bloody visions of a werewolf-like creature. Has her burgeoning sexuality transformed her into a monster?

The short answer is: no. The long answer: after 110 tedious minutes with little to show but interminable "arty" close-ups and mundane slice-of-life sequences … who cares?

The film's sole point of excitement/interest—the creature—appears only briefly in two flash-and-you'll-miss-it moments, plus one slightly longer sequence in which the beast bloodily attacks Jack (in what turns out to be a dream) after the girls' first failed attempt at lesbian lovemaking. Seen only in a few fleeting glimpses, the beast looks more like a giant mutant rat-monster, with lumpy, malformed head and oversized teeth, than a werewolf. In fact, nothing in the film ties the (imaginary) creature to the wolf (or *any* animal, for that matter)—it's just a vaguely bestial monster conjured from Diane's troubled imagination. And there's no metamorphosis: the beast just pops up out of nowhere, with the implication that it is Diane transformed.

"[Writer/director] Brad [Gray's] opening statement was, 'I'm using the word 'werewolf,' but I want you to reinterpret 'werewolf,'" recounted the movie's creature creator, Gabe Bartalos (*Frankenhooker, Bad Biology*). In fact, during *Jack & Diane*'s roll-out on the festival circuit, Gray intentionally *mis*labeled it a "lesbian werewolf film." Explained the director, "If I said it was about a monster, it could be an octopus, you know? But If I mentioned that the creature might be a werewolf, people could say, 'OK, it's on two legs, blah blah blah…' That was the word Gabe and I used early on, but we never talked about it being a werewolf, really. That was just a way of letting people understand what we were trying to do." Ok, *not* a lesbian werewolf movie, but what is it exactly? How about an awkward coming-of-age love story between two teen girls in the Big Apple—with the rocky moments in their love affair underscored by the occasional fleeting appearance of the malformed monster. "If you only want to see a horror movie," warned Gray, "you're really going to hate this, just to be honest," since it's really a "sweet love story." A love story, yes; sweet, not so much, especially given the two girls' vulgarity (vomiting, urinating and defecating being frequent topics of conversation). Such slice-of-scatological-life storytelling may be relatively "realistic," but it's far from "sweet." Comprised of scene after sleep-inducing scene of the duo staring awkwardly at each other, masturbating (fully clothed), arguing, or choosing what to wear—and filled with far too many pretentiously shot hand-held extreme close-ups right out of film school vérité 101—*Jack & Diane* remains a pointless slice of uninteresting life that not even an imaginary monster can liven up.

With quotes from: "Love Transforms *Jack & Diane*," by Michael Gingold, *Fangoria* 318.

Kibakichi

(2004; GP Museum/Saiko Films; Japan) Original Language Title: *Kibakichi: Bakko-yokaiden*; Alternate Title: *Werewolf Warrior*; Director: Tomo'o Haraguchi.

"A long time ago," begins the film's opening narration, "humans and monsters named yokai lived in harmony, without interfering in each other's lives. But as time went by, humans forgot their fears." The humans determined to exterminate the yokai, with the surviving monsters finally fleeing to the mountains or disguising themselves as "men, women or the elderly to hide within the human world." In 1700s feudal Japan, a lone warrior dressed in skins walks the countryside. In a scene right out of a classic chambara (samurai/swordplay film), a group of bandits attack the solitary wanderer in a field. After this introductory sword battle between the Mysterious Stranger and the outlaws, ending in severed limbs and arterial spray, the film slows to a crawl for the next half-hour as the brooding loner Kibakichi (Ryûji Harada) makes his way to a rundown village, where he drinks and visits the gambling dens that appear to be its sole industry. Fortunately, things are not quite what they seem (triggered by a very creepy supernatural attack on a disgruntled gambler in the building's green-lit basement), and the villagers are revealed to be "yokai," various monsters from Japanese folklore who take on human guise to lure local yakuza (gangsters) to their deaths (feeding on their flesh). Kibakichi is not what he seems either, for he is one of only two survivors of a slaughtered tribe of beast-people. When the local human ruling clan decides to dispense with the yokai, utilizing their newfound weaponry (an early machine gun) to slaughter the supernatural folk, Kibakichi transforms into his beastial form to take bloody revenge on the duplicitous humans.

A mix of arty cinematography (slow-motion shots of swaying trees; endless close-ups of the brooding protagonist) and nightmarish exploitation (a basement room full of skulls and half-eaten corpses; various severed limbs and arterial blood spray), *Kibakichi* never fully gels. Casting the strange creatures in a more sympathetic light than the criminal human trash upon which they feed (and the duplicitous clan of ruling humans, who promise to set up a safe haven for the persecuted yokai but intend to first use them to get rid of their enemies and then kill the monsters off), the film aligns viewer sympathies firmly with the weird yokai. But apart from a quintet of spider-ladies (who pose as geishas before revealing their true form and sucking the life from a band of yakuza), the various yokai look more goofy than terrifying (frog-faced water dwellers; elephant-nosed woman; big-headed cyclops). Even the stoic, near-silent hero with a tragic past offers a rather ridiculous appearance. Transforming into beast mode only at the film's climax, Kibakichi looks like a bare-chested wookie with long, pointy ears and a generally human face. "I made the werewolf like a Japanese *kaiju* [giant monster] suit," said makeup artist-turned-director Tomo'o Haraguchi. "This means that the actor could get into the outfit in five minutes. However, touch-up makeup took an additional hour…. We took a full-body cast of Harada and then applied the same materials and styles I used in the 1980s when doing similar work." It shows.

"Although he looks like one, Kibakichi and his kind are not werewolves in the Western sense," admitted Haraguchi. "Kibakichi does not transform by the light of the full moon. And unlike Oliver Reed fare and other werewolf movies, you won't find any religious connections, due to the simple fact that we didn't have Christianity in Japan at that period in our history. It's different in that werewolves in *Kibakichi* transform when their feelings run high." Despite Haraguchi labeling his hero a "werewolf," the film itself offers no direct link to wolves (or *any* animal, for that matter); and no one ever uses the "w" (or "l") word.

Fortunately, this movie's (non)werewolf energetically attacks and leaps (almost flying at times) with supernatural vigor at the over-the-top, no-holds-barred climax. Here the beast-man single-handedly decimates the band of gun-wielding human villains in a bloody and energized display of wirework and stylized violence that helps overcome the film's occasional tedium and disjointed feel.

With quotes from: "*Kibakichi*: The Fur Flies," by Norman England, *Fangoria* 244.

Kibakichi 2

(2004; GP Museum/Saiko Films; Japan) Original Language Title: *Kibakichi: Bakko-yokaidan 2*; Director: Daiji Hattori.

Released a mere three months after the first *Kibakichi*, this direct sequel picks up where the first film left off, with the lone warrior Kibakichi (Ryûji Harada again) wandering into a new town (this one populated by humans rather than yokai) engulfed in a wave of senseless killings perpetrated by the mad and seemingly invincible swordsman Sakuramaru. Befriended by a beautiful and kind blind girl, Kibakichi determines to stop this "hooligan's" (as one character labels him) reign of terror.

"For *Kibakichi 2*, I was involved in the planning, but I couldn't direct," explained the first film's writer-director, Tomo'o Haraguchi. "I just couldn't fit it into my schedule. I wanted to, but I also thought it might be better if more than one director shoots all of them." Consequently, Haraguchi's assistant, Daiji Hattori, stepped into Haraguchi's shoes; unfortunately, Hattori proved wholly unable to fill them. Gone were the original's sometimes-beautiful cinematography, stylized horror set-pieces, and startlingly energetic violence; replaced by comic-book lighting, cheesy artifice (featuring cartoonish characters on stage-like sets), and what appears to be dance choreography in place of violent action. With disjointed, pointless plotting in which characters behave oddly, with little apparent motivation, the sequel feels as if the filmmakers tried to create a more intimate, character-driven tale—one which falls flat because of their inability to flesh out the principals. If anything, the stoic Kibakichi acts even more deadpan and taciturn here than in the original, becoming little more than a sword-wielding somnambulist. The mad Sakuramaru, who appears to engage in violence simply for violence's sake, remains so unmotivated and undefined that he becomes a mere cipher with an oversized sword. And the mysterious, face-painted "Mr. Dugan," with his monk's robes and deep demonic voice, appears out of nowhere half-way through the film to shadow Kibakichi and finally confront him at the climax (transforming into a ridiculous-looking green-faced monster with a glowing unicorn horn) and reveal his out-of-left-field plan to kill the "human-wolf" and then rule the world!

Unlike in the first film, which made no reference to wolves or werewolves, characters here label Kibakichi a "human-wolf." But just like the original, Kibakichi transforms into his hairy "wolf" form only at the very end, when he briefly fights the other survivor of his clan's slaughter, the beautiful Anju. Most disappointingly, this slow-motion battle between the two "human-wolfs" in their hirsute form comes off like a stylized ballet performance rather than a vicious duel between beasts. Perfunctory, pointless, and pretentious ("Our souls—where are they heading to?" asks a wistful Kibakichi for no apparent reason as pink cherry blossoms fill the air), the climactic confrontation becomes laughable.

Smaller of scale and looking far cheaper than the first film, *Kibakichi 2* stands as a slapdash, inferior-in-every-way follow-up to the admittedly uneven but still entertaining original.

With quotes from: "*Kibakichi*: The Fur Flies," by Norman England, *Fangoria* 244.

Kibakichi: Bakko-yokaiden see *Kibakichi*

Kibakichi 2: Bakko-yokaiden see *Kibakichi 2*

Kiss Meets the Phantom of the Park

(1978; Hanna-Barbera) Director: Gordon Hessler.

If you truly "wanna rock 'n' roll all night / and party every day…" then you'd best skip this ridiculous, tedious, and sorely dated made-for-TV vanity project for the '70s megaband Kiss. If you're a card-carrying, face-painted member of the "Kiss Army," however, then by all means seek out this smelly slice of seventies cheese.

Set in a state of the art amusement park, the goofy plot focuses on the park's chief engineer, Abner Devereaux (Anthony Zerbe), a brilliant inventor who has created a passel of lifelike cybernetic exhibits (including a Chamber of Horrors populated by classic monsters Dracula, the Mummy, the Hunchback, the Frankenstein Monster, and the Wolf Man). Devereaux goes off the rails when the park's owner slashes his research and development budget in order to fund a publicity-garnering rock concert by the group Kiss ("the biggest band in the world" says the overenthusiastic owner). Devereaux transforms several people into human automatons to do his bidding (via tiny devices attached to their necks), sends his real androids to attack the band members, and even creates robotic doubles of Kiss, with the cybernetic imposters programmed to incite a riot among the 8,000 concert-goers that will destroy the park.

Taking a page from the recently-released *Kiss* comic book, each of the bandmates possess superpowers (imbued by magic talismans): Ace Frehley (aka Space Ace) shoots lasers and can teleport, Paul Stanley (Starchild) can shoot lightning from one eye as well as read minds, Peter Criss (aka Cat Man) possesses cat-like abilities, and Gene Simmons (Demon) has super strength and can spit fire. With these abilities they battle Devereaux's robots, including a band of samurais, karate experts, and even sumo wrestlers(!); the various classic monster denizens of the Chamber of Horrors exhibit (including a shaggy, sport coat–wearing wolfman that gnaws on Simmons' platform shoe until the rocker shakes him off and beats him about the head and shoulders); and a gaggle of white-maned werewolves that look like a cross between the Wolf Man and a yeti in silver spandex jumpsuits(!). The brief confrontations, all half-speed punches and kicks (not to mention the old knocking two heads together gag), are about as convincing as the bandmates' acting. Though all four Kiss members received a thespian crash-course, it didn't help. It must have been a real trial for the actual actors in the film, as even an old pro like Anthony Zerbe (*The Omega Man*, *Rooster Cogburn*, *License to Kill*), who at this point must have wondered why his career had up and left without him, can't do much more than offer a half-hearted caricature of a mild-mannered mad scientist.

Directed by veteran Gordon Hessler (*The Oblong Box*, *Scream and Scream Again*, *The Golden Voyage of Sinbad*), the two-million-dollar production was shot over five weeks at Magic Mountain Amusement Park in California. By all accounts, no Kiss member was pleased with the result, feeling that the film made them look like buffoons (it did) and purportedly forbidding anyone working for the band to even mention the production for years afterwards. And for those not enamored of silly shenanigans perpetrated by self-absorbed, thespian-challenged glam rockers hiding their limited talent behind a trowelful of makeup and stage pyrotechnics, it would be wise to follow the band's lead and try to forget all about when *Kiss Meets the Phantom of the Park*.

Kyûketsuki Hantâ D see *Vampire Hunter D*

Lastikman: Unang Banat

(2004; Viva Films; Philippines) Director: Mac C. Alejandre.

Based on a popular Filipino comic book hero created in 1964 by Mars Ravelo, and patterned after DC Comics' Plastic Man, this decently-budgeted (for the Philippines, anyway) adaptation failed to cross over to English-speaking markets. Consequently, the more subtler pleasures of seeing a rubbery-armed teenaged superhero battle a vengeful villainess with a dozen toothy tentacles—*and*, more to the point, a *werewolf*—remain elusive to those not fluent in Tagalog.

Tree-loving teen Adrian (Mark Bautista) is seriously beaten by a band of illegal loggers, only for his favorite rubber tree to magically wrap him in its tendrils, raise his body up, and cover him with white goo (super-sap?). He awakens in the morning to find his wounds healed and an ability to stretch his limbs like a rubber band (and even form them into different shapes, like a big mallet with which to bean a pair of punks). He becomes a costumed superhero dubbed Lastikman by the Manila newspapers and spends his nights thwarting criminals. Meanwhile, back at his rustic barrio, the superstitious inhabitants accuse a reclusive woman of witchcraft after one little boy suffers an epileptic seizure. Storming her shack, they shoot and kill both her daughters and mortally wound her near that very same rubber tree, which imbues her with similar powers. However, maddened by hate, she dubs herself Lastika and seeks vengeance on all mankind, leading to a showdown between the two elastic beings. Oh, and concurrently, a pair of werewolves—father and teenage son—stalk the Manila streets.

Lastikman: Unang Banat (loosely translated as *Lastikman: Stretched Taut*) won the Best Visual Effects award at the 2004 Metro Manila Film Festival. Apparently competition was light that year, since most of said (CGI) effects look flat and cartoonish, with Lastikman using his elongated arms to swing between buildings like Spiderman, shaping his whole body into a rubber boat to save a drowning child, and foiling various robbers and rapists by slapping guns out of their hands from thirty feet away and comically upending them into trash barrels. In between these less-than-convincing elastic feats of derring-do the juvenile cast talk, go to discos, talk some more, play a few pranks, and talk—for over two hours. The only respite from the tedium comes in the form of the two werewolves and their uneasy father-son relationship. You see, dad enjoys the stalk and the kill, and relishes his lycanthropic power (which culminates in the film's one truly shocking scene, in which the monster attacks and kills an eight-year-old girl, biting into her stomach and consuming her insides [thankfully *suggested* rather than shown]); while his son chains himself up in their dilapidated mansion each full moon in order to restrain the beast within. While Lastikman finally meets the elder killer werewolf at the 90-minute mark, rescuing a female victim from its clawed clutches, their encounter remains inconclusive and the monster gets away. It comes down to a crowd of locals armed with metal pipes to stop the werewolf, finally beating it to death after it kills the little girl. When his son reads the newspaper headline "Dog-like Creature Killed" the next day, he abandons his humanity and decides to embrace his inner beast, leading to the death of Lastikman's own father. Oddly, the film ends with the young werewolf still at large as Lastikman rubber-bands off to help avert some new disaster (perhaps preparing the way for a sequel that never came).

The werewolf sidebar (coming at the 45-minute mark) remains the film's most (only) effective element, with the conflict between *pere et fils* bringing into stark relief the lycanthropy as gift vs. lycanthropy as curse dichotomy. The monsters themselves look like one might expect from a low-rent superhero movie, with the creatures' impressive physiques (hair covered limbs, bare rippled stomach and muscular chest) topped by a beastly visage—blackish skin, bright green eyes, flat bat nose, sharp fangs. A fringe of long hair ringing their faces, particularly under the chin, offers an unfortunate were–mountain man connotation.

Obeying the lunar laws of lycanthropy, these werewolves change only during the full moon. However, silver remains a non-issue (the father-wolf is beaten to death with ordinary pipes by an angry mob), and they obviously retain much of their human personality while in wolfish form (at one point the lycan-dad rescues his cowering wereson when the latter is cornered by police).

This was the third film adaptation to feature the character of Lastikman, after the 1968 *Lastikman* and a 2003 version of the same name starring Vic Sotto. Lastikman even had his own television series on Filipino TV in 2007–08. *Lastikman: Unang Banat* was the first (and last, to date) to feature a werewolf, however.

The Legend of Wolf Mountain

(1992; Majestic Entertainment/Hemdale) Alternate Title: *Wolf Mountain*. Director: Craig Clyde.

Aimed squarely at the pre-teen set, this "family adventure" tale sees a trio of twelve-year-olds kidnapped by a pair of escaped criminals needing a getaway vehicle (the kids were in the car they boosted). Heading up into the mountains, the convicts release the children on Wolf Mountain, then head off. When the bad guys return after the road dead ends, the kids have set a trap (pointed sticks in the dirt road) that blows their tires. With one of the criminals (Robert D'Zar) now determined to kill the three young witnesses, they give chase through the wilderness. But the legendary "guardian spirit" of the mountain—a wolf named Simco that sometimes takes the form of a Native American warrior—aids the trio. "I keep evil from the resting place of my ancestors," he telepathically tells the girl, Kerrie [Nicole Lund]. There is evil stalking you in this place; I will help." Apparently, Kerrie "has lived before. You are a guardian spirit now," explains Simco. Though the other two tykes see the wolf, only Kerrie can see its Indian warrior form because she is "one with the earth, and the earth is our mother; and you are one of her children." (The other two kids are *not* the earth's children?) Mystical claptrap aside, through Simco's guidance, encounters with various forest animals (deer, woodchuck, rabbit and even a skunk) seem to imbue Kerrie with a sixth sense that lets her know which direction to go, when the bad guys are near, and even how to start a fire without matches. Using their own resourcefulness and the occasional aid of Simco, the trio evade their pursuers, steal the convicts' loot, and even lay traps for them until the police and local rangers (led by Bo Hopkins as Kerrie's father) can catch up with the criminals and rescue the kids.

Not a werewolf per se but a mystical Native American being (he appears and disappears like a ghost), Simco takes the form of a (beautiful) gray wolf who keeps an eye on the three kids. "You are in your world," Simco tells Kerrie, "and I am from mine. I cannot take this form for very long." That said, his appearances are corporeal enough, as he helps to pull one of the kids up from the brink of a precipice at one point, and even goes mano-a-mano with the bad guy at film's end. We first see Simco's metamorphosis via a simple dissolve when the image of the wolf fades to reveal a kneeling native warrior. One more transformation occurs later, this one equally simple but far more dynamic as the wolf trots behind a tree and the Indian brave emerges from the other side.

Though simplistic in both plot and characterization (D'Zar plays the worst of the two escapees like a villainous cartoon; Hopkins ambles through his role in such a laid-back fashion you'd never know his daughter was in mortal danger; and a collecting-his-paycheck Mickey Rooney, as a concerned rancher joining in the search, cameos to no great effect), the film offers enough suspense and clever set-pieces to hold one's interest (even for those old enough to drive). And despite the overdone mystical mumbo-jumbo and the concluding clichéd plea for "protecting the land" right out of The Conservationists' Handbook, *The Legend of Wolf Mountain* makes a decent case for at least respecting Mother Nature … not to mention Indian wolf spirits.

Licántropo: El Asesino de la Luna llena

(1996; Videokine/Television Espanola; Spain) Alternate Titles: *Lycanthrope: The Full Moon Killer* (translated English title); *Lycantropus: The Moonlight Murders* (unofficial English title). Director: Francisco R. Gordillo.

This eleventh entry in Paul Naschy's Waldemar Daninsky/Werewolf series played on Spanish television (which partly financed the project) but was never officially released in English, apart from bootleg fan-subbed versions under the titles *Lycanthrope: The Full Moon Killer* (a direct translation of the Spanish moniker) and *Lycantropus: The Moonlight Murders*. Naschy penned the script (using his real name of Jacinto Molina) while recovering from a major heart attack and subsequent triple-bypass surgery. "To take my mind off things," he wrote in his autobiography, "I started to write a Waldemar Daninsky script entitled *Licantropo*. It was just to kill a little of the nostalgia I felt. I still had no intentions of returning to the film business." Later, producer Primitivo Rodriguez read the script. "He liked it and he told me he'd try to get it off the ground." Given the lackluster results, he needn't have bothered.

During World War II, a Nazi colonel falls in love with a gypsy woman, who gives birth to triplets, the third of which is destined to become a werewolf. "You bear in your womb the child of a man of another race," accuses the xenophobic Gypsy patriarch. "You will have triplets, and you know well what fate awaits the third." (Apparently every third triplet born to mixed-race parents is destined to become a werewolf. Who knew?) After delivery, her tribesmen kill the first two, but the third baby is spirited away and placed with the wealthy Polish Daninsky family. (Note: all this is told rather than shown.) Years later, Waldemar Daninsky (Naschy) has become a successful horror novelist, but periodic pains in his chest signal that the curse has surfaced, and on nights of the full moon he transforms into a savage werewolf. It all comes to a head when a local serial killer, whose victims look like they have been attacked by an animal, finally encounters the very monster he emulates; while Waldemar's concerned friend (and doctor) arms herself with silver bullets.

Unlike most of Naschy's earlier Daninsky outings, *Licantropo* drags. The first half of the film focuses on the college-age protagonists (including Waldemar's daughter and her friends) and their petty squabbles, spiced only by a couple of abrupt murders (in which the attacker remains unseen, presumably so that we don't know if it's human or werewolf). This results in a frustratingly slow pace not helped by far too much footage devoted to the subsequent police investigation (in which the flummoxed—and obviously desperate—coppers consult with Waldemar because he wrote a fictional book called *The Psychopath*!). Naschy tosses in a few of his favorite tropes, such as the pentagram ("The five-pointed star is the emblem of their tragic destiny" reads Waldemar's doctor friend in a handy book on lycanthropy), silver bullets, and the fact that "they can only be destroyed and freed from their terrible curse by great love." But it all seems shopworn and halfhearted.

"Although *Licantropo* carries on the Waldemar Daninsky saga," observed Naschy, "quite a few elements set it apart from the previous films. For instance, there aren't any mythological creatures, such as vampires, that accompanied Waldemar in other installments." Perhaps this is what sinks *Licantropo* into the mire of dullness. A garden variety

Spanish poster for Paul Naschy's *eleventh* Waldemar Daninsky werewolf entry, which never saw legitimate release outside its native country.

serial killer (who, ironically, employs a garden trowel to do his dirty work, and who is revealed to be exactly who you thought it might be) makes for a mundane substitute for Daninsky's prior supernatural opponents. But at least the werewolf, like in many of Naschy's earlier efforts, gets to play hero at the climax by taking out the deranged murderer (though, again, this pales in comparison to the many vampires, demons, mummies, and even Yeti he'd battled in previous pictures).

When we finally get to see the *licantropo*, he proves just as disappointing as his human competitor. Clad in slacks and a sweater, Naschy sports long sideburns, fangs, a widow's peak toupee and very little else makeup-wise. He's basically an elderly version of Henry Hull's *Werewolf of London*, though less satanic looking. "One of the chief strengths of *Wolf* [a film made around the same time as this one], which I thought was let down by a bad script," opined Naschy without a trace of irony, "was that Jack Nicholson's makeup wasn't over the top—I find that lighter makeup much more frightening, because it makes the wolfman more human, more credible." Well, more human perhaps. In any case, this first attack sees him summarily grab a man and bite his throat, resulting in his victim's prompt collapse and a bit of stage blood on the wolfman's lips. The perfunctory scene offers little energy and no excitement.

In *Licantropo* Naschy looks old and rather unwell. Perhaps his recent heart surgery not only leaked into his script (Waldemar sees his doctor several times about his mysterious chest pains, which herald the coming transformations) but his appearance and acting—the metamorphoses always begin with Waldemar clutching his chest in agony. "I remember one scene," recounted director Francisco Gordillo, "where he's sitting in his office as the transformation starts, and it's a long traveling shot with the camera following as he drags himself across the room, convulsing and clawing at the air, screaming and howling with this unbearable pain racking his body. We all just stood there hypnotized watching this—and then when I yelled 'Cut!' Naschy just froze for a moment, and then he slowly turned to me and said, 'You know, I even spooked myself that time!'" Perhaps because it hit a little too close to home.

Naschy barely refers to this film in his autobiography, mentioning it only in passing as "the disappointing *Licantropo*," and railing against the movie's producer, Primitivo Rodriguez, for "ousting" Naschy as president of the Spanish Film Writers' Guild (a post he held for six years). "Some friend he turned out to be," sneered Naschy bitterly. Unhappy with the many alterations made to his script—and the final, tepid result—he labeled the largely sex-and-blood-free feature "a de-caffeinated movie for general audiences."

Director Francisco R.(odriguez) Gordillo had little experience to bring to the production apart from kinship to producer Primitivo (his brother), having worked as assistant director on the barely released vanity project *Black Jack* back in 1981, and having directed one obscure "thriller," *El Cepo*, that same year. "I was never a really big horror buff," admitted Gordillo, "but I always loved the feel of those old Hollywood film noir pictures, so maybe some of that is reflected in this film." And maybe not.

Shot in six weeks in and around Madrid, *Licantropo*'s $2 million budget (at least according to Naschy) makes it the most expensive film in the Daninsky series. It does sport some decent production values, with true night-for-night, atmospheric photography augmented by bluish backlighting and a prowling camera. And unlike the crude dissolves generally seen in his previous efforts, this werewolf transforms via then-state-of-the-art CGI in a surprisingly smooth and fluid morphing effect (particularly given that CGI was then in its infancy). "We could afford to do the man-into-werewolf transformations by computer morphing," enthused Naschy.

Still, despite such technical innovations, *Licantropo* lacks heart—the very thing that sets most of Naschy's films apart. Due to its stodgy, muddled script, dearth of interesting characterizations, and listless, Henry Hull–lite werewolf, this *Licantropo* closed out the Daninsky saga not with a howl but a whimper. Note: One more (sad) stop awaited Naschy's beloved Waldemar character—but he had to leave his homeland to make it. Unfortunately, the tawdry, California-lensed sexploitationer *Tomb of the Werewolf* proved a mere concluding footnote.

With quotes from: *Memoirs of a Wolfman*, by Paul Naschy; "*Lycantropus*: Paul Naschy Howls Again," by Mike Hodges, *Fangoria* 165.

La Loba

(1965; Sotomayor/Columbia; Mexico; b&w) Director: Rafael Baledón.

La Loba ("The She-Wolf") opens with a shuddery bang as the lid of a sarcophagus in a lonely graveyard slides open to reveal a pair of clawed, hairy hands. Then, by the light of the full moon, out crawls a hairy figure. Creeping among the shadowy trees, the creature comes upon a man beside his campfire and acrobatically leaps, snarling and biting, upon the screaming victim. The beast-creature soon claims two more—a man and a woman—pouncing upon them to savage the woman to death, leaving the man bleeding but alive. Finally, the monster returns to its tomb, emerging from a connecting secret passage into a bedroom, where it lays down and transforms into a beautiful, naked woman!

Said woman is Clarisa (Kitty de Hoyos), grown daughter of Professor Fernandez (José Elias Moreno), cursed to transform into a she-wolf during the full moon. When a suitor arrives to ask for her hand, he is attacked and bitten by the wolf woman. The Professor works to save his life, but the man has contracted the curse as well. Meanwhile, the earlier survivor has been hunting the creature that killed his wife, utilizing a werewolf-tracking dog. It all comes to a death-filled end during the next full moon when the two werewolves escape their confines to decimate the household before meeting their fates.

The first film to feature an on-camera female werewolf transformation (and daringly—if coyly—flirt with the notion of nudity), *La Loba* stands on its two lycan-legs as a superior specimen not only of vintage Mexican horror, but of classic werewolf cinema as well. It is atmospheric (the fog-shrouded graveyard, shadow-filled woodlands, and imposing hacienda all create an oppressive, near–Gothic atmosphere), fast-paced (these werewolves attack frequently and viciously), and beautifully filmed (courtesy of talented cinematographer Raúl Martínez Solares, under the concise direction of Rafael Baledón).

Baledón fills his film with impressive shots of the she-beast moving rapidly through the forest. This werewolf doesn't simply lope through the woodlands, it leaps and bounds off logs, at times even catapulting through the air in an impressive acrobatic display. The mobile camera follows the characters and heightens suspense, even producing the occasional shock—such as when a man lies prone on an operating table before abruptly sitting up to reveal his snarling werewolf visage staring straight into the camera in a startling and unnerving display. And the frequent up-angle shots and shadowy lighting accentuate the story's dark sense of impending doom.

Baledón handles the pivotal transformation scenes with equal aplomb. Locked in her room when the changes begin, Clarisa sports hairy clawed hands and sharp fangs in her shapely mouth. Then (taking a page from the original *Wolf Man*), the camera focuses on her feet as we see them darken and (via some effective time-lapse photography) grow hairy, with misshapen claws in place of toenails. (Unfortunately, in a momentary misstep, Baledón reveals her still-bare legs, making it look like she's wearing a pair of unruly fur slippers). After a shot of the full moon, Baledón recovers by focusing on her head and bare shoulders as she lay gasping on the carpet, while fur grows (via dissolves) on her bare back. Her still-beautiful face is now framed by long hair and large wolf's ears. As the kicker, this all comes via the point of view of a small, terrified child peeking out unobserved from under the bed where she'd hidden, adding a sense of mortal danger to the weird transformation.

La Loba's behind-the-scenes personnel proved to be a who's who of Mexican horror cinema. Costa Rican–born screenwriter Ramón Obón concocted many of the classics of Mexi-horror, including *The Vampire* (1957) and its sequel *The Vampire's Coffin* (1958), *The Black Pit of Dr. M* (1959), and *The World of the Vampires* (1961). Tragically, Obón died in 1965 at the young age of 47. Near-ubiquitous cinematographer Solares (with nearly 300 credits to his name!) had filmed a werewolf before in 1959's *Casa del Terror* (which became the bastardized *Face of the Screaming Werewolf* five years later), and shone light on multiple wolfmen in the entertaining *Santo and Blue Demon vs. the Monsters* (1970). Solares also shot (figuratively speaking) a were-*ape* in *Night of the Bloody Apes* (1968). Director Rafael Baledón was responsible for one of the best Mexihorrors of the time, the excellent *Curse of the Crying Woman* (1963).

As the doomed *La Loba*, sexy Kitty de Hoyos remains one of the most stunning she-wolves in cinema. Her perfect face, with its large eyes, dark lashes, aquiline nose and sensuous mouth, remains largely unaffected by the subtle makeup, making her a vicious yet still fetching wolf-woman. The long blonde wolf hair covering much of her body does just enough to suggest a gorgeous figure, barely concealing her nakedness. Curiously, this female lycanthrope sports a small tail as well (unlike her pants-wearing male counterpart).

The male werewolf is not nearly so attractive, looking like an escapee from Dr. Moreau's island, with his fright-wig hair, scraggly overgrown beard, mouthful of oversized teeth and fangs, and fur-covered torso, arms and feet.

Both these lycanthropes attack with animal ferocity, clawing, slashing, and biting, all while emitting menacing growls and vicious snarls. Grappling with bloody, clawed hands, they rend and tear at their victims, leaving shockingly (for the time) bloody corpses, which the camera often reveals in close-up (even focusing on a gaping wound at one point). This was strong stuff for the 1960s, much less the generally conservative 1960s *Mexico*.

Bullets have no apparent effect on these supernatural creatures, but a silver knife is another matter—as is a well-trained attack dog. For the exciting climax, Baledón cuts back and forth between *la loba* and *el hombre lobo* violently attacking several human foes, culminating in the wolfman engaging in a fight to the death with the werewolf-hunting hound. The film closes with an almost romantic sense of tragedy, as the dying she-wolf (wounded by the silver knife) crawls to the body of her stricken wolfman mate. Lying together, the two return (via simple dissolves) to their human forms and finally find peace in death. Even the victorious dog gets in on the tragedy act when it goes to lie forlornly next to the body of his fallen master, slain by the wolfman.

Besides the beautiful presence of Kitty de Hoyo, *La Loba* sports the authoritative yet haunted playing of José Elias Moreno as the doomed girl's anguished father. Having assayed the title role in the outlandish 1959 Mexican psychotronic oddity *Santa Claus* (in which Kris Kringle matches wits with a horned devil named "Pitch"!), Moreno went on to scientifically create his own were-creature as the scientist who inadvertently transforms his own son into a were-ape during the *Night of the Bloody Apes* (1968).

Sadly, *La Loba* has yet to howl outside of Spanish-speaking territories, though Columbia did allow a limited release in 1966 to a few select Spanish-language theaters in the U.S.

The sexy Kitty de Hoyos as *La Loba* (The She-Wolf) (Mexican lobby card).

Un Lobisomem na Amazônia

(2005; Diler & Associados; Brazil) Alternate Title: *A Werewolf in the Amazon* (unofficial). Director: Ivan Cardoso.

"Believe it or not!!!" shouts the poster (in Portuguese) for this obscure Brazilian oddity that has yet to receive a legitimate English-language release (available only in fan-subbed grey-market form). For those, er, lucky enough to run across it, I think "not"—as there's *nothing* believable about *Un Lobisomen na Amazonia* (aka *A Werewolf in the Amazon*). That said, there's still plenty of offbeat entertainment to be found in this laughably potty potted-plant jungle.

Opening on a terrified woman fleeing through the forest only to be brutally attacked by an unseen beast, *A Werewolf in the Amazon* then segues into a sexy shower scene that morphs into a *Psycho* homage (complete with Herrmann-esque music riffs), ending in a topless lesbian embrace. Whew! The plot proper has a group of vacationing twenty-somethings trek into the Amazon jungle to enjoy some local hallucinogenic tea, heedless of the vicious murders committed in the area by what appears to be a mysterious animal. But their surreal hallucinations (including a singing Inca performing a rumba number!) soon give way to real horror as they're gruesomely killed by a roving werewolf. The two survivors, J.P. (Erandro Mesquita) and the gorgeous Natasha (Danielle Winits), end up prisoners of Dr. Moreau (Paul Naschy) at his nearby secret jungle lab. Moreau has a basement full of "half-man half-beast monsters," and is served by a bevy of blonde Amazons (girls he's drugged and hypnotized into thinking they're a tribe of warrior women!). Oh, and Moreau also carries the sign of the pentagram on his chest (which we see in a rather embarrassing sex scene between the balding and overweight 70-year-old Naschy and an Amazonian hottie), meaning he's also a werewolf. With Moreau intent on setting up Natasha as the new Amazon Queen (thinking this will somehow alleviate his "curse"), can J.P. and the bumbling inspector on the case (also imprisoned by Moreau) stop the madman before he creates an army of beast-creatures to take over the world?

Obviously tongue-in-cheek, this wild mixture of classic horror, jungle videography (though well lit, it was obviously shot digitally), cheesy soundstage sets (that jarringly contrast with the real jungle daytime scenes), various T&A moments, gruesome gore (including severed heads and limbs), a nonsensical musical number, and a plot straight out of the pulps, *A Werewolf in the Amazon* barely hangs together. It also, however, rarely fails to entertain with its lively kitchen-sink approach and kitschy sensibilities.

Then, of course, there's the werewolf. Looking very much like Naschy's famous Waldemar Daninsky (right down to the black shirt and pants, and copious drool), this lycanthrope attacks its victims with vigor upon the nights of the full moon, adhering to the expected lycan-lore (including death by silver dagger). Naschy, *El Hombre Lobo* himself, who played everything from Dracula to Fu Manchu over the previous four decades, here adds another famous character to his stable—Dr. Moreau (from H.G. Wells' *The Island of Dr. Moreau*). He plays it straight, mustering up as much intensity and conviction as his abilities allow (meaning he comes off as more sincere than convincing). Oddly, while everyone else in the film speaks Portuguese, Naschy delivers his lines in his native tongue, Spanish (accompanied by Portuguese subtitles)—and no character in the film seems to notice. But then, when one deals with *A Werewolf in the Amazon*, a few language peccadilloes are the *least* of one's worries.

Lost Boys: The Thirst

(2010; Warner Home Video) Alternate Title: *Lost Boys 3: The Thirst*. Director: Dario Piana.

This second direct-to-video sequel to the popular '80s vampire flick *The Lost Boys* (1987) sees Corey Feldman return as one half of the vampire-killing Frog Brothers. With his brother Alan having previously been turned, Edgar (Feldman) teams up with his perky comic book shop employee friend Zoe (Casey B. Dolan) to track down the "alpha vampire" who intends to create an army of the undead via a series of raves, starting right there in Frog's home town of San Cazador, California. When Corey Feldman is your "asskicking vampire killer," you know the proceedings are not to be taken seriously. Consequently, *The Thirst* offers more knowing winks and lame one-liners than genuine scares or moments of frisson. The sexy vamps, the techno-music, the competent but uninspired special effects have all been done before and far better (see just about any *Buffy the Vampire Slayer* TV episode).

Lycanthropy rears its hirsute head only at the very last, and that simply as a final throwaway gag. After the undead have been subdued and all is right with the surfer-dude world of San Cazador, Frog pops 'round to see Zoe at the comic shop and tells her he's been reading up on other aspects of the supernatural. In fact, he's learned that female werewolves, "she wolves," for instance, can transform any time

In 2005 Paul Naschy left his native Spain to become *A Werewolf in the Amazon* (*Un Lobisomem na Amazônia*) (Brazilian poster).

they want, not just under the full moon. "A very interesting theory," responds Zoe, who turns away from Frog and towards the camera, a knowing smile on her lips and her eyes glowing like those of a ... well, a wolf. Roll credits. Despite this suggestion of a new turn for the franchise, to date no further *Lost Boys* installments (vampiric or lycanthropic) have materialized.

Lost Boys 3: The Thirst see **Lost Boys: The Thirst**

Le Loup des Malveneur

(1943; Realisation d'Art Cinematografique; France; b&w) Director: Guilluame Radot.

This obscurity from Occupied France produced during World War II (whose title translates as "The Wolf of the Malveneurs") centers on the reclusive Malveneur family, who keep to their hilltop chateau while the superstitious villagers below whisper of legends and wolves, including a family curse involving a Malveneur ancestor who sold his soul to the Devil and would transform into a wolf at night. Said legendary werewolfery serves only as distant backdrop to familial drama, and no beast (wolf *or* werewolf) ever puts in a personal appearance. Instead, family intrigue and budding romance take center stage, with elements such as a mysteriously missing husband, a frail wife (who soon succumbs to a deadly heart condition), a domineering older sister obsessed with the family estate, and a fresh-faced young governess who comes to the chateau and becomes smitten with a charming local artist.

Some surprisingly mobile camerawork and the occasional off-kilter angle fail to breathe much life into the listless proceedings, and the viewer must make do with some pastoral scenery, a picturesque chateau, and a climactic revelation of madness. In any case, *Le Loup des Malveneur* never saw an English-language release.

Lycanthrope

(1999; Dead Alive Productions) Alternate Title: *Bloody Moon*. Director: Bob Cook.

Despite its title and misleading poster (featuring a nude woman juxtaposed with a red-eyed wolf's head), no werewolf appears in this bloodless low-budget direct-to-video effort. What does appear is said nude, and Robert Carradine as a government agent sent to investigate trouble at a scientific outpost in the Amazon jungle. It seems the depletion of the ozone layer has caused one man to become an animalistic killer that several characters fatuously label a "lycanthrope."

Lycanthrope: The Full Moon Killer see **Licantropo: El Asesino de la Luna Ilena**

Lycanthropy

(2006; ImageWorks; UK) Director: Kevin McDonagh.

Filmed in Birmingham, England (though for all the filmmakers make of the location, it could be anywhere), this low-budget, direct-to-video thriller attempts to tie lycanthropy to drugs—a premise pregnant with possibilities that, unfortunately, first-time director-producer-co-writer Kevin McDonagh botches completely. (*Full Eclipse* did far more with this intriguing notion ten years earlier.)

After a young female drug addict named Zoey is murdered (in a "frenzied attack ... looks like she's been bitten or clawed"), police detective Alex Taylor (George Calil) investigates, leading him to a hedonistic, fetish-focused nightclub. As he becomes more and more embroiled in the seedy scene, Taylor ultimately discovers a new drug, "a regular cocktail of steroids and a hybrid of a fungus called ergot," which causes its small circle of users "to think they're animals who think a bit like humans."

Obvious, grainy digital photography; poorly modulated sound; hand-held camerawork that generates more seasickness than immediacy; a plethora of too-close close-ups (to hide the cheesiness of the sets?); no-name actors who think that shaking one's head while talking adds gravitas to dull dialogue (the only actor of note—and the only one that makes any notable impression—is David Bradley, "Argus Filch" in the *Harry Potter* films, who cameos as the crotchety club owner); a lame, tame, grandmother-safe fetish club setting; and loads of protracted, uninteresting conversations lose whatever needle of interest the concept might have held in this haystack of boredom.

After the opening murder (consisting of a few confusing hand-held shots and some blood spattering an alleyway), nothing of interest happens for the next 50 largely-pointless minutes as we follow the dour detective about on his investigation: talking to the victim's roommate; interviewing her musician ex-boyfriend; visiting the fetish club she frequented; stopping in at a punk clothing shop; checking out a fleapit hotel she'd patronized; playing squash with his co-worker.... Finally there comes a second murder. But it's simply a quick foot chase in which several girls from the club run down some doctor who'd been treating Zoey, concluding with one girl grabbing his lapels and pretending to bite his neck. Brief and perfunctory, this second killing lacks (ahem) bite.

Lip service to the titular "lycanthropy" finally comes into play 70 minutes in when Taylor has a friend analyze a strange substance found in Zoey's tissue, revealing the new, ergot-based drug. "If this stuff ever hits the streets," warns his friend, "we're in shitsville." Taylor then spends time reading up on the history of werewolves before telling his incredulous superior, "I don't think these people were killed by an animal; I think they were killed by people who *thought* they were animals."

Ergot (the original source from which LSD was first isolated) is a real fungus that grows on rye which can cause hallucinations, convulsions, and even death. (Ergot extract is used in pharmaceuticals as a vasoconstrictor to treat migraine headaches and excessive bleeding after childbirth.) Ergot poisoning was fairly common in Medieval Europe due to the consumption of contaminated rye bread. It has been historically linked to witchcraft (some claim it was at the root of the Salem Witch Trials) and lycanthropy, with victims suffering "bad trips" in which they believed themselves to be werewolves.

"These people think they're werewolves," continues Taylor. "I think we've got a new drug on our hands.... The drug's making them incredibly strong, psychotic. I think they killed the girl because she wanted to leave the pack. They killed the doctor because he was trying to cure her." So what we have here is a case of lycanthropy-tinged-psychosis-by-fungal-PCP (or something), though without this "illuminating" dialogue one would never know, given that the few users don't behave psychotically (or lycan-like) at all (apart form the single neck-biting incident) and never allude to any transformation, physical change or animal attributes.

After these "revelations," there follows another stretch of nothing until the small-scale climax in a cramped apartment, which leaves in doubt the detective's status—and the wisdom of the viewer for sticking with this inept, pointless, dull time-waster.

Lycantropus: The Moonlight Murders see *Licántropo: El Asesino de la Luna Ilena*

Mad at the Moon

(1992; Spectacor Films/Republic) Director: Martin Donovan.

This werewolf western (a real rarity in lycan-cinema) turns out to be something of a cheat, not only werewolf-wise (with the lycanthrope transforming only in his own mind) but in the horror department as well. In a small frontier town a young woman, Jenny (Mary Stuart Masterson), at the urging of her overbearing mother, reluctantly agrees to marry a timid farmer, James Miller (Stephen Blake), after Jenny's true love, Miller Brown (Hart Bochner), the town rogue and bastard half-brother to James, rejects her. Following a disastrous wedding night, things go from bad to worse when James locks himself out of the house and seemingly transforms into a beast during the full moon. Terrified, Jenny finally comes back to him—on the condition that someone will stay with her during the next full moon. That someone she chooses, not so surprisingly, is Miller Brown. In the end, as Brown grapples with James, Jenny finally goes to her husband and calms him, love apparently conquering all, including his "moon sickness."

Focusing on (dull) soap-opera drama, little of significance happens until the 50-minute mark, when the diffident husband boards up the house and orders his startled wife to bar the door and keep him outside. That night he groans and growls in front of the full moon, then tries to get into the house like a snarling animal. Though Argentinean-born director Martin Donovan creates some impressive shots of James silhouetted against the huge moon, and there's some suggestion of hairy hands, when, at film's end, his "werewolf" face finally comes into view, it's simply his normal visage. The transformation occurs only in James' "moon-sick" mind.

It appears that the sight of the full moon is the trigger for James' madness. At the start of the climactic night the orb is initially hidden behind some storm clouds, and James notes hopefully, "Maybe it's not comin' out tonight." But, alas, the clouds part, and James once again succumbs to his "moon sickness." Earlier, James tried to explain his condition to the concerned townsfolk (after Jenny has spilled the lycan-beans). "Some folks got palsy," says James, "some sleep sickness, and some epilepsy. I kept my affliction hidden all my life. I suffer from moon sickness—I always have." How did this come about? "One night the moon came out and bewitched me," he states rather unhelpfully.

Frustratingly slow, and filled with long stretches of the actors staring pointedly at each other or even at nothing at all, *Mad at the Moon* often appears too "arty" for its own good. The odd lighting (including the natural light dwindling to a harsh spotlight on James as he relates his story), and the actors pointedly posing, simply calls attention to the too-precious techniques. Werewolf fans (and, indeed, most viewers) will come away *Mad at* more than *the Moon*.

Mad Monster Party?

(1967; Embassy) Director: Jules Bass.

Although beloved by a generation of monster movie fans (including filmmaker Tim Burton) with fond memories of its Halloween season TV broadcasts, the charms of *Mad Monster Party?* may escape those who don't view it through the rose-colored glasses of childhood nostalgia.

Rankin-Bass Productions shot this monster-themed children's movie in its trademark "Animagic" process, using stop-motion puppets like those seen in its popular Christmas specials *Rudolph the Red-Nosed Reindeer* and *Santa Claus Is Coming to Town*. Rather than cute reindeer and jolly old elves, however, the puppets here consist of classic *monsters* (albeit kid-friendly caricatures): Dracula, the Frankenstein Monster (and his Mate), the Mummy, the Invisible Man, Dr. Jekyll and Mr. Hyde, the Creature (as in *Black Lagoon*), the Hunchback of Notre Dame, a Kong-like giant gorilla dubbed "It," and, of course, the Werewolf. Designed by *Mad Magazine* artist Harvey Kurtzman, these eight-inch figures cost about $5,000 each to create.

Dr. Frankenstein (voiced by the original Monster himself, Boris Karloff), head of the "Worldwide Organization of Monsters," calls all the creatures to his private island for a special meeting to reveal his latest discovery (a powerful explosive that "disintegrates matter") and announce his retirement. "I've grown a little tired of this horror business—" he explains to his beautiful assistant Francesca, "doing bad for others and rarely getting any bad in return." The good doctor intends to hand over his title and secrets to his unwitting nephew Felix Flanken, but Dracula, aided by the duplicitous Francesca, intends to dispose of Felix and so take over Frankenstein's position and power.

The monstrous spotlight falls mainly on lead villain Dracula and his opponents-turned-allies the Frankenstein Monster and his Mate, as well as zombie toady Yetch. The rest of the creatures, including the Werewolf, simply round out the roster to serve up the occasional monster-specific pun or gag. Upon the Werewolf's arrival at Castle Frankenstein, for instance, Dracula embraces his pal, saying, "Wolfy, you old dog! This convention is going to be a howling success." During the dinner party free-for-all, the Werewolf snatches a bone off a living skeleton musician (of the rock group "Little Tibia and the Fibias") and runs off with it. That night in bed, the Werewolf noisily howls in his sleep, so that his exasperated roommate the Invisible Man ties a gag around the sleeping beast's muzzle. And when the Werewolf jumps out at Felix in the jungle, the bumbler mistakes him for a dog, picks up a stick, and tosses it—sending the Werewolf scurrying to fetch it. That's about it for this rather non-threatening manbeast, who never transforms, remaining in his werewolf guise the entire time. Said guise consists of a grinning dog-face, long hairy arms (which he uses to walk on all fours like an ape), an even longer tail, and big wolf feet. He also sports a tattered shirt and vest, short pants, and a gold earring in his left ear(!).

Leading the voice talent is the incomparable Boris Karloff, whose playful delivery sets the perfect tone. Vocal artist and impressionist Alan Swift provides celebrity voices for several of the monsters—Bela Lugosi for Dracula (naturally), Peter Lorre for the zombie servant Yetch, Sidney Greenstreet for the Invisible Man (why?), and Jimmy Stewart for the hapless Felix. (The Werewolf merely howls and snuffles on occasion.) Singer Gale Garnett ("We'll Sing in the Sunshine") voices Francesca. Full of jokes that largely fall flat, and featuring far too much Phyllis Diller (as the Bride of Frankenstein) for one sitting, *Mad Monster Party?* tries to make up for what it lacks in wit with a half-dozen forgettable songs that simply serve to pad out an already too-long running time.

Mad Monster Party? made a brief and unsuccessful theatrical run (mostly playing kiddie matinees) before quickly dropping from sight. Resurfacing on television, however, it became an October staple for many local networks. "We had a ball making *Mad Monster Party?*" recalled producer Arthur Rankin, Jr. "It was one of three films we made with [executive producer] Joseph E. Levine [head of Embassy Pictures]. He was a very colorful fellow. We had a good time and we all made a few pennies." Not to be a *Party*-pooper, but today *Mad Monster Party?* stands more as a monster-filled curio than a truly entertaining feature.

With quotes from: "The Mad, Mad, Mad Monsters of Rankin/Bass," by Rick Goldschmidt, *Monsterscene* 9.

The Maltese Bippy

(1969; MGM) Director: Norman Panama.

Dan Rowan and Dick Martin were two nightclub comedians who attained TV stardom with their groundbreaking *Rowan and Martin's Laugh-In* (1968–73). The zany variety show proved to be one of the top hits of the time, adding to the pop culture zeitgeist such catchphrases as "Sock it to me!" "Verrry interrresting—but stupid!" and "You bet your sweet bippy!" The latter informed the nonsensical title of this picture, which, unfortunately for the duo (and the viewer), failed to capture the madcap, irreverent spirit of the show, and flopped both with critics and audiences.

Rowan and Martin play Sam and Ernest, two small-time sex-movie makers whose rocky partnership is strained to the breaking point when Sam moves in with Ernest in the big old house (next to a cemetery) Ernest has bought. The mysterious neighbors, the Eastern European Ravenwoods, including Mischa (Fritz Weaver) and sultry sister Carlotta (Julie Newmar), seem to be werewolves who want to bring Ernest into their pack. This explains Ernest's recent odd behavior ("I feel like dropping down on all fours and licking your hand," he says at one point, "I also have an uncontrollable urge to bark"), for which he seeks help from psychiatrist Dr. Strauss. The good doctor reads a book on lycanlore that claims they can draw out "the evil creature that has chosen you to be one of its kind" by fashioning a werewolf trap "from a circle of horse hair with three drops of human blood." Along with this esoteric (and bizarre) bit of lore, he reads that "the werewolf is vulnerable only to a silver bullet in the brain." So a trap they set. But not all is as it seems…

Beginning like a legit (if silly) werewolf tale, the lycan-bubble bursts half-way through when we learn it's all a hoax, a plot—a silly, convoluted, impractical plot—to get at a cache of jewels hidden on Ernest's property. "I may be a dum-dum, but I'm not a werewolf," realizes a relieved Ernest. The only actual werewolf footage comes from a two-minute sequence in which Ernest dreams he transforms—via a few cutaways—while brushing his teeth. Looking just as silly as the rest of the movie, the Ernie-wolf sports a built-up dog nose, protruding fangs, and bushy beard to match his hairy hands. The suit-wearing lycanthrope runs down the street, chased by an angry mob (in speeded-up, Keystone Cops fashion), then flees from a pack of stray dogs while riding a scooter. Finally, the werewolf climbs a building, only to be scared off the ledge by his partner Sam in Dracula drag. This silly non sequitur sequence adds nothing to either the movie's plotting or its entertainment value.

About the only saving grace in the entire farce is Dick Martin's low-key, likable playing and the beautiful Julie Newmar occasionally gliding about. At film's end, after numerous double-crosses involving just about every character seen so far (plus a few new ones), resulting in a kitchen full of corpses, the moviemakers not only break the fourth wall, they toss what's left of it into a landfill—by literally rewinding the film to try out *three different endings*. Desperation anyone?

With its murder mystery/old dark house/hoary horror movie premise, goofy gags, and handful of lame jokes ("What the hell, I can always get a distemper shot," says Sam when he decides to date Carlotta), *The Maltese Bippy* comes off like a subpar episode of *The Munsters* stretched to 90 minutes, but without the charming characters and occasional funny bit. Bad movie? You bet your sweet bippy.

Meng Gui Zue Tang see *The Haunted Cop Shop II*

Meridian

(1990; Full Moon Entertainment) Alternate Title: *Meridian: Kiss of the Beast*. Director: Charles Band.

When Katherine (Sherilyn Fenn) returns to her ancestral castle home in Italy to claim her inheritance and assume the mantle of "Lady of the Castle," she encounters a traveling circus whose destiny and

Tellingly, this silly promo for Rowan & Martin's *The Maltese Bippy* is funnier than anything in the movie itself (courtesy Ted Okuda).

hers seem intertwined. She invites the small troupe to dinner at her castle, but their leader, Lawrence (Malcolm Jamieson), drugs her and her friend Gina (Charlie Spradling) to take advantage of more than their hospitality. It turns out Lawrence has an identical twin, Oliver, who transforms into a hairy beast when he has sex with the woozy Katherine. Oliver was cursed 400 years before by Katherine's sorcerer ancestor, after Lawrence (pretending to be Oliver) had killed the sorcerer's daughter. Now, admits Oliver, "when I love, I become a *creature* that no one could love in return." But can Katherine indeed love him and so end the curse? And, more to the point, why on earth would she *want* to, given the date-rape circumstances of their first meeting?! Yikes.

Filmed in Italy (primarily at the Castello di Giovi) by the prolific Charles Band for his Full Moon Entertainment company (which specialized in such low-budget horror fare as the *Trancers, Subspecies* and *Puppet Master* films), *Meridian* is not only a slap in the face to women everywhere (and just plain decency), it's a smack to the jaw of werewolf cinema. Band's Gothic-romantic take on the "Beauty and the Beast" story (though it's more like "Beauty and the *Breasts*," given the [over]exposure of the two female leads and lengthy soft-core date-rape scenes) does indeed offer a man transforming into a hirsute beast (and back again), but this "creature" (no one ever uses the "W" word) retains all its mental (and emotional) faculties. So the metamorphosis remains only skin deep. And apart from its appearance (a hairy, hump-backed biped with elongated features and pointy ears), nothing else ties the monster to lycanthropy—no lunar cycles, no silver, no pentagram, and, most importantly, no wolfishness. On the plus side, the film does "borrow" the intriguing notion that the beast can only be killed by a woman who loves it enough to understand (à la 1941's *The Wolf Man*); and the idea of sexual arousal triggering the transformation into an animal is rife with philosophical possibilities—which the filmmakers simply let lie.

Beyond its disappointing creature, *Meridian* also suffers from sluggish pacing, strained acting, and a general air of overwrought romanticism (not helped by Band's annoying penchant for slo-mo photography). Apparently lead actress Sherilyn Fenn was no more impressed by *Meridian* than most viewers who caught it during its innumerable late-night cable channel showings in the early 1990s. When asked twenty years later what she thought of the film, she merely replied, "That was my chance to go to Italy." Well, as least somebody got *something* out of it. For those who care, Charles Band did finally direct a full-on (if diminutive and comical) werewolf—in 1997's *The Creeps*.

With quotes from: "Interview: Sherilyn Fenn," by Aaron Duenas, thedeathrattle.net.

Meridian: Kiss of the Beast see **Meridian**

Mexican Werewolf in Texas

(2005; Maverick Entertainment) Director: Scott Maginnis.

Don't be fooled by the title. The low-budget (about $300,000) *Mexican Werewolf in Texas* features no werewolf in any shape or form, focusing instead on the legendary Mexican beast chupacabra. In the tiny nowheresville Texas town of Furlough ("goat capitol of the world"), a mysterious creature decimates the goat population, slaughtering most of the animals and drinking their blood, before moving on to the human inhabitants. When the local sheriff and various yahoos fail to stop the beast, it's up to a handful of teens to face down and dispatch the dreaded "goat-sucker."

Beginning promisingly enough with a frenetic attack by the monster (played by a man on all fours in a hairy suit topped by a wickedly-fanged, skull-like canine head), propman-turned-writer/director Scott Maginnis soon loses his way, as the film devolves into one meandering moronic incident after another (party in the desert; the arrival of a crazy "chupacabra hunter" who thinks aliens control the beast; idiot deputy leading a group of camouflage-wearing locals on an inept night-time hunt; various teens sneaking out to try and catch the beast—multiple times; the local mortician dressing up in furs for his own nefarious purpose). Sprinkled among the tepid time-killer scenes are the occasional chupacabra attacks, which, despite (or even because of) the rapid editing and handheld camerawork, become repetitive and predictable. Most disappointing of all, of course, is the fact there's no manbeast, just an awkward animal. (A *were*-chupacabra might have upped the interest level considerably.) But even had it foregone its misleading moniker and been titled something like "Chupacabra in Texas," this *Mexican* (non-)*Werewolf* would still be a dog.

The Midnight Hour

(1985; ABC) Alternate Title: *In the Midnight Hour*. Director: Jack Bender.

This made-for-TV ABC Halloween special is another of those catch-all monster romps that just happens to feature a werewolf among its myriad monsters. This time the lycanthrope appears, along with vampires, witches, a Phantom of the Opera clone, and a whole gaggle of zombies, when a group of high-schoolers read from an old parchment that inadvertently summons demons and raises the dead. As the monsters commit mayhem throughout their small New England town (which has an extensive history of witchcraft, naturally) and gradually turn its inhabitants into creatures like themselves, it's up to the Smart Teen (with help from a sympathetic, perky 1950s cheerleader returned from her premature grave) to find a way to reverse the spell and save what's left of their burg. The werewolf first appears atop a mausoleum in the cemetery, howling at the moon while the graves around him disgorge their grotesque residents. In full hairy body suit, it sports a rather unremarkable and un–wolf-like face, so that it might just as easily be a yeti or even a wookie. It moves swiftly but rather awkwardly on all fours when it unconvincingly attacks a night watchman. However, this results in the man quickly transforming (off camera, unfortunately) into a more traditional (clothes-wearing) wolfman. Disappointingly, neither hairy beast does much throughout the film, with the bulk of the story focusing on the vampires and ghouls, and the fates of the various teens and townsfolk—not to mention the burgeoning romance between the lead protagonist and his newfound (and newly resurrected) girlfriend. The wolfman meets his abrupt demise via a silver bullet fired by the protagonist (who dipped bullets in melted silver he purloined from his dad's dental office), while the fate of the original beast remains unknown (though presumably it disappeared along with the rest of the monsters when the spell was reversed at film's end).

With a few recognizable faces, such as Kevin McCarthy, Dick Van Patten, and Kurtwood Smith, along with the up-and-coming Lavar Burton and Shari Belafonte as two of the teens (not to mention the voice of Wolfman Jack introducing some appropriate Golden Oldie tunes on the radio/soundtrack), *The Midnight Hour* offers what one might expect from a family-friendly Halloween mash-up, with far more comical gags than frights. (The nadir comes when the head vamp leads her undead converts in a choreographed *dance routine* at the local Halloween party!) But credit veteran TV director Jack

Bender for at least generating a few creepy moments, with various ghouls staggering through the foggy night or looming out of the darkness to menace the populace. And while of course good conquers evil in the end, scripter William Bleich (1980's *The Hearse*) eschews the saccharine to provide a closing that, while not unexpected, still remains bittersweet.

Mo gao yi zhang see *Return of the Demon*

The Monster Club

(1981; ITC Films; UK) Director: Roy Ward Baker.

Shot in five weeks at EMI Elstree studios in the Spring of 1980, *The Monster Club* was Vincent Price's first horror film in six years. (It was also the only time the horror star played a vampire on the big screen, *and* the only time he appeared in a [pseudo-]werewolf film. His illustrious co-star, John Carradine, on the other hand, was a long-time werewolf veteran, having starred in both *House of Frankenstein* and *House of Dracula*, as well as playing a werewolf himself in *The Howling*.) "I see *Monster Club* as a sort of vampire disco, as a fun picture for children," announced Price to the London *Daily Mail* on May 20, 1981. "It is scary but not frightening. My vampire, for instance, is quite kindly ... and I have insisted on a line in the script to explain that I have retractable teeth. This had to be written in because I found I couldn't talk with the vampire fangs in my mouth." Given some of the dialogue he's forced to spout, Price may very well have longed for those fangs after all.

Comprised of three stories and a wraparound, *The Monster Club* begins when vampire Erasmus (Vincent Price) bites famous horror author R. Chetwynd-Hayes (John Carradine) and then takes him to the private "Monster Club" as a way to show his appreciation. There Erasmus regales the writer with a trio of tales involving a "Shadmock," whose whistle means death; an old-school vampire making his way in modern England; and an American filmmaker searching for "a strange, eerie, lonely, half-deserted village in which to make an atmospheric horror film," who runs across a hamlet populated by flesh-eating ghouls. In between we're treated to some alternately amusing and awful byplay between Price and Carradine, and some alternately catchy and awful "rock" numbers (four, to be precise) at the Club.

Produced by one-time Amicus head honcho Milton Subotsky, *The Monster Club* plays like a low-rent, tongue-in-cheek Amicus-lite anthology, with the middle vampire story played strictly for laughs. Also laughable are the various monsters populating the disco dance floor of the Monster Club, their cheesy dime-store rubber masks looking phony and ridiculous. "Subotsky found a milkman who had a hobby of making masks," commented a disappointed Price long after the fact. "They were terrible, just terrible ... like amateur night." Indeed. "Shadmock" remains too one-note and predictable to be fully engaging, and "Vampire" is a strictly one-joke tale stretched far too long. The final tale offers some creepy atmosphere but little else.

The Monster Club Secretary is a suit-and-bow-tie-wearing werewolf, complete with golden locks and a little dog nose that makes him look more like a mutant Pomeranian than a man-wolf. He appears briefly in two scenes at the club—at the intro before the second story, and at the end when Erasmus proposes Hayes be accepted as a member of the Monster Club (because, after all, humans, with their "guns and tanks and bombs and airplanes and extermination camps and poison gas and daggers and swords and bayonets and booby traps and atomic bombs and flying missiles" are the most monstrous creatures of all).

Director Roy Ward Baker (*The Vampire Lovers* [1970], *Dr. Jekyll and Sister Hyde* [1971], *The Vault of Horror* [1973]) had been working in television for the previous four years and hadn't helmed a feature since *The Legend of the Seven Golden Vampires* in 1974. "*The Monster Club* was an awful failure," Baker conceded. "Quite frankly, I was frightened of it going in, because the script wasn't any good.... I was able to do a bit photographically with the Stuart Whitman ['Ghoul'] segment, but the other episodes were pretty straightforward."

Released in the UK in 1981 with an "A" rating (suitable for children over 4), *The Monster Club* failed to find a distributor in the U.S. market (which, perhaps, was just as well).

With quotes from: *Vincent Price: The Art of Fear*, by Denis Meikle; "Roy Ward Baker: Life After Hammer," by Steve Swires, *Fangoria* 117.

Vampire Erasmus (Vincent Price, right) and the lycanthropic club secretary (Roger Sloman, left) show horror author (and human—"the most monstrous creature of all") R. Chetwynd-Hayes (John Carradine) the delights of *The Monster Club*.

Monster Mash: The Movie

(1995; Greenhouse Film Group) Alternate Title: *Frankenstein Sings*. Directors: Joel Cohen, Alec Sokolow.

"The Smash Hit Song Is Now a Smash Hit Movie!" touted advertisements for *Monster Mash: The Movie*. Well, not really. This horror comedy-musical based on the Bobby "Boris" Pickett novelty song "Monster Mash" and the unsuccessful 1967 stage musical *I'm Sorry the Bridge Is Out, You'll Have to Spend the Night* (also by Pickett and Sheldon Allman) was anything but a "smash hit," disappearing into the video ether soon after its release (despite a later re-release under the new title *Frankenstein Sings*). A *Rocky Horror Picture Show* wannabe, it just never caught on—perhaps because it's not half as clever or funny as it obviously wants to be.

A teen couple, Mary and Scott (Ian Bohen and Candace Cameron), dressed as Romeo and Juliet on their way to a Halloween party, experience car trouble and seek help at the nearby mansion of Dr. Frankenstein (Bobby Pickett). Also at the creepy estate are Dracula and his wife, Igor the hunchback, a mummy who thinks he's Elvis, a trio of delectable vampire dancer-nymphets, Frankenstein's monstrous creation, and Wolfgang the werewolf and his gypsy mother. The good doctor decides to do a bit of brain transplanting (à la *House of Frankenstein*), with Scott's cranium a prime target; while the Count, in search of virgin blood, sets his fanged sights on Mary.

The humor consists of silly pratfalls (the Frankenstein Monster continually hitting his head on the low door frames), poor puns (Dr. Frankenstein admits of his brain-swapping experiments that "There's really no reason to do it, but a mind is a terrible thing to waste"), and lame jokes ("You have violated the seven seals of the Jackals," protests the Elvis mummy's "manager," before adding, "including Latoya"). The creatures fare no better, with Dracula played like a smarmy lounge lizard, the cartoonish Frankenstein Monster appearing as a cross between the Universal creature and the Wicked Witch of the West, and the mummy looking like an Elvis impersonator wrapped in toilet paper. Fortunately, John Kassir (voice of the Cryptkeeper from TV's *Tales from the Crypt*) plays Igor with a bit of pathos (and even some wit), while Bobby Pickett occasionally amuses as the exasperated Dr. Frankenstein while affecting a passable Boris Karloff accent.

In between the sight (*sans* fright) gags are a sextet of songs, everything from Igor's rendition of "Play Your Hunch" to Dracula's "Eternity Blues." Apart from Bobby Pickett's own "Monster Mash" sung round the dinner table, however, none of them are memorable, including "Things a Mother Goes Through," belted out Bette Midler–style by Wolfie's mother (John Waters regular Mink Stole): "Now I don't mean to be so bitter, but you're really quite a hound / Find yourself a mate, have a litter, settle down / If the moon comes out don't squeal, she's your missus not your meal / The things a mother goes through."

"Wolfie" (as his mother calls him) the werewolf (Adam Shankman) fares less well than the rest, as he plays the butt of a few jokes in a couple of scenes and then disappears. At the beginning he's a rather shy young man who occasionally emits a bark and awkwardly tries to make conversation with Mary ("Do you believe in puppy love?" he asks her, while later commiserating, "Men are such dogs"). "I've got a very delicate skin condition," admits Wolfie. "Eczema?" asks Mary. "More like Chia Pet," answers Wolfie. When Dr. F proclaims, "Your son is a werewolf," his mother defensively retorts, "We prefer 'canine-ally challenged.'"

Just like in *House of Frankenstein*, this mad doctor has promised to help cure the werewolf but drags his feet, preferring to focus on his own experiments. "You promised you'd help," protests Wolfie's mother at one point, to which Dr. F dismissively retorts, "Here, give him this chew stick and keep him off the rug. Now, if you'll excuse me, I'm busy."

As the night wears on and the moon rises during dinner, Wolfie sports a black dog nose and halo of dark fur around his face (in a kind of dark-haired version of the Cowardly Lion). Then, as dinner concludes, he's suddenly a (real) dog. Wolfie then scampers off in canine form and disappears from the story.

Treating its viewers little better than its monsters—by bombarding them with (now-dated) pop-culture references, lame jokes, poor puns and terrible songs—*Monster Mash* makes a hash of its efforts to artificially create a cult movie. My advice: just listen to the Bobby "Boris" Pickett song for the umpteenth time instead.

Monsterwolf

(2010; Active Entertainment) Director: Todor Chapkanov.

In this made-for-TV movie, some illegal drilling in rural Louisiana uncovers not oil but an ancient Indian artifact. Soon the workers of the nefarious oil company begin dying, ripped to pieces by what appears to be a huge mutant wolf. Said *Monsterwolf* turns out to be the manifestation of the spirit protector of the local Native American tribe, whose land the evil corporation intends to steal.

Filled with characterizations as cartoonish as its poor CGI effects, *Monsterwolf* turns out to be a monster disappointment not only in the entertainment department but in its werewolfery. The titular invincible beast is more spirit than lycan (it magically appears and disappears seemingly at will) and never transforms into anything other than its long-toothed, snarling self. Though ancient legend has it that the tribe's greatest warrior utilized powerful magic to release his "inner animal" and so became the beast, we see this miraculous transformation only as a stylized animated cartoon flashback! And, relates the tribal elder telling the story, "he can never change back."

With its vapid love story, muddled mumbo-jumbo, and lack of "were" in its wolf, this *Monsterwolf* turns out to be a *Monster*dog.

The Mortal Instruments: City of Bones

(2013; Sony/Screen Gems) Director: Harald Zwart.

Based on the first book of the *Mortal Instruments* young adult fantasy series by author Cassandra Clare, *The Mortal Instruments: City of Bones* follows the plight of teenager Clary (Lily Collins), who discovers that she is descended from a line of half-angel warriors called Shadowhunters who are sworn to protect the human race in a war against demons, "a war that can never be won but must always be fought." With a hidden magical chalice as the McGuffin, Clary joins with a small group of Shadowhunters to battle demons, vampires and a rogue Shadowhunter who has aligned himself with the forces of Evil.

City of Bones apes both the *Harry Potter* and *Twilight* franchises in its attempt to create yet another tween/teen cash cow. Like in the *Potter* series, a magical world exists side-by-side with the normal, and only those with special powers can see the fantastical beings and baroque buildings within it. The Shadowhunters even refer to normal humans as "Mundanes" (like the "Muggles" of *Harry Potter*). And like the other series it strains to emulate, this *City* is full of tween-targeted romance focusing on a young girl torn between two hunks who manage to shed their shirts at regular intervals. Fortunately, Lily Collins makes a far more engaging heroine than *Twilight*'s vapid Kristen Stewart. All this second-hand borrowing, however, as well as convoluted over-plotting and a heavy reliance on CGI effects, leaves *City of*

Bones an overcrowded and unoriginal mess that failed miserably in becoming the Next Big Thing.

Shot in Ontario, Canada, and New York City, *City of Bones* cost an estimated $60 million to produce, with Sony reportedly spending *another* $60 million on marketing alone. The film took in only $31 million domestically, however, with another $49 million worldwide, leaving Sony holding the bag for a $40 million loss. A sequel, based on the second book, *City of Ashes*, had been announced even before the release of *City of Bones* but was put on hold after the first film failed to set the box office alight.

In *The Mortal Instruments: City of Bones*, the werewolf plays a decidedly minor role, both as a general figure and a specific character. Clary's mother's boyfriend, Luke, is the only foregrounded werewolf character, but he appears in his bestial form in only two brief scenes. Disappointingly, there's no onscreen transformation, and no exploration/explanation of the lycanthropes' characteristics or behavior, leaving us to infer that these werewolves can change at will and retain their human thought processes (given that at one point Luke and his fellow lycans come to the "rescue" of Clary at the vampires' lair). But we also see Luke entering a padded room with a timer lock in his basement, which suggests just the opposite—that he has little control over the change and what he does when in wolf form. The werewolves do feature at the climax, when they arrive at the Shadowhunters' headquarters to help battle a horde of invading demons, but, with some vague reference to an ancient pact, they disappointingly remain in human form. Onscreen for mere seconds as werewolves, these friendly lycanthropes, taking yet another page out of the *Twilight* series, appear as oversized (black) wolves. Consequently, the film's sole intriguing werewolf-centric moment comes as a comedic exchange between Clary and (human) Luke when they get into his truck after Clary learns the truth about his wolfish nature. "Go ahead," Clary quips, "you can hang your head out the window if you need to." At this, an affronted Luke snaps, "I'm a *werewolf*—not a golden retriever!" Perfunctory and muddled, this *City* throws nary a *Bone* to its lycanthropes—or its viewers.

Mortal Kombat: Annihilation

(1997; New Line Cinema) Director: John R. Leonetti.

Based on a series of video games, this first sequel to the 1995 film *Mortal Kombat* centers on a group of human fighters, including Liu Kang (the Mortal Kombat tournament winner from the original), who must band together to try and defeat the evil Outworld lord Shao Kahn. Kahn intends to merge the Outworld with Earth in six days and thus destroy mankind. At one point Liu Kang's mentor sends the champion to the "Hopi Mesa" in search of the shaman "Nightwolf" (played by Cherokee actor "Litefoot," nee Gary Paul Davis). A shapeshifter, Nightwolf first appears in full wolf form, leaping at a startled Liu Kang before morphing into his human guise and boasting, "Pretty cool, huh? It's my animality." This one brief shot of a wolf and the subsequent two-second CGI transformation is all the werewolfery on offer in *Mortal Kombat: Annihilation*, as Nightwolf merely delivers a few lines and then bonks Liu Kang on the head to send him on a trio of "dream tests" that will purportedly prepare him for the coming confrontation. The shapeshifter then disappears from the narrative altogether, never to be seen again.

Though the first *Mortal Kombat* proved a financial hit (grossing $122 million worldwide), *Mortal Kombat: Annihilation* failed to meet expectations (earning little more than a third of the original's take), leaving plans for more films in the franchise consigned to the cinematic scrapheap. And it's not hard to see why. A ridiculously simplistic yet disjointed story aimed strictly at the gaming crowd (the original at least attempted to draw in the casual moviegoer); poorly realized CGI and cheesy effects (despite its mid-range $30-million budget); characters that preen and pose to laughable effect (played by actors that do the same); overwrought yet impossibly banal dialogue (sample: "I have come to the eternal palace because your sacred rules have been broken"); mindless, repetitive and tiresome fight scenes full of leaping, twirling, spinning and little else; and a horrible techno-dance soundtrack all work to *Annihilate* any chance the film might have had. In essence, it's simply unwatchable.

Munster, Go Home!

(1966; Universal) Director: Earl Bellamy.

The Munsters, a situation comedy produced by Universal Studios and featuring cartoonish parodies of its classic monster characters, debuted on CBS in 1964. After a successful first season, the series was overshadowed by ABC's new hit *Batman* during its second campaign and cancelled after 70 episodes. *Munster, Go Home!*, a Technicolor theatrical feature, was Universal's first attempt to resurrect the franchise.

The film reunites a houseful of amiable creatures: Herman Munster (Fred Gwynne), aka the Frankenstein Monster; Lily Munster (Yvonne De Carlo) and Grandpa (Al Lewis), a pair of vampires; Lily's niece, Marilyn (Debbie Watson), the only non-monstrous Munster; and Herman and Lily's son Eddie (Butch Patrick), a supposed werewolf. Despite all its macabre trappings, conceptually *The Munsters* strongly resembled *The Beverly Hillbillies* (another CBS series), with nearly all its humor arising from the displacement of an eccentric multigenerational family into an environment ill-prepared to cope with them. Like the Clampetts, the Munsters consider themselves normal, well-adjusted citizens. They try to be good neighbors and often wonder why other people act so strangely in their presence. *Munster, Go Home!* brings this similarity with *The Beverly Hillbillies* into even sharper relief via a plot that sees Herman Munster coming into unexpected wealth, then loading up his family and moving not to Beverly Hills, but to an English manor.

A wealthy, distant British uncle dies and leaves Herman the family estate and title of Lord Munster. While Herman, Lily, Grandpa, Eddie and Marilyn board a transatlantic liner, Herman's English cousins plot to bump Herman off and claim the fortune for themselves. Later, Herman and Grandpa discover that someone is operating a counterfeit ring out of Munster Manor. The whole business concludes with a slapstick auto race.

Werewolf-wise, apart from a pair of slightly pointed ears, Little Eddie's appearance—with his greenish complexion, and normal teeth and hair (apart from a vampire-like widow's peak)—has nothing lycanthropic about it. Nor does Eddie engage in any wolfish behavior, apart from sleeping with a wolfman doll he dubs "Wolf Wolf." Consequently, the only werewolfery in the film comes from an amusing bit in which Grandpa (a mad scientist as well as vampire) accidentally takes a "Wolf Pill" instead of a seasickness remedy while onboard the ship bound for England. Realizing his mistake, he heads for his cabin, but too late—he exits into the corridor as a four-legged wolf (played by a real one). The crew spots the stray "dog," and Grandpa-wolf ends up in the ship's kennel (cage number 13, naturally). With Grandpa now facing a six-month quarantine upon docking, as per British regulations, Herman goes to spring him from the kennel. In the movie's one laugh-out-loud moment, they smuggle Wolfpa off the boat by having Lily wear him around her neck like a fur piece! Once on the dock, Grandpa spies a cat and races after it, only for the pill to wear off, leaving him on all fours wondering why he was chasing a feline. Later, during the climactic road race, a stranded Grandpa takes another "Wolf pill" (on purpose this time) in order to make it cross-country in time for the race—only to be chased by a pack of hounds and a group of British fox-hunters on horseback! The next thing we know, Grandpa is back to human form and treed by the hounds.

Munster, Go Home! plays like an extended episode of the TV series, with Gwynne, De Carlo, Lewis and Patrick simply carrying forward their shtick from the show. While it inspires the occasional smirk or odd chuckle, it mostly results in frowns and groans at the obvious and generally unfunny jokes (Lily affectionately calling Herman "Sugarfang"; Grandpa admiring the dank catacombs under the manor and saying, "I must ask Freddy where he gets his slime—it looks imported").

Perhaps because the series had so recently flopped, or more likely because it's simply not very funny, *Munster, Go Home!* sank like a stone at the box office. Yet, despite the film's failure and the brevity of their life on CBS, the Munsters refused to stay dead. The series gained great popularity in syndication and enjoyed numerous other revivals, beginning with an animated series, *The Mini-Munsters*, in 1973 and continuing with *The Munsters' Revenge* (1981), which reunited the original cast. Eventually, Universal decided to produce *The Munsters Today*, a syndicated series featuring a new cast, which ran from 1988 to 1991 (two episodes longer than the first series) and also spawned two more telefilms, *Here Come the Munsters* (1995) and *The Munsters' Scary Little Christmas* (1996).

The Munsters' Revenge

(1981; Universal) Director: Don Weis.

This second Munsters telefilm (based on the short-lived-but-popular-in-syndication TV series) was created to kickstart a possible series revival. Universal purportedly paid Fred Gwynne an exorbitant amount to entice the reluctant actor back to the role of Herman Munster. And so worried was CBS that this NBC-backed movie would be successful that they scheduled a showing of the perennial favorite *The Wizard of Oz* (1939) to play opposite. None of them need have bothered, really, given the result of this poor effort. Though loaded with affection for the characters, and focusing more on the goofy antics of Herman and Grandpa (Al Lewis), *The Munsters' Revenge* failed to jumpstart anything more than Gwynne's bank account. (Though Universal *did* eventually revive the concept, it came seven years later and with an all-new cast.)

The Munsters' Revenge sees the lovable ghoulish family visiting their local wax museum's Chamber of Horrors, only to see wax effigies of themselves among the grotesque exhibits. Which is all fine and dandy until it comes to light that these are not wax figures but robots, which the nefarious owner (played by a supercilious Sid Caesar) sends out to commit all manner of mayhem as he trains them to steal the treasures of the pharaohs from the National Museum. Can Herman and Grandpa, blamed for the "stealing and terrorizing" perpetrated by their robot doubles, foil the upcoming heist and clear their good name? It's no spoiler to proclaim, "Of course they can!"

Besides the robotic Herman and Grandpa, the criminal robo-gang includes versions of Quasimodo, the Creature from the Black Lagoon (an excellent facsimile), and the Wolf Man (sporting a not-so-excellent Don Post–level mask and gloves). With the focus on the Munster figures, this android lycan remains just one of the background creatures (whose portrayers try valiantly to keep as still as statues but generally fail miserably). Apart from some good chemistry between the two leads (not Herman and Lily but *Herman and Grandpa*), a few amusing moments (such as when the duo dresses in drag as female waitresses) and the occasional chuckle-inducing bit of dialogue ("Grandpa, she's only a robot—that woman can't talk," to which Grandpa replies, "I know—*those* are the best kind"), *The Munsters' Revenge* offers little more than corny jokes and weak nostalgia for a simpler tele-time.

The Munsters' Scary Little Christmas

(1996; MCA Television/Universal) Director: Ian Emes.

This fourth (and final, to date) telefilm based on the beloved 1960s sitcom *The Munsters* features a brand new cast (different from both the original series, the 1980s revival *The Munsters Today*, and the three made-for-TV movies) going through the usual Munsters motions. Which means a plethora of often groan-inducing dialogue and sight gags, including the good-hearted, child-like Herman (a Frankenstein Monster figure) frightening nearly everyone he meets (including a gaggle of caroling nuns), and Herman, in searching for his keys, lamenting, "Sometimes I swear I'd lose my head if it wasn't bolted on."

The overstuffed plot sees the Christmas-loving Munster family worried over little Eddie's lack of enthusiasm about the upcoming holiday. Downcast Eddie is homesick for Transylvania and has lost his *joie de vivre* (or *joie de morte*, as the case may be). So the family decides to do all they can to lift the little guy's spirits: Herman attempts to find a second job so he can buy Eddie that new Marquis DeSade Torture Dungeon playset; Lily enters she and Eddie in the neighborhood house-decorating contest; Marilyn organizes a Christmas party by inviting all their ghoulish relations from the Old Country; and Grandpa determines to use his alchemic skills to make it snow (in Southern California). Of course, Grandpa's experiments go awry, and he accidentally transports Santa(!) and two disgruntled elves to his basement laboratory (with an astonished Mr. Kringle amusingly exclaiming, "Where the fa-la-la am I?!"). Hijinks ensue, as the Munsters try to figure a way to get Santa back to the North Pole by Christmas Eve, with the two party-loving elves doing everything in their power to stay in SoCal (including turning Santa into a giant fruitcake at one point). But with everyone banding together, including Eddie, who's reclaimed his yuletide spirit, they manage to save Christmas after all, Munster-style.

Though for fans of the original series there's no getting past the fact that Fred Gwynne, Yvonne DeCarlo, Al Lewis, et al. are irreplaceable, the new actors do a passable job of imitating the originals. (Note: The movie was originally set to feature the principal players from the previous year's TV movie *Here Come the Munsters*, but a salary dispute resulted in complete re-casting.) The only one in *Scary Little Christmas* with any Munsters experience is Sandy Baron (memorable as the "far-out" DJ annoying Boris Karloff in *Targets*) as Grandpa; Baron had created the role of Yorga, Grandpa's older brother, for *The Munsters Today* series back in the late 1980s.

Filmed in Australia, with the New South Wales historic Heathcote Hall, an 1887 Gothic-style mansion, standing in for 1313 Mockingbird Lane, *The Munsters' Scary Little Christmas* offers decent production values and some amusing visuals (highlighted by the horror-themed Christmas decorations, such as an animatronic guillotine chopping the heads off snowmen, and "Randolph the Rabid Reindeer"). But the myriad silly subplots and cardboard characters (including a cranky neighbor intent on winning the decorations contest by hook or by crook) makes it tough going for anyone not enamored of bad puns.

First aired on the Fox Network on December 17, 1996, *The Munsters'*

Scary Little Christmas qualifies as a "pseudowolf" entry not because of the Eddie character (though he sports pointy ears, and someone refers to him as a "wolf boy," little Eddie Munster does not appear to be a true werewolf; in fact, he seems more vampiric than lycan, even complaining about the harsh California sunshine and sporting a Dracula-like widow's peak) but because one of the out-of-town guests at the Munsters' climactic Christmas party is a lycanthrope. First seen (like several other monstrous relations, such as a mummy and a Creature from the Black Lagoon wannabe) opening up his mailbox to retrieve the Munsters' invitation, this lycanthrope never makes it past the status of background player, appearing for only a few seconds at the final party (which itself lasts all of two minutes), where we see the tuxedo-sporting wolfman dance and later raise his glass with the rest in a Christmas toast. Which is unfortunate, as the creature's sole close-up (creatively shot from inside his mailbox) reveals a hairy-faced, beetle-browed, canine-nosed man-wolf with an impressive set of fangs jutting from his lower molars. It's just too bad he never gets to really howl in this overcrowded scenario.

Nazareno Cruz y el Lobo

(1975; Producciones del Plata; Argentina) Director: Leonardo Favio.

In this tragic romantic fantasy from Argentina (whose title translates as "Nazareno Cruz and the Wolf"), a rancher's newborn son, the titular Nazareno Cruz (Juan José Camero), is cursed (due to the fact he is the *seventh* son) to "be fed by the Devil's breast." Baptized with a holy name ("The Nazarene Cross"), Nazareno grows up with no ill effects, becoming a handsome, likable young man. But when he falls in love with blonde beauty Griselda (Marina Magali), the curse inside him begins to stir. Warned by his mother and godmother, as well as a sinister stranger with supernatural powers, to forsake his love, Nazareno refuses and continues seeing Griselda. Consequently, on the next full moon Nazareno transforms into a wolf, killing a shepherd and some livestock. The villagers then mount a hunt for Nazareno, who avoids the mob but falls down a hole. At the bottom he meets an old woman, a shapeshifting witch (or "nahual") who inexplicably transforms into a goat, snake, chicken and fox in quick succession. She leads him to a cavern of Devil worshippers and strange sights, lorded over by the mysterious stranger himself—the Devil—who talks with Nazareno at length before returning him to the surface to rejoin Griselda and meet his tragic lover's fate.

A beautifully shot art film by acclaimed Argentinean director Leonardo Favio (winner of several of his country's Oscar equivalents), *Nazareno* offers intriguing characters, earthy surroundings, and beautiful imagery to go with its stately pace and sometimes surrealistic symbolism (at one point Nazareno is startled by a snake sitting atop a chicken—which precipitates his plunge down the hole to Hell ... or something). Frequent depth of field changes (often revealing animals in the foreground—frogs, lizards, birds—representing, perhaps, man's link to, or *true*, nature?), mobile camerawork (including spinning turns and 360 degree pans), and evocative lighting that captures the beauty and wonder of the natural countryside make *Nazareno* a visual delight.

Director Favio is not above utilizing a bag full of cinema-tricks to get his ideas—and moods—across. Slow-motion shots of the couple embracing and spinning joyously through superimposed flames as angelic chorus music swells on the soundtrack represent the couple's all-consuming passion. Later, a tear dissolving into a fresh mountain stream, followed by images of the naked couple kissing beneath the water, reveal the quenching of that fire.

Half-way into the film the curse takes hold and Nazareno transforms. Disappointingly, the change comes abruptly and with little preamble. Nazareno suddenly awakens under the full moon and begins moving about on all fours, panting like a dog. An abrupt cut then shows a black wolf (looking more like a German Shepherd) in Nazareno's place, which pads off into the darkness. After the attack on the farmer, a few further shots of the wolf moving through the waving grasslands are the only other manifestations of Nazareno's werewolf, as the symbolic coming-of-age romantic tragedy of the tale takes precedence over all else.

Nazareno Cruz y el Lobo became the most successful picture of all time in its home country, and was even the Argentinean entry for the Best Foreign Language Film at the 48th Academy Awards. It failed to make the cut as a nominee, however. Worse, the poetic, fascinating *Nazareno Cruz y el Lobo* failed to land an English-language distributor and remains largely unseen in non–Spanish speaking territories.

Necroville

(2007; Cinema Guild/Shock-O-Rama) Directors: Billy Garberina, Richard Griffin.

In the New Mexican town of Necroville, monsters are everywhere, becoming both a dangerous threat and an everyday annoyance. After being fired from their video store jobs, best friends Jack (Billy Garberina) and Alex (Adam Jarmon Brown) hire on at the Zom-B-Gone company. As the cheesy TV commercial states, the company "provides extermination—including living dead, lycanthropes, nosferatu, mutated fish men, extraterrestrial nuisances, occult and paranormal phenomenon, chupacabra, loud college parties, and many many more." Armed with guns, baseball bats, stakes and holy water, the two blue-collar boys punch in to punch out zombies, vampires, and (in one brief scene) werewolves. But when an old nemesis of Jack's returns to town as a near-unstoppable "Master Vampire" and sets his bloodsucking sights on Jack's shrewish girlfriend (Brandy Bluejacket), will the two friends be able to stop this powerful creature? And will Jack even *want* to?

The film's conceit (and source of whatever humor it possesses) comes from the notion of the humdrum reality of monstrous creatures becoming mere commonplace annoyances. At one point Jack's nagging girlfriend complains about how long it took him to buy her cigarettes. At this, Jack peevishly declares, "Main Street was overrun. They re-routed traffic. I swear, between the zombie swarms and those fucking orange barrels, you can't get anywhere in this town in less than twenty minutes."

Fifty minutes into this no-budget horror-comedy, Jack and Alex run across a pack of six werewolves chowing down on a hapless victim—during the *day* of the full moon (the micro-budget obviously didn't allow for more expensive night shooting). At this, Jack blows a dog whistle to get the werewolves' attention, and when they attack, the duo takes them out with a machine gun (loaded with silver bullets) and a silver spear. As co-director, co-scripter and star Billy Garberina said on the DVD commentary track, "In keeping with the commonplace nuisance of the monsters in Necroville, I really liked the idea of just kind of dispatching the werewolves—in just kind of a nonchalant way—in a hail of silver bullets." With the lycanthropes played strictly for laughs, the amateurish makeup consists of long beards, blackened eye makeup and rubbery dog noses (with nary a claw nor fang in sight). The entire werewolf interlude lasts less than two minutes.

While a few sequences remain mildly diverting (such as when the pair burst into a nest of vampires only to discover they're about to stake a bunch of pretentious, fang-sporting "goth kids"), the bulk of the impoverished production consists of the two "best friends" continually bitching and sniping at one another (often arguing about Jack's domineering girlfriend) in between scenes that come off as just plain stupid (dancing zombies) or tasteless (the Master Vampire sucking the brains out of a baby's skull through a straw). The disappointing climax consists of a small-scale, half-speed kung-fu battle between Jack and the Master Vampire on a rooftop, which finally ends when Alex has the bright idea of *urinating* on the bloodsucker after drinking holy water (demonstrating the film's level of maturity).

Shot in seventeen days in 2005 in and around Albuquerque, New Mexico, for about $9,000 (but not released until two years later), *Necroville* remains watchable only for Garberina's obvious enthusiasm and likable presence as Jack. Coming off like a (very) low-rent Bruce Campbell, Garberina's exaggerated exasperation raises a few chuckles (unlike the deadpan delivery of his snarky co-star—and co-writer— Adam Jarmon Brown). What little interest a viewer can muster in the characters or plot stems from Garberina's crude yet engaging portrayal. Too much fake-looking grue, rubber limbs, and expletives in place of meaningful dialogue drown the film's clever central concept, so that *Necroville* remains just another disappointing home-grown horror. For the discerning genre (and werewolf) fan, not only would you not want to live here, it's not even a nice place to visit.

The Nightmare Before Christmas

(1993; Touchstone) Alternate Title: *Tim Burton's The Nightmare Before Christmas* Director: Henry Selick.

This wildly imaginative stop-motion musical fantasy produced and co-written by Tim Burton originated as a three-page poem written by Burton in 1982 while he worked as a Disney animator. Burton took the project back to Disney years later, with the studio ultimately releasing it under their Touchstone banner (feeling it was too dark for the kiddie-centric "Disney" label). Burton was unable to direct it himself due to commitments to *Batman Returns*, but served as producer as well as creating the characters and story. With a budget of $18 million, this *Nightmare* was anything but, earning the studio $50 million upon its initial release, and half-again as much upon subsequent reissues.

Jack Skellington, pumpkin king of Halloween Town, has grown weary of the same ol' hauntings and scares. During his wanderings he stumbles across a magical portal that transports him to Christmas Town. Enchanted with the notion of Christmas, he determines that "This year, Christmas will be ours!" To this end he kidnaps "Sandy Claws" (as he mislabels him) and puts the denizens of Halloween Town—witches, vampires, ghosts, mummies, etc.—to work making toys. Come Christmas Eve, Jack mounts his coffin-sleigh (pulled by skeletal reindeers) and takes to the skies. But rather than bringing joy to the world's children, Jack inadvertently delivers only terror with his presents of shrunken heads, bloodsucking wooden ducks and killer dolls. Finally realizing he's suited more for scares than Santa, can he rescue the real Saint Nick (who's fallen into the evil clutches of "Oogey Boogey," the dreaded Boogeyman) and save Christmas?

Among the various devils, killer clowns and bat-creatures of Halloween Town is a rather fierce-looking (for a stop-motion puppet, anyway) werewolf. Standing upright in a ragged, too-small flannel shirt, he sports a full wolf's head with an elongated snout and mouth lined with oversized teeth. Disappointingly, he serves as mere background dressing (like so many of the other creatures), receiving only a few close-ups and the occasional banal line like "Here comes Jack."

Apart from one howl of anguish when it's thought that Jack has met his doom, the lycanthrope evinces no wolfish behavior, and there's nary a transformation in sight (he apparently keeps his lupine form year round).

Nights of the Werewolf

(1968; Spain/France; unreleased) Original Language Title: *Los Noches del Hombre Lobo*. Director: René Govar.

Frustratingly for fans of Spain's Paul Naschy, this second entry in his long-running Waldemar Daninsky/Wolfman series was never released (doubts remain as to whether it was even finished). Naschy himself is unsure if a complete print of the film (co-written by and starring Naschy) even exists. "That picture was shot in Paris with a fairly good budget for its time," he said. "I remember including some scenes of the Wolf Man on the Parisian rooftops surrounded by the fog. The film ran into serious economic problems which resulted in lawsuits; but the most unfortunate thing was that the director, René Govar, was killed in a car accident shortly after filming was completed.... I left after my work was finished; but owing to the legal problems resulting from Govar's death, the film was impounded.... It really is a 'damned' film." Naschy's description of this "damned" movie is tantalizing: "The film told the story of a professor who discovers that one of his pupils suffers from the curse of lycanthropy. Under the guise of helping him, the professor instead uses him as an instrument of revenge. He dominates the pupil during his transformations by means of sound waves, and in this manner causes him to act against the people he wants to get rid of."

With quotes from: "Interview: Paul Naschy," and "Filmography: Paul Naschy," by Jose Luis Gonzalez and Michael Secula, *Videooze* 6/7.

Los Noches del Hombre Lobo see *Nights of the Werewolf*

Orgy of the Dead

(1965; F.O.G. Distributors) Alternate Title: *Orgy of the Vampires*. Director: Stephen C. Apostolof (as A.C. Stephen).

A horror writer and his girlfriend visit a cemetery where they're taken captive by the "Master of the Dead" (Criswell) and the "Princess of Darkness" (Fawn Silver), who force them to watch various zombie women called up from the netherworld to dance topless. The most famous of the horror-themed "nudie-cuties" of the era, *Orgy of the Dead* has very little plot to get in the way of the various bored-looking strippers performing their desultory acts on the cheap graveyard soundstage. Penned by the notorious Ed Wood, Jr. (*Plan Nine from Outer Space*), this atrocious "adult" film (in its copious nudity if not its puerile approach) offers little more than a few moments of unintentional amusement via Wood's risible dialogue: "I am Criswell! For years I have told the almost unbelievable, related the unreal and showed it to be more than a fact. Now I tell the tale of the threshold people, so astounding that some of you may faint!" (an introductory quote cribbed nearly word for word from Wood's earlier opus, 1959's *Night of the Ghouls*).

A half-hour into the film, and for no particular reason, two servants to the Prince of Darkness show up—a poorly-costumed mummy and a sweat-stained werewolf (John Andrews in crude Chaney-esque makeup, with shocks of gray running through his coarse hair—a *geriatric* wolf man perhaps?). The mummy speaks (offering a few bad Cleopatra jokes) but the wolfman only howls (in a painfully high-pitched voice). For the few scenes in which they briefly appear, this monstrous odd couple calmly watch the various dancers along with their masters, with the wolfish voyeur occasionally gesturing and pointing, and doing precious little else.

"What attracted me to *Orgy of the Dead*," said director Stephen Apostolof, "was that it was all dancers, there was no 'body contact,' and it was relatively very inexpensive." It certainly looks it. Despite the plethora of pulchritude on display, *Orgy of the Dead* only manages to make eyelids droop rather than temperatures rise.

With quotes from: "Interview with Director Stephen Apostolof," *Orgy of the Dead* Rhino DVD.

Orgy of the Vampires see *Orgy of the Dead*

Power Corps see *Recon 2020: The Caprini Massacre*

Ragewar see *The Dungeonmaster*

Recon 2020: The Caprini Mission

(2004; Critical Mass/Maverick Entertainment; Canada) Alternate Title: *Power Corps*. Director: Christian Viel.

In the near future, a mysterious alien race called the Ma'Har ("using the accumulated knowledge from decades of abductions and probings") have decimated Earth and its inhabitants. Now (according to the film's opening scrawl), "remnants of the human race used what they learned from the various alien technologies to take to the stars where the last of human soldiers [sic] carry out dangerous missions against the deadly Ma'Har armada." One such mission involves a small platoon of Galactic Marine Infantry sent to reconnoiter an imperiled colony on a planet in the Caprini System.

Structured (and filmed) very much like a first-person shooter game, the GMIs encounter one bizarre and deadly peril after another, including mutant bugs (via poor CGI), gun-toting cyborgs, zombies, vampires, a huge three-headed dinosaur (even poorer CGI) and a werewolf! Apparently, the Ma'Hars "found a way to use humans against themselves by genetically altering their bodies into biological weapons based on human myths" (as one character so helpfully explains). Oh, and there's a group of *Road Warrior*–reject "pirates" tailing the marines as well. As one sardonic soldier states, "So we're stuck on this madhouse planet with werewolves, zombies, scavengers, and some fucking maniac who has a grudge against the Corps. I'd say we hit the jackpot this time, boys."

Loud, frenetic, and packed with low-budget action (these resourceful space marines never seem to run out of bullets or explosives), *Recon 2020*'s ambition frequently outstrips its resources, with the alien planet consisting of abandoned factories and dirty, graffiti-covered warehouses; while the marines are decked out in what looks to be modified paintball gear. And though much of the film consists of repetitive footage of the squaddies making their way through the various corridors and derelict buildings, wary of the next ambush of cyborgs and zombies and vampires (oh my), there's generally something menacing just around the next corner to pop out and keep things lively. Among said menaces is a solitary werewolf, who briefly leaps upon one soldier before running off without doing any real damage. Later it reappears to jump another soldier, but this time the marines immediately shoot it dead (with one quipping, "Man bites dog; woof"). Upon its demise, the wolfman immediately (CGI) morphs back into human form. Looking like a cross between the cowardly lion and a shaggy escapee from a roadshow production of *Cats*, this "genetically-altered" lycanthrope remains onscreen for a total of about 20 seconds.

Made for the amazingly low sum of 50,000 Canadian dollars (roughly $38,000 American), *Recon 2020* was shot entirely in Montreal, Canada, over 13 days on the Sony Mini-Digital Video format and edited on a Macintosh computer. French-Canadian director/producer/screenwriter/editor/camera operator Christian Viel was nothing if not committed to his overly-ambitious project, literally setting himself on fire for his film (he played one of two scientists engulfed in flames during the opening credits sequence). Describing his *Recon* series (two more features followed) as "popcorn movies in the style of the Cannon movies from the eighties on which I grew up," Viel observed, "As far as my films are concerned, people either love them with a passion or hate them with equal passion. At least they leave nobody indifferent, which I think would be the worst. In the end it's only a person's opinion. Same as the films are only a person's expression or perception of a reality or lack thereof." In the case of the action-filled but ridiculous cinematic video game that is *Recon 2020*, it's definitely a "lack thereof."

Two slightly-bigger-budgeted (but werewolf-free) sequels followed—*Recon 2022: The Mezzo Incident* (2007) and *Recon 2023: The Gauda Prime Conspiracy* (2009).

With quotes from: "Satanic Christian," by CCF, pollystaffle.com, June 2006.

Return from the Past see *Dr. Terror's Gallery of Horrors*

Return of the Demon

(1987; Fortune Star; Hong Kong) Original Language Title: *Mo gao yi zhang*. Director: Wong Ying.

This schizophrenic Hong Kong horror-comedy vacillates between slapstick antics and gruesome horror to a near-alarming degree, sometimes even within the same scene. Pratfalls and "piss" jokes alternate with oogey brain-spilling and eerie zombie attacks, creating an uneasy mix that literally explodes in a violent finale in which everyone ends up either maimed or dead. The story has a small group of treasure-hunters inadvertently releasing an evil sorcerer (referred to as "the Monster") from a stone Buddha. Said sorcerer intends to reincarnate and secure immortality by eating the brains (and reanimating the corpses) of 49 people born in a specific month. A 280-year-old good wizard, "the Master," and his young apprentice aid the hapless heroes in tracking the Monster.

Werewolfery (sort of) enters the picture as a brief comical interlude in which the Master casts a spell involving a dog in order to gain the powers of the animal (primarily the ability to track and follow the Monster's scent). During a frantic montage, the spell goes as follows (in its awkwardly subtitled form): "Just trim a tuff [tuft] of fur to put on the forehead. And wrap with a red string on my body. And put my born [birth] information on his [the dog's] body. Mix my blood with the dog's. He drinks a sip. I drink a sip. Burning some celestial money. Lit on [light] the candle. Walk on the magic bridge. And the person must be crowned by a virgin boy."

And voila! Though played for laughs (at one point the Master lifts his leg on a tree and chases after a female dog in heat), there's danger in this spell. "When I become a dog I will go crazy in a full-moon night," he warns, indicating the dog hair pasted on his forehead must be removed before said moon rises. When the little band falls foul of a sadistic local magistrate, who incarcerates them for the Monster's brain-sucking crimes, circumstances result in the Master transforming into a wolfman (or were-hound, perhaps). The lycanthrope makes its appearance in dramatic enough fashion. We see the Master huddled on the floor, his back to us. Then a close-up of his outstretched hands show them to be covered in coarse hair and ending in claws. Suddenly his face lifts into frame, and in extreme close-up his eyes abruptly open—revealing the startlingly bright red pupils. His lips suddenly part in a snarl, exposing a mouth full of wicked fangs. After this shocking introduction, and a few impressive bits of savagery (with the creature bursting through iron bars and slashing big chunks from a wooden pillar), however, the sequence devolves into a series of goofy antics, speeded-up photography, and a running gag involving a fake bone. Equally unfortunate is the lack of visual metamorphosis, with the transformation from man to beast taking place off-screen. And he's no Lon Chaney, Jr., either. Though the bright red pupils are an arresting touch, the long hair sprouting from his cheeks and the lack of fur around his eyes, temples and forehead makes him look like a mountain man desperately in need of a shave. The episode concludes when Our Heroes finally trap the marauding manbeast in a set of stocks and remove the tuft of dog hair pasted on his forehead. "Take off his fur and he'll return to be a human," instructs the Master's apprentice. At this the wolfman passes out, and the scene shifts to the merry band hitting the road again, with the Master back to normal (again, no costly, time-consuming transformation needed…).

With the brief, comical werewolfery concluded, the film quickly moves on to the next set-piece (involving a haunted house, an amorous ghost and hundreds of eggs!) before charging into its creepy, gory and violent climax at the Monster's zombie-infested lair. Though no classic of that peculiar cinematic subset that is 1980s Hong Kong horror, *Return of the Demon* fills the bill well enough. But for the werewolf fan, and those viewers more enamored of less-frantic Western horror conventions, *Return of the Demon* remains a puzzling, disappointing, and exhausting experience.

Rider of the Skulls

(1965; Derechos Reservados Televisa S.A./Columbia; Mexico; b&w) Original Language Title: *El Charro de las Calaveras*. Director: Alfredo Salazar.

A werewolf *Western*? Check. A *Mexican* lycanthrope? *Si*. The *oddest* wolfman transformation in celluloid history? *Absolutamente*. The outré 1965 south-of-the-border monster mash anthology *Rider of the Skulls* (*El Charro de las Calaveras*) offers all this and so much more.

Back in the Old (Mexican) West, a werewolf (David Silva, who played an inspector in the engagingly bizarre 1962 offering *The Brainiac*) terrorizes a village. Into the hamlet gallops the Rider of the Skulls (voiced by Dagoberto Rodriguez but represented in the physical action by rough-and-tumble former wrestler Fernando Oses), a mask-wearing, gun-toting, horseback-riding hero (kind of a sombrero-sporting Lone Ranger) dressed all in black and sworn "to fight evil in all its forms." Why does he wear a mask? "My identity doesn't matter," he says. "I represent justice; justice doesn't have a face." But the rampaging lycanthrope terrorizing the town does, and a rather unusual one at that. Long hair, mammoth eyebrows, protruding fangs, huge pointy wolf-ears, and veined wrinkly skin (as well as hairy arms and hands ending in sharp, 2-inch fingernail-claws) provide this wolf man's decidedly demonic look (well, as demonic-looking as a crude rubber and paper maché mask can be). With the Rider on his trail, the werewolf claims two victims, terrifies his own stepson, and reveals himself to be the owner of the very hacienda at which the Rider is staying. Ultimately, the Rider tracks the beast to a rock quarry, where the wolf man finally tumbles over the edge. The now orphaned boy (his mother was killed by the werewolf), along with a bumbling hired hand (the comic relief), follow the Rider to his next two adventures, first facing down a vampire in another town, and finally vanquishing a headless horseman.

Director/screenwriter Alfredo Salazar (brother of actor/producer/director Abel [*The Brainiac*] Salazar) shot *Rider of the Skulls* as three separate "mini" films, thus explaining the repetitive structure of the three monster-du-jour segments. Though this might indicate it was meant as separate episodes for television, that's not necessarily so, as union regulations in Mexico at that time often limited studios to filming shorts. Producers got around this by combining their half-hour episodes at a later date to create full-length feature films. A number of features were created this way, including the quartet of *Nostradamus* vampire movies starring Germán Robles.

Prolific screenwriter Alfredo Salazar, after twenty years of scribbling such delirious Mexi-horror "classics" as *The Aztec Mummy* trilogy, *The Man and the Monster*, *The World of the Vampires*, and numerous Santo outings (including *Santo and Blue Demon vs. Dracula and the Wolfman*), takes the directorial reins for the first time with *Rider of the Skulls* (and even puts in a Hitchcock-like cameo as a victim of the vampire in the second tale). And while Salazar adds few flourishes to this obviously impoverished production (spending a lot of time filming medium-shots out of doors on dusty roads and fields, and in rundown buildings), he at least keeps things moving at a *rapido* pace, allowing little time to question the sheer absurdity of it all. For instance, in a nonsensically bizarre—but decidedly novel—twist on the classic werewolf transformation scene, the man stares at the moon outside his window, curses his fate, and then collapses to the floor where (via two simple dissolves) his body becomes first a skeleton(!) and then the (fully clothed) wolfman. Salazar seemed very pleased with this wacky take on lycanthropic metamorphosis, for he repeats it not one, not two, but *three* more times (all within the space of 20 minutes).

Things don't become any less *loco* as the tale gallops along. At one point the local witch aids the Rider by resurrecting a dead victim of the werewolf. The gruesome cadaver sits up in his coffin to regale the Rider about the werewolf's origin (unhelpfully admitting that "nobody knows where it came from") and reveal the beast's human identity. Later, the Rider catches sight of and chases the wolf man across an open field, relentlessly firing at the beast (he's either a terrible shot or the bullets have no effect, since he's only 20 feet behind the monster). Suddenly—and inexplicably—the Rider falls into a concealed pit. Instantly aware of this, the werewolf turns back and starts hurling oversized rocks down upon the trapped Rider! This all appears in the film's first third, with subsequent wackiness arriving in the form of a cape-wearing vampire with a dried-apple monkey face; a talking head in a box; and a headless horseman who, after reattaching his wayward cranium, rails against God Himself when a bolt of lightning takes out his two skeletal henchmen. *Ay Caramba!*

Of course, such outré inventiveness is often abetted (though not aided) by mere incompetence. For instance, the monsters' masks appear no less phony for their uniqueness. The third segment's paper maché head in a box, whose mouth moves like a hand-puppet when it talks, takes the cheesiness to a whole new level. Despite the monsters prowling at night and characters often commenting on the "late hour," the action obviously takes place midday, with only the weakest of not-fooling-anyone day-for-night filters employed. At one point, while chasing the wolfman away yet again, the Rider states, "The werewolf won't show up for the next 15 days—not until the next full moon." Apparently, math is not his strong suit, as the full moon comes only once a month, not twice (blue moons excepted).

Additionally, due to its tripartite nature, *Rider of the Skulls* becomes rather repetitious in structure: initial monster attack; arrival of Our Hero; several inconclusive fisticuff-filled confrontations between Rider and monster; culminating in a final decisive battle resulting in the fiend's demise.

Continuity between segments (much like the werewolf itself) seems to fall by the wayside as well. For example, the boy's name inexplicably changes from "Perico" in the werewolf episode to "Juanito" in the vampire story (though the comical sidekick remains "Cleofas"). And the skull emblems on the Rider's costume metamorphose from a simplistic skull-and-crossbones image on the sleeves in the first segment to more artistically-rendered skull-only patches that migrate to the chest in the second segment. When the heroine of the vampire story asks Juanito if he's ever seen the Rider's face, Juanito answers, "No, I don't think anyone has ever seen it"—despite the fact that at the close of the werewolf episode mere minutes before, the rider unveiled his face to the boy and Cleofas (who even commented on how handsome the hero looks).

Even traditional werewolf lore can't escape Salazar's screenwriting peccadilloes. After the wolfman transforms back to his human form, he laments, "I've killed her" (referring to his latest victim), obviously remembering exactly what he did as the beast; most screen werewolves have no recollection of their actions in bestial guise. And while guns and knives seemingly have little effect, a simple fall down a thirty-foot embankment is enough to send this manbeast to his everlasting rest.

Though it's not all delirious *durazno y crema* (peaches and cream), *Rider of the Skulls* still offers dollops aplenty for those enamored of south-of-the-border monster thrills, and anyone who enjoys a huge helping of the offbeat with their horror.

A werewolf terrorizes the Mexican countryside in the delirious south-of-the-border monster mash-up *Rider of the Skulls* (Mexican poster).

Romasanta

(2004; Filmax International; Spain/UK) Alternate Titles: *Werewolf Hunter: The Legend of Romasanta* (U.S. DVD); *Werewolf Manhunt* (U.S. DVD); *Werewolf Hunter* (U.S. video); *Romasanta: The Werewolf Hunt* (UK DVD); Director: Paco Plaza.

"In 1851 the very first serial killer in Europe was caught and brought to trial for dozens of murders," begins the opening written narration. "He had a very unusual defense.... He claimed he was a werewolf." Based on the real-life figure of Manuel Blanco Romasanta, Spain's first documented serial killer, *Romasanta* stars Julian Sands as a traveling peddler and man of letters who first charms his female victims, then cruelly kills and robs them (even using the fat from their bodies to make high-quality soap to sell). When an accomplice, Antonio (John

Sharian), whom Romasanta holds in thrall ("He made me a wolf ... he makes me hunt like a wolf and kill like a wolf"), falls into the hands of the law, it leads to the apprehension of Romasanta himself. (Producer Brian Yuzna initially wanted Paul Naschy[!] for the role of Antonio, but was unable to procure his services.) Claiming to be cursed, Romasanta inspires a superstition vs. science debate during his trial. It all comes to a head when his former lover, Barbara (Elsa Pataky), the sister of one of his victims, visits the killer in prison to seek revenge ... with a silver knife.

Authentic period settings and costumes perfectly captures the time period, while Julian Sands offers a riveting portrayal of the mysterious, enigmatic killer. And the werewolf-vs.-mental illness angle brought to the fore during the trial scenes (illustrated, sometimes gruesomely, by a number of suspenseful flashbacks) keeps interest high. (In a stranger-than-fiction scenario, *Romasanta* co-scripter Alfredo Conde is a real-life descendent of one of the doctors involved in the original "Werewolf of Alleriz" case.)

Accused of murdering 15 people, Romasanta admits it, stating, "I had no choice. It's well known where I come from that the Devil has a claim on the ninth-born son, and I was my father's ninth-born son." This marks a rather arbitrary change from the accepted Galacian folklore of the *seventh* son, who can either be born normal or as a *lobishome* (werewolf). Despite this "Devil's claim," however, Romasanta (like many killers) doesn't see himself as particularly evil. "Evil?" he asks. "A wolf kills through instinct; it's in his nature." Of course, a wolf doesn't systematically rob his prey nor make soap from its body, either ...

The Age of Enlightenment brought with it the incorporation of hypnosis and psychiatry into the medical field—and into the courtroom—two concepts utilized in the film (as well as the original real-life court case). The notion is personified in the figure of "Professor Phillips" (David Grant), who testifies before the court that "this so-called 'curse' is nothing more than a severe mental disorder which in modern medical terms we refer to as lycanthropy. It's an uncontrollable impulse that transforms an ordinary man into a wild and dangerous animal—a lycanthrope or 'wolfman,' to call it by its more sensationalist and populist name." The professor also believes that this condition can be cured. How such a cure could be affected, however, remains unclear. What the film *does* suggest, though, is the rather romantic/cinematic notion that *love* might just be the balm (be it for lycanthropy or mental illness). "With [Barbara]," declares Romasanta, "I felt human for the first time in my life. I experienced emotions, perhaps love. And so for a few precious days my curse left me, and I lived as a man."

Romasanta—a film about a man who only *thinks* he's a werewolf—features one of the most visually effective transformation sequences in cinema. It begins as Antonio, in wolf form, lies panting in the rain. In close-up we see the animal's hair appear to slough off and melt away, with the skin beneath rippling and changing color, and a cowl forming over the pulsating skin. The now-hairless wolf muzzle shortens, the wolf's paw stretches into human-like fingers flexing forward. Then, as the rain beats down, the now-human hands rip through the gooey, placenta-like covering to reveal the human head beneath, mouth wide open in a violent cry of anguish as it peels away the supernatural skin. It's a startling and affecting physical transformation whose physical effects work looks altogether too real. And, ironically, it occurs merely as a deluded imagining.

"I didn't want to do a movie where a man gets bitten by a wolf, and, as a result, the wretched guy has to do evil things," stated director Paco Plaza. "That's why we did our transformation the other way round; it's a wolf turning into a man. That's how Romasanta saw himself, so it was important not to show a poor unwilling victim but rather a merciless being who only cares about himself and his own gain and feels neither remorse nor guilt—a guy who assumes his nature and enjoys it." As Antonio says, "Romasanta is not a man; he's a wolf who becomes human to murder and seduce his victims." Either way, the film suggests, it's immaterial. Man or wolf, Romasanta remains a true monster.

Known as the "Werewolf of Alleriz," the real Romasanta admitted in 1853 (not 1851) to killing 13 (not 15) people. He did indeed deny responsibility because he was cursed to turn into a wolf. He was initially sentenced to death for his crimes, but Queen Isabella II personally commuted the sentence to life imprisonment on the urging of the Spanish Minister of Justice, acting on behalf of a French hypnotist named Mr. Phillips who claimed Romasanta was suffering from monomania and so was not responsible for his actions. According to newspaper reports of the time, Romasanta died in the Ceuta prison in 1863 of stomach cancer (with a silver knife nowhere in sight).

During his trial, the real Romasanta made the following statement: "The first time I transformed, I was in the mountains of Couso. I came across two ferocious-looking wolves. I suddenly fell to the floor, and began to feel convulsions, I rolled over three times, and a few seconds later I myself was a wolf. I was out marauding with the other two for five days, until I returned to my own body, the one you see before you today, Your Honour. The other two wolves came with me, who I thought were also wolves, changed into human form. They were from Valencia. One was called Antonio and the other Don Genaro. They too were cursed ... we attacked and ate a number of people because we were hungry." The prosecutor, Luciano Bastida Hernáez, asked Romasanta to demonstrate the transformation for the court. At this, Romasanta answered that the curse only lasted for thirteen years and that he was now cured because that time had expired the previous week. Indeed.

With quotes from: "Howling for *Werewolf Hunter*," by Mike Hodges, *Fangoria* 248; "The Wolfman of Allariz," *Spain Features: Profiles*.

Romasanta: The Werewolf Hunt see *Romasanta*

Samson in the Wax Museum

(1963; Filmadora Panamerica S.A./Trans-International Films; Mexico; b&w) Original Language Title: *Santo en el Museo de Cera*; Alternate Title: *Santo in the Wax Museum*. Directors: Alfonso Corona Blake, Manuel San Fernando (English language version).

It's *Mystery of the Wax Museum* gone south, south of the border, that is—as well as south of believability, since the film's hero is that purveyor of Truth, Justice and the Mexican Way, the silver-masked, crime-fighting professional wrestler Santo (don't let the dubbing of the character "Samson" fool you—a Santo by any other name wrestles just as sweetly). Here Santo/Samson investigates a series of disappearances revolving around a sinister wax museum run by Dr. Karol (Claudio Brook). *Samson in the Wax Museum* sports a rather intriguing mystery motif in its first half, in which the police, Samson and the viewer receive evidence both for *and* against Dr. Karol's guilt. Along with the eerie atmosphere in Karol's cavern-like "museum" housing his weird, monstrous figures—many of which, including a wolfman—come to life to attack Our Hero, this initial ambivalence keeps the viewer off balance and interested. Of course, after 45 minutes the picture spoils it all by revealing the identity of the villain who transforms people into disfigured "monsters" with his flesh-eroding and trance-inducing serum.

Disappointingly, the faux monsters look like cut-rate *Island of Lost Souls* rejects (brawny man with unconvincing pig-snout, scraggly-faced wolfman, etc.), and they do very little until the climax, when, after turning on their creator, they briefly menace Samson before the Silver Masked Man dumps a vat of boiling wax over them. And the film makes up for its wrestling-free first third by tossing in a number of ringside scenes towards the middle and end, spoiling the picture's rhythm (though presumably giving the Santo enthusiasts what they really want). But for said Santo fans (and we know who we are), one could do worse than spend 90 minutes in this *Wax Museum*.

Samson vs. the Vampire Women

(1962; Filmadora Primamaricana S.A./Trans-International Films; Mexico; b&w) Original Language Title: *El Santo contra las Mujeres Vampiros*. Director: Alfonso Corona Blake, Manuel San Fernando (English Language Version).

The best of the three Santo (ne Samson) movies dubbed into English and released on the Saturday matinee circuit and then to television in the 1960s (*Invasion of the Zombies* and *Samson in the Wax Museum* being the other two), *Samson vs. the Vampire Women* stars that most famous of all Mexican masked wrestler heroes, El Santo (changed to "Samson" in the English dubbing), as the main opposition to a coven of vampire women (led by Lorena Velásquez). The bloodsuckers have awakened after 200 years to seek a new Queen of the Vampires (an innocent girl chosen at birth and destined to take her place among the undead upon her twenty-first birthday). Diana (María Duval), daughter of Professor Roloff (Augusto Benedico), is the chosen unfortunate, and it's up to Roloff's friend Samson (with a little help from the police) to take time out of his ringside activities and foil the bloodsuckers' plans.

Actress Lorena Velásquez (who also starred with the masked wrestler in *Invasion of the Zombies*, and who played a wrestler herself in several pictures, including *The Wrestling Women vs. the Aztec Mummy*) appeared on Britain's *Incredibly Strange Film Show* in 1989. About El Santo, she said: "He represented justice. He was the Mexican Schwarzenegger. And he was a very nice man, very kind man, very good actor—well, *not* very good, but he represented justice and this was very important for the people." Indeed, one doesn't watch a Santo movie to see classical thesping, but to watch an icon of Truth, Justice and the Mexican Way take out bad guys and monsters.

This film presents a rather unique take on vampirism. When the female vampires drink blood, they transform from grotesque hags into diaphanous-gowned, leggy beauties who pray to Satan, even conjuring up the "Lord of Darkness" himself (in silhouette, anyway)—aligning vampirism with Satanism. And this evil cult is definitely a Matriarchy (with hints of lesbianism, as they seem to prefer biting women),

Though prominent in this Spanish poster, the werewolf barely appears in Samson in the Wax Museum.

adding a bit of subtext to the tale by pitting Samson, the ultimate defender of Patriarchal society, against this aberration of matriarchal "deviants."

But lest one become lost in subtextual musings on women's liberation and alternate sexuality, the movie periodically reminds the viewer of what it's *really* all about, as Samson tackles a vampire opponent in the ring (a male minion who's secretly taken a wrestler's place). After the vampire-wrestler fails to kill Samson ("He's using karate!" Our Hero exclaims), Samson unmasks him—revealing the hirsute face of a *werewolf*, who then proceeds to escape by transforming into a bat! Though odd in the extreme, this scene is nothing if not novel. (Unfortunately, that's all we see of this unique were-vamp.)

And novel may be the operative word for *Samson vs. the Vampire*

Women, which provides enough cobwebbed lairs, low-key lighting, and hideous dried crones transforming into beautiful vampire women to keep any Mexi-movie enthusiast satisfied. As the Professor so earnestly exclaims at picture's end, "God bless Samson!"

El Santo contra las Mujeres Vampiros see *Samson vs. the Vampire Women*

Santo en el Museo de Cera see *Samson in the Wax Museum*

Santo in the Wax Museum see *Samson in the Wax Museum*

Saturday the 14th Strikes Back

(1988; Concorde) Director: Howard R. Cohen.

What could be worse than a nitwit pastiche of horror-comedy clichés and goofy non-sequiturs (i.e., the tepid 1981 spoof *Saturday the 14th*)? Its even more puerile and nonsensical "sequel" *Saturday the 14th Strikes Back*, that's what. More of a vapid remake than a true follow-up, *Strikes Back* (produced by Roger Corman's wife Julie for their indy company Concorde Pictures; the Cormans should be *ashamed*) replaces the first film's ancient book of evil that summons monsters with a simple crack in the basement floor that *leaks* monsters. Shy sixteen-year-old Eddie Baxter (Jason Presson) discovers that the basement of the old mansion his family has just inherited houses a fissure that emits a mysterious mist. Through this mist comes a bevy of monsters (both supernatural and human, including William Burke, Lizzie Borden, and Genghis Kahn), who take up residence in the house, waiting for the fateful upcoming Saturday the 14th when Evil can then take over the world. Worse than that, Eddie discovers that he has been chosen to be their new "Prince of Darkness"! Can Eddie, with the help of his senile old grandfather (an obviously down-on-his-heels Ray Walston), stop the Evil before it spreads?

Unlike in the first, lycan-less *Saturday the 14th*, among the monsters that arrive in Eddie's basement about half-way through this tedious exercise in sequel silliness is a suit-wearing, talking werewolf (played by dancer/actor Tommy Rall [*Kiss Me Kate, Seven Brides for Seven Brothers*] in his final screen role). His kid-friendly, non-threatening appearance consists of a brownish face, dainty fangs, and long mane of fluffy gray hair. On screen for little more than a minute, this lazy lycan does nothing more than stand around in the basement and dance a bit at the Monster Party the denizens throw there.

The film's meandering plot is comprised of unfunny, loosely-connected and often pointless gags with no real punchline, with the "lowlights" being: Eddie's uncle with a miniature submarine in his stomach that causes him to emit various nautical sounds whenever he opens his mouth; a cookie-eating puppet-monster under the bed; sleepwalking family members creating chocolate pudding sculptures; a plumber turned into a chicken; *The Hills Have Eyes'* Michael Berryman as a sparsely-wrapped, makeup-less mummy; and a vampire musical number in which the undead chanteuse laments a bloodsucker's limited diet (actually the sole mildly amusing moment in the whole picture). The cheat "climax," in which Evil is supposedly released on the world, consists of newsreel stock footage and clips from other (better) New World/Concorde films, including *Rock 'n' Roll High School, Grand Theft Auto, Avalanche,* and *Deathsport*. Couple all this with childish characterizations (the family eats nothing but cookies and sweets [leaving Gramps longing for some simple bacon and eggs] even *before* the evil house makes them all "weird"), and *Saturday the 14th Strikes Back* becomes nigh on unwatchable. You'd do better spending the next Saturday the 14th washing your hair.

Scooby-Doo and the Ghoul School

(1988; Hanna-Barbera) Director: Ray Patterson.

The popular *Scooby-Doo, Where Are You?* cartoon series began in 1969 and featured four teenagers and their talking Great Dane Scooby-Doo, who rode around in their van (dubbed "The Mystery Machine") and solved supernatural mysteries. These "meddling kids" proved so popular in Saturday morning syndication that Hanna-Barbera ran through a number of series iterations through 1979 until they revamped the show in 1980 by jettisoning all the human characters, save Scooby's beatnik buddy Shaggy, and adding an articulate pup named Scrappy-Doo (Scooby's annoying nephew). While the various supernatural shenanigans investigated by the original "Mystery, Inc." gang invariably turned out to be hoaxes perpetrated by greedy villains wearing monster masks, the *Scooby-Doo and Scrappy-Doo* series offered *real* supernatural creatures. *Scooby-Doo and the Ghoul School*, a 1988 made-for-television feature produced by Hanna-Barbera for syndication eschews the mystery angle of the original Scooby-Doo series to follow the formula created in the newer *Scooby-Doo and Scrappy-Doo* efforts that aired from 1979 to 1985.

Shaggy (voiced by Casey Kasem) has taken a job as gym teacher at "Miss Grimwood's Finishing School for Ghouls" (thinking it a school for *girls*). But upon arriving with his talking canine pals Scooby and Scrappy, Shaggy soon realizes it's a school for young *monsters*, including the daughters of Dracula, the Frankenstein Monster, the Mummy, a ghostly phantom, and a werewolf. The first half of the film consists of Shaggy and Scooby overcoming their initial fright to ultimately train the young ghouls for their upcoming annual volleyball match with the boys' military academy next door. The latter half offers a villainous four-armed witch who kidnaps the quintet of young monsterettes in a plan to turn them evil and become "the most powerful witch in Monsterdom." It's up to Shaggy, Scooby and Scrappy, with help from the boys at the academy, to save the little monsters from an evil fate.

Covered in brown fur, and sporting pointy ears, tiny fangs and a mop of curly orange hair, "Winnie" the werewolf looks cute as a were-button in her pale dress and big blue bow. Upbeat and energetic, she runs on all fours and makes comments like, "I'm so happy I could howl" (often doing just that). She remains in her werewolf form throughout (even during the day), never transforming into a human. At one point, during the school's annual Parents' Day on Halloween, the various monster parents come for a visit, including "Papa Werewolf," who looks fairly impressive with his full wolf's head topping a muscular, furry torso. After the party, Papa tells his daughter it's time for him to leave: "The moon is going down, I'd better run too" (this being the only allusion to any lunar ties).

Filled with juvenile silliness (such as a baby dragon named "Matches" that constantly gives Scooby the hot seat; or a supercilious military headmaster oblivious to the ghoul school's "special" qualities) and bad puns (at one point Shaggy, trapped in a well with a water monster, exclaims, "Zoinks! I don't think the Well Dweller means well"), the over-frantic, flatly-animated *Scooby-Doo and the Ghoul School* will delight only those viewers under the age of ten—or those who have a mighty strong sense of childish nostalgia.

Scooby-Doo! And the Goblin King

(2008; Hanna-Barbera/Warner Bros.) Director: Joe Sichta.

The twelfth direct-to-video Scooby-Doo feature produced by Warner Bros. Animation, *Scooby-Doo! And the Goblin King* is the fifth Scooby movie in which the monsters are real rather than human villains in costumes. At the local Halloween carnival, the Mystery, Inc. gang (Scooby, Shaggy, Daphne, Fred, and Velma) run afoul of a two-bit magician whose search for "real" magic leads him to steal the powers of a fairy (a Tinkerbell-like sprite) on Halloween night. Seeking to solidify his newfound magical abilities, the magician intends to secure the fabled scepter of the Goblin King. "He who holds the Goblin Scepter holds the magic of Halloween in his grasp," he reads in an ancient tome. Meanwhile, a trick-or-treating Shaggy and Scooby stumble into the house of a *good* magician, who warns them of what may happen in the future, with the evil magician transforming Fred, Daphne and Velma into monsters: Fred becomes a vampire, Daphne a witch, and Velma an eyeglass-sporting *werewolf* who howls at the moon. The friendly mage then sends the pair on a quest to the Netherworld to retrieve the Goblin Scepter before dawn. Upon arriving (via a creepy skeletal-looking train that travels through the sky), Shaggy and Scooby immediately run afoul of a huge cockney guarding a graveyard who then transforms into a hulking wolfman. With a toothy wolf's head and imposing, muscular, hair-covered physique, the lycanthrope snarls, "Time for a late night snack." But the quick-thinking Shaggy claims that he, too, is a werewolf, and pulls his head and arms back into his shirt while Scooby sticks *his* head and arms through the holes and growls convincingly. The duped, none-too-bright wolfman then invites his newfound lycan-brother into his mausoleum bar to meet the rest of the monsters partying on Halloween.

Subsequent adventures on their quest include a comical interlude with a trio of witches (one voiced by Lauren Bacall); an exciting encounter with a truly frightening Headless Horseman; and a confrontation with the goblin hordes. With the film's animation being a vast improvement over the 1980s-level work on previous Scooby-Doo installments (there's some real depth to the imaginative surroundings), and a better level of "punny" jokes and gags, *Scooby-Doo! And the Goblin King* stands head and Scooby-shoulders over its earlier brethren. And apart from Casey Kasem (as Shaggy), the film features some heavy-hitters in the voice artistry department, including Jay Leno, Lauren Bacall, James Belushi, and Tim Curry (as the Goblin King *and* the Boneyard Werewolf). Of course, there's still plenty of too-silly shenanigans and a trio of foolish songs to slow things down, but at least there's no Scrappy-Doo.

Scream of the Wolf

(1974; ABC-TV) Director: Dan Curtis.

This *ABC Movie of the Week* entry produced and directed by TV horror specialist Dan Curtis (*Dark Shadows, The Night Stalker, Trilogy of Terror*) focuses on a Malibu, California, community terrorized by a rash of brutal killings in which the victims are torn apart by a wolf-like creature. Big-game hunter-turned-adventure novelist John Weatherby (Peter Graves), called in to consult by his friend the sheriff, remains puzzled. "The tracks go from four feet to two feet to nothing, period!" Soon the press begins printing headlines like "'WEREWOLF' KILLER STILL AT LARGE," and Weatherby seeks out his reclusive friend and former hunting partner, Byron (Clint Walker), for help in stalking the beast. But Byron (who, incidentally, had earlier been bitten by a wolf himself) isn't interested. "In a way, these killings may be of benefit to everybody," Byron opines, believing that the anger and fear in the community will make its all-too-civilized citizens "feel alive—perhaps for the first time in years." It turns out the disturbed Byron keeps a wolf in his basement that he has trained "to kill another kind of prey," after which he places altered footprints at the scene to suggest a werewolf attack. Why? "To give these rustic clods some reason for existence. To fill their empty minds with so much terror that even *they* come alive. And to bring my old friend back to me again."

Curtis handles the "werewolf" attacks well, generating tension with point-of-view camerawork for the stalk through mist-shrouded woodlands and shadowy home invasions. We never see the beast—the camera abruptly rushes in, glass shatters, the victim screams, and the screen fades to black. Foggy nights, key lighting, and low angles generate tension. Unfortunately, theses sequences come few and far between, with the majority of the telefilm's running time taken up with Weatherby puzzling over the mystery, the sheriff searching for clues, and repeated visits to Byron to try to talk him into helping. But with the periodic attacks, the werewolf mystery angle (Byron's quietly suspicious manservant serves as a likely suspect), Walker's menacingly creepy portrayal, and the various twists and turns (including the exciting—if brief—concluding hunt), *Scream of the Wolf* holds one's interest better than most made-for-TV movies from the 1970s.

The Screaming Dead see Dracula, Prisoner of Frankenstein

Sexbomb

(1989; Populuxe Pictures) Director: Jeff Broadstreet.

This hit-and-miss (mostly miss) low-budget spoof of low-budget moviemaking stars down-on-his-luck former horror star Robert Quarry (*Count Yorga, Vampire, Dr. Phibes Rises Again, Sugar Hill*) as a tyrannical movie mogul named King Faraday (sound it out—it's one of this T&A flick's *better* jokes, actually). Deep in production on his latest opus, *I Rip Your Flesh with Pliers*, Faraday bullies everyone around him, including his sexbomb of a wife, Candy (Delia Sheppard), who's intent on murdering him for his money. She attempts to enlist the aid of a hapless screenwriter Faraday has just hired to pen a new picture, *Werewolves in Heat*, leading to various shenanigans, including encounters with comical mobsters.

Several scenes revolve around the faux werewolf flick (its laughable six-day shooting schedule is only three days shorter than that of the real *Sexbomb* itself!), showcasing a horny beast whose headpiece looks like a live-action Wile E. Coyote. One of the movie's better gags involves an air-bladder effect, à la *The Howling*, gone laughably wrong. Additionally, *Werewolves in Heat* lead actress Phoebe (played by frequently topless '80s scream queen Linnea Quigley, at the time utilizing the pretentious single-moniker sobriquet of "Linnea"—though Cher she ain't) brings her "spiritual adviser and psychic nutritionist," Brother Ron (R.C. Rosenbalm), to the set. "You know what causes lycanthropy," rhetorically asks Brother Ron, "improper diet." Ron knows this because he claims to have been a werewolf in a previous life. "Luckily I was able to subsist on a bean-curd human flesh substitute," he explains, "or I could have incurred a substantial karmic penalty." Ron states that "the werewolf craves human flesh, but that's the worst thing for him. Cannibalism is devastating to the human immune system. The lycanthrope thinks he's a wolf, but in reality he's a human undergoing a violent allergic reaction." Lycanthropy as allergy—a novel (and amusing) notion. Of *Werewolves in Heat*, Ron concludes,

She

(1988; Trans World Entertainment; Italy) Director: Avi Nesher.

This post-holocaust fantasy/adventure mishmash stars Sandahl Bergman, fresh from her supporting sword-and-sandal role in the much bigger (and better) *Conan the Barbarian* (1982), as the sword-wielding "She, Goddess of the Urich," leader of a band of female warriors. When wanderer Tom's sister is kidnapped by the evil Norks, he (along with his friend Dick) and She (accompanied by her right-hand woman Shandra) reluctantly team up to find the "Valley of Nork" and rescue the girl.

Structured as an episodic (though decidedly small-scale) quest story, *She* puts its protagonists through all manner of bizarre trials and tribulations, including violent encounters with mummy-wrapped mutants; sadistic, telekinetic monks; a band of Road Warrior wannabes; a mad doctor and his tutu-wearing assistant; self-replicating, impersonation-happy sailor boys obsessed with pop-culture references; knights; punks; and even a robotic Frankenstein Monster. Among the many encounters is a brief interlude in which the two heroes run across an oasis of civilization that appears to be a cross between a Roman villa and a hippie commune. By day the gentle inhabitants frolic by the pool, play with balloons, and recite poetry. But at night they transform into hairy, fanged beast-creatures that attack Tom and Dick. Fortunately, She and her companion arrive and quickly dispatch (with ordinary swords) the cannibalistic creatures (whose kitchen is stocked with human body parts).

The interlude lasts barely two minutes, and it remains unclear whether these beings are true werewolves. The sparse makeup—heavy brows, tufts of facial hair, and a mouthful of bad teeth—coupled with the notion of (off-screen) transformation, vaguely suggest lycanthropy; but nothing ties the monsters to wolves (or any other animal), and the "W" word is conspicuous solely by its absence. "What was that?!" demands Dick after the last of the monsters have been dispatched, a pertinent question for which he—and we—receive no answer.

Sometimes goofy, sometimes stupid, but always cheerfully cheesy, and permeated by early '80s sensibilities (big blonde hairdos, Valley Girl accents, and ersatz '80s rock soundtrack—by Rick Wakeman, no less), *She*'s kitchen-sink, tongue-in-cheek approach remains moderately entertaining despite itself.

She-Wolf of London

(1946; Universal) Director: Jean Yarbrough. Alternate Title: *The Curse of the Allenbys* (UK).

Though it begins as a straightforward horror film, with talk of a female werewolf stalking the local park in turn-of-the-century London ("The papers are full of it," pronounces one character in an accidentally amusing turn of phrase), *She-Wolf of London* soon devolves into a tepid drive-the-heiress-mad drawing-room melodrama, full of talky scenes of the mousey, insipid heroine (played by a mousey, insipid June Lockhart) wringing her hands and declaring that she can't go through with her nuptials because of her family "curse." Said curse involves an ancestral affinity for wolves and changing into them.

High-strung Phyllis Allenby (June Lockhart), engaged to marry intrepid lawyer Barry Lanfield (Don Porter), soon thinks the "legend of the Allenby curse" has struck home when she awakens from troubling dreams to find her dressing gown muddy and blood dried on her hands. It's giving nothing away to reveal that the kindly aunt has been committing the murders and planting the damning evidence to convince Phyllis of her lycanthropic culpability. (The screenwriters tip their hand about ten minutes in when the aunt, serving as Phyllis' guardian, discloses that she and her daughter are actually unrelated to the heiress and will be out on their ears once Phyllis marries next week.) The film's centerpiece (the one attack we [sort of] see) shows the "She-Wolf" stalking a Scotland Yard inspector who's come too close to the truth. As she glides through the mist in her hooded robe (looking more like Little Red Riding Hood than a vicious lycanthrope), we can plainly see a woman's face beneath the barely obfuscating cowl. And this She-Wolf carefully creeps rather than savagely stalks, revealing still further her prosaic *human* origin, and ultimately offering little to the discerning viewer apart from a plethora of palaver and soundstage fog.

Journeyman director Jean Yarbrough (*The Devil Bat* [1940], *King of the Zombies* [1941], *House of Horrors* [1946]) took less than two weeks to shoot *She-Wolf of London*, but he still came in three days *over* schedule and had to work cast and crew on Christmas Eve for retakes. Remembered Don Porter, "They closed the set so people couldn't get away and go to all the Christmas parties on the other sets. We damned near starved to death. We smuggled in some sandwiches, and finally they got the process right. I was focused and got the words right. The director said, 'Cut! Print! That's a wrap!' and before I could get out of the buggy and help June [Lockhart], the set was cleared ... everybody left!" And such an early exit isn't a bad idea for viewers of this fangless *She-Wolf* either.

With quotes from: *Universal Horrors*, by Michael Brunas, John Brunas and Tom Weaver.

Shopping for Fangs

(1997; Margin Films) Directors: Quentin Lee, Justin Lin.

"Discover your dark side," advises the poster for co-directors Quentin Lee and Justin Lin's low-budget take on Asian American disaffection in modern SoCal. *Shopping for Fangs* follows the intersecting paths of dissatisfied housewife Katherine, provocative lesbian waitress Trinh (who hides behind ever-present blonde wig and sunglasses), and ordinary office worker Phil, who comes to believe he's a werewolf. Phil (Radmar Agano Jao) has girl troubles (i.e., he can't find one). When he suddenly begins experiencing weird hair growth, his doctor tells him it may be linked to an increased level of testosterone and intimates that he needs to "release that tension."

Phil's sister's live-in boyfriend Matt is a writer whose latest project is a book about lycanthropy. He plants the seed in Phil's mind that werewolves are indeed real (though not of the classic man-wolf variety). He cites the case of one of his research subjects, "Tracy": "She can run a mile in three minutes flat. She makes a living being a stunt person—no one can understand why she never gets hurt." When Phil, worried that he's killed someone (though this remains inconclusive), asks how to lift the "curse," Matt tells him that "people with lycanthropy usually don't want to give up the power—it's a privilege to be chosen." (Said "power" remains frustratingly undefined, however, as does why or how one is "chosen.") He continues, "Contrary to popular belief, the only time a werewolf kills—which is rare—is when there's an element of danger that threatens their own existence. It's a survival of the fittest instinct." Then he adds, "But we all have that," leading one to conclude that werewolves are little different from "normal" people. When Phil asks, "How do they cope with the uncontrollable rage?" Matt answers, "Like the rest of us—they just do." Phil's "uncontrollable rage" never manifests further than mildly insulting his boss and head-butting a punk trying to rob a grocery store. "Just because you have a little facial hair does not mean you're a werewolf," exclaims Phil's exasperated sister. Disappointingly, the viewer can only agree.

"*Shopping for Fangs* is about finding connections," said co-director Quentin Lee, "which is a theme that threads through all my movies." Said connections come in surprising and even disturbing ways, but often at the price of a leisurely pace and general dullness that may very well exasperate those viewers expecting something a little more cinematic. Filmed for less than $100,000 in 21 days in Los Angeles in a cinema verité style (hand-held camerawork, frequent close-ups, minimal background music), *Shopping for Fangs* features far too many scenes of dull conversations and characters doing ordinary, everyday things (shopping, working, or, in Phil's case, shaving). Also frustrating is the flat playing of Jeanne Chinn as Katherine, whose breathy-yet-toneless delivery and general lack of expression makes her into an Asian Meg Tilly. But what initially appears to be amateurish acting takes on far different shadings by film's end, which provides the patient viewer with a surprising and clever payoff. "Justin and I set off to make something different that would shake up the genre of Asian American films from *Joy Luck Club* and ching-chong Asian Americana," commented Lee. "We didn't know much then and really wanted to make our first feature. We were rebelling with a cause." While they may indeed have rebelled with this Asian American art-house effort, *Shopping* remains disappointingly *Fang*-less in regards to werewolves.

With quotes from: "Cinema Asian America: Filmmaker Quentin Lee Discusses *Shopping for Fangs*," by Chi-Hui Yang.

Skinwalker: Curse of the Shaman

(2005; Second 8 Productions) Director: Steve Stevens, Jr.

Brooke and A.J. (Amanda Paytas and Timothy Parham), two college students making a documentary on myths, investigate a small-town curse that appears to have claimed the lives of six teenagers (children of a group of youths who accidentally killed a Native American medicine man back in 1969). In uncovering the terrifying truth about

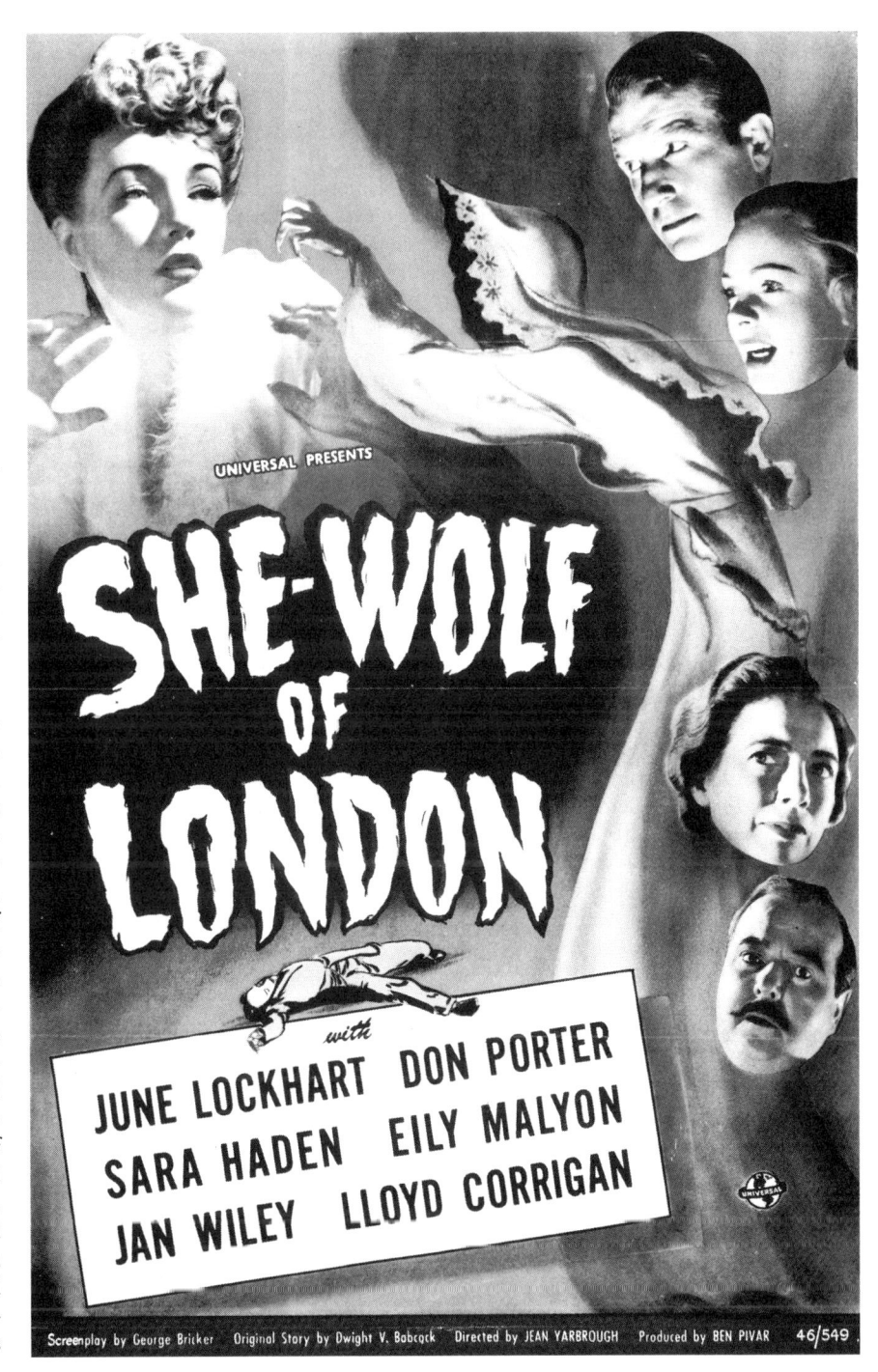

Despite its title, the *She-Wolf of London* isn't one (American one-sheet poster).

the recent disappearances, Brooke learns of her own terrible connection to the curse. It turns out the now-grown grandson of the dead man has become a "skinwalker" and has enacted belated revenge, with Brooke now in his vengeful sights.

It would be charitable indeed to label *Skinwalker* a werewolf film, as this maddened shaman transforms into something that looks like a cross between a demon and a zombie rather than a wolf or wolfman. No one, least of all the skinwalker himself, mentions any animal affinity, and the creature's distorted, ridged, funhouse face and mouthful of scraggly, pointed teeth, along with its skeletal-looking frame, carries little canine connection (apart from a pair of pointy ears). The only information about this creature comes when the shaman, in human form, confesses, "I'm a skinwalker—I'm limited by boundaries." Nothing about tribal history or any spiritual connection to animals, only an admission that his territory is apparently delineated by the supernatural equivalent of a doggy's "Invisible Fence."™

Shot on digital video in the desert near Action, California, with a budget of about $20,000, one wonders where even that much money went—unless to pay the salaries of the two professional actors making cameos in this amateurish mess, Celeste Yarnall (*Beast of Blood*, *The Velvet Vampire*, both 1971) and *Star Trek*'s "Scotty" himself, 84-year-old James Doohan (sadly making his final acting appearance before his death this same year). The cheap shot-on-video look offers scenes alternately over- and under-lit. Little happens for the first hour, with the bulk of the "action" consisting of the two students interviewing the various grieving and regretful parents (as well as a local prospector, embarrassingly enacted by Hollywood fringe player Johnny Legend). The occasional split-second flashback to mutilated bodies serves only to expose the amateurish nature of the (not-so) special effects, until the final 10 minutes when a few bits of more clearly-shown cheesy gore "rewards" the patient (or foolish) viewer. There's no onscreen transformation, which is probably just as well given the level of technical effects.

"I'd rent digital horror movies all over the shelves at Blockbuster and Hollywood Video," recalled director Steve Stevens about the genesis of his first (and only, to date) feature, "and I was like, I know I can make a movie this good or better. Most have no story, bad acting, and the lighting and sound are bad. We made *Skinwalker* for less than $20,000, and I've seen digital movies with five times our budget that I can't get through the first ten minutes. I'm very happy with my first attempt." Well, that makes one.

With quotes from: "Shapeshifters, Zombies Dominate 2004 *Hollywood Investigator* Halloween Horror Film Awards," by Thomas M. Sipos, hollywoodinvestigator.com.

Sogni d'Oro

(1981; Opera Film/Rai; Italy) Director: Nanni Moretti.

Translating as "Sweet Dreams," the Italian art-house comedy-drama *Sogni d'Oro* follows arrogant, neurotic, unlikable filmmaker Michelle Apicella (writer-director Nanni Moretti himself) as he defends his position as *the* country's serious young filmmaker while attempting to make a movie about Sigmund Freud and his mother. Sometimes surreal, often silly, and always satirical, the film has little cohesion (being a series of vignettes that touch on—and skewer—the director's insecurities and problematic relationships with friends, colleagues, mother and other women). Whatever message(es) Moretti might have intended become lost in a miasma of parodic set-pieces and outright non sequiturs, as typified by the film's final, out-of-nowhere scene (the reason for its inclusion here).

Lasting little more than a minute, the final sequence has Michelle meeting his former girlfriend in a restaurant after she's been away for two years. She tells him how she's changed, and become more self-assured and independent. Suddenly, Michelle knocks over a glass, and we see his reaching hand covered in hair. She looks up, and the camera reveals long, scraggly hair and heavy eyebrows covering most of his pasty face (no fangs or nose-piece are evident, however). She screams, and he shouts, "Yes, I am a monster! And I love you!" She flees, and he follows into the night, screaming, "I don't want to die!" Roll credits.

Make of that what you will…

Son of Dracula

(1974; Cinemation Industries; UK) Alternate Title: *Count Downe*. Director: Freddie Francis.

A musical-horror-comedy, advertised as "The First Rock-and-Roll Dracula Movie!" with "7 Hit Songs" ("Daybreak," "Remember," "Jump Into the Fire," "Down," "Without You," "Moonbeam," and "At My Front Door"), *Son of Dracula* remains a mess from start to finish. The mess begins when Dracula's son, calling himself Count Downe (Harry Nilsson), comes to London for his coronation as "Overlord of the Netherworld." But upon meeting a beautiful young girl (Suzanna Leigh), the Count decides to give up his immortality and become human so that he can love fully. He seeks help from the duplicitous Dr. Frankenstein (Freddie Jones), who has designs on the crown himself. But Merlin the magician (Ringo Starr) has been watching over all and soon sets things right.

Among the "Netherworld" denizens who put in brief appearances are various ghouls, a hunchbacked dwarf, a medusa, a Frankenstein's Monster—and a werewolf, first seen when the Count goes out for a stroll in a London cemetery. There, a young woman laying flowers on a tomb is suddenly attacked by the manbeast. The Count draws his sword cane and stabs the wolfman in the shoulder, sending the creature scurrying away. (Of course, the Count then puts the bite on the rescued damsel himself.) As befitting an early '70s production full of rock stars and musicians, this classic-style wolfman sports big hair and stylish threads. Unfortunately, he does little else throughout the film, appearing only a few times as background dressing and once to quickly throttle the Count's servant. Such brevity in this awful production, however, could easily be taken for a blessing rather than a curse.

When David Bowie declined the lead role, producer Ringo Starr cast his longtime friend Harry Nilsson (Starr served as Best Man at Nilsson's wedding) in the role of Count Downe, which proved to be a huge mistake, as the singer/songwriter's detached demeanor and deadpan delivery (not to mention his curly red hair and bushy beard) makes the Count a veritable non-presence. Add in an embarrassing turn by Ringo himself as Merlin (complete with wizard's robes, pointy hat, and a ridiculous long white beard and frizzy fright wig), and even the *real* thespians in the company, including a hammy Freddie Jones, a slumming Dennis Price, and a bewildered Suzanna Leigh, can't save the silly production.

Little enough happens as the Count mostly ambles about between performing a quartet of musical numbers (with several notable rockers playing his backup band, including John Bonham, Peter Frampton, and Keith Moon). A half-hearted stab at skullduggery comes towards the end when Dr. Frankenstein plots to destroy the trusting Count and take his place as Overlord of the Underworld. But any chance for excitement or suspense is quashed more quickly than Dr. F's planned coup.

Director Freddie Francis (*The Skull* [1965], *Dracula Has Risen from the Grave* [1968]) directed a lycanthrope nearly a decade earlier in *Dr. Terror's House of Horrors* (1964), and went on to make a third werewolf film—1974's *Legend of the Werewolf*. Of the three, *Son of Dracula* stands head and shoulders *below* the rest (in fact, it may very well be Francis' worst film ever, beating out such unworthy contenders as *They Came from Beyond Space* [1967] and *The Vampire Happening* [1971]). "It was one of the strangest films I was ever involved with," recalled Francis about *Son of Dracula*. "Ringo sent me the script, which I have to say was more than a little odd." Indeed.

Though completed in November 1972, *Son of Dracula* took a year-and-a-half to see a spotty release before quickly sinking from view.

Harry Nilsson released a similarly titled album in conjunction with the movie, but it fared no better with the public.

With quotes from: *The Unholy Three*, by John Hamilton.

Stephen King's It see *It*

Tales of the Night

(2011; Gkids/Studio Canal; France) Original Language Title: *Les Contes de la Nuit*. Director/Animator: Michel Ocelot.

This collection of six stories brought to life via the shadow puppet–like animation of renowned French animator Michel Ocelot, in which black silhouettes move in front of colorful, at times kaleidoscopic, backgrounds, begins with a werewolf tale. An old man, a boy and a girl, all fascinated by movies, meet at an old theater to concoct and act out tales of imagination. "In an abandoned cinema every night," the man explains, "we'd talk, we'd dream, we'd work. We'd get into disguises and live new adventures." The first story, the medieval-set "Night of the Werewolf," has "the noble knight Jan" set to marry a princess. But Jan has a problem, and when his fiancée balks at the apparent lack of trust he places in her (he tells her they cannot be together that full-moon evening but refuses to say why), he finally confesses, "I am a werewolf. When the moon is full, this chain, which you see I always wear, starts to burn intolerably. I take it off and—and I'm transformed into a wolf. In the morning I have to put the chain back on to become a man again. If I cannot find the chain I shall stay a wolf forever." Though she claims she wants to help her betrothed, that night the duplicitous princess steals his necklace after he transforms and drops it down a deep well. She then claims that the "black wolf" of the forest has killed and eaten Jan, and organizes a hunt for the beast. But the princess' younger sister, who truly loves Jan (unlike her sibling, who thinks of him as a monster and only wants his wealth and estate), learns the secret of the wolf when it saves her from a bear, and tricks her sister into revealing the truth. Retrieving the necklace from the well, the younger sister places it around the wolf's neck, and Jan reappears, now aware of the identity of his *true* love.

Lasting a brief 11 minutes, the story, based on a classic medieval folk tale, is short, sweet, and beautifully rendered, with simple yet stunning forest backgrounds. Before the story begins, the boy and the old man banter about the direction their tale will take. "What if I was a werewolf," ponders the boy, to which the old man dismisses, "A pathetic freak." "Pathetic?" asks the boy, before positing, "As a werewolf everyone would be afraid of me; I'd like that." The old man still isn't convinced, saying, "In legend he's portrayed as a monster in pain, a slave to the full moon and his urge to kill." To this the boy responds, "Perhaps I wouldn't have to kill." And he doesn't, for in wolf form Jan seems to retain his human faculties and kindness, harming no one and instead acting as hero by battling a bear for the life of the girl.

The remaining five stories also feature striking visuals, exotic settings, and simplistic yet effective story lines, covering everything from a Caribbean-set jaunt to the underworld "Country of the Dead," to battling a dragon in an Aztec city of gold, to the Africa savanna and "Tom Tom Boy," to the Tibetan tale of "The Boy Who Never Lied," to the sorcerer-and-fairy-filled "The Young Doe and the Architect's Son." Charming in subject matter as well as presentation, these *Tales of the Night* are tales well worth hearing (and seeing).

Tales of the Third Dimension

(1984; E.O. Corp.) Directors: Thom McIntyre, Worth Keeter, Irl Dixon.

With this three-part horror anthology, North Carolina movie mogul Earl Owensby (whose 1970s and '80s efforts played mostly on the Southern drive-in circuit) returned to the werewolf well (sort of) once more after producing (and starring in) 1979's *Wolfman*. Owensby also mined the then-popular (and short-lived) 3D revival here, as the obviously-if-nonsensically-named *Tales of the Third Dimension* was one of six Earl Owensby Corporation films shot in that dubious format.

Each of the three *Tales* begins with an animatronic skeleton (named Igor) delivering *Twilight Zone*–style introductions (complete with Rod Serling impersonation) while a bevy of goofy-looking puppet vultures, modeled on The Three Stooges and Laurel and Hardy, make supposed "comedic" interjections. (For instance, following the vampire/werewolf story, the "Hardy" vulture says, "I hope you learned a lesson from this," to which the "Laurel" buzzard responds, "I certainly did—werewolves are hard to house train.") At one point Igor announces: "You've reached that final crossroad and entered another dimension, a dimension from which there is no return, no escape. A dimension of sight, sound, mind, body, et cetera, et cetera, et cetera. It's the beginning of the end. There's no turning back now. Welcome to *Tales of the Third Dimension*." Oddly, this "welcome" comes only after the film is two-thirds finished; though Igor and his fowl wisenheimers bookend each and every episode, the movie's title doesn't appear until just before the *final* tale.

Tales of the Third Dimension starts promisingly enough on a fog-shrouded, dilapidated graveyard set in which a coffin eerily rises from the earth in front of a gravestone. The lid opens and a suited skeleton—Igor—sits up to address the viewer.

The tongue-in-cheek tone of the introduction carries forward into the first episode, "Young Blood," in which a stereotypical vampire couple (the "Count" and "Countess," naturally) intend to adopt a child. The adoption agency sends a Ms. Marquette and her assistant Dudley to interview the prospective parents, with the woman mesmerized by the Count, while Dudley appears suspicious of the Transylvanian-accented, cape-wearing, haunted house–inhabiting duo. Ultimately, Ms. Marquette delivers a young boy to the couple, with the Count rewarding the entranced woman by draining her dry. Meanwhile, upstairs the boy gazes out the window at the full moon, and we see his hand darken and transform before he rushes past the camera to fling himself under the covers of his bed, making growling and whimpering noises. When the Count slowly draws back the blanket, the boy, now fully transformed, springs upon him. With the camera now outside, gazing at the (model) mansion, we hear a howl and the screams of the Countess. Then, back in the boy's room, the shadow of a wolf on the wall becomes the shadow of the boy, and we see the Count and Countess lying dead. Dudley soon arrives at the house, and the human-once-more boy asks, "Can we go home now, Dad?" Dudley answers, "Of course, son; I think we're quite finished here." Back in the cemetery, Igor pontificates, "Everyone with even a rudimentary grasp of life's system of checks and balances knows vampires are no match for a werewolf. Everyone, it appears, except for vampires."

Utilizing lycanthropy merely as the punch line to a rather protracted joke, the segment never offers a good look at either the interim wolf-boy (just the blur of a hairy hand and head as he streaks past the camera) or the fully-transformed werewolf (a split-second shot of a snarling muzzle and ungainly wolf paw). Even more disappointingly, the notion of a father using his werewolf son as some sort of vampire exterminator brings up all sorts of issues that remain wholly unexplored.

After this rather unsatisfying first episode, the *Tales* continue with

"The Guardians," an atmospheric story of grave robbing that ends in an anticlimactic encounter with a few desultory rodents. Fortunately, after two tepid tales comes the final story, "Visions of Sugar Plums"—the *real* reason to seek out this Southern drive-in obscurity. "Sugar Plums" centers on a pair of children dropped off at their kindly grandmother's house the week before Christmas while their parents vacation in Hawaii. The loving and affectionate Granny, however, has run out of her medication and takes a turn for the homicidal, talking to her deceased husband, eating flies, popping rat poison into the hot cocoa, and finally chasing her grandkids through the house on her electric wheelchair with a shotgun! It all culminates in a truly surprising and audacious ending perfectly in keeping with the holiday spirit. Though such outrageous inventiveness didn't spread to the other two episodes, "Visions of Sugar Plums" ultimately makes this *Dimension* one worth visiting.

The Teeth of the Night see Vampire Party

The Tenement

(2003; Brain Damage Films) Director: Glen Baisley.

What could be worse than a no-budget, poorly scripted, terribly acted horror anthology filmed in Putnam County, New York? A no-budget, poorly scripted, terribly acted horror anthology filmed in Putnam County, New York, that is *two hours long*. Welcome to *The Tenement*, whose residents consist of a horror movie–loving mama's boy who snaps and turns killer; a couple with a mute teenage daughter obsessed with dancing to the radio and who supernaturally turns the auditory tables on an attacker; a serial killer who finds love in the unlikeliest of places; and a socially awkward shut-in who, after an animal attack, becomes a murderer and cannibal under the impression he's a werewolf.

Of the four stories (five if you count the wraparound involving the Tenement building's mysterious owner and a previous resident there for a visit), the werewolf tale "Full Moon Rising" remains one of the more coherent (if meandering). Jimmy Wayne Garrick (Mike Lane), walking home in the dark after an uncomfortable group therapy session, hears a howl and deep growling before an indistinct shape savages his arm (accompanied by a cheap color-spectrum effect to signify a monster p.o.v., and one split-second shot of what looks like a malamute trotting behind him). Tedious, largely pointless scenes of Jimmy's psychiatric appointments (with nothing but two straight-backed chairs in front of a cheap computer desk to designate his shrink's office), a trip to a doctor to examine his arm (where the impossibly young-looking MD laughs at her own joke about Jimmy becoming a werewolf), and *two* protracted instances of Jimmy making monster faces in his bathroom mirror (in homage to *An American Werewolf in London*) do nothing except indicate Jimmy's belief he was attacked by a wolf and stretch the running time. Jimmy goes shopping at a Halloween store, then dons some plastic fangs, sheds his clothes, and tries to frighten an old lady in the park. Disgusted at being flashed, she simply hits Jimmy and chases him away. But soon some real murders occur, and Jimmy begins scarfing raw hamburger and biting out the jugular of his sole friend. The next night, a full moon, Jimmy goes to drown his sorrows at a strip club, where he murders the silicone sister giving him a private lap dance by slashing her with his claws (curiously, his face remains unchanged). A security camera captures the murder on tape, and the police take Jimmy into custody the next day. He claims to have no memory of the killing—until the cops produce a pair of werewolf gloves modified with deadly steel blades they found at his apartment. Sentenced to life in an institution for the criminally insane, the episode's final scene has a pair of *real* wolfmen (complete with hairy faces and hands) entering Jimmy's cell to tell him, "You've drawn too much attention to us; it must end" as Jimmy screams in terror and the full moon shines.

One-man-band (director-producer-writer-cameraman) Glen Baisley's script opens the door to some potentially intriguing psychological aspects of lycanthropy here, but fails to cross the threshold. Instead, it settles for a few cheap laughs and a bit of wobbly T&A. The best it can do is a rather less-than-incisive observation by Jimmy's psychiatrist that Jimmy is becoming "delusional" and is on the verge of "a psychotic episode." Then, turning off his recorder, the doc mutters, "Fuckin' nuts is what he is."

Beyond its lycan-lite tack, the cheap video look, flat lighting, echoing sound, amateurish acting, silly script and mundane direction (full of long takes and uninteresting camera work) make this a *Tenement* few would ever want to visit.

The Three Faces of Terror

(2004; Istituto Luce; Italy) Original Language Title: *I Tre Volte del Terrore*; Director: Sergio Stivaletti.

Special effects artist Sergio Stivaletti created monsters and corpses for such Italian horror classics as Lamberto Bava's *Demons* (1985), Dario Argento's *Opera* (1987) and Michele Soavi's *Cemetery Man* (1994). In 1997 he turned his hand to directing with *The Wax Mask* (a clip of which plays on a black-and-white television set in *Three Faces*' werewolf segment). *The Three Faces of Terror* was his sophomore directorial feature effort—and his final one, to date. Two men and a woman on a train encounter a mysterious hypnotist named Dr. Price (John Phillip Law), who, with his gold orb, shows a "vision" to each one. Two of these tales involve a model running afoul of a mad plastic surgeon, and three friends encountering a flesh-eating lake monster. The other story, however, titled "L'Anello della Luna" (The Ring of the Moon), sees Marco (Riccardo Serventi Longhi) rob an ancient Etruscan tomb, where he removes a wolf's head ring from the hand of the decayed mummy. Trying it on for size the next day, he finds he can't take it off, and cuts his finger attempting to remove it (with the ring magically absorbing his blood). That night (a full moon), Marco becomes agitated, his eyes begin to glow, and he slaughters his partner with a cleaver before transforming into a hulking werewolf, killing a man at his own swimming pool and trapping his victim's bikini-clad girlfriend in a car. Back on the train, Dr. Price tells the trio that his orb "has the ability to read people's past." Suddenly Price disappears, and the worried woman proclaims, "At the end of my vision I was dead. But we're alive, alive!" Or are they? (The answer will *not* surprise you.)

"We wanted to pay homage to movies like Mario Bava's *Black Sabbath* and *Dr. Terror's House of Horrors* by Freddie Francis, which is a cult movie for me and Sergio," explained Antonio Tentori (*Dracula 3D*), who co-wrote the screenplay with director Stivaletti. "We have been friends since the '80s, and together we wrote many screenplays that never made it to filming. We were able to realize this one because it was a really low-budget project; we took inspiration, even in the title, from the aforementioned anthology films." (The Italian title for *Black Sabbath* translates as "The Three Faces of Fear.") They took a little more than "inspiration" from *Dr. Terror's*, actually, for they lifted the entire premise—a mysterious man on a train relating the fates of several passengers who are already dead and on their way to their "final destination." Unfortunately, the toneless John Phillip Law (*Danger: Diabolik, Barbarella* [both 1968]) is no Peter Cushing (Dr. Terror himself), and Stivaletti's cheesy light-show effects and ridiculous 2001-esque coda fails to come close to Freddie Francis' eerie and impactful denouement from the original.

"We built the story around John Phillip Law," recalled Tentori, "he had agreed to do the movie, and we wrote four different characters for him." Too bad Tentori and Stivaletti failed to imbue any of the four with real characterization. But poor scripting and a wooden "star" proved to be the least of their problems. Lethargic pacing, cipher-like characters, awkward acting (heightened by Stivaletti forcing his Italian thespians to speak in stilted English, their accents so thick that one can barely make out the banal dialogue), uninspired direction that desperately apes much better filmmakers (right down to a bright Bava-esque color scheme and Argento-heavy camera angles), and the bizarre decision to end each of the three tales before their climaxes (cutting back to the characters on the train each time before finally bundling the three stories' finales all together at the end) nearly make this *The Three Faces of* Awful.

Fortunately, the movie has one card up its sleeve: Sergio Stivaletti. Not Stivaletti the derivative director, and not Stivaletti the stilted screenwriter, but Stivaletti the superb special effects artist. He supervised the movie's effects himself and these prove to be the film's major (sole) asset.

Gooey face removals, realistic severed limbs, an impressive giant lake monster, and, best of all, a powerful werewolf (complete with excellent transformation) help hide the acne scars in these Three Faces.

The striking-looking werewolf blends human and wolf features into a monstrous hybrid, with a long lupine muzzle filled with oversized fangs topped by a human-looking forehead and eyes. Its muscular chest surrounded by hair, and its massive, shaggy arms suggest power, while its oversized mouth opens and roars impressively. The transformation scene remains remarkable for such an obviously impoverished shot-on-digital-video job. Staggering through the night, Marco comes upon a private swimming pool where a man offers some wine to his gorgeous girlfriend in the water. Diving into the pool to slake his ungodly thirst, Marco begins to writhe and thrash, with the startled—and angry—pool owner grabbing him by the arm to try and remove him. Suddenly, blood pours forth from Marco's mouth, and in close-up we watch as his teeth are painfully pushed out by the fangs sprouting underneath. Another close-up shows Marco's fingernails digging into the man's arm, as claws extend from under the nails to skewer the man's skin. Marco's ears stretch into wolfish shapes, and his face bulges outwards into a muzzle, looking painfully real in this very visceral and effective metamorphosis. "I believe Sergio did an amazing job with almost no budget," enthused Tentori. And looking at this lycan-scene, one can only agree—and wish that such quality had bled over to the rest of this subpar film.

A couple of in-jokes help a little (such as putting an Italian poster for *Frankenstein Meets the Wolf Man* on Marco's bedroom wall, and beginning the plastic surgery tale with the heroine acting on a movie set—"Demons 7," with director Lamberto Bava cameoing as himself), but it's really the clever, gory effects and monsters that make these *Three Faces* even halfway attractive.

With quotes from: "Written in Blood," by Roberto E. D'Onofrio, *Gorezone* 33.

Tim Burton's The Nightmare Before Christmas see *The Nightmare Before Christmas*

Totally Awesome

(2006; VH1/Paramount; U.S./Canada) Director: Neal Brennan.

This made-for-TV spoof of 1980s teen flicks (shot in Vancouver, Canada) follows the Gunderson kids, 17-year-old Charlie (Mikey Day), 16-year-old Lori (Dominique Swain) and 11-year-old Max (Trevor Heins), as they move from Pittsburgh to California where they must cope with the bogus cliques, bodacious bitches and jerky jocks of high school in the 1980s. In among the spandex, hair feathers, and Devo hats are riffs on everything from *Footloose* and *Dirty Dancing* to *Pretty in Pink* and even *Soul Man* (featuring a hilarious turn by *30 Rock*'s Tracy Morgan).

Though overlong and frequently hit-and-miss in its comedy, *Totally Awesome* definitely hits with a ... totally awesome one-minute parody of *Teen Wolf*. In the cafeteria on Charlie's first day at Taylor High, he's introduced to Nick (Richard DeKlerk)—just as someone spills milk on Nick, causing him to lose control and transform (via a few simple cutaways) into a werewolf! "Oh my God," shouts one student unnecessarily, "Nick is turning into a werewolf again!" As Nick rampages through the cafeteria, knocking lunch trays out of students' hands and thoughtlessly tossing garbage cans, another high schooler asks, "Why would they let a werewolf go to our school?" Why indeed. Suddenly, the guidance counselor shows up and tries to placate the angry teen wolf with, "Let's talk about this." But the teencanthrope tackles the man and viciously rips into his throat, sending bright red stage blood flying. "Hey," shouts a student, "the werewolf just killed Mr. Phillips!" before adding, "Good kill, wolf!" At this, the approving onlookers begin chanting "Wolf, Wolf, Wolf!" causing the puzzled—and obviously pleased—werewolf to look up, flesh dangling from his mouth, and happily join in the chant. Brilliant. With his pointy elf ears, funny nose, delicate canines and long, straight beard, this teen wolf looks more like a ZZ Top troll than a savage wolfman—which makes it all the more amusing when he sends the blood spraying in an over-the-top display as he rips into his victim. The werewolf turns up only once more—when he appears out of nowhere to attack Charlie's threatening nemesis, BMOC Kipp, at film's end, with similar splattery results.

Transylmania

(2009; Full Circle Releasing) Directors: David Hillenbrand, Scott Hillenbrand.

In this broad, hit-and-miss horror spoof, a group of American college students spend a semester at a university in Romania (housed in an impressive and forbidding castle) where they run afoul of vampires *and* the mad scientist/dwarf college dean. Taking potshots at everything from *Frankenstein* and *The Hunchback of Notre Dame* to *The Brain That Wouldn't Die* and *Van Helsing*, with some *Animal House* thrown in for good measure, most of the gags (running or otherwise) are too repetitious and puerile to leave an impression, and the stereotypical characters (hot girl, stoners, nerd, etc.) add nothing to the dull mix. Some of the more successful comedy bits feature a student posing as a vampire hunter to impress Romanian chicks, a pair of potheads paying for drinks and lap dances by using "American blue jeans" as currency, and an inspired epilogue in which female vampire hunter Teodora Van Sloan (Musetta Vander) has moved to America, joined the Brisby County Sheriff's Department, and is featured on the reality show *Cuffed*. "The fools in my precinct refuse to believe me," she tells the camera. "But they will see—*this* is the home of the leader of the werewolves." Next she bursts into a trailer and starts shooting at the occupant—a long-haired, bearded hippie she mistakes for a lycanthrope.

Transylvania 6-5000

(1985; New World Pictures) Director: Rudy DeLuca.

Transylvania 6-5000 is the first and only feature directed by writer/actor Rudy DeLuca, who helped pen Mel Brooks' *Young Frankenstein* and *High Anxiety*. And given the result, *Transylvania 6-5000* merely underscores the comic genius that is Mel Brooks. Rambling and unfunny, the tedious film was shot by DeLuca in the former Yugoslavia, with the city of Zagreb standing in for Transylvania.

Two tabloid reporters, Jack (Jeff Goldblum) and Gil (Ed Begley, Jr.), journey to Transylvania to scare up a story on "Frankenstein" (after a supposed sighting), only to find a modernized land that scoffs at the idea of monsters. Of course, the locals, including the mayor (Jeffrey Jones) and his butler Fejos (Michael Richards), act mysteriously, and encounters with the Frankenstein Monster, a mummy, a vampiress, and a werewolf are in the (tarot) cards. In the end, however, prosaic rather than supernatural explanations are the order of the day, all under the aegis of a local (semi-mad) doctor attempting to cure the afflicted.

This limp horror-comedy (offering only the slightest bit of either horror or comedy) sees Jeff Goldblum at his smirkiest, Ed Begley, Jr., at his goofiest, and Michael Richards (of later *Seinfeld* fame) at his pratfalliest. None of this is a good thing, particularly in such a drawn-out, tiresome scenario. About the only thing worth watching is a young Geena Davis literally vamping it up in a sexy Vampirella-esque costume.

At one point the reporters go to see an old gypsy woman who tells them, "The creature walks as a man by day, but as the full moon rises he becomes a wolf. He is a werewolf. You must find him, destroy him and put him out of his torment." As they leave, she announces, "He goes by the name of Lawrence Malbot; he is my son." That night (a full moon, of course) they follow Malbot from his house into the woods. He disappears into some bushes amidst a chorus of grunts and growls. The duo creep forward and tentatively part the shrubbery to reveal ... Malbot snogging a local lass. "Who sent you?!" he cries, dismayed. "My wife?" Gil reassures him with, "I'm terribly sorry, we thought you were an animal." "He is," snarks the girl.

But there's further werewolfery (sort of) to come when Jack and Gil later search the woods for a missing girl. Jack hears more grunts and growls emanating from some brush. Remembering their earlier embarrassing encounter, he shrugs it off—just as a wolfman leaps from the bushes with a yell. After screaming like a girl, Jack says, "Down boy, down." But the wolfman grabs him in a bear hug. Just then Gil arrives on the scene and jumps onto the werewolf's back, with the beast-man fleeing, carrying Gil off into the forest with him.

Looking more like Jo-Jo the Dogfaced Boy than a savage werewolf, this lycanthrope sports long hair all over his head, face and hands, with nary a fang or claw in sight. It turns out that this gypsy's son (Larry Malbot *Junior*) is no cursed wolfman after all, but one who "has a

This lackluster horror-comedy provides prosaic explanations for its "monsters," including a werewolf who turns out to be just a man desperately in need of electrolysis.

rare condition called hyperdrycosis" that causes excessive hair growth. "I've been trying to give him electrolysis," announces the local mad medico as explanation.

The movie's level of "wit" can be summed up by the scene in which the local doctor (who goes a little mad whenever in his lab), annoyed with his hirsute patient, orders his minions to "Get him back in the cage before I send him to the pound." At this, the annoyed wolfman retorts, "I'll tear every bit of hair *you* have out of your ass." Further "funny" business comes with the Hairy One sprucing up with hairspray while looking into a hand mirror and singing to himself, "Oh yeah, I'm going into town."

The most interesting thing about this comic misfire is its genesis, as *Transylvania 6-5000* was the first (and only, to date) commercial feature completely funded by a *chemical company*. Dow Chemicals had some cash frozen in Yugoslavian banks and decided to finance a movie to free up these dinars (the local currency). Consequently, the big-business conglomerate partnered with New World Pictures, and a terrible horror-comedy was born. When released in the U.S., the movie made over $7 million in a 700-theater wide release before word of mouth rightly put a stake through its fiscal heart. Unfortunately, it was too late for this author, who had already plunked down his $3 and wasted 93 minutes of his life. The film's trailer suggests, "For a good time, call *Transylvania 6-5000*." Better yet, don't.

According to writer-director Rudy De Luca, he wanted former *Bosom Buddies* co-stars Tom Hanks and Peter Scolari for the lead roles played by Jeff Goldblum and Ed Begley, Jr., but New World Pictures didn't want to take a chance on an "unknown" like Hanks. Prescient they were not.

I Tre Volte del Terrore see The Three Faces of Terror

Trick 'r Treat

(2007; Warner Bros.) Director: Michael Dougherty.

Four terror tales entwine and blend together into one of cinema's best horror anthologies—the clever, funny, and frightening ode to Halloween that is *Trick 'r Treat*. In the small town of Warren Valley, Ohio, which goes all out with its yearly Halloween carnival, a high school principal by day/serial killer by night uses the festival as cover to hunt and claim his victims; a group of tweeners receive terrifying comeuppance for their mean-spirited Halloween prank; a cantankerous old grinch receives a visit from a grotesque little pumpkin-headed demon who painfully teaches him the true meaning of Halloween, and a quartet of party-happy twenty-something girls turn out to be far more than they seem ... *werewolves*.

The lycan-story focuses on the nervous, unsure Laurie (Anna Paquin, of *True Blood* fame), whose big sister and several friends determine to help her finally find her "first" ("If you just tried a little harder you wouldn't be a virgin at 22," one admonishes). Dressed in a Little Red Riding Hood costume, Laurie wanders the carnival searching in vain for a Mr. Right to take to the party at "Sheep's Meadow." Finally trudging alone into the forest to join her compatriots, she's followed by a hooded figure whose sharp fangs have already claimed one young victim. But when the killer attacks her in the woods, the tables turn as she and her kindred begin to change. For it's not her first sexual conquest she-wolf Laurie intends to make this Halloween night, but her first kill...

The striking woodland transformation scene begins with the girls sensually wriggling and writhing before one's skin suddenly splits up the back, revealing moist fur beneath. Others peel the skin off their arms like gloves, and off their legs like stockings, to release clawed, hairy limbs. Before long the gaping jaws of their elongated wolf heads chow down on their dates. (It's little wonder these werewolves look as impressive—and frightening—as they do, given that Tatopoulis Studios created the beasts, the same outfit that came up with the *Underworld* lycans, some of the best of the decade.) Apart from its gruesome surprise twist in having the protagonists become ravening monsters, this story offers a nod to feminism, with the females turning the tables on the traditional male predators (both sexually—in the form of their oversexed "dates"—and literally: Laurie's stalker turns out to be Principal Wilkins from the serial killer episode, who has donned a vampire outfit to continue his killing at the town carnival). She-wolf power!

Animator-turned-screenwriter (*X-Men 2*, *Superman Returns*) Michael Dougherty's directorial debut, the Vancouver-lensed *Trick 'r Treat* is not your average anthology. Cleverly constructed so that the four storylines intersect at various times along unexpected paths, à la *Pulp Fiction* (with the film showing these temporal intersections from various points of view), the four tales were originally to have been directed by four different genre veterans: John Carpenter, Tobe Hooper, George Romero and Stan Winston. But when that fell through, and Bryan Singer (director of the *X-Men* franchise) came on as producer, *Trick 'r Treat* scripter Dougherty (a good friend of Singer's) took up the director's baton himself—and ran with it. Which is just as well, as having four different helmers with four different styles might have creating some jarring clashes and destroyed the overall tone. Dougherty made an amazingly self-assured debut, utilizing mobile camerawork, p.o.v. shots, creepy ambiance, and, above all, sardonic humor to brilliantly capture the Halloween spirit—and its attendant fun, laughs and *fear*. (Sadly, as of this writing, Dougherty has directed only one other feature, *Krampus*, another holiday-themed horror; though *Trick 'r Treat 2* has been announced...)

Uniquely, *Trick 'r Treat*'s four tales mirror "how our lives progress," observed Dougherty. "The first story is very much about a father and a son—a 6-year-old boy. Then when you get to the next one, it's a bunch of kids who are between 12 and 15, and about what it's like to roam on your own and be up to no good. Then the next one involves a group of characters in their 20s, and that's when Halloween becomes about sex, and it's about getting hot costumes and finding someone to hook up with and getting drunk and going to parties. And then the final story is very much the lonely, crotchety old man we're all destined to become—maybe—and what it's like to deal with and celebrate Halloween by yourself in the later years." So *Trick 'r Treat* is not merely a slice-of-life (or sliced-*up* life) snapshot, but a spooky Halloween paean to life's *progression*—with serial killers, zombies, demons, and werewolves, of course.

About the film's "mascot" who appears at some point in each episode like some Halloween guardian angel (or devil)—the demonic little "Sam" (as dubbed by Dougherty), a child-sized, pumpkin-headed imp in footie pajamas with a burlap sack over its deformed head, wielding a razor sharp, half-bitten sucker and razor-blades hidden inside candy bars—the writer-director said, "I wanted to create a character that, to me, embodied everything the holiday is about: He's creepy but he's cute; he's mischievous but he's deadly. To me the holiday is about these separate ideas: the cute, the creepy; the scary, the funny—they all come together on one night."

Definitely coming out more on the side of "creepy" than cute, many of the movie's victims are, shockingly, *children* (though plenty of adults meet their fates as well). "Something that we do in the film—it sounds really bad when you put it out there, but it's done in a very Edward Gorey way—is we kill a lot of kids.... It's like Gorey's *The Gashlycrumb*

Tinies, in a weird way. I remember reading that for the first time; I was like nine years old. I was so horrified, but laughing my ass off about how he kills off a kid in every single letter of the alphabet. That was a huge inspiration." Such a horrifyingly refreshing approach establishes the notion that *no one* is safe on Halloween—or at least no one who disregards the holiday's ancient traditions.

Though Warner Bros. invested $12 million in this scary love letter to All Hallows Eve, they ended up shamefully neglecting it. *Trick 'r Treat* was originally announced as an October 2007 release but never made it into commercial theaters, playing only a few film festivals before debuting on DVD in 2009, almost two years later. This Halloween-themed anthology gem deserved far better.

With quotes from: "*Trick 'r Treat*: Don't Open the Door!" by Dayna Van Buskirk, *Fangoria* 266.

Twisted Tales

(1994; Brimstone) Directors: Rita Klus, Mick McCleery, Keven J. Lindenmuth.

This shot-on-video, micro-budget horror anthology (not to be confused with the 1996 Australian television series, the 2005 BBC series, nor the 2013 American teen mystery/drama of the same name) by filmmaking friends Rita Klus, Nick McCleery and Kevin (*Rage of the Werewolf*) Lindenmuth offers a trio of supernatural stories. The first, "Nothing but the Truth," stands as a cautionary tale of a compulsive liar whose tall tales come back to haunt him. The second, "The Shooting," centers on a traumatic killing and its apparitional aftermath; while the third, "Hungry Like a ... BAT?" sees a man trying to cope with being not only a werewolf but a vampire as well. Charlie (Mick McCleery) seeks the solace of a psychiatrist in order to relate his tale of supernatural woe. It seems that a year ago, while camping in Europe, he was attacked by a vampire *and* a werewolf, both on the same night. And now he worries that he might harm the attractive neighbor who's just moved into his building...

Anthologies generally live and die by the quality of their wraparound story that ties the disparate episodes together. Consequently, it's perhaps telling that *Twisted Tales* doesn't even *have* one, with the three stories simply spliced together to create something of feature length (or close, as it comes in at a scant 70 minutes). Likewise, the nuggets of a few clever ideas lie buried beneath the cheap camcorder photography, uneven sound quality, rubber Halloween masks and props, cramped New York apartment settings, and amateurish acting.

Directed, written, shot and edited by Keven Lindenmuth, "Hungry Like a ... BAT?" offers the novel notion of a man suffering not only from the curse of lycanthropy but of vampirism as well. "I can't use silverware," he complains. "And it's bad enough that I change into this snarling beast every full moon. But what really is a pain in the ass is I can't go out in the daytime!" Besides these minor inconveniences, Charlie (actually rather well played by Lindenmuth regular Mick McCleery, who also directed the film's second—and weakest—segment, "The Shooting") suffers from feelings of disassociation and alienation. He tried to adjust to his new supernatural status by first joining a group of vampires. But when they see him transform during a full moon, they snub him for being "too uncivilized" ("bunch of fuckin' snobs," Charlie snarls). Then he joined "a pack of werewolves in Canada," but they kicked him out because he only drank blood. Unfortunately, such a potentially amusing scenario sinks under the weight of some terrible acting (Theresa Oliva, who plays Charlie's psychiatrist, looks—and acts—like she's still in high school) and even worse effects. The big transformation sequence begins when Charlie looks out a window at the full moon, then instantaneously metamorphoses (off-screen) to reveal ... a man sporting a rubber mask with elongated snout and oversized teeth topped by thick crepe hair. The subsequent attack is no better, as the masked man ... er, werewolf pulls the victim out of frame, a scream sounds, and a spritz of stage blood hits the lampshade.

The impoverished *Twisted Tales* arose because of homegrown horror auteur Lindenmuth's trials and tribulations on his first feature. "Right after I shot my first film, *Vampires & Other Stereotypes*," admitted Lindenmuth, "I shot and edited the anthology *Twisted Tales*, primarily because I needed a break from that particular film." Quite tellingly, the bloopers and outtakes that roll under the drawn-out end credits of *Twisted Tales* demonstrate that the cast and crew had far more fun making the shoestring production than any viewer might have watching it.

With quotes from: *How to Make Movies*, by Kevin J. Lindenmuth.

Urufi Gai: Moero Ôkami-Otoko see Wolfguy: Enraged Lycanthrope

Vampire Hunter D

(1985; Ashi; Epic/Sony/Movic) Original Language Title: *Kyûketsuki Hantâ D*. Director: Toyoo Ashida.

Japanese anime is definitely an acquired taste, one not so easily acquired back in the 1980s before the animated art form became all the rage. One of the first anime films released outside of Japan, *Vampire Hunter D* tells the story of Doris, who, in a world ruled by the supernatural, enlists the aid of a roving Vampire Hunter, "D," to free her from the thrall of the local vampire lord, the evil 10,000-year-old Count Magnus Lee (named in homage to Hammer *Dracula* star Christopher Lee).

"This story takes place in the distant future," begins the opening written narration, "when mutants and demons slither through a world of darkness." In terms of technique, however, *Vampire Hunter D* points more towards the past, as the flat animation, stilted dialogue, and static posing conjures up memories of the late-'60s *Speed Racer* (one almost expects Chim Chim to pop up among the various mist-monsters, giant centipedes and blob creatures). Even original author Hideyuki Kikuchi, upon whose novel the film was based, complained of the animated movie's "cheapness." With its tragic hero "D" (a half-vampire tormented by his bloodsucking lineage and tendencies), innocent teen ingénue Doris (who, rather disturbingly, features into two instances of gratuitous underage cartoon nudity), and Doris' annoying little brother (shades of *Speed Racer*'s Spridle!), *Vampire Hunter D* offers little in the way of character, leaving only the monsters to hold one's interest. Unfortunately, the occasionally imaginative creature is often undone by the repetitive and static animation. To top it off, the film, for no discernible reason, goes all *2001: A Space Odyssey* at the end, but without the thought-provoking symbolism—or any point at all, really.

Among the various mutant monsters and supernatural creatures comes one blink-and-you'll-miss-it werewolf at the film's opening. After Doris chases down and kills a dinosaur-like beast in her field, a huge werewolf suddenly rises up, lifting her wounded horse in its jaws. "Oh my god, a werewolf!" Doris exclaims, and the beast's huge hand reaches towards her, only to delicately pull the cross from her neck with a solitary claw. The werewolf then leaps away, carrying the horse with it, leaving the girl at the mercy of its master, the vampire Magnus Lee, who soon appears to drink from her now-unprotected neck. Over in seconds, this marks the only appearance of any werewolf—all the more disappointing due to its gigantic size and menacing look (standing twelve feet tall on two powerful legs, with its wolf head adorned with two blazing red eyes).

With quotes from: *Watching Anime, Reading Manga: 25 Years of Essays and Reviews*, by Fred Patten.

Vampire Hunter D: Bloodlust

(2000; Madhouse Studios; Japan) Original Language Title: *Banpaia Hantâ D*. Director: Yoshiaki Kawajiri.

Based on the third novel of Hideyuki Kikuchi's *Vampire Hunter D* series, *D—Demon Deathchase*, this anime stands miles above the original 1985 *Vampire Hunter D*—both in terms of animation/visual quality and character/story content. It's even superior in its strikingly unique werewolf concept (though lycanthropy still remains a decidedly minor, cameo element).

Thousands of years into the future, vampires have fallen on hard times, their power and numbers dwindling due to the efforts of bounty hunters like "D," a half-vampire/half-human "Dunpeal." When a rich man's daughter is taken by the vampire lord Meier Link, the concerned father independently hires both D and a team of hunters, led by the Markus brothers, to retrieve her. But all is not as it seems, and the hunters must battle not only the vampire but a cadre of supernatural bodyguards, as well as "Carmilla, the Bloody Countess," to learn the truth.

Among said bodyguards is the vampire's coach-driver, who turns out to be a werewolf. At one point he transforms into the expected wolf-headed creature walking on two legs—but with a novel characteristic: a huge set of fanged jaws, with which he rends his victims, protrudes from his abdomen! Unfortunately, this bizarre-yet-novel mutant lycanthrope appears in only two brief scenes, leaving his character as underdeveloped as it is underutilized.

The film itself, however, remains a sumptuous feast for the eyes of animation lovers, with some epically cinematic set-pieces taking place among its imaginative settings and baroque backgrounds. And the various twists and turns the plot takes, along with more mature characters and themes than those found in the first *Vampire Hunter D*, keep the mind involved as well as the eye.

Production began on this belated follow-up film in 1997, with the project aimed at the American market (even in Japan it was shown in English with Japanese subtitles). Even so, *Vampire Hunter D: Bloodlust* played in only six theaters in the U.S., grossing a mere $151,000.

Vampire Party

(2008; SND/Dark Sky Films; Luxembourg/Belgium/France) Original Language Title: *Les Dents de la Nuit*. Alternate Title: *The Teeth of the Night*. Directors: Stephen Cafiero, Vincent Lobelle.

In this lightweight but amusing French horror-comedy, a trio of party-loving friends scores tickets to the "ultimate" party of the year—which turns out to be hosted by vampires. Now trapped in an isolated castle as human menu items on the bloodsuckers' yearly feast, the three friends must join up with several other partygoers to try and escape the horde of hungry nosferatu.

At one point, one unsuspecting female protagonist hooks up with a handsome fellow guest—who turns out to be not only a vampire, but a vampire-werewolf hybrid. Leading her to a sumptuous upstairs bedroom, he suddenly starts sniffing her all over. When she balks at this weird behavior, he explains, "I can't help it, my mother's a werewolf," and then proceeds to pee all around the bed, stating, "If I don't mark my territory, I'm blocked." The were-vamp then transforms. With the camera behind him, looking towards the astonished girl, pointy ears suddenly sprout from his head before the camera reveals a hirsute face, dog nose and fangs. As he leaps at her, she shoves a pillow into his mouth and escapes into the bathroom. There she finds a handful of other guests hiding out. The duplicitous were-vamp sheepishly apologizes to his intended lunch through the door, assuring her he'll behave, and she responds, "I'll let you in; but don't jump on me—I don't want fur on my dress." When she opens the door and he goes for her once more, the guests all leap upon the manbeast and knock him out with an iron. Then the victim-to-be finishes him off by stabbing him repeatedly with the wooden handle of a toilet brush, causing his body to burst into flames (he is, after all, half-vampire). It makes for a brief but rather funny pseudowolf interlude.

With its cast of ditzy but likable characters, its authentic castle location, professional production values, and some clever gags (including a cute-yet-creepy animated credits sequence reminiscent of *Abbott and Costello Meet Frankenstein*), this *Vampire Party* is one that horror buffs with a sense of humor would do well to attend.

Vampires Suck

(2010; 20th Century–Fox). Directors: Jason Friedberg, Aaron Seltzer.

When a film's trailer opens with "From the guys who couldn't sit through another vampire movie comes a story of one woman's journey to find love," you know that this will not be another of those trendy, angsty, romantic vamp flicks. With *Vampires Suck*, the parody-purveying partnership of Jason Friedberg and Aaron Seltzer (co-writers of the *Scary Movie* franchise, and writer/directors of *Epic Movie*, *Meet the Spartans*, and *Disaster Movie*) take on one of the most successful recent franchises in history by creating a hit-and-miss spoof of the painful angst-fest that is *The Twilight Saga* films. Since *Vampires Suck* specifically mocks the first two entries—*Twilight* and *New Moon*, there's not much emphasis on werewolfery. Jacob (the love-interest lycanthrope from the series, here played with amusing accuracy by Cris Riggi) only wolfs out for one (particularly funny) scene, though the occasional ridiculous reference to his "condition" arises here and there. For instance, when Becca (and the viewer) first meets Jacob, he inexplicably scratches his ear with his foot, pees on a fire hydrant, and breaks off his conversation to chase a passing cat. Later, when Becca tells the lovesick lothario, "You're like my little gay brother," Jacob dejectedly trots off—sporting a tail. And when the sheriff pursues the three evil vampires through the woods, the tracking animal on the end of his leash isn't a dog but Jacob on all fours. Finally, when Jacob tries to teach Becca how to ride a motorcycle, the now-buffed-up Jacob sports clawed hands, a dog nose and pointy ears, noting he's gone through some "changes" since his "bar mitzvah." He even takes off his shirt to reveal a hairy chest—and two rows of teats. The sole transformation scene comes when Becca is menaced by an evil, dreadlock-sporting vampire, and Jacob arrives to save her. But rather than the horse-sized savage wolf of the original films, he metamorphoses into a pint-sized *Chihuahua*. When the bloodsucker just laughs at the tiny were-dog, Jacob calls his beefy, shirtless, short-shorts-sporting pack members to back him up—who suddenly break into a gay-themed dance routine (prancing to "It's Raining Men"). But in the end (and after their dance number) they get the job done by ripping the vampire limb from limb while in hunky human form.

Vampires Suck follows the general plot lines of the first two *Twilight* films fairly closely, aping entire scenes and set-pieces, though (thankfully) condensing and taking the occasional ludicrous liberty (including appropriating the old *Mad Magazine* movie parody name-change trick by altering the setting from Forks, Washington, to "Sporks," and turning Edward Cullen into the apropos "Edward Sullen"). And like those *Mad* spoofs, some of the jokes land as knock-out punches while others miss their mark entirely. In the latter category, for example, are inexplicable out-of-nowhere bits involving Alice in Wonderland and Buffy the Vampire Slayer, and some clunker dialogue like Edward's "Strangely, the only thing that does keep aging [on vampires] is your ass—it gets pretty wrinkly over time." But for every gag or bit of dialogue that falls flat, there's another just around the corner that succeeds in either its parodic cleverness or laugh-out-loud ludicrousness. For instance, on Becca's MP3 player are "Bite Me Mix," "I Hate Life Mix," "Loathe Ya Mix," and "Teen Angst Mix." Then Becca describes herself to her new school chum by saying, "Actually, I'm more of the humorless type, kind of a sourpuss, really. Full of insecurities, with no great personality, yet every hot guy finds me irresistible." Spot-on. Then there's the crude but laugh-out-loud moment when the smitten Edward watches over the sweetly sleeping Becca and oh-so-earnestly says to himself, "Just you breathing is the greatest gift you could give me"—right before Becca farts in his face to send him reeling backwards out the open window.

Panned by most critics, *Vampires Suck* received four Golden Raspberry Award nominations, including Worst Picture, Worst Director, and Worst Screenplay—but then so did *The Twilight Saga: Eclipse*. Even so, *Vampires Suck* took in $36 million domestically (against a purported $20 million budget) and earned over $80 million worldwide, demonstrating that 1) while critics may have lost their sense of humor, audiences haven't; and 2) discerning viewers can see through the overblown absurdity of the *Twilight* phenomenon and appreciate a sometimes silly yet often dead-on spoof of same (or maybe they just like fart jokes…).

Vampiros en la Habana

(1985; ICAIC/Durniok; Cuba) Director: Juan Padrón.

The first (and only, to date) *Cuban* werewolf turned out to be … a cartoon. A subversive, adult-oriented feature (with political, as well as sexual, references … and nudity) by celebrated Cuban cartoonist and animator Juan Padrón, *Vampiros en la Habana* ("Vampires in Havana") follows the trials and tribulations of Joseph Emmanuel von Dracula (aka "Pepe") who, in 1930s Havana, plays trumpet (performed by jazz great Arturo Sandoval, who defected in 1990, becoming a U.S. citizen nine years later) and works with his fellow revolutionaries to try and overthrow the repressive government of General Machado while also wooing his beloved Lola. If that weren't enough, Pepe soon learns that he's a *vampire* (a grandson of Dracula, in fact), whose Uncle, Bernhardt Amadeus von Dracula, had developed a potion that allows vampires to walk in the sunlight, using Pepe as his unwitting test subject from an early age. With Pepe being the proof of his formula's efficacy, Von Dracula now intends to give it to the vampire world. However, two undead factions have other plans—a Chicago vampire-gangster cartel, led by Johni Terrori (who wants to suppress the formula and so maintain their monopoly on indoor beach resorts for vampires), and the European vampire alliance (who intend to market what they've dubbed "Vampisun" to cement their financial empire)—and they converge on Havana to secure Von Dracula's formula, with Pepe caught in the middle.

Though a vampire rather than werewolf show (after all, it's not called "*Hombre lobo* en la Habana"), a spindly-legged, long-nosed, lolling-tongued lycanthrope appears briefly midway through the movie. As the vampires search for the on-the-lam Pepe, a scraggly wolf-dog with a cigarette dangling from its mouth spies on Pepe's hideout through a window. A stray mutt sniffs its butt, receiving a swift kick of annoyance for its unwanted attentions, before the wolf lopes over to Johni Terrori, stands on its hind legs, scratches its ear, and then (after a quick slap from its impatient master) transforms into a big-nosed, heavily mustachioed man in cap and red sweater. Never speaking (as either wolf or man), this were-minion appears only twice more, once to sniff out Pepe's trail again (as a human), then in wolf form to flee from a pack of amorous street dogs who apparently have more on their canine minds than sniffing posteriors. Sprinting away from the pack, the beast-creature runs right in front of a car. "It's only a dog," says the driver dismissively after running over the animal, to which a bystander observes, "A dog with *shoes*?" Under the bumper lay the fully clothed dead body of the mustachioed man.

The colorful animation (reminiscent of a *Rocky and Bullwinkle* cartoon), action-filled scenario (including chases and shootouts between the rebel group and police, as well as the two vampire factions, who employ stake-shooting guns and silver bullets that apparently work on vampires), and *rapido* pace—not to mention the frequently amusing comedic asides (one thirsty Eurovamp protests, "Not Cubans, please, they taste of sugar")—make this a worthwhile trip to "the Pearl of the Antilles," vampiros and all.

La Venganza de Huracán Ramirez

(1967; Cinematografica Roma SA; Mexico) Director: Joselito Rodriguez.

Huracán Ramirez was one of the most popular masked Mexican wrestlers of the 1950s, '60s and '70s, standing tall alongside such luchadore icons as El Santo, Blue Demon and Mil Máscaras. And like his contemporaries, Ramirez starred in a number of popular films. Unlike his wrasslin' brethren, however, Ramirez faced only human villains rather than the assorted madmen, monsters and space aliens battled by Santo, Blue and Mil. The sole exception (out of eight films) being *La Venganza de Huracán Ramirez*.

Wrestler-cum-mad scientist "Professor Landru" (Jean Safont) experiments with a serum derived from animals in an attempt to transfer their savage qualities to himself and so defeat his arch-rival in the ring, Huracán Ramirez (David Silva when not sporting a mask, Daniel Garcia when in Huracán mode). When none of his dirty tricks work, Landru finally disguises himself as the masked wrestler "Vampiro Sangriento" to go at Ramirez once more in the ring. Landru injects himself with even more serum, giving him superhuman strength. Despite this, Ramirez still triumphs, and when he unmasks his opponent, Landru sports the hirsute face of a werewolf (shades of *Sampson vs. the Vampire Women*). Through a series of grimacing-faced dissolves, Landru transforms back to his human form, then collapses, killed by an overdose of his own mad concoction. While this werewolf afterthought remains as nebulous as it is brief (nothing ties the serum to a wolf—apart from the beast-man's traditional appearance—as the doc experiments mostly with dogs and cats), it still makes for a startling (if cheesy) coda.

Though the film devotes far too much time to the non-wrestling characters' palaver and silly antics (including a pie fight!), the encroaching ennui is regularly chased away by three brutal and exciting free-for-all wrestling bouts (including one in which a cheating opponent tries to burn out Ramirez' eyes with a handful of flame[!], then chloroforms Huracán's partner to the point that the groggy wrestler attacks Ramirez[!!]); a colorful musical number set in a swinging sixties record store (Mexican style); and several scenes of the evilly grinning Landru in his basement lab filled with bubbling beakers, snakes, spiders, vermin, and even a Gila monster. Unfortunately, Ramirez' *Venganza* was for Spanish-speaking territories only, having never received an English-language release.

The 41-year-old Daniel Garcia was not the only luchadore to wrestle under the famous mask and moniker of "Huracán Ramirez," but he was the most prolific, playing the role in the ring for over two decades and appearing in five of the eight Huracán Ramirez movies. A frequent tag-team partner and friend of the great El Santo, Garcia saw his youngest daughter marry the wrestler Axxel, grandson of El Santo.

Waxwork

(1988; Vestron) Director: Anthony Hickox.

"More fun than a barrel of mummies," claims the film's trailer. While this seriously overstates the case, this mired-in-the-1980s nostalgia-fest does indeed offer up the occasional homage-and-gore-soaked bit of "fun" for the diehard genre fan (most of it revolving around some over-the-top, comedic gore, and the re-creation of far better horror movie scenarios, such as Hammer's *The Mummy* and *Night of the Living Dead*). Something of a pseudo-anthology film (a quintet of brief, self-contained tales lie buried within the overarching storyline), *Waxwork* centers on the mysterious eponymous establishment that springs up seemingly overnight in a suburban neighborhood. Sinister owner Mr. Lincoln (a bored looking David Warner) invites a gaggle of college students, led by *Gremlins*' Zach Galligan, to a "private showing" at midnight. When someone steps into the wax tableau (and they always do), they're magically transported into that time and place to become victims of the various evil creatures, including vampires, zombies, the Marquis de Sade, a mummy, and a werewolf.

The first of the living waxwork stories begins when one of the half-dozen obnoxious spoiled preppies, Tony (Dana Ashbrook of *Return of the Living Dead II* and TV's *Twin Peaks*), drops his lighter into the werewolf exhibit and steps across the rope to retrieve it, thereby stepping into another world that sees him sporting peasant garb in a spooky nighttime forest. Inside a nearby rustic cabin he finds a man (John Rhys-Davies) who seems to know him and spouts cryptic warnings like "The full moon has already risen" and "In a few moments I dare not think what could happen." Tony humors him and steps outside to get some wood for a fire (because "it's cold in here"). Tony fails to take it all seriously, however, and once outside rails to no one in particular, "I'm stuck it his cold place—nowhere to go and *no cigarettes*! What am I supposed to do—entertain this asshole?! Do I get a pretty woman in my illusion? No. I get a *dick*. This sucks, man." Meanwhile, back in the house, the man sits at his table, digging divots into the wood with his transformed fingernails. Tony returns with an armful of logs, only to be confronted by the now-fully-transformed werewolf. A p.o.v. shot has the camera rushing towards Tony, who yelps, drops the wood, and scurries away. A brief close-up of a wolfish face then gives way to more lupine p.o.v. as Tony grabs up a bone from the table and tosses it (like you would to a dog)—to no effect. "Good boy ... stay," Tony gibbers as he frantically grabs up whatever comes to hand (a large ladle) and runs about the cabin. But the beast bites his arm just as an elderly hunter (Nelson Welch) and his young assistant bursts through the door. "We're too late—give me the silver bullets." As the hunter fumbles with the shells, his helper (James Hickox, brother of director Anthony Hickox) distracts the manbeast by hitting it with a chair. The monster disdainfully dusts off its shoulder before grabbing the young man's head with his clawed hands and pulling his victim apart. "The werewolf literally tears someone open from the top of his head to the base of his spine—just tears the guy in half and eats what's inside. It's a lovely family movie, you know," joked FX artist Bob Keen. It is indeed a startlingly gruesome scene (though Keen exaggerates when he says the beast eats his victim, as no noshing takes place).

Meanwhile, Tony begins to writhe in pain ("Oh, that's gotta hurt!" he cries) while bone-crunching noises on the soundtrack herald his imminent transformation. After a cut to the hunter reloading, Tony now sports fangs. After another cutaway to the hunter cocking his rifle, Tony now sports hair on his face and clawed hands. A few air bladders bubble beneath the skin of his forehead (à la Rob Bottin's groundbreaking effects for *The Howling*) before the hunter shoots the half-transformed Tony. Back in the real world, Tony is now a figure in the display, a victim of the werewolf. The entire episode lasts all of six minutes, with the lycan–business end taking up just half of that.

"For the werewolf we used *The Howling* type, not the Lon Chaney, Jr., version," said Hickox. And while not up to the high standards of Rob Bottin's game-changing creations, it's a decent stab at a Big Bad Wolf: a hair-covered biped topped by an oversized, evil-looking demonic wolf's head that includes angry eyes, a canine muzzle, and a mouth full of oversized fangs. Completing the lycan-picture is a set of large ears that, unfortunately, move more comically than naturally

The *Waxwork* werewolf comes to life (courtesy FX artist Bob Keen).

(perhaps fitting for a monster segment that's part scary *Howling* and part smart-ass *Scream*).

Waxwork is not a cute movie," claims Hickox, which one can't disagree with given its myriad grue-fueled moments (that include a man strapped to a table, still conscious and aware, with half his leg literally gnawed to the bone). "It's action. It's time travel, it's horror and comedy, and it's as bloody as I could get it." It's also not a very good movie. First-time writer-director Anthony Hickox (son of *Theater of Blood* director Douglas Hickox) penned the script in three days—and it shows. Besides the dearth of character development and far too much unfunny dialogue, the scenario itself fails to hold together, not so much for the outlandish premise (a Satanist plots to bring to life all the classic monsters, which will somehow raise the dead and destroy the world) but because of the nonsensical actions of the clichéd characters. They smoke and act like jaded noir figures, but they're just shallow, college-age ciphers. Even the normally likable Zach Galligan plays a whiny hipster-wannabe rich boy who gets pushed around not only by his mother but by his bitchy girlfriend. Hickox doesn't help matters by dressing David Warner like Willy Wonka, and backing it all with a cheesy synth score. Though Hickox' sequel-heavy career never climbed much higher than *Waxwork* (with films like *Sundown: The Vampire in Retreat* [1989], *Hellraiser III* [1992] and *Warlock: The Armageddon* [1993] being "highlights"), he did helm one subsequent full-on werewolf movie (arguably his best): the superior made-for-cable *Full Eclipse* (1993).

Though intermittently entertaining when in the alternate waxworlds, the poor script transforms the film into an uneven, ridiculous mishmash. Even talented veteran thespians like John Rhys-Davies, David Warner and *Howling* veteran Patrick Macnee can't breathe much life into this *Waxwork*. "In a climactic battle reminiscent of the outrageousness of Monty Python or *Casino Royale*'s finale," enthused Hickox about his goofy free-for-all conclusion, "300 extras, led by Patrick Macnee, arrive to save the world." Too bad they couldn't to the same for the movie.

Hickox (and Galligan) returned three years later for *Waxwork II: Lost in Time*, a more overtly comedic follow-up that, while still not "more fun than a barrel of mummies," proved more fun than its predecessor. (Particularly amusing is a spot-on homage to the Robert Wise ghost classic *The Haunting* that goes hilariously off the rails.) No lycanthropes rear their hirsute head, however.

With quotes from: "Making the *Waxwork*," by Larry Barsky, *Fangoria* 78.

Werewolf Hunter see Romasanta

Werewolf Hunter: The Legend of Romasanta see Romasanta

A Werewolf in the Amazon see Un Lobisomem na Amazônia

Werewolf Manhunt see Romasanta

Werewolf Warrior see Kibakichi

What We Do in the Shadows

(2014; Unison Films; New Zealand) Directors: Jemaine Clement, Taika Waititi.

This witty mockumentary stars writer-directors Jemaine Clement (one half of the folk-comedy duo Flight of the Conchords) and Taika Waititi (*Eagle vs. Shark*) as Vladislav and Viago, two vampires who share their flat with bad boy Deacon and ghoulish Petyr. Trying to get by in the ever-changing New World of Wellington, New Zealand, these Old World bloodsuckers must contend with technology, household chores, nosy (but friendly) police, a vampire hunter and such frustrations as trying to convince a perplexed nightclub bouncer that they must be *invited* inside. They also have two brief run-ins with a band of werewolves.

The first encounter, played strictly for laughs, has our merry band of bloodsuckers out on the town when Vlad notes, "We're just about to walk past some werewolves, so some shit might go down." As they pass the half-dozen average-looking blokes, smartass Deacon quips, "Look out guys, don't catch fleas." At this the two groups posture and exchange insults ("Why don't you go smell your own crotches"), with Deacon even pretending to throw a stick (causing one to give chase, as his mates admonish, "Nathan, it's not real"). When several of the lycanthropes start growling, the others hold them back, with the alpha instructing, "Hey, hey—do the breathing. Count to ten, mate."

The second encounter sees actual transformations (a few split-second shots of hairy faces and fangs), as it's the night of the full moon. After attending a vampire party, the gang comes across the werewolf group preparing to chain themselves to trees ("Declan, that tree's far too thin," admonishes the bossy alpha, "you know how big you get when you transform"). "Don't hassle us tonight," warns their leader, and adds, "By the way, I find that offensive" (indicating Vlad's fur coat). Organizing his brood, the alpha instructs, "Take all the clothes off you wanna keep, everyone" ("Take that Army surplus jacket off—you've only just bought that, Nathan"). But it's too late, and the distracted werewolves transform. This results in a brief, two-minute melee in which the hair-covered, bi-pedal beasts attack.

"Every single wolf is different," observed co-writer-director Jermaine Clement of the film's lycanthropes, before admitting, "They were actually cobbled together with what we could afford and what we could get people to help make." They are indeed different, one walking on extended legs, for example, another looking more gorilla-like (complete with elongated arms). The chaotic, hand-held photography (one of the werewolves even takes down a cameraman) that captures the melee in long shots, silhouette, and extreme close-ups (highlighted by a truly frightening wolf face—slavering jaws agape—rushing out of the darkness directly into the camera) not only heightens the sense of violent chaos but effectively obscures the "cobbled together" nature of the creatures, making this one of the edgier and more disturbing sequences in the otherwise comedic scenario.

"Being chased by vampires was a recurring nightmare of mine," commented Clement on the film's genesis, "so I wanted to do a vampire thing, and it was Taika's idea that it should be a mockumentary. I thought it was a great concept, because you can't make a documentary about [vampires]." Shot in the camera crew/interview-style of a Christopher Guest parody (*Best in Show* [2000], *A Mighty Wind* [2003]), with healthy dollops of capture-the-moment chuckles à la television's *The Office* and *Modern Family*, *What We Do in the Shadows* is filled not only with macabre humor (neatfreak Viago—who lays down newspapers and towels before biting a victim—seems to hit the artery every time, sending bloody spray everywhere) but witty satirical jibes at everything from relationships to religion to vanity to basic human interactions. From the very opening, in which a "flatmate meeting" in the kitchen sees the group discussing Deacon not having done the bloody (in the literal sense of the word) dishes in five years, the cleverness of juxtaposing the preternatural with the mundane highlights the humor of the human condition. "Vampires don't do dishes!" exclaims the indignant bloodsucker, and the sequence closes with the cowed Deacon at the sink wiping a glass and grumbling "This is bullshit" in his Hungarian accent.

The characters, led by the quartet of vampire archetypes (Vladislav, a Vlad-the-Impaler type; elegant, foppish Viago, cast in the *Interview with the Vampire* mold; rough-and-tumble *Lost Boys*–ish Deacon; and *Nosferatu*-like Petyr) all come off as quite likable and even sweet (apart from the mute Petyr, who stays mostly in the crypt-like basement), despite the occasional throat-ripping. And with their various hang-ups and foibles, they seem painfully, humorously human.

With its biting satire (pun intended) on the human condition, the clever, subtle, and very very funny *What We Do in the Shadows* shows that no one, not even centuries-old vampires, can wholly escape their all-too-human flaws.

With quotes from: "*What We Do in the Shadows*: Old Blood in New Zealand," by Samuel Zimmerman, *Fangoria* 339.

The Widderburn Horror see *House of the Black Death*

Wilczyca

(1982; Zespol Filmowy Silesia; Poland) Director: Marek Piestrak.

A rare Polish horror film, *Wilczyca* (which translates as "She-wolf") has yet to see an English language release. In the mid–1800s, cavalry officer Kacper (Krzysztof Janinski) returns to his farm after a long absence fighting the Prussians only to find his unfaithful wife Maryna (Iwona Bielska) dying. Worse, the ungodly woman has burned the family crucifix and sold her soul to the Devil, promising to return after death as a wolf. When she dies, Kacper's older brother, who had been taking care of the farm and had witnessed Maryna's fall from grace, insists they drive a stake through her body. Dismayed, Kacper leaves the farm in his brother's hands to go work as gamekeeper on the estate of his former commander, Count Ludwik. When the Prussians invade again, the weak-willed Ludwik takes Kacper and flees, leaving Ludwik's duplicitous wife Julia behind. But not only the enemy pursues them; seemingly a large wolf dogs their trail...

Though overlong, with far too much time taken up with the Count's faithless, bitter young wife (looking just like Maryna, as if the evil dead woman's spirit has infested the evil living Countess) taking up with the handsome Prussian officer who temporarily occupies the estate, *Wilczyca*'s too-stately pace is leavened with the occasional bit of Gothic atmosphere or horrific shock. A nighttime flight through the bleak, foggy, wintry landscape, all mysterious shadows and howling winds, ends with the discovery of a hanged corpse. At one point, Kacper's brother arrives and relates how Prussian artillery disturbed the graves in the cemetery; Maryna's coffin contained only the splintered remains of the wooden stake—her body had disappeared. That night he awakened to the sight of Maryna's decomposing corpse (a truly effective—and horrific—makeup job) advancing upon him.

Crude yet haunting poster for the folklore-heavy period werewolf entry *Wilczyca*, which failed to escape the confines of its native Poland into English-language territories.

The film looks polished, filled with authentic period costumes and settings, and boasting fluid camerawork (the camera moving frantically through the forest as Kacper hunts the wolf, for instance). Krzysztof Janinski makes for an almost too-stoic protagonist, however. Fortunately, his humorless portrayal is more than offset by the near-animalistic, vibrant playing of Iwona Bielska (as both the diabolical Maryna and the wicked Countess).

Though slight on werewolf scenes (the wolf is only glimpsed fleetingly in the forest; and while noises and footprints indicate its presence, it never attacks anyone), *Wilczycy* offers a few moments of lycan-interest. In a scene taken directly from folklore, Kacper shoots the wolf in the forest and follows the trail of blood only to find the Countess bandaging her wounded hand (though she doesn't seem particularly bothered by the wound, and only smiles at the nonplussed Kacper).

At one point the local doctor, an expert in "esoteric knowledge," uses a voodoo-like process in which he stabs a portrait of Maryna with a knife—drawing blood from the image and causing pain to the Countess at the same time—to prove the supernatural link between the possessed Julia and Maryna. The doctor then provides Kacper with a silver bullet, with which Kacper shoots Julia in the *eye*, triggering a brief but surprisingly gory sequence during which he dispatches two guards (chopping off one's arm with a sword and slashing the other's throat). Shot while fleeing on horseback, Kacper escapes to an uncertain fate. Months later the Count returns to his estate and insists upon the exhumation of his wife's body. Opening Julia's coffin, he cries out in horror to see the skeletal remains of a *wolf*.

The film's director, Marek Piestrak, made a sequel of sorts in 1990 titled *Powrot Wilczycy* ("Return of the She-Wolf") in which lightning strikes Julia's grave, resulting in subsequent werewolf attacks. Exceedingly obscure, the follow-up apparently never made it outside Poland.

Wolf Blood see Wolfblood: A Tale of the Forest

Wolf Girl see Blood Moon

Wolf Mania see The Feral Man

Wolf Mountain see The Legend of Wolf Mountain

The Wolf of the Malveneurs see Le Loup des Malveneur

Wolfblood: A Tale of the Forest

(1925; Lee-Bradford Corporation) Alternate Title: *Wolf Blood*; Directors: Bruce Mitchell and George Chesebro.

Though some sources cite this as the earliest extant werewolf film (beating out *Werewolf of London* by a full decade), it's not. While it offers an intriguing premise, a picturesque snapshot of the logging industry in the 1920s, and even a few eerie special effects (involving a pack of "phantom" wolves), the story's lycanthrope is merely a man who goes crazy, hallucinates, and suspects he's become "a thing that is neither man nor beast!" (as he so agonizingly describes it). "Deep in the vastness of the great Canadian forest," proclaims the films opening title card, stands Ford Logging Company Camp No. 1, run by crack foreman and all round swell guy Dick Bannister (co-director George Chesebro, who went on to appear in literally hundreds of B-Westerns, often as a heavy or in bit parts; *Wolfblood* was his only directing credit). Due to the evil machinations of his unscrupulous counterpart at the rival Consolidated Lumber Company, Bannister ends up injured and bleeding to death. To save his life, the camp surgeon transfuses the blood of a wolf (the only available donor) into Bannister's veins. The Doc recalls a passage from a medical textbook that reads: "And it is a fact that Dr. d'Ore has successfully transfused into man animal blood. The question still remains, however, whether following such transfusion the character, nature and desire of the human subject may partake of the nature of the animal whose blood was used." Bannister recovers (amazingly), but when he learns the truth about his treatment, he cracks. "To Bannister's mind," reads a title card, "weakened from the loss of blood at the time of his injury, came the remembrance of the weird tales of the loup garou of the Far North—the Wolf in human form!" Thinking he's killed a man while possessed of his now-bestial nature (he hasn't), Bannister conjures up a phantom wolf pack in his tortured mind and nearly follows them over a cliff—stopped only in the nick of time by "the power of a great love!" provided by Bannister's new love interest (played by Marguerite Clayton).

Offering what one might expect from a modest mid-twenties production—flowery, melodramatic acting; cramped sets; a surfeit of medium shots with a locked-down camera; superficial characters (stalwart hero, swooning heroine, evil villain); jazz-era flapper parties (complete with comments on the evils of bootleg liquor); and a love-triangle storyline that neatly resolves itself in the end—*Wolfblood* also provides some impressive woodland photography, a pack of semi-transparent wolves (a neat optical effect) roaming the forest of Bannister's unhinged mind, and the intriguing psychological conflict of a man overwhelmed by superstition and the power of suggestion. While no long-lost silent classic—and not really a werewolf movie—*Wolfblood* shows that not all lycanthro-centric stories need fur and fangs to hold one's interest.

Wolfen

(1981; Orion/Warner Bros.) Director: Michael Wadleigh.

Though often characterized as such, *Wolfen* is not a werewolf film. *Time Out* magazine labeled it a "werewolf movie," while Roger Ebert claimed that *Wolfen* "is not about werewolves but is about the possibility that Indians and wolves can exchange souls." Neither is correct. (According to director Michael Wadleigh, *Wolfen* is not even a horror movie but rather a "political thriller.") While the notion of "shapeshifting" arises ("We do it for kicks," says a local Native American), and at one point the film's protagonist, police detective Dewey (Albert Finney), comes to half-suspect former Indian activist Eddie Holt (Edward James Olmos) of transforming into a wolf to carry out a series of killings, shapeshifting turns out to be "all in the head," as Holt himself states. What's *not* all in the head is a pack of super-intelligent wolves secretly preying on the "sick and unwanted" (i.e., homeless people) in the urban wasteland of the South Bronx, New York. When an uber-rich developer breaks ground on a new construction project designed to clean up the inner-city wasteland, the wolves protect their hunting grounds by killing him and several others involved, leading to Dewey's investigation. As Holt explains after a shaken Dewey finally sees these elusive creatures with his own eyes, "It's not wolves, it's 'Wolfen.' [Centuries ago] the smartest ones, they went underground, into the new wilderness—your cities—into the slum areas, the graveyard of your fucking species."

Co-written and directed by former documentary filmmaker Michael Wadleigh (*Woodstock* [1970]), *Wolfen* (Wadleigh's first—and last—dramatic feature) takes a realistic approach not only to its menace but to its characters, populating the scenario with quirky people played by engaging actors like Gregory Hines and Albert Finney. (Reportedly, Dustin Hoffman actively sought the role of Dewey but was rejected by Wadleigh, who wanted to work with Finney, his favorite actor.) The script also takes great pains to highlight the plight of the Native Americans (who, in New York City, work the high construction sites, like bridges and skyscrapers) and even draws parallels between them and the wolves themselves. "Wolves and Indians evolved and were destroyed simultaneously," explains an eccentric animal expert. "Their societies are practically one and the same. They're tribal, they look out for their own, they don't overpopulate." But it's not all political overtones and historical exposition, as *Wolfen* goes for the jugular (sometimes literally) more than once during its startlingly visceral moments.

An exceedingly well-shot film, *Wolfen* originated the innovative and striking thermographic/chromatic visuals employed to represent the wolves' point of view, a technique subsequently employed by a number of films, most notably the *Predator* series. Wadleigh recalled, "We kept playing around with various things, infrared photography and reprinting the colored layers and so on. [Steadicam operator] Garret [Brown], who not only invented the Steadicam but is considered the best operator by everybody, is 6 feet 8 inches tall and a very athletic guy who can run like crazy. He is also very smart, and so the first thing we got was the terrific Steadicam photography that makes you think there's a mind behind the point of view, that we are actually looking out of somebody or something's eyes." Indeed, the way the camera tracks and moves at wolf's-eye level, gliding across open spaces and darting behind objects to keep out of sight, coupled with the oddly textured and strangely colored visuals, makes for some uncanny—and unnerving—moments.

Extra precautions were taken while shooting with real wolves—much to Wadleigh's disgust. "The paranoia of human beings is extreme," scoffed the director. "I mean, wolves are presented in all the movies as evil, and we have associated them in our mythologies with the Devil and all of that kind of thing, but there are relatively few instances of a pack of wolves wiping out a human being." While filming in New York City, "they had like a dozen armed policemen—you know, sharpshooters—positioned all over the place because the wolves were considered wild, uncontrollable animals. The police had their orders to shoot to kill if a wolf got out of the enclosure. They weren't about to have one running around New York City! We all thought that was amusing, we who were used to dealing with animals. Their paranoia was, to my mind, unjustified." No wolfish difficulties ever arose.

Wolfen cost a reported $15 million to produce—a hefty sum in 1981. Unfortunately, Orion/Warner Bros. marketed it as an outright horror shocker ("They can tear the scream from your throat; there is no defense," warned the advertising), and it failed to even make back its costs, grossing a little over $10 million upon initial release. Cerebral. Moody. Startling. Unsettling. *Wolfen* is all those things and more; but it's just not really a werewolf movie.

With quotes from: "Wolfen," by Roger Ebert, rogerebert.com; "Wolfen: A Political Animal, Parts 1 and 2," by Michael Doyle, *Fangoria* 301 and 302.

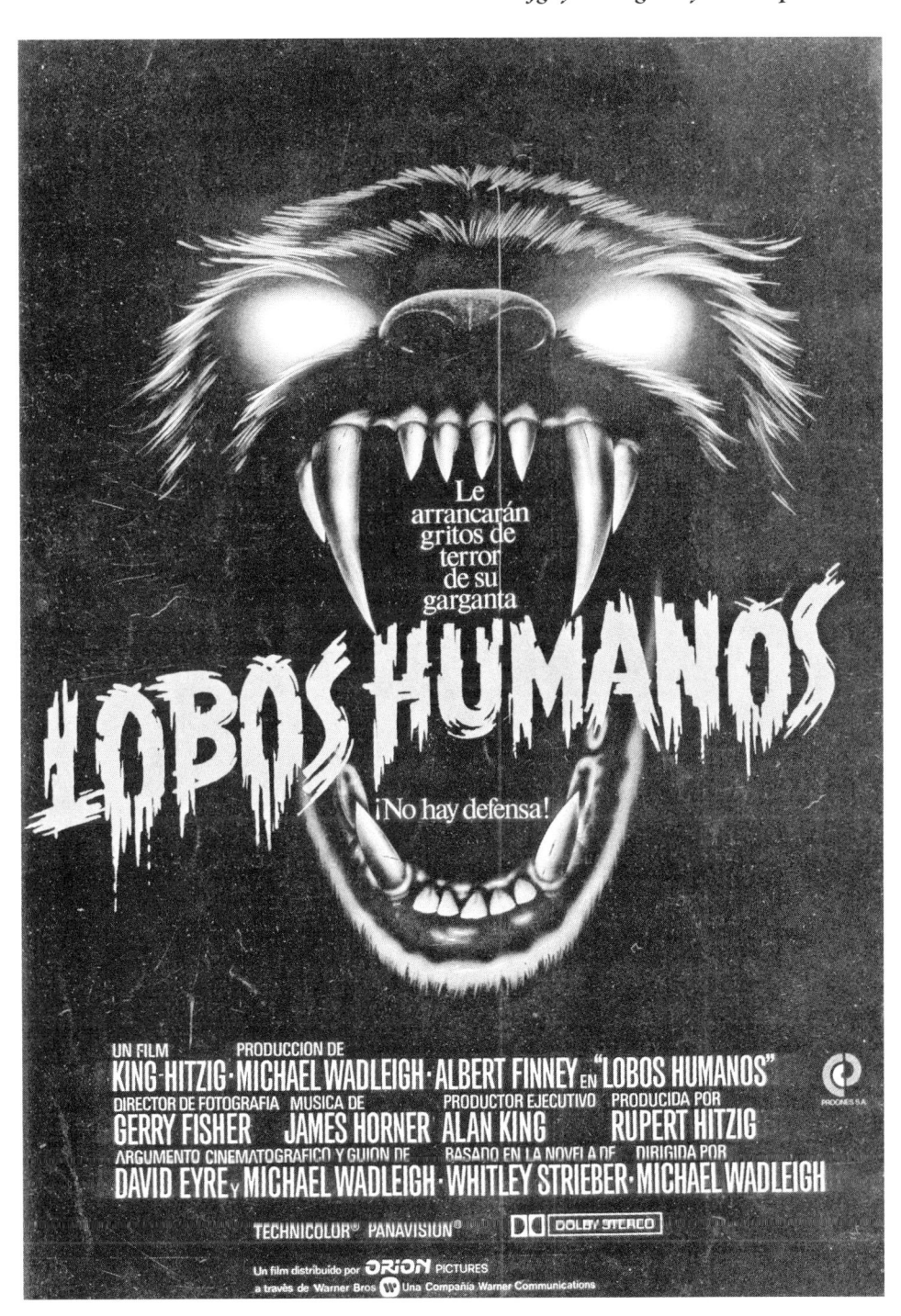

Though, strictly speaking, *not* a werewolf film, the thought-provoking, gripping *Wolfen* remains a watershed genre entry (Spanish poster).

Wolfguy: Enraged Lycanthrope

(1975; Toei; Japan) Original Language Title: *Urufi Gai: Moero Ôkami-Otoko*. Director: Kazuhiko Yamaguchi.

A reporter witnesses a man on the streets of Tokyo slashed to death by an invisible tiger(!). Upon investigating, the newsman engages in a karate battle with a group of gangsters, is shot, and makes his escape with the help of a mysterious woman on a motorcycle. She takes him home, strips off her leathers, and licks the blood from his hand before seducing him ("I'm just a woman who wants a man who's an animal!").

And this occurs all within the first 15 minutes of the obscure (to Westerners, anyway) *Wolfguy: Enraged Lycanthrope*.

Japanese hard man (and martial arts superstar) Sonny Chiba (*The Streetfighter* [1974]) plays "Wolf" Inugami, the hard-bitten reporter drawn into this bizarre world of tiger curses, Yakuza (Japanese gangsters), crooked politicians, covert government agencies, and despicable record executives who destroy young singers' careers and lives. But the topper: Inugami just happens to be the last surviving member of a clan of werewolves. And he'll need all his lupine skills to survive…

Strangely, this "last wolf" (as his dying mother labels him in flashback) never transforms physically. Rather than manifesting in outward signs (hair, claws, fangs), lycanthropy remains internalized as a latent power (increased strength, agility and healing). And this hidden power waxes and wanes with the moon—so much so that at the height of the full moon Inugami becomes impervious to bullets. And in a crude, over-the-top (and novel) sequence, at one point the to-all-appearances mortally wounded Inugami smiles grimly as the exposed innards spilling from his torn stomach literally ooze back *into* his body while the gaping wound miraculously heals!

Nor does this "wolfguy" lose any of his human mental facilities during the lunar cycle. Far from transforming into an animal, Inugami remains the most human—and humane—character in the film, attacking only those that threaten him, and doing everything he can to protect the weak (which includes a drink-addled witness and a junkie victim).

In a wild turn of the plot screw, it turns out Inugami's motorcycle-riding, sex-starved savior works for the clandestine "J.C.I.A.," who want to harness Inugami's supernatural powers—either by inducing him to join their ranks or by creating their own "wolfguy" by transfusing Inugami's blood into one of their assassins. Though the operation initially seems to work ("The transfusion of your blood made me a werewolf too," crows the now-supernaturally-strong assassin), the newly-minted wolfman soon collapses, coughing up blood. Apparently, "the mixing of wolf blood with human blood resulted in sepsis." It appears that only nature (through heredity) can create a werewolf, not science.

Wolfguy: Enraged Lycanthrope's outré twists and turns and gonzo '70s sensibilities, chock full of post–Watergate cynicism, marital arts battles, gunfights, bright orange stage blood, and nudity (with various women throwing themselves at Inugami—animal magnetism, perhaps?), make this a uniquely memorable, fast-paced, and outrageous slice of '70s import cheese, topped by the imposing presence of the intense-yet-likable Sonny Chiba. Unfortunately (and surprisingly, given that it stars the iconic Chiba), to date, this *Wolfguy* has never seen a legitimate English-language release.

The Wolves of Kromer

(1998; First Run Features; UK) Director: Will Gould.

Though occasionally tagged as a werewolf film, the gay-themed *The Wolves of Kromer* is more allegorical fantasy than horror movie. Rather than lycanthropes, the titular "wolves" that inhabit the woodlands around the rural English village of Kromer are a pack of attractive young gay men that wear fur coats over their bare chests, go about shoeless, and enjoy frolicking at the local lake. The repressed villagers, led by the hypocritical, vitriolic vicar ("They only bring disease and spread trouble wherever they go"), see them as dangerous outsiders and even determine to hunt them down. The film focuses on two story lines that ultimately intertwine—one involving a family whose matriarch is bumped off by her long-time servant (looking all the world like a female Boris Karloff); the other following the burgeoning, rocky relationship between a newcomer wolf and his more experienced lover.

Apart from their alternate sexuality (and odd

Sonny Chiba takes action as *Wolfguy: Enraged Lycanthrope* (Japanese poster).

Three of *The Wolves of Kromer*, more a gay-themed allegorical fantasy than werewolf movie.

mode of dress), what sets these "wolves" apart from the locals are two physical traits—pointy ears and a tail (neither of which, however, are presented particularly realistically nor even commented upon). And these wolves never transform, nor do they prey on anyone; in fact, they're far less violent than the homophobic villagers. The only "change" comes when they reach puberty and their "wolfish" nature surfaces. "Mom used to tell me to tuck my tail into my jeans," relates newcomer Seth, "and Dad used to make jokes about boys like me. It's like they just hoped it would go away."

A unique, even clever, conceptualization (adapted from screenwriter Charles Lambert's own play of the same name), *The Wolves of Kromer* posits werewolfery (or, more accurately, just plain wolfery) as a metaphor for homosexuality, casting much of the "human" population as either self-absorbed neutrals, ignorant xenophobes or violent hypocrites (as personified by the shotgun-wielding clergyman). Avoiding the pitfall of preachiness, scripter Lambert, first (and last)-time director Will Gould, and the talented cast leaven the social commentary with bits of black humor that help liven up the sometimes slow pace and dearth of activity. Though not for everyone, the bizarre *Wolves of Kromer* makes for an intriguing, amusing, and even rewarding pseudowolf entry with more metaphorical bite than most.

OTHER WERE-BEASTS

Listed here are those movies that feature a were-*something*, rather than a were*wolf*—such as were-cats (*Cat People*), snake-women (*The Reptile*), were-reindeer (*The White Reindeer*) and even Jellyfish-men (*Sting of Death*). In order to qualify for inclusion, the afflicted must transform back and forth between his or her human and bestial form; i.e., their new shape is not permanent (which excludes such efforts as *The Alligator People*, *Night of the Cobra Woman*, *The Beast Within*, and the various *Beauty and the Beast* adaptations). Also, the were-creature must have some sort of animal affiliation (simply transforming periodically into a nondescript—though entertainingly bizarre—monster like *The Brainiac* or *Voodoo Woman* doesn't cut the were-mustard).

Anchorman 2: The Legend Continues

(2013; Paramount) Director: Rawson Marshall Thurber.

In this uneven-but-still-funny sequel to the hilariously non–P.C. *Anchorman: The Legend of Ron Burgundy* (2004), Will Ferrell returns as the self-absorbed San Diego news anchor who, with his unlikely news team, rules the San Diego airwaves in the 1970s. But after he's fired (for gross incompetence, naturally) by his boss, legendary newsman Mack Tannen (Harrison Ford), he ends up in New York on the first 24-hour news network (GNN), becoming a national star despite himself, only to fall fast and hard while learning a few lessons about what's really important in life ... or something. The film climaxes with a ridiculous and hilarious pitched battle in Central Park between Burgundy and his crew and just about every other news team in American (and Canada). Mack Tannen shows up and, commenting on the "early rising moon," suddenly transforms into a "were-hyena," bursting out of his suit in a brief but impressive CGI display before joining battle. Though a split-second throwaway gag (like so many jokes in the film), this amusing moment of metamorphosis (made doubly so by the participation of pop-culture acting legend Harrison Ford) underlines the undeniable appeal of lycanthropy in modern cinema.

The Bat People

(1974; American International Pictures) Alternate Titles: *It Lives by Night*, *It's Alive*; Director: Jerry Jameson.

"After the sun has set and the night wind has died comes the hour of the Bat People!" So proclaimed the ads for this mostly-forgotten mid–1970s AIP entry in the eco-monster sweepstakes, which tries for a more philosophical bent in its depiction of "civilized" man returning to nature—by periodically transforming into a bloodthirsty man-bat! While on a delayed honeymoon, a young doctor and his wife tour a local cave and are attacked by a bat. After being bitten, the doc soon begins experiencing violent seizures and blackouts, the result of him temporarily metamorphosing into a bat-monster who kills several people. The tortured doc ultimately comes to take a different view of his affliction, and leaves a recorded message for his wife. Reflecting the ecological-minded, consciousness-raising times (it *was* the '70s, after all), he tells her, "Many will deny the phenomenon—the miracle—which has forever altered my being.... Now the metamorphosis is swift, smooth, painless, natural. I welcome it." He goes on to explain that "something within my psyche has emerged, has helped me reach a new consciousness, a sharp awareness of truth, untouched by human greed or ambition. Free from the negative, the hypocrite, I'm part of everything now. I'm journeying to a belonging." Apparently he has become the first Zen were-beast. In any case, it all ends on an enigmatic, even philosophical note, as the wife, apparently infected as well, dispatches the unctuous sheriff on their trail (via a horde of killer bats) and goes to join her bat-husband in the caves.

Though novel in approach (and in its choice of were-monsters), *The Bat People* remains a decidedly minor and mostly forgotten film (one that performed poorly at the box office back in the day). Its slow build-up, glacial pacing, and sparsity of true horror (the attacks are all filmed from the beast's point of view, so we see only the cringing victim, and never any actual bloodshed or violence) all work against its more thoughtful, character-driven approach. Fortunately, the two leads, Stewart Moss and Marianne McAndrew, form a convincing and likable couple, possibly helped along by the fact that they were man-and-wife in real life. Both actors worked primarily in television, as did director Jerry Jameson (though he did pilot *Airport '77* and help *Raise the Titanic* in 1980).

One of *The Bat People* (Stewart Moss).

Jameson keeps the were-bat coyly hidden until the climax, with only a webbed, hairy hand indicating the occasional transformation. When finally revealed, the clothes-wearing monster sports a flattened bat-nose; discolored fangs; dark, ridged skin; coarse hair; and pointy ears. This unique yet slightly ridiculous creation was the first feature work of future Oscar-winning makeup maestro Stan Winston (*Jurassic Park*, *Terminator 2*, *Aliens*, etc.). Fortunately, Winston got a *lot* better.

Long on pathos but short on activity, the minor, eco-friendly *The Bat People* rightly remains in the shadows of '70s horror. Still, it features a unique were-creature, some involving acting, *and* a gratuitous though always welcome (to this author, anyway) vintage skiing sequence. Love those long-and-straight K2s…

The Blood Beast Terror see The Vampire-Beast Craves Blood

Blood Freak

(1972; Variety Films) Directors: Brad F. Grinter, Steven Hawkes.

A young drifter named Herschell (co-producer/director/writer Steve Hawkes) meets a pair of sisters—one spouts Bible quotes and the other is into the "far out" drug scene. Herschell tries some form of super-marijuana, which turns him into an instant drug addict. After landing a job at a local turkey farm, Herschell eats some experimental turkey meat and periodically transforms into a capon-monster with the body of a man and the head of a mutant turkey! He goes about making gobbling noises and killing female druggies to drink their tainted blood. In the end Herschell realizes it's all been a drug-induced hallucination and seeks redemption from his wild ways in the bosom of the Lord. The onscreen narrator (co-director Brad Grinter) drives the moral home for us high-risk viewers: "This has been a story based partly on fact, partly on probability." Indeed.

Okay, this just *has* to be a send-up, right? Wrong—it's the first ever anti-drug religious gore movie! Said gore consists of several incompetent throat slashings (complete with watery blood and the *same* looped scream) and Turkey-Herschell lopping off a pusher's leg with a table saw (the sole non-derisive moment in the film, since the victim is obviously a one-legged actor with a prosthetic device). The rest of the picture proves just as inept, from the flat-as-road-kill emoting by the various non-actors, to the ill-lit shaky-cam home-movie photography, to the insipid musical score (by the film's multi-tasking editor, no less), to the pacing that couldn't outrun an Alaskan glacier (at one point we watch Herschell smoke a joint *in real time*). And don't forget that mutant paper maché turkey head, with its oversized beak and bulbous eyes making it look like Big Bird gone bad.

At one point Herschell says, "I spent some time in Vietnam in the hospital. I've been burned pretty bad." Indeed he had. Herschell was played by the only professional actor in the cast, Steve Hawkes (well, he had made a couple of Italian pseudo–Tarzan films, anyway). "On October 31st, 1970," related Hawkes, "during the filming of *Tarzan and the Brown Prince*, I was burned over 90 percent of my body. And guess who saved my life? A Lion named Samson. He dragged me out of the burning fire and ripped off the ropes I was staked down with. Then I realized what the animals were all about. The love that I have for them cannot be measured by anything that life offers…. That's why if there ever was such a man as Tarzan, I'm probably the closest one to him." True to his sentiments, for years Hawkes ran a private sanctuary for big cats in Florida before running into financial difficulties.

With quotes from: "Steve Hawkes Interview," by Matt Winans, Tarzanmovieguide.com.

Bride of the Gorilla

(1951; Realart) Director: Curt Siodmak.

A jungle/ape variation on *The Wolf Man* (which *Bride* writer-director Curt Siodmak had scripted ten years earlier), *Bride of the Gorilla* stars Raymond Burr as Barney Chavez, the manager of an Amazonian plantation who kills his boss and marries the beautiful widow (Barbara Payton). A native servant places a curse upon Barney, causing him to transform into a gorilla at inopportune moments and roam the jungle.

"It was a marvelous idea," opined Siodmak. "So he's a murderer,

Ad for *Blood Freak*, cinema's only were-*turkey*.

Wolf Man scripter Curt Siodmak wrote and directed *Bride of the Gorilla* a decade later, a simian take on the werewolf theme.

but his conscience doesn't permit that, so every time he looks in the mirror he sees an animal. Because an animal can kill without being punished, he's free of guilt. *They* made a gorilla out of it—I didn't even want to show that. *They* called the film *Bride of the Gorilla*; my title was *The Face in the Water*." ("[Producer] Jack [Broder] wanted an exploitation title," explained Herman Cohen, who served as Broder's assistant, "and I came up with *Bride of the Gorilla*.")

For most of the film Siodmak shows the ape solely from Barney's point of view (watching the backs of his hands transform into hairy, wrinkled paws, and seeing his reflection as that of an animal), intimating that it's all in Barney's tortured mind. Towards the end, however, full shots of the beast (gorilla-man Steve Calvert in his ape suit) lumbering through the jungle put paid this intriguing notion. But Siodmak's script fails to play up Barney's feelings of guilt anyway, so the writer-director's "marvelous idea" was really a moot point.

Raymond Burr brings a raw, dangerously elemental edge to his portrayal of the murderous foreman. Yet when he speaks of the jungle and his newfound senses ("I heard something strange and beautiful—a voice, calling me; I couldn't resist going out there"), his tone becomes almost poetic, and one can see the genuine longing in his eyes. "Oh, [Burr] was so professional," said Cohen. "And a wonderful guy. Raymond was a hell of an actor. Great actor, great voice, and I knew he was gonna become something."

Bride of the Gorilla co-stars the original Wolf Man himself—Lon Chaney, Jr.—here miscast and giving a stiff, stilted performance as a "native" commissioner. "It wasn't a bad picture," concluded Cohen. Indeed, with a bit more subtlety in both presentation and acting, it could have become a *good* picture.

With quotes from: *Interviews with B Science Fiction Movie Makers*, by Tom Weaver; *Attack of the Monster Movie Makers*, by Tom Weaver.

Captive Wild Woman

(1943; Universal) Director: Edward Dmytryk.

In the mid–1940s Universal's stable of monsters were tiring, unable to cross the finish line without help, resulting in the teaming and re-teaming of their classic monsters (including the Wolf Man) in features like *Frankenstein Meets the Wolf Man* and the two *House* films. In this climate of quiet desperation the studio sought a fresh thoroughbred to inject new life into the horror race. They found it in a little franchise filly called "Paula the Ape Woman." Paula ambled through three features before she died of ennui. Though the last two pictures, *Jungle Woman* (1944) and *Jungle Captive* (1945), proved to be tired, repetitive potboilers, the first, *Captive Wild Woman*, was something else entirely.

John Carradine plays a respected scientist who, through some ambiguous use of "gland extracts," turns a man in an ape suit (Ray "Crash" Corrigan) into the beautiful Acquanetta (marking this as the first *reverse* were-beast flick). He dubs his new creation Paula Dupree and takes her back to visit the circus from which she was stolen. There she proves a "natural," since all the animals seem to fear her. Consequently, animal trainer Fred Mason (Milburn Stone), unaware that Paula is actually his missing ape, Cheela, incorporates her into his new and dangerous act—mixing lions and tigers in the same ring. The trouble is, "terrific emotion destroys the new tissue in [Paula's] gland growths," causing her to periodically revert back to a half-simian

The Captive Wild Woman (Aquanetta) mid-transformation.

form. And Fred's fiancée (Evelyn Ankers) inspires in Paula just such a "terrific emotion" in the form of violent jealousy.

Not the best of plots, nor the biggest of budgets (much of the time is filled with stock footage of famous lion-tamer Clyde Beatty), but this fun cheapie packs its brief 60 minute running time with plenty of vintage thrills. The film begins with an exciting sequence in which a tiger gets loose on the shipyard docks and is promptly cornered by Fred. From then on it never lets up, alternating thrilling lion and tiger taming footage of Beatty from *The Big Cage* (1933) with laboratory chills, presided over by the ever-villainous John Carradine at his subdued best.

Carradine is excellent as the brilliant but amoral scientist, turning in an even-tempered, effective characterization that's a far cry from his many desultory Poverty Row portrayals. Milburn Stone (later to achieve modest fame playing "Doc" on TV's *Gunsmoke*) as Fred, and Evelyn Ankers as his fiancée, are solid audience identification figures, making their characters both approachable and likable.

As the titular creature, the exotic Acquanetta (a model turned actress inexplicably dubbed the "Venezuelan Volcano"—though she was actually from an Arapaho Indian reservation in Wyoming) looks striking as the gorilla-turned-woman who possesses a strange "animal magnetism." She's not asked to do much more than stand about with an intent look on her beautiful face (though at one point she does manage to effectively convey an ill-controlled rage). This is just as well, since she subsequently proved herself (in films like *Dead Man's Eyes* and *Captive Wild Woman*'s first sequel, *Jungle Woman*) to be an actress of decidedly limited range.

Captive Wild Woman boasts some deft transformation scenes in which original Wolf Man–creator Jack P. Pierce performs his usual top-flight job of turning men (or in this case, women) into monsters. Via filters to show Acquanetta's face suddenly darken (à la 1931's *Dr. Jekyll and Mr. Hyde*) and effective dissolves (à la 1941's *The Wolf Man*), Paula loses her humanity right before our very eyes. "Jack Pierce was a nice man," recalled Acquanetta, "but it took hours to do the make-up. Hair all over the place, and then they put those big false teeth on top of your teeth [groans], and then it took twelve hours to get it off!" (This last was no doubt a bit of playful hyperbole on the actress' part,

as it generally took 1 to 2 hours to remove Pierce's heavy make-up.)

Shaggy in ape form and sexy in human guise (thanks to the dark beauty of the "Venezuelan Volcano"), Paula made for an acceptable Jekyll/Hyde animal update. And, at least for her debut outing, this longshot came in a winner. Sure *Captive Wild Woman* is horror hokum, but it's exciting, vintage 1940s hokum nonetheless.

With quotes from: "Acquanetta," by J. F. Parda, *The Exploitation Journal* 15.

The Cat Creature

(1973; ABC-TV) Director: Curtis Harrington.

Given this telefilm's personnel, both behind and in front of the camera, *The Cat Creature* should have been a far better were-beast entry than the barely mediocre movie it turned out to be. Written by revered horror writer Robert Bloch (*Torture Garden*, *The House That Dripped Blood*, the novel *Psycho*), directed by cult favorite Curtis Harrington (*Night Tide*, *Queen of Blood*, *What's the Matter with Helen?*), and filled with excellent character actors like Gale Sondergaard (1939's *The Cat and the Canary*), Keye Luke (numerous *Charlie Chans*, *Gremlins*), John Carradine (*Captive Wild Woman*, *House of Frankenstein*, *House of Dracula*), Kent Smith (the frustrated husband from the original *Cat People*), Milton Parsons (*The Monster That Challenged the World*) and John Abbott (*Cry of the Werewolf*), *The Cat Creature* proves to be about as terrifying as, well, a house cat.

When a wealthy collector dies, an appraiser (Kent Smith) comes to his mansion to take inventory and discovers a basement filled with Egyptian artifacts, including a mysterious sarcophagus containing a mummy wearing a golden cat amulet. After a thief (Keye Luke) steals the necklace, the mummy disappears, and a cat attacks and kills the appraiser (all in shadow). The thief takes his loot to "The Sorcerer's Shop," run by former fence Hester Black (Gail Sondergaard), who, realizing it's stolen, sends him packing. Lt. Marco (Stuart Whitman) investigates the murder, aided by local college professor (and Egyptologist) Roger Edmonds (David Hedison). Roger tells Marco that "the priests of Bast believed that in return for human sacrifices, the goddess could grant them eternal life. And they were also supposed to have the power to turn into cats." Meanwhile, a young woman, Rena (Meredith Baxter), takes a job at The Sorcerer's Shop and becomes romantically involved with Roger. More cat-killings (with the victims "nearly drained of blood") occur as the search for the missing amulet continues. Roger finally comes to realize that the "amulet was placed on the mummy's throat for the same reason a stake is driven through a vampire's heart—to keep it from rising and resuming an unnatural life, nourished by blood." And much to his dismay, he concludes that Rena is the missing mummy ("No wonder you're afraid of cats," he tells her, "they recognize you for what you are—the priestess of Bast").

Much of the blame for the film's flatness can be laid, like a mangled mouse, at the feet of screenwriter Robert Bloch, whose teleplay meanders turgidly at times and features several just-plain-lazy plot contrivances. For instance, Lt. Marco decides to stake out the shop and asks Rena to keep the store open after hours in the hopes that Ms. Black (who now has the amulet) will return for the cash she keeps there—when it would make more sense to just close up as usual and then wait for Black (who'd be more likely to return when no one was there anyway). And after finally recovering the missing amulet, the lieutenant reluctantly hands over the precious necklace (an important piece of evidence) to Roger to take away in order to decipher the hieroglyphics on the back—when a photocopy, or even just writing the few symbols down on a piece of paper, would have sufficed. But then he wouldn't possess the real thing for the climactic confrontation with Rena—to which he foolishly goes alone.

But at least Bloch offers a few fine bits of dialogue, including a passage on shapeshifting delivered with convincing gravitas by the baritone-voiced John Abbott (as Roger's colleague): "Vampires turn into bats in the wilds of Transylvania. Man assumes the shape of wolves in Germany, of foxes in China. In Africa men turn into leopards. The Arctic Eskimos believe their wizards can transform into bears…. Why is it that since the beginning of time people of every culture, living 10,000 miles apart, with no possible connection, have always maintained the same belief—that under certain conditions man can take the form of an animal? Behind every universal legend lies a universal reality." And at film's end, Rena finally admits to her true nature and delivers a powerful, pathos-laden soliloquy: "You don't know what it's like to be buried away alone in the darkness, century upon century of blackness, paralyzed and unable to move or breathe—yet conscious of every crawling moment."

Director Curtis Harrington's heart didn't appear to be fully in this production. (Thinking of himself as a feature director, he generally looked down on television work, despite this medium providing most of his employment over the course of his career.) The problem of making an ordinary house cat (even a black one) appear frightening seemed too difficult a task for the director. Harrington takes a halfhearted stab at it by mostly filming the little beast in shadow, but it's still just an ordinary *cat's* shadow. And he neglects to shoot any cat's-eye-view footage or provide low-angle shots, with the camera (and audience) too often just looking down on the little house pet. As presented, it's just not particularly menacing. And Harrington tends to succumb to directorial laziness at times, such as when Roger finally puts two and two together (and comes up with 'Rena is the cat-creature'). Harrington illustrates this eureka moment with a standard montage of previous scenes and dialogue (just in case viewers had dozed off during the film's many dull stretches, perhaps, or maybe to eat up some more running time).

Disappointingly, there's nary a transformation in sight, with the felonious feline just appearing out of nowhere to hypnotize or stalk its victim. Only at the end, during the big reveal that Rena is actually the reanimated mummy/cat-creature (which will come as a surprise to only the most somnambulant of viewers), does a metamorphosis take place—sort of. Rejecting her offer of "the secret of immortality," Roger pushes Rena away. Suddenly she's gone, but a cat (or at least its shadow) stalks through the room. The kitty leaps on Roger, who struggles with it mightily (if unconvincingly), wrestles it into his arms, places the amulet around its furry neck, and pushes it away. Abruptly rising up into frame, Rena—now decked out in her golden Egyptian priestess finery—opens her mouth to ridiculously emit cat snarls, and turns to stagger onto the terrace. A glowing light transforms her into a walking mummy, which the dozen or so cats who've gathered there suddenly attack, leaving only a pile of dust, bones, and wrappings.

On the plus side, Gail Sondergaard brings a sinister air of mystery to her shop owner character, Stuart Whitman makes a welcome no-nonsense skeptic, and the various supporting players add color to the sometimes drab proceedings. Unfortunately, the bland Meredith Baxter (later Meredith Baxter Birney) makes for a poor cat-creature indeed. Harrington recalled in his autobiography that the ABC executives originally wanted Patty Duke (who'd recently appeared in a highly-rated show and so offered a good "TVQ") for the role of the "beautiful, dark, exotic, sexually alluring girl." Harrington was aghast, feeling Duke to be a "short, dwarfish, unsexy and unattractive character actress." After his protests, "they came back with Meredith Baxter [*Ben*, 1972], an actress who was popular at portraying ordinary middle-class American girls … [but] was at least reasonably pretty." Unfortunately, she proved to be little *more* than that, bringing no real presence or depth to her pivotal role (nor even any chemistry between herself and romantic interest David Hedison). She only comes alive at the close—due mostly to Bloch's incisive dialogue.

In the end, rather than a ferocious were-beast, this *Cat Creature* turns out to be a disappointingly harmless pussycat.

With quotes from: *Nice Guys Don't Work in Hollywood*, by Curtis Harrington.

Cat Girl

(1957; Anglo-Amalgamated/AIP; UK/U.S.) Director: Alfred Shaughessey.

An obvious takeoff on Val Lewton's stylish 1942 classic *Cat People* (right down to aping the original's suspenseful city-street stalking sequence and having the big cat killed by a car at the end), *Cat Girl*, a British/American co-production between Anglo-Amalgamated and American International Pictures (who put up $25,000 and a script by Lou Rusoff in exchange for the Western Hemisphere distribution rights), barely qualifies as a "were-creature" film. For that matter, this artless, stodgy, dour derivative barely qualifies as *entertainment*.

After being summoned to her ancestral home by her estranged uncle, Leonora (Barbara Shelley) seemingly inherits the family's 700-year-old curse in which her soul becomes entwined with that of a leopard. After the big cat he kept in the basement kills her uncle, the roving beast now begins acting on *her* violent desires (including attacking her philandering husband and menacing the wife of Leonora's old flame). Not really a were-beast in the strictest sense of the term, Leonora controls and shares experiences with the wild cat rather than actually transforming into one. At one point Leonora says of her late uncle, "He was a werewolf. At night, when darkness came, his soul entered into the body of a leopard. He stalked the forest for prey, looking for things to kill and devour." Though misusing the "werewolf" term here, *Cat Girl* does feature a (sort of) transformation in which Leonora sees herself changing into a leopard-woman, her hands becoming clawed paws and her face turning into a fuzzy leopard countenance. Later, she tells her old boyfriend Brian (who also happens to be the psychiatrist trying to help her), "I saw myself [change] in the mirror!" At this, Brian explains, "Your sick mind created an image for you." And that indeed turns out to be the case, for she never changes again (even failing to transform when she tries to prove herself to the doubting Brian).

With its lumbering lack of action (the few animal attacks occur off-screen), cheesy production values (blurry camerawork during the metamorphosis scene hides the sub-par stuffed-animal leopard makeup), a dearth of likable characters (even Brian, the ostensible hero, appears stiff and overbearing), and a central figure who acts far too cold and passionless to engender any sympathy (Barbara Shelley, an excellent actress when given decent material, would go on to far better things, like 1960's *Village of the Damned* and various Hammer films), *Cat Girl* has little to recommend. In America, AIP fobbed off this dour, humorless and small-scale production onto unsuspecting audiences as the bottom half of a double-bill with the far more entertaining *The Amazing Colossal Man*.

Cat People

(1942; RKO; b&w) Director: Jacques Tourneur.

Eyeing the profits made by Universal with their relatively inexpensive horror productions, RKO hired David O. Selznick's personal assistant/story editor/jack-of-all-cinema-trades Val Lewton as a producer and put him in charge of a B-picture unit that was to make horror movies on budgets of less than $150,000 and based on "pre-tested" titles provided by the studio. First up: *Cat People* (an obvious nod to the mega-success of *The Wolf Man*). Ironically, Lewton was an ailurophobe (afraid of cats) whose were-cat story "The Bagheeta" had been published in the July 1930 issue of *Weird Tales*. Lewton, a well-read, literary-minded man (who'd penned several novels) eschewed the more obvious terrors of Universal's fright factory to produce a series of "thinking man's" horrors—intelligent, suggestive thrillers whose scripts (often retooled, or pseudonymously written outright, by an uncredited Lewton himself) plumbed the depths of the human psyche more than the outer reaches of the preternatural (though the two sometimes crossed). What resulted were nine of the finest horror films of the 1940s.

Cat People follows the trials and tribulations of newlyweds Oliver (Kent Smith) and Irena (Simone Simon), whose marriage has hit a snag from the outset: Irena is so terrified of intimacy that she can't even *kiss* her new husband, much less share his bed. Serbian-born, she comes from a village with a terrible legend in which the women transform into murderous panthers whenever aroused by anger or desire. After psychiatrist Dr. Judd (Tom Conway) fails to help her, the jealous Irena ends up stalking Oliver's beautiful co-worker Alice (Jane Randolph) before the curse leads her to her doom.

As Irena relates of her village's horrible history, "People bowed down to Satan and said their masses to him. They had become witches and were evil." This evilness took the form of "cat-women." As Dr. Judd reiterates what she's told him under hypnosis, "The cat-women of your village ... who, in jealousy or anger or under their own corrupt passions, can change into great cats like panthers. And if one of these women were to fall in love, and if the lover were to kiss her, take her into his embrace, she would be driven by her own evil to kill him."

Although obviously influenced by the previous year's *The Wolf Man* (the film even indirectly references that lycanthropic groundbreaker when Dr. Judd skeptically responds to Alice's warning with, "Oh, you want me to carry some means of protection—a gun, perhaps, with a silver bullet?"), *Cat People* takes a more subtle and suggestive (in more ways than one, given its focus on sexual frustration) path. The film only reveals its were-panther as shadows and sound until eight minutes from the end when it finally provides a glimpse of it (a black leopard) in all its night-black feline glory. The transformation, too, remains suggested rather than shown, first by a set of muddy paw prints that abruptly become a woman's shoe prints; then when a subtle lighting change darkens Irena's face, causing Judd to back away in horror before the huge cat attacks. But these remain no less effective for their subtlety.

Though a polished production, with director Jacques Tourneur making good use of standing sets and evocative lighting (courtesy of cinematographer Nicolas Musuraca), *Cat People* remains too prosaic for its own good, both in its focus on mundane activity (Irena's multiple visits to the zoo; the couple's banal—and chaste—interactions; Oliver's frequent talks with Alice at work, at home, in a coffee shop, etc.) and in its two rather uninteresting leads. The coquettish, lightweight Simone Simon and the dull, coltish Kent Smith spark no chemistry between them, so one wonders how (and why) they fall so hard—and abruptly—in love. Acting-wise, the film's vibrancy stems solely from the plucky Jane Randolph and the urbane Tom Conway—two secondary support figures.

And near the film's end, Irena suddenly—and unconvincingly—overcomes her overwhelming fear far too easily when Dr. Judd, at only their second meeting, tells her to simply forget about the legends that obsess her (he must be some psychiatrist). Of course, it's too late, since, after Irena sets a romantic candle-lit dinner in obvious anticipation of their coming consummation, Oliver abruptly tells her that he now loves Alice, leading to the fateful climactic tragedy. Then there's the rather hokey moment when Irena, in cat form, traps Oliver and Alice in their office, and Oliver grabs up a t-square, brandishes it like a cross, and calmly intones, "In the name of God, leave us in peace." And she does.

Much of *Cat People*'s vaunted reputation is built upon the two justly famous stalking set-pieces, both masterful sequences of suspense and barely-suppressed terror—Irena following Alice through the park, ending in the famous Lewton "bus" (when, tension at its height, a bus suddenly enters the frame accompanied by the startling hiss of its air brakes), and the atmospheric pool sequence in which a prowling presence traps a terrified Alice alone in the water. (This sprang from a real-life incident involving director Jacques Tourneur when years before he was swimming alone at a friend's pool—a friend who owned a pair of pet cheetahs. "And one day I'll be damned if one of the cheetahs wasn't out of his cage and starting to prowl around and growl in a low way," recounted the director. "And I thought, 'Oh my God, here I am feeling naked; I can't scream,' and I was going around in circles in the nude.... Luckily, the cheetah was afraid of the water. And eventually, from way back on the property somewhere, the gardener came with a rake and shooed the cheetah back.")

Not quite the perfect classic some make it out to be, the flawed but still impressive *Cat People* was shot in a scant three weeks for a mere $134,959 (coming in $7,000 under budget). A huge financial success, the film made $4 million during the first two years of its release, reportedly saving RKO from bankruptcy. Its unexpected success launched a mini-horror cycle, with Lewton's "B" unit making one fine inexpensive horror film after another, among them such well-respected classics as *I Walked with a Zombie*, *The Body Snatcher* (featuring arguably Boris Karloff's greatest performance) and the original's sequel, *Curse of the Cat People* (a superior effort offering a touching tale of childhood fantasy in place of the metamorphic horror of the original)

With quotes from: *The Celluloid Muse*, by Charles Higham and Joel Greenberg.

Cat People

(1982; Universal) Director: Paul Schrader.

"*Cat People* is not a horror movie," announced director Paul Schrader (screenwriter of *Taxi Driver*). "It's an erotic fantasy." Well, yes, it is fairly erotic (thanks to the willingness of the undeniably sexy Nastassia Kinski to show off her waifish body). But this 40-years-later remake of the classic Val Lewton–produced *Cat People* (1942) features such scenes as a zoo attendant (Ed Begley, Jr.) having his arm graphically torn out by the roots, and a man transform into a powerful leopard to attack the hero. So it's rather disingenuous when Schrader says, "I don't want people to consider this a horror or a special effects film. Not only would that be a false impression but it would link the movie to a genre that is dying out."

Dying out? Prescient, Schrader was not. "Not only am I not of that

Ad for the erotically-charged 1982 remake of *Cat People*.

genre," he insisted, "but I wouldn't want to be identified as being of that genre even if I was!"

Fortunately, Schrader's disdain for "horror" didn't prevent him from ringing as much terror and suspense as he could from this stylish but only partly satisfying tale of a shy young woman, Irena (Nastassia Kinski), journeying to New Orleans to reunite with her long-lost brother Paul (Malcolm McDowell). She soon gets a job at the local zoo, and falls for curator Oliver (John Heard). But Paul reveals his true purpose in tracking down his sister—he intends to make her his lover. They are from a long line of cat-people who can only mate with their own kind—otherwise, they transform into black leopards, "and before we can become human again we must kill…"

"There's very little similarity between our movie and the original *Cat People*," claimed executive producer Jerry Bruckheimer. Even so, the remake effectively replicates a number of key sequences from the original: Irena's chance meeting with her "sister" cat-woman; the stalk through the park, culminating in the famous "bus" moment; and the terrifying pool scene (this time with a *topless* heroine). "What we've done is gone back to the first film and taken the original *Cat People* legend out of that plotline," continued Bruckheimer. "We've expanded it, *showing* what the first film only spoke about." That being the notion that sex literally brings out the beast in (cat) people, emphasizing the transformative properties of lust (or love).

"I didn't consider it a classic," dismissed Schrader of the original 1942 *Cat People*. "I think it's very well directed but you can see that it's a back-lot, low-budgeted quickie. With the exception of Simone Simon, it's badly acted." Obviously Schrader never heard the proverb about glass houses, for, with the exception of the perennially-intense Malcolm McDowell, it's actually the remake that's "badly acted." As Oliver, John Heard strains for likability but more often comes across as broody and distant. Nominal heroine Annette O'Toole (as coworker Alice, Oliver's *human* love-interest) seems more shallow than concerned, and more doormat than character. Most damaging of all, Nastassia Kinski lacks the depth necessary for such a complex role as Irena. Kinski's general blankness simply can't navigate her character's arc—from naïve to coquettish to terrified to menacing.

Well-produced and atmospherically photographed, the film features two very different transformation scenes, both equally effective. The first plays out as Oliver enters a darkened room to find Paul sitting in a corner's semi-darkness. Paul, his shrouded features indistinct but seeming strange, gives a strangled shout and begins to crawl forward, his eyes glowing. With the camera overhead, he passes into deep shadow and emerges the other side as a panther (his clothes having conveniently vanished). The second metamorphosis comes when Irena finally makes love with Oliver and transforms afterwards. We see her first writhe in an interim stage, her face distorted and angular; then her head gruesomely splits open as the panther beneath the skin bursts forth and roars. Though one is subtle and one grotesque, both transformations remain startling in their suddenness and terrifying in their execution.

Unlike the highly suggestive—and successful—original, the more explicit *Cat People* remake failed to connect with the public. Shot from April to June on location in New Orleans in 1981, *Cat People* cost $18 million to produce but grossed a mere $7 million domestically. Perhaps, as Val Lewton posited back in 1942, sometimes less truly *is* more.

In 2009, Quentin Tarantino coopted David Bowie's haunting "Cat People Theme" for a pivotal sequence in his brilliantly imaginative, Oscar-nominated *Inglourious Basterds*.

With quotes from: "The Cat People Conspiracy," by Ed Naha, *Starlog* 59.

The Catman of Paris

(1946; Republic) Director: Lesley Selander.

Paris, 1895: When a prominent police archivist is murdered, "clawed to ribbons as if by a cat," the Prefect of Police (Fritz Feld) immediately concludes that it's a "supernatural matter" and a "catman" is on the prowl. "You may scoff," he tells his doubting colleague, "but you cannot alter the fact that human beings have been known to take the forms of certain animals—for example, werewolves and vultures and cats. There have been cat-people. These things are a matter of record." (Hmmm, one wonders what sort of "records" are kept by the Paris police.) When his compatriot objects with, "Oh, not record, merely legend," the Prefect shoots back, "Practically the same thing." So much for the science of police detection in the 1890s! In any case, suspicion falls on famous author Charles Regnier (Carl Esmond), whose latest book eerily mirrors facts from a sealed case upon which the archivist was working. Charles, who "had a long siege of tropical fever" during his recent exotic travels, begins suffering blackouts (presaged by a montage of blowing snow, lightning and stormy seas—all photographed in negative), and after his bloody gloves are found alongside the murdered body of his clinging fiancée, whom he'd attempted to break away from, it becomes clear that he is indeed the Catman of Paris, and he goes on the run.

Given its genteel time period and setting (all high-society drawing rooms and elegant cafés), and the well-mannered cast of characters, the horror quotient in *The Catman of Paris* remains rather neutered, relying on shadow and suggestion, and not even revealing the titular terror until the final reel. Still, this being a Republic film (home of the action-packed serial of the 1940s and early '50s), it offers a few instances of slam-bang action, including a vigorous barroom brawl (1890s style) and a high-speed carriage chase culminating in a fairly spectacular crash. And at a mere 65 minutes, it has little time to wear out its welcome, while providing not only a novel were-beast but a genuinely surprising twist ending.

Clad in fancy evening clothes, opera cloak and top hat, this dapper were-cat is the best dressed monster this side of a Dracula flick. Of course, we see nothing of this creature—apart from one slightly hairy hand—until the climactic confrontation. Finally revealed, the catman cuts a striking, if subtle, figure of menace, with heavy eyebrows, satanic facial hair, pointy ears, and fangs, not to mention some wicked-looking elongated fingernails. Though a supposed cat-creature, he apparently can curb his animal instincts, as he carefully selects his victims and behaves quite normally—at least until close enough to use his claws.

The explanation for this catman remains rather vague—something to do with reincarnation dating all the way back to ancient Rome, and periodic appearances of the creature during certain "astrological conjunctions." At the close of the film, the dying catman speaks. "Death has been denied me," he says, "until I have fulfilled the cycle of my destiny. This is my last reincarnation." In other words, it's his ninth and final life.

Though it turned out he did an adequate job, *Catman of Paris* director Lesley Selander seemed an unlikely candidate to pilot a were-beast movie, having made something of a name for himself as a low-budget *Western* specialist. Born in turn-of-the-century Los Angeles, Selander entered the film industry right out of high school as a lab technician. Graduating from assistant to full cameraman, and then to assistant director on films like *The Thin Man* (1934) and *Night at the Opera* (1935), Selander, with the backing of his friend Buck Jones, finally got his chance to direct features in 1936. Over the next thirty-one years he helmed over 150 films, most of them oaters (often starring Jones, Tim Holt, or William Boyd—Selander directed *twenty-five* "Hopalong Cassidy" features!). Selander also worked extensively in television, supervising 60 *Lassie* episodes, and becoming a regular fixture on *Laramie* and *Cannonball*. Though he rarely left the cinematic saddle, Selander did hitch up to the horror/sci-fi post on two other occasions—for *The Vampire's Ghost* (1946) and *Flight to Mars* (1951). He died in 1979 at age 79.

Chillerama

(2011; Image) Directors: Adam Green, Joe Lynch, Adam Rifkin, Tim Sullivan.

Here's a cinematic first—a were*bear*. But this unique werebeast is not merely a man who transforms into a grizzly, but a man who turns into a slightly bear-faced (well, dark nose, hairy visage and fangs, anyway), black-leather-and-studs-wearing gay "daddy bear"! "I Was a Teenage Werebear," the second story of this four-part comic-horror anthology, is about a "closeted kid who meets these other closeted kids, who when aroused turn into leather daddy werebears." (In the gay community, the term "bear" is slang for big, hairy, burly men.) Director Tim Sullivan (*2001 Maniacs*), an openly gay filmmaker, decided to make a gay-themed camp horror-musical. Riffing on everything from *Rebel Without a Cause* and *Grease* to *The Lost Boys* and *The Twilight Saga*, "Teenage Werebear" tells the tale of high-schooler Ricky (played by gay porn star Sean Paul Lockhart, aka Brent Corrigan, dubbed "the Traci Lords of the gay industry"), who, confused over his sexual identity, falls in with a trio of local toughs. More than merely leather-jacketed teddy boys, they're also werebears, and their leader passes on the curse (blessing?) to Ricky when he literally bites him on the ass during a wrestling bout. Ricky must then deal with his "urges," deciding to defend the rest of his schoolmates against the violent werebears and so promote acceptance for all. Filled with songs like "Love Bit Me on the Ass" and "Do the Werebear (and Let the Werebear Do You)," this segment offers clever homages (including directly referencing *The Wolf Man* when "Nurse Maleva" informs Ricky, "Where I am from there is an old saying: 'Even a boy who thinks he's straight yet shaves his balls by night / May become a werebear

The elegant *Catman of Paris* (Carl Esmond).

when the hormones rage and the latent urge takes flight"), over-the-top gore, and chuckles galore along with its well-disguised plea for sexual tolerance.

Chillerama began with filmmaker friends Adam Rifkin and Tim Sullivan deciding to make a horror anthology called *Famous Monsters of Filmland*, to be based on the classic monster mag they both loved growing up. Each short would be dedicated to a different era: "The Diary of Anne Frankenstein" (the 1940s), "I Was a Teenage Vampire" (the 1950s), "Zombie Drive-In" (the 1960s) and "Werewolf of Alcatraz" (the 1970s). But a deal with the magazine fell through, and the idea was shelved until the pair met fellow filmmakers Adam Green and Joe Lynch. The quartet then decided to revive the notion as an independent production, with budget constraints necessitating a few changes. "Werewolf of Alcatraz" was dropped in favor of "Wadzilla"; "I Was a Teenage Vampire" became "I Was a Teenage Werebear"; and "Zombie Drive-In" morphed into the "Zom-B-Movie" wraparound story (set at a drive-in on its closing night). A fifth segment, the totally tasteless and thankfully truncated "Deathication," was also added as a kicker for "Zom-B-Movie."

In describing the finished film, co-director Adam Green noted that "Adam Rifkin is doing a segment called '*Wadzilla*,' which is basically a take on '50s giant monster movies. It's [about] a guy that goes to get his sperm count raised, and it creates one big sperm that attacks New York City. Tim Sullivan is doing something called '*I was a Teenage Werebear…*' and his has kind of a *Rebel Without a Cause*–type feel. My segment is called '*The Diary of Anne Frankenstein.*' It's a black and white movie about Hitler trying to create the perfect killing machine to win the war…. The final one is being done by Joe Lynch. His is like a zombie movie with a twist—they're more like sex zombies than zombies that just want to eat you."

With its obvious affection for both the horror genre and drive-in milieu, wacky and often dead-on satire, and clever homages coming fast and furious, *Chillerama* is what a Troma film might look like with more talent, more wit and more budget. And while some might dismiss this as merely an amalgam of bad taste, those with an appreciation of outré humor, meta-cinema, and the nostalgic drive-in experience will pump their fist with delight—just like the faux audience at *Chillerama*'s clever film-within-a-film finale.

With quotes from: "Is Hollywood Ready for a Gay Male Adult Actor in Mainstream Roles?" by Lee Stranahan, *The Huffington Post*; "*Hatchet 2* Director Adam Green on His New Anthology Movie Chillerama," by Clark Collis, *Entertainment Weekly*.

Conan the Barbarian

(1982; Universal) Director: John Milius.

Based on the popular character created by 1930s pulp-fiction writer Robert E. Howard, *Conan the Barbarian* is certainly the biggest-budgeted, and arguably the best, sword-and-sorcery film ever made. Filming at Shepperton Studios in England and on location in Spain lasted five months, with more than 1500 extras to add that epic feel. A single temple set cost $350,000 to construct, while Conan's two swords (wielded by an up-and-coming Arnold Schwarzenegger) cost $10,000 each. Then there was the 36-foot-long mechanical giant snake which set the production back a cool twenty grand. The movie made Schwarzenegger a bankable star (and increased his personal bank account by $250,000).

The simple (though sprawling) story sees evil sorcerer Thulsa Doom (James Earl Jones) and his band of savage warriors decimate a village in the north, killing all the adults and enslaving the children. One such child, Conan, grows to become a mighty gladiator (Schwarzenegger). Escaping his enslavement, he joins forces with a pair of thieves and a friendly wizard to seek revenge on Thulsa Doom, who now leads a powerful snake cult intent on controlling the known world.

Among the evil sorcerer's powers are hypnotic mind control and the ability to transform himself into a man-sized snake (which he does at about the 90 minute mark in order to flee an attack on his throne room by Conan and co.). In a simple but visually convincing (and exceedingly creepy) sequence, Thulsa Doom's face appears to elongate (an effect achieved by pushing against the inside of a very lifelike James Earl Jones rubber mask), his hands draw up into the sleeves of his robe, and an oversized snake head sits beneath his elaborate headdress. Now a big boa constrictor, he slithers down the throne to escape through a small opening in the wall behind. (The next we see of Thulsa Doom he's back in human guise.)

Costing a hefty-for-the-time $20 million, *Conan* cleaved a profitable path through the box office, taking in nearly $69 million worldwide. With ancillary rentals and sales, that figure rose to over $300 million over the next 25 years. An inferior (and snake-less) sequel, *Conan the Destroyer*, was released in 1984.

Cult of the Cobra

(1955; Universal International) Director: Francis D. Lyon.

Six G.I.s sightseeing in Burma (in 1945, the day before they're discharged), secretly observe a meeting of "Lamians"—the sinister and secret Cult of the Cobra. Inadvertently disrupting the ceremony, the soldiers flee, and an angry high priest (an unbilled Edward C. Platt) vows that the Cobra Goddess will strike them down. The men return to Manhattan, where one (Marshall Thompson) falls for a strangely-accented neighbor (Faith Domergue), who turns out to be a Lamian capable of transforming herself into a venomous cobra—in which guise she disposes of the interlopers one by one. As Paul (Richard Long) tells the others, "For thousands of years people have believed in metamorphosis. You can laugh if you want to, but the changing of man into an animal is part of the folklore of many countries." Indeed.

Heavy on atmosphere and strong on suggestion (the attacks consist of a cobra shadow rising up over the victim and some snake's-eye-view shots, including an imaginative distorted "bubble" effect borrowed from 1953's *It Came from Outer Space* to simulate snake-vision), *Cult* tries hard to emulate the Val Lewton films of the Forties—but doesn't quite succeed. With a more prosaic script that lacks the adult, sexual undercurrents of the Lewton classics (like *Cat People*) and rather bland characters (played by a group of rather bland actors destined for careers in television), *Cult of the Cobra* stands as a serviceable but unremarkable horror entry from Universal in the sci-fi-heavy 1950s.

"For hundreds of years," intones the money-hungry turncoat Lamian who takes the soldiers to the secret ceremony, "there have been those in every generation who have the power to change from humans into snakes. These are used as the instruments of the cult's vengeance." As this shapeshifting "instrument," Faith Domergue tries hard to evoke the right blend of beauty, exoticism and mysticism. She even becomes convincingly conflicted about her "mission" when she experiences real feelings towards Marshall Thompson's character, but it's too little and too late to make much of an impact. It takes over an hour for the film to offer us a first transformation, with this miraculous occurrence revealed merely in silhouette, as her shadow on the wall changes—via a simple dissolve—into that of a cobra. Though perhaps on the coy side, such a simple technique works far better than the sole on-screen transformation, which occurs at film's end when the dead snake unconvincingly dissolves, accompanied by a shimmering light, into the form of the woman—complete with fancy evening gown, shiny jewelry, and satin wrap intact.

True to the movie's tale of a "curse," two of the film's protagonists, Richard Long and David Janssen, died young; while two others, Thompson and Jack Kelly, didn't exactly live to a ripe old age either. (Then again, you could make those same TV star/early grave statements about the actor who *invoked* the curse, Ed Platt, who co-starred on *Get Smart* and died in his 50s).

Curse of the Black Widow

(1977; ABC-TV) Alternate Title: *Love Trap*; Director: Dan Curtis.

Private investigator Mark Higby (Tony Franciosa) becomes drawn into a series of bizarre murders of men in which the victims are "completely drained of blood" and injected with spider venom through two huge puncture wounds. The killings seem to revolve around the Lockridge family, particularly fraternal twin sisters Leigh (Donna Mills) and Laura (Patty Duke Astin). Higby's investigation reveals that back in 1947 the twins' mother had survived a plane crash that killed their father, only to give birth to the girls in the wilderness. Before being rescued, however, one of the infants had been bitten numerous times by spiders. But which twin might be involved—and who is the mysterious dark-haired, heavily-accented beauty seen before each attack?

At the center of this film's web sits one of the most unusual were-beasts ever seen on the screen: a were-spider. Spiders (and insects) invoke unreasoning fear in many people. (This terror of the eight-legged even made Stephen King's list of ten key fears at the heart of horror fiction and cinema: "fear of the dark, fear of 'squishy' things, fear of deformity, fear of snakes, fear of rats, fear of closed-in spaces, fear of insects and spiders, fear of death, fear of other people, and fear for someone.") The film ties its unique were-creature to Native American legend. As Higby reads from a book, "Some Northern California Indians believed it was a curse of some kind transmitted down through the female line. It may lie dormant for years until triggered by a certain kind of spider venom. Once bitten by the spider, the woman periodically, but only during the cycle of the full moon, makes the transformation into an incredibly large spider." Unfortunately, a television budget precluded any elaborate on-camera metamorphosis, and director Dan Curtis must make do with a tight close-up of a woman's eye as the iris takes on a bizarre hue, and shapes within it appear to swirl and move, before the camera shifts to an eight-legged (or, in this case, eight-eyed—one scene has an astounded Higby pointing out how a black widow has "eight eyes") p.o.v. shot of the terrified victim du jour. Higby also learns that "the legend says they are virtually indestructible while in the form of a spider. Nothing can kill them—except fire." Cue the predictable climactic conflagration.

Competently directed (Dan Curtis knew his way around a television camera, having produced or directed, or both, such tele-classics as *The Night Stalker* and *Trilogy of Terror*), atmospherically photographed (the spider's cobwebbed lair, strewn with corpses both skeletal and fresh, is like a living nightmare), and well-acted, the movie's true *Curse* stems from its sluggish pacing and meandering script, with Higby continually trying to discover various events and details that were long ago made obvious to the viewer. This becomes doubly disappointing when considering that one of the film's two screenwriters, Robert Blees (who adapted his own story, with help from later Oscar-winner Earl Wallace [1985's *Witness*], into the teleplay), had earlier penned a classic 1950s Big Bug movie in *The Black Scorpion* (1957), as well as two other genre winners, *Dr. Phibes Rises Again* and *Frogs* (both 1972). Then there's the giant arachnid. While the grotesque creature (seen only at film's end) looks terrifying enough when emerging from the shadows and advancing towards the camera, once completely out in the open, it looks—and acts (given the way it seems to float about, obviously on wires)—like an oversized balloon prop.

The excellent cast do what they can with what they're given, particularly Tony Franciosa as the likable "hero" Higby (whose revolted reactions to normal-sized spiders, much less gigantic ones, are anything *but* heroic); and the comical chemistry between Higby and his dubious Girl Friday "Flaps" (Roz Kelly) enlivens some of the more mundane moments.

With a tighter script and some better effects work, *Curse of the Black Widow* might have become a made-for-TV terror classic from the halcyon tele-terror days of the 1970s. As is, it's merely a sometimes diverting, sometimes desultory throwback to '50s B-monster movies

Though not as goofy looking as this ad might suggest, the oversized were-spider afflicted with the *Curse of the Black Widow* remains less than convincing when it finally rears its ugly eight-eyed head.

(but with one last clever coda that could only come from the more nihilistic 1970s).

With quotes from: "Why We Crave Horror Movies," by Stephen King, in *The Prose Reader: Essays for Thinking, Reading and Writing, 6th Edition.*

Death Curse of Tartu

(1967; Thunderbird International Pictures) Director: William Grefé.

Written (in 24 hours!) and directed (in seven days for $27,000!!) by William Grefé, the man who brought us *Stanley* (1972) and *Mako: The Jaws of Death* (1976), not to mention *Tartu*'s co-feature, *Sting of Death* (about a jellyfish-man!!!), this Florida-lensed indy follows a group of archeology students into the Everglades to excavate an ancient Seminole Indian burial site. "My grandfather and the elder members of my tribe say that 400 years ago a witchdoctor named Tartu had power to turn himself into a wild creature," warns their native guide. "When he died, he swore if anyone would disturb the burial ground he would change himself into a wild beast and kill them." And Tartu proceeds to do just that—as a snake, alligator and shark(!).

Composed mostly of lengthy sequences of canoeing, airboating and hiking through the 'Glades, *Tartu* sports so much padding it could play in the NFL. The amateurish performances by a cast of unknowns, and the less-than-scintillating dialogue ("Man, this is groovy," enthuses one student when they find a carved stone tablet), do nothing to alleviate the tedium. At an hour and twenty-three minutes, *Death Curse of Tartu* is about an hour too long, its pace as sluggish as an Everglade current.

Devil's Partner

(1961; Filmgroup) Director: Charles R. Rondeau.

Filmed in 1958, this low-budget independent horror film didn't see release until 1961 when Roger and Gene Corman's Filmgroup acquired it as double-feature support for their *Creature from the Haunted Sea*. Though small scale, the rather eerie and well acted (and refreshingly non-"scientific," given the atomic-obsessed times) *Devil's Partner* actually proved superior to its better-known co-feature.

In the desert town of Furnace Flats (population 1505), an old man sells his soul to the Devil (by signing a goat's skin in blood) and then drops dead. Soon after, the old coot's nephew, Nick (Ed Nelson), arrives to take possession of his uncle's rundown shack and ingratiate himself with the locals. Despite the 100 degree heat, the handsome, charming Nick never breaks a sweat, and it quickly becomes apparent that Nick is actually the old man made younger through his diabolical pact. His powers allow him to force a man's dog to attack its owner, and to transform himself (off-screen) into a stallion to trample the town drunk (who's seen too much) or become a rattlesnake to menace the film's nominal hero. Nick accomplishes these feats by sacrificing a goat and daubing the blood on the magical hexagon he's painted on the shack floor. Like the lycanthrope legends of the Middle Ages, his metamorphic powers arise from Satanic witchcraft.

The first (and only) were-beast double feature: *Death Curse of Tartu*, featuring a shapeshifting witch-doctor who transforms into snake, alligator and shark(!); and *Sting of Death*, about a jellyfish-man(!!).

Director Charles Rondeau made only a handful of low-budget features (with *Devil's Partner* his only horror entry) before turning to television, where he forged an extensive twenty-year career helming episodes of everything from *77 Sunset Strip* and *Bonanza* to *Wonder Woman* and *B.J. and the Bear*. *Devil's Partner* star Ed Nelson (who receives a special "Introducing" credit—despite the fact he'd played significant roles in nearly a dozen films to this point, including *Attack of the Crab Monsters*, *Invasion of the Saucer-Men*, *Night of the Blood Beast* and *The Brain Eaters*) characterized Rondeau as a "big guy, pretty much of a bullshitter [*laughs*]," but here Rondeau cuts through the bull to deliver an atmospheric, intimate little supernatural thriller. Though perhaps predictable, the various earnest, likable players, including Nelson, Jean Allison and Edgar Buchanan, make it a painless seventy-minute time-killer. While it's never going to drive such superior Satanic fare as *The Seventh Victim*, *Rosemary's Baby*, or even *The Devil's Rain* from one's mind, you could do far worse than to shake hands with the *Devil's Partner*.

With quotes from: *Attack of the Monster Movie Makers*, by Tom Weaver.

47 Ronin

(2013; Universal) Director: Carl Rinsch.

Inspired by the real-life Japanese story of a group of early 18th century master-less samurai who banded together to avenge their lord, this big-budget American iteration filmed in Hungary, England and Japan stars Keanu Reeves as Kai, an outcast half-breed raised by a group of magic-wielding forest "demons" who imbue Kai with amazing fighting skills. When Kai flees his otherworldly life, he is taken in by the local lord. But during a visit by the Shogun, Kai's master is tricked by sorcery into perpetrating a dishonorable act, for which the lord must commit seppuku (ritual suicide). A year later, the lord's former samurai gather together, rescue Kai from his bondage (he'd been sold into slavery upon the death of his lord), and set about exacting revenge on the rival lord and his witch concubine who orchestrated their master's downfall.

Said witch, played by the beautiful Rinko Kikuchi, twice transforms into a white fox in order to spy on her master's enemies. Though the CGI animal never looks completely realistic, this doesn't detract from the notion, as it's not a "normal" fox after all (it even sports one blue and one green eye, just like the witch-woman). The sole brief transformation sequence is cleverly handled (again via CGI), with the fox trotting down a castle corridor towards the camera. As it passes under our vision and out of view behind us, its tail transforms into the trailing green robes of the witch woman, with the camera smoothly flipping upside-down to show the now-human sorceress moving off down the corridor.

Showcasing a Japan filled with magic, demons and ghosts, as well as traditional samurai and political/romantic court intrigue, the film is beautifully shot, offering impressive vistas and imaginative action that matches its fantastical creatures. Surprisingly, it did not take the expected Hollywood route and instead remained true to the chambara (sword fighting) subgenre from which it drew its inspiration, keeping the often tragic tenets of bushido, the samurai code of honor, front and center in the story. Despite much violence and deadly swordplay, the film eschews the bloody gashes and arterial spray of the typical chambara and offers little onscreen blood (no doubt to keep its PG-13 rating).

The tale of "The 47 Ronin" had been adapted to film at least half-a-dozen times in Japan, but none of them went the fantasy route like this one, nor did any of them have 175 million dollars(!) to play with. Though the movie earned $150 million worldwide, *47 Ronin* proved a financial disaster for Universal (it would have needed to make twice that just to break even), given its mammoth cost (an amazing amount of money to be entrusted to a first-time director; Carl Rinsch had only made a few shorts up to his being handed the reigns of this cinematic colossus).

Gomar: The Human Gorilla see *Night of the Bloody Apes*

La Horripilante Bestia Humana see *Night of the Bloody Apes*

Horror and Sex see *Night of the Bloody Apes*

Hyenas

(2011; Grindstone Entertainment/Lionsgate) Director: Eric Weston.

Hyenas have traditionally been looked down upon in the hierarchy of the Animal Kingdom, perhaps due to their scavenger nature (a misnomer, really, as hyenas actually kill up to 95 percent of the food they consume) or their awkward, heavy-haunch appearance. Traditionally the object of fear or loathing, hyenas seem a natural for the "were" treatment. Unfortunately, this disappointing initial dip into the were-hyena pool does the much-maligned African predator no favors, and perhaps even sinks the notion before it has a chance to swim.

After his wife and baby are killed and eaten by a band of were-hyenas on a dark road at night, Gannon (Costas Mandylor) partners with hyena hunter "Crazy Briggs" (Meshach Taylor) to track down and destroy the roving clan. With some local white and Hispanic teen gang members caught in the mix, the hunters finally trail the hyenas to their lair in an abandoned copper mine for an explosive finish.

Hyenas proves poor in all departments, from the plastic acting of heroine Amanda Aardsma ("Miss Teenage California" of 1994) to the cartoonish CGI hyenas that even the SyFy Channel would be ashamed to show. Director Eric Weston (who did far better with his only other film of note, 1981's *Evilspeak*) does little to help matters. For instance, he introduces "Crazy Briggs" by having him sit at a campfire and talk directly to the camera. This breaking of the fourth wall comes off as amateurish and hokey at best, and stupid and lazy at worst.

The nature of these bizarre beasts is explored only in one brief dialogue exchange:

BRIGGS: "I suppose you heard of a werewolf.... My ancestors tell a folk tale of these mystery beasts that lived all over Africa.... They hunt and kill humans for food."
GANNIN: "African werewolves?"
BRIGGS: "More hideous than that. These creatures live somewhere between Earth and the Underworld. Science calls them 'cryptohumans'" [a nonsensical, made-up term].

Briggs concludes, "Seems like the white slavers brought back a little bit more than they bargained for. These hyenas are looking for easier prey—the new white meat [chuckles]." While implying that the hyenas might be some form of supernatural punishment for the injustice of slavery—racial avengers, as it were—the film just as quickly drops this intriguing notion to focus on the more mundane conflict between the white and Hispanic teen gang members (though even this goes no further than some mild name-calling ["Beaners" vs.

"Crackers"] and one brief fistfight). Most curiously, since were-hyenas were apparently imported from Africa, and the condition appears to be hereditary in nature (no one is ever "turned," only eaten), it seems rather odd that the clan features only one black member…

When not yawning during the pointless, time-killing teen scenes (including a ridiculous interlude when the gang induces a new initiate to go on a literal snipe hunt), the inept monster moments will have you derisively laughing like … well, a hyena.

It Lives by Night see *The Bat People*

It's Alive see *The Bat People*

Jungle Captive

(1945; Universal) Alternate Title: *Wild Jungle Captive* (reissue title). Director: Harold Young.

In this third and final entry in Universal's Paula the Ape Woman series begun with the far better *Captive Wild Woman*, yet another mad doctor, Stendahl (Otto Kruger), steals the corpse of Paula Dupree (aka the Ape Woman) in order to test out his new technique in restoring life. It works, but Paula is in her Ape Woman form, and Stendahl, determined to make her human again, kidnaps his own female assistant to use her blood—and eventually her *brain*—in his experiments.

Though far, far better than the previous entry (the scraping-the-bottom-of-the-barrel *Jungle Woman*), the repetitive and obviously tired-out *Jungle Captive* adds nothing new to the Ape Woman mythos. In fact, Paula (played by Vicky Lane, replacing Acquanetta from the first two entries) spends most of the picture either dead or recuperating on an operating table, only getting up and about on a couple of rare occasions (to murder a dog—off-screen, and then, at the end, her own savior, the mad Stendahl) before being laid to rest (for the final time, it turns out) by a policeman's bullet. But at least we get to see her once in a while, which was not the case with the desultory *Jungle Woman*). The make-up looks menacing, and we're even treated to two transformation sequences—sort of, as both times we see only her hand change into the clawed, hairy paw of a hybrid beast, and the footage is cribbed from *Captive Wild Woman* anyway. This was the final Universal monster makeup provided by the great Jack Pierce (who created the hirsute appearances of both the *Werewolf of London* and *The Wolf Man*, not to mention the *Frankenstein* monster and *The Mummy*). The studio fired Pierce (after a quarter-century of faithful service) in 1946, largely because they felt his methods were too slow and antiquated.

Jungle Woman

(1945; Universal). Director: Reginald LeBorg.

"Venezuelan Volcano" Acquanetta returns as Paula Dupree, the Ape Woman, in this first sequel to Universal's *Captive Wild Woman*. First announced as *Jungle Queen* before morphing into *Jungle Girl*, it acquired its final moniker in February 1944 during shooting. Clumsily set up in flashback (that even features flashbacks *within* flashbacks), the story has a new (and far less mad) doctor, Dr. Fletcher (J. Caroll Naish), taking the bullet-riddled body of Cheela the ape back to his lab, where he "detects a faint respiration" and revives it. (It's sadly indicative of this shoestring production's ambition that this is simply *told* to us during a coroner's inquest rather than shown.) Soon Cheela disappears and Paula Dupree (Cheela's human form) walks out of the woods to become Fletcher's new patient. When Paula falls for Fletcher's daughter's fiancé, it brings out the beast in her, and, two attempted and one completed murders later, the Ape Woman meets her demise at Fletcher's hands.

Veteran "B" moviemaker and Universal house director Reginald LeBorg (*The Mummy's Ghost*, *Weird Woman* [both 1944], *Voodoo Island* [1957]) was less than impressed with his assignment here. "It was an atrocious script," opined LeBorg, "and a silly idea anyway. But again, I was under contract. If I had refused it, I would have been suspended without pay." LeBorg decided to go a more psychological (or "Lewtonesque," if you will) route with his new 12-day wonder, and so kept the Ape Woman completely off-screen until the final brief reveal at film's end (in which an entire coroner's inquest tramps down to the morgue to view Paula's body—only to discover the half-human/half-beast Ape Woman on the slab). "I think that was the only way to make the script palatable," said LeBorg. "I tried that especially because I think you have suspense that way. If you'd seen the Ape Woman immediately, you wouldn't care about it anymore. The story was so bad, I felt I had to do something. If I gave it away in the first reel, I would have no more picture." Of course, here LeBorg apparently forgets that the ten minutes of "flashback" footage from *Captive Wild Woman* replayed at the film's beginning does indeed feature Paula in her monstrous form. So much for "suspense." Consequently, LeBorg effectively shot his picture in the foot by keeping the movie's primary asset off-screen for the rest of the time. But LeBorg was right in one respect—after the *Captive Wild Woman* redux footage ended, he really had "no more picture."

The ten minutes of footage "borrowed" from *Captive Wild Woman* provides what little excitement this desultory sequel can muster. And until the final scene, it is only in these stolen sequences that we see Paula in either her full hirsute form (an obvious ape suit) or her impressive Jack Pierce–created were-ape makeup. This leaves only scene after scene of Fletcher trying to discover what we already know, and a mass of dull palaver to fill its hour-long running time.

In this sequel, Acquanetta finally gets to speak (she remained mute in *Captive Wild Woman*). Unfortunately, her alternately lifeless and amateurishly strident delivery makes one wish she couldn't. Of the neophyte actress, LeBorg said, "She was a beginner. It was not easy, but she was trying." But even someone of the quality of J. Carrol Naish (Academy Award nominee for both 1943's *Sahara* and 1945's *A Medal for Benny*) could do little with the desultory script. (Sample dialogue: "She isn't just an ordinary girl, she's a horrible creature.") "J. Carrol Naish," recalled Acquanetta, "was one of the nicest. It's a simple word, 'nice,' but it means a lot. He was one of the nicest persons I've ever met in my entire life. He was a gentleman, always, and he was very bright. He understood acting. He never achieved his full potential. He should have been a star." Naish went on to bigger and hairier things this same year in Universal's werewolf entry *House of Frankenstein*, in which he created a genuinely moving portrayal in the form of the sympathetic hunchback Daniel.

With its lack of action, lack of were-monster (and nary a transformation in sight), and lack of quality in general, *Jungle Woman* appears to be an instance of Universal just flogging a dead horse (or, in this case, Ape Woman). Apparently said horse wasn't *quite* dead, however, as *Jungle Captive*, the third and final entry in the "Paula, the Ape Woman" series, followed in 1945.

With quotes from: *Universal Horrors*, by Michael Brunas, John Brunas, and Tom Weaver; "Interview: Reginald LeBorg," by Bernie O'Heir, *Cinemacabre* 7; "The Exotic Lives of Acquanetta," by John and Micael Brunas, *Scarlet Street* 15.

Kvitebjørn Kong Valemon see *The Polar Bear King*

Love Trap see *Curse of the Black Widow*

The Mummy and the Curse of the Jackals

(1969/86; Vega International Pictures/Academy Home Entertainment)

Shot in 1969 but unreleased (for reasons obvious to anyone who's ever seen it) until the I'll-stock-anything-on-tape video store boom of the mid–80s, the derivative, nonsensical, amateurish *Mummy and the Curse of the Jackals* stars low-rent leading man Anthony Eisley as a Las Vegas archeologist who discovers two Egyptian mummies—one a still-beautiful princess and the other a '40s Universal knockoff named "Sirahk" ("Kharis" spelled backwards). Eisley succumbs to the titular "curse" and transforms into a jackal-man during the full moon. The princess revives, as does the mummy, who goes on a brief rampage before the jackal-man and the bandaged one face off in a laughable showdown.

Featured in a couple of scenes is John Carradine collecting yet another I've-gotta-support-my-ex-wives paycheck. Lon Chaney, Jr., reportedly turned down the role of the mummy. Watching the Kharis clone shambling down a crowded Vegas street, with bemused bystanders gawking, laughing and even following behind the silly-suited actor, it's little wonder why.

Though *Jackals* offers the occasional unintentional chuckle ("We can't just stand by and let a 4,000-year-old mummy and a jackal-man take over the city," deadpans Carradine), its dull pacing and incoherence (reportedly, it was never even finished) makes it tough going even for the so-bad-it's-good crowd. Worst of all, the were-jackal appears more like a poodle in need of a groomer than a demonic denizen of the Egyptian underworld. Veteran B-Western director Oliver Drake "was quite senile at the time," related Eisley. "The director was sort of losing his faculties, and I realized after a few days that he really didn't know what the hell was going on at all times." And neither will the viewer.

With quotes from: *Interviews with B Science Fiction and Horror Movie Makers*, by Tom Weaver.

Night of the Bloody Apes

(1968; Cinematográfica Calderon/Jerand Films; Mexico) Original Language Title: *La Horripilante Bestia Humana*. Alternate Titles: *Gomar: The Human Gorilla; Horror and Sex.* Director: René Cardona.

A scientist (Armando Silvestre) places the heart and blood of a gorilla into the body of his dying son Julio (Augustin Martinez Solares), resulting in Julio's transformation into a hideous ape-man (looking more Neanderthal than simian). While the father searches for a cure, Julio escapes and goes on a sex-murder rampage ("the lust of a man in the body of a beast!" as the film's trailer so delicately puts it).

The pajama-clad were-ape from the Mexican oddity *Night of the Bloody Apes*.

Though this were-gorilla ("a horrible half-beast, half-human," proclaims the investigating police lieutenant hero) results not from a supernatural curse but from science (a point hammered home by the inclusion of some in-your-face real-life heart surgery footage), Julio reverts back to his human form but transforms twice more to continue his brutal, bestial pursuits.

One of the most unusual Latino immigrants to slip past the border guards of 1960s cinema (though released in Mexico in 1968, the film didn't reach American theaters until 1972), *Night of the Bloody Apes* possessed all the peculiar proclivities of Mexi-movies of the time (the heroine, for instance, is a mask-wearing professional *wrestler*) while also offering a shockingly sleazy sex-and-gore quotient unheard of in the more innocent black-and-white south-of-the-border efforts made earlier in the decade. The heroine displays her charms in not one but *two* gratuitous stepping-out-of-the-shower scenes. Then there's the gore. The angry ape-man gruesomely rips out a victim's throat; gouges out a man's eyeball with this thumb; repeatedly stabs a man in the chest with the victim's own knife; literally rips the head off another (in extreme close-up); and tears off a person's scalp. (The cheeky promotional department suggested theaters give fans the opportunity to pick out their own free miniature rubber organs in the lobby. Now *that's* entertainment.) It all serves to make this Ed-Wood-Meets-Herschell-Gordon-Lewis-in-Tijuana travesty a risible yet oddly compelling bit of Mexi-trash (though the production values here—meager as they are—appear miles above anything enjoyed by Wood or Lewis). And, like so much of the output of those two no-budget "auteurs," *Night of the Bloody Apes* offers enough eccentricities, shocks and bizarre ineptitude to hold one's interest. Though far from a good movie, *Night of the Bloody Apes* remains a bloody entertaining one.

The Polar Bear King

(1991; Capella International; Norway/Germany/Sweden) Original Language Title: *Kvitebjørn Kong Valemon*. Director: Ola Solum.

Based on Norwegian folklore, the Scandinavian production *The Polar Bear King* announces its fairy-tale intentions from its opening narration: "Once upon a time, far far away, a magical adventure took place in a world of eternal ice and snow known as 'the Winterland.'" There the king's 17-year-old daughter (Maria Bonnevie) dreams (literally) of a flower-filled land of "eternal warmth and fertility." In this very place, "Summerland," lives Prince Valemon (Tobias Hoesl), newly made king after his father's death. An evil sorceress (Anna-Lotta Larsson) appears and demands to be made his bride so that together they might rule the world. When Valemon refuses, the witch places a curse upon him: "I'll turn you into a huge wild bear for seven years. Only at midnight will you be human. *No* woman will be your bride; who could love such an animal? But you mustn't be seen as a man. If you are, then you will be mine—forever!" With that, she disappears in a puff of smoke, and the young king is now a fierce-looking polar bear, growling and pawing in protest. Soon, "Valemon desperately journeyed northward to the Winterland, searching for someone who could love and understand a polar bear," as the narrator informs us. Encountering the Winterland princess, he tells her of his woes (yes, even in polar bear form he can speak), and she falls in love with him. Finally overcoming her father the king's opposition, she rides south to Summerland on the bear's back to take up residence in his castle as his bride. Over the years he comes to her every night at midnight (making sure that she never sees him as a man in the light), resulting in the birth of three children. But when her curiosity proves too much and she finally gazes upon her husband's sleeping face three months shy of the seven-year-deadline, the witch reappears to whisk Valemon to her clifftop castle in preparation to make him her own. The princess, aided by such magical items as scissors that create clothes, a tablecloth that conjures food, and boots that allow the wearer to walk straight up sheer walls, must then try to reach the castle, stop the upcoming wedding (apparently bigamy was not a consideration in Summerland), and reunite with her love. It all culminates in the expected "happily ever after" ending.

Some beautiful winter landscapes and settings, including the princess' village, with its ice-block gateway and sinuous, lantern-lit pathway, and the amazingly realistic animatronic polar bear (courtesy of Jim Henson's Creature Shop), with its expressive articulated mouth and eyes, are about all the film has to offer the discerning viewer. Neither the script nor actors add anything to the simplistic fairy-tale characters (good princess, evil witch, patient prince, loving father). As a consequence, anyone over the age of 10 will have difficulty relating to, or becoming involved with, the tale.

Apart from the impressive bear, the effects (what there are of them) prove as simplistic as the characters. Even the witch's much-anticipated demise proves anti-climactic, as she simply fades away in a less-than-explosive puff of smoke. Most disappointingly, the filmmakers never even attempt to show the man-bear's nightly transformation.

Despite the story's potentially dark themes, the movie takes a light approach, eschewing any potential for horror or suspense in even the most bizarre and disturbing aspects of the tale (including an appearance by the Devil himself, who looks like a goofy fop in a silly hat). Consequently, *The Polar Bear King* remains rather uninvolving for anyone whose age has reached double digits.

The picture also downplays the tragic, even horrific alienation inherent in its central concept by allowing the beast the powers of speech (and so letting him readily communicate—and connect—with other people), and also by having the princess instantly fall in love with the big bear (literally recognizing in his eye—through a cheesy superimposition—the flower-filled land of her dreams). Without the tension of possible misunderstanding and loss, the story becomes a mere rote tale of the two lovers waiting out the seven years. Ultimately, despite its novel (and convincingly conceived) polar were-bear, this shallow and juvenile *King* wears merely a paper crown.

The Reptile

(1966; Hammer/Seven Arts; UK) Director: John Gilling.

Something of a yardstick for were-snake movies, *The Reptile* adds some welcome Hammer polish to an admittedly suspect subset. Shot nearly back-to-back with, and on the same sets as, *The Plague of the Zombies* (with some of the same cast and crew, including director John Gilling), *The Reptile* (like most Hammer productions) looks far more sumptuous than its low (100,000 pound) budget should allow.

Newlyweds Harry and Valerie Spalding (Ray Barrett and Jennifer Daniel) inherit a cottage in a remote Cornish village following the mysterious death of Harry's brother, Charles. The surly locals put it down to "the Black Death" (so named because of the victims' darkened, swollen faces—which strangely echo the effects of a King Cobra bite). The Spalding cottage sits adjacent to the sprawling estate of the reclusive Dr. Franklyn (Noel Willman), who seems overprotective of (and perhaps abusive toward) his adult daughter Anna (Jacqueline Pearce). Harry ultimately learns—much to his regret—that Anna is a shape-shifting snake-woman, victim of a curse inflicted by a snake-worshipping Malaysian sect, the "Ourang Sancto," who objected to Dr. Franklyn's investigation of its rituals.

Structured very much like a mystery for its first hour, *The Reptile* suffers from a slow pace, as Harry and co. uncover clues about the sinister deaths. Fortunately, it picks up around the hour mark once the snake-woman finally comes into full view and, excepting a late-hour fillip in which Franklyn feels obliged to engage in some lengthy soul-baring exposition, races towards its fiery conclusion.

The snake-woman's first appearance in abrupt close-up, accompanied by her hideous hissing, highlights Roy Ashton's impressive makeup—the scaly, papery, greenish skin; round, lidless, reptilian eyes; and prominent, venom-dripping fangs, her tongue moving rapidly between them. She strikes quickly, then sinuously backs away through a door, hissing all the while. It's a startling introduction to cinema's most effective were-snake.

We never see the actual metamorphosis, however (perhaps for budgetary reasons)—she's either Anna or the snake-woman, appearing suddenly to deadly effect. And just what triggers the transformation remains a mystery, though one suspects the vindictive, sinister servant (referred to only as "Malay") has something to do with it.

"A lot of research went into the appearance of the Reptile," recounted Ashton (who five years earlier had transformed Oliver Reed into a savage lycanthrope for *The Curse of the Werewolf*). "Again I consulted anatomical authorities, drew snakes many times and constructed a model adapting the plate-like build-up of reptilian scales to the bones of the human head. There is a clear similarity of the human head to the structure of a snake's skull." The makeup, which "took, I should say, one hour to apply," was quite an ordeal for Jacqueline Pearce. "It was not fun," complained the actress. "It was very painful and uncomfortable, as well as being very creepy and claustrophobic."

More remarkable even than Roy Ashton's unique, fierce-looking snake-woman is the marked xenophobia slithering throughout Anthony Hinds' (aka John Elder) screenplay. Villagers shun outsiders and complain that their Cornish hamlet was a delightful place until Those People arrived with their foreign ways. Dr. Franklyn brought disaster upon himself and his daughter by investigating, and eventually adopting, foreign customs and beliefs. And the "Malay" lurking about Franklyn's manor house making threatening statements such as "You will be punished to the end of your miserable life" looms as the story's true villain, an inscrutable Asian fiend who takes sadistic pleasure in the prolonged tormenting of the doctor and his daughter. As a perhaps unconscious reaction to the radicalism and sweeping social changes of the Sixties, this reactionary *Reptile* can be seen as a cinematic snake in the grass.

With quotes from: *Greasepaint and Gore*, by Bruce Sachs and Russell Wall.

Roger Corman Presents: The Wasp Woman see *The Wasp Woman*, 1995

Scooby-Doo on Zombie Island

(1998; Hanna-Barbera/Warner Bros.)

The first in a long line of direct-to-video Scooby-Doo cartoon features, *Scooby-Doo on Zombie Island* sees Scooby and Shaggy reunite with Fred, Daphne, and Velma to help Daphne, now a successful television reporter, find some *real* ghosts for her new TV show. After several supernatural menaces turn out to be phonies (in a clever and concise montage), just like in their old mystery-busting days, the gang journeys to New Orleans and the surrounding bayou country, where they learn of the private Moonscar Island and its supposedly haunted house on a pepper plantation (which gives rise to all manner of hot pepper gags involving the ever-hungry Shaggy and Scooby). The island's owner, Simone (voiced by Adrienne Barbeau), and her servant Lena offer the ghost-hunters their hospitality, and soon the "Mystery, Inc." gang are enmeshed in genuine ghostly goings-on, as well as several confrontations with *zombies* who rise from their watery graves. These walking cadavers (of pirates, Confederate soldiers, and even some camera-packing tourists), though frightening, turn out to be merely the undead victims of Simone and Lena, who are 200-year-old *werecats*. Two centuries ago, a group of pirates invaded the island, leading to the demise of nearly all the colonists there, a group of peaceful, cat-god worshiping farmers. Survivors Simone and Lena prayed to their cat-god for the means to exact revenge. "We became cat creatures," reveals Simone, "and destroyed the pirates." Ever since, however, "every harvest moon I must drain the life force of victims lured to my island to preserve my immortality."

The werecat duo transform into their cat-creature guises at will, and take two distinct forms. The first, in which they can still speak as humans, combines their human faces with cat features—pointed ears, cat's eyes, fangs, claws and a tail. Once they go full-on cat-creature, however, fur sprouts over their entire bodies, and their heads become those of evil-looking felines. With the zombies' help (they have risen to try and warn the gang of the life-stealing shapeshifters) and the use of some voodoo dolls (Simone and Lena utilize the magical dolls to imprison and control their intended victims), the gang prevents the werecats from absorbing the needed life force, ending their existence and the curse.

With some mobile, atmospheric animation (featuring better backgrounds than those seen in the original series) and mood-enhancing music, the film significantly ups the creep factor while still focusing on the comical antics of the beloved characters. Though for the first half the self-aware movie entertainingly plays with the *Scooby-Doo* trope of the expected villain-in-a-mask denouement, it's still somewhat

Ad for Hammer's were-snake opus *The Reptile*.

disconcerting for those of us who grew up watching "those meddling kids" unmask villain after villain on Saturday mornings to see them finally meet some *real* monsters.

The Secret of Roan Inish

(1995; Samuel Goldwyn Company; USA/Ireland) Director: John Sayles.

Shortly after the close of World War II, ten-year-old Fiona (Jeni Courtney) is sent by her widower father to live with her grandparents on the west coast of Ireland. There, as she reconnects with her past, she discovers her four-year-old brother, who disappeared three years prior during an evacuation (his cradle literally floating out to sea), alive and living on the abandoned familial isle of Roan Inish, seemingly looked after by the seals inhabiting the island.

Local legend states that these animals are actually "selkies," half-human, half-seal creatures who can shed their skin to take on human form. Fiona's cousin (who some say is "tetched" in the head) tells her a story of an ancestor that one day witnessed a seal changing into a beautiful woman. Sneaking close, the young man took possession of the discarded seal skin, thereby forcing the selkie to remain a woman. They fell in love and married, and she bore him a number of children before the seal-woman inadvertently found her hidden seal skin and was drawn back to the sea as a seal.

The flashback tale of the selkie lasts only a few minutes, but the transformation scene is well-staged to show her literally peeling off her seal skin like a wetsuit, revealing the glistening naked human form beneath (or a modest portion, anyway, this being a family-friendly film).

Filled with Irish character actors acting like Irish characters, and lacking a central antagonist (much less outright villain), this *Secret* is all sweetness and leprechaun light, a near-magical celebration of the Old Ways and the Simple Man's love for, and relationship with, nature (specifically the sea). But this being a John Sayles movie (both in writing and directing), it's also a cleverly constructed, brilliantly scripted character study, one of self-discovery as the various protagonists reconnect with their roots.

The Shaggy D.A.

(1976; Buena Vista)

Rather than a best-of-show relation, this belated, ill-conceived follow-up to Disney's 1959 hit *The Shaggy Dog* turned out to be nothing more than a stray cinematic cur. Teenager Wilby Daniels from the original *Shaggy Dog* has grown up, gotten married, had a son of his own, and practices as a lawyer. Wilby (Dean Jones) decides to run against corrupt incumbent "Honest John Slade" (Keenan Wynn) for the position of District Attorney. Unfortunately, just as his campaign gets rolling, thieves steal a magical Borgia ring from the local museum—the same ring that transformed Wilby into a shaggy dog 17 years earlier. Now whenever someone reads the ring's Latin inscription aloud, Wilby turns into a sheepdog once again (inhabiting the body of the local ice cream vendor's dog, Elwood). As Wilby, his wife and young son set about trying to retrieve the ring (which changes hands several times) and stop the inconvenient transformations, Slade conspires with his criminal cohort to secure the ring himself and put an end to Wilby's campaign ... for good.

The sequel alters the shapeshifting mythology slightly from the original film, in which Wilby read the magical inscription once and then suffered from random temporary transformations (lasting several hours) until freed from the spell by performing an heroic deed. Here the grown Wilby changes whenever someone reads the inscription aloud, with the metamorphosis lasting only a few minutes. The notion of Wilby "possessing" an existing dog's body, however, remains the same; Wilby sprouts increasingly hairy phases, and the real Elwood's body vanishes as Wilby takes over Elwood's form. As Wilby tries to tell his initially disbelieving wife, "There was a big shaggy dog next door and I *became* that dog."

Apart from the impressive makeup dissolves that puts the more primitive original transformation sequences to shame, *The Shaggy D.A.* is a mere flea on the back of the original. Though *The Shaggy Dog*'s broad comedy antics were anything but subtle, the tired, unfunny shenanigans perpetrated by *The Shaggy D.A.* (including a pie fight and the dog skating in a roller derby match—complete with uniform) would embarrass even a '70s sitcom. In fact, *The Shaggy D.A.*, with its cartoonish characters, silly script, and sorry slapstick, offers little more than an extended episode of *Gilligan's Island*. Dean Jones' shrill performance leaves little to hang one's dog collar on (his rather cold portrayal is a far cry from the likable Tommy Kirk of the original, or even the flustered yet well-meaning Fred MacMurray), and the supporting players add nothing. The only cast member offering any warmth at all is the desperate-to-do-*something*-with-this-awful-material Tim Conway as the hapless ice cream man whose repeated efforts to make some quick cash with "the world's only talking dog" end only in disaster.

Not only can Wilby speak in his natural human voice while in dog form (via a terrible effect which sees the same shot of the dog opening its mouth run backwards and forwards ad naseam), he can also talk with—and hear—his fellow canines. Summing up the movie's juvenile approach is a scene in which Wilby winds up at the pound with a band of other mutts who speak in *celebrity* voices! Edward G. Robinson, Peter Lorre, Mae West, Humphrey Bogart, etc., all get together to bust outta da joint. Sad. Packed with stale "comedy," with nary a fresh laugh—or thought—in sight, the hoary *Shaggy D.A.* makes the original *Shaggy Dog* look like a prize-winning pooch.

The Shaggy Dog

(1959; Buena Vista; b&w) Director: Charles Barton.

"This is a shaggy dog story," begins ubiquitous 1950s narrator Paul Frees (who also makes a rare onscreen appearance in the film as a psychiatrist). "It could have happened anywhere or to anyone." Well, anyone who stumbles across a magic ring that creates were-dogs, anyway. This live-action Disney comedy (released by the company's Buena Vista distribution arm) follows the misadventures of teenager Wilby Daniels (Disney star Tommy Kirk), who accidentally ends up with a magical ring employed by the Borgias after a visit to the local museum. Thanks to this sorcerer's bauble ("The Borgias dabbled in black magic," informs the kindly museum curator, played by the cherubic Cecil Kellaway), Wilby now periodically transforms into a Bratislavian sheepdog.

There seems to be no rhyme nor reason for just when Wilby transforms—or for how long—apart from the arbitrary dictates of the script, which includes him becoming a dog at his first formal dance, resulting in comedic hijinks; and later changing back to human at an inopportune moment when a pair of spies have just finished discussing their plans to steal an "underwater hydrogen missile" from the local munitions plant. While in dog-form, Wilby retains his full faculties, and can even speak with his own voice (resulting in a running gag involving an incredulous local beat cop). Leavening the comical antics (highlighted by the Shaggy Dog driving a hot rod down the street during a car chase) is a bit of teen romance (in which Wilby and his suave best friend vie for the favors of Francesca, the new girl on the block, whose dog's body Wilby inhabits when he transforms); a dash of chilling atmosphere at the creepy museum; a modicum of suspense via the spy plotting and capture of Wilby; and even a few surprisingly dark elements (such as when Wilby's younger brother betrays his father by refusing to corroborate the man's shaggy dog story, resulting in a near-heartbreaking reaction from Fred MacMurray; and then having the heroine's own father turn out to be a ruthless, villainous spy—therapy anyone?), *The Shaggy Dog* has a little something for everyone. Of course, it also has a painfully artificial *Leave It to Beaver* '50s sensibility, a surfeit of silly slapstick comedy, and wave after wave of even broader acting (one can't help but feel that poor Fred MacMurray, as Wilby's befuddled father, was completely wasted in his one-dimensional, double-take-filled roll of blustering victim of circumstance).

The transformations take place in stages, with Wilby's hair suddenly sporting a few tufts of dog fur, then showing his whole head (and hands) covered in sheepdog hair (with nose nicely blackened), and finally (after a shot of the real sheepdog de-materializing) displaying Wilby in full canine mode (typically bemoaning his new appearance in a mirror). "Apparently you've become involved with some old spell cast upon this ring, probably by one of the Borgias," the curator rather nonchalantly explains to the canine Wilby after his first transformation. "Shapeshifting was the medieval art of borrowing somebody else's body to live in for a while." Consequently, during those times when Wilby takes his new shape, he actually subsumes—and inhabits—the body of Francesca's real sheepdog. This offers a rather unique take on the astral projection angle of lycanthropy, with the added fillip of corporeal possession. But lest one read too much into this, remember this is, after all, merely a *Shaggy Dog* story. "An act of heroism might break the spell," adds the professor helpfully, for no earthly reason than to provide an out for Our Hero at film's end.

In trying to explain the situation to the authorities, Wilby's father exclaims, "Don't be ridiculous—my son isn't any werewolf! He's just a big, baggy, stupid-looking, shaggy dog!" Disney's ad campaign promoting their shaggy dog story as "a new kind of HORROR movie" suggests that the studio was well aware of the recent massive success of AIP's *I Was a Teenage Werewolf*. And a few rather chilling scenes in the museum, complete with low-key lighting and talk of black magic, only reinforce such a notion.

Shaggy Dog director Charles Barton made a name for himself as a comedy director at Universal in the 1940s and '50s, where he oversaw nine Abbott and Costello features, including the werewolf outing *Abbott and Costello Meet Frankenstein*, generally considered the team's best.

Costing less than a million dollars to produce, *The Shaggy Dog* grossed more than $9 million upon its initial release, making it the most successful film of the year. Surprisingly, it took Disney over a decade-and-a-half to mount a sequel, *The Shaggy D.A.* (1976).

The Shaggy Dog

(2006; Disney) Director: Brain Robbins.

Tim Allen takes over for Fred McMurray in Disney's $50 million update of their 1959 family favorite. Unfortunately, the over-ingratiating, one-note Allen makes a poor substitute for the likable McMurray. As the workaholic Deputy DA who's bitten by a 300-year-old super-intelligent Tibetan sheepdog held captive by a nefarious genetics lab, Allen begins exhibiting canine traits (scratching, panting, and chasing cats on all fours) before morphing fully into a sheep dog. Rather than exploring the terror and alienation such a metamorphosis would engender (this ain't Kafka, after all, but a kid-targeted Disney movie), the film focuses on the dog–Allen discovering just how distant he has become from his wife and children. "I'm not a bad dog," he says to himself, "but I'm a terrible man. I've *got* to make this better." While the first few transformations come unbidden, the final change from man to dog occurs when he pays a homeless man to throw a stick for him to fetch, the doggy behavior triggering the transformation. "I can't believe that worked," he marvels, without irony, as neither can we. He always reverts back to human after he sleeps or meditates (lowering his heart rate).

Saccharine and predictable, *The Shaggy Dog*'s one bright spot comes in the form of the acerbic Robert Downey, Jr., as the sinister head of the genetics lab, whose condescending comments and pointed quips ("Be back to cut you up like a birthday cake later," he tosses back over his shoulder at the captured canine at one point) remain the only truly amusing parts of the picture. Despite the fact the film was a moderate financial success, grossing $87 million worldwide, this *Shaggy Dog* is indeed just that—a dog.

Shapeshifter see Shifter

Shifter

(1999; Full Moon; Canada/Romania) Alternate Title: *Shapeshifter*. Director: Philippe Browning.

Shot in Bucharest, Romania, this family-friendly Canadian-Romanian co-production stars the never-heard-from-before-or-since Paul Nolan as the teenage Alex, who must rescue his good-guy-spy parents from the clutches of a plutonium-stealing madman while also thwarting the magical powers of the evil "Cyberwitch." Alex does so with the help of a 363-year-old man named Django with a magical rock and "glass harmonica," who brings out Alex's latent shapeshifting abilities. Alex transforms into a dog (a German shepherd), a bird, and a mythological griffin (in which form he literally flies his parents to safety). A muddled mess, with time-traveling avatars from the future, a ridiculous *Tron*-like segment in which Alex becomes "pure digital matter," and a rescue by a band of "Little People," *Shifter* gets nearly everything wrong, from the banal characters and toneless acting (apart from Catherine Blythe as the snarlingly over-the-top Cyberwitch) to the poor CGI effects and near-complete waste of the shapeshifting notion. Granted, the film is aimed at a younger audience, so one's expectations must be adjusted accordingly; but such an inclusive kitchen-sink approach should have offered at least a modicum of excitement. Unfortunately, like a poorly-baked cake with too many ingredients, *Shifter* comes out as just formless and bland.

Sleepwalkers

(1992; Columbia) Alternate Title: *Stephen King's Sleepwalkers*. Director: Mick Garris.

"In some ways it's a little bit like *The Howling*," proclaimed director Mick Garris in describing this tale of feline shapeshifters who feed off the life force of young virgins. Hmmm. Apart from replacing *The Howling*'s extensive coven of werewolves with a pair of cat-monsters, and substituting *The Howling*'s well-drawn characterizations and excellent physical transformations with wise-cracking cyphers and simplistic computer-generated metamorphoses, and turning the werewolves' greatest fear (silver) into the sleepwalkers' intense phobia of common house cats (apparently the only thing that can kill them), *Sleepwalkers* indeed *might* be seen as "a little bit like *The Howling*." But probably not.

The film opens by offering a faux "Encyclopedia of Arcane Knowledge" entry: "Sleepwalker n. Nomadic shape-shifting creatures with human and feline origins. Vulnerable to the deadly scratch of the cat, the sleepwalker feeds upon the life-force of virginal human females. Probably the source of the vampire legend." Not to mention the werewolf myth. Teenager Charles (Brian Krause) and his mother (Alice Krige) arrive in a small Indiana town, intent on slaking their thirst for virginal life forces. Charles sets his predatory sights on "good girl" Tanya (Madchen Amick), but must first deal with various obstacles, like a nosy teacher, a suspicious policeman, and a gaggle of local cats who can see them for the monsters they are.

The oogey, incestuous mother-son relationship between Charles and his mom makes it hard to sympathize with the lad, though for the first half of the picture such empathy-building seems to be the intent, as Charles only reluctantly "courts" the virginal heroine at the sometimes violent urgings of his shut-in mother, and even shows concern for her when he brings her home to meet mom. But once Charles finally gets Tanya alone, he suddenly (and literally) morphs into a wise-cracking monster intent on draining her life force. "I don't think you're entering into the spirit of this," he cheekily tells the struggling Tanya. "Why don't you just think of yourself as *lunch*!" Later, when a cop comes to the girl's aid, Charles pops up behind him and shoves a pencil into the policeman's ear with a gleeful, "Cop kabob!"

Apart from the occasional "gotcha" moment, some impressive cat action (a horde of killer kitties finally brings down these monsters), and a few spot-the-horror-filmmaker cameos—Clive Barker, Tobe Hooper, Stephen King, and, best of all, werewolf movie veterans Joe (*The Howling*) Dante and John (*An American Werewolf in London*) Landis all show up in bit parts just for fun—*Sleepwalkers* remains an occasionally disturbing, sometimes silly (these cat-creatures not only change their shape to look human, they can make themselves—and even their cars—*invisible*!), but mostly disappointing entry in the shapeshifter sweepstakes. With Stephen King adapting his own novel for the screen, *Sleepwalkers* just goes to show that even the world's most successful writer can't win Best of (cat) Show every time.

With quotes from: "Sleepwalkers Awaken," by Bill Warren, *Fangoria* 111.

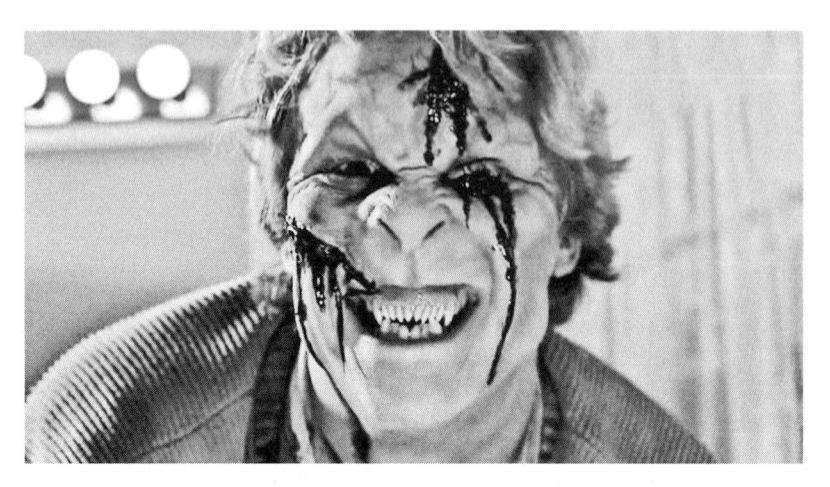

Brian Krause as one of *Sleepwalkers*' life-draining cat-creatures.

The Snake Woman

(1961; Caralan Productions Ltd.; UK) Alternate Title: *Terror of the Snake Woman*. Director: Sidney J. Furie.

Taking a page from *Cult of the Cobra* (1955), and prefiguring Hammer's *The Reptile* (1966), *The Snake Woman* tells the story of a herpetologist (John Cazabon) in a small turn-of-the-century English village who injects his wife with snake venom in order to cure her insanity. The unorthodox treatment works, but it also affects the woman's unborn baby. The wife dies in childbirth; the midwife labels the cold-blooded, lidless newborn "the Devil's offspring"; and the fearful torch-wielding villagers set fire to the house, killing the herpetologist. Fortunately (or *unfortunately*, as it turns out), the baby is whisked away by the doctor and delivered into the hands of a friendly shepherd. Twenty years later the village is plagued by a rash of mysterious snakebite deaths, and a Scotland Yard detective (John McCarthy) arrives to investigate. As the torpid tale crawls along to its foregone conclusion, he runs across the beautiful and mysterious Atheris (Susan Travers), who can transform herself into a King Cobra at will.

Plagued by a pace more sluggish than a serpent in December, *The Snake Woman* just coils up and lies there for most of its (blessedly brief) 68-minute running time. Cramped sets (including sparse studio-bound "moors"), lengthy and pointless talking head scenes, mundane staging (Sidney Furie offers up drab direction more along the lines of his earlier *Dr. Blood's Coffin* than his later, more stylish films like *The Ipcress File* and *The Entity*), melodramatic *over*acting (particularly from Elsie Wagstaff as the cartoonish "witch"), and a predictable story do nothing to warm up this *Snake Woman*. Scenes of victims being stalked by a literal snake in the grass offer little suspense, particularly when the "special effects" consist of alternating footage of a live snake with that of a rubber one, with nary a transformation scene in sight (excepting one simple and unconvincing superimposition at the very end). And the potentially fascinating character of Atheris remains completely undeveloped, as she's given little dialogue and even less personality, denying the story much of its pathos and leaving only the "mystery" angle to engage viewer interest—of which there is none (neither mystery *nor* interest).

Spookies

(1986; Sony) Directors: Eugenie Joseph, Thomas Doran, Brendan Faulkner.

With a title like *Spookies*, one might expect a comedic horror parody along the lines of, say, *Saturday the 14th* or *The Creeps*. So it comes as a surprise when the goofy chuckles fail to materialize, replaced instead by the occasional cringe (as some grotesque monster oozes goo over a protagonist) or jaw-dropping wince (as a hook-handed ghoul *buries a 12-year-old alive*). Apart from its title, there's nothing "cute" about *Spookies*, a tale of two carloads of "partiers" who stumble across a sorcerer's creepy mansion and meet their fate one by one at the hands (and claws) of various creatures conjured by the magician.

Begun in 1984 under the title "Twisted Souls" by first-time filmmakers Brendan Faulkner and Thomas Doran (who shot at the John Jay Estate, a 24-room Colonial mansion in Rye, New York; Jay was the first Chief Justice of the Supreme Court and the second governor of New York), the low-budget ($300,000) *Spookies* ended up in post-production hell—to the point where producer/financier Michael Lee took the film away from Faulkner and Doran. Lee hired Genie ("Eugenie') Joseph, an editor at Troma who got her start in porn, to "save" the production. Joseph kept about 45 minutes of footage (primarily the monster and effects shots) and scrapped the rest, changing (some might say muddling) the storyline by writing and filming a whole new subplot in which the sorcerer sacrifices his unwanted "guests" in order to revive his reluctant lady love, who ultimately runs afoul of a gaggle of zombies when she tries to escape. Joseph also added the preamble concerning an odd, cat-faced, hook-handed ghoul who chases down doomed little Billy after his haunted birthday celebration.

Not surprisingly, with the original *Evil Dead*–like demon and monster infestation melded onto the tale of a sorcerer trying to revive—and woo—the reticent object of his passion, the film's disparate tones never quite gel (and one is never sure just who pulls the strings, the Ouija board–conjured demon or the sorcerer, as each has scenes in which they appear to summon up Dark Forces). Likewise, the cadre of unlikable, bickering protagonists have an obvious history and back story that we never see (no doubt covered in the discarded original footage), making their sometimes stupid behavior that much more inexplicable. In essence, *Spookies* is a storytelling mess. But it's a gory, scary, Halloween funhouse sort of mess that, through its audacious creepiness and sheer volume of monster mayhem, still manages to entertain.

Among the various demons, slime monsters, and scythe-wielding angels of death is an encounter with an exotic-looking Asian woman who transforms into a giant spider and literally sucks the life out of a victim, leaving him a deflated husk. The unique, impressive metamorphosis comes in several stages. She first raises her arms up in front of her face, drawing her diaphanous black shroud over her. When she lowers her arms, she's transformed into a wrinkled, distorted, horrible travesty of humanity. She obscures her visage a second time, and now she sports a veined, rounded head along with her hideous countenance. Then giant, spindly spider legs slowly emerge from her side before her head splits open and expands into the body of a fanged, bulbous arachnid. It's an inventive, skin-crawling change.

Of course, balancing out effectively horrific sequences like this is a tussle with a group of grotesque sludge monsters that rise out of the cellar floor and proceed to break wind at every step. According to co-director Brendan Faulkner, it was producer Lee who added the ridicu-

American poster for the self-explanatory *The Snake Woman*.

lous scatological sound effects. "The backer [Lee] had a thing about bowel movements," said Faulkner. "He used to walk up to people and say 'Pull my finger,' and he would fart. At one time he wanted to call the movie *Bowel Erupters*.... [Original co-director] Tom Doran, the major architect of the Muck Men scene, was absolutely horrified when he heard the farting."

Though it bombed abysmally in theaters (grossing less than $18,000), *Spookies* made between two and three *million* dollars on video and became a mainstay on USA Network's *Up All Night*. Perhaps "pull my finger" *can* work after all…

With quotes from: "The Strange Saga of *Spookies*," by Max Evry, thedissolve.com.

Stephen King's Sleepwalkers see Sleepwalkers

Sting of Death

(1967; Thunderbird International Pictures) Director: William Grefé.

"Special Singing Guest Star NEIL SEDAKA," proclaims the posters for *Sting of Death*. Yes, *that* Neil Sedaka gives us a rousing rendition of "Do the Jellyfish" (via vinyl; the chart-topper did not deign to appear onscreen) in this no-budget, Florida-lensed Sixties drive-in obscurity about a biologist in the Florida Everglades whose home/research lab is invaded not only by a group of partying young people (friends of his daughter's), but by a jellyfish-man who kills with his long, ropey stingers. According to director William Grefé, producer Richard S. Flink simply threw some quick cash at Sedaka (in Miami at the time working a nightclub gig) to come up with a song. But you gotta love lyrics like: "Wella, I'm-a saying fella / Forget your Cinderella / And do the jella / The jillajalla jella / It's really swella / To do the Jalla Jellyfish!"

And there's plenty more to love in this cheesy, entertaining-in-the-right-frame-of-mind throwback to the Fifties' mutant monster movie craze. Enhancing the ambiance: Beach Party–style poolside dancing; a semi-nude scene involving a cutie and a barely opaque shower door; and the nihilistic notion that nearly all of the gyrating groovers end up *dead*! *Sting of Death* opens with an unseen creature (apart from its crusty "hand") pulling a sunbathing co-ed off a dock, then swimming along underwater, towing the dead girl by her hair(!) as the credits roll. Later, we meet a disfigured scientist's helper named Egon (John Vella doing his best crazed Cameron Mitchell impersonation) whose deformed eye-socket alternately contains and lacks an orb from shot to shot; a boatload of partying university students twisting, arm-waving and chicken-clucking to the aforementioned dance-craze-sensation-that-failed-to-sweep-the-nation; and the jelly-fish man lurking in the pool during the dance party … with *nobody noticing*. "Highlights" include the partygoers attacked by a school (herd, pride, gaggle?) of little colored plastic bags (aka jellyfish) floating on top of the water; a paper maché underwater cave set (built in a local TV station studio) filled with out-of-date, obviously-not-up-to-code electrical equipment; and one of the goofiest, laugh-out-loud monsters since *The Brainiac*.

"What we did when we designed the costume was copy from photographs of an actual Portuguese man-of-war, a very deadly jellyfish," related creature-creator (and wearer) Doug Hobart. "We combined images of a man with the jellyfish, and it was a super concept indeed.… The monster suit cost around 300 dollars to make. We made it in a two week period, and it looked quite good for the time and funds involved." Well, *that's* debatable. In fact, it looks just like what it is—a man in a crusty, dirty wetsuit and flippers, with plastic cords hanging from his shoulders and a clear hefty-bag inflated over his head (the human face shows nice and clear through the jellyfish casing).

Unfortunately, an overabundance of mundane dialogue and amateurish acting float through the production like student bodies after a jellyfish attack. The film's idiotic science seems more magical than scientific, with the solitary sop to explanatory exposition being one line about "sea water, electricity and human blood mixed with chemicals" explaining how the human antagonist dipping his head into a tank containing a Portuguese man-of-war magically transforms him into a jellyfish hybrid. Even so, the world's first (and only) jellyfish-monster movie manages to entertain through sheer audacity and the fact that it's not nearly as dull as its better-known double-bill co-feature, the dreadful *Death Curse of Tartu*.

With quotes from: "Jellyfish-Man … an Interview with Doug Hobart," by Paul Parla, *Scary Monsters* 26.

Terror of the Snake Woman see The Snake Woman

Track of the Moon Beast

(1978; Cinema Shares International) Director: Richard Ashe.

An asteroid (represented by a flaming charcoal briquette) flies through space to collide with the moon, sending a meteor shower of moon fragments mixed with asteroid bits to earth. On a New Mexican mountaintop, one of these "lunar meteorites" grazes the temple of young mineralogist Paul Carlson. Paul later develops nausea and dizziness and, worse, transforms into a lizard-man when the moon rises! Like the skeptical Sheriff asks, "You mean this energy or whatever it is can turn a human into a monster? Like in those werewolf tales—when there's a full moon in Transylvania?"

With the were-lizard kept off-screen and unseen for most of the film (only one brief attack scene displays the "demon lizard monster" suit to any degree, with the rest represented by monster-point-of-view photography), we only get one (botched) transformation sequence. Strapped to a hospital table, actor Chase Cordell undergoes a set of simple dissolves (à la the original *The Wolf Man*), but the inept special effects crew can't keep Cordell's head in the same place, so it looks more like a series of disjointed overlapping phantom images than a monstrous metamorphosis.

"There was a [film] company that was looking around for a property because they had been in contact with something like the New Mexico Film Development Board or something to that effect," recalled co-screenwriter Charles Sinclair (*The Green Slime*) about the project's genesis. "The state government of New Mexico had decided that it would be nice to have them come down and make movies there to spread the economy around and all that. They were offering location assistance, and everything you could offer a film company." So Sinclair sat down with his writing partner Bill Finger and banged out the script over a single weekend. Given the result, no doubt the members of the New Mexico Film Development Board were not amused.

Shot in September 1972 (with a working title of *The Lunar Analog*) on location in New Mexico, the movie took six years to see the light of day (or moon), and then bypassed theaters to go straight to television. And it's not hard to see why, given its slow pace, banal dialogue, murky photography, awful performances from actors never heard from before or since, desultory direction (from first—and last—time director Richard Ashe), and *Star Trek*–level lizard-man. For the discerning viewer, this *Track* is one best avoided.

"I almost literally forgot about the movie," said Sinclair. "[My son] phoned me one night and said, 'Guess what? *Track of the Moon Beast* is coming up on an obscure TV channel.' I said, 'Great, I've never seen it.' I looked in on it that night, and thought, 'Oh my god, did I have a hand in this thing?'"

With quotes from: "On the *Track of the Moonbeast*: An Interview with Charles Sinclair," by Brian Albright, regionalhorrorfilms.blogspot.com.

The Two Little Bears

(1961; 20th Century–Fox; b&w) Director: Randall F. Hood.

Intending to cash in on the success of Disney's *The Shaggy Dog* (1959), this forgotten family feature has two young brothers, age six and seven, obsessed with becoming bears. Donning their bear costumes for Halloween, they go to visit an old "witch" (actually an itinerant phony fortune teller), who tells them that indeed they could transform into bears by donning an animal pelt, rubbing their face with a special salve, and reciting a magic ditty. Finding some smelly homemade "freckle cream" their older sister's boyfriend had given her, they mistake it for a gift from the "witch," don their bear costumes and say some magic words. Well ... it works, and the two happily scamper off for a few tame adventures as bear cubs. Of course, things soon go awry, and they end up taken by rangers up into the mountains, where they join a real mamma bear in a cave to hibernate. Unfortunately, whenever they sleep the spell wears off, so they soon awaken as boys again and must make their way back down the mountain through a snowstorm. That sole sequence of suspense over, the film then winds down with the boys' dad, whom everyone thinks is crazy after he's attempted to get help for his two cubs ... er, kids, is pilloried in front of the local school board (he's principal of the town's grammar school). But the boys ultimately show that belief can work miracles, and they all live happily ever after ... bearly (ouch). As Dad proudly tells his two tykes at film's end, it wasn't the suits or the salve or the magic words ... no, "you had something *special* that, more than anything else, helped you to change: You both *believed.*"

An unavoidable air of late '50s/early '60s sitcom blankets this production, from the suburban middle-class sets and small-town nuclear-family focus, to the casting of Eddie Albert (*Green Acres*) as the likable dad and *The Beverly Hillbillies'* Nancy Culp as a very Miss Hathaway–esque schoolteacher (not to mention Eddie Munster himself, Butch Patrick, as one of the boys). Nothing much of import happens over its 80-odd minutes, and the cuteness factor of the two well-trained bear cubs trumps all.

"One minute they're loveable kids...," proclaims the film's poster, "the next minute they're live, cute cubs!" And thanks to the simplest of dissolves, that indeed proves to be the case. The movie's only special effects consist of a man in an obvious bear suit (playing a grown momma bear that takes the two boy-cubs under her paw, even telling them the story of "Goldibear and the Three People") and some admittedly impressive real-life bear-cub wrangling (featuring the cute cubs climbing out windows, sliding down drainpipes, opening cabinet doors, etc.).

"Wait'll you hear Brenda Lee give out with the songs!" proclaims the film's advertising. Well, the two non sequitur numbers she performs in the movie (plus the odd opening credit warble) are simply not worth the wait. But at least they're better than her (ahem) toneless acting as the boys' teenage sis (inexplicably, the only member of the family sporting a Southern accent!). The remainder of the cast (including a wasted Soupy Sales in his film debut as the friendly local cop) are competent but unremarkable—excepting Milton Parsons as Dr. Fredricks, "one of the few authorities in America on hysteric lycanthropic manifestations." Upon examining the "crazy" father, the doc offers, "In Vienna we had several cases in the black forest. However, in those cases we treated the *wolf*—er, the man who *thought* he was a wolf; not the father of the bears—er, the boys who *think* they are the bears. It's very confusing, isn't it?" Parsons' slow, deliberate delivery and quirky inflections (not to mention his cadaverous appearance) at least make his character stand out from the cookie-cutter crowd. Unfortunately, he only appears in two scenes. (Parsons lent his singular presence to yet another werebeast flick the following decade, 1973's *The Cat Creature*.)

Bland, forgettable and harmless, *The Two Little Bears* stands as the vanilla wafer of werebeast movies.

Valkoinen Peura see The White Reindeer

The Vampire-Beast Craves Blood

(1968/69; Tigon/Pacemaker Pictures; UK) Alternate Title: *The Blood Beast Terror* (UK); Director: Vernon Sewell.

The Death's Head Vampire (the film's shooting title) began filming on August 7, 1967, in the tiny Goldhawk Studios in Shepherd's Bush, London. Set in Victorian England, the ludicrous story has an entomologist (Robert Flemyng) seeking to create a giant (male) moth in order to pacify and curtail the bloodlust of his moth-monster daughter (whom he has also created), a beautiful girl who periodically transforms into a giant death's head moth and sucks the blood from her would-be lovers. A police inspector (Peter Cushing) and his long-suffering Sergeant (Glynn Edwards) must discover the absurd truth and lure this murderous monster moth to the flame (literally).

Made by Tony Tenser's Tigon film company (a sort of bargain basement Hammer that bankrolled such pictures as *Witchfinder General*, *Blood on Satan's Claw* and *The Creeping Flesh*), *The Vampire-Beast Craves Blood* (released in the U.S. on a double bill with *Curse of the Blood-Ghouls*, a re-titled *Slaughter of the Vampires*) is by far Tigon's most tepid terror offering. Slow, desultory and, oh yes, bloody awful are adjectives that readily spring to mind.

Tenser managed to secure the services of the once-great Basil Rathbone to play the mad moth-maker, but the 75-year-old actor died on July 21 and was replaced by Robert Flemyng (*The Horrible Dr. Hichcock* himself). Though Rathbone would have undoubtedly brought a touch of his trademark class to the role, there was little to work with in Peter Bryan's script. While Bryan was (partly) responsible for penning such winners as *The Brides of Dracula* and *The Plague of the Zombies*, his screenplay for *Vampire-Beast* falls more in line with his later efforts like the terrible *Trog* and *Seven Deaths in a Cat's Eye*. "They'll never believe this at the Yard," opines the Sergeant at film's end, to which the Inspector replies, "They'll never believe it *anywhere.*" Indeed. (Note: According to Tenser, this clever retort wasn't even in the script, but was ad-libbed by star Peter Cushing. "He [Cushing] rewrote a lot of his dialogue," reported Tenser.)

While the Victorian-era costumes and settings evoke a nicely nostalgic atmosphere, nothing much of interest takes place; and Vernon Sewell's (*Curse of the Crimson Altar*) indifferent direction fails to improve the lugubrious pacing. Worst of all is the titular terror itself, which looks (in the few brief flashes Sewell dares show us) like a pathetic papier-mâché copy of *The Wasp Woman*.

Peter Cushing does what he can with his underdeveloped Inspector character, adding bits of business here and there in a vain attempt to liven up the proceedings, but it was obviously a lost cause. In fact, Cushing labeled *Vampire-Beast* his worst film, and it's a tough point to argue. Author Jonathan Rigby, in his excellent *English Gothic*, quotes actor Roy Hudd (who, in two scenes, stole the show playing the irascible morgue attendant) as recalling, "I was called for make-up and there, in the next chair, was the great man himself. 'Good morning,' he said, 'I'm Peter Cushing'—as if I didn't know. 'Have you seen the script?' he asked. 'Not very good, is it?' 'Well...' I blustered. 'No, we can do better than that.' 'Can we? How can we make it funnier,' asked the great man.... That was the start. Together we rejigged the whole two scenes." Too bad they couldn't have rejigged the entire script.

374 • *Wallace & Gromit: The Curse of the Were-Rabbit*　　　　　　　　OTHER WERE-BEASTS

The Vampire-Beast Craves Blood ... because she's a were-*moth*. Odd, hokey poster for the odd, hokey film that Peter Cushing labeled his worst.

With quotes from: *Beasts in the Cellar: The Exploitation Film Career of Tony Tenser*, by John Hamilton; *English Gothic*, by Jonathan Rigby.

Wallace & Gromit: The Curse of the Were-Rabbit

(2005; Aardman/Dreamworks; UK) Directors: Nick Park, Steve Box.

Directors Nick Park and Steve Box jokingly referred to *Wallace & Gromit: The Curse of the Were-Rabbit* as the world's "first vegetarian horror film." A feature-length stop-motion animation movie based on the beloved British Wallace & Gromit shorts, *Curse of the Were-Rabbit* sees cheese-loving inventor Wallace and his highly intelligent (and blessedly silent) dog Gromit running a "humane pest-control" service in which they guard the prized vegetables of the local gardeners intent on entering the "Giant Vegetable Competition" against unwanted lepus invaders. Using such devices as the "Bun-Vac 6000" ("capable of 125 rpm—rabbits per minute"), the duo store the myriad captured bunnies in their basement. Needing a solution to their overcrowding problem, Wallace determines to "brainwash the bunnies—rabbit rehabilitation"—and condition them not to eat vegetables. But something goes wrong with his brainwave transference device when he adds "just a little lunar power to enhance the mind waves," resulting in a 10-foot-tall, buck-toothed, cotton-tailed monster who pillages the prized produce under the light of the full moon. But with Wallace and Gromit hot on his cotton-tail, the monstrous marauder turns out not to be their experimental subject bunny, but Wallace himself! Can Gromit keep his friend from eating all the veg in the village, and, more importantly, keep the local hunting enthusiast from blasting Wallace while in were-rabbit form?

Since this were-creature turns out to be the alter-ego of the kind and gentle Wallace, the hulking were-rabbit attacks only vegetables. It also howls at the moon like a wolf. "The beast lurks within us all," observes the local Vicar, who consults his "Book of Monsters" to learn that a were-rabbit can only be killed by a bullet of pure gold—"twenty-four *carrot*."

Full of endearing characters and clever antics, the film was a financial and critical success, grossing over $192 million (on a $30 million budget) and winning the Academy Award for Best Animated Feature. With its impeccably detailed and imaginative animation, *Wallace & Gromit: The Curse of the Were-Rabbit* remains highly entertaining for both children and adults. As Wallace might say, "Cracking film, Gromit."

The Wasp Woman

(1959; Filmgroup) Director: Roger Corman.

Susan Cabot plays Janice Starlin, the 40-something owner of a cosmetics firm whose sales have plummeted since Jan pulled her aging image off her products. Desperate to regain her youthful appearance and save her business, she engages the services of scientist Eric

Zinthrop (Michael Mark), who's developed an extract from wasp enzymes that actually rejuvenates tissue. She insists that Zinthrop use her as his human guinea pig, and the experimental formula does indeed restore her beauty. It also periodically changes her into a bloodthirsty wasp-monster.

Producer-director Roger Corman shot *The Wasp Woman* in less than two weeks for about $50,000. There wasn't much time (or money) for frills or attention to detail (at one point Zinthrop makes a guinea pig younger—by transforming it into a *white rat*!). And considerable running time is eaten up by Starlin's concerned co-workers creeping about trying to find proof that Zinthrop is a charlatan. Since we already know he's *not*, much of the film becomes a pointless—and tedious—exercise. What *The Wasp Woman* has going for it is some naturalistic acting and an occasional flourish from director Corman. He cleverly stages the wasp woman attacks in semi-darkness, for instance, with the indistinct figure rushing *at* the camera, the movement adding menace to the moment. And the frantic buzzing noise on the soundtrack that accompanies the attacks enhances the sense of danger.

Star Susan Cabot's projected veneer of no-nonsense businesswoman jibes nicely with the desperate vulnerability—stemming from her fear of aging—that she hides beneath the facade. And when in wasp form, Cabot (who wore the rather unconvincing mask and claws herself, and did all her own stunts—including spitting out chocolate syrup upon the necks of her victims as she pretended to bite them) moves with a rapid, frantic motion that transforms her slight frame into a dynamo of frightening energy. "Since I'm small," said Cabot, "I'm five-foot-two, another challenge was figuring out a way to attack six-foot-four-inch men and make it look credible. The only way I felt I could convincingly down a bigger person was through swiftness—by coming at them so fast, like a bolt of lightening, and staying right on target. It worked." Indeed it did.

On December 10, 1986, Susan Cabot, age 59, was bludgeoned to death with a weight-lifting bar by her own son Timothy, age 22, in the bedroom of her Encino home. After the defense cited emotional instability (characterizing Cabot as an overprotective, disturbed mother), and steroid and experimental hormone use (Timothy was born dwarfed), Timothy Scott Roman received a three-year suspended sentence and was placed on probation. It proved a sad, untimely end for a talented actress who deserved better than being remembered simply as *The Wasp Woman*.

With quotes from: *Interviews with B Science Fiction and Horror Movie Makers*, by Tom Weaver.

In 1959's *The Wasp Woman* an experimental cosmetic formula involving wasp enzymes transforms Susan Cabot into a killer were-wasp that looks *nothing* like the monster on this creepy half-sheet poster.

The Wasp Woman

(1995; New Horizons) Alternate Title: *Roger Corman Presents: The Wasp Woman*. Director: Jim Wynorski.

Though Roger Corman's original *Wasp Woman* may have been cheap, it was never cheesy, thanks largely to its economical but effective direction and the naturalistic playing of its underrated cast, headed by Susan Cabot in the title role. Unfortunately, the same can *not* be said for this unnecessary remake (for which Corman served as executive producer), as director Jim Wynorski is no Roger Corman, and star Jennifer Rubin is no Susan Cabot.

Faithfully following the original, the 1995 *Wasp Woman* focuses on the 40-something Janet Starlin (Rubin sporting unflattering—and unconvincing—aging makeup), who's faced with having to step down as the face of her cosmetics company. Desperate to rejuvenate her looks, she talks experimental scientist Dr. Zinthrop (Daniel Travanti) into testing his wasp enzyme extract on her. The result: she now looks twenty years younger. *And* she occasionally transforms into a giant wasp monster (primarily during sex) to cocoon and kill her lovers/victims.

Mundanely shot on a few overlit and ordinary sets, *The Wasp Woman* lacks any significant visual character, much like it lacks any *actual* characters. As Starlin, Jennifer Rubin's too-flat delivery and toneless personality fails to engender sufficient sympathy to carry the role. And the various underlings and bimbos surrounding her (played by low-budget '90s regulars like Jay Richardson and Maria Ford) make even less impression.

The primitive, unconvincing CGI morphing effects for the instantaneous transformations are matched by the ludicrous, unwieldy giant wasp-monster—with breasts—that lumbers in place, doing very little. And the perfunctory ending, culminating in an explosion at the ubiquitous Bronson Caverns in the Hollywood Hills (home to *Robot Monster* and a zillion other low-budget productions) remains the anticlimactic icing on this tasteless cake. The only "innovation" displayed by this pointless remake is the addition of some gratuitous nudity—about what one might expect from the director of *The Bare Wench Project* (2000), *The Witches of Breastwick* (2005), and *Cleavagefield* (2009).

The White Reindeer

(1952; Coronet/Luomi Filmi; Finland; b&w) Original Language Title: *Valkoinen Peura*. Director: Erik Blomberg.

The first fictional feature of Finnish documentary filmmaker Erik Blomberg, *The White Reindeer* (which Blomberg co-scripted with his actress wife Mirjami Kuosmanen), set (and filmed) in Finnish Lapland, stars Kuosmanen as newlywed Pirita, who attempts to keep her hard-working husband, reindeer herder Aslak, close to home by visiting the local shaman for a love potion. But something goes terribly wrong when, while casting the spell, the shaman leaps back in horror and labels her a "witch!" (Pirita's mother had died in childbirth, apparently under a curse.) The result: Pirita periodically transforms into a "bewitched" white reindeer that leads men to their deaths.

Filled with striking visuals—astoundingly beautiful stark snowy landscapes, huge reindeer herds, and even an unsettling reindeer graveyard surrounding a pagan "Great Altar" (with antlers eerily poking up through the snow)—*The White Reindeer* is most remarkable in its depiction of the harsh realities of life above the Arctic Circle. The hardy Lapps traverse the snow-and-ice landscape either on skis or in toboggans pulled by reindeer; and their simple pleasures include singing and reindeer races. The story itself, based upon a Lapp folk tale, is matched in its simplicity by the film's sparse dialogue and Silent era–style acting. But it's the visuals that catch one's attention—and at times even one's breath—as director Blomberg juxtaposes his well-composed landscape shots with moments of near–Gothic cinema. For instance, when Pirita transforms for the first time, she rises up in front of the outdoor fire, the eerie low-key lighting casting unnatural-looking shadows over her face. Then she suddenly leaps out of frame, with the next shot revealing the white reindeer landing in the snow. Though lacking any overt special effects, the transformation remains no less effective for its simplicity.

It remains ambiguous as to what triggers the change in Pirita. Nor is it clear whether she embraces the metamorphosis. At times she seems distraught over what she's done in her "bewitched reindeer" form, while at others she appears to revel in it (even sporting vampiric fangs in one scene, as her "witch" half seemingly takes over). It's as if she has two personalities—the innocent Pirita and the evil witch. In any case, once the villagers arm themselves with spears to use against the white reindeer/witch ("You can only kill a witch with cold iron"), a terrified Pirita goes to the Great Altar and pleads, "Powerful spirit of the Alter—take back the spell. Release me from witchcraft." But

French film card for the Finnish *White Reindeer*, the only movie to date featuring a were-*reindeer*. Pictured: Mirjami Kuosmanen as Pirita (in human form) (courtesy Nicholas Schlegel).

it's no use; her insecurities and poor judgment have led her down this path, and she rises up once again as the white reindeer to meet her fate.

The White Reindeer won an award at the 1953 Cannes Film Festival (for best "Mythical Film"), and later, upon its 1957 (limited) U.S. release, earned a Golden Globe award for Best Foreign Film. Unfortunately, this unique, bewitching movie has all but disappeared from view in the States, never receiving a home video release, with only a European DVD to mark its presence.

Wild Jungle Captive see *Jungle Captive*

Wolfhound

(2002; Califilm) Director: Donovan Kelly.

Wolfhound takes place in "an enchanted village with a secret" (according to the film's trailer)—the secret being that it has literally gone to the dogs. American-raised writer Calum Kennedy (Allen Scolti) returns with his wife and two small children to the place of his birth, the Irish village of Wolfshead, to work on his latest book. Taking up residence on his deceased parents' farm, Calum notices a large number of Irish wolfhounds roaming the land, and falls prey to visions of a dog transforming into a beautiful woman. But these are no hallucination, for the residents of Wolfshead are indeed shapeshifters (most of them of the canine variety, though the local babysitter morphs into a crow), and the locals, led by the seductive Siobahn (Julie Cialini), conspire to bring Calum back to his canine heritage.

A movie about were*dogs*? Yes indeed. While the Irish wolfhound is one of the more imposing breeds size-wise, the animals' rather sweet-looking faces and curly-haired coats make them a less-than-menacing monster. Donovan Kelly, making his directorial debut (*and apparent swan song*), desperately tries to make his hounds look sinister via slo-mo shots and extreme close-ups of their eyes and teeth. It doesn't work. Failing that, Kelly (purportedly aided by sexploitation veteran Jim Wynorski) tosses in copious quantities of gratuitous nudity and softcore sex, spearheaded by Julie Cialini (*Playboy*'s 1995 Playmate of the Year) as Siobahn (though at one point a pair of gorgeous lesbians appear literally from nowhere to beef up yet another torrid tryst). Cialini was hired, no doubt, more for her willingness to display her body than any acting talent (of which she displays woefully little). And it's rather amusing to realize that this supposed Irish rose (and shapeshifting "wolfhound") speaks like an American cheerleader and sports bikini tan lines.

Worst of all, this erotic shaggy dog story wanders about chasing its tale but ultimately goes nowhere—as exemplified by the disappointingly perfunctory climactic were-dogfight and unsatisfying non-ending. It comes when the village alpha male menaces Calum's bewildered wife, and Calum must go nose-to-nose (or snout-to-snout) with the brute. But rather than staging a supernatural hound-vs.-hound battle, they grapple in standard human form, with the occasional near-subliminal shot of red-lit dog snouts and teeth interspersed to remind viewers that they're actually were-beasts and not just a pair of ordinary pugilists. Though offering plenty of pulchritude, *Wolfhound*, with its meandering story, unfortunate choice of were-creatures, poor staging and dearth of exciting action, truly turns out to be a dog.

Appendix A: Film Chronology

Only full-fledged werewolf films are included here, with their initial release dates in parentheses (along with their U.S. premiers for foreign films).

1935
Werewolf of London (May 9)

1941
The Wolf Man (December 12)

1942
The Mad Monster (May 8)
The Undying Monster (November 27)

1943
Frankenstein Meets the Wolf Man (March 5)

1944
Return of the Vampire (January 1)
Cry of the Werewolf (August 17)
House of Frankenstein (December 15)

1945
House of Dracula (December 7)

1948
Abbott and Costello Meet Frankenstein (June 15)

1956
The Werewolf (July)

1957
I Was a Teenage Werewolf (June 19)
Daughter of Dr. Jekyll (July 28)

1961
The Curse of the Werewolf (May 1 [UK]; June 7 [USA])
Werewolf in a Girls' Dormitory (November 9 [Italy]; June 5, 1963 [USA])

1962
House on Bare Mountain (September 11)

1963
Face of the Screaming Werewolf (November 30)

1968
Frankenstein's Bloody Terror (July 29 [Spain]; October 8, 1971 [USA])

1969
Blood of Dracula's Castle (May 14)
Dracula, the Dirty Old Man (December 11)

1970
Assignment Terror (February 27 [Germany]; 1972 [USA TV])
Santo and Blue Demon vs. the Monsters (May 14 [Mexico])

1971
The Werewolf vs. the Vampire Woman (May 17 [Spain]; 1972 [USA])
Werewolves on Wheels (October 27)

1972
The Fury of the Wolfman (February 7 [Spain]; 1974 [USA TV])
Moon of the Wolf (September 26 [TV])
Dr. Jekyll and the Werewolf (November 13 [Spain]; 1973 [USA])

1973
Santo and Blue Demon vs. Dracula and the Wolf Man (July 26 [Mexico])
The Boy Who Cried Werewolf (August 1)
Curse of the Devil (September 21 [Spain]; May 1977 [USA])
The Werewolf of Washington (October)

1974
Blood (March)
The Beast Must Die (April)

1975
The Werewolf of Woodstock (January 4 [TV])
Night of the Howling Beast (January 9 [Spain]; 1977 [USA])
Legend of the Werewolf (October 27 [UK])

1976
The Legend of the Wolf Woman (March 18 [Italy]; June 1977 [USA])
Santo vs. the She-Wolves (May 13 [Mexico]; August 1978 [USA])

1978
Death Moon (May 31 [TV])

1979
Wolfman (September 21)

1981
The Howling (April 10)
The Craving (April 10 [Spain]; 1985 [USA])
An American Werewolf in London (August 21)
Full Moon High (October 9)

1984
The Company of Wolves (September 15 [Canada]; April 19, 1985 [USA])
Monster Dog (December [Italy]; 1986 [USA video])

1985
Ladyhawke (March 27 [France]; April 12 [USA])
Teen Wolf (August 23)
Howling II... Your Sister Is a Werewolf (August 28 [France]; January 1986 [USA])
Silver Bullet (October 11)

1987
Werewolf (July 11 [TV])
The Monster Squad (August 14)
Howling III: The Marsupials (November 13)
Teen Wolf Too (November 20)

1988
Lone Wolf (August 16 [video])
Scooby-Doo and the Reluctant Werewolf (September 14 [TV])

Howling IV: The Original Nightmare (November [video])

1989

Red Riding Hood (March 15 [video])
My Mom's a Werewolf (May)
Night Shadow

1990

Howling V: The Rebirth (February 22 [video])

1993

Full Eclipse (November 27 [TV])
Plenilunio

1994

Wolf (June 17)
Moonchild

1995

Project: Metalbeast (January [video])
The Howling: New Moon Rising (October 24 [video])

1996

Werewolf (January 21)
Bad Moon (November 1)

1997

Wilderness (April 23 [Sweden]; May 2001 [USA video])
House of Frankenstein (November 2 & 3 [TV])
An American Werewolf in Paris (October 31 [UK]; December 12 [USA])

1998

The Strangers (June 10 [video])
The Werewolf Reborn! (October 20 [video])

1999

Rage of the Werewolf (October 18)

2000

Alvin and the Chipmunks Meet the Wolfman! (August 29 [video])
Monster Mash (August 29 [video])
Ginger Snaps (September 10 [Canada]; April 21, 2001 [USA])

2001

The Curse (October 26)
Blood of the Werewolf

2002

Dog Soldiers (May 10 [UK]; October 15 [USA TV])
Wolves of Wall Street (December 31)

2003

Darkwolf (April 15 [video])
Underworld (September 19)
Eyes of the Werewolf

2004

Ginger Snaps 2: Unleashed (January 30 [Canada]; April 13 [USA video])
Van Helsing (May 7)
Tomb of the Werewolf (June 8 [video])
Ginger Snaps Back: The Beginning (July 10 [Canada]; September 7 [USA video])

2005

Werewolf in Bangkok (January 13)
Cursed (February 25)
The Beast of Bray Road (September 1)

2006

Creature of the Night (January 1 [video])
Underworld: Evolution (January 20)
Wild Country (February 24 [Scotland]; December 2008 [USA video])
An Erotic Werewolf in London (March 6 [UK video]; June 24, 2008 [USA video])
Horrors of War (March 25)
Red Riding Hood (June 27 [video])
The Feeding (July 11 [TV])
Skinwalkers (August 10)
Bloodz vs. Wolvez (September 12 [video])
Werewolf in a Womens Prison (October 19)
Big Bad Wolf (October 25)

2007

Blood and Chocolate (January 26)
Nature of the Beast (October 21 [TV])
Werewolf: The Devil's Hound (December 4 [video])
Curse of the Wolf

2008

Never Cry Werewolf (May 11 [TV])
Audie & the Wolf (August 14)
Ski Wolf (November 11 [video])

2009

Underworld: Rise of the Lycans (January 23)
War Wolves (March 8 [TV])
Thor: Hammer of the Gods (April 11)
House of the Wolf Man (October 1)
Zombie Werewolves Attack! (October 3)
Dark Moon Rising (October 10)
Wolvesbayne (October 18 [TV])
The Twilight Saga: New Moon (November 16)
Werewolf Fever (November)

2010

The Wolfman (February 12)
Neowolf (April 20 [video])
The Twilight Saga: Eclipse (June 30)
Night Wolf (August 28 [UK]; April 2012 [USA video])
The Hair of the Beast (October 1 [Canada])
Half Moon (October 1)
The Boy Who Cried Werewolf (October 23 [TV])
Red: Werewolf Hunter (October 30 [TV])

2011

Red Riding Hood (March 11)
Dylan Dog: Dead of Night (March 15 [Italy]; April 29 [USA])
Game of Werewolves (October 7 [Spain]; June 2012 [USA])
Monster Brawl (July 23 [Canada]; March 30, 2012 [USA])
The Big Bad (September 10)
The Howling Reborn (October 18 [video])
The Twilight Saga: Breaking Dawn Part One (November 18)
Death Hunter: Werewolves vs. Vampires (December 15 [video])

2012

Underworld: Awakening (January 20)
Strippers vs. Werewolves (April 27 [UK])
President Wolfman (September 28)
Werewolf: The Beast Among Us (October 9 [video])
A Werewolf Boy (October 31 [South Korea]; April 25, 2013 [USA])
The Twilight Saga: Breaking Dawn Part Two (November 6)
Love Bite (November 9 [UK])

2013

Battledogs (April 6 [TV])
Iron Wolf (September 13 [Germany]; July 14, 2014 [UK video])
Wer (November 16 [Japan]; August 19, 2014 [USA internet])

2014

Late Phases (March 9)
WolfCop (June 6)
Light of Blood (July 6 [video])
Blood Moon (August 25 [UK]; September 1 [USA video])
Sabrina, Secrets of a Teenage Witch: A Witch and the Werewolf (September 9 [video])
Werewolf Rising (September 22 [UK video]; October 14 [USA video])
Wolves (November 14)

2015

Dark Moon Rising (August 4)
Blood Moon (September 1 [video])
Howl (October 16 [video])
Crying Wolf (December 10)

2016

Little Dead Rotting Hood (January 5 [video])
Uncaged (February 2 [video])

Appendix B: Film Series and Subsets

Listed here are those film series or subsets (consisting of at least three movies) that deal with werewolves. Entries are listed chronologically. Note: Some series, like Universal's Larry Talbot/Wolf Man and the *Ginger Snaps* films, maintain continuity (sort of) from one movie to the next. Others, such as Paul Naschy's Waldemar Daninsky films and *The Howling* series, offer entries that are completely independent from one another. Then there are certain protagonists who encounter werewolves over a run of films, such as El Santo, Blue Demon and, yes, even Scooby-Doo. Also included are a few lycan-cinema groupings that, while featuring unrelated entries produced by different companies, form their own mini-subset due to format ("Anthologies," "Animated") or content ("Red Riding Hood"). A * indicates a Pseudowolves entry.

Animated
Mad Monster Party? (1967)*
Vampire Hunter D (1985)*
Scooby-Doo and the Ghoul School (1988)*
The Nightmare Before Christmas (1993)*
Alvin and the Chipmunks Meet the Wolfman! (2000)
Monster Mash (2000)
Vampire Hunter D: Bloodlust (2000)*
Scooby-Doo! and the Reluctant Werewolf (2002)
Hellboy Animated: Blood and Iron (2007)*
Scooby-Doo! And the Goblin King (2008)*
The Haunted World of El Superbeasto (2009)*
Tales of the Night (2011)*
Big Top Scooby-Doo! (2012)*
Hotel Transylvania (2012)*
Sabrina, Secrets of a Teenage Witch: A Witch and the Werewolf (2014)

Anthologies
Dr. Terror's House of Horrors (1965)*
Rider of the Skulls (1965)*
Dr. Terror's Gallery of Horrors (1967)*
The Monster Club (1981)*
The Company of Wolves (1984)
Tales of the Third Dimension (1984)*
Deadtime Stories (1986)*
Waxwork (1988)*
Twisted Tales (1994)*
Blood of the Werewolf (2001)
Exhumed (2003)*
The Tenement (2003)*
CreepTales (2004)*
Evil Deeds (2004)*
The Three Faces of Terror (2004)*
Fright Club (2006)*
Trick 'r Treat (2007)*

Blue Demon
Blue Demon: El Demonio Azul (1964)*
Santo and Blue Demon vs. the Monsters (1970)
Santo and Blue Demon vs. Dracula and the Wolf Man (1973)

Waldemar Daninsky
Frankenstein's Bloody Terror (1968)
Nights of the Werewolf (1968)* (unfinished/unreleased)
Assignment Terror (1970)
The Fury of the Wolfman (1972) (filmed before but released after *The Werewolf vs. Vampire Woman*)
The Werewolf vs. the Vampire Woman (1971)
Dr. Jekyll and the Werewolf (1972)
Curse of the Devil (1973)
Night of the Howling Beast (1975)
The Craving (1981)
The Beast and the Magic Sword (1983)*
Howl of the Devil (1987)*
Licántropo: El Asesino de la Luna Ilena (1996)*
Tomb of the Werewolf (2004)

Ginger Snaps
Ginger Snaps (2000)
Ginger Snaps 2: Unleashed (2004)
Ginger Snaps Back: The Beginning (2004)

The Howling
The Howling (1981)
Howling II… Your Sister Is a Werewolf (1985)
Howling III: The Marsupials (1987)
Howling IV: The Original Nightmare (1988)
Howling V: The Rebirth (1990)
Howling VI: The Freaks (1991)
The Howling: New Moon Rising (1995)
The Howling Reborn (2011)

The Munsters
Munsters, Go Home! (1966)*
The Munsters' Revenge (1981)*
The Munsters Scary Little Christmas (1996)*

Red Riding Hood
The Company of Wolves (1984)
Deadtime Stories (1986)*
Red Riding Hood (1989)
Red Riding Hood (2006)
Fright Club (2006)*
Red: Werewolf Hunter (2010)
Red Riding Hood (2011)
Little Dead Rotting Hood (2016)

El Santo
Samson vs. the Vampire Women (1962)*
Samson in the Wax Museum (1963)*
Santo and Blue Demon vs. the Monsters (1970)
Santo and Blue Demon vs. Dracula and the Wolf Man (1973)
Santo vs. the She-Wolves (1976)

Scooby-Doo
Scooby-Doo and the Ghoul School (1988)*
Scooby-Doo and the Reluctant Werewolf (2001)
Scooby-Doo and the Goblin King (2008)*
Big-Top Scooby Doo (2012)*

Lawrence Talbot
The Wolf Man (1941)
Frankenstein Meets the Wolf Man (1943)
House of Frankenstein (1944)
House of Dracula (1945)
Abbott and Costello Meet Frankenstein (1948)
The Wolfman (2010)

The Twilight Saga
The Twilight Saga: New Moon (2009)
The Twilight Saga: Eclipse (2010)
The Twilight Saga: Breaking Dawn Part 1 (2011)
The Twilight Saga: Breaking Dawn Part 2 (2012)

Underworld
Underworld (2003)
Underworld: Evolution (2006)
Underworld: Rise of the Lycans (2009)
Underworld: Awakening (2012)

BIBLIOGRAPHY

"Adam Arkin." Buddy TV, http://www.buddytv.com/info/adam-arkin-info.aspx (accessed 7/27/2013).

Adams, Michael. *Showgirls, Teen Wolves, and Astro Zombies: A film Critic's Year-Long Quest to Find the Worst Movie Ever Made*. New York: Itbooks, 2010.

Aguilar, Carlos. *El Cine Fantastico y de Terror Espanol, 1900–1983*. San Sebastian, Spain: Donostia Kultura, 1999.

Albright, Brian. "On the Track of the Moonbeast: An Interview with Charles Sinclair." *The Dead Next Door: A Field Guide to Regional Horror Films*, http://regionalhorrorfilms.blogspot.com/2011/01/on-track-of-moonbeast-interview-with.html (accessed 6/4/2014).

"*Las Alegres Vampiras de Vögel*," Cinemadrome.yuku.com, June 28, 2014, http://cinemadrome.yuku.com/topic/1562/LAS-ALEGRES-VAMPIRAS-DE-VOGEL#.VLtq6EfF_K0 (accessed 1/17/2015).

Alexander, Chris. "An English Rose Among *Dark Shadows*." *Fangoria* 313 (May 2012).

_____. "The Sultan of Sleaze Lives!" *Fangoria* 294 (June 2010).

_____. "A Wolf in Rea's Clothing." *Fangoria* 301 (March 2011).

Allen, Christine. "*The Curse*: Blood Moon Rising." *Fangoria* 225 (August 2003).

"Anchor Bay Films 'Bays' at the Moon with *The Howling Reborn* on Blu-Ray and DVD." Anchorbayentertainment.com, August 24, 2011 press release, http://www.anchorbayentertainment.com/news.aspx?id=50bcf950-b8c7-4c6b-b230-61f35441ce08 (accessed 12/19/2014).

Andersen, Craig. "Where Are the Wolves?" *Fangoria* 329 (January 2013).

Anderson, Travis. "Interview: Director Jared Cohn Talks *Little Dead Rotting Hood*." Shocktillyoudrop.com, January 16, 2016, http://www.shocktillyoudrop.com/news/features/395257-interview-director-jared-cohn-talks-little-dead-riding-hood/?utm_source=rss&utm_medium=rss&utm_campaign=interview-director-jared-cohn-talks-little-dead-riding-hood (accessed 3/22/2016).

Arena, James. *Fright Night on Channel 9*. Jefferson, NC: McFarland, 2012.

Armstrong, Chad. "Interview with *Little Dead Rotting Hood*'s Jared Cohn." Leglesscorpse.com, January 11, 2016, http://leglesscorpse.us/interview-with-little-dead-rotting-hoods-jared-cohn/ (accessed 3/22/2016).

Armstrong, Vic, with Robert Sellers. *The True Adventures of the World's Greatest Stuntman: My Life as Indiana Jones, James Bond, Superman and Other Movie Heroes*. London: Titan Books, 2011.

Balbo, Lucas. "Paul Naschy: Spain's Greatest Horror Star." *Psychotronic* 7.

Barsky, Larry. "Making the *Waxwork*." *Fangoria* 78 (October 1988).

Beahm, Justin. "The Man Behind the Mask." *Fangoria* 307 (October 2011).

Benardello, Karen. "Interview: Joe Nimziki Talks *The Howling: Reborn*." shockya.com, October 14, 2011, http://www.shockya.com/news/2011/10/14/interview-joe-nimziki-talks-the-howling-reborn/#ixzz3MdWRZGjt (accessed 12/22/2014).

Bene, Jason. "Friedman's Frights." *Fangoria* 331 (March 2014).

Bernstein, Abbie. "Giving 'Em Helsing." *Fangoria* 232 (May 2004).

_____. "International House of Monsters." *Fangoria* 232 (May 2004).

_____. "*Van Helsing* Steps Up to Bat." *Fangoria* 231 (April 2004).

Blellk, Alain. "*The Brothers Grimm*: A Gilliam Fairy Tale." AWN.com, August 25, 2005, http://www.awn.com/vfxworld/brothers-grimm-gilliam-fairy-tale (accessed 11/27/2015).

Brimstone Media Productions. "Interview with Santo Marotta." Lindenmuth.com, http://www.lindenmuth.com/interview_marotta.shtml (accessed 8/16/2014).

Brooks, Conrad. "Peter Coe Interview." *Cult Movies* 8 (1993).

Brosnan, John. *The Horror People*. New York: St. Martin's Press, 1976.

Brown, Dudley. "Carolinas Filmmaker Earl Owensby Is the Reel Deal." Goupstate.com, January 21, 2010, http://www.goupstate.com/article/20100131/ARTICLES/1311032?template=printart (accessed 10/20/2013).

Brown, Todd. "Director James Isaac Talks *Skinwalkers*." Twitchfilm.com, November 9, 2005, http://twitchfilm.com/2005/11/director-james-isaac-talks-skinwalkers.html (accessed 7/7/2014).

Brunas, John, and Michael Brunas. "The Exotic Lives of Acquanetta." *Scarlet Street* 15 (Summer 1994).

Brunas, Michael, John Brunas, and Tom Weaver. *Universal Horrors*. Jefferson, NC: McFarland, 1990.

Budrewicz, Matty. "Cops and Werewolves: A *Full Eclipse* Retrospective with Director Anthony Hickox." UK Horror Scene, April 26, 2014, http://www.ukhorrorscene.com/tag/bruce-payne/ (accessed 8/9/2015).

Buncombe, Andrew. "*Deliverance*: Billy's Back with His Banjo." *The Independent*, November 16, 2003.

Canby, Vincent. "Ladyhawke." *The New York Times*, April 12, 1985.

Carnell, Thom. "*Animals* in Heat." *Fangoria* 294 (June 2010).

_____. "I, Monster Maker." *Fangoria* 230 (March 2004).

_____. "*Underworld Awakening*: Black Leather and Bloodsucking." *Fangoria* 310 (February 2012).

Cauthen, Shawn. "Learn About All the Special Effects That Went into *The Twilight Saga: Breaking Dawn Part Two*." ScreenSlam.com, November 1, 2012, http://www.screenslam.com/learn-about-all-the-special-effects-that-went-into-the-twilight-saga-breaking-dawn-part-2/ (accessed 9/28/2013).

Cawson, Frank. *The Monsters in the Mind: The Face of Evil in Myth, Literature, and Contemporary Life*. Sussex, Great Britain: Book Guild, 1995.

CCF. "Satanic Christian." Pollystaffle.com, June 2006, http://www.pollystaffle.com/questionsandanswers/christianviel.shtml (accessed 7/19/2014).

Coll, Patrick G., Geraldine O'Sullivan, Patrick A. Browne. "Lycanthropy Lives On." *British Journal of Psychiatry*, 1975, vol. 147, 201–202.

Collins, L.H., M.R. Dunlap, C. Joan (eds.). *Charting a New Course for Feminist Psychology*. Santa Barbara: Greenwood Publishing, 2002.

Collis, Clark. "*Hatchet 2* Director Adam Green on His New Anthology Movie *Chillerama*." *Entertainment Weekly*, October 11, 2010, http://popwatch.ew.com/2010/10/11/chillerama-hatchet-2-adam-green/ (accessed 8/9/2013).

Collura, Scott. "Exclusive: Zombie Talks T Rex," IGN.com, March 20, 2009 (accessed 9/10/2013).

Conley, Gary. "An Interview with Jessi Gotta and Bryan Enk." Roguecinema.com, http://www.roguecinema.com/an-interview-with-jessi-gotta-and-bryan-enk-by-cary-conley.html (accessed 4/19/2015).

Corliss, Richard, and James Inverne. "Terry's Flying Circus." Time.com, August 1, 2005, http://content.time.com/time/magazine/article/0,9171,1088723-1,00.html (accessed 11/27/2015)

Cotton, Mike. "House Party." Wizarduniverse.com, April 4, 2007, http://web.archive.org/web/20071211040830/http://www.wizarduniverse.com/magazine/wizard/004090803.cfm (accessed 7/15/2014).

"Crew Needed: *Audie and the Wolf*, Shoots April 9-May 3, CA." studentfilmmakers.com, March 1, 2007, http://www.studentfilmmakers.com/

forums/showthread.php/2732-Crew-Needed-Audie-and-the-Wolf-Shoots-April-9-May-3-CA (accessed 1/18/2016).
Crisafulli, Chick. "The Modern Legends of *Wolf*." *Fangoria* 134 (July 1994).
_____. "Who's Afraid of Nichols' *Wolf*." *Fangoria* 131 (April 1994).
Crow, Thomas. "*Bad Moon* Rising." *Fangoria* 158 (November 1996).
Crowell, Aaron, and Nathan Hanneman. "*The Monster Squad* 20 Years Later: Wolfman's Still Got Nards." *HorrorHound* 6 (Summer 2007).
Cuenca, Jose Ignacio. "The Howl from Overseas." *Fangoria* 134 (July 1994).
Cullum, Paul. "Death Race 2000." *L.A. Weekly*, January 13, 2006, http://www.laweekly.com/news/death-race-2000-2141452 (accessed 7/3/2015).
Curci, Loris. *Shock Masters of the Cinema*. Key West, FL: Fantasma Books, 1996.
Cybulski, Angela. *Werewolves: Fact or Fiction?* Farmington Hills, MI: Greenhaven Press, 2004.
"*DarkWolf*, a New Breed." *DarkWolf* DVD (Twentieth Century–Fox Home Entertainment, 2003).
Dart, Allan. "Size Doesn't Matter." *Fangoria* 202 (May 2001).
Davis, Mike. "*President Wolfman*: Making of a Green Movie." *Presidentwolfman*, November 3, 2011–March 17, 2014, http://presidentwolfman.com/ (accessed October 11, 2014).
Day, Kristian. "Pet Sounds: The Music of *Howling II*." *Fangoria* 340 (March 2015).
Del Valle, David. "Dr. Phibes Regrets: He Is Unable to Lunch Today...Madam." *Little Shoppe of Horrors* 29 (October 2012).
_____. "John Brahm: The Last Interview." Sumishta.com, July 1979, http://www.sumishta.com/pages/johnbrahminterview.html (accessed 11/21/2013).
Di Lauro, Janet. "Who's New—Mac Attack!" *Soap Opera World*, April 9, 1991.
Dickson, Evan. "Writer Eric Stolze Talks *Late Phases*." Collider.com, December 5, 2014, http://collider.com/eric-stolze-late-phases-interview/ (accessed 3/18/2015).
Dillman, Bradford. *Are You Anybody? An Actor's Life*. Santa Barbara: Fithian Press, 1997.
"Director Talks *Big Bad Wolf* Gore." HorrorDigital.com, http://www.horrordvds.com/vb3forum/showthread.php?t=27913 (accessed 3/16/2015).
Dixon, Wheeler Winston. *The Films of Freddie Francis*. Metuchen, NJ: Scarecrow Press, 1991.
_____. *Voices from Twentieth-Century Cinema*. Carbondale and Edwardsville: Southern Illinois University Press, 2001.
D'Onofrio, Roberto E. "Written in Blood: From Dario Argento to Lucio Fulci, Screenwriter Antonio Tentori Has Penned for Italy's Best." *Gorezone* 33 (December 2014).
Doyle, Michael. "*Wolfen*: A Political Animal, Part 1." *Fangoria* 301 (March 2011).
_____. "*Wolfen*: A Political Animal, Part 2." *Fangoria* 302 (April 2011).
Duenas, Aaron. "Interview: Sherilyn Fenn." *The Death Rattle*, February 22, 2010, http://www.thedeathrattle.net/2010/02/interview-sherilyn-fenn.html (accessed 7/8/2014).
Earnshaw, Tony. "An American Werewolf's Girl." *Fangoria* 313 (May 2012).
Ebert, Roger. "Wolfen." Rogerebert.com, January 1, 1981, http://www.rogerebert.com/reviews/wolfen-1981 (accessed 8/18/2013).
Edelstein, David. "The Love Bug." *Rolling Stone* 484 (October 9, 1986).

Edwards, Kathryn A., ed. *Werewolves, Witches and Wandering Spirits: Traditional Beliefs and Folklore in Early Modern Europe*. Kirksville, MS: Truman State University Press, 2002.
Ehrenreich, Barbara. *Blood Rites: Origins and History of the Passions of War*. New York: Free Press, 1997.
Ellis, Shaun. "As 400 wolves lay siege to a village... Have these ruthless killers lost their fear of humans?" DailyMail.com, February 10, 2011, http://www.dailymail.co.uk/sciencetech/article-1355435/As-400-wolves-lay-siege-village—Have-ruthless-killers-lost-fear-humans.html (accessed 5/10/2014).
England, Norman. "*Kibakichi*: The Fur Flies." *Fangoria* 244 (June 2005).
Essman, Scott. "Wolf Men: Jack Pierce's Incarnations of the Wolf Man." *Monsters from the Vault*, vol. 18, no. 32 (Summer 2013).
Etingoff, Kim. *The Making of a Monster: Vampires and Werewolves*. Broomall, PA: Mason Crest, 2011.
Everitt, David. "Stephen King's *Silver Bullet*." *Fangoria* 48 (1985).
Evry, Max. "The Strange Saga of *Spookies*." *The Dissolve*, October 15, 2014, https://thedissolve.com/features/oral-history/788-the-strange-saga-of-spookies/ (accessed 10/14/15).
Fairburn, Sean. "*Red Riding Hood* HD Tech Report." *Highdef*, Vol. 5, no. 4.
Falcone, Joseph. "Interview with David Hayter for his film *Wolves*." Gonewiththemovies.com, December 27, 2014, http://gonewiththemovies.com/interviews/tadff-david-hayter.php#.Vqp9jOgrLcs (accessed 1/28/2016).
Fallon, John. "The Arrow Interviews...Kane Hodder." JoBlo.com, 2002, http://www.joblo.com/arrow/interview82.htm (accessed 1/19/2015).
Fan Girl Next Door. "Exclusive Interview: Kevin Sorbo." House of Horrors.com, September 14, 2008, http://houseofhorrors.com/crypt/pages2/publish/Interviews_20/Exclusive_Interview_KEVIN_SORBO_printer.shtml (accessed 8/22/2014).
"The Feral Man Speaks: Interview with Brett Kelly." *The Feral Man* DVD, Tempe Video, 2005.
Ferrante, Anthony C. "*Howling VII*: Long in the Tooth?" *Fangoria* 134 (July 1994).
Fischer, Dennis. "The Amicus Empire: An Interview with Milton Subotsky." *Filmfax* 42 (December/January 1994).
_____. *Horror Film Directors, 1931–1990*. Jefferson, NC: McFarland, 1991.
_____. "An Interview with the Outspoken Sultan of Speculation: Curt Siodmak." *Filmfax* 13 (December 1988).
_____. "An Interview with the Outspoken Sultan of Speculation: Curt Siodmak, Part Two." *Filmfax* 14 (March/April 1989).
Ford, Joseph. "Wikinews Interviews Author and Filmmaker Peter John Ross." wikinews.org, March 25, 2008, https://en.wikinews.org/wiki/Wikinews_interviews_author_and_filmmaker_Peter_John_Ross (accessed 1/20/2016).
Frost, Brian J. *The Essential Guide to Werewolf Literature*. Madison: University of Wisconsin Press, 2003.
Gaita, Paul. "*Blood & Chocolate*: Young Werewolves in Love." *Fangoria* 260 (February 2007).
Gambin, Lee. *Massacred by Mother Nature: Exploring the Natural Horror Film*. Baltimore, MD: Midnight Marquee Press, 2012.
Gambin, Lee, and Ki Wone. "Back to the Colony." *Fangoria* 307 (October 2011).

Gilchrist, Todd. "FilmDistrict Takes on *The Devil Inside* Director's *Wer*." *The Hollywood Reporter*, February 7, 2012, http://www.hollywoodreporter.com/news/devil-inside-wer-william-brent-bell-filmdistrict-287811 (accessed 10/18/2014).
Gingold, Michael. "The American Werewolf That Wasn't." *Fangoria* 134 (July 1994).
_____. "Dead in Cold Climates." *Fangoria* 324 (June 2013).
_____. "*FDR: American Badass*: New Dealing with Werewolves." *Fangoria* 317 (October 2012).
_____. "*Late Phases* and Hairy Faces." *Fangoria* 338 (December 2014).
_____. "Love Transforms *Jack & Diane*." *Fangoria* 318 (November 2012).
_____. "*Red Riding Hood* Grows Up." *Fangoria* 301 (March 2011).
"Girls Get Their Teeth Into a Hairy Moment." *The Herald* (London), June 28, 2001, http://www.heraldscotland.com/sport/spl/aberdeen/girls-get-their-teeth-into-a-hairy-moment-1.182165 (accessed 4/22/2015).
Godfrey, Linda S. *Hunting the American Werewolf: Beast Men in Wisconsin and Beyond*. Madison, WI: Trails Books, 2006.
Goldberg, Lee. "Rutger Hauer, Knight Wolf to a Ladyhawke." *Starlog* 95 (June 1985).
Goldschmidt, Rick. "The Mad, Mad, Mad Monsters of Rankin/Bass." *Monsterscene* 9 (Fall 1996).
González, José Luis, and Michael Secula. "Interview: Paul Naschy." *Videooze*, 6/7 (Fall 1994).
_____. "Paul Naschy Filmography." *Videooze* 6/7 (Fall 1994).
Goodwin, Cliff. *Evil Spirits: The Life of Oliver Reed*. London: Virgin Books, 2000.
Gourley, Jack. "Lon Chaney Jr., Part Two." *Filmfax* 21 (1990).
Gourley, Jack, and Gary Dorst. "A Man, a Myth, and Many Monsters: Lon Chaney Jr." *Filmfax* 20 (May 1990).
Grippo, Pattye. "Felicia Day Interview." *Pazsaz Entertainment Network*, October 25, 2010, http://articles.pazsaz.com/redtr.html (accessed 10/31/2014).
Guillen, Michael. "Hunks of Horror: *Dark Moon Rising* (aka *Wolf Moon*)—Interview with Chris Diveccio." Twitchfilm.com, July 1, 2010, http://twitchfilm.com/2010/07/hunks-of-horror-dark-moon-rising-aka-wolf-moon—interview-with-chris-divecchio.html (accessed 8/27/2014).
Haberman, Chris. "*Cirque du Freak the Vampire's Assistant* Comes to Town." *Fangoria* 288 (November 2009).
Hallenbeck, Bruce G. "Anthony Hinds, Prince of Hammer: Part Two." *Fangoria* 75 (July 1988).
Hamilton, John. *Beasts in the Cellar: The Exploitation Film Career of Tony Tenser*. Godalming, England: FAB Press, 2005.
_____. *The Unholy Three: Screen Villains and English Gentlemen—George Couloris, Andre Morell, Dennis Price*. Baltimore, MD: Midnight Marquee Press, 2009.
Harmon, Jessica. "*Dark Moon Rising* Director Thanks *Twilight* Franchise, Kristen Stewart in Exclusive Interview." Moviepilot.com, June 30, 2015, http://moviepilot.com/posts/2015/07/01/dark-moon-rising-director-thanks-twilight-franchise-kristen-stewart-in-exclusive-interview-3349554?lt_source=external,manual (accessed 10/19/2015).
Harrington, Curtis. *Nice Guys Don't Work in Hollywood: The Adventures of an Aesthete in the Movie Business*. Chicago: Drag City, Inc., 2013.

Hart, Donna. "Humans as Prey." *The Chronicle of Higher Education* (April 21, 2006): B10–11.

Hawker, Philippa. "Christopher Lee: Dracula, Nazi Hunter and Much More Says Filmmaker Philippe Mora." *Sydney Morning Herald*, June 12, 2015, http://www.smh.com.au/entertainment/movies/christopher-lee-dracula-nazi-hunter-and-much-more-says-filmmaker-philippe-mora-20150612-ghmi57.html (accessed 6/23/2015).

Helms, Michael. "*Underworld Rise of the Lycans*: Bloody Beginnings." *Fangoria* 280 (February 2009).

Henderson, Lisle. "*Howl* and *The Seasoning House* Director Paul Hyett." Theslaughteredbird.com, October 26, 2015, http://theslaughteredbird.com/interview-howl-the-seasoning-house-director-paul-hyett/ (accessed 12/16/2015).

Higham, Charles, and Joel Greenberg. *The Celluloid Muse: Hollywood Directors Speak*. New York: New American Library, 1969.

Hodges, Mike. "Howling for *Werewolf Hunter*." *Fangoria* 248, November 2005.

———. "*Lycantropus*: Paul Naschy Howls Again." *Fangoria* 165, August 1997.

———. "A Spanish Werewolf in L.A." *Fangoria* 234 (July 2004).

Hood, Robert. "Interview with House of the Wolfman's Ron Chaney." *Undead Backbrain*, July 20, 2010, http://roberthood.net/blog/index.php/2010/07/20/update-house-of-the-wolf-man/ (accessed 8/15/2015).

Horn, Kristian. "AICN Horror Talks with Lowell Dead About His New Horror Comedy *WolfCop*." *Ain't It Cool News*, June 6, 2013, http://www.aintitcool.com/node/62747 (accessed 4/1/2015).

House on Bare Mountain pressbook. Olympic International Films, 1962.

Hurlburt, Roger. "Spoof of Spooks? In 'Transylvania,' Nothing Is Amusing." Sun-Sentinel.com, November 12, 1985, http://articles.sun-sentinel.com/1985-11-12/features/8502200300 (accessed 9/27/2013).

"Interview: Dominik Starck (BGT-Exclusive)." Bereitsgetestet.de, http://bereitsgetestet.de/index.php/interviews/70-interview-dominik-starck-bgt-exklusiv.html (accessed 4/22/2016).

"An Interview with Gustavo Perez." *Light of Blood* DVD. Cult Movie Mania Releasing, 2014.

"Interview with *13 Hrs and Strippers vs. Werewolves* Director Jonathan Glendening." LoveHorror.com, March 16, 2012, http://lovehorror.co.uk/q-a-with-jonathan-glendening (accessed 4/4/2014).

Jackson, B. Gelman. "The Life Story of Lon Chaney, Jr." *Monster Fantasy* 1, no. 4 (1975).

Janisse, Kier-La. "Jack's Journey into Perversion." *Fangoria* 325 (August 2013).

"Jeff Leroy: Making Movies for Blu-Ray Drive-Ins." *Guestar, Blog of the Missed*, May 3, 2010, http://guestar.wordpress.com/2010/05/03/jeff-leroy-making-movies-for-blu-ray-drive-ins/ (accessed 6/16/2014).

JimmyO. "Int: Christa Campbell." *Arrow in the Head*, April 8, 2008, http://www.joblo.com/horror-movies/news/interview-christa-campbell (accessed 4/24/2015).

Johnson, Aidan, and Michael Gingold. "Interview with a Vampire Director." *Fangoria* 325 (August 2013).

Johnson, Tom, and Mark A. Miller. *The Christopher Lee Filmography*. Jefferson, NC: McFarland, 2004.

Jones, Alan. "The Bark & Bite of *Dog Soldiers*." *Fangoria* 212 (May 2002).

———. "Notes from the *Underworld*." *Fangoria* 226 (September 2003).

———. "*Underworld*: Love Be Damned." *Fangoria* 222 (May 2003).

Jones, Beth. "Wolf's Tale." *The Roanoke Times*, www.roanoke.com, September 2, 2004, http://www.roanoke.com/webmin/features/wolf-s-tale/article_59d4ed46-55ed-5059-8a66-91cb0a08b288.html (accessed 4/11/2015).

Jones, Stephen. *The Illustrated Werewolf Movie Guide*. London: Titan Books, 1996.

Kaiser, Matthew. "Interview with *Howl* Director Paul Hyett." Punchdrunkmovies.com, http://punchdrunkmovies.com/index.php/hudak-thinks-this-is-cool/27-interviews-1/interviews/4370-interview-with-howl-director-paul-hyett (accessed 12/16/2015).

Kay, Tony. "Piranhas and Werewolves and Rats... OH MY! An Interview with Belinda Balaski." *Shock Cinema* 33 (July 2007).

Keck, Paul. E., Harrison G. Pope, James I. Hudson, Susan L. McElroy, Aaron R. Kulick. "Lycanthropy: Alive and Well in the Twentieth Century." *Psychological Medicine*, vol. 18, 1988, 113–120. Cambridge University Press.

King, Stephen. "Why We Crave Horror Movies." *The Prose Reader: Essays for Thinking, Reading and Writing*, 6th Edition, Kim Flachmann and Michael Flachmann, eds. Upper Saddle River, NJ: Prentice Hall, 2002.

Konow, David. *Reel Terror: The Scary, Bloody, Gory, Hundred-Year History of Classic Horror Films*. New York: Thomas Dunne Books, 2012.

Labbe, Rod. "Directing in the Shadows." *Fangoria* 313 (May 2012).

"Ladyhawke." Rutger Hauer Official Website. http://www.rutgerhauer.org/plots/ladyh.php (accessed 6/21/2013).

"Ladyhawke." *Time Out*, http://www.timeout.com/london/film/ladyhawke (accessed 6/21/2013).

Laemmle, Carl. "A Message from the President of Universal Pictures." Universal Pictures, April 1935.

Landis, John. *Monsters in the Movies: 100 Years of Cinematic Nightmares*. London: Darling Kindersley Ltd., 2011.

———. "Trailers from Hell: *Curse of the Werewolf*." Trailersfromhell.com, 2013.

Lavagnini, Massimo F. "Maestro... di Silvestro." *Nocturno* vol. 2, no. 4 (September 1997).

Lee, Christopher. *Lord of Misrule: The Autobiography of Christopher Lee*. London: Orion Books, Ltd., 2003.

Leibe, Jessica. "Under a New Moon." *Fangoria* 288 (November 2009).

Lindenmuth, Kevin J. *How to Make Movies: Low-Budget/No-Budget Indie Experts Tell All*. Jefferson, NC: McFarland, 2013.

———. *The Independent Film Experience: Interviews with Directors and Producers*. Jefferson, NC: McFarland, 2002.

Loftus, Elizabeth F. *Eyewitness Testimony*. Cambridge, MA: Harvard University Press, 1996.

Los Angeles Times. "Forrest J Ackerman Dead at 92." *Los Angeles Times*, December 5, 2008, http://herocomplex.latimes.com/uncategorized/forrest-j-acker/ (accessed 7/3/2013).

Luster, Shannon, and Sharon Jordan. "The Master of On-Screen Chemistry: Randal Kleiser." *Cultscoop Magazine*, http://www.cultmachine.com/cultnik/cult/Randal_Kleiser/Randal_Kleiser.html (accessed 11/25/2015).

"The Making of Underworld." *Underworld* DVD. Sony Pictures Home Entertainment, 2004.

Mank, Gregory William. *It's Alive: The Classic Cinema Saga of Frankenstein*. New York: A.S. Barnes and Company, 1981.

———. *The Very Witching Time of Night: Dark Alleys of Classic Horror Cinema*. Jefferson, NC: McFarland, 2014.

"Matthew Lillard: Biography," *Internet Movie Data Base*, http://www.imdb.com/name/nm0000498/bio?ref_=nm_ov_bio_sm (accessed 10/22/2014).

McClelland, Doug. *The Golden Age of B Movies*. New York: Bonanza Books, 1978.

McDonagh, Maitland. "Scare Sisters." *Fangoria* 102 (May 1991).

McDonnell, David. "When the American Werewolf Howled." *Fangoria* 129 (December 1993).

McDonough, Jimmy. *The Ghastly One: The Sex-Gore Netherworld of Filmmaker Andy Milligan*. Chicago: A Capella Books, 2001.

McVicar, W. Brice. "Bad Mood Rising." *Fangoria* 307 (October 2011).

———. "*Monster Brawl*: Gruesome Grappling." *Fangoria* 302 (April 2011).

———. "Tales of the Brothers Gore." *Gorezone* 29 (2013).

Medina, Victor. "Q&A: David Hayter Talks *Wolves*, *Metal Gear*, and *X-Men*." Cinelinx.com, October 30, 2014, http://www.cinelinx.com/interviews/item/6643-q-a-david-hayter-talks-wolves-metal-gear-and-x-men.html (accessed 1/28/2016).

Meikle, Denis. *Vincent Price: The Art of Fear*. London: Reynolds and Hearn, 2003.

Memmott, Carol. "Damon, Prague, Star in 'Grimm' Fairy Tale." Usatoday.com, April 11, 2004, http://usatoday30.usatoday.com/life/movies/news/2004-04-11-damon-prague_x.htm (accessed 11/27/2015).

Miller, James. "Interview: Ilona Massey." *Varulven* 4 (April 1972).

Moore, Anne. "*Full Eclipse*: Police Lycanthropy." *Fangoria* 129 (December 1993).

———. "Theories of *Evolution*." *Fangoria* 250 (February 2006).

Moore, David J. "Howling for More: *Werewolf the Beast Among Us*." *Fangoria* 317 (October 2012).

Moran, Brian. "Director Gilberto Martinez Solares." *Santo Street* 18 (2000).

———. "Investigating 'Investigador' Capulina." *Santo Street* 14 (Summer 1997).

———. "Meet the True Blue Demon." *Santo Street* 7 (October 1995).

Naha, Ed. "The *Cat People* Conspiracy." *Starlog* 59 (June 1982).

Naschy, Paul. *Memoirs of a Wolfman*. Trans. by Mike Hodges. Baltimore, MD: Midnight Marquee Press, 2000.

Nicoll, Gregory. "The Comeback Kid." *Fangoria* 76 (August 1988).

Night of the Howling Beast pressbook. Constellation Films Inc., 1976.

"*Night Shadow* Reviews and Ratings," *Internet Movie Data Base*, June 1, 2005, http://www.imdb.com/title/tt0097973/reviews?ref_=tt_urv (accessed 1/7/2015).

Noll, Richard, ed. *Vampires, Werewolves, and Demons: Twentieth Century Reports in the Psychiatric Literature*. New York: Bruner/Mazel, 1996.

Nutman, Philip. "Chris Tucker in the Company of Wolves." *Fangoria* 42 (March 1985).

O'Heir, Bernie. "Interview: Reginald LeBorg." *Cinemacabre* 7 (1988).

Oliphant, Roland. "Wolf Attacks Lead to a State of Emergency in Russia's Siberia Region." *The Telegraph*, January 6, 2013, http://www.telegraph.co.uk/news/worldnews/europe/russia/9783783/Wolf-attacks-lead-to-state-of-emergency-in-Russias-Siberia-region.html (accessed 5/10/2015).

Pappademus, Alex. "We Are All Teenage Werewolves." *New York Times Magazine*, May 20, 2011, http://www.nytimes.com/2011/05/22/magazine/we-are-all-teenage-werewolves.html?_r=0 (accessed 1/24/2016).

Parda, J.F. "Acquanetta." *The Exploitation Journal* 15 (Summer 1993).

Parker, Andrew. "Interview: Chris Green." *Notes from the Toronto Underground*," October 28, 2010, http://notesfromthetorontounderground.blogspot.com/2010/10/interview-chris-green-zombie-werewolves.html (accessed 11/17/2013).

Parla, Paul. "Jellyfish-Man ... an Interview with Doug Hobart." *Scary Monsters* 26 (March 1998).

Parla, Paul, and Donna Parla. "Cult of *The Werewolf*: An Interview with Steven Ritch." *Filmfax* 62 (August/September 1997).

Patrick, Holly. "*Love Bite*: Ed Speleers and Luke Pasqualino Interviewed by Holly Patrick." *The Fan Carpet*, November 4, 2012, https://www.youtube.com/watch?v=s8y9d40orhE (accessed 8/30/2015).

Patten, Fred. *Watching Anime, Reading Manga: 25 Years of Essays and Reviews*. Stone Bridge Press: 2004.

"Paul Naschy: Memoirs of a Wolfman." *Dr. Jekyll and the Werewolf* DVD, Mondo Macabro.

Pierce, Dale. "Horror with a Spanish Twist: Paul Naschy." *Filmfax* 33.

Plante, Bob. "Motorcycle Maniacs, Fantastic Fights: John 'Bud' Cardos." *Psychotronic Video* 24 (1997).

Powell, W. Andrew. "*Wolves* Interview with Writer and Director David Hayter." Thegate.ca, November 19, 2014, http://www.thegate.ca/film/022464/wolves-interview-writer-director-david-hayter/ (accessed 1/28/2016).

Quammen, David. *Monster of God: The Man-Eating Predator in the Jungles of History and the Mind*. New York: W.W. Norton, 2003.

Rabkin, William. "*The Monster Squad*." *Fangoria* 66 (August 1987).

_____. "*The Monster Squad* and Me." *Fangoria* 67 (September 1987).

Radish, Christina. "Brandon Routh and Sam Huntington Exclusive Interview *Dylan Dog*." collider.com, April 27, 2011, http://collider.com/brandon-routh-sam-huntington-interview-dylan-dog-2/ (accessed 1/22/2106).

_____. "Director Catherine Hardwicke Exclusive Interview: *Red Riding Hood*." Collider.com, March 9, 2011, http://collider.com/catherine-hardwicke-interview-red-riding-hood/ (accessed 3/21/2015).

_____. "Director Kevin Munroe Exclusive Interview, *Dylan Dog*." April 28, 2011, http://collider.com/kevin-munroe-interview-dylan-dog/ (accessed 1/22/2016).

Radner, Gilda. *It's Always Something*. New York: Simon & Schuster, 1989.

Rice, Anne. "Whither the Werewolf." *The New York Times Book Review*, April 5, 1987, p. 33.

Rigby, Jonathan. *English Gothic: A Century of Horror Cinema*. London: Reynolds & Hearn, Ltd., 2000.

Rollans, Scott. "Berger Sez Bigger's Not Better." *Fangoria* 230 (March 2004).

_____. "*Ginger Snaps II: Unleashed*—Howling for More." *Fangoria* 230 (March 2004).

_____. "*Ginger Snaps Back*: Historical Howls." *Fangoria* 236 (September 2004).

Ross, John Peter. *Tales from the Front Line of Indy Filmmaking*. Pickerington, OH: Sonnyboo Publishing, 2007.

Rotton, J., and I. W. Kelly. "Much Ado About the Full Moon: A Meta-Analysis of Lunar-Lunacy Research." *Psychological Bulletin* 97 (1985), 286–306.

Rowe, Michael. "*Ginger Snaps*." *Fangoria* 234 (July 2004).

_____. "*Skinwalkers*: Werewolf Wars." *Fangoria* 262 (April 2007).

Sachs, Bruce, and Russell Wall. *Greasepaint and Gore: The Hammer Monsters of Roy Ashton*. Sheffield, England: Tomahawk Press, undated.

Sailsbury, Mark. "Faces of *The Wolfman*." *Fangoria* 291 (March 2010).

_____. "A Lycanthropic Sequel in Limbo." *Fangoria* 129 (December 1993).

_____. "Makeup Effects Lab: Baker's New Recipe." *Fangoria* 291 (March 2010).

_____. "The New Breed of Werewolf FX." *Fangoria* 134 (July 1994).

_____. "*The Wolfman*: Hair Today, Gore Tomorrow." *Fangoria* 290 (February 2010).

_____. "*The Wolfman*: New Moon Rising." *Fangoria* 279 (January 2008).

Sano, Ruben (trans. Rogelio Agrasanchez, Jr.). "On Monsters and Imposters: Santo's Final Say." *Santo Street* 13 (Spring 1997), originally in *Cine* 26 (June 1980).

Santos. "Interview: Sybil Danning." horrornews.net, October 22, 2010, http://horrornews.net/18234/interview-sybil-danning-halloween-battle-beyond-the-stars-howling-2/ (accessed 1/6/2016).

Savello, Danny. "A Werewolf Prepares: Nina Foch." *Scarlet Street* 33 (1999).

Schlegel, Nicholas G. *Sex, Sadism, Spain, and Cinema: The Spanish Horror Film*. Lanham, MD: Rowman & Littlefield, 2015.

Seat42F. "*Nature of the Beast* Autumn Reeser Interview." Seat42F.com, October 20, 2007, http://www.seat42f.com/nature-of-the-beast-autumn-reeser.html (accessed 3/3/2015).

Senn, Bryan. Ted A. Bohus phone interview. June 12, 2015.

_____. Freddie Francis interview. May 1995.

_____. Cortlandt Hull email interview. January 2016.

_____. Ricardo Islas email interview. January 2015.

_____. Kevin McCarthy interview, May 1996.

_____. William Ragsdale interview. October 4, 2014.

_____. Fred Olen Ray email interview. October 29, 2015.

_____. Curt Siodmak interview. May 1993.

_____. Gloria Stuart interview. May 1993.

_____. Jack Taylor email interview. March 30, 2015.

_____. Robert Tinnell interview. May 1997.

_____. Carrie Vaughn interview. February 7, 2014.

_____. George Willis interview. February 7, 2014.

Senn, Bryan, Richard Sheffield, and Jim Clatterbaugh. "El Vampiro Speaks! An Interview with Mexican Horror Star German Robles." *Monsters from the Vault* 24 (2008).

Sergio. "Monster Dog." SickthingsUK, May 1997, http://www.sickthingsuk.co.uk/content.php?id=film/f-monsterdog.php (accessed 12/21/2013).

Serino, Jack. "*Red Riding Hood*." *Highdef*, Vol. 5, no. 4.

Shapiro, Marc. "The *Cursed* Is Over?" *Fangoria* 241 (March 2005).

_____. "*Cursed*: Where Wolf?" *Fangoria* 237 (October 2004).

_____. "*Fright Night Part 2* Bares Its Fangs." *Fangoria* 76 (August 1988).

_____. "Second Time Hairy." *Fangoria* 241 (March 2005).

Siegemund-Broka, Austin. "Universal Adds *American Werewolf in London* to Halloween Horror Nights." Hollywoodreporter.com, August 11, 2014, http://www.hollywoodreporter.com/heat-vision/universal-adds-american-werewolf-london-724618 (accessed 10/9/2014).

Simpson, James. "*Werewolf Rising* Special Part 2: The BC Furtney Interview." Ukhorrorscene.com, August 15, 2014, http://www.ukhorrorscene.com/werewolf-rising-special-part-2-bc-furtney-interview/ (accessed 1/17/2015).

Simpson, M.J. "Aaaaaagh, *Wilderness*." *Wilderness* DVD, Fangoria Films, 2001.

_____. "Interview: Charles Band Part II." *MJ Simpson: Film Reviews and Interviews*, January 31, 2013, http://mjsimpson-films.blogspot.com/2013/01/charles-band-part-2.html (accessed 12/14/2014).

_____. *Urban Terrors: New British Horror Cinema, 1997–2008*. Bristol, England: Hemlock Books, 2012.

Siodmak, Curt. *Wolf Man's Maker: Memoir of a Hollywood Writer*. Lanham, MD: The Scarecrow Press, 2001.

Sipos, Thomas M. "Shapeshifters, Zombies Dominate 2004 *Hollywood Investigator* Halloween Horror Film Awards." *Hollywood Investigator*, http://www.hollywoodinvestigator.com/2004/horrorfilm2004.htm (accessed 6/6/2014).

Sites, Brandon. "Interview with Actor Bradley Stryker from *The Brotherhood* and *Final Stab*." Brandonsites.blogspot.com, http://brandonsites.blogspot.com/2010/10/interview-with-actor-bradley-stryker-of.html (accessed 10/19/2015).

_____. "Interview with Jason Toler of *Half Moon*." Brandonsites.blogspot.com, http://brandonsites.blogspot.com/2011/03/interview-with-jason-toler-of-half-moon.html (accessed 4/2/2015).

Slater, Jay. "Rats and Creeping Flesh: Claudio Fragasso Interviewed." *Darkside* 73 (June/July 1998).

Slifkin, Irv. "*Communion*, an Interview with Writer Director Philippe Mora." Moviefanfare.com, June 16, 2010, http://www.moviefanfare.com/philippe-mora/ (accessed 1/6/2016).

Smith. "Icons of Fright Interview with Robert Angelo Masciontonio." Iconsoffright.com, September 23, 2012, http://iconsoffright.com/2012/09/23/icons-of-fright-interview-wrobert-angelo-masciantonio/ (accessed 2/13/2014).

Smith, Cynthia Leitich. "Author Update: Annette Curtis Klause." *Cynsations*, January 14, 2006, http://cynthialeitichsmith.blogspot.com/2006/01/author-update-annette-curtis-klause.html (accessed 10/20/2015).

Smith, Don G. *Lon Chaney, Jr.: Horror Film Star, 1906–1973*. Jefferson, NC: McFarland, 1996.

Spiderbaby, Lianne. "Danning with Praise." *Fangoria* 302 (April 2011).

Spiegel, Janel. "Interview: Jeremy Wooding—Director (*Blood Moon*)." www.horrornews.net, August 20, 2015, http://horrornews.net/101197/interview-jeremy-wooding-director-blood-moon/ (accessed 12/16/2015).

Standish, David. "Playboy Interview: Kurt Vonnegut Jr." *Playboy* (July 1973).

Stedeford, Victoria. "Rosie Pearson, *Crying Wolf* Interview." Youtube.com, August 14, 2014, https://www.youtube.com/watch?v=nRLJROnqaoY (accessed 3/22/2016).

Stevens, Anthony. *Aridadne's Clue: A Guide to the Symbols of Humankind*. Princeton, NJ: Princeton University Press, 1999.

Stranahan, Lee. "Is Hollywood Ready for a Gay Male Adult Actor in Mainstream Roles?" *The Huffington Post*, November 2011, http://www.huffingtonpost.com/lee-stranahan-is-hollywood-ready-for-a-_b_790154.html (accessed 8/9/2013).

"*Strippers vs. Werewolves* World Premier Interviews," April 26, 2012, http://www.heyuguys.co.uk/strippers-vs-werewolves-premiere-interviews/ (accessed 4/4/2014).

Summers, Montague. *The Werewolf*. London: Kegan Paul, Trench, Trubner & Co., 1933.

Sunshine, Linda (ed.). *Van Helsing: The Making of the Legend*. New York: Newmarked Press, 2004.

Swires, Steve. "Kerwin Mathews: Part II." *Starlog* 120 (July 1987).

_____. "Nathan Juran." *Starlog* 141 (April 1989).

_____. "Roy Ward Baker: Life After Hammer." *Fangoria* 117 (October 1992).

Terenzio, Maurice. "The Interview of a Lifetime with John Howard." *Filmfax* 31 (February/March 1992).

Tessnear, Michael. "Earl Owensby, Studio Owe $40k in Taxes." *Shelby Star*, February 20, 2013, http://www.shelbystar.com/news/local/earl-owensby-studio-owe-40k-in-taxes-1.99103?page=7 (accessed 10/20/2013).

Thomas, Bob. *Bud & Lou: The Abbott and Costello Story*. New York: Lippincott, 1977.

Tohill, Cathal, and Pete Tombs. *Immoral Tales: European Sex and Horror Movies, 1956–1984*. New York: St. Martin's Griffin, 1995.

Toffolo, Matthew. "Interview with Chris Green." *WILDsound Horror Film Festival*, October 26, 2010, http://www.youtube.com/watch?v=PA4-1-nwhzs&feature=channel (accessed 11/17/2013).

Trivedi, Sachin. *Little Dead Rotting Hood*: A Reimagining of the Red Riding Hood Story—Exclusive Interview with Writer Gabriel Campisi." Ibtimes.com, January 18, 2016, http://www.ibtimes.com.au/little-dead-rotting-hood-reimagining-red-riding-hood-story-exclusive-interview-writer-gabriel (accessed 3/22/2016).

Trout, Paul A. *Deadly Powers: Animal Predators and the Mythic Imagination*. New York: Prometheus Books, 2011.

Tudor, Andrew. *Monsters and Mad Scientists: A Cultural History of the Horror Movie*. Cambridge, MA: Basil Blackwell, Inc., 1989.

Van Buskirk, Dayna. "*Trick 'r Treat*: Don't Open the Door!" *Fangoria* 266 (September 2007).

Vermette, Al J. "Master of Monsters." *Werewolf Cafe*, October 8, 2006, http://www.werewolfcafe.com/movies.php (accessed 7/26/2014).

Vié, Caroline. "French Kills with *An American Werewolf in Paris*." *Fangoria* 167 (October 1997).

_____. "Monster Invasion: *An American Werewolf in Paris*." *Fangoria* 162 (May 1997).

Vraney, Mike. "Cult Movies Interview: Bob Cresse." *Cult Movies* 9 (1993).

Waddell, Calum. *Minds of Fear: A Dialogue with 30 Modern Masters of Horror!* Baltimore: Luminary Press/Midnight Marquee, 2005.

Waiter, Stanley. "Horror in Print: Gary Brandner." *Fangoria* 72 (March 1988).

Warren, Bill. "Sleepwalkers Awaken." *Fangoria* 111 (April 1992).

Weaver, Tom. *Attack of the Monster Movie Makers: Interviews with 20 Genre Giants*. Jefferson, NC: McFarland, 1994.

_____. *Earth vs. the Sci-Fi Filmmakers: Twenty Interviews*. Jefferson, NC: McFarland, 2005.

_____. "I Remember Bela! Earl Bellamy on Bela Lugosi." *VideoScope* 44 (Fall 2002).

_____. *Interviews with B Science Fiction and Horror Movie Makers: Writers, Producers, Directors, Actors Moguls and Makeup*. Jefferson, NC: McFarland, 1988.

_____. *John Carradine: The Films*. Jefferson, NC: McFarland, 1999.

_____. *Science Fiction and Fantasy Film Flashbacks*. Jefferson, NC: McFarland, 1998.

_____. *Science Fiction Stars and Horror Heroes: Interviews with Actors, Directors, Producers and Writers of the 1940s through 1960s*. Jefferson, NC: McFarland, 1991.

Weaver, Tom, and Michael Brunas. "Siodmak's Brain." *Fangoria* 44 (March 1985).

"Wehrwolves." *Household Words*, vol. 15, no. 370 (April 25, 1857).

Wells, Mitchell. "Ohio Based Feature Film *Horrors of War*." *Horror Society*, October 8, 2007, www.horrorsociety.com (accessed 6/20/2013).

The Werewolf pressbook. Columbia Pictures, 1956.

"*Werewolf of London*: Universal's Supreme Shocker Revisited!" *Famous Monsters of Filmland* 86 (September 1971).

Whipple, G.M. "The Obtaining of Information: Psychology of Observation and Report." *Psychological Bulletin* 15 (1918): 217–248.

Whittington, James. "Exclusive Interview with Director Jeff Burr: Part III." *HorrorChannel*, May 31, 2010, http://www.horrorchannel.co.uk/articles.php?feature=1563&category=5&archive=2010 (accessed 12/14/2014).

Williams, Owen. "Night Visions 2012: Juan Martinez Moreno and *Attack of the Werewolves*." Empireonline.com, November 3, 2012, http://www.empireonline.com/empireblogs/words-from-the-wise/post/p1313 (accessed 7/12/2014).

Williams, Sharon. "Stephen King's Silver Bullet." *Monsterland* 6 (December 1985).

Wilson, Staci Layne. "Exclusive Interview with David B. Hayter on *Wolves*." Dreadcentral.com, October 15, 2015, http://www.dreadcentral.com/news/73396/exclusive-interview-david-b-hayter-wolves/ (accessed 1/28/2016).

Winans, Matt. "Steve Hawkes Interview," *Tarzan Movie Guide*, March 27, 2000, http://www.tarzanmovieguide.com/hawkes.htm.

Wloszczyna, Susan. "What Does the Future Hold for Bella, Edward in *Breaking Dawn*?" USAToday.com, January 7, 2011, http://usatoday30.usatoday.com/life/movies/news/2011-01-07-breakingdawn07_ST_N.htm (accessed 9/22/2013).

Wolfman, The. "Director Adrian Garcia Bogliano and Star Nick Damici Talk *Late Phases*." TheWolfmanCometh.com, March 14, 2014, http://thewolfmancometh.com/2014/03/21/director-adrian-garcia-bogliano-and-star-nick-damici-talk-late-phases-interview-sxsw-14/ (accessed 3/18/2015).

"The Wolfman of Allariz." *Spain Features: Profiles*, Nov 13, 2007, http://www.typicallyspanish.com/spain-archive/profiles/The_Wolfman_of_Allariz.shtml (accessed 11/10/14).

Woodward, Ian. *The Werewolf Delusion*. New York: Paddington Press, 1979.

Wooley, John, and Micheal H. Price. "Forgotten Horrors: *Werewolves on Wheels*." *Fangoria* 242 (April 2005).

Yang, Chi-Hui. "Cinema Asian America: Filmmaker Quentin Lee Discusses *Shopping for Fangs*." *Cinema Asian America*, Xfinity on Demand, September 18, 2012, http://xfinity.comcast.net/blogs/tv/2012/09/18/cinema-asian-america-filmmaker-quentin-lee-discusses-shopping-for-fangs/ (accessed 10/26/2014).

Yanes, Nicholas. "Interview: Jonathan Sothcott Discusses Indie Movie Making, Chata Pictures and His Film *Strippers vs. Werewolves*." Scifipulse.net, October 2012, http://scifipulse.net/2012/10/interview-jonathan-sothcott-discusses-indie-movie-making-chata-pictures-and-his-film-%E2%80%9Cstrippers-vs-werewolves%E2%80%9D/ (accessed 4/4/2014).

Yim, Vince. "*Underworld Evolution*: Monsters in Love and War." *Fangoria* 249 (January 2006).

"Your [sic] Watching Caught in Clapper." *Children of the Night* DVD, Brain Damage Films, 2006.

Zimmerman, Samuel. "What We Do in the Shadows: Old Blood in New Zealand." *Fangoria* 339 (February 2014).

Zombie King. "Interview: Brian Singleton, Director of *Werewolf Fever*!" ZombieInfo.com, August 12, 2011, http://www.zombieinfo.com/2011/08/interview-brian-singleton-director-of-werewolf-fever-and-forest-of-the-dead-and-and-and/ (accessed 3/27/2014).

INDEX

Numbers in ***bold italics*** refer to pages with photographs.

Aardsma, Amanda 363
Aarniokoski, Doug 272
Abbott, Bud 21
Abbott, John 57, 355, 356
Abbott and Costello Meet Frankenstein 1, 10, 15, 21–23, **22**, 112, 116, 122, 158, 159, 195, 211, 246, 273, 296, 300, 369
Abbott and Costello Meet the Killer, Boris Karloff 23
Abbott and Costello Meet the Mummy 23
ABC Movie of the Week 160, 333
The ABCs of Death 141
ABC's Wide World of Entertainment (TV series) 240
The Abominable Dr. Phibes 303
Abraham Lincoln: Vampire Hunter 294
The Abyss 263
Ackerman, Forest J 164, 275, 286
Acquanetta **355**, 355, 364
Adam-12 (series) 76
Adams, Jane 111
Adamson, Al 45, 46
Agar, John 73–74
Agutter, Jenny 24, 26
AIP see American International Pictures
Airplane! 162, 175
Alazraki, Benito 297
Albert, Eddie 373
Alda, Rutanya 142
Las Alegres Vampiras de Vögel 272
Alexander, Monique 204
Alfred Hitchcock Presents 74
Alien 27, 52, 158, 166
Aliens 80
Allen, Claude "Pappy" 135
Allen, David 292
Allen, Tim 369
Allison, Jean 363
Al-Quasri, Abdul Fattah 300
Alvin and the Chipmunks Meet Frankenstein 23
Alvin and the Chipmunks Meet the Wolfman! 23–24
The Amazing Colossal Man 356
The Amazing Transparent Man 74
American Drive-In 302
American International Pictures 137, 356
American Pie (film series) 165

An American Werewolf in London 1, 8, 12, **13**, 14, 21, 24–27, **25**, 28, 31, 33, 52, 53, 54, 59, 66, 74, 75, 81, 82, 84, 96, 101, 102, 123, 124, 132, 143, 149, 159, 162, 163, 200, 211, 219, 226, 233, 235, 243, 246, 255, 258, 260, 261, 264, 283, 285, 293, 338
An American Werewolf in London XXX Porn Parody 15
An American Werewolf in Paris 27–28
Amicus 37, 289
The Amityville Curse 150
Anaconda 80
Anchor Bay 135
Anchorman: The Legend of Ron Burgundy 352
Anchorman 2: The Legend Continues 352
Anders, Donna 250
Anderson, Harry 309
Andrews, Tige 241
Angel Warriors 2 see *Werewolves on Wheels*
Angels from Hell 76
Animal House 26, 339
Animals 272–273
Ankers, Evelyn **15**, 91, 258, 355
Ankrum, Morris 307
Annett, Paul 36, 37
Annie Oakley (TV series) 133
Anoushka 83, 84
Anthony, Lysette 201
Ants 76
The Ape Man 152, 186, 279
Apostolof, Stephen 327
Aquí Huela a Muerto… (Ipues yo no he Sido!) 273
Aquilar, Carlos 248
Argento, Dario 256
Arizona Werewolf see *Werewolf* (1996 film)
Arkin, Adam 96, 97
Arkin, Alan 96
Arkoff, Samuel Z. 334
Armstrong, Vic 219, 264–265
Arrested Development (series) 203
Arsenic and Old Lace (play) 111, 186
Arthur, Robert 21
Ashe, Richard 372
Asher, William 275
Ashley, John 307

Ashton, Roy 64–65, 65, 367
Assignment Terror 28–30, **29**, 61, 97, 248
The Astro-Zombies 47
Asylum (film) 289
The Asylum (production company) 35, 38, 149
At the Earth's Core 168
Atom Age Vampire 16
The Atomic Submarine 73
Attack of the 50 Foot Woman (1958) 50
Attack of the Mayan Mummy 86, 87
Attack of the 60 Foot Centerfold 204
Attack of the Werewolves see *Game of Werewolves*
Attack the Block 246
Attenbury, Malcolm 307
Attias, Daniel 195, 196
Atwill, Lionel 85, 113
Aubert, Lenore 22
Audette, Robert "Odi" 230
Audette, Robin 230
Audie & the Wolf 2, 31–32
El Aullido del Diablo see *Howl of the Devil*
Aured, Carlos 63
Auto de fey 64
Autrey, Gene 133
Avalanche 332
Avco Embassy 97, 124
The Awful Dr. Orlof 291
Axxel 345

Bacall, Lauren 333
Bacchus, John 47
Back to the Future 162, 202
Bad Moon 32–34, **33**
"Bad Moon Rising" (song) 24, 128
Bagdasarian, Ross, Jr. 23
Bagdasarian, Ross, Sr. 23
"The Bagheeta" (short story) 357
Baisley, Glen 338
Baker, Rick 12, 14, **25**, 26, 68, 123, 159, 211, 226, 255, 258, 261, **263**, 263, 263–264, 264
Baker, Roy Ward 321
Bakshi, Ralph 303–304
Balaski, Belinda 241
Baledón, Rafael 314, 315
Ballard, Lucien 218
Band, Charles 242, 243, 284, 292, 320

The Band from Hell see *Neowolf*
Banpaia Hantâ D see *Vampire Hunter D: Bloodlust*
Barbeau, Adrienne 220, 221
Barber, Sandy 262
Barker, Clive 370
Baron, Sandy 324
Barri, Barta 157
Bartalos, Gabe 310
Barton, Charles 21, 22, 122, 369
Basic Instinct 256
The Bat People 352–353, **352**
Batbabe: The Dark Nighty 65
Bateman, Jason 202, 203
Bateman, Kent 202
Batman (TV series) 323
Batman Returns 326
Battle Beyond the Stars 125
Battledogs 34–35, **35**, 149
Bauer, Steven 246
Bava, Lamberto 339
Bava, Mario
Baxley, Paul 50
Baxter, Meredith 356
Beach Babes from Beyond 267
The Beast (1975 film) 15
The Beast and the Magic Sword see *La Bestia y la Espada Mágica*
Beast from 20,000 Fathoms 46
The Beast Must Die 35–37, **36**, 130
The Beast of Bray Road 37–38, 149, 269
The Beast of the Yellow Night 16
The Beast Within (1982) 16
Beast Within (2016) see *Uncaged*
Beaton, Stephanie 84, **85**
Beatty, Clyde 355
Beckinsale, Kate 212, **212**, 213, 214
Beetlejuice 162
Begley, Ed Jr. 340
Belaski, Belinda 24
Bell, William Brent 222, 223
Bellamy, Earl 186
Bellamy, Ralph 258
Belushi, James 333
Bender, Jack 320–321
Bent, Richard 199
Berardi, Dennis 197, 198
Berger, Howard 51, 106
Bergman, Ingrid 180
Bergman, Sandahl 334
Berkoff, Steve 201
The Best Exotic Marigold Hotel 216

389

La Bestia y la Espada Mágica 56, 273–274, **274**
The Beverly Hillbillies (TV series) 323
Beverly Hills 90210 (series) 196
Beyond the Time Barrier 74
Biddle, Adam 121
Biedrzyńska, Adrianna *see* Miles, Adrianna
Bielska, Iwona 347
The Big Bad 38–40
Big Bad Wolf (2006) 40–41
The Big Cage 355
The Big Chill 41
Big Fish 274–275
Big Top Pee-wee 181
Big Top Scooby Doo! 23, 82, 275
Big Trouble in Little China 170
Bigfoot vs. D.B. Cooper 267
Bikini Beach 275
Bikini Girls on Dinosaur Planet 84
Bikini Planet 84
Billy the Kid vs. Dracula 44, 288
The Birds 70, 166
Birney, Meredith Baxter *see* Baxter, Meredith
Bishop, Wes 46, 119
Bissell, Whit 138–139
Black, Shane 158, 159, 160
Black, Tori 108–109
Black Caesar 95
The Black Cat (1934) 74
Black Christmas 154
The Black Harvest of Countess Dracula see *Curse of the Devil*
Black Jack 314
Black Park 120, 145
The Black Room 90
Black Roses 300
Black Sabbath 338
The Black Scorpion 361
The Black Sleep 73
Black Sunday (1960) 54
Black Werewolf see *The Beast Must Die*
Blair, Linda 299
Blair, Selma 304
Blakely, Susan 164
Blasco, Joe 241
Blees, Robert 361
Bleich, William 321
The Blob (1958) 137
Bloch, Robert 355, 356
Blomberg, Erik 376
Blood (1974) 12, 41–42, **42**, 178
Blood and Chocolate 2, 42–44, **43**, 51
The Blood Beast Terror see *The Vampire-Beast Craves Blood*
Blood Freak 353, **353**
Blood Moon (1971) see *The Werewolf vs. the Vampire Woman*
Blood Moon (2001) 167, 275–276
Blood Moon (2014) 44–45
Blood of Dracula 137
Blood of Dracula's Castle 2, 45–46
Blood of Ghastly Horror 45
Blood of the Man Devil see *House of the Black Death*
Blood of the Werewolf 46–47, 178
Blood on Satan's Claw 373
Blood Orgy of the She Devils 147
Blood Rites: Origins and History of the Passions of War 19n20

Blood Sisters see *Sisters*
The Blood Suckers see *Dr. Terror's Gallery of Horrors*
Bloodbath in Psycho Town 177
Bloodspit 276
Bloodthirsly Butchers 178
Bloody Moon see *Lycanthrope*, 1999
Bloodz vs. Wolvez 47–48
Blucas, Marc 272
Blue Demon 191–192, 192, 276, 277, **277**, 344
Blue Demon: El Demonio Azul 276–277, **277**
Blue Demon vs. the Satanic Power 191
Blue Demon y Zovek en la Invasión de los Muertos 277–278
Blue Eyes of the Broken Doll 63
The Blue Lagoon 181, 182
"Blue Moon" (song) 24
Blue Velvet 180
Bluebeard (1944) 74
The Blues Brothers 26
Blythe, Catherine 369
The Bob Newhart Show (series) 164
The Body Snatcher 357
Bogliano, Adrian Garcia 141, 142, 143
Bohus, Ted A. 150
Bolt, Ben 253
Bonanza (series) 138
Bonham, John 336
Bonneywell, David 253
Bonns, Miguel Iglesias 169–170
The Boogie Man Will Get You 186
Borel, Annik 147
Borland, Ros 253
Born to Fight (2004) 235
El Bosque del Lobo 248, 278
Bostwick, Barry 176–177, 294
Bottin, Rob 12, 121, 122, 123, 125, 130, 135, 258, 261, 345
Bowie, David 336, 358
Box, Steve 374
The Boy Who Cried Werewolf (1973) 10, 11, 48–50, **49**
The Boy Who Cried Werewolf (2010) 50–51
The Boy's Club 102
Bradley, David 317
Brahm, John 218
Brambilla, Marco 28
Brandner, Gary 125, 127
Brascia, Dominick 301
Brawith, Garrett 294
Brazil 278
Breaking Wind 278
Brenna, Kevin 130
Bricker, Jack 309
Bride of Frankenstein 237, 279
Bride of the Gorilla 257, 353–354, **354**
Brides of Dracula 295, 373
Brimstone Productions 47
Brinegar, Paul **306**
Broadchurch (series) 45
Broder, Jack 354

Broderick, Matthew 141
Brogan, Ron 289
Bronson Canyon (nee Bronson Caverns) 81, 376
The Brood 154
Brooks, Adam 180
Brooks, Conrad 286, 297
Brooks, Elisabeth 122
Brooks, Mel 1, 96, 340
The Brotherhood 267
Brotherhood of the Wolf 15, 246
The Brothers Gore 155
The Brothers Grimm (film) 43, 82, 278–279
Brown, Adam Jarmon 326
Brown, Clancy 281
Brown, Dyann 150
Brown, Erin *see* Mundae, Misty Mundae
Brown, Garret 349
Brown, Z. Winston *see* Bacchus, John
Browning, Tod 132, 158, 188
Bruckheimer, Jerry 358
Bruckner, Agnes 42
Brückner, David 139, 140
Bryan, Peter 373
Bryan, Zachary 204
Bryanston Pictures 42
Buchanan, Edgar 363
Buechler, John 71, 176
Buenas Noches Señor Monstruo 279–280
Buffy the Vampire Slayer (series) 196, 246, 316
Bug 161
Bureau, Stephane J. 108
Burke, Malik 48
Burman, Tom 50
Burns, Tim 27
Burr, Jeff 243
Burr, Raymond 354
Burton, Tim 274, 275, 286, 318, 326
Buscemi, Steve 304
Busey, Gary 195
Bussey, Billy 117
Butch Camp 177
Butler, Kent 286
Buzzi, Ruth 164

The Cabin in the Woods 280, **280**
Cabot, Susan 375, 376
Cabrera, Martin 173–174
Cabrera, Norman 309
Caddyshack 162, 197
Caesar, Sid 324
Cafagna, Ashley 243
Cage, Nicholas 299
Caine, Darian 65
Callas, John 150
Calthorpe, Isabella 172
Calvert, Steve 354
Campbell, Bruce 80
Campbell, Christa 32
Campbell, Clay 187
Campisi, Gabriel 149
Campos, Antonio *see* Viruta
Canby, Vincent 141
Cannom, Greg 116, 226
Cannon Movie Tales: Red Riding Hood see *Red Riding Hood* (1989
Captive Wild Woman 91, 152, 354–355, **355**, 364

Capulina 280, 281
Capulina Contra las Momias 280
Capulina Contra los Monstruos 280–281
Capulina Contra los Vampiros 280
Cardona, René, Jr. 283
Cardona, René, Sr. 283
Cardona, René, III 283
Cardos, John "Bud" 46, 288
Carmen, Julie 298
Carnell, Melissa 244
Carnosaur 292
Carnosaur 2 245
Carpenter, John 124, 341
Carr, Benjamin 243
Carradine, John 46, 111, 114, 288, 289, 306, 321, **321**, 355, 365
Carrie 303
Carter, Angela 54
Carter, Helena Bonham 286
Cartwright, Veronica 166
La Casa del Terror see *Face of the Screaming Werewolf*
Casino Royale (1967) 346
Casino Royale (2006) 135
Caspary, Katrina 164
Cast a Deadly Spell 281
Castelnuovo-Tedesco, Mario 59
El Castillo de los Monstruos 281
Castle, Roy 145, 291
Castle, Shirley 74
Castle of Desire see *Tomb of the Werewolf*
The Cat Creature 355–356, 373
Cat Girl 356
Cat People (1942) 58, 356, 357, 358, 360
Cat People (1982) 50, 357–358, **358**
"Cat People Theme" (song) 358
Cat-Women of the Moon 73
Catacombs 132
Catagna, Ashley 242
Catch Me If You Can 275
Catch-22 256
The Catman of Paris 358–359, **359**
Cawson, Frank 5
Cazador de Demonios 281–282
CBS Wednesday Night Movies (TV series) 75
Cemetery Man 338
Cha Cha Cha, Nhong 235
Chabelo 282
Chabelo y Pepito Contra los Monstruos 282
Challenge 263
Chambers, John 50
Chan, Jackie 235
Chaney, Lon, Jr. **4**, **15**, 21, 21–22, **22**, 22, 53, 90, 90–91, 91, 92, 111, 112, 112–113, 113, 114, 156, 159, 161, 164, 165, 186, 236, 237, 238, 246, 256, **257**, 258, 259, 261, 263, 265, 280, 288–289, 289, 293, 306, 354, 365
Chaney, Patsy 22
Chaney, Ron 22, 116, 118
Chapkanov, Todor 204
Chapman, Michelle *see* Black, Tori
El Charro de las Calaveras see *Rider of the Skulls*
Chesebro, George 348
Chiba, Sonny 350, **350**

Index • 391

Child's Play 158
Chillerama 359–360
Chinn, Jeanne 335
Chocolate (2008) 234
Christie, Julie 183
Cialini, Julie 377
CineCoup 259
Cirque du Freak: The Vampire's Assistant 282
The Cisco Kid (TV series) 133
Clark, Dick 240, 241
Clark, Mark 18n2
Clark, Marlene 37
Clarke, Gary **306**, 307
Clay, Noel 9
Clement, Brian 293, 293–294
Clement, Jemaine 346
Cleopatra 118
The Climax 111
Clinton, Bill 162
Clinton, Hillary 162
Cloak and Shag Her 84
Close Encounters of the Third Kind 50
Cobain, Kurt 162
Cocoon: The Return 161
Coe, Peter 114
Cohen, Herman 137, 138, 139, 307, 354
Cohen, Larry 95, 96
Cohen, Lawrence D. 309
Cohlan, Randolph 170
Cohn, Jared 149
Cold Hearts 282–283
Coleman, Thomas 202
Colmillos, el Hombre Lobo 283
The Colossus of New York 74
Colton, John 237
Columbia Pictures 289
Coming Apart 238
The Company of Wolves 2, 52–54, **53**, 151, 245
Compston, Martin 252
Compton Cinema Club 178
Concklin, Eric 178–179
Concorde Pictures 38, 332
Conde, Alfredo 330
Condon, Bill 207, 207–208
Connery, Sean 141
Connors, Chuck 225
Conquest 228, 283–284
Conte, Steve 86
Les Contes de la Nuit see *Tales of the Night*
Conway, Gary 307
Conway, Tim 368
Conway, Tom 357
Cook, Jesse Thomas 154, 155
Cooper, Alice 155, 155–156, 157, 286
Coppola, Francis Ford 196
Coppola, Sofia 207
Corman, Julie 332
Corman, Roger 31, 124, 245, 251, 261, 292, 332, 375, 376
O Coronel e o Lobisomem (1979) 284
O Coronel e o Lobisomem (2005) 284
The Corpse Grinders 47
Corridors of Blood 233

Corrigan, Brent see Lockhart, Sean Paul
Costello, Lou 21, **22**
Cotton Comes to Harlem 36
Count Downe see *Son of Dracula*
Count Yorga, Vampire 36, 250
Countess Dracula's Orgy of Blood 204, 206
Courage Mountain 203
Craddock, Sandie 60
Crane, Stephen 58
Craven, Wes 27, 66, 67, 68
The Craving 2, **3**, 12, 54–56, **55**, 93, 157, 168, 206, 248, 273
Crawford, Broderick 258
Crawford, Daz 204
Creature from the Black Lagoon 138
Creature from the Haunted Sea 362
Creature of the Night 56–57
The Creeping Flesh 373
Creepozoids 267
The Creeps 243, 284–285, 320
Creepshow 293
CreepTales 285
Cresse, Bob 118, 118–119
Criss, Peter 311
Crombie, Peter 116
Crown International 46
Cry of the Banshee 16
Cry of the Werewolf 10, 57–59, **58**, 164, 182, 188, 355
The Crying Game 52, 54
Crying Wolf 59–60
Culp, Nancy 373
Cult of the Cobra 360–361
Curcio, E.J. 302
Curry, Diana 56, 57
Curry, Tim 276, 309, 333
The Curse (2001) 60–61
Curse, E.J. see Curcio, E.J.
Curse of Chucky 106
The Curse of the Allenbys see *She-Wolf of London*
Curse of the Black Widow 361–362, **361**
Curse of the Blood-Ghouls 373
Curse of the Cat People 357
Curse of the Crying Woman 315
Curse of the Demon 281
Curse of the Devil 11, 61–63, **62**, 206
Curse of the Puppet Masters 243
Curse of the Queerwolf 164, 285–286
Curse of the Undead 127
The Curse of the Werewolf 34, 63–65, **63**, 83, 95, 102, 117, 122, 143, 367
Curse of the Wolf 65–66
Cursed 2, 9, 27, 51, 66–68, **67**
Curtis, Dan 286, 333, 361
Cushing, Peter 37, 143, 145, 168, 291, 373
Cycle of the Werewolf (novella) 195
The Cyclops 74

Dabbs, Craig 117
Damici, Nick 142, 143
Damon, Matt 279
Dancy, Hugh 42
Daniels, Sean 265
Danning, Sybil 125, 125–126
Dano, Royal 160
Dante, Joe 122, 122–123, 124, 125, 129, 245, 261, 370

D'Arcy, Alex 46
The Dark 103
Dark Moon Rising (2009) 68–69, 70
Dark Moon Rising (2015) 69–70, 267
Dark Shadows (TV series) 205, 286
Dark Shadows (2012 film) 286
DarkWolf 70–72
Daudelin, Pierre 108
Daughter of Dr. Jekyll 10, 72–74, **73**
Davis, Geena 340
Davis, Mike 48, 174, 174–175, 175
Dawson, Anthony
Day, Felicia 185, 186
Day of Anger 157
The Day the Earth Stood Still 29, 250
Dead Man's Eyes 355
Dead Men Walk 152, 153
Dead Teenagers 287
Deadly Powers: Animal Predators and the Mythic Imagination 14
Deadtime Stories (1986) 287–288
Deadtime Stories (2009) 164, 288
De Alba, Aurora 91
Dean, Lowell 18, 259, 259–260, 260–261
De Anda, Gilberto 282
Death Becomes Her 180
Death Curse of Tartu 362, **362**
Death Hunter: Werewolves vs. Vampires 74–75
Death Moon see *Deathmoon*
Death Spa 164
Death Wish V 167
Deathmoon 12, 75–77, **76**
Deathrow Gameshow 164
Deathsport 332
DeCarlo, Yvonne 90, 324
De Carvalho, Jose Candido 284
DeCoteau, David 267
De Diego, Ángel Luis 56
DeEmmony, Andy 151
Deep Space 204
Deep Throat 42
The Deer Hunter 142
Deezen, Eddie 210
De Gaetano, Alessandro 176, 177
De Hoyos, Kitty 315, **315**
Dekker, Fred 158, 159, 160
Del Bosque, Francisco Javier Chapa see Zovek, Professor
Deliverance 275, 285
Delman, Jeffrey 287
Del Toro, Benicio 263, **263**, 263–264, 264
DeLuca, Rudy 340, 341
Demicheli, Tulio 30
Demolition Man 28
Demons 338
DeNiro, Robert 14
Dennis the Menace (film) 34
Denton, Jeff 38
Deported Women of the SS Special Section 147
Depp, Johnny 279, 286
Derushie, Jason see The Brothers Gore
Derushie, Jeff see The Brothers Gore
The Descent 172, 246
Detour (1945) 74

The Devil Inside 222
Devil Wolf of Shadow Mountain 288
Devil's Partner 362–363
Devil's Possessed 78, 249
The Devil's Rain 363
DeVito, Danny 274
Devonshire, Paula 106
DeWitt, Louis 73
The Diabolical Dr. Z 291
Diage, Louis 187
Diffring, Anton 37
Diller, Phyllis 318
Dillman, Bradford 161
Dimension Films 66, 68, 279
Dinowolf see *Dire Wolf*
Dire Wolf 204, 288
Di Silvestro, Rino 146–147, 147
DiVecchio, Chris 68, 69
"Do the Jellyfish" (song) 372
Dobrev, Nina 167
Docherty, John Paul 279
Dr. Blood's Coffin 370
Dr. Jekyll and Mr. Hyde (1931) 73, 355
Dr. Jekyll and the Werewolf 23, 62, 77–79, **79**, 157, 249
Dr. Jekyll and the Wolfman see *Dr. Jekyll and the Werewolf*
Dr. Jekyll vs. the Werewolf see *Dr. Jekyll and the Werewolf*
Dr. Jekyll y el Hombre Lobo see *Dr. Jekyll and the Werewolf*
Dr. Phibes Rises Again 361
Dr. Terror's Gallery of Horrors 288–289, **289**
Dr. Terror's House of Horrors 288, 289–291, **290**, 336, 338
Dog Soldiers 1, 2, **2**, 59, 79–81, **80**, 121, 171, 204, 211, 280
Dogman 88
Dolan, Timothy 182
Donahue, Troy 301
Donner, Richard 140, 141
Donovan, Martin 318
Doohan, James 336
Dooley, Shaun 45
Doom Asylum 71
Doran, Thomas 370, 371
Dougherty, Michael 341
Dow Chemicals 341
Downes, Robin 243
Downey, Robert, Jr. 369
Downey, Tom 38
Downton Abbey (TV series) 121, 151
Doyle, Ron 289
Dracula (1931 film) 188, 279
Dracula (novel) 1, 288
Dracula and Son 168
Drácula Contra Frankenstein see *Dracula, Prisoner of Frankenstein*
Dracula Has Risen from the Grave 144
Dracula Prince of Darkness 191
Dracula, Prisoner of Frankenstein 291–292, **292**
The Dracula Saga 78
Dracula (the Dirty Old Man) 81–82
Dracula 2000 16
Dracula Versus Frankenstein see *Assignment Terror*
Dracula vs. Frankenstein (1971) 45
Dracula's Castle see *Blood of Dracula's Castle*

392 • Index

Dracula's Curse 268
A Dragonfly for Each Corpse 249
Drake, Oliver 365
Dreesen, Lance W. 40, 41
Dudley, Royce 116
"Dueling Banjos" (song) 275
Duke, Patty 356
The Dungeonmaster 293–294
Durey, Jason 216
Durham, Brook 185
Dylan Dog (comic book series) 82
Dylan Dog: Dead of Night (film) 17, 82–83
D'Zar, Robert 312

Eagles of Death Metal 134
Earth vs. the Flying Saucers 225
Easy Rider 46
Easy Rider 2: The Ride Home 75
Ebert, Roger 185, 203, 348
Edwards, Kathryn 5
Edwards, William 81
Eguiluz, Enrique 92, 99
Eisley, Anthony 365
The Elephant Man 53
Elfman, Danny 264
Elliot, Leslie 178
Ellis, Shaun 7
Ellison, James 217
Elsey, Dave 264, 266
Elsey, Lou 266
Elvira, Mistress of the Dark 182
Empire Pictures 292
Encounters of the Spooky Kind 302
English, Christine 60
Englund, Robert 200, 201
Enk, Brian 39, 40
Ennis-Brown house 116, 125
The Entity 370
E.O. Motion Picture Studios 263
Epps, Omar 68
An Erotic Werewolf in London 83–84
The Erotic Witch Project 47
Escape from New York 177
Esmond, Carl **359**
The Essential Guide to Werewolf Literature 18
Estevez, Joe 227
"Eve of Destruction" (song) 250
Evil Dead 2 31
Evil Deeds 293
Evil in the Bayou 84
Evil Toons 205
Evilspeak 363
Exhumed 293–294
The Exorcist 63, 70, 145, 285
The Expendables 2 254
Eyes of the Werewolf 84–85, **85**, 233, **234**
Eyewitness Testimony 14

Face of the Screaming Werewolf 85–87, **86**, 122, 315
Fafard, Leo **259**, 260
Fairburn, Sean 181
Falcón, Fabiolo **10**, 63
Falcon Crest (series) 76
Family Ties (series) 287
Famous Monsters of Filmland (magazine) 164, 236, 275, 360
Fangoria (magazine) 102, 164, 173
Farrow, Mia 256
Father Knows Best (series) 250
Fatone, Joey 182

Faulkner, Brendan 370, 371
Favio, Leonardo 325
Fawcett, John 102, 103, 104, 105
FDR: American Badass 294
The Feeding 87–88
Feildler, Eric 129
Feldman, Corey 68
Felton, Tom 172
Fenn, Sherilyn 320
The Feral Man 294–295
Ferrer, Raphael 30
Ferris Bueller's Day Off 162
Fessenden, Larry 143
The Fighter 287
Filmgroup 362
Filmonsters 242
Finger, Bill 372
Finney, Albert 274, 348
Fischa, Michael 164
Fish, Leon 276
Fisher, Terence 64, 65, 122
Fist of the Vampire 65
Flash Gordon 52
Flemyng, Robert 373
Fletcher, Bramwell 218
Flight of the Conchords 346
Flight to Mars 359
Flink, Richard S. 372
Florey, Robert 236
The Fly (1958) 16, 186, 303
The Fly (1986) 198
Foch, Nina 58, 58–59, 182, 188
The Fog (1980) 121
Fogerty, John 128
Foley, Dave 154
Follows, Megan 195
Fonda, Jane 238
Fondacaro, Phil 284
For a Few Dollars More 157
Forberg, Stefan 139
Ford, Alan 201
Ford, Harrison 352
Foree, Ken 304
Foriscot, Emilio 92, 92–93
Fort Edmonton 106
47 Ronin 363
Fowler, Gene 137, 138, 139
Fox, Michael J. 202, 203, 211
Foxworth, Robert 76
Frade, Jose 279
Fragasso, Claudio 157
Frampton, Peter 336
Franciosa, Tony 361
Francis, Freddie 122, 143, 143–144, 145, 290, 291, 336, 339
Francis, Kevin 143, 144, 145
Franco, Jess 77, 291, 292
Frankenstein (1931) 22, 115, 160, 218, 295, 303
Frankenstein and Me 295, **295**
Frankenstein and the Werewolf Reborn! see *The Werewolf Reborn!*
Frankestein, el Vampiro y Compañía 295–297, **296**
Frankenstein Meets the Wolf Man 2, 30, 47, 85, 88–91, **89**, 111, 113, 114, 115, 116, 117, 122, 154, 155, 186, 258, 339
Frankenstein or the Modern Prometheus (novel) 1
Frankenstein Reborn! 38
Frankenstein's Bloody Terror 2, 11, 14, 15, 29, 30, 61, 91–94, **92**, 97, 97–98, 99, 206, 248

Frankenstein's Daughter 118
Frascino, Michael 166
Freaks (1932) 132, 276, 282
Freaky Fairytales see *Deadtime Stories*
Frees, Paul 368
Fregonese, Hugo 30
Frehley, Ace 311
Frid, Jonathan 286
Friday the 13th (film series) 72, 176, 301
Friday the 13th (2009) 39
Friday the 13th: A New Beginning 301
Friedberg, Jason 343
Friedman, Richard 70, 71, 72
Fright Club 297
Fright Night (1985) 16, 74, 129, 163, 167, 298
Fright Night Part 2 116, 226, 297–298, **297**, 309
Frogs 361
From Beyond 12
From Beyond the Grave 289
From Dusk Till Dawn 44, 74, 75, 143
Frost, Brian J. 18
Frost, Lee 119
The Fugitive (series) 161, 227
Fulci, Lucio 283
Full Eclipse 12, 94–95, **94**, 133, 317, 346
Full Moon High 95–97, **96**, 201
Full Moon Pictures 241, 243, 267, 284, 320
Fulton, John P. 90, 237, 256
La Furia del Hombre Lobo see *The Fury of the Wolfman*
Furie, Sidney 370
Furst, Anton 52
Furst, Griff 269
Furtney, B.C. 243, 244
The Fury of the Wolfman 61, 97–99, **98**, 248
Futurama (TV series) 23
"The Future's So Bright I Gotta Wear Shades" (song) 226

Gabriel Films 253
Gacy, John Wayne **17**
Gagnon, Philippe 107, 107–108
Galindo, Rubén 194
Gallery of Horror see *Dr. Terror's Gallery of Horrors*
Galligan, Zach 346
Gambin, Lee 10
Gamble, Mason 34
A Game of Thrones (TV series) 102
Game of Werewolves 2, **16**, 59, 71, 99–102, **100**, 108, 185
Garberina, Billy 325, 326
Garcia, Daniel 344, 345
Gardner, Bud 60
Garnett, Gale 318
Garris, Mick 369
Garry, Jacqueline 60, 61
The Gashlycrumb Tinies (book) 341–342
Gattaca 34
Gaul, Patti 41
Gausman, R.A. 90
Gauthier, Yvan 166
Gaynes, George 50

General Hospital (series) 227
Gentry, Roger 288
Gerard, Gil 288
Getz, Ben 210
The Ghastly Ones 178
The Ghost of Frankenstein 90, 112
Ghost Rock 75
Ghostbusters 46, 162
Ghosts on the Loose 186
The Ghoul (1975) 145
Giamotti, Paul 304
The Giant Claw 225
Giles, Rhett 268
Gilliam, Terry 278, 279
Gilling, John 366
Gilpin, Todd 88
Ginger Snaps 1, 2, 18, 61, 50, 51, 102–105, **103**, 105, 106, 167, 201, 236, 265, 309
Ginger Snaps Back: The Beginning 44, 68, 105, 106–107
Ginger Snaps 2: Unleashed 68, 105–106, 107
Ginsberg, Milton Moses 238, 239
Gladiator 64
Glendening, Jonathan 171–172, 172
Globus, Yoram 180
Glut, Don 204
The Godfather Part III 50
Godrey, Wyck 207
Gods and Monsters 207
Goetz, William 21
Golan, Menahem 180
Goldblum, Jeff 340
Goldhawk Studios 373
Goldwyn, Samuel 257
Gomar: The Human Gorilla see *Night of the Bloody Apes*
The Good, the Bad, and the Ugly 157, 220
Goodman, John 90
The Goonies 158
Goosebumps 298
Gordillo, Francisco 314
Gordon, Stuart 12
Gore, Tipper 162
Gorey, Edward 341–342
Gotta, Jessi 39
Gough, Michael 291
Gould, Will 351
Grace, Marlon 283
The Graduate 44, 256
Graham, Sasha 178
Grand Theft Auto 332
Grant, John 21
Graver, Gary 205
Gray, Billy 250
Gray, Brad 310
Grease 181, 359
Great Expectations (1934) 236
Green, Adam 360
Green, Chris 270
Grefé, William 372
Gremlins 162, 198
Grevioux, Kevin 211
Gries, Jonathan 159, **297**, 298
Grindhouse 51, 299
Grinter, Brad 353
Grotesque 299
Gryff, Stefan 145
Guest, Christopher 346
Gunsmoke (series) 355
Gwynne, Fred 324

Haig, Sid 304
Haim, Corey 195
The Hair of the Beast 2, 107–108, 265
Half Moon 108–109
Hall, Ken 292
Hall of the Mountain King see *Night of the Howling Beast*
Hallenbeck, Bruce G. 47
Halloween (1978) 124, 303
Halloween III: Season of the Witch 309
Halloweentown 299
Halloweentown High 299–300
Hamilton, George 238
Hammer (film company) 63, 64, 168, 289
Hammer of the Gods see *Thor: Hammer of the Gods*
The Hammond Mystery see *The Undying Monster*
Hampton, James 203
Hangover Square 218
Hanks, Tom 341
Hanna-Barbera 332
The Happy Hooker Goes to Hollywood 150
Harada, Ryûji 310
Haraguchi, Tomo'o 310, 311–312
Haram Alek 300
Hard Rock Nightmare 300–301
Hard Rock Zombies 300, 301–302
Hard Time 135
Harding, Tonya 162
Hardwicke, Catherine 183, 184, 184–185, 185
Harrington, Curtis 355, 356
Harris, Robert 238, **306**
Harrison, Jim 255
Harry O (series) 161
Harry Potter (film series) 172, 282, 302, 322
Harry Potter and the Order of the Phoenix 16
Harry Potter and the Prisoner of Azkaban 302
Hart, Donna 5
Hart, Jimmy 155
Harvey, Grant 106
Hattori, Daiji 311
Hauer, Rutger 141
Haunted Airplane 75
Haunted Cop Shop 302
The Haunted Cop Shop II 15, 302, 303
Haunted Honeymoon 303
The Haunted Palace 258
The Haunted World of El Superbeasto 303–304
The Haunting (1963) 346
Have Mercy see *Haram Alek*
Hawkes, Steve 353
Hawkins, Peter 253
Hayter, David 12, 265, 265–266, 266
Heacock, Gary R. 289
Headcrusher 172
Heard, John 358
Heartburn 256
Hebner, Joel 38
Hedren, Tippi 70
Heffron, Brian ("Blue Meanie") 65
Helen Keller vs. Nightwolves 15
Hell of the Living Dead 157

Hell Up in Harlem 95
Hellboy 304
Hellboy Animated: Blood and Iron 304
Hellboy Animated: Sword of Storms 304
The Hellcat 250
Hellfire, William 83, 84
Hellraiser 80
Hellraiser III 346
Hell's Angels on Wheels 250
Hell's Creatures see *Frankenstein's Bloody Terror*
Hemingway, Mariel 34
Hemmings, David 226, 227
Henaine, Gaspar see Capulina
Hendrix, Duke 276
Hennah, Dan 216
Henriksen, Lance 154, 155
Henry, Thomas Bowne 307
Hercules (series) 167
Here Come the Munsters 324
Here Comes the Devil 141
Hernaez, Luciano Bastida 330
Herrera, Ernesto 143
Hessler, Gordon 311
Hewitt, David L. 289
Hewitt, Jennifer Love 42
Hickox, Anthony 94, 95, 345, 346
Hickox, Douglas 346
Hickox, James 345
The Hideous Sun Demon 16
Highway to Heaven (series) 138
Hilko, Mary Kay 47
The Hills Have Eyes (1977) 67
The Hills Have Eyes Part II (1984) 150
Hindle, Art 154
Hinds, Anthony 143, 144, 145, 367
Hines, Gregory 348
Hitchcock, Alfred 127
The Hitcher (1986) 34
The Hitcher 2 245
Hitler, Adolf 19n20
Hoban, Steve 104, 265
Hobart, Doug 372
Hobson, Valerie 236–237
Hodder, Kane 71, 72, 176
Hoffman, Dustin 348
Ho-gyum, Hwang 229
Holland, Tom 298
Holliday, Geoffrey Alan 71
Hollywood Castle 204–205
Hollywood Chainsaw Hookers 205
Home Improvement (TV series) 204
Homel, Bob 49, 50
Homicidal 37
Hooper, Tobe 31, 341, 370
Hopkins, Anthony 264
Hopkins, Bo 312
Horrible Bosses 203
La Horripilante Bestia Humana see *Night of the Bloody Apes*
Horror and Sex see *Night of the Bloody Apes*
Horror Express 56
Horror of the Werewolf see *Night of the Howling Beast*
Horror Rises from the Tomb 56, 63, 307
Horrors of Spider Island 46
Horrors of War 110–111
Hostel 51

Hot Fuzz 27
Hotel Transylvania 304
Hotel Transylvania 2 304–305
Hough, John 129
House of Dark Shadows 286
House of Dracula 22, 85, 90, 91, 111–113, **112**, 116, 122, 168, 273, 321
House of Frankenstein (1944) 90, 91, 111, 112, 113, 113–115, **114**, 116, 122, 224, 249, 273, 321, 322, 364
House of Frankenstein (1997) 12, 85, 115–116
House of Psychotic Women see *Blue Eyes of the Broken Doll*
House of the Black Death 305–306, **305**
House of the Wolf Man 116–118, **117**
House of Usher 288
House on Bare Mountain 11, 118–119, **119**
House on Haunted Hill (1958) 116, 125
The House That Dripped Blood 37, 289
The House That Screamed 56
Household Words 8
How Green Was My Valley 74
How to Make a Monster 279, 306–307, **306**
Howard, Clint 32, 40, 304
Howard, John 218
Howard, Rance 32
Howard, Ron 32
Howl 120–121, **120**
Howl Con 18
Howl of the Devil 56, 307–308, **308**
The Howling (film) 1, 12, **12**, 33, 52, 53, 54, 59, 80, 81, 97, 102, 116, 121–125, **123**, 125, 127, 129, 135, 149, 150, 167, 194, 226, 241, 258, 261, 280, 321, 345, 369–370
Howling (film series) 127, 129, 130, 133, 135, 149
The Howling II (novel) 125, 129, 135
Howling II: Stirba—Werewolf Bitch see *Howling II... Your Sister Is a Werewolf*
Howling II... Your Sister Is a Werewolf (film) 58, 125–127, **126**, 127, 131, 134, 164
The Howling III (novel) 127
Howling III: The Marsupials 127–129, **128**
Howling IV: The Original Nightmare 129–130, **130**, 131, 133, 134
Howling V: The Rebirth 130–132, **131**, 133, 134
Howling VI: The Freaks 94, 132–133, 133
Howling VII see *The Howling: New Moon Rising*
The Howling: New Moon Rising 133–135
The Howling Reborn 135–137, **136**, 185
Hudd, Roy 373
Huerta, Rudolfo Guzman see El Santo
Hughes, Brendan 132
Hughes, Derek 31, 31–32
Hulette, Don 46
Hull, Cortland 236

Hull, Henry 95, 200, 233, 236, 237, **237**, 258, 283
Human Beasts 273
The Hunchback of Notre Dame (1923) 113, 339
"Hungry Like a Wolf" (song) 200
Hunter, Tab 299
Hunting the American Werewolf 1
Huntington, Sam 83
Hurt, John 304
Hybrid 308–309
Hyenas 167, 363–364
Hyett, Paul 120, 121, 246

I Am Curious Yellow 178
I Dream of Jeannie (series) 76
I Know What You Did Last Summer 66
I Married a Monster from Outer Space 139
I Married a Werewolf see *Werewolf in a Girls' Dormitory*
I Walked with a Zombie 217, 357
I Was a Teenage Frankenstein 137, 138, 307
I Was a Teenage Werewolf 2, 10, 18, 43, 50, 72, 137–139, **138**, 148, 188, 201, 223, 265, 307, 309, 369
"Identity Crisis" (song) 156
The Illustrated Werewolf Movie Guide 18n3
I'm Sorry the Bridge Is Out, You'll Have to Spend the Night (stage play) 322
Image FX 253
In the Heat of the Night 160
In the Midnight Hour see *The Midnight Hour*
The Incredible Hulk 18, 227
El Incredible Profesor Zovek 278
Independent International 30, 46, 91
The Indestructible Man 293
Indiana Jones (film series) 219
Inglourious Basterds 358
Inquisition 168
Interview with the Vampire 54, 84, 347
La Invasion de los Muertos see *Blue Demon y Zovek en la Invasion de los Muertos*
Invasion of the Body Snatchers (1956) 138
Invasion of the Body Snatchers (1978) 50
Invasion of the Saucer Men 307
Invasion of the Zombies 297, 331
Invisible Invaders 113
The Invisible Ray 71, 113
The Ipcress File 370
Iron Wolf 139–140
Irons, Jeremy 183
Irons, Max 183
Irreversible 121
Isaac, James 3, 197, 198, 199
Isabelle, Katharine 103, 106
The Island of Dr. Moreau (novel) 316
Island of Lost Souls 113
Islas, Ricardo 172, 173, 174
Ismail and Abdul Meet Frankenstein see *Haram Alek*
Ismail Yassen Meets Frankenstein see *Haram Alek*

It (1990 film) 309
It (novel) 309
It Came from Outer Space 360
It Conquered the World 307
It Lives Again 95
It Lives by Night see *The Bat People*
It's Alive (1974) 95
It's Alive see *The Bat People*
Ivanov, Sergei 199
Ivanov, Yuri 199

Jack & Diane 309–310
"Jack and Diane" (song) 309
Jack the Giant Killer (1962) 50
Jackman, Hugh 219
Jameson, Jerry 352, 353
Janinski, Krzysztof 347
Janssen, David 161, 361
Jason X 197
Jasso, José 296
Jaws 27, 70, 88, 172
Jaws 3-D 124
Jay, John 370
Jo, Sung-hee 229
Johannigmeier, Heidi 166
Johnson, Amy Jo 282
Johnson, David Leslie 183
Johnson, Steve 33, 123, 129, 130–131, 135
Johnston, Joe 264
Jones, Buck 359
Jones, Dean 368
Jones, Freddie 336
Jones, Grace 275
Jones, Paul 104, 167
Jones, Stephen 18*n*3
Jopia, Tony 59
Jordan, Neil 52, 53, 54
Joseph, Genie ("Eugenie") 371
Joshua Tree National Park 133
Joy Ride 2 245
Joyce, Michael P. 50
Judge Roy Bean (TV series) 133
Jungle Captive 354, 364
Jungle Woman 354, 355, 364
Juran, Nathan 50
Jurassic Park (film) 34
Jurassic Park (film series) 80
Justice, Victoria 50, 51

Kaba, Agim 166
Kabasinski, Len 65
Kaelin, Kato 170, 171
Kandel, Aben 139
The Karate Kid 201
Karloff, Boris 90, **92**, 111, 114, 115, 116, 157, 186, 236, 257, 275, 289, 318, 357
Karman, Janice 23
Kasem, Casey 275, 333
Kassir, John 322
Katzman, Sam 225
Keen, Bob 80, 253, 345, **345**
Keeter, Worth 261, 262
Kellaway, Cecil 368
Kelley, Vince 81
Kelly, Brett 295
Kelly, Donovan 377
Kelly, Jack 361
Kelly's Heroes 26
Kemp, Martin 201
Kemp, Will 219
Kensit, Patsy **94**
Kenton, Erle C. 113, 122

Kentucky Fried Movie 26
Kessler, Bruce 76
Khmara, Edward 141
Kibakichi 310
Kibakichi: Bakko-yokaiden see *Kibakichi*
Kibakichi 2 310–311
Kibakichi 2: Bakko-yokaiden see *Kibakichi 2*
Kick Ass 286
Kikuchi, Hideyuki 342
The Killer Shrews 107, 253
King, Stephen 158, 195, 370
King Kong (1933) 87, 225, 241
King of the Lost World 38
Kingburger Drive-In 230
Kingdom of the Spiders 46
Kinky Kong (1933) 47, 65, 115
Kinsey 207
Kinski, Nastassia 357, 358
Kirk, Tommy 368
Kiss (band) 311
Kiss Meets the Phantom of the Park 311
Kiss of the Vampire 144
Klause, Annette Curtis 42
Kleiser, Randal 181, 182
Klimovsky, León 55, 56, 77, 78, 79, 248, 249, 249–250
KNB EFX 68, 106, 106–107
Kolchak: The Night Stalker (series) 76
Komodo vs. Cobra 34
Kovaks, Leslie 46
Kraft Theatre (series) 241
Krampus 341
Kranhouse, Jon 226
Krause, Brian **370**
Kring, Timothy 203
Krueger, Michael 150
Kruger, Ehren 42, 42–43
Kubrick, Stanley 256
Kuosmanen, Mirjami 376, **376**
Kurtzman, Harvey 318
Kurtzman, Robert 143
Kvitebjørn Kong Valemon see *The Polar Bear King*
Kyûketsuki Hantâ D see *Vampire Hunter D*

Ladyhawke 2, 12, 140–141
Laemmle, Carl 237, 238
Lake Dead 167
Lakehurst, Alix 197
Lamarche, Maurice 23
Lambert, Charles 351
The Land Before Time (film series) 23
Landers, Lew 122, 186, 188
Landis, John 8, 21, 24, 25, 26, 27, 63, 80, 123, 124, 261, 370
Landon, Christopher 43
Landon, Michael 43, 138, 148, 188
Lane, Steven 135
Lane, Vicky 364
Lansbury, Angela 52
LaShelle, Joseph 139
Lass, Barbara 232
Lastikman (1968) 312
Lastikman (2003) 312
Lastikman (2007-08 series) 312
Lastikman: Unang Banat 311–312
Late Phases 2, 18, 108, 141–143
Laugh-In (series) 164

Launer, S. John **224**
Laura 139
Lautner, Taylor 278
Law, John Phillip 339
Lawler, Mike 75
Leachman, Cloris 51
Le Bar, Bob 91
LeBorg, Reginald 364
Ledger, Heath 279
Lee, Brenda 373
Lee, Christopher 125, 126, 126–127, 168, 280, 291, 342
Lee, Michael 371
Lee, Quentin 335
Leeches 267
Leena Meets Frankenstein 15
Lees, Robert 21
Legend, Johnny 336
The Legend of Hell House 129
Legend of the Werewolf 122, 143–145, **144**, 336
The Legend of the Wolf Woman 83, 145–147, **146**, 164
The Legend of Wolf Mountain 312
Leigh, Suzanna 336
Leitch, Christopher 203
Lemche, Kris 104–105
Lennay-Thivierge, Guillaume 108
Leno, Jay 333
Leo, Melissa 287
Leob, Joseph 203
Leroy, Jeff 85, 233, 234
Lesser, Len 243
Lethal Weapon (film series) 141, 158
Levesque, Michel 250, 251
Leven, Eric 207–208
Leviatán see *Monster Dog*
Levin, Henry 58
Levine, Joseph E. 318
Lewis, Al 324
Lewis, Geoffrey 160
Lewis, H.G. 126, 366
Lewton, Val 357, 358
Li, Jet 235
Licantropo: El Asesino de la Luna Ilena 205, 312–314, **313**
License to Kill 170
Lieving, Sarah 38
The Life and Crimes of Alice Cooper (record album) 156
Light of Blood 147–148
Lillard, Matthew 275
Linden, Edwin 225
Lindenmuth, Kevin J. 47, 177, 178, 342
Lionsgate 68, 171
Lips of Blood 113
Little Dead Rotting Hood 148–149
Little House on the Prarie (series) 138
"Little Red Riding Hood" (fairy tale) 40, 52, 149, 181, 182, 185
"Little Red Riding Hood" (song) 182
The Living Dead at the Manchester Morgue 56
La Loba 164, 314–315, **315**
Un Lobisomem na Amazônia 315–316, **316**
Lobos de Arga see *Game of Werewolves*
Lock, Stock and Two Smoking Barrels 200
Lockhart, Calvin 36

Lockhart, June 334
Lockhart, Sean Paul 359
The Lodger (1944) 218
Loftus, Elizabeth 11
Lon Chaney, Jr. (book) 258
Lone Wolf 149–150
Long, Richard 361
López, Javier see Chabelo
Lord of the Rings: The Return of the King 216
Loredo Western Town 44
The Lost Boys 316, 347, 359
Lost Boys: The Thirst 316–317
Lost Boys 3: The Thirst see *Lost Boys: The Thirst*
Louise, Tina 141
Le Loup des Malveneur 317
Loup-Garou 19n34
Love—American Style (series) 147
Love Bite 121, 150–151
Love Trap see *Curse of the Black Widow*
Lowe, Edward T. 113, 115
Loy, John 23
Lugosi, Bela 21, 81, 90, 111, 152, 186, 188, 236, 280
Luke, Keye 355
La Lupa Mannara see *The Legend of the Wolf Woman*
Lycanthrope (1999) 317
Lycanthrope: The Full Moon Killer see *Licantropo: El Asesino de la Luna Ilena*
Lycanthropy (2006) 317
"Lycanthropy: Alive and Well in the Twentieth Century" 13
Lycantropus see *Werewolf in a Girls' Dormitory*
Lycantropus: The Moonlight Murders see *Licantropo: El Asesino de la Luna Ilena*
Lynch, David 39
Lynch, Joe 360
Lynch, Richard 227
Lynn, George 224

Macaluso, Jerry 135
MacDonald, Lennie 129
MacDonald, Mary 90
Machete 299
MacLane, Barton 58
MacMurray, Fred 368, 369
Macnee, Patrick 346
Mad at the Moon 318
The Mad Monster 10, 122, 151–153, **152**, 205, 246, 293
Mad Monster Party? 318
Magic Mountain Amusement Park 311
Maginnis, Scott 320
The Making of a Monster: Vampires and Werewolves 1
La Maldición de la Beastia see *Night of the Howling Beast*
The Maltese Bippy 319, **319**
Malthe, Natassia **198**
The Man and the Monster 16
Man Beast 86
The Man from Planet X 74
The Man with Two Heads 178
Mander, Miles 187
Manhattan 34
Mankofsky, Isidore 251
Mapson, Darrell 171

La Marca del Hombre Lobo see *Frankenstein's Bloody Terror*
Marcus Welby, M.D. (series) 76
Mark, Michael 115
Mark of the Wolfman see *Frankenstein's Bloody Terror*
Marks, Jennifer 199
Marlowe, Scott 138
Marotta, Santo 178
Marr, Eddie 307
Mars, Kenneth 96
Marshall, Michael 106
Marshall, Neil 79, 80, 81
Marsolais, Michael 295
Martes y Trece 273
Martin, Dick 319
Martin, Megan 105
Martinez, Olivier 42
Masciantonio, Robert A. 283
Massacred by Mother Nature 10
Massey, Ilona 30, 90, 91
Massicotte, Stephen 106
Masters, Todd 133
Matheson, Richard 95
Matheson, Richard Christian 95
Mathews, Kerwin 49, 50
Matousek, Marek 109
Mattei, Bruno 157
May, Elaine 255
McAndrew, Marianne 352
McBride, Danny 214
McCallum, Neil 291
McCallum, Rick 71
McCarthy, Kevin 124
McCleery, Mick 342
McConkey, Sam 74
McCoo, Marilyn 164
McDonagh, Kevin 317
McDowell, Malcolm 358
McDowell, Roddy 298
McGarr, Eben 116, 117, 118
McGill, Bruce 294
McGill, Everett 196
McGuire, Barry 250
McHattie, Stephen 185
McMahon, Ed 96
McNeil, Scott 158
Mears, Derek 67
Mega Piranha 38
Mega Python vs. Gatoroid 149
Memoirs of a Wolfman 3
Men in Black 261
Meng gui zue tang see *The Haunted Cop Shop II*
Mennie, Dana 68, 69
Mennie, Julie Snider 68
Mercero, Antonio 279
Meridian 116, 284, 319–320
Mesa of Lost Women 152
Metalbeast see *Project: Metalbeast*
Mexican Werewolf in Texas 320
Meyer, Stephenie 207, 209
Michael Collins 54
The Midnight Hour 320–321
Mifune, Toshiro 274
Mighty Morphin Power Rangers (series) 282
Mignola, Mike 304
Mikels, Ted V. 47
Mil Máscaras 344
Miles, Adrianna 228
Milicevic, Ivana 135
Miller, Dick 122
Miller, Ken 138

Miller, Romeo 149
Milligan, Andy 41, 178, 179, 179–180, 180
Mindkiller 150
The Mini-Munsters (TV series) 324
Mishkin, William 178
Miss Werewolf 15
The Mist 51
Mr. Vampire 302
Mitler, Matt 287
Mitra, Rhona 216
Mo gao yi zhang see *Return of the Demon*
Modern Family (series) 346
Moffit, John 241
Molina, Jacinto see Naschy, Paul
Molina, Sergio 307
Moll, Richard 292, 293
La Momia Azteca 86–87
Monkey Planet (novel) 125
Monster Among the Girls see *Werewolf in a Girls' Dormitory*
Monster Brawl 2, 153–155, **154**, 185, 265
The Monster Club 10, 321, **321**
Monster Dog 155–157, **156**, 286
Monster Mash (film) 157–158
"Monster Mash" (song) 158, 322
Monster Mash: The Movie 322
The Monster Squad 2, 12, 158–160, **159**
Monsters (TV series) 109, 150
Monsters and Mad Scientists: A Cultural History of the Horror Movie 9
The Monsters in the Mind: The Face of Evil in Myth, Literature, and Contemporary Life 5
Monsterwolf 204, 269, 322
Los Monstruos del Terror see *Assignment Terror*
Monteith, Corey 309
Monti, Aldo 189
Monty Python and Holy Grail 278
Moody, Ron 145
Moon, Keith 336
Moon of the Wolf 160–162, **161**
"Moon Child" (song) 162
"Moon Shadow" (song) 24
Moonchild 162
"Moondance" (song) 24
Moor, Paul 88
Moore, Julianne 281
Mora, Philippe 125, 126, 127, 128–129, 129
Moreno, Alejandro Munoz (Blue Demon) 192
Moreno, José Elias 315
Moreno, Juan Martinez 101, 102
Moretti, Nanni 336
Moretz, Chloe Grace 286
Morgan, Tracy 339
Morneau, Louis 245, 246
Morot, Adrian 135
Morrow, Gary **92**
The Mortal Instruments: City of Bones 322–323
Mortal Kombat 323
Mortal Kombat: Annihilation 323
Moss, Stewart 352, **352**
Motel Hell 75
Movie Tales film series 180
Muldoon, Patrick 149
Muller, Barbara 30–31

The Mummy (1932) 218
The Mummy (1958) 345
The Mummy (1999) 80, 219, 263
The Mummy and the Curse of the Jackals 81, 365
The Mummy's Revenge 63
Mundae, Misty 84
Munro, Caroline 59
Munroe, Kevin 82, 83
Munster, Go Home! 323–324
The Munsters (series) 323
The Munsters' Revenge 324
The Munsters' Scary Little Christmas 324, 324–325
The Munsters Today (series) 324
Murder, She Wrote (series) 241
Murray, Bill 197
Murray, Billy 201
Musuraca, Nicolas 357
Mute Witness 28
My Dinner with Andre 108
My Mom's a Werewolf 149, 162–164, **163**
My Soul to Take 67
Myers, Mark 283
Mystery of Edwin Drood 236
Mystery Science Theater 3000 (TV series) 228
Myton, Fred 153

Nadley, Aaron 187–188
Nagy, Imre 92
Naish, J. Carrol 114, 364
Nall, Roger 133, 134, 134–135, 135
Nannuzzi, Armand 196
Naschy, Paul 3, 11, 28–29, 30, 54, 55, 56, 62–63, 63, 77, 78, 79, **79**, 89, 92, 93, 93–94, 97, **98**, 99, 102, 122, 148, 168, 169, 204, 205–206, 206, 243, **248**, 248, 249, 273, 273, **274**, 274, 279, 307, 308, 313, 313–314, 314, 316, 326, 330
National Velvet 74
Nature of the Beast 164–165
Naughton, David 24, **25**, 26, 40
La Nave de los Monstruos 191
The Navy vs. the Night Monsters 118
Nazareno Cruz y el Lobo 325
NBC Today (series) 175
Necroville 325–326
Neill, Roy William 90, 122
Nelson, Craig T. 100
Nelson, David "The Rock" 15, 287
Nelson, Ed 363
Nemesis 228
Neowolf 165–166, 176, 177
Neufeld, Sigmund 151, 153
Neufeld, Sigmund, Jr. 153
Neuk-dae-so-nyeon see *A Werewolf Boy*
Neumann, F. 91
Neumann, Kurt 186, 236
Never Cry Werewolf 2, 166–168
Never Say Never Again 141
The Neverending Story 15
New World Pictures 124, 341
Newcomb, Jaime 150
Newfield, Sam 122, 151, 153
Newmar, Julie 319
Nhong Werewolf see *Werewolf in Bangkok*
Nichols, Mike 17, 256

Nicholson, Jack 69, 138, 255, **255**, 256, 258, 274–275, 313–314
Nicotero, Greg 51, 68
Nier, Jens 139
Night at the Museum 2 135
Night Drop see *Night Shadow*
Night Fangs 172
Night of Dark Shadows 286
Night of the Bloody Apes 315, 365–366, **365**
Night of the Creeps 158, 160, 162
Night of the Ghouls 326
Night of the Howling Beast 2, 93, 98, 168–170, **169**, 236
Night of the Living Dead (1968) 12, 31, 79, 94, 121, 172, 194, 230, 277, 295, 345
The Night of the Werewolf see *The Craving*
Night Shadow 170–171
The Night Stalker 225, 361
Night Vision 150
Night Wolf 2, 171–172, 200
The Nightmare Before Christmas 326
Nightmare in Blood 50
Nightmare in Wax 45, 46
A Nightmare on Elm Street (1984) 27, 66, 121
Nightmare on Elm Street 5 133
Nights of the Werewolf 30, 97, 326
Nighy, Bill 216
Niles, Chuck 86
Nilsson, Harry 336, 337
Nimziki, Joe 135
Ninja: Prophecy of Death 65
Nixon, Richard 238
La Noche de Walpurgis see *The Werewolf vs. the Vampire Woman*
Los Noches del Hombre Lobo see *Nights of the Werewolf*
Noll, Richard 5–6, **6**
Northern Exposure (series) 196
Nosferatu 347
"Not Somebody Else" (song) 51
NSYNC 182
The Nude Vampire 113
NYPD Blue (series) 176

Oberst, Bill, Jr. 244
Obón, Ramón 314
The O.C. (series) 165
Ocelot, Michel 337
O'Connell, L.W. 58, 188
O'Connor, Brian Scott 222
The Odd Couple (series) 147
The Office (series) 346
Oland, Warner 236, 237
The Old Dark House (1932) 116, 258, 303
Oldman, Gary 183, 284
Olea, Pedro 248
Oliva, Theresa 342
Olivas, Antonio 297
Olivier, Jackeline **234**
O'Malley, B. Scott 31
The Omen (1976) 141
"One Less Bell to Answer" (song) 164
Ong-Bak 234
Ooms, Amanda 253, 254, **254**
Opera 338
O'Quinn, Terry 196
Orgasm Torture in Satan's Rape Clinic 84

Orgy of the Dead 119, 326–327
Orgy of the Vampires see *Orgy of the Dead*
Orphan Black (series) 103
Oses, Fernando 328
O'Shane, Gene 46
O'Toole, Annette 358
Otterson, Jack 256
Ouspenskaya, Maria 122, 256
Owensby, Earl 261, **262**, 262, 262–263, 263, 337
Oxley, Ron 141

Pacheco, Frank 278
Padrón, Juan 344
Palacios, Ricardo 157
Palazzolo, Michael 285, 286
Panescu, Vlad 243
Panic Beats 274
Pappademas, Alex 104
Pappy and Harriet's Pioneertown Palace 133, 134
Paragon International 46
Pare, Michael 34
Park, Bo-yeong 229
Park, Nick 374
Parker, Eddie 90
Parker, Gregory C. 247
Parker, Lara 286
Parker, Steve 38
Parks, Michael 240
Parsons, Alan 141
Parsons, Milton 355, 373
Parsons, Stephen W. 125
Pasqualino, Luke 151
Passenger 57 94
Pate, Michael 127
Patrick, Butch 324, 373
Patrick, George 232
Patterson, Ross 294
Patton, Scott 106
Paul 203
Payne, Bruce 94, 95, 133
Pearce, Jacqueline 367
Pearson, Rosie 60
Pegg, Simon 27
Pena, Cindy 297
The People Who Own the Dark 78, 249
Pepin, Megan 166
Perello, Hope 132, 133
Perez, Gustavo 147, 148
Periano, Louie "Butchie" 42
Perkins, Emily 103, 105, 106, 309
Perlman, Ron 304
Perro, Carlos 102
Persecution 145
Pertwee, Sean 79, 81, 121
Pester, Jan 253
Peterman, Matthew 223
Petersen, Curtis 167
Peterson, Cassandra 182
Petrie, Daniel 161
Petty, Tom 205
Pfeifer, Michelle 141, 256
Phantom of the Mall: Eric's Revenge 71
Phantom of the Opera (1962) 279
Pharaoh's Curse 73
Phillips, Simon 201
Pickett, Bobby "Boris" 322
The Picture of Dorian Gray (1945) 188
Pierce, Jack P. 14, 21, 91, 121, 233, 236, 256, 257–258, 258, 264, 355, 364
Pierce-Roberts, Tony 212
Pigozzi, Luciano 232
Pindar, Christian 247
Pinder, Lucy 201
Pioneertown 133
Piranha (1978) 124, 161
Pirro, Mark 164, 285
The Pit and the Pendulum 288
The Plague of the Zombies 366, 373
The Plainsman 217
Plan 9 from Outer Space 118, 197
Planet of the Apes (1968) 50, 177, 303
Planet of the Werewolves see *Rage of the Werewolf*
Planet Terror 110
Plant, Robert 134
Platt, Ed 361
Play-Mate of the Apes 47
Plaza, Paco 330
Plenilunio 2, 172–174
Plunder Road 224
Poffo, Lanny 65
Le Poil de la Bête see *The Hair of the Beast*
Polanski, Roman 232
The Polar Bear King 366
Police Story (series) 147
A Polish Vampire in Burbank 164, 285
Pollexfen, Jack 74
Poltergeist 180
Pons, Jaime Jiménez 194
Pope Paul VI 92
Porada, Renee 66
Porky's 162
porphyria 222, 223
Porter, Don 334
The Poseidon Adventure (1972) 121
Posse 94
Powell, Andrew 141
Power Corps. see *Recon 2020: The Caprini Massacre*
Practical Magic 180
Predator 160, 349
President Wolfman 48, 174–175, **175**
Price, Dennis 291, 336
Price, Justin 69, 70
Price, Vincent 21, 168, 258, 321, **321**
Pringle, Robert 135
Producers Releasing Corporation 151
Professor Zovek see Zovek
Project: Metalbeast 12, 71, 175–177
The Protector 234
Pryce, Jonathan 279
Psycho (1960) 61, 315
Punky Brewster 50
Puppetmaster 132

Q, the Winged Serpent 95
Quammen, David 4
Quan, Stuart 170
Quarry, Robert 36, 333, 334
Quest for Fire 52
The Questor Tapes 75
Quigley, Linnea 333

Rabin, Jack 73
Radice, Marco 59
Radner, Gilda 303
Rage of the Werewolf 12, 47, 177–178
Ragewar see *The Dungeonmaster*
Raging Phoenix 234
Ragsdale, William 167, 298
Rains, Claude 256, 257, 264
A Raisin in the Sun 161
Rall, Tommy 332
Rambaldi, Carlo 195, 196
Ramirez, Huracán 344, 345
Randolph, Jane 357
Rankin, Arthur Jr. 318
Rankin-Bass Productions 318
Raso, Michael 83
Rathbone, Basil 373
The Rats Are Coming! The Werewolves Are Here! 12, 41, 178–180, **179**
Rats, Night of Terror 157
Ravelo, Mars 311
The Raven (1935) 186
The Raven (1963) 288
Ravenous 44
Ray, Aldo 170
Ray, Christina 106
Ray, Fred Olen 204, 205, 206, 288
Raymond, Paula 46
Rea, Stephen 52, 54, 213, 245
Re-Animator 12, 110
Reaves, Michael 95
Rebel Without a Cause 359
Recon 2020: The Caprini Mission 327
Recon 2022: The Mezzo Incident 327
Recon 2023: the Gauda Prime Conspiracy 327
Red, Eric 32–33, 33, 34
Red Dwarf (series) 151
Red Eye 67
Red Riding Hood (1989) 180–181
Red Riding Hood (2006) 181–182
Red Riding Hood (2011) 2, 182–185, **184**
Red: Werewolf Hunter 185–186, **186**
Redden, Billy 275
Reed, Oliver 63–64, **63**, 64, 65, 95, 117, 143
The Reels 128
Reeser, Autumn 165
Regaliz 279, 280
Regehr, Duncan 159
Reicher, Frank 115
Reid, Tim 309
Reilly, Paul C., Jr. 150
Reiter, Mimi 19n20
Renaud, Gilles 107
Rennie, Michael 29, 30
The Reptile 144, 366–367, **367**
Requiem for a Vampire 113
La Residencia 248
Resident Evil Apocalypse 167
El Retorno de Walpurgis see *Curse of the Devil*
El Retorno del Hombre Lobo see *The Craving*
Return from the Past see *Dr. Terror's Gallery of Horrors*
The Return of Dracula 191
Return of the Demon 327–328
Return of the Jedi 198
The Return of the Living Dead 162
Return of the Secaucus Seven 31
The Return of the Vampire 2, 10, 58, 59, 81, 122, 182, 186–188, **187**, 211, 223, 246
Return of the Wolfman see *The Craving*
The Return of Walpurgis see *Curse of the Devil*
Reynolds, Burt 295
Reynolds, Debbie 299
Rhys-Davies, John 346
Rice, Anne 10
Richards, Ariana 34
Richards, Michael 340
Richardson, Jay 205
Rickles, Don 275
Ride the Wild Stud 81
Rider of the Skulls 44, 328–329, **329**
Rifkin, Adam 360
Riggi, Chris 343
Rikert, Dustin 74, 75
Rikert, Wade 75
Rinaldo, Frederic 21
Rinsch, Carl 363
Rintoul, David **144**, 145
Rio Brava 79
Ritch, Steven 224, **224**
Ritchie, Guy 200
Ritter, John 309
Rivero, George (Jorge) 228
RKO 357
Robbins, Daniel 210
Roberts, Eric 69, 267
Roberts, Jennifer 137
Robinson, George 90, 113
Robles, Germán 281
Rochon, Debbie 178
Rock, Kevin 130, 134
Rock 'n' Roll High School 332
Rock 'n' Roll Nightmare 300
The Rockford Files (series) 76
Rocknrolla 200
The Rocky Horror Picture Show 176
Rodriguez, Dagoberto 328
Rodriguez, Miguel Angel 283
Rodriguez, Primitivo 313, 314
Rodriguez, Robert 299
Roger Corman Presents: The Wasp Woman see *The Wasp Woman*, 1995
Rogers, Roy 133, 134
Rollin, Jean 113
Roman, Timothy Scott 375
Romanek, Mark 264
Romasanta (2004 film) 278, 329–330
Romasanta, Manuel Blanco 278, 329, 330
Romasanta: The Werewolf Hunt see *Romasanta*
Romero, George 12, 31, 288, 341
Rondeau, Charles 363
Rooney, Mickey 312
Rosemary's Baby 363
Rosenberg, Max 289
Rosenblat, Michael 202
Ross, Harry 152
Ross, Peter John 110
Ross, Ryan 166
Rossellini, Isabella 180
Rossellini, Roberto 180
Routh, Brandon 83
Rowan, Dan 319
Rowan and Martin's Laugh-In (TV series) 319
Rowe, Freddie 130

Rubin, Jennifer 376
Ruiz, Jose Luis 93
Rumpelstiltskin (1987) 180
Rusoff, Lou 356
Rusoff, Ted 156
Russek, Jorge 194
Russell, Kurt 141
Russo, Danny 38
Ryan, Max 68–69

Sabo, Timothy E. 176
Sabrina, Secrets of a Teenage Witch (TV series) 188
Sabrina, Secrets of a Teenage Witch: A Witch and the Werewolf (film) 188–189
The Sadistic Baron Von Klaus 291
Sáenz de Heredia, Álvaro 273
Sainz, Salvador 308
Salazar, Abel 281
Salazar, Alfredo 328
Sales, Soupy 373
Samson in the Wax Museum 193, 330–331, **331**
Samson vs. the Vampire Women 193, 331–332, 344
Sanchez, Victoria 276
Sanders, George 217
Sanders, Tom 183
Sandler, Adam 304
Sandoval, Arturo 344
Sands, Julian 330
Santa Barbara Studios 28
Santa Claus (1959) 315
Santa Monica Sound Stage 46
El Santo 191, 191–192, 192, 193, 194, 228, 276, 331, 344, 345
Santo and Blue Demon vs. Dracula and the Wolf Man 189–191, **190**, 192, 193, 328
Santo and Blue Demon vs. the Monsters 87, 189, 193, 315
El Santo contra las Mujeres Vampiros see *Samson vs. the Vampire Women*
Santo en el Museo de Cera see *Samson in the Wax Museum*
Santo vs. las Lobas see *Santo vs. the She-Wolves*
Santo vs. the She-Wolves 58, 164, 192–194, **193**
Santo y Blue Demon contra los Monstruous see *Santo and Blue Demon vs. the Monsters*
Santo y Blue Demon vs. Drácula y el Hombre Lobo see *Santo and Blue Demon vs. Dracula and the Wolf Man*
Sarandon, Chris 167, 298
Sarno, Robert 125
Satana, Tura 304
Satan's Sadists 250
Saturday Night Fever 202
Saturday the 14th 332
Saturday the 14th Strikes Back 332
Saved by the Bell (series) 242
Saving Private Ryan 79, 183
Sawyer, Mark 84
Saxon, John 164, 220, 221
Sayles, John 31, 122, 124, 368
Scared Stiff 71
Scheer, Philip 138, 307

Schell, Carl 233
Schell, Maximillian 233
Schenck, George 76
Schlegel, Nicholas 92, 249
Schrader, Paul 357–358
Schulman, Nina 238
Schumacher, Martha 195
Schwarzenegger, Arnold 360
Schwimmer, David 256
Scolari, Peter 341
Scooby-Doo and the Ghoul School 332
Scooby-Doo and Scrappy-Doo (TV series) 332
Scooby-Doo! And the Goblin King 333
Scooby-Doo and the Reluctant Werewolf 194–195
Scooby-Doo on Zombie Island 195, 367–368
Scooby-Doo, Where Are You? (TV series) 332
Scott, Katherine Leigh 286
Scott, Leigh 37, 38, 268, 269
Scott, Rick 171
Scott, Ron 81
Scream 27, 66, 67, 260
Scream of the Wolf 333
Scream 3 68
The Screaming Dead see *Dracula, Prisoner of Frankenstein*
Scrooged 50
Sealey, Scott 50
Sears, Fred F. 223, 225
Seaver, Chris 196, 197
The Secret of Roan Inish 368
Sedaka, Neil 372
"See Me in the Mirror" (song) 156
Selander, Lesley 359
Selby, David 286
Seltzer, Aaron 343
Sentner, Nico 139
Sergevici, Viorel 243
Serino, Jack 181
The Serpent and the Rainbow 66
Serrador, Narciso Ibanez 248
Seven Deaths in a Cat's Eye 373
The Seventh Victim 363
The Seventh Voyage of Sinbad 50
Sewell, Vernon 373
Sex Galaxy 175
Sex, Sadism, Spain and Cinema 92
Sexbomb 333–334
Sexual Freedom in Denmark 178
Seyfried, Amanda 183
Sgt. Pepper's Lonely Hearts Club Band (film) 157
Shadow of a Doubt 32
Shadow of the Werewolf see *The Werewolf vs. the Vampire Woman*
The Shaggy D.A. (1976) 368, 369
The Shaggy Dog (1959) 368–369, 373
The Shaggy Dog (2006) 369
Shah, Krishna 302
Shapeshifter see *Shifter*
Sharknado 38, 149
Shaun of the Dead 27, 31, 102, 216
Shaw, Joseph 110
Shayne, Robert 307
She (1988) 334
The She Creature 307
She Wolf see *The Legend of the Wolf Woman*

She-Wolf of London (film) 334, **335**
She-Wolf of London (series) 52
She Wore a Yellow Ribbon 74
Sheen, Charlie 227
Sheen, Martin 227
Sheen, Michael 207, 212, 216
Sheets, Todd 162
Sheffer, Craig **35**
Shelley, Barbara 356
Sherlock Holmes (2009 film) 246
Sherman, Sam 30, 46, 92
Shields, Arthur 74
Shields, Brooke 51
Shields, Samantha 252
Shifter 369
The Shining (1980) 256, 303
Shopping for Fangs 334–335
Shuler, Lauren 141
Silva, David 328, 344
Silver Bullet 1, 2, 12, 142, 195–196
Silverado 41
Simmons, Gene 311
Simon, Simone 357, 358
Simon, King of the Witches 76
The Simpsons (TV series) 23
Sinclair, Charles 372
Singer, Bryan 341
Singleton, Brian 230, 230–231, 232
Singleton, Mark 230, 231, **231**
Siodmak, Curt 4–5, 10, 16, 18, 85, 89–90, 90, 91, 256, 257, 258, 259, 353–354
Sirk, Douglas 74
Siskel, Gene 203
Sisters 37
Sisto, Rocco 181
Sivilli, Dominick 39
The Six Million Dollar Man (series) 167, 256
Ski Wolf 196–197
Skin Walkers see *Skinwalkers*
Skinner, R.J. 155
Skinwalker: Curse of the Shaman 335–336
Skinwalkers 2, 3, 167, 197–199, **198**
Skipp, John 273
Skull Forest 65
Slaughter of the Vampires see *Curse of the Blood-Ghouls*
Sleepwalkers 369–370, **370**
Sloman, Roger **321**
Smirk, Sneer and Scream: Great Acting in Horror Cinema 18n2
Smith, Brian 14
Smith, Don G. 258
Smith, Jono 44
Smith, Kavan 185
Smith, Kent 355, 357
The Snake Woman 370, **371**
Snatch 200
Snegoff, Tony 133
Sogni d'Oro 336
Solares, Agustin Martinez 189
Solares, Agustin Martinez, Jr. 189
Solares, Gilberto Martinez 87, 189
Solares, Raúl Martinez 189, 314, 314–315
Soler, Julián 281
Sommers, Stephen 219, 220
Son of Dracula (1943) 186
Son of Dracula (1974) 336–337
Son of Dracula (record album) 337
Son of Frankenstein 113, 117
Son of Kong 225

Sondergaard, Gale 355, 356
Song, Joong-ki 229
Sons of the Pioneers 133
The Sopranos (series) 181, 196
Sorbo, Kevin 167
Sormare, Peter 279
Sothcott, Jonathan 200, 201
The Soul of a Monster **58**
Spader, James 256
Spease, Matt 293
Spector, Craig 273
Speed Racer (series) 342
Speelers, Ed 121, 151
Spencer, Brenton 167
Spielberg, Steven 196, 274–275
Spiritism 297
Spookies 370–372
Ssssss 50
Stagecoach (1939) 44
Stanley, Paul 311
Stansbury, Hope 178, 179
Star Wars FAQ 18n2
Starck, Dominik 139
Starr, Ringo 336
Starship Invasions 168
Stebbings, Peter 167
Steele, Barbara 91
Steele, Brian 212, 215, 216
Stephen King's It see *It*
Stephen King's Silver Bullet see *Silver Bullet*
Stephen King's Sleepwalkers see *Sleepwalkers*
Stephenson, Geoffrey 126
Stern, Tom 27–28
Sterne, David 44
Stevens, Andrew 241
Stevens, Anthony 5
Stevens, Onslow 111
Stevens, Stella 241
Stevens, Steve 336
Stevenson, Robert Louis 77
Stewart, Kristin 69, 183, 207, 208, 322
Sting of Death **362**, 372
Stivaletti, Sergio 338, 339
Stockwell, Dean 174, **175**, 238, 239
Stole, Mink 322
Stolze, Eric 141, 142
Stone, Christopher 124
Stone, Evan 204
Stone, Milburn 355
Stone, Sharon 256
Storaro, Vittorio 111
Stormare, Peter 82
Strachen, Craig 252, 253
Strange, Glenn 22, 152–153, **152**
The Strange Case of Dr. Jekyll and Mr. Hyde (novel) 1, 77
Strange Love of the Vampires 78
The Strangers (1998) 199
Straw Dogs 156
Strick, Wesley 255
Strippers vs. Werewolves 200–201, 252
Stryker, Bradley 267
Stuart, Gloria 258
Stumar, Charles 237
Stumar, John 188
Suarez, Carlos 193
Subotsky, Milton 36–37, 37, 289, 291, 321
Sudden Birth 175
Sullivan, Brett 105, 106

398 • Index

Sullivan, Tim 84, 359, 360
Summers, Montague 6
Sundown: The Vampire in Retreat 346
Sundstrom, Neal 131–132
Supercroc 38
Superman (1978) 141
Superman Returns 83
Survival of the Dead 167
Sutherland, Donald 238, 291
Swamp Zombies 65
Swan, Paul 47
Sweet Sixteen 252
Sweet Sugar 251
Swift, Alan 318
Sybil 161
SyFy Channel 35, 88, 166, 185, 203, 204, 220, 269

Tabb, Michael 246
Talbot, Gloria 74
Tales from the Crypt 37, 289, 293
Tales from the Dark Side (TV series) 109
Tales of the Night 337
Tales of the Third Dimension 337–338
Tarantino, Quentin 39, 44, 358
Targets 324
Tarzan and the Brown Prince 353
Tatopoulos, Patrick 211, 214, 216
Tatopoulos Studios 215, 341
Taxi Driver 357
Taylor, Jack 77, 78, 291
Taylor, Robert 30
Team America: World Police 23
Teen Wolf 50, 66, 149, 162, 201–202, **202**, 202, 203, 211, 339
Teen Wolf Too 149, 162, 202–203
Teenage Caveman 137
Teenage Zombies 86
The Teeth of the Night see *Vampire Party*
Ten Little Indians 37, 130
The Tenement (2003) 338
Tenser, Tony 373
Tentori, Antonio 338, 339
Terror of the She Wolf see *The Legend of the Wolf Woman*
Terror of the Snake Woman see *The Snake Woman*
Tesoro, Ashley 243
The Texas Chain Saw Massacre 31, 42, 84, 145
They Saved Hitler's Brain 46, 303
Thibault, Carl 159
The Thin Man (film series) 101
The Thing (1951) 173, 288
The Thing (1982) 121, 124
The Thing (2011) 167
Thir13en Ghosts 243
13 Hrs. see *Night Wolf*
This Is Spinal Tap 205
This Island Earth 303
This Isn't The Twilight Saga Eclipse 15
Thomas, Eddie Kaye 165
Thomas, Harry 118
Thomas, Michael R. 117
Thomas, Richard 309
Thomerson, Tim 220
Thompson, Marshall 361
Thor 203
Thor: Hammer of the Gods 203–204

The Three Faces of Terror 338–339
300 135
Thriller (series) 74, 218
Thring, Frank 127
Thurston, Helen 22
Tierney, Lawrence 196
Tigon Film Company 373
Tim Burton's The Nightmare Before Christmas see *The Nightmare Before Christmas*
Time Bandits 278
The Time Machine (2002) 279
Time Out magazine 141
Tin Tan 86, 87
Tinnell, Robert 295
Tippett, Phil 208, 209
Tippett Studio 207
Tohill, Cathal 92
Toler, Jason 108–109, 109
Tom Savini Ltd. 283
Tomb of the Werewolf 11, 56, 204–206, **205**, 288, 314
Tombs, Pete 92
Torrez, Tyger 297
Torture Dungeon 178
Torture Garden 289
Totally Awesome 339
Tourneur, Jacques 357
Tower of London (1939) 113
The Towering Inferno 121
Track of the Moon Beast 241, 372–373
Trailer Park of Terror 182
Transylmania 339–340
Transylvania 6-5000 340–341, **340**
A Transylvanian Werewolf in America see *Full Moon High*
I Tre Volte del Terrore see *The Three Faces of Terror*
Trejo, Danny 278, 304
Tremors 34, 281
Trentham, Barbara 76
Trick or Treat (1986) 300
Trick 'r' Treat 50, 341–342
Trilogy of Terror 361
The Trip 251
Trog 373
Troll 2 157
Troma 276
Tromeo and Juliet 178
Tron (1982) 292
Trout, Paul A. 4, 5, 14
Truck Turner 147
Tucker, Christopher 52, 53–54
Tudor, Andrew 9
Turner, Clive 129, 130, 132, 133, 134, 135
Twenty Million Miles to Earth 50
Twilight 183, 209, 210, 343, 343–344
Twilight (film series) 17, 42, 69, 89, 92, 135, 136, 182–183, 184, 207, 208, 282, 322, 343, 344, 359
The Twilight Saga: Breaking Dawn Part One 206–207, 278
The Twilight Saga: Breaking Dawn Part Two 207–208
The Twilight Saga: Eclipse 210, 278, 344
The Twilight Saga: New Moon 207, 208, 209–210, 282, 343, 343–344
Twilight Zone (TV series) 109, 218
Twilight Zone: The Movie 95

Twins of Evil 129
Twisted Tales (1994) 342
2 Headed Shark Attack 149
The Two Little Bears 373
2001: A Space Odyssey 342
Two Weeks Notice 46
Tyburn Film Company 143, 145
Tyson, Richard 40
Tyxe 150

Ulloa, Alejandro 56
Ulmer, Edward G. 73, 74
Ulrich, Skeet 68
Unapix 61
Uncaged (2008) see *Never Cry Werewolf*
Uncaged (2016) 210–211
Under the Bed 141
Underworld (film) 211–213, 215, 218
Underworld (film series) 18, 47, 71, 89, 92, 187, 246, 341
Underworld: Awakening **212**, 213, 213–214, 216, 245
Underworld: Evolution 9, 212, 213, 214–215, **215**, 216
Underworld: Rise of the Lycans 2, 213, 215–216
The Undying Monster 10, 216–218, **217**
The Uninvited (1944) 188
Universal Studios Hollywood 8, 215
The Unliving see *Tomb of the Werewolf*
Urban Terrors 81
Urufi Gai: Moero Okami-Otoko see *Wolfguy: Enraged Lycanthrope*

Valdés, Manuel "Loco" 296
Valentine, Scott 287
Valerie (series) 203
Valkoinen Peura see *The White Reindeer*
Valley of the Headhunters 224
The Vampire Bat 113
The Vampire-Beast Craves Blood 373–374, **374**
Vampire Circus 158
Vampire Hunter D 342–343
Vampire Hunter D: Bloodlust 343
Vampire Party 343
Vampire Weekend 134
Vampires & Other Stereotypes 342
The Vampire's Coffin 281
The Vampire's Ghost 57, 359
The Vampire's Night Orgy 78
Vampires Suck 278, 343–344
Vampiros en la Habana 344
Vampiyaz 47
Van Helsing 116, 213, 218–220, **219**, 226, 246, 339
Van Peebles, Mario 94
Van Sant, Gus 207
Van Sloan, Edward 303
Vaughan, Tim 254
Vaughn, Carrie 8, 13
The Vault of Horror 289
Vegoda, Joe 289
Velásquez, Lorena 331
Vella, John 372
La Venganza de Huracán Ramirez 344–345
Vengeance of the Zombies 78, 249

Vera, Victoria 157
Verdugo, Elena 113–114, 114
Vergara, Enrique 276
Vernon, Howard 291
Victor, Katherine 306
Viel, Christian 327
Village of the Damned (1995) 34
Viruta 280, 281
Visconti, Luchino 140–141
Von Garnier, Katja 43, 44
Vonnegut, Kurt 99

Wadleigh, Michael 348, 349
Waggner, George 90, 122, 256
Wagstaff, Elsie 370
Waititi, Taika 346
Wakeman, Rick 334
Walker, Stuart 236, 237
The Walking Dead (1936) 228
Walking Tall (1973) 263
Wallace, Dee 123, 124, 304
Wallace, Earl 361
Wallace, Marcia 164
Wallace, Tommy Lee 298, 309
Wallace & Gromit (film series) 101, 374
Wallace & Gromit: The Curse of the Were-Rabbit 374
Waller, Anthony 28
Walston, Ray 332
Walters, Bruce 28
Walton, Karen 105
War Wolves 220–221, **221**
Ward, Fred 281
Warhol, Andy 127
Warlock: The Armageddon 346
Warner, David 345, 346
Warren, Jerry 38, 86, 87, 122, 306
Warren, John F. 74
Warren, Val 275
The Wasp Woman (1959) 374–375, **375**
The Wasp Woman (1995) 376
Watchmen (film) 265
Watergate 238, 239
The Wax Mask 338
Waxwork 94, 167, 345–346, **345**
Waxwork II: Lost in Time 346
Wayne, John 44
Weaver, Dennis 241
Weaver, Rob 241
Weiner, Zachary 210
Weinstein, Bob 66, 279
Weinstein, Harvey 66, 279
Weiss, Michael T. 129
Weitz, Chris 209, 282
Weitz, Paul 282
Wells, H.G. 79
Wer 221–223, **222**
The Werewolf (1913 film) 10
The Werewolf (1956 film) 2, 10, 72, 148, 187, 223–225, **224**
Werewolf (1975 film) see *Night of the Howling Beast*
Werewolf (1987 film) 116, 166, 225–227, **226**
Werewolf (1996 film) 12, 227–228
Werewolf (series) 225, 227, 288
The Werewolf and the Yeti see *Night of the Howling Beast*
A Werewolf Boy 228–230, **229**
Werewolf by Night 6
Werewolf Fever 230–232, **231**, 265
Werewolf Hunter see *Romasanta*

Werewolf Hunter: The Legend of Romasanta see *Romasanta*
Werewolf in a Girls' Dormitory 232–233, **232**, 272
Werewolf in a Women's Prison 85, 233–234, **234**
Werewolf in Bangkok 234–236
A Werewolf in the Amazon see *Un Lobisomem na Amazônia*
Werewolf Manhunt see *Romasanta*
The Werewolf of Fever Swamp (novel) 298
Werewolf of London 2, 10, 14, 34, 57, 82, 85, 95, 97, 158, 168, 178, 186, 200, 225, 233, 236–238, **237**, 246, 256, 257, 258, 273, 283
The Werewolf of Paris (novel) 10, 257
The Werewolf of Washington 11, 174, **175**, 238–240, **239**
The Werewolf of Woodstock 11, 195, 240–241, **240**
The Werewolf Reborn! 12, 241–243, **242**
Werewolf Rising 243–244
Werewolf Shadow see *The Werewolf vs. the Vampire Woman*
Werewolf Terror see *Iron Wolf*
Werewolf: The Beast Among Us 121, 244–246, **245**
Werewolf: The Devil's Hound 247
The Werewolf vs. the Vampire Woman 2, 54, 55, 56, 61, 78, 93, 157, 206, 247–250, **248**, 292, 292
Werewolf Warrior see *Kibakichi*
Werewolf Woman see *The Legend of the Wolf Woman*
Werewolf Women of the SS (faux trailer) 299
Werewolves: Fact or Fiction? 1
"Werewolves of London" (song) 69
Werewolves on Wheels 11, 164, 250–251, **251**
Westmore, Bud 21
Weston, Eric 363

Whale, James 303
What We Do in the Shadows 346–347
Whipple, G.M. 14
White, Cameron 69
White, William 306
The White Reindeer 376–377, **376**
Whitman, Jack 76
Whitman, Stuart 356
Whitney, John 110, 111
Whitton, Billy 81
Who Can Kill a Child? 56
Who's Afraid of Virginia Woolf? 256
The Widderburn Horror see *House of the Black Death*
Wiehl, Christopher 282
Wilczyca 347–348, **347**
The Wild Angels 250
The Wild Bunch 194
Wild Country 252–253, **252**
Wild Jungle Captive see *Jungle Captive*
The Wild One 250
Wilder, Gene 238, 303
Wilderness (1997) 2, 253–254, **254**
Willard 178
Williamson, Kevin 66, 67, 68
Willis, George 9–10, 215
Willis, Matt 187, 223
Wilson, Sheldon 185
Windsor, Romy 129
Winston, Stan 159, **159**, 198, 341, 353
Wise, Greg 116
Wise, Ray 294
Wiseman, Len 211, 212, 214, 214–215, 215, 216
Wiseman, Matthew 203
Witchfinder General 373
The Wizard of Oz (1939) 207, 324
Wolf 12, 17, 69, 255–256, **255**, 258, 313–314
Wolf Blood see *Wolfblood: A Tale of the Forest*
Wolf Creek 75

Wolf Girl see *Blood Moon*
The Wolf Man (1941) 1, 2, **4**, 9, 10, 14, **15**, 18, 22, 23, 24, 30, 34, 39, 47, 49, 50, 57, 64, 66, 85, 88–89, 90, 91, 92, 113, 121, 122, 137, 151, 152, 161, 164, 182, 188, 210, 217, 218, 219, 220, 221, 225, 226, 236, 237, 238, 239, 242, 246, 256–259, **257**, 261, 262, 263, 264, 270, 279, 285, 295, 320, 353, 355, 357, 359
Wolf Mania see *The Feral Man*
Wolf Moon see *Dark Moon Rising*, 2009
Wolf Mountain see *The Legend of Wolf Mountain*
The Wolf of the Malveneurs see *Le Loup des Malveneur*
The Wolf of Wall Street 266
Wolfblood: A Tale of the Forest 10, 348
WolfCop 2, 14, 17, 18, 259–261, **259**, 265
Wolfen 12, 348–349, **349**
Wolfguy: Enraged Lycanthrope 349–350, **350**
Wolfhound 377
Wolfman (1979) 261–263, **262**, 337
Wolfman (2010) 2, 44, 244, 263–265, **263**
Wolfman Never Sleeps see *The Fury of the Wolfman*
Wolfman: The Beast Among Us see *Werewolf: The Beast Among Us*
Wolves 2, 12, 17, 265–266
The Wolves of Kromer 350–351, **351**
Wolves of Wall Street 266–267
Wolvesbayne 35, 267–269, **268**
The Woman in Black (2012) 45
Women in Cell Block 7 147
Woo, John 94
Wood, Ed, Jr. 99, 326, 366
Wooding, Jeremy 44, 45
Woodruff, Tom, Jr. 282
Woodward, Ian 7

Woolley, Stephen 52
The Worst Horror Movie Ever Made 15, 287
Worth, Michael 220–221
The Wrestling Women vs. the Aztec Mummy 331
Wright, Edgar 27
Wright, Frank Lloyd 116
Wright, Richard 213, 216
Wrightman, Alan 45
Wrong Turn 4 106
Wynn, Keenan 275
Wynorski, Jim 376, 377

XFX Company 33
X-Men (film series) 219, 265

Yarbrough, Jean 334
Yarnall, Celeste 336
Yassen, Ismail 300
Yellen, Alexander 35
York, John J. 227
Yorn, Rick 263
Young Frankenstein 1, 51, 96
Young Lady Chatterley 150
Yucca Valley 133
Yuzna, Brian 330

Zabalza, José Maria 97, 99
Zahlava, Bruce 129
Zarindast, Tony 227, 228
Zebub, Bill 15
Zepeda, Gerardo 278
Zerbe, Anthony 311
Ziffle, Emersen 14, 260
Zombie, Rob 299, 303, 303–304
Zombie, Sheri Moon 303
Zombie Farm 172
Zombie Werewolves Attack! 269–272, **270**
Zombies of War see *Horrors of War*
Zombiez 47
Zovek 277, 278
Zucco, George 153
Zulu 79